Lecture Notes in Computer Science   4424

Commenced Publication in 1973
Founding and Former Series Editors:
Gerhard Goos, Juris Hartmanis, and Jan van Leeuwen

T0205311

Orna Grumberg   Michael Huth (Eds.)

Tools and Algorithms for the Construction and Analysis of Systems

13th International Conference, TACAS 2007
Held as Part of the Joint European Conferences
on Theory and Practice of Software, ETAPS 2007
Braga, Portugal, March 24 - April 1, 2007
Proceedings

 Springer

Volume Editors

Orna Grumberg
Technion
Israel Institute of Technology
Haifa 32000, Israel
E-mail: orna@cs.technion.ac.il

Michael Huth
Imperial College London
United Kingdom
E-mail: M.Huth@doc.imperial.ac.uk

Library of Congress Control Number: 2007922076

CR Subject Classification (1998): F.3, D.2.4, D.2.2, C.2.4, F.2.2

LNCS Sublibrary: SL 1 – Theoretical Computer Science and General Issues

ISSN   0302-9743
ISBN-10   3-540-71208-9 Springer Berlin Heidelberg New York
ISBN-13   978-3-540-71208-4 Springer Berlin Heidelberg New York

Springer is a part of Springer Science+Business Media

springer.com

© Springer-Verlag Berlin Heidelberg 2007
Printed in Germany

Typesetting: Camera-ready by author, data conversion by Scientific Publishing Services, Chennai, India
Printed on acid-free paper   SPIN: 12029204   06/3142   5 4 3 2 1 0

Foreword

ETAPS 2007 is the tenth instance of the European Joint Conferences on Theory and Practice of Software, and thus a cause for celebration.

The events that comprise ETAPS address various aspects of the system development process, including specification, design, implementation, analysis and improvement. The languages, methodologies and tools which support these activities are all well within its scope. Different blends of theory and practice are represented, with an inclination towards theory with a practical motivation on the one hand and soundly based practice on the other. Many of the issues involved in software design apply to systems in general, including hardware systems, and the emphasis on software is not intended to be exclusive.

History and Prehistory of ETAPS

ETAPS as we know it is an annual federated conference that was established in 1998 by combining five conferences [Compiler Construction (CC), European Symposium on Programming (ESOP), Fundamental Approaches to Software Engineering (FASE), Foundations of Software Science and Computation Structures (FOSSACS), Tools and Algorithms for Construction and Analysis of Systems (TACAS)] with satellite events.

All five conferences had previously existed in some form and in various colocated combinations: accordingly, the prehistory of ETAPS is complex. FOSSACS was earlier known as the Colloquium on Trees in Algebra and Programming (CAAP), being renamed for inclusion in ETAPS as its historical name no longer reflected its contents. Indeed CAAP's history goes back a long way; prior to 1981, it was known as the Colleque de Lille sur les Arbres en Algebre et en Programmation. FASE was the indirect successor of a 1985 event known as Colloquium on Software Engineering (CSE), which together with CAAP formed a joint event called TAPSOFT in odd-numbered years. Instances of TAPSOFT, all including CAAP plus at least one software engineering event, took place every two years from 1985 to 1997 inclusive. In the alternate years, CAAP took place separately from TAPSOFT.

Meanwhile, ESOP and CC were each taking place every two years from 1986. From 1988, CAAP was colocated with ESOP in even years. In 1994, CC became a "conference" rather than a "workshop" and CAAP, CC and ESOP were thereafter all colocated in even years.

TACAS, the youngest of the ETAPS conferences, was founded as an international workshop in 1995; in its first year, it was colocated with TAPSOFT. It took place each year, and became a "conference" when it formed part of ETAPS 1998. It is a telling indication of the importance of tools in the modern field of informatics that TACAS today is the largest of the ETAPS conferences.

The coming together of these five conferences was due to the vision of a small group of people who saw the potential of a combined event to be more than the sum of its parts. Under the leadership of Don Sannella, who became the first ETAPS steering committee chair, they included: Andre Arnold, Egidio Astesiano, Hartmut Ehrig, Peter Fritzson, Marie-Claude Gaudel, Tibor Gyimothy, Paul Klint, Kim Guldstrand Larsen, Peter Mosses, Alan Mycroft, Hanne Riis Nielson, Maurice Nivat, Fernando Orejas, Bernhard Steffen, Wolfgang Thomas and (alphabetically last but in fact one of the ringleaders) Reinhard Wilhelm.

ETAPS today is a loose confederation in which each event retains its own identity, with a separate programme committee and proceedings. Its format is open-ended, allowing it to grow and evolve as time goes by. Contributed talks and system demonstrations are in synchronized parallel sessions, with invited lectures in plenary sessions. Two of the invited lectures are reserved for "unifying" talks on topics of interest to the whole range of ETAPS attendees. The aim of cramming all this activity into a single one-week meeting is to create a strong magnet for academic and industrial researchers working on topics within its scope, giving them the opportunity to learn about research in related areas, and thereby to foster new and existing links between work in areas that were formerly addressed in separate meetings.

ETAPS 1998–2006

The first ETAPS took place in Lisbon in 1998. Subsequently it visited Amsterdam, Berlin, Genova, Grenoble, Warsaw, Barcelona, Edinburgh and Vienna before arriving in Braga this year. During that time it has become established as the major conference in its field, attracting participants and authors from all over the world. The number of submissions has more than doubled, and the numbers of satellite events and attendees have also increased dramatically.

ETAPS 2007

ETAPS 2007 comprises five conferences (CC, ESOP, FASE, FOSSACS, TACAS), 18 satellite workshops (ACCAT, AVIS, Bytecode, COCV, FESCA, FinCo, GT-VMT, HAV, HFL, LDTA, MBT, MOMPES, OpenCert, QAPL, SC, SLA++P, TERMGRAPH and WITS), three tutorials, and seven invited lectures (not including those that were specific to the satellite events). We received around 630 submissions to the five conferences this year, giving an overall acceptance rate of 25%. To accommodate the unprecedented quantity and quality of submissions, we have four-way parallelism between the main conferences on Wednesday for the first time. Congratulations to all the authors who made it to the final programme! I hope that most of the other authors still found a way of participating in this exciting event and I hope you will continue submitting.

ETAPS 2007 was organized by the Departamento de Informática of the Universidade do Minho, in cooperation with

- European Association for Theoretical Computer Science (EATCS)
- European Association for Programming Languages and Systems (EAPLS)
- European Association of Software Science and Technology (EASST)
- The Computer Science and Technology Center (CCTC, Universidade do Minho)
- Camara Municipal de Braga
- CeSIUM/GEMCC (Student Groups)

The organizing team comprised:

- João Saraiva (Chair)
- José Bacelar Almeida (Web site)
- José João Almeida (Publicity)
- Luís Soares Barbosa (Satellite Events, Finances)
- Victor Francisco Fonte (Web site)
- Pedro Henriques (Local Arrangements)
- José Nuno Oliveira (Industrial Liaison)
- Jorge Sousa Pinto (Publicity)
- António Nestor Ribeiro (Fundraising)
- Joost Visser (Satellite Events)

ETAPS 2007 received generous sponsorship from Fundação para a Ciência e a Tecnologia (FCT), Enabler (a Wipro Company), Cisco and TAP Air Portugal.

Overall planning for ETAPS conferences is the responsibility of its Steering Committee, whose current membership is:

Perdita Stevens (Edinburgh, Chair), Roberto Amadio (Paris), Luciano Baresi (Milan), Sophia Drossopoulou (London), Matt Dwyer (Nebraska), Hartmut Ehrig (Berlin), José Fiadeiro (Leicester), Chris Hankin (London), Laurie Hendren (McGill), Mike Hinchey (NASA Goddard), Michael Huth (London), Anna Ingólfsdóttir (Aalborg), Paola Inverardi (L'Aquila), Joost-Pieter Katoen (Aachen), Paul Klint (Amsterdam), Jens Knoop (Vienna), Shriram Krishnamurthi (Brown), Kim Larsen (Aalborg), Tiziana Margaria (Göttingen), Ugo Montanari (Pisa), Rocco de Nicola (Florence), Jakob Rehof (Dortmund), Don Sannella (Edinburgh), João Saraiva (Minho), Vladimiro Sassone (Southampton), Helmut Seidl (Munich), Daniel Varro (Budapest), Andreas Zeller (Saarbrücken).

I would like to express my sincere gratitude to all of these people and organizations, the programme committee chairs and PC members of the ETAPS conferences, the organizers of the satellite events, the speakers themselves, the many reviewers, and Springer for agreeing to publish the ETAPS proceedings. Finally, I would like to thank the organizing chair of ETAPS 2007, João Saraiva, for arranging for us to have ETAPS in the ancient city of Braga.

Edinburgh, January 2007   Perdita Stevens
                                          ETAPS Steering Committee Chair

Preface

This volume contains the proceedings of the 13th International Conference on Tools and Algorithms for the Construction and Analysis of Systems (TACAS 2007) which took place in Braga, Portugal, March 26-30, 2007.

TACAS is a forum for researchers, developers and users interested in rigorously based tools and algorithms for the construction and analysis of systems. The conference serves to bridge the gaps between different communities that share common interests in, and techniques for, tool development and its algorithmic foundations. The research areas covered by such communities include but are not limited to formal methods, software and hardware verification, static analysis, programming languages, software engineering, real-time systems, communications protocols and biological systems. The TACAS forum provides a venue for such communities at which common problems, heuristics, algorithms, data structures and methodologies can be discussed and explored. In doing so, TACAS aims to support researchers in their quest to improve the utility, reliability, flexibility and efficiency of tools and algorithms for building systems. The specific topics covered by the conference included, but were not limited to, the following: specification and verification techniques for finite and infinite-state systems; software and hardware verification; theorem-proving and model-checking; system construction and transformation techniques; static and run-time analysis; abstraction techniques for modeling and validation; compositional and refinement-based methodologies; testing and test-case generation; analytical techniques for secure, real-time, hybrid, critical, biological or dependable systems; integration of formal methods and static analysis in high-level hardware design or software environments; tool environments and tool architectures; SAT solvers; and applications and case studies.

TACAS traditionally considers two types of papers: research papers that describe in detail novel research within the scope of the TACAS conference; and short tool demonstration papers that give an overview of a particular tool and its applications or evaluation. TACAS 2007 received 170 research and 34 tool demonstration submissions (204 submissions in total), and accepted 45 research papers and 9 tool demonstration papers. Each submission was evaluated by at least three reviewers. Submissions co-authored by a Program Committee member were neither reviewed, discussed nor decided on by any Program Committee member who co-authored a submission. After a 35-day reviewing process, the program selection was carried out in a two-week electronic Program Committee meeting. We believe that this meeting and its detailed discussions resulted in a strong technical program. The TACAS 2007 Program Committee selected K. Rustan M. Leino (Microsoft Research, USA) as invited speaker, who kindly agreed and gave a talk entitled "Verifying Object-Oriented Software: Lessons and Challenges," reporting on program verification of modern software from the perspective of the Spec# programming system. These proceedings also include the title and abstract of an ETAPS "unifying" talk entitled "There and Back Again: Lessons Learned on the Way to the Market," in which Rance Cleaveland reports about his experience of commercializing formal modeling and verification technology, and how this has changed his view of mathematically oriented software research.

As TACAS 2007 Program Committee Co-chairs we thank the authors and co-authors of all submitted papers, all Program Committee members, subreviewers, and especially our Tool Chair Byron Cook and the TACAS Steering Committee for guaranteeing such a strong technical program. Martin Karusseit gave us prompt support in dealing with the online conference management service. The help of Anna Kramer at the Springer Editorial Office with the general organization and the production of the proceedings was much appreciated. TACAS 2007 was part of the 10th European Joint Conference on Theory and Practice of Software (ETAPS), whose aims, organization and history are detailed in the separate foreword by the ETAPS Steering Committee Chair. We would like to express our gratitude to the ETAPS Steering Committee, particularly its Chair Perdita Stevens, and the Organizing Committee — notably João Saraiva — for their efforts in making ETAPS 2007 a successful event.

Last, but not least, we acknowledge Microsoft Research Cambridge for kindly agreeing to sponsor seven awards (2000 GBP split into seven parts) for students who co-authored and presented their award-winning paper at TACAS 2007. The quality of these papers, as judged in their discussion period, was the salient selection criterion for these awards.

January 2007   Orna Grumberg and Michael Huth

Organization

TACAS Steering Committee

Ed Brinksma	ESI and University of Twente (The Netherlands)
Rance Cleaveland	University of Maryland and Fraunhofer USA Inc(USA)
Kim Larsen	Aalborg University (Denmark)
Bernhard Steffen	University of Dortmund (Germany)
Lenore Zuck	University of Illinois (USA)

TACAS 2007 Program Committee

Christel Baier	TU. Dresden, Germany
Armin Biere	Johannes Kepler University, Linz, Austria
Jonathan Billington	University of South Australia, Australia
Ed Brinksma	ESI and University of Twente, The Netherlands
Rance Cleaveland	University of Maryland and Fraunhofer USA Inc, USA
Byron Cook	Microsoft Research, Cambridge, UK
Dennis Dams	Bell Labs, Lucent Technologies, Murray Hill, USA
Marsha Chechik	University of Toronto, Canada
Francois Fages	INRIA Rocquencourt, France
Kathi Fisler	Worcester Polytechnic, USA
Limor Fix	Intel Research Laboratory, Pittsburgh, USA
Hubert Garavel	INRIA Rhône-Alpes, France
Susanne Graf	VERIMAG, Grenoble, France
Orna Grumberg	TECHNION, Israel Institute of Technology, Israel
John Hatcliff	Kansas State University, USA
Holger Hermanns	University of Saarland, Germany
Michael Huth	Imperial College London, UK
Daniel Jackson	Massachusetts Institute of Technology, USA
Somesh Jha	University of Wisconsin at Madison, USA
Orna Kupferman	Hebrew University, Jerusalem, Israel
Marta Kwiatkowska	University of Birmingham, UK
Kim Larsen	Aalborg University, Denmark
Michael Leuschel	University of Düsseldorf, Germany
Andreas Podelski	University of Freiburg, Germany
Tiziana Margaria-Steffen	University of Potsdam, Germany
Tom Melham	Oxford University, UK
CR Ramakrishnan	SUNY Stony Brook, USA
Jakob Rehof	University of Dortmund and Fraunhofer ISST, Germany
Natarajan Shankar	SRI, Menlo Park, USA
Lenore Zuck	University of Illinois, USA

Additional Reviewers

Parosh Abdulla	Erika Ábrahám	Cyrille Artho
Domagoj Babic	Marco Bakera	Ittai Balaban
Bernd Beckert	Gerd Behrmann	Jens Bendisposto
Josh Berdine	Marco Bernardo	Tanya Berger-Wolf
Christian Bessière	Per Bjesse	Dragan Bosnacki
Juliana Bowles	Marius Bozga	Laura Brandán Briones
Manuela L. Bujorianu	Thomas Chatain	Krishnendu Chatterjee
Aziem Chawdhary	Alessandro Cimatti	Koen Lindström Claessen
Christopher Conway	Patrick Cousot	Frank de Boer
Leonardo de Moura	Alexandre David	Conrado Daws
Giorgio Delzano	Henning Dierks	Zinovy Diskin
Dino Distefano	Daniel Dougherty	Bruno Dutertre
Niklas Een	Jochen Eisinger	Cindy Eisner
Sandro Etalle	Kousha Etessami	Azaleh Farzan
Harald Fecher	Bernd Finkbeiner	Maarten Fokkinga
Marc Fontaine	Martin Fränzle	Lars Frantzen
Goran Frehse	Joern Freiheit	Guy Gallasch
Yuan Gan	Dan Geiger	Naghmeh Ghafari
Mihaela Gheorghiu	Georges Gonthier	Alexey Gotsman
Michael Greenberg	Marcus Groesser	Roland Groz
Dimitar Guelev	Sumit Gulwani	Arie Gurfinkel
Peter Habermehl	Rémy Haemmerlé	Matt Harren
Tom Hart	Monika Heiner	Noomene Ben Henda
Marc Herbstritt	Tamir Heyman	Josef Hooman
Hardi Hungar	Radu Iosif	Franjo Ivancic
Florent Jacquemard	Himanshu Jain	David N. Jansen
Thierry Jéron	Barbara Jobstmann	Narendra Jussien
Toni Jussila	Joost-Pieter Katoen	Victor Khomenko
Joachim Klein	Piotr Kordy	Eric Koskinen
Steve Kremer	Sriram Krishnamachari	Daniel Kroening
Kelvin Ku	Hillel Kugler	Wouter Kuijper
Viktor Kuncak	Marcos E. Kurbán	Marcel Kyas
Shuvendu Lahiri	Charles Lakos	Anna-Lena Lamprecht
Frédéric Lang	Rom Langerak	Richard Lassaigne
Axel Legay	Jerome LeRoux	Tal Lev-Ami
Nimrod Lilith	Lin Liu	Yoad Lustig
Angelika Mader	Stephen Magill	Thomas Mailund
Oded Maler	Shahar Maoz	Jelena Marincic
Joao Marques-Silva	Thierry Massart	Radu Mateescu
Frédéric Mesnard	Roland Meyer	Marius Mikucionis
Laurent Mounier	Anca Muscholl	Alan Mycroft
Ralf Nagel	Kedar Namjoshi	Shiva Nejati
Dejan Nickovic	Brian Nielsen	Gethin Norman

Ulrik Nyman
Ernst-Rüdiger Olderog
Matthew Parkinson
Lee Pike
Erik Poll
Shaz Qadeer
Zvonimir Rakamaric
Arend Rensink
Oliver Roux
Andrey Rybalchenko
Gwen Salaün
Wolfgang Schubert
Koushik Sen
Sharon Shoham
Jocelyn Simmonds

Ana Sokolova
Maria Sorea
Bernhard Steffen
Greogoire Sutre
Hayo Thielecke
Christian Topnik
Rachel Tzoref
Somsak Vanit-Anunchai
Jacques Verriet
Horst Voigt
Uwe Waldmann
Martin Wehrle
Georg Weissenbacher
Thomas Wies
Verena Wolf
Avi Yadgar
Karen Yorav
Aleksandr Zaks

Iulian Ober
Rotem Oshman
Corina Pasareanu
Nir Piterman
Olivier Ponsini
Sophie Quinton
Jacob Illum Rasmussen
Pierre-Alain Reynier
Oliver Ruething
Tarek Sadani
German Puebla Sanchez
Stefan Schwoon
Wendelin Serwe
Marcus Siegle
Carsten Sinz

Sylvain Soliman
Scott Smolka
Marielle Stoelinga
Don Syme
Ashish Tiwari
Tayssir Touili
Sebastian Uchitel
Moshe Vardi
Marie Vidal
Tomas Vojnar
Xu Wang
Ou Wei
Bernd Westphal
Daniel Willems
Olaf Wolkenhauer
Alex Yakovlev
Greta Yorsh
Lijun Zhang

Peter O'Hearn
David Parker
Larry Paulson
Daniel Plagge
Riccardo Pucella
Harald Raffelt
Clemens Renner
Jan-Willem Roorda
Theo C. Ruys
Hassen Saidi
Lutz Schroeder
Helmut Seidl
Saad Sheikh
Joao Margues Silva
Viorica
Sofronie-Stokkermans
Kim Solin
Biblav Srivastava
Zhendong Su
Mana Taghdiri
Christophe Tollu
Jan Tretmans
Viktor Vafeiadis
Helmut Veith
Willem Visser
Björn Wachter
Heike Wehrheim
Christioph Weidenbach
Jon Whittle
Christian Winkler
Tao Xie
Hongseok Yang
Cong Yuan

Table of Contents

Invited Contributions

Software Verification

Probabilistic Model Checking and Markov Chains

Static Analysis

Markov Chains and Real-Time Systems

Timed Automata and Duration Calculus

Assume-Guarantee Reasoning

Biological Systems

Abstraction Refinement

Message Sequence Charts

Automata-Based Model Checking

Specification Languages

Security

Software and Hardware Verification

Decision Procedures and Theorem Provers

Model Checking

Infinite-State Systems

THERE AND BACK AGAIN:
Lessons Learned on the Way to the Market

Rance Cleaveland

Department of Computer Science, University of Maryland &
Fraunhofer USA Center for Experimental Software Engineering &
Reactive Systems Inc.
rance@cs.umd.edu

Abstract. In 1999 three formal-methods researchers, including the speaker, founded a company to commercialize formal modeling and verification technology for envisioned telecommunications customers. Eight years later, the company sells testing tools to embedded control software developers in the automotive, aerospace and related industries. This talk will describe the journey taken by the company during its evolution, why this journey was both less and more far than it seems, and how the speaker's views on the practical utility of mathematically oriented software research changed along the way.

O. Grumberg and M. Huth (Eds.): TACAS 2007, LNCS 4424, p. 1, 2007.

Verifying Object-Oriented Software:
Lessons and Challenges

K. Rustan M. Leino

Microsoft Research, Redmond, WA, USA
leino@microsoft.com

Abstract. A program verification system for modern software uses a host of technologies, like programming language semantics, formalization of good programming idioms, inference techniques, verification-condition generation, and theorem proving. In this talk, I will survey these techniques from the perspective of the Spec# programming system, of which I will also give a demo. I will reflect on some lessons learned from building automatic program verifiers, as well as highlight a number of remaining challenges.

O. Grumberg and M. Huth (Eds.): TACAS 2007, LNCS 4424, p. 2, 2007.
© Springer-Verlag Berlin Heidelberg 2007

Shape Analysis by Graph Decomposition

R. Manevich[1,*], J. Berdine[3], B. Cook[3], G. Ramalingam[2], and M. Sagiv[1]

[1] Tel Aviv University
{rumster,msagiv}@post.tau.ac.il
[2] Microsoft Research India
grama@microsoft.com
[3] Microsoft Research Cambridge
{bycook,jjb}@microsoft.com

Abstract. Programs commonly maintain multiple linked data structures. Correlations between multiple data structures may often be *non-existent or irrelevant to verifying that the program satisfies certain safety properties or invariants*. In this paper, we show how this *independence* between different (singly-linked) data structures can be utilized to perform shape analysis and verification more efficiently. We present a new abstraction based on decomposing graphs into sets of subgraphs, and show that, in practice, this new abstraction leads to very little loss of precision, while yielding substantial improvements to efficiency.

1 Introduction

We are interested in verifying that programs satisfy various safety properties (such as the absence of null dereferences, memory leaks, dangling pointer dereferences, etc.) and that they preserve various data structure invariants.

Many programs, such as web-servers, operating systems, network routers, etc., commonly maintain multiple linked data-structures in which data is added and removed throughout the program's execution. The Windows IEEE 1394 (firewire) device driver, for example, maintains separate cyclic linked lists that respectively store bus-reset request packets, data regarding CROM calls, data regarding addresses, and data regarding ISOCH transfers. These lists are updated throughout the driver's execution based on events that occur in the machine. Correlations between multiple data-structures in a program, such as those illustrated above, may often be *non-existent or irrelevant to the verification task of interest*. In this paper, we show how this *independence* between different data-structures can be utilized to perform verification more efficiently.

Many scalable heap abstractions typically maintain no correlation between different *points-to* facts (and can be loosely described as *independent attribute abstractions* in the sense of [7]). Such abstractions are, however, not precise enough to prove that programs preserve data structure invariants. More precise abstractions for the heap that use shape graphs to represent *complete* heaps [17], however, lead to exponential blowups in the state space.

---

* This research was partially supported by the Clore Fellowship Programme. Part of this research was done during an internship at Microsoft Research India.

In this paper, we focus on (possibly cyclic) singly-linked lists and introduce an approximation of the *full heap abstraction* presented in [13]. The new *graph decomposition abstraction* is based on a decomposition of (shape) graphs into sets of (shape) subgraphs (without maintaining correlations between different shape subgraphs). In our initial empirical evaluation, this abstraction produced results almost as precise as the full heap abstraction (producing just one false positive), while reducing the state space significantly, sometimes by exponential factors, leading to dramatic improvements to the performance of the analysis. We also hope that this abstraction will be amenable to abstraction refinement techniques (to handle the cases where correlations between subgraphs are necessary for verification), though that topic is beyond the scope of this paper.

One of the challenges in using a subgraph abstraction is the design of safe and precise transformers for statements. We show in this paper that the computation of the most precise transformer for the graph decomposition abstraction is FNP-complete.

We derive efficient, polynomial-time, transformers for our abstraction in several steps. We first use an observation by Distefano et al. [3] and show how the most precise transformer can be computed more efficiently (than the naive approach) by: (a) identifying *feasible combinations of subgraphs referred to by a statement*, (b) composing only them, (c) transforming the composed subgraphs, and (d) decomposing the resulting subgraphs. Next, we show that the transformers can be computed in polynomial time by omitting the feasibility check (which entails a possible loss in precision). Finally, we show that the resulting transformer can be implemented in an *incremental* fashion (i.e., in every iteration of the fixed point computation, the transformer reuses the results of the previous iteration).

We have developed a prototype implementation of the algorithm and compared the precision and efficiency (in terms of both time and space) of our new abstraction with that of the full heap abstraction over a standard suite of shape analysis benchmarks as well as on models of a couple of Windows device drivers. Our results show that the new analysis produces results as precise as the full heap-based analysis in almost all cases, but much more efficiently.

A full version of this paper contains extra details and proofs [11].

2   Overview

In this section, we provide an informal overview of our approach. Later sections provide the formal details.

Fig. 1 shows a simple program that adds elements into independent lists: a list with a head object referenced by a variable h1 and a tail object referenced by a variable t1, and a list with a head object referenced by a variable h2 and a tail object referenced by a variable t2. This example is used as the running example throughout the paper. The goal of the analysis is to prove that the data structure invariants are preserved in every iteration, i.e., at label L1 variables h1

```
//@assume h1!=null && h1==t1 && h1.n==null && h2!=null && h2==t2 && h2.n==null
//@invariant Reach(h1,t1) && Reach(h2,t2) && DisjointLists(h1,t1)
EnqueueEvents() {
L1:   while (...) {
          List temp = new List(getEvent());
          if (nondet()) {
L2:         t1.n = temp;
L3:         t1 = temp;
          } else {
            t2.n = temp;
            t2 = temp;
      } } }
```

Fig. 1. A program that enqueues events into one of two lists. `nondet()` returns either `true` or `false` non-deterministically.

and `t1` and variables `h2` and `t2` point to disjoint acyclic lists, and that the head and tail pointers point to the first and last objects in every list, respectively.

The shape analysis presented in [13] is able to verify the invariants by generating, at program label L1, the 9 abstract states shown in Fig. 2. These states represent the 3 possible states that each list can have: a) a list with one element, b) a list with two elements; and c) a list with more than two elements. This analysis uses a *full heap abstraction*: it does not take advantage of the fact that there is no interaction between the lists, and explores a state-space that contains all 9 possible combinations of cases $\{a, b, c\}$ for the two lists.

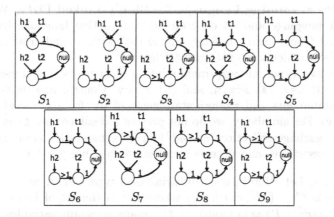

Fig. 2. Abstract states at program label L1, generated by an analysis of the program in Fig. 1 using a powerset abstraction. Edges labeled 1 indicate list segments of length 1, whereas edges labeled with >1 indicate list segments of lengths greater than 1.

The shape analysis using a *graph decomposition abstraction* presented in this paper, represents the properties of each list separately and generates, at program label L1, the 6 abstract states shown in Fig. 3. For a generalization of this program to k lists, the number of states generated at label L1 by using a graph decomposition abstraction is $3 \times k$, compared to 3^k for an analysis using a full heap abstraction, which tracks correlations between properties of all k lists.

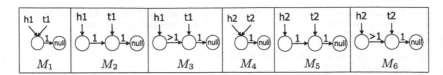

Fig. 3. Abstract states at program label L1, generated by an analysis of the program in Fig. 1 using the graph decomposition abstraction

In many programs, this exponential factor can be significant. Note that in cases where there is no *correlation* between the different lists, the new abstraction of the set of states is as precise as the full heap abstraction: e.g., Fig. 3 and Fig. 2 represent the same set of concrete states.

We note that in the presence of pointers, it is not easy to decompose the verification problem into a set of sub-problems to achieve similar benefits. For example, current (flow-insensitive) alias analyses would not be able to identify that the two lists are disjoint.

3   A Full Heap Abstraction for Lists

In this section, we describe the concrete semantics of programs manipulating singly-linked lists and a full heap abstraction for singly-linked lists.

A Simple Programming Language for Singly-Linked Lists. We now define a simple language and its concrete semantics. Our language has a single data type *List* (representing a singly-linked list) with a single reference field **n** and a data field, which we conservatively ignore.

There are five types of heap-manipulating statements: (1) x=new List(), (2) x=null, (3) x=y, (4) x=y.n, and (5) x.n=y. Control flow is achieved by using **goto** statements and **assume** statements of the form **assume(x==y)** and **assume(x!=y)**. For simplicity, we do not present a deallocation, **free(x)**, statement and use garbage collection instead. Our implementation supports memory deallocation, assertions, and detects (mis)use of dangling pointers.

Concrete States. Let *PVar* be a set of variables of type *List*. A concrete program state is a triple $C = (U^C, env^C, n^C)$ where U^C is the set of heap objects, an environment $env^C : PVar \cup \{null\} \rightarrow U^C$ maps program variables (and *null*) to heap objects, and $n^C : U^C \rightarrow U^C$, which represents the n field, maps heap objects to heap objects. Every concrete state includes a special object v_{null} such that $env(null) = v_{null}$. We denote the set of all concrete states by *States*.

Concrete Semantics. We associate a transition function $[\![st]\!]$ with every statement st in the program. Each statement st takes a concrete state C, and transforms it to a state $C' = [\![st]\!](C)$. The semantics of a statement is given by a pair (*condition, update*) such that when the condition specified by *condition* holds the state is updated according to the assignments specified by *update*. The concrete semantics of program statements is shown in Tab. 1.

Table 1. Concrete semantics of program statements. Primed symbols denote post-execution values. We write x,y, and x' to mean $env(x)$, $env(y)$, and $env'(x)$, respectively.

Statement	Condition	Update
x=new List()		$x' = v_{new}$, where v_{new} is a fresh List object
		$n' = \lambda v . (v = v_{new} ?\ null\ :\ n(v))$
x=null		$x' = null$
x=y		$x' = y$
x=y.n	$y \neq null$	$x' = n(y)$
x.n=y	$x \neq null$	$n' = \lambda v . (v = x ?\ y\ :\ n(v))$
assume(x!=y)	$x \neq y$	
assume(x==y)	$x = y$	

3.1   Abstracting List Segments

The abstraction is based on previous work on analysis of singly-linked lists [13]. The core concepts of the abstraction are *interruptions* and *uninterrupted list*. An object is an *interruption* if it is referenced by a variable (or *null*) or shared (i.e., has two or more predecessors). An uninterrupted list is a path delimited by two interruptions that does not contain interruptions other than the delimiters.

Definition 1 (Shape Graphs). *A shape graph $G \doteq (V^G, E^G, env^G, len^G)$ is a quadruple where V^G is a set of nodes, E^G is a set of edges, $env^G : PVar \cup \{null\} \rightarrow V^G$ maps variables (and null) to nodes, and $len^G : E^G \rightarrow$ pathlen assigns labels to edges. In this paper, we use pathlen $= \{1, >1\}$.*[1]

We denote the set of shape graphs by SG_{PVar}, omitting the subscript if no confusion is likely, and define equality between shape graphs by isomorphism. We say that a variable x points to a node $v \in V^G$ if $env^G(x) = v$.

We now describe how a concrete state $C \doteq (U^C, env^C, n^C)$ is abstracted into a shape graph $G \doteq (V^G, E^G, env^G, len^G)$ by the function $\beta^{FH} : States \rightarrow SG$. First, we remove any node in U^C that is not reachable from a (node pointed-to by a) program variable. Let $PtVar(C)$ be the set of objects pointed-to by some variable, and let $Shared(C)$ the set of heap-shared objects. We create a shape graph $\beta^{FH}(C) \doteq (V^G, E^G, env^G, len^G)$ where $V^G \doteq PtVar(C) \cup Shared(C)$, $E^G \doteq \{(u, v) \mid (u, \ldots, v)$ is an uninterrupted list$\}$, env^G restricts env^C to V^G, and $len^G(u, v)$ is 1 if the uninterrupted list from u to v has one edge and >1 otherwise. The abstraction function α^{FH} is the point-wise extension of β^{FH} to sets of concrete states[2]. We say that a shape graph is *admissible* if it is in the image of β^{FH}.

---

[1] The abstraction in [13] is more precise, since it uses the abstract lengths $\{1, 2, > 2\}$. We use the lengths $\{1, > 1\}$, which we found to be sufficiently precise, in practice.

[2] In general, the point-wise extension of a function $f : D \rightarrow D$ is a function $f : 2^D \rightarrow 2^D$, defined by $f(S) \doteq \{f(s) \mid s \in S\}$. Similarly, the extension of a function $f : D \rightarrow 2^D$ is a function $f : 2^D \rightarrow 2^D$, defined by $f(S) \doteq \bigcup_{s \in S} f(s)$.

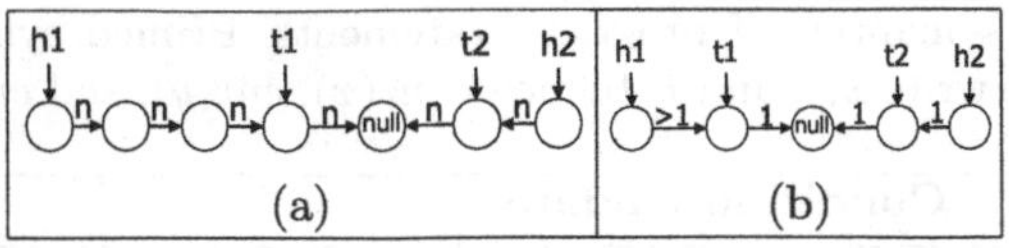

Fig. 4. (a) A concrete state, and (b) The abstraction of the state in (a)

Proposition 1. *A shape graph is admissible iff the following properties hold: (i) Every node has a single successor; (ii) Every node is pointed-to by a variable (or null) or is a shared node, and (iii) Every node is reachable from (a node pointed-to by) a variable.*

We use Prop. 1 to determine if a given graph is admissible in linear time and to conduct an efficient isomorphism test for two shape graphs in the image of the abstraction. It also provides a bound on the number of admissible shape graphs: $2^{5n^2+10n+8}$, where $n \doteq |PVar|$.

Example 1. Fig. 4(a) shows a concrete state that arises at program label L1 and Fig. 4(b) shows the shape graph that represents it.   □

Concretization. The function $\gamma^{FH} : SG \rightarrow 2^{States}$ returns the set of concrete states that a shape graph represents: $\gamma^{FH}(G) \doteq \{C \mid \beta^{FH}(C) = G\}$. We define the concretization of sets of shape graphs by using its point-wise extension. We now have the Galois Connection $\langle 2^{States}, \alpha^{FH}, \gamma^{FH}, 2^{SG} \rangle$.

Abstract Semantics. The most precise, a.k.a *best*, abstract transformer [2] of a statement is given by $[\![st]\!]^{\#} \doteq \alpha^{FH} \circ [\![st]\!] \circ \gamma^{FH}$. An efficient implementation of the most precise abstract transformer is shown in the full version [11].

4   A Graph Decomposition Abstraction for Lists

In this section, we introduce the abstraction that is the basis of our approach as an approximation of the abstraction shown in the previous section. We define the domain we use—2^{ASSG}, the powerset of atomic shape subgraphs—as well as the abstraction and concretization functions between 2^{SG} and 2^{ASSG}.

4.1   The Abstract Domain of Shape Subgraphs

Intuitively, the graph decomposition abstraction works by decomposing a shape graph into a set of *shape subgraphs*. In principle, different graph decomposition strategies can be used to get different abstractions. However, in this paper, we focus on decomposing a shape graph into a set of subgraphs induced by its *(weakly-)connected components*. The motivation is that different weakly connected components mostly represent different "logical" lists (though a single list may occasionally be broken into multiple weakly connected components during a sequence of pointer manipulations) and we would like to use an abstraction that decouples the different logical lists. We will refer to an element of SG_{PVar} as a shape graph, and an element of SG_{Vars} for any $Vars \subseteq PVar$ as a shape subgraph. We denote the set of shape subgraphs by SSG and define $Vars(G)$ to be the set of variables that appear in G, i.e., mapped by env^G to some node.

4.2 Abstraction by Graph Decomposition

We now define the decomposition operation. Since our definition of shape graphs represents *null* using a special node, we identify connected components *after excluding the null node*. (Otherwise, all *null*-terminated lists, i.e. all acyclic lists, will end up in the same connected component.)

Definition 2 (Projection). *Given a shape subgraph $G \doteq (V, E, env, len)$ and a set of nodes $W \subseteq V$, the subgraph of G induced by W, denoted by $G|_W$, is the shape subgraph (W, E', env', len'), where $E' \doteq E \cap (W \times W)$, $env' \doteq env \cap (Vars(G) \times W)$, and $len' \doteq len \cap (E' \times pathlen)$.*

Definition 3 (Connected Component Decomposition). *For a shape subgraph $G \doteq (V, E, env, len)$, let $R \doteq E'^*$ be the reflexive, symmetric, transitive closure of the relation $E' \doteq E \setminus \{(v_{null}, v), (v, v_{null}) \mid v \in V\}$. That is, R does not represent paths going through null. Let $[R]$ be the set of equivalence classes of R. The connected component decomposition of G is given by*

$$Components(G) \doteq \{G|_{C'} \mid C' = C \cup \{v_{null}\}, C \in [R]\} \ .$$

Example 2. Referring to Fig. 2 and Fig. 3, we have $Components(S_2) = \{M_1, M_5\}$.

Abstracting Away Null-value Correlations. The decomposition *Components* manages to decouple distinct lists in a shape graph. However, it fails to decouple lists from null-valued variables.

```
if (?) x = new List() else x = null;
y = new List();
```

                    (a)   (b)

Fig. 5. (a) A code fragment; and (b) Shape subgraphs arising after executing y=new List(). M_1: y points to a list and x is not null, M_2: y points to a list and x is null; and M_3: x points to a list and y is not null.

Example 3. Consider the code fragment shown in Fig. 5(a) and the shape subgraphs arising after y=new List(). y points to a list (with one cell), while x is *null* or points to another list (with one cell). Unfortunately, the y list will be represented by two shape subgraphs in the abstraction, one corresponding to the case that x is *null* (M_2) and one corresponding to the case that x is not *null* (M_1). If a number of variables can be optionally null, this can lead to an exponential blowup in the representation of other lists! Our preliminary investigations show that this kind of exponential blow-up can happen in practice. □

The problem is the occurrence of shape subgraphs that are isomorphic except for the *null* variables. We therefore define a coarser abstraction by decomposing the set of variables that point to the *null* node. To perform this further decomposition, we define the following operations:

- *nullvars* : $SSG \to 2^{PVar}$ returns the set of variables that point to *null* in a shape subgraph.
- *unmap* : $SSG \times 2^{PVar} \to SSG$ removes the mapping of the specified variables from the environment of a shape subgraph.
- *DecomposeNullVars* : $SSG \to 2^{SSG}$ takes a shape subgraph and returns: (a) the given subgraph without the null variables, and (b) one shape subgraph for every null variable, which contains just the null node and the variable:

$$DecomposeNullVars(G) \doteq \{unmap(G, nullvars(G))\} \cup$$
$$\{unmap(G|_{v_{null}}, Vars(G) \setminus \{var\} \mid var \in nullvars(G)\} \ .$$

In the sequel, we use the point-wise extension of *DecomposeNullVars*.

We define the set *ASSG* of *atomic* shape subgraphs to be the set of subgraphs that consist of either a single connected component or a single *null*-variable fact (i.e., a single variable pointing to the *null* node). Non-atomic shape subgraphs correspond to conjunctions of atomic shape subgraphs and are useful intermediaries during concretization and while computing transformers.

The abstraction function $\beta^{GD} : SG \to 2^{ASSG}$ is given by

$$\beta^{GD}(G) \doteq DecomposeNullVars(Components(G)) \ .$$

The function $\alpha^{GD} : 2^{SG} \to 2^{ASSG}$ is the point-wise extension of β^{GD}. Thus, $ASSG = \alpha^{GD}(SG)$ is the set of shape subgraphs in the image of the abstraction.

Note: We can extend the decomposition to avoid exponential blowups created by different sets of variables pointing to the same (non-*null*) node. However, we believe that such correlations are significant for shape analysis (as they capture different states of a single list) and abstracting them away can lead to a significant loss of precision. Hence, we do not explore this possibility in this paper.

4.3   Concretization by Composition of Shape Subgraphs

Intuitively, a shape subgraph represents the set of its super shape graphs. Concretization consists of connecting shape subgraphs such that the intersection of the sets of shape graphs that they represent is non-empty. To formalize this, we define the following binary relation on shape subgraphs.

Definition 4 (Subgraph Embedding). *We say that a shape subgraph* $G' \doteq (V', E', env', len')$ *is embedded in a shape subgraph* $G \doteq (V, E, env, len)$, *denoted*

$G' \sqsubseteq G$, *if there exists a function* $f : V \to V'$ *such that: (i)* $(u, v) \in E$ *iff* $(f(u), f(v)) \in E'$; *(ii)* $f(env(x)) = env'(x)$ *for every* $x \in Vars(G)$; *and (iii) for every* $x \in Vars(G') \setminus Vars(G)$, $f^{-1}(env'(x)) \cap V = \emptyset$ *or* $env'(x) = env'(null)$.[3]

Thus, for any two atomic shape subgraphs G and G', $G' \sqsubseteq G$ iff $G = G'$.

We make $\langle SSG, \sqsubseteq \rangle$ a complete partial order by adding a special element $\bot$ to represent infeasible shape subgraphs, and define $\bot \sqsubseteq G$ for every shape subgraph G. We define the operation *compose* : $SSG \times SSG \to SSG$ that accepts two shape subgraphs and returns their greatest lower bound (w.r.t. to the $\sqsubseteq$ ordering). The operation naturally extends to sets of shape subgraphs.

Example 4. Referring to Fig. 2 and Fig. 3, we have $S_1 \sqsubseteq M_1$ and $S_1 \sqsubseteq M_4$, and *compose*$(M_1, M_4) = S_1$. $\square$

The concretization function $\gamma^{GD} : 2^{ASSG} \to 2^{SG}$ is defined by

$$\gamma^{GD}(XG) \doteq \{G \mid G = compose(Y), Y \subseteq XG, \text{ G is admissible}\} \ .$$

This gives us the Galois Connection $\langle 2^{SG}, \alpha^{GD}, \gamma^{GD}, 2^{ASSG} \rangle$.

Properties of the Abstraction. Note that there is neither a loss of precision nor a gain in efficiency (e.g., such as a reduction in the size of the representation) when we decompose a single shape graph, i.e., $\gamma^{GD}(\beta^{GD}(G)) = \{G\}$. Both potentially appear when we abstract a set of shape graphs by decomposing each graph in a set. However, when there is no logical correlation between the different subgraphs (in the graph decomposition), we will gain efficiency without compromising precision.

Example 5. Consider the graphs in Fig. 2 and Fig. 3. Abstracting S_1 gives $\beta^{GD}(S_1) = \{M_1, M_4\}$. Concretizing back, gives $\gamma^{GD}(\{M_1, M_4\}) = \{S_1\}$. Abstracting S_5 yields $\beta^{GD}(S_5) = \{M_2, M_5\}$. Concretizing $\{M_1, M_2, M_4, M_5\}$ results in $\{S_1, S_2, S_4, S_5\}$, which overapproximates $\{S_1, S_5\}$. $\square$

5   Developing Efficient Abstract Transformers for the Graph Decomposition Abstraction

In this section, we show that it is hard to compute the most precise transformer for the graph decomposition abstraction in polynomial time and develop sound and efficient transformers. We demonstrate our ideas using the statement t1.n=temp in the running example and the subgraphs in Fig. 6 and Fig. 3.

An abstract transformer $T_{st} : 2^{ASSG} \to 2^{ASSG}$ is *sound* for a statement st if for every set of shape subgraphs XG the following holds:

$$(\alpha^{GD} \circ [\![st]\!]^{\#} \circ \gamma^{GD})(XG) \subseteq T_{st}(XG) \ . \tag{1}$$

---

[3] We define $f^{-1}(x) \doteq \{y \in V \ . \ f(y) = x\}$.

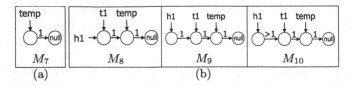

Fig. 6. (a) A subgraph at label L2 in Fig. 1, and (b) Subgraphs at L3 in Fig. 1

5.1   The Most Precise Abstract Transformer

We first show how the *most precise transformer* $[\![st]\!]^{GD} \doteq \alpha^{GD} \circ [\![st]\!]^{\#} \circ \gamma^{GD}$ can be computed *locally*, without concretizing complete shape graphs. As observed by Distefano et al. [3], the full heap abstraction transformer $[\![st]\!]^{\#}$ can be computed by considering only the *relevant* part of an abstract heap. We use this observation to create a local transformer for our graph decomposition abstraction.

The first step is to identify the subgraphs "referred" to by the statement *st*. Let *Vars(st)* denote the variables that occur in statement *st*. We define:

- The function $modcomps_{st} : 2^{SSG} \rightarrow 2^{SSG}$ returns the shape subgraphs that have a variable in *Vars(st)*: $modcomps_{st}(XG) \doteq \{G \in XG \mid Vars(G) \cap Vars(st) \neq \emptyset\}$.
- The function $samecomps_{st} : 2^{SSG} \rightarrow 2^{SSG}$ returns the complementary subset: $samecomps_{st}(XG) \doteq XG \setminus modcomps_{st}(XG)$.

Example 6. $modcomps_{\texttt{t1.n=temp}}(\{M_1, \dots, M_7\}) = \{M_1, M_2, M_3, M_7\}$ and $samecomps_{\texttt{t1.n=temp}}(\{M_1, \dots, M_7\}) = \{M_4, M_5, M_6\}$.   □

Note that the transformer $[\![st]\!]^{\#}$ operates on *complete* shape graphs. However, the transformer can be applied, in a straightforward fashion, to any shape *subgraph* G as long as G contains all variables mentioned in *st* (i.e., $Vars(G) \supseteq Vars(st)$). Thus, our next step is to compose subgraphs in $modcomps_{st}(XG)$ to generate subgraphs that contain all variables of *st*. However, not every set of subgraphs in $modcomps_{st}(XG)$ is a candidate for this composition step.

Given a set of subgraphs XG, a set $XG' \subseteq XG$, is defined to be *weakly feasible* in XG if $compose(XG') \neq \bot$. Further, we say that XG' is *feasible* in XG if there exists a subset $XR \subseteq XG$ such that $compose(XG' \cup XR)$ is an admissible shape graph (i.e., $\exists G \in SG : XG' \subseteq \alpha^{GD}(G) \subseteq XG$).

Example 7. The subgraphs M_1 and M_7 are feasible in $\{M_1, \dots, M_7\}$, since they can be composed with M_4 to yield an admissible shape graph. However, M_1 and M_2 contain common variables and thus $\{M_1, M_2\}$ is not (even weakly) feasible in $\{M_1, \dots, M_7\}$. In Fig. 7, the shape subgraphs M_1 and M_4 are weakly-feasible but not feasible in $\{M_1, \dots, M_5\}$ (there is no way to compose subgraphs to include w, since M_1 and M_2 and M_3 and M_4 are not weakly-feasible.).   □

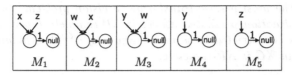

Fig. 7. A set of shape subgraphs over the set of program variables {x,y,z,w}

Let st be a statement with $k \doteq |Vars(st)|$ variables ($k \leq 2$ in our language). Let $M^{(\leq k)}$ denote all subsets of size k or less of a set M. We define the transformer for a heap-mutating statement st by:

$$T_{st}^{GD}(XG) \doteq \textbf{let } Y = \{[\![st]\!]^{\#}(G) \mid M = modcomps_{st}(XG), R \in M^{(\leq k)},$$
$$G = compose(R), Vars(st) \subseteq Vars(G),$$
$$R \text{ is feasible in } XG\}$$
$$\textbf{in } samecomps_{st}(XG) \cup \alpha^{GD}(Y) \ .$$

The transformer for an assume statement st is slightly different. An assume statement does not modify incoming subgraphs, but filters out some subgraphs that are not consistent with the condition specified in the assume statement. Note that it is possible for even subgraphs in $samecomps_{st}(XG)$ to be filtered out by the assume statement, as shown by the following definition of the transformer:

$$T_{st}^{GD}(XG) \doteq \textbf{let } Y = \{[\![st]\!]^{\#}(G) \mid R \in XG^{(\leq k+1)},$$
$$G = compose(R), Vars(st) \subseteq Vars(G),$$
$$R \text{ is feasible in } XG\}$$
$$\textbf{in } \alpha^{GD}(Y) \ .$$

Example 8. The transformer $T_{\texttt{t1.n=temp}}^{GD}$: (a) composes subgraphs: $compose(M_1, M_7)$, $compose(M_2, M_7)$, and $compose(M_3, M_7)$; (b) finds that the three pairs of subgraphs are feasible in $\{M_1, \ldots, M_7\}$; (c) applies the local full heap abstraction transformer $[\![\texttt{t1.n=temp}]\!]^{\#}$, producing M_8, M_9, and M_{10}, respectively; and (d) returns the final result: $T_{\texttt{t1.n=temp}}^{GD}(\{M_1, \ldots, M_7\}) = \{M_4, M_5, M_6\} \cup \{M_8, M_9, M_{10}\}$. □

Theorem 1. *The transformer T_{st}^{GD} is the most precise abstract transformer.*

Although T_{st}^{GD} applies $[\![st]\!]^{\#}$ to a polynomial number of shape subgraphs and $[\![st]\!]^{\#}$ itself can be computed in polynomial time, the above transformer is still exponential in the worst-case, because of the difficulty of checking the feasibility of R in XG. In fact, as we now show, it is impossible to compute the most precise transformer in *polynomial time*, unless P=NP.

Definition 5 (Most Precise Transformer Decision Problem). *The decision version of the most precise transformer problem is as follows: for a set of atomic shape subgraphs XG, a statement st, and an atomic shape subgraph G, does G belong to $[\![st]\!]^{GD}(XG)$?*

Theorem 2. *The most precise transformer decision problem, for the graph decomposition abstraction presented above, is NP-complete (even when the input set of subgraphs is restricted to be in the image of α^{GD}). Similarly, checking if XG' is feasible in XG is NP-complete.*

Proof (sketch). By reduction from the EXACT COVER problem: given a universe $U = \{u_1, \ldots, u_n\}$ of elements and a collection of subsets $A \subseteq 2^U$, decide whether there exists a subset $B \subseteq A$ such that every element $u \in U$ is contained in exactly one set in B. EXACT COVER is known to be NP-complete [4].   □

5.2   Sound and Efficient Transformers

We safely replace the check for whether R is feasible in XG by a check for whether R is weakly-feasible (i.e., whether $compose(R) \neq \perp$) and obtain the following transformer. (Note that a set of subgraphs is weakly-feasible iff no two of the subgraphs have a common variable; hence, the check for weak feasibility is easy.) For a heap-manipulating statement st, we define the transformer by:

$$\widehat{T_{st}^{GD}}(XG) \doteq \text{let } Y = \{[\![st]\!]^{\#}(G) \mid M = modcomps_{st}(XG), R \in M^{(\leq k)},$$
$$G = compose(R) \neq \perp, Vars(st) \subseteq Vars(G)\}$$
$$\text{in } samecomps_{st}(XG) \cup \alpha^{GD}(Y) \ .$$

For an assume statement st, we define the transformer by:

$$\widehat{T_{st}^{GD}}(XG) \doteq \text{let } Y = \{[\![st]\!]^{\#}(G) \mid R \in XG^{(\leq k+1)},$$
$$G = compose(R) \neq \perp, Vars(st) \subseteq Vars(G)\}$$
$$\text{in } \alpha^{GD}(Y) \ .$$

By definition, (1) holds for $\widehat{T_{st}^{GD}}$. Thus, $\widehat{T_{st}^{GD}}$ is a sound transformer.

We apply several engineering optimizations to make the transformer $\widehat{T_{st}^{GD}}$ efficient in practice: (i) by preceding statements of the form x=y and x=y.n with an assignment x=null, we specialize the transformer to achieve linear time complexity; (ii) we avoid unnecessary compositions of shape subgraphs for statements of the form x.n=y and assume(x==y), when a shape subgraph contains both x and y; and (iii) assume statements do not change subgraphs, therefore we avoid performing explicit compositions and propagate atomic subgraphs.

5.3   An Incremental Transformer

The goal of an *incremental* transformer is to compute $\widehat{T_{st}^{GD}}(XG \cup \{D\})$ by reusing $\widehat{T_{st}^{GD}}(XG)$. We define the transformer for a heap-manipulating statement st by:

$$\widehat{T_{st}^{GD}}(XG \cup \{D\}) \doteq \text{if } D \in modcomps_{st}(\{D\})$$
$$\text{let } Y = \{[\![st]\!]^{\#}(G) \mid M = modcomps_{st}(XG \cup \{D\}),$$
$$R \in M^{(\leq k)}, D \in R,$$
$$G = compose(R) \neq \perp, Vars(st) \subseteq Vars(G)\}$$

$$\text{in } \widehat{T_{st}^{GD}}(XG) \cup \alpha^{GD}(Y)$$
$$\textbf{else}$$
$$\widehat{T_{st}^{GD}}(XG) \cup \{D\} \ .$$

Here, if the new subgraph D is not affected by the statement, we simply add it to the result. Otherwise, we apply the local full heap abstraction transformer only to subgraphs composed from the new subgraph (for sets of subgraphs not containing D, the result has been computed in the previous iteration).

For an assume statement st, we define the transformer by:

$$\widehat{T_{st}^{GD}}(XG \cup \{D\}) \doteq \textbf{let } Y = \{[\![st]\!]^{\#}(G) \mid R \in (XG \cup \{D\})^{(\leq k+1)},$$
$$D \in R, G = compose(R) \neq \bot, Vars(st) \subseteq Vars(G)\}$$
$$\textbf{in } \widehat{T_{st}^{GD}}(XG) \cup \alpha^{GD}(Y) \ .$$

Again, we apply the transformer only to (composed) subgraphs containing D.

6   Prototype Implementation and Empirical Results

Implementation. We implemented the analyses based on the full heap abstraction and the graph decomposition abstraction described in previous sections in a system that supports memory deallocation and assertions of the form `assertAcyclicList(x)`, `assertCyclicList(x)`, `assertDisjointLists(x,y)`, and `assertReach(x,y)`. The analysis checks null dereferences, memory leakage, misuse of dangling pointers, and assertions. The system supports non-recursive procedure calls via call strings and unmaps variables as they become dead.

Example Programs. We use a set of examples to compare the full heap abstraction-based analysis with the graph decomposition-based analysis. The first set of examples consists of standard list manipulating algorithms operating on a single list (except for **merge**). The second set of examples consists of programs manipulating multiple lists: the running example, testing an implementation of a queue by two stacks[4], joining 5 lists, splitting a list into 5 lists, and two programs that model aspects of device drivers. We created the serial port driver example incrementally, first modeling 4 of the lists used by the device and then 5.

Precision. The results of running the analyses appear in Tab. 2. The graph decomposition-based analysis failed to prove that the pointer returned by `getLast` is non-null[5], and that a dequeue operation is not applied to an empty queue in `queue_2_stacks`. On all other examples, the graph decomposition-based analysis has the same precision as the analysis based on the full heap abstraction.

---

[4] `queue_2_stacks` was constructed to show a case where the graph decomposition-based analysis loses precision—determining that a queue is empty requires maintaining a correlation between the two (empty) lists.

[5] A simple feasibility check while applying the transformer of the assertion would have eliminated the subgraph containing the null pointer.

Performance. The graph decomposition-based analysis is slightly less efficient than the analysis based on the full heap abstraction on the standard list examples. For the examples manipulating multiple lists, the graph decomposition-based analysis is faster by up to a factor of 212 (in the `serial_5_lists` example) and consumes considerably less space. These results are also consistent with the number of states generated by the two analyses.

Table 2. Time, space, number of states (shape graphs for the analysis based on full heap abstraction and subgraphs for the graph decomposition-based analysis), and number of errors reported. Rep. Err. and Act. Err. are the number of errors reported, and the number of errors that indicate real problems, respectively. #Loc indicates the number of CFG locations. F.H. and G.D. stand for full heap and graph decomposition, respectively.

Benchmark (#Loc)		Time (sec.)		Space (Mb.)		#States		R. Err./A. Err.	
		F.H.	G.D.	F.H.	G.D.	F.H.	G.D.	F.H.	G.D.
create	(11)	0.03	0.19	0.3	0.3	27	36	0/0	0/0
delete	(25)	0.17	0.27	0.8	0.9	202	260	0/0	0/0
deleteAll	(12)	0.05	0.09	0.32	0.36	35	64	0/0	0/0
getLast	(13)	0.06	0.13	0.42	0.47	67	99	0/0	1/0
getLast_cyclic	(13)	0.08	0.09	0.39	0.41	53	59	0/0	0/0
insert	(23)	0.14	0.28	0.75	0.82	167	222	0/0	0/0
merge	(37)	0.34	0.58	2.2	1.7	517	542	0/0	0/0
removeSeg	(23)	0.19	0.33	0.96	1.0	253	283	0/0	0/0
reverse	(13)	0.09	0.12	0.47	0.46	82	117	0/0	0/0
reverse_cyclic	(14)	0.14	0.36	0.6	1.4	129	392	0/0	0/0
reverse_pan	(12)	0.2	0.6	0.9	2.2	198	561	0/0	0/0
rotate	(17)	0.05	0.08	0.3	0.4	33	50	0/0	0/0
search_nulldref	(7)	0.06	0.1	0.4	0.4	48	62	1/1	1/1
swap	(13)	0.05	0.09	0.3	0.4	35	62	0/0	0/0
enqueueEvents	(49)	0.2	0.2	1.2	0.7	248	178	0/0	0/0
queue_2_stacks	(61)	0.1	0.2	0.6	0.7	110	216	0/0	1/0
join_5	(68)	12.5	0.5	67.0	2.4	14,704	1,227	0/0	0/0
split_5	(47)	28.5	0.3	126.2	1.7	27,701	827	0/0	0/0
1394diag	(180)	26.2	1.8	64.7	8.5	10,737	4,493	0/0	0/0
serial_4_lists	(248)	36.9	1.7	230.1	11.7	27,851	6,020	0/0	0/0
serial_5_lists	(278)	552.6	2.6	849.2	16.4	89,430	7,733	0/0	0/0

7   Related Work

Single-graph Abstractions. Some early shape analyses used a single shape graph to represent the set of concrete states [8,1,16]. As noted earlier, it is possible to generalize our approach and consider different strategies for decomposing shape graphs. Interestingly, the single shape graph abstractions can be seen as one extreme point of such a generalized approach, which relies on a decomposition of a graph into its set of edges. The decomposition strategy we presented in this paper leads to a more precise analysis.

Partially Disjunctive Heap Abstraction. In previous work [12], we described a heap abstraction based on merging sets of graphs with the same set of nodes into one (approximate) graph. The abstraction in the current paper is based on decomposing a graph into a set of subgraphs. The abstraction in [12] suffers from the same exponential blow-ups as the full heap abstraction for our running example and examples containing multiple independent data structures.

Heap Analysis by Separation. Yahav et al. [18] and Hackett et al. [6] decompose heap abstractions to separately analyze different parts of the heap (e.g., to establish the invariants of different objects). A central aspect of the separation-based approach is that the analysis/verification problem is itself decomposed into a set of problem instances, and the heap abstraction is specialized for each problem instance and consists of one sub-heap consisting of the part of the heap relevant to the problem instance, and a coarser abstraction of the remaining part of the heap ([6] uses a points-to graph). In contrast, we simultaneously maintain abstractions of different parts of the heap and also consider the interaction between these parts. (E.g., it is possible for our decomposition to dynamically change as components get connected and disconnected.)

Application to Other Shape Abstractions. Lev-Ami et al. [9] present an abstraction that could be seen as an extension of the full heap abstraction in this paper to more complex data structures, e.g., doubly-linked lists and trees. We believe that applying the techniques in this paper to their analysis is quite natural and can yield a more scalable analysis for more complex data structures. Distefano et al. [3] present a full heap abstraction based on separation logic, which is similar to the full heap abstraction presented in this paper. We therefore believe that it is possible to apply the techniques in this paper to their analysis as well. TVLA[10] is a generic shape analysis system that uses canonical abstraction. We believe it is possible to decompose logical structures in a similar way to decomposing shape subgraphs and extend the ideas in this paper to TVLA.

Decomposing Heap Abstractions for Interprocedural Analysis. Gotsman et al. [5] and Rinetzky et al. [14,15] decompose heap abstractions to create procedure summaries for full heap+ abstractions. This kind of decomposition, which does not lead to loss of precision (except when cutpoints are abstracted), is orthogonal to our decomposition of heaps, which is used to reduce the number of abstract states generated by the analysis. We believe it is possible to combine the two techniques to achieve a more efficient interprocedural shape analysis.

Acknowledgements. We thank Joseph Joy from MSR India for helpful discussions on Windows device drivers.

References

1. D. R. Chase, M. Wegman, and F. Zadeck. Analysis of pointers and structures. In *Proc. Conf. on Prog. Lang. Design and Impl.*, New York, NY, 1990. ACM Press.
2. P. Cousot and R. Cousot. Abstract interpretation: a unified lattice model for static analysis of programs by construction or approximation of fixpoints. In *Conference Record of the Fourth Annual ACM SIGPLAN-SIGACT Symposium on Principles of Programming Languages*, Los Angeles, California, 1977. ACM Press, New York, NY.
3. D. Distefano, P. W. O'Hearn, and H. Yang. A local shape analysis based on separation logic. In *In Proc. 13th Intern. Conf. on Tools and Algorithms for the Construction and Analysis of Systems (TACAS'06)*, 2006.
4. M. R. Garey and D. S. Johnson. *Computers and Intractability, A Guide to the Theory of NP-Completeness.* W. H. Freeman and Company, New York, 1979.
5. A. Gotsman, J. Berdine, and B. Cook. Interprocedural shape analysis with separated heap abstractions. In *Proceedings of the 13th International Static Analysis Symposium (SAS'06)*, 2006.
6. B. Hackett and R. Rugina. Region-based shape analysis with tracked locations. In *Proc. Symp. on Principles of Prog. Languages*, 2005.
7. N. D. Jones and S. S. Muchnick. Complexity of flow analysis, inductive assertion synthesis, and a language due to dijkstra. In *Program Flow Analysis: Theory and Applications*, chapter 12. Prentice-Hall, Englewood Cliffs, NJ, 1981.
8. N. D. Jones and S. S. Muchnick. Flow analysis and optimization of Lisp-like structures. In S. S. Muchnick and N. D. Jones, editors, *Program Flow Analysis: Theory and Applications*, chapter 4. Prentice-Hall, Englewood Cliffs, NJ, 1981.
9. T. Lev-Ami, N. Immerman, and M. Sagiv. Abstraction for shape analysis with fast and precise transformers. In *CAV*, 2006.
10. T. Lev-Ami and M. Sagiv. TVLA: A system for implementing static analyses. In *Proc. Static Analysis Symp.*, 2000.
11. R. Manevich, J. Berdine, B. Cook, G. Ramalingam, and M. Sagiv. Shape analysis by graph decomposition. 2006. Full version.
12. R. Manevich, M. Sagiv, G. Ramalingam, and J. Field. Partially disjunctive heap abstraction. In *Proceedings of the 11th International Symposium, SAS 2004*, Lecture Notes in Computer Science. Springer, August 2004.
13. R. Manevich, E. Yahav, G. Ramalingam, and M. Sagiv. Predicate abstraction and canonical abstraction for singly-linked lists. In *Proceedings of the 6th International Conference on Verification, Model Checking and Abstract Interpretation, VMCAI 2005*. Springer, January 2005.
14. N. Rinetzky, J. Bauer, T. Reps, M. Sagiv, and R. Wilhelm. A semantics for procedure local heaps and its abstractions. In *32nd Annual ACM SIGPLAN-SIGACT Symposium on Principles of Programming Languages (POPL'05)*, 2005.
15. N. Rinetzky, M. Sagiv, and E. Yahav. Interprocedural shape analysis for cutpoint-free programs. In *12th International Static Analysis Symposium (SAS)*, 2005.
16. M. Sagiv, T. Reps, and R. Wilhelm. Solving shape-analysis problems in languages with destructive updating. *ACM Transactions on Programming Languages and Systems*, 20(1), January 1998.
17. M. Sagiv, T. Reps, and R. Wilhelm. Parametric shape analysis via 3-valued logic. *ACM Transactions on Programming Languages and Systems*, 2002.
18. E. Yahav and G. Ramalingam. Verifying safety properties using separation and heterogeneous abstractions. In *Proceedings of the ACM SIGPLAN 2004 conference on Programming language design and implementation*, 2004.

A Reachability Predicate for Analyzing Low-Level Software

Shaunak Chatterjee[1], Shuvendu K. Lahiri[2], Shaz Qadeer[2], and Zvonimir Rakamarić[3]

[1] Indian Institute of Technology, Kharagpur
[2] Microsoft Research
[3] University of British Columbia

Abstract. Reasoning about heap-allocated data structures such as linked lists and arrays is challenging. The *reachability* predicate has proved to be useful for reasoning about the heap in type-safe languages where memory is manipulated by dereferencing object fields. Sound and precise analysis for such data structures becomes significantly more challenging in the presence of low-level pointer manipulation that is prevalent in systems software.

In this paper, we give a novel formalization of the reachability predicate in the presence of internal pointers and pointer arithmetic. We have designed an annotation language for C programs that makes use of the new predicate. This language enables us to specify properties of many interesting data structures present in the Windows kernel. We present preliminary experience with a prototype verifier on a set of illustrative C benchmarks.

1 Introduction

Static software verification has the potential to improve programmer productivity and reduce the cost of producing reliable software. By finding errors at the time of compilation, these techniques help avoid costly software changes late in the development cycle and after deployment. Many successful tools for detecting errors in systems software have emerged in the last decade [2,16,10]. These tools can scale to large software systems; however, this scalability is achieved at the price of precision. Heap-allocated data structures are one of the most significant sources of imprecision for these tools. Fundamental correctness properties, such as control and memory safety, depend on intermediate assertions about the contents of data structures. Therefore, imprecise reasoning about the heap usually results in a large number of annoying false warnings increasing the probability of missing the real errors.

The *reachability predicate* is important for specifying properties of *linked* data structures. Informally, a memory location v is reachable from a memory location u in a heap if either $u = v$ or u contains the address of a location x and v is reachable from x. Automated reasoning about the reachability predicate is difficult for two reasons. First, reachability cannot be expressed in first-order

O. Grumberg and M. Huth (Eds.): TACAS 2007, LNCS 4424, pp. 19–33, 2007.

logic, the input language of choice for most modern and scalable automated theorem provers. Second, it is difficult to precisely specify the update to the reachability predicate when a heap location is updated.

Previous work has addressed these problems in the context of a reachability predicate suitable for verifying programs written in high-level languages such as Java and C# [22,18,1,17,5]. This predicate is inadequate for reasoning about low-level software, which commonly uses programming idioms such as internal pointers (addresses of object fields) and pointer arithmetic to move between object fields. We illustrate this point with several examples in Section 2.

The goal of our work is to build a scalable verifier for systems software that can reason precisely about heap-allocated data structures. To this end, we introduce in this paper a new reachability predicate suitable for verifying low-level programs written in C. We describe how to automatically compute the precise update for the new predicate and a method for reasoning about it using automated first-order theorem provers. We have designed a specification language that uses our reachability predicate, allows succinct specification of interesting properties of low-level software, and is conducive to modular program verification. We have implemented a modular verifier for annotated C programs called HAVOC (Heap-Aware Verifier Of C). We report on our preliminary encouraging experience with HAVOC on a set of small but interesting C programs.

1.1 Related Work

HAVOC is a static assertion checker for C programs in the same style that ESC/Java [15] is a static checker for Java programs, and Spec# [4] is a static checker for C# programs. However, HAVOC is different in that it deals with the low-level intricacies of C and provides reachability as a fundamental primitive in its specification language. The ability to specify reachability properties also distinguishes HAVOC from other assertion checkers for C such as CBMC [9] and SATURN [23]. The work of McPeak and Necula [20] allows reasoning about reachability, but only indirectly using ghost fields in heap-allocated objects. These ghost fields must be updated manually by the programmer whereas HAVOC provides the update to its reachability predicate automatically.

There are several verifiers that do allow the verification of properties based on the reachability predicate. TVLA [19] is a verification tool based on abstract interpretation using 3-valued logic [22]. It provides a general specification logic combining first-order logic with reachability. Recently, they have also added an axiomatization of reachability in first-order logic to the system [18]. However, TVLA has mostly been applied to Java programs and, to our knowledge, cannot handle the interaction of reachability with pointer arithmetic.

Caduceus [14] is a modular verifier for C programs. It allows the programmer to write specifications in terms of arbitrary recursive predicates, which are axiomatized in an external theorem prover. It then allows the programmer to interactively verify the generated verification conditions in that prover. HAVOC only allows the use of a fixed set of reachability predicates but provides much more automation than Caduceus. All the verification conditions generated by

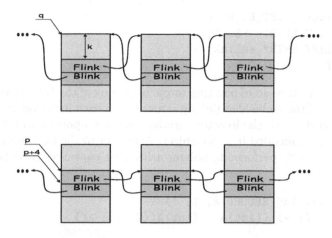

Fig. 1. Doubly-linked lists in Java and C

HAVOC are discharged automatically using SMT (satisfiability modulo-theories) provers. Unlike Caduceus, HAVOC understands internal pointers and the use of pointer arithmetic to move between fields of an object.

Calcagno et al. have used separation logic to reason about memory safety and absence of memory leaks in low-level code [7]. They perform abstract interpretation using rewrite rules that are tailored for "multi-word lists", a fixed predicate expressed in separation logic. Our approach is more general since we provide a family of reachability predicates, which the programmer can compose arbitrarily for writing richer specifications (possibly involving quantifiers); the rewriting involved in the generation and validation of verification conditions is taken care of automatically by HAVOC. Their tool can infer loop invariants but handles procedures by inlining. In contrast, HAVOC performs modular reasoning, but does not infer loop invariants.

2   Motivation

Consider the two doubly-linked lists shown in Figure 1. The list at the top is typical of high-level object-oriented programs. The linking fields Flink and Blink point to the *beginning* of the successor and predecessor objects in the list. In each iteration of a loop that iterates over the linked list, the iterator variable points to the beginning of a list object whose contents are accessed by a simple field dereference. Existing work would allow properties of this linked list to be specified using the two reachability predicates R_{Flink} and R_{Blink}, each of which is a binary relation on *objects*. For example, $R_{\text{Flink}}(a, b)$ holds for objects a and b if $a.\text{Flink}^i = b$ for some $i \geq 0$.

The list at the bottom is typical of low-level systems software. Such a list is constructed by embedding a structure LIST_ENTRY containing the two fields, Flink and Blink, into the objects that are supposed to be linked by the list.

```
typedef struct _LIST_ENTRY {
  struct _LIST_ENTRY *Flink;
  struct _LIST_ENTRY *Blink;
} LIST_ENTRY;
```

The linking fields, instead of pointing to the beginning of the list objects, point to the beginning of the embedded linking structure. In each iteration of a loop that iterates over such a list, the iterator variable contains a pointer to the beginning of the structure embedded in a list object. A pointer to the beginning of the list object is obtained by performing pointer arithmetic captured with the following C macro.

```
#define CONTAINING_RECORD(a, T, f) \
            (T *) ((int)a - (int)&((T *)0)->f)
```

This macro expects an internal pointer a to a field f of an object of type T and returns a typed pointer to the beginning of the object.

There are two good engineering reasons for this ostensibly dangerous programming idiom. First, it becomes possible to write all list manipulation code for operations such as insertion and deletion separately in terms of the type LIST_ENTRY. Second, it becomes easy to have one object be a part of several different linked lists; there is a field of type LIST_ENTRY in the object corresponding to each list. For these reasons, this idiom is common both in the Windows and the Linux operating system[1].

Unfortunately, this programming idiom cannot be modeled using the predicates R_{Flink} and R_{Blink} described earlier. The fundamental reason is that these lists may link objects via pointers at a potentially non-zero offset into the objects. Different data structures might use different offsets; in fact, the offset used by a particular data structure is a crucial part of its specification. This is in stark contrast to the first kind of linked lists in which the linking offset is guaranteed to be zero.

The crucial insight underlying our work is that for analyzing low-level software, *the reachability predicate must be a relation on pointers rather than objects*. A pointer is a pair comprising an object and an integer offset into the object, and the program memory is a map from pointers to pointers. We introduce an integer-indexed set of binary reachability predicates: for each integer n, the predicate R_n is a binary relation on the set of pointers. Suppose n is an integer and p and q are *pointers*. Then $R_n(p, q)$ holds if and only if either $p = q$, or recursively $R_n(*(p + n), q)$ holds, where $*(p + n)$ is the pointer stored in memory at the address obtained by incrementing p by n.

Our reachability predicate captures the insight that in low-level programs a list of pointers is constructed by performing an alternating sequence of pointer arithmetic (with respect to a constant offset) and memory lookup operations. For example, let p be the address of the Flink field of an object in the linked list at the bottom of Figure 1. Then, the forward-going list is captured by the

---

[1] In Linux, the CONTAINING_RECORD macro corresponds to the list_entry macro.

```
typedef struct { int data; LIST_ENTRY link; } A;

struct { LIST_ENTRY a; } g;

requires BS(&g.a) && B(&g.a, 0) == &g.a
requires forall(x, list(g.a.Flink, 0), x == &g.a || Off(x) == 4)
requires forall(x, list(g.a.Flink, 0), x == &g.a || Obj(x) != Obj(&g.a))
modifies decr(list(g.a.Flink, 0), 4)
ensures forall(x, list(g.a.Flink, 0), x == &g.a || deref(x-4) == 42)

void list_iterate() {
  LIST_ENTRY *iter = g.a.Flink;
  while (iter != &(g.a)) {
    A *elem = CONTAINING_RECORD(iter, A, link);
    elem->data = 42;
    iter = iter->Flink;
  }
}
```

Fig. 2. Example

pointer sequence $p, *(p + 0), *(*(p + 0) + 0), \ldots$. Similarly, assuming that the size of a pointer is 4, the backward-going list is captured by the pointer sequence $p, *(p + 4), *(*(p + 4) + 4), \ldots$.

The new reachability predicate is a generalization of the existing reachability predicate and can just as well describe the linked list at the top of Figure 1. Suppose the offset of the Flink field in the linked objects is k and q is the address of the start of some object in the list. Then, the forward-going list is captured by $q, *(q+k), *(*(q+k)+k), \ldots$ and the backward-going list is captured by $q, *(q + k + 4), *(*(q + k + 4) + k + 4), \ldots$.

2.1 Example

We illustrate the use of our reachability predicate in program verification with the example in Figure 2. The example has a type A and a global structure g with a field a. The field a in g and the field link in the type A have the type LIST_ENTRY, which was defined earlier. These fields are used to link together in a circular doubly-linked list the object g and a set of objects of type A. The field a in g is the dummy head of this list. The procedure list_iterate iterates over this list setting the data field of each list element to 42.

In addition to verifying the safety of each memory access in list_iterate, we would like to verify two additional properties. First, the only parts of the caller-visible state modified by list_iterate are the data fields of the list elements. Second, the data field of each list element is 42 when list_iterate terminates.

To prove these properties on list_iterate, it is crucial to have a precondition stating that the list of objects linked by the Flink field of LIST_ENTRY is circular.

To specify this property, we extend the notion of well-founded lists, first described in an earlier paper [17], to our new reachability predicate. The predicate R_n is well-founded with respect to a set BS of *blocking pointers* if for all pointers p, the sequence $*(p + n), *(*(p + n) + n), \ldots$ contains a pointer in BS. This member of BS is called the *block* of p with respect to the offset n and is denoted by $B_n[p]$. Typical members of BS include pointer values that indicate the end of linked lists, e.g., the null pointer or the head &g.a of the circular lists in our example.

Our checker HAVOC enforces a programming discipline associated with well-founded lists. HAVOC provides an *auxiliary* variable BS whose value is a set of pointers and allows program statements to add or remove pointers from BS. Further, each heap update in the program is required to preserve the well-foundedness of R_n with respect to each offset n of interest.

The first precondition of list_iterate uses the notion of well-foundedness to express that &g.a is the head of a circular list. In this precondition, B(&g.a,0) refers to B_0[&g.a]. We use B_0 to specify that the circular list is formed by the Flink field, which is at offset 0 within LIST_ENTRY. The second precondition illustrates how facts about an entire collection of pointers are expressed in our specification language. In this precondition, the expression list(g.a.Flink,0) refers to the finite and non-empty set of pointers in the sequence g.a.Flink,*(g.a.Flink + 0), ... upto but excluding the pointer B_0(g.a.Flink). Also, the function Off retrieves the offset (or the second component) from a pointer. This precondition states that the offset of each pointer in list(g.a.Flink,0), excluding the dummy head, is equal to 4, the offset of the field sequence link.Flink in the type A. The third precondition uses the function Obj, which retrieves the object (or the first component) from a pointer. This precondition says that the object of each pointer, excluding the dummy head, in list(g.a.Flink,0) is different from the object of the dummy head.

The modifies clause illustrates yet another constructor of a set of pointers provided by our language. If S is a set of pointers, then $\text{decr}(S, n)$ is the set of pointers obtained by decrementing each pointer in S by n. The modifies clause captures the update of the data field at relative offset -4 from the members of list(g.a.Flink,0).

The postcondition of the procedure introduces the operator deref, which returns the content of the memory at a pointer address. This postcondition says that the value of the data field of each object in the list, excluding the dummy head, is 42.

Using loop invariants provided by us (not shown in the figure), HAVOC is able to verify that the implementation of this procedure satisfies its specification. Note that in the presence of potentially unsafe pointer arithmetic and casts, it is nontrivial to verify that the heap update operation elem->data := 42 does not change the linking structure of the list. Since HAVOC cannot rely on the static type of the variable elem, it must prove that the offset of elem before the operation is 0 and therefore the operation cannot modify either linking field.

```
typedef struct { int x; int y[10]; } DATA;
```

```
DATA *create() {                      procedure create() returns d:ptr {
  int a;                                var a:ptr;
                                        a := call malloc(4);
  DATA *d =                             d := call malloc(44);
    (DATA *) malloc(sizeof(DATA));
  init(d->y, 10, &a);                   call init(PLUS(d, Ptr(null,4)),
                                                  Ptr(null,10), a);
  d->x = a;                             Mem[PLUS(d, Ptr(null,0))] := Mem[a];
                                        call free(a);
  return d;
}                                     }

void init(int *in, int size,          procedure init(in:ptr, size:ptr,
            int *out) {                              out:ptr) {
  int i;                                var i:ptr;
  i = 0;                                i := Ptr(null,0);
  while (i < size) {                    while (LT(i, size)) {
    in[i] = i;                            Mem[PLUS(in, i)] := i;
    *out = *out + i;                      Mem[out] := PLUS(Mem[out], i);
    i++;                                  i := PLUS(i, Ptr(null,1));
  }                                     }
}                                     }
```

Fig. 3. Translation of C programs

3 Operational Semantics of C

Our semantics for C programs depends on three fundamental types, the uninterpreted type **ref** of object references, the type **int** of integers, and the type **ptr** = **ref** × **int** of pointers. Each variable in a C program, regardless of its static type, contains a pointer value. A *pointer* is a pair containing an object reference and an integer offset. An integer value is encoded as a pointer value whose first component is the special constant **null** of type **ref**. The constructor function Ptr : **ref** × **int** → **ptr** constructs a pointer value from its components. The selector functions Obj : **ptr** → **ref** and Off : **ptr** → **int** retrieve the first and second component of a pointer value, respectively.

The heap of a C program is modeled using two map variables, Mem and Alloc, and a map constant Size. The variable Mem maps pointers to pointers and intuitively represents the contents of the memory at a pointer location. The variable Alloc maps object references to the set {UNALLOCATED, ALLOCATED, FREED} and is used to model memory allocation. The constant Size maps object references to positive integers and represents the size of the object. The procedure call malloc(n) for allocating a memory buffer of size n returns a pointer $Ptr(o, 0)$ where o is an object such that Alloc$[o]$ = UNALLOCATED before the call and Size$[o] \geq n$. The procedure modifies Alloc$[o]$ to be ALLOCATED. The procedure call free(p) for freeing a memory buffer whose address is contained in p requires that `Alloc[Obj(p)] == ALLOCATED` and `Off(p) == 0` and updates `Alloc[Obj(p)]` to `FREED`. The full specification of `malloc` and `free` is given in a detailed report [8].

HAVOC takes an annotated C program and translates it into a BoogiePL [11] program. BoogiePL has been designed to be an intermediate language for program verification tools that use automated theorem provers. This language is simple and has well-defined semantics. The operational semantics of C, as interpreted by HAVOC, is best understood by comparing a C program with its BoogiePL translation. Figure 3 shows two procedures, `create` and `init`, on the left and their translations on the right. The example uses the C struct type `DATA`.

Note that variables of both static type `int` and `int*` in C are translated uniformly as variables of type `ptr`. The translation of the first argument `d->y` of the call to `init` shows that we treat field accesses and pointer arithmetic uniformly. Since the field `y` is at an offset 4 in `DATA`, we treat `d->y` as `d+4`. The translation uses the function `PLUS` to model pointer arithmetic and the function `LT` to model arithmetic comparison operations on the type `ptr`. The definitions of these functions are also given in the detailed report [8].

The example also shows how we handle the `&` operator. In the procedure `create`, the address of the local variable `a` is passed as an out-parameter to the procedure `init`. Our translation handles this case by allocating `a` on the heap. Note that our translator allocates a static variable on the heap only if the program takes the address of that variable. For example, there is no heap allocation for the local variable `i` in the procedure `init`. To prevent access to the heap-allocated object corresponding to a local variable of a procedure, it is freed at the end of the procedure.

4   Reachability and Pointer Arithmetic

We now give the formal definition of our new reachability predicate in terms of the operational semantics of C as interpreted by HAVOC. As in our previous work [17], we define the reachability predicate on well-founded heaps. Let the heap be represented by the function $\text{Mem} : \text{ptr} \to \text{ptr}$ and let $\text{BS} \subseteq \text{ptr}$ be a set of pointers. We define a sequence of functions $f^i : \text{int} \times \text{ptr} \to \text{ptr}$ for $i \geq 0$ as follows: for all $n \in \text{int}$ and $u \in \text{ptr}$, we have $f^0(n, u) = u$ and $f^{i+1}(n, u) = \text{Mem}[f^i(n, u) + n]$ for all $i > 0$. Then Mem is *well-founded* with respect to the set of *blocking pointers* BS and *offset* n if for all $u \in \text{ptr}$, there is $i > 0$ such that $f^i(n, u) \in \text{BS}$. If a heap is well-founded with respect to BS and n, then the function idx_n maps a pointer u to the least $i > 0$ such that $f^i(n, u) \in \text{BS}$. Using these concepts, we now define for each $n \in \text{int}$, a predicate $\text{R}_n \subseteq \text{ptr} \times \text{ptr}$ and a function $\text{B}_n : \text{ptr} \to \text{ptr}$.

$$\text{R}_n[u, v] \equiv \exists i.\ 0 \leq i < idx_n(u) \land v = f^i(n, u)$$
$$\text{B}_n[u] \equiv f^{idx_n(u)}(n, u)$$

Suppose a program performs the operation `Mem[x] := y` to update the heap. Then HAVOC performs the *most precise* update to the predicate R_n and the function B_n by automatically inserting the following code just before the operation.

$$
\begin{aligned}
n \in \quad & int \\
e \in \quad & Expr ::= n \mid \texttt{x} \mid \texttt{addr}(\texttt{x}) \mid e + e \mid e - e \mid \texttt{deref}(e) \mid \texttt{block}(e,n) \mid \\
& \quad \texttt{old}(\texttt{x}) \mid \texttt{old\_deref}(e) \mid \texttt{old\_block}(e,n) \\
S \in \quad & Set ::= \{e\} \mid \texttt{BS} \mid \texttt{list}(e,n) \mid \texttt{old\_list}(e,n) \mid \texttt{array}(e,n,e) \\
\phi \in \quad & Formula ::= \texttt{alloc}(e) \mid \texttt{old\_alloc}(e) \mid \texttt{Obj}(e) == \texttt{Obj}(e) \mid \texttt{Off}(e) < \texttt{Off}(e) \mid \\
& \quad \texttt{in}(e,S) \mid \; ! \; \phi \mid \phi \; \&\& \; \phi \mid \texttt{forall}(\texttt{x},S,\phi) \\
C \in \quad & CmpdSet ::= S \mid \texttt{incr}(C,n) \mid \texttt{decr}(C,n) \mid \texttt{deref}(C) \mid \texttt{old\_deref}(C) \\
& \quad \texttt{union}(C,C) \mid \texttt{intersection}(C,C) \mid \texttt{difference}(C,C)
\end{aligned}
$$

Fig. 4. Annotation language

$$
\begin{aligned}
& \texttt{assert}(R_n[\texttt{y}, \texttt{x} - n] \Rightarrow \texttt{BS}[\texttt{y}]) \\
& B_n := \lambda\, \texttt{u} : \texttt{ptr}. \; R_n[\texttt{u}, \texttt{x} - n]? \; (\texttt{BS}[\texttt{y}] \; ? \; \texttt{y} \; : \; B_n[\texttt{y}]) : B_n[\texttt{u}] \\
& R_n := \lambda\, \texttt{u}, \texttt{v} : \texttt{ptr}. \\
& \qquad R_n[\texttt{u}, \texttt{x} - n] \\
& \qquad ? \; (R_n[\texttt{u}, \texttt{v}] \wedge \neg R_n[\texttt{x} - n, \texttt{v}]) \;\; \vee \;\; \texttt{v} = \texttt{x} - n \;\; \vee \;\; (\neg \texttt{BS}[\texttt{y}] \wedge R_n[\texttt{y}, \texttt{v}]) \\
& \qquad : \; R_n[\texttt{u}, \texttt{v}]
\end{aligned}
$$

The assertion enforces that the heap stays well-founded with respect to the blocking set BS and the offset n. The value of $B_n[\texttt{u}]$ is updated only if $\texttt{x} - n$ is reachable from $\texttt{u}$ and otherwise remains unchanged. Similarly, the value of $R_n[\texttt{u}, \texttt{v}]$ is updated only if $\texttt{x} - n$ is reachable from $\texttt{u}$ and otherwise remains unchanged. These updates are generalizations of the updates provided in our earlier paper [17] to account for pointer arithmetic.

We note that the ability to provide such updates as described above guarantees that if a program's assertions —preconditions, postconditions, and loop invariants— are quantifier-free, then its verification condition is quantifier-free as well. This property is valuable because the handling of quantifiers is typically the least complete and efficient aspect of all theorem provers that combine first-order reasoning with arithmetic.

5   Annotation Language

Our annotation language has three components: basic expressions that evaluate to pointers, set expressions that evaluate to sets of pointers, and formulas that evaluate to boolean values. The syntax for these expressions is given in Figure 4.

The set of basic expressions is captured by *Expr*. The expression $\texttt{addr}(\texttt{x})$ represents the address of the variable $\texttt{x}$. The expression $\texttt{x}$ represents the value of $\texttt{x}$ in the post-state and $\texttt{old}(\texttt{x})$ refers to the value of $\texttt{x}$ in the pre-state of the procedure. The expressions $\texttt{deref}(e)$ and $\texttt{old\_deref}(e)$ refer to the value stored in memory at the address e in the post-state and pre-state, respectively. The expressions $\texttt{block}(e, n)$ and $\texttt{old\_block}(e, n)$ represent $B_n[e]$ in the post-state and pre-state of the procedure, respectively.

The set expressions are divided into the basic set expressions in *Set* and the compound set expressions in *CmpdSet*. The expression $\texttt{array}(e_1, n, e_2)$ refers to the set of pointers $\{e_1, e_1 + n, e_1 + 2 * n, \ldots, e_1 + \texttt{Off}(e_2) * n\}$. The expressions

```
// translation of requires φ
requires ‖φ‖

// translation of ensures ψ
ensures ‖ψ‖

// translation of modifies C
modifies Mem
ensures forall x:ptr::        old(Alloc)[Obj(x)]  == UNALLOCATED ||
                              old(‖in(x,C)‖) ||
                              old(Mem)[x]  == Mem[x]

modifies R_n
ensures forall x:ptr::        old(Alloc)[Obj(x)]  == UNALLOCATED ||
                              exists y:ptr:: old(R_n)[x,y] && old(‖in(y + n, C)‖) ||
                              forall z:ptr:: old(R_n)[x,z]  == R_n[x,z]

modifies B_n
ensures forall x:ptr::        old(Alloc)[Obj(x)]  == UNALLOCATED ||
                              exists y:ptr:: old(R_n)[x,y] && old(‖in(y + n, C)‖) ||
                              old(B_n)[x]  == B_n[x]

// translation of frees D
modifies Alloc
ensures forall o:ref::        old(Alloc)[o]  == UNALLOCATED ||
                              (old(‖in(Ptr(o,0), D)‖) &&
                              Alloc[Obj(x)] != UNALLOCATED) ||
                              Alloc[x]  == old(Alloc)[x]
```

Fig. 5. Translation of requires ϕ, ensures ψ, modifies C, and frees D

$\text{list}(e, n)$ and $\text{old\_list}(e, n)$ represent the list of pointers described by the reachability predicate R_n in the post-state and pre-state, respectively. The compound set expressions include $\text{incr}(C, n)$ and $\text{decr}(C, n)$ which respectively increment and decrement each element of C by n, and $\text{deref}(C)$ and $\text{old\_deref}(C)$ which read the contents of memory at the members of C in the post-state and pre-state, respectively. The expressions $\text{union}(C, C)$, $\text{intersection}(C, C)$, and $\text{difference}(C, C)$ provide the basic set-theoretic operations.

HAVOC is designed to be a modular verifier. Consequently, we allow each procedure to be annotated by four possible specifications, requires ϕ, ensures ψ, modifies C, and frees D, where $\phi, \psi \in$ *Formula* and $C, D \in$ *CmpdSet*. The default value for ϕ and ψ is *true*, and for C and D is $\emptyset$. The translation of these specifications is given in Figure 5. The translation refers to the translation function $\| \circ \|$, which is defined in the Appendix of the detailed report [8]. We also allow each loop to be annotated with a formula representing its invariant.

In Figure 5, the translation of requires ϕ and ensures ψ is obtained in a straightforward fashion by applying the translation function $\| \circ \|$ to ϕ and ψ respectively. Then, there are four pairs of modifies and ensures clauses. The translation of modifies C is captured by the first three pairs and the translation of frees D is captured by the fourth pair. Our novel use of set expressions in these specifications results in a significant reduction in the annotation overhead at the C level.

The first pair of **modifies** and **ensures** clauses in Figure 5 states that the contents of Mem remains unchanged at each pointer that is allocated and not a member of C in the pre-state of the procedure. The second pair is parameterized by an integer offset n and specifies the update of R_n. Similarly, the third pair specifies the update of B_n. Based on the set C provided by the programmer in the **modifies** clause, one such pair is automatically generated for each offset n of interest. The postcondition corresponding to R_n says that if the set of pointers reachable from any pointer x is disjoint from the set $decr(C, n)$, then that set remains unchanged by the execution of the procedure. The postcondition corresponding to B_n says that if the set of pointers reachable from any pointer x is disjoint from the set $decr(C, n)$, then $B_n[x]$ remains unchanged by the execution of the procedure. These two postconditions are guaranteed by our semantics of reachability and the semantics of the **modifies** clause. Consequently, HAVOC only uses these postconditions at call sites and does not attempt to verify them. The set D in the annotation **frees** D is expected to contain only pointers with offset 0. Then, the fourth pair states that the contents of **Alloc** remain unchanged at each object that is allocated and is such that a pointer to the beginning of that object is not a member of D in the pre-state of the procedure.

6   Implementation

We have developed HAVOC, a prototype tool for verifying C programs annotated with specifications in our annotation language. We use the ESP [10] infrastructure to construct the control flow graph and parse the annotations. HAVOC translates an annotated C program into an annotated BoogiePL program as described in Section 3. The BOOGIE verifier generates a verification condition (VC) from the BoogiePL description, which implies the partial correctness of the BoogiePL program. The VC generation in BOOGIE is performed using a variation [3] of the standard *weakest precondition* transformer [13]. The resulting VC is checked for validity using the Simplify theorem prover [12].

6.1   Proving Verification Conditions

The verification condition generated is a formula in first-order logic with equality, augmented with the following theories:

1. The theory of integer linear arithmetic with symbols $+, \leq$ and constants $\ldots, -1, 0, 1, 2, \ldots$.
2. The theory of arrays with the **select** and **update** symbols [21].
3. The theory of *pairs*, consisting of the symbols for the pair constructor **Ptr**, and the selector functions **Obj** and **Off**.
4. The theory of the new reachability predicate, consisting of the symbols R_n, B_n, BS and Mem.

$$\forall u : \mathtt{ptr}. \ u = \mathtt{Ptr}(\mathtt{Obj}(u), \mathtt{Off}(u))$$
$$\forall x : \mathtt{ref}, i : \mathtt{int}. \ x = \mathtt{Obj}(\mathtt{Ptr}(x, i))$$
$$\forall x : \mathtt{ref}, i : \mathtt{int}. \ i = \mathtt{Off}(\mathtt{Ptr}(x, i))$$

Fig. 6. Axioms for the theory of pairs

To verify the verification conditions, the SIMPLIFY theorem prover requires axioms about the theory of pairs and the theory of reachability. The axioms for the theory of pairs are fairly intuitive and are given in Figure 6. The axioms for the theory of reachability are given in Figure 7. Note that the symbol $+$ in Figure 7 is the addition operation on pointers. We have overloaded $+$ for ease of exposition. The first axiom defines that $R_n[u, v]$ is true if and only if either $v = u$, or the pointer $\mathtt{Mem}[u + n]$ is not a blocking pointer in BS and $R_n[\mathtt{Mem}[u + n], v]$ is true. The second axiom similarly defines $B_n[u]$. We call these two axioms the base axioms of reachability because they attempt to capture the recursive definitions of R_n and B_n.

$$R_n[u, v] \Leftrightarrow (v = u \lor (\neg\mathtt{BS}[\mathtt{Mem}[u + n]] \land R_n[\mathtt{Mem}[u + n], v]))$$
$$v = B_n[u] \Leftrightarrow (\mathtt{BS}[\mathtt{Mem}[u + n]] \ ? \ v = \mathtt{Mem}[u + n] : v = B_n[\mathtt{Mem}[u + n]])$$

$$R_n[u, v] \land R_n[v, w] \Rightarrow R_n[u, w]$$
$$\mathtt{BS}[u] \land R_n[v, u] \Rightarrow u = v$$
$$R_n[u, v] \Rightarrow B_n[u] = B_n[v]$$
$$u = \mathtt{Mem}[u + n] \Rightarrow \mathtt{BS}[u]$$
$$\neg\mathtt{BS}[\mathtt{Mem}[u + n]] \Rightarrow R_n[\mathtt{Mem}[u + n]] = R_n[u] \setminus \{u\}$$

Fig. 7. Derived axioms for the theory of reachability predicate. The variables u, v and w are implicitly universally quantified.

It is well known that the reachability predicate (ours as well as the classic one) cannot be expressed in first-order logic [6]. Hence, similar to our previous work [17], we provide a sound but (necessarily) incomplete axiomatization of the theory by providing a set of derived axioms following the base axioms in Figure 7. Since the definitions of R_n and B_n are well-founded, these derived axioms can be proved from the base axioms using well-founded induction. The derived axioms are subtle generalizations of similar axioms presented for well-founded lists without pointers [17]. They have sufficed for all the examples in this paper.

7   Evaluation

In this section, we describe our experience applying HAVOC to a set of examples. These examples illustrate the use of pointer arithmetic, internal pointers, arrays, and linked lists in C programs. For each of these examples, we prove a variety of partial correctness properties, including the absence of null dereferences.

Figure 8 lists the examples considered in this paper. `iterate` is the example from Figure 2 in Section 2. `iterate_acyclic` and `array_iterate` are versions

Example	Time(s)
iterate	1.8
iterate_acyclic	1.7
array_iterate	1.4
slist_add	1.5
reverse_acyclic	2.0

Example	Time(s)
array_free	2.5
slist_sorted_insert	16.43
dlist_add	38.9
dlist_remove	45.4
allocator	901.8

Fig. 8. Results of assertion checking. SIMPLIFY was used as the theorem prover. The experiments were conducted on a 3.2GHz, 2GB machine running Windows XP.

of iterate for an acyclic list and an array, respectively. reverse_acyclic performs in-place reversal of an acyclic singly-linked list; we verify that the output list is acyclic and contains the same set of pointers as the input list. The example slist_add adds a node to an acyclic singly-linked list. dlist_add and dlist_remove are the insertion and deletion routines for cyclic doubly-linked lists used in the Windows kernel. The examples using doubly-linked lists require the use of R_0 and R_4 to specify the lists reachable through the Flink and Blink fields of the LIST_ENTRY structure. The example slist_sorted_insert inserts a node into a sorted (by the data field) linked list; we verify that the output list is sorted. This example illustrates the use of arithmetic reasoning (using $\leq$) on the data fields. The example array_free takes as input an array a of pointers, and iterates over the array to free the pointers that are not null. We check that an object is freed at most once. To verify this property, we needed to express the invariant that if i is distinct from j, then the pointers a[i] and a[j] are aliased only if they both point to null.

The final example allocator is a low-level storage allocator that closely resembles the malloc_firstfit_acyclic example described by Calcagno et al. [7]. The allocator maintains a list of free blocks within a single large object; each node in the list maintains a pointer to the next element of the list and the size of the free block in the node. Allocation of a block may result in either removing a node (if the entire free block at the node is returned) from the list, or readjusting the size of the free block (in case only a chunk of the free block is returned). We check two main postconditions: (i) the allocated block (when a non null pointer is returned) is a portion of some free block in the input list, and (ii) the free blocks of the output list do not overlap. This example required the use of R_0 to specify the list of free blocks.

Figure 8 gives the running times taken by SIMPLIFY to discharge the verification conditions. The examples involving singly-linked lists and arrays take only a few seconds. The examples involving doubly-linked lists take much longer because they make heavy use of quantifiers to express the invariant that connects the forward-going and backward-going links in a doubly-linked list. The allocator example makes heavy use of arithmetic as well as quantifiers, and therefore takes the longest to verify.

Interestingly, HAVOC revealed a bug in our implementation of the allocator. This bug was caused by an interaction between pointer casting and pointer arithmetic. Instead of the following correct code

```
return ((unsigned int) cursor) + sizeof(RegionHeader);
```

we had written the following incorrect code

```
return (unsigned int) (cursor + sizeof(RegionHeader));
```

Note that the two are different because the size of **RegionHeader**, the static type of **cursor**, is different from the size of **unsigned int**. We believe that such mistakes are common when dealing with low-level C code, and our tool can provide great value in debugging such programs.

8   Conclusions and Future Work

In this work, we introduced a new reachability predicate suitable for reasoning about data structures in low-level systems software. Our reachability predicate is designed to handle internal pointers and pointer arithmetic on object fields. It is a generalization of the classic reachability predicate used in existing verification tools. We have designed an annotation language for C programs that allows concise specification of properties of lists and arrays. We have also developed HAVOC, a verifier for C programs annotated with assertions in our specification language.

We believe that HAVOC is a good foundation for building powerful safety checkers for systems software based on automated first-order theorem proving. We are currently working to extend HAVOC with techniques for inference and abstraction to enable its use on realistic code bases inside Windows.

Acknowledgements. Our formalization of the C memory model has been deeply influenced by discussions with Madan Musuvathi. We are grateful to Stephen Adams, Henning Rohde, Jason Yang and Zhe Yang for their help with the ESP infrastructure. Rustan Leino answered numerous questions about Simplify and Boogie. Finally, we thank Tom Ball and Rustan Leino for providing valuable feedback on the paper.

References

1. I. Balaban, A. Pnueli, and L. D. Zuck. Shape analysis by predicate abstraction. In *Verification, Model checking, and Abstract Interpretation (VMCAI '05)*, LNCS 3385, pages 164–180, 2005.
2. T. Ball, R. Majumdar, T. Millstein, and S. K. Rajamani. Automatic predicate abstraction of C programs. In *Programming Language Design and Implementation (PLDI '01)*, pages 203–213, 2001.
3. M. Barnett and K. R. M. Leino. Weakest-precondition of unstructured programs. In *ACM SIGPLAN-SIGSOFT Workshop on Program Analysis For Software Tools and Engineering (PASTE '05)*, pages 82–87, 2005.
4. M. Barnett, K. R. M. Leino, and W. Schulte. The Spec# programming system: An overview. In *Construction and Analysis of Safe, Secure and Interoperable Smart Devices*, LNCS 3362, pages 49–69, 2005.

5. J. Bingham and Z. Rakamarić. A logic and decision procedure for predicate abstraction of heap-manipulating programs. In *Verification, Model Checking, and Abstract Interpretation (VMCAI '06)*, LNCS 3855, pages 207–221, 2006.
6. E. Börger, E. Grädel, and Y. Gurevich. *The Classical Decision Problem*. Springer-Verlag, 1997.
7. C. Calcagno, D. Distefano, P. W. O'Hearn, and H. Yang. Beyond reachability: Shape abstraction in the presence of pointer arithmetic. In *Static Analysis Symposium (SAS '06)*, LNCS 4134, pages 182–203, 2006.
8. S. Chatterjee, S. K. Lahiri, S. Qadeer, and Z. Rakamarić. A reachability predicate for analyzing low-level software. Technical Report MSR-TR-2006-154, Microsoft Research, 2006.
9. E. Clarke, D. Kroening, N. Sharygina, and K. Yorav. Predicate abstraction of ANSI–C programs using SAT. *Formal Methods in System Design (FMSD)*, 25:105–127, September–November 2004.
10. M. Das, S. Lerner, and M. Seigle. ESP: Path-sensitive program verification in polynomial time. In *Programming Language Design and Implementation (PLDI '02)*, pages 57–68, 2002.
11. R. DeLine and K. R. M. Leino. BoogiePL: A typed procedural language for checking object-oriented programs. Technical Report MSR-TR-2005-70, Microsoft Research, 2005.
12. D. L. Detlefs, G. Nelson, and J. B. Saxe. Simplify: A theorem prover for program checking. Technical report, HPL-2003-148, 2003.
13. E. W. Dijkstra. Guarded commands, nondeterminacy and formal derivation of programs. *Communications of the ACM*, 18:453–457, 1975.
14. J. Filliâtre and C. Marché. Multi-prover verification of C programs. In *International Conference on Formal Engineering Methods (ICFEM '04)*, LNCS 3308, pages 15–29, 2004.
15. C. Flanagan, K. R. M. Leino, M. Lillibridge, G. Nelson, J. B. Saxe, and R. Stata. Extended static checking for Java. In *Programming Language Design and Implementation (PLDI'02)*, pages 234–245, 2002.
16. T. A. Henzinger, R. Jhala, R. Majumdar, and G. Sutre. Lazy abstraction. In *Principles of Programming Languages (POPL '02)*, pages 58–70, 2002.
17. S. K. Lahiri and S. Qadeer. Verifying properties of well-founded linked lists. In *Principles of Programming Languages (POPL '06)*, pages 115–126, 2006.
18. T. Lev-Ami, N. Immerman, T. W. Reps, S. Sagiv, S. Srivastava, and G. Yorsh. Simulating reachability using first-order logic with applications to verification of linked data structures. In *Conference on Automated Deduction (CADE '05)*, LNCS 3632, pages 99–115, 2005.
19. T. Lev-Ami and S. Sagiv. TVLA: A system for implementing static analyses. In *Static Analysis Symposium (SAS '00)*, LNCS 1824, pages 280–301, 2000.
20. S. McPeak and G. C. Necula. Data structure specifications via local equality axioms. In *Computer-Aided Verification (CAV '05)*, LNCS 3576, pages 476–490, 2005.
21. G. Nelson and D. C. Oppen. Simplification by cooperating decision procedures. *ACM Transactions on Programming Languages and Systems (TOPLAS)*, 2(1):245–257, 1979.
22. S. Sagiv, T. W. Reps, and R. Wilhelm. Solving shape-analysis problems in languages with destructive updating. *ACM Transactions on Programming Languages and Systems (TOPLAS)*, 20(1):1–50, 1998.
23. Y. Xie and A. Aiken. Scalable error detection using boolean satisfiability. In *Principles of Programming Languages (POPL '05)*, pages 351–363, 2005.

Generating Representation Invariants of Structurally Complex Data

Muhammad Zubair Malik, Aman Pervaiz, and Sarfraz Khurshid

The University of Texas at Austin, 1 University Station C5000, Austin, TX 78712
{mzmalik,pervaiz,khurshid}@ece.utexas.edu

Abstract. Generating likely invariants using dynamic analyses is becoming an increasingly effective technique in software checking methodologies. This paper presents Deryaft, a novel algorithm for generating likely *representation invariants* of structurally complex data. Given a small set of concrete structures, Deryaft analyzes their key characteristics to formulate local and global properties that the structures exhibit. For effective formulation of structural invariants, Deryaft focuses on graph properties, including reachability, and views the program heap as an edge-labeled graph.

Deryaft outputs a Java predicate that represents the invariants; the predicate takes an input structure and returns true if and only if it satisfies the invariants. The invariants generated by Deryaft directly enable automation of various existing frameworks, such as the Korat test generation framework and the Juzi data structure repair framework, which otherwise require the user to provide the invariants. Experimental results with the Deryaft prototype show that it feasibly generates invariants for a range of subject structures, including libraries as well as a stand-alone application.

1 Introduction

Checking programs that manipulate dynamically-allocated, structurally complex data is notoriously hard. Existing dynamic and static analyses [19, 4, 8, 20, 2, 10] that check non-trivial properties of such programs impose a substantial burden on the users, e.g., by requiring the users to provide invariants, such as loop or representation invariants, or to provide complete executable implementations as well as specifications.

We present Deryaft, a novel framework for generating representation invariants of structurally complex data given a (small) set of structures. The generated invariants serve various purposes. Foremost, they formally characterize properties of the given structures. More importantly, they facilitate the use of various analyses. To illustrate, consider test generation using a constraint solver, such as Korat [4], which requires the user to provide detailed invariants. Deryaft enables using just a handful of small structures to allow these solvers to efficiently enumerate a large number of tests and to systematically test code. The generated invariants can similarly be used directly in other tools, such as ESC/Java [8], that are based on the Java Modeling Language [17], which uses Java expressions, or simply be used as assertions for runtime checking, e.g., to check if a public method establishes the class invariant. The invariants even enable non-conventional assertion-based analyses, such as repair of structurally complex data, e.g., using the Juzi framework [15].

O. Grumberg and M. Huth (Eds.): TACAS 2007, LNCS 4424, pp. 34–49, 2007.

Given a set of structures, Deryaft inspects them to formulate a set of hypotheses on the underlying structural as well as data constraints that are likely to hold. Next, it checks which hypotheses actually hold for the structures. Finally, it translates the valid hypotheses into a Java predicate that represents the structural invariants of the given structures. The predicate takes an input structure, traverses it, and returns true if and only if the input satisfies the invariants.

Deryaft views the program heap as an edge-labeled graph whose nodes represent objects and whose edges represent fields [14] and focuses on generating graphs properties, which include reachability. To make invariant generation feasible, Deryaft incorporates a number of heuristics, which allow it to hone on relevant properties. For non-linear structures, Deryaft also conjectures properties about lengths of paths from the root, and *completeness* of acyclic structures. Thus, it conjectures local as well as global properties. In addition to properties of structure, Deryaft also conjectures properties among data values in the structures. For example, it conjectures whether the key in a node is larger than all the keys in the node's left sub-tree, or whether the value of a field represents a function of the number of nodes in the structure.

The undecidability of the problem that Deryaft addresses necessitates that its constraint generation, in general, cannot be sound and complete [7]. The generated constraints are sound with respect to the set of given structures. Of course, unseen structures may or may not satisfy them. Deryaft's generation is not complete: it may not generate all possible constraints that hold for the given set of structures. We provide a simple API for allowing users to systematically extend the pool of invariants Deryaft hypothesizes.

Even though Deryaft requires a small set of structures to be given, if a method that constructs structures is given instead, Deryaft can use the method in place of the structures. For example, consider a method that adds an element to a binary search tree. Exhaustive enumeration of small sequences of additions of say up to three arbitrarily selected elements, starting with an empty tree, automatically provides a set of valid binary search trees (assuming the implementation of add is correct) that Deryaft requires.

Deryaft's approach has the potential to change how programmers work. Test-first programming [3] already advocates writing tests before implementations. Having written a small test suite, the user can rely on Deryaft to generate an invariant that represents a whole class of valid structures; Korat can use this invariant to enumerate a high quality test suite; Juzi can use the same invariant to provide data structure repair. Thus, Deryaft facilitates both systematic testing at compile-time as well as error recovery at runtime.

We make the following contributions:

- **Algorithm.** Deryaft is a novel algorithm for generating representation invariants of structurally complex data from a given small set of structures;
- **Java predicates.** Deryaft generates invariants as Java predicates that can directly be used in other applications, e.g., for test generation and error recovery;
- **Experiments.** We present experiments using our prototype to show the feasibility of generating invariants for a variety of data structures, including libraries as well as a stand-alone application.

2   Example

We present an example to illustrate Deryaft's generation of the representation invariant of acyclic singly-linked lists. Consider the following class declaration:

```
public class SinglyLinkedList {
    private Node header; // first list node
    private int size;    // number of nodes in the list

    private static class Node {
        int elem;
        Node next;
    }
}
```

A list has a `header` node, which represents the first node of the list, and caches the number of nodes it contains in the `size` field. Each node has an integer element `elem` and a `next` field, which points to the next node in the list.

Assume that the class `SinglyLinkedList` implements acyclic lists, i.e., there are no directed cycles in the graph reachable from the `header` node of any valid list. Figure 1 shows a set of three lists, one each with zero, one and three nodes, which are all acyclic. Given a set of these lists, i.e., a reference to a `HashSet` containing the three list objects shown, Deryaft generates the representation invariant shown in Figure 2.

The method `repOk` performs two traversals over the structure represented by `this`. First, `repOk` checks that the structure is acyclic along the `next` field. Second, it checks that the structure has the correct value for the `size` field. The acyclicity checks that there is a unique path from `header` to every reachable node, while the check for `size` simply computes the total number of reachable nodes and verifies that number.

To illustrate how Deryaft automates existing analyses, consider enumeration of test inputs using the Korat framework, which requires the user to provide a `repOk` and a bound on input size. To illustrate, given the `repOk` generated by Deryaft, and a bound of 5 nodes with integer elements ranging from 1 to 5, Korat takes 1.9 seconds to generate all 3905 nonisomorphic lists with up to 5 nodes. Using the inputs that Korat enumerates, any given implementation of the list methods can be tested systematically.

Notice that neither the generation of `repOk` nor the enumeration of test inputs required an a priori implementation of *any* method of the class `SinglyLinkedList`. Indeed once such methods are written, they can be checked using a variety of frameworks

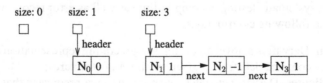

Fig. 1. Three acyclic singly-linked lists, one each containing zero, one, and three nodes, as indicated by the value of the `size` field. Small hollow squares represent the list objects. The labeled arrows represent the fields `header` and `next`. N_0, N_1, N_2, and N_3 represent the identities of node objects. The nodes also contain the integer elements, which for the given three lists range over the set {-1, 0, 1}.

```
public boolean repOk() {
    if (!acyclicCore(header)) return false;
    if (!sizeOk(size, header)) return false;
    return true;
}

private boolean acyclicCore(Node n) {
    Set<Node> visited = new HashSet<Node>();
    LinkedList<Node> worklist = new LinkedList<Node>();
    if (n != null) {
        worklist.addFirst(n);
        visited.add(n);
    }
    while (!worklist.isEmpty()) {
        Node current = worklist.removeFirst();
        if (current.next != null) {
            if (!visited.add(current.next)) {
                //re-visiting a previously visited node
                return false;
            }
            worklist.addFirst(current.next);
        }
    }
    return true;
}

private boolean sizeOk(int s, Node n) {
    Set<Node> visited = new HashSet<Node>();
    LinkedList<Node> worklist = new LinkedList<Node>();
    if (n != null) {
        worklist.addFirst(n);
        visited.add(n);
    }
    while (!worklist.isEmpty()) {
        Node current = worklist.removeFirst();
        if (current.next != null) {
            if (visited.add(current.next)) {
                worklist.addFirst(current.next);
            }
        }
    }
    return (s == visited.size());
}
```

Fig. 2. Invariant generated by Deryaft. The method `repOk` represents the structural invariants of the given set of list structures. The method `acyclicCore` uses a standard work-list based graph traversal algorithm to visit all nodes reachable from n via the field `next` and returns true if and only if the structure is free of cycles. The method `sizeOk` performs a similar traversal to checks that the number of nodes reachable from n equals s.

that make use of the representation invariants, which traditionally have been provided by the user but can now be generated using Deryaft.

In case a partial implementation of the class `SinglyLinkedList` is available, Deryaft is able to utilize that. For example, assume that we have an implementation of the instance method `add`:

```
void add(int i) { ... }
```

which adds the given integer i at the head of the list `this`. Given `add`, it is trivial to automatically synthesize a driver program that repeatedly invokes `add` to enumerate all lists within a small bound, e.g., with up to 3 nodes, using the integer elements {-1, 0, 1}. These lists then serve as the set of input structures for Deryaft.

3 Deryaft

This section describes Deryaft. We first describe an abstract view of the program heap.
Next, we define core and derived sets. Then, we characterize the invariants that Deryaft
can generate. Finally, we describe how its algorithm works and illustrate it.

3.1 Program Heap as an Edge-Labeled Graph

We take a *relational view* [14] of the program heap: we view the heap of a Java program
as an edge-labeled directed graph whose nodes represent objects and whose edges represent fields. The presence of an edge labeled f from node o to v says that the f field of
the object o points to the object v (or is null) or has the primitive value v. Mathematically, we treat this graph as a set (the set of nodes) and a collection of relations, one for
each field. We partition the set of nodes according to the declared classes and partition
the set of edges according to the declared fields; we represent null as a special node.
A particular program state is represented by an assignment of values to these sets and
relations. Since we model the heap at the concrete level, there is a straightforward isomorphism between program states and assignments of values to the underlying sets and
relations.

To illustrate, recall the class declaration for SinglyLinkedList from Section 2.
The basic model of heap for this example consists of three sets, each corresponding to
a declared class or primitive type:

```
SinglyLinkedList
Node
int
```

and four relations, each corresponding to a declared field:

```
header: SinglyLinkedList x Node
size: SinglyLinkedList x int
elem: Node x int
next: Node x Node
```

The "size: 3" list from Figure 1 can be represented using the following assignment
of values to these sets and relations:

```
SinglyLinkedList = { L0 }
Node = { N1, N2, N3 }
int = { -1, 0, 1 }

header = { <L0, N0> }
size = { <L0, 3> }
elem = { <N1, 1>, <N2, -1>, <N3, 0> }
next = { <N1, N2>, <N2, N3>, <N3, null> }
```

Deryaft assumes (without loss of generality) that each structure in the given set has
a unique root pointer. Thus, the abstract view of a structure is a *rooted* edge-labeled
directed graph, and Deryaft focuses on generating properties of such graphs, including
properties that involve reachability, e.g., acyclicity.

3.2 Core and Derived Fields

Deryaft partitions the set of reference fields declared in the classes of objects in the
given structures into two sets: *core* and *derived*. For a given set, S, of structures, let F
be the set of all reference fields.

```
Set coreFields(Set ss) {
    // post: result is a set of core fields with respect to the
    //        structures in ss

    Set cs = allClasses(ss);
    Set fs = allReferenceFields(cs);
    foreach (Field f in fs)
        Set fs' = fs - f;
        boolean isCore = false;
        foreach (Structure s in ss) {
            if (reachable(s, fs') != reachable(s, fs)) {
                isCore = true;
                break;
            }
        }
        if (!isCore) fs = fs';
    }
    return fs;
}
```

Fig. 3. Algorithm to compute a core set. The method allClasses returns the set of all classes of objects in structures in ss. The method allReferenceFields returns the set of all reference fields declared in classes in cs. The method reachable returns a set of objects reachable from the root of s via traversals only along the fields in the given set.

Definition 1. *A subset $C \subseteq F$ is a core set with respect to S if for all structures $s \in S$, the set of nodes reachable from the root r of s along the fields in C is the same as the set of nodes reachable from r along the fields in F.*

In other words, a core set preserves reachability in terms of the set of nodes. Indeed, the set of all fields is itself a core set. We aim to identify a *minimal* core set, i.e., a core set with the least number of fields.

To illustrate, the set containing both the reference fields header and next in the example from Section 2 is a minimal core set with respect to the given set of lists.

Definition 2. *For a core set C, the set of fields $F - C$ is a derived set.*

Since elem in Section 2 is a field of a primitive type, the SinglyLinkedList example has no fields that are derived.

Our partitioning of reference fields is inspired by the notion of a *back-bone* in certain data structures [19].

Algorithm. The set of core fields can be computed by taking each reference field in turn and checking whether removing all the edges corresponding to the field from the graph changes the set of nodes reachable from root. Figure 3 gives the pseudo-code of an algorithm to compute core fields.

3.3 Properties of Interest

We consider *global* as well as *local* properties of rooted edge-labeled directed graphs, which are likely representatives of structurally complex data. The properties are divided into various categories as follows.

Global: reachability. Reachability properties include the *shape* of the structure reachable from root along some set of reference fields. The shapes can be *acyclic* (i.e., there is a unique path from the root to every node), *directed-acyclic* (i.e., there are no directed cycles in the graph), *circular* (i.e., all the graph nodes of a certain type are linked in a cycle), or *arbitrary*. Note that any acyclic graph is also directed-acyclic.

To illustrate, the property *acyclic*(header, {next}), i.e, the structure reachable from header along the field next is acyclic, holds for all the lists shown in Figure 1.

Global: primitive fields. In reasoning about graphs, the notion of a cardinality of a set of nodes occurs naturally. We consider properties relating values of integer fields and cardinalities of sets of reachable objects. For example, the property *equals*(size, *reachable*(header, next).*cardinality*()) checks whether size is the cardinality of the set of objects reachable from header following zero or more traversals of next.

Global: path lengths. For non-linear structures, such as trees, we consider properties that relate lengths of different paths from root. For example, the property *balanced* represents that no simple path from the root differs in length from another simple path by more than one. For binary trees, this property represents a *height-balanced* tree.

Local: reference fields. In edge-labeled graphs that are not acyclic (along the set of all fields), local properties that relate different types of edges are likely. To illustrate, consider a graph where if an edge connects a node n of type N to a node m of type M, there is a corresponding edge that connects m to n. We term such properties *two-cycles*. For a doubly-linked list, next and previous form a two-cycle.

Another local property on reference fields is whether a particular node always has an edge of a particular type from it to null.

Local: primitive fields. Another category of local properties pertains to primitive values. For example, in a binary tree, the value in a node might be greater than the values in the node's children. We consider local properties that relate a node's value to it's successors along reference fields.

3.4 Algorithm

Given a set of structures, Deryaft traverses the structures to formulate a set of hypotheses. Next, it checks which of the hypotheses actually hold for the given structures. Finally, it translates the valid hypotheses into a Java predicate that represents the structural invariants of the given structures, i.e., it generates a method that takes an input structure, traverses it, and returns true if and only if the input satisfies the invariants.

To make invariant generation feasible, a key heuristic that Deryaft incorporates to focus on relevant properties is: hypothesize properties about reachability, such as acyclicity or circularity, only for the fields in the core set; and hypothesize local properties that relate derived fields and core fields, e.g., whether a derived field forms two-cycles with some core fields.

Figure 4 presents the Deryaft algorithm using Java-like pseudo-code. To minimize the number of properties that are checked on the given structures, the checkProperties does not check a property p if a property q that contradicts p is already known to be true, e.g., if acyclic holds then circular (for the same set of fields) is not checked.

```
String deryaft(Set structs) {
    // post: result is a string representation of a Java method
    //       that represents the structural invariants of the
    //       given structures

    Set classes = allClasses(structs);
    Set fields = allFields(structs);
    Set core = coreFields(fields);
    Set derived = derivedFields(fields, core);
    Set relevantGlobal =
            globalProperties(structs, core, classes);
    Set relevantLocal =
            localProperties(structs, derived, classes);
    Set propertiesThatHold =
            checkProperties(relevantGlobal, structs);
    propertiesThatHold.addAll(
            checkProperties(relevantLocal, structs));
    simplify(propertiesThatHold);
    return generateInvariants(propertiesThatHold);
}
```

Fig. 4. The Deryaft algorithm. The methods `allClasses` and `allFields` respectively return a set of all classes and a set of all fields from the given set of structures. The method `coreFields` (`derivedFields`) returns the set of core (derived) fields. The methods `globalProperties` (`localProperties`) compute sets of relevant global (local) properties. The method `checkProperties` returns a subset of given properties, which hold for all given structures. The method `simplify` removes redundant constraints. The method `generateInvariants` generates a Java predicate that corresponds to the given properties.

To minimize the number of checks in the generated repOk, the `simplify` method removes redundant properties from set of properties that actually hold, e.g., if a graph is acyclic, there is no need to generate a check for directed-acyclic.

In summary, the algorithm performs the following five key steps:

– Identification of core and derived fields;
– Formulation of global and local properties that are relevant;
– Computation of properties that actually hold;
– Minimization of properties; and
– Generation of Java code that represents properties.

3.5 Illustration: Binary Tree Representation of Heaps

To illustrate the variety of invariants that Deryaft can generate, we next present a case study on generating invariants of the heap data structure, which is also called a priority queue [5]. We consider a binary tree representation of heaps.

The following class declares a binary tree with parent pointers:

```
public class BinaryTree {
    Node root;  // first node in the tree
    int size;   // number of nodes in the tree

    private static class Node {
        Node left;
        Node right;
        Node parent;
        int key;
    }
}
```

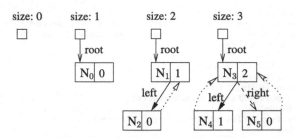

Fig. 5. Four heaps represented using binary trees, one each containing zero, one, two and three nodes, as indicated by the value of the `size` field. Small hollow squares represent the `BinaryTree` objects. The labeled arrows represent the fields `root`, `left`, `right`. The dotted arrows with hollow heads represent `parent` fields, which have not been labeled for clarity. N_0, ..., N_5 represent the identities of node objects. The nodes also contain the integer keys, which for the given four heaps range over the set $\{0, 1, 2\}$.

Consider a binary tree representation of heap, which requires: acyclicity along `left` and `right`; correctness of `parent` and `size`; heap property: the key of a node is greater than any key in a left or right child; and nearly complete binary tree.

Consider the heaps represented in Figure 5. As an example execution of the algorithm for computing the core fields (Figure 3), consider computing the set with respect to these structures. The algorithm initially sets `fs` to $\{$`left, right, parent`$\}$, i.e., the set that contains all the fields that represent homogeneous relations. Removing `left` from the set changes reachability, e.g., in the case of the structure with three nodes and therefore `left` is core; similarly `right` is core; however, removing `parent` does not effect the reachability in any of the given structures and therefore `parent` is not core.

As an example execution of the `deryaft` algorithm (Figure 4), consider computing the representation invariants for the given structures. The formulation of relevant global properties gives:

$-acyclic($`root`$, \{$`left, right`$\})$
$-directed\text{-}acyclic($`root`$, \{$`left, right`$\})$
$-circular($`root`$, \{$`left, right`$\})$
$-equals($`size`$, reachable($`root`$, \{$`left, right`$\}).cardinality())$
$-equals($`size` $+ 1, reachable($`root`$, \{$`left, right`$\}).cardinality())$
$-height\text{-}difference($`root`$, \{$`left, right`$\}, x)$
$-nearly\text{-}complete($`root`$, \{$`left, right`$\})$

The formulation of relevant local properties gives:

$-two\text{-}cycle($`root, parent, left`$)$
$-two\text{-}cycle($`root, parent, right`$)$
$-is\text{-}null($`root, parent`$)$
$-\{<, \leq, >, \geq\}($`root`$, \{$`left`$\})$
$-\{<, \leq, >, \geq\}($`root`$, \{$`right`$\})$

```
public boolean repOk() {
    if (!acyclicCore(root)) return false;
    if (!sizeOk(size, root)) return false;
    if (!nearlyComplete(root)) return false;
    if (!parentNull(root)) return false;
    if (!parentTwoCycleLeft(root)) return false;
    if (!parentTwoCycleRight(root)) return false;
    if (!greaterThanLeft(root)) return false;
    if (!greaterThanRight(root)) return false;
    return true;
}

private boolean parentNull(Node n) {
    return (n.parent == null);
}

private boolean parentTwoCycleLeft(Node n) {
    Set<Node> visited = new HashSet<Node>();
    LinkedList<Node> worklist = new LinkedList<Node>();
    if (n != null) {
        worklist.addFirst(n);
        visited.add(n);
    }
    while (!worklist.isEmpty()) {
        Node current = worklist.removeFirst();
        if (current.left != null) {
            if (current.left.parent != current) return false;
            if (visited.add(current.left)) {
                worklist.addFirst(current.left);
            }
        }
        if (current.right != null) {
            if (visited.add(current.right)) {
                worklist.addFirst(current.right);
            }
        }
    }
    return true;
}
```

Fig. 6. Code snippet of heap invariant generated by Deryaft

The computation of properties that actually hold gives:

$-acyclic(\text{root}, \{\text{left}, \text{right}\})$

$-directed\text{-}acyclic(\text{root}, \{\text{left}, \text{right}\})$

$-equals(\text{size}, reachable(\text{root}, \{\text{left}, \text{right}\}).cardinality())$

$-height\text{-}difference(\text{root}, \{\text{left}, \text{right}\}, 1)$

$-nearly\text{-}complete(\text{root}, \{\text{left}, \text{right}\})$

$-two\text{-}cycle(\text{root}, \text{parent}, \text{left})$

$-two\text{-}cycle(\text{root}, \text{parent}, \text{right})$

$-is\text{-}null(\text{root}, \text{parent})$

$-\{>, \geq\}(\text{root}, \{\text{left}\})$

$-\{>, \geq\}(\text{root}, \{\text{right}\})$

Removal of redundant properties gives:

$-acyclic(\text{root}, \{\text{left}, \text{right}\})$

$-equals(\text{size}, reachable(\text{root}, \{\text{left}, \text{right}\}).cardinality())$

$-nearly\text{-}complete(\text{root}, \{\text{left}, \text{right}\})$

$-two\text{-}cycle$(root, parent, left)
$-two\text{-}cycle$(root, parent, right)
$-is\text{-}null$(root, parent)
$-greater\text{-}than$(root, {left})
$-greater\text{-}than$(root, {right})

Deryaft's code generation takes these resulting properties and generates Java code, which performs appropriate traversals to check the properties. Figure 6 gives a code snippet of Deryaft's output. The method repOk represents the structural invariants of the given heaps. It invokes several helper methods to perform several traversals on the input structure to determine the structure's validity. The method acyclicCore returns true if and only if the input structure is free of cycles along the fields left and right. The method parentNull checks that the parent of n is null. The method parentTwoCycleLeft checks that for each node n, if n has a left child m, m's parent is n, i.e., parent and left form a two-cycle; parentTwoCycleRight checks that for each node n, if n has a right child m, m's parent is n. The method sizeOk checks the number of nodes reachable from n equals s. The method greaterThanLeft checks that for any node n, if n has a left child m, n's key is greater than m's key; the method greaterThanRight checks that for any node n, if n has a right child m, n's key is greater than m's key.

4   Experiments

This section describes Deryaft's generation of structural invariants for seven subjects, which include some structures library classes as well as a standalone application. For each subject, we constructed by hand five small representative structures and gave them as inputs to Deryaft. For all subjects, Deryaft correctly generated all the standard data structure invariants. The subjects were as follows.

Singly-linked acyclic list. A list object has a header node; each list node has a next field. Integrity constraint is acyclicity along next.

Ordered list. An ordered list is a singly-linked acyclic list, whose nodes have integer elements. Integrity constraints are acyclicity and an (ascending or descending) ordering on the elements.

Doubly-linked circular list. A list object has a header node; each list node has a next and a previous field. Integrity constraints are circularity along next and the transpose relation between next and previous. This subject is based on the library class java.util.LinkedList.

Binary search tree. A binary search tree object has a root node; each node has a left and a right child node, a parent, and an integer key. Integrity constraints are acyclicity along left and right, correctness of parent as well as correct ordering of keys: for each node, its key is larger than any of the keys in the left sub-tree and smaller than any of the keys in the right-sub tree.

AVL tree. An AVL tree [5] is a height-balanced binary search tree. Integrity constraints are the binary search tree constraints as well as the height-balance constraint.

Heap array. Heap arrays provide an array-based implementation of the binary heap data structure that is also commonly known as a priority queue. A heap has a capacity that is the length of the underlying array and a `size` that is the number of elements currently in the heap. For a heap element at index i, its left child is at index $2 * i + 1$ and the right child is at index $2 * i + 2$. Integrity constraints are `size <= capacity` and the heap satisfies the *max-heap* (respectively *min-heap*) property: an element is larger (respectively smaller) than both its children.

Intentional name. The Intentional Naming System [1] (INS) is a service location system that allows client applications to specify *what* they are looking for without having to know *where* it may be situated in a dynamic network. A key data structure in INS is an *intentional name*—a hierarchical arrangement of *attribute-value pairs* that describe service properties. Clients use these names to locate services, while services use them as advertisements.

An intentional name can be implemented using the class `AVPair` that has two `String` fields `attribute` and `value` and a `Vector<AVPair>` field `children`. Structural integrity constraints for `AVPair` are: (1) attribute and value of the root are `null`; (2) the children of a node have unique attributes; and (3) the structure is acyclic along the `children` field.

5   Discussion

This section discusses current limitations of Deryaft and future work.

Limitations. Constraint generation using a given set of structures has two limitations. One, the set may not be representative of the class of desired structures. Two, not all relevant properties can feasibly be identified, e.g., conjecturing all possible relations among integer fields is infeasible even using simple arithmetic operators. Deryaft's current generation algorithm therefore, focuses on structural properties which involve reference fields, which can naturally be viewed as edges in a graph, and simple constraints on primitive data. In future, we plan to explore more complex relations among primitive as well as reference fields.

Our Deryaft implementation is under construction. The prototype at this stage can handle a class of structures similar to the ones illustrated in this paper.

Optimization of Repeated Traversals. The `repOk` code that Deryaft outputs typically performs several traversals over a given structure. While an optimization of these traversals might not produce a noticeable speed-up in code generation due to the small size of given structures, optimizations may be quite important in the context of where the generated code is to be used. In fact, based on the usage context, very different optimizations may be necessary.

Consider the case for structure enumeration using a constraint solver. It is well-known that the performance of constraint solvers, such as propositional satisfiability (SAT) solvers, depends crucially on the formulation of given invariants—the same holds for Korat and the Alloy Analyzer [18]. In fact, repeated traversals which may seemingly be slow, may actually elicit faster generation.

The case for assertion evaluation is usually different: generated code that minimizes the number of traversals is likely to improve the time to check the assertion. Thus, it is natural to extend Deryaft to incorporate information about the context to tune its generation to the intended use.

Introduction of New Invariants. It would be useful to build an extensible invariant generation system, where new invariants that involve new operators can be plugged into the invariant generator. This would enable not only focused generation on the particular domain of interest, but also generation of a wider class of invariants. Such extensibility requires a language for expressing invariants.

Integration with Other Software Analysis Frameworks. We have given an example of how Korat can be used for input enumeration using invariants generated by Deryaft. We plan to fully integrate Deryaft's algorithm with various existing frameworks.

Static Analysis for Optimizing Generation. While in the presence of a partial implementation we may not require the user to provide a set of structures, we can use the implementation in a different way as well: a static analysis of the code, say the method that adds a node to a heap, can help formulate the likely invariants more accurately.

6   Related Work

Dynamic analyses Our work is inspired by the Daikon invariant detection engine [7], which pioneered the notion of dynamically detecting likely program invariants in the late 90s and has since been adapted by various other frameworks [12, 11]. Deryaft differs from Daikon in three key aspects. First, the model of data structures in Daikon uses arrays to represent object fields. While this representation allows detecting invariants of some data structures, it makes it awkward as to how to detect invariants that involve intricate global properties, such as relating lengths of paths. Deryaft's view of the heap as an edge-labeled graph and focus on generic graph properties enables it to directly capture a whole range of structurally complex data. Second, Deryaft employs specific heuristics that optimize generation of invariants for data structures, e.g., the distinction between core and derived fields allows it to preemptively disallow hypothesizing relations among certain fields. We believe this distinction, if adopted, can optimize Daikon's analysis too. Third, Deryaft generates invariants in Java, which can directly be plugged into a variety of tools, such as the Korat testing framework [4] and the Juzi [15] repair framework.

We have conducted some intial experiments to compare the output of Daikon with Deryaft. Daikon does not seem to generate rich data structure invariants for the subjects we have presented in this paper. For example, for the `SinglyLinkedList` class (Section 2), using the lists shown in Figure 1, Daikon generates the following class invariant for `SinglyLinkedList`:

```
/*@ invariant this.header.next.next != null; */
/*@ invariant this.header.next.elem == -1; */
/*@ invariant this.header.elem == 0 || this.header.elem == 1; */
/*@ invariant this.size == 0; */
```

and the following for `Node`:

```
/*@ invariant this.next == null; */
/*@ invariant this.elem == -1 || this.elem == 0 || this.elem == 1; */
```

Even using a larger test suite with 100 randomly generated lists using the API methods of `SinglyLinkedList`, we were not able to generate more precise invariants with

Daikon. We believe that Daikon experts can set its parameters so that it generates a richer class of invariants.

In previous work [16], we developed aDeryaft, a tool for assisting Alloy [13] users build their Alloy specifications. aDeryaft generates first-order logic formulas that represent structural invariants of a given set of Alloy instances. This paper extends both the design and implementation of aDeryaft by (1) supporting all of Java data-types (including arrays), which significantly differ from Alloy's relational basis, (2) extending the class of invariants supported and (3) evaluating using a wide class of subject structures, including those from a stand-alone application.

Static analyses Researchers have explored invariant generation using static analyses for over three decades. There is a wide body of research in the context of generating loop invariants [9,6,23,21] using recurrence equations, abstract interpretation with widening, matrix theory for Petri nets, constraint-based techniques etc. Most of these analyses are limited to relations between primitive variables.

Shape analyses [10, 20, 19, 2] can handle structural constraints using abstract heap representations, predicate abstraction etc. However, shape analyses typically do not consider rich properties of data values in structures and mostly abstract away from the data. Moreover, none of the existing shape analyses can feasibly check or detect rich structural invariants, such as height-balance for binary search trees, which involve complex properties that relate paths.

Combined dynamic/static analyses Some recent approaches combine static and dynamic analyses for inferring API level specifications [22, 25].

Invariant generation has also been used in the context of model checkers to explain the absence of counterexamples, while focusing on integer variables [24].

7 Conclusions

Dynamically detecting likely invariants, as pioneered by Daikon, is becoming immensely popular. In this paper, we focused on generating *representation invariants of structurally complex data*, given a small set of concrete structures. We presented Deryaft, a novel invariant generation algorithm. Deryaft analyzes the key characteristics of the given structures to formulate local and global properties that the structures have in common. A key idea in Deryaft is to view the program heap as an edge-labeled graph, and hence to focus on properties of graphs, including reachability. Deryaft partitions the set of edges into *core* and *derived* sets and hypothesizes different classes of properties for each set, thereby minimizing the number of hypotheses it needs to validate.

Deryaft generates a Java predicate that represents the properties of given structures, i.e., it generates a method that takes an input structure, traverses it, and returns true if and only if the input satisfies the properties. Even though Deryaft does not require an implementation of any methods that manipulate the given structures, in the presence of such an implementation, it can generate the invariants without a priori requiring a given set of structures. The invariants generated by Deryaft enable automation of various software analyses. We illustrated how the Korat framework can use these invariants to enumerate inputs for Java programs and to check their correctness.

Acknowledgments

We thank the anonymous reviewers and Darko Marinov for useful comments. This work was funded in part by the Fulbright Program and the NSF Science of Design Program (award #0438967).

References

1. William Adjie-Winoto, Elliot Schwartz, Hari Balakrishnan, and Jeremy Lilley. The design and implementation of an intentional naming system. In *Proc. 17th ACM Symposium on Operating Systems Principles (SOSP)*, Kiawah Island, December 1999.
2. Ittai Balaban, Amir Pnueli, and Lenore D. Zuck. Shape analysis by predicate abstraction. In *Proc. 6th International Conference on Verification, Model Checking and Abstract Interpretation*, Paris, France, 2005.
3. Kent Beck and Erich Gamma. Test infected: Programmers love writing tests. *Java Report*, 3(7), July 1998.
4. Chandrasekhar Boyapati, Sarfraz Khurshid, and Darko Marinov. Korat: Automated testing based on Java predicates. In *Proc. International Symposium on Software Testing and Analysis (ISSTA)*, July 2002.
5. Thomas H. Cormen, Charles E. Leiserson, and Ronald L. Rivest. *Introduction to Algorithms*. The MIT Press, Cambridge, MA, 1990.
6. P. Cousot and N. Halbwachs. Automatic discovery of linear restraints among variables of a program. In *Proc. 5th Annual ACM Symposium on the Principles of Programming Languages (POPL)*, Tucson, Arizona, 1978.
7. Michael D. Ernst. *Dynamically Discovering Likely Program Invariants*. PhD thesis, University of Washington Department of Computer Science and Engineering, August 2000.
8. Cormac Flanagan, K. Rustan M. Leino, Mark Lillibridge, Greg Nelson, James B. Saxe, and Raymie Stata. Extended static checking for Java. In *Proc. ACM SIGPLAN 2002 Conference on Programming language design and implementation*, 2002.
9. Steven M. German and Ben Wegbreit. A synthesizer of inductive assertions. *IEEE Trans. Software Eng.*, 1(1), 1975.
10. Rakesh Ghiya and Laurie J. Hendren. Is it a tree, a DAG, or a cyclic graph? A shape analysis for heap-directed pointers in C. In *POPL '96: Proceedings of the 23rd ACM SIGPLAN-SIGACT symposium on Principles of programming languages*, 1996.
11. Neelam Gupta and Zachary V. Heidepriem. A new structural coverage criterion for dynamic detection of program invariants. In *Proc. 18th Conference on Automated Software Engineering (ASE)*, San Diego, CA, October 2003.
12. Sudheendra Hangal and Monica S. Lam. Tracking down software bugs using automatic anomaly detection. In *ICSE '02: Proceedings of the 24th International Conference on Software Engineering*, 2002.
13. Daniel Jackson. *Software Abstractions: Logic, Language and Analysis*. The MIT Press, Cambridge, MA, 2006.
14. Daniel Jackson and Alan Fekete. Lightweight analysis of object interactions. In *Proc. Fourth International Symposium on Theoretical Aspects of Computer Software*, Sendai, Japan, October 2001.
15. Sarfraz Khurshid, Iván García, and Yuk Lai Suen. Repairing structurally complex data. In *Proc. 12th SPIN Workshop on Software Model Checking*, San Francisco, CA, 2005.
16. Sarfraz Khurshid, Muhammad Zubair Malik, and Engin Uzuncaova. An automated approach for writing Alloy specifications using instances. In *2nd International Symposium on Leveraging Applications of Formal Methods, Verification and Validation*, Paphos, Cyprus, 2006.

17. Gary T. Leavens, Albert L. Baker, and Clyde Ruby. Preliminary design of JML: A behavioral interface specification language for Java. Technical Report TR 98-06i, Department of Computer Science, Iowa State University, June 1998.
18. Darko Marinov, Sarfraz Khurshid, Suhabe Bugrara, Lintao Zhang, and Martin Rinard. Optimizations for compiling declarative models into boolean formulas. In *8th Intl. Conference on Theory and Applications of Satisfiability Testing (SAT)*, 2005.
19. Anders Moeller and Michael I. Schwartzbach. The pointer assertion logic engine. In *Proc. SIGPLAN Conference on Programming Languages Design and Implementation*, Snowbird, UT, June 2001.
20. Mooly Sagiv, Thomas Reps, and Reinhard Wilhelm. Solving shape-analysis problems in languages with destructive updating. *ACM Transactions on Programming Languages and Systems (TOPLAS)*, January 1998.
21. Sriram Sankaranarayanan, Henny B. Sipma, and Zohar Manna. Non-linear loop invariant generation using groebner bases. In *POPL '04: Proceedings of the 31st ACM SIGPLAN-SIGACT symposium on Principles of programming languages*, 2004.
22. Mana Taghdiri. Inferring specifications to detect errors in code. In *Proceedings of the 19th IEEE International Conference on Automated Software Engineering*, Washington, DC, 2004.
23. Ashish Tiwari, Harald Rue, Hassen Saidi, and Natarajan Shankar. A technique for invariant generation. In *Proc. 7th Conference on Tools and Algorithms for Construction and Analysis of Systems (TACAS)*, London, UK, 2001.
24. M. Vaziri and G. Holzmann. Automatic detection of invariants in spin. In *Proc. SPIN Workshop on Software Model Checking*, November 1998.
25. John Whaley, Michael C. Martin, and Monica S. Lam. Automatic extraction of object-oriented component interfaces. In *Proc. International Symposium on Software Testing and Analysis (ISSTA)*, July 2002.

Multi-objective Model Checking of Markov Decision Processes

K. Etessami[1], M. Kwiatkowska[2], M.Y. Vardi[3], and M. Yannakakis[4]

[1] LFCS, School of Informatics, University of Edinburgh
[2] School of Computer Science, Birmingham University
[3] Dept. of Computer Science, Rice University
[4] Dept. of Computer Science, Columbia University

Abstract. We study and provide efficient algorithms for multi-objective model checking problems for Markov Decision Processes (MDPs). Given an MDP, M, and given multiple linear-time (ω-regular or LTL) properties φ_i, and probabilities $r_i \in [0, 1]$, $i = 1, \ldots, k$, we ask whether there exists a strategy σ for the controller such that, for all i, the probability that a trajectory of M controlled by σ satisfies φ_i is at least r_i. We provide an algorithm that decides whether there exists such a strategy and if so produces it, and which runs in time polynomial in the size of the MDP. Such a strategy may require the use of both randomization and memory. We also consider more general multi-objective ω-regular queries, which we motivate with an application to assume-guarantee compositional reasoning for probabilistic systems.

Note that there can be trade-offs between different properties: satisfying property φ_1 with high probability may necessitate satisfying φ_2 with low probability. Viewing this as a multi-objective optimization problem, we want information about the "trade-off curve" or *Pareto curve* for maximizing the probabilities of different properties. We show that one can compute an approximate Pareto curve with respect to a set of ω-regular properties in time polynomial in the size of the MDP.

Our quantitative upper bounds use LP methods. We also study qualitative multi-objective model checking problems, and we show that these can be analysed by purely graph-theoretic methods, even though the strategies may still require both randomization and memory.

1 Introduction

Markov Decision Processes (MDPs) are standard models for stochastic optimization and for modelling systems with probabilistic and nondeterministic or controlled behavior (see [Put94, Var85, CY95, CY98]). In an MDP, at each state, the controller can choose from among a number of actions, or choose a probability distribution over actions. Each action at a state determines a probability distribution on the next state. Fixing an initial state and fixing the controller's strategy determines a probability space of infinite runs (trajectories) of the MDP. For MDPs with a single objective, the controller's goal is to optimize the value of an objective function, or payoff, which is a function of the entire trajectory.

O. Grumberg and M. Huth (Eds.): TACAS 2007, LNCS 4424, pp. 50–65, 2007.
© Springer-Verlag Berlin Heidelberg 2007

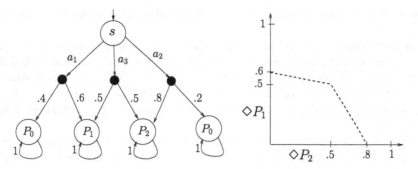

Fig. 1. An MDP with two objectives, $\Diamond P_1$ and $\Diamond P_2$, and the associated Pareto curve

Many different objectives have been studied for MDPs, with a wide variety of applications. In particular, in verification research linear-time model checking of MDPs has been studied, where the objective is to maximize the probability that the trajectory satisfies a given ω-regular or LTL property ([CY98, CY95, Var85]).

In many settings we may not just care about a single property. Rather, we may have a number of different properties and we may want to know whether we can simultaneously satisfy all of them with given probabilities. For example, in a system with a server and two clients, we may want to maximize the probability for both clients 1 and 2 of the temporal property: "every request issued by client i eventually receives a response from the server", $i = 1, 2$. Clearly, there may be a trade-off. To increase this probability for client 1 we may have to decrease it for client 2, and vice versa. We thus want to know what are the simultaneously *achievable* pairs (p_1, p_2) of probabilities for the two properties. More specifically, we will be interested in the "trade-off curve" or *Pareto curve*. The Pareto curve is the set of all achievable vectors $p = (p_1, p_2) \in [0, 1]^2$ such that there does not exist another achievable vector p' that *dominates* p, meaning that $p \leq p'$ (coordinate-wise inequality) and $p \neq p'$.

Concretely, consider the very simple MDP depicted in Figure 1. Starting at state s, we can take one of three possible actions $\{a_1, a_2, a_3\}$. Suppose we are interested in LTL properties $\Diamond P_1$ and $\Diamond P_2$. Thus we want to maximize the probability of reaching the two distinct vertices labeled by P_1 and P_2, respectively. To maximize the probability of $\Diamond P_1$ we should take action a_1, thus reaching P_1 with probability 0.6 and P_2 with probability 0. To maximize the probability of $\Diamond P_2$ we should take a_2, reaching P_2 with probability 0.8 and P_1 with probability 0. To maximize the *sum* total probability of reaching P_1 or P_2, we should take a_3, reaching both with probability 0.5. Now observe that we can also "mix" these pure strategies using randomization to obtain any convex combination of these three value vectors. In the graph on the right in Figure 1, the dotted line plots the Pareto curve for these two properties.

The Pareto curve $\mathcal{P}$ in general contains infinitely many points, and it can be too costly to compute an exact representation for it (see Section 2). Instead of computing it outright we can try to *approximate* it ([PY00]). An ϵ-*approximate Pareto curve* is a set of achievable vectors $\mathcal{P}(\epsilon)$ such that for every achievable vector r there is some vector $t \in \mathcal{P}(\epsilon)$ which "almost" dominates it, meaning $r \leq (1 + \epsilon)t$.

In general, given a labeled MDP M, k distinct ω-regular properties, $\Phi = \langle \varphi_i \mid i = 1, \ldots, k \rangle$, a start state u, and a strategy σ, let $\mathrm{Pr}_u^\sigma(\varphi_i)$ denote the probability that starting at u, using strategy σ, the trajectory satisfies φ_i. For a strategy σ, define the vector $t^\sigma = (t_1^\sigma, \ldots, t_k^\sigma)$, where $t_i^\sigma = \mathrm{Pr}_u^\sigma(\varphi_i)$, for $i = 1, \ldots, k$. We say a value vector $r \in [0,1]^k$ is *achievable* for Φ, if there exists a strategy σ such that $t^\sigma \geq r$.

We provide an algorithm that given MDP M, start state u, properties Φ, and rational value vector $r \in [0,1]^k$, decides whether r is achievable, and if so produces a strategy σ such that $t^\sigma \geq r$. The algorithm runs in time polynomial in the size of the MDP. The strategies may require both randomization and memory. Our algorithm works by first reducing the achievability problem for multiple ω-regular properties to one with multiple reachability objectives, and then reducing the multi-objective reachability problem to a multi-objective linear programming problem. We also show that one can compute an ϵ-approximate Pareto curve for Φ in time polynomial in the size of the MDP and in $1/\epsilon$. To do this, we use our linear programming characterization for achievability, and use results from [PY00] on approximating the Pareto curve for multi-objective linear programming problems.

We also consider more general *multi-objective queries*. Given a boolean combination B of quantitative predicates of the form $\mathrm{Pr}_u^\sigma(\varphi_i) \Delta p$, where $\Delta \in \{\leq, \geq, <, >, =, \neq\}$, and $p \in [0,1]$, a *multi-objective query* asks whether there exists a strategy σ satisfying B (or whether *all* strategies σ satisfy B). It turns out that such queries are not really much more expressive than checking achievability. Namely, checking a fixed query B can be reduced to checking a fixed number of *extended achievability* queries, where for some of the coordinates t_i^σ we can ask for a strict inequality, i.e., that $t_i^\sigma > r_i$. (In general, however, the number and size of the extended achievability queries needed may be exponential in the size of B.) A motivation for allowing general multi-objective queries is to enable *assume-guarantee compositional reasoning* for probabilistic systems, as explained in Section 2.

Whereas our algorithms for quantitative problems use LP methods, we also consider qualitative multi-objective queries. These are queries given by boolean combinations of predicates of the form $\mathrm{Pr}_u^\sigma(\varphi_i) \Delta b$, where $b \in \{0, 1\}$. We give an algorithm using purely graph-theoretic techniques that decides whether there is a strategy that satisfies a qualitative multi-objective query, and if so produces such a strategy. The algorithm runs in time polynomial in the size of the MDP. Even for satisfying qualitative queries the strategy may need to use both randomization and memory.

In typical applications, the MDP is far larger than the size of the query. Also, ω-regular properties can be presented in many ways, and it was already shown in [CY95] that the query complexity of model checking MDPs against even a single LTL property is 2EXPTIME-complete. We remark here that, if properties are expressed via LTL formulas, then our algorithms run in polynomial time in the size of the MDP and in 2EXPTIME in the size of the query, for deciding arbitrary multi-objective queries, where both the MDP and the query are part of the input. So, the worst-case upper bound is the same as with a single LTL objective. However, to keep our complexity analysis simple, we focus in this paper on the model complexity of our algorithms, rather than their query complexity or combined complexity.

Due to lack of space in the proceedings, many proofs have been omitted. Please see [EKVY07] for a fuller version of this paper, containing an appendix with proofs.

Related work. Model checking of MDPs with a single ω-regular objective has been studied in detail (see [CY98, CY95, Var85]). In [CY98], Courcoubetis and Yannakakis also considered MDPs with a single objective given by a positive weighted sum of the probabilities of multiple ω-regular properties, and they showed how to efficiently optimize such objectives for MDPs. They did not consider tradeoffs between multiple ω-regular objectives. We employ and build on techniques developed in [CY98].

Multi-objective optimization is a subject of intensive study in Operations Research and related fields (see, e.g., [Ehr05, Clí97]). Approximating the Pareto curve for general multi-objective optimization problems was considered by Papadimitriou and Yannakakis in [PY00]. Among other results, [PY00] showed that for multi-objective linear programming (i.e., linear constraints and multiple linear objectives), one can compute a (polynomial sized) ϵ-approximate Pareto curve in time polynomial in the size of the LP and in $1/\epsilon$.

Our work is related to recent work by Chatterjee, Majumdar, and Henzinger ([CMH06]), who considered MDPs with multiple discounted reward objectives. They showed that randomized but memoryless strategies suffice for obtaining any achievable value vector for these objectives, and they reduced the multi-objective optimization and achievability (what they call *Pareto realizability*) problems for MDPs with discounted rewards to multi-objective linear programming. They were thus able to apply the results of [PY00] in order to approximate the Pareto curve for this problem. We work in an undiscounted setting, where objectives can be arbitrary ω-regular properties. In our setting, strategies may require both randomization and memory in order to achieve a given value vector. As described earlier, our algorithms first reduce multi-objective ω-regular problems to multi-objective reachability problems, and we then solve multi-objective reachability problems by reducing them to multi-objective LP. For multi-objective reachabilility, we show randomized memoryless strategies do suffice. Our LP methods for multi-objective reachability are closely related to the LP methods used in [CMH06] (and see also, e.g., [Put94], Theorem 6.9.1., where a related result about discounted MDPs is established). However, in order to establish the results in our undiscounted setting, even for reachability we have to overcome some new obstacles that do not arise in the discounted case. In particular, whereas the "discounted frequencies" used in [CMH06] are always well-defined finite values under all strategies, the analogous undiscounted frequencies or "expected number of visits" can in general be infinite for an arbitrary strategy. This forces us to preprocess the MDPs in such a way that ensures that a certain family of undiscounted stochastic flow equations has a finite solution which corresponds to the "expected number of visits" at each state-action pair under a given (memoryless) strategy. It also forces us to give a quite different proof that memoryless strategies suffice to achieve any achievable vector for multi-objective reachability, based on the convexity of the memorylessly achievable set.

Multi-objective MDPs have also been studied extensively in the OR and stochastic control literature (see e.g. [Fur80, Whi82, Hen83, Gho90, WT98]). Much of this work is typically concerned with discounted reward or long-run average reward models, and does not focus on the complexity of algorithms. None of this work seems to directly imply even our result that for multiple reachability objectives checking achievability of a value vector can be decided in polynomial time, not to mention the more general results for multi-objective model checking.

2   Basics and Background

A finite-state MDP $M = (V, \Gamma, \delta)$ consists of a finite set V of states, an action alphabet Γ, and a transition relation δ. Associated with each state v is a set of enabled actions $\Gamma_v \subseteq \Gamma$. The transition relation is given by $\delta \subseteq V \times \Gamma \times [0,1] \times V$. For each state $v \in V$, each enabled action $a \in \Gamma_v$, and every state $v' \in V$, we have exactly one transition $(v, \gamma, p_{(v,\gamma,v')}, v') \in \delta$, for some probability $p_{(v,\gamma,v')} \in [0,1]$, such that $\sum_{v' \in V} p_{(v,\gamma,v')} = 1$. Thus, at each state, each enabled action determines a probability distribution on the next state. There are no other transitions, so no transtitions on disabled actions. We assume every state v has some enabled action, i.e., $\Gamma_v \neq \emptyset$, so there are no dead ends. For our complexity analysis, we assume of course that all probabilities $p_{(v,\gamma,v')}$ are rational. A labeled MDP $M = (V, \Gamma, \delta, l)$ has, in addition a set of propositional predicates $Q = \{Q_1, \ldots, Q_r\}$ which label the states. We view this as being given by a labelling function $l : V \mapsto \Sigma$, where $\Sigma = 2^Q$. There are other ways to present MDPs, e.g., by separating controlled and probabilistic nodes into distinct states. The different presentations are equivalent and efficiently translatable to each other. For a labeled MDP $M = (V, \Gamma, \delta, l)$ with a given initial state $u \in V$, which we denote by M_u, runs of M_u are infinite sequences of states $\pi = \pi_0 \pi_1 \ldots \in V^\omega$, where $\pi_0 = u$ and for all $i \geq 0$, $\pi_i \in V$ and there is a transition $(\pi_i, \gamma, p, \pi_{i+1}) \in \delta$, for some $\gamma \in \Gamma_{\pi_i}$ and some probability $p > 0$. Each run induces an ω-word over Σ, namely $l(\pi) \doteq l(\pi_0) l(\pi_1) \ldots \in \Sigma^\omega$.

A *strategy* is a function $\sigma : (V\Gamma)^* V \mapsto \mathcal{D}(\Gamma)$, which maps a finite history of play to a probability distribution on the next action. Here $\mathcal{D}(\Gamma)$ denotes the set of probability distributions on the set Γ. Moreover, it must be the case that for all histories wu, $\sigma(wu) \in \mathcal{D}(\Gamma_u)$, i.e., the probabilty distribution has support only over the actions available at state u. A strategy is *pure* if $\sigma(wu)$ has support on exactly one action, i.e., with probability 1 a single action is played at every history. A strategy is *memoryless* (stationary) if the strategy depends only on the last state, i.e., if $\sigma(wu) = \sigma(w'u)$ for all $w, w' \in (V\Gamma)^*$. If σ is memoryless, we can simply define it as a function $\sigma : V \mapsto \mathcal{D}(\Gamma)$. An MDP M with initial state u, together with a strategy σ, naturally induces a Markov chain M_u^σ, whose states are the histories of play in M_u, and such that from state $s = wv$ if $\gamma \in \Gamma_v$, there is a transition to state $s' = wv\gamma v'$ with probability $\sigma(wv)(\gamma) \cdot p_{(v,\gamma,v')}$. A run θ in M_u^σ is thus given by a sequence $\theta = \theta_0\theta_1 \ldots$, where $\theta_0 = u$ and each $\theta_i \in (V\Gamma)^*V$, for all $i \geq 0$. We associate to each history $\theta_i = wv$ the label of its last state v. In other words, we overload the notation and define $l(wv) \doteq l(v)$. We likewise associate with each run θ the ω-word $l(\theta) \doteq l(\theta_0)l(\theta_1)\ldots$. Suppose we are given φ, an LTL formula or Büchi automaton, or any other formalism for expressing an ω-regular language over alphabet Σ. Let $L(\varphi) \subseteq \Sigma^\omega$ denote the language expressed by φ. We write $\Pr_u^\sigma(\varphi)$ to denote the probability that a trajectory θ of M_u^σ satitisfies φ, i.e., that $l(\theta) \in L(\varphi)$. For generality, rather than just allowing an initial vertex u we allow an initial probability distribution $\alpha \in \mathcal{D}(V)$. Let $\Pr_\alpha^\sigma(\varphi)$ denote the probability that under strategy σ, starting with initial distribution α, we will satify ω-regular property φ. These probabilities are well defined because the set of such runs is Borel measurable (see, e.g., [Var85, CY95]).

As in the introduction, for a k-tuple of ω-regular properties $\Phi = \langle \varphi_1, \ldots, \varphi_k \rangle$, given a strategy σ, we let $t^\sigma = (t_1^\sigma, \ldots, t_k^\sigma)$, with $t_i^\sigma = \Pr_u^\sigma(\varphi_i)$, for $i = 1, \ldots, k$. For MDP M and starting state u, we define the *achievable* set of value vectors with respect to Φ to be $U_{M_u,\Phi} = \{r \in \mathbb{R}_{\geq 0}^k \mid \exists\sigma \text{ such that } t^\sigma \geq r\}$. For a set $U \subseteq \mathbb{R}^k$, we define a subset $\mathcal{P} \subseteq U$ of it, called the *Pareto curve* or the *Pareto set* of U, consisting of the set of *Pareto optimal* (or *Pareto efficient*) vectors inside U. A vector $v \in U$ is called *Pareto optimal* if $\neg\exists v'(v' \in U \wedge v \leq v' \wedge v \neq v')$. Thus $\mathcal{P} = \{v \in U \mid v \text{ is Pareto optimal}\}$. We use $\mathcal{P}_{M_u,\Phi} \subseteq U_{M_u,\Phi}$ to denote the Pareto curve of $U_{M_u,\Phi}$.

It is clear, e.g., from Figure 1, that the Pareto curve is in general an infinite set. In fact, it follows from our results that for general ω-regular objectives the Pareto set is a convex polyhedral set. In principle, we may want to compute some kind of exact representation of this set by, e.g., enumerating all the vertices (on the upper envelope) of the polytope that defines the Pareto curve, or enumerating the facets that define it. It is not possible to do this in polynomial-time in general. In fact, the following theorem holds (the proof is omitted here):

Theorem 1. *There is a family of MDPs, $\langle M(n) \mid n \in \mathbb{N} \rangle$, where $M(n)$ has n states and size $O(n)$, such that for $M(n)$ the Pareto curve for two reachability objectives, $\Diamond P_1$ and $\Diamond P_2$, contains $n^{\Omega(\log n)}$ vertices (and thus $n^{\Omega(\log n)}$ facets).*

So, the Pareto curve is in general a polyhedral surface of superpolynomial size, and thus cannot be constructed exactly in polynomial time. We show, however, that the Pareto set can be efficiently *approximated* to any desired accuracy $\epsilon > 0$. An ϵ-*approximate Pareto curve*, $\mathcal{P}_{M_u,\Phi}(\epsilon) \subseteq U_{M_u,\Phi}$, is any achievable set such that $\forall r \in U_{M_u,\Phi} \ \exists t \in \mathcal{P}_{M_u,\Phi}(\epsilon)$ such that $r \leq (1+\epsilon)t$. When the subscripts M_u and Φ are clear from the context, we will drop them and use U, $\mathcal{P}$, and $\mathcal{P}(\epsilon)$ to denote the achievable set, Pareto set, and ϵ-approximate Pareto set, respectively.

We also consider general *multi-objective queries*. A *quantitative predicate* over ω-regular property φ_i is a statement of the form $\Pr_u^\sigma(\varphi_i)\Delta p$, for some rational probability $p \in [0,1]$, and where Δ is a comparison operator $\Delta \in \{\leq, \geq, <, >, =\}$.

Suppose B is a boolean combination over such predicates. Then, given M and u, and B, we can ask whether there exists a strategy σ such that B holds, or whether B holds for all σ. Note that since B can be put in DNF form, and the quantification over strategies pushed into the disjuction, and since ω-regular languages are closed under complementation, any query of the form $\exists \sigma B$ (or of the form $\forall \sigma B$) can be transformed to a disjunction (a negated disjunction, respectively) of queries of the form:

$$\exists \sigma \bigwedge_i (\mathrm{Pr}_u^\sigma(\varphi_i) \geq r_i) \wedge \bigwedge_j (\mathrm{Pr}_u^\sigma(\psi_j) > r_j') \tag{1}$$

We call queries of the form (1) *extended achievability queries*. Thus, if the multi-objective query is fixed, it suffices to perform a fixed number of extended achievability queries to decide any multi-objective query. Note, however, that the number of extended achievability queries we need could be exponential in the size of B. We do not focus on optimizing query complexity in this paper.

A motivation for allowing general multi-objective queries is to enable *assume-guarantee compositional reasoning* for probabilistic systems. Consider, e.g., a probabilistic system consisting of the concurrent composition of two components, M_1 and M_2, where output from M_1 provides input to M_2 and thus controls M_2. We denote this by $M_1 \triangleright M_2$. M_2 itself may generate outputs for some external device, and M_1 may also be controlled by external inputs. (One can also consider symmetric composition, where outputs from both components provide inputs to both. Here, for simplicity, we restrict ourselves to asymmetric composition where M_1 controls M_2.) Let M be an MDP with separate input and output action alphabets Σ_1 and Σ_2, and let φ_1 and φ_2 denote ω-regular properties over these two alphabets, respectively. We write $\langle \varphi_1 \rangle_{\geq r_1} M \langle \varphi_2 \rangle_{\geq r_2}$, to denote the assertion that *"if the input controller of M satisfies φ_1 with probability $\geq r_1$, then the output generated by M satisfies φ_2 with probability $\geq r_2$"*. Using this, we can formulate a general compositional assume-guarantee proof rule:

$$\frac{\langle \varphi_1 \rangle_{\geq r_1} M_1 \langle \varphi_2 \rangle_{\geq r_2}}{\langle \varphi_1 \rangle_{\geq r_1} \ M_1 \triangleright M_2 \ \langle \varphi_3 \rangle_{\geq r_3}}$$

Thus, to check $\langle \varphi_1 \rangle_{\geq r_1} M_1 \triangleright M_2 \langle \varphi_3 \rangle_{\geq r_3}$ it suffices to check two properties of smaller systems: $\langle \varphi_1 \rangle_{\geq r_1} M_1 \langle \varphi_2 \rangle_{\geq r_2}$ and $\langle \varphi_2 \rangle_{\geq r_2} M_2 \langle \varphi_3 \rangle_{\geq r_3}$. Note that checking $\langle \varphi_1 \rangle_{\geq r_1} M \langle \varphi_2 \rangle_{\geq r_2}$ amounts to checking that there does not exist a strategy σ controlling M such that $\mathrm{Pr}_u^\sigma(\varphi_1) \geq r_1$ and $\mathrm{Pr}_u^\sigma(\varphi_2) < r_2$.

We also consider *qualitative multi-objective queries*. These are queries restricted so that B contains only *qualitative predicates* of the form $\mathrm{Pr}_u^\sigma(\varphi_i) \Delta b$, where $b \in \{0, 1\}$. These can, e.g., be used to check qualitative assume-guarantee conditions of the form: $\langle \varphi_1 \rangle_{\geq 1} M \langle \varphi_2 \rangle_{\geq 1}$. It is not hard to see that again, via

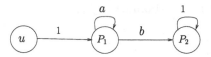

Fig. 2. The MDP M'

boolean manipulations and complementation of automata, we can convert any qualitative query to a number of queries of the form:

$$\exists \sigma \bigwedge_{\varphi \in \Phi} (\mathrm{Pr}_u^\sigma(\varphi) = 1) \wedge \bigwedge_{\psi \in \Psi} (\mathrm{Pr}_u^\sigma(\psi) > 0)$$

where Φ and Ψ are sets of ω-regular properties. It thus suffices to consider only these qualitative queries.

In the next sections we study how to decide various classes of multi-objective queries, and how to approximate the Pareto curve for properties Φ. Let us observe here a difficulty that we will have to deal with. Namely, in general we will need both randomization and memory in our strategies in order to satisfy even simple qualitative multi-objective queries. Consider the MDP, M', shown in Figure 2, and consider the conjunctive query: $B \equiv \mathrm{Pr}_u^\sigma(\Box\Diamond P_1) > 0 \wedge \mathrm{Pr}_u^\sigma(\Box\Diamond P_2) > 0$. It is not hard to see that starting at state u in M' any strategy σ that satisfies B must use both memory and randomization. Each predicate in B can be satisfied in isolation (in fact with probability 1), but with a memoryless or deterministic strategy if we try to satisfy $\Box\Diamond P_2$ with non-zero probability, we will be forced to satisfy $\Box\Diamond P_1$ with probability 0. Note, however, that we can satisfy both with probability > 0 using a strategy that uses both memory and randomness: namely, upon reaching the state labeled P_1 for the first time, with probability $1/2$ we use move a and with probability $1/2$ we use move b. Thereafter, upon encountering the state labeled P_1 for the nth time, $n \geq 2$, we deterministically pick action a. This clearly assures that both predicates are satisfied with probability $= 1/2 > 0$.

3   Multi-objective Reachability

In this section, as a step towards quantitative multi-objective model checking problems, we study a simpler multi-objective reachability problem. Specifically, we are given an MDP, $M = (V, \Gamma, \delta)$, a starting state u, and a collection of target sets $F_i \subseteq V$, $i = 1, \ldots, k$. The sets F_i may overlap. We have k objectives: the i-th objective is to maximize the probability of $\Diamond F_i$, i.e., of reaching some state in F_i. We assume that the states $F = \bigcup_{i=1}^k F_i$ are all absorbing states with a self-loop. In other words, for all $v \in F$, $(v, a, 1, v) \in \delta$ and $\Gamma_v = \{a\}$.[1]

We first need to do some preprocessing on the MDP, to remove some useless states. For each state $v \in V \setminus F$ we can check easily whether there exists a

---

[1] The assumption that target states are absorbing is necessary for the proofs in this section, but it will of course follow from the model checking results in Section 5, which build on this section, that multi-objective reachability problems for arbitrary target states can also be handled with the same complexities.

Objectives $(i = 1, \ldots, k)$:   **Maximize** $\sum_{v \in F_i} y_v$;

Subject to:

$$\sum_{\gamma \in \Gamma_v} y_{(v,\gamma)} - \sum_{v' \in V} \sum_{\gamma' \in \Gamma_{v'}} p_{(v',\gamma',v)} y_{(v',\gamma')} = \alpha(v) \qquad \text{For all } v \in V \setminus F;$$
$$y_v - \sum_{v' \in V \setminus F} \sum_{\gamma' \in \Gamma_{v'}} p_{(v',\gamma',v)} y_{(v',\gamma')} \qquad = 0 \qquad \text{For all } v \in F;$$
$$y_v \qquad \geq 0 \qquad \text{For all } v \in F;$$
$$y_{(v,\gamma)} \qquad \geq 0 \qquad \text{For all } v \in V \setminus F \text{ and } \gamma \in \Gamma_u;$$

Fig. 3. Multi-objective LP for the multi-objective MDP reachability problem

strategy σ such that $Pr_v^\sigma(\Diamond F) > 0$: this just amounts to whether there exists a path from v to F in the underlying graph of the MDP. Let us call a state that does not satisfy this property a *bad* state. Clearly, for the purposes of optimizing reachability objectives, we can look for and remove all bad states from an MDP. Thus, it is safe to assume that bad states do not exist.[2] Let us call an MDP with goal states F *cleaned-up* if it does not contain any bad states.

Proposition 1. *For a cleaned-up MDP, an initial distribution $\alpha \in \mathcal{D}(V \setminus F)$, and a vector of probabilities $r \in [0, 1]^k$, there exists a (memoryless) strategy σ such that $\bigwedge_{i=1}^k \Pr_\alpha^\sigma(\Diamond F_i) \geq r_i$ if and only if there exists a (respectively, memoryless) strategy σ' such that $\bigwedge_{i=1}^k \Pr_\alpha^{\sigma'}(\Diamond F_i) \geq r_i \wedge \bigwedge_{v \in V} \Pr_v^{\sigma'}(\Diamond F) > 0$.*

Now, consider the multi-objective LP described in Figure 3.[3] The set of variables in this LP are as follows: for each $v \in F$, there is a variable y_v, and for each $v \in V \setminus F$ and each $\gamma \in \Gamma_v$ there is a variable $y_{(v,\gamma)}$.

Theorem 2. *Suppose we are given a cleaned-up MDP, $M = (V, \Gamma, \delta)$ with multiple target sets $F_i \subseteq V$, $i = 1, \ldots, k$, where every target $v \in F = \bigcup_{i=1}^k F_i$ is an absorbing state. Let $\alpha \in \mathcal{D}(V \setminus F)$ be an initial distribution (in particular $V \setminus F \neq \emptyset$). Let $r \in (0, 1]^k$ be a vector of positive probabilities. Then the following are all equivalent:*

(1.) There is a (possibly randomized) memoryless strategy σ such that

$$\bigwedge_{i=1}^k (\Pr_\alpha^\sigma(\Diamond F_i) \geq r_i)$$

---

[2] Technically, we would need to install a new "dead" absorbing state $v_{dead} \notin F$, such that all the probabilities going into states that have been removed now go to v_{dead}. For convenience in notation, instead of explicitly adding v_{dead} we treat it as implicit: we allow that for some states $v \in V$ and some action $a \in \Gamma_v$ we have $\sum_{v' \in V} p_{(v,\gamma,v')} < 1$, and we implicitly assume that there is an "invisible" transition to v_{dead} with the residual probability, i.e., with $p_{(v,\gamma,v_{dead})} = 1 - \sum_{v' \in V} p_{(v,\gamma,v')}$. Of course, v_{dead} would then be a "bad" state, but we can ignore this implicit state.

[3] We mention without further elaboration that this LP can be derived, using complementary slackness, from the dual LP of the standard LP for single-objective reachability obtained from Bellman's optimality equations, whose variables are x_v, for $v \in V$, and whose unique optimal solution is the vector x^* with $x_v^* = \max_\sigma \Pr_v^\sigma(\Diamond F)$ (see, e.g., [Put94, CY98]).

(2.) There is a feasible solution y' for the multi-objective LP in Fig. 3 such that

$$\bigwedge_{i=1}^{k} (\textstyle\sum_{v \in F_i} y'_v \geq r_i)$$

(3.) There is an arbitrary strategy σ such that

$$\bigwedge_{i=1}^{k} (Pr_\alpha^\sigma(\Diamond F_i) \geq r_i)$$

Proof

(1.) $\Rightarrow$ (2.). Since the MDP is cleaned up, by Proposition 1 we can assume there is a memoryless strategy σ such that $\bigwedge_{i=1}^{k} \Pr_\alpha^\sigma(\Diamond F_i) \geq r_i$ and $\forall v \in V$ $Pr_v^\sigma(\Diamond F) > 0$. Consider the square matrix P^σ whose size is $|V \setminus F| \times |V \setminus F|$, and whose rows and columns are indexed by states in $V \setminus F$. The (v, v')'th entry of P^σ, $P^\sigma_{v,v'}$, is the probability that starting in state v we shall in one step end up in state v'. In other words, $P^\sigma_{v,v'} = \sum_{\gamma \in \Gamma_v} \sigma(v)(\gamma) \cdot p_{v,\gamma,v'}$.

For all $v \in V \setminus F$, let $y'_{(v,\gamma)} = \sum_{v' \in V \setminus F} \alpha(v') \sum_{n=0}^{\infty} (P^\sigma)^n_{v',v} \sigma(v)(\gamma)$. In other words $y'_{(v,\gamma)}$ denotes the "expected number of times that, using the strategy σ, starting in the distribution α, we will visit the state v and upon doing so choose action γ". We don't know yet that these are finite values, but assuming they are, for $v \in F$, let $y'_v = \sum_{v' \in V \setminus F} \sum_{\gamma' \in \Gamma_{v'}} p_{(v',\gamma',v)} y'_{(v',\gamma')}$. This completes the definition of the entire vector y'.

Lemma 1. *The vector y' is well defined (i.e., all entries $y'_{(v,\gamma)}$ are finite). Moreover, y' is a feasible solution to the constraints of the LP in Figure 3.*

Now we argue that $\sum_{v \in F_i} y'_v = \Pr_\alpha^\sigma(\Diamond F_i)$. To see this, note that for $v \in F$, $y'_v = \sum_{v' \in V \setminus F} \sum_{\gamma' \in \Gamma_{v'}} p_{(v',\gamma',v)} y'_{(v',\gamma')}$ is precisely the *"expected number of times that we will transition into state v for the first time"*, starting at distribution α. The reason we can say "for the first time" is because only the states in $V \setminus F$ are included in the matrix P^σ. But note that this italicised statement in quotes is another way to define the probability of eventually reaching state v. This equality can be establish formally, but we omit the formal algebraic derivation here. Thus $\sum_{v \in F_i} y'_v = \Pr_\alpha^\sigma(\Diamond F_i) \geq r_i$. We are done with (1.) $\Rightarrow$ (2.).

(2.) $\Rightarrow$ (1.). We now wish to show that if y'' is a feasible solution to the multi-objective LP such that $\sum_{v \in F_i} y''_v \geq r_i > 0$, for all $i = 1, \ldots, k$, then there exists a memoryless strategy σ such that $\bigwedge_{i=1}^{k} \Pr_\alpha^\sigma(\Diamond F_i) \geq r_i$.

Suppose we have such a solution y''. Let $S = \{v \in V \setminus F \mid \sum_{\gamma \in \Gamma_v} y''_{(v,\gamma)} > 0\}$. Let σ be the memoryless strategy, given as follows. For each $v \in S$

$$\sigma(v)(\gamma) := \frac{y''_{(v,\gamma)}}{\sum_{\gamma' \in \Gamma_v} y''_{v,\gamma'}}$$

Note that since $\sum_{\gamma \in \Gamma_v} y''_{(v,\gamma)} > 0$, $\sigma(v)$ is a well-defined probability distribution on the moves at state $v \in S$. For the remaining states $v \in (V \setminus F) \setminus S$, let $\sigma(v)$ be an arbitrary distribution in $\mathcal{D}(\Gamma_v)$.

Lemma 2. *This memoryless strategy σ satisfies $\bigwedge_{i=1}^{k} Pr_\alpha^\sigma(\Diamond F_i) \geq r_i$.*

Proof. The proof is in [EKVY07]. Here we very briefly sketch the argument. We can think of a feasible solution y'' to the LP constraints as defining a "stochastic flow", whose "source" is the initial distribution $\alpha(v)$, and whose sinks are F. By flow conservation, vertices $v \in V \setminus F$ that have positive outflow (and thus positive inflow) must all be reachable from the support of α, and must all reach F, and can not reach any vertex with zero outflow. The strategy σ is obtained by normalizing the outflow on each action at the states with positive outflow. It can be shown that, using σ, the expected number of times we choose action γ at vertex v is again given by $y''_{(v,\gamma)}$. Therefore, since transitions into the states $v \in F$ from $V \setminus F$ are only crossed once, the constraint defining the value y''_v yields $y''_v = \Pr^\sigma_\alpha(\lozenge\{v\})$. □

This completes the proof that (2.) ⇒ (1.).

(3.) ⇔ (1.). Clearly (1.) ⇒ (3.), so we need to show that (3.) ⇒ (1.).

Let U be the set of achievable vectors, i.e., all k-vectors $r = \langle r_1 \ldots r_k \rangle$ such that there is a (unrestricted) strategy σ such that $\bigwedge_{i=1}^k \Pr^\sigma_\alpha(\lozenge F_i) \geq r_i$. Let $U^\odot$ be the analogous set where the strategy σ is restricted to be a possibly randomized but memoryless (stationary) strategy. Clearly, U and $U^\odot$ are both downward closed, i.e., if $r \geq r'$ and $r \in U$ then also $r' \in U$, and similarly with $U^\odot$. Also, obviously $U^\odot \subseteq U$. We characterized $U^\odot$ in (1.) ⇔ (2.), in terms of a multi-objective LP. Thus, $U^\odot$ is the projection of the feasible space of a set of linear inequalities (a polyhedral set), namely the set of inequalities in the variables y given in Fig. 3 and the inequalities $\sum_{v \in F_i} y_v \geq r_i$, $i = 1, \ldots, k$. The feasible space is a polyhedron in the space indexed by the y variables and the r_i's, and $U^\odot$ is its projection on the subspace indexed by the r_i's. Since the projection of a convex set is convex, it follows that $U^\odot$ is convex.

Suppose that there is a point $r \in U \setminus U^\odot$. Since $U^\odot$ is convex, this implies that there is a separating hyperplane (see, e.g., [GLS93]) that separates r from $U^\odot$, and in fact since $U^\odot$ is downward closed, there is a separating hyperplane with non-negative coefficients, i.e. there is a non-negative "weight" vector $w = \langle w_1, \ldots, w_k \rangle$ such that $w^T r = \sum_{i=1}^k w_i r_i > w^T x$ for every point $x \in U^\odot$.

Consider now the MDP M with the following undiscounted reward structure. There is 0 reward for every state, action and transition, except for transitions to a state $v \in F$ from a state in $V \setminus F$; i.e. a reward is produced only once, in the first transition into a state of F. The reward for every transition to a state $v \in F$ is $\sum \{w_i \mid i \in \{1, \ldots, k\} \ \& \ v \in F_i\}$. By the definition, the expected reward of a policy σ is $\sum_{i=1}^k w_i \Pr^\sigma_\alpha(\lozenge F_i)$. From classical MDP theory, we know that there is a memoryless strategy (in fact even a deterministic one) that maximizes the expected reward for this type of reward structure. (Namely, this is a positive bounded reward case: see, e.g., Theorem 7.2.11 in [Put94].) Therefore, $\max\{w^T x \mid x \in U\} = \max\{w^T x \mid x \in U^\odot\}$, contradicting our assumption that $w^T r > \max\{w^T x \mid x \in U^\odot\}$. □

Corollary 1. *Given an MDP $M = (V, \Gamma, \delta)$, a number of target sets $F_i \subseteq V$, $i = 1, \ldots, k + k'$, such that every state $v \in F = \bigcup_{i=1}^{k+k'} F_i$ is absorbing, and an initial state u (or even initial distribution $\alpha \in \mathcal{D}(V)$):*

(a.) Given an extended achievability query for reachability, $\exists \sigma B$, where

$$B \equiv \bigwedge_{i=1}^{k} (Pr_u^{\sigma}(\Diamond F_i) \geq r_i) \wedge \bigwedge_{j=k+1}^{k+k'} (Pr_u^{\sigma}(\Diamond F_j) > r_j),$$

we can in time polynomial in the size of the input, $|M|+|B|$, decide whether $\exists \sigma \, B$ is satisfiable and if so construct a memoryless strategy that satisfies it.

(b.) For $\epsilon > 0$, we can compute an ϵ-approximate Pareto curve $\mathcal{P}(\epsilon)$ for the multi-objective reachability problem with objectives $\Diamond F_i$, $i = 1, \ldots, k$, in time polynomial in $|M|$ and $1/\epsilon$.

4   Qualitative Multi-objective Model Checking

Theorem 3. *Given an MDP M, an initial state u, and a qualitative multi-objective query B, we can decide whether there exists a strategy σ that satisfies B, and if so construct such a strategy, in time polynomial in $|M|$, and using only graph-theoretic methods (in particular, without linear programming).*

Proof. (Sketch) By the discussion in Section 2, it suffices to consider the case where we are given MDP, M, and two sets of ω-regular properties Φ, Ψ, and we want a strategy σ such that

$$\bigwedge_{\varphi \in \Phi} Pr_u^{\sigma}(\varphi) = 1 \wedge \bigwedge_{\psi \in \Psi} Pr_u^{\sigma}(\psi) > 0$$

Assume the properties in Φ, Ψ are all given by (nondeterministic) Büchi automata A_i. We will use and build on results in [CY98]. In [CY98] (Lemma 4.4, page 1411) it is shown that we can construct from M and from a collection A_i, $i = 1, \ldots, m$, of Büchi automata, a new MDP M' (a refinement of M) which is the "product" of M with the *naive determinization* of all the A_i's (i.e., the result of applying the standard subset construction on each A_i, without imposing any acceptance condition).[4] This MDP M' has the following properties. For every subset R of $\Phi \cup \Psi$ there is a subset T_R of corresponding "target states" of M' (and we can compute this subset efficiently) that satisfies the following two conditions:

(I) If a trajectory of M' hits a state in T_R at some point, then we can apply from that point on a strategy μ_R (which is deterministic but uses memory) which ensures that the resulting infinite trajectory satisfies all properties in R almost surely (i.e., with conditional probability 1, conditioned on the initial prefix that hits T_R).

---

[4] Technically, we have to slightly adapt the constructions of [CY98], which use the convention that MDP states are either purely controlled or purely probabilistic, to the convention used in this paper which combines both control and probabilistic behavior at each state. But these adaptations are straightforward.

(II) For every strategy, the set of trajectories that satisfy all properties in R and do not infinitely often hit some state of T_R has probability 0.

We now outline the algorithm for deciding qualitative multi-objective queries.

1. Construct the MDP M' from M and from the properties Φ and Ψ.
2. Compute T_Φ, and compute for each property $\psi_i \in \Psi$ the set of states T_{R_i} where $R_i = \Phi \cup \{\psi_i\}$.[5]
3. If $\Phi \neq \emptyset$, prune M' by identifying and removing all "bad" states by applying the following rules.
   (a) All states v that cannot "reach" any state in T_Φ are "bad".[6]
   (b) If for a state v there is an action $\gamma \in \Gamma_v$ such that there is a transition $(v, \gamma, p, v') \in \delta$, $p > 0$, and v' is bad, then remove γ from Γ_v.
   (c) If for some state v, $\Gamma_v = \emptyset$, then mark v as bad.
   Keep applying these rules until no more states can be labelled bad and no more actions removed for any state.
4. Restrict M' to the reachable states (from the initial state u) that are not bad, and restrict their action sets to actions that have not been removed, and let M'' be the resulting MDP.
5. If ($M'' = \emptyset$ or $\exists \psi_i \in \Psi$ such that M'' does not contain any state of T_{R_i})
   then return No.
   Else return Yes.

Correctness proof: In one direction, suppose there is a strategy σ such that $\bigwedge_{\varphi \in \Phi} \Pr_u^\sigma(\varphi) = 1 \wedge \bigwedge_{\psi \in \Psi} \Pr_u^\sigma(\psi) > 0$. First, note that there cannot be any finite prefix of a trajectory under σ that hits a state that cannot reach any state in T_Φ. For, if there was such a path, then all trajectories that start with this prefix go only finitely often through T_Φ. Hence (by property (II) above) almost all these trajectories do not satisfy all properties in Φ, which contradicts the fact that all these properties have probability 1 under σ. From the fact that no path under σ hits a state that cannot reach T_Φ, it follows by an easy induction that no finite trajectory under σ hits any bad state. That is, under σ all trajectories stay in the sub-MDP M''. Since every property $\psi_i \in \Psi$ has probability $\Pr_u^\sigma(\psi_i) > 0$ and almost all trajectories that satisfy ψ_i and Φ must hit a state of T_{R_i} (property (II) above), it follows that M'' contains some state of T_{R_i} for each $\psi_i \in \Psi$. Thus the algorithm returns Yes.

In the other direction, suppose that the algorithm returns Yes. First, note that for all states v of M'', and all enabled actions $\gamma \in \Gamma_v$ in M'', all transitions $(v, \gamma, p, v') \in \delta$, $p > 0$ of M' must still be in M'' (otherwise, γ would have been removed from Γ_v at some stage using rule 3(b)). On the other hand, some states may have some missing actions in M''. Next, note that all bottom strongly

---

[5] Actually these sets are all computed together: we compute maximal *closed* components of the MDP, determine the properties that each component *favors* (see Def. 4.1 of [CY98]), and tag each state with the sets for which it is a target state.

[6] By "reach", we mean that starting at the state $v = v_0$, there a sequence of transitions $(v_i, \gamma, p_i, v_{i+1}) \in \delta$, $p_i > 0$, such that $v_n \in T_\Phi$ for some $n \geq 0$.

connected components (bscc's) of M'' (to be more precise, in the underlying one-step reachability graph of M'') contain a state of T_Φ (if $\Phi = \emptyset$ then all states are in T_Φ), for otherwise the states in these bsccs would have been eliminated at some stage using rule 3(a).

Define the following strategy σ which works in two phases. In the first phase, the trajectory stays within M''. At each control state take a random action that remains in M'' out of the state; the probabilities do not matter, we can use any non-zero probability for all the remaining actions. In addition, at each state, if the state is in T_Φ or it is in T_{R_i} for some property $\psi_i \in \Psi$, then with some nonzero probability the strategy decides to terminate phase 1 and move to phase 2 by switching to the strategy μ_Φ or μ_{R_i} respectively, which it applies from that point on. (Note: a state may belong to several T_{R_i}'s, in which case each one of them gets some non-zero probability - the precise value is unimportant.)

We claim that this strategy σ meets the desired requirements - it ensures probability 1 for all properties in Φ and positive probability for all properties in Ψ. For each $\psi_i \in \Psi$, the MDP M'' contains some state of T_{R_i}; with nonzero probability the process will follow a path to that state and then switch to the strategy μ_{R_i} from that point on, in which case it will satisfy ψ_i (property (I) above). Thus, all properties in Ψ are satisfied with positive probability.

As for Φ (if $\Phi \neq \emptyset$), note that with probability 1 the process will switch at some point to phase 2, because all bscc's of M'' have a state in T_Φ. When it switches to phase 2 it applies strategy μ_Φ or μ_{R_i} for some $R_i = \Phi \cup \{\psi_i\}$, hence in either case it will satisfy all properties of Φ with probability 1.   ⊓

5   Quantitative Multi-objective Model Checking

Theorem 4

(1.) *Given an MDP M, an initial state u, and a quantitative multi-objective query B, we can decide whether there exists a strategy σ that satisfies B, and if so construct such a strategy, in time polynomial in $|M|$.*

(2.) *Moreover, given ω-regular properties $\Phi = \langle \varphi_1, \ldots, \varphi_k \rangle$, we can construct an ϵ-approximate Pareto curve $P_{M_u,\Phi}(\epsilon)$, for the set of achievable probability vectors $U_{M_u,\Phi}$ in time polynomial in M and in $1/\epsilon$.*

Proof. (Sketch.) For (1.), by the discussion in Section 2, we only need to consider extended achievability queries, $B \equiv \bigwedge_{i=1}^{k'} \mathrm{Pr}_u^\sigma(\varphi_i) \geq r_i \wedge \bigwedge_{j=k'+1}^{k} \mathrm{Pr}_u^\sigma(\varphi_j) > r_j$, where $k \geq k' \geq 0$, and for a vector $r \in (0,1]^k$. Let $\Phi = \langle \varphi_1, \ldots, \varphi_k \rangle$. We are going to reduce this multi-objective problem with objectives Φ to the quantitative multi-objective reachability problem studied in Section 3. From our reduction, both (1.) and (2.) will follow, using Corollary 1. As in the proof of Theorem 3, we will build on constructions from [CY98]: form the MDP M' consisting of the product of M with the naive determinizations of the automata A_i for the properties $\varphi_i \in \Phi$. For each subset $R \subseteq \Phi$ we determine the corresponding subset T_R of target states in M'.[7]

---

[7] Again, we don't need to compute these sets separately. See Footnote 5.

Construct the following MDP M''. Add to M' a new absorbing state s_R for each subset R of Φ. For each state u of M' and each maximal subset R such that $u \in T_R$ add a new action γ_R to Γ_u, and an new transition $(u, \gamma_R, 1, s_R)$ to δ. With each property $\varphi_i \in \Phi$ we associate the subset of states $F_i = \{s_R \mid \varphi_i \in R\}$. Let $\overline{F} = \langle \Diamond F_1, \ldots, \Diamond F_k \rangle$. Let u^* be the initial state of the product MDP M'', given by the start state u of M and the start states of all the naively determinized A_i's. Recall that $U_{M_u,\Phi} \subseteq [0,1]^k$ denotes the achievable set for the properties Φ in M starting at u, and that $U_{M''_{u^*},\overline{F}}$ denotes the achievable set for $\overline{F}$ in M'' starting at u^*.

Lemma 3. $U_{M_u,\Phi} = U_{M''_{u^*},\overline{F}}$. *Moreover, from a strategy σ that achieves r in $U_{M_u,\Phi}$, we can recover a strategy σ' that achieves r in $U_{M''_{u^*},\overline{F}}$, and vice versa.*

It follows from the Lemma that: there exists a strategy σ in M such that $\bigwedge_{i=1}^{k'} \mathrm{Pr}_u^\sigma(\varphi_i) \geq r_i \wedge \bigwedge_{j=k'+1}^{k} \mathrm{Pr}_u^\sigma(\varphi_j) > r_j$ if and only if there exists a strategy σ' in M'' such that $\bigwedge_{i=1}^{k'} \mathrm{Pr}_{u^*}^\sigma(\Diamond F_i) \geq r_i \wedge \bigwedge_{j=k'+1}^{k} \mathrm{Pr}_{u^*}^\sigma(\Diamond F_j) > r_j$. Moreover, such strategies can be recovered from each other. Thus (1.) and (2.) follow, using Corollary 1. $\qquad\square$

6 Concluding Remarks

We mention that although our quantitative upper bounds use LP methods, in practice there is a way to combine efficient iterative numerical methods for MDPs, e.g., based on value iteration, with our results in order to approximate the Pareto curve for multi-objective model checking. This is because the results of [PY00] for multi-objective LPs only require a black-box routine that optimizes (exactly or approximately) positive linear combinations of the LP objectives. We omit the details of this approach.

An important extension of the applications of our results is to extend the asymmetric assume-guarantee compositional reasoning rule discussed in Section 2 to a general compositional framework for probabilistic systems. It is indeed possible to describe symmetric assume-guarantee rules that allow for general composition of MDPs. A full treatment of the general compositional framework requires a separate paper, and we plan to expand on this in follow-up work.

Acknowledgements. We thank the Newton Institute, where we initiated discussions on the topics of this paper during the Spring 2006 programme on Logic and Algorithms. Several authors acknowledge support from the following grants: EPSRC GR/S11107 and EP/D07956X, MRL 2005-04; NSF grants CCR-9988322, CCR-0124077, CCR-0311326, and ANI-0216467, BSF grant 9800096, Texas ATP grant 003604-0058-2003, Guggenheim Fellowship; NSF CCF-04-30946.

References

[Clí97]   J. Clímaco, editor. *Multicriteria Analysis.* Springer-Verlag, 1997.

[CMH06]   K. Chatterjee, R. Majumdar, and T. Henzinger. Markov decision processes with multiple objectives. In *Proc. of 23rd Symp. on Theoretical Aspects of Computer Science*, volume LNCS 3884, pages 325–336, 2006.

[CY95]   C. Courcoubetis and M. Yannakakis. The complexity of probabilistic verification. *Journal of the ACM*, 42(4):857–907, 1995.

[CY98]   C. Courcoubetis and M. Yannakakis. Markov decision processes and regular events. *IEEE Trans. on Automatic Control*, 43(10):1399–1418, 1998.

[Ehr05]   M. Ehrgott. *Multicriteria optimization.* Springer-Verlag, 2005.

[EKVY07]   K. Etessami, M. Kwiatkowska, M. Vardi, & M. Yannakakis. Multi-Objective Model Checking of Markov Decision Processes. Fuller version of this conference paper with proofs. http://homepages.inf.ed.ac.uk/kousha/homepages/tacas07long.pdf

[Fur80]   N. Furukawa. Characterization of optimal policies in vector-valued Markovian decision processes. *Mathematics of Operations Research*, 5(2):271–279, 1980.

[Gho90]   M. K. Ghosh. Markov decision processes with multiple costs. *Oper. Res. Lett.*, 9(4):257–260, 1990.

[GLS93]   M. Grötschel, L. Lovász, and A. Schrijver. *Geometric Algorithms and Combinatorial Optimization.* Springer-Verlag, 2nd edition, 1993.

[Hen83]   M. I. Henig. Vector-valued dynamic programming. *SIAM J. Control Optim.*, 21(3):490–499, 1983.

[Put94]   M. L. Puterman. *Markov Decision Processes.* Wiley, 1994.

[PY00]   C. Papadimitriou and M. Yannakakis. On the approximability of trade-offs and optimal access of web sources. In *Proc. of 41st IEEE Symp. on Foundations of Computer Science*, pages 86–92, 2000.

[Var85]   M. Vardi. Automatic verification of probabilistic concurrent finite-state programs. In *Proc. of 26th IEEE FOCS*, pages 327–338, 1985.

[Whi82]   D. J. White. Multi-objective infinite-horizon discounted Markov decision processes. *J. Math. Anal. Appl.*, 89(2):639–647, 1982.

[WT98]   K. Wakuta and K. Togawa. Solution procedures for multi-objective Markov decision processes. *Optimization. A Journal of Mathematical Programming and Operations Research*, 43(1):29–46, 1998.

PReMo:
An Analyzer for Probabilistic Recursive Models

Dominik Wojtczak and Kousha Etessami

School of Informatics, University of Edinburgh

Abstract. This paper describes PReMo, a tool for analyzing Recursive
Markov Chains, and their controlled/game extensions: (1-exit) Recursive
Markov Decision Processes and Recursive Simple Stochastic Games.

1 Introduction

Recursive Markov Chains (RMCs) [4,5] are a natural abstract model of probabilistic procedural programs and other systems involving recursion and probability. They are formally equivalent to probabilistic Pushdown Systems (pPDSs)
([2,3]), and they define a class of infinite-state Markov chains that generalize a
number of well studied stochastic models such as Stochastic Context-Free Grammars (SCFGs) and Multi-Type Branching Processes. In a series of recent papers
([4,5,6,7]), the second author and M. Yannakakis have developed algorithms for
analysis and model checking of RMCs and their controlled and game extensions:
1-exit Recursive Markov Decision Processes (1-RMDPs) and 1-exit Recursive
Simple Stochastic Games (1-RSSGs). These extensions allow modelling of nondeterministic and interactive behavior.

In this paper we describe PReMo, a software tool for analysing models based
on RMCs, 1-RMDPs, and 1-RSSGs. PReMo allows these models to be specified in several different input formats, including a simple imperative-style language for specifying RMCs and RSSGs, and an input format for SCFGs. For
RMCs/RSSGs, PReMo generates a graphical depiction of the model, useful for
visualizing small models (see Figure 1). PReMo has implementations of numerical algorithms for a number of analyses of RMCs and 1-RSSGs. From an RMC,
PReMo generates a corresponding system of nonlinear polynomial equations,
whose Least Fixed Point (LFP) solution gives precisely the termination probabilities for vertex-exit pairs in the RMC. For 1-RSSGs, it generates a system
of nonlinear min-max equations, whose LFP gives the *values* of the termination
game starting at each vertex. Computation of termination probabilities is a key
ingredient for model checking and other analyses for RMCs and pPDSs ([4,5,2]).
PReMo provides a number of optimized numerical algorithms for computing termination probabilities. Methods provided include both dense and sparse versions
of a decomposed Newton's method developed in [4], as well as versions of value
iteration, optimized using nonlinear generalizations of Gauss-Seidel and SOR
techniques. The latter methods also apply to analysis of 1-RSSGs.

In addition to computing termination probabilities, PReMo can compute the
(maximum/minimum/game) *expected termination time* in 1-RMCs, 1-RMDPs,

O. Grumberg and M. Huth (Eds.): TACAS 2007, LNCS 4424, pp. 66–71, 2007.

```
A(2,2);
B(1,2);

A {
    L1(A);
    L2(B);
    entry 0:
        0.5: goto L3; 0.5: call L2(0);
    entry 1:
        0.3: call L1(0); 0.7: call L1(1);
    L1 {
        exit 0:
            0.8: goto L3; 0.2: call L2(0);
        exit 1:
            1.0: return 1;
    }
    L2 {
        exit 0:
            1.0: goto L3;
        exit 1:
            1.0: return 0;
    }
    L3 {
        0.5: return 0; 0.5: return 1;
    }
}

B {
    L4(A);
    entry 0:
        0.3: call L4(0); 0.3: call L4(1); 0.4: goto L5;
    L4 {
        exit 0:
            0.5: return 0; 0.5: return 1;
        exit 1:
            0.5: return 0; 0.5: goto L5;
    }
    L5 {
        0.4: goto L5; 0.6: return 1;
    }
}
```

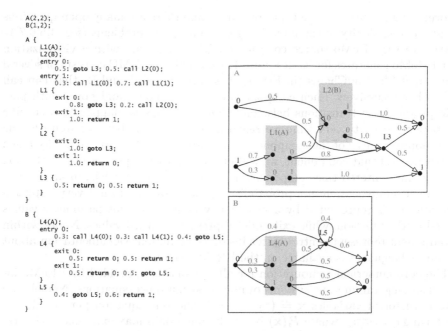

Fig. 1. Source code of an RMC, and its visualization generated by PReMo

and 1-RSSGs. It does so by generating a different monotone system of linear (min-max) equations, whose LFP is the value of the game where the objectives of the two players are to maximize/minimize the expected termination time (these expected times can be infinity). (This analysis extends, to a game setting, the expected reward analysis for pPDSs (equivalently, RMCs) studied in [3]. The generalization works for 1-RMDPs and 1-RSSGs, which correspond to controlled/game versions of *stateless* pPDSs, also known as pBPAs. We do not explicate the theory behind these game analyses here. It is a modification of results in [6,7], and will be explicated elsewhere.)

PReMo is implemented entirely in Java, and has the following main components: (1) A parsers for text descriptions of RMCs, RSSGs, and SCFGs, using one of several input formats; (2) A menu-driven GUI (using the Standard Widget Library(SWT)), with an editor for different input formats, and menu choices for running different analyses with different methods; (3) A graphical depiction generator for RMCs and RSSGs, which produces output using the dot format. (4) *Optimized solvers:* Several solvers are implemented for computation of termination probabilities/values for RMCs and 1-RSSGs, and also computation of expected termination times for 1-RMCs, 1-RMDPs, 1-RSSGs. We conducted a range of experiments. Our experiments indicate very promising potential for several methods. In particular, our decomposed Sparse Newton's method performed very well on most models we tried, up to quite large sizes. Although these numerical methods appear to work well in practice on most instances, there are no theoretical guarantees on their performance, and there are many open questions about the complexity of the underlying computational problems (see [4,5,6,7]).

We can see PReMo source code for an RMC, together with a visualization that PReMo generates for it, in Figure 1. Informally, an RMC consists of several component Markov Chains (in Fig. 1, these are named A and B) that can call each other recursively. Each component consists of nodes and boxes with possible probabilistic transitions between them. Each box is mapped to a specific component so that every time we reach an entry of this box, we jump to the corresponding entry of the component it is mapped to. When/if we finally reach an exit node of that component, we will jump back to a respective exit of the box that we have entered this component from. This process models, in an obvious way, function invocation in a probabilistic procedural program. Every potential function call is represented by a box. Entry nodes represent parameter values passed to the function, while exit nodes represent returned values. Nodes within a component represent control states inside the function. Documentation about the input languages is available on the PReMo web page.

The core numerical computation for all the analyses provided by PReMo involves solving a monotone systems of nonlinear min-max equations. Namely, we have a vector of variables $\mathbf{x} = (x_1, \ldots, x_n)$, and one equation per variable of the form $x_i = P_i(\mathbf{x})$, where $P_i(\mathbf{x})$ is a polynomial-min-max expression with rational coefficients. In vector notation, this system of equations can be denoted $\mathbf{x} = P(\mathbf{x})$. The goal is to find the Least Fixed Point solution, i.e., the least nonnegative solution, $\mathbf{q}^* \in \mathbb{R}_{\geq 0}^n$, of these equations, which is $\lim_{k \to \infty} P^k(\mathbf{0})$. In brief, the solvers in PReMo work as follows (see [4,6] for more background). First, we decompose the equations into SCCs and calculate the solution "bottom-up", solving the Bottom SCCs first and plug in the solution as constants in higher SCCs. To solve each SCC, PReMo provides several methods:

Value iteration: nonlinear Jacobi & Gauss-Seidel. Optimized forms of nonlinear *value iteration* have been implemented for computing the LFP of $\mathbf{x} = P(\mathbf{x})$. Jacobi, or basic iteration, just computes $\mathbf{x}^0 = \mathbf{0}, \mathbf{x}^1, \mathbf{x}^2, \ldots$, where $\mathbf{x}^i = P(\mathbf{x}^{i-1})$. Gauss-Seidel iteration optimizes this slightly: inductively, having computed x_j^{k+1} for $j < i$, let $x_i^{k+1} := P_i(x_1^{k+1}, \ldots, x_{i-1}^{k+1}, x_i^k, x_{i+1}^k, \ldots, x_n^k)$. Successive Overrelaxation (SOR) is an "optimistic" modification of Gauss-Seidel, which isn't guaranteed to converge in our case.

Dense and sparse decomposed Newton's method. Newton's method attempts to compute solutions to $F(\mathbf{x}) = \mathbf{0}$. In n-dimensions, it works by iterating $\mathbf{x}^{k+1} := \mathbf{x}^k - (F'(\mathbf{x}^k))^{-1}F(\mathbf{x}^k)$ where $F'(\mathbf{x})$ is the *Jacobian* matrix of partial derivatives of F. In our case we apply this method for $F(\mathbf{x}) = P(\mathbf{x}) - \mathbf{x}$. It was shown in [4] that if the system is decomposed into SCCs appropriately, convergence to the LFP is guaranteed, if we start with $\mathbf{x}^0 = \mathbf{0}$. The expensive task at each step of Newton is the matrix inversion $(F'(\mathbf{x}^k))^{-1}$. Explicit matrix inversion is too expensive for huge matrices. But this matrix is typically sparse for RMCs, and we can handle much larger matrices if instead of inverting $(F'(\mathbf{x}^k))$ we solve the following equivalent sparse linear system of equations: $(F'(\mathbf{x}^k))(\mathbf{x}^{k+1} - \mathbf{x}^k) = F(\mathbf{x}^k)$ to compute the value of $\mathbf{x}^{k+1} - \mathbf{x}^k$, and then add $\mathbf{x}^k$ to obtain $\mathbf{x}^{k+1}$. We used the solver library MTJ (Matrix Toolkit for Java) and tried various sparse linear solvers. Our Dense Newton's method uses LU decomposition to invert $(F'(\mathbf{x}^k))$.

Iterative numerical solvers can only converge to within some error to the actual solution. PReMo provides different mechanisms for users to choose when to stop the iteration: absolute tolerance, relative tolerance, and a specified number of iterations. In, e.g., the absolute tolerance mode, the algorithm stops after the first iteration when the absolute difference in the value for all variables changed less than a given $\epsilon > 0$. This does not in general guarantee closeness to the actual solution, but it behaves well in practice.

2   Experimental Results

We ran a wide range of experiments on a Pentium 4 3GHz with 1GB RAM, running Linux Fedora 5, kernel 2.6.17, using Java 5.0. Please see our fuller report [9] for more details about our experimental results.

SCFGs generated from the Penn Treebank NLP corpora. We checked the *consistency*[1] of a set of large SCFGs, with 10,000 to 50,000 productions, used by the Natural Language Processing (NLP) group at University of Edinburgh and derived by them from the Penn Treebank NLP corpora. These SCFGs were assumed to be consistent by construction. Our most efficient method (Sparse Newton) solved all these SCFGs in a few seconds (see Table 1). Two out of seven SCFGs were (very) inconsistent, namely those derived from the **brown** and **switchboard** corpora of Penn Treebank, with termination probabilities as low as 0.3 for many nonterminals. This inconsistency was a surprise to our NLP colleagues, and was subsequently identified by them to be caused by annotation errors in Penn Treebank itself ([1]). Note that both dense and sparse versions of decomposed Newton's method are by far the fastest. Since the largest SCCs are no bigger than 1000 vertices, dense Newton also worked on these examples. Most of the time for Newton's method was in fact taken up by the initialization phase, for computing all the partial derivatives in entries of the Jacobian $F'(\mathbf{x})$. We thus optimized the computation of the Jacobian in several ways.

Randomly generated RMCs and 1-RSSGs. We tested PReMo on randomly generated RMCs of different sizes, ranging from 10,000 to 500,000 nodes (variables). In random large instances, with very high probability most nodes are in one huge SCC with small diameter ("small world phenomenon"). Dense Newton's method did not work at all on these huge SCCs, because inverting such large matrices is too costly, but both Gauss-Seidel and Sparse Newton did very well. In particular, Sparse Newton handled instances with 500,000 variables in ~ 45 seconds. For random 1-RSSGs, although we have no Newton's method available for 1-RSSGs, value iteration performed well (see [9]).

Quicksort. For expected termination time analyses, we considered a toy model of randomized Quicksort, using a simple hierarchical 1-RMC. The model has

---

[1] An SCFG is called *consistent* if starting at all nonterminals in the grammar, a random derivation terminates, and generates a finite string, with probability 1.

Table 1. Performance results for checking consistency of SCFGs derived from Penn Treebank. Time is in seconds. In parentheses is the number of iterations for the biggest SCC. Stopping condition: absolute tolerance $\epsilon = 10^{-12}$. SCFG was declared "consistent" if all nonterminals had termination probability $\geq (1 - 10^{-4})$. The SCFGs brown and swbd failed consistency by a wide margin.

name	#prod	max-scc	Jacobi	Gauss Seidel	SOR ω=1.05	DNewton	SNewton
brown	22866 ✗	448	312.084(9277)	275.624(7866)	diverge	2.106(8)	2.115(9)
lemonde	32885 ✓	527	234.715(5995)	30.420(767)	diverge	1.556(7)	2.037(7)
negra	29297 ✓	518	16.995(610)	4.724(174)	4.201(152)	1.017(6)	0.499(6)
swbd	47578 ✗	1123	445.120(4778)	19.321(202)	25.654(270)	6.435(6)	3.978(6)
tiger	52184 ✓	1173	99.286(1347)	16.073(210)	12.447(166)	5.274(6)	1.871(6)
tuebadz	8932 ✓	293	6.894(465)	1.925(133)	6.878(461)	0.477(7)	0.341(7)
wsj	31170 ✓	765	462.378(9787)	68.650(1439)	diverge	2.363(7)	3.616(8)

n components, Q_i, $i = 1, \ldots, n$, corresponding to invocations of Quicksort on arrays of size i. Component Q_i takes time i to pivot and split the entries, and then recurses on the two partitions. This is modeled by transitions of probability $1/(i-1)$, for each $d \in \{1, \ldots, i-1\}$, to two sequential boxes labeled by Q_d and Q_{i-d}. We computed expected termination time for various sizes n. We also tried letting the pivot be controlled by the *minimizer* or *maximizer*, and we computed optimal expected running time for such 1-RMDPs, in order to consider best-case and worst-case running times of Quicksort. As expected, the results fitted the well-known theoretical analysis of $\Theta(n \log n)$ and $\Theta(n^2)$ for running times of randomized/best-case, and worst-case Quicksort, respectively.

3   Future Work

The next important step is to extend the RMC language to allow variables and conditional branching, i.e., probabilistic Boolean Programs. We are working toward implementation of a full-fledged linear-time model checker for RMCs. This is a major challenge because there are very difficult numerical issues that have to be overcome in order to enable general model checking. PReMo 1.0 is available at: http://homepages.inf.ed.ac.uk/s0571094/PReMo

Acknowledgements. Thanks to Mihalis Yannakakis: the second author's work on analysis of RMCs/RSSGs, on which PReMo is based, is joint work with him. Thanks to Mark-Jan Neiderhof and Giorgio Satta for pointing us in the direction of large SCFG libraries used in NLP, and telling us about their own current work on implementing these methods [8]. Thanks to Amit Dubey and Frank Keller for providing us SCFGs from their NLP work.

References

1. A. Dubey and F. Keller. *personal communication*, 2006.
2. J. Esparza, A. Kučera, and R. Mayr. Model checking probabilistic pushdown automata. In *Proc. LICS'04*, 2004.

3. J. Esparza, A. Kučera, and R. Mayr. Quantitative Analysis of Probabilistic Pushdown Automata: Expectations and Variances. In *Proc. LICS'05*, 2005.
4. K. Etessami and M. Yannakakis. Recursive markov chains, stochastic grammars, and monotone systems of nonlinear equations. In *Proc. STACS'05*, 2005.
5. K. Etessami and M. Yannakakis. Algorithmic verification of recursive probabilistic state machines. In *Proc. TACAS'05*, 2005.
6. K. Etessami and M. Yannakakis. Recursive markov decision processes and recursive stochastic games. In *Proc. ICALP'05*, 2005.
7. K. Etessami and M. Yannakakis. Efficient qualitative analysis of classes of recursive markov decision processes and simple stochastic games. In *Proc. STACS'06*, 2006.
8. M. J. Neiderhof and G. Satta. Using Newton's method to compute the partition function of a PCFG, 2006. *unpublished draft manuscript.*
9. D. Wojtczak and K. Etessami. PReMo: an analyzer for Probabilistic Recursive Models. Fuller report, with more experimental data. http://homepages.inf.ed.ac.uk/s0571094/PReMo/tacas07premo-long.pdf

Counterexamples in Probabilistic Model Checking

Tingting Han and Joost-Pieter Katoen

Software Modelling and Verification, RWTH Aachen, Germany
Formal Methods and Tools, University of Twente, The Netherlands
{tingting.han,katoen}@cs.rwth-aachen.de

Abstract. This paper considers algorithms for counterexample generation for (bounded) probabilistic reachability properties in fully probabilistic systems. Finding the strongest evidence (i.e, the most probable path) violating a (bounded) until-formula is shown to be reducible to a single-source (hop-constrained) shortest path problem. Counterexamples of smallest size that are mostly deviating from the required probability bound can be computed by adopting (partially new hop-constrained) k shortest paths algorithms that dynamically determine k.

1 Introduction

A major strength of model checking is the possibility to generate counterexamples in case a property is violated. The shape of a counterexample depends on the checked formula and the used temporal logic. For logics such as LTL, typically paths through the model suffice. The violation of linear-time safety properties is indicated by finite path fragments that end in a "bad" state. Liveness properties, instead, require infinite paths ending in a cyclic behavior indicating that something "good" will never happen. LTL model checkers usually incorporate breadth-first search algorithms to generate *shortest* counterexamples, i.e., paths of minimal length. For branching-time logics such as CTL, paths may act as counterexample for a subclass of universally quantified formulae, ACTL∩LTL, to be exact. To cover a broader spectrum of formulae, though, more advanced structures such as trees of paths [11], proof-like counterexamples [18] (for ACTL\LTL) or annotated paths [26] (for ECTL) are used.

Counterexamples are of utmost importance in model checking: first, and for all, they provide diagnostic feedback even in cases where only a fragment of the entire model can be searched. They constitute the key to successful abstraction-refinement techniques [10], and are at the core of obtaining feasible schedules in e.g., timed model checking [8]. As a result, advanced counterexample generation and analysis techniques have intensively been investigated, see e.g., [21,7,13].

This paper considers the generation of counterexamples in probabilistic model checking. Probabilistic model checking is a technique to verify system models in which transitions are equipped with random information. Popular models are discrete- and continuous-time Markov chains (DTMCs and CTMCs, respectively), and variants thereof which exhibit nondeterminism. Efficient model-checking algorithms for these models have been developed, have been implemented in a variety of software tools, and have been applied to case studies from various application areas ranging from randomized distributed algorithms, computer systems and security protocols to biological

O. Grumberg and M. Huth (Eds.): TACAS 2007, LNCS 4424, pp. 72–86, 2007.
© Springer-Verlag Berlin Heidelberg 2007

systems and quantum computing. The crux of probabilistic model checking is to appropriately combine techniques from numerical mathematics and operations research with standard reachability analysis. In this way, properties such as "the (maximal) probability to reach a set of goal states by avoiding certain states is at most 0.6" can be automatically checked up to a user-defined precision. Markovian models comprising millions of states can be checked rather fast.

In probabilistic model checking, however, counterexample generation is almost not developed; notable exception is the recent heuristic search algorithm for CTMCs and DTMCs [3,4] that works under the assumption that the model is unknown. Instead, we consider a setting in which it has already been established that a certain state refutes a given property. This paper considers algorithms and complexity results for the generation of counterexamples in probabilistic model checking. The considered setting is probabilistic CTL [19] for discrete-time Markov chains (DTMCs), a model in which all transitions are equipped with a probability. In this setting, typically there is no single path but rather a *set* of paths that indicates why a given property is refuted. We concentrate on properties of the form $\mathcal{P}_{\leqslant p}(\Phi\,\mathcal{U}^{\leqslant h}\Psi)$ where p is a probability and h a (possibly infinite) bound on the maximal allowed number of steps before reaching a goal (i.e., a Ψ-) state. In case state s refutes this formula, the probability of all paths in s satisfying $\Phi\,\mathcal{U}^{\leqslant h}\Psi$ exceeds p. We consider two problems that are aimed to provide useful diagnostic feedback for this violation: generating strongest evidences and smallest, most indicative counterexamples.

Strongest evidences are the most probable paths that satisfy $\Phi\,\mathcal{U}^{\leqslant h}\Psi$. They "contribute" mostly to the property refutation and are thus expected to be informative. For unbounded until (i.e., $h=\infty$), determining strongest evidences is shown to be equivalent to a standard single-source shortest path (SP) problem; in case h is bounded, we obtain a special case of the (resource) constrained shortest path (CSP) problem [2] that can be solved in $\mathcal{O}(hm)$ where m is the number of transitions in the DTMC. Alternatively, the Viterbi algorithm can be used for bounded h yielding the same time complexity.

Evidently, strongest evidences may not suffice as true counterexamples, as their probability mass lies (far) below p. As a next step, therefore, we consider the problem of determining most probable subtrees (rooted at s). Similar to the notion of shortest counterexample in LTL model checking, we consider trees of *smallest size* that exceed the probability bound p. Additionally, such trees, of size k, say, are required to *maximally* exceed the lower bound, i.e., no subtrees should exist of size at most k that exceed p to a larger extent. The problem of generating such *smallest, most indicative counterexamples* can be casted as a k shortest paths problem. For unbounded-until formulae (i.e., $h=\infty$), it is shown that the generation of such smallest counterexamples can be found in pseudo-polynomial time by adopting k shortest paths algorithms [15,24] that compute k on the fly. For bounded until-formulae, we propose an algorithm based on the recursive enumeration algorithm of Jiménez and Marzal [20]. The time complexity of this adapted algorithm is $\mathcal{O}(hm+hk\log(\frac{m}{n}))$, where n is the number of states in the DTMC.

Finally, we show how the algorithms for $\mathcal{P}_{\leqslant p}(\Phi\,\mathcal{U}^{\leqslant h}\Psi)$ can be exploited for generating strongest evidences and counterexamples for lower bounds on probabilities, i.e., $\mathcal{P}_{\geqslant p}(\Phi\,\mathcal{U}^{\leqslant h}\Psi)$.

2 Preliminaries

DTMCs. Let AP denote a fixed, finite set of atomic propositions ranged over by $a, b, c, \ldots$. A (labelled) *discrete-time Markov chain* (DTMC) is a Kripke structure in which all transitions are equipped with discrete probabilities such that the sum of outgoing transitions of each state equals one. Formally, DTMC $\mathcal{D} = (S, \mathbf{P}, L)$ where S is a finite set of states, $\mathbf{P} : S \times S \to [0,1]$ is a stochastic matrix, and $L : S \to 2^{AP}$ is a labelling function which assigns to each state $s \in S$ the set $L(s)$ of atomic propositions that are valid in s. A state s in $\mathcal{D}$ is called absorbing if $\mathbf{P}(s,s) = 1$. W.l.o.g. we assume a DTMC to have a unique initial state.

Definition 1 (Paths). *Let* $\mathcal{D} = (S, \mathbf{P}, L)$ *be a DTMC.*

- *An* infinite path *σ in $\mathcal{D}$ is an infinite sequence $s_0 \cdot s_1 \cdot s_2 \cdot \ldots$ of states such that $\mathbf{P}(s_i, s_{i+1}) > 0$ for all $i \geqslant 0$.*
- *A* finite path *in $\mathcal{D}$ is a finite prefix of an infinite path.*

For state s and finite path $\sigma = s_0 \cdot s_1 \cdot \ldots \cdot s_n$ with $\mathbf{P}(s_n, s) > 0$, let $\sigma \cdot s$ denote the path obtained by extending σ by s. Let $|\sigma|$ denote the length of the path σ, i.e., $|s_0 \cdot s_1 \cdot \ldots \cdot s_n| = n$, $|s_0| = 0$ and $|\sigma| = \infty$ for infinite σ. For $0 \leqslant i \leqslant |\sigma|$, $\sigma[i] = s_i$ denotes the $(i{+}1)$-st state in σ. $Path(s)$ denotes the set of all infinite paths that start in state s and $Path_{fin}(s)$ denotes the set of all finite paths of s.

A DTMC $\mathcal{D}$ enriched with an initial state s_0 induces a probability space. The underlying σ-algebra from the basic cylinder is induced by the finite paths starting in s_0. The probability measure $\mathrm{Pr}_{s_0}^{\mathcal{D}}$ (briefly Pr) induced by $(\mathcal{D}, s_0)$ is the unique measure on this σ-algebra where:

$$\mathrm{Pr}\{\underbrace{\sigma \in Path(s_0) \mid s_0 \cdot s_1 \cdot \ldots \cdot s_n \text{ is a prefix of } \sigma\}}_{\text{basic cylinder of the finite path } s_0 \cdot s_1 \cdot \ldots \cdot s_n} = \prod_{0 \leqslant i < n} \mathbf{P}(s_i, s_{i+1}).$$

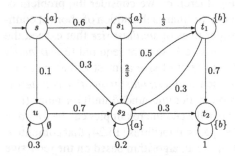

Fig. 1. An example DTMC

Example 1. Fig. 1 illustrates a simple DTMC with initial state s. $AP = \{a, b\}$ and L is given through the subsets of AP labelling the states as $L(s) = L(s_i) = \{a\}$, for $1 \leqslant i \leqslant 2$; $L(t_1) = L(t_2) = \{b\}$ and $L(u) = \emptyset$. t_2 is an absorbing state. $\sigma_1 = s \cdot u \cdot s_2 \cdot t_1 \cdot t_2$ is a finite path with $\mathrm{Pr}\{\sigma_1\} = 0.1 \times 0.7 \times 0.5 \times 0.7$ and $|\sigma_1| = 4$, $\sigma_1[3] = t_1$. $\sigma_2 = s \cdot (s_2 \cdot t_1)^\omega$ is an infinite path.

PCTL. Probabilistic computation tree logic (PCTL) [19] is a probabilistic extension of CTL in which state-formulae are interpreted over states of a DTMC and path-formulae are interpreted over paths in a DTMC. The syntax of PCTL is as follows:

$$\Phi ::= \mathsf{tt} \mid a \mid \neg \Phi \mid \Phi \wedge \Phi \mid \mathcal{P}_{\trianglelefteq p}(\phi)$$

where $p \in [0, 1]$ is a probability, $\trianglelefteq \in \{<, \leqslant, >, \geqslant\}$ and ϕ is a path formula defined according to the following grammar:

$$\phi ::= \Phi \mathcal{U}^{\leqslant h} \Phi \mid \Phi \mathcal{W}^{\leqslant h} \Phi$$

where $h \in \mathbb{N} \cup \{\infty\}$. The path formula $\Phi \mathcal{U}^{\leqslant h} \Psi$ asserts that Ψ is satisfied within h transitions and that all preceding states satisfy Φ. For $h=\infty$ such path-formulae are standard (unbounded) until-formulae, whereas in other cases, these are bounded until-formulae. $\mathcal{W}^{\leqslant h}$ is the weak counterpart of $\mathcal{U}^{\leqslant h}$ which does not require Ψ to eventually become true. For the sake of simplicity, we do not consider the next-operator. The temporal operators $\Diamond^{\leqslant h}$ and $\Box^{\leqslant h}$ are obtained as follows:

$$\mathcal{P}_{\trianglelefteq p}(\Diamond^{\leqslant h}\Phi) = \mathcal{P}_{\trianglelefteq p}(\text{tt}\,\mathcal{U}^{\leqslant h}\,\Phi) \quad \text{and} \quad \mathcal{P}_{\trianglelefteq p}(\Box^{\leqslant h}\Phi) = \mathcal{P}_{\trianglelefteq p}(\Phi \mathcal{W}^{\leqslant h}\text{ff})$$

Note that ff $= \neg$tt. Some example formulae are $\mathcal{P}_{\leqslant 0.5}(a\mathcal{U}b)$ asserting that the probability of reaching a b-state via an a-path is at most $\frac{1}{2}$, and $\mathcal{P}_{>0.001}(\Diamond^{\leqslant 50}error)$ stating that the probability for a system error to occur within 50 steps exceeds 0.001. Dually, $\mathcal{P}_{\leqslant 0.999}(\Box^{\leqslant 50}\neg error)$ states that the probability for no error in the next 50 steps is at most 0.999.

Semantics. Let DTMC $\mathcal{D} = (S, \mathbf{P}, L)$. The semantics of PCTL is defined by a satisfaction relation, denoted $\models$, which is characterized as the least relation over the states in S (paths in $\mathcal{D}$, respectively) and the state formulae (path formulae) satisfying:

$$s \models \text{tt} \quad \text{iff} \quad true \qquad s \models a \quad \text{iff} \quad a \in L(s) \qquad s \models \neg\Phi \quad \text{iff} \quad \text{not}\,(s \models \Phi)$$
$$s \models \Phi \wedge \Psi \quad \text{iff} \quad s \models \Phi \text{ and } s \models \Psi \qquad s \models \mathcal{P}_{\trianglelefteq p}(\phi) \quad \text{iff} \quad Prob(s, \phi) \trianglelefteq p$$

Let $Path(s, \phi)$ denote the set of infinite paths that start in state s and satisfy ϕ. Formally, $Path(s, \phi) = \{\sigma \in Path(s) \mid \sigma \models \phi\}$. Here, $Prob(s, \phi) = \Pr\{\sigma \mid \sigma \in Path(s, \phi)\}$ denotes the probability of $Path(s, \phi)$. Let σ be an infinite path in $\mathcal{D}$. The semantics of PCTL path formulae is defined as:

$$\sigma \models \Phi \mathcal{U}^{\leqslant h}\Psi \quad \text{iff} \quad \exists i \leqslant h \text{ such that } \sigma[i] \models \Psi \text{ and } \forall j : 0 \leqslant j < i.(\sigma[j] \models \Phi)$$
$$\sigma \models \Phi \mathcal{W}^{\leqslant h}\Psi \quad \text{iff} \quad \text{either } \sigma \models \Phi \mathcal{U}^{\leqslant h}\Psi \text{ or } \sigma[i] \models \Phi \text{ for all } i \leqslant h$$

For finite path σ, $\models$ is defined in a similar way by changing the range of i to $i \leqslant \min\{h, |\sigma|\}$. Let $Path_{fin}(s, \phi)$ denote the set of finite paths starting in s that fulfill ϕ.

The until and weak until operators are closely related. This follows from the following equations. For any state s and all PCTL-formulae Φ and Ψ we have:

$$\mathcal{P}_{\geqslant p}(\Phi \mathcal{W}^{\leqslant h}\Psi) \equiv \mathcal{P}_{\leqslant 1-p}((\Phi \wedge \neg\Psi)\mathcal{U}^{\leqslant h}(\neg\Phi \wedge \neg\Psi))$$
$$\mathcal{P}_{\geqslant p}(\Phi \mathcal{U}^{\leqslant h}\Psi) \equiv \mathcal{P}_{\leqslant 1-p}((\Phi \wedge \neg\Psi)\mathcal{W}^{\leqslant h}(\neg\Phi \wedge \neg\Psi))$$

For the rest of the paper, we explore counterexamples for PCTL formulae of the form $\mathcal{P}_{\leqslant p}(\Phi \mathcal{U}^{\leqslant h}\Psi)$. In Section 7, we will show how to generate counterexamples for formulae of the form $\mathcal{P}_{\geqslant p}(\Phi \mathcal{U}^{\leqslant h}\Psi)$.

3 Strongest Evidences and Counterexamples

Let us first consider what a counterexample in our setting actually is. To that end, consider the formula $\mathcal{P}_{\leqslant p}(\phi)$, where we denote $\phi = \Phi \mathcal{U}^{\leqslant h} \Psi$ ($h \in \{\infty\} \cup \mathbb{N}$) for the rest of the paper. It follows directly from the semantics that:

$$s \nvDash \mathcal{P}_{\leqslant p}(\phi) \quad \text{iff} \quad \text{not } (Prob(s, \phi) \leqslant p) \quad \text{iff} \quad \Pr\{\sigma \mid \sigma \in Path(s, \phi)\} > p.$$

So, $\mathcal{P}_{\leqslant p}(\phi)$ is refuted by state s whenever the total probability mass of all ϕ-paths that start in s exceeds p. This indicates that a counterexample for $\mathcal{P}_{\leqslant p}(\phi)$ is in general a *set* of paths starting in s and satisfying ϕ. As ϕ is an until-formula whose validity (regardless of the value of h) can be witnessed by finite state sequences, *finite* paths do suffice in counterexamples. A counterexample is defined as follows:

Definition 2 (Counterexample). *A counterexample for $\mathcal{P}_{\leqslant p}(\phi)$ in state s is a set C of finite paths such that $C \subseteq Path_{fin}(s, \phi)$ and $\Pr(C) > p$.*

A counterexample for state s is thus a set of finite paths that all start in s. We will not dwell further upon how to represent this set, being it a finite tree (or dag) rooted at s, or a bounded regular expression (over states), and assume that an abstract representation as a set suffices. Note that the measurability of counterexamples is ensured by the fact that they just consist of finite paths; hence, $\Pr(C)$ is well-defined. Let $CX_p(s, \phi)$ denote the set of all counterexamples for $\mathcal{P}_{\leqslant p}(\phi)$ in state s. For $C \in CX_p(s, \phi)$ and C's superset $C': C \subseteq C' \subseteq Path_{fin}(s, \phi)$, it follows that $C' \in CX_p(s, \phi)$, since $\Pr(C') \geqslant \Pr(C) > p$. That is to say, any extension of a counterexample C with paths in $Path_{fin}(s, \phi)$ is a counterexample.

Definition 3 (Minimal counterexample). *$C \in CX_p(s, \phi)$ is a minimal counterexample if $|C| \leqslant |C'|$, for any $C' \in CX_p(s, \phi)$.*

Note that what we define as being minimal differs from minimality w.r.t. $\subseteq$. As a counterexample should exceed p, a maximally probable ϕ-path is a strong evidence for the violation of $\mathcal{P}_{\leqslant p}(\phi)$. For minimal counterexamples such maximally probable paths are essential.

Definition 4 (Strongest evidence). *A strongest evidence for violating $\mathcal{P}_{\leqslant p}(\phi)$ in state s is a finite path $\sigma \in Path_{fin}(s, \phi)$ such that $\Pr\{\sigma\} \geqslant \Pr\{\sigma'\}$ for any $\sigma' \in Path_{fin}(s, \phi)$.*

Dually, a strongest evidence for violating $\mathcal{P}_{\leqslant p}(\phi)$ is a strongest witness for fulfilling $\mathcal{P}_{>p}(\phi)$. Evidently, a strongest evidence does not need to be a counterexample as its probability mass may be (far) below p.

As in conventional model checking, we are not interested in generating arbitrary counterexamples, but those that are easy to comprehend, and provide a clear evidence of the refutation of the formula. So, akin to shortest counterexamples for linear-time logics, we consider the notion of a smallest, most indicative counterexample. Such counterexamples are required to be succinct, i.e., minimal, allowing easier analysis of the cause of refutation, and most distinctive, i.e., their probability should mostly exceed p among all minimal counterexamples.

Definition 5 (Smallest counterexample). $C \in CX_p(s, \phi)$ *is a smallest (most indicative) counterexample if it is minimal and* $\Pr(C) \geqslant \Pr(C')$ *for any minimal counterexample* $C' \in CX_p(s, \phi)$.

The intuition is that a smallest counterexample is mostly deviating from the required probability bound given that it has the smallest number of paths. Thus, there does not exist an equally sized counterexample that deviates more from p. Strongest evidences, minimal counterexamples or smallest counterexamples may not be unique, as paths may have equal probability. As a result, not every strongest evidence is contained in a minimal (or smallest) counterexample. Whereas minimal counterexamples may not contain any strongest evidence, any smallest counterexample contains at least one strongest evidence. Using some standard mathematical results we obtain:

Lemma 1. *A smallest counterexample for* $s \not\models \mathcal{P}_{\leqslant p}(\phi)$ *is finite.*

Remark 1 (Finiteness). For until path formulae, smallest counterexamples are always *finite* sets of paths if we consider *non-strict* upper-bounds on the probability, i.e., probability bounds of the form $\leqslant p$. In case of strict upper-bounds of the form $< p$, finiteness of counterexamples is no longer guaranteed as C for which $\Pr(C)$ equals p is a smallest counterexample, but may contain infinitely many paths. For instance, consider the following DTMC:

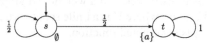

The violation of $\mathcal{P}_{<1}(\lozenge a)$ in state s can only be shown by an infinite set of paths, viz. all paths that traverse the self-loop at state s arbitrarily often.

Example 2. Consider the DTMC in Fig. 1, for which s violates $\mathcal{P}_{\leqslant \frac{1}{2}}(a\mathcal{U}b)$. Evidences are, amongst others, $\sigma_1 = s \cdot s_1 \cdot t_1$, $\sigma_2 = s \cdot s_1 \cdot s_2 \cdot t_1$, $\sigma_3 = s \cdot s_2 \cdot t_1$, $\sigma_4 = s \cdot s_1 \cdot s_2 \cdot t_2$, and $\sigma_5 = s \cdot s_2 \cdot t_2$. Their respective probabilities are 0.2, 0.2, 0.15, 0.12 and 0.09. Paths σ_1 and σ_2 are strongest evidences. The set $C_1 = \{\sigma_1, \ldots, \sigma_5\}$ with $\Pr(C_1) = 0.76$ is a counterexample, but not a minimal one, as the removal from either σ_1 or σ_2 also yields a counterexample. $C_2 = \{\sigma_1, \sigma_2, \sigma_4\}$ is a minimal but not a smallest counterexample, as $C_3 = \{\sigma_1, \sigma_2, \sigma_3\}$ is minimal too with $\Pr(C_3) = 0.56 > 0.52 = \Pr(C_2)$. C_3 is a smallest counterexample.

In the remainder of the paper, we consider the strongest evidence problem (SE), that for a given state s with $s \not\models \mathcal{P}_{\leqslant p}(\phi)$, determines the strongest evidence for this violation. Subsequently, we consider the corresponding smallest counterexample problem (SC). For both cases, we distinguish between until-formulae for which $h=\infty$ (unbounded until) and $h \in \mathbb{N}$ (bounded until) as distinctive algorithms are used for these cases.

4   From a DTMC to a Weighted Digraph

Prior to finding strongest evidences or smallest counterexamples, we modify the DTMC and turn it into a weighted digraph. Let $Sat(\Phi) = \{s \in S \mid s \models \Phi\}$ for any Φ. Due to the bottom-up traversal of the model-checking algorithm over the formula $\phi = \Phi \mathcal{U}^{\leqslant h}\Psi$, we may assume that $Sat(\Phi)$ and $Sat(\Psi)$ are known.

Step 1: Adapting the DTMC. First, we make all states in the DTMC $\mathcal{D} = (S, \mathbf{P}, L)$ that neither satisfy Φ nor Ψ absorbing. Then we add an extra state t so that all outgoing transitions from a Ψ-state are replaced by a transition to t with probability 1. State t can thus only be reached via a Ψ-state. The obtained DTMC $\mathcal{D}' = (S', \mathbf{P}', L')$ has state space $S \cup \{t\}$ for $t \notin S$. The stochastic matrix $\mathbf{P}'$ is defined as follows:

$\mathbf{P}'(s, s) = 1$ and $\mathbf{P}'(s, s') = 0$ for $s' \neq s$ \qquad if $s \notin Sat(\Phi) \cup Sat(\Psi)$ or $s = t$

$\mathbf{P}'(s, t) = 1$ and $\mathbf{P}'(s, s') = 0$ for $s' \neq t$ \qquad if $s \in Sat(\Psi)$

$\mathbf{P}'(s, s') = \mathbf{P}(s, s')$ for $s' \in S$ and $\mathbf{P}'(s, t) = 0$ \quad otherwise

$L'(s) = L(s)$ for $s \in S$ and $L'(t) = \{at_t\}$, where $at_t \notin L(s')$ for any $s' \in S$, i.e., at_t uniquely identifies being at state t. Remark that all the $(\neg \Phi \wedge \neg \Psi)$-states could be collapsed into a single state, but this is not further explored here. The time complexity of this transformation is $\mathcal{O}(n)$ where $n = |S|$. It is evident that the validity of $\Phi \mathcal{U}^{\leqslant h} \Psi$ is not affected by this amendment of the DTMC. By construction, any finite path $\sigma \cdot t$ in $\mathcal{D}'$ satisfies $(\Phi \vee \Psi) \mathcal{U}^{\leqslant h+1} at_t$ and has the form $s_0 \cdot \ldots \cdot s_i \cdot s_{i+1} \cdot t$ where $s_j \models \Phi$ for $0 \leqslant j \leqslant i < h$, $s_{i+1} \models \Phi$; the prefix σ (in $\mathcal{D}$) satisfies $\Phi \mathcal{U}^{\leqslant h} \Psi$ where σ' and σ are equally probable.

Step 2: Conversion into a weighted digraph. As a second preprocessing step, the DTMC obtained in the first phase is transformed into a weighted digraph. Recall that a weighted digraph is a tuple $\mathcal{G} = (V, E, w)$ where V is a finite set of vertices, $E \subseteq V \times V$ is a set of edges, and $w : E \to \mathbb{R}_{\geqslant 0}$ is a weighted function.

Definition 6. *[Weighted digraph of a DTMC] For DTMC $\mathcal{D} = (S, \mathbf{P}, L)$, the weighted digraph $\mathcal{G}_D = (V, E, w)$ where:*

$$V = S \quad and \quad (v, v') \in E \text{ iff } \mathbf{P}(v, v') > 0 \quad and \quad w(v, v') = \log(\mathbf{P}(v, v')^{-1}).$$

Note that $w(s, s') \in [0, \infty)$ if $\mathbf{P}(s, s') > 0$. Thus, we indeed obtain a non-negatively weighted digraph. Note that this transformation can be done in $\mathcal{O}(m)$, where $m = |\mathbf{P}|$, i.e., the number of non-zero elements in $\mathbf{P}$.

A path σ from s to t in $\mathcal{G}$ is a sequence $\sigma = v_0 \cdot v_1 \cdot \ldots \cdot v_j \in V^+$, where $v_0 = s, v_j = t$ and $(v_i, v_{i+1}) \in E$, for $0 \leqslant i < |\sigma|$. As for paths in DTMCs, $|\sigma|$ denotes the length of σ. The *distance* of finite path $\sigma = v_0 \cdot v_1 \cdot \ldots \cdot v_j$ in graph $\mathcal{G}$ is $d(\sigma) = \sum_{i=0}^{j-1} w(v_i, v_{i+1})$. Due to the fact that multiplication of probabilities in $\mathcal{D}$ corresponds to addition of weights in $\mathcal{G}_D$, and that weights are based on taking the logarithm of the reciprocal of the transition probabilities in $\mathcal{D}$, distances in $\mathcal{G}$ and path-probabilities in DTMC $\mathcal{D}$ are related as follows:

Lemma 2. *Let σ and σ' be finite paths in DTMC $\mathcal{D}$ and its graph $\mathcal{G}_D$. Then:*

$$\Pr\{\sigma'\} \geqslant \Pr\{\sigma\} \quad iff \quad d(\sigma') \leqslant d(\sigma).$$

The correspondence between path probabilities in the DTMC and distances in its weighted digraph as laid down in the following lemma, constitutes the basis for the remaining algorithms in this paper.

Lemma 3. *For any path σ from s to t in DTMC $\mathcal{D}$, $k > 0$, and $h \in \mathbb{N} \cup \{\infty\}$: σ is a k-th most probable path of at most h hops in $\mathcal{D}$ iff σ is a k-th shortest path of at most h hops in $\mathcal{G}_D$.*

5 Finding Strongest Evidences

Unbounded until. Based on the results of Lemma 3 where $k = 1$ and $h = \infty$, we consider the well-known shortest path problem. Recall that:

Definition 7 (SP problem). *Given a weighted digraph $\mathcal{G} = (V, E, w)$ and $s, t \in V$, the shortest path (SP) problem is to determine a path σ from s to t such that $d(\sigma) \leqslant d(\sigma')$ for any path σ' from s to t in $\mathcal{G}$.*

From Lemma 3 together with the transformation of a DTMC into a weighted digraph, it follows that there is a polynomial reduction from the SE problem for unbounded until to the SP problem. As the SP problem is known to be in PTIME, it follows:

Theorem 1. *The SE problem for unbounded until is in PTIME.*

Various efficient algorithms [14,9,12] exist for the SP problem, e.g., when using Dijkstra's algorithm, the SE problem for unbounded until can be solved in time $\mathcal{O}(m + n \log n)$ if appropriate data structures such as Fibonacci heaps are used.

Bounded until. Lemma 3 for $k = 1$ and $h \in \mathbb{N}$ suggests to consider the hop-constrained SP problem.

Definition 8 (HSP problem). *Given a weighted digraph $\mathcal{G} = (V, E, w)$, $s, t \in V$ and $h \in \mathbb{N}$, the hop-constrained SP (HSP) problem is to determine a path σ in $\mathcal{G}$ from s to t with $|\sigma| \leqslant h$ such that $d(\sigma) \leqslant d(\sigma')$ for any path σ' from s to t with $|\sigma'| \leqslant h$.*

The HSP problem is a special case of the constrained shortest path (CSP) problem [25,2], where the only constraint is the hop count.

Definition 9 (CSP problem). *Given a weighted digraph $\mathcal{G} = (V, E, w)$, $s, t \in V$ and resource constraints λ^i, for $1 \leqslant i \leqslant c$. Edge $e \in E$ uses $r^i(e) \geqslant 0$ units of resource i. The (resource) constrained shortest path problem (CSP) is to determine a shortest path σ in $\mathcal{G}$ from s to t such that $\sum_{e \in \sigma} r^i(e) \leqslant \lambda^i$ for $1 \leqslant i \leqslant c$.*

The CSP problem is NP-complete, even for a single resource constraint [2]. However, if each edge uses a constant unit of that resource (such as the hop count), the CSP problem can be solved in polynomial time, cf. [17], problem [ND30]. Thus:

Theorem 2. *The SE problem for bounded until is in PTIME.*

For $h \geqslant n-1$, it is possible to use Dijkstra's SP algorithm (as for unbounded until), as a shortest path does not contain cycles. If $h < n-1$, however, Dijkstra's algorithm does not guarantee to obtain a shortest path of at most h hops. We, therefore, adopt the Bellman-Ford (BF) algorithm [9,12] which fits well to our problem as it proceeds by increasing hop count. It can be readily modified to generate a shortest path within a given hop count. In the sequel of the paper, this algorithm is generalized for computing smallest counterexamples. The BF-algorithm is based on a set of recursive equations; we extend these with the hop count h. For $v \in V$, let $\pi_h(s, v)$ denote the shortest path from s to v of at most h hops (if it exists). Then:

$$\pi_h(s, v) = \begin{cases} s & \text{if } v = s \text{ and } h \geqslant 0 \quad (1a) \\ \bot & \text{if } v \neq s \text{ and } h = 0 \quad (1b) \\ \arg\min_u\{d(\pi_{h-1}(s, u) \cdot v) \mid (u, v) \in E\} & \text{if } v \neq s \text{ and } h > 0 \quad (1c) \end{cases}$$

where $\perp$ denotes nonexistence of such a path. The last clause states that $\pi_h(s, v)$ consists of the shortest path to v's predecessor u, i.e., $\pi_{h-1}(s, u)$, extended with edge (u, v). Note that $\min_u\{d(\pi_{h-1}(s, u) \cdot v) \mid (u, v) \in E\}$ is the distance of the shortest path; by means of arg, the path is obtained. It follows (cf. [22]) that equation $(1a)\sim(1c)$ characterizes the shortest path from s to v in at most h hops, and can be solved in time $\mathcal{O}(hm)$. As $h < n-1$, this is indeed in PTIME. Recall that for $h \geqslant n-1$, Dijkstra's algorithm has a favorable time complexity.

Exploiting the Viterbi algorithm. An alternative to using the BF algorithm is to adopt the *Viterbi algorithm* [16,27]. In fact, to apply this algorithm the transformation into a weighted digraph is not needed. The Viterbi algorithm is a dynamic programming algorithm for finding the most likely sequence of hidden states (i.e., a finite path) that result in a sequence of observed events (a trace), especially in the context of hidden Markov models. Let $\mathcal{D}$ be a DTMC that is obtained after the first step described in Section 4, and suppose that $L(s)$ contains the set of atomic propositions that are valid in s and all subformulae of the formula under consideration. (Note that these labels are known due to the recursive descent nature of the PCTL model checking algorithm.) Let $tr(\sigma)$ denote the projection of a path $\sigma = s_0 \cdot s_1 \cdot \ldots \cdot s_h$ on its trace, i.e., $tr(\sigma) = L(s_0) \cdot L(s_1) \cdot \ldots \cdot L(s_h)$. $\sigma\downarrow_i$ denotes the prefix of path σ truncated at length i (thus ending in s_i), formally, $\sigma\downarrow_i = \sigma[0] \cdot \sigma[1] \cdot \ldots \cdot \sigma[i]$. Thus, $tr(\sigma\downarrow_i) = L(s_0) \cdot L(s_1) \cdot \ldots \cdot L(s_i)$. $\gamma\downarrow_i$ denotes the prefix of trace γ with length i. Let $\rho(\gamma, i, v)$ denote the probability of the most probable path $\sigma\downarrow_i$ whose trace equals $\gamma\downarrow_i$ and reaches state v. $\rho(\gamma, i, v)$ can be formally defined as follows:

$$\rho(\gamma, i, v) = \max_{tr(\sigma\downarrow_i)=\gamma_i} \prod_{j=0}^{i-1} \mathbf{P}(s_j, s_{j+1}) \cdot \mathbf{1}_v(s_i),$$

where $\mathbf{1}_v(s_i)$ is the characteristic function of v, i.e., $\mathbf{1}_v(s_i)$ returns 1, if $s_i = v$, and 0 otherwise. The Viterbi algorithm provides an algorithmic solution to compute $\rho(\gamma, i, v)$:

$$\rho(\gamma, i, v) = \begin{cases} 1 & \text{if } s = v \text{ and } i = 0 \\ 0 & \text{if } s \neq v \text{ and } i = 0 \\ \max_{u \in S} \rho(\gamma, i-1, u) \cdot \mathbf{P}(u, v) & \text{otherwise} \end{cases}$$

By computing $\rho(\Phi^h\Psi, h, s_h)$, the Viterbi algorithm determines the most probable h-hop path $\sigma = s_0 \cdot s_1 \cdot \ldots \cdot s_h$ that generates the trace $\gamma = L'(s_0)L'(s_1)\ldots L'(s_h) = \Phi^h\Psi$ with length $(h+1)$. Here, $L'(s) = L(s) \cap \{\Phi, \Psi\}$, i.e., L' is the labelling restricted to the subformulae Φ and Ψ. For our SE problem for bounded until, the trace of the most probable hop-constrained path from s to t is among $\{\Psi at_t, \Phi\Psi at_t, \ldots, \Phi^h\Psi at_t\}$. The self-loop at vertex t with probability one ensures that all these paths have length $h+1$ while not changing their probabilities. For instance, the path with trace $\Phi^i\Psi at_t$ can be extended so that the trace becomes $\Phi^i\Psi at_t^{h+1-i}$, where $i \leqslant h$. Since the DTMC is already transformed as in Step 1, we can obtain the most probable path for $\Phi\mathcal{U}^{\leqslant h}\Psi$ by computing $\rho((\Phi\vee\Psi\vee at_t)^{h+1} at_t, h+1, t)$ using the Viterbi algorithm. The time complexity is $\mathcal{O}(hm)$, as for the BF algorithm.

6 Finding Smallest Counterexamples

Recall that a smallest (most indicative) counterexample is a minimal counterexample, whose probability—among all minimal counterexamples—deviates maximally from the required probability bound. In this section, we investigate algorithms and complexity bounds for computing such smallest counterexamples. First observe that any smallest counterexample that contains, say k paths, contains the k most probable paths. This follows from the fact that any non-k most probable path can be exchanged with a more probable path, without changing the size of the counterexample, but by increasing its probability.

Unbounded until. Lemma 3 is applicable here for $k > 1$ and $h = \infty$. This suggests to consider the k shortest paths problem.

Definition 10 (KSP problem). *Given a weighted digraph $\mathcal{G} = (V, E, w)$, $s, t \in V$, and $k \in \mathbb{N}$, the k shortest paths (KSP) problem is to find k distinct shortest paths between s and t in $\mathcal{G}$, if such paths exist.*

Theorem 3. *The SC problem for unbounded until is a KSP problem.*

Proof. We prove that a smallest counterexample of size k, contains k most probable paths. It is proven by contradiction. Let C be a smallest counterexample for ϕ with $|C| = k$, and assume C does not contain the k most probable paths satisfying ϕ. Then there is a path $\sigma \notin C$ satisfying ϕ such that $\Pr\{\sigma\} > \Pr\{\sigma'\}$ for some $\sigma' \in C$. Let $C' = C \setminus \{\sigma'\} \cup \{\sigma\}$. Then C' is a counterexample for ϕ, $|C| = |C'|$ and $\Pr(C) > \Pr(C')$. This contradicts C being a smallest counterexample. $\square$

The question remains how to obtain k. Various algorithms for the KSP problem require k to be known a priori. This is inapplicable in our setting, as the number of paths in a smallest counterexample is implicitly provided by the probability bound in the PCTL-formula and is not known in advance. We therefore consider algorithms that allow to determine k on the fly, i.e., that can halt at any k and resume if necessary. A good candidate is Eppstein's algorithm [15]. Although this algorithm has the best known asymptotic time complexity, viz. $\mathcal{O}(m+n \log n+k)$, in practice the recursive enumeration algorithm (REA) by Jiménez and Marzal [20] prevails. This algorithm has a time complexity in $\mathcal{O}(m+kn \log \frac{m}{n})$ and is based on a generalization of the recursive equations for the BF-algorithm. Besides, it is readily adaptable to the case for bounded h, as we demonstrate below. Note that the time complexity of all known KSP algorithms depends on k, and as k may be exponential, their complexity is *pseudo-polynomial*.

Bounded until. Similar to the bounded until case for strongest evidences, we now consider the KSP problem where the path length is constrained, cf. Lemma 3 for $h \in \mathbb{N}$.

Definition 11 (HKSP problem). *Given a weighted digraph $\mathcal{G} = (V, E, w)$, $s, t \in V$ and $h, k \in \mathbb{N}$, the hop-constrained KSP (HKSP) problem is to determine k shortest paths each of length at most h between s and t.*

Similar to Theorem 3 we obtain:

Theorem 4. *The SC problem for bounded until is a HKSP problem.*

To our knowledge, algorithms for the HKSP problem do not exist. In order to solve the HKSP problem, we propose a new algorithm that is strongly based on Jiménez and Marzal's REA algorithm [20]. The advantage of adapting this algorithm is that k can be determined on the fly, an essential characteristic for our setting. The algorithm is a conservative extension of the REA algorithm.

For $v \in V$, let $\pi_h^k(s, v)$ denote the k-th shortest path from s to v of length at most h (if it exists). As before, we use $\perp$ to denote the non-existence of a path. We establish the following equations:

$$
\pi_h^k(s, v) = \begin{cases}
s & \text{if } k = 1, v = s \text{ and } h \geqslant 0 & (2a) \\
\perp & \text{if } (k > 1, v = s, h = 0) \text{ or } (v \neq s, h = 0) & (2b) \\
\arg\min_\sigma \{d(\sigma) \mid \sigma \in Q_h^k(s, v)\} & \text{otherwise} & (2c)
\end{cases}
$$

where $Q_h^k(s, v)$ is a set of candidate paths among which $\pi_h^k(s, v)$ is chosen. The candidate sets are defined by:

$$
Q_h^k(s, v) = \begin{cases}
\{\pi_{h-1}^1(s, u) \cdot v \mid (u, v) \in E\} \\
\quad \text{if } k = 1, v \neq s \text{ or } k = 2, v = s \\
(Q_h^{k-1}(s, v) - \{\pi_{h-1}^{k'}(s, u) \cdot v\}) \cup \{\pi_{h-1}^{k'+1}(s, u) \cdot v\} \\
\quad \text{if } k > 1 \text{ and } u, k' \text{ are the node and index,} \\
\quad \text{such that } \pi_h^{k-1}(s, v) = \pi_{h-1}^{k'}(s, u) \cdot v
\end{cases} \tag{3}
$$

Path $\pi_{h-1}^{k'+1}(s, u) \cdot v = \perp$ occurs when $Q_{h-1}^{k'+1}(s, u) = \emptyset$. Note that $\perp \cdot v = \perp$ for any $v \in V$. $Q_h^k(s, v) = \emptyset$ if it only contains $\perp$.

If $k=1$, the shortest path to v's predecessor u is extended with the edge to v. In the latter clause, $\pi_{h-1}^{k'}(s, u)$ denotes the selected $(k-1)$-st shortest path from s to u, where u is the direct predecessor of v. Paths in $Q_h^k(s, v)$ for $k > 1$ are thus either candidate paths for $k-1$ where the selected path is eliminated (first summand) or the $(k'+1)$-st shortest path from s to u extended with edge (u, v) (second summand). Note that for the source state s, there is no need to define $Q_h^k(s, s)$ as $\pi_h^k(s, s)$ is defined by equations $(2a)$ and $(2b)$, which act as termination conditions. In a similar way as in [20] it can be proven that:

Lemma 4. *The equations $(2a)$-$(2c)$ and (3) characterize the hop-constrained k shortest paths from s to v in at most h hops.*

The adapted REA. The adapted REA for computing the k shortest paths from s to t which each consist of at most h hops is sketched as follows. The algorithm is based on the recursive equations given just above.

(i) Compute $\pi_h^1(s, t)$ by the BF algorithm and set $k := 1$.

(ii) Repeat until $\displaystyle\sum_{i=1}^k \Pr\{\pi_h^i(s, t)\} > p$:

   (a) Set $k := k+1$ and compute $\pi_h^k(s, t)$ by invoking *NextPath(v, h, k)*.

For $k>1$, and once $\pi_h^1(s, v), \ldots, \pi_h^{k-1}(s, v)$ are available, *NextPath(t, h, k)* computes $\pi_h^k(s, v)$ as follows:

1. If $h \leqslant 0$, goto step 4.
2. If $k=2$, then set $Q[v, h] := \{\pi_{h-1}^1(s, u) \cdot v \mid (u, v) \in E \text{ and } \pi_h^1(s, v) \neq \pi_{h-1}^1(s, u) \cdot v\}$.
3. Let u and k' be the node and index such that $\pi_h^{k-1}(s, v) = \pi_{h-1}^{k'}(s, u) \cdot v$.
   (a) If $\pi_{h-1}^{k'+1}(s, u)$ has not yet been computed, invoke *NextPath*$(u, h-1, k'+1)$.
   (b) If $\pi_{h-1}^{k'+1}(s, u)$ exists, then insert $\pi_{h-1}^{k'+1}(s, u) \cdot v$ in $Q[v, h]$.
4. If $Q[v, h] \neq \emptyset$, then select and delete a path with minimum weight from $Q[v, h]$ and assign it to $\pi_h^k(s, v)$, else $\pi_h^k(s, v)$ does not exist.

In the main program, first the shortest path from s to t is determined using, e.g., the BF-algorithm. The intermediate results are recorded. Then, the k shortest paths are determined iteratively using the subroutine *NextPath*. The computation terminates when the total probability mass of the k shortest paths so far exceeds the bound p. Recall that p is the upper bound of the PCTL formula to be checked. Note that $Q[v, h]$ in the algorithm corresponds to $Q_h^k(s, v)$, where k is the parameter of the program. In steps 2 through 3, the set $Q_h^k(s, v)$ is determined from $Q_h^{k-1}(s, v)$ according to equation (3). In the final step, $\pi_h^k(s, v)$ is selected from $Q_h^k(s, v)$ according to equation (2c).

To determine the computational complexity of the algorithm, we assume the candidate sets to be implemented by heaps (as in [20]). The k shortest paths to a vertex v can be stored in a linked list, where each path $\pi_h^k(s, v) = \pi_{h-1}^{k'}(s, u) \cdot v$ is compactly represented by its length and a back pointer to $\pi_{h-1}^{k'}(s, u)$. Using these data structures, we obtain:

Theorem 5. *The time complexity of the adapted REA is* $\mathcal{O}(hm + hk \log(\frac{m}{n}))$.

Note that the time complexity is pseudo-polynomial due to the dependence on k which may be exponential in n. As in our setting, k is not known in advance, this can not be reduced to a polynomial time complexity.

7   Lower Bounds on Probabilities

For the violation of PCTL formulae with lower bounds, i.e., $s \not\models \mathcal{P}_{\geqslant p}(\Phi \mathcal{U}^{\leqslant h} \Psi)$, the formula and model will be changed so that the algorithms for finding strongest evidences and smallest counterexamples for PCTL can be applied.

Unbounded until. For $h = \infty$, we have:

$$\mathcal{P}_{\geqslant p}(\Phi \mathcal{U} \Psi) \equiv \mathcal{P}_{\leqslant 1-p}(\underbrace{(\Phi \wedge \neg \Psi)}_{\Phi^*} \mathcal{W} \underbrace{(\neg \Phi \wedge \neg \Psi)}_{\Psi^*}) \equiv \mathcal{P}_{\leqslant 1-p}(\underbrace{(\Phi \wedge \neg \Psi)}_{\Phi^*} \mathcal{U}(at_u \vee at_b)),$$

where at_u and at_b are two new atomic propositions such that (i) $s \models at_u$ iff $s \models \Psi^*$ (ii) $s \models at_b$ iff $s \in B$ where B is a bottom strongly connected component (BSCC) such that $B \subseteq Sat(\Phi^*)$, or shortly $s \in B_{\Phi^*}$. A BSCC B is a maximal strong component that has no transitions that leave B.

Algorithmically, the DTMC is first transformed such that all the $(\neg \Phi^* \wedge \neg \Psi^*)$-states are made absorbing. Note that once those states are reached, $\Phi^* \mathcal{W} \Psi^*$ will never be satisfied. As a second step, all the Ψ^*-states are labelled with at_u and made absorbing. Finally, all BSCCs are obtained and all states in B_{Φ^*} are labelled with at_b. The obtained DTMC now acts as the starting point for applying all the model transformations and algorithms in Section 4-6 to generate a counterexample for $\mathcal{P}_{\leqslant 1-p}(\Phi^* \mathcal{U}(at_u \vee at_b))$.

Bounded until. For $h \in \mathbb{N}$, identifying all states in BSCC B_{Φ^*} is not sufficient, as a path satisfying $\square^{\leqslant h}\Phi^*$ may never reach such BSCC. Instead, we transform the DTMC and use:

$$\mathcal{P}_{\geqslant p}(\Phi\mathcal{U}^{\leqslant h}\Psi) \equiv \mathcal{P}_{\leqslant 1-p}(\underbrace{(\Phi \wedge \neg\Psi)}_{\Phi^*}\mathcal{U}^{=h}(at_u \vee at_h)),$$

where at_u and at_h are new atomic propositions such that at_u is labelled as before and $s' \models at_h$ iff there exists $\sigma \in Path_{fin}(s)$ such that $\sigma[h] = s'$ and $\sigma \models \square^{\leqslant h}\Phi^*$.

Algorithmically, the $(\neg\Phi^* \wedge \neg\Psi^*)$-states and Ψ^*-states are made absorbing; besides, all Ψ^*-states are labelled with at_u. As a second step, all the Φ^*-states that can be reached in exactly h hops are computed by e.g., a breadth first search (BFS) algorithm. The obtained DTMC now acts as the starting point for applying all the model transformations and algorithms in Section 4-6 to generate a counterexample for $\mathcal{P}_{\leqslant 1-p}(\Phi^*\mathcal{U}^{=h}(at_u \vee at_h))$. Finite paths of exactly h paths suffice to check the validity of $\sigma \models \square^{\leqslant h}\Phi^*$, thus $\Phi^*\mathcal{U}^{=h}at_h$ (not $\Phi^*\mathcal{U}^{\leqslant h}at_h$) is needed; besides the validity is unaffected if we change $\Phi\mathcal{U}^{\leqslant h}at_u$ into $\Phi\mathcal{U}^{=h}at_u$, since all at_u states are absorbing. Note that it is very easy to adapt the strongest evidences and smallest counterexamples algorithms for $\mathcal{U}^{\leqslant h}$ to those for $\mathcal{U}^{=h}$ – only the termination conditions need a slight change. The time complexity remains the same.

In the above explained way, counterexamples for (bounded) until-formulae with a lower bound on their probability are obtained by considering formulae on slightly adapted DTMCs with upper bounds on probabilities. Intuitively, the fact that s refutes $\mathcal{P}_{\geqslant p}(\Phi\mathcal{U}^{\leqslant h}\Psi)$ is witnessed by showing that violating paths of s are too probable, i.e., carry more probability mass than p. Alternatively, *all* paths starting in s that satisfy $\Phi\mathcal{U}^{\leqslant h}\Psi$ could be determined as this set of paths has a probability less than p.

8   Conclusion

Summary of results. We have investigated the computation of strongest evidences (maximally probable paths) and smallest counterexamples for PCTL model checking of DTMCs. Relationships to various kinds of shortest path problems have been established. Besides, it is shown that for the hop-constrained strongest evidence problem, the Viterbi algorithm can be applied. Summarizing we have obtained the following connections and complexities:

counterexample problem	shortest path problem	algorithm	time complexity
SE (until)	SP	Dijkstra	$\mathcal{O}(m + n \log n)$
SE (bounded until)	HSP	BF/Viterbi	$\mathcal{O}(hm)$
SC (until)	KSP	Eppstein	$\mathcal{O}(m + n \log n + k)$
SC (bounded until)	HKSP	adapted REA	$\mathcal{O}(hm + hk \log(\frac{m}{n}))$

where n and m are the number of states and transitions, h is the hop bound, and k is the number of shortest paths.

Extensions. The results reported in this paper can be extended to (weak) until-formulae with minimal or interval bounds on the number of allowed steps. For instance, strongest evidences for $s \not\models \mathcal{P}_{\leqslant p}(\Phi \mathcal{U}^{[h,h']} \Psi)$ with $0 < h \leqslant h'$ can be obtained by appropriately combining maximally probable paths from s to states at distance h from s, and from those states to Ψ-states. Similar reasoning applies to the SC problem. For DTMCs with rewards, it can be established that the SE problem for violating reward- and hop-bounded until-formulae boils down to solving a non-trivial instance of the CSP problem. As this problem is NP-complete, efficient algorithms for finding counterexamples for PRCTL [5], a reward extension to PCTL, will be hard to obtain.

Further research. Topics for further research are: succinct representation and visualization of counterexamples, experimental research of the proposed algorithms in probabilistic model checking and considering loopless paths (see e.g., [23]).

Related work. The SE problem for timed reachability in CTMCs is considered in [3]. Whereas we consider the generation of strongest evidences once a property violation has been established, [3] assumes the CTMC to be unknown. The SE problem for CTMCs is mapped onto an SE problem on (uniformised) DTMCs, and heuristic search algorithms (Z*) are employed to determine the evidences. The approach is restricted to bounded until and due to the use of heuristics, time complexities are hard to obtain. In our view, the main advantage of our approach is the systematic characterization of generating counterexamples in terms of shortest path problems. Recently, [4] generalizes the heuristic approach to obtain failure subgraphs, i.e., counterexamples. To our knowledge, smallest counterexamples have not been considered yet.

Acknowledgement. Christel Baier and David N. Jansen are kindly acknowledged for their useful remarks on the paper. This research has been financially supported by the NWO project QUPES and by 973 and 863 Program of China (2002CB3120022005AA113160, 2004AA112090, 2005AA113030) and NSFC (60233010, 60273034, 60403014).

References

1. A.V. Aho, J.E. Hopcroft and J.D. Ullmann. The design and analysis of computer algorithms. Addison-Wesley, 1974.
2. R.K. Ahuja, T.L. Magnanti and J.B. Orlin. *Network Flows: Theory, Algorithms and Applications*, Prentice Hall, Inc., 1993.
3. H. Aljazzar, H. Hermanns and S. Leue. Counterexamples for timed probabilistic reachability. FORMATS 2005, LNCS 3829: 177-195, 2005.
4. H. Aljazzar and S. Leue. Extended directed search for probabilistic timed reachability. FORMATS 2006, LNCS 4202: 33-51, 2006.
5. S. Andova, H. Hermanns and J.-P. Katoen. Discrete-time rewards model-checked. FORMATS 2003, LNCS 2791: 88-104, 2003.
6. C. Baier, J.-P. Katoen, H. Hermanns and V. Wolf. Comparative branching-time semantics for Markov chains. *Inf. Comput.* 200(2): 149-214 (2005).
7. T. Ball, M. Naik and S. K. Rajamani. From symptom to cause: localizing errors in counterexample traces. POPL: 97-105, 2003.

8. G. Behrmann, K. G. Larsen and J. I. Rasmussen. Optimal scheduling using priced timed automata. *ACM SIGMETRICS Perf. Ev. Review* 32(4): 34-40 (2005).
9. R. Bellman. On a routing problem. *Quarterly of Appl. Math.*, 16(1): 87-90 (1958).
10. E.M. Clarke, O. Grumberg, S. Jha, Y. Lu and H. Veith: Counterexample-guided abstraction refinement. CAV, LNCS 1855: 154-169, 2000.
11. E.M. Clarke, S. Jha, Y. Lu and H. Veith. Tree-like counterexamples in model checking. LICS: 19-29 (2002).
12. T.H. Cormen, C.E. Leiserson, R.L. Rivest and C. Stein. *Introduction to Algorithms*, 2001. Section 24.1: The Bellman-Ford algorithm, pp.588-592.
13. L. de Alfaro, T.A. Henzinger and F. Mang. Detecting errors before reaching them. CAV, LNCS 2725: 186-201, 2000.
14. E.W. Dijkstra. A note on two problems in connection with graphs. *Num. Math.*, 1:395-412 (1959).
15. D. Eppstein. Finding the k shortest paths. *SIAM J. Comput.* 28(2): 652-673 (1998).
16. G.D. Forney. The Viterbi algorithm. *Proc. of the IEEE* 61(3): 268-278 (1973).
17. M.R. Garey and D.S. Johnson. *Computers and Intractability, A Guide to the Theory of NP-Completeness*, Freeman, San Francisco, 1979.
18. A. Gurfinkel and M. Chechik. Proof-like counter-examples. TACAS, LNCS 2619: 160-175, 2003.
19. H. Hansson and B. Jonsson. A logic for reasoning about time and reliability. *Formal Asp. Comput.* 6(5): 512-535 (1994).
20. V.M. Jiménez and A. Marzal. Computing the K shortest paths: A new algorithm and an experimental comparison. WAE 1999, LNCS 1668: 15-29, 1999.
21. H. Jin, K. Ravi and F. Somenzi. Fate and free will in error traces. *STTT* 6(2): 102-116 (2004).
22. E.L. Lawler. *Combinatorial Optimization: Networks and Matroids*. Holt, Reinhart, and Winston, 1976.
23. E.Q.V. Martins and M.M.B. Pascoal. A new implementation of Yen's ranking loopless paths algorithm. *4OR* 1(2): 121-133 (2003).
24. E.Q.V. Martins, M.M.B. Pascoal and J.L.E. Dos Santos. Deviation algorithms for ranking shortest paths. *Int. J. Found. Comput. Sci.* 10(3): 247-262 (1999).
25. K. Mehlhorn and M. Ziegelmann. Resource constrained shortest paths. ESA 2000, LNCS 1879: 326-337, 2000.
26. S. Shoham and O. Grumberg. A game-based framework for CTL counterexamples and 3-valued abstraction-refinement. CAV, LNCS 2725: 275-287, 2003.
27. A.J. Viterbi. Error bounds for convolutional codes and an asymptotically optimum decoding algorithm. *IEEE Trans. on Inf. Theory* 13(2):260-269, 1967.

Bisimulation Minimisation Mostly Speeds Up Probabilistic Model Checking

Joost-Pieter Katoen[1,2], Tim Kemna[2], Ivan Zapreev[1,2], and David N. Jansen[1,2]

[1] Software Modeling and Verification Group, RWTH Aachen, Germany
[2] Formal Methods and Tools, University of Twente, The Netherlands

Abstract. This paper studies the effect of bisimulation minimisation in model checking of monolithic discrete-time and continuous-time Markov chains as well as variants thereof with rewards. Our results show that—as for traditional model checking—enormous state space reductions (up to logarithmic savings) may be obtained. In contrast to traditional model checking, in many cases, the verification time of the original Markov chain exceeds the quotienting time plus the verification time of the quotient. We consider probabilistic bisimulation as well as versions thereof that are tailored to the property to be checked.

1 Introduction

Probabilistic model checking enjoys a rapid increase of interest from different communities. Software tools such as PRISM [31] (with about 4,000 downloads), MRMC [29], and LiQuor [4] support the verification of Markov chains or variants thereof that exhibit nondeterminism. They have been applied to case studies from areas such as randomised distributed algorithms, planning and AI, security, communication protocols, biological process modeling, and quantum computing. Probabilistic model checking engines have been integrated in existing tool chains for widely used formalisms such as stochastic Petri nets [11], Statemate [9], and the stochastic process algebra PEPA [24], and are used for a probabilistic extension of Promela [4].

The typical kind of properties that can be checked is time-bounded reachability properties—"Does the probability to reach a certain set of goal states (by avoiding bad states) within a maximal time span exceed $\frac{1}{2}$?"—and long-run averages—"In equilibrium, does the likelihood to leak confidential information remain below 10^{-4}?" Extensions for cost-based models allow for checking more involved properties that refer to e.g., the expected cumulated cost or the instantaneous cost rate of computations. Intricate combinations of numerical or simulation techniques for Markov chains, optimisation algorithms, and traditional LTL or CTL model-checking algorithms result in simple, yet very efficient verification procedures. Verifying time-bounded reachability properties on models of tens of millions of states usually is a matter of seconds.

Like in the traditional setting, probabilistic model checking suffers from state space explosion: the number of states grows exponentially in the number of system components and cardinality of data domains. To combat this problem,

O. Grumberg and M. Huth (Eds.): TACAS 2007, LNCS 4424, pp. 87–101, 2007.

various techniques have been proposed in the literature. Variants of binary decision diagrams (multi-terminal BDDs) have been (and still are) successfully applied in PRISM [31] to a range of probabilistic models, abstraction-refinement has been applied to reachability problems in MDPs [12], partial-order reduction techniques using Peled's ample-set method have been generalised to MDPs [19], abstract interpretation has been applied to MDPs [36], and various bisimulation equivalences and simulation pre-orders allow model aggregation prior to model checking, e. g., [7,39]. Recently proposed techniques include abstractions of probabilities by intervals combined with three-valued logics for DTMCs [15,25,26], stochastic ordering techniques for CSL model checking [8], abstraction of MDPs by two-player stochastic games [32], and symmetry reduction [33].

The purpose of this paper is to empirically investigate the effect of strong bisimulation minimisation in probabilistic model checking. We hereby focus on fully probabilistic models such as discrete-time and continuous-time Markov chains (DTMCs and CTMCs, for short), and variants thereof with costs. The advantages of probabilistic bisimulation [34] in this setting are manifold. It preserves the validity of PCTL [20] and CSL [2,6] formulas, variants of CTL for the discrete- and continuous-time probabilistic setting, respectively. It implies ordinary lumpability of Markov chains [10], an aggregation technique for Markov chains that is applied in performance and dependability evaluation since the 1960s. Quotient Markov chains can be obtained in a fully automated way. The time complexity of quotienting is logarithmic in the number of states, and linear in the number of transitions—as for traditional bisimulation minimisation—when using splay trees (a specific kind of balanced tree) for storing partitions [14]. Besides, probabilistic bisimulation can be used for obtaining (coarser) abstractions that are tailored to the properties of interest (as we will see), and enjoys the congruence property for parallel composition allowing compositional minimisation. We consider explicit model checking as the non-trivial interplay between bisimulation and MTBDDs would unnecessarily complicate our study; such symbolic representations mostly grow under bisimulation minimisation [23].

Thanks to extensive studies by Fisler and Vardi [16,17,18], it is known that bisimulation minimisation for LTL model checking and invariant verification leads to drastic state space reductions (up to logarithmic savings) but at a time penalty: the time to minimise and model check the resulting quotient Kripke structure significantly exceeds the time to verify the original model. This paper considers these issues in probabilistic (i. e., PCTL and CSL) model checking. To that end, bisimulation minimisation algorithms have been realised in the prototypical explicit-state probabilistic model checker MRMC, several case studies have been considered that are widely studied in the literature (and can be considered as benchmark problems), and have been subjected to various experiments. This paper presents our results. As expected, our results show that enormous state space reductions (up to logarithmic savings) may be obtained. In contrast to the results by Fisler and Vardi [16,17,18], the verification time of the original Markov chain mostly *exceeds* the quotienting time plus the verification time of the quotient. This effect is stronger for probabilistic bisimulation that is tailored to the property to be checked and for model checking Markov chains with costs (i. e., rewards). This is due to the fact that probabilistic model checking is more time-consuming than traditional model checking, while minimization w. r. t. probabilistic bisimulation is only slightly slower than for traditional bisimulation.

The paper is organised as follows. Section 2 introduces the considered probabilistic models. Section 3 considers probabilistic bisimulation and the algorithms used. Section 4 presents the considered case studies, the obtained results, and analyses these results. Section 5 concludes the paper.

2   Preliminaries

DTMCs. Let AP be a fixed, finite set of *atomic propositions*. A (labelled) DTMC $\mathcal{D}$ is a tuple $(S, \mathbf{P}, L)$ where S is a finite set of *states*, $\mathbf{P} : S \times S \rightarrow [0, 1]$ is a *probability matrix* such that $\sum_{s' \in S} \mathbf{P}(s, s') = 1$ for all $s \in S$, and $L : S \rightarrow 2^{AP}$ is a *labelling* function which assigns to each state $s \in S$ the set $L(s)$ of atomic propositions that hold in s. A path through a DTMC is a sequence[1] of states $\sigma = s_0 s_1 s_2 \ldots$ with $\mathbf{P}(s_i, s_{i+1}) > 0$ for all i. Let $Path^{\mathcal{D}}$ denote the set of all paths in DTMC $\mathcal{D}$. $\sigma[i]$ denotes the $(i{+}1)$th state of σ, i. e., $\sigma[i] = s_i$.

The logic PCTL. Let $a \in AP$, probability $p \in [0, 1]$, $k \in \mathbb{N}$ (or $k = \infty$) and $\bowtie$ be either $\leq$ or $\geq$. The syntax of Probabilistic CTL (PCTL) [20] is defined by:

$$\Phi ::= \text{tt} \mid a \mid \Phi \wedge \Phi \mid \neg \Phi \mid \mathcal{P}_{\bowtie p}(\Phi \, \mathcal{U}^{\leq k} \, \Phi).$$

A state s satisfies $\mathcal{P}_{\bowtie p}(\Phi \, \mathcal{U}^{\leq k} \, \Psi)$ if $\{ \sigma \in Path^{\mathcal{D}}(s) \mid \sigma \models \Phi \, \mathcal{U}^{\leq k} \, \Psi \}$ has a probability that satisfies $\bowtie p$. A path σ satisfies $\Phi \, \mathcal{U}^{\leq k} \, \Psi$ if within k steps a Ψ-state is reached, and all preceding states satisfy Φ. That is, if $\sigma[j] \models \Psi$ for some $j \leq k$, and $\sigma[i] \models \Phi$ for all $i < j$. We define the abbreviation $\Diamond^{\leq k}\Phi := \text{tt} \, \mathcal{U}^{\leq k} \, \Phi$. The unbounded until formula that is standard in temporal logics is obtained by taking $k = \infty$, i. e., $\Phi \, \mathcal{U} \, \Psi = \Phi \, \mathcal{U}^{\leq \infty} \, \Psi$.[2]

Given a set F of PCTL formulas, we denote with PCTL_F the smallest set of formulas that contains F and is closed under the PCTL operators $\wedge$, $\neg$, and $\mathcal{U}$.

Verifying hop-constrained probabilistic reachability. PCTL model checking [20] is carried out in the same way as verifying CTL by recursively computing the set $Sat(\Phi) = \{ s \in S \mid s \models \Phi \}$. The probability of $\{ \sigma \mid \sigma \models \Phi \, \mathcal{U}^{\leq k} \, \Psi \}$ is the least solution of the following linear equation system. Let $S_1 = \{ s \mid s \models \Psi \}$, $S_0 = \{ s \mid s \models \neg \Phi \wedge \neg \Psi \}$, and $S_? = \{ s \mid s \models \Phi \wedge \neg \Psi \} = S \setminus (S_1 \cup S_0)$.

$$Prob^{\mathcal{D}}(s, \Phi \, \mathcal{U}^{\leq k} \, \Psi) = \begin{cases} 1 & \text{if } s \in S_1 \\ \sum_{s' \in S} \mathbf{P}(s, s') \cdot Prob^{\mathcal{D}}(s', \Phi \, \mathcal{U}^{\leq k-1} \, \Psi) & \text{if } s \in S_? \wedge k > 0 \\ 0 & \text{otherwise} \end{cases}$$

---

[1] In this paper, we do not dwell upon the distinction between finite and infinite paths.
[2] For simplicity, we do not consider the next operator.

One can simplify this system by replacing S_0 by $U_0 = S_0 \cup \{ s \in S_? \mid \neg \exists \sigma \in$ $Path^{\mathcal{D}}(s) : \sigma \models \Phi \, \mathcal{U} \, \Psi \}$. If $k = \infty$, one may also replace S_1 by $U_1 = S_1 \cup \{ s \in$ $S_? \mid \forall \sigma \in Path^{\mathcal{D}}(s) : \sigma \models \Phi \, \mathcal{U} \, \Psi \}$. The sets U_0 and U_1 can be found via a simple graph analysis (a depth-first search) in time $O(|S| + |\mathbf{P}|)$.

Alternatively, the probabilities can be calculated by making the states $s \notin S_?$ absorbing as follows. For DTMC $\mathcal{D} = (S, \mathbf{P}, L)$ and $A \subseteq S$, let $\mathcal{D}[A]$ be the DTMC $(S, \mathbf{P}[A], L)$ where the states in A are made absorbing: If $s \in A$, then $\mathbf{P}[A](s, s) = 1$ and $\mathbf{P}[A](s, s') = 0$ for $s' \neq s$. Otherwise, $\mathbf{P}[A](s, s') = \mathbf{P}(s, s')$. Let $\pi^{\mathcal{D}}(s \overset{k}{\rightsquigarrow} s')$ denote the probability of being in state s' after exactly k steps in DTMC $\mathcal{D}$ when starting in s. Then:

$$Prob^{\mathcal{D}}(s, \Phi \, \mathcal{U}^{\leq k} \, \Psi) = \sum_{s' \in S_1} \pi^{\mathcal{D}[S_0 \cup S_1]}(s \overset{k}{\rightsquigarrow} s').$$

Calculating $Prob^{\mathcal{D}}(s, \Phi \, \mathcal{U}^{\leq k} \, \Psi)$ thus amounts to computing $(\mathbf{P}[S_0 \cup S_1])^k \cdot \iota_{S_1}$, where $\iota_{S_1}(s) = 1$ if $s \in S_1$, and 0 otherwise.

CTMCs. A (labelled) CTMC $\mathcal{C}$ is a tuple $(S, \mathbf{P}, E, L)$ where $(S, \mathbf{P}, L)$ is a DTMC and $E : S \to \mathbb{R}_{\geq 0}$ provides the *exit rate* for each state. The probability of taking a transition from s within t time units equals $1 - e^{-E(s) \cdot t}$. The probability of taking a transition from state s to state s' within time t is given by: $\mathbf{P}(s, s') \cdot (1 - e^{-E(s) \cdot t})$.

A path through a CTMC is a sequence of states and sojourn times $\sigma = s_0 \, t_0 \, s_1 \, t_1 \ldots$ with $\mathbf{P}(s_i, s_{i+1}) > 0$ and $t_i \in \mathbb{R}_{\geq 0}$ for all i. Let $Path^{\mathcal{C}}$ denote the set of all paths in CTMC $\mathcal{C}$.

Uniformisation. In a *uniform* CTMC, the exit rate of all states is the same. A non-uniform CTMC can be uniformized by adding self loops as follows: let $\mathcal{C} = (S, \mathbf{P}, E, L)$ be a CTMC and choose $\tilde{E} \geq \max_{s \in S} E(s)$. Then, $Unif_{\tilde{E}}(\mathcal{C}) = (S, \mathbf{P}', E', L)$ where $E'(s) = \tilde{E}$ for all s, $\mathbf{P}'(s, s') = E(s) \mathbf{P}(s, s') / \tilde{E}$ if $s \neq s'$ and $\mathbf{P}'(s, s) = 1 - \sum_{s' \neq s} \mathbf{P}'(s, s')$. The probability to be in a given state at a given time in the uniformized CTMC is the same as the one in the original CTMC.

The logic CSL. Continuous stochastic logic (CSL, [6]) is similar to PCTL. For a, p and $\bowtie$ as before, time bounds $t_1 \in [0, \infty)$ and $t_2 \in [t_1, \infty]$, the syntax is:

$$\Phi ::= \text{tt} \mid a \mid \Phi \wedge \Phi \mid \neg \Phi \mid \mathcal{P}_{\bowtie p}(\Phi \, \mathcal{U}^{[t_1, t_2]} \, \Phi) \mid \mathcal{S}_{\bowtie p}(\Phi)$$

A state s satisfies $\mathcal{P}_{\bowtie p}(\Phi \, \mathcal{U}^{[t_1, t_2]} \, \Psi)$ if the set of timed paths $\{ \sigma \in Path^{\mathcal{C}}(s) \mid \sigma \models \Phi \, \mathcal{U}^{[t_1, t_2]} \, \Psi \}$ has a probability $\bowtie p$. A timed path satisfies $\Phi \, \mathcal{U}^{[t_1, t_2]} \, \Psi$ if within time $t \in [t_1, t_2]$ a Ψ-state is reached, and all preceding states satisfy Φ. We will mostly let $t_1 = 0$ and denote this as $\Phi \, \mathcal{U}^{\leq t_2} \, \Psi$. A state s satisfies the formula $\mathcal{S}_{\bowtie p}(\Phi)$ if the steady-state probability to be in a Φ-state (when starting in s) satisfies the constraint $\bowtie p$.

CSL model checking [2,6] can be implemented as follows. The operator $\mathcal{S}$ can be solved by a (standard) calculation of the steady-state probabilities together with a graph analysis. For the time-bounded until operator, note that, after uniformisation the probability to take k steps within time t does not depend on the actual states visited. This probability is Poisson distributed, and the probability to satisfy the until formula within k steps is calculated using the PCTL algorithm. The total probability is an infinite sum over all k, which can be approximated well.

Rewards. A discrete-time Markov reward model (DMRM) $\mathcal{D}_r$ is a tuple $(\mathcal{D}, r)$ where $\mathcal{D}$ is a DTMC and $r : S \to \mathbb{R}_{\geq 0}$ is a *reward* assignment function. The quantity $r(s)$ indicates the reward that is earned on leaving state s. Rewards could also be attached to edges in a DTMC, but this does not increase expressivity. A path through a DMRM is a path through its DTMC, i.e., sequence of states $\sigma = s_0 \, s_1 \, s_2 \ldots$ with $\mathbf{P}(s_i, s_{i+1}) > 0$ for all i.

Let a, p and k be as before, and $r \in \mathbb{R}_{\geq 0}$ be a nonnegative reward bound. The two main operators that extend PCTL to Probabilistic Reward CTL (PRCTL) [1] are $\mathcal{P}_{\bowtie p}(\Phi \, \mathcal{U}_{\leq r}^{\leq k} \, \Psi)$ and $\mathcal{E}_{\leq r}^{=k}(\Phi)$. The until-operator is equipped with a bound on the maximum number (k) of allowed hops to reach the goal states, and a bound on the maximum allowed cumulated reward (r) before reaching these states. Formula $\mathcal{E}_{\leq r}^{=k}(\Phi)$ asserts that the expected cumulated reward in Φ-states until the k-th transition is at most r. Thus, in order to check the validity of this formula for a given path, all visits to Φ-state are considered in the first k steps and the total reward that is obtained in these states; the rewards earned in other states or earned in Φ-states after the first k steps are not relevant. Whenever the expected value of this quantity over all paths that start in state s is at most r, state $s \models \mathcal{E}_{\leq r}^{=k}(\Phi)$.

A continuous-time Markov reward model (CMRM) $\mathcal{C}_r$ is a tuple $(\mathcal{C}, r)$ where $\mathcal{C}$ is a CTMC and $r : S \to \mathbb{R}_{\geq 0}$ is a reward assignment function (as before). The quantity $r(s)$ indicates that if t time units are spent in state s, a reward $r(s) \cdot t$ is acquired. A path through a CMRM is a path through its underlying CTMC. Let $\sigma = s_0 \, t_0 \, s_1 \, t_1 \ldots$ be a path. For $t = \sum_{j=0}^{k-1} t_j + t'$ with $t' \leq t_k$ we define $r(\sigma, t) = \sum_{j=0}^{k-1} t_j \cdot r(s_j) + t' \cdot r(s_k)$, the cumulative reward along σ up to time t.

CSRL [5] is a logic that extends CSL with one operator $\mathcal{P}_{\bowtie p}(\Phi \, \mathcal{U}_{\leq r}^{\leq t} \, \Psi)$ to express time- and reward-bounded properties. Checking this property of a CMRM is difficult. One can either approximate the CMRM by a discretisation of the rewards or compute for each (untimed) path the probability to meet the bound and sum them up. Reward-bounded until properties of a CMRM can be checked via a transformation of rewards into exit rates and checking a corresponding time-bounded until property [5].

3   Bisimulation

Bisimulation. Let $\mathcal{D} = (S, \mathbf{P}, L)$ be a DTMC and R an equivalence relation on S. The quotient of S under R is denoted S/R. R is a *strong bisimulation* on $\mathcal{D}$ if for $s_1 \, R \, s_2$:

$$L(s_1) = L(s_2) \quad \text{and} \quad \mathbf{P}(s_1, C) = \mathbf{P}(s_2, C) \text{ for all } C \text{ in } S/R.$$

s_1 and s_2 in $\mathcal{D}$ are strongly bisimilar, denoted $s_1 \sim_d s_2$, if there exists a strong bisimulation R on $\mathcal{D}$ with $s_1 \; R \; s_2$. Strong bisimulation [10,24] for CTMCs, that implies ordinary lumpability, is a mild variant of the notion for the discrete-time probabilistic setting: in addition to the above, it is also required that the exit rates of bisimilar states are equal: $E(s_1) = E(s_2)$.

Measure-driven bisimulation. Requiring states to be equally labelled with all atomic propositions is rather strong if one is interested in checking formulas that just refer to a (small) subset of propositions, or more generally, sub-formulas. The following notion weakens the labelling requirement in strong bisimulation by requiring equal labellling for a set of PCTL formulas F. Let $\mathcal{D} = (S, \mathbf{P}, L)$ be a DTMC and R an equivalence relation on S. R is a F-*bisimulation* on $\mathcal{D}$ if for $s_1 \; R \; s_2$:

$$s_1 \models \Phi \Longleftrightarrow s_2 \models \Phi \text{for all } \Phi \in F$$
$$\mathbf{P}(s_1, C) = \mathbf{P}(s_2, C) \text{ for all } C \in S/R.$$

States s_1 and s_2 are F-bisimilar, denoted $s_1 \sim_F s_2$, if there exists an F-bisimulation R on $\mathcal{D}$ with $s_1 \; R \; s_2$. F-bisimulation on CTMCs (for a set of CSL formulas F) is defined analogously [5]. Note that strong bisimilarity is F-bisimilarity for $F = AP$.

Preservation results. Aziz et al. [3] have shown that strong bisimulation is sound and complete with respect to PCTL (and even PCTL*):

Proposition 1. *Let $\mathcal{D}$ be a DTMC, R a bisimulation and s an arbitrary state of $\mathcal{D}$. Then, for all PCTL formulas Φ, $s \models_{\mathcal{D}} \Phi \Longleftrightarrow [s]_R \models_{\mathcal{D}/R} \Phi$.*

This result can be generalised to F-bisimulation in the following way:

Proposition 2. *Let $\mathcal{D}$ be a DTMC, R an F-bisimulation and s an arbitrary state of $\mathcal{D}$. Then, for all PCTL$_F$ formulas Φ, $s \models_{\mathcal{D}} \Phi \Longleftrightarrow [s]_R \models_{\mathcal{D}/R} \Phi$.*

Similar results hold for CSL and bisimulation on CTMCs [6], for PRCTL on DMRM, and for CSRL on CMRM.

Bisimulation minimisation. The preservation results suggest that one can verify properties of a Markov chain on a bisimulation quotient. The next issue to consider is how to obtain the quotient. An often used algorithm (called *partition refinement*) is based on *splitting:* Let Π be a partition of S. A splitter for some block $B \in \Pi$ is a block $Sp \in \Pi$ such that the probability to enter Sp is not the same for each state in B. In this case, the algorithm splits B into subblocks such that each subblock consists of states s with identical $\mathbf{P}(s, Sp)$. This step is repeated until a fixpoint is reached. The final partition is the coarsest bisimulation that respects the initial partition. The worst-case time complexity of this algorithm is $O(|\mathbf{P}| \log |S|)$ provided that splay trees are used to store blocks [14]. These data structures are adopted in our implementation.[3]

Initial partition. The choice of initial partition in the partition refinement algorithm determines what kind of bisimulation the result is. If we group states labelled with the same atomic propositions together, the result is the strong bisimulation quotient $S/\sim_d$. If we choose the initial partition according to the satisfaction of formulas in F, the resulting partition is the F-bisimulation quotient $S/\sim_F$. To get the smallest bisimulation quotient, it is important to start with a coarse initial partition. Instead of only calculating the strong bisimulation quotient, we will also use measure-driven bisimulation for a suitable set F.

A naive approach for formula $\mathcal{P}_{\bowtie p}(\Phi\,\mathcal{U}\,\Psi)$ is to choose $F = \{\,\Psi, \Phi \wedge \neg\Psi\,\}$. In fact, $\mathcal{P}_{\bowtie p}(\Phi\,\mathcal{U}\,\Psi)$ is not in PCTL_F, but the equivalent formula $\mathcal{P}_{\bowtie p}(\Phi\wedge\neg\Psi\,\mathcal{U}\,\Psi)$ is. This yields an initial partition consisting of the sets $S_1 = Sat(\Psi)$, $S_? = Sat(\Phi\wedge\neg\Psi)$ and $S_0 = S\backslash(S_1\cup S_?)$ (cf. Section 2). Note that selecting $F = \{\,\Psi, \Phi\,\}$ would lead to a less efficient initial partition with four blocks instead of three. We improve this initial partition by replacing S_0 by $U_0 = Sat(\mathcal{P}_{\leq 0}(\Phi\,\mathcal{U}\,\Psi))$ and S_1 by U_1, which is essentially[4] $Sat(\mathcal{P}_{\geq 1}(\Phi\,\mathcal{U}\,\Psi))$. (Defining U_0 and U_1 as satisfaction sets of some formula has the advantage that we can still use Proposition 2.) The sets of states U_0 and U_1 can be collapsed into single states u_0 and u_1, respectively. This results in the initial partition $\{\,\{u_0\}, \{u_1\}, S\setminus(U_0\cup U_1)\,\}$.

For bounded until, one can still use U_0, but not U_1, since the fact that (almost) all paths satisfy $\Phi\,\mathcal{U}\,\Psi$ does not imply that these paths reach a Ψ-state within the step or time bound. Therefore, for this operator the initial partition is $\{\,\{u_0\}, \{s_1\}, S\setminus(U_0\cup S_1)\,\}$ with u_0 as before and s_1 the collapsed state for S_1.[5] Thus, for bounded until the measure-driven initial partition is finer than for unbounded until. In the experiments reported in the next section, the effect of the granularity of the initial partition will become clear.

4   Experiments

To study the effect of bisimulation in model checking, we realised the minimisation algorithms in MRMC and applied them to a variety of case studies, most of which can be obtained from the PRISM webpage.[6] We used PRISM to specify the models and generate the Markov chains. Subsequently, the time and memory requirements have been considered for verifying the chains (by MRMC), and for minimising plus verifying the lumped chain (both by MRMC). All experiments were conducted on a 2.66 GHz Pentium 4 processor with 1 GB RAM running Linux. All reported times are in milliseconds and are obtained by taking the average of running the experiment 10 times.

---

[3] In practice, an implementation using red-black trees is often slightly faster, although this raises the theoretical complexity to $O(|\mathbf{P}| \log^2 |S|)$, cf. [13, Section 3.4].

[4] Up to states s where the set $\{\,\sigma \in Path^{\mathcal{D}}(s) \mid \sigma \not\models \Phi\,\mathcal{U}\,\Psi\,\}$ is only almost empty.

[5] For the sake of brevity, we omit the details for the optimal initial partition for time-bounded until-formulas of the form $\mathcal{U}^{[t_1, t_2]}$ with $0 < t_1$.

[6] see http://www.cs.bham.ac.uk/dxp/prism/index.php.

4.1 Discrete Time

Crowds protocol [38]. This protocol uses random routing within a group of nodes (a crowd) to establish a connection path between a sender and a receiver. Routing paths are reconstructed once the crowd changes; the number of such new route establishments is R, and is an important parameter that influences the state space. Random routing serves to hide the secret identity of a sender. The table below summarises the results for checking $\mathcal{P}_{\leq p}(\Diamond observe)$ where *observe* characterises a situation in which the sender's id is detected. The parameter N in the first column is the number of honest crowd members; our models include $N/5$ dishonest members. The second column shows parameter R. The next three columns indicate the size of the state space of the DTMC (i. e., $|S|$), the number of transitions (i. e., the number of non-zero entries in $\mathbf{P}$), and the verification time. The next three columns indicate the number of states in the quotient DTMC, the time needed for obtaining this quotient, and the time to check the validity of the same formula on the quotient. The last two columns indicate the reduction factor for the number of states and total time. Note that we obtain large state space reductions. Interestingly, in terms of time consumption, quotienting obtains a reduction in time of about a factor 4 to 7.

		original DTMC			lumped DTMC			red. factor	
N	R	states	transitions	ver. time	blocks	lump time	ver. time	states	time
5	3	1198	2038	3.2	53	0.6	0.3	22.6	3.7
5	4	3515	6035	11	97	2.0	0.5	36.2	4.4
5	5	8653	14953	48	153	6.0	0.9	56.6	6.9
5	6	18817	32677	139	209	14	1.4	90.0	9.0
10	3	6563	15143	24	53	4.6	0.2	124	4.9
10	4	30070	70110	190	97	29	0.5	310	6.4
10	5	111294	261444	780	153	127	0.9	727	6.1
10	6	352535	833015	2640	221	400	1.4	1595	6.6
15	3	19228	55948	102	53	23	0.2	363	4.4
15	4	119800	352260	790	97	190	0.5	1235	4.1
15	5	592060	1754860	4670	153	1020	0.9	3870	4.6
15	6	2464168	7347928	20600	221	4180	1.5	11150	4.9

Leader election [28]. In this protocol, N nodes that are arranged in an unidirectional ring select an identity randomly according to a uniform distribution on $\{1, \ldots, K\}$. By means of synchronous message passing, processes send their identity around the ring. The protocol terminates once a node has selected a unique id (the node with the highest unique id becomes the leader); if no such node exists, the protocol restarts. The property of interest is the probability to elect a leader within a certain number of rounds: $\mathcal{P}_{\leq q}(\Diamond^{\leq (N+1)\cdot 3} leader\ elected)$. The obtained results are summarised in the table below. For a fixed N, the number of blocks is constant. This is due to the fact that the initial state is the only probabilistic state and that almost all states that are equidistant w. r. t. this initial state are bisimilar. For $N = 4$, no gain in computation time is obtained due to the relatively low number of iterations needed in the original DTMC. When N increases, bisimulation minimisation also pays off timewise; in this case a small reduction of the time is obtained (more iterations are needed due to the bound in the until-formula that depends on N).

N	K	original DTMC states	transitions	ver. time	lumped DTMC blocks	lump time	ver. time	red. factor states	time
4	2	55	70	0.02	10	0.05	0.01	5.5	0.4
4	4	782	1037	0.4	10	0.5	0.01	78.2	0.8
4	8	12302	16397	7.0	10	9.0	0.01	1230	0.8
4	16	196622	262157	165.0	10	175	0.01	19662	0.9
5	2	162	193	0.1	12	0.1	0.02	13.5	0.9
5	4	5122	6145	2.8	12	2.9	0.02	427	0.9
5	6	38882	46657	28	12	26	0.02	3240	1.1
5	8	163842	196609	140	12	115	0.02	13653	1.2

Cyclic polling server [27]. This standard example in performance analysis considers a set of stations that are allowed to process a job once they possess the token. The single token circulates among the stations. The times for passing a token to a station and for serving a job are all distributed exponentially. We consider the DTMC that is obtained after uniformisation, and check the formula: $\mathcal{P}_{\bowtie p}(\bigwedge_{j\neq 1}^{N} \neg serve_j \; \mathcal{U} \; serve_1)$, i.e. with probability $\bowtie p$ station 1 will be served before any other station, as well as a time-bounded version thereof.[7] Ordinary (strong) bisimulation yields no state-space reduction. The results for measure-driven bisimulation minimisation are summarised below. In checking the bounded until formula, we used the naive initial partition $\{\{s_0\}, \{s_1\}, S_?\}$. The improved initial partition with $\{u_0\}$ would have led to almost the same number of blocks as the unbounded until, e.g. 46 instead of 151 blocks for $N = 15$. For both formulas, large reductions in state space size as well as computation time are obtained; the effect of $\{u_0\}$ on the number of blocks is also considerable.

N	original DTMC states	transitions	time $\mathcal{U}^{\leq t}$	time $\mathcal{U}$	time-bounded until lumped DTMC blocks	time	red. factor states	time	unbounded until lumped DTMC blocks	time	red. factor states	time
4	96	368	1.4	2.1	19	0.4	5.1	3.5	12	0.9	8	2.3
6	576	2784	10	11	34	1.2	16.9	8.3	18	1.4	32	7.9
8	3072	17920	62	52	53	4.0	58	15.5	24	2.9	128	17.9
12	73728	577536	3050	3460	103	120	716	25.4	36	55	2048	62.9
15	737280	6881280	39000	32100	151	1590	4883	24.5	45	580	16384	55.3

Randomised mutual exclusion [37]. In this mutual exclusion algorithm, N processes make random choices based on coin tosses to ensure that they can all enter their critical sections eventually, although not simultaneously. The following table summarizes our results for verifying the property that process 1 is the first to enter the critical section, i.e., the PCTL formula $\mathcal{P}_{\leq q}(\bigwedge_{j\neq 1}^{N} \neg enter_j \; \mathcal{U} \; enter_1)$.

N	original DTMC states	transitions	ver. time	strong bisimulation lumped DTMC blocks	lump time	ver. time	red. factor states	time	F-bisimulation lumped DTMC blocks	time	red. factor states	time
3	2368	8272	3.0	1123	8.0	1.6	2.1	0.3	233	2.9	10.2	1.0
4	27600	123883	47.0	5224	192	19	5.3	0.4	785	29	35.2	1.6
5	308800	1680086	837	18501	2880	120	16.7	0.3	2159	507	143	1.7
6	3377344	21514489	9589	−	$> 10^7$	−	−	−	5166	7106	653	1.4

Due to the relatively high number of transitions, quotienting the DTMC according to *AP*-bisimilarity is computationally expensive, and takes significantly

---

[7] For the sake of comparison, the unbounded until-formula is checked on the uniformised and not on the embedded DTMC.

more time than verifying the original DTMC. However, measure-driven bisimilarity yields a quotient that is roughly an order of magnitude smaller than the quotient under AP-bisimilarity. Due to the coarser initial partition, this quotient is constructed rather fast. In this case, verifying the original model is more time consuming.

4.2 Continuous Time

Workstation cluster [22]. This case study considers a system consisting of two clusters of workstations connected via a backbone. Each cluster consists of N workstations, connected in a star topology with a central switch that provides the interface to the backbone. Each component can break down according to a failure distribution. A single repair unit is available to repair the failed components. The number of correctly functioning workstations determines the level of quality of service (QoS). The following two tables summarise the results for checking the probability that:

- In the long run, premium QoS will be delivered in at least 70% of the cases;
- QoS drops below minimum QoS within 40 time-units is at most 0.1;
- QoS goes from minimum to premium between 20 and 40 time units.

The last property involves a sequence of two transient analyses on different CTMCs. The results for the long-run property:

	original CTMC			lumped CTMC			red. factor	
N	states	transitions	ver. time	blocks	lump time	ver. time	states	time
8	2772	12832	3.6	1413	12	130	2	0.03
16	10132	48160	21	5117	64	770	2	0.03
32	38676	186400	114	19437	290	215	2	0.2
64	151060	733216	730	75725	1360	1670	2	0.2
128	597012	2908192	6500	298893	5900	14900	2	0.2
256	2373652	11583520	103000	1187597	25400	175000	2	0.2

The plain verification time of the quotient is larger than of the original CTMC, despite a state space reduction of a factor two. This is due to the fact that the subdominant eigenvalues of the Gauss-Seidel iteration matrices differ significantly—the closer this value is to one, the slower the convergence rate for the iterative Gauss-Seidel method. For instance for $N = 8$, the values of the original (0.156) and the quotient (0.993) are far apart and the number of iterations needed differ for about two orders of magnitude. The same applies for $N = 16$. These differences are much smaller for larger values of N.

The results for time-bounded reachability:

					time-bounded until $[0, 40]$			time-bounded until $[20, 40]$		
	original CTMC				lumped CTMC		red. factor	lumped CTMC		red. factor
N	states	transitions	ver. time $\mathcal{U}^{\leq 40}$	ver. time $\mathcal{U}^{[20,40]}$	blocks	time	states	time	blocks	time	states	time
8	2772	12832	36	49	239	16.3	11.6	2.2	386	24.0	7.2	2.0
16	10132	48160	360	480	917	70	11.0	5.1	1300	96.0	7.8	5.0
32	38676	186400	1860	2200	3599	300	10.7	6.2	4742	430	8.2	5.1
64	151060	733216	7200	8500	14267	1810	10.6	4.0	18082	2550	8.4	3.3
128	597012	2908192	29700	33700	56819	9300	10.5	3.2	70586	12800	8.5	2.6
256	2373652	11583520	121000	143000	226787	45700	10.5	2.6	278890	60900	8.5	2.3

These results are obtained using a measure-driven bisimulation. In contrast, for an *AP*-bisimulation, we only obtained a 50% state-space reduction. For measure-driven bisimulation another factor 4–5 reduction is obtained. The reduction factors obtained for this case study are not so high, as its formal (stochastic Petri net) specification already exploits some lumping; e. g., workstations are modeled by anonymous tokens.

IEEE 802.11 group communication protocol [35]. This is a variant of the centralized medium access protocol of the IEEE 802.11 standard for wireless local area networks. The protocol is centralized in the sense that medium access is controlled by a fixed node, the Access Point (AP). The AP polls the wireless stations, and on receipt of a poll, stations may broadcast a message. Stations acknowledge the receipt of a message such that the AP is able to detect whether or not all stations have correctly received the broadcast message. In case of a detected loss, a retransmission by the originator takes place. It is assumed that the number of consecutive losses of the same message is bounded by *OD*, the omission degree. This all refers to time-critical messages; other messages are sent in another phase of the protocol. The property of interest is, as in [35] and other studies of this protocol, the probability that a message originated by the AP is not received by at least one station within the duration of the time-critical phase, i. e., $t = 2.4$ milliseconds, i. e., $\mathcal{P}_{\bowtie p}(\Diamond^{\leq 24000} fail)$ where *fail* identifies all states in which more than *OD* losses have taken place. The following table reports the results for the verification of this property for different values of *OD* and the minimization results for a measure-driven bisimulation.

	original CTMC			lumped CTMC		red. factor	
OD	states	transitions	ver. time	blocks	lump + ver. time	states	time
4	1125	5369	121.9	71	13.5	15.9	9.00
12	37349	236313	7180	1821	642	20.5	11.2
20	231525	1590329	50133	10627	5431	21.8	9.2
28	804837	5750873	195086	35961	24716	22.4	7.9
36	2076773	15187833	5103900	91391	77694	22.7	6.6
40	3101445	22871849	7725041	135752	127489	22.9	6.1

We obtain a state space reduction of about a factor 22, which results in an efficiency improvement of a factor 5 to 10. The reason that the verification times are rather excessive for this model stems from the fact that the time bound (24000) is very large, resulting in many iterations. These verification times can be improved by incorporating an on-the-fly steady-state detection procedure [30], but this is not further considered here.

Simple P2P protocol [33]. This case study describes a simple peer-to-peer protocol based on BitTorrent—a "torrent" is a small file which contains metadata about the files to be shared and about the host computer that coordinates the file distribution. The model comprises a set of clients trying to download a file that has been partitioned into *K* blocks. Initially, there is a single client that has already obtained all blocks and *N* additional clients with no blocks. Each client can download a block (lasting an exponential delay) from any of the others but they can only attempt four concurrent downloads for each block. The following table summarises our minimisation results using AP-bisimilarity in columns 3 through 6. The property of interest is the probability that all blocks are downloaded within 0.5 time units. The last columns list the results for a recently proposed symmetry reduction technique for probabilistic systems [33] that has been realised in PRISM.

	original CTMC		bisimulation minimisation				symmetry reduction			
			lumped CTMC			red. factor	reduced CTMC		red. factor	
N	states	ver. time	blocks	lump time	ver. time	states	time	states	red. time	ver. time	states	time
2	1024	5.6	56	1.4	0.3	18.3	3.3	528	12	2.9	1.93	0.38
3	32768	410	252	170	1.3	130	2.4	5984	100	59	5.48	2.58
4	1048576	22000	792	10200	4.8	1324	2.2	52360	360	820	20.0	18.3

We observe that bisimulation minimisation leads to a significantly stronger state-space reduction than symmetry reduction. For $N = 3$ and $N = 4$, bisimulation minimisation leads to a state-space reduction of more than 23 and 66 times, respectively, the reduction of symmetry reduction. Symmetry reduction is—as expected—much faster than bisimulation minimisation, but this is a somewhat unfair comparison as the symmetries are indicated manually. These results suggest that it is affordable to first apply a (fast) symmetry reduction, followed by a bisimulation quotienting on the obtained reduced system. Unfortunately, the available tools did not allow us to test this idea.

4.3 Rewards

This section reports on the results for bisimulation minimisation for Markov reward models. Note that the initial partitions need to be adapted such that only states with equal reward are grouped. We have equipped two DTMCs and one CTMC with a reward assignment function r:

- Crowds protocol (DMRM): the reward indicates the number of messages sent;
- Randomised mutual exclusion protocol (DMRM): the reward indicates the number of attempts that have been undertaken to acquire access to the critical section;
- Workstation cluster (CMRM): the reward is used to measure the repair time.

Recall that for DMRMs, $r(s)$ indicates the reward that is earned on leaving a state, while for CMRMs, $r(s) \cdot t$ is the earned reward when staying t time-units in s. The experiments are focused on verifying time- and reward-bounded until-formulas. For DMRMs, these formulas are checked using a path graph generation algorithm as proposed in [1] which has a time complexity in $O(k \cdot r \cdot |S|^3)$, where k and r are the time-bound and reward-bound, respectively. For CMRMs, we employed the discretization approach by Tijms and Veldman as proposed in [21] which runs in time $O(t \cdot r \cdot |S|^3 \cdot d^{-2})$ where d is the step size of the discretisation. In our experiments, the default setting is $d = \frac{1}{32}$.

For the Crowds protocol (for $R = 3$), we checked the probability that the sender's id is discovered within 100 steps and maximally two messages, i.e., $\mathcal{P}_{\leq p}(\diamond_{\leq 2}^{\leq 100} observe)$. In case of the randomised mutual exclusion protocol, we checked $\mathcal{P}_{\leq q}(\bigwedge_{j\neq 1}^{N} \neg enter_j \ \mathcal{U}_{\leq 10}^{\leq 50} \ enter_1)$, i. e., maximally 10 attempts are allowed to enter the critical section. Finally, for the workstation cluster, we checked the change of providing minimum QoS to premium QoS within maximally 5 time units of repair (and 10 time units). All results are listed in the following table.

Due to the prohibitive (practical) time-complexity, manageable state space sizes are (much) smaller than for the case without rewards. Another consequence of these large verification times, bisimulation minimisation is relatively cheap, and results in possibly drastic time savings, as for the Crowds protocol.

	Crowds protocol with rewards						
	original DTMC			lumped DTMC		red. factor	
N	states	transitions	ver. time	blocks	lump + ver. time	states	time
5	1198	2038	2928	93	44.6	12.88	65.67
10	6563	15143	80394	103	73.5	63.72	1094.49
15	19228	55948	1004981	103	98.7	186.68	10182.13
20	42318	148578	5174951	103	161	410.85	32002.61
	Randomised mutual exclusion protocol with rewards						
2	188	455	735	151	616	1.25	1.19
3	2368	8272	60389	1123	19010	2.11	3.18
4	27600	123883	5446685	5224	298038	5.28	18.28
5	308800	1680086	$> 10^7$	18501	3664530	16.69	–
	Workstation cluster with rewards						
2	276	1120	278708	147	55448	1.88	5.03
3	512	2192	849864	268	151211	1.91	5.62
4	820	3616	2110095	425	347324	1.93	6.08
5	1200	5392	$> 10^7$	618	2086575	1.94	–
6	1652	7520	$> 10^7$	847	3657682	1.95	–

5 Concluding Remarks

Our experiments confirm that significant (up to logarithmic) state space reductions can be obtained using bisimulation minimisation. The appealing feature of this abstraction technique is that it is fully automated. For several case studies, also substantial reductions in time have been obtained (up to a factor 25). This contrasts results for traditional model checking where bisimulation minimisation typically outweighs verifying the original system. Time reduction strongly depends on the number of transitions in the Markov chain, its structure, as well as on the convergence rate of numerical computations. The P2P protocol experiment shows encouraging results compared with symmetry reduction [33] (where symmetries are detected manually). For measure-driven bisimulation for models without rewards, this speedup comes with no memory penalty: the peak memory use is typically unchanged; for ordinary bisimulation some experiments showed an increase of peak memory up to 50 %. In our case studies with rewards, we experienced a 20–40 % reduction in peak memory use.

We plan to further investigate combinations of symmetry reduction with bisimulation minimisation, and to extend our experimental work towards MDPs and simulation preorders.

Acknowledgement. This research has been performed as part of the MC=MC project that is financed by the Netherlands Organization for Scientific Research (NWO), and the project VOSS2 that is financed by NWO and the German Research Council (DFG).

References

1. Andova, S., Hermanns, H., Katoen, J.-P.: Discrete-time rewards model-checked. In Larsen, K. G., et al. (eds.): *FORMATS. LNCS*, Vol. 2791. Springer, Berlin (2003) 88–104
2. Aziz, A., Sanwal, K., Singhal, V., Brayton, R.: Model-checking continuous time Markov chains. *ACM TOCL* **1** (2000) 162–170
3. Aziz, A., Singhal, V., Balarin, F., Brayton, R. K., Sangiovanni-Vincentelli, A. L.: It usually works: the temporal logic of stochastic systems. In Wolper, P. (ed.): *CAV. LNCS*, Vol. 939. Springer, Berlin (1995) 155–165
4. Baier, C., Ciesinski, F., Größer, M.: ProbMela and verification of Markov decision processes. *Performance Evaluation Review* **32** (2005) 22–27
5. Baier, C., Haverkort, B., Hermanns, H., Katoen, J.-P.: On the logical characterisation of performability properties. In Montanari, U., et al. (eds.): *ICALP. LNCS*, Vol. 1853. Springer, Berlin (2000) 780–792
6. Baier, C., Haverkort, B., Hermanns, H., Katoen, J.-P.: Model-checking algorithms for continuous-time Markov chains. *IEEE TSE* **29** (2003) 524–541
7. Baier, C., Katoen, J.-P., Hermanns, H., Wolf, V.: Comparative branching-time semantics for Markov chains. *Information and Computation* **200** (2005) 149–214
8. Ben Mamoun, M., Pekergin, N., Younès, S.: Model checking of continuous-time Markov chains by closed-form bounding distributions. In: *QEST*. IEEE CS, Los Alamitos (2006) 189–198
9. Böde, E., Herbstritt, M., Hermanns, H., Johr, S., Peikenkamp, T., Pulungan, R., Wimmer, R., Becker, B.: Compositional performability evaluation for STATEMATE. In: *QEST*. IEEE CS, Los Alamitos (2006) 167–178
10. Buchholz, P.: Exact and ordinary lumpability in finite Markov chains. *Journal of Applied Probability* **31** (1994) 59–75
11. D'Aprile, D., Donatelli, S., Sproston, J.: CSL model checking for the GreatSPN tool. In Aykanat, C., et al. (eds.): *Computer and Information Sciences, ISCIS. LNCS*, Vol. 3280. Springer, Berlin (2004) 543–553
12. D'Argenio, P. R., Jeannet, B., Jensen, H. E., Larsen, K. G.: Reachability analysis of probabilistic systems by successive refinements. In de Alfaro, L., et al. (eds.): *PAPM–PROBMIV. LNCS*, Vol. 2165. Springer, Berlin (2001) 39–56
13. Derisavi, S.: *Solution of Large Markov Models using Lumping Techniques and Symbolic Data Structures*. PhD thesis, Univ. of Illinois at Urbana-Champaign (2005)
14. Derisavi, S., Hermanns, H., Sanders, W. H.: Optimal state-space lumping in Markov chains. *IPL* **87** (2003) 309–315
15. Fecher, H., Leucker, M., Wolf, V.: Don't know in probabilistic systems. In Valmari, A. (ed.): *Model Checking Software. LNCS*, Vol. 3925. Springer, Berlin (2006) 71–88
16. Fisler, K., Vardi, M. Y.: Bisimulation minimization in an automata-theoretic verification framework. In Gopalakrishnan, G., et al. (eds.): *FMCAD. LNCS*, Vol. 1522. Springer, Berlin (1998) 115–132
17. Fisler, K., Vardi, M. Y.: Bisimulation and model checking. In Pierre, L., et al. (eds.): *CHARME. LNCS*, Vol. 1703. Springer, Berlin (1999) 338–342
18. Fisler, K., Vardi, M. Y.: Bisimulation minimization and symbolic model checking. *Formal Methods in System Design* **21** (2002) 39–78
19. Groesser, M., Baier, C.: Partial order reduction for Markov decision processes: a survey. In de Boer, F. S., et al. (eds.): *FMCO. LNCS*, Vol. 4111. Springer, Berlin (2006) 408–427

20. Hansson, H., Jonsson, B.: A logic for reasoning about time and reliability. *Formal Aspects of Computing* **6** (1994) 512–535
21. Haverkort, B., Cloth, L., Hermanns, H., Katoen, J.-P., Baier, C.: Model checking performability properties. In: *DSN*. IEEE CS, Los Alamitos (2002) 103–112
22. Haverkort, B. R., Hermanns, H., Katoen, J.-P.: On the use of model checking techniques for quantitative dependability evaluation. In: *19th IEEE Symposium on Reliable Distributed Systems*. IEEE CS, Los Alamitos (2000) 228–237
23. Hermanns, H., Kwiatkowska, M., Norman, G., Parker, D., Siegle, M.: On the use of MTBDDs for performability analysis and verification of stochastic systems. *J. of Logic and Alg. Progr.* **56** (2003) 23–67
24. Hillston, J.: *A Compositional Approach to Performance Modelling.* Cambridge University Press (1996)
25. Huth, M.: An abstraction framework for mixed non-deterministic and probabilistic systems. In Baier, C., et al. (eds.): *Validation of Stochastic Systems. LNCS*, Vol. 2925. Springer, Berlin (2004) 419–444
26. Huth, M.: On finite-state approximants for probabilistic computation tree logic. *TCS* **346** (2005) 113–134
27. Ibe, O. C., Trivedi, K. S.: Stochastic Petri net models of polling systems. *IEEE J. on Selected Areas in Communications* **8** (1990) 1649–1657
28. Itai, A., Rodeh, M.: Symmetry breaking in distributed networks. *Information and Computation* **88** (1990) 60–87
29. Katoen, J.-P., Khattri, M., Zapreev, I. S.: A Markov reward model checker. In: *QEST*. IEEE CS, Los Alamitos (2005) 243–244
30. Katoen, J.-P., Zapreev, I. S.: Safe on-the-fly steady-state detection for time-bounded reachability. In: *QEST*. IEEE CS, Los Alamitos (2006) 301–310
31. Kwiatkowska, M., Norman, G., Parker, D.: Probabilistic symbolic model checking with PRISM: a hybrid approach. *Int. J. on STTT* **6** (2004) 128–142
32. Kwiatkowska, M., Norman, G., Parker, D.: Game-based abstraction for Markov decision processes. In: *QEST*. IEEE CS, Los Alamitos (2006) 157–166
33. Kwiatkowska, M., Norman, G., Parker, D.: Symmetry reduction for probabilistic model checking. In Ball, T., et al. (eds.): *CAV. LNCS*, Vol. 4144. Springer, Berlin (2006) 234–248
34. Larsen, K. G., Skou, A.: Bisimulation through probabilistic testing. *Information and Computation* **94** (1991) 1–28
35. Massink, M., Katoen, J.-P., Latella, D.: Model checking dependability attributes of wireless group communication. In: *DSN*. IEEE CS, Los Alamitos (2004) 711–720
36. Monniaux, D.: Abstract interpretation of programs as Markov decision processes. *Science of Computer Programming* **58** (2005) 179–205
37. Pnueli, A., Zuck, L.: Verification of multiprocess probabilistic protocols. *Distributed Computing* **1** (1986) 53–72
38. Reiter, M. K., Rubin, A. D.: Crowds: anonymity for web transactions. *ACM Transactions on Information and System Security* **1** (1998) 66–92
39. Sproston, J., Donatelli, S.: Backward bisimulation in Markov chain model checking. *IEEE TSE* **32** (2006) 531–546

Causal Dataflow Analysis for Concurrent Programs

Azadeh Farzan and P. Madhusudan

Department of Computer Science,
University of Illinois at Urbana-Champaign
{afarzan,madhu}@cs.uiuc.edu

Abstract. We define a novel formulation of dataflow analysis for concurrent programs, where the flow of facts is along the *causal* dependencies of events. We capture the control flow of concurrent programs using a Petri net (called the *control net*), develop algorithms based on partially-ordered unfoldings, and report experimental results for solving causal dataflow analysis problems. For the subclass of distributive problems, we prove that complexity of checking data flow is linear in the number of facts and in the *unfolding* of the control net.

1 Introduction

Advances in multicore technology and the wide use of languages that inherently support threads, such as Java, foretell a future where concurrency will be the norm. Despite their growing importance, little progress has been made in static analysis of concurrent programs. For instance, there is no standard notion of a control-flow graph for concurrent programs, while the analogous notion in sequential programs has existed for a long time [10]. Consequently, dataflow analysis problems (arguably the simplest of analysis problems) have not been clearly understood for programs with concurrency.

While it is certainly easy to formulate dataflow analysis for concurrent programs using the *global product state space* of the individual threads, the usefulness of doing so is questionable as algorithms working on the global state space will not scale. Consequently, the literature in flow analysis for threaded programs concentrates on finding tractable problem definitions for dataflow analysis. A common approach has been to consider programs where the causal relation between events is *static* and apparent from the structure of the code (such as fork-join formalisms), making feasible an analysis that works by finding fixpoints on the *union* of the individual sequential control flow graphs. These approaches are often highly restrictive (for example, they require programs to have no loops [23] or at least to have no loops with concurrent fork-join constructs [13,14]), and cannot model even simple shared-memory program models. In fact, a coherent

O. Grumberg and M. Huth (Eds.): TACAS 2007, LNCS 4424, pp. 102–116, 2007.
© Springer-Verlag Berlin Heidelberg 2007

formulation of control-flow that can capture programs with dynamic concurrency (including those with shared memory) and a *general definition* of dataflow analysis problems for these programs has not been formulated in the literature (see the end of this section for details on related work).

The goals of this paper are (a) to develop a formal *control-flow* model for programs using Petri nets, (b) to propose a novel definition of dataflow analyses based on *causal flows* in a program, (c) to develop algorithms for solving causal flow analyses when the domain of flow facts is a finite set $\mathbb{D}$ by exploring the partially-ordered runs of the program as opposed to its interleaved executions, and (d) to provide provably efficient algorithms for the class of *distributive* CCD problems, and support the claim with demonstrative experiments. The framework we set forth in this paper is the first one we know that defines a formal general definition of dataflow analysis for concurrent programs.

We first develop a Petri net model that captures the control flow in a concurrent program, and give a translation from programs to Petri nets that explicitly abstracts data and captures the control flow in the program. These nets, called *control nets*, support dynamic concurrency, and can model concurrent constructs such as lock-synchronizations and shared variable accesses. In fact, we have recently used the same model of control nets to model and check *atomicity* of code blocks in concurrent programs [7]. We believe that the control net model is an excellent candidate for capturing control flow in concurrent programs, and can emerge as the robust analog of *control-flow graphs* for sequential programs.

The causal concurrent dataflow (CCD) framework is in the flavor of a *meet-over-all-paths* formulation for sequential programs. We assume a set of dataflow facts $\mathbb{D}$ and each statement of the program is associated with a *flow transformer* that changes a subset of facts, killing some old facts and generating new facts. However, we demand that the flow transformers respect the concurrency in the program: we require that if two *independent* (concurrent) statements transform two subsets of facts, D and D', then the sets D and D' must be *disjoint*. For instance, if there are two local variable accesses in two different threads, these statements are independent, and cannot change the same dataflow fact, which is a very natural restriction. For example, if we are tracking *uninitialized variables*, two assignments in two threads to local variables do affect the facts pertaining to these variables, but do not modify the same fact. We present formulations of most of the common dataflow analysis problems in our setting.

The structural restriction of requiring transformers to respect causality ensures that dataflow facts can be inferred using partially ordered traces of the control net. We define the dataflow analysis problem as *a meet over partially ordered traces* that reach a node, rather than the traditional meet-over-paths definition. The meet-over-traces definition is crucial as it preserves the concurrency in the program, allowing us to exploit it to solve flow analysis using *partial-order* based methods, which do not explore all interleavings of the program.

Our next step is to give a solution for the general causal dataflow analysis problem when the set of of facts $\mathbb{D}$ is finite by reducing the problem to a reachability problem of a Petri net, akin to the classic approach of reducing meet-over-paths to graph reachability for sequential recursive programs [21]. Finally, the reachability/coverability problem is solved using the optimized partial-order *unfolding* [16,6] based tool called PEP [9].

For the important subclass of *distributive* dataflow analysis problems, we develop a more efficient algorithm for checking flows. If N is the control net of a program and the size of its finite unfolding is n, we show that any distributive CCD problem over a domain $\mathbb{D}$ of facts results in an augmented net of size $n|\mathbb{D}|$ (and hence in an algorithm working within similar bounds of time and space). This is a very satisfactory result, since it proves that the causal definition does not destroy the concurrency in the net (as that would result in a blow-up in n), and that we are exploiting distributivity effectively (as we have a linear dependence on $|\mathbb{D}|$). The analogous result for sequential recursive programs also creates an augmented graph of size $n|\mathbb{D}|$, where n is the size of the control-flow graph.

Related Work. Although the majority of flow analysis research has focused on sequential software [1,19,17,20], flow analysis for concurrent software has also been studied to some extent. Existing methods for flow-sensitive analyses have at least one of the following restrictions: (a) the programs handled have simple static concurrency and can be handled precisely using the union of control flow graphs of individual programs, or (b) the analysis is sound but not complete, and solves the dataflow problem using heuristic approximations.

A body of work on flow-sensitive analyses exists in which the model for the program is essentially a collection of CFGs of individual threads (tasks, or components) together with additional edges among the CFGs that model inter-thread synchronization and communication [15,18,22]. These analyses are usually restricted to a class of behaviors (such as detecting deadlocks) and their models do not require considering the set of interleavings of the program. More general analyses based on the above type of model include [12] which presents a *unidirectional* bit-vector dataflow analysis framework based on abstract interpretation (where the domain $\mathbb{D}$ is a *singleton*). This framework comes closest to ours in that it explicitly defines a meet-over-paths definition of dataflow analysis, can express a variety of dataflow analysis problems, and gives sound and complete algorithms for solving them. However, it cannot handle dynamic synchronization mechanisms (such as locks), and the restriction to having only one dataflow fact is crucially (and cleverly) used, making multidimensional analysis impossible. For example, this framework cannot handle the problem of solving *uninitialized variables*. See also [23] for dataflow analysis that uses flow along causal edges but disallows loops in programs and requires them to have static concurrency. The works in [13,14] use the extension of the static single assignment form [3] for concurrent programs with emphasis on optimizing concurrent programs as opposed to analyzing them.

In [4], concurrent models are used to represent interleavings of programs, but the initial model is coarse and refined to obtain precision, and efficiency is gained by sacrificing precision. Petri nets are used as control models for Ada programs in [5], although the modeling is completely different form ours. In [2], the authors combine reachability analysis with symbolic execution to prune the infeasible paths in order to achieve more effective results.

This paper presents only the gist of the definitions and proofs. For more detailed definitions of Petri nets, unfoldings, the framework for backward flow analyses and the non-distributive framework, for further examples and detailed proofs, we refer the reader to the technical report [8].

2   Preliminaries

A Simple Multithreaded Language. We base our formal development on the language SML (Simple Multithreaded Language). Figure 1 presents the syntax of SML. The number of threads in an SML program is fixed and preset. There are two kinds of variables: local and global, respectively identified by the sets *LVar* and *GVar*. All variables that appear at the definition list of the program are global and shared among all threads. Any other variable that is used in a thread is assumed to be local to the thread.

We assume that all variables are integers and are initialized to zero. We use small letters (capital letters) to denote local (global, resp.) variables. *Lock* is a global set of locks that the threads can use for synchronization purposes through acquire and release primitives. The semantics of a program is the obvious one and we do not define it formally.

$$
\begin{array}{lll}
P ::= \textsf{defn thlist} & & \text{(program)} \\
\textsf{thlist} ::= \textsf{null} \mid \textsf{stmt} \parallel \textsf{thlist} & & \text{(thread list)} \\
\textsf{defn} ::= \textsf{int } Y \mid \textsf{lock } l \mid \textsf{defn ; defn} & & \text{(variable declaration)} \\
\textsf{stmt} ::= \textsf{stmt ; stmt} \mid x := e \mid \textsf{skip} & & \\
\quad \mid \textsf{while } (b) \; \{ \textsf{ stmt } \} \mid \textsf{acquire}(l) \mid \textsf{release}(l) & & \\
\quad \mid \textsf{if } (b) \; \{ \textsf{ stmt } \} \textsf{ else } \{ \textsf{ stmt } \} & & \text{(statement)} \\
e ::= i \mid x \mid Y \mid e + e \mid e * e \mid e/e & & \text{(expression)} \\
b ::= \textsf{true} \mid \textsf{false} \mid e \; op \; e \mid b \vee b \mid \neg b & & \text{(boolean expression)}
\end{array}
$$

$$op \in \{<, \leq, >, \geq, =, ! =\}$$
$$x \in \text{LVar}, Y \in \text{GVar}, i \in \text{Integer}, l \in \text{Lock}$$

Fig. 1. SML syntax

Petri Nets and Traces

A Petri net is a triple $N = (P, T, F)$, where P is a set of places, T (disjoint from P) is a set of transitions, and $F \subseteq (P \times T) \cup (T \times P)$ is the flow relation.

For a transition t of a (Petri) net, let $^\bullet t = \{p \in P | (p,t) \in F\}$ denote its set of pre-conditions and $t^\bullet = \{p \in P | (t,p) \in F\}$ its set of post-conditions. A marking of the net is a subset M of positions of P.[1] A marked net is a structure (N, M_0), where N is a net and M_0 is an initial marking. A transition t is *enabled* at a marking M if $^\bullet t \subseteq M$. The transition relation is defined on the set of markings: $M \xrightarrow{t} M'$ if transition t is enabled at M and $M' = (M \setminus {}^\bullet t) \cup t^\bullet$. Let $\xrightarrow{*}$ denote the reflexive and transitive closure of $\longrightarrow$. A marking M' *covers* a marking M if $M \subseteq M'$. A *firing sequence* is a finite sequence of transitions $t_1 t_2 \ldots$ provided we have a sequence of markings $M_0 M_1 \ldots$ and for each i, $M_i \xrightarrow{t_{i+1}} M_{i+1}$. We denote the set of firing sequences of (N, M_0) as $FS(N, M_0)$. Given a marked net (N, M_0), $N = (P, T, F)$, the *independence* relation of the net I_N is defined as $(t, t') \in I$ if the neighborhoods of t and t' are disjoint, i.e. $(^\bullet t \cup t^\bullet) \cap (^\bullet t' \cup t'^\bullet) = \emptyset$. The *dependence* relation D_N is defined as the complement of I_N.

Definition 1. *A trace of a marked net (N, M_0) is a labeled poset $Tr = (\mathcal{E}, \preceq, \lambda)$ where $\mathcal{E}$ is a finite or a countable set of events, $\preceq$ is a partial order on $\mathcal{E}$, called the* causal order, *and $\lambda : \mathcal{E} \longrightarrow T$ is a labeling function such that the following hold:*

- *$\forall e, e' \in \mathcal{E}, e \prec\!\!\!\cdot\; e' \Rightarrow \lambda(e) D_N \lambda(e')$.[2] Events that are immediately causally related must correspond to dependent transitions.*
- *$\forall e, e' \in \mathcal{E}, \lambda(e) D_N \lambda(e') \Rightarrow (e \preceq e' \lor e' \preceq e)$. Any two events with dependent labels must be causally related.*
- *If σ is a linearization of Tr then $\sigma \in FS(N, M_0)$.*

For any event e in a trace $(\mathcal{E}, \preceq, \lambda)$, define $\downarrow e = \{e' \in \mathcal{E} \mid e' \preceq e\}$ and let $\Downarrow e = \downarrow e \setminus \{e\}$.

3   The Control Net of a Program

We model the flow of control in SML programs using Petri nets. We call this model the *control net* of the program. The control net formally captures the concurrency between threads using the concurrency constructs of a Petri net, captures synchronizations between threads (e.g.. locks, accesses to global variables) using appropriate mechanisms in the Petri net, and formalizes the fact that data is abstracted in a sound manner.

We describe the main ideas of this construction but skip the details (see [8] for details). Transitions in the control net correspond to program statements, and places are used to control the flow, and to model the interdependencies and synchronization primitives. Figure 2 illustrates a program and its control net.

---

[1] Petri nets can be more general, but in this paper we restrict to 1-safe Petri nets where each place gets at most one token.

[2] $\prec\!\!\!\cdot$ is the immediate causal relation defined as: $e \prec\!\!\!\cdot\; e'$ iff $e \prec e'$ and there is no event e'' such that $e \prec e'' \prec e'$.

There is a place l associated to each lock l which initially has a token in it. To acquire a lock, this token has to be available which then is taken and put back when the lock is released.

For each global variable Y, there are n places $Y_1, \ldots, Y_n$, one per thread. Every time the thread T_i reads the variable Y (Y appears in an expression), it takes the token from the place Y_i and puts it back immediately. If T_i wants to write Y (Y is on the left side of an assignment), it has to take one token from each place Y_j, $1 \leq j \leq n$ and put them all back. This ensures correct causality: two read operations of the same variable by different threads will be independent (as their neighborhoods will be disjoint), but a read and a write, or two writes to a variable are declared dependent.

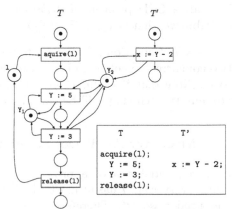

Fig. 2. Sample Net Model

4   Causal Concurrent Dataflow Framework

We now formulate our framework for dataflow analysis of concurrent programs based on causality, called the CAUSAL CONCURRENT DATAFLOW (CCD) framework.

A property space is a *subset lattice* $(\mathcal{P}(\mathbb{D}), \sqsubseteq, \sqcup, \bot)$ where $\mathbb{D}$ is a finite set of *dataflow facts*, $\bot \subseteq \mathbb{D}$, and where $\sqcup$ and $\sqsubseteq$ can respectively be $\cup$ and $\subseteq$, or $\cap$ and $\supseteq$. Intuitively, $\mathbb{D}$ is the set of dataflow facts of interest, $\bot$ is the initial set of facts, and $\sqcup$ is the *meet* operation that will determine how we combine dataflow facts along different paths reaching the same control point in a program. "May" analysis is formulated using $\sqcup = \cup$, while "must" analysis uses the $\sqcup = \cap$ formulation. The property space of an IFDS (interprocedural finite distributive subset) problem [21] for a sequential program (i.e. the subset lattice) is exactly the same lattice as above.

For every transition t of the control net, we associate two subsets of $\mathbb{D}$, D_t and D_t^*. Intuitively, D_t^* is the set of dataflow facts relevant at t, while $D_t \subseteq D_t^*$ is the subset of relevant facts that t may modify when it executes. The *transformation function* associated with t, f_t, maps every subset of D_t to a subset of D_t, reflecting how the dataflow facts change when t is executed.

Definition 2. *A causal concurrent dataflow (CCD) problem is a tuple* $(N, \mathcal{S}, \mathcal{F}, \mathcal{D}, \mathcal{D}^*)$ *where:*

- $N = (P, T, F)$ *is the control net model of a concurrent program,*
- $\mathcal{S} = (\mathcal{P}(\mathbb{D}), \sqsubseteq, \sqcup, \bot)$ *is a property space,*
- $\mathcal{D} = \{D_t\}_{t \in T}$ *and* $\mathcal{D}^* = \{D_t^*\}_{t \in T}$, *where each* $D_t \subseteq D_t^* \subseteq \mathbb{D}$.

- $\mathcal{F}$ *is a set of functions* $\{f_t\}_{t \in T} : 2^{D_t} \rightarrow 2^{D_t}$ *such that:*
  (*) $\forall t, t' : (t, t') \in I_N \Rightarrow (D_t \cap D_{t'}^* = D_t^* \cap D_{t'} = \emptyset).$[3]

We call a CCD problem *distributive* if all transformation functions in $\mathcal{F}$ are distributive, that is $\forall f_t \in \mathcal{F}, \ \forall X, Y \subseteq D_t : f_t(X \sqcup Y) = f_t(X) \sqcup f_t(Y)$.

Remark 1. Condition (*) above is to be specially noted. It demands that for any two concurrent events e and e', e cannot change a dataflow fact that is relevant to e'. Note that if e and e' are events in a trace such that $D_{\lambda(e)} \cap D_{\lambda(e')}^*$ is non-empty, then they will be causally related.

4.1 Meet over All Traces Solution

In a sequential run of a program, every event t has at most one predecessor t'. Therefore, the set of dataflow facts that hold before the execution of t (let us call this $in(t)$) is exactly the set of dataflow facts that hold after the execution of t' ($out(t')$). This is not the case for a trace (a partially ordered run). Consider the example in Figure 3. Assume t_1 generates facts d_1 and d_2, t_2 generates d_3

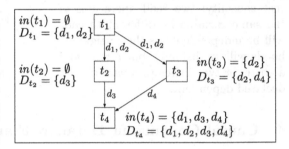

Fig. 3. Flow of facts over a trace

and t_3 kills d_2 and generates d_4. The corresponding D_t sets appear in the Figure. Trying to evaluate the "*in*" set of t_4, we see three important scenarios: (1) t_4 inherits *independent* facts d_3 and d_4 respectively from its immediate predecessors t_2 and t_3, (2) t_4 inherits fact d_1 from t_1 which is not its immediate predecessor, and (3) t_4 does not inherit d_2 from t_1 because t_3, which is a (causally) later event and the last event to modify d_2, kills d_2.

This example demonstrates that in a trace the immediate causal predecessors do not specify the "*in*" set of an event. The indicating event is actually the (causally) last event that can change a dataflow fact (eg. t_3 for fact d_2 in computing $in(t_4)$). We formalize this concept by defining the operator $maxc_{\preceq}^d(Tr)$, for a trace $Tr = (E, \preceq, \lambda)$ as $maxc_{\preceq}^d(Tr) = max_{\preceq}(\{e \mid e \in E \wedge d \in D_{\lambda(e)}\})$. Note that this function is undefined on the empty set, but well-defined on non-empty sets because all events that affect a dataflow fact d are causally related due to (*) in Definition 2.

Remark 1 suggests that for each event e it suffices to only look at the facts that are in the "*out*" set of events in $\Downarrow e$ (events that are causally before e), since events that are concurrent with e will not change any fact that's relevant to e.

---

[3] And hence $D_t \cap D_{t'} = \emptyset$.

Definition 3. *For any trace* $Tr = (E, \preceq, \lambda)$ *of the control net and for each event* $e \in E$, *we define the following dataflow sets:*

$$\begin{cases} in^{Tr}(e) = \bigcup_{d \in D^*_{\lambda(e)}} (out^{Tr}(maxc^d_{\preceq}(\Downarrow e)) \cap \{d\})) \\ out^{Tr}(e) = f_{\lambda(e)}(in^{Tr}(e) \cap D_{\lambda(e)}) \end{cases}$$

where $in^{Tr}(e)$ *(respectively* $out^{Tr}(e)$*) indicates the set of dataflow facts that hold before (respectively after) the execution of event* e *of trace* Tr.

In the above definition, $maxc^{d_i}_{\preceq}(\Downarrow e))$ may be undefined (if $\Downarrow e = \emptyset$), in which case we assume $in^{Tr}(e)$ evaluates to the empty set.

We can now define the **meet over all traces** solution for a program Pr, assuming the $T(N)$ denotes the set of all traces induced by the control net N.

Definition 4. *The set of dataflow facts that hold before the execution of a transition* t *of a control net* N *is* $MOT(t) = \bigcup_{Tr \in T(N), e \in Tr, \lambda(e) = t} in^{Tr}(e)$.

The above formulation is the concurrent analog of the meet-over-all-paths formulation for sequential programs. Instead of the above definition, we could formulate the problem as a meet-over-all-paths problem, where we take the meet over facts accumulated along the *sequential runs* (interleavings) of the concurrent program. However, due to the restriction (*) in Definition 2, we can show that the dataflow facts accumulated at an event of a trace is precisely the same as that accumulated using any of its linearizations. Consequently, for dataflow problems that respect causality by satisfying the condition (*), the meet-over-all-paths and the meet-over-traces formulations coincide. The latter formulation however yields faster algorithms based on partial-order methods based on unfoldings to solve the dataflow analysis problem.

4.2   Formulation of Specific Problems in the CCD Framework

A wide variety of dataflow analysis problems can be formulated using the CCD framework, including reaching definitions, uninitialized variables, live variables, available expressions, copy constant propagation, very busy expressions, etc. Some of these are *backward flow analysis* problems that can be formulated using an adaptation of CCD for backward flows. Due to lack of space, we detail only a couple of representative forward flow problems here; formulation of several others, including formulation of backward flows can be found in [8].

Reaching Definitions. The reaching definitions analysis determines: *"For each control point, which relevant assignments may have been made and not overwritten when program execution reaches that point along some path"*. The relevant assignments are the assignments to variables that are referred to in that control point. Given the control net $N = (P, T, F)$ for a program Pr, define $Defs = \{(v, t) \mid t \in T, v \in (\text{GVar} \cup \text{LVar}), \text{and } v \text{ is assigned in } t\}$. The property space is $(Defs, \subseteq, \cup, \emptyset)$, where presence of (v, t) in $D^{in}(t')$ means that the definition of v at t may reach t'.

Let $D_t = \{(v, t') \mid v$ is assigned in $t\}$; $D_t^* = \{(v, t') \mid v$ is assigned or accessed by $t\}$.

For each transition t and each set $S \subseteq D_t$:

$$f_t(S)(= \begin{cases} S & \text{if } t \text{ is not an assignment} \\ S - \{(v, t') \mid t' \in T\} \cup \{(v, t)\} & \text{if } t \text{ is of the form } \mathtt{v} := \mathtt{e} \end{cases}$$

The construction of the control net ensures that two accesses of a variable v where one of them is a write, are dependent (neighborhoods intersect). This guarantees that the condition (*) of Definition 2 holds, i.e. our formulation of reaching-definitions ensures that information is inherited only from causal predecessors. Note that the above formulation is also distributive.

Available Expressions. The available expressions analysis determines: *"For a program point containing $x := Exp(x_1, \ldots, x_k)$ whether Exp has already been computed and not later modified on all paths to this program point"*.

In the standard (sequential) formulation of available expressions analysis, dataflow facts are defined as pairs (t, Exp), where Exp is computed at t. This formulation does not work for the concurrent setting. To see why consider the trace on the right where x is a local variable in T and Y is a global variable. Events e_2 and e_3 are independent (concurrent), but they both can change (kill) the dataflow fact associated with $x + Y$, which is not in accordance with the condition (*) of Definition 2. The natural remedy is to divide this fact into two facts, one for x and another for Y. Let us call these two facts $x + Y : x$ and $x + Y : Y$. The fact $x + Y : x$ (respectively $x + Y : Y$) starts to hold when the expression $x + Y$ is com-

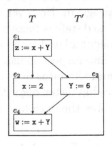

puted, and stops to hold when a definition to x (respectively Y) is seen. The problem is that $x + Y$ holds when $x + Y : x$ holds **and** $x + Y : Y$ holds, which makes the framework *non-distributive*. Although we can solve non-distributive problems in the CCD framework (see Appendix), distributive problems yield faster algorithms (see Section 5).

The analysis can however be formulated as a distributive CCD problem by looking at the dual problem; that is, for *unavailability* of expressions. The dataflow fact $x + Y$ indicates the expression being unavailable, and accordingly the presence of $x + Y : x$ or $x + Y : Y$ can make it hold. We are now in a distributive framework. Assume EXP presents the set of all expressions appearing in the program code, and define $\mathbb{D} = \{exp : x_i \mid exp \in EXP \wedge x_i$ appears in $exp\}$. The property space is the subset lattice $(\mathbb{D}, \subseteq, \cup, \mathbb{D})$, where presence of exp in $D^{in}(t')$ means that exp is unavailable at t. We have $D_t = D_t^* = \{exp : x \mid x$ is assigned in t or exp appears in $t\}$. For each transition t and each set $S \subseteq \mathbb{D}$:

$$f_t(S) = \begin{cases} S & t \text{ is not an assignment} \\ S \cup \{exp' : x \mid \forall exp' \in EXP, x \in V(exp')\} \\ \quad - \{exp : y \mid y \in V(exp)\} & t \text{ is } x := exp \end{cases}$$

where $V(exp)$ denotes the set of variables that appear in exp.

5   Solving the Distributive CCD Problem

In this section, we show how to solve a dataflow problem in the CCD framework. The algorithm we present is based on augmenting a control net to a larger net based on the dataflow analysis problem, and reducing the problem of checking whether a dataflow fact holds at a control point to a reachability problem on the augmented net. The augmented net is carefully constructed so as to not destroy the concurrency present in the system (crucially exploiting the condition (*) in Definition 2). Reachability on the augmented net is performed using net unfoldings, which is a partial-order based approach that checks traces generated by the net as opposed to checking linear runs.

Due to space restrictions, we present only the solution for the distributive CCD problems where the meet operator is union, and we prove upper bounds that compare the unfolding of the augmented net with respect to the size of the unfolding of the original control net.

In order to track the dataflow facts, we enrich the control net so that each transition performs the transformation of facts as well. We introduce new places which represent the dataflow facts. The key is then to model the transformation functions, for which we use *representation relations* from [21].

Definition 5. *The representation relation of a distributive function $f : 2^D \to 2^D$ ($D \subseteq \mathbb{D}$) is $R_f \subseteq (D \cup \{\bot\}) \times (D \cup \{\bot\})$, a binary relation, defined as follows:*

$$R_f = \{(\bot, \bot)\} \ \cup \ \{(\bot, d) \mid d \in f(\emptyset)\} \ \cup \ \{(d, d') \mid d' \in f(\{d\}) \wedge \ d' \notin f(\emptyset)\}$$

The relation R_f captures f faithfully in that we can show that $f(X) = \{d' \in D \mid (d, d') \in R_f, \text{ where } d = \bot \text{ or } d \in X\}$, for any $X \subseteq D$.

Given a CCD framework $(N, \mathcal{S}, \mathcal{F}, \mathcal{D}, \mathcal{D}^*)$ with control net $N = (P, T, F)$, we define the net representation for a function f_t as below:

Definition 6. *The net representation of f_t is a Petri net $N_{f_t} = (P_{f_t}, T_{f_t}, F_{f_t})$ defined as follows:*

- *The set of places is $P_{f_t} = {}^\bullet t \cup t^\bullet \cup \{\bot_m \mid m \in [1, n]\} \cup \bigcup_{d_i \in D_t} \{p_i, \overline{p}_i\}$ where a token in p_i means the dataflow fact d_i holds, while a token in $\overline{p}_i$ means that d_i does not hold, and n is the number of dataflow facts.*
- *The set of transitions T_f contains exactly one transition per pair $(d_i, d_j) \in R_{f_t}$, and is defined as:*

$$T_{f_t} = \left\{ s^t_{(\bot, \bot)} \right\} \cup \left\{ s^t_{(\bot, j)} \mid (\bot, d_j) \in R_{f_t} \right\} \cup \left\{ s^t_{(i, j)} \mid (d_i, d_j) \in R_{f_t} \right\}$$

Note that if $D_t = \emptyset$ then $T_{f_t} = \left\{ s^t_{(\bot, \bot)} \right\}$.

– *The flow relation is defined as follows:*

$$F_{f_t} = \bigcup_{s \in T_{f_t}} \left(\bigcup_{p \in {}^\bullet t} \{(p,s)\} \cup \bigcup_{p \in t^\bullet} \{(s,p)\} \right) \cup \bigcup_{d_k \in D_t} \left\{ (\bar{p}_k, s^t_{(\perp,\perp)}), (s^t_{(\perp,\perp)}, \bar{p}_k) \right\}$$

$$\cup \bigcup_{(\perp,d_j) \in R_{f_t}} \left(\left\{ (\perp_m, s^t_{(\perp,j)}) \mid t \in T_m \right\} \cup \left\{ (s^t_{(\perp,j)}, p_j) \right\} \right.$$

$$\cup \bigcup_{d_k \in D_t} \left\{ (\bar{p}_k, s^t_{(\perp,j)}) \right\} \cup \bigcup_{k \neq j} \left\{ (s^t_{(i,j)}, \bar{p}_k) \right\} \right)$$

$$\cup \bigcup_{\substack{(d_i,d_j) \in R_{f_t} \\ i \neq j}} \left(\left\{ (p_i, s^t_{(i,j)}), (s^t_{(i,j)}, p_j), (\bar{p}_j, s^t_{(i,j)}), (s^t_{(i,j)}, \bar{p}_i) \right\} \right)$$

$$\cup \bigcup_{(d_i,d_i) \in R_{f_t}} \left(\left\{ (p_i, s^t_{(i,i)}), (s^t_{(i,i)}, p_i) \right\} \right)$$

The idea is that each transition $s^t_{(i,j)}$ is a copy of transition t that, besides simulating t, models one pair (d_i, d_j) of the relation R_{f_t}, by taking a token out of place p_i (meanwhile, also checking that nothing else holds by taking tokens out of each $\bar{p}_k$, $k \neq i$) and putting it in p_j (also returning all tokens $\bar{p}_k$, $k \neq j$). Thus if d_i holds (solely) before execution of t, d_j will hold afterwards. The transitions $s^t_{\perp,j}$ generate new dataflow facts, but consume the token $\perp_m$ associated with the thread. We will engineer the net to initially contain only one $\perp_m$ marking (for some thread m), and hence make sure that only one fact is generated from $\perp$.

For every t, transitions $s^t_{(i,j)}$ are in *conflict* since they have ${}^\bullet t$ as common predecessors. This means that only one of them can execute at a time, generating a single fact. If we assume that initially nothing holds (i.e., initial tokens are in every $\bar{p}_i$'s and no initial tokens in any of the p_i's), then since each transition consumes one token and generates a new token, the following invariant always holds for the system: "At any reachable marking of the augmented net, exactly one position p_i corresponding to some dataflow fact d_i holds". We use this observation later to argue the complexity of our analysis.

Definition 7. *The augmented marked net $N^{\mathcal{S},\mathcal{F}}$ of a CCD problem $(N, \mathcal{S}, \mathcal{F})$ is defined as $\bigcup_{f \in \mathcal{F}} N_f$ where the union of two nets $N_1 = (P_1, T_1, F_1)$ and $N_2 = (P_2, T_2, F_2)$ is defined as $N_1 \cup N_2 = (P_1 \cup P_2, T_1 \cup T_2, F_1 \cup F_2)$. It is assumed that N_f's have disjoint set of transitions, and only the common places are identified in the union. Furthermore we add a new position p^*, make each $\bar{p}_i$ initial, and also introduce n initial transitions t^*_m, one for each thread, that removes p^* and puts a token in $\perp_m$ and a token in the initial positions of each thread.*

The above construction only works when $\perp = \emptyset$. When $\perp = D_0$, for some $D_0 \subseteq \mathbb{D}$, we will introduce a new initial set of events (all in conflict) that introduce nondeterministically a token in some $p_i \in D_0$ and remove $\bar{p}_i$.

The problem of computing the *MOT* solution can be reduced to a *coverability* problem on the augmented net. To be more precise, fact d_i *may* hold before the execution of transition t of the control net if and only if $\{p_i, p_t\}$ is coverable from the initial marking of the control net where p_t is the local control place associated to transition t in its corresponding thread.

Theorem 1. *A dataflow fact d_i holds before the execution of a transition t in the control net N of a program if and only if $d_i \in D_t^*$ and the marking $\{p_i, p_t\}$ is coverable from the initial marking in the augmented net $N^{S,F}$ constructed according to Definition 7.*

Checking coverability: While there are many tools that can check reachability/coverability properties of Petri nets, tools that use *unfolding* techniques [16,6] of nets are particularly effective, as they explore the state space using partially ordered unfoldings and give automatic reduction in state-space (akin to partial-order reduction for model checking of concurrent systems). We assume the reader is familiar with net unfoldings and refer to [6] for details.

Complexity of distributive CCD: Algorithms for Petri nets which use finite unfoldings essentially produces a finite unfolding of the net, from which coverability of one position can be checked in linear time. For every transition $t' \in T_{f_t}$ and every fact $d_i \in D_t^*$, we can create a new transition whose preconditions are those of t' plus p_i, and outputs a token in a new position (t, d_i). By Theorem 1, coverability of this single position is equivalent to fact d_i holding at t. Furthermore, we can argue that the unfolding of this net introduces at most $n|\mathbb{D}|$ new events compared to the unfolding of the augmented net.

Let us now analyze the size of the unfolding of the augmented net in terms of the size of the unfolding of the original control net; let us assume the latter has n events. We can show that (a) every marking reachable by a local configuration of the control net has a corresponding event in its finite unfolding that realizes this marking, and (b) that for every marking reached by a local configuration of the control net, there are at most $|\mathbb{D}|$ corresponding local configurations in the augmented net (at most one for each dataflow fact), and this covers all local configurations of the augmented net. Since the number of events in the unfolding is bounded by the number of markings reachable by local configurations, it follows that the size of the unfolding of the augmented net is at most $|\mathbb{D}|$ times that of the control net. This argues the efficacy of our approach in preserving the concurrency inherent in the control net and in exploiting distributivity to its fullest extent.

Theorem 2. *Let (N, S, F) be a distributive CCD problem, with $S = (\mathcal{P}(\mathbb{D}), \subseteq , \cup, \perp)$. Let n be the size of the unfolding of N. Then the size of the unfolding of the augmented net $N^{S,F}$ (and even the complexity of checking whether a fact holds at a control point) is at most $O(n|\mathbb{D}|)$.*

6   Experiments

We have applied the techniques from Section 5 to perform several dataflow analyses for concurrent programs. Unfortunately, there is no standard benchmark for concurrent dataflow programs. We have however experimented our algorithms with sample programs for the primary dataflow analysis problems, and studied performance when the number of threads is increased.

The motive of the experiments is to exhibit in practice the advantages of concurrent dataflow that exploit the causal framework set forth in this paper. While the practical efficacy of our approach on large programs is still not validated, we believe that setting up a general framework with well-defined problems permitting reasonable algorithms is a first step towards full-scale flow analysis. Algorithms that work on large code may have to implement approximations and heuristics, and we believe that the our framework will serve as a standard for correctness.

In many of our examples, there is an exponential increase in the set of reachable states as one increases the number of threads, but the partial order methods inherent to these techniques substantially alleviate the problem. We use the PEP tool [9] to check the coverability property on the augmented net to answer the relevant coverability queries.

For each example, we have included the sizes of the unfolding for the program's control net and of the augmented net (see Table 1). The *construction* time refers to the time to build the unfolding, and the *checking* time refers to the time for a single fact checking. Note the huge differences between the two times in some cases, and also note that the unfolding is only built once and is then used to answer several coverability queries. All experiments were performed on a Linux machine with a 1.7GHz processor and 1GB of memory. The numbers are all in seconds (with a precision of 0.01 seconds).

Uninitialized Variables. This set of examples contains a collection of n threads with n global variables $X^0, \ldots, X^n$. One uninitialized variable X^0 in one thread can consequently make all X^is uninitialized. Concurrency results in many possible interleavings in this example, a few of which can make a certain variable X^j uninitialized.

Reaching Definitions. This example set demonstrates how our method can successfully handle synchronization mechanisms. There are two types of threads: (1) those which perform two consequent writes to a global variable Y, and (2) those which perform a read of Y. There are two variations of this example: (1) where none of the accesses is protected

T	T'
acquire(1);	acquire(1)
Y := 1;	x := Y + 1;
Y := 2;	release(1)
release(1);	

by a lock, which we call RD, and (2) where the read, and the two writes combined are protected by the same lock, which we call RDL (the code on the right). The main difference between the two versions is that Y := 1 will reach the read in the lock-free version, but cannot reach it in the presence of the locks. In a setting with one copy of T' and n copies of T, there are $2n$ definitions where only n of them can reach the line x := Y + 1 of T'.

Table 1. Programs and Performances

Example	$|\mathbb{D}|$	#Threads	Unfolding Control Net	Unfolding Augmented Net	Checking Time (sec)	Construction Time (sec)
UV(10)	11	11	906	4090	< 0.01	<0.01
UV(20)	21	21	3311	16950	< 0.01	0.70
UV(60)	61	61	40859	156390	0.01	60.11
RD(3)	4	6	410	1904	< 0.01	0.03
RD(4)	5	8	1545	9289	0.01	1.5
RD(5)	6	10	5596	41186	0.01	133.16
RDL(3)	6	4	334	1228	< 0.01	0.01
RDL(4)	8	5	839	3791	< 0.01	29
RDL(5)	10	6	2024	10834	< 0.01	5.35
RDL(6)	12	7	4745	29333	0.01	121.00
AE(50)	2	50	250	650	< 0.01	< 0.01
AE(150)	2	150	750	1950	< 0.01	0.34
AE(350)	2	350	1750	4550	< 0.01	4.10

Available Expressions. The example set AE shows how the unfolding method can fully benefit from concurrency. The threads here do not have any dependencies. Each thread defines the same expression X + Y twice, and therefore, the expression is always available for the second instruction of each thread. Table 1 shows that in the case of zero dependencies, the size of the unfolding grows linearly with the number of threads (understandably so since new threads do not introduce new dataflow facts).

7   Conclusions

The main contribution of this paper lies in the definition of a framework that captures dataflow analysis problems for concurrent program using partial orders that preserves the concurrency in the system. The preserved concurrency has been exploited in the partial-order based analysis, but could instead have been exploited in other ways, for example using partial-order reduction strategies as those used in SPIN.

As for future directions, the first would be to study *local* or *compositional* methods to solve the CCD problems and deploy them on large real world programs. This would have to handle (approximately) complex data such as pointers and objects. Our algorithms do not work for programs with *recursion*, and it is well known that dataflow analysis for concurrent programs with recursion quickly leads to undecidability. Structural restrictions like nested locking (see [11]) would be worth studying to obtain decidable fragments. Studying a framework based on computing *minimal fixpoints* for concurrent programs would be also interesting. Extending our approach to decide flow problems with *infinite domains of finite height* is challenging as well (they can be handled in the sequential setting [20]).

References

1. Alfred V. Aho, Ravi Sethi, and Jeffrey D. Ullman. *Compilers: principles, techniques, and tools.* Addison-Wesley Longman Publishing Co., Inc., 1986.
2. A. T. Chamillard and Lori A. Clarke. Improving the accuracy of petri net-based analysis of concurrent programs. In *ISSTA*, pages 24–38, 1996.
3. Ron Cytron, Jeanne Ferrante, Barry K. Rosen, Mark N. Wegman, and F. Kenneth Zadeck. Efficiently computing static single assignment form and the control dependence graph. *ACM Trans. Program. Lang. Syst.*, 13(4):451–490, 1991.
4. M. Dwyer, L. Clarke, J. Cobleigh, and G. Naumovich. Flow analysis for verifying properties of concurrent software systems, 2004.
5. Matthew B. Dwyer and Lori A. Clarke. A compact petri net representation and its implications for analysis. *IEEE Trans. Softw. Eng.*, 22(11):794–811, 1996.
6. J. Esparza, S. Römer, and W. Vogler. An improvement of McMillan's unfolding algorithm. *Formal Methods in System Design*, 20:285–310, 2002.
7. A. Farzan and P. Madhusudan. Causal atomicity. In *CAV*, LNCS 4144, pages 315 – 328, 2006.
8. A. Farzan and P. Madhusudan. Causal dataflow analysis for concurrent programs. Technical Report UIUCDCS-R-2007-2806, CS Department, UIUC, 2007.
9. B. Grahlmann. The PEP tool. In *CAV*, pages 440–443, 1997.
10. M. Hecht. *Flow Analysis of Computer Programs.* Elsevier Science Inc., 1977.
11. V. Kahlon, F. Ivancic, and A. Gupta. Reasoning about threads communicating via locks. In *CAV*, volume LNCS 3576, pages 505–518, 2005.
12. Jens Knoop, Bernhard Steffen, and Jürgen Vollmer. Parallelism for free: Efficient and optimal bitvector analyses for parallel programs. *TOPLAS*, 18(3):268–299, May 1996.
13. Jaejin Lee, Samuel P. Midkiff, and David A. Padua. Concurrent static single assignment form and constant propagation for explicitly parallel programs. In *Languages and Compilers for Parallel Computing*, pages 114–130, 1997.
14. Jaejin Lee, David A. Padua, and Samuel P. Midkiff. Basic compiler algorithms for parallel programs. In *PPoPP*, pages 1–12, 1999.
15. Stephen P. Masticola and Barbara G. Ryder. Non-concurrency analysis. In *PPOPP*, pages 129–138, 1993.
16. K. McMillan. A technique of state space search based on unfolding. *Formal Methods in System Design*, 6(1):45–65, 1995.
17. S. S. Muchnick. *Advanced Compiler Design and Imlementation.* Morgan Kaufmann, 1997.
18. Gleb Naumovich and George S. Avrunin. A conservative data flow algorithm for detecting all pairs of statements that may happen in parallel. In *SIGSOFT/FSE-6*, pages 24–34, 98.
19. F. Nielson and H. Nielson. Type and effect systems. In *Correct System Design*, pages 114–136, 1999.
20. T. Reps, S. Schwoon, S. Jha, and D. Melski. Weighted pushdown systems and their application to interprocedural dataflow analysis. *Sci. Comput. Program.*, 58(1-2):206–263, 2005.
21. Thomas Reps, Susan Horwitz, and Mooly Sagiv. Precise interprocedural dataflow analysis via graph reachability. In *POPL*, pages 49–61, 1995.
22. Alexandru Salcianu and Martin Rinard. Pointer and escape analysis for multithreaded programs. In *PPoPP*, pages 12–23. ACM Press, 2001.
23. Eric Stoltz and Michael Wolfe. Sparse data-flow analysis for dag parallel programs, 1994.

Type-Dependence Analysis and Program Transformation for Symbolic Execution

Saswat Anand, Alessandro Orso, and Mary Jean Harrold

College of Computing, Georgia Institute of Technology
{saswat,orso,harrold}@cc.gatech.edu

Abstract. Symbolic execution can be problematic when applied to real applications. This paper addresses two of these problems: (1) the constraints generated during symbolic execution may be of a type not handled by the underlying decision procedure, and (2) some parts of the application may be unsuitable for symbolic execution (e.g., third-party libraries). The paper presents *type-dependence analysis*, which performs a context- and field-sensitive interprocedural static analysis to identify program entities that may store symbolic values at run-time. This information is used to identify the above two problematic cases and assist the user in addressing them. The paper also presents a technique to transform real applications for efficient symbolic execution. Instead of transforming the entire application, which can be inefficient and infeasible (mostly for pragmatic reasons), our technique leverages the results of type-dependence analysis to transform only parts of the program that may interact with symbolic values. Finally, the paper discusses the implementation of our analysis and transformation technique in a tool, STINGER, and an empirical evaluation performed on two real applications. The results of the evaluation show the effectiveness of our approach.

1 Introduction

Testing is one of the most commonly used techniques to gain confidence in the correct behavior of software. Because manual generation of test inputs is time consuming and usually results in inadequate test suites, researchers have proposed automated techniques for test-input generation. One of these techniques, symbolic execution, generates test-inputs by interpreting a program over symbolic values and solving constraints that lead to the execution of a specific program path. Although symbolic execution was first introduced in the mid 1970s [15], the dramatic growth in the computational power of the average machine and the availability of increasingly powerful decision procedures in recent years have renewed interest in using symbolic execution for test-input generation (e.g., [2,11,19,25,28]).

Despite the fact that symbolic execution is well understood, and performing symbolic execution on simple programs is straightforward, problems arise when attempting to symbolically execute real applications. In this paper, we address two such problems. The first problem concerns the capabilities of the underlying decision procedure used to check satisfiability and solve path conditions. If the

O. Grumberg and M. Huth (Eds.): TACAS 2007, LNCS 4424, pp. 117–133, 2007.

underlying decision procedure is incapable of (or inefficient in) handling the types of constraints produced during symbolic execution, users must rewrite parts of the program so that the offending constraints are not produced. However, this rewriting requires a user to identify those parts of the program that may generate problematic constraints, which is a difficult task. The second problem concerns the flow of symbolic values outside the boundaries of the software being symbolically executed. In these cases (e.g., when a symbolic value is passed as a parameter to an external library call), the execution must abort because external code cannot handle symbolic values. In real applications, there can be many instances of this problem, such as calls to native methods in Java, unmanaged code in the .NET framework, and third-party pre-compiled libraries. To address this issue, users must replace the calls to external components that may be reached by symbolic values with calls to stubs that model the components' behaviors. Like the first problem, performing this transformation requires manual intervention: the users must identify the external calls that may be problematic before actually performing symbolic execution.

In some studies on symbolic execution [25,28], the two problems do not arise because of the types of programs used (e.g., implementations of data structures). In other studies where these problems arise, researchers have taken various approaches to address them. Some researchers proposed approaches that replace symbolic values with concrete values whenever the symbolic values cannot be handled by the decision procedure or by an external component [10,19]; these approaches make the technique incomplete, in that it may fail to generate test inputs for a feasible program path. Other researchers proposed approaches based on "trial and error" [3]—every time the symbolic execution cannot continue because of a call to an external-library function with one or more symbolic parameters, the users are notified and must modify the code appropriately; although this solution may eventually lead to a successful execution, it can be inefficient when the interaction with the user is frequent. Yet other researchers proposed to use decision procedures for bit vectors that use boolean satisfiability (SAT) solvers [2]. Such decision procedures (e.g., STP [9]) can theoretically handle most types of constraints that may arise in a program under the assumption of finite representation of numbers. However, they are inefficient in handling linear integer arithmetic constraints, when compared to decision procedures specifically designed for this domain, such as Omega [17] and Yices [6].

To facilitate symbolic execution of real applications, where the previously described problems are frequently encountered, we present a new approach. Our approach is based on the insight that both of these problems are caused by the flow of symbolic values to *problematic variables*, such as parameters of library calls or operands of expressions that cannot be handled by the underlying decision procedure. Our approach is based on a novel static analysis, called type-dependence analysis, that identifies problematic variables before performing symbolic executions. Our type-dependence analysis formulates the problem of identifying variables that may assume symbolic values as a value-flow analysis problem. The analysis is context- and field-sensitive, which has the advantage of providing fairly precise results. The benefit of our analysis is that it can automatically detect parts of the program that may be problematic for symbolic execution (e.g., a modulo operation that involves at least one symbolic operand). For any such part, the analysis reports to the users the identified problem, together with contextual information, to help them understand the issue and perform necessary program changes.

In this paper, we also present a technique that leverages the results of the analysis to transform applications and prepare them for symbolic execution. The basic idea behind the transformation is to replace concrete types with symbolic types and concrete operators with operators that work over symbolic values [14]. Naively applying such transformation to the entire application leads to two problems. First, in practice, execution engines such as the Java virtual machine make implicit assumptions about the internal structures of some components. Transforming such components is thus problematic. Second, symbolic operations are more expensive than their concrete counterparts, even when they operate on concrete values (the extra overhead is incurred in checking whether a value is symbolic or concrete). Therefore, transforming those components of the program that may not interact with symbolic values introduces inefficiencies. Because type-dependence analysis can identify which variables may be symbolic, our technique avoids transforming parts of the code that have no interactions with symbolic values, thus improving both applicability and efficiency of symbolic execution.

To evaluate our type-dependence analysis and transformation technique, we implemented them in a tool, called STINGER, that works on Java and is integrated in Java Pathfinder [13], and used the tool to perform an empirical evaluation on two real programs. To the best of our knowledge, the programs that we used are considerably larger than those used in previous studies on symbolic execution. The results of the studies show that our analysis can be effective in (1) statically identifying areas of the code that would be problematic for symbolic execution, (2) providing useful feedback to the users to guide them in the resolution of the problems, and (3) limiting the transformation necessary for symbolic execution.

The main contributions of the paper are

- A context- and field-sensitive static flow analysis that can identify the variables in a program that may hold symbolic values, given a set of symbolic inputs. The analysis results enable static identification of program segments that are potentially problematic for symbolic execution and can guide users in transforming the program to eliminate the problems.
- A general transformation technique that leverages the type-dependence analysis to transform programs into "symbolic programs" (i.e., programs whose execution essentially performs symbolic execution of the original program).
- A tool, STINGER, that implements our approach for Java and is integrated in Java Pathfinder.
- A set of empirical studies, performed on two real programs, whose results show the usefulness of our approach.

2 Type-Dependence Analysis

This section presents our type-dependence analysis, which computes the set of program entities that may store symbolic values when a program is symbolically executed. We target a typical scenario in which the user selects a set of variables to hold symbolic input values for a program and then symbolically executes the program. In this context, the type of the selected variables and of other variables that can hold values derived from these selected variables must be symbolic.

```
public class Object{
    public static native Object clone ();
}
public class M extends Object{
    int m;
    M(int x){ this.m = x; }
    int getM(){ return this.m; }
    static native boolean isPrime(int x);
    public static void main(String[] arg){
        int s = Symbolic.integer ();
        M a = new M(s); M b = new M(4);
        int p = a.getM(); int q = b.getM();
        if(isPrime(p) && q % 3 == 0)
            M c = (M) a.clone ();
    }
}
```

Fig. 1. Motivating example

Before discussing the details of our analysis, we introduce a motivating example that illustrates some of the issues that the analysis can help to address. Suppose that we want to symbolically execute the Java program shown in Fig. 1, and that s represents the (symbolic) input to the program (as shown by the assignment of Symbolic.integer() to s). On initial inspection, the program contains three potentially-problematic cases: the use of the modulo (%) operation, which is not supported by many decision procedures; the invocation of native method clone; and the invocation of native method isPrime. However, a more careful inspection reveals that the first two cases are not problematic: the modulo operator never operates on symbolic values and native method clone can access only fields of class Object,[1] none of which may store symbolic values. As for the third potentially-problematic case, a symbolic value is passed as an argument to native method isPrime and is likely to be problematic because the method expects a concrete value. Our type-dependence analysis can discover that the first two cases are not problematic but the third case is. For this third case, the analysis can provide context information to help the user understand the problem and address it.

We call our analysis type-dependence analysis because it identifies type dependence between variables. We define type dependence as follows: For a given

---

[1] This conclusion is based on the common assumption that native methods do not use dynamic type discovery and thus access only fields of declared types of their parameters [23].

(assignment)	$\mathtt{p = x} \Longrightarrow p \leftarrow x$
(binop)	$\mathtt{p = x \oplus y} \Longrightarrow p \leftarrow x, p \leftarrow y$
(load)	$\mathtt{p = o.f} \Longrightarrow p \xleftarrow{get[f]} o$
(store)	$\mathtt{o.f = x} \Longrightarrow o \xleftarrow{put[f]} x$
(return)	$\mathtt{return\ x} \Longrightarrow R_m \leftarrow x$, where m is the concerned method
(array-new)	$\mathtt{a = new\ t[size]} \Longrightarrow a \xleftarrow{put[length]} size$
(array-assign1)	$\mathtt{a[i] = x} \Longrightarrow a \xleftarrow{put[elem]} x$
(array-assign2)	$\mathtt{p = a[i]} \Longrightarrow p \xleftarrow{get[elem]} a$
(array-length)	$\mathtt{p = a.length} \Longrightarrow p \xleftarrow{get[length]} a$
(invocation)	$\mathtt{x = a.foo(a_1,\dots,a_n)} \Longrightarrow x \leftarrow R_{foo}, P^1_{foo} \leftarrow a_1, \dots, P^n_{foo} \leftarrow a_n$

Fig. 2. Rules for building the type-dependence graph

type-correct program, an entity x is *type dependent* on an entity y iff x's type may need to be changed as a consequence of a change in y's type to maintain type correctness. Our type-dependence analysis computes a conservative approximation of the type-dependence relation between a given set of entities and the other entities in the program. The type-dependence analysis is an instance of the more general value-flow analysis, which identifies whether the value of an entity x can flow to an another entity y in the program. In the definition of our analysis, we leverage techniques for demand-driven interprocedural analysis [12] and cloning-based interprocedural analysis [27], and techniques that use binary decision diagrams for scaling interprocedural analysis [1,27].

Type-dependence analysis consists of two phases. The first phase builds a *Type-Dependence Graph (TDG)* for the program, which encodes direct type-dependence information between program entities. The second phase performs Context-Free Language (CFL) reachability [18] on the TDG to identify transitive type dependences.

2.1 Building the TDG

In the first phase, the analysis builds the Type-Dependence Graph (TDG), a directed graph (N, E). N is a set of nodes, each of which represents one of several entities: a static field, a local variable of a method, a field of primitive type, a parameter of a method, or the return value of a method. E is a set of directed edges. An edge $x \leftarrow y$ in E indicates that there is a direct type dependence between the entity represented by y and the entity represented by x (i.e., x is directly type-dependent on y).

To build the TDG, our analysis processes each program statement once and adds an edge to the graph for each relevant statement, according to the rules shown in Fig. 2. Note that the rules apply only to non-constant right-hand side values—the analysis does not add nodes or corresponding edges to the TDG for constant entities. In the figure, $o.f$ represents field f of object o; P^i_m represents the ith parameter of method m; R_m represents the return value of method m.

$$\frac{p \leftarrow x,\ x \in Sym}{p \in Sym}$$

$$\frac{p \xleftarrow{get[f_1]} q,\ y \xleftarrow{put[f_2]} x,\ f_1 = f_2,\ alias(y, q),\ x \in Sym}{p \in Sym}$$

Fig. 3. Context-insensitive inference rules for type dependence analysis.

For the definition of the rules, the analysis treats arrays as objects with two fields, *elem* and *length*, that represent all array elements and the length of the array, respectively. For space reasons, rules for statements involving static field references, unary operations, and casting are not shown; they are analogous to the assignment rule.

2.2   Performing CFL-Reachability on the TDG

In the second phase, the analysis performs CFL-reachability [18] on the TDG with a user-specified set of variables selected to be symbolic, Sym_0, and computes set Sym, which contains all local variables, static fields, formal parameters, and return values of scalar types that are type-dependent on variables in Sym_0. Instance fields and entities of array-types that are type-dependent on variables in Sym_0 are then computed from Sym; due to space constraint, this is described in Appendix A. The analysis initializes Sym to Sym_0 and applies a set of inference rules until a fix point on Sym is reached. For clarity, we first present a context-insensitive version of our analysis and then describe how it can be extended to be context-sensitive.

The context-insensitive version of our analysis is represented by the two inference rules in Fig. 3. The first rule states that an entity p is added to the Sym set if there is another entity x in Sym on which p is directly type dependent. The second rule captures transitive type dependence through heap aliases. It states that entity p must be added to Sym if there is another entity x in Sym and two object references y and q such that (1) p is directly type dependent on a field f of q, (2) the same field f of y is directly type dependent on x, and (3) y and q may point to the same object (expressed using the notation $alias(y, q)$). Without loss of generality, our analysis assumes that may-alias information is computed on demand by some points-to analysis (e.g., [22]).

Our analysis is *field-sensitive*—in the second rule, the labels $get[f_1]$ and $put[f_2]$ must refer to the same fields. This is in contrast to a *field-based* analysis, which does not distinguish between different fields of an object. Field sensitivity cannot be achieved through simple reachability. It requires our analysis to perform CFL reachability by matching $get[]$ and $put[]$ labels (two matching labels must refer to the same field), while identifying all nodes reachable from the initial set Sym_0,

The context-insensitive analysis described above may compute unnecessarily-large Sym sets. In the example in Fig. 1, for instance, the analysis would not distinguish between the two calls to the getM method and, thus, would not be able to detect that variable q is not type-dependent on variable s. To improve the precision of the analysis, we define a context-sensitive version of the TDG using an approach similar to method cloning [27]. First, we create multiple nodes for each entity—one for each calling context of the method that contains the entity. The only exceptions are entities that correspond to global variables (e.g., static fields in Java) that are represented with a single node in the context-sensitive TDG. Second, we create copies of the TDG's edges so that if an edge exists between two nodes, there is an edge between corresponding (context-specific) copies of the nodes. Note that each copy of an invocation edge is an inter-context edge—an edge that connects nodes that belong in different contexts.

Because cloning-based approaches can lead to an exponential explosion in the size of the graphs, we use Binary Decision Diagrams (BDDs) to represent context-sensitive TDGs [16,27]. In addition, we adopt the k-CFA approach [21], which limits the context of a call to the top k elements of the call stack.

After building the context-sensitive TDG, our analysis uses a context-sensitive version of the inference rules described in Fig. 3 to compute Sym. We obtain the context-sensitive inference rules by modifying the context-insensitive rules: we identify each entity in the rule with respect to a specific context c. The context-sensitive version of the first rule in Fig. 3, for instance, is

$$\frac{p^c \leftarrow x^c, \ x^c \in Sym}{p^c \in Sym}$$

3 Program Transformation

One common way to perform symbolic execution of a program is to first transform the program so that it can operate on both symbolic and concrete values, and then execute it.[2] A naive program transformation technique would change the types of all program entities to symbolic types, and change all operations over concrete values to operations over symbolic values. In practice, this approach is not feasible for two reasons. First, execution engines typically make implicit assumptions about the types of some entities (e.g., fields of certain classes), and these assumptions would be violated by the transformation. Second, treating all variables in a program as symbolic can be inefficient (compared to having only a small subset of symbolic variables and executing parts of the programs not affected by those variables normally). In this section, we present a program-transformation technique that leverages the results of type-dependence analysis to transform, in an automated way, only a subset of the program. By doing this, our technique mitigates (when it does not completely eliminate) the two problems mentioned above.

Our technique supports two operators that enable selective program transformations: box and unbox. The *box* operator converts a concrete value to a corresponding symbolic value. The *unbox* operator converts a symbolic value

---

[2] There are also other approaches not based on transformation (e.g., [5,8]).

```
public class M {
    int m;
    Expression m_JPF_;
    M(int x) { this(Symbolic.makeSymbolic(x));}
    int getM() { return Symbolic.makeConcrete_int(getM_JPF_());}
    static native boolean isPrime(int i);
    M(Expression x) { this.m_JPF_ = x; }
    Expression getM_JPF_() { return this.m_JPF_; }
    static native boolean isPrime_JPF_(Expression expression);
    public static void main(String[] strings) {
        M a = new M(Symbolic.symbolic_int());
        M b = new M(4);
        Expression p = a.getM_JPF_();
        int q = b.getM();
        if (isPrime_JPF_(p) && q % 3 == 0)
            M c = (M) a.clone();
    }
}
```

Fig. 4. Transformed version of the example from Fig. 1.

created by the box operator to the corresponding concrete value. These operators are needed to handle program entities that must be of symbolic types for
type correctness, but may store either symbolic and concrete values depending on
contexts. The operators let these entities store (boxed) concrete values whenever
necessary. The technique automatically adds to the program appropriate boxing
and unboxing operators to enable assignments between entities of symbolic and
concrete types. Note that unboxing a symbolic value (i.e., a symbolic value that
is not the result of a boxing operation) would cause a run-time error. However,
the transformation technique guarantees that such a situation will never occur
due to its use of the results of the conservative type-dependence analysis.

Before presenting the formal definition of the transformation, we illustrate
some features of our approach by showing, in Fig. 4, the transformed version of
the example program from Fig. 1. In the code, **Expression** represents the type
of symbolic expressions, and methods **makeSymbolic** and **makeConcrete_int**
represent box and unbox operators, respectively. For each field that may store a
symbolic value, such as m, the transformation adds a new field of symbolic type.
Similarly, for each method that may operate on symbolic values, a new method
is added that may take symbolic values as arguments and/or return symbolic
values. Note that because the analysis determines that variable q can never
store a symbolic value at runtime, q's type is unchanged, and the % operation
is not replaced by its corresponding symbolic operation. In contrast, p's type
is changed to **Expression** because the analysis determines that it may store
a symbolic value. When a symbolic version of a method is created, only those
calls that may pass and/or receive symbolic values are changed to invoke the
new method. In the example, for instance, **getM_JPF_()** is called on a because a
symbolic value may be returned by the method at that callsite. Conversely, the
call to **getM()** on b is unchanged, as only concrete values are returned at the
corresponding callsite.

Source language

$l \in$ Local, $f \in$ Field, $r \in$ RefType

$n \in$ NumType $n ::=$ int | short | char | long | byte | float | double

$\tau \in$ Type $\quad \tau ::= n \mid$ boolean $\mid r \mid \tau[\,]$

$i \in$ Immediate $i ::= l \mid$ const

$e \in$ Expr $\quad e ::= i \mid i_1$ binop $i_2 \mid$ unop $i \mid l.f^{(\tau)} \mid (\tau)\, i \mid l[i]^{(\tau)} \mid l.\text{length}^{(\tau)} \mid$ new $\tau[i]$

$s \in$ Stmt) $\quad s ::= l = e \mid l.f = i \mid l[i_1]^{(\tau)} = i_2$

binop $\in \{+, -, *, /, \%, =, >, \geq, <, \leq, \neq\}$
unop $\in \{-, !\}$

Extension for symbolic execution

$\tilde{l} \in$ SymLocal, $\tilde{f} \in$ SymField

$\tilde{\tau} \in$ SymType $\quad \tilde{\tau} ::=$ EXPR | EXPRARRAY | BOOLARRAY | REFARRAY

$\tilde{i} \in$ SymImmediate $\tilde{i} ::= \tilde{l}$

$\tilde{e} \in$ SymExpr $\quad \tilde{e} ::= \text{box}^{\tilde{\tau}}(e) \mid \tilde{i} \mid \text{symbinop}(\tilde{e}_1, \tilde{e}_2) \mid \text{symunop } \tilde{i} \mid l.\tilde{f} \mid \text{cast}^{\tau}(\tilde{e}) \mid$
$\qquad \text{array\_get}^{\tilde{\tau}}(\tilde{l}, \tilde{e}) \mid \text{array\_len}^{\tilde{\tau}}(\tilde{l}) \mid \text{new\_array}^{\tilde{\tau}}(\tilde{e})$

$\tilde{s} \in$ SymStmt $\quad \tilde{s} ::= \tilde{l} = \tilde{e} \mid l = \text{unbox}^{\tilde{\tau}}(\tilde{e}) \mid a.\tilde{f} = \tilde{e} \mid \text{array\_set}^{\tilde{\tau}}(\tilde{l}, \tilde{e}_1, \tilde{e}_2)$

symbinop $\in \{ \_\text{plus}, \_\text{minus}, \_\text{mul}, \_\text{div}, \_\text{mod}, \_\text{eq}, \_\text{gt}, \_\text{ge}, \_\text{lt}, \_\text{le}, \_\text{ne} \}$
symunop $\in \{ \_\text{neg}, \_\text{not} \}$

Fig. 5. Source language and its extensions for symbolic execution

3.1   Source and Target Languages

For the sake of clarity, we define our transformation on a subset of Java, referred to as *source* language, that contains only those Java features relevant to the transformation. The transformation of a program in *source* language produces a program in *target* language. Fig. 5 presents the source language and its extensions for symbolic execution. The target language is the union of the source language and its extensions.

Both the source and the target languages are statically and explicitly typed according to Java's type rules. Types in the source language include all types supported by Java. The target language supports four symbolic types, namely EXPR, EXPRARRAY, BOOLARRAY, and REFARRAY, that represent types of symbolic expressions, arrays of symbolic expressions, arrays of boolean values, and arrays of references, respectively. Each of the symbolic array types can also have symbolic length. The correspondence between concrete and symbolic types (for concrete types that have a corresponding symbolic type) is defined by function $stype : \text{Type} \to \text{SymType}$.

$$stype(\tau) \;\; = \text{EXPR} \qquad \tau \in \text{NumType} \qquad stype([\,]\text{boolean}) = \text{BOOLARRAY}$$
$$stype([\,]\tau) = \text{EXPRARRAY} \; \tau \in \text{NumType} \qquad stype([\,]r) \qquad = \text{REFARRAY}$$

Expressions include local variables, constants, unary and binary operations, field references, casts, array references, array length and array allocation expressions. In the source language, τ represents the element type of array l in terms $l[i]^{(\tau)}$ and $l.\texttt{length}^{(\tau)}$, and the type of field f in term $l.f^{(\tau)}$.

In the target language, there is one syntactic category for each category in the source language, represented by the same symbol with a tilde on the top. In addition, for each unary, binary, and comparison operators in the source language, the target language provides a corresponding operator that operates on symbolic values. In the definition of the language extensions, we use the following terminology (where $\tilde{\tau}$ denotes the type of array element): $\texttt{array\_get}^{\tilde{\tau}}(\tilde{l}, \tilde{e})$ is an operation that returns the $\tilde{e}^{th}$ element of symbolic array $\tilde{l}$; $\texttt{array\_len}^{\tilde{\tau}}(\tilde{l})$ returns the length of $\tilde{l}$; $\texttt{new\_array}^{\tilde{\tau}}(\tilde{e})$ allocates a symbolic array of size $\tilde{e}$; and $\texttt{array\_set}^{\tilde{\tau}}(\tilde{l}, \tilde{e}_1, \tilde{e}_2)$ stores symbolic expression $\tilde{e}_2$ as the element at index $\tilde{e}_1$ of array $\tilde{l}$. The box operator is represented by $box^{\tilde{\tau}}(e)$, which transforms the concrete value e into the corresponding symbolic value of type $\tilde{\tau}$. Analogously, $unbox^{\tilde{\tau}}(\tilde{e})$ indicates the transformation of the symbolic value contained in $\tilde{e}$, of type $\tilde{\tau}$, into its original concrete value and type.

3.2   Transformation

The transformation is performed in two steps. In the first step, new fields, methods, and local variables of symbolic types are added to the program. For each field that may store symbolic values, the transformation adds a new field with corresponding symbolic type. For each method m that may operate on symbolic values, the transformation adds a new method m_s, which may potentially have parameters and return value of symbolic types. Also, for each of m's local variables v, if v may store symbolic values, a local variable of corresponding symbolic type is added to m_s; otherwise, the original v is added to m_s. Finally, all statements of m are moved to m_s, and m is transformed into a proxy that invokes m_s and performs boxing and unboxing of parameters and/or return values as needed. Note that, even if the analysis is context-sensitive, it generates at most one variant of each method because the results of the analysis are unified over all contexts.

In the second step of the transformation, statements in the newly-added methods are transformed according to the rules provided in Fig. 6. Note that Fig. 6 does not include transformation rules that involve arrays, which are provided in Fig. 8 (see Appendix A). Each rule defines how a specific statement in the source language is transformed and is applicable only if the respective guard is satisfied. The rules use the following notations:

- For a given local variable or field x that may store symbolic values, $\bar{x}$ represents the corresponding entity of symbolic type added by the transformation in the first step. If x cannot store a symbolic value, then $\bar{x}$ simply represents the original entity. In particular, if x is a constant, $\bar{x}$ always represents x.
- $\bar{\tau}$, represent the symbolic type corresponding to a concrete type τ, as defined by function $stype$.
- For an expression e of concrete type τ, $< e >$ represents $box^{\bar{\tau}}(e)$ (i.e., e boxed as a value of its corresponding symbolic type). For an expression $\tilde{e}$ of a symbolic type, $< \tilde{e} >$ represents $\tilde{e}$ itself.

Original statement	Transformed statement	Guard	
$[l = i]$	$[\bar{l} = <\bar{i}>]$	$\bar{l} \neq l$	(1)
$[l = i_1 \text{ binop } i_2]$	$[\bar{l} = \text{box}^{\text{EXPR}}(i_1 \text{ binop } i_2)]$	$\bar{l} \neq l, \bar{i_1} = i_1, \bar{i_2} = i_2$	(2)
	$[\bar{l} = \text{symbinop}(<\bar{i_1}>, <\bar{i_2}>)]$	$\bar{i_1} \neq i_1 \text{ or } \bar{i_2} \neq i_2$	(3)
$[l = \text{unop } i]$	$[\bar{l} = \text{box}^{\text{EXPR}}(\text{unop } i)]$	$\bar{l} \neq l, \bar{i} = i$	(4)
	$[\bar{l} = \text{symunop}(\bar{i})]$	$\bar{i} \neq i$	(5)
$[l.f = i]$	$[l.\bar{f} = <\bar{i}>]$	$\bar{f} \neq f$	(6)
$[l_1 = l_2.f^{(\tau)}]$	$[\bar{l_1} = <l_2.\bar{f}>]$	$\bar{l_1} \neq l_1$	(7)
	$[\bar{l_1} = \text{unbox}^{\tau}(l_2.\bar{f})]$	$\bar{l_1} = l_1, \bar{f} \neq f$	(8)
$[l_1 = (\tau) \, l_2]$	$[\bar{l_1} = \text{box}^{\tau}((\tau) \, l_2)]$	$\bar{l_1} \neq l_1, \bar{l_2} = l_2$	(9)
	$[\bar{l_1} = \text{cast}^{\tau}(\bar{l_2})]$	$\bar{l_1} \neq l_1, \bar{l_2} \neq l_2$	(10)

Fig. 6. Transformation rules for program statements

For space reasons, we discuss transformation rules for only two types of statements: assignments of a local variable or constant to a local variable and assignments of a field to a local variable. According to Rule 1, assignment statements of the form $l = i$ are transformed only if l may store a symbolic value. If so, a local variable of symbolic type that corresponds to l, $\bar{l}$, is added and becomes the l-value of the transformed statement. If i is a non-constant local variable and has a corresponding local variable of symbolic type, $\bar{i}$, $\bar{i}$ becomes the r-value of the transformed statement. Otherwise, if i is either a constant or a local variable without a corresponding local of symbolic type, i's value is boxed and assigned to $\bar{l}$.

We discuss rules for statements of type $l_1 = l_2.f^{(\tau)}$ because they make use of the unbox operator. There are two rules that involve these statements. In the first case (Rule 7), l_1 has a corresponding local of symbolic type, $\bar{l_1}$, which becomes the l-value of the transformed statement. If field f has a corresponding field of symbolic type, $\bar{f}$, the value of $\bar{f}$ of l_2 is assigned to $\bar{l_1}$; otherwise, the value of field f of l_2 is boxed and assigned to $\bar{l_1}$. In the second case (Rule 8), where l_1 does not have a corresponding local of symbolic type, but f has a corresponding field of symbolic type, $l_2.f$'s value is unboxed and assigned to l_1.

4 Empirical Studies

To assess the effectiveness of our approach, we implemented our type-dependence analysis and automatic transformation technique in a tool named STINGER (Symbolic-execution based Test INput GenEratoR), and used STINGER to perform a set of empirical studies. STINGER works on Java bytecode, leverages the SOOT framework [24], and is integrated with Java Pathfinder [13]. The type-dependence analysis is implemented using Jedd [16], a Java language extension that supports use of binary decision diagrams to store and manipulate relations. STINGER inputs a program in Java bytecode, the initial set of program entities specified to be symbolic (called Sym_0 in Section 2), and a specification of the capabilities of the decision procedure used by the symbolic executor (in terms of supported operators). Given these inputs, STINGER performs two tasks: (1) it performs type-dependence analysis and identifies and reports the two kinds of problematic cases considered (i.e., constraints that cannot be handled by the decision procedure and symbolic values that may flow outside the scope of the software being symbolically executed); (2) it performs an automated translation of the program and generates skeleton stubs for the problematic cases identified, which the user is expected to complete with appropriate code.

We used STINGER to investigate three research questions:

RQ1: How effective is our technique in identifying parts of the code responsible for constraints that cannot be handled by the decision procedure in use?

RQ2: How often do symbolic values flow outside the boundaries of the program being symbolically executed? When that happens, can our analysis correctly identify and report problematic cases beforehand?

RQ3: To what extent can the use of our analysis reduce the transformation needed to perform symbolic execution?

Empirical Setup. As subjects for our studies, we used two freely-available Java programs: NANOXML and ANTLR. NANOXML (http://nanoxml.cyberelf.be/) is an XML-parsing library that consists of approximately 6KLOC. We selected NANOXML because it is small yet not trivial, and lets us evaluate our technique and inspect our results in detail. ANTLR (http://www.antlr.org/) is a widely-used language-independent lexer and parser generator that consists of 46KLOC. ANTLR was selected because it is a relatively large and complex software that can provide more confidence in the generality of our results. NANOXML inputs a file containing an XML document, and ANTLR inputs a file containing the grammar of a language. We changed both applications so that they input an array of symbolic characters *arr* instead of reading from a file. We then ran STINGER and specified *arr* as the only element in the initial set of symbolic entities. STINGER produced, for each program, a report and a transformed version of the program.

4.1   Results and Discussion

To address our research questions, we ran STINGER on the subjects, and measured several statistics as shown in Fig. 7. In the figure, the number of methods includes both methods of the application and methods in the Java standard library, which may also need to be transformed when symbolically executing a program. We first discuss the results for each research question independently, and then discuss the precision of the analysis.

RQ1. STINGER finds 48 (for NANOXML) and 82 (for ANTLR) cases that would be problematic for our decision procedure of choice [6]. In this context, the problematic cases are those that involve bit-wise and modulo operations over symbolic values. These problematic cases reside in 10 and 23 methods of NANOXML and ANTLR, respectively. These cases would be reported to the user, who would then

	Statistics	NanoXML	Antlr
RQ1	No. of problematic operations	48	82
	No. of methods with problematic operations	10	23
RQ2	No. of native calls that may be reached by symbolic values	3	8
	Total no. of native calls	27	48
RQ3	No. of methods transformed	89	253
	No. of reachable methods	438	1176
	No. of statements transformed	1253	4052
	No. of statements in all transformed methods	2642	8547

Fig. 7. Empirical results

need to modify the methods (or replace them with stubs) to eliminate the problem. After inspecting STINGER's report, we found that many of these problematic constraints arise because of the use of modulo operators in classes HashMap and HashTable. Replacing these classes with another implementation of a map, such as TreeMap, eliminates the problem. The remaining problematic methods were methods operating on characters (e.g., to change a character from upper to lower case). We were able to rewrite these methods and eliminate the use of bit-wise operators in them by assuming that the input characters are ASCII characters.

RQ2. For the two subject programs, the only instances of symbolic values that may flow outside the boundaries of the program consist of calls to native methods. STINGER determines that for 3 of the 27 (for NanoXML) and for 8 of the 48 (for Antlr) calls to native methods, a symbolic value may actually be passed as a parameter, either through a primitive value or as a field of an object. Based on these results we first observe that, for the two (real) applications considered, symbolic values may indeed cross the program boundaries and create problems for symbolic execution. We also observe that our technique is successful in identifying such problematic cases and in identifying methods that, although potentially problematic, are guaranteed to never be actually reached by symbolic values. For NanoXML and Antlr, our analysis lets users focus their attention on only 15% of the potentially-problematic calls.

RQ3. Our analysis discovers that symbolic values are confined within approximately one fifth of the total number of methods for both subjects. Furthermore, within methods that may handle symbolic values, less than half of the statements are actually affected by these values. Our translator is therefore able to transform the program so that half of the statements can be executed without incurring any overhead due to symbolic execution.

Precision. Our analysis is conservative and can be imprecise in some cases (i.e., it may conclude that a variable may store symbolic values even if it never does so in reality). Although context-sensitivity increases the precision significantly, the underlying points-to analysis does not scale beyond 2-cfa for our subjects, and STINGER can thus produces imprecise results. For example, for NanoXML, we found that many standard library classes are unnecessarily transformed because of the imprecision of the analysis. We believe that this imprecision could be reduced by using a demand-driven, highly-precise points-to analysis.

5   Related Work

Our work is related to approaches that provide tool support for abstraction in model checking (e.g., [4,7]). In [4], type inference is used to identify a set of variables that can be removed from a program when building a model for model checking. In [7], a framework for type inference and subsequent program transformation is proposed. In both approaches, the type-inference algorithm used is not as precise as our type-dependence analysis. Precision is crucial for our goal of reducing manual intervention and reducing the transformations that must be performed. However, unlike our work, where only one kind of abstraction (concrete to symbolic) is supported, the framework in [7] allows multiple user-defined abstractions.

Our approach to symbolic execution (i.e., execution of a transformed program) is also used in several other approaches (e.g., [2,11,19]). These approaches, however, transform the entire program, whereas our technique leverages type-dependence analysis to transform only the parts of the program actually affected by the symbolic execution. In this way, our technique reduces both the manual intervention and the amount program transformation needed. Also related to ours is the technique presented in [5], which is based on executing the program symbolically. The technique differs from our approach because it does not transform the program, but executes it using a virtual machine with a special semantics that support symbolic values.

Finally, being our type-dependence analysis a specific instance of flow analysis, it bears similarity to other approaches based on flow analysis, such as taint analysis [20] and information-flow analysis [26]. Our demand-driven formulation of type-dependence analysis is similar to the formulation of points-to analysis in [22], and our cloning-based approach to interprocedural analysis and use of binary decision diagrams to make context-sensitive analysis scale were studied in [27] and [1], respectively.

6   Conclusion

In this paper, we address two problems that hinder the application of symbolic execution to real software: (1) the generation of constraints that the decision procedure in use cannot handle and (2) the flow of symbolic values outside the program boundary. We present type-dependence analysis, which automatically and accurately identifies places in the program where these two problems occur, and a technique that uses the analysis results to help users address the identified problems. We also present a program-transformation technique that leverages the analysis results to selectively transform applications into applications that can be symbolically executed. We have implemented the analysis and transformation techniques in a tool, STINGER, that is integrated with Java

Pathfinder's symbolic execution engine. In our empirical evaluation, we applied STINGER to two Java applications. The results show that the problems that we target do occur in real applications, at least for the subjects considered, and that our analysis can identify these problems automatically and help users to address them. Moreover, we show that our analysis is precise enough to allow for transforming only the part of the code actually affected by symbolic values at runtime.

In future work, we plan to use STINGER for generating test inputs for real software and investigate techniques for guiding symbolic execution to exercise new program behaviors (e.g., coverage of specific program states). In this paper, we consider program boundaries defined by pragmatic reasons, such as interfaces with external libraries. In the future, we will investigate the application of our approach to cases where the boundaries are defined by the user (e.g., to exclude part of the system and thus reduce the state space to explore).

References

1. M. Berndl, O. Lhoták, F. Qian, L. Hendren, and N. Umanee. Points-to analysis using BDDs. In *PLDI*, pages 103–114, 2003.
2. C. Cadar, V. Ganesh, P. M. Pawlowski, D. L. Dill, and D. R. Engler. EXE: Automatically generating inputs of death. In *CCS*, pages 322–335, 2006.
3. C. Cadar, P. Twohey, V. Ganesh, and D. R. Engler. EXE: A system for automatically generating inputs of death using symbolic execution. Technical Report CSTR 2006-01, Stanford University., 2006.
4. D. Dams, W. Hesse, and G. J. Holzmann. Abstracting C with abC. In *CAV*, pages 515–520, 2002.
5. X. Deng, J. Lee, and Robby. Bogor/Kiasan: A k-bounded symbolic execution for checking strong heap properties of open systems. In *ASE*, pages 157–166, 2006.
6. B. Dutertre and L. de Moura. A Fast Linear-Arithmetic Solver for DPLL(T). In *CAV*, pages 81–94, 2006.
7. M. B. Dwyer, J. Hatcliff, R. Joehanes, S. Laubach, C. S. Pasareanu, Robby, H. Zheng, and W. Visser. Tool-supported program abstraction for finite-state verification. In *ICSE*, pages 177–187, 2001.
8. C. Flanagan, K. R. M. Leino, M. Lillibridge, G. Nelson, J. B. Saxe, and R. Stata. Extended static checking for Java. In *PLDI*, pages 234–245, 2002.
9. V. Ganesh and D. Dill. System Description of STP. http://www.csl.sri.com/users/demoura/smt-comp/descriptions/stp.ps.
10. P. Godefroid, N. Klarlund, and K. Sen. DART: directed automated random testing. In *PLDI*, pages 213–223, 2005.
11. W. Grieskamp, N. Tillmann, and W. Schulte. XRT–exploring runtime for .NET architecture and applications. *Electr. Notes Theor. Comp. Sci.*, 144(3):3–26, 2006.
12. S. Horwitz, T. W. Reps, and S. Sagiv. Demand interprocedural dataflow analysis. In *FSE*, pages 104–115, 1995.
13. Java PathFinder. http://javapathfinder.sourceforge.net.
14. S. Khurshid, C. Pasareanu, and W. Visser. Generalized symbolic execution for model checking and testing. In *TACAS*, pages 553–568, 2003.
15. J. C. King. Symbolic execution and program testing. *CACM*, 19(7):385–394, 1976.

16. O. Lhoták and L. J. Hendren. Jedd: a BDD-based relational extension of Java. In *PLDI*, pages 158–169, 2004.
17. W. Pugh. The Omega test: a fast and practical integer programming algorithm for dependence analysis. In *SC*, pages 4–13, 1991.
18. T. W. Reps. Program analysis via graph reachability. In *ILPS*, pages 5–19, 1997.
19. K. Sen, D. Marinov, and G. Agha. CUTE: a concolic unit testing engine for C. In *FSE*, pages 263–272, 2005.
20. U. Shankar, K. Talwar, J. S. Foster, and D. Wagner. Detecting format-string vulnerabilities with type qualifiers. In *USENIX Security Symposium*, pages 201–218, 2001.
21. O. Shivers. Control-flow analysis in Scheme. In *PLDI*, pages 164–174, 1988.
22. M. Sridharan, D. Gopan, L. Shan, and R. Bodík. Demand-driven points-to analysis for Java. In *OOPSLA*, pages 59–76, 2005.
23. E. Tilevich and Y. Smaragdakis. Transparent program transformations in the presence of opaque code. In *GPCE*, pages 89–94, 2006.
24. R. Vallée-Rai, L. Hendren, V. Sundaresan, P. Lam, E. Gagnon, and P. Co. Soot - a Java optimization framework. In *CASCON*, pages 125–135, 1999.
25. W. Visser, C. S. Pasareanu, and S. Khurshid. Test input generation with Java PathFinder. In *ISSTA*, pages 97–107, 2004.
26. D. M. Volpano, C. E. Irvine, and G. Smith. A sound type system for secure flow analysis. *Journal of Computer Security*, 4(2/3):167–188, 1996.
27. J. Whaley and M. S. Lam. Cloning-based context-sensitive pointer alias analysis using binary decision diagrams. In *PLDI*, pages 131–144, June 2004.
28. T. Xie, D. Marinov, W. Schulte, and D. Notkin. Symstra: A framework for generating object-oriented unit tests using symbolic execution. In *TACAS*, pages 365–381, 2005.

A   Type-Dependence Analysis for Fields and Entities of Array-Types

Sym, computed by the fix-point algorithm described in section 2, contains only local variables, static fields, formal parameters, and return values of scalar types that are type-dependent on variables in Sym_0. In this section, we describe how type-dependent instance fields and entities of array-types are computed from *Sym*.

The type-dependent instance fields are represented by the set $\{f \text{ s.t. } y \xleftarrow{put[f]} x, x \in Sym\}$. In other words, a field f is type-dependent on a variable in Sym_0 if the value of a local variable x that is type-dependent on Sym_0 is stored into field f of some reference variable y. To compute the type-dependent entities of array-types, the algorithm first computes a set of program statements that allocate arrays Arr_s, as follows:

$$Arr_s = \{s \text{ s.t. } s \in pt(a), a \xleftarrow{put[elem]} x \text{ or } a \xleftarrow{put[length]} x \text{ in TDG}, x \in Sym\}$$

A statement that allocates an array a is in Arr_s if either (1) a may store a value that is not type-compatible with a's current element-type, or (2) *length* of a may not be of integer type as a result of change in the types of variables in

Sym_0. $pt(a)$ returns all of the statements that allocates arrays to which a local variable a of array-type may point-to at run-time. After computing Arr_s, the entities of array-type that are type-dependent on variables in Sym_0 are given by the set $\{v \text{ s.t. } pt(v) \cap Arr_s \neq \Phi\}$. In other words, an entity of array-type is type-dependent on a variable in Sym_0 if it may store an array allocated by one of the statements in Arr_s.

B   Transformation Rules

Fig. 8 shows the transformation rules for statements referencing arrays.

Original statement		
Transformed statement	Guard	
$[s : l = \texttt{new } \tau[i]]$		
$[\bar{l} = \texttt{new\_array}^{\tau}(< \bar{i} >)]$	$s \in Arr_s$	(11)
$[l_1 = l_2.\texttt{length}^{(\tau)}]$		
$[\overline{l_1} = \texttt{box}^{\text{EXPR}}(l_2.\texttt{length})]$	$\overline{l_1} \neq l_1, \overline{l_2} = l_2$	(12)
$[l_1 = \texttt{unbox}^{\text{EXPR}}(\texttt{array\_len}^{\tau}(\overline{l_2}))]$	$\overline{l_1} = l_1, \overline{l_2} \neq l_2$	(13)
$[\overline{l_1} = \texttt{array\_len}^{\tau}(\overline{l_2})]$	$\overline{l_1} \neq l_1, \overline{l_2} \neq l_2$	(14)
$[l[i_1]^{(\tau)} = i_2]$		
$[\texttt{array\_set}^{\tau}(< \bar{l} >, < \overline{i_1} >, < \overline{i_2} >)]$	$\tau \in \text{NumType}, \bar{l} \neq l \text{ or } \overline{i_1} \neq i_1$	(15)
$[\texttt{array\_set}^{\tau}(< \bar{l} >, < \overline{i_1} >, i_2)]$	$\tau \in \text{RefType or } \tau = \text{boolean}, \bar{l} \neq l \text{ or } \overline{i_1} \neq i_1$	(16)
$[l_1 = l_2[i]^{(\tau)}]$		
$[\overline{l_1} = \texttt{box}^{\tau}(l_2[i])]$	$\overline{l_1} \neq l_1, \overline{l_2} = l_2, \bar{i} = i$	(17)
$[\overline{l_1} = \texttt{array\_get}^{\tau}(< \overline{l_2} >, < \bar{i} >)]$	$\tau \in \text{NumType}, \overline{l_2} \neq l_2 \text{ or } \bar{i} \neq i, \overline{l_1} \neq l_1$	(18)
$[l_1 = \texttt{unbox}^{\text{EXPR}}(\texttt{array\_get}^{\tau}(< \overline{l_2} >, < \bar{i} >))]$	$\tau \in \text{NumType}, \overline{l_2} \neq l_2 \text{ or } \bar{i} \neq i, \overline{l_1} = l_1$	(19)
$[l_1 = \texttt{array\_get}^{\tau}(< \overline{l_2} >, < \bar{i} >)]$	$\tau = \text{boolean}, \overline{l_2} \neq l_2 \text{ or } \bar{i} \neq i$	(20)
$[l_1 = (\tau) \texttt{ array\_get}^{\tau}(< \overline{l_2} >, < \bar{i} >)]$	$\tau \in \text{RefType}, \overline{l_2} \neq l_2 \text{ or } \bar{i} \neq i$	(21)

Fig. 8. Tranformation Rules (Continuation from Fig. 6.)

JPF–SE: A Symbolic Execution Extension to Java PathFinder

Saswat Anand[1], Corina S. Păsăreanu[2], and Willem Visser[2]

[1] College of Computing, Georgia Institute of Technology
saswat@cc.gatech.edu
[2] QSS and RIACS, NASA Ames Research Center, Moffett Field, CA 94035
{pcorina,wvisser}@email.arc.nasa.gov

Abstract. We present JPF–SE, an extension to the Java PathFinder Model Checking framework (JPF) that enables the symbolic execution of Java programs. JPF–SE uses JPF to generate and explore symbolic execution paths and it uses off-the-shelf decision procedures to manipulate numeric constraints.

1 Introduction

Explicit state model checking tools, such as Java PathFinder (JPF) [5,12], are becoming effective in detecting subtle errors in complex concurrent software, but they typically can only deal with closed systems. We present here JPF–SE, a symbolic execution extension to Java PathFinder, that allows model checking of concurrent Java programs that take inputs from unbounded domains.

JPF–SE enables symbolic execution of Java programs during explicit state model checking, which has the following unique characteristics: (a) checks the behavior of code using symbolic values that represent data for potentially infinite input domains, instead of enumerating and checking for small concrete data domains (b) takes advantage of the built-in capabilities of JPF to perform efficient search through the program state space: systematic analysis of different thread interleavings, heuristic search, state abstraction, symmetry and partial order reductions (c) enables modular analysis: checking programs on un-specified inputs enables the analysis of a compilation unit in isolation (d) automates test input generation for Java library classes [13] (e) uses annotations in the form of method specifications and loop invariants to prove light-weight properties of Java programs [8] and (f) uses a common interface to several well-known decision procedures to manipulate symbolic numeric constraints; JPF–SE can be extended easily to handle other decision procedures.

2 JPF–SE Overview

Java PathFinder. JPF [5,12] is an explicit-state model checker for Java programs that is built on top of a customized Java Virtual Machine. By default,

O. Grumberg and M. Huth (Eds.): TACAS 2007, LNCS 4424, pp. 134–138, 2007.

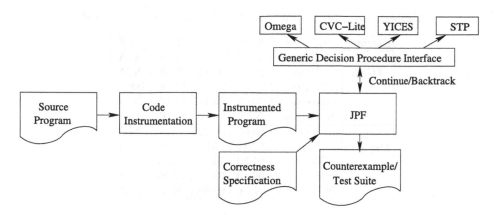

Fig. 1. Tool Architecture

JPF stores all the explored states, and it backtracks when it visits a previously explored state. The user can also customize the search (using heuristics) and it can specify what part of the state to be stored and used for matching.

Symbolic Execution. Symbolic execution [7] is a technique that enables analysis of programs that take un-initialized inputs. The main idea is to use *symbolic values*, instead of actual (concrete) data, as input values and to represent the values of program variables as symbolic expressions. As a result, the outputs computed by a program are expressed as a function of the symbolic inputs. The state of a symbolically executed program includes the (symbolic) values of program variables, a *path condition* and a program counter. The path condition accumulates constraints which the inputs must satisfy in order for an execution to follow the corresponding path.

JPF–SE Architecture. In previous work, we presented a framework that uses JPF to perform symbolic execution for Java programs [6, 8]. It has now been added to the JPF open-source repository [5] and is illustrated in Figure 1. Programs are instrumented to enable JPF to perform symbolic execution; concrete types are replaced with corresponding symbolic types and concrete operations are replaced with calls to methods that implement corresponding operations on symbolic expressions. Whenever a path condition is updated, it is checked for satisfiability using an appropriate decision procedure. If the path condition is unsatisfiable, the model checker backtracks. The approach can be used for finding counterexamples to safety properties and for test input generation (that satisfy a testing criterion, such as branch coverage).

Symbolic State Space Exploration. JPF–SE exploits JPF's ability to explore arbitrary program control flow (loops, recursion, method invocation), but performing symbolic execution on a program with loops (or recursion) may result in an infinite number of symbolic states. JPF–SE uses two complementary techniques to address this problem: (a) for systematic state space exploration JPF–SE puts a *bound* on the size of the program inputs and/or the search depth,

Table 1. Comparative Results. "N/A" indicates not supported.

Example	Interface	Omega	CVCL	YICES	STP
TCAS	File	00:15	00:26	N/A	N/A
	Pipe	00:04	00:12	N/A	N/A
	Native	00:03	00:13	00:06	00:31
	Native table	00:01	00:11	00:05	N/A
	Native inc	N/A	00:03	00:01	N/A
TreeMap	File	02:02	06:02	N/A	N/A
	Pipe	07:42	13:04	N/A	N/A
	Native	01:39	06:11	03:06	>60:00
	Native table	00:40	05:10	02:36	N/A
	Native inc	N/A	02:58	00:33	N/A

and (b) JPF–SE provides automated tool support for *abstracting* and *comparing* symbolic states, to determine if a symbolic state has been visited before, in which case the model checker will backtrack (see [1] for details).

Decision Procedures. JPF–SE uses the following decision procedures; they vary in the types of constraints they can handle and their efficiency. **Omega library** [9] – supports linear integer constraints. **CVC-Lite** [3] – supports integer, rational, bit vectors, and linear constraints. **YICES**[1] [4] – supports types and operations similar to those of CVC-Lite. **STP**[2] [2] – supports operations over bit vectors. In the JPF–SE interface, all integers are treated as bit vectors of size 32. Recently, we have also added a constraint solver, **RealPaver** [10], that supports linear and non-linear constraints over floating point numbers.

Generic Decision Procedure Interfaces. JPF–SE provides three interfaces with decision procedures. They vary in their degree of simplicity and efficiency. In the **file** based interface, the decision procedure is started for each query and a query is sent (and result received) via a file. This interface is the simplest to use and extend, but in general it is slow. With the **pipe** interface, the decision procedure is run concurrently with JPF and the communication is accomplished over a pipe. Although this does not suffer the process startup cost of the file approach it is harder to use and extend and it is operating system and language specific. With the **native** interface, JPF communicates directly with the decision procedure through a Java Native Interface (JNI). This mode is most difficult to implement among the three, but is usually much faster.

There are two optimizations available for the native interface: a table-based approach for efficient storing of the path condition that allows sharing of common sub-expressions and if the decision procedure supports incremental constraint analysis, the path condition is not sent all at once but rather just the new constraint that should be added/removed before checking satisfiability.

---

[1] SMT competition 2006 winner in all categories but one.
[2] SMT competition 2006 winner for QF_UFBV32 (Quantifier Free, Uninterpreted Functions, Bit Vector).

Experience with Different Decision Procedures. The interfaces for communications with the decision procedures is defined such that it is straightforward to connect a new tool. As a consequence, JPF–SE is well suited for performance comparisons across a wide array of examples. We show in Table 1 the runtime results (in mins:secs) for generating all reachable states while running JPF–SE with varying decision procedure configurations over two examples: TCAS from the Siemens Suite and on the TreeMap example from [13]. TCAS is small (only 2694 queries) but contains many constraints that are both satisfiable and unsatisfiable; TreeMap produces many queries (83592), but they are all satisfiable.

The preliminary results indicate that the native interfaces are the fastest and both the optimizations (where applicable) improve the performance further. For this reason YICES and STP are only used through the native interface.

3   Conclusion and Future Work

We have presented JPF–SE, an extension to JPF that enables symbolic execution of Java programs to be performed during model checking. JPF–SE uses JPF to generate and explore symbolic states and it uses different decision procedures to manipulate numeric constraints. JPF–SE has been applied to checking concurrent Java programs and to generating test inputs for Java classes. In the future we plan to extend JPF–SE's code instrumentation package, which currently handles only numeric values, to handle symbolic complex data structures. We also plan to add compositional reasoning for increased scalability and to interface with tools using the SMT-LIB standard [11] (through file and pipe).

Acknowledgements

We thank Sarfraz Khurshid and Radek Pelánek for contributing to this work.

References

1. S. Anand, C. Pasareanu, and W. Visser. Symbolic execution with abstract subsumption checking. In *Proc. SPIN*, 2006.
2. C. Cadar, V. Ganesh, P. M. Pawlowski, D. L. Dill, and D. R. Engler. Exe: Automatically generating inputs of death. In *Computer and Comm. Security*, 2006.
3. CVCL. http://www.cs.nyu.edu/acsys/cvcl/.
4. B. Dutertre and L. de Moura. A Fast Linear-Arithmetic Solver for DPLL(T). In *Proceedings of CAV*, volume 4144 of *LNCS*, pages 81–94. Springer-Verlag, 2006.
5. Java PathFinder. http://javapathfinder.sourceforge.net.
6. S. Khurshid, C. Pasareanu, and W. Visser. Generalized symbolic execution for model checking and testing. In *Proc. TACAS'03*, Warsaw, Poland, April 2003.
7. J. C. King. Symbolic execution and program testing. *Commun. ACM*, 19(7), 1976.
8. C. Pasareanu and W. Visser. Verification of java programs using symbolic execution and invariant generation. In *Proc of SPIN'04*, volume 2989 of *LNCS*, 2004.

9. W. Pugh. The Omega test: A fast and practical integer programming algorithm for dependence analysis. *Commun. ACM*, 31(8), Aug. 1992.
10. realPaver.   http://www.sciences.univ-nantes.fr/info/perso/permanents/granvil/ realpaver/.
11. SMT-LIB. http://combination.cs.uiowa.edu/smtlib/.
12. W. Visser, K. Havelund, G. Brat, S. J. Park, and F. Lerda. Model checking programs. *Automated Software Engineering Journal*, 10(2), April 2003.
13. W. Visser, C. Pasareanu, and R. Pelanek. Test input generation for java containers using state matching. In *Proc. ISSTA*, 2006.

A Symbolic Algorithm for
Optimal Markov Chain Lumping

Salem Derisavi

Department of Systems and Computer Engineering
Carleton University, Ottawa, Canada
derisavi@sce.carleton.ca

Abstract. Many approaches to tackle the state explosion problem of
Markov chains are based on the notion of lumpability, which allows computation of measures using the quotient Markov chain, which, in some
cases, has much smaller state space than the original one. We present,
for the first time, a symbolic algorithm and its implementation for the
lumping of Markov chains that are represented using Multi-Terminal Binary Decision Diagrams. The algorithm is optimal, i.e., generates the
smallest possible quotient Markov chain. Our experiments on various
configurations of two example models show that the algorithm (1) handles significantly larger state spaces than an explicit algorithm, (2) is in
the best case, faster than an efficient explicit algorithm while not prohibitively slower in the worst case, and (3) generates quotient Markov
chains that are several orders of magnitude smaller than ones generated
by a model-dependent symbolic lumping algorithm.

1 Introduction

Markov chains (MCs) are among the fundamental mathematical structures used
for performance and dependability modeling of communication and computer
systems. As the size of an MC usually grows exponentially with the size of
the corresponding high-level model, one often encounters the inevitable state
explosion problem, which often makes solution of the MC intractable. Many
approaches to alleviate or circumvent this problem are implicitly or explicitly
based on the notion of *lumpability* [17], which allows computation of measures
of the original MC using the solution of a *lumped* (or *quotient*) MC, which, in
some cases, is much smaller than the original one.

Even a lumped MC can be extremely large, and therefore, its *explicit* (e.g.,
sparse matrix) representation may not fit in memory. Symbolic data structures
such as Multi-Terminal Binary Decision Diagrams (MTBDDs) [7] and Matrix
Diagrams (MDs) [6] are two of the widely-used approaches that enable us to
represent large MCs using less memory than the explicit approach. Nowadays,
algorithms that directly generate symbolic representations of MCs from the high-
level model are commonplace.

In one form of classification, there are three types of lumping algorithms:
state-level, model-level, and *compositional*. State-level algorithms work directly

O. Grumberg and M. Huth (Eds.): TACAS 2007, LNCS 4424, pp. 139–154, 2007.

Table 1. Examples of previous work on lumping algorithms in probabilistic settings

	state-level	model-level	compositional
explicit	[9, 5]	[20] Stochastic Activity Networks	[12] Interactive Markov chains
symbolic	[14]	[10] state-sharing composed models [18] PRISM models	[11] Markov chains represented by matrix diagrams

on the MC (i.e., at the level of the states) and do not use information from the high-level model. They are *optimal*, i.e., they generate the smallest possible lumped MC, are restricted neither to a specific high-level formalism nor to a specific type of symmetry, and are often slower than the other two types.

Both model-level and compositional algorithms exploit information from the high-level model specification to generate lumped MCs. Neither types are optimal because the optimal lumping cannot be computed directly from the high-level model. Finally, both types address a specific (set of) formalism(s). Model-level algorithms are distinguished by the fact that they exploit a restricted type of user-specified symmetry while compositional algorithms apply a state-level algorithm to individual components of a compositional model.

Not all model-level algorithms can automatically find and exploit all types of symmetries. Therefore, the fact that the main source of lumpability is symmetry in the high-level model specification does *not* imply that model-level algorithms are in general preferred over state-level algorithms, as one may argue. Moreover, there are situations in which only state-level algorithms are applicable. For example, consider an MC that is transformed by a model checking algorithm.

Table 1 shows examples of previous work on lumping algorithms for stochastic/probabilistic models, e.g., Markov chains, Markov decision processes. It classifies them also based on whether they use explicit or symbolic representation. Fairly related to MC lumping, is lumping of non-probabilistic models, a.k.a. bisimulation minimization. Bouali et. al. [2] were the first to apply symbolic BDD-based techniques. Wimmer et. al. [22] improve upon [2] by presenting a general BDD-based algorithm that computes some of the popular bisimulations.

The shaded area in Table 1 indicates where our new algorithm fits. This paper gives, to our knowledge for the first time, a symbolic MTBDD-based MC lumping algorithm and its implementation. In [14], an algorithm based on DNBDDs (Decision-Node BDDs) is given without a concrete implementation or runtime analysis. Our algorithm is (1) symbolic, and hence, it can handle much larger state spaces than explicit algorithms, (2) optimal, i.e., generates the smallest possible lumped MC, (3) state-level, i.e., does not rely on the high-level model, and (4) faster than the efficient explicit algorithm of [9] in the best case, and not prohibitively slower in the worst case we experimented.

The rest of the paper is organized as follows: Section 2 gives an overview of CTMCs[1] (Continuous Time Markov Chains), lumpability of CTMCs, the explicit lumping algorithm of [9] which is the basis of our new algorithm, and MTBDDs. Sections 3 and 4 put forward the new contributions of this paper. The former

---

[1] Although the paper is focused on CTMCs, the algorithms can be adapted for DTMCs (Discrete Time Markov Chains) in a very straightforward manner.

explains how we transformed the explicit algorithm to a symbolic algorithm that is not so fast. The latter presents two techniques that dramatically improve the running time of our algorithm. In Section 5, we compare the running time of our symbolic algorithm, the explicit state-level algorithm of [9], and the symbolic model-level algorithm of [18] by applying them to several configurations of two example models. We finally conclude in Section 6.

2   Background

2.1   Notation, CTMC, and Lumpability

All matrices are real-valued and typeset with bold characters. All sets are finite and typeset with roman characters. We consider a CTMC $M = (S, \mathbf{R})$ with state space S and state transition rate matrix $\mathbf{R} : S \times S \to \mathbb{R}^{\geq 0}$ where $\mathbf{R}(s, s) = 0$ for all $s \in S$. The generator matrix $\mathbf{Q} : S \times S \to \mathbb{R}$ is defined as $\mathbf{Q}(s, s) = -\sum_{s' \in S} \mathbf{R}(s, s')$ and $\mathbf{Q}(s, t) = \mathbf{R}(s, t)$ for all $s, t \in S$ and $s \neq t$. Let $n = |S|$ and m denote the number of non-zero entries of $\mathbf{R}$. For a matrix $\mathbf{A}$ and $C \subseteq S$, we define $\mathbf{A}(s, C) = \sum_{s' \in C} \mathbf{A}(s, s')$ and $\mathbf{A}(C, s') = \sum_{s \in C} \mathbf{A}(s, s')$. Consider a partition $\Pi = \{C_1, \dots, C_{\tilde{n}}\}$ of S. Sets $C_1, \cdots, C_{\tilde{n}}$ are the equivalence classes, or in short, *classes* of Π. We use $[s]_{\Pi}$ to denote the class of Π that contains $s \in S$. Partition Π' is a *refinement* of Π (or *finer* than Π) if every class of Π' is a subset of some class of Π. In that case, Π is said to be *coarser* than Π'.

Often, the final goal of a CTMC analysis is not the computation of the steady-state or transient probability of its states. Instead, it is the computation of high-level measures such as performability. Many of those high-level measures can be computed using reward values associated with states (i.e., rate rewards) and the stationary and transient probability distribution [16]. In this paper, we do not concern ourselves with those details as they do not contribute to the main ideas of our algorithm. However, we will briefly explain how to adapt the algorithm to take rate rewards and initial probability distribution into account.

Sometimes, the desired measures can be obtained from a smaller (lumped) CTMC using less time and space. The lumped CTMC is constructed through a partition (or equivalence relation) on the state space of the original CTMC. For that to be possible, the original CTMC should satisfy a set of conditions with respect to that partition. Following [4], two of the most important sets of conditions (and the types of lumping they lead to) on the generator matrix $\mathbf{Q}$ are outlined in Definition 1. Often, it is necessary to check the lumpability conditions in terms of $\mathbf{R}$ instead of $\mathbf{Q}$. Theorem 1 serves that purpose. Finally, the lumped (or quotient) CTMC is obtained using Theorem 2. For more details on the properties of ordinary and exact lumping see [4].

Definition 1. *Consider a CTMC $M = (S, \mathbf{R})$, its corresponding $\mathbf{Q}$ matrix, and a partition Π of S. Then, with respect to Π, M is*
1. *ordinarily lumpable iff $\forall C, C' \in \Pi$, $s, \hat{s} \in C$: $\mathbf{Q}(s, C') = \mathbf{Q}(\hat{s}, C')$, and*
2. *exactly lumpable iff $\forall C, C' \in \Pi$, $s, \hat{s} \in C$: $\mathbf{Q}(C', s) = \mathbf{Q}(C', \hat{s})$.*

Theorem 1 (Theorem 2.1 of [8]). *Consider a CTMC $M = (S, \mathbf{R})$. With respect to a partition Π, M is*
1. *ordinarily lumpable iff $\forall C \neq C' \in \Pi$, $s, \hat{s} \in C$: $\mathbf{R}(s, C') = \mathbf{R}(\hat{s}, C')$.*
2. *exactly lumpable if $\forall C, C' \in \Pi$, $s, \hat{s} \in C$: $\mathbf{R}(s, S) = \mathbf{R}(\hat{s}, S) \wedge \mathbf{R}(C', s) = \mathbf{R}(C', \hat{s})$.*

Theorem 2 (Theorems 2.2 and 2.3 of [8]). *Let CTMC $M = (S, \mathbf{R})$ be ordinarily or exactly lumpable with respect to a partition Π of S. Then $\widetilde{M} = (\widetilde{S}, \widetilde{\mathbf{R}})$ is the lumped (or, quotient) CTMC such that*

$$\widetilde{S} = \{\text{arbitrary element of } C \,|\, C \in \Pi\}$$

$$\widetilde{\mathbf{R}}(\tilde{s}, \tilde{s}') = \begin{cases} \mathbf{R}(\tilde{s}, [\tilde{s}']_\Pi) & \text{(ordinary)} & \text{if } \tilde{s} \neq \tilde{s}' \\ \mathbf{R}([\tilde{s}]_\Pi, \tilde{s}') & \text{(exact)} & \text{if } \tilde{s} \neq \tilde{s}' \\ 0 & \text{(both)} & \text{if } \tilde{s} = \tilde{s}' \end{cases}$$

Note that although $\widetilde{S}$ depends on the arbitrarily selected element of each class of Π, all possible lumped CTMCs will be "equivalent".

2.2 Explicit State-Level Lumping Algorithm

The basis of our new symbolic algorithm is the efficient lumping algorithm of [9]. It is an optimal and explicit state-level algorithm for ordinary lumping. In [8], we extended the algorithm to Markov reward processes (i.e., CTMCs augmented with rate rewards and initial probability distribution) and also to exact lumping. Since we discuss both ordinary and exact lumping, we will use the extended version of [8] in this paper.

Figure 1(a) shows the explicit lumping algorithm. ExpLumpCTMC (Exp stands for explicit) takes the original CTMC M and returns the quotient CTMC $\widetilde{M}$. It works in two stages. First, ExpCoarsestPart computes the coarsest partition Π with respect to which M is lumpable by repetitive refinements of Π^{ini}. To extend our algorithm to Markov reward processes we only need to set the initial partition Π^{ini} such that all states with the same value (of rate reward or initial probability) are in the same class. If rate rewards and initial probability distribution are not considered, we set $\Pi^{\text{ini}} = \{S\}$. In the second stage (line 2), ExpCompQuot computes the quotient $\widetilde{M}$ according to Theorem 2.

ExpCoarsestPart maintains L, a list of potential *splitters*. Each refinement iteration of ExpCoarsestPart (line 3-5) refines Π with respect to a potential splitter B. ExpSplit splits each class C of Π into classes $C_1', \ldots, C_\alpha'$ (line 3-4) as follows. For ordinary lumping, the states of C are grouped based on their total outgoing rates to B (line 2_o of ExpComputeKeys) and for exact lumping they are grouped based on their total incoming rates from B (line 2_e). More formally,

$$\forall 1 \leq i, j \leq \alpha, s \in C_i', s' \in C_j' : \mathbf{k}(s) = \mathbf{k}(s') \Leftrightarrow i = j \tag{1}$$

The algorithm works correctly regardless of the selection of C_i' in line 5 of Ex-pSplit. If we choose C_i' to be the largest among $C_1', \ldots, C_\alpha'$, it is proved that the

ExpLumpCTMC(M)	ExpSplit(Π, B, L)
1 $\Pi :=$ ExpCoarsestPart($S, \mathbf{R}, \Pi^{\text{ini}}$)	1 **foreach** $C \in \Pi$
2 $(\widetilde{S}, \widetilde{\mathbf{R}}) :=$ ExpCompQuot($S, \mathbf{R}, \Pi$)	2 $\mathbf{k} :=$ ExpComputeKeys($\mathbf{R}, C, B$)
3 **return** $\widetilde{M} = (\widetilde{S}, \widetilde{\mathbf{R}})$	3 $\{C'_1, \dots, C'_\alpha\} :=$ refinement of C
	according to Eq. (1)
ExpCoarsestPart($S, \mathbf{R}, \Pi^{\text{ini}}$)	4 $\Pi := \Pi \cup \{C'_1, \dots, C'_\alpha\} - C$
1 $\Pi := \Pi^{\text{ini}}$	5 $L := L \cup \{C'_1, \dots, C'_\alpha\} -$ arbitrary C'_i
2 $L := \Pi^{\text{ini}}$	ExpComputeKeys($\mathbf{R}, C, B$)
3 **while** $L \neq \emptyset$	1 **foreach** $s \in C$
4 $B :=$ Pop(L)	2_o $\mathbf{k}(s) := \mathbf{R}(s, B)$
5 ExpSplit(Π, B, L)	2_e $\mathbf{k}(s) := \mathbf{R}(B, s)$
6 **return** Π	3 **foreach** $s \in S - C$
	4 $\mathbf{k}(s) := 0$
	5 **return** $\mathbf{k}$

(a) Explicit lumping algorithm

SymLumpCTMC(M)	SymComputeKeys($\mathcal{R}, C, \mathcal{B}$)
1 $\beta(\Pi) :=$ SymCoarsPart($\mathcal{S}, \mathcal{R}, \beta(\Pi^{\text{ini}})$)	1_o $\mathcal{R}_o :=$ Apply($\times, \mathcal{R},$ Apply($\times, C,$ Permute($\mathcal{B}$)))
2 $(\widetilde{\mathcal{R}}, \widetilde{\mathcal{S}}) :=$ SymCompQuot($\mathcal{S}, \mathcal{R}, \beta(\Pi)$)	1_e $\mathcal{R}_e :=$ Apply($\times, \mathcal{R},$ Apply($\times, \mathcal{B},$ Permute(C)))
3 **return** $\widetilde{M} = (\widetilde{\mathcal{R}}, \widetilde{\mathcal{S}})$	2_o $\mathcal{K}_o :=$ SumC($\mathcal{R}_o$)
SymCoarsestPart($\mathbf{R}, S, \beta(\Pi^{\text{ini}})$)	2_e $\mathcal{K}_e :=$ SumC($\mathcal{R}_e$)
1 $\beta(\Pi) := \beta(\Pi^{\text{ini}})$	3_o **return** $\mathcal{K}_o$
2 **for** $sc := 0$ **to** $|\Pi| - 1$	3_e **return** $\mathcal{K}_e$
3 $\mathcal{B} :=$ GetClass($\beta(\Pi), sc$)	SymCompQuot($\mathcal{S}, \mathcal{R}, \beta(\Pi)$)
4 SymSplit($\beta(\Pi), \mathcal{B}$)	1 $\widetilde{\mathcal{S}}(s) := 0$; $\widetilde{\mathcal{R}}(s, t) := 0$;
5 **return** $\beta(\Pi)$	2 **for** $c := 0$ **to** $|\Pi| - 1$
SymSplit($\beta(\Pi), \mathcal{B}$)	3_o $C_c :=$ GetClass($\beta(\Pi), c$)
1 **for** $c := 0$ **to** $|\Pi| - 1$	3_e $C_c :=$ Permute(GetClass($\beta(\Pi), c$))
2 $C :=$ GetClass($\beta(\Pi), c$)	4 $\mathcal{X}_c := \{$arbitrary element of $C_c\}$
3 $\mathcal{K} :=$ SymComputeKeys($\mathcal{R}, C, \mathcal{B}$)	5 $\widetilde{\mathcal{S}} :=$ Apply($+, \widetilde{\mathcal{S}}, \mathcal{X}_c$)
4 $T := \{$leaves of $\mathcal{K}\}$	6 $\mathcal{R}' :=$ Apply($\times, \widetilde{\mathcal{R}}, \widetilde{\mathcal{S}}$)
5 $\alpha := 1$	7 **for** $c := 0$ **to** $|\Pi| - 1$
6 **foreach** $x \in T$	8_o $\mathcal{R}'' :=$ SumC(Apply($\times, \mathcal{R}',$ Permute(C_c)))
7 $C'_\alpha :=$ Apply($=, \mathcal{K}, x$)	8_e $\mathcal{R}'' :=$ SumR(Apply($\times, \mathcal{R}',$ Permute(C_c)))
8 $\alpha := \alpha + 1$	9 $\mathcal{R}'' :=$ Apply($\times, \mathcal{R}'',$ Permute($\mathcal{X}_c$))
9 ReplaceClass($\beta(\Pi), c, C'_1$)	10 $\widetilde{\mathcal{R}} :=$ Apply($+, \widetilde{\mathcal{R}}, \mathcal{R}''$)
10 **for** $i := 2$ **to** α	11 **return** $(\widetilde{\mathcal{S}}, \widetilde{\mathcal{R}})$
11 AddClass($\beta(\Pi), C'_i$)	

(b) Symbolic lumping algorithm

Fig. 1. Explicit lumping algorithm for Markov chains

algorithm runs in $O(m \lg n)$ time [9]. The algorithm finishes when Π is refined with respect to all potential splitters. See [8] for more details.

2.3   Multi-Terminal Binary Decision Diagram

BDDs (Binary Decision Diagrams) [3] are a data structure for compact representation of binary functions of k binary variables, i.e., $\{0,1\}^k \rightarrow \{0,1\}$. MTB-DDs [7] are a variation of BDDs used to represent finite-ranged functions of k binary variables, i.e., $\{0,1\}^k \rightarrow A$ where A is a finite set.

MTBDDs are widely used to represent transition matrices of MCs and we follow that in this paper. To that purpose, the MTBDD uses $2L$ binary variables $vr_1, \dots, vr_L$ and $vc_1, \dots, vc_L$ that encode the row index and the column index, respectively. Although the variable ordering can be arbitrary, we consider the *interleaved ordering* in which the top-down order of the variables is $vr_1, vc_1, vr_2, vc_2, \dots, vr_L, vc_L$. Interleaved ordering often leads to smaller

MTBDDs for MCs that are generated from high-level models [13]. We denote the set of all possible row and column indices (states) by $S_r = \bigtimes_{i=1}^{L} vr_i$ and $S_c = \bigtimes_{i=1}^{L} vc_i$. We use calligraphic letters to denote the MTBDD representation of matrices and sets (described below). We denote an element of $\mathcal{R}$ by $\mathcal{R}(s,t)$ where $s \in S_r$ and $t \in S_c$ are encodings of states.

Our implementation is based on the CUDD package [21], a widely-used and efficient package for the manipulation of MTBDDs. In an MTBDD-based implementation, such as CUDD, the same set of MTBDD variables are used to represent all entities, that is, matrices and sets of states. In our symbolic algorithm, we will need to represent states using either the variable set $vr_1, \ldots, vr_L$ (*row encoding*) or $vc_1, \ldots, vc_L$ (*column encoding*). We define $\mathcal{B}$ representing a set B such that $\forall\, t \in S_c : \mathcal{B}(s,t) = [s \in B]$ (row encoding) or $\forall\, t \in S_r : \mathcal{B}(t,s) = [s \in B]$ (column encoding), in which $[s \in B] = 1$ if $s \in B$ and $[s \in B] = 0$ otherwise. Since $\mathcal{B}(s,t)$ (resp. $\mathcal{B}(t,s)$) does not depend on t in row (resp. column) encoding we use $\mathcal{B}(s)$ as a shorthand. PERMUTE($\mathcal{B}$), used in Fig. 1(b), switches the encoding of the set $\mathcal{B}$ from row encoding to column encoding or vice versa. By default, sets are represented using row encoding.

3   Transforming the Algorithm from Explicit to Symbolic

To transform the explicit algorithm of Figure 1(a) to a symbolic one, we need to replace both its explicit data structures and also its explicit operations with symbolic counterparts. We already know how to symbolically represent matrices and sets of states. In this section, we first present a new approach for the symbolic representation of partitions. Then, we show how to replace the set of splitters L by partition $\varPi$, thereby representing the set of splitters symbolically. Finally, we explain how the various explicit operations of Figure 1(a) are done symbolically.

3.1   Symbolic Representation of Partitions

The challenges in the symbolic representation of partition $\varPi$ are that 1) $|\varPi|$ can be very large, and 2) $\varPi$ is updated frequently during the execution of the algorithm and modifying a symbolic data structure in an "explicit" manner is often very inefficient. Our new symbolic approach for partition representation tries to address these challenges. Of equal importance are its properties that we exploit in Section 4 to improve the running time of our symbolic algorithm. Conceptually, our partition representation technique does not need to be based on a symbolic data structure. However, it will be very inefficient otherwise.

Before we explain our new approach, we give a quick overview of other studied approaches. The first obvious method is to store each class of a partition as a BDD. Another technique, given in [1], is to assign an extra set of BDD variables to denote class indices. In particular, $s \in C_i$ iff $\mathcal{P}(s,i) = 1$ where $\mathcal{P}$ is the BDD representation of $\varPi$. Yet another approach is to use a BDD $\mathcal{P}$ such that $\mathcal{P}(s,t) = 1$ iff $\exists\, C \in \varPi : s \in C \wedge t \in C$.

Representation. Let $\Pi = \{C_0, \ldots, C_{d-1}\}$ be a partition of $S \neq \emptyset^2$. We define a family of sets $\beta(\Pi) = \{P_0, \ldots, P_{k-1}, S\}$ to represent Π as follows: $s \in P_i$ $(0 \leq i < k)$ iff the ith bit of the binary representation of the index of $[s]_\Pi$ is one. In other words,

$$P_i = \bigcup_{i^{\text{th}} \text{ bit of } j \text{ is one}} C_j \quad \text{and} \quad S - P_i = \bigcup_{i^{\text{th}} \text{ bit of } j \text{ is zero}} C_j. \quad (2)$$

We will use (MT)BDDs to represent members of $\beta(\Pi)$. The important point here is that we can represent Π with $k+1 = \lceil \lg d \rceil + 1$ instead of d (MT)BDDs.

Example. Let $S = \{1, \ldots, 8\}$, $\Pi = \{C_0, C_1, C_2, C_3\}$, $C_0 = \{2, 3, 8\}$, $C_1 = \{1\}$, $C_2 = \{4, 7\}$, and $C_3 = \{5, 6\}$. Then, $\beta(\Pi) = \{P_0, P_1, S\}$ in which $P_0 = \{1, 5, 6\}$ and $P_1 = \{4, 5, 6, 7\}$.

Partition Manipulation. In the explicit algorithm, we access Π through getting its classes and update Π through adding/removing classes to/from it. In the following, we describe how to symbolically perform those manipulations by one access procedure GETCLASS, and two update procedures REPLACECLASS, and ADDCLASS. Let Π' be the modified partition after an update procedure is performed on Π. Using Eq. (2) to compute the symbolic representation of Π', i.e., $\beta(\Pi')$, after each update procedure would take $O(2^k)$ set operations. In the following, we show how to compute it directly from the symbolic representation of Π, i.e., $\beta(\Pi)$ using only $O(k)$ set operations.

1. GETCLASS$(\beta(\Pi), j)$ returns C_j. Let $(b_{k-1} \cdots b_1 b_0)_2$ be the binary representation of j $(0 \leq j < d)$. Then, using Eq. (2), we have

$$\text{GETCLASS}(\beta(\Pi), j) = C_j = \bigcap_{i=0}^{k-1} D_i \quad \text{where } D_i = \begin{cases} S - P_i & \text{if } b_i = 0 \\ P_i & \text{if } b_i = 1 \end{cases} \quad (3)$$

   Using GETCLASS, line 1 of EXPSPLIT is symbolically performed in lines 1-2 of SYMSPLIT.

2. REPLACECLASS$(\beta(\Pi), l, C_l')$ replaces $C_l \in \Pi$ with C_l' such that $\Pi' = (\Pi - \{C_l\}) \uplus \{C_l'\} = \{C_0, \ldots, C_{l-1}, C_l', C_{l+1}, \ldots C_{d-1}\}^3$. We have $S' = (S - C_l) \uplus C_l'$, and by Eq. (2),

$$P_i' = \begin{cases} P_i & \text{if } i\text{th bit of } l \text{ is zero} \\ (P_i - C_l) \uplus C_l' & \text{if } i\text{th bit of } l \text{ is one} \end{cases}$$

3. ADDCLASS$(\beta(\Pi), C_d)$ adds C_d to Π where C_d is non-empty set disjoint with all members of Π. Obviously, we have $S' = S \uplus C_d$, and by Eq. (2),

$$P_i' = \begin{cases} P_i & \text{if } i\text{th bit of } d \text{ is zero} \\ P_i \uplus C_d & \text{if } i\text{th bit of } d \text{ is one} \end{cases}$$

---

[2] Although in a strict mathematical sense, the classes of a partition are not ordered, we assign them a total order here.

[3] $\uplus$ is the disjoint union operation.

For $d = 2^k$, assume $P_k = \emptyset$. Using REPLACECLASS and a sequence of AD-DCLASS operations, line 4 of EXPSPLIT is symbolically performed in lines 9-11 of SYMSPLIT.

3.2 Replacing Explicit L by Symbolic Π

In our new symbolic algorithm, we need to have a symbolic representation of L that is efficient to update. Knowing that (1) similar to Π, L is a set of sets of states, and (2) updates of L is very similar to updates of Π (compare lines 4 and 5 of EXPSPLIT), we will show how we have modified our algorithm such that we do not need to explicitly store L. Instead, we use the symbolic representation of Π and an index to emulate a list of potential splitters.

Consider Fig. 1. We have removed L from EXPCOARSESTPART (lines 2-5) and EXPSPLIT (line 5) and replaced it by an index sc in SYMCOARSESTPART (lines 2-3). In line 2 of SYMCOARSESTPART, sc iterates through all classes of Π. During the running time of the algorithm, classes are possibly added to (the end of) Π. Therefore, $\mathcal{B}$, in line 3 of SYMCOARSESTPART, will take on the value of all those new classes, one at a time. Note that the set of potential splitters processed by SYMSPLIT may be different from the one processed by EXPSPLIT. However, we will prove that SYMCOARSESTPART still works correctly by showing that the different sets of splitters that EXPCOARSESTPART and SYMCOARSESTPART see have the same refinement effect on Π.

Lemma 1. *Assume $C \subseteq S$ and $\{C'_1, \ldots, C'_\alpha\}$ be a partition of C. Then, splitting a partition Π of S with respect to any α members of $T = \{C, C'_1, \ldots, C'_\alpha\}$ leads to the same refinement of Π.*

Proof. We give the proof for ordinary lumping. The arguments for exact lumping are similar. According to Eq. (1), for any splitter $B \in T$, $\mathbf{R}(s, B)$ determines how the blocks of Π are partitioned. Moreover, for any state $s \in S$, we have $\mathbf{R}(s, C'_1) + \cdots + \mathbf{R}(s, C'_\alpha) = \mathbf{R}(s, C)$. Therefore, given any α terms of the equality, the $(\alpha + 1)$-st term is implicit. Hence, splitting with respect to any $B \in T$ does not further refine a partition that has already been refined with respect to the other α members of T.

Theorem 3. *The sequence of splitters seen by SYMCOARSESTPART leads to the correct refinement of Π.*

Proof. We need to show that each time a block $\mathcal{C}$ is partitioned into $C'_1, \ldots, C'_\alpha$, at least α members of $\{\mathcal{C}, C'_1, \ldots, C'_\alpha\}$ have already been or will be seen by SYM-COARSESTPART. Assume the algorithm is at the beginning of line 9 of SYM-SPLIT. There are two cases. If $sc \leq c$, then SYMCOARSESTPART has not yet seen $\mathcal{C}$ as a splitter, and lines 9-11 replace $\mathcal{C}$ with $\{C'_1, \ldots, C'_\alpha\}$. All those α sets will be seen as splitters in future iterations of SYMCOARSESTPART. If $sc > c$, then SYMCOARSESTPART has already used $\mathcal{C}$ as a splitter, and lines 9-11 add $\alpha - 1$ sets, i.e., $\{C'_2, \ldots, C'_\alpha\}$, to the end of Π. All of those sets will be seen by SYMCOARSESTPART in its future iterations.

3.3 Symbolic Procedures: SymComputeKeys and SymSplit

Let $B, C \subseteq S$. EXPCOMPUTEKEYS computes $\mathbf{R}(s, B)$ for ordinary lumping and $\mathbf{R}(B, s)$ for exact lumping for each $s \in C$. In order to compute $\mathbf{R}(s, B)$ and $\mathbf{R}(B, s)$ symbolically, we define $\mathcal{R}_o^{C,B}$ and $\mathcal{R}_e^{C,B}$ as follows:

$$\mathcal{R}_o^{C,B}(s,t) = r \text{ iff } \mathcal{R}(s,t) = r \wedge C(s) = 1 \wedge B(t) = 1 \quad \text{(ordinary lumping)}$$
$$\mathcal{R}_e^{C,B}(s,t) = r \text{ iff } \mathcal{R}(s,t) = r \wedge B(s) = 1 \wedge C(t) = 1 \quad \text{(exact lumping)}$$

In other words, $\mathcal{R}_o^{C,B}$ (resp. $\mathcal{R}_e^{C,B}$) is the same as $\mathcal{R}$ except that its set of rows and columns are restricted to C and B (resp. B and C) respectively. $\mathcal{R}_o^{C,B}$ and $\mathcal{R}_e^{C,B}$ are computed in lines 1_o and 1_e of SYMCOMPUTEKEYS, the symbolic version of EXPCOMPUTEKEYS. SYMCOMPUTEKEYS uses APPLY$(\bowtie, \mathcal{X}, \mathcal{Y})$ which is provided by the CUDD package and returns an MTBDD $\mathcal{Z}$ such that $\mathcal{Z}(s,t) = \mathcal{X}(s,t) \bowtie \mathcal{Y}(s,t)$ where $\bowtie$ is an arithmetic or logical operator. For logical operators, APPLY returns an MTBDD with only 0 and 1 terminals.

Now, we define MTBDDs $\mathcal{K}_o^{C,B}(s,t)$ and $\mathcal{K}_e^{C,B}(s,t)$ as follows:

$$\forall t \in S_c : \mathcal{K}_o^{C,B}(s,t) = \sum_{t' \in S_c} \mathcal{R}_o^{C,B}(s,t') = \sum_{t' \in B} \mathcal{R}_o^{C,B}(s,t') = \mathbf{R}(s,B)$$
$$\forall s \in S_r : \mathcal{K}_e^{C,B}(s,t) = \sum_{s' \in S_r} \mathcal{R}_e^{C,B}(s',t) = \sum_{s' \in B} \mathcal{R}_e^{C,B}(s',t) = \mathbf{R}(B,t).$$

Since $\mathcal{K}_o^{C,B}(s,t) = \mathbf{R}(s,B)$ and $\mathcal{K}_e^{C,B}(s,t) = \mathbf{R}(B,t)$, $\mathcal{K}_o^{C,B}$ and $\mathcal{K}_e^{C,B}$ are in fact the MTBDD representations of $\mathbf{k}$ in Section 2.2. Thus, they are the key to partition C into $\{C_1', \dots, C_\alpha'\}$ according to Eq. (1). They are computed symbolically using SUMC and SUMR. For an MTBDD $\mathcal{A}$, SUMC$(\mathcal{A})$ returns $\mathcal{A}'$ such that $\forall t \in S_c : \mathcal{A}'(s,t) = \sum_{t' \in S_c} \mathcal{A}(s,t')$. Similarly, SUMR$(\mathcal{A})$ returns $\mathcal{A}'$ such that $\forall s \in S_r : \mathcal{A}'(s,t) = \sum_{s' \in S_r} \mathcal{A}(s',t)$. SUMC and SUMR are implemented using Cudd addExistAbstract function of the CUDD package. Lines 4-8 of SYMSPLIT show how to symbolically derive $C_1', \dots, C_\alpha'$ from C. Line 4 is done using a depth first traversal of $\mathcal{K}$.

Note that if there is no transition from any state in C (resp. B) to any state in B (resp. C), then $\mathcal{R}_o^{C,B}$ (resp. $\mathcal{R}_e^{C,B}$), and therefore, $\mathcal{K}_o^{C,B}$ (resp. $\mathcal{K}_e^{C,B}$) are zero-valued MTBDDs. Hence, C will not be split. The second technique in Section 4 exploits that observation to improve the running time of the symbolic algorithm.

So far, we have transformed all data structures and operations of the explicit procedures of Figure 1(a) to symbolic ones in their corresponding symbolic procedures. That gives us the completely symbolic algorithm of Figure 1(b).

4 Improving the Symbolic Algorithm Running Time

The properties of our partition representation method enable us to improve the running time of the symbolic algorithm developed in Section 3. In this section, we present two techniques T1 and T2 that utilize those properties. Both techniques use relatively small additional memory to gain significant speed improvements.

Based on the combination of the techniques, we distinguish three versions of our algorithm: V1 uses neither techniques, V2 uses T1 only, and V3 uses both T1 and T2. In the following, we present the arguments only for ordinary lumping and they are straightforwardly adaptable to the case of exact lumping. We will compare the performance of the three versions in Section 5.

4.1   T1: Computing GetClass($\beta(\Pi), j + 1$) from GetClass($\beta(\Pi), j$)

The main loops of SYMCOARSESTPART and SYMSPLIT compute all classes of Π using GETCLASS. T1 is an algorithm that computes those classes more efficiently than naively applying Eq. (3) for each class. To do so, T1 exploits the similarity between the computation of all pairs of consecutive classes of Π.

Figure 2 shows the *Class Computation Tree* (CCT) for Π. The tree shows the sequence of set operations that GETCLASS executes for all classes of Π according to Eq. (3)[4]. It has $k + 1$ levels numbered top-down from 0 to k, and hence, has at most $2^{k+1} - 1$ nodes. We denote the root node by r. A non-root node $v \neq r$ is connected to its parent $p(v)$ by an edge with label $e(v) \subseteq S$. For a non-leaf node u at level i, we denote its left and right children by u_l and u_r. We define $e(u_l) = S - P_i$ and $e(u_r) = P_i$. A path from r to v corresponds to a set expression $E(v)$ defined recursively as follows:

$$E(r) = S, \text{ and } E(v) = E(p(v)) \cap e(v). \tag{4}$$

For example, in Fig. 2, we have $E(u') = S \cap (S - P_0) = (S - P_0)$ and $E(v_0) = S \cap (S - P_0) \cap \ldots \cap (S - P_{k-1})$. Indexing the leaf nodes from left to right starting from 0, we observe that for a leaf node v_j with index j, $E(v_j)$ yields the jth class of Π, i.e., $E(v_j) = C_j = \text{GETCLASS}(\beta(\Pi), j)$.

For any leaf node v, the number of set intersections in $E(v)$, and hence, the number of times GETCLASS performs set intersection, is k. Hence, calling GETCLASS for all classes of Π requires $k \cdot d = \Theta(d \lg d)$ set intersections in which $d = |\Pi|$.

Now consider two classes $C_j, C_{j'} \in \Pi$ ($j' = j + 1$ is a special case) and their corresponding leaf nodes v_j and $v_{j'}$ (See Figure 2). We observe that set expressions $E(v_j)$ and $E(v_{j'})$ have a common prefix subexpression which is determined by the lowest common ancestor node x of v_j and $v_{j'}$. Hence, by storing $E(x)$ at x during the computation of $C_j = E(v_j)$, we can compute $C_{j'} = E(v_{j'})$ with smaller number of set intersections than what would be necessary for its computation from scratch using Eq. (3).

Making the above observation, we propose the following method to compute all classes of Π in order of their indices: perform a depth first traversal of the CCT such that the left subtree is visited before the right subtree. At each non-root node v compute $E(v)$ using Eq. (4) and store it as an MTBDD. The number of set intersections performed is the number of edges of the CCT which is at most $2^{k+1} - 2 \in \Theta(d)$. Note that we do not need to store $E(v)$ for all nodes; storing one per level suffices.

In summary, T1 reduces the number of set operations necessary to compute all classes of Π from $\Theta(d \lg d)$ to $\Theta(d)$ using $k + 1$ extra MTBDDs.

---

[4] The tree is not generated or stored by the algorithm.

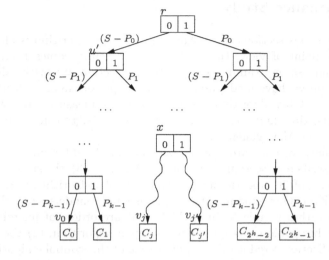

Fig. 2. Class Computation Tree (CCT)

4.2   T2: Fast Detection and Skipping of Stable Classes

SYMSPLIT splits each class $C \in \Pi$ with respect to the splitter $\mathcal{B}$. However, if there is no transition from any state in C to any state in $\mathcal{B}$, then C will not be split into smaller subclasses. Therefore, executing lines 2-11 of SYMSPLIT can be skipped for classes such as C. We call C *stable* with respect to $\mathcal{B}$.

T2 is a technique for efficient detection of stable classes. It enables the main loop of SYMSPLIT to skip over those classes, thereby reducing SYMSPLIT's running time. CTMCs generated from high-level models often have sparse transition matrices. For such CTMCs, the ratio of stable classes (with respect to a given $\mathcal{B}$) to the total number of classes is often close to 1. Therefore, T2 yields a considerable speedup.

Let B' be the set of states that have at least one transition to any state in B, i.e., $B' = \{s' | \exists s \in B, \mathbf{R}(s', s) \neq 0\}$. Observe that C is stable with respect to B iff $B' \cap C = \emptyset$. Therefore, the problem is reduced to evaluating whether $B' \cap C = \emptyset$. If $B' = \emptyset$ every class $C \in \Pi$ is stable with respect to B. In the following, we assume that $B' \neq \emptyset$.

Using the *modified CCT*, a slight modification of the CCT, we can efficiently compute $B' \cap C$ for all $C \in \Pi$. The modified CCT uses the following equation to compute the set expression $E'(v)$ corresponding to a node v: $E'(r) = B'$ and $E'(v) = E'(p(v)) \cap e(v)$ for $v \neq r$. Thus, $E'(v_j) = B' \cap C_j$ for a leaf node v_j with index j. Finally, checking for emptiness of an MTBDD takes constant time.

A significant improvement is achieved by observing that if $E'(v)$ is empty, so is $E'(v')$ for all descendants v' of v. Thus, we can prune the tree at node v, thereby saving time on its traversal.

5   Performance Study

While the previous sections show that our symbolic algorithm is efficient from a theoretical point of view, the evidence of its utility comes from its implementation and use on example models. In this section, we briefly describe the implementation we have made, and compare its performance with implementations of other related algorithms. The performance measures that we compare are mainly the time and space requirements of the algorithms and the size of lumped MCs that they generate.

In particular, we compare the performance of the different versions of the algorithm described in Section 4 (that is, V1, V2, and V3), the state-level explicit algorithm (EA) of [9], and the model-level symbolic algorithm of Kwiatkowska et. al. [18] (KA). Our experiments on two example models show that (1) our symbolic algorithm is able to lump MCs that are orders of magnitude larger than what is lumpable using an explicit lumping algorithm, (2) the techniques explained in Section 4 reduce the running time of the symbolic algorithm by up to 3 orders of magnitude, (3) in the best case we tried, V3, the fastest version of our symbolic algorithm outperforms EA, and in the worst case, it is not prohibitively slower than EA, and (4) KA is a few orders of magnitude faster than V3 while V3 generates lumped MCs that are (sometimes several) orders of magnitude smaller.

5.1   Implementation and Example Models

To generate both the MTBDD and sparse matrix representations of the input Markov chains, we use the probabilistic model checking tool PRISM [15]. All the code involved in the experiments was compiled using gcc 3.4.4. All experiments were conducted on a Pentium 4 2.66 GHz CPU with 1 GB of RAM.

We consider two example models from the literature to study the performance of the algorithms: A fault-tolerant parallel computer system (FPCS) [19] and a peer-to-peer (P2P) protocol based on BitTorrent [18]. For the first model, we converted the SAN (Stochastic Activity Network) specification to the PRISM specification. For the second model, we used the PRISM specification given in http://www.cs.bham.ac.uk/~dxp/prism/casestudies/peer2peer.php.

Both models have two parameters N_1 and N_2. For FPCS, they denote the number of computers in the system and the number of memory modules in each computer, respectively. For P2P, they represent the number of clients and the number of blocks of the file to be transmitted, respectively.

5.2   Results

Comparison of V1, V2, V3, and EA. EA is theoretically the fastest explicit state-level lumping algorithm given so far[5]. We applied the ordinary lumping algorithm of V1, V2, V3, and EA on a number of configurations of FPCS and

---
[5] We are not aware of a study that compares the practical performance of various explicit state-level algorithms.

Table 2. Performance Results

(a) Performance comparison of symbolic and explicit algorithms

	Config (N_1,N_2)	# of states		# of nodes		total running time (sec)				peak # of nodes		
		n	$\tilde{n}$	η	$\tilde{\eta}$	V1	V2	V3	EA	V1	V2	V3
FPCS	(2,2)	1.58e4	703	5960	4979	1.83e2	4.00e1	7.50e0	5.20e-1	2.58e4	2.58e4	2.75e4
	(3,1)	2.30e4	969	14370	9079	1.00e3	1.90e2	2.90e1	8.80e-1	6.42e4	6.42e4	6.86e4
	(2,3)	2.57e5	2145	9114	13731	1.20e4	1.50e3	7.80e1	1.00e1	6.82e4	6.82e4	7.09e4
	(3,2)	1.89e6	9139	34122	43134	TL	TL	4.20e3	9.40e1	TL	4.68e5	4.78e5
	(2,4)	3.80e6	5151	12314	34318	TL	2.60e4	5.80e2	1.80e2	TL	1.62e5	1.65e5
	(2,5)	5.26e7	10585	15468	70809	TL	2.30e5	3.00e3	ML	TL	3.49e5	3.54e5
	(3,3)	1.24e8	47905	53177	151368	TL	TL	1.15e5	ML	TL	TL	2.56e6
P2P	(3,5)	3.28e4	56	2451	1751	3.40e0	2.72e0	1.70e0	8.38e-1	2.36e4	2.73e4	2.83e4
	(4,5)	1.05e6	126	11941	5914	8.04e1	5.17e1	2.03e1	3.84e1	1.18e5	1.43e5	1.50e5
	(5,5)	3.36e7	196	26266	10975	7.43e2	4.13e2	1.37e2	ML	3.63e5	4.44e5	4.68e5
	(6,5)	1.07e9	266	40591	20212	3.64e3	1.91e3	5.56e2	ML	8.56e5	1.06e6	1.12e6
	(7,5)	3.44e10	336	54916	26182	1.18e4	6.22e3	1.64e3	ML	1.54e6	1.83e6	1.93e6
	(8,5)	1.10e11	406	69241	36153	4.43e4	2.53e4	1.14e4	ML	2.65e6	3.37e6	3.51e6

(b) Comparison of V3, Kwiatkowska's algorithm and their combination

Model	Config (N_1,N_2)	# of states			# of nodes			running times (sec)		
		n	$\tilde{n}_{\mathrm{KA}}$	$\tilde{n}_{\mathrm{V3}}$	η	$\tilde{\eta}_{\mathrm{KA}}$	$\tilde{\eta}_{\mathrm{V3}}$	V3	KA	Comb.
P2P	(3,5)	3.28e4	5.98e3	56	2451	12518	1751	1.70e0	1.15e-1	2.15e0
	(4,5)	1.05e6	5.24e4	126	11941	42166	5914	2.03e1	4.90e-1	2.56e1
	(5,5)	3.36e7	3.77e5	196	26266	101630	10975	1.37e2	1.30e0	1.68e2
	(6,5)	1.07e9	2.32e6	266	40591	189704	20212	5.56e2	3.05e0	7.09e2
	(7,5)	3.44e10	1.26e7	336	54916	306123	26182	1.64e3	5.11e0	2.26e3
	(8,5)	1.10e11	6.15e7	406	69241	449599	36153	1.14e4	9.17e0	1.48e4

P2P. The results are given in Table 2(a). Columns 3 to 6 give the number of states and MTBDD nodes of the original (input) and the lumped (output) MCs. Times shown in columns 7 to 10 include both the partition computation and the quotient construction times. The last three columns give the maximum number of live MTBDD nodes during the runtime of V1, V2, and V3. ML (Memory Limit) and TL (Time Limit) mean that the corresponding data is not available because the algorithm ran out of memory and its running time exceeded 3 days ($\approx 2.5 \times 10^5$ seconds), respectively.

Since all algorithms are optimal, they generate the same lumped MCs, and for V1-V3, with the same MTBDD representations. It has been observed (e.g., see [13]) that lumping often increases the size of the MTBDD representation, i.e., $\eta < \tilde{\eta}$. The reason is that the structure regularity of the MTBDD of the lumped MC is lost. In our experiments, that holds true when $\tilde{n}$ is sufficiently large.

From Table 2(a) we can see how effective T1 and T2, the improvement techniques described in Section 4, are. Based on all experiments, V3 is faster than V2 by a factor of 1.6 to 76 and V2 is faster than V1 by a factor of 1.3 to 10. Since T1 saves time on computing all classes of Π and T2 does so by skipping stable classes of Π, their effects grow as $|\Pi|$ and $\tilde{n}$ increase (note that $|\Pi| \leq \tilde{n}$ during the runtime of the algorithm). That is the reason why the speedup factors are less for P2P than FPCS and for each model the speedup factors increase as $\tilde{n}$ grows. Overall, the combination of T1 and T2 achieve a speedup of 2 to 700, depending on the input MC. Note that their combined memory overhead, in terms of the number of alive nodes, is very low (at most 32%) relative to the speedup they cause.

Those improvements significantly pale the speed disadvantage that V3 has compared to EA. We observed that if the structure of input MTBDD is sufficiently regular and the CTMC is significantly lumpable, V3 outperforms EA. In configuration (4,5) of P2P, V3 is 1.9 times faster than EA. We anticipate that the ratio of V3's speed to EA's would increase for larger P2P models if EA did not run out of memory. The reason is that V3's running time is growing slower than n while EA's would increase at least as fast as n. Although V3 is 45 times slower than EA on one of the experiments, its main advantage comes from its ability to handle MCs that are several orders of magnitude larger.

SYMCOMPQUOT of Fig. 1(b) has two explicit loops over states of the lumpable partition. Therefore, one may not consider it as a "very symbolic" algorithm or may have suspicion about its efficiency. Based on our measurements (not shown in Table 2(a)), SYMCOMPQUOT never takes more than 23% of the total running time of the symbolic algorithm for the FPCS model. The corresponding number for the P2P model is 6%.

Comparison and Combination of Two Symbolic Algorithms. Finally, we compare the performance of V3 against another symbolic algorithm. We are not aware of any other *state-level* symbolic lumping algorithm. However, we think that it is informative to compare our algorithm to the MTBDD-based *model-level* lumping algorithm of Kwiatkowska et. al. [18]. Kwiatkowska's algorithm (KA) exploits a special type of symmetry, i.e., symmetry among identical components.

Table 2(b) shows the results of our experiments with V3 and KA[6]. In general, $\tilde{n}_{KA} \neq \tilde{n}_{V3}$ since KA is not optimal, and therefore, may not generate the smallest quotient CTMC for all inputs. Based on the results given in Table 2(b), we observe that (1) KA is a few orders of magnitude faster than our algorithm because it gets symmetry information from the high-level specification of the model and not from the CTMC, (2) $\tilde{n}_{V3}$ is (sometimes, several) orders of magnitude smaller than $\tilde{n}_{KA}$ because V3 is optimal, (3) V3 may additionally lead to a much smaller MTBDD representation ($\tilde{\eta}_{KA} \gg \tilde{\eta}_{V3}$) as is the case for all instances of P2P model we tried. Obviously, (2) generally holds for models that are lumpable due to symmetries other than those exploited by KA. For models that have no symmetries but those exploitable by KA, KA is much more efficient than V3 in that it would generate the (same) smallest quotient MC much faster.

In explicit lumping algorithms, we observe the same trend when comparing state-level and model-level algorithms: the former are slower but may generate much smaller quotient CTMCs. Since the running time of explicit state-level algorithms are at least linear in n, it will be beneficial to combine the the state-level and the model-level algorithms, i.e., to apply them in sequence. First, the

---

[6] We did not include the FPCS model in Table 2(b) because KA does not currently support exploiting the hierarchical symmetries of the FPCS model. However, we believe that the theory and implementation of KA are extendible to hierarchical symmetries in a straightforward manner as in [10].

model-level algorithm quickly produces a partially lumped CTMC. Then, the state-level algorithm takes the result and produces the optimally lumped CTMC much faster than what it would take the state-level algorithm to optimally lump the original CTMC.

The last column of Table 2(b) shows the total running time of applying KA and V3 in sequence. As we can see, in the case of symbolic algorithms, the combination is always slower than V3. That is not a surprising result because the running time of a symbolic state-level algorithm (e.g., V3) does not depend on the size of the state space of the input CTMC. Rather, it depends on the structure regularity and the number of nodes of the input MTBDD; the former is diminished and the latter is increased by the model-level algorithm ($\widetilde{\eta}_{KA} \gg \eta$).

6 Conclusion and Future Work

In this paper, we developed the first symbolic state-level lumping algorithm for Markov chains using a new partition representation technique whose properties enabled us to improve the running time of the algorithm by up to three orders of magnitude. In the worst case we experimented, our symbolic algorithm was less than two orders of magnitude slower than an efficient explicit algorithm. In the best case, the former was even faster by a factor of 1.9. The natural strength of our algorithm is its ability to lump CTMCs with state spaces that are several orders of magnitude larger than what the explicit algorithm can.

We also compared our state-level symbolic algorithm with Kwiatkowska's symbolic model-level algorithm. We observed in our experiments that although our algorithm is a few orders of magnitude slower, it generates lumped CTMCs that are several orders of magnitude smaller. Finally, we combined the two symbolic algorithms. Unlike the explicit case, the combination is always slower than the state-level algorithm due to loss of structure regularity and increase in size of the MTBDD representation by the model-level algorithm.

There is no study that shows the effect of the various partition representation methods on the performance of (Markov chain) lumping algorithms. This paper is a first step toward that study. We also would like to investigate whether our partition representation method benefits other symbolic algorithms. Finally, we intend to integrate the algorithm into PRISM.

Acknowledgments. We would like to thank Holger Hermanns for pointing out some of the previous work, Dave Parker, Gethin Norman, and Marta Kwiatkowska for their technical support with the PRISM tool and and the P2P model, Shravan Gaonkar for his helpful comments on the manuscript, and last but not least, the reviewers for their very useful feedback.

References

1. E. Böde, M. Herbstritt, H. Hermanns, S. Johr, T. Peikenkamp, R. Pulungan, R. Wimmer, and B. Becker. Compositional performability evaluation for STATE-MATE. In *Proc. of QEST*, USA, Sep. 2006.

2. A. Bouali and R. de Simone. Symbolic bisimulation minimisation. In *Proc. of CAV*, volume 663 of *LNCS*, pages 96–108. Springer, 1992.
3. R. E. Bryant. Graph-based algorithms for Boolean function manipulation. *IEEE Trans. Comp.*, 35(8):677–691, Aug. 1986.
4. P. Buchholz. Exact and ordinary lumpability in finite Markov chains. *Journal of Applied Probability*, 31:59–74, 1994.
5. P. Buchholz. Efficient computation of equivalent and reduced representations for stochastic automata. *Int. Journal of Comp. Sys. Sci. & Eng.*, 15(2):93–103, 2000.
6. G. Ciardo and A. S. Miner. A data structure for the efficient Kronecker solution of GSPNs. In *Proc. of PNPM*, pages 22–31, 1999.
7. E. Clarke, M. Fujita, P. McGeer, K. McMillan, J. Yang, and X. Zhao. Multiterminal binary decision diagrams: An efficient data structure for matrix representation. *Formal Methods in System Design*, 10(2/3):149–169, 1997.
8. S. Derisavi. *Solution of Large Markov Models Using Lumping Techniques and Symbolic Data Structures*. PhD thesis, U. of Illinois at Urbana-Champaign, 2005.
9. S. Derisavi, H. Hermanns, and W. H. Sanders. Optimal state-space lumping in Markov chains. *Information Processing Letters*, 87(6):309–315, September 2003.
10. S. Derisavi, P. Kemper, and W. H. Sanders. Symbolic state-space exploration and numerical analysis of state-sharing composed models. *Linear Algebra and Its Applications*, 386:137–166, July 15, 2004.
11. S. Derisavi, P. Kemper, and W. H. Sanders. Lumping matrix diagram representations of markovian models. In *Proc. of DSN*, pages 742–751, Japan, 2005.
12. H. Hermanns. *Interactive Markov Chains and the Quest for Quantified Quality*, volume 2428 of *LNCS*. Springer, 2002.
13. H. Hermanns, J. Meyer-Kayser, and M. Siegle. Multi terminal binary decision diagrams to represent and analyse continuous time Markov chains. In *Proc. of 3rd Meeting on Numerical Solution of Markov Chains (NSMC)*, pages 188–207, 1999.
14. H. Hermanns and M. Siegle. Bisimulation algorithms for stochastic process algebras and their bdd-based implementation. In *ARTS*, pages 244–264, 1999.
15. A. Hinton, M. Kwiatkowska, G. Norman, and D. Parker. PRISM: A tool for automatic verification of probabilistic systems. In H. Hermanns and J. Palsberg, editors, *Proc. of TACAS '06*, volume 3920 of *LNCS*, pages 441–444. Springer, 2006.
16. R. A. Howard. *Dynamic Probabilistic Systems, Volume II: Semi-Markov and Decision Processes*. Wiley, New York, 1971.
17. J. G. Kemeney and J. L. Snell. *Finite Markov Chains*. D. Van Nostrand Company, Inc., 1960.
18. M. Kwiatkowska, G. Norman, and D. Parker. Symmetry reduction for probabilistic model checking. In T. Ball and R. Jones, editors, *Proc. of CAV*, volume 4114 of *LNCS*, pages 234–248. Springer-Verlag, 2006.
19. W. H. Sanders and L. M. Malhis. Dependability evaluation using composed SAN-based reward models. *J. of Para. and Dist. Comp.*, 15(3):238–254, July 1992.
20. W. H. Sanders and J. F. Meyer. Reduced base model construction methods for stochastic activity networks. *IEEE J. on Selected Areas in Comm.*, 9(1):25–36, Jan. 1991.
21. F. Somenzi. CUDD: Colorado University decision diagram package. public software, Colorado Univeristy, Boulder, http://vlsi.colorado.edu/ fabio/.
22. R. Wimmer, M. Herbstritt, H. Hermanns, K. Strampp, and B. Becker. Sigref - a symbolic bisimulation tool box. In *Proc. of ATVA '06*, China, 2006. to appear.

Flow Faster: Efficient Decision Algorithms for Probabilistic Simulations[*]

Lijun Zhang[1], Holger Hermanns[1], Friedrich Eisenbrand[2],
and David N. Jansen[3,4]

[1] Department of Computer Science, Saarland University, Saarbrücken, Germany
[2] Department of Mathematics, University of Paderborn, Germany
[3] Department of Computer Science, University of Twente, Enschede, The Netherlands
[4] Software Modeling and Verification Group, RWTH Aachen, Germany

Abstract. Abstraction techniques based on simulation relations have become an important and effective proof technique to avoid the infamous state space explosion problem. In the context of Markov chains, strong and weak simulation relations have been proposed [17,6], together with corresponding decision algorithms [3,5], but it is as yet unclear whether they can be used as effectively as their non-stochastic counterparts. This paper presents drastically improved algorithms to decide whether one (discrete- or continuous-time) Markov chain strongly or weakly simulates another. The key innovation is the use of parametric maximum flow techniques to amortize computations.

1 Introduction

To compare the stepwise behaviour of states in transition systems, simulation relations ($\precsim$) have been widely considered [18,16]. Simulation relations are preorders on the state space such that if $s \precsim s'$ ("s' simulates s") state s' can mimic all stepwise behaviour of s; the converse, i. e., $s' \precsim s$ is not guaranteed, so state s' may perform steps that cannot be matched by s. Thus, if $s \precsim s'$ then every successor of s has a corresponding related successor of s', but the reverse does not necessarily hold. In the context of model checking, simulation relations can be used to combat the well-known state space explosion problem, owed to the preservation of certain classes of temporal formulas. For instance, if $s \precsim s'$ then for all *safe* CTL* formulas Φ (formulas with universal path-quantifiers only) it follows that $s' \models \Phi$ implies $s \models \Phi$ [9].

Verification of stochastic systems faces very similar state space explosion problems. Therefore, simulation preorders [17,6] have been proposed for discrete- and continuous-time Markov chains (DTMCs and CTMCs). In correspondence to the non-probabilistic setting, these preorders preserve fragments of PCTL [14] and CSL [2,4]. They provide the principal ingredients to perform abstraction of Markov chains, while preserving *safe* fragments of the respective logics. However,

---

[*] This work is supported by the NWO-DFG bilateral project VOSS and by the DFG as part of the Transregional Collaborative Research Center SFB/TR 14 AVACS.

O. Grumberg and M. Huth (Eds.): TACAS 2007, LNCS 4424, pp. 155–169, 2007.

it is as yet unclear whether these relations can be used with similar effectiveness as in the non-probabilistic setting. One prerequisite is the availability of efficient decision procedures for simulation in finite-state models.

Let n denote the number of states, and m denote the number of transitions. For strong simulation preorder, Baier *et al.* [3] introduced a polynomial decision algorithm with complexity $\mathcal{O}(n^7/\log n)$, by tailoring a network flow algorithm to the problem, embedded into an iterative refinement loop. This technique can not be applied to *weak* simulations [7] directly. In [5], Baier *et al.* proved that probabilistic weak simulation is decidable in polynomial time by reducing it to a linear programming (LP) problem.

In this paper, we present drastically improved algorithms. For strong simulation, the core observation is that the networks on which the maximum flows are calculated, are very similar across iterations of the refinement loop. We exploit this by adaptation of the parametric maximum flow algorithm [10] to solve the maximum flows for the arising sequences of similar networks, arriving at an overall time complexity $\mathcal{O}(m^2 n)$.

For weak simulation, adapting the maximum flow idea is not straightforward. This is because successor states might need to be *split* into two fragments and one does not a priori know how to split them. Nevertheless, we manage to incorporate the parametric maximum flow algorithm into a decision algorithm with complexity $\mathcal{O}(m^2 n^3)$.

The algorithms are developed for both discrete- and continuous-time Markov chains. Especially in the very common case, where the state fanout of a model is bounded by a constant k (and hence $m \le kn$), our strong simulation algorithm has complexity $\mathcal{O}(n^2)$ which is faster by a factor of $n^5/\log n$ in comparison to the existing algorithm. This complexity corresponds to the best algorithms for deciding strong simulation over non-probabilistic systems [15,11]. As we will discuss the weak simulation algorithm even leads to an improvement in the order of n^{10} for CTMCs (and n^9 for DTMCs), compared to the one using a polynomial LP routine [20]. Remarkably, our algorithm is polynomial in the RAM-model of computation while no known LP-based algorithm is. We argue that especially for CTMCs, which have a very broad spectrum of applications ranging from disk storage dimensioning to gene regulatory networks, the availability of such algorithms can become a key ingredient to fight the state space explosion problem.

The paper proceeds by first giving necessary definitions and background in Section 2. Section 3 presents algorithms for deciding strong simulations while Section 4 focuses on algorithms for weak simulations. Section 5 concludes the paper.

2   Preliminaries

This section recalls the definitions of fully probabilistic systems, discrete- and continuous-time Markov chains, strong and weak simulations on these models [7]. We also review the preflow algorithm to solve maximum flow problems [13].

Models. Let X, Y be finite sets. For $f : X \to \mathbb{R}$, let $f(A)$ denote $\sum_{x \in A} f(x)$ for all $A \subseteq X$. If $f : X \times Y \to \mathbb{R}$ is a two-dimensional function, let $f(x, A)$ denote $\sum_{y \in A} f(x, y)$ for all $x \in X$ and $A \subseteq Y$, and $f(A, y)$ denote $\sum_{x \in A} f(x, y)$ for all $y \in Y$ and $A \subseteq X$. Let AP be a fixed, finite set of atomic propositions.

Definition 1. *A labeled fully probabilistic system (FPS) is a tuple $\mathcal{D} = (S, \mathbf{P}, L)$ where S is a finite set of states, $\mathbf{P} : S \times S \to [0, 1]$ is a probability matrix satisfying $\mathbf{P}(s, S) \in [0, 1]$ for all $s \in S$, and $L : S \to 2^{AP}$ is a labeling function.*

A state s is called stochastic if $\mathbf{P}(s, S) = 1$, absorbing if $\mathbf{P}(s, S) = 0$, and sub-stochastic otherwise.

Definition 2. *A labeled discrete-time Markov chain (DTMC) is a FPS $\mathcal{D} = (S, \mathbf{P}, L)$ where s is either absorbing or stochastic for all $s \in S$.*

Definition 3. *A labeled continuous-time Markov chain (CTMC) is a tuple $\mathcal{C} = (S, \mathbf{R}, L)$ with S and L as before, and a rate matrix $\mathbf{R} : S \times S \to \mathbb{R}_{\geq 0}$.*

The embedded DTMC of $\mathcal{C} = (S, \mathbf{R}, L)$ is defined by $emb(\mathcal{C}) = (S, \mathbf{P}, L)$ with $\mathbf{P}(s, s') = \mathbf{R}(s, s')/\mathbf{R}(s, S)$ if $\mathbf{R}(s, S) > 0$ and 0 otherwise. We will also use $\mathbf{P}$ for a CTMC directly, without referring to its embedded DTMC explicitly.

A distribution μ on S is a function $\mu : S \to [0, 1]$ satisfying the condition $\mu(S) \leq 1$. We let $Dist(S)$ denote the set of distributions over the set S. μ is called stochastic if $\mu(S) = 1$. If it is not stochastic, we use an auxiliary state (not a *real* state) $\perp \notin S$ and set $\mu(\perp) = 1 - \mu(S)$. Further, for a given FPS, let $\mathbf{P}(s, \cdot)$ denote the distribution defined by the transition probability matrix $\mathbf{P}$ for all $s \in S$. Let $\mathbf{P}(s, \perp) = 1 - \mathbf{P}(s, S)$ for all $s \in S$, and let $S_\perp$ denote the set $S \cup \{\perp\}$. For $s \in S$, let $post(s)$ denote $\{s' \in S \mid \mathbf{P}(s, s') > 0\}$, i.e., the set of successor states of s. Let $post_\perp(s)$ denote $\{s' \in S_\perp \mid \mathbf{P}(s, s') > 0\}$, i.e., $post(s)$ plus the auxiliary state $\perp$ in case that $\mathbf{P}(s, \perp) > 0$. For CTMC $\mathcal{C} = (S, \mathbf{R}, L)$, let $post(s) = \{s' \in S \mid \mathbf{R}(s, s') > 0\}$ for all $s \in S$.

For a given FPS, DTMC or CTMC, its *fanout* is defined by $\max_{s \in S} |post(s)|$, the number of states is usually denoted by n, and the number of transitions is denoted by m. For $s \in S$, $reach(s)$ denotes the set of states that are reachable from s with positive probability. For a relation $R \subseteq S \times S$ and $s \in S$, let $R[s]$ denote the set $\{s' \in S \mid (s, s') \in R\}$, and $R^{-1}[s]$ denote the set $\{s' \in S \mid (s', s) \in R\}$. If $(s, s') \in R$, we write also $s \, R \, s'$.

Simulation relations. Strong simulation is based on the notion of a *weight function*. We recall the definition here from [17], adapted to FPS as in [7].

Definition 4. *Let $\mu, \mu' \in Dist(S)$ and $R \subseteq S \times S$. A weight function for (μ, μ') w.r.t. R, denoted by $\mu \sqsubseteq_R \mu'$, is a function $\Delta : S_\perp \times S_\perp \to [0, 1]$ such that $\Delta(s, s') > 0$ implies $s \, R \, s'$ or $s = \perp$, $\mu(s) = \Delta(s, S_\perp)$ for $s \in S_\perp$ and $\mu'(s') = \Delta(S_\perp, s')$ for $s' \in S_\perp$.*

Strong simulation requires similar states to be related via weight functions on their distributions [17].

Definition 5. *Let* $\mathcal{D} = (S, \mathbf{P}, L)$ *be an FPS.* $R \subseteq S \times S$ *is a* strong simulation *on* $\mathcal{D}$ *iff for all* s_1, s_2 *with* $s_1 \, R \, s_2$: $L(s_1) = L(s_2)$ *and* $\mathbf{P}(s_1, \cdot) \sqsubseteq_R \mathbf{P}(s_2, \cdot)$. *We say that* s_2 strongly simulates s_1 *in* $\mathcal{D}$, *denoted by* $s_1 \precsim_d s_2$, *iff there exists a strong simulation* R *on* $\mathcal{D}$ *such that* $s_1 \, R \, s_2$.

For CTMCs we say that s_2 strongly simulates s_1 if, in addition to the DTMC conditions, s_2 can move stochastically *faster* than s_1 [7], which manifests itself by a slower rate.

Definition 6. *Let* $\mathcal{C} = (S, \mathbf{R}, L)$ *be a* CTMC. $R \subseteq S \times S$ *is a* strong simulation *on* $\mathcal{C}$ *iff for all* s_1, s_2 *with* $s_1 \, R \, s_2$: $L(s_1) = L(s_2)$, $\mathbf{P}(s_1, \cdot) \sqsubseteq_R \mathbf{P}(s_2, \cdot)$ *and* $\mathbf{R}(s_1, S) \leq \mathbf{R}(s_2, S)$. *We say that* s_2 strongly simulates s_1 *in* $\mathcal{C}$, *denoted by* $s_1 \precsim_c s_2$, *iff there exists a strong simulation* R *on* $\mathcal{C}$ *such that* $s_1 \, R \, s_2$.

We now recall the notion of weak simulation on FPSs. Intuitively, s_2 weakly simulates s_1 if they have the same labels, and if their successor states can be grouped into sets U_i and V_i for $i = 1, 2$, satisfying certain conditions. We can view steps to V_i as *stutter* steps while steps to U_i are *visible* steps. It is then required that there exists a weight function for the conditional distributions: $\frac{\mathbf{P}(s_1, \cdot)}{K_1}$ and $\frac{\mathbf{P}(s_2, \cdot)}{K_2}$ where K_i intuitively correspond to the probability of performing a visible step from s_i. For reasons explained in [7], the definition needs to account for states which partially belong to U_i and partially to V_i. Technically, this is achieved by functions δ_i that distribute s_i over U_i and V_i in the definition below [7].

Definition 7. *Let* $\mathcal{D} = (S, \mathbf{P}, L)$ *be an FPS. The relation* $R \subseteq S \times S$ *is a* weak simulation *on* $\mathcal{D}$ *iff for all* s_1, s_2 *with* $s_1 \, R \, s_2$: $L(s_1) = L(s_2)$ *and there exist functions* $\delta_i : S_\perp \to [0, 1]$ *and sets* $U_i, V_i \subseteq S_\perp$ *(for* $i = 1, 2$*) with*

$$U_i = \{u_i \in post_\perp(s_i) \mid \delta_i(u_i) > 0\} \quad and \quad V_i = \{v_i \in post_\perp(s_i) \mid \delta_i(v_i) < 1\}$$

such that

1. *(a)* $v_1 \, R \, s_2$ *for all* $v_1 \in V_1 \setminus \{\perp\}$, *and (b)* $s_1 \, R \, v_2$ *for all* $v_2 \in V_2 \setminus \{\perp\}$
2. *there exists a function* $\Delta : S_\perp \times S_\perp \to [0, 1]$ *such that:*
   (a) $\Delta(u_1, u_2) > 0$ *implies* $u_1 \in U_1, u_2 \in U_2$ *and either* $u_1 \, R \, u_2$ *or* $u_1 = \perp$,
   (b) if $K_1 > 0$ *and* $K_2 > 0$ *then for all states* $w \in S_\perp$:

$$K_1 \cdot \Delta(w, U_2) = \mathbf{P}(s_1, w)\delta_1(w) \quad and \quad K_2 \cdot \Delta(U_1, w) = \mathbf{P}(s_2, w)\delta_2(w)$$

   where $K_i = \sum_{u_i \in U_i} \delta_i(u_i) \cdot \mathbf{P}(s_i, u_i)$ *for* $i = 1, 2$.
3. *for* $u_1 \in U_1 \setminus \{\perp\}$ *there exists a path fragment* $s_2, w_1, \ldots, w_n, u_2$ *with positive probability such that* $n \geq 0$, $s_1 \, R \, w_j$ *for* $0 < j \leq n$, *and* $u_1 \, R \, u_2$.

We say that s_2 weakly simulates s_1 in $\mathcal{D}$, denoted $s_1 \precapprox_d s_2$, iff there exists a weak simulation R on $\mathcal{D}$ such that $s_1 \, R \, s_2$.

Condition (3.) will in the sequel be called the *reachability condition*. If $U_2 = \emptyset$ and $U_1 \neq \emptyset$, which implies that $K_1 > 0$ and $K_2 = 0$, the reachability condition guarantees that for any visible step $s_1 \to u_1$ with $u_1 \in U_1$, s_2 can reach a state u_2 which simulates u_1 while passing only through states simulating s_1.

Weak simulation on DTMCs arises as a special case of the above definition, as a DTMC is an FPS (where each state is absorbing or stochastic). Weak simulation for CTMCs is defined as follows.

Definition 8 ([7,6]). *Let $C = (S, \mathbf{R}, L)$ be a CTMC. $R \subseteq S \times S$ is a weak simulation on C iff for $s_1 R s_2$: $L(s_1) = L(s_2)$ and there exist functions $\delta_i : S \to [0, 1]$ and sets $U_i, V_i \subseteq S_\perp$ (for $i = 1, 2$) satisfying conditions (1.) and (2.) of Definition 7 and the rate condition holds: (3') $K_1 \cdot \mathbf{R}(s_1, S) \leq K_2 \cdot \mathbf{R}(s_2, S)$.*

We say that s_2 weakly simulates s_1 in C, denoted $s_1 \precsim_c s_2$, iff there exists a weak simulation R on C such that $s_1 R s_2$.

In this definition, the rate condition *(3')* replaces the reachability condition of the preceding definition. We refer to [7] for a discussion of subtleties in this definition.

Simulation up to R. For an arbitrary relation R on the state space S of an FPS with $s_1 R s_2$, we say that s_2 simulates s_1 strongly up to R, denoted $s_1 \precsim_R s_2$, if $L(s_1) = L(s_2)$ and $\mathbf{P}(s_1, \cdot) \sqsubseteq_R \mathbf{P}(s_2, \cdot)$. Otherwise we write $s_1 \not\precsim_R s_2$. Note that $s_1 \precsim_R s_2$ does not imply $s_1 \precsim_d s_2$ unless R is a strong simulation, since only the first step is considered for $\precsim_R$. Likewise, we say that s_2 simulates s_1 weakly up to R, denoted by $s_1 \precsim_R s_2$, if there are functions δ_i, sets U_i, V_i as required by Definition 7 for this pair. Otherwise, we write $s_1 \not\precsim_R s_2$. Similar to strong simulation up to R, $s_1 \precsim_R s_2$ does not imply $s_1 \precsim_d s_2$, since no conditions are imposed on pairs in R different from (s_1, s_2). These conventions extend to DTMCs and CTMC in the obvious way.

Preflow algorithm. We briefly recall the preflow algorithm [13, p. 925] for finding the maximum flow over the network $\mathcal{N} = (V, E, u)$ where V is a finite set of vertices and $E \subseteq V \times V$ is a set of edges. V contains a distinguished *source* vertex $\nearrow$ and a distinguished *sink* vertex $\searrow$. $u : E \to \mathbb{R}_{>0}$ is the capacity function. We extend the capacity function to all vertex pairs: $u(v, w) = 0$ if $(v, w) \notin E$. A *flow* f on $\mathcal{N}$ is a function $f : V \times V \to \mathbb{R}$ that satisfies:

1. $f(v, w) \leq u(v, w)$ for all $(v, w) \in V \times V$ *capacity constraints*
2. $f(v, w) = -f(w, v)$ for all $(v, w) \in V \times V$ *antisymmetry constraint*
3. $f(v, V) = 0$ at vertices $v \in V \setminus \{\nearrow, \searrow\}$ *conservation rule*

The value of a flow function f is given by $f(\nearrow, V)$. A *maximum flow* is a flow of maximum value.

A *preflow* is a function $f : V \times V \to \mathbb{R}$ satisfying (1.) and (2.) above, and the relaxation of (3.): $f(V, v) \geq 0$ for all $v \in V \setminus \{\nearrow\}$. The *excess* $e(v)$ of a vertex v is defined by $f(V, v)$. A vertex $v \notin \{\nearrow, \searrow\}$ is called *active* if $e(v) > 0$. Observe that a flow is a preflow in which no vertex v is active for $v \in V \setminus \{\nearrow, \searrow\}$. A pair (v, w) is a *residual edge* of f if $f(v, w) < u(v, w)$. The set of residual edges w.r.t. f is denoted by E_f. The *residual capacity* $u_f(v, w)$ of the residual edge (v, w) is defined by $u(v, w) - f(v, w)$. If (v, w) is not a residual edge, it is called *saturated.* A *valid distance function* (called *valid labeling* in [13]) d is a function

SIMREL$_s(\mathcal{D})$
1   $R, R_{new} \leftarrow \{(s_1, s_2) \in S \times S \mid L(s_1) = L(s_2)\}$
2   **do**
3       $R \leftarrow R_{new}$ and $R_{new} \leftarrow \emptyset$
4   **for** $((s_1, s_2) \in R)$
5   **if** $(s_1 \precsim_R s_2)$
6               $R_{new} \leftarrow R_{new} \cup \{(s_1, s_2)\}$.
7   **until**$(R_{new} = R)$
8   **return** R

Fig. 1. Basic algorithm to decide strong simulation

$V \rightarrow \mathbb{R}_{\geq 0} \cup \{\infty\}$ satisfying: $d(\nearrow) = |V|$, $d(\searrow) = 0$ and $d(v) \leq d(w) + 1$ for every residual edge (v, w). A residual edge (v, w) is *admissible* if $d(v) = d(w) + 1$.

We initialise the preflow f by: $f(v, w) = u(v, w)$ if $v = \nearrow$ and 0 otherwise. The distance function d is initialised by: $d(v) = |V|$ if $v = \nearrow$ and 0 otherwise. The *preflow algorithm* maintains the preflow f and the valid distance function d. If there is an active vertex v such that (v, w) is admissible, it pushes $\min\{e(v), u_f(v, w)\}$ flows from v toward the sink along the admissible edge (v, w). If v is active but there are no admissible edges leaving it, the *relabeling* of v sets the distance of v equal to $\min\{d(w) + 1 \mid (v, w) \in E_f\}$. If there are no active vertices, the preflow f is a maximum flow.

3   Algorithms for Deciding Strong Simulation

We recall first the basic algorithm to decide strong simulation preorder. Then, we refine this algorithm to deal with strong simulations on FPSs, DTMCs and CTMCs respectively.

Basic algorithm to decide strong simulation. The algorithm in [3], depicted as SIMREL$_s$ in Fig. 1, takes as a parameter a model, which, for now, is an FPS $\mathcal{D}$. The subscript 's' stands for strong simulation; later, a very similar algorithm, i.e., SIMREL$_w$, will be used for weak simulation. To calculate the strong simulation relation for $\mathcal{D}$, the algorithm starts with the trivial relation $R_{init} = \{(s_1, s_2) \in S \times S \mid L(s_1) = L(s_2)\}$ and removes each pair (s_1, s_2) if s_2 cannot strongly simulate s_1 up to the current relation R, i.e., $s_1 \not\precsim_R s_2$. This proceeds until there is no such pair left, i.e., $R_{new} = R$. Invariantly throughout the loop it holds that R is coarser than $\precsim_d$. Hence, we obtain the strong simulation preorder $\precsim_d = R$, once the algorithm terminates.

The decisive part of the algorithm is the check whether $s_1 \precsim_R s_2$ in line 5. The answer is computed with the help of a maximum flow computation on a particular network $\mathcal{N}(\mathbf{P}(s_1, \cdot), \mathbf{P}(s_2, \cdot), R)$ constructed out of $\mathbf{P}(s_1, \cdot)$, $\mathbf{P}(s_2, \cdot)$ and R. This network is constructed via a graph containing a copy $\bar{t} \in \overline{S_\perp}$ of each state $t \in S_\perp$ where $\overline{S_\perp} = \{\bar{t} \mid t \in S_\perp\}$ as follows: Let $\nearrow$ (the source) and $\searrow$ (the sink) be two additional vertices not contained in $S_\perp \cup \overline{S_\perp}$. For functions

$\mu, \mu' : S \to \mathbb{R}_{\geq 0}$ and a relation $R \subseteq S \times S$ we define the network $\mathcal{N}(\mu, \mu', R) = (V, E, u)$ with the set of vertices

$$V = \{\nearrow, \searrow\} \cup \{s \in S_\perp \mid \mu(s) > 0\} \cup \{\overline{s} \in \overline{S_\perp} \mid \mu'(s) > 0\}$$

and the set of edges E is defined by

$$E = \{(s, \overline{t}) \mid (s, t) \in R \vee s = \perp\} \cup \{(\nearrow, s)\} \cup \{(\overline{t}, \searrow)\}$$

where $s, t \in S_\perp$ with $\mu(s) > 0$ and $\mu'(t) > 0$. The capacity function u is defined as follows: $u(\nearrow, s) = \mu(s)$ for all $s \in S_\perp$, $u(\overline{t}, \searrow) = \mu'(t)$ for all $t \in S_\perp$, $u(s, \overline{t}) = \infty$ for all $(s, t) \in E$ and $u(v, w) = 0$ otherwise. This network is a bipartite network, where the vertices can be partitioned into two subsets $V_1 := \{s \in S_\perp \mid \mu(s) > 0\} \cup \{\searrow\}$ and $V_2 := \{\overline{s} \in \overline{S_\perp} \mid \mu'(s) > 0\} \cup \{\nearrow\}$ such that all edges have one endpoint in V_1 and another in V_2. For two states s_1, s_2 of an FPS or a CTMC, we let $\mathcal{N}(s_1, s_2, R)$ denote the network $\mathcal{N}(\mathbf{P}(s_1, \cdot), \mathbf{P}(s_2, \cdot), R)$.

The following lemma expresses the crucial relationship between maximum flows and weight functions on which the algorithm is based. It is a direct extension of [3, Lemma 5.1] now accounting for sub-stochasticity.

Lemma 1. *Let S be a finite set of states and R be a relation on S. Let $\mu, \mu' \in Dist(S)$. Then, $\mu \sqsubseteq_R \mu'$ iff the maximum flow in $\mathcal{N}(\mu, \mu', R)$ is 1.*

Thus we can decide $s_1 \precsim_R s_2$ by computing the maximum flow in $\mathcal{N}(s_1, s_2, R)$. Using the best known flow algorithm for this type of networks [8,12], one obtains the overall complexity $\mathcal{O}(n^7 / \log n)$ for the algorithm SIMREL$_s$ [3]. The space complexity is $\mathcal{O}(n^2)$.

An improved algorithm for FPSs. We first analyse the behaviour of SIMREL$_s$ in more detail. We consider an arbitrary pair (s_1, s_2), and assume that (s_1, s_2) stays in relation R throughout the iterations, until the pair is either found not to satisfy $s_1 \precsim_R s_2$ or the algorithm terminates with a fix-point. If we let $l_{(s_1, s_2)}$ denote the number of iterations until either of these happens, then altogether $l_{(s_1, s_2)}$ maximum flow algorithms are run for this pair. However, the networks $\mathcal{N}(s_1, s_2, \cdot)$ constructed in successive iterations are very similar, and may often be identical across iterations: They differ from iteration to iteration only by deletion of some edges induced by the successive clean up of R. For our particular pair (s_1, s_2) the network might not change at all in some iterations, because the deletions from R do not affect their direct successors. We are going to exploit this observation by an algorithm that re-uses the already computed maximum flows, in a way that whatever happens is good: If no changes occur to $\mathcal{N}(s_1, s_2, \cdot)$, then the maximum flow is equal to the one in the last iteration. If changes occur, the preflow algorithm can be applied to get the new maximum flow very fast, using the maximum flow constructed in the last iteration as a preflow.

To understand the algorithm, we look at the network $\mathcal{N}(s_1, s_2, R_{init})$. Let $D_1, \ldots, D_k$ be pairwise disjoint subsets of R_{init}, which correspond to the pairs deleted from R_{init} in iteration i. Let $\mathcal{N}(s_1, s_2, R_i)$ denote $\mathcal{N}(s_1, s_2, R_{init})$ if $i = 1$, and $\mathcal{N}(s_1, s_2, R_{i-1} \setminus D_{i-1})$ if $1 < i \leq k + 1$. Let f_i denote the maximum flow of the network $\mathcal{N}(s_1, s_2, R_i)$ for $i = 1, \ldots, k + 1$. We address the problem of checking $|f_i| = 1$ for all $i = 1, \ldots, k+1$. Very similar to the *parametric maximum algorithm* [10, p. 34], our algorithm $\text{SMF}_{(s_1, s_2)}$ (*sequence of maximum flows*) for the pair (s_1, s_2) consists of initialising the preflow $f_{(s_1, s_2)}$ and the distance function $d_{(s_1, s_2)}$ as for the preflow algorithm, setting $i = 0$, and repeating the following steps at most k times:

$\text{SMF}_{(s_1, s_2)}$
1. Increase i by 1. If $i = 1$ go to step 2. Otherwise, for all pairs $(u_1, u_2) \in D_{i-1}$, set $f_{(s_1, s_2)}(u_1, \overline{u_2}) = 0$ and replace the flow $f_{(s_1, s_2)}(\overline{u_2}, \backslash)$ by $f_{(s_1, s_2)}(\overline{u_2}, \backslash)$ $-f_{(s_1, s_2)}(u_1, \overline{u_2})$. Set $\mathcal{N}(s_1, s_2, R_i) = \mathcal{N}(s_1, s_2, R_{i-1} \setminus D_{i-1})$. Let $f_{(s_1, s_2)}$ and $d_{(s_1, s_2)}$ be the resulting flow and final valid distance function.
2. Apply the preflow algorithm to calculate the maximum flow for $\mathcal{N}(s_1, s_2, R_i)$ with preflow $f_{(s_1, s_2)}$ and distance function $d_{(s_1, s_2)}$.
3. If $|f_{(s_1, s_2)}| < 1$ return false for all $j \geq i$. Otherwise, return true and continue with step 1.

To understand this algorithm, assume $i > 1$. At step (1.), before we remove the edges D_{i-1} from the network $\mathcal{N}(s_1, s_2, R_{i-1})$, we modify the flow $f_{(s_1, s_2)}$, which is the maximum flow of the network $\mathcal{N}(s_1, s_2, R_{i-1})$, by

- setting $f_{(s_1, s_2)}(u_1, \overline{u_2}) = 0$ for all deleted edges $(u_1, u_2) \in D_{i-1}$, and
- modifying $f_{(s_1, s_2)}(\overline{u_2}, \backslash)$ such that the flow $f_{(s_1, s_2)}$ becomes consistent with the flow conservation rule.

The excess $e(v)$ is increased if there exists w such that $(v, w) \in D_{i-1}$, and unchanged otherwise. Hence, the modified flow is a preflow. The distance function $d_{(s_1, s_2)}$ keeps valid, since by removing the set of edges D_{i-1}, no new residual edges are induced. This guarantees that, at step (2.), the *preflow algorithm* finds a maximum flow over the network $\mathcal{N}(s_1, s_2, R_i)$. If $|f_{(s_1, s_2)}| < 1$ at some iteration i, then $|f_{(s_1, s_2)}| < 1$ for all iterations $j \geq i$ because more edges will be deleted in subsequent iterations. Therefore, at step (3.), the algorithm returns true and continues with step (1.) if $|f_{(s_1, s_2)}| = 1$, otherwise, returns false for all subsequent iterations. We derive the complexity of the algorithm as follows:

Lemma 2. *Let $D_1, \ldots, D_k$ be pairwise disjoint subsets of $R_{init} \cap post(s_1) \times post(s_2)$. Let f_i denote the flow constructed at the end of step (2.) in iteration i. Assume that $|post(s_1)| \leq |post(s_2)|$. The algorithm $\text{SMF}_{(s_1, s_2)}$ correctly computes maximum flow f_i for $\mathcal{N}(s_1, s_2, R_i)$ where $i = 1, \ldots, k + 1$, and runs in time $\mathcal{O}(|post(s_1)||post(s_2)|^2)$.*

The improved algorithm SIMREL'_s for FPSs is depicted in Fig. 2. The variable l (line 2) denotes the number of iterations of the until-loop, and the set D (line 9) contains edges removed from R. For every pair $(s_1, s_2) \in R_{init}$, the network $\mathcal{N}(s_1, s_2, R_{init})$ (line 4), the flow function $f_{(s_1, s_2)}$ and the distance function $d_{(s_1, s_2)}$ are initialised as for the preflow algorithm (line 5). At line 6 a set

$$\textbf{Listener}_{(s_1, s_2)} = \{(u_1, u_2) \mid u_1 \in pre(s_1) \wedge u_2 \in pre(s_2) \wedge L(u_1) = L(u_2)\}$$

SIMREL'$_s$($\mathcal{D}$)

1    $R, R_{new} \leftarrow \{(s_1, s_2) \in S \times S \mid L(s_1) = L(s_2)\}$
2    $l \leftarrow 0$ // auxiliary variable to count the number of iterations.
3   **for** $((s_1, s_2) \in R)$
4   Construct the initial network $\mathcal{N}(s_1, s_2, R_{init}) := \mathcal{N}(s_1, s_2, R)$
5   Initialise the flow function $f_{(s_1, s_2)}$ and the distance function $d_{(s_1, s_2)}$
6   **Listener**$_{(s_1, s_2)} \leftarrow \{(u_1, u_2) \mid u_1 \in pre(s_1) \wedge u_2 \in pre(s_2) \wedge L(u_1) = L(u_2)\}$
7   **do**
8        $l++$
9        $D \leftarrow R \backslash R_{new}$ and $R \leftarrow R_{new}$ and $R_{new} \leftarrow \emptyset$
10   **for** $((s_1, s_2) \in D)$
11   **for** $((u_1, u_2) \in$ **Listener**$_{(s_1, s_2)})$
12               $D_l^{(u_1, u_2)} \leftarrow D_l^{(u_1, u_2)} \cup \{(s_1, s_2)\}$
13   **for** $((s_1, s_2) \in R)$
14   **if** (SMF$_{(s_1, s_2)}$ returns true on the set $D_l^{(s_1, s_2)}$)
15               $R_{new} \leftarrow R_{new} \cup \{(s_1, s_2)\}$.
16   **until**($R_{new} = R$)
17   **return** R

Fig. 2. Efficient algorithm for deciding strong simulation

is saved, where $pre(s) = \{t \in S \mid \mathbf{P}(t, s) > 0\}$. The set **Listener**$_{(s_1, s_2)}$ contains all pairs (u_1, u_2) such that the network $\mathcal{N}(u_1, u_2, R)$ contains the edge $(s_1, \overline{s_2})$. In lines 10–12, the pair (s_1, s_2) is inserted into the set $D_l^{(u_1, u_2)}$ if $(s_1, s_2) \in D$ and $(u_1, u_2) \in$ **Listener**$_{(s_1, s_2)}$. $D_l^{(u_1, u_2)}$ contains edges which should be removed to update the network for (u_1, u_2) in iteration l. At line 14, the algorithm SMF$_{(s_1, s_2)}$ constructs the maximum flow for the set $D_l^{(s_1, s_2)}$. Note that l corresponds to i in SMF. The initialisation of SMF corresponds to lines 4–5. In the first iteration (in which $D_1^{(s_1, s_2)} = \emptyset$), SMF$_{(s_1, s_2)}$ skips the computations in step (1.) and proceeds directly to step (2.), in which the maximum flow f_1 for $\mathcal{N}(s_1, s_2, R_{init})$ is constructed. In iteration $l > 1$, SMF$_{(s_1, s_2)}$ takes the set $D_l^{(s_1, s_2)}$, updates the flow f_{l-1} and the network, and constructs the maximum flow f_l for the network $\mathcal{N}(s_1, s_2, R_l)$. If SMF$_{(s_1, s_2)}$ returns true, (s_1, s_2) is inserted into R_{new} and survives this iteration.

Lemma 3. SIMREL'$_s$($\mathcal{D}$) *runs in time* $\mathcal{O}(m^2 n)$ *and in space* $\mathcal{O}(m^2)$. *If the fanout is bounded by a constant, it has complexity* $\mathcal{O}(n^2)$, *both in time and space.*

Algorithm for DTMCs and CTMCs. We now consider how to handle DTMCs and CTMCs. Since each DTMC is a special case of an FPS the algorithm SIMREL'$_s$ applies directly. For CTMCs, we replace line 1 of the algorithm by

$$R, R_{new} \leftarrow \{(s_1, s_2) \in S \times S \mid L(s_1) = L(s_2) \wedge \mathbf{R}(s_1, S) \leq \mathbf{R}(s_2, S)\}$$

to check the rate condition of Definition 6. We arrive at the same complexity.

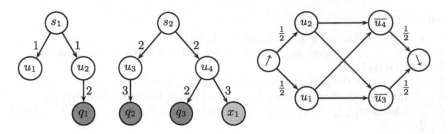

Fig. 3. A CTMC example

Example 1. Consider the CTMC in Fig. 3 (it has 10 states) where labels are indicated by shades of grey. Consider the pair $(s_1, s_2) \in R_{init}$. The network $\mathcal{N}(s_1, s_2, R_1)$ is depicted on the right of the figure. Assume that we get the maximum flow f_1 which sends $\frac{1}{2}$ flow along the path $\nearrow, u_2, \overline{u_4}, \searrow$ and $\frac{1}{2}$ along $\nearrow, u_1, \overline{u_3}, \searrow$. Hence, the check for (s_1, s_2) is successful in the first iteration. The checks for the pairs (u_1, u_3), (u_1, u_4) and (u_2, u_3) are also successful in the first iteration. However, the check for the pair (u_2, u_4) is unsuccessful, as no successor of u_2 has the same label as x_1. In the second iteration, the network $\mathcal{N}(s_1, s_2, R_2)$ is obtained from $\mathcal{N}(s_1, s_2, R_1)$ by deleting the edge $(u_2, \overline{u_4})$. In $\mathcal{N}(s_1, s_2, R_2)$, the flows on $(u_2, \overline{u_4})$ and $(\overline{u_4}, \searrow)$ are set to 0, and the vertex u_2 has a positive excess $\frac{1}{2}$. Applying the preflow algorithm, we push the excess from u_2, along $\overline{u_3}, u_1, \overline{u_4}$ to $\searrow$. We get a maximum flow f_2 for $\mathcal{N}(s_1, s_2, R_2)$ which sends $\frac{1}{2}$ flow along the path $\nearrow, u_2, \overline{u_3}, \searrow$ and $\frac{1}{2}$ along $\nearrow, u_1, \overline{u_4}, \searrow$. Hence, the check for (s_1, s_2) is also successful in the second iteration. Once the fix-point is reached, R still contains (s_1, s_2).

4   Algorithms for Deciding Weak Simulation

We now turn our attention to algorithms to decide weak simulation $\precsim_c$. We first focus on FPSs before addressing DTMCs and CTMCs. The theoretical complexity of the algorithms for DTMCs and CTMCs are the same as the one for FPSs (except for bounded fanout). Nevertheless, we shall present dedicated algorithms for DTMCs and CTMCs, because their specific properties can be exploited for significant improvements in practice.

An algorithm for FPSs. The basic weak simulation algorithm $\mathrm{SIMREL}_w(\mathcal{D})$ is obtained by replacing line 5 of $\mathrm{SIMREL}_s(\mathcal{D})$ in Fig. 1 by: **if** $(s_1 \precsim_R s_2)$. Thus instead of checking the pairs w.r.t. $\precsim_R$ we check them w.r.t. $\precsim_R$. The latter check is performed by $\mathrm{WS}(\mathcal{D}, s_1, s_2, R)$, shown in Fig. 4.

Here, line 1 corresponds to the case that s_1 has only *stutter* steps, i.e., $K_1 = 0$: Assuming $post(s_1) \subseteq R^{-1}[s_2]$ we choose $U_1 = \emptyset, V_1 = post_\perp(s_1)$ and $U_2 = post(s_2), V_2 = \{\perp\}$ to fulfill the conditions in Definition 7. Hence, $s_1 \precsim_R s_2$. If line 3 is reached in WS, s_1 has at least one *visible* step, and all successors of s_2 can simulate s_1. In this case we need to check the reachability condition (3.) of Definition 7, which is performed in lines 3–6. Line 7 of the algorithm is only

$\text{WS}(\mathcal{D}, s_1, s_2, R)$

1   **if** $(post(s_1) \subseteq R^{-1}[s_2])$ **return true**
2   **if** $(post(s_2) \subseteq R[s_1])$
3   **if** $(\exists s \in reach(s_2)$, such that $s \notin R[s_1])$ **return true**
4        $U_1 \leftarrow \{s'_1 \in post(s_1) \mid s'_1 \notin R^{-1}[s_2]\}$
5   **if** $(\forall u_1 \in U_1. \exists s \in reach(s_2)$, such that $s \in R[u_1])$ **return true**
6   **else return false**
7   **return** $\text{WSFPS}(\mathcal{D}, s_1, s_2, R)$

Fig. 4. Algorithm to check whether $s_1 \precsim_R s_2$

touched if the checks in line 1 and 2 both return false. In this case, more work
is needed, and this work is delegated to a parametric maximum flow algorithm,
which is called by $\text{WSFPS}(\mathcal{D}, s_1, s_2, R)$.

To understand the details of this algorithm, we require a bit of notation.
We focus on a particular pair $(s_1, s_2) \in R$, where R is the current relation. We
partition the set $post_\perp(s_i)$ into MU_i (for: must be in U_i) and PV_i (for: potentially
in V_i). The set PV_1 consists of those successors of s_1 which can be either put into
U_1 or V_1 or both. For technical reasons, we assume additionally that $\perp \in PV_1$ if
s_1 is not stochastic. Hence,

$$PV_1 = post_\perp(s_1) \cap (R^{-1}[s_2] \cup \{\perp\})$$

The set MU_1 equals $post_\perp(s_1) \backslash PV_1$ which consists of the successor states which
can only be placed in U_1. The sets PV_2 and MU_2 are defined similarly:

$$PV_2 = post_\perp(s_2) \cap (R[s_1] \cup \{\perp\})$$

and $MU_2 = post_\perp(s_2) \backslash PV_2$. Obviously, $\delta_i(u) = 1$ for $u \in MU_i$ for $i = 1, 2$.

We write $\gamma\mathbf{P}$ to denote a distribution $\mathbf{P}$ scaled by a constant $\gamma \in \mathbb{R}_{>0}$.
If s_1, s_2 and R are clear from the context, we let $\mathcal{N}(\gamma)$ denote the network
$\mathcal{N}(\mathbf{P}(s_1, \cdot), \gamma\mathbf{P}(s_2, \cdot), R)$. We say a flow function f of $\mathcal{N}(\gamma)$ is valid for $\mathcal{N}(\gamma)$ iff f
saturates all edges $(\top, u_1)$ with $u_1 \in MU_1$ and all edges $(\overline{u_2}, \bot)$ with $u_2 \in MU_2$.
For $\gamma \in \mathbb{R}_{>0}$, we address the problem of checking whether there exists a valid
flow f for $\mathcal{N}(\gamma)$. This is a *feasible flow problem* with lower bounds (f saturates
edges to MU_1 and from MU_2) and upper bounds (the capacities) on the flows.
It can be solved by applying a simple transformation to the graph (in time
$\mathcal{O}(|MU_1| + |MU_2|)$), solving the maximum flow problem for the transformed
graph, and checking whether the flow is large enough. Details are, for example,
described in [1, p. 169–170].

If there exists a valid flow f for $\mathcal{N}(\gamma)$, we say that γ is valid for $\mathcal{N}(\gamma)$. The
following lemma shows that the algorithm $\text{WSFPS}(\mathcal{D}, s_1, s_2, R)$ can be reduced
to checking whether there exists a valid γ for $\mathcal{N}(\gamma)$.

Lemma 4. *If* $\text{WS}(\mathcal{D}, s_1, s_2, R)$ *reaches line 7,* $s_1 \precsim_R s_2$ *iff there exists a valid*
γ *for* $\mathcal{N}(\gamma)$.

In the network $\mathcal{N}(\gamma)$ the capacities of the edges leading to the sink are an increasing function of a real-valued parameter γ. $\mathcal{N}(\gamma)$ is a *parametric network*[1] as described in [10, p. 33]. We recall briefly the *breakpoints* [10, p. 37–42] of $\mathcal{N}(\gamma)$. Let $\kappa(\gamma)$ denote the *minimum cut capacity function*, which is the capacity of a minimum cut as a function of γ. A breakpoint is a value γ_0 at which the slope of $\kappa(\gamma)$ changes. $\kappa(\gamma)$ is a piecewise-linear concave function with at most $|V| - 2$ breakpoints where $|V|$ denotes the number of vertices of $\mathcal{N}(\gamma)$. The $|V| - 1$ or fewer line segments forming the graph of $\kappa(\gamma)$ correspond to $|V| - 1$ or fewer distinct cuts. The same minimum cut can be chosen on the same slope of $\kappa(\gamma)$, and at breakpoints certain edges become saturated or unsaturated. As we expect, it is sufficient to consider only the breakpoints of $\mathcal{N}(\gamma)$:

Lemma 5. *There exists a valid γ for $\mathcal{N}(\gamma)$ iff one of the breakpoints of $\mathcal{N}(\gamma)$ is valid.*

All of the breakpoints can be obtained by the *breakpoint algorithm* [10, p. 40], which we embed into our algorithm WsFps as follows:

    WsFps$(\mathcal{D}, s_1, s_2, R)$
1. Compute all of the breakpoints $b_1 < b_2 < \ldots < b_j$ of $\mathcal{N}(\gamma)$.
2. Return true, iff for some $i \in \{1, \ldots, j\}$, b_i is valid for $\mathcal{N}(b_i)$.

The following lemma gives the correctness of the algorithm Ws:

Lemma 6. Ws$(\mathcal{D}, s_1, s_2, R)$ *returns true iff $s_1 \stackrel{\scriptscriptstyle\searrow}{\approx}_R s_2$.*

For each given breakpoint, we need to solve one feasible flow problem to check whether it is valid. So overall we apply at most $|V| - 2$ times feasible flow algorithms for all breakpoints. Applying a binary search method over the breakpoints, a better bound can be achieved where only $\log(|V|)$ maximum flow problems need to be solved. This allows us to achieve the following complexity result:

Lemma 7. SimRel$_w(\mathcal{D})$ *runs in time $\mathcal{O}(m^2 n^3)$ and in space $\mathcal{O}(n^2)$. If the fanout g is bounded by a constant, the time complexity is $\mathcal{O}(n^5)$.*

An algorithm for DTMCs. Let $\mathcal{D} = (S, \mathbf{P}, L)$ be a DTMC. We exploit the absence of sub-stochasticity in DTMC to arrive at an improved algorithm, in which we achieve the effect of WsFps$(\mathcal{D}, s_1, s_2, R)$ via only one maximum flow problem.

    Let H denote the sub-relation $R \cap [(post(s_1) \cup \{s_1\}) \times (post(s_2) \cup \{s_2\})]$ which is the local fragment of the relation R. Now let $A_1, A_2, \ldots A_h$ enumerate the classes of the equivalence relation $(H \cup H^{-1})^*$ generated by H where h denotes the number of classes. W.l.o.g., we assume in the following that A_h is the equivalence class containing s_1 and s_2, i.e., $s_1, s_2 \in A_h$. The following lemma gives some properties of the sets A_i provided that $s_1 \stackrel{\scriptscriptstyle\searrow}{\approx}_R s_2$:

---

[1] In [10, p. 33], the capacities leading to \ is a non-increasing function of γ. As indicated in [10, p. 36], if we reverse the directions of all the edges and exchange the source and sink, the algorithms presented there can be used directly.

WsDTMC$(\mathcal{D}, s_1, s_2, R)$
1   Construct the partition $A_1, \ldots, A_h$
2   **if** $(h = 1)$ **return** WsFps$(\mathcal{D}, s_1, s_2, R)$
3   **foreach** $i \leftarrow 1, 2, \ldots h - 1$
4   **if** $(\mathbf{P}(s_1, A_i) = \mathbf{P}(s_2, A_i) = 0)$ **raise error**
5   **else if** $(\mathbf{P}(s_1, A_i) = 0$ or $\mathbf{P}(s_2, A_i) = 0)$ **return false**
6   **else** $\gamma_i \leftarrow \frac{\mathbf{P}(s_1, A_i)}{\mathbf{P}(s_2, A_i)}$
7   **if** $(\gamma_i \neq \gamma_j$ for some $i, j < h)$ **return false**
8   **return true** iff γ_1 is valid for $\mathcal{N}(\gamma_1)$.

Fig. 5. Algorithm to check whether $s_1 \precsim_R s_2$ tailored to DTMCs

Lemma 8. *For* $(s_1, s_2) \in R$, *assume that there exists a state* $s_1' \in post(s_1)$ *such that* $s_1' \notin R^{-1}[s_2]$, *and* $s_2' \in post(s_2)$ *such that* $s_2' \notin R[s_1]$. *Let* $A_1, \ldots, A_h$ *be the sets constructed for* (s_1, s_2) *as above. If* $s_1 \precsim_R s_2$, *the following hold:*

1. $\mathbf{P}(s_1, A_i) > 0$ *and* $\mathbf{P}(s_2, A_i) > 0$ *for all* $i < h$
2. $\gamma_i = \frac{K_1}{K_2}$ *for all* $i < h$ *where* $\gamma_i = \frac{\mathbf{P}(s_1, A_i)}{\mathbf{P}(s_2, A_i)}$

The algorithm WsDTMC is presented in Fig. 5. The partition $A_1, \ldots, A_h$ is constructed in line 1. If $h = 1$ (line 2), it is reduced to WsFps$(\mathcal{D}, s_1, s_2, R)$. Lines 3–7 follows directly from Lemma 8. Line 8 follows from the following lemma, which is the counterpart of Lemma 4:

Lemma 9. *Assume* WsDTMC$(\mathcal{D}, s_1, s_2, R)$ *reaches line 7 and* $h > 1$, $s_1 \precsim_R s_2$ *iff* γ_1 *is valid for* $\mathcal{N}(\gamma_1)$.

One might expect that this lemma allows us to establish a better time bound for DTMCs in the order of $\log n$. This is indeed the case if $h > 1$ for each pair (s_1, s_2) in the initial R_{init}, which is a peculiar structural restriction: the labels of at least one successor of s_1 or s_2 must differ from $L(s_1)$ (or s_2). In this special case we can even establish the time bound $\mathcal{O}(m^2 n)$, the same as for strong simulation.

An algorithm for CTMCs. We now discuss how to handle CTMCs. Recall that in Definition 8, we have the rate condition $(3')$: $K_1 \mathbf{R}(s_1, S) \leq K_2 \mathbf{R}(s_2, S)$. To determine the weak simulation $\precsim_c$, we simplify the algorithm for DTMCs as follows. If $K_1 > 0$ and $K_2 = 0$, we must have $s_1 \not\precsim_R s_2$ because of the rate condition. Hence, the check of the reachability condition in lines 2–6 of the algorithm Ws$(\mathcal{C}, s_1, s_2, R)$ can be skipped. At line 7 the algorithm WsDTMC$(\mathcal{C}, s_1, s_2, R)$ is called as before. To check the additional rate condition in WsDTMC we use the following lemma:

Lemma 10. *Assume that* $s_1 \precsim_R s_2$ *in* $emb(\mathcal{C})$ *and there exists* $s_1' \in post(s_1)$ *such that* $s_1' \notin R^{-1}[s_2]$. *We let* γ_{min} *denote the minimal valid breakpoint for* $\mathcal{N}(\gamma_{min})$ *in* $emb(\mathcal{C})$. *Then,* $s_1 \precsim_R s_2$ *in* $\mathcal{C}$ *iff* $\gamma_{min} \leq \mathbf{R}(s_2, S)/\mathbf{R}(s_1, S)$.

To check the rate condition for the case $h > 1$, we replace line 8 of the algorithm WsDTMC by:

return true iff $\gamma_1 \leq \mathbf{R}(s_2, S)/\mathbf{R}(s_1, S)$ and γ_1 is valid for $\mathcal{N}(\gamma_1)$

In case $h = 1$, WsDTMC calls WsFPs$(\mathcal{C}, s_1, s_2, R)$ in line 2. We replace line 2 of WsFPs by:

Return true iff, for some $i \in \{1, \ldots, j\}$, $b_i \leq \mathbf{R}(s_2, S)/\mathbf{R}(s_1, S)$ and b_i is valid for $\mathcal{N}(b_i)$

to check the rate condition. The existential quantifier corresponds to the minimal valid breakpoint requirement. Similar to FPSs, a binary search method over the breakpoints can be used to find the minimal valid breakpoint. As checking the reachability condition is not required for CTMCs, we get even a better bound for sparse CTMCs:

Lemma 11. *If the fanout g of CTMC $\mathcal{C}$ is bounded by a constant, the time complexity is $\mathcal{O}(n^4)$.*

5   Conclusions

We have introduced efficient algorithms to decide simulation on Markov models. For sparse models where the fanout is bounded by a constant, we achieve the complexities $\mathcal{O}(n^2)$ for strong and $\mathcal{O}(n^4)$ for weak simulation relations on CTMCs, and $\mathcal{O}(n^5)$ for DTMCs, respectively. If instead one uses the original algorithm for weak simulation combined with the polynomial method to solve such an LP ($\mathcal{O}(n^{10} \cdot r)$) [20], one would obtain a time complexity of $\mathcal{O}(n^{14} \cdot r)$ where r is the maximal binary encoding length of a coefficient of the LP. The weak simulation algorithm is polynomial in the RAM-model of computation while no known linear programming based algorithm is.

We believe that the strong and weak simulation algorithms are core contributions in the quest for model checking techniques of ever larger Markov chains. Currently, the main bottleneck is the prohibitively unstructured computations required in the numerical solution phase, resulting in the need to store an n-dimensional vector of floating point values in memory without much chance for an efficient symbolic representation [19].

At first sight our situation is worse, since we have to keep flows in the order of m^2 across the iterations of our algorithm. But since these flows are resulting from very local computations (on bipartite, loop-free networks of diameter 3), they are much more structured, making it possible to utilise symbolic and hashing techniques effectively in their internal representation. We therefore expect that the algorithms in this paper can effectively be employed to reduce the – otherwise prohibitive – size of a Markov chain prior to numerically checking a safe temporal logic formula. By doing so, we trade time against memory, because the direct numerical solution is practically of quadratic complexity (in n) – but only if the above vector fits in memory.

Acknowledgments. The authors are grateful to Björn Wachter (Saarland University) for helpful comments at an early state of this paper.

References

1. R. K. Ahuja, T. L. Magnanti, J. B. Orlin: Network Flows: theory, algorithms, and applications. Prentice Hall, 1993
2. A. Aziz, K. Sanwal, V. Singhal, R. K. Brayton: Verifying Continuous Time Markov Chains. In CAV (1996) 269–276
3. C. Baier, B. Engelen, M. E. Majster-Cederbaum: Deciding Bisimilarity and Similarity for Probabilistic Processes. J. Comput. Syst. Sci. **60(1)** (2000) 187–231
4. C. Baier, B. R. Haverkort, H. Hermanns, J.-P. Katoen: Model-Checking Algorithms for Continuous-Time Markov Chains. IEEE Trans. Software Eng. **29(6)** (2003) 524–541
5. C. Baier and H. Hermanns and J.-P. Katoen: Probabilistic weak simulation is decidable in polynomial time. Inf. Process. Lett. **89(3)** (2004) 123–130
6. C. Baier, J.-P. Katoen, H. Hermanns, B. Haverkort: Simulation for Continuous-Time Markov Chains. In CONCUR (2002) 338–354
7. C. Baier, J.-P. Katoen, H. Hermanns, V. Wolf: Comparative branching-time semantics for Markov chains. Inf. Comput **200(2)** (2005) 149–214
8. J. Cheriyan, T. Hagerup, K. Mehlhorn: Can a Maximum Flow be Computed in $\mathcal{O}(nm)$ Time? In Proc. ICALP (1990) 235–248
9. E. M. Clarke, O. Grumberg, D. E. Long: Model Checking and Abstraction. ACM Transactions on Programming Languages and Systems **16(5)** (1994) 1512–1542
10. G. Gallo, M. D. Grigoriadis, R. E. Tarjan: A fast parametric maximum flow algorithm and applications. SIAM J. Comput. **18(1)** (1989) 30–55
11. R. Gentilini, C. Piazza, A. Policriti: From Bisimulation to Simulation: Coarsest Partition Problems. J. Autom. Reasoning **31(1)** (2003) 73–103
12. A. V. Goldberg: Recent Developments in Maximum Flow Algorithms (Invited Lecture). In SWAT (1998) 1–10
13. A. V. Goldberg, R. E. Tarjan: A new approach to the maximum-flow problem. J. ACM **35(4)** (1988) 921–940
14. H. Hansson, B. Jonsson: A Logic for Reasoning about Time and Reliability. Formal Asp. Comput. **6(5)** (1994) 512–535
15. M. R. Henzinger, T. A. Henzinger, P. W. Kopke: Computing Simulations on Finite and Infinite Graphs. In FOCS (1995) 453–462
16. B. Jonsson: Simulations Between Specifications of Distributed Systems. In CONCUR (1991) 346–360
17. B. Jonsson, K. G. Larsen: Specification and Refinement of Probabilistic Processes. In LICS (1991) 266–277
18. R. Milner: Communication and Concurrency. Prentice Hall, 1989
19. D. Parker: Implementation of Symbolic Model Checking for Probabilistic Systems. University of Birmingham, 2002
20. A. Schrijver: Theory of Linear and Integer Programming. Wiley, 1986

Model Checking Probabilistic Timed Automata with One or Two Clocks*

Marcin Jurdziński[1], François Laroussinie[2], and Jeremy Sproston[3]

[1] Department of Computer Science, University of Warwick, Coventry CV4 7AL, UK
[2] Lab. Spécification & Verification, ENS Cachan – CNRS UMR 8643, France
[3] Dipartimento di Informatica, Università di Torino, 10149 Torino, Italy
mju@dcs.warwick.ac.uk, fl@lsv.ens-cachan.fr,
sproston@di.unito.it

Abstract. Probabilistic timed automata are an extension of timed automata with discrete probability distributions. We consider model-checking algorithms for the subclasses of probabilistic timed automata which have one or two clocks. Firstly, we show that PCTL probabilistic model-checking problems (such as determining whether a set of target states can be reached with probability at least 0.99 regardless of how nondeterminism is resolved) are PTIME-complete for one clock probabilistic timed automata, and are EXPTIME-complete for probabilistic timed automata with two clocks. Secondly, we show that the model-checking problem for the probabilistic timed temporal logic PTCTL is EXPTIME-complete for one clock probabilistic timed automata. However, the corresponding model-checking problem for the subclass of PTCTL which does not permit both (1) punctual timing bounds, which require the occurrence of an event at an exact time point, and (2) comparisons with probability bounds other than 0 or 1, is PTIME-complete.

1 Introduction

Model checking is an automatic method for guaranteeing that a mathematical model of a system satisfies a formally-described property [8]. Many real-life systems, such as multimedia equipment, communication protocols, networks and fault-tolerant systems, exhibit *probabilistic* behaviour. This leads to the study of *probabilistic model checking* of probabilistic models based on Markov chains or Markov decision processes [25,12,9,7,10,6]. Similarly, it is common to observe complex *real-time* behaviour in systems. Model checking of (non-probabilistic) continuous-time systems against properties of timed temporal logics, which can refer to the time elapsed along system behaviours, has been studied extensively in, for example, the context of *timed automata* [3,4], which are automata extended with *clocks* that progress synchronously with time. Finally, certain systems exhibit both probabilistic *and* timed behaviour, leading to the development of model-checking algorithms for such systems [2,12,10,15,5,19].

In this paper, we aim to study model-checking algorithms for *probabilistic timed automata* [13,15], a variant of timed automata extended with discrete probability distributions, or (equivalently) Markov decision processes extended with clocks. Probabilistic

---

* Supported in part by EPSRC project EP/E022030/1, Miur project Firb-Perf, and EEC project Crutial.

O. Grumberg and M. Huth (Eds.): TACAS 2007, LNCS 4424, pp. 170–184, 2007.
© Springer-Verlag Berlin Heidelberg 2007

Table 1. Complexity results for model checking probabilistic timed automata

	One clock	Two clocks
Reachability, PCTL	P-complete	EXPTIME-complete
PTCTL$^{0/1}[\leq, \geq]$	P-complete	EXPTIME-complete
PTCTL$^{0/1}$	EXPTIME-complete	EXPTIME-complete
PTCTL$[\leq, \geq]$	P-hard, in EXPTIME	EXPTIME-complete
PTCTL	EXPTIME-complete	EXPTIME-complete

timed automata have been used to model systems such as the IEEE 1394 root contention protocol, the backoff procedure in the IEEE 802.11 Wireless LANs, and the IPv4 link local address resolution protocol [14]. The temporal logic that we use to describe properties of probabilistic timed automata is PTCTL (Probabilistic Timed Computation Tree Logic) [15]. The logic PTCTL includes operators that can refer to bounds on exact time and on the probability of the occurrence of events. For example, the property "a request is followed by a response within 5 time units with probability 0.99 or greater" can be expressed by the PTCTL property $request \Rightarrow \mathbb{P}_{\geq 0.99}(\mathsf{F}_{\leq 5} response)$. The logic PTCTL extends the probabilistic temporal logic PCTL [12,7], and the real-time temporal logic TCTL [3].

In the non-probabilistic setting, timed automata with one clock have recently been studied extensively [17,21,1]. In this paper we consider the subclasses of probabilistic timed automata with one or two clocks. While probabilistic timed automata with a restricted number of clocks are less expressive than their counterparts with an arbitrary number of clocks, they can be used to model systems with simple timing constraints, such as probabilistic systems in which the time of a transition depends only on the time elapsed since the last transition. Conversely, one clock probabilistic timed automata are more natural and expressive than Markov decision processes in which durations are associated with transitions (for example, in [11,19]). We note that the IEEE 802.11 Wireless LAN case study has two clocks [14], and that an abstract model of the IEEE 1394 root contention protocol can be obtained with one clock [23].

After introducing probabilistic timed automata and PTCTL in Section 2 and Section 3, respectively, in Section 4 we show that model-checking properties of PCTL, such as the property $\mathbb{P}_{\geq 0.99}(\mathsf{F} target)$ ("a set of target states is reached with probability at least 0.99 regardless of how nondeterminism is resolved"), is PTIME-complete for one clock probabilistic timed automata, which is the same as for probabilistic reachability properties on (untimed) Markov decision processes [22]. We also show that, in general, model checking of PTCTL on one clock probabilistic timed automata is EXPTIME-complete. However, inspired by the efficient algorithms obtained for non-probabilistic one clock timed automata [17], we also show that, restricting the syntax of PTCTL to the sub-logic in which (1) punctual timing bounds and (2) comparisons with probability bounds other than 0 or 1, are disallowed, results in a PTIME-complete model-checking problem. In Section 5, we show that reachability properties with probability bounds of 0 or 1 are EXPTIME-complete for probabilistic timed automata with two or more clocks, implying EXPTIME-completeness of all the model-checking problems that we consider for this class of models. Our results are summarized in Table 1, where $0/1$

denotes the sub-logics of PTCTL with probability bounds of 0 and 1 only, and $[\leq, \geq]$ denotes the sub-logics of PTCTL in which punctual timing bounds are disallowed. The EXPTIME-hardness results are based on the concept of *countdown games*, which are two-player games operating in discrete time in which one player wins if it is able to make a state transition after *exactly* c time units have elapsed, regardless of the strategy of the other player. We believe that countdown games may be of independent interest. Note that we restrict our attention to probabilistic timed automata in which positive durations elapse in all loops of the system.

2 Probabilistic Timed Automata

Preliminaries. We use $\mathbb{R}_{\geq 0}$ to denote the set of non-negative real numbers, $\mathbb{N}$ to denote the set of natural numbers, and AP to denote a set of atomic propositions. A (discrete) probability *distribution* over a countable set Q is a function $\mu : Q \to [0, 1]$ such that $\sum_{q \in Q} \mu(q) = 1$. For a function $\mu : Q \to \mathbb{R}_{\geq 0}$ we define $\text{support}(\mu) = \{q \in Q \mid \mu(q) > 0\}$. Then for an uncountable set Q we define $\text{Dist}(Q)$ to be the set of functions $\mu : Q \to [0, 1]$, such that $\text{support}(\mu)$ is a countable set and μ restricted to $\text{support}(\mu)$ is a (discrete) probability distribution.

We now introduce *timed Markov decision processes*, which are Markov decision processes in which rewards associated with transitions are interpreted as time durations.

Definition 1. *A* timed Markov decision process *(TMDP)* $\mathsf{T} = (S, s_{init}, \to, lab)$ *comprises a (possibly uncountable) set of states S with an initial state $s_{init} \in S$; a (possibly uncountable) timed probabilistic, nondeterministic transition relation $\to \subseteq S \times \mathbb{R}_{\geq 0} \times \text{Dist}(S)$ such that, for each state $s \in S$, there exists at least one tuple $(s, \_, \_) \in \to$; and a labelling function $lab : S \to 2^{AP}$.*

The transitions from state to state of a TMDP are performed in two steps: given that the current state is s, the first step concerns a nondeterministic selection of $(s, d, \nu) \in \to$, where d corresponds to the duration of the transition; the second step comprises a probabilistic choice, made according to the distribution ν, as to which state to make the transition to (that is, we make a transition to a state $s' \in S$ with probability $\nu(s')$). We often denote such a transition by $s \xrightarrow{d, \nu} s'$.

An infinite or finite *path* of the TMDP T is defined as an infinite or finite sequence of transitions, respectively, such that the target state of one transition is the source state of the next. We use $Path_{fin}$ to denote the set of finite paths of T, and $Path_{ful}$ the set of infinite paths of T. If ω is a finite path, we denote by $last(\omega)$ the last state of ω. For any path ω, let $\omega(i)$ be its $(i+1)$th state. Let $Path_{ful}(s)$ refer to the set of infinite paths commencing in state $s \in S$.

In contrast to a path, which corresponds to a resolution of nondeterministic and probabilistic choice, an *adversary* represents a resolution of nondeterminism *only*. Formally, an adversary of a TMDP T is a function A mapping every finite path $\omega \in Path_{fin}$ to a transition $(last(\omega), d, \nu) \in \to$. Let Adv be the set of adversaries of T. For any adversary $A \in Adv$, let $Path_{ful}^A$ denote the set of infinite paths resulting from the choices of distributions of A, and, for a state $s \in S$, let $Path_{ful}^A(s) = Path_{ful}^A \cap Path_{ful}(s)$. Then we can define the probability measure $Prob_s^A$ over $Path_{ful}^A(s)$ (for details, see, for example, [15]). Note that, by defining adversaries as functions from finite paths, we permit adversaries to be dependent on the history of the system. Hence, the choice made by an adversary at a certain point in system execution can depend on the sequence of states visited, the nondeterministic choices taken, and the time elapsed from each state, up to that point.

We distinguish the two classes of TMDP. *Discrete TMDPs* are TMDPs in which (1) the state space S is finite, and (2) the transition relation $\rightarrow$ is finite and of the form $\rightarrow \subseteq S \times \mathbb{N} \times \text{Dist}(S)$. In discrete TMDPs, the delays are interpreted as discrete jumps, with no notion of a continuously changing state as time elapses. The size $|\mathsf{T}|$ of a discrete TMDP T is $|S| + | \rightarrow |$, where $| \rightarrow |$ includes the size of the encoding of the timing constants and probabilities used in $\rightarrow$: the timing constants are written in binary, and, for any $s, s' \in S$ and (s, d, ν), the probability $\nu(s')$ is expressed as a ratio between two natural numbers, each written in binary. We let T^u be the untimed Markov decision process (MDP) corresponding to the discrete TMDP T, in which each transition $(s, d, \nu) \in \rightarrow$ is represented by a transition (s, ν). We define the accumulated duration $\text{DiscDur}(\omega, i)$ along the infinite path $\omega = s_0 \xrightarrow{d_0, \nu_0} s_1 \xrightarrow{d_1, \nu_1} \cdots$ of T until the $(i+1)$-th state to be the sum $\sum_{0 \leq k < i} d_k$. A discrete TMDP is *structurally non-Zeno* when any finite path of the form $s_0 \xrightarrow{d_0, \nu_0} s_1 \cdots \xrightarrow{d_n, \nu_n} s_{n+1}$, such that $s_{n+1} = s_0$, satisfies $\sum_{0 \leq i \leq n} d_i > 0$. *Continuous TMDPs* are infinite-state TMDPs in which any transition $s \xrightarrow{d, \nu} s'$ describes the continuous passage of time, and thus a path $\omega = s_0 \xrightarrow{d_0, \nu_0} s_1 \xrightarrow{d_1, \nu_1} \cdots$ describes implicitly an infinite set of visited states. In the sequel, we use continuous TMDPs to give the semantics of probabilistic timed automata.

Syntax of Probabilistic Timed Automata. Let $\mathcal{X}$ be a finite set of real-valued variables called *clocks*, the values of which increase at the same rate as real-time. The set $\Psi_{\mathcal{X}}$ of *clock constraints* over $\mathcal{X}$ is defined as the set of conjunctions over atomic formulae of the form $x \sim c$, where $x, y \in \mathcal{X}$, $\sim \in \{<, \leq, >, \geq, =\}$, and $c \in \mathbb{N}$.

Definition 2. *A probabilistic timed automaton (PTA)* $\mathsf{P} = (L, \bar{l}, \mathcal{X}, inv, prob, \mathcal{L})$ *is a tuple consisting of a finite set L of locations with the initial location $\bar{l} \in L$; a finite set $\mathcal{X}$ of clocks; a function $inv : L \rightarrow \Psi_{\mathcal{X}}$ associating an invariant condition with each location; a finite set $prob \subseteq L \times \Psi_{\mathcal{X}} \times \text{Dist}(2^{\mathcal{X}} \times L)$ of probabilistic edges such that, for each $l \in L$, there exists at least one $(l, \_, \_) \in prob$; and a labelling function $\mathcal{L} : L \rightarrow 2^{AP}$.*

A probabilistic edge $(l, g, p) \in prob$ is a triple containing (1) a source location l, (2) a clock constraint g, called a *guard*, and (3) a probability distribution p which assigns probability to pairs of the form (X, l') for some clock set X and target location l'. The behaviour of a probabilistic timed automaton takes a similar form to that of a timed automaton [4]: in any location time can advance as long as the invariant holds, and a probabilistic edge can be taken if its guard is satisfied by the current values of the clocks. However, probabilistic timed automata generalize timed automata in the sense that, once a probabilistic edge is nondeterministically selected, then the choice of which clocks to reset and which target location to make the transition to is *probabilistic*.

The size $|\mathsf{P}|$ of the PTA P is $|L| + |\mathcal{X}| + |inv| + |prob|$, where $|inv|$ represents the size of the binary encoding of the constants used in the invariant condition, and

$|prob|$ includes the size of the binary encoding of the constants used in guards and the probabilities used in probabilistic edges. As in the case of TMDPs, probabilities are expressed as a ratio between two natural numbers, each written in binary.

A PTA is *structurally non-Zeno* [24] if, for every sequence $X_0, (l_0, g_0, p_0), X_1,$ $(l_1, g_1, p_1), \cdots, X_n, (l_n, g_n, p_n)$, such that $p_i(X_{i+1}, l_{i+1}) > 0$ for $0 \leq i < n$, and $p_n(X_0, l_0) > 0$, there exists a clock $x \in \mathcal{X}$ and $0 \leq i, j \leq n$ such that $x \in X_i$ and $g_j \Rightarrow x \geq 1$ (that is, g_j contains a conjunct of the form $x \geq c$ for some $c \geq 1$). We use 1C-PTA (resp. 2C-PTA) to denote the set of structurally non-Zeno PTA with only one (resp. two) clock(s).

Semantics of Probabilistic Timed Automata. We refer to a mapping $v : \mathcal{X} \to \mathbb{R}_{\geq 0}$ as a *clock valuation*. Let $\mathbb{R}_{\geq 0}^{\mathcal{X}}$ denote the set of clock valuations. Let $\mathbf{0} \in \mathbb{R}_{\geq 0}^{\mathcal{X}}$ be the clock valuation which assigns 0 to all clocks in $\mathcal{X}$. For a clock valuation $v \in \mathbb{R}_{\geq 0}^{\mathcal{X}}$ and a value $d \in \mathbb{R}_{\geq 0}$, we use $v + d$ to denote the clock valuation obtained by letting $(v + d)(x) = v(x) + d$ for all clocks $x \in \mathcal{X}$. For a clock set $X \subseteq \mathcal{X}$, we let $v[X := 0]$ be the clock valuation obtained from v by resetting all clocks within X to 0; more precisely, we let $v[X := 0](x) = 0$ for all $x \in X$, and let $v[X := 0](x) = v(x)$ for all $x \in \mathcal{X} \setminus X$. The clock valuation v *satisfies* the clock constraint $\psi \in \Psi_{\mathcal{X}}$, written $v \models \psi$, if and only if ψ resolves to true after substituting each clock $x \in \mathcal{X}$ with the corresponding clock value $v(x)$.

Definition 3. *The semantics of the probabilistic timed automaton* $\mathsf{P} = (L, \bar{l}, \mathcal{X}, inv,$ $prob, \mathcal{L})$ *is the continuous TMDP* $\mathsf{T}[\mathsf{P}] = (S, s_{init}, \to, lab)$ *where:*

- $S = \{(l, v) \mid l \in L \text{ and } v \in \mathbb{R}_{\geq 0}^{\mathcal{X}} \text{ s.t. } v \models inv(l)\}$ *and* $s_{init} = (\bar{l}, \mathbf{0})$;
- $\to$ *is the smallest set such that* $((l, v), d, \mu) \in \to$ *if there exist* $d \in \mathbb{R}_{\geq 0}$ *and a probabilistic edge* $(l, g, p) \in prob$ *such that:*
  1. $v + d \models g$, *and* $v + d' \models inv(l)$ *for all* $0 \leq d' \leq d$;
  2. *for any* $(X, l') \in 2^{\mathcal{X}} \times L$, *we have that* $p(X, l') > 0$ *implies* $(v + d)[X := 0] \models inv(l')$;
  3. *for any* $(l', v') \in S$, *we have that* $\mu(l', v') = \sum_{X \in \mathsf{Reset}(v, d, v')} p(X, l')$, *where* $\mathsf{Reset}(v, d, v') = \{X \subseteq \mathcal{X} \mid (v + d)[X := 0] = v'\}$.
- *lab is such that* $lab(l, v) = \mathcal{L}(l)$ *for each state* $(l, v) \in S$.

Given a path $\omega = (l_0, v_0) \xrightarrow{d_0, \nu_0} (l_1, v_1) \xrightarrow{d_1, \nu_1} \cdots$ of $\mathsf{T}[\mathsf{P}]$, for every i, we use $\omega(i, d)$, with $0 \leq d \leq d_i$, to denote the state $(l_i, v_i + d)$ reached from (l_i, v_i) after delaying d time units. Such a pair (i, d) is called a *position* of ω. We define a total order on positions: given two positions $(i, d), (j, d')$ of ω, the position (i, d) precedes (j, d') — denoted $(i, d) \prec_{\omega} (j, d')$ — if and only if either $i < j$, or $i = j$ and $d < d'$. Furthermore, we define the accumulated duration $\mathsf{CtsDur}(\omega, i, d)$ along the path ω until position (i, d) to be the sum $d + \sum_{0 \leq k < i} d_k$.

3   Probabilistic Timed Temporal Logic

We now proceed to describe a *probabilistic, timed* temporal logic which can be used to specify properties of probabilistic timed automata [15].

Definition 4. *The formulae of* PTCTL *(Probabilistic Timed Computation Tree Logic) are given by the following grammar:*

$$\phi ::= a \mid \phi \wedge \phi \mid \neg \phi \mid \mathbb{P}_{\bowtie\zeta}(\phi \mathsf{U}_{\sim c}\phi)$$

where $a \in AP$ *is an atomic proposition,* $\bowtie \in \{<, \leq, \geq, >\}$*,* $\sim \in \{\leq, =, \geq\}$*,* $\zeta \in [0, 1]$ *is a probability, and* $c \in \mathbb{N}$ *is a natural number.*

We use standard abbreviations such as true, false, $\phi_1 \vee \phi_2$, $\phi_1 \Rightarrow \phi_2$, and $\mathbb{P}_{\bowtie\zeta}(\mathsf{F}_{\sim c}\phi)$ (for $\mathbb{P}_{\bowtie\zeta}(\text{true}\mathsf{U}_{\sim c}\phi)$). Formulae with "always" temporal operators $\mathsf{G}_{\sim c}$ can also be written; for example $\mathbb{P}_{\geq\zeta}(\mathsf{G}_{\sim c}\phi)$ can be expressed by $\mathbb{P}_{\leq 1-\zeta}(\mathsf{F}_{\sim c}\neg\phi)$. The modalities U, F and G without subscripts abbreviate $\mathsf{U}_{\geq 0}$, $\mathsf{F}_{\geq 0}$ and $\mathsf{G}_{\geq 0}$, respectively. We refer to PTCTL properties of the form $\mathbb{P}_{\bowtie\zeta}(\mathsf{F}a)$ or $\neg\mathbb{P}_{\bowtie\zeta}(\mathsf{F}a)$ as *(untimed) reachability properties*. When $\zeta \in \{0, 1\}$, these properties are referred to as *qualitative reachability properties*.

We define PTCTL$[\leq, \geq]$ as the sub-logic of PTCTL in which subscripts of the form $= c$ are not allowed in modalities $\mathsf{U}_{\sim c}, \mathsf{F}_{\sim c}, \mathsf{G}_{\sim c}$. We define PTCTL$^{0/1}[\leq, \geq]$ and PTCTL$^{0/1}$ as the qualitative restrictions in which probability thresholds ζ belong to $\{0, 1\}$. Furthermore PCTL is the sub-logic in which there is no timing subscript $\sim c$ associated with the modalities $\mathsf{U}, \mathsf{F}, \mathsf{G}$. The size $|\Phi|$ of Φ is defined in the standard way as the number of symbols in Φ, with each occurrence of the same subformula of Φ as a single symbol.

We now define the satisfaction relation of PTCTL for discrete and continuous TMDPs.

Definition 5. *Given a discrete TMDP* $\mathsf{T} = (S, s_{init}, \rightarrow, lab)$ *and a* PTCTL *formula* Φ*, we define the satisfaction relation* $\models_\mathsf{T}$ *of* PTCTL *as follows:*

$$
\begin{aligned}
s &\models_\mathsf{T} a & &\text{iff } a \in lab(s) \\
s &\models_\mathsf{T} \Phi_1 \wedge \Phi_2 & &\text{iff } s \models_\mathsf{T} \Phi_1 \text{ and } s \models_\mathsf{T} \Phi_2 \\
s &\models_\mathsf{T} \neg\Phi & &\text{iff } s \not\models_\mathsf{T} \Phi \\
s &\models_\mathsf{T} \mathbb{P}_{\bowtie\zeta}(\varphi) & &\text{iff } Prob_s^A\{\omega \in Path_{ful}^A(s) \mid \omega \models_\mathsf{T} \varphi\} \bowtie \zeta, \; \forall A \in Adv \\
\omega &\models_\mathsf{T} \Phi_1 \mathsf{U}_{\sim c}\Phi_2 & &\text{iff } \exists i \in \mathbb{N} \text{ s.t. } \omega(i) \models_\mathsf{T} \phi_2, \text{ DiscDur}(\omega, i) \sim c, \\
& & &\text{and } \omega(j) \models_\mathsf{T} \phi_1, \; \forall j < i \, .
\end{aligned}
$$

Definition 6. *Given a continuous TMDP* $\mathsf{T} = (S, s_{init}, \rightarrow, lab)$ *and a* PTCTL *formula* Φ*, we define the satisfaction relation* $\models_\mathsf{T}$ *of* PTCTL *as in Definition 5, except for the following rule for* $\Phi_1 \mathsf{U}_{\sim c}\Phi_2$*:*

$$\omega \models_\mathsf{T} \Phi_1 \mathsf{U}_{\sim c}\Phi_2 \text{ iff } \exists \text{ position } (i, \delta) \text{ of } \omega \text{ s.t. } \omega(i, \delta) \models_\mathsf{T} \phi_2, \text{ CtsDur}(\omega, i, \delta) \sim c,$$
$$\text{and } \omega(j, \delta') \models_\mathsf{T} \phi_1, \; \forall \text{ positions } (j, \delta') \text{ of } \omega \text{ s.t. } (j, \delta') \prec_\omega (i, \delta) \, .$$

When clear from the context, we omit the T subscript from $\models_\mathsf{T}$. We say that the TMDP $\mathsf{T} = (S, s_{init}, \rightarrow, lab)$ satisfies the PTCTL formula Φ, denoted by $\mathsf{T} \models \Phi$, if and only if $s_{init} \models \Phi$. Furthermore, the PTA P satisfies Φ, denoted by $\mathsf{P} \models \Phi$, if and only if $\mathsf{T[P]} \models \Phi$. Given an arbitrary structurally non-Zeno PTA P, model checking PTCTL formulae is in EXPTIME [15] (the algorithm consists of executing a standard polynomial-time model-checking algorithm for finite-state probabilistic systems [7,6] on the exponential-size region graph of P). Qualitative reachability problems are EXPTIME-complete for PTA with an arbitrary number of clocks [20].

4 Model Checking One Clock Probabilistic Timed Automata

In this section we consider the case of 1C-PTA. We will see that model checking PCTL and PTCTL$^{0/1}[\leq, \geq]$ over 1C-PTA is P-complete (where the lower bound follows from the fact that qualitative reachability properties are P-hard for MDPs [22]), but remains EXPTIME-complete for the logic PTCTL$^{0/1}$. First we have the following result about the model-checking of PCTL formulae.

Proposition 1. *The PCTL model-checking problem for 1C-PTA is P-complete.*

4.1 Model Checking PTCTL$^{0/1}[\leq, \geq]$ on 1C-PTA

In this section, inspired by related work on timed concurrent game structures [16], we first show that model-checking PTCTL$^{0/1}[\leq, \geq]$ properties of discrete TMDPs can be done efficiently. Then, in Theorem 1, using ideas from the TMDP case, we show that model checking PTCTL$^{0/1}[\leq, \geq]$ on 1C-PTA can also be done in polynomial time.

Proposition 2. *Let* $\mathsf{T} = (S, s_{init}, \rightarrow, lab)$ *be a structurally non-Zeno discrete TMDP and* Φ *be a* PTCTL$^{0/1}[\leq, \geq]$ *formula. Deciding whether* $\mathsf{T} \models \Phi$ *can be done in time* $O(|\Phi| \cdot |S| \cdot | \rightarrow |)$.

Proof (sketch). The model-checking algorithm is based on several procedures to deal with each modality of PTCTL$^{0/1}[\leq, \geq]$. The boolean operators and the PCTL modalities (without timed subscripts) can be handled in the standard manner, with the PCTL properties verified on the untimed MDP T^u corresponding to T. For formulae $\mathbb{P}_{\bowtie\zeta}(\Phi_1 \mathsf{U}_{\sim c}\Phi_2)$, we assume that the truth values of subformulae Φ_1 and Φ_2 are known for any states of T. First, given that the TMDP is structurally non-Zeno, we have the equivalences $\mathbb{P}_{\leq 0}(\Phi_1 \mathsf{U}_{\sim c}\Phi_2) \equiv \neg\mathsf{E}\Phi_1\mathsf{U}_{\sim c}\Phi_2$ and $\mathbb{P}_{\geq 1}(\Phi_1 \mathsf{U}_{\sim c}\Phi_2) \equiv \mathsf{A}\Phi_1\mathsf{U}_{\sim c}(\mathbb{P}_{\geq 1}(\Phi_1\mathsf{U}\Phi_2))$, where E (resp. A) stands for the existential (resp. universal) quantification over paths which exist in the logic TCTL. Thus we can apply the procedure proposed for model checking TCTL formulae – running in time $O(|S| \cdot | \rightarrow |)$ – over weighted graphs [18] (in the case of $\mathbb{P}_{\geq 1}(\Phi_1 \mathsf{U}_{\sim c}\Phi_2)$, by first obtaining the set of states satisfying $\mathbb{P}_{\geq 1}(\Phi_1\mathsf{U}\Phi_2)$, which can be done on T^u in time $O(\sum_{(s,d,\nu)\in\rightarrow} |\mathsf{support}(\nu)|))$.

The problem of verifying the remaining temporal properties of PTCTL$^{0/1}[\leq, \geq]$ can be considered in terms of turn-based 2-player games. Such a game is played over the space $S \cup \rightarrow$, and play proceeds as follows: from a state $s \in S$, player P_n chooses a transition $(s, d, \nu) \in\rightarrow$; then, from the transition (s, d, ν), player P_p chooses a state $s' \in \mathsf{support}(\nu)$. The duration of the move from s to s' via (s, d, ν) is d. Notions of strategy of each player, and winning with respect to (untimed) path formulae of the form $\Phi_1\mathsf{U}\Phi_2$, are defined as usual for 2-player games.

For the four remaining formulae, namely $\mathbb{P}_{\bowtie\zeta}(\Phi_1 \mathsf{U}_{\sim c}\Phi_2)$ for $\bowtie\zeta \in \{> 0, < 1\}$, and $\sim \in \{\leq, \geq\}$, we consider the functions $\alpha, \beta, \gamma, \delta : S \rightarrow \mathbb{N}$, for representing minimal and maximal durations of interest. Intuitively, for a state $s \in S$, the value $\alpha(s)$ (resp. $\gamma(s)$) is the minimal (resp. maximal) duration that player P_p can ensure, regardless of the counter-strategy of P_n, along a path prefix from s satisfying $\Phi_1\mathsf{U}\Phi_2$ (resp. $\Phi_1\mathsf{U}(\mathbb{P}_{>0}(\Phi_1\mathsf{U}\Phi_2)))$. Similarly, the value $\beta(s)$ (resp. $\delta(s)$) is the minimal (resp. maximal) duration that player P_n can ensure, regardless of the counter-strategy of P_p, along a path prefix from s satisfying $\Phi_1 U \Phi_2$ (resp. $\Phi_1 U(\neg \mathbb{P}_{<1}(\Phi_1 U \Phi_2)))$. [1]

Using the fact that the TMDP is structurally non-Zeno, for any state $s \in S$, we can obtain the following equivalences: $s \models \mathbb{P}_{>0}(\Phi_1 U_{\le c} \Phi_2)$ if and only if $\alpha(s) \le c$; $s \models \mathbb{P}_{<1}(\Phi_1 U_{\le c} \Phi_2)$ if and only if $\beta(s) > c$; $s \models \mathbb{P}_{>0}(\Phi_1 U_{\ge c} \Phi_2)$ if and only if $\gamma(s) \ge c$; $s \models \mathbb{P}_{<1}(\Phi_1 U_{\ge c} \Phi_2)$ if and only if $\delta(s) < c$. The functions $\alpha, \beta, \gamma, \delta$ can be computed on the 2-player game by applying the results of [16] on timed concurrent game structures: for each temporal operator $\mathbb{P}_{\bowtie \zeta}(\Phi_1 U_{\sim c} \Phi_2)$, this computation runs in time $O(|S| \cdot | \to |)$.   □

We use Proposition 2 to obtain an efficient model-checking algorithm for 1C-PTA.

Theorem 1. *Let* $P = (L, \bar{l}, \mathcal{X}, inv, prob, \mathcal{L})$ *be a 1C-PTA and* Φ *be a* PTCTL$^{0/1}[\le, \ge]$ *formula. Deciding whether* $P \models \Phi$ *can be done in polynomial time.*

Proof (sketch). Our aim is to label every state (l, v) of $T[P]$ with the set of subformulae of Φ which it satisfies (as $|\mathcal{X}| = 1$, recall that v is a single real value). For each location $l \in L$ and subformula Ψ of Φ, we construct a set $Sat[l, \Psi] \subseteq \mathbb{R}_{\ge 0}$ of intervals such that $v \in Sat[l, \Psi]$ if and only if $(l, v) \models \Psi$. We write $Sat[l, \Psi] = \bigcup_{j=1,...,k} \langle c_j; c'_j \rangle$ with $\langle \in \{[, (\} \text{ and } \rangle \in \{],)\}$. We consider intervals which conform to the following rules: for $1 \le j \le k$, we have $c_j < c'_j$ and $c_j, c'_j \in \mathbb{N} \cup \{\infty\}$, and for $1 \le j < k$, we have $c'_j < c_{j+1}$. We will see that $|Sat[l, \Psi]|$ – *i.e.* the number of intervals corresponding to a particular location – is bounded by $|\Psi| \cdot 2 \cdot |prob|$.

The cases of obtaining the sets $Sat[l, \Psi]$ for boolean operators and atomic propositions are straightforward, and therefore we concentrate on the verification of subformulae Ψ of the form $\mathbb{P}_{\bowtie \zeta}(\Phi_1 U_{\sim c} \Phi_2)$. Assume that we have already computed the sets $Sat[\_, \_]$ for Φ_1 and Φ_2. Our aim is to compute $Sat[l, \Psi]$ for each location $l \in L$.

There are several cases depending on the constraint "$\bowtie \zeta$". The equivalence $\mathbb{P}_{\le 0}(\Phi_1 U_{\sim c} \Phi_2) \equiv \neg E \Phi_1 U_{\sim c} \Phi_2$ can be used to reduce the "≤ 0" case to the appropriate polynomial-time labeling procedure for $\neg E \Phi_1 U_{\sim c} \Phi_2$ on one clock timed automata [17]. In the "≥ 1" case, the equivalence $\mathbb{P}_{\ge 1}(\Phi_1 U_{\sim c} \Phi_2) \equiv A \Phi_1 U_{\sim c}(\mathbb{P}_{\ge 1}(\Phi_1 U \Phi_2))$ relies on first computing the state set satisfying $\mathbb{P}_{\ge 1}(\Phi_1 U \Phi_2)$, which can be handled using a qualitative PCTL model-checking algorithm, applied to a discrete TMDP built from P, $Sat[l, \Phi_1]$ and $Sat[l, \Phi_2]$, in time $O(|P| \cdot |prob| \cdot (|\Phi_1| + |\Phi_2|))$, and second verifying the formula $A \Phi_1 U_{\sim c}(\mathbb{P}_{\ge 1}(\Phi_1 U \Phi_2))$ using the aforementioned method for one clock timed automata.

For the remaining cases, our aim is to construct a (finite) discrete TMDP $T^r = (S^r, \_, \to^r, lab^r)$, which represents partially the semantic TMDP $T[P]$, for which the values of the functions α, β, γ and δ of the proof of Proposition 2 can be computed, and then use these functions to obtain the required sets $Sat[\_, \Psi]$ (the initial state of T^r is irrelevant for the model-checking procedure, and is therefore omitted). The TMDP T^r will take a similar form to the region graph MDP of PTA [15], but will be of reduced

---

[1] If there is no strategy for player P_p (resp. player P_n) to guarantee the satisfaction of $\Phi_1 U \Phi_2$ along a path prefix from s, then we let $\alpha(s) = \infty$ (resp. $\beta(s) = \infty$). Similarly, if there is no strategy for player P_p (resp. player P_n) to guarantee the satisfaction of $\Phi_1 U(\mathbb{P}_{>0}(\Phi_1 U \Phi_2))$ (resp. $\Phi_1 U(\neg \mathbb{P}_{<1}(\Phi_1 U \Phi_2)))$ along a path prefix from s, then we let $\gamma(s) = -\infty$ (resp. $\delta(s) = -\infty$).

size (the size will be independent of the magnitude of the constants used in invariants and guards): this will ensure a procedure running in time polynomial in $|\mathsf{P}|$.

We now describe the construction of T^r. In the following we assume that the sets $\mathrm{Sat}[l, \Phi_i]$ contain only closed intervals and that the guards and invariant of the PTA contain non-strict comparisons (and possibly intervals of the form $[b; \infty)$). The general case is omitted for reasons of space. Formally we let $\mathbb{B} = \{0\} \cup \mathrm{Cst}(\mathsf{P}) \cup \bigcup_{i \in \{1,2\}} \bigcup_{l \in L} \mathrm{Cst}(\mathrm{Sat}[l, \Phi_i])$, where $\mathrm{Cst}(\mathsf{P})$ is the set of constants occurring in the clock constraints of P, and where $\mathrm{Cst}(\mathrm{Sat}[l, \Phi_i])$ is the set of constants occurring as endpoints of the intervals in $\mathrm{Sat}[l, \Phi_i]$. Moreover for any right-open interval $[b; \infty)$ occurring in some $\mathrm{Sat}[l, \_]$, we add the constant $b + c + 1$ in $\mathbb{B}$. We enumerate $\mathbb{B}$ as $b_0, b_1, \dots b_M$ with $b_0 = 0$ and $b_i < b_{i+1}$ for $i < |\mathbb{B}|$. Note that $|\mathbb{B}|$ is bounded by $4 \cdot |\Psi| \cdot |prob|$. For any interval $(b_i; b_{i+1})$ and clock constraint $\psi \in \Psi_\mathcal{X}$, we let $(b_i; b_{i+1}) \models \psi$ if $v \models \psi$ for all $v \in (b_i; b_{i+1})$.

Considering the discrete TMDP corresponding to $\mathsf{T}[\mathsf{P}]$ restricted to states (l, b_i), with $b_i \in \mathbb{B}$, is sufficient to compute the values of functions α, β, γ and δ in any state (l, b_i). However, this does not allows us to deduce the value for any intermediate states in $(b_i; b_{i+1})$: indeed some probabilistic edges enabled from b_i may be disabled inside the interval. Therefore, in T^r, we have to consider also (l, b_i^+) and (l, b_{i+1}^-) corresponding respectively to the leftmost and rightmost points in $(b_i; b_{i+1})$ (when $i < M$). Then S^r is defined as the pairs (l, b_i) with $b_i \in \mathbb{B}$ and $b_i \models inv(l)$, and (l, b_i^+) and (l, b_{i+1}^-) with $b_i \in \mathbb{B}$, $i < M$ and $(b_i; b_{i+1}) \models inv(l)$. Note that the truth value of any invariant is constant over such intervals $(b_i; b_{i+1})$. Moreover note that all $\mathsf{T}[\mathsf{P}]$ states of the form (l, v) with $v \in (b_i; b_{i+1})$ satisfy the same boolean combinations of Φ_1 and Φ_2, and *enable the same probabilistic edges*. For any $(l, g, p) \in prob$, we write $b_i^+ \models g$ (and $b_{i+1}^- \models g$) when $(b_i; b_{i+1}) \models g$. Similarly, we write $b_i^+ \models inv(l)$ (and $b_{i+1}^- \models inv(l)$) when $(b_i; b_{i+1}) \models inv(l)$. We also consider the following ordering $b_0 < b_0^+ < b_1^- < b_1 < b_1^+ < \cdots < b_M^- < b_M < b_M^+$. We now define the set $\to^r$ of transitions of T^r as the smallest set such that $((l, \lambda), d, \nu) \in \to^r$, where $\lambda \in \{b_i^-, b_i, b_i^+\}$ for some $b_i \in \mathbb{B}$, if there exists $\lambda' \geq \lambda$, where $\lambda' \in \{b_j^-, b_j, b_j^+\}$ for some $b_j \in \mathbb{B}$, and $(l, g, p) \in prob$ such that:

- $d = b_j - b_i$, $\lambda' \models g$, and $\lambda'' \models inv(l)$ for any $\lambda \leq \lambda'' \leq \lambda'$;
- for each $(X, l') \in \mathrm{support}(p)$, we have $0 \models inv(l')$ if $X = \{x\}$, and $\lambda' \models inv(l')$ if $X = \emptyset$;
- for each $(l', \lambda'') \in S^r$, we have $\nu(l', \lambda'') = \nu_0(l', \lambda'') + \nu_\lambda(l', \lambda'')$, where $\nu_0(l', \lambda'') = p(l', \{x\})$ if $\lambda'' = [0, 0]$ and $\nu_0(l', \lambda'') = 0$ otherwise, and $\nu_\lambda(l', \lambda'') = p(l', \emptyset)$ if $\lambda'' = \lambda'$ and $\nu_\lambda(l', \lambda'') = 0$ otherwise.

Finally, to define lab^r, for a state (l, b_i), we let $a_{\Phi_j} \in lab^r(l, b_i)$ if and only if $b_i \in \mathrm{Sat}[l, \Phi_j]$, for $j \in \{1, 2\}$. The states (l, b_i^+) and (l, b_{i+1}^-) are labeled depending on the truth value of the Φ_j's in the interval $(b_i; b_{i+1})$: if $(b_i; b_{i+1}) \subseteq \mathrm{Sat}[l, \Phi_j]$, then $a_{\Phi_j} \in lab^r(l, b_i^+)$ and $a_{\Phi_j} \in lab^r(l, b_{i+1}^-)$. Note that given the "closed intervals" assumption made on $\mathrm{Sat}[l, \Phi_j]$, we have $lab^r(l, b_i^+) \subseteq lab^r(l, b_i)$ and $lab^r(l, b_{i+1}^-) \subseteq lab^r(l, b_i)$. Note that the fact that P is structurally non-Zeno means that T^r is structurally non-Zeno. The size of T^r is in $O(|\mathsf{P}|^2 \cdot |\Psi|)$.

Now we can apply the algorithms defined in the proof of Proposition 2 and obtain the value of the coefficients α, β, γ or δ for the states of T^r. Our next task is to define functions $\overline{\alpha}, \overline{\beta}, \overline{\gamma}, \overline{\delta} : S \to \mathbb{R}_{\geq 0}$, where S is the set of states of $\mathsf{T}[P]$, which are analogues of α, β, γ or δ defined on $\mathsf{T}[P]$. Our intuition is that we are now considering an infinite-state 2-player game, with players P_n and P_p, as in the proof of Proposition 2, over the state space of $\mathsf{T}[P]$. Consider location $l \in L$. For $b \in \mathbb{B}$, we have $\overline{\alpha}(l, b) = \alpha(l, b)$, $\overline{\beta}(l, b) = \beta(l, b)$, $\overline{\gamma}(l, b) = \gamma(l, b)$ and $\overline{\delta}(l, b) = \delta(l, b)$. For intervals of the form $(b_i; b_{i+1})$, the functions $\overline{\alpha}$ and $\overline{\delta}$ will be decreasing (with slope -1) throughout the interval, because, for all states of the interval, the optimal choice of player P_n is to delay as much as possible inside any interval. Hence, the value $\overline{\alpha}(l, v)$ for $v \in (b_i; b_{i+1})$ is defined entirely by $\alpha(l, b_{i+1}^-)$ as $\overline{\alpha}(l, v) = \alpha(l, b_{i+1}^-) - b_{i+1} + b_i + v$. Similarly, $\overline{\delta}(l, v) = \delta(l, b_{i+1}^-) - b_{i+1} + b_i + v$.

Next we consider the values of $\overline{\beta}$ and $\overline{\gamma}$ over intervals $(b_i; b_{i+1})$. In this case, the functions will be constant over a portion of the interval (possibly an empty portion, or possibly the entire interval), then decreasing with slope -1. The constant part corresponds to those states in which the optimal choice of player P_n is to take a probabilistic edge, whereas the decreasing part corresponds to those states in which it is optimal for player P_n to delay until the end of the interval. The value $\overline{\beta}(l, v)$ for $v \in (b_i; b_{i+1})$ is defined both by $\beta(l, b_i^+)$ and $\beta(l, b_{i+1}^-)$ as $\overline{\beta}(l, v) = \beta(l, b_i^+)$ if $b_i < v \leq b_{i+1} - (\beta(l, b_i^+) - \beta(l, \beta_{i+1}^-))$, and as $\overline{\beta}(l, v) = \beta(l, \beta_{i+1}^-) - (v - \beta(l, b_i^+))$ otherwise. An analogous definition holds also for $\overline{\gamma}$.

From the functions $\overline{\alpha}$, $\overline{\beta}$, $\overline{\gamma}$ and $\overline{\delta}$ defined above, it becomes possible to define $\mathsf{Sat}[l, \Psi]$ by keeping in this set of intervals only the parts satisfying the thresholds $\leq c$, $> c$, $\geq c$ and $< c$, respectively, as in the proof of Proposition 2. We can show that the number of intervals in $\mathsf{Sat}[l, \Psi]$ is bounded by $2 \cdot |\Psi| \cdot |prob|$. For the case in which a function $\overline{\alpha}$, $\overline{\beta}$, $\overline{\gamma}$ or $\overline{\delta}$ is decreasing throughout an interval, then an interval in $\mathsf{Sat}[l, \Phi_1]$ which corresponds to several consecutive intervals in T^r can provide at most one (sub)interval in $\mathsf{Sat}[l, \Psi]$, because the threshold can cross at most once the function in at most one interval. For the case in which a function $\overline{\beta}$ or $\overline{\gamma}$ combines a constant part and a part with slope -1 within an interval, the threshold can cross the function in several intervals $(b_i; b_{i+1})$ contained in a common interval of $\mathsf{Sat}[l, \Phi_1]$. However, such a cut is due to a guard $x \geq k$ of a given transition, and thus the number of cuts in bounded by $|prob|$. Moreover a guard $x \leq k$ may also add an interval. Thus the number of new intervals in $\mathsf{Sat}[q, \Psi]$ is bounded by $2 \cdot |prob|$.

In addition to these cuts, any interval in $\mathsf{Sat}[l, \Phi_2]$ may provide an interval in $\mathsf{Sat}[l, \Psi]$. This gives the $2 \cdot |\Psi| \cdot |prob|$ bound for the size of $\mathsf{Sat}[l, \Psi]$. $\qquad\square$

Corollary 1. *The* $\mathrm{PTCTL}^{0/1}[\leq, \geq]$ *model-checking problem for 1C-PTA is P-complete.*

4.2 Model Checking $\mathrm{PTCTL}^{0/1}$ on 1C-PTA

We now consider the problem of model-checking $\mathrm{PTCTL}^{0/1}$ properties on 1C-PTA. An EXPTIME algorithm for this problem exists by the definition of a MDP analogous to the region graph used in non-probabilistic timed automata verification [15]. We now show that the problem is also EXPTIME-hard by the following three steps. First we introduce *countdown games*, which are a simple class of turn-based 2-player games with discrete timing, and show that the problem of deciding the winner in a countdown game is EXPTIME-complete. Secondly, we reduce the countdown game problem to the

$\text{PTCTL}^{0/1}$ problem on TMDPs. Finally, we adapt the reduction to TMDPs to reduce also the countdown game problem to the $\text{PTCTL}^{0/1}$ problem on 1C-PTA.

A *countdown game* C consists of a weighted graph (S, T), where S is the set of *states* and $T \subseteq S \times \mathbb{N} \setminus \{0\} \times S$ is the *transition relation*. If $t = (s, d, s') \in T$ then we say that the *duration* of the transition t is d. A configuration of a countdown game is a pair (s, c), where $s \in S$ is a state and $c \in \mathbb{N}$. A *move* of a countdown game from a configuration (s, c) is performed in the following way: first player 1 chooses a number d, such that $0 < d \le c$ and $(s, d, s') \in T$, for some state $s' \in S$; then player 2 chooses a transition $(s, d, s') \in T$ of duration d. The resulting new configuration is $(s', c - d)$. There are two types of *terminal* configurations, i.e., configurations (s, c) in which no moves are available. If $c = 0$ then the configuration (s, c) is terminal and is a *winning configuration for player 1*. If for all transitions $(s, d, s') \in T$ from the state s, we have that $d > c$, then the configuration (s, c) is terminal and it is a *winning configuration for player 2*. The algorithmic problem of *deciding the winner* in countdown games is, given a weighted graph (S, T) and a configuration (s, c), where all the durations of transitions in C and the number c are given in binary, to determine whether player 1 has a winning strategy from the configuration (s, c). If the state from which the game is started is clear from the context then we sometimes specify the initial configuration by giving the number c alone.

Theorem 2. *Deciding the winner in countdown games is* EXPTIME-*complete.*

Proof (sketch). Observe that every configuration of a countdown game played from a given initial configuration can be written down in polynomial space and every move can be computed in polynomial time; hence the winner in the game can be determined by a straightforward alternating PSPACE algorithm. Therefore the problem is in EXPTIME because APSPACE = EXPTIME.

We now prove EXPTIME-hardness by a reduction from the acceptance of a word by a linearly-bounded alternating Turing machine. Let $M = (\Sigma, Q, q_0, q_{acc}, Q_\exists, Q_\forall, \Delta)$ be an alternating Turing machine, where Σ is a finite alphabet, $Q = Q_\exists \cup Q_\forall$ is a finite set of states partitioned into existential states $Q_\exists$ and universal states $Q_\forall$, $q_0 \in Q$ is an initial state, $q_{acc} \in Q$ is an accepting state, and $\Delta \subseteq Q \times \Sigma \times Q \times \Sigma \times \{L, R\}$ is a transition relation. Let $B > 2 \cdot |Q \times \Sigma|$ be an integer constant and let $w \in \Sigma^n$ be an input word. W.l.o.g. we can assume that M uses exactly n tape cells when started on the word w, and hence a configuration of M is a word $b_0 b_1 \cdots b_{n-1} \in (\Sigma \cup Q \times \Sigma)^n$. Let $\langle \cdot \rangle : (\Sigma \cup Q \times \Sigma) \to \{0, 1, \ldots, B - 1\}$ be an injection. For every $a \in \Sigma \cup Q \times \Sigma$, it is convenient to think of $\langle a \rangle$ as a B-ary digit, and we can encode a configuration $u = b_0 b_1 \cdots b_{n-1} \in (\Sigma \cup Q \times \Sigma)^n$ of M as the number $N(u) = \sum_{i=0}^{n-1} \langle b_i \rangle \cdot B^i$.

Let $i \in \mathbb{N}$, $0 \le i < n$, be a tape cell position, and let $a \in \Sigma \cup Q \times \Sigma$. We define a countdown game $\text{Check}^{i,a}$, such that for every configuration $u = b_0 \cdots b_{n-1}$ of M, player 1 has a winning strategy from the configuration $(s_0^{i,a}, N(u))$ of the game $\text{Check}^{i,a}$ if and only if $b_i = a$. The game $\text{Check}^{i,a}$ has states $S = \{ s_0^{i,a}, \ldots, s_n^{i,a} \}$, and for every k, $0 \le k < n$, we have a transition $(s_k^{i,a}, d, s_{k+1}^{i,a}) \in T$, if:

$$d = \begin{cases} \langle a \rangle \cdot B^k & \text{if } k = i, \\ \langle b \rangle \cdot B^k & \text{if } k \ne i \text{ and } b \in \Sigma \cup S \times \Sigma. \end{cases}$$

There are no transitions from the state $s_n^{i,a}$. Observe that if $b_i = a$ then the winning strategy for player 1 in game $\text{Check}^{i,a}$ from $N(u)$ is to choose the transitions $(s_k^{i,a}, b_k \cdot B^k, s_{k+1}^{i,a})$, for all k, $0 \le k < n$. If, however, $b_i \ne a$ then there is no way for player 1 to count down from $N(u)$ to 0 in the game $\text{Check}^{i,a}$.

Now we define a countdown game $\mathcal{C}_M$, such that M accepts $w = \sigma_0\sigma_1 \ldots \sigma_{n-1}$ if and only if player 1 has a winning strategy in $\mathcal{C}_M$ from configuration $(q_0, N(u))$, where $u = (q_0, \sigma_0)\sigma_1 \ldots \sigma_{n-1}$ is the initial configuration of M with input w. The main part of the countdown game $\mathcal{C}_M$ is a gadget that allows the game to simulate one step of M. Note that one step of a Turing machine makes only local changes to the configuration of the machine: if the configuration is of the form $u = \mathbf{a}_0 \ldots \mathbf{a}_{n-1} = \sigma_0 \ldots \sigma_{i-1}(q,\sigma_i)\sigma_{i+1} \ldots \sigma_{n-1}$, then performing one step of M can only change entries in positions $i - 1$, i, or $i + 1$ of the tape. For every tape position i, $0 \le i < n$, for every triple $\tau = (\sigma_{i-1}, (q,\sigma_i), \sigma_{i+1}) \in \Sigma \times (Q \times \Sigma) \times \Sigma$, and for every transition $t = (q, \sigma, q', \sigma', D) \in \Delta$ of machine M, we now define the number $d_t^{i,\tau}$, such that if $\sigma_i = \sigma$ and performing transition t at position i of configuration u yields configuration $u' = \mathbf{b}_0 \ldots \mathbf{b}_{n-1}$, then $N(u) - d_t^{i,\tau} = N(u')$. For example, assume that $i > 0$ and that $D = L$; we have that $\mathbf{b}_k = \mathbf{a}_k = \sigma_k$, for all $k \notin \{i - 1, i, i + 1\}$ and $\mathbf{b}_{i+1} = \mathbf{a}_{i+1} = \sigma_{i+1}$. Moreover we have that $\mathbf{b}_{i-1} = (q', \sigma_{i-1})$, and $\mathbf{b}_i = \sigma'$. We define $d_t^{i,\tau}$ as follows:

$$d_t^{i,\tau} = ((\langle\mathbf{b}_{i-1}\rangle - \langle\mathbf{a}_{i-1}\rangle) \cdot B^{i-1} + (\langle\mathbf{b}_i\rangle - \langle\mathbf{a}_i\rangle) \cdot B^i$$
$$= ((\langle(q',\sigma_{i-1})\rangle - \langle\sigma_{i-1}\rangle) \cdot B^{i-1} + (\langle\sigma'\rangle - \langle(q,\sigma_i)\rangle) \cdot B^i.$$

The gadget for simulating one transition of M from a state $q \in Q \setminus \{q_{acc}\}$ has three layers. In the first layer, from a state $q \in Q \setminus \{q_{acc}\}$, player 1 chooses a pair (i, τ), where i, $0 \le i < n$, is the position of the tape head, and $\tau = (\mathbf{a}, \mathbf{b}, \mathbf{c}) \in \Sigma \times (Q \times \Sigma) \times \Sigma$ is his guess for the contents of tape cells $i - 1$, i, and $i + 1$. In this way the state (q, i, τ) of the gadget is reached, where the duration of this transition is 0. Intuitively, in the first layer player 1 has to declare that he knows the position i of the head in the current configuration as well as the contents $\tau = (\mathbf{a}, \mathbf{b}, \mathbf{c})$ of the three tape cells in positions $i - 1$, i, and $i + 1$. In the second layer, in a state (q, i, τ) player 2 chooses between four successor states: the state $(q, i, \tau, *)$ and the three subgames $\text{Check}^{i-1,a}$, $\text{Check}^{i,b}$, and $\text{Check}^{i+1,c}$. The four transitions are of duration 0. Intuitively, in the second layer player 2 verifies that player 1 declared correctly the contents of the three tape cells in positions $i - 1$, i, and $i + 1$. Finally, in the third layer, if $q \in Q_\exists$ (resp., $q \in Q_\forall$), then from a state $(q, i, \tau, *)$ player 1 (resp., player 2) chooses a transition $t = (q, \sigma, q', \sigma', D)$ of machine M, such that $\mathbf{b} = (q, \sigma)$, reaching the state $q' \in Q$ of the gadget, with a transition of duration $d_t^{i,\tau}$.

Note that the gadget described above violates some conventions that we have adopted for countdown games. Observe that durations of some transitions in the gadget are 0 and the duration $d_t^{i,\tau}$ may even be negative, while in the definition of countdown games we required that durations of all transitions are positive. In order to correct this we add the number B^n to the durations of all transitions described above. This change requires a minor modification to the subgames $\text{Check}^{i,a}$: we add an extra transition $(s_n^{i,a}, B^n, s_n^{i,a})$. We need this extra transition because instead of starting from $(q_0, N(u))$ as the initial configuration of the game $\mathcal{C}_M$, where u is the initial configuration of M running on w, we are going to start from the configuration $(q_0, B^{3n} + N(u))$. In this way the countdown game can perform a simulation of at least B^n steps of M; note that B^n is an upper bound on the number of all configurations of M.

W.l.o.g., we can assume that whenever the alternating Turing machine M accepts an input word w then it finishes its computation with blanks in all tape cells, its head in position 0, and in the unique accepting state q_{acc}; we write u_{acc} for this unique accepting configuration of machine M. Moreover, assume that there are no transitions from q_{acc} in M. In order to complete the definition of the countdown game G_M, we add a transition of duration $N(u_{acc})$ from the state q_{acc} of game C_M.   □

Proposition 3. *The* $\text{PTCTL}^{0/1}$ *model-checking problem for structurally non-Zeno discrete TMDPs is EXPTIME-complete.*

Proof. An EXPTIME algorithm can be obtained by employing the algorithms of [19]. We now prove EXPTIME-hardness of $\text{PTCTL}^{0/1}$ model checking on discrete TMDPs by a reduction from countdown games. Let $C = (S, T)$ be a countdown game and $(\bar{s}, c)$ be its initial configuration. We construct a TMDP $T_{C,(\bar{s},c)} = (S, s_{init}, \rightarrow, lab)$ such that player 1 wins C from $(\bar{s}, c)$ if and only if $T_{C,(\bar{s},c)} \models \neg\mathbb{P}_{<1}(\mathsf{F}_{=c}\mathtt{true})$. Let $S = \mathsf{S}$ and $s_{init} = \bar{s}$. We define $\rightarrow$ to be the smallest set satisfying the following: for each $\mathsf{s} \in \mathsf{S}$ and $d \in \mathbb{N}_{>0}$, if $(\mathsf{s}, d, \mathsf{s}') \in \mathsf{T}$ for some $\mathsf{s}' \in \mathsf{T}$, we have $(\mathsf{s}, d, \nu) \in\rightarrow$, where ν is an arbitrary distribution over S such that $\text{support}(\nu) = \{\mathsf{s}' \mid (\mathsf{s}, d, \mathsf{s}') \in \mathsf{T}\}$. The labelling condition lab is arbitrary. Then we can show that player 1 wins from the configuration $(\bar{s}, c)$ if and only if there exists an adversary of $T_{C,(\bar{s},c)}$ such that a state is reached from $s_{init} = \bar{s}$ after exactly c time units with probability 1. The latter is equivalent to $s_{init} \models \neg\mathbb{P}_{<1}(\mathsf{F}_{=c}\mathtt{true})$.   □

We now show that the proof of Proposition 3 can be adapted to show the EXPTIME-completeness of the analogous model-checking problem on 1C-PTA.

Theorem 3. *The* $\text{PTCTL}^{0/1}$ *model-checking problem for 1C-PTA is EXPTIME-complete.*

Proof. Recall that there exists an EXPTIME algorithm for model-checking $\text{PTCTL}^{0/1}$ properties on PTA; hence, it suffices to show EXPTIME-hardness for $\text{PTCTL}^{0/1}$ and 1C-PTA. Let C be a countdown game with an initial configuration $(\bar{s}, c)$. We construct the 1C-PTA $\mathsf{P}^{1C}_{C,(\bar{s},c)} = (L, \bar{l}, \{x\}, inv, prob, \mathcal{L})$ which simulates the behaviour of the TMDP $T_{C,(\bar{s},c)}$ of the proof of Proposition 3 in the following way. Each state $\mathsf{s} \in \mathsf{S}$ of $T_{C,(\bar{s},c)}$ corresponds to two distinct locations l^1_{s} and l^2_{s} of $\mathsf{P}^{1C}_{C,(\bar{s},c)}$, and we let $L^i = \{l^i_{\mathsf{s}} \mid \mathsf{s} \in \mathsf{S}\}$ for $i \in \{1, 2\}$. Let $\bar{l} = l^1_{\bar{s}}$. For every transition $(\mathsf{s}, d, \nu) \in\rightarrow$ of $T_{C,(\bar{s},c)}$, we have the probabilistic edges $(l^1_{\mathsf{s}}, x = 0, p^1), (l^2_{\mathsf{s}}, x = d, p^2) \in prob$, where $p^1(\{x\}, l^2_{\mathsf{s}}) = 1$, and $p^2(\{x\}, l^1_{\mathsf{s}'}) = \nu(\mathsf{s}')$ for each location s'. For each state $\mathsf{s} \in \mathsf{S}$, let $inv(l^1_{\mathsf{s}}) = (x \leq 0)$ and $inv(l^2_{\mathsf{s}}) = (x \leq d)$. That is, the PTA $\mathsf{P}^{1C}_{C,(\bar{s},c)}$ moves from the location l^1_{s} to l^2_{s} instantaneously. Locations in L^1 are labelled by the atomic proposition a, whereas locations in L^2 are labelled by $\emptyset$. Then we can observe that $\mathsf{P}^{1C}_{C,(\bar{s},c)} \models \neg\mathbb{P}_{<1}(\mathsf{F}_{=c}a)$ if and only if $T_{C,(\bar{s},c)} \models \neg\mathbb{P}_{<1}(\mathsf{F}_{=c}\mathtt{true})$. As the latter problem has been shown to be EXPTIME-hard in the proof of Proposition 3, we conclude that model checking $\text{PTCTL}^{0/1}$ on 1C-PTA is also EXPTIME-hard.   □

5 Model Checking Two Clocks Probabilistic Timed Automata

We now show EXPTIME-completeness of the simplest problems that we consider on 2C-PTA.

Theorem 4. *Qualitative probabilistic reachability problems for 2C-PTA are EXPTIME-complete.*

Proof. EXPTIME algorithms exist for probabilistic reachability problems on PTA, and therefore it suffices to show EXPTIME-hardness. We proceed by reduction from count-down games. Let $\mathcal{C}$ be a countdown game with initial configuration $(\bar{s}, c)$, and let $\mathsf{P}^{1C}_{\mathcal{C},(\bar{s},c)} = (L, \bar{l}, \{x\}, inv, prob, \mathcal{L})$ be the 1C-PTA constructed in the proof of Theorem 3. We define the 2C-PTA $\mathsf{P}^{2C}_{\mathcal{C},(\bar{s},c)} = (L \cup \{l^*\}, \bar{l}, \{x, y\}, inv', prob', \mathcal{L}')$ in the following way. The set of probabilistic edges $prob'$ is obtained by adding to $prob$ the following: for each location $l \in L$, we extend the set of outgoing probabilistic edges of l with $(l, y = c, p^{l^*})$, where $p^{l^*}(\emptyset, l^*) = 1$; to make $prob'$ total, we also add $(l^*, \texttt{true}, p^{l^*})$. For each $l \in L$, let $inv'(l) = inv(l)$, and let $inv'(l^*) = \texttt{true}$. Finally, we let $\mathcal{L}'(l^*) = a$, and $\mathcal{L}(l) = \emptyset$ for all $l \in L$. Then $\mathsf{P}^{2C}_{\mathcal{C},(\bar{s},c)} \models \neg \mathbb{P}_{<1}(\mathsf{F}a)$ if and only if $\mathsf{P}^{1C}_{\mathcal{C},(\bar{s},c)} \models \neg \mathbb{P}_{<1}(\mathsf{F}_{=c}a)$. The EXPTIME-hardness of the latter problem has been shown in the proof of Theorem 3, and hence checking qualitative probabilistic reachability properties such as $\neg \mathbb{P}_{<1}(\mathsf{F}a)$ on 2C-PTA is EXPTIME-hard.   □

Corollary 2. *The* PCTL, PTCTL$^{0/1}[\leq, \geq]$, PTCTL$^{0/1}$, PTCTL$[\leq, \geq]$ *and* PTCTL *model-checking problems for 2C-PTA are EXPTIME-complete.*

References

1. P. A. Abdulla, J. Deneux, J. Ouaknine, and J. Worrell. Decidability and complexity results for timed automata via channel machines. In *Proc. of the 32nd Int. Coll. on Aut., Lang. and Progr. (ICALP'05)*, volume 3580 of *LNCS*, pages 1089–1101. Springer, 2005.
2. R. Alur, C. Courcoubetis, and D. L. Dill. Model-checking for probabilistic real-time systems. In *Proc. of the 18th Int. Coll. on Aut., Lang. and Progr. (ICALP'91)*, volume 510 of *LNCS*, pages 115–136. Springer, 1991.
3. R. Alur, C. Courcoubetis, and D. L. Dill. Model-checking in dense real-time. *Inf. and Comp.*, 104(1):2–34, 1993.
4. R. Alur and D. L. Dill. A theory of timed automata. *Theo. Comp. Sci.*, 126(2):183–235, 1994.
5. C. Baier, B. Haverkort, H. Hermanns, and J.-P. Katoen. Model-checking algorithms for continuous-time Markov chains. *IEEE Trans. on Soft. Enginee.*, 29(6):524–541, 2003.
6. C. Baier and M. Kwiatkowska. Model checking for a probabilistic branching time logic with fairness. *Distributed Computing*, 11(3):125–155, 1998.
7. A. Bianco and L. de Alfaro. Model checking of probabilistic and nondeterministic systems. In *Proc. of the 15th Conf. on Found. of Software Technol. and Theor. Comp. Sci. (FSTTCS'95)*, volume 1026 of *LNCS*, pages 499–513. Springer, 1995.
8. E. M. Clarke, O. Grumberg, and D. Peled. *Model checking*. MIT Press, 1999.
9. C. Courcoubetis and M. Yannakakis. The complexity of probabilistic verification. *Journal of the ACM*, 42(4):857–907, 1995.

10. L. de Alfaro. *Formal verification of probabilistic systems*. PhD thesis, Stanford University, Department of Computer Science, 1997.

11. L. de Alfaro. Temporal logics for the specification of performance and reliability. In *Proc. of the 14th An. Symp. on Theor. Aspects of Comp. Sci. (STACS'97)*, volume 1200 of *LNCS*, pages 165–176. Springer, 1997.

12. H. A. Hansson and B. Jonsson. A logic for reasoning about time and reliability. *Formal Aspects of Computing*, 6(5):512–535, 1994.

13. H. E. Jensen. Model checking probabilistic real time systems. In *Proc. of the 7th Nordic Work. on Progr. Theory*, pages 247–261. Chalmers Institute of Technology, 1996.

14. M. Kwiatkowska, G. Norman, D. Parker, and J. Sproston. Performance analysis of probabilistic timed automata using digital clocks. *Formal Meth. in Syst. Design*, 29:33–78, 2006.

15. M. Kwiatkowska, G. Norman, R. Segala, and J. Sproston. Automatic verification of real-time systems with discrete probability distributions. *Theo. Comp. Sci.*, 286:101–150, 2002.

16. F. Laroussinie, N. Markey, and G. Oreiby. Model checking timed ATL for durational concurrent game structures. In *Proc. of the 4th Int. Conf. on Formal Modelling and Analysis of Timed Systems (FORMATS'06)*, volume 4202 of *LNCS*, pages 245–259. Springer, 2006.

17. F. Laroussinie, N. Markey, and P. Schnoebelen. Model checking timed automata with one or two clocks. In *Proc. of the 15th Int. Conf. on Concurrency Theory (CONCUR'04)*, volume 3170 of *LNCS*, pages 387–401. Springer, 2004.

18. F. Laroussinie, N. Markey, and P. Schnoebelen. Efficient timed model checking for discrete-time systems. *Theo. Comp. Sci.*, 353(1–3):249–271, 2005.

19. F. Laroussinie and J. Sproston. Model checking durational probabilistic systems. In *Proc. of the 8th Int. Conf. on Foundations of Software Science and Computation Structures (FoSSaCS'05)*, volume 3441 of *LNCS*, pages 140–154. Springer, 2005.

20. F. Laroussinie and J. Sproston. State explosion in almost-sure probabilistic reachability. To appear in *IPL*, 2007.

21. S. Lasota and I. Walukiewicz. Alternating timed automata. In *Proc. of the 8th Int. Conf. on Foundations of Software Science and Computation Structures (FoSSaCS'05)*, volume 3441 of *LNCS*, pages 299–314. Springer, 2005.

22. C. Papadimitriou and J. Tsitsiklis. The complexity of Markov decision processes. *Mathematics of Operations Research*, 12(3):441–450, 1987.

23. M. Stoelinga. *Alea Jacta est: Verification of probabilistic, real-time and parametric systems*. PhD thesis, Institute for Computing and Information Sciences, University of Nijmegen, 2002.

24. S. Tripakis, S. Yovine, and A. Bouajjani. Checking timed Büchi automata emptiness efficiently. *Formal Meth. in Syst. Design*, 26(3):267–292, 2005.

25. M. Y. Vardi. Automatic verification of probabilistic concurrent finite-state programs. In *Proc. of the 16th An. Symp. on Foundations of Computer Science (FOCS'85)*, pages 327–338. IEEE Computer Society Press, 1985.

Adaptor Synthesis for Real-Time Components[*]

Massimo Tivoli[1], Pascal Fradet[2], Alain Girault[2], and Gregor Goessler[2]

[1] University of L'Aquila[**]
Dip. Informatica, via Vetoio 1, 67100 L'Aquila, Italy
tivoli@di.univaq.it
[2] INRIA Rhône-Alpes - POP ART project
655 avenue de l'Europe, 38330 Montbonnot, France
{Pascal.Fradet,Alain.Girault,Gregor.Goessler}@inrialpes.fr

Abstract. Building a real-time system from reusable or COTS components introduces several problems, mainly related to compatibility, communication, and QoS issues. We propose an approach to automatically derive adaptors in order to solve black-box integration anomalies, when possible. We consider black-box components equipped with an expressive interface that specifies the interaction behavior with the expected environment, the component clock, as well as latency, duration, and controllability of the component's actions. The principle of adaptor synthesis is to coordinate the interaction behavior of the components in order to avoid possible mismatches, such as deadlocks. Each adaptor models the correct assembly code for a set of components. Our approach is based on labeled transition systems and Petri nets, and is implemented in a tool called SynthesisRT. We illustrate it through a case study concerning a remote medical care system.

1 Introduction

Due to their increasing complexity, control systems are nowadays often designed in a modular approach by means of libraries of building blocks. This has lead to a need of a component-based approach for building real-time systems out of a set of already implemented components. Building a real-time system from reusable or *Commercial-Off-The-Shelf* (COTS) components introduces several problems, mainly related to compatibility, communication, and quality of service (QoS) issues [2,10,11,12,18]. Indeed, incompatibilities between the components may arise and make their composition impossible.

In this paper, we show how to deal with these problems within a lightweight component model where components follow a data-flow interaction model. Each component declares input and output ports which are the points of interaction with other components and/or the execution environment. Input (resp., output) ports of a component are connected to output (resp., input) ports of a different

---

[*] This work has been partially funded by the ALIDECS project and the ARTIST II European network of excellence.

[**] This work has been done while the first author was a postdoctoral fellow in the POP ART project team at INRIA Rhône-Alpes.

O. Grumberg and M. Huth (Eds.): TACAS 2007, LNCS 4424, pp. 185–200, 2007.

component through synchronous links. In our framework, a component interface includes a formal description of the *interaction protocol* of the component with its expected environment in terms of sequences of writing and reading actions to and from ports. The interface language is expressive enough to specify QoS constraints such as writing and reading *latency, duration,* and *controllability,* as well as the component's *clock* (*i.e.,* its activation frequency). In order to deal with incompatible components (*e.g.,* clock inconsistency, read/write latency/duration inconsistency, mismatching interaction protocols, *etc.*) we synthesize component *adaptors* interposed between two or more interacting components. An adaptor is a component that mediates the interaction between the components it supervises, in order to harmonize their communication. Each adaptor is automatically derived by taking into account the interface specification of the components it supervises. The adaptor synthesis allows the developer to automatically and *incrementally* build *correct-by-construction* systems from third-party components, hence reducing time-to-market and improving reusability. The space complexity of the synthesis algorithm is exponential in the number of states of the automaton modeling the interaction protocol of each component. Thus, incrementality is crucial to manage the complexity of real systems.

We have formalized the adaptor synthesis algorithm by using Petri nets [16] theory, and we address its correctness in a companion paper [19]. Moreover, in order to realize the whole approach, we have implemented a tool, called *Synthesis Real Time* (SynthesisRT) [19], which we have used on a case study concerning a remote medical care system (RMCS).

The remainder of the paper is organized as follows. Section 2 introduces the notions of latency, duration, controllability, and local/global time/clock. Section 3 provides an informal overview of our method. Section 4 presents our component specification formalism and its semantics in terms of *Labeled Transition Systems* (LTSs). Section 5 formalizes the technical core of adaptor synthesis. Section 6 describes our method at work on the RMCS case study. Finally, Section 7 summarizes our work and presents related work and future extensions.

2   Background

In this section, we introduce the background notions used by our framework.

2.1   Context

We want to build component-based real-time systems by assembling third-party black-box components. Black-box means that the component source code is not available to the system designer. Each component is equipped with a rich interface that describes its behavior as well as real-time properties. According to the *"design by contract"* approach [18], such an interface specification is given by the component developer, who is aware of the information needed. An interface includes:

- A behavioral interface specification. This specification is given in terms of a *Labeled Transition System* (LTS) that models the sequences of actions that the component performs when it interacts with its environment. As it is explained below, this LTS contains also timing information.
- A periodic clock that, for reuse purposes, is instantiated at assembly-time. It specifies a sequence of instants by an infinite stream of boolean values: 1 denotes an instant where the component is *enabled* (it can perform an action or let the time elapse) and 0 denotes an instant where then component is *disabled*. A periodic clock can be finitely represented by its periodic sub-stream (*e.g.*, the clock $(10)^\omega$ represents the infinite stream $10101010101010\ldots$). The global time is defined by the clock $(1)^\omega$ that is called the *base clock*. The clock of each component defines a time that is *local* to the component. It characterizes the component speed and can be seen as a sub-clock of the base clock. For hierarchies of components, the local clock of each component is a sub-clock of the clock of its super-component. We refer the reader to [5] for a comprehensive presentation of the periodic clock concept.
- A latency (a natural number) for each action. It specifies the number of *global* time units that can pass before the action is performed. In other words, the component may choose to synchronize with its environment to perform the corresponding action any time before the latency is elapsed.
- A duration (an interval of natural numbers) for each action. It specifies the *local* time units needed for the action execution. For instance, a duration $[1,2]$ indicates that the action may require one or two instants where the component is enabled to complete. Contrary to the latency, the precise duration cannot be chosen. The component must synchronize correctly with its environment for every possible execution time specified by its duration.
- A controllability tag for each action. An uncontrollable action (*i.e.*, tagged with u) cannot be disabled. For example, inputs coming from a sensor are often considered as uncontrollable since they must be accepted and treated by the component. In contrast, controllable actions (without a tag) can be safely disabled (*e.g.*, by a supervisor or an adaptor), for instance to prevent a deadlock.

2.2   Architectural Model

In this section, we provide an overview of our architectural model using a small example. Figure 1 shows the architectural specification of a black-box component C_1, with a clock port w_1, which interacts with its environment through the input port a and the output port b.

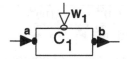

Fig. 1. Architectural schema of component C_1

In general, a component can have several input and output ports. Components are connected to each other through their ports and interact *synchronously*. An input port of a component can be connected to an output port of a different component. Input (resp., output) ports support a *reading* (resp., *writing*) operation. Synchronous communication implies that reading and writing operations among connected ports are blocking actions. In other words, connected components are forced to synchronize on complementary read/write operations. E.g., let the input port p_1 and the output port p_2 be connected: a reading from p_1 has to synchronize with a writing to p_2. This style of communication is not a limitation because it is well known that, with the introduction of a buffer component, we can always simulate an asynchronous system by a synchronous one [13].

The clock port of a component can be seen as a special input port whose current value (either 1 or 0) depends on the periodic clock that has been assigned to the component and on the current instant of the global time. It is not connected to other ports since it serves only to assign a periodic clock to the component at assembly-time.

3   Overview

In this section, we informally describe the main steps of our method as illustrated in Figure 2. Although we took inspiration from [3], our synthesis algorithm is very different from theirs as it is discussed in Section 7.

We take as input the architectural specification of the network of components to be composed and the component interface specifications. The behavioral models of the components are generated in form of LTSs that make the elapsing of

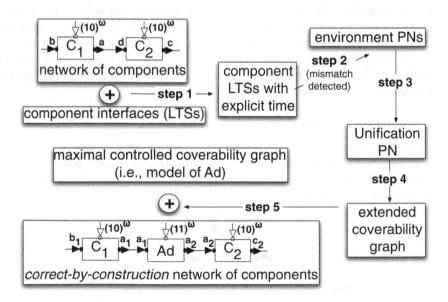

Fig. 2. Main steps of adaptor synthesis for real-time components

time explicit (step 1). Connected ports with different names are renamed such that complementary actions have the same label in the component LTSs (see actions a and d in Figure 2). Possible mismatches/deadlocks are checked by looking for possible sink states into the parallel composition of the LTSs. The adaptor synthesis process starts only if such deadlocks are detected.

The synthesis first proceeds by constructing a Petri net (PN) representation of the environment expected from a component in order to avoid deadlocks (step 2). It consists in complementing the actions in the component LTSs that are performed on connected ports, considering the actions performed on unconnected ports as internal actions. A buffer storing read and written values is modeled as a place in the environment PN for each IO action. Each such PN represents a partial view of the adaptor to be built. It is partial since it reflects the expectation of a single component. In particular, a write (resp. read) action gives rise to a place (buffer) without outgoing (resp. incoming) arcs.

The partial views of the adaptor are composed together by building causal dependencies between the reading/writing actions and by unifying time-elapsing transitions (step 3). Furthermore, the places representing the same buffer are merged in one single place. This *Unification PN* desynchronizes emission from reception using buffers. However, the unification PN may include behaviors that deadlock and/or require unbounded buffers. In order to obtain the most permissive and correct adaptor, we generate an extended version of the graph usually known in PNs theory as the coverability graph [8] (step 4).

Our method automatically restricts the behavior of the adaptor modeled by the extended coverability graph in order to keep only the behaviors that are deadlock-free and that use finite buffers (*i.e.*, bounded interactions). This is done by automatically constructing, if possible, an "instrumented" version of our extended coverability graph, called the *Controlled Coverability Graph (CCG)*. The CCG is obtained by pruning from the extended coverability graph both the *sinking* paths and the *unbounded* paths, by *controller synthesis* [17] (step 5). This process also performs a *backwards propagation* in order to correctly take into account the case of sinking and unbounded paths originating from the firing of uncontrollable transitions.

If it exists, the maximal CCG generated is the LTS modeling the behavior of the correct (*i.e.*, deadlock-free and bounded) adaptor. This adaptor models the correct-by-construction assembly code for the components in the specified network. If it does not exist, a correct adaptor assembling the components given as input to our method cannot be derived, and hence our method does not provide any assembly code for those components.

4   The Interface Specification and Its Translation

In this section, we present the interface specification language by continuing the small example introduced before (the component C_1 described in Section 2.2). We have defined a higher-level language, called DLiPA [19], based on process

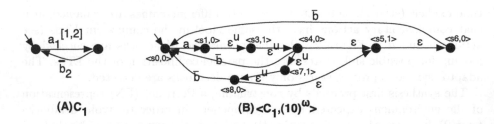

(A) C_1 (B) $<C_1,(10)^\omega>$

Fig. 3. (A) Behavioral interface of C_1 and (B) its semantic model with respect to $(10)^\omega$

algebra. In this paper, we start from an LTS, a form that DLiPA processes can be easily translated into.

Our source LTSs are labeled with actions of the form $x_l^{\{u\} \ [i,j]}$ where x denotes the action (read or write), l its allowed latency, $[i,j]$ its duration, and u, if present, the uncontrollability of the action.

Figure 3.(A) gives the interface specification of the component C_1 as an LTS. From its initial state (denoted by an incoming arrow without source state), C_1 performs an action a (*i.e.*, it reads from port a) followed by an action $\bar{b}$ (*i.e.*, it writes to port b) that returns to the initial state. All C_1 actions are controllable (no u tag). The action a has latency 1, *i.e.*, its execution can be delayed by one global time unit at most. Moreover, a has duration $[1,2]$ meaning that its execution can take either one or two local time units. Similarly, the execution of $\bar{b}$ can be delayed by two global time units at most and takes no time.

Figure 3.(B) presents the semantic model of C_1 that has been derived by taking into account the interface specification of Figure 3.(A) and a periodic clock, here $(10)^\omega$, which has been assigned to C_1. This semantics is noted $\langle C_1, (10)^\omega \rangle$. It is an LTS modeling the interaction behavior of C_1 with its expected environment and making time elapsing explicit. The clock $(10)^\omega$ has been assigned by the designer of the system to be assembled and it represents the required component activation frequency. The LTS of $\langle C_1, (10)^\omega \rangle$ is produced by compiling latency and duration information into *abstract* actions ε representing time elapsing. Each state of the LTS is named by a pair made of a label (*e.g.*, $s0$) and a global time instant (*e.g.*, 0). These instants refer to the finite representation of the assigned periodic clock, *i.e.*, they are the instants $0, \ldots, l-1$ where l is the length of the clock's period. In our example, where the clock is $(10)^\omega$, the instant 0 represents instants where C_1 is enabled (*i.e.*, it can perform some action or let the time elapse) whereas the instant 1 represents instants where C_1 is disabled (*i.e.*, it can only let the time elapse).

A transition labeled by a concrete action (*e.g.*, a) is instantaneous: it represents the starting point for the execution of the action. For example, the transition $\langle s0,0 \rangle \xrightarrow{a} \langle s1,0 \rangle$ in Figure 3.(B) means that C_1 starts to read from port a. A transition labeled by an abstract action ε or ε^u lets the time elapse: it represents a tick of the global clock (*e.g.*, $\langle s1,0 \rangle \xrightarrow{\varepsilon^u} \langle s3,1 \rangle$ in Figure 3.(B)).

Latency is translated using the controllable action ε. For instance an action x with latency 1 is translated into two sequences of transitions: one sequence performing x immediately and another sequence performing x after an ε-transition. If one branch leads to a deadlock, the environment (i.e., the adaptor to be synthesized) may choose the other one by synchronizing only with it.

Duration is translated using the uncontrollable action ε^u. For instance, assuming the clock $(1)^\omega$, an action x with duration $[1,2]$ is translated into the transition x followed by the branching between one or two ε^u-transitions. The uncontrollability enforces the composition with the environment to be compatible with both time-elapsing possibilities. Note that, since duration refers to local time and the semantics refers to the global time, the previous example with a clock $(10)^\omega$ would be translated into the transition x followed by the branching between two or four ε^u-transitions depending on the clock instant (assuming the action x is enabled initially).

In the LTS of Figure 3.(B) (i.e., $\langle C_1, (10)^\omega \rangle$), a duration unit is represented by two ε^u-transitions. Note also that the local clock influences the actual latency. For instance, according to clock $(10)^\omega$, C_1 either executes b immediately (from the time it is enabled) or waits exactly two global time units to execute it: a one time unit wait leads to a state where the component is disabled and b cannot be performed. Analogously, in order to represent the latency of a, an ε-transition should be produced from the initial state. However, this transition is pruned since it is controllable and leads to a sink state (only a read from a is permitted but it is disabled).

To define the semantics of a system (i.e., a network of components), we put in parallel the semantic models of the components by forcing the synchronization on complementary concrete actions and on abstract actions. Components synchronize *pairwise* on complementary concrete actions by producing, for each synchronizing pair $b/\overline{b}$, a τ-transition at the level of the composed system, where τ denotes an internal action. Components synchronize, *altogether*, on time-elapsing transitions by producing a time-elapsing transition at the level of the system. Whenever two or more components have a mismatching interaction due to some behavioral inconsistency, a deadlock occurs in the composed system (i.e., a sink state is produced in the LTS of the system). This is precisely what we avoid thanks to our adaptor synthesis method, presented in the next section. We refer to [19] for further details.

5   Adaptor Synthesis

In this section, we illustrate our method using another small example and formalize part of it. For space reasons, we focus only on the formalization of the Unification PN (see Definition 1) and we omit other formal details that will be illustrated through the explanatory example.

5.1   Unification PN Generation

Let us suppose that the designer wants to build an assembly S formed by two components C_1 and C_2 whose semantic models are shown in Figure 4.

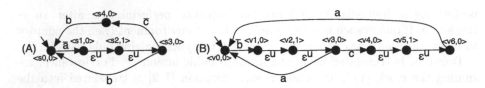

Fig. 4. *After step 1:* (A) $\langle C_1, (11)^\omega \rangle$; (B) $\langle C_2, (10)^\omega \rangle$

Note that the periodic clocks of C_1 and C_2 have the same length. This is required in order to perform the generation of the Unification PN. This requirement is not a limitation since, although the designer can specify clocks with different length, they can be always rewritten in such a way that they have the same length by taking the least common multiple of the different lengths. In Figures 5.(A) and 5.(B) we show respectively the PNs modeling the environment expected from $\langle C_1, (11)^\omega \rangle$ and $\langle C_2, (10)^\omega \rangle$ in order not to block.

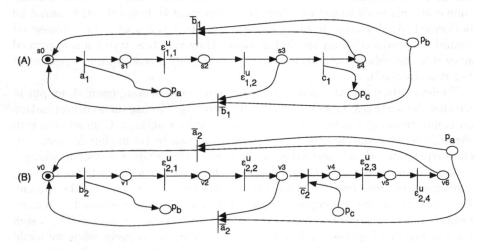

Fig. 5. *After step 2:* Component PNs - (A) PN_1; (B) PN_2

For technical reasons, the actions have been relabeled. Since, now, all the latencies and durations have been made explicit through ε-transitions, the indexing that has been used for the action labels must not be confused with the one used above to specify the latency. We recall that each environment PN is a partial view of the adaptor to be built since it reflects the expectation of only one component. In particular, for each state in the component LTS, there is a place in the environment PN. The initial marking puts a token in the place corresponding to the initial state. For each transition labeled with a concrete action in the component LTS, there is a transition labeled with the *complementary* action in the environment PN. The transition label is such that it contains the information concerning which component has performed the corresponding action (through a suitable indexing: *e.g.*, subscript 1 for C_1 and 2 for C_2).

For each component writing action to an output port x, a place p_x is produced and an arc from the corresponding transition to p_x is added. It corresponds to the fact that, in order to synchronize with a component, the adaptor reads and stores values into an internal buffer. A stored value will be written as output as soon as the adaptor synchronizes with a component that expects to read this value. Component reading actions are handled in a complementary way. In this way, the adaptor desynchronizes the received events from their emission, hence solving mismatches arising from the fact that different components perform complementary actions at different instants.

For a time-elapsing transition in the component LTS, the corresponding transitions, places, and arcs are generated in the environment PN as it is shown in Figure 5. That is, a correct environment for a component has to let the time elapse whenever the component lets the time elapse as well.

Actions that do not force the component to synchronize with the environment can be freely performed; the adaptor must not preempt them and produces an internal action whenever they occur (there is no such action in our example). We refer the reader to [19] for a formal definition of environment PN.

After the partial views of the adaptor have been built, they are composed in order to obtain the Unification PN. In Figure 6 we show the Unification PN (i.e., $PN_{1,2}$) that has been obtained after the unification of PN_1 and PN_2. The Unification PN $PN_{1,2}$ is automatically derived from the union of PN_1 and PN_2 plus a unification operation of their time-elapsing transitions. Informally, casual dependencies between the reading and writing of data are generated by performing the union of the sets of places, arcs, and transitions, except for the arcs and transitions concerning the elapsing of time. Time-elapsing transitions are composed using the synchronous product. Figure 6 shows the obtained time-elapsing transitions as dashed and grey arrows. For readability issues, we have

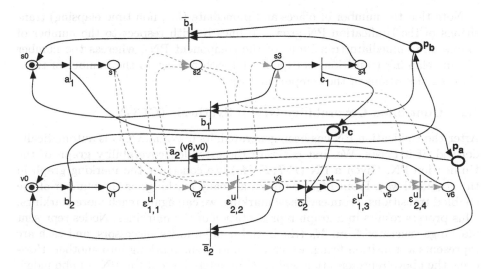

Fig. 6. *After step 3:* $PN_{1,2}$: the Unification PN for PN_1 and PN_2

drawn only the fireable transitions. For example, the first time-elapsing transition of PN_1 composed with the first time-elapsing transition of PN_2 is fireable. Note that the first time-elapsing transition of PN_1 composed with the third time-elapsing transition of PN_2 is fireable as well (after PN_1 has performed one loop). The step to derive the unification PN is formalized by Definition 1:

Definition 1 (Unification PN). *Let* $PN_i = (P_i, T_i, F_i, M_0^i)$ *(where* $i = 1, \ldots, n$, P_i *is the set of places,* T_i *is the set of transitions,* F_i *is the set of arcs, and* M_0^i *is the initial marking) be the PN modeling the environment expected from the component* C_i. *The* Unification PN *is the Petri Net* $UPN = (P, T, F, M_0)$, *where:*

- $P = \bigcup_{i=1}^{n} P_i$;
- $T = \bigcup_{i=1}^{n} T_i' \cup \{\varepsilon_{k_1,\ldots,k_n}^u \mid \forall i = 1, \ldots, n . \varepsilon_{i,k_i}^x \in T_i \wedge \exists i . \varepsilon_{i,k_i}^u \in T_i\} \cup \{\varepsilon_{k_1,\ldots,k_n} \mid \forall i = 1, \ldots, n . \varepsilon_{i,k_i} \in T_i\}$, *where* T_i' *is* T_i *without time-elapsing transitions and the superscript* x *is either equal to 'u' or is empty;*
- $F = \bigcup_{i=1}^{n} F_i' \cup \bigcup_i \{(p, \varepsilon_{k_1,\ldots,k_n}^u), (\varepsilon_{k_1,\ldots,k_n}^u, p') \mid p, p' \in P_i \wedge (p, \varepsilon_{i,k_i}^x) \in F_i \wedge (\varepsilon_{i,k_i}^x, p') \in F_i \wedge \varepsilon_{k_1,\ldots,k_n}^u \in T\} \cup \{(p, \varepsilon_{k_1,\ldots,k_n}), (\varepsilon_{k_1,\ldots,k_n}, p') \mid p, p' \in P_i \wedge (p, \varepsilon_{i,k_i}) \in F_i \wedge (\varepsilon_{i,k_i}, p') \in F_i \wedge \varepsilon_{k_1,\ldots,k_n} \in T\}$, *where* F_i' *is* F_i *without arcs to or from time-elapsing transitions, and the superscript* x *is either equal to 'u' or is empty;*
- *for each* $p \in P$ *if* $\exists i . M_0^i(p) = 1$ *then* $M_0(p) = 1$, *otherwise* $M_0(p) = 0$.

The following is an upper-bound estimation of the size of the Unification PN in terms of its number of places and transitions:

$$|P| = \sum_{i=1}^{n} |P_i|$$
$$|T| = \sum_{i=1}^{n} |T_i'| + \prod_{i=1}^{n} |T_i^{te}| \text{ where } T_i^{te} \text{ is the set of time-elapsing transitions}$$
of PN_i

Note that the number of places and immediate (*i.e.*, non time-elapsing) transitions of the Unification PN grows up linearly with respect to the number of places and immediate transitions of the component PNs; whereas the number of time-elapsing transitions is exponential with respect to the number of time-elapsing transitions of the component PNs.

5.2   Controlled Coverability Graph Synthesis (CCG)

After the Unification PN has been generated, its maximal CCG is automatically derived, if it exists. We first generate the extended coverability graph of the Unification PN. Given a PN (P, T, F, M_0), we construct the marking graph in the standard way. From M_0, we obtain as many markings as the number of the enabled transitions. From each new marking, we can again reach more markings. This process results in a graph representation of the markings. Nodes represent markings generated from M_0 (the initial node) and its successors, and each arc represents a transition firing, which transforms one marking into another. However, the above representation will grow infinitely large if the PN is unbounded. To keep it finite, we introduce a special symbol ω to indicate a possibly infinite number of tokens in some place. ω can be thought of as "infinity". It has the properties that for each integer n, $\omega > n$, $\omega \pm n = \omega$, and $\omega \geq \omega$. Given markings M and M' such that: (1) M' is reachable from M, and (2) $\forall p, M'(p) \geq M(p)$ (i.e., M is coverable by M'), then, for each place q such that $M'(q) > M(q) \geq 1$, we replace $M'(q)$ by ω in the extended coverability graph. This is the same criterion as the *termination criterion* used by Cortadella et al. to identify *irrelevant markings* [6]. They conjecture that this criterion is *complete* [6], meaning that if a bounded and non-blocking execution exists, it will be represented in the extended coverability graph.

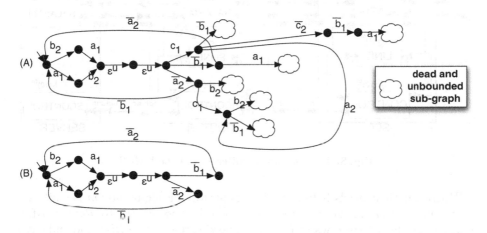

Fig. 7. *After step 4:* (A) extended coverability graph of $PN_{1,2}$; *After step 5:* (B) its *controlled* version

By continuing our example, we partially show the extended coverability graph of $PN_{1,2}$ in Figure 7.(A). The cloud-nodes are portions of the coverability graph made only of paths whose nodes are either *dead* or contain *unbounded* markings. Informally, a dead (resp., unbounded) marking is a node without successors (resp., that represents a marking in which some place has stored a potentially infinite number of tokens) or whose successors always lead to dead (resp., unbounded) markings. We refer to [19] for a formal definition of dead and unbounded markings, and of CCG.

In Figure 7.(B), we show the maximal CCG of $PN_{1,2}$. The maximal CCG is the most permissive one among all possible CCGs. Informally, it is obtained from Figure 7.(A) by pruning the transitions that lead inevitably to cloud-nodes and that are controllable. The pruning of controllable transitions, as well as the "most permissive" notion, is borrowed from Discrete Controller Synthesis [17].

6   Case Study: A Remote Medical Care System

We now apply our approach to a case study, borrowed with minor modifications from [4]: a *Remote Medical Care System* (RMCS). The RMCS provides monitoring and assistance to disabled people. A typical service is to send relevant information to a local phone-center so that medical or technical assistance can be timely notified of critical circumstances. The RMCS can be built from eight COTS components (*Alarm, Line, Control, RAlarm*, etc.) assembled into three composite components: *User, Router*, and *Server* (see Figure 8). Using our adaptor synthesis method and its associated tool (SynthesisRT), it has been possible to incrementally and automatically assemble a correct by construction RMCS.

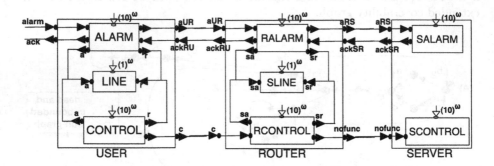

Fig. 8. The software architecture of the RMCS

When a patient needs help (*i.e.*, the uncontrollable signal *alarm* is emitted), *User* sends either an alarm ($\overline{aUR}$) or a check message ($\overline{c}$) to *Router*. After sending an alarm, *User* waits for an acknowledgment (*ackRU*) and indicates the conclusion of the alarm dispatching to the patient (*ack*). *Router* waits for check or alarm messages from *User* (*c* or *aUR*). It forwards alarm messages to *Server* (*aRS*) and checks the state of *User* through the check message (*c*). *Server* dispatches the alarm requests (*aRS*).

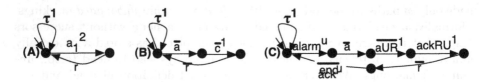

Fig. 9. Behavioral specification of (A) *Line*, (B) *Control*, and (C) *Alarm*

Router and *Server* are connected through a dedicated line (modeled by the component *SLine*) that is always available. Conversely, *User* and *Router* are connected through a usual phone line (modeled by the component *Line*) that can be busy.

For space reasons, we only show the part of the case study that concerns the assembly of the correct-by-construction version of *User*. We refer to [19] for a complete description of both the case study and our SynthesisRT tool. *User* models the logic of the control device provided to patients in order to dispatch alarms. It is an assembly of the three components *Control*, *Alarm*, and *Line*. Figure 9 provides the interface specifications of these components. From these behavioral specifications, SynthesisRT automatically derives the corresponding LTSs. Then, the CADP toolbox [9] is used to derive the LTS representing *User*[1]. CADP allows us to detect possible deadlocks and to exhibit deadlocking traces. For instance, in *User*, an alarm request can deadlock whenever *Alarm* receives an alarm request from the patient and *Control* gets the *Line* to send a check message to *Router*. Figure 10 represents a deadlocking trace where, after an alarm request, *Control* and *Line* synchronize (producing a τ) and let time elapse (*i.e.*, perform a and $\bar{c}$) whereas *Alarm* is still waiting on action $\bar{a}$ that should be performed immediately (no latency).

Fig. 10. A deadlocking trace of *User*

An adaptor is therefore required to avoid deadlocks in *User*. SynthesisRT automatically derives the environment PNs of *Line*, *Control*, and *Alarm*, as well as their Unification PN. The Unification PN is encoded in a file that can be fed to the TINA tool [1]. TINA is used to automatically derive the extended coverability graph of the generated Unification PN. The coverability graph is generated in 0.061 seconds on a Macbook Pro; it is unbounded and has 348 states, 763 transitions, 197 unbounded markings/states and no dead marking/state. This means that the message reordering has been sufficient to solve the detected deadlock, but it can still lead to some buffer overflows.

At this point, SynthesisRT is used again to automatically derive, from the uncontrolled coverability graph, its corresponding maximal CCG that prevents the reaching of the unbounded states. The maximal CCG is the LTS of the synthesized adaptor (Ad_{user}) that allows one to correctly assemble *User*. In our example, the adaptor is generated in 0.127 seconds but it is too large to be presented here; it has 116 states and 242 transitions. The deadlock is solved by Ad_{user} using message buffering and reordering. More precisely, when *Line* and *Control* perform a and $\bar{c}$, Ad_{user} synchronizes with *Alarm* on the line request $\bar{a}$. It stores the received request in a buffer in order to forward it when the line is released by *Control*. Then, the execution of *Alarm* can proceed and reach a point where it can let the time elapse, as required by *Control* and *Line*.

So, by putting Ad_{user} in parallel with *Line*, *Control*, and *Alarm*, we obtain the correct-by-construction version of the composite component *User*. We have also used SynthesisRT to derive three other adaptors: Ad_{router} (interposed between *RAlarm*, *SLine*, and *RControl*), Ad_{rs} (interposed between the adapted router and *Server*) and Ad_{rmcs} (interposed between the adapted composite router/server component and the adapted user component). Through the

---

[1] Referring to Figure 2, steps 1, 3, and 5 are performed with SynthesisRT, step 2 with CADP, and step 4 with TINA.

synthesis of these four adaptors, we have incrementally and automatically built a correct-by-construction RMCS.

7   Conclusion

In this paper, we have described an adaptor-based approach to assemble correct by construction real-time components that take into account interaction protocols, timing information, and QoS constraints. Our approach focuses on detection, correction, and prevention of deadlocks and unbounded buffers due to mismatching protocols. The main idea is to build a model of the environment of the component and to extract a controlled version (an adaptor) preventing deadlocks and unbounded buffers. In the general case, the space complexity of the synthesis algorithm is exponential in the number of states of the component LTSs. We have validated the approach by means of a case study.

Our work is related to several techniques in different research areas. In control theory, a related technique is *discrete controller synthesis* [17]. The objective is to restrict the system behavior so that it satisfies a *specification*. This is achieved by automatically synthesizing a suitable controller w.r.t. the specification. Beyond restricting the system behavior, our approach also extends it to resolve possible mismatches. For instance, while the approach in [17] performs only deadlock prevention, our approach performs also deadlock correction.

Another related work in synchronous programming is the synchronizing of different clocks. In [5], each input and output port is associated with a periodic clock. Adaptation is performed at the level of each connection between ports using finite buffers. It is sufficient to look at the clocks of two connected ports and to introduce a delay by interposing a *node buffer* between the two ports. In our context, adaptation must be performed at the component level by taking into account several dimensions of the specification: the component clock, the interaction protocol, the latency, duration, and controllability of each action. For this reason, introducing delays is not sufficient and, *e.g.*, the reordering or inhibition of actions may be necessary.

Related work in *interface automata* theory [7] also uses LTSs to model the input/output behavior of components. When composing two LTSs, they derive a constraint on their environment such that deadlocks are avoided, but they do not produce an adaptor to solve the incompatibilities between the two components.

Related work in component adaptation [3] and component interface compatibility [15] has shown how to automatically generate the behavioral model of an adaptor from: (i) a partial specification of the interaction behavior of the components and (ii) an abstract specification of the adaptor. In contrast with our work, they do not deal with real-time attributes. Although we took inspiration from [3] with respect to the PN encoding into the TINA tool and the use of CADP, our synthesis algorithm is very different from theirs since they do not have to take into account time-elapsing actions. Moreover, both techniques in [3] and [15] consider all component actions to be controllable, and neither considers the problem of synthesizing an adaptor model that ensures to always have bounded buffers.

Our approach focuses only on the automatic generation of the behavioral model of the correct adaptor. Future work shall consider the generation of the adaptor's actual code using, e.g., synchronous languages such as Signal, Lustre, or Esterel. So far, the clocks are fixed before synthesizing the adaptor. Changing a component clock means re-executing the synthesis algorithm. An interesting extension would be to automatically derive clock-independent adaptors. A component clock would become a function of the adaptor clock. When the adaptor clock is instantiated, the component clocks will be instantiated as well to obtain a correct-by-construction assembly. Another possible future work is to study and formalize component architectures for which incremental adaptor synthesis is equivalent to a centralized adaptor synthesis.

References

1. B. Berthomieu, P. Ribet, and F. Vernadat. Construction of abstract state spaces for Petri nets and time Petri nets. *International Journal of Production Research*, 42(14), 2004. TINA web page: http://www.laas.fr/tina/.
2. B. Boehm and C. Abts. COTS integration: Plug and pray? *IEEE Computer*, 32(1), 1999.
3. C. Canal, P. Poizat, and G. Salaün. Synchronizing behavioural mismatch in software composition. In *FMOODS*, volume 4037 of *LNCS*, 2006.
4. M. Cioffi and F. Corradini. Specification and analysis of timed and functional TRMCS behaviors. In *Proc. of the 10th IWSSD*, 2000.
5. A. Cohen, M. Duranton, C. Eisenbeis, C. Pagetti, F. Plateau, and M. Pouzet. Synchronization of periodic clocks. In *Proc. of the 5th EMSOFT*, 2005.
6. J. Cortadella, A. Kondratyev, L. Lavagno, C. Passerone, and Y. Wanatabe. Quasi-static scheduling of independant tasks for reactive systems. *IEEE Trans. on Computer-Aided Design of Integrated Circuits and Systems*, 24(10):1492–1514, Oct. 2005.
7. L. de Alfaro and T. Henzinger. Interface automata. In *Annual Symposium on Foundations of Software Engineering, FSE'01*, pages 109–120. ACM, 2001.
8. A. Finkel. The minimal coverability graph for Petri nets. In *Proc. of the 12th APN*, volume 674 of *LNCS*, 1993.
9. H. Garavel, F. Lang, and R. Mateescu. An overview of CADP 2001. *EASST Newsletter*, 4, 2002. http://www.inrialpes.fr/vasy/cadp.
10. D. Garlan, R. Allen, and J. Ockerbloom. Architectural mismatch: Why reuse is so hard. *IEEE Software*, 12(6), 1995.
11. P. Inverardi, D. Yankelevich, and A. Wolf. Static checking of system behaviors using derived component assumptions. *ACM TOSEM*, 9(3), 2000.
12. N. Kaveh and W. Emmerich. Object system. *8th FSE/ESEC*, 2001.
13. R. Milner. *Communication and Concurrency*. Prentice Hall, 1989.
14. T. Murata. Petri nets: Properties, analysis and applications. *Proceedings of the IEEE*, 77(4), 1989.
15. R. Passerone, L. de Alfaro, T. Henzinger, and A. Sangiovanni-Vincentelli. Convertibility verification and converter synthesis: Two faces of the same coin. In *ICCAD*, 2002.

16. C. Petri. *Kommunikation mit Automaten*. PhD thesis, University of Bonn, 1962.
17. P. Ramadge and W. Wonham. The control of discrete event systems. *Proceedings of the IEEE*, 1(77), 1989.
18. C. Szyperski. *Component Software. Beyond Object Oriented Programming*. Addison Wesley, 1998.
19. M. Tivoli, P. Fradet, A. Girault, and G. Gössler. Adaptor synthesis for real-time components. Research report, INRIA, 2007, to appear.

Deciding an Interval Logic
with Accumulated Durations*

Martin Fränzle[1] and Michael R. Hansen[2],**

[1] Dpt. Informatik, C. v. Ossietzky Universität Oldenburg, Germany
fraenzle@informatik.uni-oldenburg.de
[2] Informatics and Math. Modelling, Technical University of Denmark
mrh@imm.dtu.dk

Abstract. A decidability result and a model-checking procedure for a rich subset of Duration Calculus (DC) [19] is obtained through reductions to first-order logic over the real-closed field and to Multi-Priced Timed Automata (MPTA) [13]. In contrast to other reductions of fragments of DC to reachability problems in timed automata, the reductions do also cover constraints on positive linear combinations of accumulated durations. By being able to handle accumulated durations under chop as well as in arbitrary positive Boolean contexts, the procedures extend the results of Zhou et al. [22] on decidability of linear duration invariants to a much wider fragment of DC.

Keywords: Real-time systems, metric-time temporal logic, decidability, model-checking, multi-priced timed automata.

1 Introduction

The Duration Calculi (DC) are a family of metric-time temporal logics facilitating reasoning about embedded real-time systems at a high level of abstraction from operational detail [21,19]. Its major ingredients permitting such abstractness are, on one hand, that it is an interval-based [10] rather than a situation-based temporal logic [14] and, on the other hand, the notion of an accumulated duration of a predicate being true over some observation interval. While the former permits a less state-based style of specification, the latter supports abstraction from the fine-granular distribution of interesting or critical situations along the time line. An example is the accumulated runtime of some task in a multitasking environment, where the time instants where the task actually is run are of minor importance, provided the accumulated duration of running it before its deadline is sufficient for its completion.

---

* This work has been supported by the German Research Council (DFG) as part of the Transregional Collaborative Research Center "Automatic Verification and Analysis of Complex Systems" (SFB/TR 14 AVACS, www.avacs.org) and by Velux Fonden, Søborg, Denmark, through the Velux Visiting Professors Programme.
** This work has been partially funded by The Danish Council for Strategic Research under project **MoDES**.

O. Grumberg and M. Huth (Eds.): TACAS 2007, LNCS 4424, pp. 201–215, 2007.

While the abstractness supported by DC is desirable for system specification and analysis, it proved to be a burden for automatic verification support. Both the satisfiability problem and the model-checking problem wrt. timed automata of most non-trivial fragments of DC are known to be undecidable [20,19]. In the dense-time setting with finitely variable models as interpretation, decidability has in general only been obtained by either dropping metric time altogether [20] or by dropping accumulated durations and, furthermore, seriously restricting the use of negation or chop (DC's only modality) [5,12,8,6]. The only notable exception is [22], where a conjunction of *linear duration invariants* is automatically checked on the possible runs of a timed transition table, where transition occurrences are constrained by upper and lower bounds on the residence time in the source state. Linear duration invariants are, however, an extremely small fragment of DC: They are formulae $c_0 \leq \ell \Rightarrow \sum_{i=1}^n c_i \int P_i \leq c_{n+1}$ expressing that the weighted sum $\sum_{i=1}^n c_i \int P_i$ of the accumulated durations $\int P_i$ of some mutually exclusive state properties P_i is always less than c_{n+1}, provided the length of the observation interval exceeds c_0. Furthermore, the automaton model dealt with is very restrictive: by only featuring timing bounds on the residence time in the source state of a transition, it is considerably less expressive than timed transition systems with clocks [1,4]. In particular, it is not closed under, e.g., parallel composition.

Within this paper, we do complement the aforementioned decidability results by procedures that are able to

1. check satisfiability of formulae featuring multiple different accumulated durations within subformulae which, furthermore, may occur under arbitrarily nested chop and within complex Boolean contexts, provided the chop modalities occur in positive context, and to
2. check whether every run of a timed automaton A satisfies $\neg\phi$, where ϕ is a formula as described under point (1). This model-checking problem is usually written $A \models \neg\phi$, and in this special form ϕ is a specification of an undesired situation, and $A \models \neg\phi$ asserts that no run of A exist which exhibits the undesired situation. This idea is, for example, pursued in [15,11], where ϕ can have the restricted form of a *DC implementable* [16], thus abandoning accumulated durations and replacing chop by more restricted, operationally inspired operators. We extend their work by allowing formulae featuring accumulated durations and arbitrary positive chop.

For the decidability results concerning satisfiability of formulae, our construction builds on a small model property permitting the reduction of model construction for DC to satisfiability of first-order logic over the reals with addition $FOL(\mathbb{R}, +, \leq)$. The model-checking results are obtained through a reduction to Multi-Priced Timed Automata (MPTA) [13], where weighted sums of accumulated durations are encoded by prices. The syntactic structure of the formula to be checked reflects in the structure of the MPTA generated, where conjunction and disjunction map to the corresponding operations on automata, while the chop modality yields concatenation.

Structure of the paper: In Sect. 2, we introduce Duration Calculus and the relevant notions of satisfiability and satisfiability over length-bounded models. Section 3 provides the decidability result concerning satisfiability, while Sect. 5 provides the corresponding result for the model-checking problem. In between, Sect. 4 reviews multi-priced timed automata, as defined by Rasmussen and Larsen in [13]. Section 6, finally, discusses how close these results are to the decidability borderline.

2 Duration Calculus

Duration Calculus (abbreviated DC in the remainder) is a real-time logic that is developed for reasoning about durational constraints on time-dependent Boolean-valued states. Since its introduction in [21], many variants of DC have been defined [19]. In this paper we aim at a subset involving durational constraints, which can be supported by automated reasoning.

2.1 Syntax

The syntax of DC used in this paper is defined below. We shall define two syntax categories: *state expressions*, ranged over by $S, S_1, S_2, \ldots$, and *formulae*, ranged over by $\phi, \phi_1, \psi, \psi_1, \ldots$. State expressions are Boolean combinations of state variables, and they describe combined states of a system at a given point in time. Formulae can be considered as truth-valued functions on time intervals, i.e. for a given time interval, a formula is either true or false.

The abstract syntax for state expressions and formulae is defined by:

$$S ::= 0 \mid 1 \mid P \mid \neg S \mid S_1 \vee S_2$$
$$\phi ::= \ell \bowtie k \mid \lceil S \rceil \mid \sum_{i=1}^{m} c_i \int S_i \bowtie k \mid \neg \phi \mid \phi \vee \psi \mid \phi \wedge \psi \mid \phi \frown \psi,$$

where ℓ is a special symbol denoting the interval length, P ranges over state variables, $k, m, c_i \in \mathbb{N}$, and $\bowtie \in \{<, \leq, =, \geq, >\}$.

In the remainder, we will call any formula built according to the above syntax a *DC formula*. The subset of DC formulae where the chop modality "$\frown$" do only occur under a positive number of negations is denoted DC_{pos}. $\text{DC}_{\setminus \neg}$ will name the set of all negation-free (at formula level) DC formulae. Finally, DC_{ub} contains all $\text{DC}_{\setminus \neg}$ formulae which contain only upper bound constraints on durations, i.e. where $\bowtie \in \{<, \leq\}$, and where exactly one duration constraint is a strict inequality.

2.2 Semantics

An interpretation $\mathcal{I}$ associates a function $P_{\mathcal{I}} : \mathbb{R}_{\geq 0} \to \{0, 1\}$ with every state variable P, where $\mathbb{R}_{\geq 0}$ models the dense time line such that interpretations yield time-dependent, Boolean-valued valuations of state variables. We impose the *finite variability restriction* that $P_{\mathcal{I}}$ has at most a finite number of discontinuity points in any interval $[a, b]$.

The semantics of a state expression S, given an interpretation $\mathcal{I}$, is a function: $\mathcal{I}[\![S]\!] : \mathbb{R}_{\geq 0} \to \{0, 1\}$, which is defined inductively as follows:

$$\mathcal{I}[\![0]\!](t) = 0 \qquad\qquad \mathcal{I}[\![\neg S]\!](t) = \begin{cases} 0 \text{ if } \mathcal{I}[\![S]\!](t) = 1 \\ 1 \text{ if } \mathcal{I}[\![S]\!](t) = 0 \end{cases}$$

$$\mathcal{I}[\![1]\!](t) = 1$$

$$\mathcal{I}[\![P]\!](t) = P_{\mathcal{I}}(t) \qquad \mathcal{I}[\![S_1 \vee S_2]\!](t) = \begin{cases} 0 \text{ if } \mathcal{I}[\![S_1]\!](t) = \mathcal{I}[\![S_2]\!](t) = 0 \\ 1 \text{ otherwise.} \end{cases}$$

We shall use the abbreviation $S_{\mathcal{I}} \stackrel{\text{df}}{=} \mathcal{I}[\![S]\!]$.

Satisfaction of formulae ϕ is defined over pairs $(\mathcal{I}, [a, b])$ of an interpretation $\mathcal{I}$ and a time interval $[a, b]$ with $a, b \in \mathbb{R}_{\geq 0}$. Such a pair $(\mathcal{I}, [a, b])$ is called an *observation*. The satisfaction relation $\mathcal{I}, [a, b] \models \phi$ is defined recursively, where $\mathcal{I}$ is an interpretation, $[a, b]$ is an interval, and ϕ is a formula:

$$
\begin{array}{lll}
\mathcal{I}, [a, b] \models \ell \bowtie k & \text{iff} & b - a \bowtie k \\
\mathcal{I}, [a, b] \models \lceil S \rceil & \text{iff} & a < b \text{ and } \int_a^b S_{\mathcal{I}}(t)dt = b - a \\
\mathcal{I}, [a, b] \models \sum_{i=1}^m c_i \int S_i \bowtie k & \text{iff} & \sum_{i=1}^m c_i \int_a^b S_{i\mathcal{I}}(t)dt \bowtie k \\
\mathcal{I}, [a, b] \models \neg \phi & \text{iff} & \mathcal{I}, [a, b] \not\models \phi \\
\mathcal{I}, [a, b] \models \phi \vee \psi & \text{iff} & \mathcal{I}, [a, b] \models \phi \text{ or } \mathcal{I}, [a, b] \models \psi \\
\mathcal{I}, [a, b] \models \phi \wedge \psi & \text{iff} & \mathcal{I}, [a, b] \models \phi \text{ and } \mathcal{I}, [a, b] \models \psi \\
\mathcal{I}, [a, b] \models \phi \frown \psi & \text{iff} & \mathcal{I}, [a, m] \models \phi \text{ and } \mathcal{I}, [m, b] \models \psi, \\
& & \text{for some } m \in [a, b].
\end{array}
$$

Whenever $\mathcal{I}, [a, b] \models \phi$ holds we say that ϕ is *true* in $[a, b]$ wrt. $\mathcal{I}$. A formula ϕ is said to be *valid* (written $\models \phi$) if $\mathcal{I}, [a, b] \models \phi$ holds for all interpretations $\mathcal{I}$ and all intervals $[a, b]$. Furthermore, a formula ϕ is *satisfiable* if $\mathcal{I}, [a, b] \models \phi$ for some observation $(\mathcal{I}, [a, b])$. Given $k \in \mathbb{N}$, we say that ϕ is *k-bounded satisfiable* if there is an interpretation $\mathcal{I}$ with at most k discontinuity points[1] and an interval $[a, b]$ such that $\mathcal{I}, [a, b] \models \phi$. In this case, we say that observation $(\mathcal{I}, [a, b])$ is a *k-bounded model* of ϕ.

Since every occurrence of a state variable is within the scope of an integral, we can form equivalence classes of interpretations, where no formula can distinguish between interpretations belonging to the same class. This leads to the following definition and lemma:

Definition 1. *Two interpretations $\mathcal{I}, \mathcal{I}'$ are called* equivalent *in $[a, b]$, written $\mathcal{I} \approx_{[a,b]} \mathcal{I}'$, if $P_{\mathcal{I}}$ and $P_{\mathcal{I}'}$ disagree on at most a finite number of points in $[a, b]$, for every state variable P.*

Lemma 1. *For any formula ϕ, interpretations $\mathcal{I}, \mathcal{I}'$ and interval $[a, b]$:*

$$\text{If } \mathcal{I} \approx_{[a,b]} \mathcal{I}', \text{ then } \mathcal{I}, [a, b] \models \phi \text{ iff } \mathcal{I}', [a, b] \models \phi.$$

---

[1] Formally speaking, $\mathcal{I}$ is a vector of functions $P_{\mathcal{I}}$ and has no discontinuity points itself. By the discontinuity points of $\mathcal{I}$ we mean the set $\{t \in \mathbb{R} \mid P \text{ is state variable}, P_{\mathcal{I}} \text{ has a discontinuity point in } t\}$ of all discontinuity points of the individual $P_{\mathcal{I}}$.

3   Decidability of the Satisfiability Problem

It has been observed previously, e.g. by Guelev (personal communication, 1997) and by Hoenicke [11], that for fixed $k \in \mathbb{N}$, the k-bounded satisfiability problem for Duration Calculus (as defined in Sect. 2) is decidable via a reduction to first-order logic over the reals with addition $FOL(\mathbb{R}, +, <)$, whose decidability is classical [18].

Lemma 2. *Let $k \in \mathbb{N}$ and ϕ a DC formula.*

1. *It is decidable whether ϕ is k-bounded satisfiable.*
2. *If ϕ is k-bounded satisfiable then ϕ is satisfiable.*
3. *If ϕ is satisfiable then there exists $l \in \mathbb{N}$ such that ϕ is l-bounded satisfiable.*
4. *There is no algorithm which, given a satisfiable formula ϕ, computes the bound l from item 3.*

Proof. A proof of (1) can be found in [11, p.24ff]. (2) and (3) are obvious from the definitions. (4) is a consequence of the general undecidability results of Duration Calculus (e.g., [20,19]) and the decidability result stated in (1). ☐

Item 4 of Lemma 2 shows that k-bounded satisfiability is much more limited than satisfiability in general and that, consequently, the corresponding decidability results are of limited value. For full DC, they do only provide a semi-decision procedure for (unbounded) satisfiability, based on testing increasing k in Lemma 2 (1) and exploiting the correspondences from Lemma 2 (2 and 3).

We shall show below that formulae of $\mathrm{DC_{pos}}$ have a small-model property permitting effective computation of a bound on the length of minimal models of satisfiable formulae. According to Lemma 2 (1), this implies decidability of the satisfiability problem. The main idea behind this result is that the truth value of a formula $\phi \in \mathrm{DC_{pos}}$ for an observation $(\mathcal{I}, [a, b])$ is invariant to reshuffling of certain segments of $\mathcal{I}$ in $[a, b]$.

To explain this, let $(\mathcal{I}_1, [a_1, b_1])$ and $(\mathcal{I}_2, [a_2, b_2])$ be observations. Then *observation concatenation* $a : (\mathcal{I}_1, [a_1, b_1]) \frown (\mathcal{I}_2, [a_2, b_2])$ denotes the (set of)[2] observations $(\mathcal{I}', [a, a + b_1 - a_1 + b_2 - a_2])$ with $\mathcal{I}'$ for all state variables P satisfying $\forall t \in [0, b_1 - a_1).P_{\mathcal{I}_1}(a_1 + t) = P_{\mathcal{I}'}(a + t)$ and $\forall t \in (0, b_2 - a_2].P_{\mathcal{I}_2}(a_2 + t) = P_{\mathcal{I}'}(a + b_1 - a_1 + t)$. We shall omit repeated $a :$ in repeated concatenations $a : (a : \mathcal{I}_1 \frown \mathcal{I}_2) \frown \mathcal{I}_3$.

Lemma 3. *Let ϕ be a chop-free formula and $(\mathcal{I}, [a, b]) = a : \mathcal{O}_1 \frown \mathcal{O}_2 \frown \cdots \frown \mathcal{O}_k$ be a concatenation of observations $\mathcal{O}_i$. Then*

$$a : (\mathcal{O}_1 \frown \mathcal{O}_2 \frown \cdots \frown \mathcal{O}_k), [a, b] \models \phi \text{ iff } a : (\mathcal{O}_{i_1} \frown \mathcal{O}_{i_2} \frown \cdots \frown \mathcal{O}_{i_k}), [a, b] \models \phi \ ,$$

for any permutation $i_1, i_2, \ldots i_k$ of $1, 2, \ldots, k$.

---

[2] Note that interpretation outside the observation interval is irrelevant to the semantics of DC such that the fact that concatenation actually yields a set is irrelevant in practice.

Proof. The proof is by induction on the structure of ϕ. The base case $\ell \sim k$ is simple, since the truth value depends on the interval $[a, b]$ only. The other two base cases: $\lceil S \rceil$ and $\sum_{i=1}^{m} c_i \int S_i \bowtie k$, are simple since their truth values are defined in terms of integrals of state expressions, and such integrals are invariant to the reshuffling. The inductive steps for the propositional connectives are straightforward. $\square$

This lemma provides a small-model property for any chop-free formula ϕ. Suppose that ϕ contains n state variables, and that $(\mathcal{I}, [a, b])$ is a model of ϕ. There are 2^n different truth assignments to n Boolean variables, and the above lemma allows us to reshuffle the segments of $\mathcal{I}$ in $[a, b]$ to arrive at a 2^n-bounded model of ϕ.

Corollary 1. *If a chop-free formula ϕ is satisfiable then it has a 2^n-bounded model, where n is the number of state variables occurring in ϕ*

To show the small model property for $\mathrm{DC_{pos}}$, we first introduce another operator to DC: In a *timed chop* $\phi \frown_c \psi$, where $c \in \mathbb{R}_{\geq 0}$, the chop point is confined to occur exactly at time c:

$$\mathcal{I}, [a, b] \models \phi \frown_c \psi \text{ iff } a \leq c \leq b \text{ and } \mathcal{I}, [a, c] \models \phi \text{ and } \mathcal{I}, [c, b] \models \psi.$$

It is obvious that a DC formula $\phi \in \mathrm{DC_{pos}}$ is satisfiable iff there is some satisfiable formula ψ which is syntactically equal to ψ except that all chops have been replaced by timed chops. For such a ψ, we can now show that ψ, if satisfiable, has a model of length linear in the number of (timed) chops in ψ.

Lemma 4. *If ψ does not contain an untimed chop and is satisfiable then ψ is $2^n(m+1)$-bounded satisfiable, where m is the number of (timed) chops in ψ and n is the number of state variables occurring in ψ.*

Proof. sketch: Between chop points —which are now fixed to constant occurrence times and thus cannot permute—, one can reshuffle the segments in $\mathcal{I}$ arbitrarily, thus ending up with at most 2^n segments between each two chops according to Corollary 1. Since there are m chop points, there are $m + 1$ such segments. $\square$

As chop is a relaxation of timed chop, all models of ψ are also models of ϕ. Therefore, the above result generalizes to DC formulae with untimed chop:

Corollary 2. *If a formula $\phi \in DC_{pos}$ is satisfiable then it has a $2^n(m+1)$-bounded model, where m is the number of chops in ϕ and n is the number of state variables occurring in ϕ.*

Proof. As $\mathrm{DC_{pos}}$ contains the duals of all operators except chop,[3] we can rewrite ϕ to negation-free form $\phi' \in \mathrm{DC_{\backslash \neg}}$. If ϕ' is satisfiable then it has at least one satisfiable counterpart ψ containing only timed chops. According to the previous Lemma, ψ has a $2^n(m+1)$-bounded model. As satisfaction of timed chop implies satisfaction of chop, and due to monotonicity of all other operators in the negation-free fragment $\mathrm{DC_{\backslash \neg}}$, this model is also a model of ϕ' and thus ϕ. $\square$

---

[3] For $\lceil S \rceil$, we have the duality $\lceil S \rceil = \neg(\ell = 0 \vee \int \neg S > 0)$. All other dualities are the classical ones from predicate logics.

As a consequence, we obtain decidability of the satisfiability problem of DC:

Theorem 1. *It is decidable whether a formula $\phi \in DC_{pos}$ is satisfiable.*

Proof. According to Corollary 2, in order to check for satisfiability of ϕ it suffices to check whether ϕ has a $2^n(m+1)$-bounded model, where m is the number of chops in ϕ and n is the number of state variables occurring in ϕ. Lemma 2 (1) shows decidability of $2^n(m+1)$-bounded satisfiability. □

As $\neg$after rewriting to negation-free form $DC_{\backslash\neg}$— there are no negations in our fragment of DC, the $FOL(\mathbb{R}, +, <)$ formula constructed turns out to be in the existential fragment of $FOL(\mathbb{R}, +, <)^4$. Its size is linear in $|\phi|$ and in the bound $k = 2^n(m+1)$ of model construction. For a fixed number n of state variables, it is thus worst-case quadratic in $|\phi|$. As deciding the existential fragment of $FOL(\mathbb{R}, +, <)$ is NP-complete, this implies that satisfiability of DC formulae with a fixed number of state variables is in NP. Without a bound on the number of variables, it obviously is singly exponential.

4 Priced Timed Automata

In this section, we review the definition of *Linearly Multi-Priced Timed Automata* (*MPTA*) together with the theorems that we shall use in order to establish our decidability result for DC. The presentation of MPTA is based on [13]. MPTA are an extension of timed automata [1,4], where *prices* are associated with edges and locations. The cost of taking an edge is the price of that edge, and the cost of staying in a location is given by the product of the *cost-rate* for that location and the time spent in the location.

Let $\mathbb{C}$ be a finite set of clocks. An *atomic constraint* is a formula of the form: $x \bowtie n$, where $x \in \mathbb{C}$, $\bowtie \in \{\leq, =, \geq, <, >\}$, and $n \in \mathbb{N}$. A *clock constraint* over $\mathbb{C}$ is a conjunction of atomic constraints. Let $B(\mathbb{C})$ denote the set of clock constraints over $\mathbb{C}$ and let $B(\mathbb{C})^*$ denote the set of clock constraints over $\mathbb{C}$ involving only upper bounds, i.e. $\leq$ or $<$. Furthermore, let $2^{\mathbb{C}}$ denote the power set of $\mathbb{C}$.

A *clock valuation* $v : \mathbb{C} \to R_{\geq 0}$ is a function assigning a non-negative real number with each clock. The valuation v *satisfies* a clock constraint $g \in B(\mathbb{C})$, if each conjunct of g is true in v. In this case we write $v \in g$. Let $\mathbb{R}_{\geq 0}^{\mathbb{C}}$ denote the set of all clock valuations.

Definition 2 (cf. [13]). *A multi-priced timed automaton A over clocks $\mathbb{C}$ is a tuple (L, l_0, E, I, P), where L is a finite set of locations, l_0 is the initial location, $E \subseteq L \times B(\mathbb{C}) \times 2^{\mathbb{C}} \times L$ is the set of edges, where an edge contains a source, a guard, a set of clocks to be reset, and a target. $I : L \to B(\mathbb{C})^*$ assigns invariants to locations, and $P : (L \cup E) \to \mathbb{N}^m$ assigns a vector of prices to both locations and edges. In the case of $(l, g, r, l') \in E$, we write $l \xrightarrow{g,r} l'$.*

In order to give semantics to linearly multi-priced timed automata, the notion of a multi-priced transition system is introduced. A *multi-priced transition system*

---
[4] Also known as "LinSAT", featuring powerful tool support, e.g. [3,9].

is a structure $T = (S, s_0, \Sigma, \longrightarrow)$, where S is a, possibly infinite, set of states, $s_0 \in S$ is the initial state, Σ is a finite set of labels, and $\longrightarrow$ is a partial function from $S \times \Sigma \times S$ to $\mathbb{R}_{\geq 0}^m$, defining the possible transitions and their associated costs. The notation $s \xrightarrow{a}_p s'$ means that $\longrightarrow (s, a, s')$ is defined and equal to p. An *execution* of T is a finite sequence $\alpha = s_0 \xrightarrow{a_1}_{p_1} s_1 \xrightarrow{a_2}_{p_2} s_2 \cdots s_{n-1} \xrightarrow{a_n}_{p_n} s_n$, and the associated *cost* of α is $\mathrm{cost}(\alpha) = \sum_{i=1}^n p_i$.

For a given state s and a vector $u = (u_1, \dots, u_{m-1}) \in \mathbb{R}_{\geq 0}^{m-1}$, let $\mathrm{mincost}_{T,u}(s)$ denote the *minimum cost* wrt. the last component of the price vector of reaching s while respecting the upper bound constraints to the other prices which are given by u. This is defined as the infimum of the cost of all executions ending in s and respecting price constraint u, i.e.

$$\mathrm{mincost}_{T,u}(s) = \inf \left\{ \mathrm{cost}(\alpha)_m \; \middle| \; \begin{matrix} \alpha \text{ an execution of } T \text{ ending in } s, \\ \forall i \in \mathbb{N}_{<m}.\mathrm{cost}(\alpha)_i \leq u_i \end{matrix} \right\}.$$

Furthermore, for a set of states $G \subseteq S$, let $\mathrm{mincost}_{T,u}(G)$ denote the minimal cost of reaching some state in G while respecting the upper price bounds u.

The semantics of a linearly multi-priced timed automaton $A = (L, l_0, E, I, P)$ is a *multi-priced transition system* $T_A = (S, s_0, \Sigma, \longrightarrow)$, where

- $S = L \times \mathbb{R}_{\geq 0}^{\mathcal{C}}$,
- $s_0 = (l_0, v_0)$, where v_0 is the (clock) valuation assigning 0 to every clock,
- $\Sigma = E \cup \{\delta\}$, where δ indicates a delay and $e \in E$ the edge taken, and
- the partial transition function $\longrightarrow$ is defined as follows:
  - $(l, v) \xrightarrow{\delta}_p (l, v + d)$ if $\forall e.0 \leq e \leq d : v + e \in I(l)$, and $p = d \cdot P(l)$,
  - $(l, v) \xrightarrow{e}_p (l', v')$ if $(l, g, r, l') \in E, v \in g, v' = v[r \mapsto 0]$ and $p = P(e)$,
  where $v + d$ means the clock valuation where the value of x is $v(x) + d$, for $x \in \mathbb{C}, d \in R_{\geq 0}$, and $v[r \mapsto 0]$ is the valuation which is as v except that clocks in r are mapped to 0.

In case T_A performs a δ step $(l, v) \xrightarrow{\delta}_p (l, v + d)$, we say that the *duration of the step* is d. All other steps, i.e. those labelled $e \in E$, have duration 0.

The main results that we shall exploit concerning linearly multi-priced timed automata is that the minimum cost of reaching some target location is computable for any (set of) target location(s) and any upper bound on the remaining prices: Given an MPTA $A = (L, l_0, E, I, P)$, a target $G \subset L$, and some cost constraint $u \in \mathbb{R}_{\geq 0}^{m-1}$, we define the *minimum cost* $\mathrm{mincost}_{A,u}(G)$ to be $\mathrm{mincost}_{T_A,u}(G \times \mathbb{R}_{\geq 0}^{\mathcal{C}})$.

Theorem 2 ([13]). *For any MPTA $A = (L, l_0, E, I, P)$, any set $G \subset L$, and any cost constraint $u \in \mathbb{R}_{\geq 0}^{m-1}$, the minimum cost $\mathrm{mincost}_{A,u}(G)$ is computable.*

5   Encoding of DC$_{\mathrm{ub}}$ Formulae by MPTA

Within this section, we will provide an encoding of DC$_{\mathrm{ub}}$ formulae ϕ by MPTA representing their models. The encoding will be such that each model of ϕ

corresponds to a run of the corresponding MPTA with the associated costs representing and satisfying the duration constraints in ϕ. In detail, we shall represent each formula ϕ by a tuple $(L, s, E, I, P, f, \Lambda)$ denoted A_ϕ, where (L, s, E, I, P) is a multi-priced timed automaton, f is a special *final location* to be reached, and Λ is a function associating a DC state-expression S with every location. The construction will be such that the automaton will not be allowed to spend positive time in the final location, and the intuition is that the satisfying observations of ϕ are represented by the set of executions of A_ϕ ending in f. Subformulae of the form $\sum_{i=1}^{m} c_i \int S_i \bowtie k$ will, however, receive a special treatment. The intuition about the automaton for such a formula is that its executions ending in f can generate all possible interpretations to the state variables and that the value of the expression $\sum_{i=1}^{m} c_i \int S_i$ is the cost of the execution, and a bounding of the cost or an analysis of the minimal cost of executions can be used to decide satisfaction of $\sum_{i=1}^{m} c_i \int S_i \bowtie k$.

5.1   The Construction

In the construction we shall use the following conventions:

- the cost of an edge is always 0,
- the cost-rate of a location is 0 unless otherwise stated,
- the invariant of a location is true unless otherwise stated,
- the mark of a location l is the state expression 1, i.e. $\Lambda(l) = 1$, unless otherwise stated.

In the following we assume that the formula ϕ under consideration contains n distinct state variables $P_1, \ldots, P_n$ and m subformulae $\sum_{i=1}^{m_j} c_{i,j} \int S_{i,j} \bowtie_j k_j$, where $\bowtie_m = <$ and $\bowtie_j = \leq$ for every $j < m$. We shall give a recursive construction of an automaton which follows the structure of the formula. The base cases are $\ell \bowtie k$, $\lceil S \rceil$ and $\sum_{i=1}^{m_j} c_i \int S_i \bowtie_j k_j$.

The case $\phi = \ell \bowtie k$. Let $A_\phi = (L, s, E, I, P, f, \Lambda)$, where

- $L = \{s, f\}$,
- $E = \{(s, x \bowtie k, \{x\}, f)\}$, and
- $I(f) = x \leq 0$.

This automaton is depicted in Fig. 1(a).

The case $\phi = \lceil S \rceil$. Let $A_\phi = (L, s, E, I, P, f, \Lambda)$, where

- $L = \{s, l_1, f\}$,
- $E = \{e_1, e_2, e_3\}$, where $e_1 = (s, \text{true}, \{\}, l_1)$, $e_2 = (l_1, y > 0, \{y\}, s)$, and $e_3 = (l_1, x > 0, \{x\}, f)$,
- $I(s) = y \leq 0$ and $I(f) = x \leq 0$, and
- $\Lambda(l_1) = S$.

This automaton is depicted in Fig. 1(b).

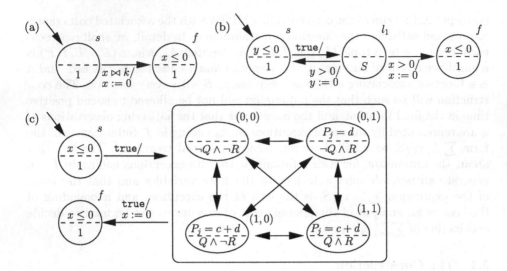

Fig. 1. MPTA encoding of atomic formulae: (a) $\ell \bowtie k$, (b) $\lceil S \rceil$, (c) $c \int Q + d \int Q \vee R \bowtie k$. State decorations above the dashed line denote invariants and cost assignments (both omitted if trivial), while those below the dashed line denote the labeling function Λ.

The case $\phi = \sum_{i=1}^{m_j} c_{i,j} \int S_{i,j} \bowtie_j k_j$. Let $A_\phi = (L, s, E, I, P, f, \Lambda)$, where $L = \{s, f\} \cup \{0,1\}^n$ and E, I, P and Λ are defined below. Each n-tuple in $\{0,1\}^n$ is a bit-vector $\boldsymbol{b} = (b_1, \ldots, b_n)$ and the idea with this is that $b_i = 1$ iff the value of P_i is 1 in that state.

The set of edges $E = E_1 \cup E_2 \cup E_3$ is defined as the union of three sets, where

- $E_1 = \{(s, \text{true}, \emptyset, \boldsymbol{b}) \mid \boldsymbol{b} \in \{0,1\}^n\}$,
- $E_2 = \{(\boldsymbol{b}, \text{true}, \emptyset, \boldsymbol{b}') \mid \boldsymbol{b}, \boldsymbol{b}' \in \{0,1\}^n \wedge \boldsymbol{b} \neq \boldsymbol{b}'\}$, and
- $E_3 = \{(\boldsymbol{b}, \text{true}, \{x\}, f) \mid \boldsymbol{b} \in \{0,1\}^n\}$.

For $\boldsymbol{b} \in \{0,1\}^n$, we define two sets: $\boldsymbol{b}^+ = \{l \in \mathbb{N} \mid 1 \leq l \leq n \wedge b_l = 1\}$ and $\boldsymbol{b}^- = \{l \in \mathbb{N} \mid 1 \leq l \leq n \wedge b_l = 0\}$. Let $F(\boldsymbol{b})$ denote the state expression:

$$\bigwedge_{l \in \boldsymbol{b}^-} \neg P_l \wedge \bigwedge_{l \in \boldsymbol{b}^+} P_l \,.$$

For each state expression $S_{i,j}$ occurring in the summation $\sum_{i=1}^{m_j} c_{i,j} \int S_{i,j}$, we define the cost rate as follows:

$$C(\boldsymbol{b})(S_{i,j}) = \begin{cases} c_{i,j}, & \text{if } F(\boldsymbol{b}) \Rightarrow S_{i,j}, \\ C(\boldsymbol{b})(S_{i,j}) = 0 & \text{otherwise.} \end{cases}$$

The invariants of locations are as follows: $I(s) = x \leq 0, I(f) = x \leq 0$, and for all other locations the invariant is true.

The cost assignment $P : L \cup E \to \mathbb{N}^m$ is defined as follows:

$$P(l)_k = \begin{cases} 0 & \text{if } l = s \text{ or } l = f \text{ or } k \neq j \text{ or } l \in E \\ \sum_{i=1}^{m_j} C(l)(S_{i,j}) & \text{otherwise.} \end{cases}$$

The definition of the labelling function Λ is $\Lambda(l) = 1$ iff $l = s$ or $l = f$ and $F(l)$ otherwise. An example of this automaton construction is shown in Fig. 1(c).

We now consider the recursive cases: $\phi \vee \psi$, $\phi \wedge \psi$ and $\phi \frown \psi$. In these cases, we will assume that the automata $A_\phi = (L_1, s_1, E_1, I_1, P_1, f_1, \Lambda_1)$ and $A_\psi = (L_2, s_2, E_2, I_2, P_2, f_2, \Lambda_2)$, have disjoint sets of locations and clocks, respectively.

The case $\phi \vee \psi$. Assume that s and f are two new locations and that x is a new clock. Let $A_{\phi \vee \psi} = (L, s, E, I, P, f, \Lambda)$, where

- $L = \{s, f\} \cup L_1 \cup L_2$,
- $E = \{e_1, e_2, e_3, e_4\} \cup E_1 \cup E_2$, where $e_1 = (s, \text{true}, \{\}, s_1)$, $e_2 = (s, \text{true}, \{\}, s_2)$, $e_3 = (f_1, \text{true}, \{x\}, f)$, and $e_4 = (f_2, \text{true}, \{x\}, f)$.
- $I(s) = I(f) = x \leq 0$, $I(l) = I_1(l)$, for $l \in L_1$, and $I(l) = I_2(l)$, for $l \in L_2$,
- $P(l) = P_1(l)$, for $l \in L_1$, and $P(l) = P_2(l)$, for $l \in L_2$, and
- $\Lambda(l) = \Lambda_1(l)$, for $l \in L_1$, and $\Lambda(l) = \Lambda_2(l)$, for $l \in L_2$.

The case: $\phi \wedge \psi$. Let $A_{\phi \wedge \psi} = (L, (s_1, s_2), E, I, P, (f_1, f_2), \Lambda)$, where

- $L = \{(l_1, l_2) \in L_1 \times L_2 \mid \Lambda_1(l_1) \wedge \Lambda_2(l_2) \text{ is satisfiable}\}$,
- $E = \left\{ ((l_1, l_2), g_1 \wedge g_2, r_1 \cup r_2, (l_1', l_2')) \;\middle|\; \begin{array}{l} (l_1, l_2), (l_1', l_2') \in L \\ \wedge (l_1, g_1, r_1, l_1') \in E_1 \\ \wedge (l_2, g_2, r_2, l_2') \in E_2 \end{array} \right\} \quad \cup$

$\{((l_1, l_2), g_1, r_1, (l_1', l_2)) \mid (l_1, l_2), (l_1', l_2) \in L \wedge (l_1, g_1, r_1, l_1') \in E_1 \} \cup$
$\{((l_1, l_2), g_1, r_1, (l_1, l_2')) \mid (l_1, l_2), (l_1, l_2') \in L \wedge (l_2, g_2, r_2, l_2') \in E_2 \}$

- $I(l_1, l_2) = I_1(l_1) \wedge I_2(l_2)$, for $(l_1, l_2) \in L$,
- $P(l_1, l_2)_k = P_1(l_1)_k + P_2(l_2)_k$, for $(l_1, l_2) \in L$ and $1 \leq k \leq m$ and
- $\Lambda(l_1, l_2) = \Lambda_1(l_1) \wedge \Lambda_2(l_2)$, for $(l_1, l_2) \in L$.

The case: $\phi \frown \psi$. Let $A_{\phi \frown \psi} = (L_1 \cup L_2, s_1, E, I, P, f_2, \Lambda)$, where

- $E = \{(f_1, \text{true}, C_2, s_2)\} \cup E_1 \cup E_2$, where C_2 is the set of clocks used by A_ψ,
- $I(l) = I_1(l)$, for $l \in L_1$, and $I(l) = I_2(l)$, for $l \in L_2$,
- $P(l) = P_1(l)$, for $l \in L_1$, and $P(l) = P_2(l)$, for $l \in L_2$.
- $\Lambda(l) = \Lambda_1(l)$, for $l \in L_1$, and $\Lambda(l) = \Lambda_2(l)$, for $l \in L_2$.

Note that the transition from f_1 to s_2 has to be taken immediately when f_1 is reached, as the clock constraints imposed in $I_1(f_1)$ does not permit durational stays in f_1.

5.2   Correspondence Between Interpretations of Formulae and Runs of Corresponding MPTA

The above construction yields a correspondence between satisfiability of the encoded DC formula and existence of runs in A_ϕ featuring adequate prices. In order to show this, we shall first establish a connection between DC observations and the runs of automata.

Let $A = (L, s, E, I, P, f, \Lambda)$ and $\alpha = s_0 \xrightarrow{a_1}_{p_1} s_1 \xrightarrow{a_2}_{p_2} s_2 \cdots s_{n-1} \xrightarrow{a_n}_{p_n} s_n$ be a run of (L, s, E, I, P). The *duration* of α, written $\Delta(\alpha)$, is the sum of all the durations of steps in α. We shall below define the set of DC observations generated by run α as a set of interpretations observed over the interval $[0, \Delta(\alpha)]$. We first define anchored concatenation $(\mathcal{I}_1, [0, e_1]) \frown (\mathcal{I}_2, [0, e_2])$ of observations $(\mathcal{I}_1, [0, e_1])$ and $(\mathcal{I}_2, [0, e_2])$ as the set of observations $0 : (\mathcal{I}_1, [0, e_1]) \frown (\mathcal{I}_2, [0, e_2])$, as defined on page 205. This definition extends to sets of observations: $S_1 \frown S_2 = \bigcup_{\mathcal{O}_1 \in S_1, \mathcal{O}_2 \in S_2} \mathcal{O}_1 \frown \mathcal{O}_2$.

Based on this, we will now define $Intp(\alpha)$ in two steps: First, we define $Intp(s_i)$ for each step in $\alpha = s_0 \xrightarrow{a_1}_{p_1} s_1 \ldots$. Then, we concatenate these observations. For each step s_i in α, the set $Intp(s_i)$ of interpretations over that state is defined by:

$$Intp(s_i) = \{(\mathcal{I}, [0, 0]) \mid \mathcal{I} \text{ an arbitrary interpretation}\}$$
$$\text{if } i = 0 \text{ or if } s_i \text{ is reached via an edge } e \in E \text{ in } \alpha,$$
$$Intp(s_i) = \{(\mathcal{I}, [0, d]) \mid \mathcal{I}, [0, d] \models \lceil \Lambda(l_i) \rceil \}$$
$$\text{if } s_i \text{ is reached by a delay transition of duration } d \text{ in } \alpha.$$

The set of observations $Intp(\alpha)$ corresponding to α is then defined as the concatenation of the individual $Intp(s_i)$:

$$Intp(\alpha) = Intp(s_0) \frown Intp(s_1) \frown \cdots \frown Intp(s_n) .$$

With the above correspondence between runs and interpretations, we can now formalize the correspondence between DC formulae and the corresponding multi-priced timed automata.

Lemma 5. *Let ϕ be a $DC_{\backslash \neg}$ formula and $A_\phi = (L, s, E, I, P, f, \Lambda)$ be the corresponding multi-priced timed automaton. Then $\mathcal{I}, [0, e] \models \phi$ iff there exists a run α of A_ϕ with $(\mathcal{I}, [0, e]) \in Intp(\alpha)$ and $\text{cost}(\alpha)_j \bowtie_j k_j$ for $1 \leq j \leq m$.*

Proof. By induction over the structure of ϕ.   □

As a consequence, we obtain a correspondence between satisfiability of the encoded DC formula and existence of runs in A_ϕ featuring adequate prices.

Theorem 3. *Let ϕ be a formula in DC_{ub}, let $A_\phi = (L, s, E, I, P, f, \Lambda)$ be the corresponding multi-priced timed automaton, and let $\boldsymbol{u} = (k_1, \ldots, k_{m-1})$. Then $\text{mincost}_{(L,s,E,I,P),\boldsymbol{u}}(f) < k_m$ iff ϕ is satisfiable.*

Proof. By the previous lemma, $\mathcal{I}, [0, b] \models \phi$ iff there is a run α of A_ϕ such that $(\mathcal{I}, [0, b]) \in Intp(\alpha)$ and $\text{cost}(\alpha)_j \bowtie_j k_j$ for $1 \leq j \leq m$. As $Intp$ is a total function, this implies that ϕ is satisfiable iff A_ϕ has run α with $\text{cost}(\alpha)_j \bowtie_j k_j$. By $\bowtie_j = \leq$, for $1 \leq j < m$, and $\bowtie_m = <$, this is the case iff $\text{mincost}_{T,\boldsymbol{u}}(s) < k_m$.   □

The above construction can also be used for model-checking timed automata wrt. negations of DC formulae. The cornerstone is to exploit an appropriate automata product between timed automata and priced timed automata to establish an automata-based verification procedure. The *model-checking problem* considered here has the form $A \models \neg\phi$, where $A = (L_1, s_1, E_1, I_1, \Lambda_1)$ is an arbitrary timed automaton (L_1, s_1, E_1, I_1), extended by a labeling $\Lambda_1 : L_1 \rightarrow S$ of locations with state expressions. We say that $A \models \neg\phi$ holds iff for each run α of A, the set[5] of all corresponding DC interpretations $Intp(\alpha)$ satisfies $\neg\phi$.

Theorem 4. *Let $A = (L_1, s_1, E_1, I_1, \Lambda_1)$ be a timed automaton (L_1, s_1, E_1, I_1) extended by a location labelling $\Lambda_1 : L_1 \rightarrow S$, let ϕ be a DC_{ub} formula, let $A_\phi = (L_2, s_2, E_2, I_2, P_2, f_2, \Lambda_2)$, and let $\boldsymbol{u} = (k_1, \ldots, k_{m-1})$. Then $A \models \neg\phi$ iff $\text{mincost}_{(L,s,E,I,P),\boldsymbol{u}}(f \times L_1) \geq k_m$, where*

- $B = (L_1, s_1, E_1, I_1, P_0, s, \Lambda_1)$ *is A converted to an MPTA by extension with the trivial cost function $P_0 \equiv \boldsymbol{0}$ and an irrelevant terminal state $s \in L_1$,*
- $(L, s, E, I, P, f, P) = A_\phi \otimes B$ *is the multi-priced automaton product from case $\phi \wedge \psi$.*

Proof. Similar to the previous theorem it can be shown that for each run α of A and each model $(\mathcal{I}, [0, b])$ of ϕ with $(\mathcal{I}, [0, b]) \in Intp(\alpha)$ it is the case that α is a run of $A_\phi \otimes B$ with $\text{cost}(\alpha)_j \bowtie_j k_j$ for $1 \leq j \leq m$. I.e., A has a run α with $Intp(\alpha) \models \phi$ iff $\text{mincost}_{(L,s,E,I,P),\boldsymbol{u}}(f \times L_1) < k_m$. Consequently, all runs of A satisfy $\neg\phi$ iff $\text{mincost}_{(L,s,E,I,P),\boldsymbol{u}}(f \times L_1) \geq k_m$.   □

Model-checking timed automata against DC_{ub} formulae is thus possible.

6   Conclusion

Within this paper, two new decision procedures for rich subsets of Duration Calculus have been devised:

1. We have shown that satisfiability of DC formulas with linear combinations of accumulated durations, yet chop confined to occur in positive context only, is decidable.
2. A model-checking procedure for timed automata against DC formula with only upper bound duration constraints and only a single, outermost negation has been established based on a reduction to multi-priced timed automata.

Both procedures do considerably extend the scope of automatic procedures for DC beyond the previous state of the art: These procedures are the first to combine reasoning over accumulated durations and over chop within automated decision procedures. Furthermore, (2.) extends model-checking procedures for timed transition systems against accumulated duration properties, as pioneered in [22], from timed transition tables with per-transition delays to timed automata with clocks.

For the first of the two procedures, it is clear that the positive decidability results marks the frontier to undecidability, as admitting chop in negative context leads to undecidability [20]. The correspondence of DC without accumulated durations to timed regular expressions [2] shown in [8], together with the lacking closure of timed regular languages under negation [1], shows that decidability is

---

[5] Note that the labeling Λ_1 may permit multiple different valuations within a single location $l \in L_1$.

even lost without nesting of chop under different polarity; negative chop itself leads to undecidability. Accordingly, the encodings of two-counter machines by DC formulas used in [20] or of stop-watch automata used in [7, App. A] to demonstrate undecidability of DC do only use negative chop.

With respect to the model-checking result, the exact borderline to undecidability is open. While one might well expect that lower bounds on accumulated durations should also be decidable, e.g. through replacing minimum price reachability in priced timed automata by maximum price reachability, the current notion of maximum price reachability in priced timed automata does not permit an adequate reduction. Being inspired by scheduling problems, the theory of priced timed automata does define the maximum price to be infinite as soon as path length in the automaton is unbounded. This does interfere with the notion of accumulated duration, as an accumulated duration may well be bounded even though the number of state changes in the run is not a priori bounded, as can be seen from the formula $\phi = (\ell < 2 \wedge \int P > 2)$. This formula is unsatisfiable, yet the automaton construction from Sect. 5 yields an automaton with unbounded path length (cf. Fig. 1(c)) such that maximum cost reachability would consider the cost P to be infinite, suggesting $\int P > 2$ to hold.

Another open question is whether the more restricted notion of chop used in Interval Duration Logic (IDL) [17] facilitates model-checking of larger formula classes. It is obvious that all the procedures detailed in this paper do also work on IDL with the appropriate minor modifications.

References

1. R. Alur and D. L. Dill. A theory of timed automata. *Theoretical Comput. Sci.*, 126(2):183–235, 1994.
2. E. Asarin, P. Caspi, and O. Maler. A Kleene theorem for timed automata. In G. Winskel, editor, *12th Annual IEEE Symposium on Logic in Computer Science (LICS'97)*. IEEE Computer Society Press, 1997.
3. G. Audemard, P. Bertoli, A. Cimatti, A. Kornilowics, and R. Sebastiani. A SAT-based approach for solving formulas over boolean and linear mathematical propositions. In A. Voronkov, editor, *Automated Deduction — CADE-18*, volume 2392 of *Lecture Notes in Computer Science*, pages 193–208. Springer-Verlag, 2002.
4. J. Bengtsson, K. Larsen, F. Larsson, P. Pettersson, and W. Yi. Uppaal – a tool suite for automatic verification of real-time systems. In R. Alur, T. Henzinger, and E. Sonntag, editors, *Hybrid Systems III – Verification and Control*, volume 1066 of *Lecture Notes in Computer Science*, pages 232–243. Springer-Verlag, 1997.
5. A. Bouajjani, Y. Lakhnech, and R. Robbana. From duration calculus to linear hybrid automata. In P. Wolper, editor, *Computer Aided Verification (CAV '95)*, volume 939 of *Lecture Notes in Computer Science*. Springer-Verlag, 1995.
6. H. Dierks. Synthesizing controllers from real-time specifications. In *Tenth International Symposium on System Synthesis (ISSS '97)*, pages 126–133. IEEE Computer Society Press, 1997.
7. M. Fränzle. *Controller Design from Temporal Logic: Undecidability need not matter*. Dissertation, Technische Fakultät der Chr.-Albrechts-Universität Kiel, Germany, 1997.

8. M. Fränzle. Model-checking dense-time duration calculus. *Formal Aspects of Computing*, 16(2):121–139, 2004.
9. M. Fränzle and C. Herde. Efficient proof engines for bounded model checking of hybrid systems. In J. Bicarregui, A. Butterfield, and A. Arenas, editors, *Proceedings Ninth International Workshop on Formal Methods for Industrial Critical Systems (FMICS 04)*, volume 133 of *Electronic Notes in Theoretical Computer Science*, pages 119–137. Elsevier Science B.V., 2005.
10. J. Halpern, B. Moszkowski, and Z. Manna. A hardware semantics based on temporal intervals. In J. Diaz, editor, *International Colloquium on Automata, Languages, and Programming (ICALP'83)*, volume 154 of *Lecture Notes in Computer Science*, pages 278–291. Springer-Verlag, 1983.
11. J. Hoenicke. *Combination of Processes, Data and Time*. Dissertation, Carl von Ossietzky Universität, Oldenburg, Germany, 2006.
12. Y. Laknech. *Specification and Verification of Hybrid and Real-Time Systems*. Dissertation, Technische Fakultät der Chr.-Albrechts-Universität Kiel, Germany, 1996.
13. K. G. Larsen and J. I. Rasmussen. Optimal conditional reachability for multipriced timed automata. In V. Sassone, editor, *Foundations of Software Science and Computation Structures (FOSSACS '05)*, volume 3441 of *Lecture Notes in Computer Science*, pages 230–244. Springer-Verlag, 2005.
14. Z. Manna and A. Pnueli. *The Temporal Logic of Reactive and Concurrent Systems*, volume 1. Springer-Verlag, 1992.
15. E.-R. Olderog and H. Dierks. Decomposing real-time specifications. In H. Langmaack, W. de Roever, and A. Pnueli, editors, *Compositionality: The Significant Difference*, Lecture Notes in Computer Science. Springer-Verlag, 1998.
16. A. P. Ravn. *Design of Embedded Real-Time Computing Systems*. Doctoral dissertation, Department of Computer Science, Danish Technical University, Lyngby, DK, Oct. 1995. Available as technical report ID-TR: 1995-170.
17. P. Sharma, P. K. Pandya, and S. Chakraborty. Bounded validity checking of interval duration logic. In *TACAS 2005*, volume 3440 of *Lecture Notes in Computer Science*. Springer-Verlag, 2005.
18. A. Tarski. A decision method for elementary algebra and geometry. RAND Corporation, Santa Monica, Calif., 1948.
19. Zhou Chaochen and M. R. Hansen. *Duration Calculus — A Formal Approach to Real-Time Systems*. EATCS monographs on theoretical computer science. Springer-Verlag, 2004.
20. Zhou Chaochen, M. R. Hansen, and P. Sestoft. Decidability and undecidability results for duration calculus. In P. Enjalbert, A. Finkel, and K. W. Wagner, editors, *Symposium on Theoretical Aspects of Computer Science (STACS 93)*, volume 665 of *Lecture Notes in Computer Science*, pages 58–68. Springer-Verlag, 1993.
21. Zhou Chaochen, C. A. R. Hoare, and A. P. Ravn. A calculus of durations. *Information Processing Letters*, 40(5):269–276, 1991.
22. Zhou Chaochen, Zhang Jingzhong, Yang Lu, and Li Xiaoshan. Linear duration invariants. In H. Langmaack, W.-P. de Roever, and J. Vytopil, editors, *Formal Techniques in Real-Time and Fault-Tolerant Systems (FTRTFT '94)*, volume 863 of *Lecture Notes in Computer Science*, pages 86–109. Springer-Verlag, 1994.

From Time Petri Nets to Timed Automata:
An Untimed Approach*

Davide D'Aprile[1], Susanna Donatelli[1], Arnaud Sangnier[2], and Jeremy Sproston[1]

[1] Dipartimento di Informatica, Università di Torino, 10149 Torino, Italy
[2] Lab. Spécification & Verification, ENS Cachan – CNRS UMR 8643, France
{daprile,susi,sproston}@di.unito.it,
sangnier@lsv.ens-cachan.fr

Abstract. Time Petri Nets (TPN) and Timed Automata (TA) are widely-used formalisms for the modeling and analysis of timed systems. A recently-developed
approach for the analysis of TPNs concerns their translation to TAs, at which
point efficient analysis tools for TAs can then be applied. One feature of much of
this previous work has been the use of timed reachability analysis on the TPN in
order to construct the TA. In this paper we present a method for the translation
from TPNs to TAs which bypasses the timed reachability analysis step. Instead,
our method relies on the reachability graph of the underlying untimed Petri net.
We show that our approach is competitive for the translation of a wide class of
TPNs to TAs in comparison with previous approaches, both with regard to the
time required to perform the translation, and with regard to the number of locations and clocks of the produced TA.

1 Introduction

As real-time systems become ever more complex and diffuse, it becomes increasingly
important to develop methods for reasoning about such systems in a formal way. Two
widely-used formalisms for the modeling and analysis of real-time systems are Time
Petri Nets (TPNs) [15] and Timed Automata (TA) [3]. TPNs and TA are dense-time
formalisms, which implies that their underlying state space is infinite, and therefore
verification techniques which enumerate exhaustively the state space cannot be applied.
In general, this difficulty is addressed by applying symbolic methods or by partitioning
the infinite state-space. With regard to TA, the well-known region graph [3] or zone-
based graph [2] techniques are two such methods, the latter of which forms the basis of
the techniques implemented in tools such as UPPAAL [4,18] and KRONOS [19,12]. With
regard to TPNs, in [5,14] an approach based on the so-called state class graph (SCG)
construction is presented. In the SCG the nodes are sets of states, represented by a pair
comprising a marking and a firing domain, where the firing domain represents the set of
times at which a transition can be fired. The SCG construction allows the verification
of untimed reachability and LTL properties [5,14], while variants of this method allow
the verification of CTL, and a subset of TCTL [1] properties [6,17].

A different approach to allow TCTL model checking of TPNs is to produce from
a TPN a timed bisimilar TA which maintains TCTL properties, and then verify it by

---

* Supported in part by Miur project Firb-Perf and EEC project Crutial.

O. Grumberg and M. Huth (Eds.): TACAS 2007, LNCS 4424, pp. 216–230, 2007.

means of model-checking tools (for example, the above cited UPPAAL and KRONOS). In the literature there are two different techniques for the translation of TPNs to TA. The first is based on the Petri net (PN) structure [8], and is generally characterized by a potentially high number of clocks in the produced TA; the second is based on exploration of the timed state space, for example in [13], in which a method based on an extended version of the SCG is used to compute the so-called state class timed automaton (SCTA), and in [10], where zone-based timed reachability analysis (see [2]) allows the construction of the so-called marking timed automaton, that in the following we will call the zone-based marking timed automaton (ZBMTA). The ZBMTA always has no more locations and edges than the SCTA, while the latter has no more clocks than the former. Finally, it should be noticed that, in [10,13], the reachability techniques for the generation of a TA are generally employed again subsequently to analyze the produced TA; this fact could increase the total verification time of the TPN under investigation.

In this paper we present a different technique for the translation of a TPN into a (strong) timed bisimilar TA, by using the reachability graph of the underlying *untimed* Petri Net to build what we have called the *marking class timed automaton* (MCTA). We will show that the SCTA, obtained by applying [13], and the MCTA, obtained by applying our approach, are incomparable in the number of locations and edges, while the MCTA produces a greater or equal number of locations and edges with respect to the ZBMTA approach, obtained by applying [10]; finally, the number of clocks may be equal to that of the SCTA, and less or equal to that of the ZBMTA. From these considerations it may be deduced that our approach represents a competitive choice for a number of classes of systems, especially when a trade-off is needed between the number of the produced locations and clocks; we will present experimental evidence to show this. The main disadvantage of our method is the requirement of boundedness of the underlying untimed PN, while [10,13] require only TPN boundedness. In order to address this problem, we give some suggestions to partially bound specific PN subnets of the TPN under investigation. In addition, because our method may explore some paths in the untimed Petri net which are unreachable in the TPN, resulting in a greater number of locations, we consider an adjustment to the MCTA construction algorithm which, for some TPNs, can alleviate this problem.

This paper is organized as follows: Section 2 provides some background, while Section 3 explains our approach to verify TPNs by translation to TA, and makes a comparison with the SCTA and ZBMTA approaches. Section 4 presents some optimization techniques: a simple method to partially resolve the above cited unreachable path problem, a variant for reducing the number of locations of the produced TA, and some ideas to address the boundedness requirements of our approach. Section 5 describes our tool, GREATSPN2TA, for the translation of TPNs to TA in the input language of the KRONOS model checker, and reports some experimental results, obtained on a set of case studies, also comparing them against the results of the tool ROMEO [9,16], which implements the SCTA and ZBMTA approaches. Section 6 concludes the paper.

2 Preliminaries

Timed Transition Systems. Let Σ be a finite set of *events*, and let $\mathbb{R}_{\geq 0}$ be the set of non-negative real numbers. A timed transition system (TTS) S is a tuple $\langle Q, q^0, \Sigma, \rightarrow \rangle$

where Q is the set of the *states*, $q^0 \in Q$ is the *initial state*, and $\rightarrow \subseteq Q \times (\Sigma \cup \mathbb{R}_{\geq 0}) \times Q$ is the set of *edges*. We use $q \xrightarrow{a} q'$ to denote $(q, a, q') \in \rightarrow$, which indicates that when the state of the system is q, it can change to q' upon *label* $a \in \Sigma \cup \mathbb{R}_{\geq 0}$. The edges labeled with an event of Σ are called *discrete edges* and the edges labeled with a non-negative real number are called *continuous edges*. A *path* is a finite or infinite sequence of edges $q_0 \xrightarrow{a_0} q_1 \xrightarrow{a_1} \cdots$. A set of states $Q' \subseteq Q$ is *reachable* from a state q if there exists a finite path $q_0 \xrightarrow{a_0} q_1 \xrightarrow{a_1} \cdots \xrightarrow{a_{n-1}} q_n$, such that $q_0 = q$ and $q_n \in Q'$.

Timed Automata. Timed Automata (TA) [3] are automata extended with clocks, which are real-valued variables, and which increase at the same rate as real-time. Let X be a set of *clocks*, and $\Phi(X)$ be the set of the *clock constraints* over X, which are defined by the following grammar: $\varphi := x \leq c | x \geq c | x < c | x > c | \varphi_1 \wedge \varphi_2$, where $x \in X$ and $c \in \mathbb{Q}_{\geq 0}$ is a non-negative rational number. A *timed automaton* A is a tuple $\langle L, l^0, \Sigma, X, I, E \rangle$ where L is a finite set of *locations*, $l^0 \in L$ is an *initial location*, I is a (total) function $L \mapsto \Phi(X)$ that associates to each location an *invariant condition* (i.e. a clock constraint), and $E \subseteq L \times \Sigma \times \Phi(X) \times 2^X \times 2^{X^2} \times L$ represents the set of the *switches*. The switch $(l, \sigma, \varphi, \lambda, \rho, l') \in E$ represents a switch from l to l' on the event σ, with the guard φ (a clock constraint) describing the set of clock values that can enable the switch, the set $\lambda \subseteq X$ describing the clocks that are set to 0 by the switch, and $\rho \subseteq X^2$ describing how clocks should be renamed when the switch is taken. The semantics of TA is defined by means of a TTS, and its definition is standard (in particular, see [7,13] for the semantics of the variant of TA with clock renaming); we omit it for reasons of space. In [3], the problems and the possible solutions regarding the infinite number of states and transitions of such a TTS are also illustrated. This leads to the use of abstraction methods, for example the *region graph* and the *zone graph*.

Time Petri Nets. A *Time Petri Net* (TPN) $\mathcal{T}$ [5,15] is a tuple $\langle P, T, W^-, W^+, M_0, (\alpha, \beta) \rangle$ where $P = \{p_1, ..., p_m\}$ is a finite set of *places*, $T = \{t_1, ..., t_n\}$ is a finite set of *transitions*, $W^- : (\mathbb{N}^P)^T$ is the *backward incidence function*, $W^+ : (\mathbb{N}^P)^T$ is the *forward incidence function*, $M_0 \in \mathbb{N}^P$ is the *initial marking*, and $\alpha \in (\mathbb{Q}_{\geq 0})^T$ and $\beta \in (\mathbb{Q}_{\geq 0} \cup \{\infty\})^T$ are the *earliest* and *latest firing time* functions.

The semantics of a TPN $\mathcal{T}$ can be represented by a TTS $S_{\mathcal{T}}$. Before introducing the semantics we define the following notation. A *marking* M is an element of $\mathbb{N}^P$. In the following, we use standard notation for markings, such as $M \geq M'$ if and only if $M(p) \geq M'(p)$ for all $p \in P$, and $M - M'$ where $M - M'(p) = M(p) - M'(p)$ for all $p \in P$. A *valuation* is a vector $v \in (\mathbb{R}_{\geq 0})^n$ such that each value v_i represents the elapsed time since the last time transition t_i was enabled, or since the launching of the system if t_i was never enabled. The initial valuation $\bar{0} \in (\mathbb{R}_{\geq 0})^n$ is defined by $\bar{0}_i = 0$, for all $1 \leq i \leq n$. A transition t is said to be *enabled for a marking* M if and only if $M \geq W^-(t)$. For all $(t_k, M, t_i) \in T \times \mathbb{N}^P \times T$, let $\uparrow enabled(t_k, M, t_i) = (M - W^-(t_i) + W^+(t_i) \geq W^-(t_k)) \wedge ((M - W^-(t_i) < W^-(t_k)) \vee (t_k = t_i))$. Intuitively, $\uparrow enabled(t_k, M, t_i) = \texttt{true}$ if and only if t_k is newly enabled after the firing of t_i in M, where a transition t_k is said to be *newly enabled* after the firing of a transition t_i in M if t_k is not enabled for the marking $M - W^-(t)$ (or if $t_i = t_k$) and it is enabled for the marking $M' = M - W^-(t) + W^+(t)$.

The TTS $S_T = \langle Q, q_0, T, \rightarrow \rangle$ associated to a TPN $T = \langle P, T, W^-, W^+, M_0, (\alpha, \beta) \rangle$ is defined by $Q = \mathbb{N}^P \times (\mathbb{R}_{\geq 0})^n$, $q_0 = (M_0, \bar{0})$, and $\rightarrow \in Q \times (T \cup \mathbb{R}_{\geq 0}) \times Q$ is the set of edges defined by:

1. The *discrete edges* are defined by, for all $t_i \in T$:

$$(M, v) \xrightarrow{t_i} (M', v') \Leftrightarrow \begin{cases} M \geq W^-(t_i) \wedge M' = M - W^-(t_i) + W^+(t_i) \\ \alpha(t_i) \leq v_i \leq \beta(t_i) \\ v'_k = \begin{cases} 0 & \text{if } \uparrow enabled(t_k, M, t_i) \\ v_k & \text{otherwise.} \end{cases} \end{cases}$$

2. The *continuous edges* are defined by, for all $\delta \in \mathbb{R}_{\geq 0}$:

$$(M, v) \xrightarrow{\delta} (M, v') \Leftrightarrow v' = v + \delta, \text{ and } \forall k \in \{1, \cdots, n\}, (M \geq W^-(t_k) \Rightarrow v'_k \leq \beta(t_k)).$$

The last condition on continuous transitions ensures that the time that elapses in a marking cannot increase to a value which would disable transitions that are enabled by the marking. For TPNs, as for TA, it is not possible to work directly on the TTS which represents the behavior of the TPN, because this TTS has infinitely many states (and infinitely many labels). Again, the use of abstraction methods permit the construction of a transition system where the labels expressing the passing of time are eliminated and where states are regrouped into classes on which the reachability analysis can be done. The *state class graph* [5] and the *zone graph* [10] are examples of such an approach. However these methods do not always give a result because, as pointed out in [5], for a TPN the problems of reachability and of boundedness are undecidable.

3 From Time Petri Nets to Timed Automata

We now describe our approach for translating a TPN model into a TA, called the marking class timed automaton (MCTA), in order to subsequently perform analysis on MCTA. Section 3.1 is devoted to this technique, also providing a proof that the TTS of the TPN and of the MCTA are timed bisimilar, while in Section 3.2 our approach is compared with those based on the SCTA and the zBMTA [13,10].

3.1 MCTA of a TPN

In this section we present the MCTA construction, where the constructed TA has an equivalent (timed bisimilar) behavior to that of a TPN. Consider the TPN $T = \langle P, T, W^-, W^+, M_0, (\alpha, \beta) \rangle$. We will "untime" the TPN T (that is, remove the timing functions (α, β)) in order to obtain a Place/Transition PN $P = \langle P, T, W^-, W^+, M_0 \rangle$. We denote by $\mathcal{R}_u(M_0) \subseteq \mathbb{N}^P$ the reachability set of P (the set of markings that P can reach from its initial marking M_0). When bounded (i.e. $(\exists k \in \mathbb{N})(\forall p \in P)(\forall M \in \mathcal{R}_u(M_0))(M(p) \leq k)$), the behavior of this PN can be represented by the *reachability graph* (RG), which is an untimed finite-state transition system $\langle Q, q_0, T, \rightarrow \rangle$ where $Q = \mathcal{R}_u(M_0)$, $q_0 = M_0$, and the edge relation $\rightarrow$ is defined by classical 1-step reachability in untimed PN: for all $M, M' \in \mathcal{R}_u(M_0)$, for all $t \in T$:

$$M \xrightarrow{t} M' \Leftrightarrow M \geq W^-(t) \text{ and } M' = M + W^+(t) - W^-(t).$$

The MCG construction. We now present the algorithm which builds the *marking class graph* (MCG) $\Gamma(\mathcal{T})$ of the TPN $\mathcal{T}$, which is a transition system $\Gamma(\mathcal{T}) = \langle C, C_0, T, \rightarrow_{mc}\rangle$. The states C of $\Gamma(\mathcal{T})$ are called *marking classes*. Each marking class is a triple of the form $\langle M, \chi, trans\rangle$, comprising a marking M of $\mathcal{T}$, a set χ of clocks, and a function $trans : \chi \rightarrow 2^T$ associating a set of transitions to each clock in χ. The initial marking class $C_0 = \langle M_0, \{x_0\}, trans_0\rangle$ is such that M_0 is the initial marking of $\mathcal{T}$, the set of clocks of C_0 is composed of a single clock x_0, and $trans_0$ is defined by $trans_0(x_0) = \{t \in T \mid t \text{ is enabled for } M_0\}$. To build the graph, we also need the notion of clock similarity (adapted from [13]), in order to group certain marking classes together. Two marking classes $C = \langle M, \chi, trans\rangle$ and $C' = \langle M', \chi', trans'\rangle$ are *clock similar*, denoted $C \approx C'$, if and only if they have the same markings, the same number of clocks and their clocks are mapped to the same transitions, written formally as:

$$C \approx C' \Leftrightarrow M = M', |\chi| = |\chi'| \text{ and } \forall x \in \chi, \exists x' \in \chi', trans(x) = trans(x').$$

The MCG construction is shown in Algorithm 1, and is a classical breadth-first graph generation algorithm which starts from the initial unexplored marking class C_0. At each step an unexplored marking class C is marked as explored, all marking classes C' reachable in one step (firing of a transition) from C are added to the set of unexplored classes, unless an equivalent one (according to clock similarity) has already been considered before. The algorithm terminates when all unexplored markings have been considered. In lines 1.6 to 1.13, the set of clocks χ' and the function $trans'$, which associates clocks to enabled transitions, are computed. We note that the construction of this graph can be done by following the different paths in the reachability graph of the underlying PN adding a clock set χ' and a relation $trans'$, and possibly "unlooping" some loops of the reachability graph when a marking is reached many times with associated marking classes which are not clock-similar.

The MCTA Construction. From the MCG defined above, it is possible to build a TA $A(\mathcal{T})$ which has the same behavior as the TPN $\mathcal{T}$, as we will show in the next section. Let $\mathcal{T} = \langle P, T, W^-, W^+, M_0, (\alpha, \beta)\rangle$ be a TPN and $\Gamma(\mathcal{T}) = \langle C, C_0, T, \rightarrow_{mc}\rangle$ its associated marking class graph. The *marking class timed automaton* (MCTA) $A(\mathcal{T})$ associated to $\mathcal{T}$ is the TA $\langle L, l_0, \Sigma, X, I, E\rangle$ defined by:

- $L = C$ is the set of the marking classes;
- $l_0 = C_0$, where C_0 is the initial marking class ($C_0 = \langle M_0, \{x_0\}, trans_0\rangle$);
- $X = \bigcup_{\langle M, \chi, trans\rangle \in C} \chi$;
- $\Sigma = T$;
- E is the set of switches defined by:

$$\forall C_i = \langle M_i, \chi_i, trans_i\rangle \in C, \forall C_j = \langle M_j, \chi_j, trans_j\rangle \in C$$
$$\exists C_i \xrightarrow{t_i}_{mc} C_j \Leftrightarrow \exists (l_i, a, \phi, \lambda, \rho, l_j) \in E \text{ such that}$$

$$\begin{cases} l_i = C_i, l_j = C_j, a = t_i, \\ \phi = (trans_i^{-1}(t_i) \geq \alpha(t_i)), \lambda = \{trans_j^{-1}(t_k) \mid \uparrow enabled(t_k, M_i, t_i) = \texttt{true}\}, \\ \forall x \in \chi_i, \forall x' \in \chi_j, \text{ such that } trans_j(x') \subseteq trans_i(x), x' \notin \lambda, \rho(x') = x; \end{cases}$$

- $\forall C_i = \langle M_i, \chi_i, trans_i\rangle \in C, I(C_i) = \bigwedge_{x \in \chi_i, t \in trans_i(x)} (x \leq \beta(t)).$

---

input : The initial marking class C_0 of a TPN $\mathcal{T}$
output: The MCG of $\mathcal{T}$

1.1 $MCG := \emptyset;\ New := C_0$;
1.2 **while** *New is not empty* **do**
1.3 $C := \text{remove}\,(New)$; (where $C = \langle M, \chi, trans \rangle$)
1.4 $Fireable(C) := \{t \mid t \text{ is enabled for } M\}$;
1.5   **for** *all transitions* $t \in Fireable(C)$ **do**
1.6 $M' := M + W^+(t) - W^-(t)$;
1.7   For each clock $x \in \chi$, remove from $trans(x)$ all the transitions t_k such that t_k is
        enabled in M and is not in $M - W^-(t)$, to obtain a relation $trans'$;
1.8   The clocks whose image by $trans'$ is empty are removed from χ, to obtain a set
        of clocks χ';
1.9   **for** *all transitions* t_k *which verify* $\uparrow enabled(t_k, M, t) = \text{true}$ **do**
1.10   **if** *a clock* x *has already been created for the computation of* C' **then**
1.11 t_k is added to $trans'(x)$;
1.12   **else**
1.13   a new clock x_n is created; n is the smallest available index among the
               clocks of χ' and $trans'(x_n) = t_k$;
1.14   **end**
1.15   **end**
1.16 $C' := \langle M', \chi', trans' \rangle$;
1.17   **if** *there is a marking class* C'' *in MCG such that* $C' \approx C''$ **then**
1.18 $MCG := MCG \cup \{C \xrightarrow{t}_{mc} C''\}$;
1.19   **else**
1.20 $MCG := MCG \cup \{C \xrightarrow{t}_{mc} C'\}$ and $\text{add}(New, C')$;
1.21   **end**
1.22   **end**
1.23 **end**

Algorithm 1. MCG construction

In order to build the MCTA of a TPN, the number of marking classes has to be bounded, otherwise the construction of the MCG will not terminate. Note that the MCG has a bounded number of marking classes if and only if the underlying untimed PN is bounded. We recall that in contrast to the case of the boundedness of TPN [5], the boundedness of a PN is decidable. We will return to boundedness issues in Section 4.3.

Bisimulation. We now define an equivalence relation between the states of the TPN $\mathcal{T}$ and the states of its associated MCTA, and we will prove that this relation is a timed bisimulation. Our results are analogous to those in the context of the SCTA [13] and the ZBMTA [10].

First, we recall the definition of timed bisimulation (see, for example, [8,13,10]). Let $S_1 = \langle Q_1, q_1^0, \Sigma_1, \rightarrow_1 \rangle$ and $S_2 = \langle Q_2, q_2^0, \Sigma_2, \rightarrow_2 \rangle$ be two TTSs. The equivalence relation $\approx \subseteq Q_1 \times Q_2$ on Q_1 and Q_2 is a *timed bisimulation* if and only if, for all $a \in \Sigma \cup \mathbb{R}_{\geq 0}$:

– if $s_1 \approx s_2$ and $s_1 \xrightarrow{a} s_1'$ then there exists $s_2 \xrightarrow{a} s_2'$ such that $s_1' \approx s_2'$;
– if $s_1 \approx s_2$ and $s_2 \xrightarrow{a} s_2'$ then there exists $s_1 \xrightarrow{a} s_1'$ such that $s_1' \approx s_2'$.

Let $\mathcal{T} = \langle P, T, W^-, W^+, M_0, (\alpha, \beta) \rangle$ be a TPN and $A(\mathcal{T})$ its associated MCTA. We consider $\overline{Q}_{\mathcal{T}}$ the set of reachable states of $\mathcal{T}$ and Q_A the set of states of $A(\mathcal{T})$. We define the relation $\simeq_{mc} \subseteq \overline{Q}_{\mathcal{T}} \times Q_A$ by the following rule. For all $s = (M, \nu_{\mathcal{T}}) \in \overline{Q}_{\mathcal{T}}$, for all $r = (C_r, \nu_A) \in Q_A$ (with $C_r = \langle M_r, \chi_r, trans_r \rangle$):

$$s \simeq_{mc} r \Leftrightarrow \begin{cases} M = M_r \text{ and} \\ \forall t \in T \text{ such that } t \text{ is enabled in } M, \\ \nu_{\mathcal{T}}(t) = \nu_A(x) \text{ with } x \in \chi_r \text{ such that } t \in trans_r(x). \end{cases}$$

Theorem 1. *The binary relation $\simeq_{mc} \subset \overline{Q}_{\mathcal{T}} \times Q_A$ is a timed bisimulation.*

If we consider a TPN $\mathcal{T} = \langle P, T, W^-, W^+, M_0, (\alpha, \beta) \rangle$ and its associated MCTA $A(\mathcal{T})$, because we have by construction $(M_0, \overline{0}) \simeq_{mc} (C_0, \overline{0})$, we conclude that a marking M is reachable from M_0 in $\mathcal{T}$ if and only if there exists a state of $A(\mathcal{T})$ whose associated marking (within the state's marking class) is M. The timed bisimulation property also allows us to obtain the set of states of $\mathcal{T}$ which satisfy a TCTL property: the TCTL property can be verified on $A(\mathcal{T})$, and the resulting set of states of $\mathcal{T}$ satisfying the property can be obtained using $\simeq_{mc}$.

Example. We now consider the application of our procedure to the TPN of Figure 1. The corresponding MCTA is given in Figure 2. The structure (locations, represented by nodes, and switches, represented by arcs) of the MCTA is derived from the MCG, which provides also the following information:

- for every location, information regarding the corresponding marking of the considered (PN underlying the) TPN, as well as information about which clock is linked to the currently enabled transitions in the corresponding state of the original model;
- for every arc, the transition which fires in the TPN.

The MCTA construction step labels the locations with invariants, while guards, clock resets and clock renaming functions are added to the arcs. Guards are written above the line labeling each arc, whereas resets and clock renaming are indicated below. Starting from the initial location C_0, we have two newly enabled transitions, t_1 and t_2, to which an unique clock, named x, is assigned; the corresponding invariants and guards, indicated on the corresponding outgoing arcs, are defined with respect to the timing intervals in the TPN under translation. When the outgoing arc labeled t_1 is taken from location C_0 to location C_1 (between time 4 and 5), the transition named t_2 is still enabled, so the clock x remains assigned to t_2, and must not be reset before entering C_1. In location C_1 the automaton cycles forever, taking the arc labeled t_2 every 1 time unit, and always resetting the clock x before entering the same location, because t_2 is always newly enabled after each firing. When the outgoing arc labeled t_2 is taken from location C_0 to location C_2 (after exactly 1 time unit), the transition named t_1 is still enabled, so the clock x remains assigned to it (and x is not reset), while the fired transition t_2 is newly enabled, and so is assigned to a new clock, y, which must be reset before entering C_2. In location C_2 the automaton can cycle every 1 time unit, resetting the clock y on every cycle, because t_2 is always newly enabled after each firing. When the outgoing arc labeled t_1 is taken from location C_2 to location C_1 (after between 4 and 5 time units since t_1 was enabled), the transition named t_2 is still enabled, but in C_1 the transition t_2

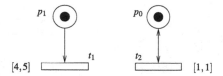

Fig. 1. A TPN model $\mathcal{T}$

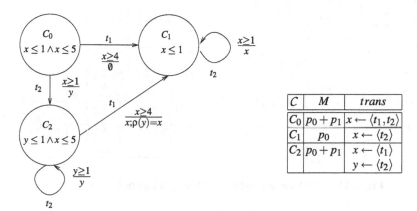

Fig. 2. The MCTA corresponding to TPN $\mathcal{T}$ in Figure 1

is already assigned to a clock named x; this implies that the clock y must be renamed to x while taking the arc. Note that the guard on the arc between C_0 and C_1 is never true, due to the invariant associated with C_0, but that C_1 is reachable via C_2.

3.2   Comparing the MCG, ESCG, and ZBMCG Approaches

In this section we compare the ESCG, MCG, and ZBMCG approaches, taking into account the cardinality of locations and edges, as well as the number of clocks of the produced TA. We recall that, with respect to the MCG, the ESCG nodes are enriched by the firing domain constraints [13], while in the ZBMCG nodes the available information regards only the reached markings [10].

We first observe that *the MCG and the ESCG approaches are incomparable with respect to the number of generated locations*. We provide two examples to substantiate this remark. Let $|MCG|_\mathcal{T}$ and $|ESCG|_\mathcal{T}$ be the cardinality of locations of the MCG and ESCG, respectively, of the TPN $\mathcal{T}$ of Figure 1. The fact that $|MCG|_\mathcal{T} = 3$ can be derived from the TA shown in Figure 2, while the ESCG construction for $\mathcal{T}$ leads to $|ESCG|_\mathcal{T} = 9$. The TA corresponding to the ESCG is shown in Figure 3. The table of Figure 3 defines, for each extended class ESC, the net marking M, the association *trans* of transitions to clocks, and the firing domains D of transitions. It is clear that, in this net, the ESCG construction distinguishes more than the MCG one. This happens because, in the ESCG, for each reachable marking there may be a number of associated firing domains. Figure 4, instead, give us an example of a TPN $\mathcal{T}$ for which $|MCG|_\mathcal{T} \geq |ESCG|_\mathcal{T}$, as shown in Figures 5 and 6. In this case, the MCG algorithm, being unable to identify unreachable paths, produces an higher number of locations, two of which

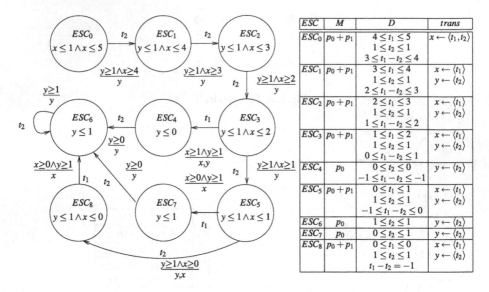

ESC	M	D	trans
ESC_0	p_0+p_1	$4\le t_1\le 5$ $1\le t_2\le 1$ $3\le t_1-t_2\le 4$	$x\leftarrow\langle t_1,t_2\rangle$
ESC_1	p_0+p_1	$3\le t_1\le 4$ $1\le t_2\le 1$ $2\le t_1-t_2\le 3$	$x\leftarrow\langle t_1\rangle$ $y\leftarrow\langle t_2\rangle$
ESC_2	p_0+p_1	$2\le t_1\le 3$ $1\le t_2\le 1$ $1\le t_1-t_2\le 2$	$x\leftarrow\langle t_1\rangle$ $y\leftarrow\langle t_2\rangle$
ESC_3	p_0+p_1	$1\le t_1\le 2$ $1\le t_2\le 1$ $0\le t_1-t_2\le 1$	$x\leftarrow\langle t_1\rangle$ $y\leftarrow\langle t_2\rangle$
ESC_4	p_0	$0\le t_2\le 0$ $-1\le t_1-t_2\le -1$	$y\leftarrow\langle t_2\rangle$
ESC_5	p_0+p_1	$0\le t_1\le 1$ $1\le t_2\le 1$ $-1\le t_1-t_2\le 0$	$x\leftarrow\langle t_1\rangle$ $y\leftarrow\langle t_2\rangle$
ESC_6	p_0	$1\le t_2\le 1$	$y\leftarrow\langle t_2\rangle$
ESC_7	p_0	$0\le t_2\le 1$	$y\leftarrow\langle t_2\rangle$
ESC_8	p_0+p_1	$0\le t_1\le 0$ $1\le t_2\le 1$ $t_1-t_2=-1$	$x\leftarrow\langle t_1\rangle$ $y\leftarrow\langle t_2\rangle$

Fig. 3. The SCTA corresponding to TPN $\mathcal{T}$ in Figure 1

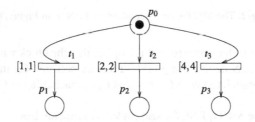

Fig. 4. A TPN model $\mathcal{T}$, with $|\text{MCG}|_{\mathcal{T}} \ge |\text{ESCG}|_{\mathcal{T}}$

are unreachable in the MCTA. In fact, the ESCG construction process, thanks to the firing domain computation, correctly "cuts off" the untakeable t_2 and t_3 transitions, and so the C_2 and C_3 locations are not reached, while this does not happen with the MCG.

Next, we observe that *the ZBMCG approach results in no more locations and switches than the MCG and ESCG approaches*. The ZBMCG method generates only those markings that are reachable in the TPN, whereas our MCG approach generates markings that are reachable in the underlying untimed PN. For this reason alone, it is easy to show an example in which the number of locations and switches produced by the ZBMCG method is less than or equal to the number of locations and switches produced by our MCG method. Now note that each location produced by the ZBMCG method corresponds to a set of locations produced by the ESCG method: the markings corresponding to the locations will be the same, but, in the case of the ESCG method, the locations are enriched with firing domains. A similar argument can be used for the switches. Taking again the TPN as in Figure 1, in Figure 7 we give the TA obtained by applying the ZBMCG technique.

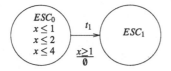

ESC	M	D	trans
ESC_0	p_0	$t_1 = 1\ t_2 = 2\ t_3 = 4$ $t_2 - t_1 = 1$ $t_3 - t_2 = 2$ $t_3 - t_1 = 3$	$x \leftarrow \langle t_1, t_2, t_3 \rangle$
ESC_1	p_1	$\emptyset$	$\emptyset$

Fig. 5. The SCTA corresponding to TPN $\mathcal{T}$ in Figure 4

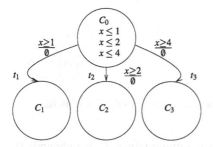

C	M	trans
C_0	p_0	$x \leftarrow \langle t_1, t_2, t_3 \rangle$
C_1	p_1	$\emptyset$
C_2	p_2	$\emptyset$
C_3	p_3	$\emptyset$

Fig. 6. The MCTA corresponding to TPN $\mathcal{T}$ in Figure 4

Despite the fact that the ESCG and the ZBMCG can result in smaller TA in terms of locations and switches or clocks than the MCG, we show in Section 5 that, when applied to a number of examples from the literature, the proposed MCG-based translation can be competitive in size and execution time.

4   Improving the Effectiveness of the MCG Approach

In this section we present some modifications of the MCG algorithm, in order to improve the effectiveness and applicability of our proposed solution.

4.1   Reducing the Number of Unreachable Locations

The first modification allows to "cut off" paths that could obviously not be taken, such as the firing of t_1 in C_0 of the example in Figures 1 and 2. As observed before in the TPN of Figure 1, when t_1 and t_2 are newly enabled only t_2 can fire. Cutting off the edge from C_0 to C_1 does not change $|\text{MCG}|_{\mathcal{T}}$ in this case, but it does for the TPN of Figure 4, because it discards the possibility of firing t_2 and t_3. Line 1.4 of the algorithm can be changed to check the earliest and latest firing time of the newly enabled transitions, and to remove from consideration transitions that are not firable:

$Fireable(C) := \{t \mid t \text{ is enabled for } M_C\} \backslash$
$\{t \mid \exists t' \in T. \exists x \in \chi_C \text{ such that } t, t' \in trans_C(x) \text{ and } \alpha(t) > \beta(t')\};$

Observe that this modification takes timing information into account, as ESCGs and ZBMCGs do, but with the difference that the check does not consider the elapsed enabling time (which is encoded in the state class domains in ESCGs, and in zones in ZBMCGs). The TPN on the left part of Figure 8 illustrates an effective case of the

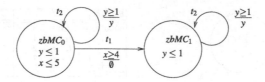

Fig. 7. The ZBMTA corresponding to TPN $\mathcal{T}$ in Figure 1

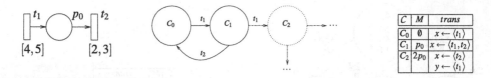

Fig. 8. A TPN model $\mathcal{T}$, for which the application of the local optimization is useful

modification of the algorithm: the original MCG is infinite (since $\mathcal{R}_u$ is unbounded), but the modified algorithm stops because, as shown on the central and right part of Figure 8, the firing of t_1 in C_1 is not considered.

4.2   Trading Clocks for Locations and Speed

Our second modification increases the number of clocks, but decreases the number of locations and the computation time. This variant to the MCTA generation proce-dure consists of the assignment of a unique clock for every enabled transition, and not a unique clock for every set of newly enabled transitions: indeed, unless two transi-tions are always enabled at the same time, it is better to associate to them two separate clocks. As a consequence the expensive check of clock similarity can be removed from the algorithm. We call MCTA^{clock} the automata obtained with such a procedure. The construction of the MCTA^{clock} of the TPN of Figure 1 results in the same TA as that corresponding to the ZBMTA and is shown in Figure 7: assigning two different clocks, x and y, to the newly enabled transitions t_1 and t_2 in location C_0 let us merge C_0 and C_2 into a unique location, decreasing from 3 to 2 the number of required locations.

4.3   Dealing with Unboundedness

Consider the TPN on the left part of Figure 9, illustrating a producers-consumers sys-tem model distributed with the ROMEO package. The set $\mathcal{R}_u$ of this net is unbounded, but the TPN itself has a bounded behavior because the consumers (top part of the net) are always faster than the producers, so that tokens never accumulate unboundedly in place $P3$. Observe that in TPN models whose boundedness depends of time, even the smallest change in the definition of the timing constraints may cause non-termination of the ESCG and ZBMCG algorithms; on the other hand such models may be of interest in many application fields. The method we propose here, inspired by similar techniques for performance evaluation of unbounded stochastic Petri Nets, is to artificially bound

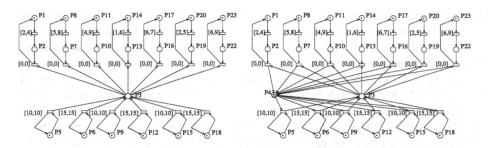

Fig. 9. An unbounded TPN (left), and the same model after the bounding procedure (right)

the net, using an initial, random guess for this bound, and then to check on the corresponding TA whether the bound is too low. We proceed as follows:

1. Compute the P-semiflows of the untimed PN.
2. If all places are covered by at least one P-semiflow, then the net is bounded and we can apply the MCG algorithm in the standard way; otherwise, for all places p_i not covered by a P-semiflow, build the complementary places $\bar{p}_i$, and set $M_0(\bar{p}_i)$ to a guessed value (we use $\bar{P}$ to denote the set of complementary places).
3. Build the MCTA using Algorithm 1.
4. Finally, check on the MCTA whether there is a reachable state of the TA of marking M, in which the complementary place is actually limiting the original timed behavior (formally, $\exists t: \forall p \in P, M(p) \geq W^-(p,t) \land \exists p \in \bar{P}, M(p) < W^-(p,t)$); if such a state exists, increase the initial guess for $M_0(\bar{p})$ and repeat.

Note that, if the TPN is unbounded, then the number of iterations is unbounded and the algorithm does not terminate (the ESCG and ZBMCG computations also do not terminate). P-semiflow and complementary places are standard PN concepts, and we do not recall them here. We only show how the net on the left part of Figure 9 is modified to obtain the net on the right part of the same figure. P-semiflow analysis reveals that place $P3$ is unbounded and the complementary place $P4$ is inserted. Choosing $M_0(P4) = 6$ bounds also $P3$ to a maximum of 6 tokens. The check on the MCTA reveals that this was a good choice, and we can safely use the MCTA built from the net on the right part of Figure 9, rather than the TPN on the left part of the figure (the underlying PN of which is unbounded), because they have the same behavior over reachable states.

5 The GREATSPN2TA Tool

In this section we present the tool GREATSPN2TA for the computation of the MCTA (or MCTA^{clock}) of a given TPN. The underlying PN is described with the tool GREATSPN [11], which is a software package for the modeling, validation and performance evaluation of distributed systems using models based on stochastic Petri nets. The produced MCTA (or MCTA^{clock}) is described in the input format of KRONOS [12], a model-checking tool for TA. In the following, we compare GREATSPN2TA to ROMEO. The software ROMEO [9] permits the state space computation of TPN, on-the-fly TCTL model-checking and the translation from TPN to TA with equivalent behavior. ROMEO incorporates two tools of interest in our context, namely GPN and MERCUTIO. Both tools transform a given TPN to the UPPAAL or KRONOS input format: the tool GPN exploits the SCTA computation, whereas MERCUTIO is based on the ZBMTA construction.

We ran MERCUTIO, GPN, and GREATSPN2TA (using also the variant GREATSPN2TA^{clock}, which implements the MCTA^{clock} construction), on a number of different models. Our experiments were executed on a 1.60 GHz Pentium 4 PC with 512 MB of RAM, running Linux. Table 1 lists, for every model, the number of locations and clocks of the TA, and the elapsed time to compute the TA. We considered two classical PN models: the dining philosophers (with 4 philosophers, *Philo4*), the slotted ring with 4 devices (*SR4*), and three models taken from the ROMEO package: a producer-consumer with 6 producers and 7 consumers (*P6C7*), and a set of parallel sequences (*Oex15*), which we have also modified so that each sequence cycles (*Oex15^{cycle}*). For *Philo4* and *Oex15^{cycle}* a number of different timings of the TPN were considered: in the *Philo4* case, we have forced one of the four philosophers to be 10, 100, or 1000 times slower during the thinking activity (so obtaining the *Timing$_{1slw-10}$*, *Timing$_{1slw-100}$*, and *Timing$_{1slw-1000}$* variants, respectively); in the *Oex15^{cycle}* case, the time intervals describing the different activities were considered totally disjoint (*Timing$_{disj}$*), partially overlapping (*Timing$_{overlapping}$*), or having the same latest firing times (*Timing$_{contained-LFT}$*). The results, shown in Table 1, provide examples of the various trade-off that the four methods offer. Due to the different characteristics of the four algorithms, we compare the tools by pairs: GREATSPN2TA with GREATSPN2TA^{clock}, GPN with MERCUTIO, GPN with GREATSPN2TA and MERCUTIO with GREATSPN2TA^{clock}.

GREATSPN2TA **and** GREATSPN2TA^{clock}. GREATSPN2TA always produces a greater number of locations and a smaller number of clocks than the GREATSPN2TA^{clock} variant: the smaller number of clocks is nevertheless paid for in terms of execution time, especially for models in which, in each state, there is an high number of enabled transitions (indeed the execution of GREATSPN2TA on *P6C7* did not terminate even after 5 minutes). The greater number of locations can be explained by recalling the discussion of Section 4.2. As expected, execution times do not change when changing the timing of transitions.

GPN **and** MERCUTIO. As already observed, GPN optimizes clocks and MERCUTIO optimizes locations: there is not a definitive winner in terms of execution times, although they are both sensitive to timings (most notably in the *Philo4* case).

GPN **and** GREATSPN2TA. For the examples considered, the two tools generate the same number of clocks. In the *P6C7* case the MCTA computation explodes while computing clock similarity, due to the high number of transitions enabled in each state. In all other cases, the execution time is smaller for GREATSPN2TA.

MERCUTIO **and** GREATSPN2TA^{clock}. MERCUTIO assigns statically one clock per transition and leaves to the TA tool (UPPAAL or KRONOS) the task of minimizing the number of clocks, while GREATSPN2TA^{clock} assigns a different clock to each enabled transition: this explains the smaller number of clocks in the GREATSPN2TA^{clock} column. As expected, the number of locations is smaller in

Table 1. Experiments results for GPN, MERCUTIO, GREATSPN2TA, and GREATSPN2TA^{clock}

Model	GPN	MERCUTIO	GREATSPN2TA	GREATSPN2TA ^{clock}
SR4	22907 loc	5136 loc	7327 loc	5136 loc
	4 clocks	33 clocks	4 clocks	8 clocks
	4.30 s	3.86 s	2.63 s	2.08 s
Philo4	4406 loc	322 loc	1161 loc	322 loc
	6 clocks	17 clocks	6 clocks	8 clocks
	1.50 s	0.16 s	0.11 s	0.07 s
Timing$_{1slw-10}$	6.7 s	6.2 s	0.11 s	0.07 s
Timing$_{1slw-100}$	> 300 s	> 300 s	0.11 s	0.07 s
Timing$_{1slw-1000}$	> 300 s	> 300 s	0.11 s	0.07 s
P6C7	11490 loc	449 loc	n.a.	896 loc
	3 clocks	21 clocks	n.a.	13 clocks
	3.44 s	4.70 s	> 300 s	1.24 s
Oex15	1048 loc	360 loc	625 loc	625 loc
	4 clocks	17 clocks	4 clocks	4 clocks
	0.36 s	0.63 s	0.12 s	0.11 s
Oex15^{cycle}	3510 loc	256 loc	369 loc	256 loc
	4 clocks	17 clocks	4 clocks	4 clocks
	3.10 s	7.9 s	0.07 s	0.06 s
Timing$_{disjoint}$	7.8 s	32.5 s	0.07 s	0.06 s
Timing$_{overlapping}$	4.7 s	32.7 s	0.07 s	0.06 s
Timing$_{contained-LFT}$	4.8 s	25.9 s	0.07 s	0.06 s

MERCUTIO (which is optimal in this respect), but its execution times can be much worse, especially when changing transition timings.

6 Conclusions

In this paper we have presented a method to translate a TPN to a TA by exploiting reachability of the underlying untimed PN of the TPN. This technique has a disadvantage that the untimed PN can be unbounded, even if the TPN is bounded; to address this issue, we have described an empirical method for bounding the PN using complementary places, and then checking if this bound is too restrictive. The experimental results show that the computation time used by our method is competitive for a number of classes of system, and the produced TA generally offer a good compromise between the number of locations and the number of clocks. In future work, we plan to address methods for obtaining information about bounds on the number of tokens in places of the TPN, which can then be used in our approach based on complementary places. We also intend to implement a translation to UPPAAL TA (which requires a translation of the MCTA, which has clock renaming, to an equivalent TA without renaming [7]), and to consider the use of clock reduction, as implemented in model-checking tools for TA, in the context of our technique.

References

1. R. Alur, C. Courcoubetis, and D. L. Dill. Model-checking in dense real-time. *Information and Computation*, 104(1):2–34, 1993.
2. R. Alur and D. Dill. Automata-theoretic verification of real-time systems. *Formal Methods for Real-Time Computing*, pages 55–82, 1996.

3. R. Alur and D. L. Dill. A theory of timed automata. *Theor. Comput. Sci.*, 126(2):183–235, 1994.
4. G. Behrmann, A. David, K. G. Larsen, J. Håkansson, P. Pettersson, W. Yi, and M. Hendriks. UPPAAL 4.0. In *Proceedings of the 3rd International Conference on Quantitative Evaluation of Systems (QEST 2006)*, pages 125–126. IEEE Computer Society Press, 2006.
5. B. Berthomieu and M. Diaz. Modeling and verification of time dependent systems using time Petri nets. *IEEE Transactions on Software Engineering*, 17(3):259–273, Mar. 1991.
6. B. Berthomieu and F. Vernadat. State class constructions for branching analysis of time Petri nets. In *Proceedings of the 9th International Conference on Tools and Algorithms for the Construction and Analysis of Systems (TACAS 2003)*, volume 2619 of *LNCS*, pages 442–457. Springer, 2003.
7. P. Bouyer, C. Dufourd, E. Fleury, and A. Petit. Updatable timed automata. *Theoretical Computer Science*, 321(2-3):291–345, 2004.
8. F. Cassez and O. H. Roux. Structural translation from time Petri nets to timed automata. *Journal of Systems and Software*, 79(10):1456–1468, 2006.
9. G. Gardey, D. Lime, M. Magnin, and O. H. Roux. Romeo: A tool for analyzing time Petri nets. In *Proceedings of the 17th International Conference on Computer Aided Verification (CAV 2005)*, volume 3576 of *LNCS*, pages 418–423. Springer, 2005.
10. G. Gardey, O. H. Roux, and O. F. Roux. State space computation and analysis of time Petri nets. *Theory and Practice of Logic Programming (TPLP). Special Issue on Specification Analysis and Verification of Reactive Systems*, 6(3):301–320, 2006.
11. GREATSPN web site. http://www.di.unito.it/~greatspn.
12. KRONOS web site. http://www-verimag.imag.fr/TEMPORISE/kronos/.
13. D. Lime and O. H. Roux. Model checking of time Petri nets using the state class timed automaton. *Journal of Discrete Events Dynamic Systems - Theory and Applications (DEDS)*, 16(2):179–205, 2006.
14. M. Menasche and B. Berthomieu. Time Petri nets for analyzing and verifying time dependent protocols. *Protocol Specification, Testing and Verification III*, pages 161–172, 1983.
15. P. M. Merlin and D. J. Farber. Recoverability of communication protocols: Implications of a theoretical study. *IEEE Trans. Comm.*, 24(9):1036–1043, Sept. 1976.
16. ROMEO web site. http://romeo.rts-software.org/.
17. J. Toussaint, F. Simonot-Lion, and J.-P. Thomesse. Time constraints verification method based on time Petri nets. In *Proceedings of the 6th IEEE Computer Society Workshop on Future Trends of Distributed Computing Systems (FTDCS'97)*, pages 262–267. IEEE Computer Society Press, 1997.
18. UPPAAL web site. http://www.uppaal.com.
19. S. Yovine. Kronos: A verification tool for real-time systems. *International Journal of Software Tools for Technology Transfer*, 1(1/2):123–133, 1997.

Complexity in Simplicity: Flexible Agent-Based State Space Exploration

Jacob I. Rasmussen, Gerd Behrmann, and Kim G. Larsen

Department of Computer Science, Aalborg University, Denmark
{illum,behrmann,kgl}@cs.aau.dk

Abstract. In this paper, we describe a new flexible framework for state space exploration based on cooperating agents. The idea is to let various agents with different search patterns explore the state space individually and communicate information about fruitful subpaths of the search tree to each other. That way very complex global search behavior is achieved with very simple local behavior. As an example agent behavior, we propose a novel anytime randomized search strategy called frustration search. The effectiveness of the framework is illustrated in the setting of priced timed automata on a number of case studies.

1 Introduction

Efficient exploration of large state spaces given as graphs is highly relevant in a number of areas, e.g. verification, model checking, planning, scheduling, etc.

For many applications we are interested in placing guarantees on systems. For verification this could be guaranteeing deadlock freedom or guaranteeing optimality in scheduling and planning. Such guarantees often require exhaustive search of the state space and algorithms for doing this are expensive in terms of time and memory usage. The high memory usage is required to keep track of all states that have been explored. Algorithms in this category often have breadth-first characteristics, such as e.g. A*, [12].

However, covering the entire state space is sometimes unnecessary or even infeasible. Many real application domains prefer algorithms to find solutions fast and then gradually improve the solution instead of guaranteeing optimality. Algorithms with such characteristics are called anytime algorithms and include genetic algorithms, [14], simulated annealing, [16], beam-stack search (a complete variant of beam search), [20], tabu search, [9,10], and others.

Other algorithms rely on heuristic information for states such as estimated distance to the goal. Such heuristic algorithms include beam search and best-first search (e.g. A*). Alternately, randomized or stochastic algorithms like Monte Carlo methods can be used when optimality does not have to be guaranteed. For a good introduction to many type of algorithms for optimization purposes, we refer the reader to [15]. For an interesting approach to LTL model checking using Monte Carlo methods, we refer the reader to [11].

When searching for solutions to optimization problems, the famous "no-free-lunch" theorem, [19], states that all optimization algorithms perform

O. Grumberg and M. Huth (Eds.): TACAS 2007, LNCS 4424, pp. 231–245, 2007.
© Springer-Verlag Berlin Heidelberg 2007

indistinguishably when averaged over all optimization problems. The theorem implies the importance of tailoring solutions to different problems as there is no single best algorithm for all problems. However, there is also the important implication that general purpose exploration engines cannot rely on a single search strategy, but need to offer a wide variety algorithms.

One way to let an exploration engine use multiple search algorithms is to run the search algorithms as co-routines in simulated parallelism. This can be a very efficient approach to searching because of the wide range of strong search algorithms that have been published. However, a weak point with this approach is that no algorithm utilizes the strength of the other algorithms, e.g. a depth-first approach could be searching a fruitful part of the state space, but might not find a good solution in reasonable time due to the search strategy, whereas a beam search performed in the same part of the state space might find good solutions immediately. In turn, beam search might never get to explore that part of the state space due to poor heuristics and/or very expensive transitions to reach that part of the state space.

Alternatively, if the algorithms are able to detect fruitful parts[1] of the state space and employ other algorithms to assist in the exploration, very complex search behaviors can be achieved using just simple and well-known algorithms.

This is exactly the approach we advocate in this paper. We propose an agent framework where individual agents use basic search algorithms (e.g. (random) depth-first search, beam search) and execute as co-routines using a given exploration engine. The agents are connected to a pool of tasks where each agent can put new tasks and get tasks. Tasks in this setting are sub-paths of the state space indicating interesting areas to search. This way an agent with a fixed search strategy that detects a potentially interesting part of the state space can put a number of tasks to the task pool and let other agents with different search strategies pick the tasks and aid in the search of the given part of the state space.

We apply our framework in the setting of priced timed automata (PTA), [17,3], an extension of timed automata, [2], that address the optimal reachability problem. PTA have proven useful for a wide range of different search problems such as model checking, [7], and scheduling, [1,5,18]. The diversity of applications and generality of the modelling language of PTA suggests that no single search algorithm is superior and, thus, could benefit from an agent-based approach to search. The framework has been applied to a number of case studies from PTA with promising results.

The rest of the paper is structured as follows: Section 2 describes the agent framework and the constituents hereof. Section 3 proposes a novel search algorithm termed frustration search and describes its incorporation in the agent framework. In Section 4, we describe the instantiation of our framework for priced timed automata and its application to a number of case studies. We finally conclude in Section 5 and indicate directions of future work.

---

[1] E.g., estimated cost of finding a solution is lower than the current best solution, or parts of the search space where deadlocks a rarely encountered.

2 Agent Framework

In this section, we propose a highly flexible agent-based framework for state space exploration. The framework has been implemented in the setting of priced timed automata, which is evaluated in Section 4.

An overview of the framework is depicted in Fig. 1. Subsequently, we describe the three components of our framework - exploration engine, agents and task store.

Exploration Engine. The framework we propose is constructed to be independent of the type of state space that is being explored. We require a front-end to the state space in terms of an exploration engine that can take states and return their successors plus meta information such as traditional heuristics (e.g. remaining costs) if the state space supports it. We assume that the given exploration engine offers a single interface function `getSuccessors(s)` that, as input, takes a state and, as output, returns a collection of successors.

Task Store. The task store is a pool of tasks available to the agents. The task store offers an interface to access the pool of tasks by means of putting (adding) new tasks to the store and getting (removing) existing tasks from the store. A task is an entry into the state space either in terms of a sub-path from the initial state or simply a reachable state. The task store is considered to have an infinite number of the initial state.

There are several choices involved in managing the store with respect to states that are added and removed. Different design considerations include:

- When agents perform a `get` call, tasks can be removed in e.g. FIFO, LIFO, most promising first, random, or some other order.
- The initial state can be returned only when there are no other tasks in the store or by some probability.
- The task store can be implemented with a fixed size where the oldest tasks are removed when the size limit is reached. This makes sense when searching for optimality since old tasks might relate to parts of the search space that are no longer promising as new better solutions might have been found since the tasks was added to the store.

Agents. The framework defines a fixed number of agents which are co-routines running in simulated parallel interacting with the exploration engine and, indirectly, with each other through the task store. The agents are simply search algorithms employing some search strategy, e.g. variants of depth-first search, beam search, etc. The configuration of agents can be either static (the collection of agents remains unchanged throughout the search) or dynamic (agents might be replaced by other types of agents depending on how they perform). Each agent A_i has a personal configuration C_i necessary to perform the given search strategy. The configuration holds information about which state to explore next and possibly a list of states waiting to be explored.

There are two aspects to bounding the overall memory consumption of the agent framework. First, each agent should have a reasonably bounded memory consumption such as some constant times the largest depth of the state space.

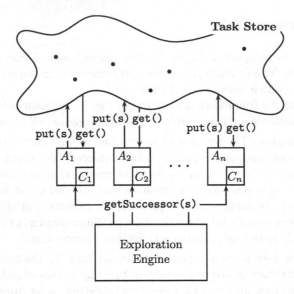

Fig. 1. The three part agent framework consisting of an exploration engine, a set of agents and a task store

This is very applicable for a large number of search algorithms such a different variants of depth-first search (e.g. random, best) and beam search.

Second, there can be no central store of states that have already been explored. This is obviously a trade-off as agents in the framework might explore states that have already been explored by itself or other agents[2]. However, together with the memory limit requirement of the agents, the main benefit is that the search framework can search indefinitely, constantly improving solutions for optimization problems.

Obviously, the behavior of a given agent setup can be described in terms of a single anytime search algorithm, however, that behavior would be inherently complex to describe and very inflexible if changes needed to be made. On the other hand, the agent framework is highly flexible to changes and agents can be added or removed to fit a certain application area.

Furthermore, the agent framework is easily distributed to a multiple processor architecture (in either a cluster, grid, or single PC) by having a number of agents running on each processor sharing a single or multiple task stores.

Note that the agent framework generalizes all of search algorithms, as any one algorithm can be implemented in a framework using a single agent.

3   Frustration Search

In this section we introduce a novel search strategy termed frustration search. Frustration search is an incomplete, randomized anytime algorithm build around

---

[2] Obviously, for cycle detection, an agent will not explore state already found on its current search path.

random depth-first search and will be discussed in detail and analyzed for time and memory usage. Furthermore, incorporation of the algorithm into the agent framework will be discussed.

Prior to describing the frustration search algorithm, we need to establish some notation to be used in this and the following section.

Preliminaries. We consider state spaces given as a weighted, potentially cyclic, digraph $\langle V, s_0, G, E, \text{Cost} \rangle$, where V is a finite set of vertices, s_0 the root vertex, $G \subseteq V$ the set of goal vertices, $E \subseteq V \times V$ the set of directed edges, and $\text{Cost} : E \to \mathbb{N}$ a weight assignment to edges. As a shorthand notation, we write $s \to s'$ to denote $(s, s') \in E$. The set of all vertices reachable from a vertex s by means of a single transition is denoted by $\text{Succ}(s)$, i.e.,

$$\text{Succ}(s) = \{ s' \mid s \to s' \}.$$

A path in a search space $\langle V, s_0, G, E, \text{Cost} \rangle$ is a sequence of states:

$$\sigma = s_1, s_2, ..., s_n$$

such that $s_1 = s_0$ and for $1 \leq i < n$, $s_i \to s_{i+1}$. If $s_i \in V$ appears in σ, we write $s_i \in \sigma$; otherwise $s_i \notin \sigma$. $\text{tail}(\sigma)$ and $\text{head}(\sigma)$ denote the first (leftmost) and last (rightmost) vertex in a path, respectively. The empty path is denoted by ϵ. The binary operator '·' denotes concatenation of paths. I.e., for two paths $\sigma_1 = s_i, ..., s_j$ and $\sigma_2 = s_k, ..., s_l$, the concatenation $\sigma_1 \cdot \sigma_2$ is given by:

$$\sigma_1 \cdot \sigma_2 = s_i, ..., s_j, s_k, ..., s_l,$$

and is only valid when $(s_j, s_k) \in E$. Furthermore, for any path σ, $\sigma \cdot \epsilon = \epsilon \cdot \sigma = \sigma$. The cost of the path σ is the sum of costs of the edges, i.e.,

$$\text{Cost}(\sigma) = \sum_{i=1}^{n-1} \text{Cost}(s_i, s_{i+1}).$$

A path $\sigma = s_1, ..., s_n$ is a solution if $s_1 = s_0$ and $s_n \in G$. The optimization problem associated with a state space is to find the solution with minimal cost.

Some heuristic search algorithms assume for every state an under-approximated cost of reaching the goal. We define such a heuristic as a function $rem : V \to \mathbb{N}$ satisfying,

$$\forall s \in V . \forall \sigma = s, ..., s' . s' \in G \implies rem(s) \leq \text{Cost}(\sigma). \tag{1}$$

In other words, rem is a valid admissible heuristic. Having no such a priori information of the state space corresponds to $rem(s) = 0$ for all states $s \in V$.

Now, we progress to describing the frustration search algorithm that is depicted in Algorithm 1. Frustration search explores different areas of the state space in a randomized fashion identically to random depth-first search, however, the extent to which a given part of the state space is explored depends on the "attractiveness" of the given part. Unattractive parts of the state space are areas with many deadlocks or states that have *rem* values that cannot improve the current best solution.

Intuitively, frustration search explores the state space while keeping track of its own frustration level. The frustration level increases when encountering deadlocked states or states that can only reach the goal with a cost much higher than current best solution. The frustration level decreases when finding goals with costs close to or better than the current best solution. Whenever the frustration level exceeds a given threshold the current part of the search space is discarded and another part is explored. How much the frustration level decreases depends on how much of the path to the current state is maintained.

The formal structure of frustration search is given in Algorithm 1, which we describe in detail below.

Lines 1-4 initialize the algorithm stating that the best found cost is infinite, the best path is not found, the frustration level is zero (empty path), and the waiting list contains only the path consisting of the initial state. The main (while) loop of the algorithm terminates when the WAITING stack is empty.

At each iteration, a path is selected from WAITING (line 6). How we proceed depends on whether the state at the head of the path is a goal state or not. In case it is, the path can fall in one of three categories compared to the current best solution: Better than, reasonably close to (say, within 10 percent), or far from (say, by more than 10 percent). In the former case, we update the current best solution to the current path, update the best cost and reset the frustration level to zero. Resetting the frustration level guarantees that the current part of the search space is searched more thoroughly. In the middle case, the frustration level is decreased slightly to search the current part of the state space more thoroughly. In the latter case, the frustration level is increased.

In case the head of the path is not a goal state, we need to compute the successors of the state at the head of the path. At line 18, we select only those successors that are neither on the path already nor unable to reach the goal within an acceptable margin of the current best solution. If the computed set of successors is empty, we increase the frustion level accordingly. Otherwise, we add the successors to the WAITING list in random order.

Lines 27 through 31 are executed regardsless of whether the head of the current path is a goal state or not. Here, the frustration level is tested against a predefined frustration threshold. If the threshold has not been exceeded, we do nothing. Otherwise, we compute a random number between zero and the size of WAITING plus one. This value determines the number of states that should be removed from the top of the WAITING list (line 30). Furthermore, the frustration level is decreased proportionally to the number of states that has been removed from WAITING.

Finally, when the WAITING list is empty the algorithm returns to line 4 and reinserts the initial state into WAITING to re-search the state space. The randomization of the algorithm guarantees a diminishingly small chance of two runs being identical.

Algorithm 1. Frustration search

proc FrustSearch ≡

```
 1:  COST ← ∞
 2:  BEST ← ε
 3:  FRUST ← 0
 4:  WAITING ← {ε · s₀}
 5:  while WAITING ≠ ∅ do
 6:      σ ← pop(WAITING)
 7:      if head(σ) ∈ G then
 8:          if Cost(σ) < COST then
 9:              COST ← Cost(σ)
10:              BEST ← σ
11:              FRUST ← 0
12:          else if Cost(σ) ≤ COST×1.10 then
13:              FRUST← dec(FRUST)
14:          else
15:              FRUST← inc(FRUST)
16:          end if
17:      else
18:          SUCC ← {s′ | s′ ∈ Succ(head(σ)), s′ ∉ σ, Cost(σ · s′) + rem(s′) ≤ COST×1.10}
19:          if SUCC ≠ ∅ then
20:              for all s′ ∈ SUCC do
21:                  push(WAITING, σ · s′)
22:              end for
23:          else
24:              FRUST ← Inc(FRUST)
25:          end if
26:      end if
27:      if FRUST ≥ MAXFRUST then
28:          RAND ← (rand mod |WAITING|+1)
29:          FRUST ← FRUST × (|WAITING|−RAND)/|WAITING|
30:          pop(WAITING, RAND)
31:      end if
32:  end while
33:  goto 4
```

MAXFRUST and how much the frustration level is incremented or decremented can be adjusted to specific applications, e.g., how often are deadlocked states expected or how often should the algorithm start over etc.

Since frustration search restarts after each termination, it only makes sense to talk about time and memory usage for each iteration (the while-loop). The worst case time behavior of frustration search ocurs when no states are ever removed from the WAITING list due to frustration. In this case, the behavior is identical to random depth-first search. Thus, the worst-case execution time is $\mathcal{O}(|V|)$ as with random depth-first search. The memory usage depends on the size of the WAITING list and will - like depth-first search - never exceed $\mathcal{O}(MaxDepth \cdot$

MaxOut), where *MaxDepth* is the maximum depth of any path of the state space[3] and *MaxOut* is the maximum number of successors of any state.

Variants of Frustration Search. The behavior of the frustration search algorithm is easily changed into different variants by changing the order in which states are added to the WAITING list. Using either the *rem* heuristic or other user defined guides, frustration search can be tailored to different kinds of problems. E.g., in Section 4, we use a variant of frustration search that sorts the successors according to the current cost plus the remaining estimate. That way, the states are searched in a best first manner with randomization as a tiebreaker. Variants of this type have no impact on the worst-case time or memory usage.

Relating to the Agent Framework. To implement frustration search in the agent framework defined in Section 2, the state inserted into the WAITING list can be taken from the task store instead of the initial state. Furthermore, tasks can be added to the task store whenever a promising goal location is found. Subpaths of this solution can be added to the task store for further investigation by other agents.

4   Framework Instantiation

In this section, we discuss ways of utilizing the agent-based architecture in scheduling using priced timed automata. We explore only static agent setups and leave dynamic setups as future work.

Timed Automata. Timed automata were first introduced by Alur and Dill in [2] as a model for describing reactive real-time systems. The benefit of using timed automata over the more expressive hybrid automata is that the model checking problem for timed automata - unlike for hybrid automata - is decidable. Decidability is achieved because the infinite state space for timed automata has a finite quotient. The finite quotient allows algorithms to reason about sets of states (a symbolic state) with equivalent behavior.

Because timed automata analysis requires representing sets of states, a symbolic state of most timed automata exploration engines has the form (l, Z) where l is discrete state information and Z is a convex polyhedron representing dense timing information. For priced timed automata (PTA), the state representation is similar except that we associate an affine cost function with the polyhedron. In minimum-cost reachability analysis we need to compute the minimum of the cost function using linear programming.

A symbolic A* algorithm for minimum-cost reachability of priced timed automata has been implemented as an extension to the symbolic state space exploration engine of the real-time verification tool UPPAAL. The result is the optimization tool UPPAAL CORA, which has been successfully applied to a number of benchmarks and industrial scheduling problems, [6]. This A* algorithm is depicted in Algorithm 2.

---

[3] A path ends whenever it encounters a state already on the path or has no successors.

Algorithm 2. Reachability algorithms used by UPPAAL CORA

```
1:  WAITING = {ε · s₀}
2:  PASSED = ∅
3:  COST = ∞
4:  while WAITING ≠ ∅ do
5:     σ ← pop(WAITING)
6:     if head(σ) ∈ G then
7:        if Cost (σ) < COST then
8:           COST = Cost (σ)
9:        end if
10:    else
11:       SUCC ← {s′ | s′ ∈ Succ(head(σ)), s′ ∉ PASSED, s′ ∉ WAITING, Cost (σ · s′)
                     +rem(s′) < COST}
12:       for all s ∈ SUCC do
13:          push(WAITING, σ · s)
14:          sort(MinCostRem, WAITING)
15:       end for
16:       add(PASSED, σ)
17:    end if
18: end while
19: return COST
```

The algorithm is a classical A^* search algorithm with a WAITING list sorted according to the cost plus remaining estimate for each state. The algorithm further keeps a PASSED list of states that have been explored. The successor computation on line 11 involves manipulation of symbolic states that are up to cubic in the number of variables used in Z. Furthermore, inclusion checking and computation of symbolic state costs involve solving linear programs.

Given the computational complexity of manipulating symbolic states, most of the work done for optimizations of (priced) timed automata involves finding better representations of Z assuming that the algorithm is fixed. In this section, we focus solely on the algorithm to explore whether an incomplete search framework like that agent framework is competitive to existing methods.

4.1 Applications

The implementation of the agent framework applied in this section uses the following search agents, referred to as 'Mix':

- *Depth-first search* (DFS): Deterministic search where states are added to the waiting list in the order provided by the exploration engine.
- *Best depth-first search* (BDFS): A variant of DFS that sorts the successors according to their expected cost (current cost plus remaining estimate). Randomization is used for tie-breaking states with equal cost.
- *Random depth-first search* (RDFS): Successors are shuffled before adding them to the waiting list.
- *Beam search* (BS): Classical beam search with a fixed beam width of 100.

- *Frustration search* (Frust): Successors are shuffled before added to the waiting list. Frustration decrement is set to 0.5 and increments to 1 with a MAXFRUST set to 1000.
- *Best frustration search* (BestFrust): Like Frust, but successors are sorted according to their cost plus remaining estimate.

The framework uses one agent of every type and creates ten copies of every job in the task store to increase the chance that every agent has a chance to explore every job.

Lacquer Scheduling. This case studies has been provided by Axxom[4] - a German company that provides scheduling software for the lacquer production industry. The scheduling problem involves fulfilling a number of orders (with deadlines) for lacquer of different colors. The lacquer production process requires the use of a number of different machines, which have to be cleaned in-between usage for lacquer of different colors. Each type of lacquer has a special recipe describing which machines to use. Costs are incurred during machine use, cleaning and storage (if recipes are fulfilled before the deadline). The Axxom case has been studied for schedulability with timed automata in [5] and for optimization in [13]. For a thorough introduction to the Axxom case study, we refer the reader to either of the two papers.

The lacquer production scheduling problem is of a size that inhibits exploration of the entire state space, and schedules used rely on suboptimal solutions. Axxom uses custom-made software for scheduling, but [13] reports that the solution found with UPPAAL CORA are comparable to those of the custom scheduling software. Thus, every advancement of the solutions found by UPPAAL CORA only make the PTA approach more competitive.

The purpose of the following experiments is twofold: First, to compare cooperating agents in a scheduling framework where guaranteeing optimality is unrealistic to other single search algorithm methods. Second, to determine how well the heuristic used in frustration search for skipping parts of the state space is to an uninformed approach. The algorithm used in [13] is ideal for such a comparison as the algorithm is a best depth-first algorithm with (random) restarting (BDFS-RR) based on a stochastic choice. We will test two agent setups with a single agent using the default variant of frustration search and a single agent using the best frustration search approach. The test setup we have used is the following:

- *Hardware:* 3.2GHz PC with 4GB RAM running Linux/Debian 3.1.
- *Models:* We have chosen the two models used in [13]. Both models have 29 orders, but the first model (6) has no costs associate with storage of lacquer whereas the second model (7) has. Model 6 has two variants depending on how machine availability is modelled. Model 6a models the availability as a fraction of the overall times where model 6b models availability according

---

[4] The case study was provided as a test bed for algorithms in the European Community Project IST-2001-35304 AMETIST.

to the work shifts provided by Axxom. The models use the guiding *rem* estimates defined in [13].

- *Instances:* For each variant of model 6, we vary the number of orders that can be active simultaneously. This heuristic was used in [13] where the limit was set to five orders, but we include 15 and 29 as well. Model 7 is the most accurate model of the case study, and we use no variant hereof even though the model is reported to be very difficult in [13].
- *Algorithms:* We use four different algorithms in our test setup: BDFS-RR, Frust, BestFrust, and Mix.
- *Duration:* For model 6, we run experiments for 10 minutes each in accordance with the tests of [13]. In that paper, problems were reported for executing model 7 for longer than 10 seconds, however, we have not experienced such problems and have performed test for 10 minutes and 2 minutes to investigate how fast solutions are found, and how much they are improved over time.
- *Repetition:* Each test is executed 10 times for every algorithm.

For the experiments with model 6(a and b) in Table 1, Mix is clearly the best algorithm for finding schedules, it is only outperformed once by BestFrust on model 6b with 15 active orders. For all other cases Mix is superior both for the best solution, worst solution and average solution. BestFrust is clearly better than BDFS-RR for all instances supporting the idea of using a more informed heuristics for skipping parts of the state space. For all instances, but one, BestFrust also outperforms Frust showing that some guiding is important for model 6. This is further supported by the fact that Frust only outperforms BDFS-RR on two instances.

Even though Mix is the superior approach, the experiments suggests that the benefits of having a mix of agents to a single BestFrust agent are negligible, but the following experiments show that this is not the case.

Table 1. Results for two versions of Axxom model 6 from [13] showing the costs of the best solutions found within 10 minutes of search

Axxom model 6a											
Agent	Mix			BestFrust			Frust			BDFS-RR		
Active orders:	29	15	5	29	15	5	29	15	5	29	15	5
Best (10^6)	2.08	1.98	1.73	2.28	2.36	1.81	3.16	2.10	2.46	-	2.61	2.03
Worst (10^6)	4.91	2.59	2.07	6.09	2.69	2.12	11.77	2.47	6.02	-	3.89	11.1
Average (10^6)	**2.89**	**2.18**	**1.90**	**3.76**	**2.54**	**1.97**	**8.61**	**2.26**	**4.59**	-	**2.91**	**4.33**

Axxom model 6b											
Agent	Mix			BestFrust			Frust			BDFS-RR		
Active orders:	29	15	5	29	15	5	29	15	5	29	15	5
Best (10^6)	6.97	7.03	6.46	7.25	6.87	6.98	7.61	8.02	7.52	7.18	7.44	7.21
Worst (10^6)	7.88	8.56	7.82	7.75	7.73	7.59	8.91	8.85	8.82	8.32	8.55	9.8
Average (10^6)	**7.41**	**7.58**	**7.34**	**7.50**	**7.37**	**7.46**	**8.33**	**8.31**	**8.11**	**7.86**	**7.93**	**8.2**

Table 2. Results for Axxom model 7 from [13] showing the best costs after 10 and 2 minutes of search

Axxom model 7								
Agent Setup	Mix		BestFrust		Frust		BDFS-RR	
Time	10min	2min	10min	2min	10min	2min	10min	2min
Best (10^6)	2.09	2.11	10.21	11.6	4.21	2.44	69.85	64.87
Worst (10^6)	6.32	14.93	17.50	25.21	10.01	15.37	87.83	94.49
Average (10^6)	**3.12**	**6.55**	**13.36**	**18.77**	**8.15**	**8.60**	**79.60**	**88.10**
Found solution	100%	100%	100%	100%	100%	100%	50%	30%

The experiments for model 7 in Table 2 show that the algorithm used in [13] was unable to find even a single solution for a significant fraction of the instances, whereas all agent setups found solution for all experiments. The solutions BDFS-RR actually found are significantly inferior to any solution found by the agent setup. For this model, Frust clearly outperforms BestFrust for both best, worst and average solutions. However, neither algorithm alone is competitive to the cooperating agent framework, which consequently finds the best solutions.

All of the experiments above support that using the agent framework for search has significant benefits for general purpose search. Furthermore, varying the search intensity in different areas of the search space with frustration search seems very fruitful.

Aircraft Landing Problem. The aircraft landing problem involves scheduling landing times for a number of aircraft onto a fixed number of runways. Each aircraft has an earliest, target, and latest landing time given by physical constraints on aircraft speed and fuel capacity. Costs are incurred for each plane deviating from the target landing time. For more information see [4,17,8].

The aircraft landing problem was first discussed in [4] where a mixed integer linear programming solution was given. In [17], the problem was solved using priced timed automata and the results obtained were highly competitive to those of [4]. The case was reused in [18] with optimizations of the algorithm used for minimum-cost reachability for PTA, and with the optimized algorithm PTA were faster than [4] at solving the case for almost every instance.

The purpose of the following experiment is to determine how efficient the agent framework (and frustration search) is at finding optimal schedules in state spaces that are small enough to be searched exhaustively. And further, how well the performance competes with a powerful complete search strategy, A*. The test setup we have used is the following:

- *Hardware:* 3.2GHz PC with 4GB RAM running Linux/Debian 3.1.
- *Models:* We have chosen the seven models used in [4,17,8]. The model uses no form of guiding with *rem* estimates.
- *Instances:* The instances for the models involves varying the number of runways until all planes can land with a total cost overhead of zero.
- *Algorithms:* We use mix of agents described in the beginning of this section together with the default A* search algorithm used in UPPAAL CORA.

Table 3. Aircraft landing problem. *: 50% of the tests completed within the time limit of 20 minutes, and the average is computed among these.

Instance			1	2	3	4	5	6	7
Runways	Algorithm								
1	Cora		0.04s	0.17s	0.11s	0.50s	1.10s	0.05s	0.07s
	Agents	Best	0.16s	2.24s	3.77s	6.01s	4.77s	0.05s	6.68s
		Worst	0.22s	3.15s	4.75s	>1200s	8.97s	0.06s	7.70s
		Average	0.18s	2.64s	4.34s	58.01s*	5.88s	0.06s	7.34s
2	Cora		0.15s	0.29s	0.25s	3.56s	4.98s	0.14s	0.35s
	Agents	Best	0.09s	0.28s	5.65s	6.14s	9.69s	2.96s	2.25s
		Worst	0.59s	4.23s	6.12s	7.23s	162.37s	13.87s	13.19s
		Average	0.19s	3.00s	5.83s	6.90s	37.33s	8.86s	4.85s
3	Cora		0.16s	0.22s	0.33s	91.43s	71.95s	0.15s	
	Agents	Best	0.67s	1.66s	7.01s	6.71s	7.12s	0.06s	
		Worst	3.06s	5.97s	7.70s	19.94s	18.43s	0.07s	
		Average	1.94s	5.27s	7.45s	9.44s	9.76s	0.07s	
4	Cora					7.60s	3.14s		
	Agents	Best				9.13s	8.48s		
		Worst				26.48s	20.93s		
		Average				12.59s	11.79s		

- *Duration:* A maximum of 20 minutes were allowed for each instance.
- *Repetition:* The agent setup was executed 10 times and the UPPAAL CORA algorithm only once as it is deterministic.

The results in Table 3 clearly indicate that for most instances the A* algorithm outperforms the agent framework. However, it is interesting to note that for the most difficult instances - 4 and 5 - the A* algorithm shows exponential growth in running time until all aircraft can be scheduled with zero cost (4 runways). However, the agent framework does not have this issue, as there appears to be no correlation between the number of runways and the time to find the optimal solution. On instances 4 and 5 with 3 runways, the agent framework clearly outperforms the A* algorithm in finding the optimal solution. On instance 5 with 2 runways, the agent framework performs significantly worse on average, but reasonably for the best case. Only for one instance - 4 with 1 runway - was the agent framework unable to find the optimal solution with the time limit. The optimum was found for 50 percent of the executions, however, all executions - even the ones that never found the optimum within the time limit - found a solution deviating only 1 percent from the optimal within 6 seconds!

Another interesting observation of the agent framework is that for the majority (~80%) of the executions, the optimum was found by agents searching subpaths created by other agents that found reasonable solutions. In many cases, the beam search agent was able to find a close to optimal solution, but did not find the optimum, and some frustration agent found the optimal solution using subpaths of the suboptimal solution. This supports the use of interacting agents to achieve complex global search behavior through simple local behavior.

5   Conclusions and Future Work

In this paper, we have investigated using sets of cooperating agents to explore large state spaces. We have tested the agent framework against complete and incomplete single algorithm methods. The results show that for state spaces that are too large to be searched exhaustively, the agent framework consistently finds good solutions that are superior to any single algorithm tested. For smaller search spaces where exhaustive search is possible, the A* algorithm performs better, however, unlike A*, the agent framework does not perform exponentially worse as the state space grows. For the most difficult problems, the agent framework performed significantly better than A*.

We also introduced frustration search as an anytime algorithm for large state spaces. The heuristic to skip parts of the state space based on frustration was shown to be superior to an uninformed stochastic heuristic. Furthermore, for the Axxom case study, frustration search alone proved competitive to the agent framework for a number of instances. Thus, frustration search seems a promising algorithm for general purpose search when exhaustive search is infeasible.

As future work, we need to explore the agent setup for a larger number of cases and compare to other frameworks for general purpose search. Furthermore, a distributed version of the agent framework needs to be implemented to take advantage of multi-processor architectures. Also, we need to investigate a more dynamic strategy for assigning agents to search problem, e.g., by adjusting the number of agents of different kinds by keeping track of how well the agents perform in the given search space.

References

1. Yasmina Abdeddaim, Abdelkarim Kerbaa, and Oded Maler. Task graph scheduling using timed automata. *Proc. of the International Parallel and Distributed Processing Symposium (IPDPS)*, 2003.
2. R. Alur and D. Dill. Automata for modelling real-time systems. In *Proc. of Int. Colloquium on Algorithms, Languages and Programming*, volume 443 of *Lectur Notes in Computer Science*, pages 322–335. Springer-Verlag, July 1990.
3. Rajeev Alur, Salvatore La Torre, and George J. Pappas. Optimal paths in weighted timed automata. In *Proc. of Hybrid Systems: Computation and Control*, volume 2034 of *Lecture Notes in Computer Science*, pages 49–62. Springer-Verlag, 2001.
4. J. E. Beasley, M. Krishnamoorthy, Y. M. Sharaiha, and D. Abramson. Scheduling aircraft landings - the static case. *Transportation Science*, 34(2):pp. 180–197, 2000.
5. G. Behrmann, E. Brinksma, M. Hendriks, and A. Mader. Scheduling lacquer production by reachability analysis – a case study. In *Workshop on Parallel and Distributed Real-Time Systems 2005*, pages 140–. IEEE Computer Society, 2005.
6. Gerd Behrmann, Kim G. Larsen, and Jacob I. Rasmussen. Optimal scheduling using priced timed automata. *SIGMETRICS Perform. Eval. Rev.*, 32(4):34–40, 2005.

7. Thomas Brihaye, Véronique Bruyère, and Jean-François Raskin. Model-checking weighted timed automata. In *Proc. of Formal Modelling and Analysis of Timed Systems*, volume 3253 of *Lecture Notes in Computer Science*, pages 277–292. Springer-Verlag, 2004.

8. Ansgar Fehnker. *Citius, Vilius, Melius - Guiding and Cost-Optimality in Model Checking of Timed and Hybrid Systems*. IPA Dissertation Series, University of Nijmegen, 2002.

9. Fred Glover. Tabu search-part I. *ORSA Jour. on Computing*, 1(3):190–206, 1989.

10. Fred Glover. Tabu search-part II. *ORSA Jour. on Computing*, 2(1):4–32, 1990.

11. R. Grosu and S. A. Smolka. Monte carlo model checking. In *Proc. of Tools and Algorithms for the Construction and Analysis of Systems*, Lecture Notes in Computer Science, pages 271–286. Springer-Verlag, 2005.

12. P. E. Hart, N. J. Nilsson, and B. Raphael. A formal basis for the heuristic determination of minimum cost paths. *IEEE Transactions on Systems Science and Cybernetics*, 4(2):100–107, 1968.

13. Martijn Hendriks. *Model Checking Timed Automata - Techniques and Applications*. IPA Dissertation Series, University of Nijmegen, 2006.

14. John H. Holland. *Adaptation in Natural and Artificial Systems*. University of Michigan Press, Ann Arbor, 1975.

15. Juraj Hromkovic and Waldyr M. Oliva. *Algorithmics for Hard Problems*. Springer-Verlag New York, Inc., Secaucus, NJ, USA, 2002.

16. S. Kirkpatrick, C. D. Gelatt, and M. P. Vecchi. Optimization by simulated annealing. *Science, Number 4598, 13 May 1983*, 220(4598):671–680, 1983.

17. Kim Larsen, Gerd Behrmann, Ed Brinksma, Ansgar Fehnker, Thomas Hune, Paul Pettersson, and Judi Romijn. As cheap as possible: Efficient cost-optimal reachability for priced timed automata. In *Proc. of Computer Aided Verification*, volume 2102 of *Lecture Notes in Computer Science*, pages 493+. Springer-Verlag, 2001.

18. J. Rasmussen, K. Larsen, and K. Subramani. Resource-optimal scheduling using priced timed automata. In *Proc. of Tools and Algorithms for the Construction and Analysis of Systems*, volume 2988 of *Lecture Notes in Computer Science*, pages pages 220–235. Springer Verlag, 2004.

19. David H. Wolpert and William G. Macready. No free lunch theorems for search. Technical Report SFI-TR-95-02-010, Santa Fe Institute, Santa Fe, NM, 1995.

20. Rong Zhou and Eric A. Hansen. Beam-stack search: Integrating backtracking with beam search. In *Proc. of International Conference on Automated Planning and Scheduling*, pages 90–98. AAAI, 2005.

On Sampling Abstraction of Continuous Time Logic with Durations

Paritosh K. Pandya[1,*], Shankara Narayanan Krishna[2], and Kuntal Loya[2]

[1] Tata Institute of Fundamental Research, India
pandya@tifr.res.in
[2] Indian Institute of Technology, Bombay, India
{krishnas,kloya}@cse.iitb.ac.in

Abstract. Duration Calculus (DC) is a real-time logic with measurement of duration of propositions in observation intervals. It is a highly expressive logic with continuous time behaviours (also called signals) as its models. Validity checking of DC is undecidable. We propose a method for validity checking of Duration Calculus by reduction to a sampled time version of this logic called Well Sampled Interval Duration Logic ($WSIDL$). This reduction relies on representing a continuous time behaviour by a well-sampled behaviour with 1-oversampling. We provide weak and strong reductions (abstractions) of logic DC to logic $WSIDL$ which respectively preserve the validity and the counter models. By combining these reductions with previous work on deciding IDL, we have implemented a tool for validity checking of Duration Calculus. This provides a partial but practical method for validity checking of Duration Calculus. We present some preliminary experimental results to measure the success of this approach.

1 Introduction

Timed behaviours capture how the system state evolves with time. Temporal logics specify properties of such behaviours. Real-time logics deal with quantitative timing properties of timed behaviours.

Timed logics can make use of various notions of time: continuous, sampled (with precise clocks) or discrete. Continuous time, where observable propositions are boolean functions of real-valued time (also called signals), corresponds most naturally to our intuitive notion of timed behaviour. Discrete time, where the set of time points is natural numbered can be appropriate when describing clocked systems such as synchronous circuits. There are other intermediate notions such as timed words [1] which take a sampled view of timed behaviour. The behaviour is given as a sequence of states where each state has a real-valued time stamp.

Real-time logics can be interpreted over these various notions of time and their properties such as expressiveness and decidability also vary accordingly. For example, the well known Metric Temporal Logic (MTL) has been shown

---

* This work was partially supported by General Motors India Science Lab sponsored project "Advanced Research on Formal Analysis of Hybrid Systems".

O. Grumberg and M. Huth (Eds.): TACAS 2007, LNCS 4424, pp. 246–260, 2007.

to be undecidable for continuous time where as it is decidable for sampled time (for finite behaviours) [11]. Unfortunately, using notions such as sampled time can also lead to counter intuitive behaviour. For example, the Duration Calculus formula $\ell = 3 \wedge \lceil P \rceil$ states that P holds invariantly for 3 time units. (This can be written in MTL as $\square_{\leq 3}P$.) The DC formula $(\ell = 1 \wedge \lceil P \rceil) ^\frown (\ell = 2 \wedge \lceil P \rceil)$ states that P holds invariantly for 1 time unit and this followed by P holding invariantly for 2 more time units. (This can be written in MTL as $\square_{\leq 1}(P \wedge (\square_{\leq 2}P))$.) Although intuitively the two properties are the same, unfortunately the two formulae are not equivalent in sampled view of time as intermediate sampling point at time 1 may not be available. With this in mind, Rabinovich and Hirschfeld [8] have argued that continuous time logics should be preferred for real-time requirements. On the other hand, sampled time logics are closer to automata theoretic models and they may have better decidability properties.

In this paper, we consider the abstraction of continuous time properties by sampled time properties while preserving validity or counter-examples. Further abstraction of sampled time properties by discrete time properties has already been considered in literature using notions such as digitization [7,3,10].

We cast our work in context of Duration Calculus [16] which was one of the early real-time logics in computer science to make use of continuous time (or signals). It is an interval temporal logic incorporating the measurement of accumulated duration for which a proposition holds in a time interval. Duration Calculus constitutes a convenient and highly expressive notation for real-time requirements. But this has also made its validity undecidable in general and hard to check in practice. Availability of effective automatic validity and model checking tools for the continuous time Duration Calculus has been a long standing quest. We provide a partial solution to this problem.

There have been many past attempts at deciding Duration Calculus (DC). A discrete time version of DC called DDC (and its extension with state quantification called $QDDC$) were shown to be decidable using a finite automata theoretic decision procedure [12]. A validity and model checking tool called DC-VALID has been built for this logic [12,13]. Pandya proposed a sampled time version of DC, called Interval Duration Logic (IDL) [14]. It was argued that this logic, although undecidable in general, is more amenable to automatic validity checking. Amongst the (partial) approaches which are available for validity checking of IDL are bounded validity checking using SMT solvers [15] and abstraction to discrete duration calculus using digitization [3,15]. Both approaches seem effective on many examples of interest. For continuous time Duration Calculus, various decidable subsets have been considered [4,2,17]. But these have not found way into credible tools.

In this paper, we propose a generic version of Duration Calculus $GDC[M]$ whose behaviours are continuous time (signals) but the behaviour is parametrized by a set of admissible time intervals M. By appropriately choosing M, we show that we can define as $GDC[M]$ most variants of DC including DC, IDL, DDC as well as a version of continuous DC without point intervals called $PLDC$, and a special case of IDL called Well Sampled IDL with

1-Oversampling ($WSIDL$). The behaviours of $WSIDL$ are obtained by sampling continuous time behaviours at all change points, all integer valued points and they are oversampled by adding one more point between two consecutive aforementioned points. Logic $WSIDL$ will play a special role in our work here.

As our main result, we show that we can give reductions (abstractions) α^+ and α^- from $PLDC$ to $WSIDL$ which respectively preserve validity and counterexamples. Moreover, we show that logics $PLDC$ and DC have the same expressive power and that there are effective translations between them. Thus, we can analyze continuous time DC properties by reduction to the sampled time logic $WSIDL$. The digitization and bounded validity checking approaches to deciding original IDL easily extend to its variant $WSIDL$. Using these, we have constructed a tool which reduces continuous DC formulae to DDC formulae preserving validity/counter examples. The discrete time validity checking tool DCVALID [12,13] can analyze the resulting formulae. This provides a partial but practical approach for automatically checking the validity of continuous time Duration Calculus formulae. To our knowledge this constitutes amongst the first tools for validity checking a continuous time real-time logic. We give some preliminary experimental results to evaluate the effectiveness of our approach. The results indicate that interesting examples from the Duration Calculus literature can be automatically verified.

The rest of the paper is organized as follows. Section 2 introduces the logic $GDC[M]$ and various Duration Calculi as its instances. The reductions from pointless DC ($PLDC$) to $WSIDL$ is given in Section 3. Section 4 establishes the equivalence of full DC and pointless DC. Section 5 gives a brief overview of past work on reducing (Well-sampled) IDL to Discrete Duration Calculus. Combining all these steps, a partial method for validity checking continuous time DC is formulated in Section 6. Section 7 describes the experimental results obtained by applying the proposed method to some problems of interest.

2   A Variety of Duration Calculi

Duration Calculus is a real-time logic which was originally defined for continuous time finitely variable behaviours [16]. Variants of DC having other forms of time (sampled time, discrete time etc) have also been investigated [14,13].

In this section, we formulate a generic Duration Calculus, GDC, whose behaviours are parametrized by a set of admissible observation intervals I. This allows us to give a uniform treatment of a variety of Duration Calculi which can all be obtained by suitably choosing I.

Let $(\Re^0, <)$ be the set of non-negative real-numbers with usual order. Let $Pvar$ be the set of observable propositions. A behaviour $\theta \in Pvar \to \Re^0 \to \{0, 1\}$. A behaviour θ is *finitely variable* if any proposition changes value only finitely often within any finite time interval. A finitely variable behaviour is called *right continuous* if the value of a proposition P at any time point is same as the value in its small right neighborhood. We omit this obvious definition. We shall restrict ourselves to finitely variable and right continuous behaviours, and denote the set of all such behaviours by BEH.

Duration calculus is an interval temporal logic with measurements over time intervals. Let $RINTV = \{[b, e] \mid b, e \in \Re^0, \ b \leq e\}$ the set of all intervals over reals. Note that these include point intervals of the form $[b, b]$. The measurement terms mt of GDC have the form $\int P$ or ℓ. The measurement term ℓ denotes the time length of an interval $[b, e]$. The measurement term $\int P$ denotes the accumulated duration for which P is true in θ in an interval $[b, e]$. Formally, the value of measurement term mt is defined as follows: $Eval(\ell)(\theta, [b, e]) = e - b$ and $Eval(\int P)(\theta, [b, e]) = \int_b^e \theta(P)dt$.

Syntax of GDC. Let P range over *Prop*, c over natural numbers, *op* over comparison operators $\{\leq, <, =, >, \geq, >\}$ and mt over measurement terms. Let D range over GDC formulae with $\top$ denoting the formula "true". The abstract syntax of GDC is given by:

$$\top \mid \lceil P \rceil \mid \lceil \rceil \mid \lceil P \rceil^0 \mid mt \ op \ c \mid D_1 \frown D_2 \mid D_1 \wedge D_2 \mid \neg D_1$$

Semantics For a given behaviour θ, the semantics of formulae is parameterized by a set I of admissible intervals, where $I \subseteq RINTV$. Let the pair (I, θ) be called a segmented behaviour or *s-behaviour*. Let M be a specified set of s-behaviours. We parametrize the semantics of logic GDC by M and denote this by $GDC[M]$. A triple $I, \theta, [b, e]$ where $(I, \theta) \in M$ and $[b, c] \subset I$ is called an *M-model*.

For $D \in GDC[M]$ and M-model $I, \theta, [b, e]$ let $I, \theta, [b, e] \models D$ denote that formula D evaluates to true in model $I, \theta, [b, e]$. Omitting the usual boolean cases, this is inductively defined below. For a proposition P and a time point $t \in \Re^0$, let $\theta, t \models P$ denote that the proposition P has value 1 at time point t in behaviour θ. We omit this straightforward definition.

$I, \theta, [b, e] \models \lceil P \rceil^0$ iff $b = e$ and $\theta, b \models P$
$I, \theta, [b, e] \models \lceil \rceil$ iff $b = e$
$I, \theta, [b, e] \models \lceil P \rceil$ iff $b < e$ and for all $t: b \leq t < e$. $\theta, t \models P$
$I, \theta, [b, e] \models mt \ op \ c$ iff $Eval(mt)(\theta, [b, e]) \ op \ c$
$I, \theta, [b, e] \models D_1 \frown D_2$ iff for some $z: b \leq z \leq e$. $[b, z] \in I$ and $[z, e] \in I$
and $I, \theta, [b, z] \models D_1$ and $I, \theta, [z, e] \models D_2$

Note that in the definition of $\frown$, an interval $[b, e] \in I$ must be chopped into *admissible* sub-intervals $[b, z], [z, e] \in I$.

Derived operators

- $\Diamond D \stackrel{\text{def}}{=} true \frown D \frown true$ holds provided D holds for some admissible subinterval.
- $\Box D \stackrel{\text{def}}{=} \neg \Diamond \neg D$ holds provided D holds for all admissible subintervals.
- Let $ext \stackrel{\text{def}}{=} \neg \lceil \rceil$. Define $Unit \stackrel{\text{def}}{=} ext \wedge \neg(ext \frown ext)$. Formula $Unit$ holds for admissible extended intervals which cannot be chopped further into smaller admissible intervals. Let $\bot \stackrel{\text{def}}{=} \neg \top$.

Prefix Validity A prefix model of $D \in GDC[M]$ is an M-model of the form $I, \theta, [0, r]$ such that $I, \theta, [0, r] \models D$. Thus, in prefix models the interval begins at initial time point 0. Also, let $(I, \theta) \models D$ iff for all $[0, r] \in I$, $(I, \theta, [0, r]) \models D$. Finally, $D \in GDC[M]$ is prefix-valid denoted $\models D$ iff $I, \theta, [0, r] \models D$ for all prefix M-models $I, \theta, [0, r]$.

2.1 Duration Calculi

A variety of duration calculi available in the literature can be defined as special cases of $GDC[M]$ by appropriately choosing the set of s-behaviors M, and by syntactically restricting the constructs available in the logic.

Continuous Time Duration Calculus (DC). This is the original Duration Calculus investigated by Zhou, Hoare and Hansen [16]. Duration calculus DC can be defined as $GDC[M_{dc}]$ where $M_{dc} = \{RINTV\} \times BEH$, i.e. in each DC model $(I, \theta, [b, e])$ the set of admissible intervals I is fixed to $RINTV$, the set of all intervals. Because of this, we shall abbreviate $RINTV, \theta, [b, e] \models D$ by $\theta, [b, e] \models_{dc} D$.

Moreover, in the original DC, the atomic formulae of the form $\lceil P \rceil^0$ are disallowed although a more restricted atomic formula $\lceil \ \rceil$ which holds for *all* point intervals is allowed. Thus, syntactically $DC \subset GDC$. It is given by the abstract syntax: $\lceil P \rceil \mid \lceil \ \rceil \mid mt \ op \ c \mid D_1 ^\frown D_2 \mid D_1 \wedge D_2 \mid \neg D_1$.

Example 1. [Gas burner] Consider the following safety conditions for a gas burner (see [16]) in DC. Let $Des1 \overset{\text{def}}{=} \Box(\lceil Leak \rceil \Rightarrow \ell \leq maxleak)$ and $Des2 \overset{\text{def}}{=} \Box(\lceil Leak \rceil ^\frown \lceil \neg Leak \rceil ^\frown \lceil Leak \rceil \Rightarrow \ell > minsep)$. The desired requirement is $Concl \overset{\text{def}}{=} \Box(\ell \leq winlen \Rightarrow \int Leak \leq leakbound)$. Then, the validity of the formula $G(maxleak, minsep, winlen, leakbound) \overset{\text{def}}{=} Des1 \wedge Des2 \Rightarrow Concl$ establishes that the requirement follows from the two safety conditions.   □

Pointless Duration Calculus (PLDC). This is a variant of DC without point intervals. Let $EXTINTV = \{[b, e] \in RINTV \mid b < e\}$ be the set of extended intervals. Then, $PLDC = GDC[M_{pl}]$ with $M_{pl} = \{EXTINTV\} \times BEH$, i.e. in each $PLDC$ model $(I, \theta, [b, e])$ the set of admissible intervals I is fixed as $EXTINTV$, the set of all non-point intervals. We abbreviate $EXTINTV$, $\theta, [b, e] \models D$ by $\theta, [b, e] \models_{pl} D$. Syntactically $PLDC \subset GDC[M_{pl}]$ given by the abstract syntax
$$\lceil P \rceil \mid mt \ op \ c \mid D_1 ^\frown D_2 \mid D_1 \wedge D_2 \mid \neg D_1.$$

Example 2. Recall that $\Diamond D \overset{\text{def}}{=} \top ^\frown D ^\frown \top$. In $PLDC$ formula $\Diamond D$ holds for an interval $[b, e]$ if some proper subinterval $[b', e']$ with $b < b' < e' < e$ satisfies D. However, in DC, the formula $\Diamond D$ holds for an interval $[b, e]$ if some subinterval $[b', e']$ with $b \leq b' \leq e' \leq e$ satisfies D.   □

Interval Duration Logic (IDL). This logic was proposed by Pandya [14] as a variant of DC with sampled time. It was argued that IDL is more amenable to validity checking. While validity of IDL is also undecidable in general, several effective techniques and tools have been developed as partial methods for validity checking of IDL. These include Bounded Model Checking [15] as well as reduction to the decidable Discrete-time Duration Calculus using digitization [3,15].

Given a behaviour θ, let $C(\theta)$ be the set of time points where the behaviour changes state (including the initial point 0). Let S_θ be such that $C(\theta) \subseteq S_\theta$ where S is a countably infinite set of sampling points which is time-divergent. Such an S_θ gives a set of sampling points such that the behaviour is over-sampled.

Let $INTV(S_\theta) = \{[b,e] \mid b, e \in S_\theta, \ b \leq e\}$ be the set of intervals spanning sampling points. Define $M_{idl} = \{(INTV(S_\theta), \theta) \mid \theta \in BEH\}$. Then, we can define $IDL = GDC[M_{idl}]$. The syntax of IDL is same as the syntax of GDC. We will abbreviate $INTV(S_\theta), \theta, [b,e] \models D$ by $S_\theta, \theta, [b,c] \models_{id} D$.

It should be noted that the original IDL [14] was formulated using finite timed-state sequences as models. Here, we reformulate this as continuous behaviour with admissible intervals spanning the sampling points. It can be shown that the two formulations are equivalent.

Well Sampled Interval Duration Logic (WSIDL). This is a special case of IDL where continuous time behaviour is sampled at every change point and at every integer valued point. Moreover the behaviour is also 1-oversampled by including the midpoint between every consecutive pair of above sampling points.

Formally, define $C(\theta)$ as a set of time points where the behaviour changes state in θ and let $\aleph$ be the set of non-negative integer valued points. Now define $S'(\theta) = \aleph \cup C(\theta)$. Also, let Mid contain the midpoints of all consecutive pairs of points in $S'(\theta)$. Define $WS(\theta) = S' \cup Mid$. The set $WS(\theta)$ is called the set of *well-sampling points with 1-oversampling*. Here, 1-oversampling refers to the fact that we add one additional point between every pair of consecutive elements of $S'(\theta)$.

Define $WSIntv(\theta) = INTV(WS(\theta))$, the set of intervals spanning elements of $WS(\theta)$. Let, $M_{wsidl} = \{(WSIntv(\theta), \theta)\}$. Define $WSIDL = GDC[M_{wsidl}]$. The syntax of $WSIDL$ is same as the syntax of GDC. Note that the set $WS(\theta)$ is uniquely defined by θ. Hence, in a $WSIDL$ model $I, \theta, [b,e]$, the set of intervals I is uniquely determined by θ as $I = WSIntv(\theta)$. Because of this, we shall abbreviate $WSIntv(\theta), \theta, [b,e] \models D$ by $\theta, [b,e] \models_{ws} D$.

Discrete Duration Calculus (DDC). This is a special case of IDL where the formulae are interpreted only over the behaviours where $C(\theta) \subseteq \aleph$, i.e. the behaviours where state changes occur only at integer valued points. Moreover, the set of sampling points are precisely the set of non-negative integers, i.e. $S(\theta) = \aleph$. Let M_{dd} be the subset of s-behaviours of M_{idl} satisfying the above condition. Then, $DDC = GDC[M_{dd}]$. We abbreviate $INTV(S(\theta)), \theta, [b,e] \models D$ by $\theta, [b,e] \models_{dd} D$.

Consider a DC behaviour θ over an interval $[1,5]$ as follows: The points marked Mid are the newly added points which lie in between either 2 change points or a change point and an integer point. The change points are marked with C, and integer points with I.

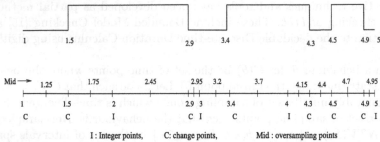

I : Integer points,   C: change points,   Mid : oversampling points

Fig. 1. A DC Behavior θ and the corresponding sampling points in $WS(\theta)$

The prefix validity of DDC (as well as its extension $QDDC$) is decidable and the logic admits a finite-automata theoretic decision procedure [12]. Based on this, a tool DCVALID has been constructed for validity and model checking of DDC formulae [12,13,9].

Example 3. Some essential features of various notions of time, can be specified by some characteristic properties.

- Let $Ax1 \stackrel{\text{def}}{=} \Box\lceil\lceil\top\rceil$. This states that every interval is extended. Clearly, $\not\models_{dc} Ax1$ but $\models_{pl} Ax1$.
- Consider the density property $Ax2 \stackrel{\text{def}}{=} \Box(ext \Rightarrow ext\,\frown ext)$. It states that any non-point interval can be chopped into two non-point intervals. Then $\models_{dc} Ax2$. However, none of the sampled logics $IDL, WSIDL, DDC$ satisfy this formula, e.g. $\not\models_{ws} Ax2$.
- The following property characterizes sampled time. Let $Ax3 \stackrel{\text{def}}{=} \Box(ext \Rightarrow ((Unit\,\frown\top)\wedge(\top\,\frown Unit)))$. Then, all the sampled logics $IDL, WSIDL, DDC$ have this axiom as valid. However, $\not\models_{dc} Ax3$.
- Let $Ax4 \stackrel{\text{def}}{=} \Box(Unit \Rightarrow \ell < 1)$. It states that each atomic extended interval is of length less than 1. This is characteristic of well sampled models with 1 oversampling. Thus, $\models_{ws} Ax4$ but $\not\models_{id} Ax4$.
- Discrete time logic DDC is characterized by validity of the following formula. $Ax5 \stackrel{\text{def}}{=} \Box(\ell = 1 \Leftrightarrow Unit)$. It states that every atomic extended interval is of unit length. Then, $\models_{dd} Ax6$ but $\not\models_{ws} Ax6$.   □

3   PLDC to WSIDL

In this section, we investigate validity/counterexample preserving reduction (abstraction) from the pointless fragment of DC, i.e. $PLDC$ to the sampled time logic with 1-oversampling, $WSIDL$. This involves reduction of both the models and the formulae.

Sampling Approximation of *DC* Models

Consider a *PLDC* model $(EXTINTV, \theta, [b, e])$. The s-behaviour $(EXTINTV, \theta)$ can be represented by a *WSIDL* s-behaviour $(WSIntv(\theta), \theta)$ as explained earlier (see Figure 1).

Definition 1 (1-Sampling). *Given PLDC model θ define a map $f : \Re^0 \rightarrow WS(\theta)$ as follows. Let $f(b) = \left\{ \begin{array}{ll} b & \text{if } b \in \mathcal{S}', \\ b_m & \text{otherwise.} \end{array} \right\}$ where b_m is the midpoint of the smallest number larger than b in $\mathcal{S}'$ and the largest number smaller than b in $\mathcal{S}'$.*

Then, f approximates every time point in θ to a sampling point in $WS(\theta)$. In Figure 1, $f(2.3) = f(2.88) = 2.45$.

Proposition 1. *We list some elementary properties of the onto map f.*

- *f is weakly monotonic, i.e. $b \leq e \Rightarrow f(b) \leq f(e)$. However, it is not strictly monotonic, i.e. $b < e$ does not ensure that $f(b) < f(e)$.*
- *$-0.5 < f(b) - b < 0.5$. This holds since $f(b)$ is either b or the midpoint of two points (on either side of b) at maximum distance 1,*
- *For any θ and any time point b, the state remains constant in the closed intervals $[f(b), b]$ and $[b, f(b)]$.*   □

Now we consider a *PLDC* interval $[b, e]$. This is mapped to its sampling approximation $[f(b), f(e)]$. The above proposition shows that an extended interval $[b, e]$ can be mapped into a point interval $[f(b), f(e)]$ with $f(b) = f(e)$.

Proposition 2. *The effect of sampling on measurements is as follows.*

- *$-1 < [eval(\ell)(\theta, [b, e]) - eval(\ell)(\theta, [f(b), f(e)])] < 1$. Also,*
- *$-1 < [eval(\int P)(\theta, [b, e]) - eval(\int P)(\theta, [f(b), f(e)])] < 1$*

Proof. We prove the first part. The proof of the second part is analogous. Let $l = e - b$ and $l' = f(e) - f(b)$. Let $\triangle e = | f(e) - e |$. If $e \in \mathcal{S}'$, then $\triangle e = 0$ else $0 \leq \triangle e < 0.5$. Similarly we have $0 \leq \triangle b < 0.5$. Thus length for the *IDL* interval $[f(b), f(e)]$ will be
$l' = f(e) - f(b) \Rightarrow l' = e \pm \triangle e - (b \pm \triangle b) \Rightarrow l' = l \pm \triangle e \pm \triangle b$
Since $| \triangle e + \triangle b | < 1, | l' - l | < 1 \Rightarrow$ There will be less than ± 1 error in the length.   □

Approximating PLDC Formulae in WSIDL

We define a strong transformation $\alpha^+ : PLDC \rightarrow WSIDL$ and a weak transformation $\alpha^- : PLDC \rightarrow WSIDL$ as follows. Both these transformations can be computed in linear time.

$PLDC$ formula D	Weak IDL formula $\alpha^-(D)$	Strong IDL formula $\alpha^+(D)$
$\lceil\lceil P\rceil$	$\lceil\lceil P\rceil \vee \lceil P\rceil^0$	$\lceil\lceil P\rceil \vee \lceil P\rceil^0$
$l = k$	$k-1 < l < k+1$	$k-1 \geq l \wedge l \geq k+1$, i.e. $\perp$
$l < k$	$l < k+1$	$l \leq k-1$
$l \leq k$	$l < k+1$	$l \leq k-1$
$l > k$	$l > k-1$	$l \geq k+1$
$l \geq k$	$l > k-1$	$l \geq k+1$
$\int P = k$	$k-1 < \int P < k+1$	$k-1 \geq \int P \wedge \int P \geq k+1$, i.e. $\perp$
$\int P < k$	$\int P < k+1$	$\int P \leq k-1$
$\int P \leq k$	$\int P < k+1$	$\int P \leq k-1$
$\int P > k$	$\int P > k-1$	$\int P \geq k+1$
$\int P \geq k$	$\int P > k-1$	$\int P \geq k+1$
$D_1 \wedge D_2$	$\alpha^-(D_1) \wedge \alpha^-(D_2)$	$\alpha^+(D_1) \wedge \alpha^+(D_2)$
$D_1 \frown D_2$	$\alpha^-(D_1) \frown \alpha^-(D_2)$	$\alpha^+(D_1) \frown \alpha^+(D_2)$
$\neg D_1$	$\neg\alpha^+(D_1)$	$\neg\alpha^-(D_1)$

One noteworthy aspect of above abstraction is that a $PLDC$ formula $mt = k$ can only be strongly approximated (using α^+) by $WSIDL$ formula $\perp$. Unfortunately, sampling does not preserve exact measurements.

Theorem 1. *For any $PLDC$ formula D and interval $[b, e] \in EXTINTV$, we have*

1. $\theta, [b, e] \models_{pl} D \;\Leftarrow\; \theta, [f(b), f(e)] \models_{ws} \alpha^+(D)$
2. $\theta, [b, e] \models_{pl} D \;\Rightarrow\; \theta, [f(b), f(e)] \models_{ws} \alpha^-(D)$

Proof. The proof is by induction on the structure of the formula D. We give some of the cases. The complete proof may be found in the full paper.

1. Let $D = \ell \; op \; k$.

   We first prove part (2), i.e. $\theta, [b, e] \models_{pl} l \; op \; k \Rightarrow \theta, [f(b), f(e)] \models_{ws} \alpha^-(l \; op \; k)$. Let $l = e-b$ and $l' = f(e)-f(b)$. From Proposition 2, we know that $\mid l-l' \mid < 1$ which implies $l' - 1 < l < l' + 1$. Then,
   $l = k \;\Rightarrow\; k-1 < l' < k+1, l < k \;\Rightarrow\; l' < k+1,$
   $l \leq k \;\Rightarrow\; l' < k+1, l > k \;\Rightarrow\; l' > k-1$
   $l \geq k \;\Rightarrow\; l' > k-1$. In each case RHS is $\alpha^-(LHS)$.

   We now prove part (1), i.e. $\theta, [b, e] \models_{pl} l \; op \; k \Leftarrow \theta, [f(b), f(e)] \models_{ws} \alpha^+(l \; op \; k)$. Let $l = e - b$ and $l' = f(e) - f(b)$. From Proposition 2, we know that $\mid l - l' \mid < 1$ which implies $l - 1 < l' < l+1$. Then, $l < k \Leftarrow l' \leq k-1$ and $l > k \Leftarrow l' \geq k+1$.

   We have already proved that $(l > k \Rightarrow l' > k - 1) \Leftrightarrow (\neg(l > k) \Leftarrow \neg(l' > k - 1)) \Leftrightarrow (l \leq k \Leftarrow l' \leq k - 1)$. Similarly we have proved that $(l < k \Rightarrow l' < k+1) \Leftrightarrow (\neg(l < k) \Leftarrow \neg(l' < k+1)) \Leftrightarrow (l \geq k \Leftarrow l' \geq k+1)$, $l = k \Leftarrow l \leq k \wedge l \geq k \Leftarrow l' \leq k - 1 \wedge l' \geq k + 1$. In each case RHS is $\alpha^+(LHS)$.

2. Let $D = \neg D_1$. We prove only the part (1).

$\theta, [f(b), f(e)] \models_{ws} \alpha^+(\neg D_1) \iff$ {Defn. α^+, Semantics}

$\theta, [f(b), f(e)] \not\models_{ws} \alpha^-(D_1) \implies$ {Induction Hyp.}

$\theta, [b, e] \not\models_{pl} D_1 \iff$ {Semantics}

$\theta, [b, e] \models_{pl} \neg D_1$

3. Let $D = D_1 \frown D_2$. We prove only part (1).

$\theta, [f(b), f(e)] \models_{ws} \alpha^+(D_1 \frown D_2) \iff$ {Defn. α^+}

$\theta, [f(b), f(e)] \models_{ws} \alpha^+(D_1) \frown \alpha^+(D_2) \iff$ {Semantics.}

$\exists m \in WS(\theta)$ s.t. $f(b) \leq m \leq f(e)$ and

$\theta, [f(b), m] \models_{ws} \alpha^+(D_1)$ and $\theta, [m, f(e)] \models_{ws} \alpha^+(D_2) \iff$

{f is Onto and monotonic}

$\exists m' \in \Re^0$ s.t. $b \leq m' \leq e$ and $f(m') = m$ and

$\theta, [f(b), f(m')] \models_{ws} \alpha^+(D_1)$ and $\theta, [f(m'), f(e)] \models_{ws} \alpha^+(D_2) \implies$

{Induction Hyp.}

$\exists m' \in \Re^0$ s.t. $b \leq m' \leq e$ and $\theta, [b, m'] \models_{pl} D_1$ and $\theta, [m', e] \models_{pl} D_2 \iff$

{Semantics of PLDC}

$\exists m' \in \Re^0$ s.t. $b < m' < e$ and

$\theta, [b, m'] \models_{pl} D_1$ and $\theta, [m', e] \models_{pl} D_2 \iff$

{Semantics of PLDC}

$\theta, [b, e] \models_{pl} D_1 \frown D_2$.

□

Corollary 1. *For any $D \in WSIDL$,*

1. $\models_{ws} \alpha^+(D) \implies \models_{pl} D$
2. $\theta, [b, e] \not\models_{ws} \alpha^-(D) \implies \theta, [b', e'] \not\models_{pl} D$ for all $b' \in f^{-1}(b)$, $e' \in f^{-1}(e)$.
   In particular, $b \in f^{-1}(b)$, $e \in f^{-1}(e)$. Hence, for any $[b, e] \in EXTINTV$
   $\theta, [b, e] \not\models_{ws} \alpha^-(D) \implies \theta, [b, e] \not\models_{pl} D$. □

Optimality of 1-Oversampling We now show that as far as preserving validity/counter examples of *PLDC* formulae is concerned, increasing the oversampling from 1 mid-point to say n intermediate points does not help in making approximations α^+ and α^- more precise. However, later in the paper we consider a *scaling* of *both model and formulae* which can improve the precision of the abstractions α^+, α^-.

We consider here a case with $n - 1$ oversampling points, where n is a natural number, greater than 1. In this general case, $f(b)$ is the oversampling point *closest* to b. Consider a *PLDC* behaviour with change points at 0, 2, 2.2, 4. Thus, we will have $(0, s_0), (1, s_0), (2, s_1), (2.2, s_2), (3, s_2), (4, s_3)$. If we decide to have $n - 1$ sample points in between, then we will have the points

$(0, s_0), (\frac{1}{n}, s_0), \ldots, ((n-1)*\frac{1}{n}, s_0), (1, s_0), (1+\frac{1}{n}, s_0), \ldots, (1+(n-1)*\frac{1}{n}, s_0), (2, s_1),$

$(2+\frac{0.2}{n}, s_1), \ldots, (2+(n-1)*\frac{0.2}{n}, s_1), (2.2, s_2), \ldots, (2.2+(n-1)*\frac{0.8}{n}, s_2), (3, s_2), (3+$

$\frac{1}{n}, s_2), \ldots, (3 + \frac{n-1}{n}, s_2), (4, s_3)$.

Now, consider the *PLDC* interval $[b, e] = [1 + \frac{n-0.7}{n}, 2.2 + \frac{(n-2)*0.8+0.6}{n}]$. The length of this interval in *PLDC* is $(2.2 - 1) + \frac{(n-2)*0.8+0.6-(n-0.7)}{n}$, which is equal to $1 + \frac{-0.3}{n}$, which is less than 1.

The corresponding approximated $WSIDL$ interval is $[f(b), f(e)] = [1 + \frac{n-1}{n}, 2.2$
$+ \frac{(n-1)*0.8}{n}] = [1 + \frac{n-1}{n}, 2 + \frac{n-0.8}{n}]$. The length of this interval is $2 - 1 + \frac{(n-0.8)-(n-1)}{n}$ which simplifies to $1 + \frac{0.2}{n}$.

Hence, for the given interval $\theta, [b, e]$ $\models_{pl} \ell < 1$ where as $\theta, [f(b), f(e)] \models_{ws} \ell > 1$. This shows that the closest approximation of $\ell < 1$ in logic $WSIDL$ which preserves models is $\alpha^-(\ell < 1) = \ell < 1 + 1$. This holds for all possible n-samplings with $n > 1$.

4   DC to PLDC

Theorem 1 allows us to abstract $PLDC$ formulae to $WSIDL$ formulae. We now show that DC and $PLDC$ have the same expressive power (modulo point intervals). We give a translations $\delta: DC \rightarrow PLDC$ and show that it preserves models.

While logic DC has point intervals, the following proposition shows that DC cannot say anything meaningful about the states at these points. It can be proved by induction on the structure of D.

Proposition 3. *If $\theta, [b, b] \models_{dc} D$ then for all $b' \in \Re^0$ and all $\theta' \in BEH$ we have $\theta', [b', b'] \models_{dc} D$.*

We first define whether a formula D is satisfiable by a point interval and denote this by $Pointsat(D)$.

Definition 2. *$Pointsat: DC \rightarrow \{\top, \bot\}$ is inductively defined as follows.*

$Pointsat(\top) = \top, \quad Pointsat(\lceil P \rceil) = \bot$
$Pointsat(mt \ op \ c) = \top \ \textbf{iff} \ (0 \ op \ c)$
$Pointsat(\neg D) = \neg Pointsat(D),$
$Pointsat(D_1 \wedge D_2) = Pointsat(D_1) \wedge Pointsat(D_2)$
$Pointsat(D_1 \frown D_2) = Pointsat(D_1) \wedge Pointsat(D_2)$

For example, by clause 3 we get that $pointsat(\ell <= 3) = (0 \leq 3) = \top$.

Proposition 4. *$Pointsat(D)$ iff $\theta, [b, b] \models_{dc} D$ for some $\theta, [b, b]$.*

Using the above we can embed DC in $PLDC$ as follows.

Definition 3. *Let $\delta: DC \rightarrow PLDC$ be inductively defined as follows. Note that size of the output of δ can be exponential in the size of input. The computation time is proportional to the output size.*

$\delta(\lceil \rceil) = \bot$
$\delta(X) = X, \ for \ X \in \{\top, \lceil P \rceil, \ell \ op \ c, \int P \ op \ c\},$
$\delta(\neg D) = \neg \delta(D), \delta(D_1 \wedge D_2) = \delta(D_1) \wedge \delta(D_2),$

$\delta(D_1 \frown D_2) = \delta(D_1) \frown \delta(D_2)$
$\qquad\qquad \vee \ \delta(D_1) \wedge Pointsat(D_2)$
$\qquad\qquad \vee \ \delta(D_2) \wedge Pointsat(D_1)$

Theorem 2. *For all $\theta \in Beh$ and $[b, e] \in EXTINTV$, we have*

$$\theta, [b, e] \models_{dc} D \quad \textbf{iff} \quad \theta, [b, e] \models_{pl} \delta(D)$$

Proof The proof is by induction on the structure of D. We prove only the case of chop here, the whole proof can be found in the full paper.

- $D = D_1 \frown D_2$. $\theta, [b, e] \models_{dc} D_1 \frown D_2$ iff $\exists m, b \leq m \leq e : \theta, [b, m] \models_{dc} D_1$ and $\theta, [m, e] \models_{dc} D_2$.

  Case 1: $b < m < e$.

  Then, $\theta, [b, m] \models_{dc} D_1$ and $\theta, [m, e] \models_{dc} D_2$. As $[b, m], [m, e] \in EXTINTV$, by the inductive hypothesis, $\theta, [b, m] \models_{pl} \delta(D_1)$ and $\theta, [m, e] \models_{pl} \delta(D_2)$. Thus, $\theta, [b, e] \models_{pl} \delta(D_1) \frown \delta(D_2)$. Conversely, if we assume that $\theta, [b, e] \models_{pl} \delta(D_1) \frown \delta(D_2)$, then $\exists m, b < m < e$ such that $\theta, [b, m] \models_{pl} \delta(D_1)$ and $\theta, [m, e] \models_{pl} \delta(D_2)$. By inductive hypothesis, this implies that $\theta, [b, m] \models_{dc} D_1$ and $\theta, [m, e] \models_{dc} D_2$.

  Case 2: $b < m = e$.

  Then, $\theta, [b, e] \models_{dc} D_1$ and $\theta, [e, e] \models_{dc} D_2$. Then $Pointsat(D_2)$, and by inductive hypothesis, we have $\theta, [b, e] \models_{pl} \delta(D_1)$. Conversely, if $\theta, [b, e] \models_{pl} \delta(D_1)$, then by inductive hypothesis, $\theta, [b, e] \models_{dc} D_1 \Rightarrow \theta, [b, e] \models D_1 \frown D_2$, for $Pointsat(D_2)$.

  Case 3: $b = m < e$. Here, $Pointsat(D_1)$. Similar to Case 2, we have $\theta, [b, e] \models_{dc} D_1 \frown D_2$ iff $\theta, [b, e] \models_{pl} \delta(D_2)$.

  Case 4: $b - m - e$. This case cannot arise as $[b, e] \in EXTINTV$. □

Corollary 2. *For any $D \in DC$,*

1. $\models_{dc} D$ *iff* $\models_{pl} \delta(D)$ *and* $Pointsat(D)$.
2. $\neg Pointsat(D)$ *then* $\theta, [b, b] \not\models_{dc} D$ *for any* $\theta, [b, b]$
3. $\theta, [b, e] \not\models_{pl} \delta(D) \Rightarrow \theta, [b, e] \not\models_{dc} D$, *for any* $[b, e] \in EXTINTV$.

Derived Modalities. Applying the translation δ to derived modality we get:

1. If $Pointsat(D)$ then

$$\delta(\Box D) = \neg(\top \frown \neg\delta(D) \frown \top)$$
$$\wedge \neg(\neg\delta(D) \frown \top) \wedge \neg(\top \frown \neg\delta(D)) \wedge \neg\delta(D)$$
$$\delta(\Diamond D) = true$$

2. If $\neg Pointsat(D)$ then

$$\delta(\Box D) = false$$
$$\delta(\Diamond D) = (\top \frown \delta(D) \frown \top)$$
$$\vee (\delta(D) \frown \top) \vee (\top \frown \delta(D)) \vee \delta(D)$$

The reverse translation of $PLDC$ into DC can be found in the full paper.

5   WSIDL to DDC

Validity of sampled time logics $WSIDL$ as well as IDL are undecidable [14] where as validity of discrete time logic DDC is decidable [12,13]. As a partial technique, Chakravorty and Pandya [3,15] have proposed strong and weak translations (abstractions) ST and WT from logic IDL to logic DDC which respectively preserve the validity and the counter examples. These reductions make use of the digitization technique [7,10]. By a small variant of this technique, we can also propose similar reductions from $WSIDL$ to DDC. We omit the details and refer the reader to the original paper [3] for details.

Theorem 3. *We can define linear time computable translations $ST : WSIDL \to DDC$ and $WT : WSIDL \to DDC$, and a linear time computable model transformation r from DDC models to $WSIDL$ models such that for any formula $D \in WSIDL$, the following holds.*

1. $\models_{ws} D \quad \Leftarrow \quad \models_{dd} ST(D)$
2. $\theta, [b, e] \not\models_{dd} WT(D) \quad \Rightarrow \quad r(\theta, [b, e]) \not\models_{ws} D.$

6   Validity Checking DC

In order to check the validity of a DC formula D first compute if $Pointsat(D) = \bot$. In this case the formula D is not valid by Corollary 2(2). Otherwise, compute the $PLDC$ formula $\delta(D)$ and proceed as follows:

1. Compute $D' = ST(\alpha^+(\delta(D))$ obtained by applying strong translations of $PLDC$ to $WSIDL$ and then strong translation of $WSIDL$ to DDC. A tool $dc2qddcstrong$ has been implemented to compute D' from D.
2. Check the validity of D' using the tool DCVALID.
3. If D' is valid, then by Theorem 3, $\alpha^+(\delta(D))$ is a valid $WSIDL$ formula and by Corollary 1, $\delta(D)$ is a valid $PLDC$ formula. Finally Corollary 2 implies that D is a valid DC formula.
4. If D' is not valid (i.e. DCVALID generates a counter example) then compute $D'' = WT(\alpha^-(\delta(D))$ obtained by first applying the weak translation from $PLDC$ to $WSIDL$ and then applying the weak translation from $WSIDL$ to DDC. A tool $dc2qddcweak$ implements translation from D to D''.
5. Validity check D'' using DCVALID. If a counter example $\theta, [b, e]$ is generated for D'' then by Theorem 3, we can infer that $\alpha^-(\delta(D))$ has a counter example $r(\theta, [b, e])$. Then, Corollary 1 implies that $r(\theta, [b, e])$ is a counter example of $\delta(D)$. Corollary 2 tells us that D also has the counter example $r(\theta, [b, e])$.
6. In case D'' is found to be valid (and earlier D' was found invalid), the method fails to conclude anything about the validity of D. However, using the well-known result on the linearity of behaviours [5], we can attempt to infer the validity of D by checking the validity of D_k obtained by suitably scaling up the constants in D by an integer $k > 1$. Theorem 4 below states that the validity of D is preserved by such transformation. The above steps must be iterated for D_k with different values of k.

Theorem 4. Let $\theta, [b, e] \models_{dc} D$ and let $k \in \Re_{>0}$. Then $\theta', [b \cdot k, e \cdot k] \models_{dc} D_k$ where D_k is the DC formula obtained from D by replacing each occurrence of $\int P$ op c by $\int P$ op $c \cdot k$ and l op c by l op $c \cdot k$ and θ' is a behaviour satisfying $\theta'(t) = \theta(\frac{t}{k})$ for all $t \in \Re^0$. □

7   Experimental Results

We first illustrate the DC validity checking method of the previous section by a simple example.

Example 4. Let $D \stackrel{\text{def}}{=} (\lceil \rceil \vee (\lceil P \rceil \frown true) \vee (\lceil \neg P \rceil \frown true))$. Formula $Ax7 \stackrel{\text{def}}{=} \Box D$ is stated as an axiom of DC [16], i.e. $\models_{dc} Ax7$. We verify its validity using the method of previous section. We have, $Pointsat(D)$ and $\delta(D) = (\ ((\lceil P \rceil \frown \top) \vee \lceil P \rceil) \vee ((\lceil \neg P \rceil \frown \top) \vee \lceil \neg P \rceil)\ )$. Taking strong translation to $WSIDL$ we obtain that $D' = \alpha^+(\delta(D))$ is $(((\lceil P \rceil^0 \vee \lceil P \rceil) \frown \top) \vee (\lceil P \rceil^0 \vee \lceil P \rceil)) \vee (((\lceil \neg P \rceil^0 \vee \lceil \neg P \rceil) \frown \top) \vee ((\lceil \neg P \rceil^0 \vee \lceil \neg P \rceil)))$. Then, $Ax7' = \alpha^+(\delta(Ax7))$ is obtained as $\neg(\top \frown \neg D' \frown \top) \wedge \neg(\top \frown \neg D') \wedge \neg(\neg D' \frown \top) \wedge D'$. This is a valid $WSIDL$ formula. We do not give the translation $Ax7''$ of this into DDC which can be found in the full paper. Our tool *dc2qddcstrong* was used to compute the full translation and resulting DDC formula was shown valid using the DCVALID tool taking a total time of 0.05 sec. □

A benchmark example of DC formula, the Gas burner problem was presented earlier in Example 1. We have checked the validity of the gas burner formula $G(maxleak, minsep, winlen, leakbound)$ for several instances of the parameters using the validity checking method of the previous section. The times taken for translating the formula into DDC as well as the validity checking time taken by the tool DCVALID are given in Table 1. The modal strength reduction technique [9] was used to optimize the performance of the DCVALID tool. The experiments were run on a 1GHz i686 PC with 1GB RAM running RedHat Linux 9.0. Both valid and invalid instances were tried. For the instance $G(2, 6, 15, 7)$ the method failed to give any result as the strong translation to DDC was invalid but the

Table 1. Results for Gas Burner

Parameters	dc2qddc Strong	DCVALID (hh:mm:ss)	Parameters	dc2qddc Strong/ Weak	DCVALID strong (hh:mm:ss)	DCVALID weak (hh:mm:ss)
Gas Burner: Valid Cases			Gas Burner: Cases with counter examples			
(4,8,30,18)	.3s	02.91s	(2,4,99,6)	.3s	1.25s	1m 22s
(20,40,120,50)	.3s	2m 28.43s	(3,3,150,36)	.3s	18m 37s	19m 31.53s
(1,4,20,12)	.3s	1.50s	(20,40,200,75)	.3s	33m 29.54s	6m 27.55s
(1,4,60,32)	.3s	14.95s	(2,4,500,15)	.3s	2h 5m 3.75s	2h 4m 8.91s
(2,4,100,53)	.3s	1m 1.62s	(5,5,350,25)	.3s	2h 13m 53s	2h 14m 12s
(2,4,300,250)	.3s	20m 39.22s	(7, 3, 175, 27)	.3s	33m 37.47s	32m 57s

weak translation gave valid formula. However, using Theorem 4, and scaling the values of constants by 2, we obtained the instance $G(4, 12, 30, 14)$, for which the strong translation resulted into a valid DDC formula, thereby confirming the validity of the original DC formula $G(2, 6, 15, 7)$.

References

1. R. Alur and D.L. Dill, Automata for modeling real-time systems, *Proc. of 17th ICALP*, LNCS 443, (1990), Springer-Verlag, pp 332-335.
2. A. Bouajjani, Y. Lakhnech and R. Robbana, From Duration Calculus to Linear Hybrid Automata, *Proc.of 7th CAV*, LNCS 939, (1995), Springer-Verlag, pp 196-210.
3. G. Chakravorty and P.K. Pandya, Digitizing Interval Duration Logic, *Proc. of 15th CAV*, LNCS 2725, (2003), Springer-Verlag, pp 167-179.
4. M. Fränzle, Model-Checking Dense-Time Duration Calculus, in *M.R. Hansen (ed.), Duration Calculus: A Logical Approach to Real-Time Systems Workshop proceedings of ESSLLI X*, 1998.
5. M. Fränzle, Take it NP-easy: Bounded Model Construction for Duration Calculus. *Proc. 7th FTRTFT*, LNCS 2469, (2002), Springer-Verlag, pp 245-264.
6. Dang Van Hung and P. H. Giang, Sampling Semantics of Duration Calculus, *Proc. 4th FTRTFT*, LNCS 1135, (1996), Springer-Verlag, pp 188-207.
7. T. A. Henzinger, Z. Manna, and A. Pnueli, What good are digital clocks?, *Proc. 19th ICALP*, LNCS 623, (1992), Springer-Verlag, pp. 545-558.
8. Y. Hirshfeld and A. Rabinovich, Logics for Real-time: Decidability and Complexity, *Fundamenta Informaticae*, 62(1), (2004), pp 1-28.
9. S. N. Krishna and P. K. Pandya, Modal Strength reduction in QDDC, *Proc. 25th FST & TCS*, LNCS 3821, (2005), Springer-Verlag, pp 444-456.
10. J. Ouaknine and J. Worrell, Revisiting Digitization, Robustness and Decidability for Timed Automata, *Proc. 18th IEEE Symposium on LICS*, (2003), pp 198-207.
11. J. Ouaknine and J. Worrell, On Decidability of Metric Temporal Logic, *Proc. 20th IEEE Symposium on LICS*, (2005), pp 188-197.
12. P.K. Pandya, Specifying and Deciding Quantified Discrete-time Duration Calculus Formulae using DCVALID: An Automata Theoretic Approach, in *Proc. RT-TOOLS'2001*, (2001).
13. P.K. Pandya, Model checking CTL*[DC], *Proc. 7th TACAS*, LNCS 2031, (2001), Springer-Verlag, pp 559-573.
14. P.K. Pandya, Interval duration logic: expressiveness and decidability, *Proc. TPTS*, ENTCS 65(6), (2002), pp 1-19.
15. B. Sharma, P.K. Pandya and S. Chakraborty, Bounded Validity Checking of Interval Duration Logic, *Proc. 11th TACAS*, LNCS 3440, (2005), Springer-Verlag, pp 301-316.
16. Zhou Chaochen, C.A.R. Hoare and A.P. Ravn, A Calculus of Durations, *Info. Proc. Letters*, 40(5), 1991.
17. Zhou Chaochen, Zhang Jingzhong, Yang Lu and Li Xiaoshan, Linear duration invariants. in *Proc. 3rd FTRTFT*, LNCS 863, (1994), Springer Verlag, pp 86-109.

Assume-Guarantee Synthesis*

Krishnendu Chatterjee[1] and Thomas A. Henzinger[1,2]

[1] University of California, Berkeley, USA
[2] EPFL, Switzerland
{c_krish,tah}@eecs.berkeley.edu

Abstract. The classical synthesis problem for reactive systems asks, given a proponent process A and an opponent process B, to refine A so that the closed-loop system $A\|B$ satisfies a given specification Φ. The solution of this problem requires the computation of a winning strategy for proponent A in a game against opponent B. We define and study the *co-synthesis* problem, where the proponent A consists itself of two independent processes, $A = A_1\|A_2$, with specifications Φ_1 and Φ_2, and the goal is to refine both A_1 and A_2 so that $A_1\|A_2\|B$ satisfies $\Phi_1 \wedge \Phi_2$. For example, if the opponent B is a fair scheduler for the two processes A_1 and A_2, and Φ_i specifies the requirements of mutual exclusion for A_i (e.g., starvation freedom), then the co-synthesis problem asks for the automatic synthesis of a mutual-exclusion protocol.

We show that co-synthesis defined classically, with the processes A_1 and A_2 either collaborating or competing, does not capture desirable solutions. Instead, the proper formulation of co-synthesis is the one where process A_1 competes with A_2 but not at the price of violating Φ_1, and vice versa. We call this *assume-guarantee synthesis* and show that it can be solved by computing secure-equilibrium strategies. In particular, from mutual-exclusion requirements the assume-guarantee synthesis algorithm automatically computes Peterson's protocol.

1   Introduction

The algorithmic *synthesis* (or control) of reactive systems is based on solving 2-player zero-sum games on graphs [11,12]. Player 1 (representing the system or controller to be synthesized) attempts to satisfy a specification Φ; player 2 (representing the environment or plant) tries to violate the specification. Synthesis is successful if a strategy for player 1 can be found which ensures that Φ is satisfied no matter what player 2 does. These games are *zero-sum*, because the objective of player 2 is $\neg\Phi$, the negation of player 1's objective. In other words, synthesis assumes the worst-case scenario that player 2 is as obstructive as possible.

In many game situations in economics, the two players do not have strictly complementary objectives. Then the appropriate notion of rational behavior is that of a Nash equilibrium. One also encounters *non-zero-sum* situations in

---

* This research was supported in part by the Swiss National Science Foundation and by the NSF grants CCR-0225610 and CCR-0234690.

O. Grumberg and M. Huth (Eds.): TACAS 2007, LNCS 4424, pp. 261–275, 2007.

computer science applications [10]. In this paper, we demonstrate that non-zero-sum situations arise in the *co-synthesis* problem. In co-synthesis, we are not asked to synthesize a single reactive process, but a system composed of several processes P_i, each with its own specification Φ_i. For instance, the design of a mutual-exclusion protocol is a co-synthesis question: each one of two processes P_1 and P_2 is supposed to satisfy certain requirements, such as mutual exclusion, bounded overtaking, and starvation freedom. In such a situation, the processes are neither collaborating nor are they strictly competitive: they are not collaborating because process P_1 cannot assume that P_2 will help establishing Φ_1; they are not strictly competitive because process P_2 will not obstruct Φ_1 at all costs, but only if doing so does not endanger Φ_2. In other words, the two processes are *conditionally competitive*: process P_1 can assume that P_2 will primarily try to satisfy Φ_2, and only secondarily try to violate Φ_1, and vice versa. This situation can be captured by 2-player games with lexicographic objectives, and Nash equilibria for such lexicographic objectives are called *secure equilibria* [4]. Formally, a pair of strategies for the two players is winning and secure if (1) both players satisfy their objectives by playing the strategies, and (2) if one player deviates from her strategy in order to harm the other player, then the other player can retaliate by violating the first player's objective. We refer to the resulting payoff profile, with both players winning, as a *winning* secure equilibrium.

We formally define the co-synthesis problem, using the automatic synthesis of a mutual-exclusion protocol as a guiding example. More precisely, we wish to synthesize two processes P_1 and P_2 so that the composite system $P_1\|P_2\|R$, where R is a scheduler that arbitrarily but fairly interleaves the actions of P_1 and P_2, satisfies the requirements of mutual exclusion and starvation freedom for each process. We show that traditional zero-sum game-theoretic formulations, where P_1 and P_2 either collaborate against R, or unconditionally compete, do not lead to acceptable solutions. We then show that for the non-zero-sum game-theoretic formulation, where the two processes compete conditionally, there exists an unique winning secure-equilibrium solution, which corresponds exactly to Peterson's mutual-exclusion protocol. In other words, Peterson's protocol can be synthesized automatically as the winning secure strategies of two players whose objectives are the mutual-exclusion requirements. This is to our knowledge the first application of non-zero-sum games in the synthesis of reactive processes. It is also, to our knowledge, the first application of Nash equilibria —in particular, the special kind called "secure"— in system design.

The new formulation of co-synthesis, with the two processes competing conditionally, is called *assume-guarantee synthesis*, because similar to assume-guarantee verification (e.g., [1]), in attempting to satisfy her specification, each process makes the assumption that the other process does not violate her own specification. The solution of the assume-guarantee synthesis problem can be obtained by computing secure equilibria in 3-player games, with the three players P_1, P_2, and R. Previously, meaningful (i.e., unique maximal) secure equilibria were known to exist only for 2-player games [4], and there it was also shown that in general such meaningful equilibria need not exist for three players. Here we

```
do                                    do
{                                     {
flag[1]:=true; turn:=2;               flag[2]:=true; turn:=1;

| while(flag[1]) nop;                 | while(flag[1]) nop;              (C1)
| while(flag[2]) nop;                 | while(flag[2]) nop;              (C2)
| while(turn=1) nop;                  | while(turn=1) nop;               (C3)
| while(turn=2) nop;                  | while(turn=2) nop;               (C4)
| while(flag[1] & turn=2) nop;        | while(flag[1] & turn=2) nop;     (C5)
| while(flag[1] & turn=1) nop;        | while(flag[1] & turn=1) nop;     (C6)
| while(flag[2] & turn=1) nop;        | while(flag[2] & turn=1) nop;     (C7)
| while(flag[2] & turn=2) nop;        | while(flag[2] & turn=2) nop;     (C8)

Cr1:=true; fin_wait; Cr1:=false;      Cr2:=true; fin_wait; Cr2:=false;
flag[1]:=false;                       flag[2]:=false;

wait[1]:=1;                           wait[2]:=1;
while(wait[1]=1)                      while(wait[2]=1)
  | nop;                                | nop;                           (C9)
  | wait[1]:=0;                         | wait[2]:=0;                    (C10)
} while(true)                         } while(true)
```

Fig. 1. Mutual-exclusion protocol synthesis

extend the theoretical results of [4] in two ways, in order to solve the assume-guarantee synthesis problem. First, we prove the existence of meaningful secure equilibria in the special case of 3-player games where the third player can win unconditionally. This special case arises in assume-guarantee synthesis, because the winning condition of the third player (i.e., the scheduler) is *fairness*. Second, we give an algorithm for answering the existence of a winning secure equilibrium (Theorem 2), and for computing the corresponding strategies (Theorem 3). These algorithms extend those of [4] from two to three players.

On large state spaces, assume-guarantee synthesis, like all algorithmic methods, can be impractical. In Section 4, we provide an *abstraction* methodology for assume-guarantee synthesis. We show how a game structure can be abstracted, independently for player 1 and player 2, so that from certain winning strategies on the two abstract games, we can infer winning secure strategies on the concrete game. To our knowledge, this is the first abstraction methodology that works with two independent abstractions of a single game structure. Single-player abstractions suffice for zero-sum games (the abstraction weakens one player and strengthens the other). However, for non-zero-sum games, the *two-abstractions* methodology suggests itself, because each abstraction focuses on the objective of a different player and may thus omit different details. In this way, both abstractions may have smaller state spaces than a combined abstraction would. Specifically, we provide proof rules for inferring winning secure strategies on a concrete 3-player non-zero-sum game from classical winning strategies on two abstract 2-player zero-sum games, for the cases of safety and Büchi objectives. In fact, in the safety case, our proof rule corresponds closely to the assume-guarantee rule of [1]. In the Büchi case, our rule provides a novel assume-guarantee rule for the verification of specifications under weak fairness.

Related work. We use non-zero-sum games in a perfect-information setting to restrict the power of an adversary in the synthesis of reactive systems. Another way to restrict the power of the adversary is to allow the adversary only a partial view of the state space. The resulting class of imperfect-information games [3,13], and more generally, distributed games [8,9], have been studied extensively in the literature, but only with zero-sum (strictly competitive) objectives. The computational complexity of imperfect-information games is typically much higher than of the perfect-information analogues, and several problems become undecidable in the distributed setting. As illustrated with the mutual-exclusion example, we believe that non-zero-sum games have their place in system synthesis, for synthesizing components with different specifications. They restrict the behaviors of the players in a natural way, by focusing on non-zero-sum objectives, without the exponential (or worse) cost of limiting information.

2   Co-synthesis

In this section we define processes, refinement, schedulers, and specifications. We consider the traditional co-operative [5] and strictly competitive [11,12] versions of the co-synthesis problem; we refer to them as *weak co-synthesis* and *classical co-synthesis*, respectively. We show the drawbacks of these formulations and then present a new formulation of co-synthesis, namely, *assume-guarantee synthesis*.

Variables, valuations, and traces. Let X be a finite set of variables such that each variable $x \in X$ has a finite domain D_x. A *valuation* v on X is a function $v : X \to \bigcup_{x \in X} D_x$ that assigns to each variable $x \in X$ a value $v(x) \in D_x$. We write V for the set of valuations on X. A *trace* on X is an infinite sequence $(v_0, v_1, v_2, \ldots) \in V^\omega$ of valuations on X. Given a valuation $v \in V$ and a subset $Y \subseteq X$ of the variables, we denote by $v \restriction Y$ the restriction of the valuation v to the variables in Y. Similarly, for a trace $\tau = (v_0, v_1, v_2, \ldots)$ on X, we write $\tau \restriction Y = (v_0 \restriction Y, v_1 \restriction Y, v_2 \restriction Y, \ldots)$ for the restriction of τ to the variables in Y. The restriction operator is lifted to sets of valuations, and to sets of traces.

Processes and refinement. For $i \in \{1, 2\}$, a *process* $P_i = (X_i, \delta_i)$ consists of a finite set X_i of variables and a nondeterministic transition function $\delta_i : V_i \to 2^{V_i} \setminus \emptyset$, where V_i is the set of valuations on X_i. The transition function maps a present valuation to a nonempty set of possible successor valuations. We write $X = X_1 \cup X_2$ for the set of variables of both processes; note that some variables may be shared by both processes. A *refinement* of process $P_i = (X_i, \delta_i)$ is a process $P_i' = (X_i', \delta_i')$ such that (1) $X_i \subseteq X_i'$, and (2) for all valuations v' on X_i', we have $\delta_i'(v') \restriction X_i \subseteq \delta_i(v' \restriction X_i)$. In other words, the refined process P_i' has possibly more variables than the original process P_i, and every possible update of the variables in X_i by P_i' is a possible update by P_i. We write $P_i' \preceq P_i$ to denote that P_i' is a refinement of P_i. Given two refinements P_1' of P_1 and P_2' of P_2, we write $X' = X_1' \cup X_2'$ for the set of variables of both refinements, and we denote the set of valuations on X' by V'.

Schedulers. Given two processes P_1 and P_2, a *scheduler* R for P_1 and P_2 chooses at each computatiuon step whether it is process P_1's turn or process P_2's turn to update its variables. Formally, the scheduler R is a function $R : V^* \rightarrow \{1, 2\}$ that maps every finite sequence of global valuations (representing the history of a computation) to $i \in \{1, 2\}$, signaling that process P_i is next to update its variables. The scheduler R is *fair* if it assigns turns to both P_1 and P_2 infinitely often; i.e., for all traces $(v_0, v_1, v_2, \ldots) \in V^\omega$, there exist infinitely many $j \geq 0$ and infinitely many $k \geq 0$ such that $R(v_0, \ldots, v_j) = 1$ and $R(v_0, \ldots, v_k) = 2$. Given two processes $P_1 = (X_1, \delta_1)$ and $P_2 = (X_2, \delta_2)$, a scheduler R for P_1 and P_2, and a start valuation $v_0 \in V$, the set of possible traces is $[\![(P_1 \| P_2 \| R)(v_0)]\!] = \{(v_0, v_1, v_2, \ldots) \in V^\omega \mid \forall j \geq 0.\ R(v_0, \ldots, v_j) = i$ and $v_{j+1} \restriction (X \setminus X_i) = v_j \restriction (X \setminus X_i)$ and $v_{j+1} \restriction X_i \in \delta_i(v_j \restriction X_i)\}$. Note that during turns of one process P_i, the values of the private variables $X \setminus X_i$ of the other process remain unchanged.

Specifications. A *specification* Φ_i for processs P_i is a set of traces on X; that is, $\Phi_i \subseteq V^\omega$. We consider only ω-regular specifications [14]. We define boolean operations on specifications using logical operators such as $\wedge$ (conjunction) and $\rightarrow$ (implication).

Weak co-synthesis. In all formulations of the co-synthesis problem that we consider, the input to the problem is given as follows: two processes $P_1 = (X_1, \delta_1)$ and $P_2 = (X_2, \delta_2)$, two specifications Φ_1 for process 1 and Φ_2 for process 2, and a start valuation $v_0 \in V$. The *weak co-synthesis* problem is defined as follows: do there exist two processes $P_1' = (X_1', \delta_1')$ and $P_2' = (X_2', \delta_2')$, and a valuation $v_0' \in V'$, such that (1) $P_1' \preceq P_1$ and $P_2' \preceq P_2$ and $v_0' \restriction X = v_0$, and (2) for all fair schedulers R for P_1' and P_2', we have $[\![(P_1' \| P_2' \| R)(v_0')]\!] \restriction X \subseteq (\Phi_1 \wedge \Phi_2)$.

Example 1 (Mutual-exclusion protocol synthesis). Consider the two processes shown in Fig. 1. Process P_1 (on the left) places a request to enter its critical section by setting `flag[1]:=true`, and the entry of P_1 into the critical section is signaled by `Cr1:=true`; and similarly for process P_2 (on the right). The two variables `flag[1]` and `flag[2]` are boolean, and in addition, both processes may use a shared variable `turn` that takes two values 1 and 2. There are 8 possible conditions C1–C8 for a process to guard the entry into its critical section.[1] The figure shows all 8×8 alternatives for the two processes; any refinement without additional variables will choose a subset of these. Process P_1 may stay in its critical section for an arbitrary finite amount of time (indicated by `fin_wait`), and then exit by setting `Cr1:=false`; and similarly for process P_2. The `while` loop with the two alternatives C9 and C10 expresses the fact that a process may wait arbitrarily long (possibly infinitely long) before a subsequent request to enter its critical section.

We use the notations $\square$ and $\Diamond$ to denote *always* (safety) and *eventually* (reachability) specifications, respectively. The specification for process P_1 consists of two parts: a safety part $\Phi_1^{\mathtt{mutex}} = \square \neg(\mathtt{Cr1} = \mathtt{true} \wedge \mathtt{Cr2} = \mathtt{true})$ and a liveness

---

[1] Since a guard may check any subset of the three 2-valued variables, there are 256 possible guards; but all except 8 can be discharged immediately as not useful.

```
do                                     do
{                                      {
flag[1]:=true; turn:=2;                flag[2]:=true; turn:=1;

while (flag[2] & turn=1) nop;          while (flag[1] & turn=2) nop;    (C8+C5)

Cr1:=true; fin_wait; Cr1:=false;       Cr2:=true; fin_wait; Cr2:=false;
flag[1]:=false;                        flag[2]:=false;

wait[1]:=1;                            wait[2]:=1;
while(wait[1]=1)                       while(wait[2]=1)
  | nop;                                 | nop;                         (C9)
  | wait[1]:=0;                          | wait[2]:=0;                  (C10)
} while(true)                          } while(true)
```

Fig. 2. Peterson's mutual-exclusion protocol

part $\Phi_1^{\text{prog}} = \Box(\text{flag}[1] = \text{true} \rightarrow \Diamond(\text{Cr1} = \text{true}))$. The first part Φ_1^{mutex} specifies that both processes are not in their critical sections simultaneously (*mutual
exclusion*); the second part Φ_1^{prog} specifies that if process P_1 wishes to enter its
critical section, then it will eventually enter (*starvation freedom*). The specifica-
tion Φ_1 for process P_1 is the conjunction of Φ_1^{mutex} and Φ_1^{prog}. The specification
Φ_2 for process P_2 is symmetric. ∎

The answer to the weak co-synthesis problem for Example 1 is "Yes." A solution
of the weak co-synthesis formulation are two refinements P_1' and P_2' of the two
given processes P_1 and P_2, such that the composition of the two refinements
satisfies the specifications Φ_1 and Φ_2 for every fair scheduler. One possible solution is as follows: in P_1', the alternatives C4 and C10 are chosen, and in P_2',
the alternatives C3 and C10 are chosen. This solution is not satisfactory, because
process P_1's starvation freedom depends on the fact that process P_2 requests to
enter its critical section infinitely often. If P_2 were to make only a single request
to enter its critical section, then the progress part of Φ_1 would be violated.

Classical co-synthesis. The *classical co-synthesis* problem is defined as follows:
do there exist two processes $P_1' = (X_1', \delta_1')$ and $P_2' = (X_2', \delta_2')$, and a valuation
$v_0' \in V'$, such that (1) $P_1' \preceq P_1$ and $P_2' \preceq P_2$ and $v_0' \upharpoonright X = v_0$, and (2) for all
fair schedulers R for P_1' and P_2', we have (a) $[\![(P_1' \parallel P_2 \parallel R)(v_0')]\!] \upharpoonright X \subseteq \Phi_1$ and
(b) $[\![(P_1 \parallel P_2' \parallel R)(v_0')]\!] \upharpoonright X \subseteq \Phi_2$.

The answer to the classical co-synthesis problem for Example 1 is "No." We
will argue later (in Example 2) why this is the case.

Assume-guarantee synthesis. We now present a new formulation of the co-
synthesis problem. The main idea is derived from the notion of secure equilibria [4]. We refer to this new formulation as the *assume-guarantee synthesis*
problem; it is defined as follows: do there exist two refiements $P_1' = (X_1', \delta_1')$ and
$P_2' = (X_2', \delta_2')$, and a valuation $v_0' \in V'$, such that (1) $P_1' \preceq P_1$ and $P_2' \preceq P_2$
and $v_0' \upharpoonright X = v_0$, and (2) for all fair schedulers R for P_1' and P_2', we have

(a) $[\![(P_1' \parallel P_2 \parallel R)(v_0')]\!] \upharpoonright X \subseteq (\Phi_2 \to \Phi_1)$ and (b) $[\![(P_1 \parallel P_2' \parallel R)(v_0')]\!] \upharpoonright X \subseteq (\Phi_1 \to \Phi_2)$ and (c) $[\![(P_1' \parallel P_2' \parallel R)(v_0')]\!] \upharpoonright X \subseteq (\Phi_1 \wedge \Phi_2)$.

The answer to the assume-guarantee synthesis problem for Example 1 is "Yes." A solution P_1' and P_2' is shown in Fig. 2. We will argue the correctness of this solution later (in Example 3). The two refined processes P_1' and P_2' present exactly Peterson's solution to the mutual-exclusion problem. In other words, Peterson's protocol can be derived automatically as an answer to the assume-guarantee synthesis problem for the requirements of mutual exclusion and starvation freedom. The success of assume-guarantee synthesis for the mutual-exclusion problem, together with the failure of the classical co-synthesis, suggests that the classical formulation of co-synthesis is too strong.

3   Game Algorithms for Co-synthesis

We reduce the three formulations of the co-synthesis problem to problems about games played on graphs with three players.

Game graphs. A *3-player game graph* $G = ((S, E), (S_1, S_2, S_3))$ consists of a directed graph (S, E) with a finite set S of states and a set $E \subseteq S^2$ of edges, and a partition (S_1, S_2, S_3) of the state space S into three sets. The states in S_i are player-i states, for $i \in \{1, 2, 3\}$. For a state $s \in S$, we write $E(s) = \{t \in S \mid (s, t) \in E\}$ for the set of successor states of s. We assume that every state has at least one outgoing edge; i.e., $E(s)$ is nonempty for all states $s \in S$. Beginning from a start state, the three players move a token along the edges of the game graph. If the token is on a player-i state $s \in S_i$, then player i moves the token along one of the edges going out of s. The result is an infinite path in the game graph; we refer to such infinite paths as plays. Formally, a *play* is an infinite sequence $(s_0, s_1, s_2, \ldots)$ of states such that $(s_k, s_{k+1}) \in E$ for all $k \geq 0$. We write Ω for the set of plays.

Strategies. A strategy for a player is a recipe that specifies how to extend plays. Formally, a *strategy* σ_i for player i is a function $\sigma_i : S^* \cdot S_i \to S$ that, given a finite sequence of states (representing the history of the play so far) which ends in a player-i state, chooses the next state. The strategy must choose an available successor state; i.e., for all $w \in S^*$ and $s \in S_i$, if $\sigma_i(w \cdot s) = t$, then $t \in E(s)$. We write Σ_i for the set of strategies for player i. Strategies in general require memory to remember some facts about the history of a play. An equivalent definition of strategies is as follows. Let M be a set called *memory*. A strategy $\sigma = (\sigma^u, \sigma^n)$ can be specified as a pair of functions: (1) a *memory-update* function $\sigma^u : S \times M \to M$ that, given the memory and the current state, updates the memory; and (2) a *next-state* function $\sigma^n : S \times M \to S$ that, given the memory and the current state, determines the successor state. The strategy σ is *finite-memory* if the memory M is finite. The strategy σ is *memoryless* if the memory M is a singleton set. Memoryless strategies do not depend on the history of a play, but only on the current state. A memoryless strategy for player i can be specified as a function $\sigma_i : S_i \to S$ such that $\sigma_i(s) \in E(s)$ for all $s \in S_i$. Given a start state $s \in S$ and three strategies $\sigma_i \in \Sigma_i$, one for each of the three players $i \in \{1,2,3\}$, there is an unique play, denoted $\omega(s, \sigma_1, \sigma_2, \sigma_3) = (s_0, s_1, s_2, \ldots)$, such that $s_0 = s$ and for all $k \geq 0$, if $s_k \in S_i$, then $\sigma_i(s_0, s_1, \ldots, s_k) = s_{k+1}$; this play is the outcome of the game starting at s *given* the three strategies σ_1, σ_2, and σ_3.

Winning. An *objective* Ψ is a set of plays; i.e., $\Psi \subseteq \Omega$. The following notation is derived from ATL [2]. For an objective Ψ, the set of *winning states* for player 1 in the game graph G is $\langle\langle 1 \rangle\rangle_G(\Psi) = \{s \in S \mid \exists \sigma_1 \in \Sigma_1. \forall \sigma_2 \in \Sigma_2. \forall \sigma_3 \in \Sigma_3. \omega(s, \sigma_1, \sigma_2, \sigma_3) \in \Psi\}$; a witness strategy σ_1 for player 1 for the existential quantifier is referred to as a *winning strategy*. The winning sets $\langle\langle 2 \rangle\rangle_G(\Psi)$ and $\langle\langle 3 \rangle\rangle_G(\Psi)$ for players 2 and 3 are defined analogously. The set of winning states for the *team* consisting of player 1 and player 2, playing against player 3, is $\langle\langle 1,2 \rangle\rangle_G(\Psi) = \{s \in S \mid \exists \sigma_1 \in \Sigma_1. \exists \sigma_2 \in \Sigma_2. \forall \sigma_3 \in \Sigma_3. \omega(s, \sigma_1, \sigma_2, \sigma_3) \in \Psi\}$. The winning sets $\langle\langle I \rangle\rangle_G(\Psi)$ for other teams $I \subseteq \{1,2,3\}$ are defined similarly. The following determinacy result follows from [6].

Theorem 1 (Finite-memory determinacy [6]). *Let Ψ be an ω-regular objective, let G be a 3-player game graph, and let $I \subseteq \{1,2,3\}$ be a set of the players. Let $J = \{1,2,3\} \setminus I$. Then (1) $\langle\langle I \rangle\rangle_G(\Psi) = S \setminus \langle\langle J \rangle\rangle_G(\neg\Psi)$, and (2) there exist finite-memory strategies for the players in I such that against all strategies for the players in J, for all states in $s \in \langle\langle I \rangle\rangle_G(\Psi)$, the play starting at s given the strategies lies in Ψ.*

Game solutions to weak and classical co-synthesis. Given two processes $P_1 = (X_1, \delta_1)$ and $P_2 = (X_2, \delta_2)$, we define the 3-player game graph $\widehat{G} = ((S, E), (S_1, S_2, S_3))$ as follows: let $S = V \times \{1,2,3\}$; let $S_i = V \times \{i\}$ for $i \in \{1,2,3\}$; and let E contain (1) all edges of the form $((v,3),(v,1))$ for $v \in V$, (2) all edges of the form $((v,3),(v,2))$ for $v \in V$, and (3) all edges of the form $((v,i),(u,3))$ for $i \in \{1,2\}$ and $u \upharpoonright X_i \in \delta_i(v \upharpoonright X_i)$ and $u \upharpoonright (X \setminus X_i) = v \upharpoonright (X \setminus X_i)$. In other words, player 1 represents process P_1, player 2 represents process P_2, and player 3 represents the scheduler. Given a play of the form $\omega = ((v_0,3),(v_0,i_0),(v_1,3),(v_1,i_1),(v_2,3),\ldots)$, where $i_j \in \{1,2\}$ for all $j \geq 0$, we write $[\omega]_{1,2}$ for the sequence of valuations $(v_0, v_1, v_2, \ldots)$ in ω (ignoring the intermediate valuations at player-3 states). A specification $\Phi \subseteq V^\omega$ defines the objective $[\![\Phi]\!] = \{\omega \in \Omega \mid [\omega]_{1,2} \in \Phi\}$. In this way, the specifications Φ_1 and Φ_2 for the processes P_1 and P_2 provide the objectives $\Psi_1 = [\![\Phi_1]\!]$ and $\Psi_2 = [\![\Phi_2]\!]$ for players 1 and 2, respectively. The objective for player 3 (the scheduler) is the fairness objective $\Psi_3 = \mathsf{Fair}$ that both S_1 and S_2 are visited infinitely often; i.e., Fair contains all plays $(s_0, s_1, s_2, \ldots) \in \Omega$ such that $s_j \in S_1$ for infinitely many $j \geq 0$, and $s_k \in S_2$ for infinitely many $k \geq 0$.

Proposition 1. *Given two processes $P_1 = (X_1, \delta_1)$ and $P_2 = (X_2, \delta_2)$, two specifications Φ_1 for P_1 and Φ_2 for P_2, and a start valuation $v_0 \in V$, the answer to the weak co-synthesis problem is "Yes" iff $(v_0,3) \in \langle\langle 1,2 \rangle\rangle_{\widehat{G}}(\mathsf{Fair} \to ([\![\Phi_1]\!] \wedge [\![\Phi_2]\!]))$; and the answer to the classical co-synthesis problem is "Yes" iff both $(v_0,3) \in \langle\langle 1 \rangle\rangle_{\widehat{G}}(\mathsf{Fair} \to [\![\Phi_1]\!])$ and $(v_0,3) \in \langle\langle 2 \rangle\rangle_{\widehat{G}}(\mathsf{Fair} \to [\![\Phi_2]\!])$.*

Example 2 (Failure of classical co-synthesis). We now demonstrate the failure of classical co-synthesis for Example 1. We show that for every strategy for process P_1, there exist *spoiling* strategies for process P_2 and the scheduler such that (1) the scheduler is fair and (2) the specification Φ_1 of process P_1 is violated. With any fair scheduler, process P_1 will eventually set `flag[1]:=true`. Whenever process P_1 enters its critical section (setting `Cr1:=true`), the scheduler assigns a finite sequence of turns to process P_2. During this sequence, process P_2 enters its critical section: it may first choose the alternative `C10` to return to the beginning of the the main loop, then set `flag[2]:=true; turn:=1;` then pass the guard `C4:` (since ($\texttt{turn} \neq 2$)), and enter the critical section (setting `Cr2:=true`). This violates the mutual-exclusion requirement $\Phi_1^{\texttt{mutex}}$ of process P_1. On the other hand, if process P_1 never enters its critical section, this violates the starvation-freedom requirement $\Phi_1^{\texttt{prog}}$ of process P_1. Thus the answer to the classical co-synthesis problem is "No."   ∎

Game solution to assume-guarantee synthesis. We extend the notion of secure equilibria [4] from 2-player games to 3-player games where player 3 can win unconditionally; i.e., $\langle\!\langle 3 \rangle\!\rangle_G(\Psi_3) = S$ for the objective Ψ_3 for player 3. In the setting of two processes and a scheduler (player 3) with a fairness objective, the restriction that $\langle\!\langle 3 \rangle\!\rangle_G(\Psi_3) = S$ means that the scheduler has a fair strategy from all states; this is clearly the case for $\Psi_3 = \mathsf{Fair}$. (Alternatively, the scheduler may not required to be fair; then Ψ_3 is the set of all plays, and the restriction is satisfied trivially.) The concept of secure equilibria is based on a lexicographic preference ordering of payoff profiles, which can be extended naturally from two to three players under the restriction that player 3 can win unconditionally. We first present the definition of secure equilibria and then characterize the winning secure equilibrium states as the winning states of certain subgames with zero-sum objectives (Theorem 2); this result is a non-trivial generalization of [4] from two to three players. We then establish the existence of finite-memory winning secure strategies (Theorem 3). This will allow us to solve the assume-guarantee synthesis problem by computing winning secure equilibria (Theorem 4).

Payoffs. In the following, we fix a 3-player game graph G and objectives Ψ_1, Ψ_2, and Ψ_3 for the three players such that $\langle\!\langle 3 \rangle\!\rangle_G(\Psi_3) = S$. Given strategies σ_i for the three players $i \in \{1, 2, 3\}$, and a state $s \in S$, the *payoff* $p_i(s, \sigma_1, \sigma_2, \sigma_3)$ for player i is 1 if $\omega(s, \sigma_1, \sigma_2, \sigma_3) \in \Psi_i$, and 0 otherwise. The payoff *profile* $(p_1(s, \sigma_1, \sigma_2, \sigma_3), p_2(s, \sigma_1, \sigma_2, \sigma_3), p_3(s, \sigma_1, \sigma_2, \sigma_3))$ consists of the payoff for each player. Since $\langle\!\langle 3 \rangle\!\rangle_G(\Psi_3) = S$, any equilibrium payoff profile will assign payoff 1 to player 3. Hence we focus on payoff profiles whose third component is 1.

Payoff-profile ordering. The preference order $\prec_i$ for player i on payoff profiles is defined by $(p_1, p_2, p_3) \prec_i (p_1', p_2', p_3')$ iff either (1) $p_i < p_i'$, or (2) $p_i = p_i'$ and $p_j + p_k > p_j' + p_k'$ for $j, k \in \{1, 2, 3\} \setminus \{i\}$ with $j \neq k$. In the case where the payoff for player 3 is 1, the player-1 preference order $\prec_1$ on payoff profiles is lexicographic: $(p_1, p_2, 1) \prec_1 (p_1', p_2', 1)$ iff either (1) $p_1 < p_1'$, or (2) $p_1 = p_1'$ and $p_2 > p_2'$; that is, player 1 prefers a payoff profile that gives her greater payoff, and if two payoff profiles match in the first component, then she prefers the payoff profile in which player 2's payoff is smaller. The preference order for player 2 is symmetric. The preference order for player 3 is such that $(p_1, p_2, 1) \prec_3 (p_1', p_2', 1)$ iff $p_1 + p_2 > p_1' + p_2'$. Given two payoff profiles (p_1, p_2, p_3) and (p_1', p_2', p_3'), we write $(p_1, p_2, p_3) = (p_1', p_2', p_3')$ iff $p_i = p_i'$ for all $i \in \{1, 2, 3\}$, and we write $(p_1, p_2, p_3) \preceq_i (p_1', p_2', p_3')$ iff $(p_1, p_2, p_3) \prec_i (p_1', p_2', p_3')$ or $(p_1, p_2, p_3) = (p_1', p_2', p_3')$.

Secure equilibria. A strategy profile $(\sigma_1, \sigma_2, \sigma_3)$ is a *secure equilibrium* at a state $s \in S$ iff the following three conditions hold:

$$\forall \sigma_1' \in \Sigma_1. \ (p_1(s, \sigma_1', \sigma_2, \sigma_3), p_2(s, \sigma_1', \sigma_2, \sigma_3), p_3(s, \sigma_1', \sigma_2, \sigma_3)) \preceq_1 p;$$
$$\forall \sigma_2' \in \Sigma_2. \ (p_1(s, \sigma_1, \sigma_2', \sigma_3), p_2(s, \sigma_1, \sigma_2', \sigma_3), p_3(s, \sigma_1, \sigma_2', \sigma_3)) \preceq_2 p;$$
$$\forall \sigma_3' \in \Sigma_3. \ (p_1(s, \sigma_1, \sigma_2, \sigma_3'), p_2(s, \sigma_1, \sigma_2, \sigma_3'), p_3(s, \sigma_1, \sigma_2, \sigma_3')) \preceq_3 p;$$

where $p = (p_1(s, \sigma_1, \sigma_2, \sigma_3), p_2(s, \sigma_1, \sigma_2, \sigma_3), p_3(s, \sigma_1, \sigma_2, \sigma_3))$. In other words, $(\sigma_1, \sigma_2, \sigma_3)$ is a Nash equilibrium with respect to the payoff-profile orderings $\preceq_i$ for the three players $i \in \{1, 2, 3\}$. For $u, w \in \{0, 1\}$, we write $S_{uw1} \subseteq S$ for the set of states s such that a secure equilibrium with the payoff profile $(u, w, 1)$ exists at s; that is, $s \in S_{uw1}$ iff there is a secure equilibrium $(\sigma_1, \sigma_2, \sigma_3)$ at s such that $(p_1(s, \sigma_1, \sigma_2, \sigma_3), p_2(s, \sigma_1, \sigma_2, \sigma_3), p_3(s, \sigma_1, \sigma_2, \sigma_3)) = (u, w, 1)$. Moreover, we write $\mathsf{MS}_{uw1}(G) \subseteq S_{uw1}$ for the set of states s such that the payoff profile $(u, w, 1)$ is a *maximal* secure equilibrium payoff profile at s; that is, $s \in \mathsf{MS}_{uw1}(G)$ iff (1) $s \in S_{uw1}$, and (2) for all $u', w' \in \{0, 1\}$, if $s \in S_{u'w'1}$, then both $(u', w', 1) \preceq_1 (u, w, 1)$ and $(u', w', 1) \preceq_2 (u, w, 1)$. The states in $\mathsf{MS}_{111}(G)$ are referred to as *winning secure equilibrium states*, and the witnessing secure equilibrium strategies as *winning secure strategies*.

Theorem 2. *Let G be a 3-player game graph G with the objectives Ψ_1, Ψ_2, and Ψ_3 for the three players such that $\langle\!\langle 3 \rangle\!\rangle_G(\Psi_3) = S$. Let*

$$U_1 = \langle\!\langle 1 \rangle\!\rangle_G(\Psi_3 \ \rightarrow \ \Psi_1);$$
$$U_2 = \langle\!\langle 2 \rangle\!\rangle_G(\Psi_3 \ \rightarrow \ \Psi_2);$$
$$Z_1 = \langle\!\langle 1, 3 \rangle\!\rangle_{G \restriction U_1}(\Psi_1 \ \wedge \ \Psi_3 \ \wedge \ \neg\Psi_2);$$
$$Z_2 = \langle\!\langle 2, 3 \rangle\!\rangle_{G \restriction U_2}(\Psi_2 \ \wedge \ \Psi_3 \ \wedge \ \neg\Psi_1);$$
$$W = \langle\!\langle 1, 2 \rangle\!\rangle_{G \restriction (S \setminus (Z_1 \cup Z_2))}(\Psi_3 \ \rightarrow \ (\Psi_1 \ \wedge \ \Psi_2)).$$

Then the following assertions hold: (1) at all states in Z_1 the only secure equilibrium payoff profile is $(1, 0, 1)$; (2) at all states in Z_2 the only secure equilibrium payoff profile is $(0, 1, 1)$; and (3) $W = \mathsf{MS}_{111}(G)$.

Proof. We prove parts (1) and (3); the proof of part (2) is similar to part (1).

Part (1). Since $\langle\!\langle 3 \rangle\!\rangle_G(\Psi_3) = S$ and $Z_1 \subseteq U_1 = \langle\!\langle 1 \rangle\!\rangle_G(\Psi_3 \rightarrow \Psi_1)$, it follows that any secure equilibrium profile in Z_1 has payoff profile of the form $(1, \_, 1)$. Since $(1, 1, 1) \prec_1 (1, 0, 1)$ and $(1, 1, 1) \prec_3 (1, 0, 1)$, to prove uniqueness it suffices to show that player 1 and player 3 can fix strategies to ensure secure equilibrium payoff profile $(1, 0, 1)$. Since $Z_1 = \langle\!\langle 1, 3 \rangle\!\rangle_{G \restriction U_1}(\Psi_1 \wedge \Psi_3 \wedge \neg\Psi_2)$, consider the strategy pair (σ_1, σ_3) such that against all player 2 strategies σ_2 and for all states $s \in Z_1$, we have $\omega(s, \sigma_1, \sigma_2, \sigma_3) \in (\Psi_1 \wedge \Psi_3 \wedge \neg\Psi_2)$. The secure equilibrium strategy pair (σ_1^*, σ_3^*) for player 1 and player 3 (along with any strategy σ_2 for player 2) is constructed as follows.

1. The strategy σ_1^* is as follows: player 1 plays σ_1 and if player 3 deviates from σ_3, then player 1 switches to a winning strategy for $\Psi_3 \to \Psi_1$. Such a strategy exists since $Z_1 \subseteq U_1 = \langle\!\langle 1 \rangle\!\rangle_G(\Psi_3 \to \Psi_1)$.

2. The strategy σ_3^* is as follows: player 3 plays σ_3 and if player 1 deviates from σ_1, then player 3 switches to a winning strategy for Ψ_3. Such a strategy exists since $\langle\!\langle 3 \rangle\!\rangle_G(\Psi_3) = S$.

Hence objective of player 1 is always satisfied, given objective of player 3 is satisfied. Thus player 3 has no incentive to deviate. Similarly, player 1 also has no incentive to deviate. The result follows.

Part (3). By Theorem 1 we have $S \setminus W = \langle\!\langle 3 \rangle\!\rangle_G(\Psi_3 \wedge (\neg\Psi_1 \vee \neg\Psi_2))$ and there is a player 3 strategy σ_3 that satisfies $\Psi_3 \wedge (\neg\Psi_1 \vee \neg\Psi_2)$ against all strategies of player 1 and player 2. Hence the equilibrium $(1, 1, 1)$ cannot exist in the complement set of W, i.e., $\mathsf{MS}_{111}(G) \subseteq W$. We now show that in W there is a secure equilibrium with payoff profile $(1, 1, 1)$. The following construction completes the proof.

1. In $W \cap U_1$, player 1 plays a winning strategy for objective $\Psi_3 \to \Psi_1$, and player 2 plays a winning strategy for objective $(\Psi_3 \wedge \Psi_1) \to \Psi_2$. Observe that $S \setminus Z_1 = \langle\!\langle 2 \rangle\!\rangle_G(\neg\Psi_1 \vee \neg\Psi_3 \vee \Psi_2)$, and hence such a winning strategy exists for player 2.

2. In $W \cap (U_2 \setminus U_1)$, player 2 plays a winning strategy for objective $\Psi_3 \to \Psi_2$, and player 1 plays a winning strategy for objective $(\Psi_2 \wedge \Psi_3) \to \Psi_1$. Observe that $S \setminus Z_2 = \langle\!\langle 1 \rangle\!\rangle_G(\neg\Psi_2 \vee \neg\Psi_3 \vee \Psi_1)$, and hence such a winning strategy exists for player 1.

3. By Theorem 1 we have $W \setminus U_1 = \langle\!\langle 2, 3 \rangle\!\rangle_G(\neg\Psi_1 \wedge \Psi_3)$ and $W \setminus U_2 = \langle\!\langle 1, 3 \rangle\!\rangle_G(\neg\Psi_2 \wedge \Psi_3)$. The strategy construction in $W \setminus (U_1 \cup U_2)$ is as follows: player 1 and player 2 play a strategy (σ_1, σ_2) to satisfy $\Psi_1 \wedge \Psi_2$ against all strategies of player 3, and player 3 plays a winning strategy for Ψ_3; if player 1 deviates, then player 2 and player 3 switches to a strategy $(\overline{\sigma}_2, \overline{\sigma}_3)$ such that against all strategies for player 1 the objective $\Psi_3 \wedge \neg\Psi_1$ is satisfied; and if player 2 deviates, then player 1 and player 3 switches to a strategy $(\overline{\sigma}_1, \overline{\sigma}_3)$ such that against all strategies for player 2 the objective $\Psi_3 \wedge \neg\Psi_2$ is satisfied. Hence neither player 1 and nor player 2 has any incentive to deviate according to the preference order $\preceq_1$ and $\preceq_2$, respectively. ∎

Alternative characterization of winning secure equilibria. In order to obtain a characterization of the set $\mathsf{MS}_{111}(G)$ in terms of strategies, we define retaliation strategies following [4]. Given objectives Ψ_1, Ψ_2, and Ψ_3 for the three players, and a state $s \in S$, the sets of *retaliation strategies* for players 1 and 2 at s are

$$\mathsf{Re}_1(s) = \{\sigma_1 \in \Sigma_1 \mid \forall \sigma_2 \in \Sigma_2. \forall \sigma_3 \in \Sigma_3. \omega(s, \sigma_1, \sigma_2, \sigma_3) \in ((\Psi_3 \wedge \Psi_2) \to \Psi_1)\};$$
$$\mathsf{Re}_2(s) = \{\sigma_2 \in \Sigma_2 \mid \forall \sigma_1 \in \Sigma_1. \forall \sigma_3 \in \Sigma_3. \omega(s, \sigma_1, \sigma_2, \sigma_3) \in ((\Psi_3 \wedge \Psi_1) \to \Psi_2)\}.$$

Theorem 3. *Let G be a 3-player game graph G with the objectives Ψ_1, Ψ_2, and Ψ_3 for the three players such that $\langle\!\langle 3 \rangle\!\rangle_G(\Psi_3) = S$. Let $U = \{s \in S \mid \exists \sigma_1 \in \mathsf{Re}_1(s). \exists \sigma_2 \in \mathsf{Re}_2(s). \forall \sigma_3 \in \Sigma_3. \omega(s, \sigma_1, \sigma_2, \sigma_3) \in (\Psi_3 \to (\Psi_1 \wedge \Psi_2))\}$. Then $U = \mathsf{MS}_{111}(G)$.*

Proof. We first show that $U \subseteq \mathsf{MS}_{111}(G)$. For a state $s \in U$, choose $\sigma_1 \in \mathsf{Re}_1(s)$ and $\sigma_2 \in \mathsf{Re}_2(s)$ such that for all $\sigma_3 \in \Sigma_3$, we have $\omega(s, \sigma_1, \sigma_2, \sigma_3) \in (\Psi_3 \rightarrow (\Psi_1 \wedge \Psi_2))$. Fixing the strategies σ_1 and σ_2 for players 1 and 2, and a winning strategy for player 3, we obtain the secure equilibrium payoff profile $(1, 1, 1)$. We now show that $\mathsf{MS}_{111}(G) \subseteq U$. This follows from the proof of Theorem 2. In Theorem 2 we proved that for all states $s \in (S \setminus (Z_1 \cup Z_2))$, we have $\mathsf{Re}_1(s) \neq \emptyset$ and $\mathsf{Re}_2(s) \neq \emptyset$; and the winning secure strategies constructed for the set $W = \mathsf{MS}_{111}(G)$ are witness strategies to prove that $\mathsf{MS}_{111}(G) \subseteq U$.   ∎

Observe that for ω-regular objectives, the winning secure strategies of Theorem 3 are finite-memory strategies. The existence of finite-memory winning secure strategies establishes the following theorem.

Theorem 4 (Game solution of assume-guarantee synthesis). *Given two processes $P_1 = (X_1, \delta_1)$ and $P_2 = (X_2, \delta_2)$, two specifications Φ_1 for P_1 and Φ_2 for P_2, and a start valuation $v_0 \in V$, the answer to the assume-guarantee synthesis problem is "Yes" iff $(v_0, 3) \in \mathsf{MS}_{111}(\widehat{G})$ for the 3-player game graph $\widehat{G}$ with the objectives $\Psi_1 = [\![\Phi_1]\!]$, $\Psi_2 = [\![\Phi_2]\!]$, and $\Psi_3 = \mathsf{Fair}$.*

Example 3 (Assume-guarantee synthesis of mutual-exclusion protocol). We consider the 8 alternatives C1–C8 of process P_1, and the corresponding spoiling strategies for process P_2 and the scheduler to violate P_1's specification. We denote by $[\rightarrow]$ a switch between the two processes (decided by the scheduler).

C1 The spoiling strategies for process P_2 and the scheduler cause the following sequence of updates:

> P_1: `flag[1]:=true; turn:=2; [→]`;
> P_2: `flag[2]:=true; turn:=1;`
> P_2: enters the critical section by passing the guard C8: (since (`turn` $\neq$ 2)). After exiting its critical section, process P_2 chooses the alternative C10 to enter the beginning of the main loop, sets `flag[2]:=true; turn:=1;` and then the scheduler assigns the turn to process P_1, which cannot enter its critical section. The scheduler then assigns turn to P_2 and then P_2 enters the critical section by passing guard C8 and this sequence is repeated forever.

The same spoiling strategies work for choices C2, C3, C6 and C7.

C4 The spoiling strategies cause the following sequence of updates:

> P_2: `flag[2]:=true; turn:=1; [→]`;
> P_1: `flag[1]:=true; turn:=2; [→]`;
> P_2: enters the critical section by passing the guard C3: (since (`turn` $\neq$ 1)). After exiting its critical section, process P_2 continues to choose the alternative C9 forever, and the scheduler alternates turn between P_1 and P_2; and process P_1 cannot enter its critical section.

The same spoiling strategies work for the choice C5.

C8 The spoiling strategies cause the following sequence of updates:

P_2: flag[2]:=true; turn:=1; [→];
P_1: flag[1]:=true; turn:=2; [→];
P_2: while(flag[2]) nop;

Then process P_2 does not enter its critical section, and neither can process P_1 enter. In this case P_2 cannot violate P_1's specification without violating her own specification.

It follows from this case analysis that no alternatives except C8 for process P_1 can witness a solution to the assume-guarantee synthesis problem. The alternative C8 for process P_1 and the symmetric alternative C6 for process P_2 provide winning secure strategies for both processes. In this example, we considered refinements without additional variables; but in general refinements can have additional variables.   ∎

4 Abstraction-Based Co-synthesis

In Section 3 we provided game-based algorithms for the three formulations of the co-synthesis problem. However, the state space of the game graph can be very large, making an algorithmic analysis often impractical. In this section we present sound proof rules (i.e., sufficient conditions) for deriving solutions to the three co-synthesis problems from the analysis of simpler game graphs, which abstracts the original game graph. We first review the appropriate notion of *game abstraction* and the corresponding proof rules for the weak and classical versions of co-synthesis. We then give proof rules for assume-guarantee synthesis in the two special but common cases where the processes have safety and Büchi objectives. In particular, we show that the solution of zero-sum games on simpler, abstract game graphs is sufficient for solving a given assume-guarantee synthesis problem: the winning strategies of two different abstract zero-sum games provide winning secure strategies for the original non-zero-sum game.

Abstraction of game graphs. Let $I \subseteq \{1, 2, 3\}$ be a set of players, and let $J = \{1, 2, 3\} \setminus I$. An *I-abstraction* for a 3-player game graph $G = ((S, E), (S_1, S_2, S_3))$ consists of a 3-player game graph $G^A = ((S^A, E^A), (S_1^A, S_2^A, S_3^A))$ and a *concretization* function $\gamma : S^A \to 2^S \setminus \emptyset$ such that the following conditions hold.

1. The abstraction preserves the player structure: for all $i \in \{1, 2, 3\}$ and $a \in S_i^A$, we have $\gamma(a) \subseteq S_i$.
2. The abstraction partitions the concrete state space: $\bigcup_{a \in S^A} \gamma(a) = S$, and for every $s \in S$ there is a unique $a \in S^A$ such that $s \in \gamma(a)$.
3. The edges for players in I are abstracted universally, and the edges for players in J are abstracted existentially:

$$E^A = \{(a, b) \mid \exists i \in I. \, a \in S_i^A \, \wedge \, \forall s \in \gamma(a). \, \exists t \in \gamma(b). \, (s, t) \in E\}$$
$$\cup \, \{(a, b) \mid \exists i \in J. \, a \in S_i^A \, \wedge \, \exists s \in \gamma(a). \, \exists t \in \gamma(b). \, (s, t) \in E\}.$$

The *abstraction* function $\alpha : S \to S^A$ is defined such that $s \in \gamma(\alpha(s))$ for all states $s \in S$. For a play $\omega = (s_0, s_1, s_2, \ldots)$ in G, the abstraction $\alpha(\omega) = (\alpha(s_0), \alpha(s_1), \alpha(s_2), \ldots)$ is a play in G^A.

Abstraction of objectives. Given an objective Ψ on the concrete game graph G, we define the following two objectives on the abstract game graph G^A:

–existential abstraction: $\alpha(\Psi) = \{\alpha(\omega) \mid \omega \in \Psi\}$;
–universal abstraction: $\beta(\Psi) = \{\tau \mid \forall \omega \in S^\omega.$ if $\tau = \alpha(\omega)$ then $\omega \in \Psi\}$.

For the players in I, the abstract objectives are obtained by universal abstraction, and for the players in J, by existential abstraction.

Proof rules for weak and classical co-synthesis. The following proposition states the basic principle behind proof rules for weak and classical co-synthesis.

Proposition 2. *[7] Given a 3-player game graph G, a set $I \subseteq \{1, 2, 3\}$ of players, an I-abstraction (G^A, γ), and an objective Ψ, let $A = \langle\!\langle I \rangle\!\rangle_{G^A}(\beta(\Psi))$. Then $\gamma(A) \subseteq \langle\!\langle I \rangle\!\rangle_G(\Psi)$.*

Proof rules for assume-guarantee synthesis. We present proof rules for assume-guarantee synthesis in two cases: for safety objectives, and for Büchi objectives (which include reachability objectives as a special case).

Safety objectives. Given a set $F \subseteq S$ of states, the *safety* objective $\Box F$ requires that the set F is never left. Formally, the safety objective $\Box F$ contains all plays $(s_0, s_1, s_2, \ldots)$ such that $s_j \in F$ for all $j \geq 0$. Given safety objectives for players 1 and 2, it is immaterial whether the scheduler (player 3) is fair or not, because if a safety objective is violated, then it is violated by a finite prefix of a play. Hence, for simplicity, we assume that the objective of player 3 is trivial (i.e., the set of all plays). The following theorem states that winning secure equilibrium states in a game graph G can be derived from winning secure equilibrium states in two simpler graphs, a $\{1\}$-abstraction G_1^A and a $\{2\}$-abstraction G_2^A. The winning secure strategies on the concrete graph can likewise be derived from the winning secure strategies on the two abstract graphs.

Theorem 5. *Let G be a 3-player game graph with two safety objectives Ψ_1 and Ψ_2 for players 1 and 2, respectively. Let (G_1^A, γ_1) be a $\{1\}$-abstraction, and let (G_2^A, γ_2) be a $\{2\}$-abstraction. Let the objective for player 1 in G_1^A and G_2^A be $\beta_1(\Psi_1)$ and $\alpha_2(\Psi_1)$, respectively. Let the objective for player 2 in G_1^A and G_2^A be $\alpha_1(\Psi_2)$ and $\beta_2(\Psi_2)$, respectively. Let the objective for player 3 in G, G_1^A, and G_2^A be the set of all plays. Let $A_1 = \mathsf{MS}_{111}(G_1^A)$ and $A_2 = \mathsf{MS}_{111}(G_2^A)$. Then $(\gamma_1(A_1) \cap \gamma_2(A_2)) \subseteq \mathsf{MS}_{111}(G)$.*

The classical assume-guarantee rule for safety specifications [1] can be obtained as a special case of Theorem 5 where all states are player-3 states (in this case, player 3 is not only a scheduler, but also resolves all nondeterminism in the two processes P_1 and P_2).

Büchi objectives. Given a set $B \subseteq S$ of states, the *Büchi* objective $\Box\Diamond B$ requires that the set B is visited infinitely often. Formally, the Büchi objective $\Box\Diamond B$ contains all plays $(s_0, s_1, s_2, \ldots)$ such that $s_j \in B$ for infinitely many $j \geq 0$. The following theorem states that winning secure equilibrium states (and the corresponding winning secure strategies) in a game graph G can be derived from a zero-sum analysis of three simpler graphs, a $\{1\}$-abstraction G_1^A, a $\{2\}$-abstraction G_2^A, and a $\{1,2\}$-abstraction $G_{1,2}^A$.

Theorem 6. *Let G be a 3-player game graph with two Büchi objectives Ψ_1 and Ψ_2 for player 1 and player 2, respectively, and the objective* Fair *for player 3. Let (G_1^A, γ_1) be a $\{1\}$-abstraction, let (G_2^A, γ_2) be a $\{2\}$-abstraction, and let $(G_{1,2}^A, \gamma_{1,2})$ be a $\{1,2\}$-abstraction. Let*

$$A_1 = \langle\!\langle 1 \rangle\!\rangle_{G_1^A}((\alpha_1(\mathsf{Fair}) \wedge \alpha_1(\Psi_2)) \rightarrow \beta_1(\Psi_1));$$
$$A_2 = \langle\!\langle 2 \rangle\!\rangle_{G_2^A}((\alpha_2(\mathsf{Fair}) \wedge \alpha_2(\Psi_1)) \rightarrow \beta_2(\Psi_2));$$
$$A_3 = \langle\!\langle 1,2 \rangle\!\rangle_{G_{1,2}^A}(\alpha_{1,2}(\mathsf{Fair}) \rightarrow (\beta_{1,2}(\Psi_1') \wedge \beta_{1,2}(\Psi_2')));$$

where $\Psi_1' = (\Psi_1 \wedge \Box\gamma_1(A_1))$ and $\Psi_2' = (\Psi_2 \wedge \Box\gamma_2(A_2))$. Then $\gamma_{1,2}(A_3) \subseteq \mathsf{MS}_{111}(G)$.

References

1. R. Alur and T.A. Henzinger. Reactive modules. In *Formal Methods in System Design*, 15:7–48, 1999.
2. R. Alur, T.A. Henzinger, O. Kupferman. Alternating-time temporal logic. *Journal of the ACM*, 49:672–713, 2002.
3. K. Chatterjee and T.A. Henzinger. Semiperfect-information games. In *FSTTCS'05*, LNCS 3821, pages 1–18. Springer, 2005.
4. K. Chatterjee, T.A. Henzinger, M. Jurdziński. Games with secure equilibria. In *LICS'04*, pages 160–169. IEEE, 2004.
5. E.M. Clarke and E.A. Emerson. Design and synthesis of synchronization skeletons using branching-time temporal logic. In *Logic of Programs'81*, LNCS 131, pages 52–71. Spinger, 1982.
6. Y. Gurevich and L. Harrington. Trees, automata, and games. In *STOC'82*, pages 60–65. ACM, 1982.
7. T.A. Henzinger, R. Majumdar, F.Y.C. Mang, J.-F. Raskin. Abstract interpretation of game properties. In *SAS'00*, LNCS 1824, pages 220–239. Springer, 2000.
8. P. Madhusudan and P.S. Thiagarajan. Distributed controller synthesis for local specifications. In *ICALP'01*, LNCS 2076, pages 396–407. Springer, 2001.
9. S. Mohalik and I. Walukiewicz. Distributed games. In *FSTTCS'03*, LNCS 2914, pages 338–351. Springer, 2003.
10. C.H. Papadimitriou. Algorithms, games, and the internet. In *STOC'01*, pages 749–753. ACM, 2001.
11. A. Pnueli and R. Rosner. On the synthesis of a reactive module. In *POPL'89*, pages 179–190. ACM, 1989.
12. P.J. Ramadge and W.M. Wonham. Supervisory control of a class of discrete-event processes. *SIAM Journal of Control and Optimization*, 25:206–230, 1987.
13. J.H. Reif. The complexity of 2-player games of incomplete information. *Journal of Computer and System Sciences*, 29:274–301, 1984.
14. W. Thomas. Languages, automata, and logic. In *Handbook of Formal Languages*, volume 3, pages 389–455. Springer, 1997.

Optimized L*-Based Assume-Guarantee Reasoning*

Sagar Chaki[1] and Ofer Strichman[2]

[1] Software Engineering Institute, Pittsburgh, USA
chaki@sei.cmu.edu
[2] Information Systems Engineering, IE, Technion, Israel
ofers@ie.technion.ac.il

Abstract. In this paper, we suggest three optimizations to the L*-based automated Assume-Guarantee reasoning algorithm for the compositional verification of concurrent systems. First, we use each counterexample from the model checker to supply multiple strings to L*, saving candidate queries. Second, we observe that in existing instances of this paradigm, the learning algorithm is coupled weakly with the teacher. Thus, the learner ignores completely the details about the internal structure of the system and specification being verified, which are available already to the teacher. We suggest an optimization that uses this information in order to avoid many unnecessary – and expensive, since they involve model checking – membership and candidate queries. Finally, and most importantly, we develop a method for minimizing the alphabet used by the assumption, which reduces the size of the assumption and the number of queries required to construct it. We present these three optimizations in the context of verifying trace containment for concurrent systems composed of finite state machines. We have implemented our approach and experimented with real-life examples. Our results exhibit an average speedup of over 12 times due to the proposed improvements.

1 Introduction

Formal reasoning about concurrent programs is particularly hard due to the number of reachable states in the overall system. In particular, the number of such states can grow exponentially with each added component. Assume-Guarantee (AG) is a method for compositional reasoning that can be helpful in such cases. Consider a system with two components M_1 and M_2 that need to synchronize on a given set of shared actions, and a property φ that the system should be verified against. In its simplest form, AG requires checking one of the components, say M_1, separately, while making some assumption on the behaviors permitted by M_2. The assumption should then be discharged when checking M_2 in order to conclude the conformance of the product machine with the property. This idea is formalized with the following AG rule:

---

* This research was supported by the Predictable Assembly from Certifiable Components (PACC) initiative at the Software Engineering Institute, Pittsburgh, USA.

$$A \times M_1 \preceq \varphi$$
$$\frac{M_2 \preceq A}{M_1 \times M_2 \preceq \varphi} \quad \text{(AG-NC)} \tag{1}$$

where $\preceq$ stands for some conformance relation[1]. For trace containment, simulation and some other known relations, AG-NC is a sound and complete rule. In this paper, we consider the case in which M_1, M_2 and φ are non-deterministic finite automata, and interpret $\preceq$ as the trace containment (i.e., language inclusion) relation.

Recently, Cobleigh et al. proposed [1] a completely automatic method for finding the assumption A, using Angluin's L* algorithm [2]. L* constructs a minimal Deterministic Finite Automaton (DFA) that accepts an unknown regular language U. L* interacts iteratively with a Minimally Adequate Teacher (MAT). In each iteration, L* queries the MAT about *membership* of strings in U and whether the language of a specific *candidate* DFA is equal to U. The MAT is expected to supply a "Yes/No" answer to both types of questions. It is also expected to provide a counterexample along with a negative answer to a question of the latter type. L* then uses the counterexample to refine its candidate DFA while enlarging it by at least one state. L* is guaranteed to terminate within no more than n iterations, where n is the size of the minimal DFA accepting U.

In this paper we suggest three improvements to the automated AG procedure. The first improvement is based on the observation that counterexamples can sometimes be reused in the refinement process, which saves candidate queries.

The second improvement is based on the observation that the core L* algorithm is completely unaware of the internal details of M_1, M_2 and φ. With a simple analysis of these automata, most queries to the MAT can in fact be avoided. Indeed, we suggest to allow the core L* procedure access to the internal structure of M_1, M_2 and φ. This leads to a tighter coupling between the L* procedure and the MAT, and enables L* to make queries to the MAT in a more intelligent manner. Since each MAT query incurs an expensive model checking run, overall performance is improved considerably.

The last and most important improvement is based on the observation that the alphabet of the assumption A is fixed conservatively to be the entire interface alphabet between M_1 and φ on the one hand, and M_2 on the other. While the full interface alphabet is always sufficient, it is often possible to complete the verification successfully with a much smaller assumption alphabet. Since the overall complexity of the procedure depends on the alphabet size, a smaller alphabet can improve the overall performance. In other words, while L* guarantees the minimality of the learned assumption DFA with respect to a given alphabet, our improvement reduces the size of the alphabet itself, and hence also the size of the learned DFA. The technique we present is based on an automated abstraction/refinement procedure: we start with the empty alphabet and keep refining it based an analysis of the counterexamples, using a pseudo-Boolean solver. The procedure is guaranteed to terminate with a minimal assumption alphabet that

---

[1] Clearly, for this rule to be effective, $A \times M_1$ must be easier to compute than $M_1 \times M_2$.

suffices to complete the overall verification. This technique effectively combines the two paradigms of automated AG reasoning and abstraction-refinement.

Although our optimizations are presented in the context of a non-circular AG rule, they are applicable for circular AG rules as well, although for lack of space we do not cover this topic in this paper. We implemented our approach in the COMFORT [3] reasoning framework and experimented with a set of benchmarks derived from real-life source code. The improvements reduce the overall number of queries to the MAT and the size of the learned automaton. While individual speedup factors exceeded 23, an average speedup of a factor of over 12 was observed, as reported in Section 6.

Related Work. The L* algorithm was developed originally by Angluin [2]. Most learning-based AG implementations, including ours, use a more sophisticated version of L* proposed by Rivest and Schapire [4]. Machine learning techniques have been used in several contexts related to verification [5,6,7,8,9]. The use of L* for AG reasoning was first proposed by Cobleigh et al. [1]. A symbolic version of this framework has also been developed by Alur et al. [10]. The use of learning for automated AG reasoning has also been investigated in the context of simulation checking [11] and deadlock detection [12]. The basic idea behind the automated AG reasoning paradigm is to learn an assumption [13], using L*, that satisfies the two premises of AG-NC. The AG paradigm was proposed originally by Pnueli [14] and has since been explored (in manual/semi-automated forms) widely. The third optimization we propose amounts to a form of counterexample-guided abstraction refinement (CEGAR). The core ideas behind CEGAR were proposed originally by Kurshan [15], and CEGAR has since been used successfully for automated hardware [16] and software [17] verification. An approach similar to our third optimization was proposed independently by Gheorghiu et. al [18]. However, they use polynomial (greedy) heuristics aimed at minimizing the alphabet size, whereas we find the optimal value, and hence we solve an NP-hard problem.

2   Preliminaries

Let λ and $\cdot$ denote the empty string and the concatenation operator respectively. We use lower letters (α, β, etc.) to denote actions, and higher letters (σ, π, etc.) to denote strings.

Definition 1 (Finite Automaton). *A finite automaton (FA) is a 5-tuple $(S, Init, \Sigma, T, F)$ where (i) S is a finite set of states, (ii) $Init \subseteq S$ is the set of initial states, (iii) Σ is a finite alphabet of actions, (iv) $T \subseteq S \times \Sigma \times S$ is the transition relation, and (v) $F \subseteq S$ is a set of accepting states.*

For any FA $M = (S, Init, \Sigma, T, F)$, we write $s \xrightarrow{\alpha} s'$ to mean $(s, \alpha, s') \in T$. Then the function δ is defined as follows: $\forall \alpha \in \Sigma . \forall s \in S . \delta(\alpha, s) = \{s' | s \xrightarrow{\alpha} s'\}$. We extend δ to operate on strings and sets of states in the natural manner. Thus, for any $\sigma \in \Sigma^*$ and $S' \subseteq S$, $\delta(\sigma, S')$ denotes the set of states of M reached by simulating σ on M starting from any $s \in S'$. The language accepted by M, denoted $\mathcal{L}(M)$, is defined as follows: $\mathcal{L}(M) = \{\sigma \in \Sigma^* \mid \delta(\sigma, Init) \cap F \neq \emptyset\}$.

Determinism. An FA $M = (S, Init, \Sigma, T, F)$ is said to be a deterministic FA, or DFA, if $|Init| = 1$ and $\forall \alpha \in \Sigma . \forall s \in S . |\delta(\alpha, s)| \leq 1$. Also, M is said to be complete if $\forall \alpha \in \Sigma . \forall s \in S . |\delta(\alpha, s)| \geq 1$. Thus, for a complete DFA, we have the following: $\forall \alpha \in \Sigma . \forall s \in S . |\delta(\alpha, s)| = 1$. Unless otherwise mentioned, all DFA we consider in the rest of this paper are also complete. It is well-known that a language is regular iff it is accepted by some FA (or DFA, since FA and DFA have the same accepting power). Also, every regular language is accepted by a unique (up to isomorphism) minimal DFA.

Complementation. For any regular language L, over the alphabet Σ, we write $\overline{L}$ to mean the language $\Sigma^* - L$. If L is regular, then so is $\overline{L}$. For any FA M we write $\overline{M}$ to mean the (unique) minimal DFA accepting $\overline{\mathcal{L}(M)}$.

Projection. The projection of any string σ over an alphabet Σ is denoted by $\sigma\downarrow_\Sigma$ and defined inductively on the structure of σ as follows: (i) $\lambda\downarrow_\Sigma = \lambda$, and (ii) $(\alpha \cdot \sigma')\downarrow_\Sigma = \alpha \cdot (\sigma'\downarrow_\Sigma)$ if $\alpha \in \Sigma$ and $\sigma'\downarrow_\Sigma$ otherwise. The projection of any regular language L on an alphabet Σ is defined as: $L\downarrow_\Sigma = \{\sigma\downarrow_\Sigma \mid \sigma \in L\}$. If L is regular, so is $L\downarrow_\Sigma$. Finally, the projection $M\downarrow_\Sigma$ of any FA M on an alphabet Σ is the (unique) minimal DFA accepting the language $\mathcal{L}(M)\downarrow_\Sigma$.

For the purpose of modeling systems with components that need to synchronize, it is convenient to distinguish between *local* and *global* actions. Specifically, local actions belong to the alphabet of a single component, while global actions are shared between multiple components. As defined formally below, components synchronize on global actions, and execute asynchronously on local actions.

Definition 2 (Parallel Composition). *Given two finite automata $M_1 = (S_1, Init_1, \Sigma_1, T_1, F_1)$ and $M_2 = (S_2, Init_2, \Sigma_2, T_2, F_2)$, their parallel composition $M_1 \times M_2$ is the FA $(S_1 \times S_2, Init_1 \times Init_2, \Sigma_1 \cup \Sigma_2, T, F_1 \times F_2)$ such that $\forall s_1, s_1' \in S_1 . \forall s_2, s_2' \in S_2, (s_1, s_2) \xrightarrow{\alpha} (s_1', s_2')$ iff for $i \in \{1, 2\}$ either $\alpha \notin \Sigma_i \wedge s_i = s_i'$ or $s_i \xrightarrow{\alpha} s_i'$.*

Trace Containment. For any FA M_1 and M_2, we write $M_1 \preceq M_2$ to mean $\mathcal{L}(M_1 \times \overline{M_2}) = \emptyset$. A counterexample to $M_1 \preceq M_2$ is a string $\sigma \in \mathcal{L}(M_1 \times \overline{M_2})$.

3   The L* Algorithm

The L* algorithm for learning DFAs was developed by Angluin [2] and later improved by Rivest and Schapire [4]. In essence, L* learns an unknown regular language U, over an alphabet Σ, by generating the minimal DFA that accepts U. In order to learn U, L* requires "Yes/No" answers to two types of queries:

1. *Membership query*: for a string $\sigma \in \Sigma^*$, 'is $\sigma \in U$?'
2. *Candidate query*: for a DFA C, 'is $\mathcal{L}(C) = U$?'

If the answer to a candidate query is "No", L* expects a counterexample string σ such that $\sigma \in U - \mathcal{L}(C)$ or $\sigma \in \mathcal{L}(C) - U$. In the first case, we call σ a *positive* counterexample, because it should be added to $\mathcal{L}(C)$. In the second case, we call σ a *negative counterexample* since it should be removed from $\mathcal{L}(C)$. As mentioned before, L* uses the MAT to obtain answers to these queries.

Observation Table. L* builds an observation table (S, E, T) where: (i) $S \subseteq \Sigma^*$ is the set of rows, (ii) $E \subseteq \Sigma^*$ is the set of columns (or experiments), and (iii) $T : (S \cup S \cdot \Sigma) \times E \to \{0, 1\}$ is a function defined as follows:

$$\forall s \in (S \cup S \cdot \Sigma). \forall e \in E. T(s, e) = \begin{cases} 1 & s \cdot e \in U \\ 0 & \text{otherwise} \end{cases} \quad (2)$$

Consistency and Closure. For any $s_1, s_2 \in (S \cup S \cdot \Sigma)$, s_1 and s_2 are equivalent (denoted as $s_1 \equiv s_2$) if $\forall e \in E. T(s_1, e) = T(s_2, e)$. A table is *consistent* if $\forall s_1, s_2 \in S. s_1 \neq s_2 \Rightarrow s_1 \not\equiv s_2$. L* always maintains a consistent table. In addition, a table is *closed* if $\forall s \in S. \forall \alpha \in \Sigma. \exists s' \in S. s' \equiv s \cdot \alpha$.

Candidate Construction. Given a closed and consistent table (S, E, T), L* constructs a candidate DFA $C = (S, \{\lambda\}, \Sigma, \Delta, F)$ such that: (i) $F = \{s \in S \mid T(s, \lambda) = 1\}$, and (ii) $\Delta = \{(s, \alpha, s') \mid s' \equiv s \cdot \alpha\}$. Note that C is deterministic and complete since (S, E, T) is consistent and closed. Since a row corresponds to a state of C, we use the terms "row" and "candidate state" synonymously.

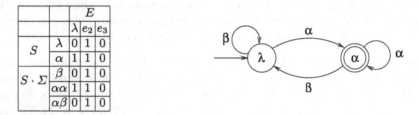

		E		
		λ	e_2	e_3
S	λ	0	1	0
	α	1	1	0
$S \cdot \Sigma$	β	0	1	0
	$\alpha\alpha$	1	1	0
	$\alpha\beta$	0	1	0

Fig. 1. An Observation Table and the Corresponding Candidate DFA

Example 1. Consider Figure 1. On the left is an observation table with the entries being the T values. Let $\Sigma = \{\alpha, \beta\}$. From this table we see that $\{e_2, \alpha, \alpha \cdot e_2, \beta \cdot e_2, \alpha\alpha, \ldots\} \in U$. On the right is the corresponding candidate DFA.   □

L* Step-By-Step. We now describe L* in more detail, using line numbers from its algorithmic description in Figure 2. This conventional version of L* is used currently in the context of automated AG reasoning. We also point out the specific issues that are addressed by the improvements we propose later on in this paper. Recall that λ denotes the empty string. After the initialization at Line 1, the table has one cell corresponding to (λ, λ). In the top-level loop, the table entries are first computed (at Line 2) using membership queries.

Next, L* closes the table by trying to find (at Line 3) for each $s \in S$, some *uncovered* action $\alpha \in \Sigma$ such that $\forall s' \in S. s' \not\equiv s \cdot \alpha$. If such an uncovered action α is found for some $s \in S$, L* adds $s \cdot \alpha$ to S at Line 4 and continues with the closure process. Otherwise, it proceeds to the next Step. Note that each $\alpha \in \Sigma$ is considered when attempting to find an uncovered action.

(1) let $S = E = \{\lambda\}$
     loop {
(2)   Update T using queries
         while (S, E, T) is not closed {
(3)   Find $(s, \alpha) \in S \times \Sigma$ such that $\forall s' \in S. s' \not\equiv s \cdot \alpha$
(4)   Add $s \cdot \alpha$ to S
         }
(5)   Construct candidate DFA C from (S, E, T)
(6)   Make the conjecture C
(7)   if C is correct return C
(8)   else Add $e \in \Sigma^*$ that witnesses the counterexample to E
     }

Fig. 2. The L* algorithm for learning an unknown regular language

Once the table is closed, L* constructs (at Line 5) a candidate DFA C using the procedure described previously. Next, at Line 6, L* conjectures that $\mathcal{L}(C) = U$ via a candidate query. If the conjecture is wrong L* extracts from the counterexample CE (returned by the MAT) a suffix e that, when added to E, causes the table to cease being closed. The process of extracting the feedback e has been presented elsewhere [4] and we do not describe it here. Once e has been obtained, L* adds e to E and iterates the top-level loop by returning to line 2. Note that since the table is no longer closed, the subsequent process of closing it strictly increases the size of S. It can also be shown that the size of S cannot exceed n, where n is number of states of the minimal DFA accepting U. Therefore, the top-level loop of L* executes no more than n times.

Non-uniform Refinement. It is interesting to note that the feedback from CE does not refine the candidate in the abstraction/refinement sense: refinement here does not necessarily add/eliminate a positive/negative CE; this occurs eventually, but not necessarily in one step. Indeed, the first improvement we propose leverages this observation to reduce the number of candidate queries. It is also interesting to note that the refinement does not work in one direction: it may remove strings that are in U or add strings that are not in U. The only guarantee that we have is that in each step at least one state is added to the candidate and that eventually L* learns U itself.

Complexity. Overall, the number of membership queries made by L* is $\mathcal{O}(kn^2 + n \log m)$, where $k = |\Sigma|$ is the size of the alphabet of U, and m is the length of the longest counterexample to a candidate query returned by the MAT [4]. The dominating fragment of this complexity is kn^2 which varies directly with the size of Σ. As noted before, the Σ used in the literature is sufficient, but often unnecessarily large. The third improvement we propose is aimed at reducing the number of membership queries by minimizing the size of Σ.

4   AG Reasoning with L*

In this section, we describe the key ideas behind the automated AG procedure proposed by Cobleigh et al. [1]. We begin with a fact that we use later on.

Fact 1. *For any FA M_1 and M_2 with alphabets Σ_1 and Σ_2, $\mathcal{L}(M_1 \times M_2) \neq \emptyset$ iff $\exists \sigma \in \mathcal{L}(M_1) . \sigma \!\downarrow_{(\Sigma_1 \cap \Sigma_2)} \in \mathcal{L}(M_2) \!\downarrow_{(\Sigma_1 \cap \Sigma_2)}$.*

Let us now restate AG-NC to reflect our implementation more accurately:

$$\frac{\begin{array}{c} A \times (M_1 \times \bar{\varphi}) \preceq \bot \\ M_2 \preceq A \end{array}}{(M_1 \times \bar{\varphi}) \times M_2 \preceq \bot} \tag{3}$$

where $\bot$ denotes a DFA accepting the empty language. The unknown language to be learned is

$$U = \mathcal{L}(\overline{(M_1 \times \bar{\varphi}) \!\downarrow_\Sigma}) \tag{4}$$

over the alphabet $\Sigma = (\Sigma_1 \cup \Sigma_\varphi) \cap \Sigma_2$ where Σ_1, Σ_2 and Σ_φ are the alphabets of M_1, M_2 and φ respectively[2]. The choice of U and Σ is significant because, by Fact 1, the consequence of Eq. 3 does not hold iff the intersection between $\overline{U} = \mathcal{L}((M_1 \times \bar{\varphi}) \!\downarrow_\Sigma)$ and $\mathcal{L}(M_2 \!\downarrow_\Sigma)$ is non-empty. This situation is depicted in Fig. 3(a). Hence, if A is the DFA computed by L* such that $\mathcal{L}(A) = U$, any counterexample to the second premise $M_2 \preceq A$ is guaranteed to be a real one. However, in practice, the process terminates after learning U itself only in the worst case. As we shall see, it usually terminates earlier by finding either a counterexample to $M_1 \times M_2 \preceq \varphi$, or an assumption A that satisfies the two premises of Eq. 3. This later case is depicted in Fig. 3(b).

MAT Implementation. The answer to a membership query with a string σ is "Yes" iff σ cannot be simulated on $M_1 \times \bar{\varphi}$ (see Eq. 4). A candidate query with some candidate A, on the other hand, is more complicated, and is described step-wise as follows (for brevity, we omit a diagram and refer the reader to the non-dashed portion of Figure 4):

Step 1. Use model checking to verify that A satisfies the first premise of Eq. 3. If the verification of the first premise fails, obtain a counterexample trace $\pi \in \mathcal{L}(A \times M_1 \times \bar{\varphi})$ and proceed to Step 2. Otherwise, go to Step 3.

---

[2] Note that we do not compute U directly because complementing M_1, a non-deterministic automaton, is typically intractable.

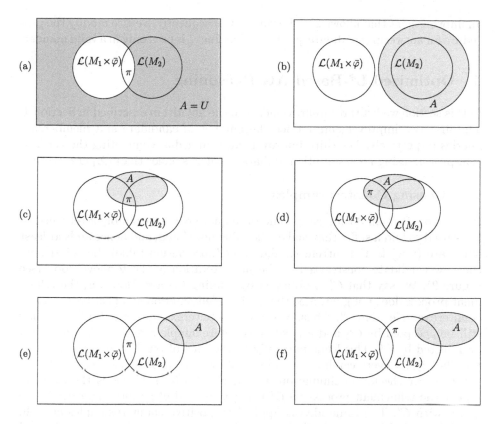

Fig. 3. Different L* scenarios. The gray area represents the candidate assumption A.

Step 2. Denote $\pi\!\downarrow_\Sigma$ by π'. Check via simulation if $\pi' \in \mathcal{L}(M_2\!\downarrow_\Sigma)$. If so, then by Fact 1, $\mathcal{L}(M_1 \times \bar{\varphi} \times M_2) \neq \emptyset$ (i.e., $M_1 \times M_2 \not\preceq \varphi$) and the algorithm terminates. This situation is depicted in Fig. 3(c). Otherwise $\pi' \in \mathcal{L}(A) - U$ is a negative counterexample, as depicted in Fig. 3(d). Control is returned to L* with π'.

Step 3. At this point A is known to satisfy the first premise. Proceed to model check the second premise. If $M_2 \preceq A$ holds as well, then by Eq. 3 conclude that $M_1 \times M_2 \preceq \varphi$ and terminate. This possibility was already shown in Fig. 3(b). Otherwise obtain a counterexample $\pi \in \mathcal{L}(M_2 \times \overline{A})$ and proceed to Step 4.

Step 4. Once again denote $\pi\!\downarrow_\Sigma$ by π'. Check if $\pi' \in \mathcal{L}((M_1 \times \bar{\varphi})\!\downarrow_\Sigma)$. If so, then by Fact 1, $\mathcal{L}(M_1 \times \bar{\varphi} \times M_2) \neq \emptyset$ (i.e., $M_1 \times M_2 \not\preceq \varphi$) and the algorithm terminates. This scenario is depicted in Fig. 3(e). Otherwise $\pi' \in U - \mathcal{L}(A)$ is a positive counterexample, as depicted in Fig. 3(f) and we return to L* with π'.

Note that Steps 2 and 4 above are duals obtained by interchanging $M_1 \times \bar{\varphi}$ with M_2 and U with $\mathcal{L}(A)$. Also, note that Fact 1 could be applied in Steps 2 and 4 above only because $\Sigma = (\Sigma_1 \cup \Sigma_\varphi) \cap \Sigma_2$. In the next section, we propose an improvement that allows Σ to be varied. Consequently, we also modify the procedure for answering candidate queries so that Fact 1 is used only in a valid manner.

5   Optimized L*-Based AG Reasoning

In this section we list three improvements to the algorithm described in Section 4. The first two improvements reduce the number of candidate and membership queries respectively. The third improvement is aimed at completing the verification process using an assumption alphabet that is smaller than $(\Sigma_1 \cup \Sigma_\varphi) \cap \Sigma_2$.

5.1   Reusing Counterexamples

Recall from Section 3 that every candidate query counterexample π returned to L* is used to find a suffix that makes the table not closed, and hence adds at least one state (row) to the current candidate C (observation table). Let C' denote the new candidate constructed in the next iteration of the top-level loop (see Figure 2). We say that C' is obtained by refining C on π. However, the refinement process does not guarantee the addition/elimination of a positive/negative counterexample from C'. Thus, a negative counterexample $\pi \in L(C) - U$ may still be accepted by C', and a positive counterexample $\pi \in U - L(C)$ may still be rejected by C'. This leads naturally to the idea of reusing counterexamples. Specifically, for every candidate C' obtained by refining on a negative counterexample π, we check, via simulation, whether $\pi \in \mathcal{L}(C')$. If this is the case, we repeat the refinement process on C' using π instead of performing a candidate query with C'. The same idea is applied to positive counterexamples as well. Thus, if we find that $\pi \notin \mathcal{L}(C')$ for a positive counterexample π, then π is used to further refine C'. This optimization reduces the number of candidate queries.

5.2   Selective Membership Queries

Recall the operation of closing the table (see Lines 3 and 4 of Figure 2) in L*. For every row s added to S, L* must compute T for every possible extension of s by a single action. Thus L* must decide if $s \cdot \alpha \cdot e \in U$ for each $\alpha \in \Sigma$ and $e \in E$ — a total of $|\Sigma| \cdot |E|$ membership queries. To see how a membership query is answered, for any $\sigma \in \Sigma^*$, let $Sim(\sigma)$ be the set of states of $M_1 \times \bar{\varphi}$ reached by simulating σ from an initial state of $M_1 \times \bar{\varphi}$ and by treating actions not in Σ as ϵ (i.e., ϵ-transitions are allowed where the actions are local to $M_1 \times \bar{\varphi}$). Then, $\sigma \in U$ iff $Sim(\sigma)$ does not contain an accepting state of $M_1 \times \bar{\varphi}$.

Let us return to the problem of deciding if $s \cdot \alpha \cdot e \in U$. Let $En(s) = \{\alpha' \in \Sigma \mid \delta(\alpha', Sim(s)) \neq \emptyset\}$ be the set of enabled actions from $Sim(s)$ in $M_1 \times \bar{\varphi}$. Now, for any $\alpha \notin En(s)$, $Sim(s \cdot \alpha \cdot e) = \emptyset$ and hence $s \cdot \alpha \cdot e$ is guaranteed to belong to U. This observation leads to our second improvement. Specifically, for every s added to S, we first compute $En(s)$. Note that $En(s)$ is computed by simulating $s|_{\Sigma_1}$ on M_1 and $s|_{\Sigma_\varphi}$ on φ separately, without composing M_1 and φ. We then make membership queries with $s \cdot \alpha \cdot e$, but only for $\alpha \in En(s)$. For all $\alpha \notin En(s)$ we directly set $T(s \cdot \alpha, e) = 1$ since we know that in this case

$s \cdot \alpha \cdot e \in U$. The motivation behind this optimization is that $En(s)$ is usually much smaller that Σ for any s. The actual improvement in performance due to this tactic depends on the relative sizes of $En(s)$ and Σ for the different $s \in S$.

5.3   Minimizing the Assumption Alphabet

As mentioned before, existing automated AG procedures use a constant assumption alphabet $\Sigma = (\Sigma_1 \cup \Sigma_\varphi) \cap \Sigma_2$. There may exist, however, an assumption A over a smaller alphabet $\Sigma_c \subset \Sigma$ that satisfies the two premises of Eq. 3. Since Eq. 3 is sound, the existence of such an A would still imply that $M_1 \times M_2 \preceq \varphi$. However, recall that the number of L* membership queries varies directly with the alphabet size. Therefore, the benefit, in the context of learning A, is that a smaller alphabet leads to fewer membership queries.

In this section, we propose an abstraction-refinement scheme for building an assumption over a minimal alphabet. During our experiments, this improvement led to a 6 times reduction in the size of the assumption alphabet. The main problem with changing Σ is of course that AG-NC is no longer complete. Specifically, if $\Sigma_C \subset \Sigma$, then there might not exist any assumption A over Σ_C that satisfies the two premises of AG-NC even though the conclusion of AG-NC holds. The following theorem characterizes this phenomenon precisely.

Theorem 1 (Incompleteness of AG-NC). *Suppose there exists a string π and an alphabet Σ_C such that:* (INC) $\pi{\downarrow}_{\Sigma_C} \in \mathcal{L}((M_1 \times \bar\varphi){\downarrow}_{\Sigma_C})$ *and* $\pi{\downarrow}_{\Sigma_C} \in \mathcal{L}(M_2{\downarrow}_{\Sigma_C})$. *Then no assumption A over Σ_C satisfies the two premises of AG-NC.*

Proof. Suppose there exists a π satisfying INC and an A over Σ_C satisfying the two premises of AG-NC. This leads to a contradiction as follows:

- *Case 1*: $\pi{\downarrow}_{\Sigma_C} \in \mathcal{L}(A)$. Since A satisfies the first premise of AG-NC, we have $\pi{\downarrow}_{\Sigma_C} \notin \mathcal{L}((M_1 \times \bar\varphi){\downarrow}_{\Sigma_C})$, a contradiction with INC.
- *Case 2*: $\pi{\downarrow}_{\Sigma_C} \notin \mathcal{L}(A)$. Hence $\pi{\downarrow}_{\Sigma_C} \in \mathcal{L}(\overline{A})$. Since A satisfies the second premise of AG-NC, we have $\pi{\downarrow}_{\Sigma_C} \notin \mathcal{L}(M_2{\downarrow}_{\Sigma_C})$, again contradicting INC.   □

We say that an alphabet Σ_C is incomplete if $\Sigma_C \neq \Sigma$ and there exists a trace π satisfying condition INC above. Therefore, whenever we come across a trace π that satisfies INC, unless $\Sigma_C = \Sigma$, we know that the current Σ_C is incomplete and must be refined. We now describe our overall procedure which incorporates testing Σ_C for incompleteness and refining an incomplete Σ_C appropriately.

Detecting Incompleteness. Our optimized automated AG procedure is depicted in Fig. 4. Initially $\Sigma_c = \emptyset^3$. Let us write π' and π'' to mean $\pi{\downarrow}_{\Sigma_C}$ and $\pi{\downarrow}_\Sigma$ respectively. The process continues as in Section 4, until one of the following two scenarios occur while answering a candidate query:

- *Scenario 1*: We reach Step 2 with a trace $\pi \in \mathcal{L}(A \times M_1 \times \bar\varphi)$. Note that this implies $\pi' \in \mathcal{L}((M_1 \times \bar\varphi){\downarrow}_{\Sigma_C})$. Now we first check if $\pi' \in \mathcal{L}(M_2{\downarrow}_{\Sigma_C})$. If not,

---

[3] We could also start with $\Sigma_c = \Sigma_\varphi$ since it is very unlikely that φ can be proven or disproven without controlling the actions that define it.

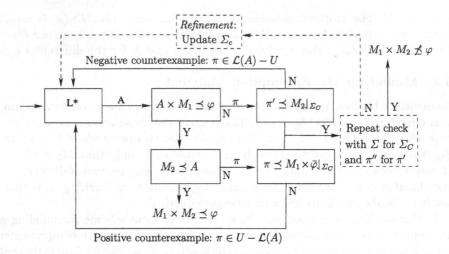

Fig. 4. Generalized AG with L*, with an abstraction-refinement loop (added with dashed lines) based on the assumption alphabet $\Sigma_c \subseteq \Sigma$. Strings π' and π'' denote $\pi{\downarrow}_{\Sigma_C}$ and $\pi{\downarrow}_{\Sigma}$ respectively.

we return π' as a negative counterexample to L* exactly as in Section 4. However, if $\pi' \in \mathcal{L}(M_2{\downarrow}_{\Sigma_C})$, then π satisfies the condition INC of Theorem 1, and hence Σ_C is incomplete. Instead of refining Σ_C at this point, we first check if $\pi'' \in \mathcal{L}(M_2{\downarrow}_{\Sigma})$. If so, then as in Section 4, by a valid application of Fact 1, $M_1 \times M_2 \npreceq \varphi$ and the algorithm terminates. Otherwise, if $\pi'' \notin \mathcal{L}(M_2{\downarrow}_{\Sigma})$, we refine Σ_C.

– *Scenario 2:* We reach Step 4 with $\pi \in \mathcal{L}(M_2 \times \overline{A})$. Note that this implies $\pi' \in \mathcal{L}(M_2{\downarrow}_{\Sigma_C})$. We first check if $\pi' \in \mathcal{L}((M_1 \times \bar\varphi){\downarrow}_{\Sigma_C})$. If not, we return π' as a positive counterexample to L* exactly as in Section 4. However, if $\pi' \in \mathcal{L}((M_1 \times \bar\varphi){\downarrow}_{\Sigma_C})$, then π satisfies INC, and hence by Theorem 1, Σ_C is incomplete. Instead of refining Σ_C at this point, we first check if $\pi'' \in \mathcal{L}((M_1 \times \bar\varphi){\downarrow}_{\Sigma})$. If so, then as in Section 4, by a valid application of Fact 1, $M_1 \times M_2 \npreceq \varphi$ and we terminate. Otherwise, if $\pi'' \notin \mathcal{L}((M_1 \times \bar\varphi){\downarrow}_{\Sigma})$, we refine Σ_C.

Note that the checks involving π'' in the two scenarios above correspond to the concretization attempts in a standard CEGAR loop. Also, Scenarios 1 and 2 are duals (as in the case of Steps 2 and 4 in Section 4) obtained by interchanging $M_1 \times \bar\varphi$ with M_2 and U with $\mathcal{L}(A)$. In essence, while solving a candidate query, an incomplete Σ_C results in a trace (specifically, π above) that satisfies INC and leads neither to an actual counterexample of $M_1 \times M_2 \preceq \varphi$, nor to a counterexample to the candidate query being solved. In accordance with the CEGAR terminology, we refer to such traces as *spurious* counterexamples and use them collectively to refine Σ_C as described next. In the rest of this section, all counterexamples we mention are spurious unless otherwise specified.

Refining the Assumption Alphabet. A counterexample arising from Scenario 1 above is said to be negative. Otherwise, it arises from Scenario 2 and is said to be positive. Our description that follows unifies the treatment of these two types of counterexamples, with the help of a common notation for $M_1 \times \bar{\varphi}$ and M_2. Specifically, let

$$M^{(\pi)} = \begin{cases} M_1 \times \bar{\varphi} & \pi \text{ is positive} \\ M_2 & \pi \text{ is negative} \end{cases}$$

We say that an alphabet Σ' eliminates a counterexample π, and denote this with $Elim(\pi, \Sigma')$, if $\pi{\downarrow}_{\Sigma'} \notin \mathcal{L}(M^{(\pi)}{\downarrow}_{\Sigma'})$. Therefore, any counterexample π is eliminated if we choose Σ_C such that $Elim(\pi, \Sigma_C)$ holds since π no longer satisfies the condition INC. Our goal, however, is to find a minimal alphabet Σ_C with this property. It turns out that finding such an alphabet is computationally hard.

Theorem 2. *Finding a minimal eliminating alphabet is NP-hard in $|\Sigma|$.*

Proof. The proof relies on a reduction from the minimal hitting set problem.

Minimal Hitting Set. A Minimal Hitting Set (MHS) problem is a pair (U, T) where U is a finite set and $T \subseteq 2^U$ is a finite set of subsets of U. A solution to (U, T) is a minimal $X \subseteq U$ such that $\forall T' \in T. X \cap T' \neq \emptyset$. It is well-known that MHS is NP-complete in $|U|$.

Now we reduce MHS to finding a minimal eliminating alphabet. Let (U, T) be any MHS problem and let $<$ be a strict order imposed on the elements of U. Consider the following problem $\mathcal{P}$ of finding a minimal eliminating alphabet. First, let $\Sigma = U$. Next, for each $T' \in T$ we introduce a counterexample $\pi(T')$ obtained by arranging the elements of U according to $<$, repeating each element of T' twice and the remaining elements of U just once. For example suppose $U = \{a, b, c, d, e\}$ such that $a < b < c < d < e$. Then for $T' = \{b, d, e\}$ we introduce the counterexample $\pi(T') = a \cdot b \cdot b \cdot c \cdot d \cdot d \cdot e \cdot e$. Also, for each counterexample $\pi(T')$ introduced, let $M(\pi(T'))$ accept a single string obtained by arranging the elements of U according to $<$, repeating each element of U just once. Thus, for the example U above, $M(\pi(T'))$ accepts the single string $a \cdot b \cdot c \cdot d \cdot e$.

Let us first show the following result: for any $T' \in T$ and any $X \subseteq U$, $X \cap T' \neq \emptyset$ iff $Elim(\pi(T'), X)$. In other words, $X \cap T' \neq \emptyset$ iff $\pi(T'){\downarrow}_X \notin \mathcal{L}(M(\pi(T')){\downarrow}_X)$. Indeed suppose that some $\alpha \in X \cap T'$. Then $\pi(T'){\downarrow}_X$ contains two consecutive occurrences of α and hence cannot be accepted by $M(\pi(T')){\downarrow}_X$. By the converse implication, if $M(\pi(T')){\downarrow}_X$ does not accept $\pi(T'){\downarrow}_X$, then $\pi(T'){\downarrow}_X$ must contain two consecutive occurrences of some action α. But then $\alpha \in X \cap T'$ and hence $X \cap T' \neq \emptyset$. The above result implies immediately that any solution to the MHS problem (U, T) is also a minimal eliminating alphabet for $\mathcal{P}$. Also, the reduction from (U, T) to $\mathcal{P}$ described above can be performed using logarithmic space in $|U| + |T|$. Finally, $|\Sigma| = |U|$, which completes our proof. $\qquad\square$

As we just proved, finding the minimal eliminating alphabet is NP-hard in $|\Sigma|$. Yet, since $|\Sigma|$ is relatively small, this problem can still be feasible in practice (as

our experiments have shown: see Section 6). We propose a solution based on a
reduction to Pseudo-Boolean constraints. Pseudo-Boolean constraints have the
same modeling power as 0-1 ILP, but solvers for this logic are typically based on
adapting SAT engines for linear constraints over Boolean variables, and geared
towards problems with relatively few linear constraints (and a linear objective
function) and constraints in CNF.

Optimal Refinement. Let Π be the set of all (positive and negative) counterexamples seen so far. We wish to find a minimal Σ_C such that: $\forall \pi \in \Pi.Elim(\pi, \Sigma_C)$.
To this end, we formulate and solve a Pseudo-Boolean constraint problem with
an objective function stating that we seek a solution which minimizes the cho-
sen set of actions. The set of constraints of the problem is $\Phi = \bigcup_{\pi \in \Pi} \Phi(\pi)$. In
essence, if $M^{[\pi]}$ is the minimal DFA accepting $\{\pi\}$, then $\Phi(\pi)$ represents symbolically the states reachable in $M^{[\pi]} \times M^{(\pi)}$, taking into account all possible
values of Σ_C. Henceforth, we continue to use square brackets when referring to
elements of $M^{[\pi]}$, and regular parenthesis when referring to elements of $M^{(\pi)}$.

We now define $\Phi(\pi)$ formally. Let $M^{[\pi]} = (S^{[\pi]}, Init^{[\pi]}, \Sigma^{[\pi]}, T^{[\pi]}, F^{[\pi]})$ and
$M^{(\pi)} = (S^{(\pi)}, Init^{(\pi)}, \Sigma^{(\pi)}, T^{(\pi)}, F^{(\pi)})$. Let $\delta^{[\pi]}$ and $\delta^{(\pi)}$ be the δ functions of
$M^{[\pi]}$ and $M^{(\pi)}$ respectively. We define a state variable of the form (s, t) for
each $s \in S^{[\pi]}$ and $t \in S^{(\pi)}$. Intuitively, the variable (s, t) indicates whether the
product state (s, t) is reachable in $M^{[\pi]} \times M^{(\pi)}$. We also define a choice variable
$s(\alpha)$ for each action $\alpha \in \Sigma$, indicating whether α is selected to be included in
Σ_C. Now, $\Phi(\pi)$ consists of the following clauses:

Initialization and Acceptance: Every initial and no accepting state is reachable:

$$\forall s \in Init^{[\pi]}.\forall t \in Init^{(\pi)}.(s, t) \qquad \forall s \in F^{[\pi]}.\forall t \in F^{(\pi)}.\neg(s, t)$$

Shared Actions: Successors depend on whether an action is selected or not:

$$\forall \alpha \in \Sigma.\forall s \in S^{[\pi]}.\forall s' \in \delta^{[\pi]}(\alpha, s).\forall t \in S^{(\pi)}.\forall t' \in \delta^{(\pi)}(\alpha, t).(s, t) \Rightarrow (s', t')$$
$$\forall \alpha \in \Sigma.\forall s \in S^{[\pi]}.\forall s' \in \delta^{[\pi]}(\alpha, s).\forall t \in S^{(\pi)}.\neg s(\alpha) \wedge (s, t) \Rightarrow (s', t)$$
$$\forall \alpha \in \Sigma.\forall s \in S^{[\pi]}.\forall t \in S^{(\pi)}.\forall t' \in \delta^{(\pi)}(\alpha, t).\neg s(\alpha) \wedge (s, t) \Rightarrow (s, t')$$

Local Actions: Asynchronous interleaving:

$$\forall \alpha \in \Sigma^{[\pi]} - \Sigma.\forall s \in S^{[\pi]}.\forall s' \in \delta^{[\pi]}(\alpha, s).\forall t \in S^{(\pi)}.(s, t) \Rightarrow (s', t)$$
$$\forall \alpha \in \Sigma^{(\pi)} - \Sigma.\forall s \in S^{[\pi]}.\forall t \in S^{(\pi)}.\forall t' \in \delta^{(\pi)}(\alpha, t).(s, t) \Rightarrow (s, t')$$

As mentioned before, the global set of constraints Φ is obtained by collecting
together the constraints in each $\Phi(\pi)$. Observe that any solution ν to Φ has
the following property. Let $\Sigma_C = \{\alpha \mid \nu(s(\alpha)) = 1\}$. Then we have $\forall \pi \in
\Pi.\mathcal{L}((M^{[\pi]}\!\downarrow_{\Sigma_C}) \times (M^{(\pi)}\!\downarrow_{\Sigma_C})) = \emptyset$. But since $\mathcal{L}(M^{[\pi]}) = \{\pi\}$, the above statement
is equivalent to $\forall \pi \in \Pi.(\pi\!\downarrow_{\Sigma_C}) \notin \mathcal{L}(M^{(\pi)}\!\downarrow_{\Sigma_C})$, which is further equivalent to
$\forall \pi \in \Pi.Elim(\pi, \Sigma_C)$. Thus, Σ_C eliminates all counterexamples. Finally, since
we want the minimal such Σ_C, we minimize the number of chosen actions via
the following objective function: $\min \sum_{\alpha \in \Sigma} s(\alpha)$.

$$\pi \quad \longrightarrow (s_0) \xrightarrow{\alpha} (s_1) \xrightarrow{\beta} (s_2)$$

$$M_1 \times \bar{\varphi} \quad \longrightarrow (t_0) \xrightarrow{\beta} (t_1) \xrightarrow{\alpha} (t_2)$$

Fig. 5. A positive counterexample π and $M^{(\pi)} = M_1 \times \bar{\varphi}$

Example 2. Consider Fig. 5, in which there is one counterexample π, and an FA $M^{(\pi)} = M_1 \times \bar{\varphi}$ on which π can be simulated if $\Sigma_c = \emptyset$. The state variables are (s_i, t_j) for $i, j \in [0..2]$ and the choice variables are $s(\alpha), s(\beta)$. The constraints are:

$$
\begin{array}{ll}
Initialization: & (s_0, t_0) \\
SharedActions: & (s_0, t_1) \rightarrow (s_1, t_2) \\
& (s_0, t_0) \wedge \neg s(\alpha) \rightarrow (s_1, t_0) \\
& (s_0, t_1) \wedge \neg s(\alpha) \rightarrow (s_1, t_1) \\
& (s_0, t_2) \wedge \neg s(\alpha) \rightarrow (s_1, t_2) \\
& (s_0, t_0) \wedge \neg s(\beta) \rightarrow (s_0, t_1) \\
& (s_1, t_0) \wedge \neg s(\beta) \rightarrow (s_1, t_1) \\
& (s_2, t_0) \wedge \neg s(\beta) \rightarrow (s_2, t_1)
\end{array}
\qquad
\begin{array}{l}
Acceptance: \neg(s_2, t_2) \\
(s_1, t_0) \rightarrow (s_2, t_1) \\
(s_1, t_0) \wedge \neg s(\beta) \rightarrow (s_2, t_0) \\
(s_1, t_1) \wedge \neg s(\beta) \rightarrow (s_2, t_1) \\
(s_1, t_2) \wedge \neg s(\beta) \rightarrow (s_2, t_2) \\
(s_0, t_1) \wedge \neg s(\alpha) \rightarrow (s_0, t_2) \\
(s_1, t_1) \wedge \neg s(\alpha) \rightarrow (s_1, t_2) \\
(s_2, t_1) \wedge \neg s(\alpha) \rightarrow (s_2, t_2)
\end{array}
$$

Since there are no local actions, these are all the constraints. The objective is to minimize $s(\alpha) + s(\beta)$. The optimal solution is $s(\alpha) - s(\beta) - 1$, corresponding to the fact that both actions need to be in Σ_C in order to eliminate π. $\quad\square$

6 Experiments

We implemented our technique in COMFORT and experimented with a set of benchmarks derived from real-life source code. All our experiments were carried out on quad 2.4 GHz machine with 4 GB RAM running RedHat Linux 9. We used PBS version 2.1[4] to solve the Pseudo-Boolean constraints. The benchmarks were derived from the source code of OpenSSL version 0.9.6c. Specifically, we used the code that implements the handshake between a client and a server at the beginning of an SSL session. We designed a suite of 10 examples, each aiming a specific property (involving a sequence of message-passing events) that a correct handshake should exhibit. For instance, the first example (SSL-1) was aimed at verifying that a handshake is always initiated by a client and never by a server.

The experiments were aimed at evaluating our proposed improvements separately, and in conjunction with each other in the context of AG-NC. The results are described in Figure 6. The columns labeled MemQ and CandQ contain the total number of membership and candidate queries respectively. The columns labeled with T_i and $\neg T_i$ contain results with/without the ith improvement for

---

[4] http://www.eecs.umich.edu/~faloul/Tools/pbs

Name	CandQ		MemQ		Alph		Time $\neg T_1$				Time T_1			
							$\neg T_2$		T_2		$\neg T_2$		T_2	
	$\neg T_1$	T_1	$\neg T_2$	T_2	$\neg T_3$	T_3	$\neg T_3$	T_3	$\neg T_3$	T_3	$\neg T_3$	T_3	$\neg T_3$	T_3
SSL-1	2.2	**2.0**	37.5	**4.5**	12	1	25.4	19.7	**12.3**	20.0	23.8	20.1	**10.5**	20.5
SSL-2	**5.0**	5.2	101.5	**11.5**	12	4	31.5	40.0	**12.6**	30.0	32.4	44.6	13.7	30.2
SSL-3	8.5	**7.5**	163.0	**28.0**	12	4	43.8	49.1	**14.5**	35.3	45.6	48.9	15.6	35.5
SSL-4	13.0	**10.5**	248.0	**56.5**	12	4	63.0	67.5	**17.4**	58.1	61.5	67.7	18.6	48.4
SSL-5	3.2	**3.0**	73.0	**9.5**	12	1	33.8	22.3	**13.6**	24.1	36.2	22.2	13.8	22.2
SSL-6	**6.8**	7.2	252.0	**36.5**	12	2	102.8	30.6	24.2	29.0	102.2	43.3	**23.1**	29.8
SSL-7	9.8	**8.0**	328.8	**52.5**	12	2	139.9	44.4	**27.8**	43.9	138.2	38.6	28.2	40.6
SSL-8	15.0	**13.0**	443.0	**77.5**	12	3	183.3	73.6	37.1	67.9	184.0	73.2	**35.8**	64.2
SSL-9	23.5	**18.2**	568.0	**109.5**	12	3	234.1	120.5	44.1	133.7	236.2	133.4	**41.0**	109.3
SSL-10	25.5	**22.0**	689.5	**128.5**	12	3	293.9	188.6	48.4	168.1	297.0	179.9	**45.9**	169.7
Avg.	10.8	**9.2**	290.0	**51.0**	12	2	115.1	65.6	25.2	61.0	115.7	67.2	**24.6**	57.1

Fig. 6. Experimental Results for Non-Circular Rule AG-NC

$i \in \{1, 2, 3\}$. The row labeled "Avg." contains the arithmetic mean for the rest of the column. Best figures are highlighted. Note that entries under MemQ and CandQ are fractional since they represent the average over the four possible values of the remaining two improvements. Specifically, these are improvements 2 and 3 for CandQ, and improvements 1 and 3 for MemQ.

We observe that the improvements lead to the expected results in terms of reducing the number of queries and the size of assumption alphabets. The second and third improvements also lead to significant reductions in overall verification time, by a factor of over 12 on an average. Finally, even though the first improvement entails fewer candidate queries, it is practically ineffective for reducing overall verification time.

References

1. Cobleigh, J.M., Giannakopoulou, D., Păsăreanu, C.S.: Learning assumptions for compositional verification. In: Proc. of TACAS. (2003)
2. Angluin, D.: Learning Regular Sets from Queries and Counterexamples. Information and Computation (2) (1987)
3. Chaki, S., Ivers, J., Sharygina, N., Wallnau, K.: The ComFoRT Reasoning Framework. In: Proc. of CAV. (2005)
4. Rivest, R.L., Schapire, R.E.: Inference of Finite Automata Using Homing Sequences. Information and Computation (2) (1993)
5. Peled, D., Vardi, M., Yannakakis, M.: Black box checking. In: Proc. of FORTE. (1999)
6. Groce, A., Peled, D., Yannakakis, M.: Adaptive Model Checking. In: Proc. of TACAS. (2002)
7. Alur, R., Cerny, P., Gupta, G., Madhusudan, P., Nam, W., Srivastava, A.: Synthesis of Interface Specifications for Java Classes. In: POPL. (2005)
8. Habermehl, P., Vojnar, T.: Regular model checking using inference of regular languages. In: Proc. of INFINITY. (2005)

9. Ernst, M., Cockrell, J., Griswold, W., Notkin, D.: Dynamically Discovering Likely Program Invariants to Support Program Evolution. In: Proc. of ICSE. (1999)

10. Alur, R., Madhusudan, P., Nam, W.: Symbolic compositional verification by learning assumptions. In: Proc. of CAV. (2005)

11. Chaki, S., Clarke, E., Sinha, N., Thati, P.: Automated Assume-Guarantee Reasoning for Simulation Conformance. In: Proc. of CAV. (2005)

12. Chaki, S., Sinha, N.: Assume-guarantee reasoning for deadlock. In: Proc. of FM-CAD. (2006)

13. Giannakopoulou, D., Păsăreanu, C., Barringer, H.: Assumption Generation for Software Component Verification. In: Proc. of ASE. (2002)

14. Pnueli, A.: In Transition from Global to Modular Temporal Reasoning About Programs. Logics and Models of Concurrent Systems (1985)

15. Kurshan, R.: Computer-Aided Verification of Coordinating Processes: The Automata-Theoretic Approach. Princeton University Press (1994)

16. Clarke, E., Grumberg, O., Jha, S., Lu, Y., Veith, H.: Counterexample-Guided Abstraction Refinement for Symbolic Model Checking. Journal of the ACM (JACM) (5) (2003)

17. Ball, T., Rajamani, S.: Generating Abstract Explanations of Spurious Counterexamples in C Programs. Technical Report MSR-TR-2002-09, Microsoft (2002)

18. Gheorghiu, M., Giannakopoulou, D., Păsăreanu, C.: Refining Interface Alphabets for Compositional Verification. In: Proc. of TACAS. (2007)

Refining Interface Alphabets for Compositional Verification

Mihaela Gheorghiu[1], Dimitra Giannakopoulou[2], and Corina S. Păsăreanu[2]

[1] Department of Computer Science, University of Toronto,
Toronto, ON M5S 3G4, Canada
mg@cs.toronto.edu
[2] RIACS and QSS, NASA Ames Research Center,
Moffett Field, CA 94035, USA
{dimitra,pcorina}@email.arc.nasa.gov

Abstract. Techniques for learning automata have been adapted to automatically infer assumptions in assume-guarantee compositional verification. Learning, in this context, produces assumptions and modifies them using counterexamples obtained by model checking components separately. In this process, the interface alphabets between components, that constitute the alphabets of the assumption automata, are fixed: they include *all* actions through which the components communicate. This paper introduces *alphabet refinement*, a novel technique that extends the assumption learning process to also infer interface alphabets. The technique starts with only a *subset* of the interface alphabet and adds actions to it as necessary until a given property is shown to hold or to be violated in the system. Actions to be added are discovered by counterexample analysis. We show experimentally that alphabet refinement improves the current learning algorithms and makes compositional verification by learning assumptions more scalable than non-compositional verification.

1 Introduction

Model checking is an effective technique for finding subtle errors in concurrent software. Given a finite model of a system and of a required property, model checking determines automatically whether the property is satisfied by the system. The limitation of this approach, known as the "state-explosion" problem [9], is that it needs to explore all the system states, which may be intractable for realistic systems.

Compositional verification addresses state explosion by a "divide and conquer" approach: properties of the system are decomposed into properties of its components and each component is then checked separately. In checking components individually, one needs to incorporate some knowledge of the contexts in which the components are expected to operate correctly. Assume-guarantee reasoning [18,23] addresses this issue by introducing assumptions that capture the expectations of a component from its environment. Assumptions have traditionally been defined manually, which has limited the practical impact of assume-guarantee reasoning.

Recent work [12,5] has proposed a framework based on learning that *fully automates* assume-guarantee model checking of safety properties. Since then, several similar frameworks have been presented [3,21,25]. To check that a system consisting of

O. Grumberg and M. Huth (Eds.): TACAS 2007, LNCS 4424, pp. 292–307, 2007.

components M_1 and M_2 satisfies a safety property P, the framework automatically guesses and refines assumptions for one of the components to satisfy P, which it then tries to discharge on the other component. The approach is guaranteed to terminate, stating that the property holds for the system, or returning a counterexample if the property is violated.

Compositional techniques have been shown particularly effective for well-structured systems that have small interfaces between components [7,15]. Interfaces consist of *all* communication points through which the components may influence each other's behavior. In the learning framework of [12] the alphabet of the assumption automata being built includes *all* the actions in the component interface. However, in a case study presented in [22], we observed that a smaller alphabet was sufficient to prove the property. This smaller alphabet was determined through manual inspection and with it, assume-guarantee reasoning achieves orders of magnitude improvement over monolithic (*i.e.*, non-compositional) model checking [22].

Motivated by the successful use of a smaller assumption alphabet in learning, we investigate here whether we can automate the process of discovering a smaller alphabet that is sufficient for checking the desired properties. Smaller alphabet means smaller interface between components, which may lead to smaller assumptions, and hence to smaller verification problems. We propose a novel technique called *alphabet refinement* that extends the learning framework to start with a small subset of the interface alphabet and to add actions into it as necessary until a required property is shown to hold or to be violated in the system. Actions to be added are discovered by analysis of the counterexamples obtained from model checking the components. We study the properties of alphabet refinement and show experimentally that it leads to time and memory savings as compared to the original learning framework [12] and monolithic model checking. The algorithm has been implemented within the LTSA model checking tool [20].

The algorithm is applicable to and may benefit any of the previous learning-based approaches [3,21,25]; it may also benefit other compositional analysis techniques. Compositional Reachability Analysis (CRA), for example, computes abstractions of component behaviors based on their interfaces. In the context of property checking [7,19], smaller interfaces may result in more compact abstractions, leading to smaller state spaces when components are put together.

The rest of the paper is organized as follows. Sec. 3 presents a motivating example. Sec. 4 summarizes the original learning framework from [12]. Sec. 5 presents the main algorithm for interface alphabet refinement. Sec. 6 discusses properties and Sec. 7 provides an experimental evaluation of the proposed algorithm. Sec. 8 surveys some related work and Sec. 9 concludes the paper. In the next section we review the main ingredients of the LTSA tool and the L* learning algorithm.

2 Background

Labeled Transition Systems (LTSs). LTSA is an explicit-state model checker that analyzes finite-state systems modeled as *labeled transition systems* (LTSs). Let $\mathcal{A}$ be the universal set of observable actions and let τ denote a special action that is unobservable.

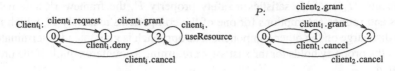

Fig. 1. Example LTS for a client (left) and a mutual exclusion property (right)

An LTS M is a tuple $\langle Q, \alpha M, \delta, q_0 \rangle$, where: Q is a finite non-empty set of states; $\alpha M \subseteq \mathcal{A}$ is a set of observable actions called the *alphabet* of M; $\delta \subseteq Q \times (\alpha M \cup \{\tau\}) \times Q$ is a transition relation, and q_0 is the initial state. An LTS M is *non-deterministic* if it contains τ-transitions or if $\exists (q, a, q'), (q, a, q'') \in \delta$ such that $q' \neq q''$. Otherwise, M is *deterministic*. We use π to denote a special *error state* that has no outgoing transitions, and Π to denote the LTS $\langle \{\pi\}, \mathcal{A}, \emptyset, \pi \rangle$. Let $M = \langle Q, \alpha M, \delta, q_0 \rangle$ and $M' = \langle Q', \alpha M', \delta', q_0' \rangle$. We say that M *transits* into M' with action a, denoted $M \xrightarrow{a} M'$, if and only if $(q_0, a, q_0') \in \delta$ and either $Q = Q', \alpha M = \alpha M'$, and $\delta = \delta'$ for $q_0' \neq \pi$, or, in the special case where $q_0' = \pi$, $M' = \Pi$.

Consider a simple client-server application (from [22]). It consists of a *server* component and two identical *client* components that communicate through shared actions. Each client sends *requests* for reservations to use a common resource, waits for the server to *grant* the reservation, uses the resource, and then *cancels* the reservation. For example, the LTS of a client is shown in Fig. 1 (left), where $i = 1, 2$. The server can *grant* or *deny* a request, ensuring that the resource is used only by one client at a time (the LTS of the server is shown in [14]).

Parallel Composition. Parallel composition "$\|$" is a commutative and associative operator such that: given LTSs $M_1 = \langle Q^1, \alpha M_1, \delta^1, q_0^1 \rangle$ and $M_2 = \langle Q^2, \alpha M_2, \delta^2, q_0^2 \rangle$, $M_1 \| M_2$ is Π if either one of M_1, M_2 is Π. Otherwise, $M_1 \| M_2$ is an LTS $M = \langle Q, \alpha M, \delta, q_0 \rangle$ where $Q = Q^1 \times Q^2, q_0 = (q_0^1, q_0^2), \alpha M = \alpha M_1 \cup \alpha M_2$, and δ is defined as follows (the symmetric version also applies):

$$\frac{M_1 \xrightarrow{a} M_1', a \notin \alpha M_2}{M_1 \| M_2 \xrightarrow{a} M_1' \| M_2} \qquad \frac{M_1 \xrightarrow{a} M_1', M_2 \xrightarrow{a} M_2', a \neq \tau}{M_1 \| M_2 \xrightarrow{a} M_1' \| M_2'}$$

Traces. A *trace* t of an LTS M is a sequence of observable actions starting from the initial state and obeying the transition relation. The set of all traces of M is called the *language* of M, denoted $\mathcal{L}(M)$. Any trace t may also be viewed as an LTS, which we call a *trace LTS*; its language consists of t and its prefixes. We denote by t both a trace and its trace LTS; the meaning should be clear from the context. For $\Sigma \subseteq \mathcal{A}$, we denote by $t \downarrow_\Sigma$ the trace obtained by removing from t all occurrences of actions $a \notin \Sigma$. Similarly, $M \downarrow_\Sigma$ is defined to be an LTS over alphabet Σ which is obtained from M by renaming to τ all the transitions labeled with actions that are not in Σ. Let t, t' be two traces. Let A, A' be the sets of actions occurring in t, t', respectively. By the *symmetric difference* of t and t' we mean the symmetric difference of sets A and A'.

Safety properties. We call a deterministic LTS not containing π a *safety LTS* (any non-deterministic LTS can be made deterministic with the standard algorithm for automata).

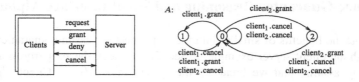

Fig. 2. Client-Server Example: complete interface (left) and derived assumption with alphabet smaller than complete interface alphabet (right).

A safety property P is specified as a *safety LTS* whose language $\mathcal{L}(P)$ defines the set of acceptable behaviors over αP. For example, the mutual exclusion property in Fig. 1 (right) captures the desired behaviour of the client-server application discussed earlier.

An LTS M satisfies P, denoted $M \models P$, iff $\forall \sigma \in M : \sigma\!\downarrow_{\alpha P} \in \mathcal{L}(P)$. For checking a property P, its safety LTS is *completed* by adding error state π and transitions on all the missing outgoing actions from all states into π; the resulting LTS is denoted by P_{err}. LTSA checks $M \models P$ by computing $M \parallel P_{err}$ and checking if π is reachable in the resulting LTS.

Assume-guarantee reasoning. In the assume-guarantee paradigm a formula is a triple $\langle A \rangle M \langle P \rangle$, where M is a component, P is a property, and A is an assumption about M's environment. The formula is true if whenever M is part of a system satisfying A, then the system must also guarantee P. In LTSA, checking $\langle A \rangle M \langle P \rangle$ reduces to checking $A \parallel M \models P$. The simplest assume-guarantee proof rule shows that if $\langle A \rangle M_1 \langle P \rangle$ and $\langle true \rangle M_2 \langle A \rangle$ hold, then $\langle true \rangle M_1 \parallel M_2 \langle P \rangle$ also holds:

$$\frac{\text{(Premise 1) } \langle A \rangle M_1 \langle P \rangle \qquad \text{(Premise 2) } \langle true \rangle M_2 \langle A \rangle}{\langle true \rangle M_1 \parallel M_2 \langle P \rangle}$$

Coming up with appropriate assumptions used to be a difficult, manual process. Recent work has proposed an off-the-shelf learning algorithm, L*, to derive appropriate assumptions *automatically* [12].

The L* learning algorithm. L* was developed by Angluin [4] and later improved by Rivest and Schapire [24]. L* learns an unknown regular language U over alphabet Σ and produces a deterministic finite state automaton (DFA) that accepts it. L* interacts with a *Minimally Adequate Teacher* that answers two types of questions from L*. The first type is a *membership query* asking whether a string $s \in \Sigma^*$ is in U. For the second type, the learning algorithm generates a *conjecture* A and asks whether $\mathcal{L}(A) = U$. If $\mathcal{L}(A) \neq U$ the Teacher returns a counterexample, which is a string s in the symmetric difference of $\mathcal{L}(A)$ and U. L* is guaranteed to terminate with a minimal automaton A for U. If A has n states, L* makes at most $n - 1$ incorrect conjectures. The number of membership queries made by L* is $O(kn^2 + n \log m)$, where k is the size of Σ, n is the number of states in the minimal DFA for U, and m is the length of the longest counterexample returned when a conjecture is made.

3   Assume-Guarantee Reasoning and Small Interface Alphabets

We illustrate the benefits of smaller interface alphabets for assume guarantee reasoning through the client-server example of Sec. 2. To check the property in a compositional way, assume that we break up the system into: $M_1 = $ Client$_1 \parallel$ Client$_2$ and $M_2 = $ Server. The *complete* alphabet of the interface between $M_1 \parallel P$ and M_2 (see Fig. 2 (left)) is: {client$_1$.cancel, client$_1$.grant, client$_1$.deny, client$_1$.request, client$_2$.cancel, client$_2$.grant, client$_2$.deny, client$_2$.request}.

Using this alphabet and the learning method of [12] yields an assumption with 8 states (see [14]). However, a (much) smaller assumption is sufficient for proving the mutual exclusion property (see Fig. 2 (right)). The assumption alphabet is {client$_1$.cancel, client$_1$.grant, client$_2$.cancel, client$_2$.grant}, which is a strict subset of the complete interface alphabet (and is, in fact, the alphabet of the property). This assumption has just 3 states, and enables more efficient verification than the 8-state assumption obtained with the complete alphabet. In the following sections, we present techniques to infer smaller interface alphabets (and the corresponding assumptions) automatically.

4   Learning for Assume-Guarantee Reasoning

We briefly present here the assume-guarantee framework from [12]. The framework uses L* to infer assumptions for compositional verification. A central notion of the framework is that of the *weakest assumption* [15], defined formally here.

Definition 1 (Weakest Assumption for Σ). *Let M_1 be an LTS for a component, P be a safety LTS for a property required of M_1, and Σ be the interface of the component to the environment. The weakest assumption $A_{w,\Sigma}$ of M_1 for Σ and for property P is a deterministic LTS such that: 1) $\alpha A_{w,\Sigma} = \Sigma$, and 2) for any component M_2, $M_1 \parallel (M_2 \downarrow_\Sigma) \models P$ iff $M_2 \models A_{w,\Sigma}$*

The notion of a weakest assumption depends on the interface between the component and its environment. Accordingly, projection of M_2 to Σ forces M_2 to communicate with our module only through Σ (second condition above). In [15] we showed that the weakest assumptions exist for components expressed as LTSs and safety properties and provided an algorithm for computing these assumptions.

The definition above refers to *any* environment component M_2 that interacts with component M_1 via an alphabet Σ. When M_2 is given, there is a natural notion of the complete *interface* between M_1 and its environment M_2, when property P is checked.

Definition 2 (Interface Alphabet). *Let M_1 and M_2 be component LTSs, and P be a safety LTS. The interface alphabet Σ_I of M_1 is defined as: $\Sigma_I = (\alpha M_1 \cup \alpha P) \cap \alpha M_2$.*

Definition 3 (Weakest Assumption). *Given M_1, M_2 and P as above, the weakest assumption A_w is defined as A_{w,Σ_I}.*

Note that, to deal with any system-level property, we allow properties in definition 2 to include actions that are not in αM_1 but are in αM_2. These actions need to be in the

Inputs: M_1, M_2, P, Σ

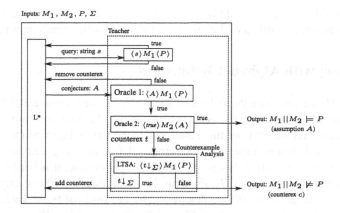

Fig. 3. Learning framework

interface since they are controllable by M_2. Moreover from the above definitions, it follows that $M_1 \parallel M_2 \models P$ iff $M_2 \models A_w$.

Learning framework. The original learning framework from [12] is illustrated in Fig. 3. The framework checks $M_1 \parallel M_2 \models P$ by checking the two premises of the assume-guarantee rule separately, and using the conjectures A from L* as assumptions. The alphabet given to the learner is fixed to $\Sigma = \Sigma_I$. The automaton A output by L* is, in the worst case, the *weakest assumption* A_w.

The Teacher is implemented using model checking. For membership queries on string s, the Teacher uses LTSA to check $\langle s \rangle M_1 \langle P \rangle$. If true, then $s \in \mathcal{L}(A_w)$, so the Teacher returns true. Otherwise, the answer to the query is false. The conjectures returned by L* are intermediate assumptions A. The Teacher implements two *oracles*: *Oracle 1* guides L* towards a conjecture that makes $\langle A \rangle M_1 \langle P \rangle$ true. Once this is accomplished, *Oracle 2* is invoked to discharge A on M_2. If this is true, then the assume guarantee rule guarantees that P holds on $M_1 \parallel M_2$. The Teacher then returns true and the computed assumption A. Note that A is not necessarily A_w, it can be *stronger* than A_w, i.e., $\mathcal{L}(A) \subseteq \mathcal{L}(A_w)$, but the computed assumption is good enough to prove that the property holds or is violated. If model checking returns a counterexample, further analysis is needed to determine if P is indeed violated in $M_1 \parallel M_2$ or if A is imprecise due to learning, in which case A needs to be modified.

Counterexample analysis. Trace t is the counterexample from Oracle 2 obtained by model checking $\langle true \rangle M_2 \langle A \rangle$. To determine if t is a real counterexample, *i.e.*, if it leads to error in $M_1 \parallel M_2 \parallel P_{err}$, the Teacher analyzes t on $M_1 \parallel P_{err}$. In doing so, the Teacher needs to first project t onto the assumption alphabet Σ, that is the interface of M_2 to $M_1 \parallel P_{err}$. Then the Teacher uses LTSA to check $\langle t \downarrow_\Sigma \rangle M_1 \langle P \rangle$. If the error state is not reached during the model checking, t is not a real counterexample, and $t \downarrow_\Sigma$ is returned to the learner L* to modify its conjecture. If the error state is reached, the model checker returns a counterexample c that witnesses the violation of P on M_1 in the context of $t \downarrow_\Sigma$. With the assumption alphabet $\Sigma = \Sigma_I$, c is guaranteed to be a real error trace on $M_1 \parallel M_2 \parallel P_{err}$ [12]. However, as we shall see in the next section, if $\Sigma \subset \Sigma_I$, c is not necessarily a real counterexample and further analysis is needed.

5 Learning with Alphabet Refinement

Let M_1 and M_2 be components, P be a property, Σ_I be the interface alphabet, and Σ be an alphabet such that $\Sigma \subset \Sigma_I$. Assume that we use the learning framework of the previous section, but we now set this smaller Σ to be the alphabet of the assumption that the framework learns. From the correctness of the assume-guarantee rule, if the framework reports true, $M_1 \parallel M_2 \models P$. When it reports false, it is because it finds a trace t in M_2 that falsifies $\langle t \downarrow_\Sigma \rangle M_1 \langle P \rangle$. This, however, does not necessarily mean that $M_1 \parallel M_2 \not\models P$. Real violations are discovered by our original framework only when the alphabet is Σ_I, and are traces t' of M_2 that falsify $\langle t' \downarrow_{\Sigma_I} \rangle M_1 \langle P \rangle$[1].

Consider again the client-server example. Assume $\Sigma = \{\text{client}_1.\text{cancel}, \text{client}_1.\text{grant}, \text{client}_2.\text{grant}\}$, which is smaller than $\Sigma_I = \{\text{client}_1.\text{cancel}, \text{client}_1.\text{grant}, \text{client}_1.\text{deny}, \text{client}_1.\text{request}, \text{client}_2.\text{cancel}, \text{client}_2.\text{grant}, \text{client}_2.\text{deny}, \text{client}_2.\text{request}\}$. Learning with Σ produces trace: $t = \langle \text{client}_2.\text{request}, \text{client}_2.\text{grant}, \text{client}_2.\text{cancel}, \text{client}_1.\text{request}, \text{client}_1.\text{grant} \rangle$. Projected to Σ, this becomes $t \downarrow_\Sigma = \langle \text{client}_2.\text{grant}, \text{client}_1.\text{grant} \rangle$. In the context of $t \downarrow_\Sigma$, $M_1 = \text{Clients}$ violates the property since $\text{Client}_1 \parallel \text{Client}_2 \parallel P_{err}$ contains the following behavior (see Fig. 2):

$$(0,0,0) \xrightarrow{\text{client}_1.\text{request}} (1,0,0) \xrightarrow{\text{client}_2.\text{request}} (1,1,0) \xrightarrow{\text{client}_2.\text{grant}} (1,2,2) \xrightarrow{\text{client}_1.\text{grant}} (2,2,error).$$

Learning therefore reports *false*. This behavior is not feasible, however, in the context of $t \downarrow_{\Sigma_I} = \langle \text{client}_2.\text{request}, \text{client}_2.\text{grant}, \text{client}_2.\text{cancel}, \text{client}_1.\text{request}, \text{client}_1.\text{grant} \rangle$. This trace requires a $\text{client}_2.\text{cancel}$ to occur before the $\text{client}_1.\text{grant}$. Thus, in the context of Σ_I the above violating behavior would be infeasible. We conclude that when applying the learning framework with alphabets smaller than Σ_I, if *true* is reported then the property holds in the system, but violations reported may be spurious.

5.1 Algorithm

We propose a technique called *alphabet refinement*, which extends the learning framework from [12] to deal with smaller alphabets than Σ_I while avoiding spurious counterexamples. The steps of the algorithm are as follows (see Fig. 4 (a)):

1. **Initialize** Σ to a set S such that $S \subseteq \Sigma_I$.
2. Use the classic learning framework for Σ. If the framework returns *true*, then report *true* and go to step 4 (END). If the framework returns false with counterexamples c and t, go to the next step.
3. Perform **extended counterexample analysis** for c. If c is a real counterexample, then report *false* and go to step 4 (END). If c is spurious, then **refine** Σ, which consists of adding to Σ actions from Σ_I. Go to step 2.
4. END of algorithm.

---

[1] In the assume guarantee triples: $t \downarrow_\Sigma$, $t' \downarrow_{\Sigma_I}$ are trace LTSs with alphabets Σ, Σ_I respectively.

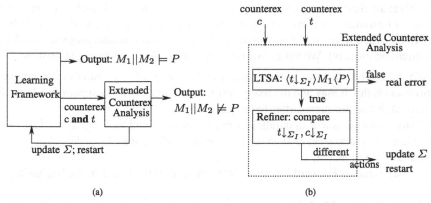

Fig. 4. Learning with alphabet refinement (a) and additional counterexample analysis (b)

When spurious counterexamples are detected, the refiner extends the alphabet with actions in the alphabet of the weakest assumption and the learning of assumptions is restarted. In the worst case, Σ_I is reached, and as proved in our previous work, learning then only reports real counterexamples. In the above high-level algorithm, the high-lighted steps are further specified in the following.

Alphabet initialization. The correctness of our algorithm is insensitive to the initial alphabet. We implement two options: 1) we set the initial alphabet to the empty set to allow the algorithm to only take into account actions that it discovers, and 2) we set the initial alphabet to those actions in the alphabet of the property that are also in Σ_I, i.e., $\alpha P \cap \Sigma_I$ (in the experiments from Sec. 7 we used the second option). The intuition for the latter option is that these interface actions are likely to be significant in proving the property, since they are involved in its definition. A good initial guess of the alphabet may achieve big savings in terms of time since it results in fewer refinement iterations.

Extended counterexample analysis. An additional counterexample analysis is appended to the original learning framework as illustrated in Fig. 4(a). The steps of this analysis are shown in Fig. 4(b). The extension takes as inputs both the counterexample t returned by Oracle 2, and the counterexample c that is returned by the original counterexample analysis. We modified the "classic" learning framework (Fig. 3) to return both c **and** t to be used in alphabet refinement (as explained below). As discussed, c is obtained because $\langle t{\downarrow}_\Sigma\rangle M_1\langle P\rangle$ does not hold. The next step is to check whether in fact t uncovers a real violation in the system. As illustrated by the client-server example, the results of checking $M_1 \parallel P_{err}$ in the context of t projected to different alphabets may be different. The correct (non-spurious) results are obtained by projecting t on the alphabet Σ_I of the weakest assumption. Counterexample analysis therefore calls LTSA to check $\langle t{\downarrow}_{\Sigma_I}\rangle M_1\langle P\rangle$. If LTSA finds an error, the resulting counterexample c is real. If error is not reached, then the counterexample is spurious and the alphabet Σ needs to be refined. Refinement proceeds as described next.

Alphabet refinement. When spurious counterexamples are detected, we need to enrich the current alphabet Σ so that these counterexamples are eventually eliminated.

A counterexample c is spurious if in the context of $t\downarrow_{\Sigma_I}$ it would not be obtained. Our refinement heuristics are therefore based on comparing c and $t\downarrow_{\Sigma_I}$ to discover actions in Σ_I to be added to the learning alphabet (for this reason c is also projected on Σ_I in the refinement process). We have currently implemented the following heuristics:

AllDiff: adds all the actions in the symmetric difference of $t\downarrow_{\Sigma_I}$ and $c\downarrow_{\Sigma_I}$; a potential problem is that it may add too many actions too soon, but if it happens to add useful actions, it may terminate after fewer iterations;

Forward: scans the traces in parallel from beginning to end looking for the first index i where they disagree; if such an i is found, both actions $t\downarrow_{\Sigma_I}(i), c\downarrow_{\Sigma_I}(i)$ are added to the alphabet;

Backward: same as Forward but scans from the end of the traces to the beginning.

5.2 Extension to n Modules

So far, we have discussed our algorithm for two components. We have extended alphabet refinement to n modules $M_1, M_2, \ldots M_n$, for any $n \geq 2$. Previous work has extended learning (without refinement) to n components [12,22]. To check if system $M_1 \parallel M_2 \parallel \ldots \parallel M_n$ satisfies P, we decompose it into: M_1 and $M_2' = M_2 \parallel \ldots \parallel M_n$ and the learning algorithm (without refinement) is invoked recursively for checking the second premise of the assume-guarantee rule.

Learning with alphabet refinement uses recursion in a similar way. At each recursive invocation for M_j, we solve the following problem: find assumption A_j and alphabet Σ_{A_j} such that the rule premises hold, *i.e.*

Oracle 1: $M_j \parallel A_j \models A_{j-1}$ and
Oracle 2: $M_{j+1} \parallel M_{j+2} \parallel \ldots \parallel M_n \models A_j$.

Here A_{j-1} is the assumption for M_{j-1} and plays the role of the property for the current recursive call. Thus, the alphabet of the weakest assumption for this recursive invocation is $\Sigma_I^j = (\alpha M_j \cup \alpha A_{j-1}) \cap (\alpha M_{j+1} \cup \alpha M_{j+2} \cup \ldots \cup \alpha M_n)$. If Oracle 2 returns a counterexample, then the counterexample analysis and alphabet refinement proceed exactly as in the 2 component case. At a new recursive call for M_j with a new A_{j-1}, the alphabet of the weakest assumption is recomputed.

6   Properties of Learning with Refinement

In this section, we discuss properties of the proposed algorithm. We present here the main results (proofs are given in [14]) We first re-state the correctness and termination of learning *without* refinement proven in [12].

Theorem 1 (Termination and correctness of learning without refinement). *Given components M_1 and M_2, and property P, the learning framework in [12] terminates and it returns true if $M_1 \parallel M_2 \models P$ and false otherwise.*

For correctness and termination of learning with alphabet refinement, we first show progress of refinement, meaning that at each refinement stage, new actions are discovered to be added to Σ.

Proposition 1 (Progress of alphabet refinement). *Let $\Sigma \subset \Sigma_I$ be the alphabet of the assumption at the current alphabet refinement stage. Let t be a trace of $M_2 \| A_{err}$ such that $t \downarrow_\Sigma$ leads to error on $M_1 \| P_{err}$ by an error trace c, but $t \downarrow_{\Sigma_I}$ does not lead to error on $M_1 \| P_{err}$. Then $t \downarrow_{\Sigma_I} \neq c \downarrow_{\Sigma_I}$ and there exists an action in their symmetric difference that is not in Σ.*

Theorem 2 (Termination and correctness of learning with alphabet refinement – 2 components). *Given components M_1 and M_2, and property P, the algorithm with alphabet refinement terminates and returns true if $M_1 \| M_2 \models P$ and false otherwise.*

Theorem 3 (Termination and correctness of learning with alphabet refinement – n components). *Given components M_1, M_2, ... M_n and property P, the recursive algorithm with alphabet refinement terminates and returns true if $M_1 \| M_2 \| ... \| M_n \models P$ and false otherwise.*

Correctness for two (and n) components follows from the assume guarantee rule and the extended counterexample analysis. Termination follows from termination of the original framework, from the progress property and also from the finiteness of Σ_I and of n. Moreover, progress implies that the refinement algorithm for two components has at most $|\Sigma_I|$ iterations.

We also note a property of weakest assumptions, namely that by adding actions to an alphabet Σ, the corresponding weakest assumption becomes *weaker*, *i.e.*, it contains more behaviors.

Proposition 2. *Assume components M_1 and M_2, property P and the corresponding interface alphabet Σ_I. Let Σ, Σ' be sets of actions such that: $\Sigma \subset \Sigma' \subset \Sigma_I$. Then: $\mathcal{L}(A_{w,\Sigma}) \subseteq \mathcal{L}(A_{w,\Sigma'}) \subseteq \mathcal{L}(A_{w,\Sigma_I})$.*

With alphabet refinement, our framework adds actions to the alphabet, which translates into adding more behaviors to the weakest assumption that L* tries to prove. This means that at each refinement stage i, when the learner is started with a new alphabet Σ_i such that $\Sigma_{i-1} \subset \Sigma_i$, it will try to learn a weaker assumption A_{w,Σ_i} than $A_{w,\Sigma_{i-1}}$, which was its goal in the previous stage. Moreover, all these assumptions are *under-approximations* of the weakest assumption A_{w,Σ_I} that is necessary and sufficient to prove the desired property. Note that at each refinement stage the learner might stop earlier, *i.e.*, before computing the corresponding weakest assumption. The above property allows re-use of learning results across refinement stages (see Sec. 9).

7 Experiments

We implemented learning with alphabet refinement in LTSA and we evaluated it on checking safety properties for the concurrent systems described below. The goal of the evaluation is to assess the effect of alphabet refinement on learning, and to compare compositional with non-compositional verification.

Models and properties. We used the following case studies. *Gas Station* [11] describes a self-serve gas station consisting of k customers, two pumps, and an operator. For

Table 1. Comparison of learning for 2-way decompositions with and without alphabet refinement

Case	k	No refinement			Refinement + bwd			Refinement + fwd			Refinement + allDiff		
		|A|	Mem.	Time	|A|	Mem.	Time	|A|	Mem.	Time	|A|	Mem.	Time
Gas Station	3	177	4.34	–	8	3.29	2.70	37	6.47	36.52	18	4.58	7.76
	4	195	100.21	–	8	24.06	19.58	37	46.95	256.82	18	36.06	52.72
	5	53	263.38	–	8	248.17	183.70	20	414.19	–	18	360.04	530.71
Chiron,	2	9	1.30	1.23	8	1.22	3.53	8	1.22	1.86	8	1.22	1.90
Property 1	3	21	5.70	5.71	20	6.10	23.82	20	6.06	7.40	20	6.06	7.77
	4	39	27.10	28.00	38	44.20	154.00	38	44.20	33.13	38	44.20	35.32
	5	111	569.24	607.72	110	–	300	110	–	300	110	–	300
Chiron,	2	9	116	110	3	1.05	0.73	3	1.05	0.73	3	1.05	0.74
Property 2	3	25	4.45	6.39	3	2.20	0.93	3	2.20	0.92	3	2.20	0.92
	4	45	25.49	32.18	3	8.13	1.69	3	8.13	1.67	3	8.13	1.67
	5	122	131.49	246.84	3	163.85	18.08	3	163.85	18.05	3	163.85	17.99
MER	2	40	6.57	7.84	6	1.78	1.01	6	1.78	1.02	6	1.78	1.01
	3	377	158.97	–	8	10.56	11.86	8	10.56	11.86	8	10.56	11.85
	4	38	391.24	–	10	514.41	1193.53	10	514.41	1225.95	10	514.41	1226.80
Rover Exec.	2	11	2.65	1.82	4	2.37	2.53	11	2.67	4.17	11	2.54	2.88

$k = 3, 4, 5$, we checked that the operator correctly gives change to a customer for the pump that he/she used. *Chiron* [11] models a graphical user interface consisting of k artists, a wrapper, a manager, a client initialization module, a dispatcher, and two event dispatchers. For $k = 2 \ldots 5$, we checked two properties: "the dispatcher notifies artists of an event before receiving a next event", and "the dispatcher only notifies artists of an event after it receives that event". *MER* [22] models the flight software component for JPL's Mars Exploration Rovers. It contains k users competing for resources managed by an arbiter. For $k = 2 \ldots 6$, we checked that communication and driving cannot happen at the same time as they share common resources. *Rover Executive* [12] models a subsystem of the Ames K9 Rover. The models consists of a main 'Executive' and an 'ExecCondChecker' component responsible for monitoring state conditions. We checked that for a specific shared variable, if the Executive reads its value, then the ExecCondChecker should not read it before the Executive clears it.

Note that the Gas Station and Chiron were analyzed before, in [11], using learning based assume guarantee reasoning (with no alphabet refinement). Four properties of Gas Station and nine properties of Chiron were checked to study how various 2-way model decompositions (i.e. grouping the modules of each analyzed system into two "super-components") affect the performance of learning. For most of these properties, learning performs better than non-compositional verification and produces small (one-state) assumptions. For some other properties, learning does not perform that well, and produces much larger assumptions. To stress-test our approach, we selected the latter, more challenging properties for our study here.

Experimental set-up and results. We performed two sets of experiments. First, we compared learning *with* different alphabet refinement heuristics to learning *without* alphabet refinement for *2-way* decompositions. Second, we compared the recursive implementation of the refinement algorithm with monolithic (non-compositional) verification, for increasing number of components. All the experiments were performed on a Dell PC with a 2.8 GHz Intel Pentium 4 CPU and a 1.0 GB RAM, running Linux Fedora

Table 2. Comparison of recursive learning with and without alphabet refinement and monolithic verification

Case	k	No refinement			Refinement + bwd			Monolithic	
		$|A|$	Mem.	Time	$|A|$	Mem.	Time	Mem.	Time
Gas Station	3	299	238.27	–	25	2.42	14.65	1.42	0.034
	4	289	298.22	–	25	3.43	23.60	2.11	0.126
	5	313	321.72	–	25	5.29	49.72	6.47	0.791
Chiron, Property 1	2	344	118.80	–	4	0.96	2.51	0.88	0.030
	3	182	114.57	–	4	1.12	2.97	1.53	0.067
	4	182	117.93	–	4	2.21	4.59	2.42	0.157
	5	182	115.10	–	4	7.77	6.97	13.39	1.22
Chiron, Property 2	2	229	134.85	–	11	1.68	40.75	1.21	0.035
	3	344	99.12	–	114	28.94	2250.23	1.63	0.068
	4	295	86.03	–	114	35.65	–	2.93	0.174
	5	295	90.57	–	114	40.49	–	15.73	1.53
MER	2	40	8.66	24.95	6	1.85	1.94	1.04	0.024
	3	440	200.55	–	8	3.12	3.58	4.22	0.107
	4	273	107.73	–	10	9.61	9.62	14.28	1.46
	5	200	83.07	–	12	18.95	23.55	143.11	27.84
	6	162	84.96	–	14	47.60	93.77	–	900

Core 4 and using Sun's Java SDK version 1.5. For the first set of experiments, for Gas Station and Chiron we used the best 2-way decompositions described in [11]. For Gas Station, the operator and the first pump are one component, and the rest of the modules are the other. For Chiron, the event dispatchers are one component, and the rest of the modules are the other. For MER, half of the users are in one component, and the other half with the arbiter in the other. For the Rover we used the two components described in [12]. For the second set of experiments, we used an additional heuristic to compute the *ordering* of the modules in the sequence $M_1, \ldots, M_n$ for the recursive learning with refinement so as to minimize the sizes of the interface alphabets $\Sigma_I^1, \ldots \Sigma_I^n$. We generated offline all possible orders with their associated interface alphabets and then chose the order that minimizes the sum $\sum_{j=1..n} |\Sigma_I^j|$.

The experimental results shown in Tables 1 and 2 are for running the learning framework with 'No refinement', and for refinement with backward ('+bwd'), forward ('+fwd') and '+allDiff' heuristics. For each run, we report $|A|$ (the *maximum* assumption size reached during learning), 'Mem.' (the *maximum* memory used by LTSA to check assume-guarantee triples, measured in MB) and 'Time' (total CPU running time, measured in seconds). Column 'Monolithic' reports the memory and run-time of non-compositional model checking. We set a limit of 30 minutes for each run. The exception is Chiron, Property 2, in our second study (Table 2) where the limit was 60 minutes (this was a challenging property and we increased the time limit in order to collect final results for our approach). The sign '–' indicates that the limit of 1GB of memory or the time limit has been exceeded. For these cases, the data is reported as it was when the limit was reached.

Discussion. The results overall show that alphabet refinement improves upon learning. Table 1 shows that alphabet refinement improved the assumption size in all cases, and in a few, up to two orders of magnitude (see Gas Station with $k = 2, 3$, Chiron, Property 3, with $k = 5$, MER with $k = 3$). It improved memory consumption in 10 out of 15 cases, and also improved running time, as for Gas Station and for MER with $k = 3, 4$ learning without refinement did not finish within the time limit, whereas with refinement it did. The benefit of alphabet refinement is even more obvious in Table 2: 'No refinement' exceeded the time limit in all but one case, whereas refinement completed in 14 of 16 cases, producing smaller assumptions and using less memory in all the cases, and up to two orders of magnitude in a few. Table 1 also indicates that the performance of the 'bwd' strategy is (slightly) better than the other refinement strategies. Therefore we used this strategy for the experiments reported in Table 2.

Table 2 indicates that learning with refinement scales better than without refinement for increasing number of components. As k increases, the memory and time consumption for 'Refinement' grows slower than that of 'Monolithic'. For Gas Station, Chiron (Property 1), and MER, for small values of k, 'Refinement' consumes more memory than 'Monolithic', but as k increases the gap is narrowing, and for the largest k 'Refinement' becomes better than 'Monolithic'. This leads to cases such as MER with $k = 6$ where, for a large enough parameter value, 'Monolithic' runs out of memory, whereas 'Refinement' succeeds.

Chiron (Property 2) was particularly challenging for learning with (or without) alphabet refinement. At a closer inspection of the models, we noticed that several modules do not influence Property 2. However, these modules do communicate with the rest of the system through actions that appear in the counterexamples reported in our framework. As a result, alphabet refinement introduces 'un-necessary' actions. If we eliminate these modules, the property still holds in the remaining system, and the performance of learning with refinement is greatly improved, e.g., for $k = 3$, the size of the largest assumption is 13 and is better than monolithic. In the future, we plan to investigate slicing techniques to eliminate modules that do not affect a given property.

8   Related Work

Several frameworks have been proposed to support assume guarantee reasoning [18,23,10,16]. For example, the Calvin tool [13] uses assume-guarantee reasoning for the analysis of Java programs, while Mocha [2] supports modular verification of components with requirements specified based in the Alternating-time Temporal logic. The practical impact of these previous approaches has been limited because they require non-trivial human input in defining appropriate assumptions.

Previous work [15,12] proposed to use L* to automate assume-guarantee reasoning. Since then, several other frameworks that use L* for learning assumptions have been developed – [3] presents a symbolic BDD implementation using NuSMV. This symbolic version was extended in [21] with algorithms that decompose models using hypergraph partitioning, to optimize the performance of learning on resulting decompositions. Different decompositions are also studied in [11] where the best two-way decompositions are computed for model-checking with the LTSA and FLAVERS tools. We follow a direction orthogonal to the latter two approaches and try to improve learning not by automating and optimizing decompositions, but rather by discovering small interface alphabets. Our approach can be combined with the decomposition approaches, by applying interface alphabet refinement in the context of the discovered decompositions.

L* has also been used in [1] to synthesize interfaces for Java classes, and in [25] to check component compatibility after component updates.

Our approach is similar in spirit to counterexample-guided abstraction refinement (CEGAR) [8]. CEGAR computes and analyzes abstractions of programs (usually using a set of abstraction predicates) and refines them based on spurious counter-examples. However, there are some important differences between CEGAR and our algorithm. Alphabet refinement works on actions rather than predicates, it is applied compositionally in an assume-guarantee style and it computes under-approximations (of assumptions) rather than behavioral over-approximations (as it happens in CEGAR). In the future, we plan to investigate more the relationship between CEGAR and our algorithm. The work of [17] proposes a CEGAR approach to interface synthesis for C libraries. This work does not use learning, nor does it address the use of the resulting interfaces in assume-guarantee verification.

A similar idea to our alphabet refinement for L* in the context of assume guarantee verification has been developed independently in [6]. In that work, L* is started with an empty alphabet, and, similarly to ours, the assumption alphabet is refined when a spurious counterexample is obtained. At each refinement stage, a new minimal alphabet is computed that eliminates all spurious counterexamples seen so far. The computation of such a minimal alphabet is shown to be NP-hard. In contrast, we use much cheaper heuristics, but do not guarantee that the computed alphabet is minimal.

The approach by [6] focuses on assume-guarantee problems involving two components and it is not clear how it extends to reasoning about n components. The experiments in [6] report on the speed-up obtained with alphabet refinement. In all the reported cases, the alphabet needed for verification is very small. It is not clear if the same speed-up would be obtained for more challenging problems with bigger alphabets that would require many stages of refinement. In our experience, the memory savings obtained by smaller assumption sizes is the most significant gain. More experimentation is needed to fully assess the benefits of alphabet refinement and the relative strengths and weaknesses of the two approaches.

9 Conclusions and Future Work

We have introduced a novel technique for automatic and incremental refinement of interface alphabets in compositional model checking. Our approach extends an existing framework for learning assumption automata in assume-guarantee reasoning. The extension consists of using interface alphabets smaller than the ones previously used in learning, and using counterexamples obtained from model checking the components to add actions to these alphabets as needed. We have studied the properties of the new learning algorithm and have experimented with various refinement heuristics. Our experiments show improvement with respect to previous learning approaches in terms of the sizes of resulting assumptions and memory and time consumption, and with respect to non-compositional model checking, as the sizes of the checked models increase.

In future work we will address further algorithmic optimizations. Currently, after one refinement stage we restart the learning process from scratch. The property formulated in Proposition 2 in Sec. 6 facilitates reuse of query answers obtained during learning.

A query asks whether a trace projected on the current assumption alphabet leads to error on $M_1 \parallel P_{err}$. If the answer is 'no', by Proposition 2 the same trace will not lead to error when the alphabet is refined. Thus, we could cache these query answers. Another feasible direction is to reuse the learning table as described in [25]. We also plan to use multiple counterexamples for refinement. This may enable faster discovery of relevant interface actions and smaller alphabets. Finally we plan to perform more experiments to fully evaluate our technique.

Acknowledgements. We thank Jamie Cobleigh for providing the models Gas station and Chiron and their decompositions. Mihaela Gheorghiu acknowledges the financial support from MCT/Nasa Ames for a Summer Research Internship, and a Graduate Award from the University of Toronto.

References

1. R. Alur, P. Cerny, P. Madhusudan, and W. Nam. "Synthesis of interface specifications for Java classes". In *Proceedings of POPL'05*, pages 98–109, 2005.
2. R. Alur, T. Henzinger, F. Mang, S. Qadeer, S. Rajamani, and S. Tasiran. "MOCHA: Modularity in Model Checking". In *Proceedings of CAV'98*, volume 1427 of *LNCS*, pages 521–525, 1998.
3. R. Alur, P. Madhusudan, and Wonhong Nam. "Symbolic Compositional Verification by Learning Assumptions". In *Proceedings of CAV05*, pages 548–562, 2005.
4. D. Angluin. "Learning regular sets from queries and counterexamples". *Information and Computation*, 75(2):87–106, November 1987.
5. H. Barringer, D. Giannakopoulou, and C. S. Păsăreanu. "Proof Rules for Automated Compositional Verification through Learning". In *Proceedings of SAVCBS'03*, pages 14–21, 2003.
6. S. Chaki and O. Strichman. "Optimized L*-based Assume-guarantee Reasoning". In *Proceedings of TACAS'07 (to appear)*, 2007.
7. S.C. Cheung and J. Kramer. Checking safety properties using compositional reachability analysis. *ACM Transactions on Software Engineering and Methodology*, 8(1):49–78, 1999.
8. E. M. Clarke, O. Grumberg, S. Jha, Y. Lu, and H. Veith. "Counterexample-Guided Abstraction Refinement". In *Proceedings of CAV'00*, volume 1855 of *LNCS*, pages 154–169, 2000.
9. E. M. Clarke, O. Grumberg, and D. Peled. *Model Checking*. MIT Press, 2000.
10. E. M. Clarke, D. E. Long, and K. L. McMillan. "Compositional Model Checking". In *Proceedings of LICS'89*, pages 353–362, 1989.
11. J. M. Cobleigh, G. S. Avrunin, and L. A. Clarke. "Breaking Up is Hard to Do: An Investigation of Decomposition for Assume-Guarantee Reasoning". In *Proceedings of ISSTA'06*, pages 97–108. ACM Press, 2006.
12. J. M. Cobleigh, D. Giannakopoulou, and C. S. Păsăreanu. "Learning Assumptions for Compositional Verification". In *Proceedings of TACAS'03*, volume 2619 of *LNCS*, pages 331–346, 2003.
13. C. Flanagan, S. N. Freund, and S. Qadeer. "Thread-Modular Verification for Shared-Memory Programs". In *Proceedings of ESOP'02*, pages 262–277, 2002.
14. M. Gheorghiu, D. Giannakopoulou, and C. S. Păsăreanu. "Refining Interface Alphabets for Compositional Verification". RIACS Technical Report, 2006.
15. D. Giannakopoulou, C. S. Pasareanu, and H. Barringer. "Assumption Generation for Software Component Verification". In *Proceedings of ASE'02*, pages 3–12. IEEE Computer Society, 2002.

16. O. Grumberg and D. E. Long. "Model Checking and Modular Verification". In *Proceedings of CONCUR'91*, pages 250–265, 1991.
17. T. A. Henzinger, R. Jhala, and R. Majumdar. "Permissive Interfaces". In *Proceedings of ESEC/SIGSOFT FSE'05*, pages 31–40, 2005.
18. C. B. Jones. "Specification and Design of (Parallel) Programs". In *Information Processing 83: Proceedings of the IFIP 9th World Congress*, pages 321–332. IFIP: North Holland, 1983.
19. J.-P. Krimm and L. Mounier. "Compositional State Space Generation from Lotos Programs". In *Proceedings of TACAS'97*, pages 239–258, 1997.
20. J. Magee and J. Kramer. *Concurrency: State Models & Java Programs*. John Wiley & Sons, 1999.
21. W. Nam and R. Alur. "Learning-Based Symbolic Assume-Guarantee Reasoning with Automatic Decomposition". In *Proceedings of ATVA'06*, volume 4218 of *LNCS*, 2006.
22. C. S. Păsăreanu and D. Giannakopoulou. "Towards a Compositional SPIN". In *Proceedings of SPIN'06*, volume 3925 of *LNCS*, pages 234–251, 2006.
23. A. Pnueli. "In Transition from Global to Modular Temporal Reasoning about Programs". In *Logic and Models of Concurrent Systems*, volume 13, pages 123–144, 1984.
24. R. L. Rivest and R. E. Shapire. "Inference of finite automata using homing sequences". *Information and Computation*, 103(2):299–347, April 1993.
25. N. Sharygina, S. Chaki, E. Clarke, and N. Sinha. "Dynamic Component Substitutability Analysis". In *Proceedings of FM'05*, volume 3582 of *LNCS*, pages 512–528, 2005.

MAVEN: Modular Aspect Verification

Max Goldman and Shmuel Katz

Technion — Israel Institute of Technology
{mgoldman,katz}@cs.technion.ac.il

Abstract. Aspects are program modules that include descriptions of key events (called joinpoints) and code segments (called advice) to be executed at those key events when the aspect is bound (woven) to an underlying system. The MAVEN tool verifies the correctness of an aspect relative to its specification, independently of any specific underlying system to which it may be woven. The specification includes assumptions about properties of the underlying system, and guaranteed properties of any system after the aspect is woven into it. The approach is based on model checking of a single state machine constructed using the linear temporal logic (LTL) description of the assumptions, a description of the joinpoints, and the state machine of the aspect advice. The tableau of the LTL assumption is used in a unique way, as a representative of any underlying system satisfying the assumptions. This is the first technique for once-and-for-all verification of an aspect relative to its specification, thereby increasing the modularity of proofs for systems with aspects.

1 Introduction

1.1 Aspect-Oriented Programming

The aspect-oriented approach to software development is one in which concerns that cut across many parts of the system are encapsulated in separate modules called *aspects*. The approach was first presented in the AspectJ [1] extension of Java, and has been generalized to a variety of languages and aspect-oriented software development techniques (see, for example, [2]). When a concern such as security or logging is encapsulated in an aspect, this aspect contains both the code associated with the concern, called *advice*, and a description of when this advice should run, called a *pointcut descriptor*. The pointcut descriptor identifies those points in the execution of a program at which the advice should be invoked, called *joinpoints*. The combination of some *base program* with an aspect (or in general, a collection of aspects), is termed an *augmented program*.

Aspects are of particular interest as a software construct because the pointcuts that govern the execution of their advice are evaluated dynamically. When a pointcut identifies joinpoints, these joinpoints are not static locations in the code; rather, in the most popular and expressive joinpoint models used by aspect-oriented programming languages, joinpoints are well-defined points during the *execution* of a program. Depending on the runtime context of a particular point, such as the methods on the program's stack, or the values currently in certain

O. Grumberg and M. Huth (Eds.): TACAS 2007, LNCS 4424, pp. 308–322, 2007.

data fields, the same static code location might match a pointcut at one time, but fail to match it at another. To give the programmer access to these dynamic data, a pointcut may also expose values of program variables to the advice.

1.2   Modular Aspectual Verification

In this work we are concerned with generic formal verification of aspects relative to a specification. The specification of an aspect consists of *assumptions* about any base program to which the aspect can reasonably be woven, and *desired properties* intended to hold for the augmented program (this terminology is applied to aspects in [3]). We view both base programs and aspect code as nondeterministic finite state machines, in which computations are infinite sequences of states within the machine. For both assumptions and desired properties to be verified we consider formulas in linear temporal logic (LTL).

Clearly, given a base program, a collection of aspects with their pointcut descriptors and advice, and a system for *weaving* together these components to produce a stand-alone augmented program, we can verify properties of this augmented system using the usual model checking techniques. Such weaving involves adding edges from joinpoint states of the base program to the initial states of the advice, and from the states at the end of an advice segment to states back in the base program. It would be preferable, however, if we could employ a modular technique in which the aspect can be considered separately from the base program. Instead of examining a particular augmented program, using a generic model of augmented program behavior will allow us to:

- obtain verification results that hold for a particular aspect with any base program from some class of programs, rather than for only one base program in particular;
- use the results to reason about the application of aspects to base programs with multiple evolving state machines describing changing configurations during execution, or to other systems not amenable to model checking; and
- avoid model checking augmented systems, which may be significantly larger than either their base systems or aspects, and whose unknown behavior may resist abstraction.

The second point above relates to object-oriented programs that create new instances of classes (objects) with associated state machine components. Often, the assumption of an aspect about the key properties of those base state machines to which it may be woven can indeed be shown to hold for every possible machine that corresponds to an object configuration of a program. For example, it may involve a so-called *class invariant*, provable by reasoning directly on class declarations, as in [4]. More details on the connections between code-based aspects (as in AspectJ) and the state machine versions are discussed in Sect. 5.

This problem of creating a single generic model that can represent any possible augmented program for an aspect woven over some class of base programs is especially difficult because of the aspect-oriented notion of *obliviousness*: base programs are generally unaware of aspects advising them, and have no control over when or how they are advised. There are no explicit markers for the transfer of control from base to advice code, nor are there guarantees about if or where advice will return control to the base program.

1.3   Results

In this paper we show how to verify once-and-for-all that for any base state machine satisfying the assumptions of an aspect, and for a weaving that adds the aspect advice as indicated in the joinpoint description, the resulting augmented state machine is guaranteed to satisfy the desired properties given in the specification. The verification algorithm is implemented in a prototype called MAVEN. A single generic state machine is constructed from the tableau of the assumption, the pointcut descriptor, and the advice state machine, and verified for the desired properties. Then, when a particular base program is to be woven with the aspect, it is sufficient to establish that the base state machine satisfies the assumptions. Thus the entire augmented program never has to be model checked, achieving true modularity and genericity in the proof. This approach is especially appropriate for aspects intended to be reused over many base programs, such as those in libraries or middleware components.

LTL model checking is based on creating a tableau state machine automaton that accepts exactly those computations that satisfy the property to be verified. Usually, the negation of this machine is then composed as a cross-product with the model to be checked. Here we use the tableau of the assumption in a unique way, as the basis of the generic model to be checked for the desired property. It represents any base machine satisfying the assumption, because the execution sequences of these base programs can be abstracted by sequences in the tableau.

The aspects treated are assumed to be *weakly invasive*, as defined in [5]. This means that when advice has completed executing, the system continues from a state that was already reachable in the original base program (perhaps for different inputs or actions of the environment). Many aspects fall into this category, including *spectative* aspects that never modify the state of the base system (logging is a good example), and *regulative* aspects that only restrict the reachable state space (for example, aspects implementing security checks). Also weakly invasive would be an aspect to enforce transactional requirements, which might roll back a series of changes so that the system returns to the state it was in before they were made. Even a 'discount policy' aspect that reduces the price on certain items in a retail system is weakly invasive, since the original price given as input could have been the discounted one.

Additionally, we assume that any executions of an augmented program that infinitely often include states resulting from aspect advice will be fair (and thus must be considered for correctness purposes). The version here does not treat multiple aspects or joinpoints influenced by the introduction of advice, although the approach can be expanded to treat such cases as well.

In the following section, needed terms and constructs are defined. Section 3 presents the algorithm, and outlines a proof of soundness in the weakly invasive aspect case. This section also uses an abstract example to illustrate the approach.

The MAVEN implementation is described in Section 4, along with descriptions of some typical aspect verifications. Section 5 details works related to the result here, and is followed by the conclusion.

2 Definitions

2.1 LTL Tableaux

Intuitively, the tableau of an LTL formula f is a state machine whose fair infinite paths are exactly all those paths which satisfy the formula f. This intuition will be realized formally in Theorem 1 below.

We define T_f, the tableau for LTL path formula f (equivalently, state formula $A f$), as given in the chapter of [6] on "Symbolic LTL Model Checking," with clarifications described in [7]. We denote $T_f = (S_T, S_0^T, R_T, L_T, F_T)$, where S_T is the set of states; S_0^T is the set of initial states, R_T is the transition relation, L_T is the labeling function, and F_T is the set of fair state sets.

If AP_f is the set of atomic propositions in f, then $L_T : S \to \mathcal{P}(AP_f)$ — that is, the labels of the states in the tableau will include sets of the atomic propositions appearing in f. A state in any machine is given a particular label if and only if that atomic proposition is true in that state. We also need:

Definition 1. *For path π, let $label(\pi)$ be the sequence of labels (subsets of AP) of the states of π. For such a sequence $l = l_0, l_1, \ldots$ and set Q, let $l|_Q = m_0, m_1, \ldots$ where for each $i \geq 0$, $m_i = l_i \sqcap Q$.*

Theorem 1. *(from [6], 6.7, Theorems 4 & 5) Given T_f, for any Kripke structure M, for all fair paths π' in M, if $M, \pi' \models f$ then there exists fair path π in T_f such that π starts in S_0^T and $label(\pi')|_{AP_f} = label(\pi)$.*

That is, for any possible computation of M satisfying formula f, there is a path in the tableau of f which matches the labels within AP_f along the states of that computation.

In the algorithm of Sect. 3, we restrict the tableau to its reachable component. Such restriction does not affect the result of this theorem, since all reachable paths are preserved, but is necessary in order to achieve useful results. This follows from the observation that the tableau for the negation of a formula has precisely the same states and transition relation, but the complementary set of initial states. Thus, any unreachable portion of the tableau is liable to contain exactly those behaviors which violate the formula of interest.

2.2 Aspects

Advice. An aspect machine $A = (S_A, S_0^A, S_{ret}^A, R_A, L_A)$ over atomic propositions AP is defined as usual for a state machine with no fairness constraint, with the following addition:

Definition 2. S_{ret}^A *is the set of* return *states of A, where $S_{ret}^A \subseteq S_A$ and for any state $s \in S_{ret}^A$, s has no outgoing edges.*

Pointcuts. Recall that a pointcut identifies the states at which an aspect's advice should be activated, and can include conditions on the present state and execution history. We do not give a prescriptive definition for pointcut descriptors; in practice they might take a number of forms, e.g., as in [8] or using variants of regular expressions. Another choice for describing pointcuts might be LTL path formulas containing only past temporal operators. For example, the descriptor $\rho_1 = a \wedge \mathsf{Y} b \wedge \mathsf{Y} \mathsf{Y} b$ would match sequences ending with a state where a is true, preceded by b, preceded by another b (operator Y is the past analogue of X). However expressed, we require that descriptors operate as follows:

Definition 3. *Given a pointcut descriptor ρ over atomic propositions AP and a finite sequence l of labels (subsets of AP), we can ask whether or not the end of l is matched by ρ.*

We define $l \models \rho$ to mean that finite label sequence l is matched by pointcut descriptor ρ in this way.

Specifications. In addition to its advice, in state machine A, and pointcut, described by ρ, an aspect has two pieces of formal specification:

- Formula ψ expresses the assumptions made by the aspect about any base machine to which it will be woven. This ψ is thus a requirement to be met by any such machine.
- Formula ϕ expresses the desired result to be satisfied by any augmented machine built by weaving this aspect with a conforming base machine. In other words, ϕ is the guarantee of the aspect.

2.3   Weaving

Weaving is the process of combining a base machine with some aspect according to a particular pointcut descriptor; the result is an augmented machine that includes the advice of the aspect.

The weaving algorithm has the following inputs:

- aspect machine $A = (S_A, S_0^A, S_{ret}^A, R_A, L_A)$ over AP,
- pointcut ρ over AP, and
- base machine $B = (S_B, S_0^B, R_B, L_B, F_B)$ over $AP_B \supseteq AP$.

And it produces as output:

- augmented machine $\widetilde{B} = (S_{\widetilde{B}}, S_0^{\widetilde{B}}, R_{\widetilde{B}}, L_{\widetilde{B}}, F_{\widetilde{B}})$.

Set AP can be thought of as the 'visible' labels of B with which the aspect is concerned; labels local to the aspect are not included.

The weaving is performed in two steps. First we construct from the base machine B a new state machine B^ρ which is *pointcut-ready* for ρ, wherein each state either definitely is or is not matched by ρ. Then we use B^ρ and A to build the final augmented machine $\widetilde{B}$.

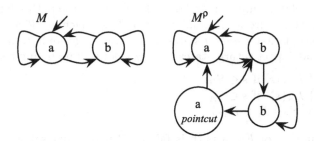

Fig. 1. Constructing a pointcut-ready machine M^ρ for the given M and LTL past formula pointcut descriptor $\rho = a \wedge Y\, b \wedge Y\, Y\, b$

Constructing a Pointcut-Ready Machine. Pointcut-ready machine $B^\rho = (S_{B^\rho}, S_0^{B^\rho}, R_{B^\rho}, L_{B^\rho}, F_{B^\rho})$ is a machine in which unwinding of certain paths has been performed, so that we can separate paths which match pointcut descriptor ρ from those that do not. The pointcut-ready machine contains states with a new label, *pointcut*, that indicates exactly those states where the descriptor has been matched.

This machine must meet the following requirements:

- $S_{B^\rho} \supseteq S_B$
- L_{B^ρ} is a function from S_{B^ρ} to $\mathcal{P}\,(AP_B \cup \{pointcut\})$
- For all finite-length paths $\pi = s_0, \ldots, s_k$ in B^ρ such that $s_0 \in S_0^{B^\rho}$, we have $label(\pi) \models \rho \Leftrightarrow s_k \models pointcut$.
- For all infinite sequences of labels $l = (\mathcal{P}(AP_B))^\omega$, there is a fair path π_{B^ρ} in B^ρ where $label(\pi_{B^\rho})|_{AP_B} = l$ if and only if there is a fair path π_B in B where $label(\pi_B) = l$.

Note that since B and B^ρ have the same paths (over AP, ignoring the added *pointcut* label), they must satisfy exactly the same LTL formulas over AP.

Figure 1 shows a simple example of this construction. Note that in state diagrams, the absence of an atomic proposition indicates that the proposition does not hold, not that the value is unknown or irrelevant. This is in contrast to a formula, where unmentioned propositions are not restricted.

Finally, note that for a pointcut descriptor that examines only the current state, the splitting and unwinding is unnecessary, and *pointcut* can be added directly to the states in which the pointcut descriptor is matched.

Constructing an Augmented Machine. We construct the components of augmented machine $\widetilde{B} = (S_{\widetilde{B}}, S_0^{\widetilde{B}}, R_{\widetilde{B}}, L_{\widetilde{B}}, F_{\widetilde{B}})$ as follows:

- $S_{\widetilde{B}} = S_{B^\rho} \cup S_A$
- $S_0^{\widetilde{B}} = S_0^{B^\rho}$

- $(s,t) \in R_{\widetilde{B}} \Leftrightarrow \begin{cases} (s,t) \in R_{B^\rho} \ \wedge\ s \not\models pointcut & \text{if } s,t \in S_{B^\rho} \\ (s,t) \in R_A & \text{if } s,t \in S_A \\ s \models pointcut \ \wedge\ t \in S_0^A \\ \qquad \wedge\ L_{B^\rho}(s)|_{AP} = L_A(t) & \text{if } s \in S_{B^\rho},\ t \in S_A \\ s \in S_{ret}^A \wedge L_A(s) = L_{B^\rho}(t)|_{AP} & \text{if } s \in S_A,\ t \in S_{B^\rho} \end{cases}$

Note that this relationship is 'if and only if.' In words, the path relation contains precisely all the edges from the pointcut-ready base machine B^ρ and from aspect machine A, except that *pointcut* states in B^ρ have edges only to matching start states in A, and aspect return states have edges to all matching base states.

$$- L_{\widetilde{B}}(s) = \begin{cases} L_{B^\rho}(s) \text{ if } s \in S_{B^\rho} \\ L_A(s) \text{ if } s \in S_A \end{cases}$$
$$- F_{\widetilde{B}} = \{F_i \cup S_A \mid F_i \in F_{B^\rho}\}$$

From the definition of $F_{\widetilde{B}}$, a path is fair in $\widetilde{B}$ if it either satisfies the original fairness constraint of the pointcut-ready machine, or if it visits some aspect state infinitely many times. A weaving is considered *successful* if every reachable node in $S_{\widetilde{B}}$ has a successor according to $R_{\widetilde{B}}$.

2.4   Weakly Invasive Aspects

As mentioned above, we show our result for the broad class of aspects which, when they return from advice, do so to a reachable state in the base machine. Without this restriction, the aspect may return to unreachable parts of the base machine whose behavior is not bound by assumption formula ψ. In this case, the augmented system contains portions with unknown behavior, and is difficult to reason about in a modular way.

Definition 4. *An aspect A and pointcut ρ are said to be weakly invasive for a base machine B if, for all states in S_{B^ρ} that are reachable by following a fair path in $\widetilde{B}$, those states were reachable by following a fair path in B^ρ.*

In particular, this means that all states to which the aspect returns are reachable in the pointcut-ready base machine. This could of course be checked directly, but would require construction of the augmented machine — precisely the operation we would like to avoid. In many cases (see [5]), the aspect can be shown weakly invasive for any base machine satisfying its assumption ψ, by using local model checking, additional information (our reasoning in the discount price example from Sect. 1.3 uses such information), or static analysis (both spectative and regulative aspects can be identified in this way).

3   Algorithm

The modular verification algorithm builds a tableau from base requirement ψ and weaves A with this tableau according to pointcut descriptor ρ, then performs model checking on the augmented tableau to verify desired result ϕ.

Algorithm. Given:

- set of atomic propositions AP;
- assumption ψ for base systems, an LTL formula over AP;
- desired result ϕ for augmented systems, an LTL formula over AP; and
- aspect machine A and pointcut descriptor ρ over AP.

Perform the following steps:

0. For all $a \in AP$, if ψ does not include a, augment ψ with a clause of the form $\cdots \wedge (a \vee \neg a)$, so that ψ contains every $a \in AP$, without altering its meaning.
1. Construct T_ψ, the tableau for ψ. Since ψ contains every AP, the result of Theorem 1 will hold when all labels in AP are considered.
2. Restrict T_ψ to only those states reachable via a fair path.
3. Weave A into T_ψ according to ρ, obtaining $\widetilde{T_\psi}$.
4. Perform model checking in the usual way to determine if $\widetilde{T_\psi} \models \phi$.

This algorithm gives us a sound proof method provided that whenever the model check of the constructed augmented tableau (in step 4 above) succeeds, then for any base system satisfying ψ, applying aspect A according to pointcut descriptor ρ will yield an augmented system satisfying ϕ. This is expressed below:

Theorem 2. *Given AP, ψ, ϕ, A, and ρ as defined, if $\widetilde{T_\psi} \models \phi$, then for any base program M over a superset of AP such that A and ρ are weakly invasive for M, if $M \models \psi$ then $\widetilde{M} \models \phi$.*

The proof is omitted for reasons of space; it can be found in [7]. It involves an inductive analysis of the paths in the augmented system $\widetilde{M}$ over an arbitrary base system M that satisfies the assumptions ψ. Each such path is shown to correspond to a path in the augmented tableau $\widetilde{T_\psi}$. If the model check in the algorithm succeeded, then all these paths satisfy ϕ, as required.

Although we make use of the entire reachable part of tableau T_ψ, it does not serve as the mechanism for performing LTL model checking, but rather forms (part of) the system to be checked. The tableau for even a complex assumption formula is likely to be much smaller than models of concrete bases systems that satisfy such assumptions. Of course, during the model checking step of the algorithm, which dominates the time and space complexity, any sound optimizations may be employed to reduce the complexity.

As a first abstract example, suppose we have an aspect with base system assumption $\psi = \mathsf{A}\,\mathsf{G}\,((\neg a \wedge b) \to \mathsf{F}\,a)$ — that is, any state satisfying $\neg a \wedge b$ is eventually followed by a state satisfying a. We would like to prove that the application of our aspect to any base system satisfying ψ will give an augmented system satisfying result $\phi = \mathsf{A}\,\mathsf{G}\,((a \wedge b) \to \mathsf{X}\,\mathsf{F}\,a)$ — that is, any state satisfying $a \wedge b$ will eventually be followed by a later state satisfying a.

Figure 2(a) shows the reachable portion of the tableau for the assumption ψ. In the diagram, shaded states are those contained in the only fairness set. The notation $\mathsf{X}g$, not formally part of the state label, designates states in the tableau which satisfy $\mathsf{X}g$ for subformula $g = \mathsf{F}\,a$ (this labeling serves only to differentiate states; other labels of this form have been omitted for clarity, and all such labels become invalid after weaving). For the example pointcut descriptor $\rho = (a \wedge b)$, this tableau machine is also pointcut-ready for ρ (since ρ references only the current state), simply by adding *pointcut* to the labels of s_3 and s_5.

Figure 2(b) shows the state machine A for the advice of our aspect. This advice will be applied at the states matched by ρ, and Fig. 2(c) gives the weaving of

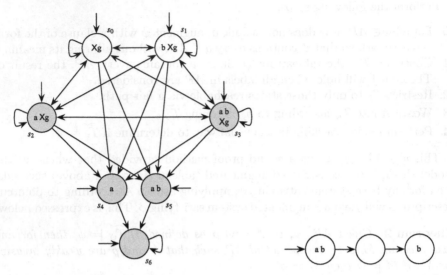

(a) The reachable portion of tableau T_ψ for $\psi = $ (b) A simple aspect machine A.
A G $((\neg a \wedge b) \rightarrow$ F $a)$

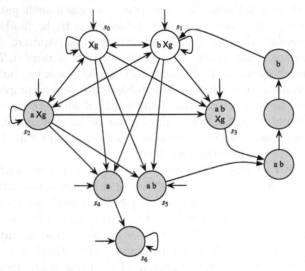

(c) Augmented   tableau $\widetilde{T_\psi}$,   satisfying ϕ =
A G $((a \wedge b) \rightarrow$ X F $a)$.

Fig. 2. Example augmented tableau

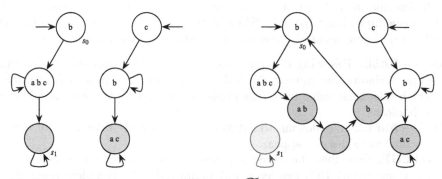

(a) One particular base machine M.   (b) $\widetilde{M}$: M woven with A according to ρ.

Fig. 3. Example weaving where $M \models \psi$ and $\widetilde{M} \models \phi$

A with T_ψ according to ρ. Model checking this augmented tableau will indeed establish that it satisfies the desired property ϕ. This result follows neither from the aspect nor base machine behavior directly, but from their combined behavior mediated by ρ. And since $\widetilde{T_\psi} \models \phi$, any $M \models \psi$ will yield $\widetilde{M} \models \phi$.

Figure 3(a) depicts a particular base machine M satisfying ψ, as could be verified by model checking. Again, the shaded states are those in the only fairness set. Although this M is small, it does contain atomic proposition c not 'visible' to the aspect, and it has a disconnected structure very unlike the tableau.

From Fig. 3(b), one sees it is indeed the case that the augmented machine $\widetilde{M}$ satisfies ϕ — but there is no need to prove this directly by model checking. This holds true even though the addition of the aspect has made a number of invasive changes to M: state s_1 is no longer reachable, because its only incoming edge has been replaced by an advice edge; a new loop through s_0 has been added, while in M there was no path visiting s_0 more than once; there is a new path connecting the previously separated left-hand component to the right-hand; and so forth. In more realistic examples, the difference in size between the augmented tableau (involving only ψ, ρ, and A) and a concrete augmented system with advice over a full base machine would be substantial.

4   MAVEN

The verification algorithm defined in the previous section has been implemented in a prototype system called MAVEN, for "Modular Aspect VerificatioN." In MAVEN, aspects are specified directly as state machines, albeit using a more convenient and expressive language than direct definition of the machine states and transitions. MAVEN operates on the level of textual input to and output from components of the NuSMV model checker [9]. NuSMV is a CTL (branching-time logic) and LTL model checker that accepts its input as textual definitions of state machine systems and their specifications. We have extended the NuSMV finite state machine language to create FSMA, for "finite state machine aspects," which describes aspects and their specifications. The language is based closely on the usual input language of NuSMV, with some added restrictions, and with a collection of new keywords used for aspect-specific declarations:

VAR – –BASE. Following this directive, one or more definitions of base machine variables can appear. NuSMV allows the user to specify variables which take their value from a symbolic set or numerical range, in addition to booleans.

VAR – –ASPECT. Following this directive, one or more definitions of aspect machine variables can appear.

POINTCUT. Describes the aspect's pointcut. Only current-state expressions are valid; (past) LTL syntax is not permitted. The complete pointcut is taken to be the disjunction of all **POINTCUT** directives; this allows the user to specify multiple logical pointcuts for the aspect.

INIT. Describes the initial states of the aspect machine.

TRANS. Gives a restriction on the set of valid transitions within the aspect machine. As in NuSMV, the conjunction of all **TRANS** directives forms the complete restriction. Unlike in NuSMV, **TRANS** is the only directive available for specifying state machine transitions in FSMA.

RETURN. Describes the return states of the aspect machine. Return states have no outgoing transitions, even if **TRANS** would indicate otherwise.

LTLSPEC – –BASE. Defines an expression which must hold as part of the base system requirement (and is used to build the tableau).

LTLSPEC – –AUGMENTED. Defines an expression which must hold as part of the augmented system result (and will be model checked).

From the definition of the **POINTCUT** directive, one limitation of MAVEN is immediately clear: only pointcuts which are restricted to examining the current state are permitted. That is, this prototype does not include the step of creating pointcut-ready machines during its weaving. However, many pointcut languages and specific applications indeed examine only the current state.

Tableau construction in MAVEN is performed by ltl2smv, an independent component of NuSMV. The ltl2smv program takes as input an LTL formula in the syntax used by NuSMV, and outputs the corresponding tableau state machine. We weave the tableau with the aspect according to the pointcut by modifying this textual representation; the result is a valid NuSMV input file representing the woven tableau and the augmented system results that must hold in it, which can be given directly to the model checker for verification.

The aspects verified while developing and testing MAVEN have not been challenging for the model checker because aspect advice typically contains only relatively short code segments. For all the correctly-specified models verified heretofore, runtime has been measured in seconds, and the number of states generated has been no more than the low thousands.

The MAVEN tool, usage instructions, and a few implemented examples, are available for download at the website noted in [7]. The examples were selected for their ability, in a simple and highly abstract way, to demonstrate real-world situations in which the verification technique is applicable and effective.

In one, the abstract example given earlier is rephrased to describe a more realistic situation: prospective base systems are known to have the property that, whenever a *request* for a status display is made when the *display* is not active at the same time, eventually the *display* will be shown. We wish to use an aspect to guarantee the new behavior that, when the *request* comes while the *display* is already active, a later status *display* will still occur, presumably with updated information. This becomes the formal specification below, which has the same structure as the example:

$$\psi = \mathsf{A} \, \mathsf{G} \, ((\neg display \wedge request) \rightarrow \mathsf{F} \, display)$$
$$\phi = \mathsf{A} \, \mathsf{G} \, ((display \wedge request) \rightarrow \mathsf{X} \, \mathsf{F} \, display)$$

The construction and model check clearly succeed.

Another example involves the notion of a retail store discount policy aspect, discussed at length in [10]. In the introduction, we noted that such an aspect, when correctly implemented, is in fact weakly invasive, even though it is altering the prices of items. We verified a concrete discount aspect whose specified goal is to implement a "50% Off the Entire Store" policy at the point of purchase. In particular, we showed both a "healthiness constraint" that assuming all prices in the underlying system are nonzero, the same is true of the augmented one, and that the new augmented system has a ceiling on its prices that is half of the previous ceiling. If the aspect code is incorrect, and zero prices can result, MAVEN reports that the aspect is not weakly invasive for the given base, because an aspect return state (one with zero price) differs from all base states, and it displays one such state, provided by NuSMV as its verification failure counterexample.

The use of such counterexamples is further investigated in an example aspect designed to alert users about the occurrence of errors, using an assumption about an existing message delivery system in the base system. By reasoning about the circumstances presented in a counterexample produced from model checking the augmented tableau, we can improve one or more of the specification, pointcut, or advice of our aspect. In general, the need to refine the specification indicates either that our original base system assumption was not strong enough, or possibly that our augmented result was too strong to prove (note that no assumptions are made about the relationship between the formulas, and we can vary them independently). Refining the pointcut can be necessary when the counterexample reveals a situation where the aspect fails to execute advice when it is needed, or activates advice in an inappropriate situation. The advice may need to be altered if the counterexample reveals circumstances under which our original implementation is inadequate; in the case where the advice model has been derived via abstraction from source code, the counterexample could indicate a place where our abstraction needs refinement.

The example fails to verify at first because the assumption is too weak, allowing multiple announcements for the same message; a revision to correct this fails due to situations with overlapping announcements. Correction now requires changing the advice, and ultimately leads to a version that passes verification. The important point is that by using the modular verification method, we were able to reason about the aspect's correctness independent of any particular base machine. Furthermore, the method has forced us to think carefully and precisely about what the aspect will assume, do, and guarantee; precision and certainty being the goal of formal analysis.

5   Related Work

The first work to separately model check the aspect state machine segments that correspond to advice is [11], where the verification is modular in the sense that base and aspect machines are considered separately. The verification method also allows for joinpoints within advice to be matched by a pointcut and themselves advised. However, the treatment there is for a particular aspect woven directly to a particular base program. Additionally, it shows only how to extend properties which hold for that base program to the augmented program (using branching-time logic CTL). A key assumption of their method is that after the aspect machine completes, the continuation is always to the state following the joinpoint in the original base program. This requirement is much stronger than the assumption used here of a weakly invasive aspect.

In [12], model checking tasks are automatically generated for the augmented system that results from each weaving of an aspect. That approach has the disadvantage of having to treat the augmented system, but offers the benefit that needed annotations and set-up need only be prepared once. That work takes advantage of the Bandera [13] system that generates input to model checking tools directly from Java code, and can be extended to, for example, the aspect-oriented AspectJ language. Bandera and other systems like Java Pathfinder [14] that generate state machine representations from code can be used to connect common high-level aspect languages to the state machines used here.

In [5] a semantic model based on state machines is given, and the treatment of code-level aspects and joinpoints defined in terms of transitions, as in AspectJ, is described. The variations needed to express in a state machine weaving the meaning of *before*, *after*, and *around* with *proceed* advice are briefly outlined.

The notion of reasoning about systems composed from two or more state machines is not new, and the most prevalent method for doing so is the assume-guarantee paradigm, which forms the basis of this work. In [15] and [16], among others, an assume-guarantee structure for aspect specification is suggested, similar to the specifications here, but model checking is not used. In [15], proof rules are developed to reason in a modular way about aspect-oriented programs modeled as alternating transition systems; the treatment is for a particular base program in combination with an aspect. And in [16], aspects are examined as transition system transformers, but a verification technique is not introduced.

In most model checking works based on assume-guarantee, the notion of compositionality is one in which two machines are composed in parallel. Composing machine M with M' yields a machine in which composed states are pairs of original states that agree on atomic propositions shared by the two machines. The work of [17] introduced tableaux to modular verification. Under the parallel composition model, no issue analogous to aspect invasiveness arises, because the machines are combined according to jointly-available states.

An alternative mode of verification for composed systems is seen in [18], treating feature-oriented programs built from collections of state machines that implement different features within a system. Consequently, that framework uses a weaving-like process of adding edges between initial and return states of individual machines, but those feature machines explicitly receive and release control over the global state, unlike the oblivious base machines here. Work on extending properties modularly for features is presented in [19].

6 Conclusion

By reusing the notion of a tableau containing all behaviors that satisfy a particular formula, we can achieve a modular verification for aspects. The approach is based on augmenting this tableau with the advice according to a pointcut descriptor and examining the result. In order to do so we must restrict our view to aspects which are weakly invasive and always return to states which were reachable in the original base system. Any computation that infinitely often visits an aspect state is considered fair, to guarantee that it is checked.

A number of directions for future work present themselves. While the current technique only addresses a single aspect and pointcut descriptor, in principle it can be extended to work for multiple aspects, given proper definitions of the weaving mechanics. Further development of how weaving is formulated will also allow treatment of aspects with advice whose addition changes the set of joinpoints. Furthermore, the entire discussion here is given in terms of states and state machines, while, as noted earlier, the usual basic vocabulary of aspect-oriented programming languages refers to events. Problems of real object systems still must be fully expressed in the state-based model checking used here.

Nevertheless, the generic method in this paper allows us for the first time to model check aspects independently of a concrete base program, and already the MAVEN modular aspect verifier can provide useful results. This technique is a significant step toward the truly modular verification of aspects.

References

1. Kiczales, G., Hilsdale, E., Hugunin, J., Kersten, M., Palm, J., Griswold, W.G.: An overview of AspectJ. In: Proceedings ECOOP 2001. LNCS 2072 (2001) 327–353 http://aspectj.org.
2. Filman, R.E., Elrad, T., Clarke, S., Akşit, M., eds.: Aspect-Oriented Software Development. Addison-Wesley, Boston (2005)
3. Sihman, M., Katz, S.: Superimposition and aspect-oriented programming. BCS Computer Journal 46(5) (2003) 529–541
4. Abraham, E., de Boer, F., de Roever, W.P., Steffen, M.: An assertion-based proof system for multithreaded java. Theoretical Computer Science 331(2-3) (2005) 251–290

5. Katz, S.: Aspect categories and classes of temporal properties. In: Transactions on Aspect Oriented Software Development, Volume 1, LNCS 3880. (2006) 106–134
6. Clarke, Jr., E.M., Grumberg, O., Peled, D.A.: Model Checking. MIT Press, Cambridge, MA (1999)
7. Goldman, M.: Modular verification of aspects. MSc thesis, Technion — Israel Institute of Technology (2006) Available at http://www.cs.technion.ac.il/Labs/ssdl/thesis/finished/2006/max.
8. Sereni, D., de Moor, O.: Static analysis of aspects. In: AOSD'03: Proc. 2nd Intl. Conf. on Aspect-oriented Software Development, ACM Press (2003) 30–39
9. NuSMV. (http://nusmv.irst.itc.it/)
10. Douence, R., Südholt, M.: A model and a tool for Event-based Aspect-Oriented Programming (EAOP). TR 02/11/INFO, Ecole des Mines de Nantes (2002)
11. Krishnamurthi, S., Fisler, K., Greenberg, M.: Verifying aspect advice modularly. In: Proc. SIGSOFT Conference on Foundations of Software Engineering, FSE'04, ACM (2004) 137–146
12. Katz, S., Sihman, M.: Aspect validation using model checking. In: Proc. of International Symposium on Verification. LNCS 2772 (2003) 389–411
13. Hatcliff, J., Dwyer, M.: Using the Bandera Tool Set to model-check properties of concurrent Java software. In Larsen, K.G., Nielsen, M., eds.: Proc. 12th Int. Conf. on Concurrency Theory, CONCUR'01. Volume 2154 of LNCS., Springer-Verlag (2001) 39–58
14. Havelund, K., Pressburger, T.: Model checking Java programs using Java PathFinder. International Journal on Software Tools for Technology Transfer (STTT) 2(4) (2000)
15. Devereux, B.: Compositional reasoning about aspects using alternating-time logic. In: Proc. of Foundations of Aspect Languages Workshop (FOAL03). (2003)
16. Sipma, H.: A formal model for cross-cutting modular transition systems. In: Proc. of Foundations of Aspect Languages Workshop (FOAL03). (2003)
17. Grumberg, O., Long, D.E.: Model checking and modular verification. ACM Transactions on Programming Languages and Systems 16(3) (1994) 843–871
18. Blundell, C., Fisler, K., Krishnamurthi, S., Hentenryck, P.V.: Parameterized interfaces for open system verification of product lines. In: Proc. 19th IEEE International Conference on Automated Software Engineering, ASE'04, Washington, DC, IEEE Computer Society (2004) 258–267
19. Guelev, D.P., Ryan, M.D., Schobbens, P.Y.: Model-checking the preservation of temporal properties upon feature integration. In: Proc. 4th Intl. Workshop on Automated Verification of Critical Systems (AVoCS). Electronic Notes in Theoretical Computer Science 128(6) (2004) 311–324

Model Checking Liveness Properties of Genetic Regulatory Networks

Grégory Batt[1], Calin Belta[1], and Ron Weiss[2]

[1] Center for Information and Systems Engineering and Center for BioDynamics,
Boston University, Brookline, MA, USA
[2] Department of Electrical Engineering and Department of Molecular Biology,
Princeton University, Princeton, NJ, USA
batt@bu.edu, cbelta@bu.edu, rweiss@princeton.edu

Abstract. Recent studies have demonstrated the possibility to build genetic regulatory networks that confer a desired behavior to a living organism. However, the design of these networks is difficult, notably because of uncertainties on parameter values. In previous work, we proposed an approach to analyze genetic regulatory networks with parameter uncertainties. In this approach, the models are based on piecewise-multiaffine (PMA) differential equations, the specifications are expressed in temporal logic, and uncertain parameters are given by intervals. Abstractions are used to obtain finite discrete representations of the dynamics of the system, amenable to model checking. However, the abstraction process creates spurious behaviors along which time does not progress, called time-converging behaviors. Consequently, the verification of liveness properties, expressing that something will eventually happen, and implicitly assuming progress of time, often fails. In this work, we extend our previous approach to enforce progress of time. More precisely, we define transient regions as subsets of the state space left in finite time by every solution trajectory, show how they can be used to rule out time-converging behaviors, and provide sufficient conditions for their identification in PMA systems. This approach is implemented in RoVerGeNe and applied to the analysis of a network built in the bacterium *E. coli*.

1 Introduction

The main goal of the nascent field of synthetic biology is to design and construct biological systems that present a desired behavior. The construction of networks of interregulating genes, so-called genetic regulatory networks, has demonstrated the feasibility of this approach [1]. However, most of the newly-created networks are non-functioning and need subsequent tuning [1]. One important reason is that large uncertainties on parameter values hamper the design of the networks. These uncertainties are caused by current limitations of experimental techniques but also by the fact that parameter values themselves vary with the ever-fluctuating extra- and intracellular environmental conditions.

In previous work [2,3], we have developed a method for the verification of dynamical properties of genetic regulatory networks with *parameter uncertainty*.

O. Grumberg and M. Huth (Eds.): TACAS 2007, LNCS 4424, pp. 323–338, 2007.
© Springer-Verlag Berlin Heidelberg 2007

In this approach, models are based on piecewise-multiaffine (PMA) differential equations, dynamical properties are specified in temporal logic, and uncertain parameters are given by intervals. Following an approach widely-used in hybrid systems theory [4], we use a time-abstracting embedding transition system in combination with discrete abstractions to obtain finite discrete representations of the dynamics of the system in state and parameter spaces, amenable to algorithmic verification by model checking [5].

In the context of gene network design, *liveness* properties, expressing that something will *eventually* happen [6], are commonly-encountered. When proving liveness properties of a dynamical system, the implicit requirement that along every behavior time progresses without upper bound plays a key role [7,8]. However, spurious, time-converging behaviors created by the abstraction process often cause the verification on the abstract system of liveness properties to fail. This problem was early recognized but is still largely unsolved for continuous and hybrid systems [7,9].

In this work, we address the above problem by enforcing progress of time in the abstract systems. First, we define transient regions as subsets of the state space that are left in finite time by every solution trajectory. Then, the simple observation that if the system remains in a transient region, the corresponding behavior is necessarily time-converging, provides us with a means to rule out time-converging behaviors in abstract systems. Finally, we propose sufficient conditions for the identification of transient regions of PMA systems. This approach has been implemented in a tool for Robust Verification of Gene Networks (RoVerGeNe), and applied to the verification of a non-trivial liveness property of a transcriptional cascade built in the bacterium *E. coli*. This case study demonstrates the practical applicability of the proposed approach.

The remainder of this paper is organized as follows. In Section 3, the biological problem is illustrated by means of an example: the analysis of the robustness of a transcriptional cascade. In Section 4, we present PMA models and briefly review the approach described in [2,3] for their analysis under parameter uncertainty. Our contribution to the verification of liveness properties is detailed in Section 5 and 6. More precisely, we show in Section 5 how transient regions can be used to rule out time-converging behaviors in discrete abstractions, and in Section 6 how transient regions can be computed for uncertain PMA systems. In Section 7, we apply the proposed approach to the analysis of the transcriptional cascade. The final section discusses the proposed approach in the context of related work.

2 Preliminaries

All the notions and notations presented here are described at length in [2]. We consider Kripke structures, also called transition systems, $T = (S, \rightarrow, \Pi, \models)$, where S is a finite or infinite set of states, $\rightarrow \subseteq S \times S$ is a total transition relation, Π is a finite set of propositions, and $\models \subseteq S \times \Pi$ is a satisfaction relation [5]. An *execution* of T is an infinite sequence $e = (s_0, s_1, \ldots)$ such that for every $i \geq 0$, $s_i \in S$ and $(s_i, s_{i+1}) \in \rightarrow$. An equivalence relation $\sim \subseteq S \times S$

is proposition- preserving if $\forall s, s' \in S$ and $\pi \in \Pi$, if $s \sim s'$ and $s \models \pi$, then $s' \models \pi$. The *quotient transition system* of $T = (S, \rightarrow, \Pi, \models)$ given a proposition-preserving equivalence relation $\sim \subseteq S \times S$ is $T/_{\sim} = (S/_{\sim}, \rightarrow_{\sim}, \Pi, \models_{\sim})$, where $S/_{\sim}$ is the set of all equivalence classes R of S, $\rightarrow_{\sim} \subseteq S/_{\sim} \times S/_{\sim}$ is such that $R \rightarrow_{\sim} R'$ iff there exist $s \in R, s' \in R'$ such that $s \rightarrow s'$, and $\models_{\sim} \subseteq S/_{\sim} \times \Pi$ is such that $R \models_{\sim} \pi$ iff there exists $s \in R$ such that $s \models \pi$. The strongly connected components of a transition system $T = (S, \rightarrow, \Pi, \models)$ are the maximal strongly connected subgraphs of the graph $(S, \rightarrow)$. We refer to [5] for the syntax and semantics of LTL formulas interpreted over executions. A transition system T satisfies an LTL formula ϕ, denoted $T \models \phi$, iff every execution of T satisfies ϕ.

Let $S \subseteq \mathbb{R}^n$. $\overline{S}$ denotes its closure in $\mathbb{R}^n$, and hull(S), its convex hull. A polytope P in $\mathbb{R}^n$ is a bounded intersection of a finite number of open or closed halfspaces. P is hyperrectangular if $P = P_1 \times \ldots \times P_n$ where $P_i = \{x_i \in \mathbb{R} \mid x = (x_1, \ldots, x_n) \in P\}$, $i \in \{1, \ldots, n\}$. The set of points $v_1, \ldots, v_p \in \mathbb{R}^n$ satisfying $\overline{P} = \text{hull}(\{v_1, \ldots, v_p\})$ and $v_i \notin \text{hull}(\{v_1, \ldots, v_{i-1}, v_{i+1}, \ldots, v_p\})$, $i \in \{1, \ldots, p\}$, is the set $\mathcal{V}_P$ of vertices of P. A facet of a full-dimensional polytope P is the intersection of P with one of its supporting hyperplanes. An affine function $f : \mathbb{R}^n \rightarrow \mathbb{R}^m$ is a polynomial of degree at most 1. A multiaffine function $f : \mathbb{R}^n \rightarrow \mathbb{R}^m$ is a polynomial in which the degree of f in any of its variables is at most 1. Stated differently, non-linearities are restricted to product of distinct variables.

Theorem 1. *[10] Let $f : \mathbb{R}^n \rightarrow \mathbb{R}^m$ be an affine function and P be a polytope in $\mathbb{R}^n$. Then, $f(\overline{P}) = \text{hull}(\{f(v) \mid v \in \mathcal{V}_P\})$.*

Theorem 2. *[11] Let $f : \mathbb{R}^n \rightarrow \mathbb{R}^m$ be a multiaffine function and P be a hyperrectangular polytope in $\mathbb{R}^n$. Then, $f(P) \subseteq \text{hull}(\{f(v) \mid v \in \mathcal{V}_P\})$.*

3 A Motivating Example: Tuning a Transcriptional Cascade

We consider the genetic regulatory network built in *E. coli* [12] and represented in Figure 1(a). It consists of 4 genes forming a cascade of transcriptional inhibitions. The network is controlled by the addition or removal of aTc that serves as controllable input. The output is the fluorescence intensity of the system, due to the fluorescent protein EYFP. The cascade is ultrasensitive: at steady-state, the output undergoes a dramatic change for a moderate change of the input in a narrow interval. The cascade is expected to present at least a 1000-fold increase of the output value for a two-fold increase of the input value, but the actual network does not meet its specifications (Figure 1(b)).

In [2,3], we investigated the possibility to tune the network by modifying some of its parameters. To do so, we built a model of the system (Figure 2(a)), identified parameter values using experimental data available in [12], specified the expected behavior in LTL (Figure 2(b)), and searched for and found parameter values for which the system satisfies its specifications (Figure 1(b)). It is important that the network presents a robust behavior, since it should behave as expected despite environmental fluctuations. So, before actually experimentally

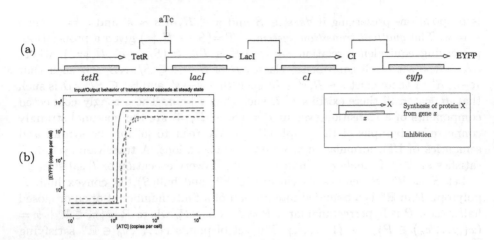

Fig. 1. (a) Synthetic transcriptional cascade. The genes *tetR*, *lacI*, *cI*, and *eyfp* code for the proteins TetR, LacI, CI, and EYFP, respectively. When a gene is expressed, the corresponding protein is produced, which inhibits the expression of a gene downstream. The input molecule, aTc, relieves the inhibition of *lacI* by TetR. (b) Steady-state I/O behavior of the cascade: measured (red dots), expected (region delimited by black dashed lines), and predicted, before (red dashed line) and after (blue solid line) tuning.

tuning the network as suggested, we would like to use our model to evaluate the robustness of the tuned system. More specifically, we would like to verify that the tuned cascade satisfies its specification for all production and degradation rate parameters varying in ±10% intervals centered at their reference values.

4   Model Checking Genetic Regulatory Networks with Parameter Uncertainty

4.1   PMA Models and LTL Specifications

We first present a formalism for modeling gene networks. The notations and terminology are adapted from [13]. We consider a network consisting of n genes. The state of the network is given by the vector $x = (x_1, \ldots, x_n)$, where x_i is the concentration of the protein encoded by gene i. The state space $\mathcal{X}$ is a hyperrectangular subset of $\mathbb{R}^n$: $\mathcal{X} = \prod_{i=1}^{n}[0, max_{x_i}]$, where max_{x_i} denotes a maximal concentration of the protein encoded by gene i. Some parameters may be *uncertain*: $p = (p_1, \ldots, p_m)$ is the vector of uncertain parameters, with values in the parameter space $\mathcal{P} = \prod_{j=1}^{m}[min_{p_j}, max_{p_j}]$, where min_{p_j} and max_{p_j} denotes a minimal and maximal value for p_j.

The dynamics of the network is given by a set of differential equations:

$$\dot{x}_i = f_i(x, p) = \sum_{j \in P_i} \kappa_i^j r_i^j(x) - \sum_{j \in D_i} \gamma_i^j r_i^j(x)\, x_i, \quad i \in \{1, \ldots, n\}, \quad (1)$$

where P_i and D_i are sets of indices, $\kappa_i^j > 0$ and $\gamma_i^j > 0$ are (*possibly uncertain*) *production* and *degradation rate parameters*, and $r_i^j : \mathcal{X} \to [0, 1]$ are continuous,

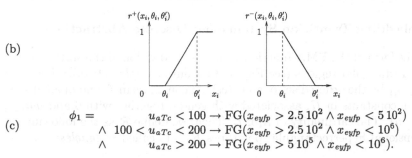

(a)

$$\dot{x}_{tetR} = \kappa_{tetR} - \gamma_{tetR}\, x_{tetR}, \tag{1'}$$

$$\dot{x}_{lacI} = \kappa_{lacI}^0 + \kappa_{lacI}(1 - r^+(x_{tetR}, \theta_{tetR}^1, \theta_{tetR}^2)\, r^-(u_{aTc}, \theta_{aTc}^1, \theta_{aTc}^2)) - \gamma_{lacI}\, x_{lacI}, \tag{2'}$$

$$\dot{x}_{cI} = \kappa_{cI}^0 + \kappa_{cI}\, r^-(x_{lacI}, \theta_{lacI}^1, \theta_{lacI}^2) - \gamma_{cI}\, x_{cI}, \tag{3'}$$

$$\dot{x}_{eyfp} = \kappa_{eyfp}^0 + \kappa_{eyfp}\, r^-(x_{cI}, \theta_{cI}^1, \theta_{cI}^2) - \gamma_{eyfp}\, x_{eyfp}, \tag{4'}$$

$(\theta_{aTc}^1, \theta_{aTc}^2) = (80, 4000)$; $(\kappa_{tetR}, \gamma_{tetR}, \theta_{tetR}^1, \theta_{tetR}^2) = (260, 0.013, 4500, 5500)$;
$(\kappa_{lacI}^0, \kappa_{lacI}, \gamma_{lacI}, \theta_{lacI}^1, \theta_{lacI}^2) = (2.4, 875.6, 0.013, 500, 4500)$; $(\kappa_{cI}^0, \kappa_{cI}, \gamma_{cI}, \theta_{cI}^1, \theta_{cI}^2) =$
$(3.9, 386, 0.013, 600, 23000)$; $(\kappa_{eyfp}^0, \kappa_{eyfp}, \gamma_{eyfp}) = (4.58, 4048, 0.013)$

(b)

(c)

$$\phi_1 = \quad u_{aTc} < 100 \rightarrow FG(x_{eyfp} > 2.5\,10^2 \wedge x_{eyfp} < 5\,10^2)$$
$$\wedge \quad 100 < u_{aTc} < 200 \rightarrow FG(x_{eyfp} > 2.5\,10^2 \wedge x_{eyfp} < 10^6)$$
$$\wedge \quad u_{aTc} > 200 \rightarrow FG(x_{eyfp} > 5\,10^5 \wedge x_{eyfp} < 10^6).$$

Fig. 2. (a) Model of the cascade. x_{tetR}, x_{lacI}, x_{cI}, x_{eyfp} denote protein concentrations, u_{aTc}, input molecule concentration, θ's, threshold parameters, κ's, production rate parameters, and γ's, degradation rate parameters. r^+ and r^- are ramp functions represented in (b). The product of ramp functions in Eq. (2') captures the assumption that the expression of *lacI* is repressed when TetR is present and aTc absent, and causes the model to be piecewise-multiaffine. Parameter values are indicated. Tuned parameters are: $\kappa_{lacI} = 2591$, $\kappa_c I = 550$, and $\kappa_{eyfp} = 8000$. (b) Increasing (r^+) and decreasing (r^-) ramp functions. (c) LTL specification of the expected behavior of the cascade represented in Figure 1(b). FGp ("eventually, p will be always true") is used to express that the property p holds at steady state. ϕ_1 is a liveness property.

piecewise-multiaffine (PMA) functions, called *regulation functions*. As seen in our example, PMA functions arise from products of ramp functions r^+ and r^- used for representing complex gene regulations or protein degradations (see Figure 2(a) Eq. (2') and Ref. [2]). The components of p are production or degradation rate parameters. With the additional assumption that r_i^j does not depend on x_i for $j \in D_i$,[1] it holds that $f = (f_1, \ldots, f_n) : \mathcal{X} \times \mathcal{P} \rightarrow \mathbb{R}^n$ is a (non-smooth) *continuous* function of x and p, a *piecewise-multiaffine* function of x, and an *affine* function of p. Note that production and degradation rate parameters may be uncertain, but regulation functions (with their threshold parameters) must be known precisely. Finally, Equation (1) is easily extended to account for constant inputs u by considering u as a new variable satisfying $\dot{u} = 0$.

A number of dynamical properties of gene networks can be specified in temporal logic by LTL formulas over atomic propositions of type $x_i < \lambda$ or $x_i > \lambda$, where $\lambda \in \mathbb{R}_{\geq 0}$ is a constant. We denote by Π the set of all such atomic

---

[1] This assumption requires that a protein does not regulate its own degradation. In practice, this assumption is generally satisfied.

propositions. A *PMA system* Σ is then defined by a piecewise-multiaffine function f defined as above and a set of atomic propositions Π: $\Sigma = (f, \Pi)$.

PMA models of gene networks were proposed in [14] (see [15] for a related, piecewise-continuous formalism). The models considered here are also related to the piecewise-affine (PA) models proposed in [16] (see also [13]). However, contrary to the step functions used in PA models, ramp functions capture the graded response of gene expression to continuous changes in effector concentrations.

4.2   Embedding Transition Systems and Discrete Abstractions

The specific form of the PMA function f suggests a division of the state space $\mathcal{X}$ into hyperrectangular regions (see Figure 3 for our example network). Let $\Lambda_i = \{\lambda_i^j\}_{j \in \{1,\dots,l_i\}}$ be the ordered set of all threshold constants in f, and of all atomic proposition constants in Π, associated with gene i, together with 0 and max_{x_i}, $i \in \{1,\dots,n\}$. The cardinality of Λ_i is l_i. Then, we define $\mathcal{R}$ as the following set of n-dimensional hyperrectangular polytopes $R \subseteq \mathcal{X}$, called *rectangles*:

$$\mathcal{R} = \{R_c \mid c = (c_1,\dots,c_n) \text{ and } \forall i \in \{1,\dots,n\} : c_i \in \{1,\dots,l_i - 1\}\},$$

where
$$R_c = \{x \in \mathcal{X} \mid \forall i \in \{1,\dots,n\} : \lambda_i^{c_i} < x_i < \lambda_i^{c_i+1}\}.$$

The union of all rectangles in $\mathcal{X}$ is denoted by $\mathcal{X}_\mathcal{R}$: $\mathcal{X}_\mathcal{R} = \cup_{R \in \mathcal{R}} R$. Note that $\mathcal{X}_\mathcal{R} \neq \mathcal{X}$. Notably, threshold hyperplanes are not included in $\mathcal{X}_\mathcal{R}$. $rect : \mathcal{X}_\mathcal{R} \to \mathcal{R}$ maps every point x in $\mathcal{X}_\mathcal{R}$ to the rectangle R such that $x \in R$. Two rectangles R and R', are said *adjacent*, denoted $R \backsim R'$, if they share a facet. Figure 3(a) shows 9 rectangles in a 2-D slice of the state space of our example network. R^1 and R^2 are adjacent (*i.e.* $R^1 \backsim R^2$), whereas R^1 and R^5 are not.

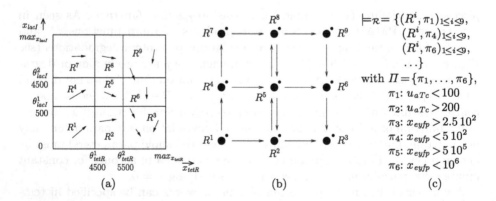

Fig. 3. Transcriptional cascade. (a) Schematic representation of the flow (arrows) in a 2-D slice of the state space. Other variables satisfy: $0 < u_{aTc} < 100$, $0 < x_{cI} < 600$, and $0 < x_{eyfp} < 250$. (b) and (c) Discrete abstraction $T_\mathcal{R}(p)$: subgraph of $(\mathcal{R}, \to_{\mathcal{R},p})$ corresponding to the region represented in (a), and satisfaction relation $\models_\mathcal{R}$. Dots denote self transitions.

Formally, we define the semantics of a PMA system Σ by means of a time-abstracting embedding transition system [4,8].

Definition 1. *Let $p \in \mathcal{P}$. The embedding transition system associated with the PMA system $\Sigma = (f, \Pi)$ is $T_\mathcal{X}(p) = (\mathcal{X}_\mathcal{R}, \rightarrow_{\mathcal{X},p}, \Pi, \models_\mathcal{X})$ defined such that:*

- $\rightarrow_{\mathcal{X},p} \subseteq \mathcal{X}_\mathcal{R} \times \mathcal{X}_\mathcal{R}$ *is the transition relation defined by $(x, x') \in \rightarrow_{\mathcal{X},p}$ iff there exist a solution ξ of (1) and $\tau \in \mathbb{R}_{>0}$ such that $\xi(0) = x$, $\xi(\tau) = x'$, $\forall t \in [0, \tau]$, $\xi(t) \in \overline{rect}(x) \cup \overline{rect}(x')$, and either $rect(x) = rect(x')$ or $rect(x) \leftrightarrow rect(x')$,*
- $\models_\mathcal{X} \subseteq \mathcal{X}_\mathcal{R} \times \Pi$ *is the satisfaction relation defined by $(x, \pi) \in \models_\mathcal{X}$ iff $x = (x_1, \ldots, x_n)$ satisfies the proposition π (of type $x_i < \lambda$ or $x_i > \lambda$) with the usual semantics.*

In $T_\mathcal{X}(p)$, a transition between two points corresponds to an evolution of the system during some time. Quantitative aspects of time are abstracted away: some time elapses, but we don't know how much. Also note that not all solution trajectories of (1) are guaranteed to be represented by our embedding. However, one can show that our embedding describes *almost all* solution trajectories of (1), which is satisfying for all practical purposes [2].

A PMA system Σ satisfies an LTL formula ϕ for a given parameter $p \in \mathcal{P}$ if $T_\mathcal{X}(p) \models \phi$, that is, if every execution of $T_\mathcal{X}(p)$ satisfies ϕ.

We use discrete abstractions [4] to obtain finite transition systems preserving dynamical properties of $T_\mathcal{X}(p)$ and amenable to algorithmic verification [5]. Let $\sim_\mathcal{R} \subseteq \mathcal{X}_\mathcal{R} \times \mathcal{X}_\mathcal{R}$ be the (proposition-preserving) equivalence relation defined by the map *rect*: $x \sim_\mathcal{R} x'$ iff $rect(x) = rect(x')$. $\mathcal{R}$ is the set of equivalence classes. Then, the discrete abstraction of $T_\mathcal{X}(p)$ is the *quotient* of $T_\mathcal{X}(p)$ given $\sim_\mathcal{R}$.

Definition 2. *Let $p \in \mathcal{P}$. The discrete abstraction of $T_\mathcal{X}(p)$ is the quotient of $T_\mathcal{X}(p)$ given $\sim_\mathcal{R}$, denoted by $T_\mathcal{R}(p) = (\mathcal{R}, \rightarrow_{\mathcal{R},p}, \Pi, \models_\mathcal{R})$.*

For the cascade, the discrete transition system $T_\mathcal{R}(p)$ is partially represented in Figure 3(b) and (c), with p denoting the tuned parameter values (Section 3). As suggested by the sketch of the flow in Figure 3(a), there exist solution trajectories reaching R^2 from R^1 without leaving $\overline{R}^1 \cup \overline{R}^2$. Consequently, there is a discrete transition from R^1 to R^2. Also, for example, rectangle R^1 satisfies the atomic proposition π_1: $u_{aTc} < 100$, that is, $(R^1, \pi_1) \in \models_\mathcal{R}$.

4.3 Model Checking Uncertain PMA Systems

Because parameter values are often uncertain, we would like to be able to test whether a PMA system Σ satisfies an LTL formula ϕ for *every* parameter in a set $P \subseteq \mathcal{P}$. This problem is defined as robustness analysis in [2,3]. Note that the problem given in Section 3 is precisely an instance of this problem.

To describe the behavior of a network for *sets* of parameters $P \subseteq \mathcal{P}$, we define the transition systems $T_\mathcal{R}^\exists(P)$ and $T_\mathcal{R}^\forall(P)$ as follows.

Definition 3. *Let* $P \subseteq \mathcal{P}$. *Then* $T_{\mathcal{R}}^{\exists}(P) = (\mathcal{R}, \to_{\mathcal{R},P}^{\exists}, \Pi, \models_{\mathcal{R}})$ *and* $T_{\mathcal{R}}^{\forall}(P) = (\mathcal{R}, \to_{\mathcal{R},P}^{\forall}, \Pi, \models_{\mathcal{R}})$, *where*

- $(R, R') \in \to_{\mathcal{R},P}^{\exists}$ *iff* $\exists p \in P$ *such that* $(R, R') \in \to_{\mathcal{R},p}$ *in* $T_{\mathcal{R}}(p)$, *and*
- $(R, R') \in \to_{\mathcal{R},P}^{\forall}$ *iff* $\forall p \in P$, $(R, R') \in \to_{\mathcal{R},p}$ *in* $T_{\mathcal{R}}(p)$.

In words, $T_{\mathcal{R}}^{\exists}(P)$ contains all the transitions present in at least one transition system $T_{\mathcal{R}}(p)$, and $T_{\mathcal{R}}^{\forall}(P)$ contains only the transitions present in all the transition systems $T_{\mathcal{R}}(p)$, $p \in P$. Informally, $T_{\mathcal{R}}^{\exists}(P)$ and $T_{\mathcal{R}}^{\forall}(P)$ can be considered as over- and under-approximations of $T_{\mathcal{R}}(p)$ when p varies, respectively.

In [2,3], we have shown the following property.

$$\text{if } T_{\mathcal{R}}^{\exists}(P) \models \phi, \text{ then for every } p \in P, \ T_{\mathcal{X}}(p) \models \phi,$$

that is, the PMA system Σ satisfies property ϕ for every parameter in P. This property is instrumental for proving robust properties of gene networks. However, note that $T_{\mathcal{R}}^{\exists}(P) \not\models \phi$ does not imply that for some, nor for every parameter, the property is false. P might still contain parameters for which the property is true, called valid parameters. So we proposed an iterative procedure that partitions P and that tests whether $T_{\mathcal{R}}^{\exists}(P') \models \phi$ for each full-dimensional subset P'. Clearly, this approach becomes very inefficient when P does not contain valid parameters, since we keep on partitioning P. This situation can be detected by means of $T_{\mathcal{R}}^{\forall}(P)$. We have shown in [2,3] that if $T_{\mathcal{R}}^{\forall}(P) \not\models \phi$, then we should stop partitioning P. So $T_{\mathcal{R}}^{\exists}(P)$ and $T_{\mathcal{R}}^{\forall}(P)$ are respectively used for proving robust properties of the system and for preserving the efficiency of the approach. Finally, we showed that $T_{\mathcal{R}}^{\exists}(P)$ and $T_{\mathcal{R}}^{\forall}(P)$ can be computed for polyhedral parameter sets using standard polyhedral operations. The robustness of a number of dynamical properties can be tested this way. However, because model checking results are almost always negative, this approach fails when applied to the verification of *liveness* properties. As we will see in the next section, this problem is due to the presence of spurious, time-converging executions in the abstract transition systems.

5   Transient Regions and Liveness Checking

The analysis of counter-examples returned by model-checkers reveals why the verification of liveness properties generally fails. For example, the execution $e_{\mathcal{R}1} = (R^1, R^1, R^1, \ldots)$ of $T_{\mathcal{R}}(p)$ (Figure 3(b)), is a counter-example of the liveness property ϕ_1 given in Figure 2(c). However, from the sketch of the flow in Figure 3(a), it is intuitively clear that the system leaves R^1 in finite time. Consequently, the execution $e_{\mathcal{R}1}$ that describes a system remaining always in R^1 conflicts with the requirement that time progresses without upper bound. Such executions are called *time-converging* [7,9][2]. Because they do not represent genuine behaviors of the system, these executions should be excluded when checking the properties of the system.

---

[2] Time-converging executions are sometimes called Zeno executions [7,9]. However, we prefer the former term since the latter is also used in a more restricted sense [17].

5.1   Time-Diverging Executions and Transient Regions

Definition 4. *Let $p \in \mathcal{P}$.*

An execution $e_{\mathcal{X}} = (x_0, x_1, \ldots)$ of $T_{\mathcal{X}}(p)$ is time-diverging iff there exists a solution ξ of (1) and a sequence of time instants $\tau = (\tau_0, \tau_1, \ldots)$ such that $\xi(\tau_i) = x_i$, for all $i \geq 0$, and $\lim_{i \to \infty} \tau_i = \infty$.

An execution $e_{\mathcal{R}} = (R_0, R_1, \ldots)$ of $T_{\mathcal{R}}(p)$ is time-diverging iff there exists a time-diverging execution $e_{\mathcal{X}} = (x_0, x_1, \ldots)$ of $T_{\mathcal{X}}(p)$ such that $x_i \in R_i$, for all $i \geq 0$.

Intuitively, an execution of the embedding transition system $T_{\mathcal{X}}(p)$ is time-diverging if it represents at least one solution on the time interval $[0, \infty)$. Also, an execution of the discrete transition system $T_{\mathcal{R}}(p)$ is time-diverging if it is the abstraction of at least one time-diverging execution of $T_{\mathcal{X}}(p)$. Here, we identify two causes for the absence of progress in the abstract system $T_{\mathcal{R}}(p)$. The first one is due to the time-abstracting semantics used. The time-elapse corresponding to a transition in $T_{\mathcal{X}}(p)$ can be infinitesimal such that the sum of all time-elapses of the transitions of an execution of $T_{\mathcal{X}}(p)$ can be finite. The second one is due to the discrete abstraction, since the abstraction process introduces the possibility to iterate infinitely on discrete states of $T_{\mathcal{R}}(p)$. While the first problem appears only for dense-time systems, the second problem is also present in untimed systems and has been studied in the model checking community [18,19]. Examples of time-converging executions of $T_{\mathcal{R}}(p)$ for our example network include $e_{\mathcal{R}1} = (R^1, R^1, R^1, \ldots)$, and $e_{\mathcal{R}2} = (R^2, R^5, R^2, R^5, R^2, \ldots)$ (Figure 3(a) and (b)).

The notion of time-diverging executions can be extended to $T_{\mathcal{R}}^{\exists}(P)$ and $T_{\mathcal{R}}^{\forall}(P)$ as follows.

Definition 5. *Let $P \subseteq \mathcal{P}$.*

An execution $e_{\mathcal{R}}$ of $T_{\mathcal{R}}^{\exists}(P)$ is time-diverging, if for some $p \in P$, $e_{\mathcal{R}}$ is an execution of $T_{\mathcal{R}}(p)$ and is time-diverging.

An execution $e_{\mathcal{R}}$ of $T_{\mathcal{R}}^{\forall}(P)$ is time-diverging, if for all $p \in P$, $e_{\mathcal{R}}$ is a time-diverging execution of $T_{\mathcal{R}}(p)$.

Finally, we define *transient regions* as subsets of the state space $\mathcal{X}$ that are left in finite time by every solution. For a reason that will become clear later, we focus on regions corresponding to unions of rectangles. As suggested by the sketch of the flow in Figure 3(a) and proved later, R^1 and $\cup_{j \in \{2,5,8\}} R^j$ are transient regions.

Definition 6. *Let $p \in \mathcal{P}$ and $U \subseteq \mathcal{X}$ be a union of rectangles $R \in \mathcal{R}$. U is transient for parameter p if for every solution ξ of (1) such that $\xi(0) \in U$, there exists $\tau > 0$ such that $\xi(\tau) \notin \overline{U}$.*

5.2   Ruling Out Time-Converging Executions

From the maximality of strongly connected components (SCCs), it follows that an infinite execution of a finite transition system remains eventually always in a unique SCC. With $T_{\mathcal{R}}$ being either $T_{\mathcal{R}}(p)$, $T_{\mathcal{R}}^{\exists}(P)$, or $T_{\mathcal{R}}^{\forall}(P)$, and $e_{\mathcal{R}}$ being an execution of $T_{\mathcal{R}}$, we denote by $SCC(e_{\mathcal{R}}) \subseteq \mathcal{X}$ the union of the rectangles of the strongly connected component of $T_\mathcal{R}$ in which $e_\mathcal{R}$ remains eventually always. Then, it is clear that if an execution $e_\mathcal{R}$ of $T_\mathcal{R}(p)$ is time-diverging, that is, represents at least a solution trajectory on a time interval $[0, \infty)$ (Definition 4), then $SCC(e_\mathcal{R})$ can not be a transient region. Proposition 1 captures this intuition and establishes a link between time-diverging executions and transient regions.

Proposition 1. *Let $p \in \mathcal{P}$. If an execution $e_\mathcal{R}$ of $T_\mathcal{R}(p)$ is time-diverging, then $SCC(e_\mathcal{R})$ is not transient for p.*

Proof. Let $p \in \mathcal{P}$ and $e_\mathcal{R} = (R_0, R_1, \ldots)$ be a time-diverging execution of $T_\mathcal{R}(p)$. By definition of $SCC(e_\mathcal{R})$, there exists $i \geq 0$ such that for every $j \geq i$, $R_j \subseteq SCC(e_\mathcal{R})$. Let $e'_\mathcal{R} = (R_i, R_{i+1}, \ldots)$ be a suffix of $e_\mathcal{R}$ and $U = \cup_{j \geq i} R_j \subseteq SCC(e_\mathcal{R})$. It holds that $e'_\mathcal{R}$ is a time-diverging execution of $T_\mathcal{R}(p)$. By Definition 4, there exists a time-diverging execution $e'_\mathcal{X} = (x_0, x_1, \ldots)$ of $T_\mathcal{X}(p)$ such that for all $j \geq 0$, $x_j \in R^{i+j} \subseteq U$. Then by Definition 4, this implies the existence of a solution ξ of (1) such that $\forall t \geq 0$, $\exists \tau \geq t$ such that $\xi(\tau) \in U$. Also, $\forall t \geq 0$, $\xi(t) \in \overline{U}$ because every rectangle visited by $\xi(t)$ is necessarily in U (Definitions 1 and 2). Consequently U is not transient for p (Definition 6). Because $U \subseteq SCC(e_\mathcal{R})$, the same necessarily holds for $SCC(e_\mathcal{R})$.

Consider again the executions $e_{\mathcal{R}1} = (R^1, R^1, R^1, \ldots)$ and $e_{\mathcal{R}2} = (R^2, R^5, R^2, R^5, R^2, \ldots)$ of $T_\mathcal{R}(p)$ (Figure 3(b)). Then, as mentioned earlier, $SCC(e_{\mathcal{R}1}) = R^1$ and $SCC(e_{\mathcal{R}2}) = \cup_{j \in \{2,5,8\}} R^j$ are transient regions for parameter p. By Proposition 1, $e_{\mathcal{R}1}$ and $e_{\mathcal{R}2}$ are consequently time-converging for p.

The following property is a generalization of Proposition 1.

Proposition 2. *Let $P \subseteq \mathcal{P}$.*
(a) If an execution $e_\mathcal{R}$ of $T_\mathcal{R}^\exists(P)$ is time-diverging, then for some $p \in P$, $SCC(e_\mathcal{R})$ is not transient for p.
(b) If an execution $e_\mathcal{R}$ of $T_\mathcal{R}^\forall(P)$ is time-diverging, then for all $p \in P$, $SCC(e_\mathcal{R})$ is not transient for p.

Proof. First note that we can not use directly Proposition 1, since by definition, $SCC(e_\mathcal{R})$ differs depending on whether $e_\mathcal{R}$ is an execution of $T_\mathcal{R}^\exists(P)$, $T_\mathcal{R}^\forall(P)$ or $T_\mathcal{R}(p)$, $p \in P$. However, with $e_\mathcal{R}$ an execution of $T_\mathcal{R}^\exists(P)$ (resp. of $T_\mathcal{R}^\forall(P)$), we can show exactly as in the proof of Proposition 1, the existence of a set U included in $SCC(e_\mathcal{R})$ and non-transient for some (resp. every) parameter $p \in P$. The conclusion follows immediately.

To summarize, let us denote by $T_\mathcal{R}$ either $T_\mathcal{R}(p)$, $T_\mathcal{R}^\exists(P)$ or $T_\mathcal{R}^\forall(P)$ and interpret "transient" as transient for p, for every $p \in P$ or for some $p \in P$, respectively. Then, using the contrapositive of Proposition 1 or 2, we obtain that given a strongly connected component of $T_\mathcal{R}$, if the corresponding region $U \subseteq \mathcal{X}$ is transient then every execution of $T_\mathcal{R}$ remaining in U (*i.e.* being eventually always in U) is time-converging and should not be taken into account when checking the properties of the system. Provided that transient regions can be identified, this suggests a method to rule out time-converging executions. To do so, we define a new atomic proposition π = 'transient' in Π and label as 'transient' all and only rectangles R in transient SCCs. Then, instead of testing whether

$$T_{\mathcal{R}} \models \phi,$$

we test whether

$$T_{\mathcal{R}} \models \phi', \quad \text{with } \phi' = \neg\text{FG}(\text{'transient'}) \to \phi.$$

The executions of $T_{\mathcal{R}}$ satisfying FG('transient') necessarily remain in a transient SCC, and are consequently time-converging (Proposition 1 or 2). So, only time-converging executions are ruled out this way. However, because Propositions 1 and 2 give only necessary conditions for an execution to be time-diverging, not all time-converging executions are guaranteed to be ruled out.

Consider again our example network. As said earlier, R^1 is a transient region. Because R^1 forms a (single-state) SCC, it is labeled 'transient' in $T_{\mathcal{R}}(p)$. Then, the execution $e_{\mathcal{R}1} = (R^1, R^1, R^1, \ldots)$, satisfying FG('transient'), is not a counterexample of ϕ'_1, and will not cause the property to be falsely invalidated anymore.

6   Transient Region Computation for PMA Systems

The approach presented in the previous section is rather general in the sense that it solely requires the capacity to characterize transient regions. In this section, we provide sufficient conditions for their identification in PMA systems. More precisely, we provide conditions for proving that regions corresponding to SCCs in the discrete abstractions are transient for a given parameter (Proposition 3), for some parameter (Proposition 5), or for all parameters in a polyhedral set (Proposition 4). Using sufficient conditions, not all transient regions are guaranteed to be identified. However, only time-converging executions will be ruled out using the approach presented in Section 5. More precisely, Propositions 3, 4 and 5 are used in combination with (the contrapositive of) Propositions 1, 2(a) and 2(b), respectively. These properties rely on the fact that in a rectangle R the function f is multiaffine and hence is a convex combination of its value at the vertices of R (Theorem 2). Our focus on PMA systems is motivated by biological applications. However, Theorem 1 for affine functions on polytopes is similar to, and in fact stronger than Theorem 2 for multiaffine functions on rectangles, such that the results in this section also hold for similarly-defined continuous, piecewise-affine systems on polytopes.

Proposition 3. *Let $p \in \mathcal{P}$ and $U \subseteq \mathcal{X}$ be a union of rectangles $R \in \mathcal{R}$. If*

$$0 \notin \text{hull}(\{f(v,p) \mid v \in \mathcal{V}_R, R \subseteq U\}),$$

then U is transient for parameter p.

Proof. Let $p \in \mathcal{P}$ and $U \subseteq \mathcal{X}$ be a union of rectangles $R \in \mathcal{R}$. Assume $0 \notin$ hull($\{f(v,p) \mid v \in \mathcal{V}_R, R \subseteq U\}$). Using the separating hyperplane theorem, there exists $\alpha \in \mathbb{R}^n$ such that for all $z \in$ hull($\{f(v,p) \mid v \in \mathcal{V}_R, R \subseteq U\}$), $\alpha^T z > 0$. For every rectangle $R \subseteq U$, $f(x,p)$ is a multiaffine function of x on $\overline{R}$, so it holds that for every $x \in \overline{R}$, $f(x,p) \in \mathrm{hull}(\{f(v,p) \mid v \in \mathcal{V}_R\})$ (Theorem 2). Then, for every $x \in \overline{U}$, $f(x,p) \in \cup_{R \subseteq U} \mathrm{hull}(\{f(v,p) \mid v \in \mathcal{V}_R\})$, which is included in $\mathrm{hull}(\{f(v,p) \mid v \in \mathcal{V}_R, R \subseteq U\})$. Consequently $\alpha^T f(x,p) > 0$. Since $\overline{U}$ is compact (union of compact sets $\overline{R}$) and f is continuous, $\alpha^T f(\overline{U},p)$ is compact, which implies that there exists $c > 0$ such that the velocity in the direction of α^T is always larger than c. Consequently, $\overline{U}$ is left in finite time.

The conditions of the above property are satisfied by R^1 and $\cup_{j \in \{2,5,8\}} R^j$, which proves that these regions are transient, as hypothesized earlier. Propositions 4 and 5 are generalizations of Proposition 3 to polyhedral parameter sets.

Proposition 4. *Let $P \subseteq \mathcal{P}$ be a polytope and $U \subseteq \mathcal{X}$ be a union of rectangles $R \in \mathcal{R}$. If $0 \notin \mathrm{hull}(\{f(v,w) \mid v \in \mathcal{V}_R, R \subseteq U, w \in \mathcal{V}_P\})$, then U is transient for all parameters $p \in P$.*

Proof. Using Proposition 3 we only have to prove that if $0 \notin \mathrm{hull}(\{f(v,w) \mid v \in \mathcal{V}_R, R \subseteq U, w \in \mathcal{V}_P\})$ then $\forall p \in P$, $0 \notin \mathrm{hull}(\{f(v,p) \mid v \in \mathcal{V}_R, R \subseteq U\})$. We prove its contrapositive. Let $p \in P$ be such that $0 \in \mathrm{hull}(\{f(v,p) \mid v \in \mathcal{V}_R, R \subseteq U\})$. Then since f is affine in p, by Theorem 1 it holds that $0 \in \mathrm{hull}(\{\mathrm{hull}(\{f(v,w) \mid w \in \mathcal{V}_P\}) \mid v \in \mathcal{V}_R, R \subseteq U\})$, or more simply $0 \in \mathrm{hull}(\{f(v,w) \mid v \in \mathcal{V}_R, R \subseteq U, w \in \mathcal{V}_P\})$. □

Proposition 5. *Let $P \subseteq \mathcal{P}$ be a polytope and $U \subseteq \mathcal{X}$ be a union of rectangles $R \in \mathcal{R}$. If for some $w \in \mathcal{V}_P$, $0 \notin \mathrm{hull}(\{f(v,w) \mid v \in \mathcal{V}_R, R \subseteq U\})$, then U is transient for some parameters $p \in P$.*

By Proposition 3, Proposition 5 is obviously sufficient for proving that a region is transient for some parameter in a polyhedral set. However, it may seem very conservative to test whether $0 \notin \mathrm{hull}(\{f(v,w) \mid v \in \mathcal{V}_R, R \subseteq U\})$ is true only at the vertices of P instead of testing whether this is true for every parameter in P. The following proposition states that this is in fact equivalent.

Proposition 6. *Let $P \subseteq \mathcal{P}$ be a polytope and $U \subseteq \mathcal{X}$ be a union of rectangles $R \in \mathcal{R}$. $\exists p \in P$ such that $0 \notin \mathrm{hull}(\{f(v,p) \mid v \in \mathcal{V}_R, R \subseteq U\})$ iff $\exists w \in \mathcal{V}_P$ such that $0 \notin \mathrm{hull}(\{f(v,w) \mid v \in \mathcal{V}_R, R \subseteq U\})$.*

Proof. The necessity is trivial. We prove sufficiency by contradiction. Let $p \in P$ and let I and J be two sets of indices labeling the vertices in $\cup_{R \subseteq U} \mathcal{V}_R$ and $\mathcal{V}_P$: $\cup_{R \subseteq U} \mathcal{V}_R = \{v_i\}_{i \in I}$ and $\mathcal{V}_P = \{w_j\}_{j \in J}$. Then, there exists $\{\mu_j\}_{j \in J}$ such that $\sum_{j \in J} \mu_j w_j = p$, with $\mu_j \geq 0$, $\forall j \in J$, and $\sum_{j \in J} \mu_j = 1$. Also, it holds that

$$\mathrm{hull}(\{f(v_i,p)\}_{i \in I}) = \mathrm{hull}(\{\textstyle\sum_{j \in J} \mu_j f(v_i,w_j)\}_{i \in I}) \quad // f \text{ is affine in } p$$

$$= \bigoplus_{j \in J} \mathrm{hull}(\{\mu_j f(v_i,w_j)\}_{i \in I}) \quad //\text{Minkowski sum of convex hulls}$$

Then, for every $w_j \in \mathcal{V}_P$, $0 \in \mathrm{hull}(\{f(v_i,w_j)\}_{i \in I})$ implies that $0 \in \mathrm{hull}(\{\mu_j f(v_i, w_j)\}_{i \in I})$. So, by definition of Minkowski sum, we have $0 \notin \mathrm{hull}(\{f(v_i,p)\}_{i \in I})$. Contradiction. □

computational		number of uncertain parameters				
time (in minutes)		0	2	5	8	11
number of	3	0.03	0.04	0.07	-	-
continuous	4	0.20	0.27	0.59	2.66	-
variables	5	2.60	3.28	6.46	29.11	207.76

Fig. 4. Computational time for the verification of a liveness property as a function of the number of variables and uncertain parameters. The 3- and 4-dimensional systems correspond to similar but shorter transcriptional cascades (see [12]).

From a computational point of view, it is important to note that the conditions in Propositions 3, 4 and 5, can be simply evaluated by solving a linear optimization problem. The implementation of the approach described in Sections 5 and 6 resulted in a new version of a publicly-available tool for Robust Verification of Gene Networks (RoVerGeNe) (http://iasi.bu.edu/~batt/rovergene/rovergene.htm). RoVerGeNe is written in Matlab and uses MPT (polyhedral operations and linear optimization), MatlabBGL (SCC computation) and NuSMV (model-checking).

7 Analysis of the Tuned Transcriptional Cascade

As explained in Section 3, in previous work we have predicted a way to tune the transcriptional cascade such that it satisfies its specifications, using a PMA model of the system. Before tuning the cascade experimentally, it is important to evaluate its robustness. To do so, we have tested whether the system satisfies the liveness property ϕ_1 (Figure 2(c)) for all of the 11 production and degradation rate parameters varying in $\pm 10\%$ intervals centered at their reference values. Because the network has no feedback loops, it is not difficult to show that oscillatory behaviors are not possible. Consequently, every (time-diverging) execution necessarily eventually remains in a single (non-transient) *rectangle*, instead of *SCC* in the general case (see Proposition 2). We have consequently applied Propositions 4 and 5 to rectangles only, to obtain tighter predictions.

Using RoVerGeNe, we have been able to prove this property in <4 hours (PC, 3.4 GHz processor, 1 Gb RAM). Given that the problem was to prove that a non-trivial property holds for every initial condition in a 5-dimensional state space (1 input and 4 state variables) and for every parameter in an 11-dimensional parameter set, this example illustrates the applicability of the proposed approach to the analysis of networks of realistic size and complexity. Computational times for smaller instances of this problem are given in Figure 4.

The same test has been performed for $\pm 20\%$ parameter variations and a negative answer has been obtained (<4 hours). We recall that from negative answers, one can not conclude that the property is false for some parameters in the set. Nevertheless, the analysis of the counter-example given by the model checker has revealed that the system can remain in a (non-transient) rectangle in which the concentration of EYFP is below the minimal value allowed by the specifications ($5 \cdot 10^5$), when the production rate constants κ_{eyfp}^0 and κ_{eyfp} are minimal and the degradation rate constant γ_{eyfp} is maximal, in the $\pm 20\%$ intervals. As a consequence, the property is not robustly satisfied by the system for $\pm 20\%$ parameter variations. This analysis illustrates that relevant constraints on parameters are identified by this approach.

8   Discussion

This work addresses the problem of the verification of liveness properties of genetic regulatory networks modeled as PMA systems. It extends previous work on the verification of PMA systems with parameter uncertainty [2,3]. Abstractions are used to obtain discrete representations of the dynamics of the system in state and parameter spaces, amenable to model checking. However, the abstractions introduce spurious behaviors along which time does not progress, called time-converging behaviors. The presence of these behaviors in the abstract systems generally causes the verification of liveness properties, expressing that something will eventually happen, to fail.

In this work, we proposed an approach to identify and rule out these behaviors, thus enforcing the progress of time in the abstract systems. We introduce the notion of transient regions as subsets of the state space that are eventually left by every solution trajectory, and established a simple relation between time-converging executions and regions corresponding to SCCs of the abstract discrete transition systems: executions that remain in a transient SCC are necessarily time-converging. Then, we provide sufficient conditions for characterizing transient regions in PMA systems. The approach is described for fixed parameters and systematically extended to deal with (polyhedral) sets of parameters. This approach is implemented in a tool called RoVerGeNe. Its capacity to provide meaningful results for non-trivial problems on networks of biological interest is illustrated on the analysis of a transcriptional cascade.

The use of model checking for the analysis of biological networks has attracted much attention [20,21,22,23,24]. The verification of true (*i.e.* unbounded) liveness properties is not possible when the semantics is based on a set of necessarily time-bounded solution trajectories obtained by numerical simulation of ordinary differential equation models [20,23]. For discrete [22,23] or hybrid [21] models, fairness properties can be added in an *ad hoc* manner for the system at hand. So, although liveness properties are commonly encountered in biological applications, no systematic approach has been proposed yet for their verification.

More generally, this work addresses the problem of the verification of liveness properties of continuous or hybrid systems having dense-time semantics. In comparison with the amount of work done for the verification of safety properties of these systems, not much work has been done for liveness properties [9]. It has been proposed that the difficulty to enforce progress of time in dense-time systems makes liveness properties comparatively more difficult to analyze [9]. Tools supporting the verification of true (*i.e.* unbounded) liveness properties of dense-time systems are Uppaal [25], TReX [18] and RED [9]. However, their applicability is limited to timed automata, which have very restricted continuous dynamics. In contrast, our approach applies to any discrete abstraction provided that transient regions can be characterized. As mentioned in Section 5, a similar problem arise in untimed systems for the verification of liveness properties when abstractions are used [18,19]. Progress of the abstract system is then enforced by the addition of fairness constraints, expressing that the system can not always remain in a given set of states. Because $\neg FG(\text{'transient'})$ $(= GF(\neg\text{'transient'})$, Section 5) is a fairness constraint, our approach precisely amounts to deduce fairness constraints from the computation of transient regions. Consequently, our work can be regarded as an extension of an approach previously proposed for untimed systems and as a first step in the direction of the verification of liveness properties for general classes of continuous or hybrid systems. We envision that the notion of transient set can play for liveness properties a role symmetrical to the well-established role of positive invariant sets for safety properties.

Acknowledgements. We would like to thank Boyan Yordanov for contributions to model development and acknowledge financial support by NSF 0432070.

References

1. Andrianantoandro, E., Basu, S., Karig, D., Weiss, R.: Synthetic biology: New engineering rules for an emerging discipline. Mol. Syst. Biol. (2006)
2. Batt, G., Belta, C.: Model checking genetic regulatory networks with applications to synthetic biology. CISE Tech. Rep. 2006-IR-0030, Boston University (2006)
3. Batt, G., Belta, C., Weiss, R.: Model checking genetic regulatory networks with parameter uncertainty. To appear in Bemporad, A., Bicchi, A., Buttazzo, G., eds.:Proc. HSCC'07. LNCS, Springer (2007)
4. Alur, R., Henzinger, T.A., Lafferriere, G.J., Pappas, G.: Discrete abstractions of hybrid systems. Proc. IEEE **88**(7) (2000) 971–984
5. Clarke, E.M., Grumberg, O., Peled, D.A.: Model Checking. MIT Press (1999)
6. Alpern, B., Schneider, F.B.: Recognizing safety and liveness. Distrib. Comput. **2**(3) (1986) 117–126
7. Henzinger, T.A., Nicollin, X., Sifakis, J., Yovine, S.: Symbolic model checking for real-time systems. Inform. and Comput. **111** (1994) 193–244
8. Tripakis, S., Yovine, S.: Analysis of timed systems using time-abstracting bisimulations. Formal Methods System Design **18**(1) (2001) 25–68
9. Wang, F., Huang, G.D., Yu, F.: TCTL inevitability analysis of dense-time systems: From theory to engineering. IEEE Trans. Softw. Eng. (2006) In press.
10. Habets, L.C.G.J.M., Collins, P.J., van Schuppen, J.H.: Reachability and control synthesis for piecewise-affine hybrid systems on simplices. IEEE Trans. Aut. Control **51**(6) (2006) 938–948
11. Belta, C., Habets, L.C.G.J.M.: Controlling a class of nonlinear systems on rectangles. IEEE Trans. Aut. Control **51**(11) (2006) 1749–1759
12. Hooshangi, S., Thiberge, S., Weiss, R.: Ultrasensitivity and noise propagation in a synthetic transcriptional cascade. Proc. Natl. Acad. Sci. USA **102**(10) (2005) 3581–3586
13. de Jong, H., Gouzé, J.L., Hernandez, C., Page, M., Sari, T., Geiselmann, J.: Qualitative simulation of genetic regulatory networks using piecewise-linear models. Bull. Math. Biol. **66**(2) (2004) 301–340

14. Belta, C., Habets, L.C.G.J.M., Kumar, V.: Control of multi-affine systems on rectangles with applications to hybrid biomolecular networks. In: Proc. CDC'02. (2002)
15. Mestl, T., Plahte, E., Omholt, S.: A mathematical framework for describing and analysing gene regulatory networks. J. Theor. Biol. **176** (1995) 291–300
16. Glass, L., Kauffman, S.A.: The logical analysis of continuous non-linear biochemical control networks. J. Theor. Biol. **39**(1) (1973) 103–129
17. Lygeros, J., Johansson, K.H., Simić, S.N., Zhang, J., Sastry, S.S.: Dynamical properties of hybrid automata. IEEE Trans. Aut. Control **48**(1) (2003) 2–17
18. Bouajjani, A., Collomb-Annichini, A., Lacknech, Y., Sighireanu, M.: Analysis of fair parametric extended automata. In Cousot, P., ed.: Proc. SAS'01. LNCS 2126, Springer (2001) 335–355
19. Dams, D., Gerth, R., Grumberg, O.: A heuristic for the automatic generation of ranking functions. In: Proc. WAVe'00. (2000) 1–8
20. Antoniotti, M., Piazza, C., Policriti, A., Simeoni, M., Mishra, B.: Taming the complexity of biochemical models through bisimulation and collapsing: Theory and practice. Theor. Comput. Sci. **325**(1) (2004) 45–67
21. Batt, G., Ropers, D., de Jong, H., Geiselmann, J., Mateescu, R., Page, M., Schneider, D.: Validation of qualitative models of genetic regulatory networks by model checking : Analysis of the nutritional stress response in *E. coli*. Bioinformatics **21**(Suppl.1) (2005) i19–i28
22. Bernot, G., Comet, J.P., Richard, A., Guespin, J.: Application of formal methods to biological regulatory networks: Extending Thomas' asynchronous logical approach with temporal logic. J. Theor. Biol. **229**(3) (2004) 339–347
23. Calzone, L., Chabrier-Rivier, N., Fages, F., Soliman, S.: Machine learning biochemical networks from temporal logic properties. In Priami, C., Plotkin, G., eds: Trans. Comput. Syst. Biol. VI. LNBI 4220, Springer (2006) 68–94
24. Eker, S., Knapp, M., Laderoute, K., Lincoln, P., Talcott, C.L.: Pathway logic: Executable models of biological networks. In Gadducci, F., Montanari, U., eds.: Proc. WRLA'02. ENTCS 71, Elsevier (2002)
25. Bengtsson, J., Larsen, K.G., Larsson, F., Pettersson, P., Wang, Y., Weise, C.: New generation of UPPAAL. In: Proc. STTT'98. (1998)

Checking Pedigree Consistency with PCS*

Panagiotis Manolios, Marc Galceran Oms, and Sergi Oliva Valls

College of Computing
Georgia Institute of Technology
Atlanta, Georgia 30332-0280 USA
{manolios,mgalceran3,soliva3}@gatech.edu

Abstract. Many important problems in bioinformatics and genetics require analyses that are NP-complete. For example, one of the basic problems facing researchers that analyze pedigrees—data that represents relationships and genetic traits of a set of individuals—is evaluating whether they are consistent with the Mendelian laws of inheritance. This problem is NP-complete and several specialized algorithms have been devised to solve the types of problems occurring in practice efficiently. In this paper, we present *PCS*, a tool based on Boolean Satisfiability (SAT) that is orders of magnitude faster than existing algorithms, and more general. In fact, *PCS* can solve real pedigree checking problems that cannot be solved with any other existing tool.

Keywords: Boolean satisfiability, SAT, Pedigree Consistency checking, bioinformatics, genetics, computational biology.

1 Introduction

Computational methods have become increasingly important in the fields of biology and genetics. In fact, the computational needs of these fields have led to grand challenge problems in computing, such as solving the protein folding problem, one of the main motivations behind IBM's Blue Gene project. Many of the problems in these domains turn out to be NP-complete, and therefore reducible to Boolean satisfiability (SAT). Given the recent improvements in SAT-solving technology, a natural question is whether SAT-based methods can be used to solve important problems arising in biology and genetics. In this paper, we provide evidence that this is in fact likely.

We focus on the pedigree consistency checking problem, a well studied and important problem. Pedigrees describe genotype information about a collection of related individuals. When we say that a pedigree is consistent, we mean that it is consistent with the laws of Mendelian inheritance. Pedigree checking is important for numerous reasons. For example, it turns out that inconsistent pedigree data can adversely affect linkage analysis, the process by which human genes are linked to traits such as the predisposition to various diseases [10, 1].

---

* This research was funded in part by NSF grants CCF-0429924, IIS-0417413, and CCF-0438871.

O. Grumberg and M. Huth (Eds.): TACAS 2007, LNCS 4424, pp. 339–342, 2007.

The consistency checking problem for pedigrees is NP-complete [1] and has been tackled in essentially two different ways. The first approach is based on specialized algorithms. This includes algorithms for dealing with the simpler "non-looping" pedigrees, e.g., by K. Lange and T. Goradia [3] and algorithms for loop-breaking, which reduce the problem to the simpler non-looping case.[1] The Pedcheck tool, developed by J. O'Connell and E. Weeks, is the best known example of this approach [8, 9]. Secondly, there is another, very recent approach by de Givry et al. that is based on the use of weighted constraint satisfaction techniques. MendelSoft is a tool implementing this approach [2].

In this paper, we describe *PCS*, a SAT-based tool that leads to orders of magnitude performance improvements over existing tools for checking pedigrees.

2   Pedigree Consistency

A *pedigree* represents family relationships among a set of individuals, as well as genotype information on the individuals. The genotype information consists of a pair of *alleles*, DNA codings appearing in given positions on chromosomes. Alleles are DNA stands that correspond to a gene, the basic unit of heredity. The pedigree is consistent, with the Mendelian laws of inheritance, if every individual inherits exactly one allele from each of its parents.

Existing systems require that all individuals in pedigrees have either two or no parents and, similarly, two or no alleles. In *PCS*, we can also handle pedigrees containing partial information, e.g., individuals with one unknown parent and/or one undefined allele are allowed. These extensions were easy to implement due to the flexibility of our approach, which involves translating the pedigree consistency checking problem to a satisfiability problem.

3   Tool Description

In this section, we give a brief overview of the internals of *PCS* [4] and also describe how *PCS* is used. *PCS* can be downloaded from http://www.cc.gatech.edu/~manolios/pcs/. The input to *PCS* is linkage-format data given in the formats describe at http://linkage.rockefeller.edu/soft/linkage/. In brief, the information for a member of the pedigree appears on one line as a sequence of integers. These integers indicate the family identifier, the member identifier, the father identifier, the mother identifier, the sex (1 for male and 2 for female), the first allele number, and the second allele number.

The pedigree data is preprocessed to rule out simple errors, e.g., we check that every member's father is a male and every member's mother is a female. We also check that in case the data is declared to be sex-linked, all males are homozygots, which means that all males have only one allele.

---

[1] Loops in pedigrees arise when there is a loop in the graph of mates, a graph whose nodes are individuals and whose edges encode the mating relationship. For example, marriage loops are formed when one individual mates with two siblings.

The main phase of *PCS* is the translation of the consistency problem into a SAT problem. We cannot describe the details of this translation here, but we note that we make essential use of the BAT tool [6, 5]. BAT implements a decision procedure for the BAT language, a powerful hardware description language. This allows us to express the consistency problem in a high-level language and to leave the details of generating reasonable CNF to BAT.

The generated CNF file can then be given to any standard SAT solver. If a satisfying assignment is found, then the problem is consistent. If the formula is unsatisfiable, then there are incompatibilities in the pedigree. In this case, it is absolutely necessary to determine the problem and to communicate it to the user. We do this by extracting an *unsatisfiable core*, an unsatisfiable subset of the clauses that will become satisfiable if any of its clauses are removed. In the worst case, this includes the set of all clauses, but in practice this is highly unlikely. By extracting an unsatisfiable core, we can determine which set of members have inconsistent genomic information and why. Instead of reporting one such error at a time, *PCS* iteratively generates unsatisfiable cores and removes the genotype information of the individuals involved until we reach a fixed point. When the fixed point is reached, we have a satisfiable problem and *PCS* generates a report outlining all of the inconsistencies found.

4   Results

We compare the performance of our approach with Pedcheck, the most widely used program for Pedigree Checking [8, 9] and with MendelSoft [2], a tool that is based on a new approach involving weighted constraint satisfaction techniques.

We use the zchaff SAT-solver [7] for satisfiability testing and for extracting unsatisfiable cores [11]. All experiments were run on an Intel 3.06GHz Xeon machine, with 512 KB of L2 cache running on a GNU/Linux OS with kernel version 2.6.9.

We used both randomly generated benchmarks and actual pedigree problems from various domains. *PCS* detected the same errors as Pedcheck and Mendel-Soft, but it was two to three orders of magnitude faster than Pedcheck and one to two orders of magnitude faster than MendelSoft.

One of the most complicated examples we used consisted of actual pedigree data from sheep. This data was obtained from a repository provided by the authors of the MendelSoft system [2]. After some preprocessing, this data set consists of 8,920 members. The data could not be handled directly by neither MendelSoft nor PedCheck. Therefore, it was partitioned into four smaller problems, entitled sheep4r_4_0, ..., sheep4r_4_3. PedCheck took over 10 hours to solve the subproblems and MendelSoft tool over an hour. *PCS* was able to solve all four problems in under 20 seconds. This includes the total time required by BAT, the SAT solver, and the unsatisfiable core generator. In addition, *PCS* can deal with the whole pedigree, sheep4r directly, without having to partition the problem into subproblems (which was done by removing parent child relationships, something that can mask inconsistencies). *PCS* was able to correctly solve this problem, which was not solvable by any other existing tool, in under a minute.

5   Conclusions

We introduced *PCS*, a SAT-based tool for checking the consistency of pedigrees. *PCS* is orders of magnitude faster than the most efficient existing algorithms. It is also more general and it is capable of easily solving real pedigree checking problems that cannot be solved with existing tools. Our work benefited greatly from the use of BAT's high-level language and the BAT decision procedure. The high-level language allowed us to think and operate at a much higher level than CNF without sacrificing efficiency, as the BAT decision procedure was able to quickly generate compact CNF optimized for current SAT solvers. Encouraged by our results, we believe that SAT-based methods should be applied to other hard problems in computational biology.

References

[1] L. Aceto, J. A. Hansen, A. Ingólfsdóttir, J. Johnsen, and J. Knudsen. The complexity of checking consistency of pedigree information and related problems. In *Proceedings of the Eighth Italian Conference on Theoretical Computer Science (ICTCS'03)*, pages 174–187, 2003.

[2] S. de Givry, I. Palhiere, Z. Vitezica, and T. Schiex. Mendelian error detection in complex pedigree using weighted constraint satisfaction techniques. In ICLP-05 workshop on Constraint Based Methods for Bioinformatics, Sitges, Spain, 2005.

[3] K. Lange and T. Goradia. An algorithm for automatic genotype elimination. *American Journal of Human Genetics*, 40(3):250–256, 1987.

[4] P. Manolios, M. G. Oms, and S. O. Valls. PCS: Pedigree Checking with SAT. 2007. Available from http://www.cc.gatech.edu/~manolios/pcs/.

[5] P. Manolios, S. K. Srinivasan, and D. Vroon. Automatic memory reductions for RTL-level verification. In *ACM-IEEE International Conference on Computer Aided Design (ICCAD 2006)*, November 2006.

[6] P. Manolios, S. K. Srinivasan, and D. Vroon. BAT: The Bit-level Analysis Tool. 2006. Available from http://www.cc.gatech.edu/~manolios/bat/.

[7] M. W. Moskewicz, C. F. Madigan, Y. Zhao, L. Zhang, and S. Malik. Chaff: Engineering an efficient SAT solver. In *Design Automation Conference (DAC'01)*, pages 530–535, 2001.

[8] J. R. O'Connell and D. E. Weeks. Pedcheck: A program for identification of genotype incompatibilities in linkage analysis. *American Journal of Human Genetics*, 63(1):259–266, 1998.

[9] J. R. O'Connell and D. E. Weeks. An optimal algorithm for automatic genotype elimination. *American Journal of Human Genetics*, 65(6):1733–1740, 1999.

[10] E. Sobel, J. C. Papp, and K. Lange. Detection and integration of genotyping errors in statistical genetics. *American Journal of Human Genetics*, 70:496–508, 2002.

[11] L. Zhang and S. Malik. Validating SAT solvers using an independent resolution-based checker: Practical implementations and other applications. In *Proceedings of the Design and Test in Europe Conference*, pages 10880–10885, March 2003.

"Don't Care" Modeling: A Logical Framework for Developing Predictive System Models*

Hillel Kugler[1], Amir Pnueli[1,2], Michael J. Stern[3], and E. Jane Albert Hubbard[1]

[1] New York University, New York, NY, USA
{kugler,amir}@cs.nyu.edu, jane.hubbard@nyu.edu
[2] The Weizmann Institute of Science, Rehovot, Israel
[3] Yale University, New Haven, CT, USA
Michael.Stern@yale.edu

Abstract. Analysis of biological data often requires an understanding of components of pathways and/or networks and their mutual dependency relationships. Such systems are often analyzed and understood from datasets made up of the states of the relevant components and a set of discrete outcomes or results. The analysis of these systems can be assisted by models that are consistent with the available data while being maximally predictive for untested conditions. Here, we present a method to construct such models for these types of systems. To maximize predictive capability, we introduce a set of "don't care" (dc) Boolean variables that must be assigned values in order to obtain a concrete model. When a dc variable is set to 1, this indicates that the information from the corresponding component does not contribute to the observed result. Intuitively, more dc variables that are set to 1 maximizes both the potential predictive capability as well as the possibility of obtaining an inconsistent model. We thus formulate our problem as maximizing the number of dc variables that are set to 1, while retaining a model solution that is consistent and can explain all the given known data. This amounts to solving a quantified Boolean formula (QBF) with three levels of quantifier alternations, with a maximization goal for the dc variables. We have developed a prototype implementation to support our new modeling approach and are applying our method to part of a classical system in developmental biology describing fate specification of vulval precursor cells in the *C. elegans* nematode. Our work indicates that biological instances can serve as challenging and complex benchmarks for the formal-methods research community.

1 Introduction

Understanding a given complex system whose behavior can be observed, but whose behavioral program is not directly available, is an important yet difficult task. Examples of such systems include complex web services, software for which only the executable binary code is available, and legacy systems where the code is available but may be written in a language that is rarely used nowadays or lacking sufficient documentation and support from the original system

---

* This research was supported in part by NIH grant R24-GM066969.

O. Grumberg and M. Huth (Eds.): TACAS 2007, LNCS 4424, pp. 343–357, 2007.

developers. Our current work was motivated by a project that uses methods from software and system design to model and analyze biological systems. The behaviors of biological systems can be observed; however, the workings of their underlying behavioral programs are not directly available, and their elucidation is the subject of much biological research.

Analysis of biological data often requires an understanding of components of pathways and/or networks and their mutual dependency relationships. Such systems are often analyzed and understood from datasets made up of the states of the relevant components and a set of discrete outcomes or results. One type of biological example of such a system relates a "genotype" (the states of a set of genes, that can be either mutated or normal) and a resulting character trait (a "phenotype"). The understanding of the behavior of these systems is often constrained by the limited set of available condition-result data. The analysis of these types of systems can be assisted by models that are consistent with the available data while being maximally predictive for untested conditions. Here, we present a method to construct such models for these types of systems. Furthermore, our approach allows identifying those additional condition-result data that can most effectively constrain the set of possible models to those that match the behavior of the system. Our approach handles models with discrete variables, thus if the actual system variables are continuous, we assume that the domain has been discretized either manually or using other computational methods.

To maximize predictive capability, we introduce a set of "don't care" (dc) Boolean variables that must be assigned values in order to obtain a concrete model. When a dc variable is set to 1, this indicates that the information from the corresponding component does not contribute to the observed result. Thus the value of 1 denotes flexibility while the value of 0 denotes inflexibility. Intuitively, increasing the number of dc variables that are set to 1 increases both the potential predictive capability as well as the possibility of obtaining an inconsistent model. We thus formulate our problem as maximizing the number of dc variables that are set to 1, while retaining a model solution that is consistent and can explain all the given data. This amounts to solving a quantified Boolean formula (QBF) with three levels of quantifier alternations, with a maximization goal for the dc variables. We first show how our problem can be solved using QBF solvers, and later demonstrate how the special structure of our QBF instances can be used to reduce the problem and allow a more efficient solution.

We are applying our method to part of a classical system in developmental biology describing fate specification of vulval precursor cells in the *C. elegans* nematode. This is a well-characterized system that provides sufficient complexity to serve as a test case for our studies. Our work indicates that biological instances can serve as challenging and complex benchmarks for the formal-methods research community.

2   Example

This section introduces the problem statement, logical representation and possible solutions through a very simple example. For ease of presentation we make some simplifying assumptions in this section [1]; the more general case can be treated by adjusting this framework.

Let Boolean variable x denote a possible genetic locus:

$$x = \begin{cases} 1 & \text{if mutated} \\ 0 & \text{if wild-type} \end{cases}$$

In this simple example we consider three possible genetic loci with corresponding variables x_1, x_2, x_3. We assume three possible phenotypic outcomes, denoted by variable $y \in \{1, 2, 3\}$. The possible phenotypic outcomes are assumed to be disjoint, thus it is not possible to measure for example both $y = 1$ and $y = 2$.

We assume two experiments were performed and show the direct logical representation:

Experiment 1. x_1 is mutated and all others are wild-type. The phenotype obtained was $y = 1$. The logical representation is:

$$x_1 = 1 \land x_2 = 0 \land x_3 = 0 \to y = 1$$

Experiment 2. x_2 is mutated and all others are wild-type. The phenotype obtained was $y = 2$. The logical representation is:

$$x_1 = 0 \land x_2 = 1 \land x_3 = 0 \to y = 2$$

We are interested in representing and understanding the connection between genotype and phenotype. For this purpose we would like to construct a model that explains experimental results, and can make predictions about new experiments.

Considering our simple example, a first attempt for a model is:

$$(x_1 = 1 \land x_2 = 0 \land x_3 = 0 \to y = 1) \land (x_1 = 0 \land x_2 = 1 \land x_3 = 0 \to y = 2)$$

The above model, being a conjunction of the two formulas representing the experimental results, is consistent with the respective experimental results, but does not provide any additional predictions about new experiments. For example, considering the experiment in which x_2 and x_3 are mutated while x_1 remains wild-type, the model predicts nothing about the phenotype y. Formally, given the assignment $x_1 = 0$, $x_2 = 1$, $x_3 = 1$ the model formula evaluates to *true* for any assignments of the phenotype y, which can be assigned to values in the range $\{1, 2, 3\}$. The meaning is that any phenotypic outcome is possible, which amounts to no prediction.

To enable prediction the model should allow generalization from the experimental results. Our second attempt for constructing a model is:

$$(x_1 = 1 \to y = 1) \land (x_2 = 1 \to y = 2)$$

---

[1] Simplifying assumptions include single variable for phenotype representation instead of cross product using several variables, single value for phenotype measurement instead of disjunction of possible outcomes.

The idea here is to generalize by recording explicitly only the information about the mutations, omitting the wild-type background. The problem is that this model is inconsistent. Specifically, for the experimental setup in which both x_1 and x_2 are mutated, obtained by assigning $x_1 = 1$, $x_2 = 1$ to the formula, no assignment to y can satisfy it since it implies both $y = 1$ and $y = 2$. Variable y denotes a phenotype output, which we assume has disjoint values, thus it is not possible to have two phenotypic outcomes simultaneously, and hence the inconsistency.

A third and final attempt is to generalize as much as possible, but avoid inconsistent models. For this goal, we add dc variables, which are Boolean variables of the form $d \in \{0, 1\}$. When $d = 1$ the phenotype of the system is unaffected by this specific mutation in a given genetic background (we "don't care" whether it is mutated or not in this situation). When $d = 0$, the mutation is important in this context.

In this formulation we construct for our example a general model as follows:

$$(x_1 = 1 \wedge x_2 <= d_1^2 \wedge x_3 <= d_1^3 \rightarrow y = 1) \wedge (x_1 <= d_2^1 \wedge x_2 = 1 \wedge x_3 <= d_2^3 \rightarrow y = 2)$$

Let us explain the formula in some more detail. Here d_i^j denotes the dc variable for locus j in experiment i. A concrete model is obtained by assigning values to all the dc variables d_i^j. The expression $x_j <= d_i^j$ allows the flexibility to determine whether or not it is important to keep variable x_j in it's "normal" restrictive setting ($x_j = 0$) for obtaining the outcome measured in experiment i. If we set the dc variable d_i^j to 1, then the expression $x_j <= d_i^j$ evaluates to $x_j <= 1$ which is equivalent to true, since x_j is a Boolean variable and the expression holds for values 0 (since $0 <= 1$) and 1 (since $1 <= 1$). In this case, the value of x_j in experiment i does not affect the phenotypic outcome. If, on the other hand, we set d_i^j to 0, the expression $x_j <= d_i^j$ evaluates to $x_j <= 0$ which, for Boolean variable x_j, is equivalent to $x_j = 0$, meaning that the value of variable x_j in experiment i is important to the phenotypic outcome.

Our first two attempts for constructing models are special cases in this formulation. If all dc variables are set to 0, this corresponds to our first model, which is not predictive, while assigning 1 to all dc variables corresponds to the second model which is inconsistent [2] . To maximize the predictiveness of consistent models, we would like to be able to maximize the number of dc variables that are set to 1, while maintaining the requirement that the model is still consistent. A model is consistent if for any assignment to the variables x_1, x_2, x_3 there exists an assignment to the phenotype variable y such that the formula evaluates to true. Intuitively, this corresponds to the fact that for any experimental setup that can be prepared in the lab some phenotype will be measured.

---

[2] In general, assigning 1 to all the dc variables gives an inconsistent model, except for the degenerate case in which there are no two experiments that differ on their phenotypic outcome.

In our example we have four dc variables : $d_1^2, d_1^3, d_2^1, d_2^3$ (two experimental setups, each having two genetic loci that potentially can be mutated without affecting the phenotypic outcome). The maximal number of dc variables that can be assigned 1 while remaining with a consistent model is 3, since assigning all 4 dc variables to 1 results in an inconsistent model. A possible solution with 3 dc variables set to 1 is $d_1^2 = 1$, $d_1^3 = 1$, $d_2^3 = 1$ and $d_2^1 = 0$. Assigning these values for the dc variables we obtain :

$$(x_1 = 1 \land x_2 <= 1 \land x_3 <= 1 \rightarrow y = 1) \land (x_1 <= 0 \land x_2 = 1 \land x_3 <= 1 \rightarrow y = 2)$$

$$= (x_1 = 1 \rightarrow y = 1) \land (x_1 = 0 \land x_2 = 1 \rightarrow y = 2)$$

Unlike the first attempted model that was consistent but not predictive, this model is consistent and allows some predictions, for example for genotype $x_1 = 0$, $x_2 = 1$, $x_3 = 1$ the predicted phenotype is $y = 2$. The maximal number of dc variables that can be assigned 1 while keeping the model consistent does not in general determine a unique solution. In our example another maximal solution is $d_2^1 = 1$, $d_1^3 = 1$, $d_2^3 = 1$ and $d_1^2 = 0$.

3   Problem Formulation

This section formalizes the concepts of logical representation and model construction that were intuitively explained through the example in Section 2. It defines the mathematical problem we are interested in and then shows how we go about solving it.

We are interested in understanding the observable behavioral outcome of a system (defined by output variables) as a function of the experimental setup (defined by input variables) . The experimental setup for the system is controlled by binary input variables $x_1, x_2, \cdots x_n$. The "normal" value of an input variable is 0, and a change to the value (for example by a genetic mutation) is specified by assigning 1 to the variable.

The outcome is represented by an output variable y, that can assume a discrete and finite [3] set of values. In the general case, the phenotypic output specified by variable y can be a result of measuring several orthogonal phenotypic outputs, designated by variables $y_1, y_2, \cdots y_m$. In this case the value of the output behavior y can be viewed as a cross product of the values of each of the orthogonal phenotypes, $y = y_1 \times y_2 \cdots \times y_m$.

Given a dataset consisting of the values for the input variables and a discrete outcome result for the output variable we construct a formula of the form:

$$((x_1 = 1 \land x_2 <= d_1^2 \land x_3 <= d_1^3 \cdots \land x_n <= d_1^n) \rightarrow y = p_1) \land \quad (1)$$

---

[3] This is a simplifying assumption. If the outcomes are continuous values we assume that the domain has been discretized according to some biological criteria either manually or using other computational methods.

$$((x_1 <= d_2^1 \land x_2 = 1 \land x_3 <= d_2^3 \cdots \land x_n <= d_2^n) \rightarrow y = p_2) \land$$

$$\vdots$$

$$((x_1 <= d_s^1 \cdots \land x_q = 1 \cdots \land x_r = 1 \cdots \land x_n <= d_s^n) \rightarrow y = p_s) \land$$

$$\vdots$$

$$((x_1 <= d_l^1 \land x_2 <= d_l^2 \land x_3 = d_l^3 \cdots \land x_n = 1) \rightarrow y = p_l)$$

Let us now explain in detail how we construct a concrete formula of the same form as Formula 1 above from the experimental datasets that are available. Each line in the formula corresponds to an experiment, composed of an experimental setup and the phenotypic outcome measured. Each line is written as a logical implication, where the left-hand side of the implication corresponds to the experimental setup defined by the input variables, while the right-hand side corresponds to the phenotypic output defined by the output variables. For a given experiment, if the input variable x_j was changed from its "normal" setting, the left-hand side will contain the conjunct $x_j = 1$, while for an input variable that was set to its "normal" value $x_j = 0$, we will introduce a new dc variable and add the conjunct $x_j <= d_i^j$. Here d_i^j denotes the dc variable corresponding to input variable j in experiment i. For experiment i, if the phenotype measured was p_i, then the right-hand side of the corresponding implication will contain the expression $y = p_i$. The notation here can handle the more general case where y is determined by the cross product of the orthogonal phenotypic outputs of variables $y_1, y_2, \cdots y_m$, in which case $p_i = (p_{i,1}, p_{i,2} \cdots p_{i,m})$ where $p_{i,k}$ is the phenotypic output for variable y_k.

Consider for example the first line from the formula. It was constructed based on an experiment in which variable x_1 was perturbed, while all the other input variables assumed their "normal" value, and the phenotypic outcome $y = p_1$ was measured. Thus the corresponding logical representation we obtain for this experiment is:

$$((x_1 = 1 \land x_2 <= d_1^2 \land x_3 <= d_1^3 \cdots \land x_n <= d_1^n) \rightarrow y = p_1)$$

Formula 1 describes the results of l different experiments. Each experiment is not necessarily restricted to single variable changes, for example, experiment s in the above formula shows a case were both input variables x_q and x_r were changed, while the other input variables remain "normal", as shown in the corresponding logical representation for the experiment:

$$((x_1 <= d_s^1 \cdots \land x_q = 1 \cdots \land x_r = 1 \cdots \land x_n <= d_s^n) \rightarrow y = p_s)$$

Our approach thus allows encoding experiments with any number of input variables changes, including double, triple and higher degrees of variable changes. It is also not necessary that all results for single variable changes appear in the formula; the formula will just encode all the information that is available in the experimental dataset. Another point worth noting is that our approach can accommodate systems where the outcome may be nondeterministic. If an experiment is repeated several times with the same experimental setup and different phenotypic outputs are observed, then the right-hand side for the corresponding experiment in the formula will be a disjunction of the observed phenotypes. Thus the notation $y = p_i$ can stand for a set of possible outcomes, where $p_i = p_i^1 \vee p_i^2 \cdots \vee p_i^k$ if k different outcomes were observed when the experiment was repeated. Our current work does not consider a probabilistic distribution related to the number of times each outcome is measured when repeating the experiment, only the set of observed outcomes.

We call a formula of the type appearing in Formula 1 a **generic model** formula, since a concrete model is obtained from it by assigning values to all the dc variables.

Definition 1. *A* **model** *is a formula obtained from a generic model formula by assigning values* 0 *or* 1 *to all the dc variables.*

When assigning values to all the dc variables to obtain a model, the formula can be simplified as follows. For each dc variable that is assigned the value 0 the expression $x_j <= d_i^j$ is replaced by $x_j = 0$, while for each dc variable that is assigned the value 1 the expression $x_j <= d_i^j$ is replaced by *true*, which is then used to further simplify the formula.

Definition 2. *The* **prediction** *that model ϕ gives about a certain experimental setup, is obtained by assigning the values of all input variables according to the experimental setup resulting in a formula ϕ' and then finding all the assignments to the output variables that satisfy formula ϕ'.*

Definition 3. *A model is* **consistent** *if for any assignment to the input variables $x_1, x_2, \cdots x_n$ there exists an assignment to the output variables $y_1, y_2, \cdots y_m$ such that the formula evaluates to true.*

Definition 4. *A model with k dc variables set to* 1 *is* **maximally predictive** *if it is consistent and any model with more than k dc variables set to* 1 *is inconsistent.*

We are interested in developing efficient algorithms for finding a maximally predictive model, a topic that is studied in the next section.

4   Solutions

According to Definition 3 checking the consistency of a model ϕ amounts to checking the satisfiability of the following quantified Boolean formula:

$$\forall x_1, x_2, \cdots x_n \exists y_1, y_2 \cdots y_m \phi$$

The intuition behind these definitions is that we require that the x_i variables are universally quantified since they are input variables representing an experimental setup that in principle can be set to any possible combination, while the existential quantification of the y_j output variables represents the fact that for any experiment that is done there will be some phenotypic output measured in the biological system.

Proposition 1. *For any given generic model formula, if there are no consistent models with exactly k dc variables set to 1, then a maximally predictive model has less than k dc variables set to 1.*

Proof. Omitted from this version of the paper due to space limitations.

Given a generic model formula, the existence of a consistent model can be formulated as a quantified Boolean formula as follows:

$$\exists d_1, d_2 \cdots d_p \forall x_1, x_2, \cdots x_n \exists y_1, y_2 \cdots y_m \phi$$

This is a quantified Boolean formula with three levels of quantifier alternations. The outermost existential quantification over the dc variables corresponds to fixing a concrete model, the universal quantification over the input variables and existential quantification over the output variables corresponds to the requirement that the fixed model is consistent.

If we encode in the formula $\chi(k)$ the requirement that exactly k dc variables are assigned to 1, then the question of the existence of a consistent model with exactly k dc variables set to 1 is reduced to the satisfiability of the formula:

$$\exists d_1, d_2 \cdots d_p \forall x_1, x_2, \cdots x_n \exists y_1, y_2 \cdots y_m \phi \wedge \chi(k)$$

Given an algorithm for checking the satisfiability of such a formula, we can use the result in Proposition 1, and perform a binary search on k, the number of dc variables set to 1, to find the maximal k for which a consistent model exists, and obtain a maximally predictive model.

4.1   Implementing the Basic Algorithm

As shown above our problem amounts to solving a quantified Boolean formula with three levels of quantifier alternations, with a maximization goal for the dc variables. We next provide some information on a direct implementation to solve our problem, using two tools, one based on a binary decision diagrams (BDDs) [1] as implemented in the TLV tool [13], the other directly on a QBF solver using the Quaffle tool [20]. As will be shown later, the special structure of our QBF instances can be used to reduce the problem and allow a more efficient solution. We still explain the direct implementation for presentation purposes; it also may be the case that for various extensions of the problem the direct solution is required.

BDD Solver. TLV [13] is a symbolic model checker that uses binary decision diagrams as the basic underlying data structure. One of the strong aspects of TLV is that it provides a high-level scripting language called TLV-basic, which is especially convenient for experimenting with the design and implementation of new verification algorithms.

We have implemented in TLV the direct algorithm based on performing a binary search on the value of k, the number of dc variables set to 1. Each iteration solves the QBF formula described above with the constraint on the value of k. Universal and existential quantification are supported as existing functions in TLV (forall, exists) and are based on direct manipulation of the BDDs. The encoding of the generic model formula in TLV is straightforward as all logical operators are directly supported. At the end of each iteration we get a BDD that represents the (possibly empty) set of all consistent models with the current value of dc variables set to 1. This turns out to be useful since at the end of the algorithm we obtain the set of all maximally predictive models. The main disadvantage of using TLV is in terms of performance. Solving QBF formulas using BDD technology is not efficient, and for this reason we have experimented with applying a QBF solver to our problem.

QBF Solver. To allow applying a QBF solver to our problem we have to encode it in one of the standard formats accepted by these tools. QBF solvers typically accept only Boolean variables, thus the output variables in our problem that are not necessarily Boolean must be encoded using several Boolean variables. The input variables and the dc variables are originally Boolean so they can be accommodated directly. Another requirement of standard formats is that the propositional part of the QBF formula is written as a CNF formula, which requires some modifications to the generic model formula. To add the constraints on the parameter k, the number of dc variables assigned to 1, we created a circuit for performing the addition of dc variables and translated the circuit to CNF using a canonical translation. We have experimented with the QBF solver Quaffle [20] on some instances we have generated manually. We are currently working on developing a program that will handle all the translations automatically, and given a generic model formula in the high level representation as that of Formula 1 and a value for the parameter k will generate an instance in the standard QBF format. This will allow a much more effective use of the QBF solvers, in fact our plan is to make these instances publicly available, since they can serve as interesting benchmarks in QBF evaluations and libraries [6].

4.2 Improved Algorithm

We now show for deterministic systems[4] how to find a maximally predictive model in a more efficient way, by reducing the original problem to that of solving a set of inequalities involving only the dc variables d_i^j where each inequality is of the form $\sum d_i^j < C$ for an integer constant C. We start with a generic model formula of the form of Formula 1 and construct the set of inequalities over the dc variables. A generic model formula is of the following form:

$$((x_1 = 1 \land x_2 <= d_1^2 \land x_3 <= d_1^3 \cdots \land x_n <= d_1^n) \to y = p_1) \land$$

---

[4] We have also extended the algorithm to deal with the general case of nondeterministic systems, allowing several phenotypic outputs for the same experimental setup. Due to space limitations and to allow a simpler presentation this extension is omitted from this version of the paper.

$$((x_1 <= d_2^1 \wedge x_2 = 1 \wedge x_3 <= d_2^3 \cdots \wedge x_n <= d_2^n) \rightarrow y = p_2) \wedge$$

$$\vdots$$

$$((x_1 <= d_l^1 \wedge x_2 <= d_l^2 \wedge x_3 = d_l^3 \cdots \wedge x_n = 1) \rightarrow y = p_l)$$

The formula is a conjunction of implications, each one appears in a separate line in the formula above, each line corresponds to an experimental setup and phenotypic outcome measured. For each pair of lines i, j if the phenotypic outputs are different, we add the following constraint:

$$\sum_{x_q=1 \text{ in line } j} d_i^q + \sum_{x_q=1 \text{ in line } i} d_j^q < C_{i,j} \tag{2}$$

Here $C_{i,j}$ is the number of dc variables appearing in the sums of the left-hand side of the inequality. This is equal to the number of input variables set to 1 in experiment i plus the number of input variables set to 1 in experiment j minus twice the number of input variables that are set to 1 in both experiments i and j. We subtract this number since if an input variable is set to 1 in both experiments i and j it was counted in the first two terms but there are no corresponding dc variables in the generic model formula since they are added only when an input variable is set to 0 in a given experiment.

Following this construction we obtain a set of inequalities on the dc variables. The input variables and output variables do not appear in these inequalities. The number of equations is at most quadratic in the number of experiments, or equivalently in the number of lines in the generic model formula. We will next prove that to find a maximally predictive model it is sufficient to solve the obtained set of inequalities under the maximization goal for the number of dc variables set to 1. Before stating and proving the relevant theorem we illustrate its application to the simple example described in Section 2.

The generic model formula we have for this example is:

$$((x_1 = 1 \wedge x_2 <= d_1^2 \wedge x_3 <= d_1^3) \rightarrow y = 1)$$
$$\wedge((x_1 <= d_2^1 \wedge x_2 = 1 \wedge x_3 <= d_2^3) \rightarrow y = 2)$$

It was derived from two experiments that have different phenotypic outputs, $y = 1$ and $y = 2$. We therefore add the following inequality:

$$d_1^2 + d_2^1 < 2$$

We ask what is the maximal k that satisfies the inequality and

$$d_1^2 + d_1^3 + d_2^1 + d_2^3 = k$$

The maximal solution is $k = 3$, and there are indeed solutions for the original formula with 3 dc variables set to 1 and no solutions with all 4 dc variables set to 1 as shown in 2.

Theorem 1. *For a given generic model formula, a model ϕ defined by an assignment D to the dc variables is consistent iff D satisfies the set of all inequalities defined in Formula 2.*

Proof. ($\Rightarrow$) Assume that the model ϕ defined by assignment D is consistent. By Definition 3 this holds if the following formula is satisfiable:

$$\forall x_1, x_2, \cdots x_n \exists y_1, y_2 \cdots y_m \phi$$

We need to show that D satisfies the set of inequalities. Assume towards contradiction that there is an inequality constructed from the pair of experiments i, j that does not hold:

$$\sum_{\substack{x_q=1 \text{ in line } j}} d_i^q + \sum_{\substack{x_q=1 \text{ in line } i}} d_j^q < C_{i,j}$$

This inequality does not hold if:

$$\sum_{\substack{x_q=1 \text{ in line } j}} d_i^q + \sum_{\substack{x_q=1 \text{ in line } i}} d_j^q = C_{i,j}$$

We get this equation only in the case that D assigns 1 to all the dc variables appearing in the left-hand side of the equation, since only then the sum of these dc variables is equal to the number of these dc variables. Consider an experimental setup that assigns the value 1 to the union of all input variables that are assigned 1 in either experiment i or experiment j (or both). All the other input variables are set to 0. This experimental setup satisfies the left-hand side of the implications for both lines i and j in the formula ϕ and thus both phenotypes defined by the right-hand side must occur, but the two original experiments i, j have different phenotypic outcomes, since only in this case we constructed the inequality. As a result for this new experimental setup no phenotype can satisfy the model ϕ, in contradiction to the assumption that ϕ is a consistent model. Thus assignment D satisfies all the inequalities defined in Formula 2.

($\Leftarrow$)

Assume that assignment D satisfies the set of all inequalities defined in Formula 2. We need to show that the model ϕ defined by assignment D is consistent. Assume towards contradiction that the model ϕ is not consistent, thus according to Definition 3 the following formula is not satisfiable:

$$\forall x_1, x_2, \cdots x_n \exists y_1, y_2 \cdots y_m \phi$$

If the formula is not satisfiable there exists an assignment for the input variables $x_1, x_2, \cdots x_n$ such that for any assignment of the output variables $y_1, y_2 \cdots y_m$ the formula evaluates to false. The formula ϕ is composed of a conjunction of implications. Consider the assignment to the input variables $x_1, x_2, \cdots x_n$ in which for any assignment to the output variables the formula evaluates to false. For this to occur there are at least two lines for which the left-hand side of the implication is satisfied and the phenotypic outcomes are different. Otherwise assigning the output variables to the unique fate defined by the left-hand side expressions that are true, will satisfy the formula. Considering these two lines, for their left-hand side expressions to hold, the dc variables for the union of input variables that are set to 1 in each of the experiments, must be set to 1 in the assignment D. Thus denoting these two lines i and j the following equation is satisfied.

$$\sum_{x_q=1 \text{ in line j}} d_i^q + \sum_{x_q=1 \text{ in line i}} d_j^q = C_{i,j}$$

And this is a direct violation of one of the inequalities defined in Formula 2:

$$\sum_{x_q=1 \text{ in line j}} d_i^q + \sum_{x_q=1 \text{ in line i}} d_j^q < C_{i,j}$$

In contradiction to our assumption that D satisfies all inequalities defined in Formula 2, therefor the model ϕ is consistent.

5   Biological Application

A great deal of biological research currently focuses on the analysis of molecular and cellular pathways and networks. An understanding of components of pathways and/or networks and their interdependencies is an important aspect of these studies. For example, a set of genes that affect a similar process (either positively or negatively) may be characterized by the effect of specific mutations of these genes on the outcome of the process. Data describing the outcome of combinations of such mutations may add additional information. Of particular interest in constructing pathways and networks is information that distinguishes between conditions in which the genotype of one genetic component in the pathway (or activity of a gene or protein component) is or is not relevant to the final outcome. Genetic epistasis analysis and analysis of modifier effects have been used to great advantage to parse many pathways [9]. With the advent of large-scale molecular-genetic data collection, the data space of genetic interactions is becoming increasingly unwieldy, even for relatively simple processes. It is, therefore, advantageous to identify methods by which dependency relationships between pathway components can be analyzed and modeled. Models of a subset of the data serve two general purposes: they may be used to predict the outcome of genetic combinations that have not been tested, and they may provide a means to readily identify the key combinatorial experiments that can be performed to distinguish between two or more equally viable models.

  We are applying our method to part of a classical system in developmental biology describing fate specification of cells in the *C. elegans* nematode. *C. elegans* is widely studied in many labs worldwide where it serves as a model organism. Various fundamental biological phenomena that also exist in higher-level organisms can be studied in effective ways in *C. elegans*. The field has taken particular advantage of the genetic approach to investigating biological processes whereby a process is perturbed by genetic mutation and the genes involved in the normal process are thereby identified. In addition, because the animals are relatively simple and the entire cell lineage is known, cell ablation experiments (in which particular cells are removed from an intact animal using a laser) have also been instrumental in discovering cell-cell interactions. The combinatorial effects of various mutations on the process that they perturb individually and the effects of combinations of mutations with cell ablations has generated a large body of complex data. Further, the molecular nature and biochemical roles of many of the gene products involved in developmental processes link the functional perturbation data to particular biochemical pathways and networks [19].

Our application focused on the process of fate specification of vulval precursor cells. The vulva is a structure through which eggs are laid. This structure derives from three cells within a set of six cells with an equivalent set of multiple developmental potentials. Due to their potential to participate in the formation of the vulva, they are known as vulval precursor cells (VPCs). Each cell has the potential to acquire either a non-vulval fate (a 3° fate) or one of two vulval cell fates (a 1° or 2° fate). The fate, 1°, 2° or 3° is expressed by the number of divisions the cells undergoes and the axis of the divisions. The fate of the VPCs is influenced by cell-cell signalling — signaling between neighboring VPCs, from the gonadal anchor cell (AC), and from the hypodermis. Vulval development was one of the first areas to which considerable effort was applied to achieve a molecular understanding of how cells acquire their particular fates. The system, though limited in cell number, provides sufficient complexity to serve as a test case for our studies [16].

The VPC system has been one of the motivations for developing the current work, after it has been modeled in a relatively detailed manner in [10,5,7]. While there are many advantages in modeling efforts such as those mentioned, in terms of the insights that are gained, one of the remaining challenges is to integrate effects of different genetic components.

As part of our initial effort to test our "don't care" modeling approach, we have encoded the results of a small subset of the experimental results on VPC fate specification as reported in one of the key publications [18] on this topic. Our output variables are of the form $y_i \in \{1, 2, 3\}$, we have six such output variable corresponding to the fates of each of the VPCs. An experiment consists of recording the results of the pattern of fate specification among the 6 VPCs after perturbations such as genetic mutations or cell ablations. In our initial evaluation we used 8 input variables corresponding to gonad ablation ($x_0 = 1$ if gonad ablated, $x_0 = 0$ if gonad intact), and the mutations *lin-12(0)*, *lin-12(d)*, *lin-15*, *lin-7*, *lin-3*, *lin-2* and *lin-10*, measured by input variables $x_1, x_2, \cdots x_7$ respectively. We have entered experimental data from [18] about set-ups when only one of the input variables was perturbed, and then using our basic algorithm implementation solved for the maximal number of dc variables that can be set to 1 and found a maximally predictive model. We then compared the predictions of the model for experiments involving perturbations to 2 or 3 of the input variables with the actual data reported in [18]. The initial results, which seem encouraging in terms of predictive capabilities and runtime performance, should be interpreted very carefully, due to the limited size of the dataset. We are in the process of evaluating the results taking into account more experiments from [18], and also experiments reported in [17,15].

6   Related Work

How to form a general description of a class of objects given a set of examples is a basic problem in machine learning and has been studied in the artificial intelligence community [12,11]. This problem is termed *Generalization* or *Inductive Learning* and is viewed as a search through the hypothesis space. The general framework considers both positive and negative training examples, while our work currently is restricted to positive examples. Our method uses the 'technological' advances made in the formal methods community using tools like BDDs [1], QBF [14] and SAT solvers based on the DPLL method [3,2] to search the hypothesis space efficiently. The connection between machine learning and circuit design is explored in [8,4] demonstrating that logic-synthesis methods can be applied effectively to certain learning problems and can compete with standard machine learning programs.

Acknowledgements. We would like to thank Dennis Shasha for helpful discussions. This research was supported in part by NIH grant R24-GM066969.

References

1. R.E. Bryant. Graph-based algorithms for Boolean function manipulation. *IEEE Transactions on Computers*, C-35(12):1035–1044, 1986.
2. M. Davis, G. Logemann, and D. Loveland. A machine program for theorem-proving. *Comm. ACM*, 5(7):394–397, 1962.
3. M. Davis and H. Putnam. A Computing Procedure for Quantification Theory. *J. ACM*, 7(3):201–215, 1960.
4. C.M. Files and M.A. Perkowski. Multi-Valued Functional Decomposition as a Machine Learning Method. In *Proc. 28th IEEE International Symposium on Multiple-Valued Logic (ISMVL'98)*, pages 173–179, Fukuoka, Japan, May 1998. IEEE Computer Society.
5. J. Fisher, N. Piterman, E.J.A. Hubbard, M.J. Stern, and D. Harel. Computational Insights into *C. elegans* Vulval Development. *Proceedings of the National Academy of Sciences*, 102(6):1951–1956, 2005.
6. E. Giunchiglia, M. Narizzano, and A. Tacchella. Quantified boolean formulas satisfiability library (qbflib), 2001. http://www.qbflib.org.
7. C.A. Giurumescu, P.W. Sternberg, and A.R. Asthagiri. Intercellular coupling amplifies fate segregation during *Caenorhabditis elegans* vulval development. *Proceedings of the National Academy of Sciences*, 103(5):1331–1336, 2006.
8. J. A. Goldman and M. L. Axtell. On Using Logic Synthesis for Supervised Classification Learning. In *Proc. 7th Int. Conference on Tools with Artificial Intelligence (ICTAI95')*, pages 198–205. IEEE Computer Society, 1995.

9. L.S. Huand and P.W. Sternberg. Genetic dissection of developmental pathways. The *C. elegans* Research Community, ed. WormBook, 2006. http://www.wormbook.org.

10. N. Kam, D. Harel, H. Kugler, R. Marelly, A. Pnueli, E.J.A. Hubbard, and M.J. Stern. Formal Modeling of C. elegans Development: A Scenario-Based Approach. In Corrado Priami, editor, *Proc. Int. Workshop on Computational Methods in Systems Biology (CMSB 2003)*, volume 2602 of *Lect. Notes in Comp. Sci.*, pages 4–20. Springer-Verlag, 2003.

11. R. S. Michalski. A Theory and Methodology of Inductive Learning. *Artificial Intelligence*, 20(2):111–161, 1983.

12. T. M. Mitchell. Generalization as Search. *Artificial Intelligence*, 18(2):203–226, 1982.

13. A. Pnueli and E. Shahar. A platform for combining deductive with algorithmic verification. In R. Alur and T. Henzinger, editors, *R. Alur and T. Henzinger, editors*, Proc. 8th Intl. Conference on Computer Aided Verification (CAV'96), *volume 1102 of* Lect. Notes in Comp. Sci., *Springer-Verlag*, pages 184–195, 1996.

14. D. P. Ranjan, D. Tang, and S. Malik. A Comparative Study of 2QBF Algorithms. In *Proc. 7th Int. Conference on Theory and Applications of Satisfiability Testing*, 2004.

15. P.W. Sternberg. Lateral inhibition during vulval induction in *Caenorhabditis elegans*. *Nature*, 335:551–554, 1989.

16. P.W. Sternberg. Vulval development. The *C. elegans* Research Community, ed. WormBook, 2005. http://www.wormbook.org.

17. P.W. Sternberg and H.R. Horvitz. Pattern formation during vulval development in *C. elegans*. *Cell*, 44:761–772, 1986.

18. P.W. Sternberg and H.R. Horvitz. The combined action of two intercellular signaling pathways specifies three cell fates during vulval induction in *C. elegans*. *Cell*, 58:679–693, 1989.

19. The *C. elegans* Research Community, ed. WormBook, 2006. www.wormbook.org.

20. L. Zhang and S. Malik. Conflict Driven Learning in a Quantified Boolean Satisfiability Solver. In *Proc. of the 2002 IEEE/ACM International Conference on Computer-aided Design (ICCAD'02)*, pages 442–449. ACM, November 2002.

Deciding Bit-Vector Arithmetic with Abstraction[*]

Randal E. Bryant[1], Daniel Kroening[2], Joël Ouaknine[3], Sanjit A. Seshia[4],
Ofer Strichman[5], and Bryan Brady[4]

[1] Carnegie Mellon University, Pittsburgh
[2] ETH Zürich
[3] Oxford University Computing Laboratory
[4] University of California, Berkeley
[5] The Technion, Haifa

Abstract. We present a new decision procedure for finite-precision bit-vector arithmetic with arbitrary bit-vector operations. Our procedure alternates between generating under- and over-approximations of the original bit-vector formula. An under-approximation is obtained by a translation to propositional logic in which some bit-vector variables are encoded with fewer Boolean variables than their width. If the under-approximation is unsatisfiable, we use the unsatisfiable core to derive an over-approximation based on the subset of predicates that participated in the proof of unsatisfiability. If this over-approximation is satisfiable, the satisfying assignment guides the refinement of the previous under-approximation by increasing, for some bit-vector variables, the number of Boolean variables that encode them. We present experimental results that suggest that this abstraction-based approach can be considerably more efficient than directly invoking the SAT solver on the original formula as well as other competing decision procedures.

1 Introduction

Decision procedures for quantifier-free fragments of first-order logic find widespread use in hardware and software verification. Current uses of decision procedures fall into one of two extremes. At one end, a Boolean satisfiability solver is directly employed as the decision procedure, with systems modeled at the bit-level. Sample applications of this kind include bounded model checking [1,2] and SAT-based program analysis [3]. At the other extreme, verifiers use decision procedures that reason over arbitrary-precision abstract types such as the integers and reals ($\mathbb{Z}$ and $\mathbb{R}$).

In reality, system descriptions are best modeled with a level of precision that is somewhere in between. System descriptions are usually at the *word-level*; i.e., they use finite-precision arithmetic and bit-wise operations on bit-vectors. The direct use of a SAT solver as cited earlier (also known as "bit-blasting") is the

---

[*] B. Brady, R. E. Bryant, and S. A. Seshia were supported in part by SRC contract 1355.001 and by the MARCO Gigascale Systems Research Center.

O. Grumberg and M. Huth (Eds.): TACAS 2007, LNCS 4424, pp. 358–372, 2007.

conceptually simplest way to implement a bit-vector decision procedure even though it ignores higher-level structure present in the original decision problem.

However, the bit-blasting approach can be too computationally expensive in practice (see, for example, [4]). There is therefore a pressing need for better decision procedures for bit-vector arithmetic.

Contribution. We present a decision procedure for quantifier-free bit-vector arithmetic that uses automatic abstraction-refinement. This procedure is now implemented in the verification system UCLID, and we shall call it by this name from hereon. Given an input bit-vector formula ϕ, UCLID first builds an under-approximation $\underline{\phi}$ from ϕ by restricting the number of Boolean variables used to encode each bit-vector variable (see details of this encoding in Section 3.1). The reduced formula is typically much smaller and easier to solve. If $\underline{\phi}$ is satisfiable, so is ϕ, and the algorithm terminates. In case the Boolean formula is found to be unsatisfiable, the SAT solver is able to output a resolution proof of this fact, from which the unsatisfiable core used in this proof can be extracted. Using this core, an over-approximation $\overline{\phi}$ is built. This over-approximation uses the full set of bits of the original vectors, but only a subset of the constraints. This subset is determined by examining the unsatisfiable core of $\underline{\phi}$. If $\overline{\phi}$ is un-satisfiable, so is ϕ, and UCLID terminates. Otherwise, the algorithm refines the under-approximation $\underline{\phi}$ by increasing, for at least one bit-vector variable, the number of Boolean variables encoding it. Specifically, the new size is implied by the value of this variable in the satisfying assignment to $\overline{\phi}$. This process is re-peated until the original formula is shown to be either satisfiable or unsatisfiable. The algorithm is trivially guaranteed to terminate due to the finite domain.

This approach has the potential of being efficient in one of the following two scenarios:

1. The bit-vector formula is satisfiable, and a solution can be represented with a small number of bits.
2. The bit-vector formula is unsatisfiable, and a relatively small number of terms in this formula participate in the proof (i.e., the proof still holds after replacing the other terms with inputs).

Whether this potential is fulfilled depends on one's ability to find such small solutions and small unsatisfiable cores[1] efficiently: For the former, we search for gradually increasing solutions in terms of the number of bits that are needed in order to represent them, and hence are guaranteed to find a small one if it exists; For the latter, modern SAT solvers are quite apt at finding small cores when they exist. In practice, as our experiments show, one of these conditions frequently holds and we are able to detect it with our tool faster than analyzing the formula head-on without any approximations.

Our approach can be seen as an adaptation to bit-vector formulas of our previ-ous work [5] on abstraction-refinement of quantifier-free Presburger Arithmetic,

---

[1] A small unsatisfiable core of the CNF encoding of a formula does not necessarily imply that a small number of terms from the original formula are necessary for the proof, but obviously the two measures are correlated.

which, in turn, was inspired by the proof-based abstraction-refinement approach to model checking proposed by McMillan and Amla [6]. Other than the different problem domain (bit-vectors vs. Presburger formulas), we also extend the theoretical framework to operate on an arbitrary circuit representation of the formula, rather than on a CNF representation. We also employ optimizations specific to bit-vector arithmetic. On the applied side, we report experimental results on a set of benchmarks generated in both hardware and software verification. Our experiments suggest that our approach can be considerably more efficient than directly invoking the SAT solver on the original formula as well as other state-of-the-art decision procedures.

Related Work. Current decision procedures for bit-vector arithmetic fall into one of three categories:

1) Bit-blasting and its variants: Many current decision procedures are based on bit-blasting the input formula to SAT, with a view of handling arbitrary bit-vector operations. The Cogent [7] procedure mentioned earlier belongs to this category. The most current version of CVC-Lite [8] pre-processes the input formula using a normalization step followed by equality rewrites before finally bit-blasting to SAT. Wedler et al. [9] have a similar approach wherein they normalize bit-vector formulas in order to simplify the generated SAT instance. STP [10] is the successor to the CVC-Lite system; it performs several array optimizations, as well as arithmetic and Boolean simplifications on the bit-vector formula before bit-blasting to MiniSat. Yices [11] applies bit-blasting to all bit-vector operators except for equality.

2) Canonizer-based procedures: Earlier work on deciding bit-vector arithmetic centered on using a Shostak-like approach of using a canonizer and solver for that theory. The work by Cyrluk et al. [12] and by Barrett et al. on the Stanford Validity Checker [13] fall into this category; the latter differs from the former in the choice of a canonical representation. These approaches are very elegant, but are restricted to a subset of bit-vector arithmetic comprising concatenation, extraction, and linear equations (not inequalities) over bit-vectors.

3) Procedures for modular and bounded arithmetic: The third category of systems focuses on techniques to handle (linear and non-linear) modular arithmetic. The most recent work in this area is by Babić and Musuvathi [14], who encode non-linear operations as non-linear congruences and make novel use of Newton's p-adic method for solving them. However, this approach does not treat some of the operations that we handle such as integer division, and seems harder to extend to new operations. Brinkmann and Drechsler [15] use an encoding of linear bit-vector arithmetic into integer linear programming with bounded variables in order to decide properties of RTL descriptions of circuit data-paths, but do not handle any Boolean operations. Parthasarathy et al. [16] build on this approach by using a lazy encoding with a modified DPLL search, but non-linear bit-vector arithmetic is not supported. Huang and Cheng [17] give an approach to solving bit-vector arithmetic based on combining ATPG with a solver for linear modular arithmetic. This approach is limited in its treatment of non-linear operations which it handles by heuristically rewriting them as linear modular arithmetic constraints.

McMillan and Amla [6] use a technique related to ours in order to accelerate model checking algorithms over finite Kripke structures. Specifically, they invoke a bounded model checker to decide which state variables should be made visible in order to generate a 'good' abstraction for the next iteration of model checking. Gupta et al. [18] propose a similar model-checking framework, which among others makes greater use of counterexamples and uses abstract models for both validation and falsification attempts. Our approach differs from both of these in the following respects: we use a bit-vector decision procedure instead of a model checker, and we seek to eliminate constraints rather than variables (or gates or latches, as the case may be).

Lahiri et al. [19] present an algorithm for deciding satisfiability of quantifier-free Presburger arithmetic that is based on alternating between an under- and an over-approximation. The under-approximation is constructed as in [5]. The over-approximation uses a Craig Interpolant.

2   Preliminaries

Boolean Satisfiability. We assume the reader is familiar with the basic terminology of propositional logic such as resolution, Conjunctive Normal Form and Tseitin encoding [20] (the linear procedure for converting an arbitrary propositional formulas to CNF based on the introduction of a new variable in each node in the DAG representation of the formula).

We remind the reader that SAT solvers can be seen as progressing by performing resolution steps. If the input formula is unsatisfiable, modern SAT solvers such as zChaff [21] and MiniSat [22] can output a *proof of unsatisfiability* [23,6] based on resolution. The leafs of such proofs (the assumptions) constitute an *unsatisfiable core*, i.e., an unsatisfiable subset of the clauses. In practice, SAT solvers tend to find small unsatisfiable cores if they exist. Indeed, in most cases in practice, formulas contain a large amount of redundant constraints.

Bit-Vector Arithmetic. While we are not aware of a standard definition of *bit-vector arithmetic* (it varies according to needs and tools), the fragment we consider here includes finite-precision integer arithmetic with linear and non-linear operators, as well as standard bit-wise operators, such as left shift, logical and arithmetic right shifts, extraction, concatenation, and so forth. In fact, the approach we use in this paper is orthogonal to the the set of operators, since it only relies on a given finite width for each variable, as well as on the existence of a propositional encoding of the formula.

At present, UCLID supports the subset of bit-vector arithmetic with the following operators: arbitrary Boolean connectives, relational operators, bitwise Boolean operators, extraction, concatenation, shifts, addition, subtraction, multiplication, division, and modulo.

Each bit-vector expression is associated with a type. The type is the width of the expression in bits and whether it is signed (two's complement encoding) or unsigned (binary encoding). Assigning semantics to this language is straightforward, e.g., as done in [15].

Note that all arithmetic operators (addition: $+$, subtraction: $-$, multiplication: $*$, division: $\div$, modulo: $\%$) are all finite-precision, and come with an associated operator width.

Example 1. The following formula is valid when interpreted over the integers:

$$(x - y > 0) \iff (x > y) \tag{1}$$

However, if x and y are interpreted as bit-vectors, this equivalence no longer holds, due to possible overflow on the subtraction operation.   □

Note also that the relational operators $>, <, \leq, \geq$, the non-linear arithmetic operators $(*, \div, \%)$ and the right-shift depend on whether an unsigned, binary encoding is used or a two's complement encoding is used. We assume that the type of the expression is clear from the context.

This paper addresses the *satisfiability problem* for bit-vector formulas: given a bit-vector formula ϕ, is there an assignment to the bits in ϕ under which ϕ evaluates to *True*? It is easy to see that this problem is NP-complete.

Notation: We henceforth denote formulas in bit-vector arithmetic as ϕ, ϕ', ϕ_1, $\phi_2, \ldots$, and Boolean formulas as β, β_1, $\beta_2, \ldots$.

3   The Decision Procedure

We now present the main contribution of this paper, a SAT-based decision procedure that operates by generating increasingly precise *abstractions* of bit-vector formulas. The input to the decision procedure is a bit-vector arithmetic formula ϕ. Let there be n bit-vector variables appearing in ϕ, denoted by $v_1, v_2, v_3, \ldots, v_n$. Each variable v_i has an associated bit-width w_i.

3.1   Overview

We first give a broad overview of our decision procedure, which is illustrated in Figure 1. Details of design decisions are described later in this section.

The decision procedure performs the following steps:

1. *Initialization:* For each variable v_i, we select a corresponding number s_i of Boolean variables to encode it with, where $0 \leq s_i \leq w_i$.
   We will call s_i the *encoding size* of bit-vector variable v_i.
2. *Generate Under-Approximation and Encode to SAT:* An under-approximation, denoted $\underline{\phi}$, is generated by restricting the values of each v_i to range over a set of cardinality 2^{s_i}. Thus, the Boolean encoding of v_i will comprise s_i Boolean variables; note, however, that the length of the vector of Boolean variables replacing v_i remains w_i.

   There are several ways to generate such an under-approximation and its Boolean encoding. One option is to encode v_i using Boolean variables on its

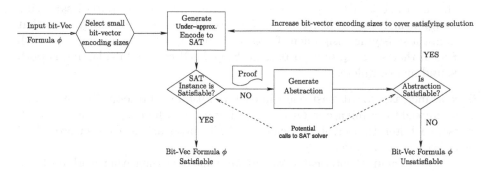

Fig. 1. Abstraction-based approach to solving bit-vector arithmetic

s_i low order bits and then zero-extend it to be of length w_i. The other is to "sign-extend" it instead. For example, if $s_i = 2$ and $w_i = 4$, the latter would generate the Boolean vector $[v_{i1}, v_{i1}, v_{i1}, v_{i0}]$ (where v_{ij} are Boolean variables). Our implementation currently uses the latter encoding, as it enables searching for solutions at both ends of the ranges of bit-vector values. Further exploration of this aspect is left to future work.

A Boolean formula β is then computed from ϕ using standard circuit encodings for bit-vector arithmetic operators. The width of the operators is left unchanged. The formula β is handed to an off-the-shelf SAT solver. The only feature required of this SAT solver is that its response on unsatisfiable formulas should be accompanied by an unsatisfiable core.

If the SAT solver reports that β is satisfiable, then the satisfying assignment is an assignment to the original formula ϕ, and the procedure terminates. However, if β is unsatisfiable, we continue on to the next step.

3. *Generate Over-Approximation from Unsatisfiable Core:* The SAT solver extracts an unsatisfiable core $\mathcal{C}$ from the proof of unsatisfiability of β. We use $\mathcal{C}$ to generate an over-approximating *abstraction* $\overline{\phi}$ of ϕ. The formula $\overline{\phi}$ is also a bit-vector formula, but typically much smaller than ϕ.

The algorithm that generates $\overline{\phi}$ is described in Section 3.2. The key property of $\overline{\phi}$ is that its translation into SAT, using the same sizes s_i as those that were used for ϕ, would also result in an unsatisfiable Boolean formula. The satisfiability of $\overline{\phi}$ is then checked using a *sound and complete decision procedure* $\mathcal{P}$ for bit-vector arithmetic, e.g., a bit-blasting approach.

If $\overline{\phi}$ is unsatisfiable, we can conclude that so is ϕ. On the other hand, if $\overline{\phi}$ is satisfiable, it must be the case that at least one variable v_i is assigned a value that is not representable with s_i Boolean variables (recall the key property enjoyed by $\overline{\phi}$ cited earlier). This larger satisfying assignment indicates the necessary increase in the encoding size s_i for v_i. Proceeding thus, we increase s_i for all relevant i, and go back to Step 2.

Remark 1. Note that in this step it would be permissible to merely use a *sound*, but not necessarily *complete*, bit-vector arithmetic decision procedure $\mathcal{P}$. In other words, we require that the outcome of $\mathcal{P}$ be correct whenever this outcome is 'Unsat', but we can tolerate spurious purported satisfying assignments. Indeed, in cases where $\mathcal{P}$ provides a satisfying assignment that is not a satisfying assignment for $\overline{\phi}$, we can simply increase s_i by 1 for each i such that $s_i < w_i$, and go back to Step 2. Of course, bit-blasting is both sound and complete.

Since s_i increases for at least one i in each iteration of this loop, this procedure is guaranteed to terminate in $O(n \cdot w_{max})$ iterations, where $w_{max} = \max_i w_i$. Of course, each iteration involves a call to a SAT solver and a decision procedure for bit-vector arithmetic.

One of the main theoretical advances we make over the earlier work on Presburger arithmetic [5] is a different method for generating the abstraction. We describe this in the following section.

3.2   Generating an Over-Approximating Abstraction

The earlier work assumed that ϕ was in conjunctive normal form (CNF), whereas our procedure works with an arbitrary directed acyclic graph (DAG) or circuit-based representation, which is the format in which the input problems are generated. While ϕ can be transformed to CNF (in two different ways, listed below), we argue below that neither of those approaches is desirable, primarily due to the presence of if-then-else (ITE) expressions at arbitrary locations in ϕ.

1) *Eliminating ITE using new variables:* By giving each ITE expression in the formula a fresh bit-vector variable name, we can eliminate all ITEs with just a linear blow-up in the formula size. However, this also introduces a number of new bit-vector variables that is linear in the size of the formula.

Note that the number of input bit-vector variables (v_i's) is usually a few orders of magnitude smaller than the size of the formula ϕ. As a result, when treating the new variables as inputs, the SAT solver's performance has been observed to suffer dramatically.

Of course, the values of these new variables are dependent on those of the v_i's, and we can therefore attempt to restrict the SAT solver from case-splitting on the bit-encodings of the new ITE variables. However, such restrictions have also been found to severely adversely affect the run-time of current SAT engines. (It amounts to changing the decision heuristic.)

2) *Direct elimination of ITE:* Another way of eliminating ITEs is to expand out the cases without introducing new variables. However, this leads to a worst-case exponential blow-up in formula size, which is commonly witnessed in practice.

We have therefore devised an abstraction-generation algorithm $\mathcal{A}$ that operates directly on the DAG representation of ϕ, denoted D_ϕ. The inputs to $\mathcal{A}$ are D_ϕ, the root node, and the unsatisfiable core $\mathcal{C}$. The output is a DAG $D_{\overline{\phi}}$ representing $\overline{\phi}$, which is an over-approximation of ϕ. Let N^ϕ and $N^{\overline{\phi}}$ be the set of nodes in D_ϕ and $D_{\overline{\phi}}$, respectively.

Before describing the algorithm, we need to describe the process of transforming the Boolean encodings of ϕ and $\overline{\phi}$ into CNF. It can be seen as a generalization of Tseitin's encoding (which introduces fresh variables for internal nodes) to the case of bit-vector formulas. Each internal node $n \in N^\phi$ is annotated with a set of CNF clauses $c(n)$ that relate the output of that node $o(n)$ to its inputs, according to the operator in the node. These output variables then appear as input to the parent nodes of n. Then a conjunction of the clauses in $\{c(n)|n \in N^\phi\}$ and one more unit clause with the variable encoding the top node, is the CNF representation of ϕ. A subset of these clauses constitutes the UNSAT core $\mathcal{C}$. These definitions and notations also apply to $D_{\bar{\phi}}$, and we will use them for both DAGs when the meaning is clear from the context. For a formula (or equivalently a set of clauses) C we denote by $vars(C)$ the set of variables that appear in C.

Procedure $\mathcal{A}$ (see Algorithm 1) recurses down the structure of D_ϕ and creates $D_{\bar{\phi}}$. It replaces a Boolean node n with a new variable and backtracks, if and only if none of the variables in $vars(c(n))$ are present in $\mathcal{C}$[2]. It uses the functions left-child(D_ϕ, n) and right-child(D_ϕ, n) to return the left and right child of n on D_ϕ, respectively.

Algorithm 1. An algorithm for abstracting an NNF formula ϕ such that only subformulas that do not contribute to the UNSAT core $\mathcal{C}$ are replaced with a new variable.

---

procedure $\mathcal{A}$(DAG D_ϕ, node n, unsat-core $\mathcal{C}$)
    if n is a leaf **then return** ;
    end if
    if n is Boolean and $vars(c(n)) \cap vars(\mathcal{C}) = \emptyset$ **then**
        Replace n in D_ϕ with a new Boolean variable;
        return ;
    end if
    $\mathcal{A}(D_\phi, \text{left-child}(D_\phi, n), \mathcal{C})$;
    $\mathcal{A}(D_\phi, \text{right-child}(D_\phi, n), \mathcal{C})$;
end procedure

The replacement of Boolean nodes with new variables can be further optimized using the "pure-literal rule": if n_ϕ is a Boolean-valued node and only appears unnegated, replace it by *True*; likewise, if n_ϕ only appears negated, replace it by *False*. In other words, in such cases no new Boolean variable is needed.

Note that the resulting DAG $D_{\bar{\phi}}$ can be embedded into D_ϕ. For each node $n \in N^\phi$ we will denote by $\bar{n}$ its counterpart in $D_{\bar{\phi}}$ before the abstraction process begins (after the abstraction some of them can be eliminated by simplifications).

The correctness of our abstraction technique is formalized by the following two theorems:

Theorem 1. $\bar{\phi}$ *is an over-approximating abstraction of* ϕ.

---

[2] The same replacement criterion can be applied to bit-vector-valued nodes, which can then be replaced with fresh bit-vector variables. Our implementation ignores this option, however, and we shall therefore also ignore this possibility in the proof.

Proof. Let α be a satisfying assignment of ϕ. We show how to construct $\bar{\alpha}$, a satisfying assignment for $\overline{\phi}$. First, for each variable $v \in vars(\phi)$ such that the (leaf) node representing v is still present in $D_{\overline{\phi}}$, define $\bar{\alpha}(v) = \alpha(v)$. Second, for each Boolean variable $b \in \{vars(\overline{\phi}) \setminus vars(\phi)\}$ (i.e., the new abstracting variables) represented by node $n \in D_{\overline{\phi}}$, define $\bar{\alpha}(b)$ to be equal to the Boolean value of the corresponding node in D_{ϕ}, as implied by α. For example, if $\alpha(b_1) =$ *True*, $\alpha(b_2) =$ *False* and the node $b_1 \vee b_2$ was replaced with a new variable b, then $\bar{\alpha}(b) =$ *True* $\vee$ *False* $=$ *True*. Clearly, $\bar{\alpha}$ satisfies $\overline{\phi}$, since every node in $D_{\overline{\phi}}$ is evaluated the same as its counterpart in D_{ϕ}. Hence, if ϕ is satisfiable, then so is $\overline{\phi}$, which implies the correctness of the Theorem. $\qquad\square$

Next, we have to prove termination. Termination is implied if we can show that any satisfying assignment to $\overline{\phi}$ requires width larger than the current one s_i (i.e., the width with which the unsatisfiable core C was derived), or, equivalently:

Theorem 2. *The SAT encoding of $\overline{\phi}$ with encoding sizes s_i is unsatisfiable.*

Proof. We will prove that the CNF encoding of $\overline{\phi}$ with sizes s_i contains the clauses of the UNSAT core C.

Three observations about this encoding are important for our proof:

1. First, for an internal node n that represents a Boolean operator, each clause in $c(n)$ contains the output variable of its node. For example, the CNF of an 'and' node $o = a \wedge b$ is $(o \vee \neg a \vee \neg b), (\neg o \vee a), (\neg o \vee b)$, and indeed o, the output variable of this node, is present in all three clauses. The same applies to the other Boolean operators. Hence, we can write $o(cl)$ for a clause cl to mean the output variable of the node that cl annotates (hence, $o(cl) \in cl$).

2. Second, the same observation applies to predicates over bit-vectors. For simplicity, we concentrate only on the bit-vector equality predicate. In such a node, each clause contains either the output variable or an auxiliary variable present only in this node. For example, the CNF of the node $o = (v_1 = v_2)$ for 2-bit bit-vectors v_1 and v_2, is the following (the first four clauses encode $x = (v_1[0] = v_2[0])$, the other clauses encode $o = x \wedge (v_1[1] = v_2[1])$ where x is the local auxiliary variable):

$$(x \vee v_1[0] \vee v_2[0]), (x \vee \neg v_1[0] \vee \neg v_2[0]),$$
$$(\neg x \vee v_1[0] \vee \neg v_2[0]), (\neg x \vee \neg v_1[0] \vee v_2[0]),$$
$$(o \vee \neg x \vee \neg v_1[1] \vee \neg v_2[1]), (o \vee \neg x \vee v_1[1] \vee v_2[1]),$$
$$(\neg o \vee v_1[1] \vee \neg v_2[1]), (\neg o \vee \neg v_1[1] \vee v_2[1]), (\neg o \vee x)$$

3. Finally, observe that resolution among clauses that relate the output and input of a node using the output variable as the resolution variable, results in a tautology. For example, recall the CNF representation of the 'and' node above: Resolving on the output variable o of that node results in a tautology. The same observation applies to other Boolean operators and equality between bit-vectors.

We use these observations for analyzing the three possible cases for a node n in D_ϕ: either it is retained in $D_{\overline{\phi}}$, replaced with a new variable, or eliminated. Our goal, recall, is to show that despite the abstraction implied by these changes to the DAG, the set of clauses that encode the new DAG $D_{\overline{\phi}}$ still contains the UNSAT core $\mathcal{C}$ of ϕ.

- *Claim*: for each node $n \in N^\phi$ for which the corresponding $\overline{n} \in N^{\overline{\phi}}$ is retained in the abstraction process, $c(n) \cap \mathcal{C} = c(\overline{n}) \cap \mathcal{C}$.

  Proof. Since n and $\overline{n}$ encode the same operator and receive the same *type* of input (e.g., if n and $\overline{n}$ represent a bit-vector operator, then their respective inputs are bit-vectors of the same width), then $c(n)$ and $c(\overline{n})$ are equivalent up to renaming of variables. Such a renaming can occur if the abstraction process replaced one of the inputs (or both with a new variable. But this means that none of these inputs are in $\mathcal{C}$, hence those clauses in $c(\overline{n})$ that contain renamed literals, are not in $\mathcal{C}$. Hence, $c(n) \cap \mathcal{C} = c(\overline{n}) \cap \mathcal{C}$.

- *Claim*: for each node $n \in N^\phi$ that was replaced with a new variable in $N^{\overline{\phi}}$, $c(n) \cap \mathcal{C} = \emptyset$.

  Proof. This is trivial by the construction of the abstraction: if any of the clauses in $c(n)$ were in $\mathcal{C}$, then this node would not be replaced with a new variable.

- *Claim*: For each node $n \in N^\phi$ whose corresponding node $\overline{n} \in N^{\overline{\phi}}$ was eliminated (i.e., the paths of this node to the root were all 'cut' by the abstraction), $c(n) \cap \mathcal{C} = \emptyset$.

  Proof. On each path from n to the root node, there exists one or more nodes other than n that were replaced with free variables. For simplicity of the proof, we will consider one such path and denote the closest node to n that was replaced with a new variable by n_c.

  We will now prove the claim by induction on the distance (in terms of number of DAG operators) from n to n_c. In the base case n is a direct child of n_c. Falsely assume that there exists a clause $cl \in c(n)$ such that $cl \in \mathcal{C}$. $c(n_c)$ contain $o(n)$, the output variable of n, and cl also contains $o(n)$ (see observations 1 and 2 above). Hence, if $cl \in \mathcal{C}$, then $o(n) \in vars(\mathcal{C})$ which contradicts the condition for abstracting n_c with a new variable.

  For the induction step falsely assume that there exists a clause $cl \in c(n)$ such that $cl \in \mathcal{C}$. By the induction hypothesis, none of the clauses in the parent node of n are in $\mathcal{C}$. Hence, only clauses from $c(n)$ can contain the output variable of cl in $\mathcal{C}$. This means that $o(cl)$ can only be resolved-on among $c(n)$ clauses. By noting that that this kind of resolution can only result in a tautology (see observation 3 above), this resolution step cannot be on the path to the empty clause in the resolution proof. This contradicts, however, the requirement that any variable in every clause that participates in a proof of the empty clause must be resolved on in order to eliminate it.

Thus, the set of clauses annotating $D_{\overline{\phi}}$ contains $\mathcal{C}$ and hence $\overline{\phi}$ is unsatisfiable.

In comparison with our previous CNF-based abstraction scheme [5], we note that, for ITE-free formulas, that approach can generate more compact abstractions, as they do not introduce new variables. However, for real-world benchmarks from both hardware and software verification, such as those discussed in the following section, we found that elimination of ITEs leads to significant space and time overheads. The approach of this paper allows us to extend the abstraction-based approach to operate on arbitrary DAG-like formulas. Moreover, we have found that the Boolean structure in the original bit-vector formula is not usually the primary source of difficulty; it is the bit-vector constraints that are the problem.

3.3   Another Step of Abstraction

It is well-known that certain bit-vector arithmetic operators, such as integer multiplication of two variables (of adequately large width), are extremely hard for a procedure based on bit blasting. However, for many problems involving these operators, it is unnecessary to reason about all of the operators' properties in order to decide the formula. Instead, using a set of rules (based on well-known rewrite rules) allows us to perform fine-grained abstractions of functions, which often suffices. Such (incomplete) abstractions can be used in the over-approximation phase of our procedure, while maintaining the overall procedure sound and complete (see Remark 1 in §3.1). This is a major advantage, because these rules can be very powerful in simplifying the formula.

Therefore, UCLID invokes a preprocessing step before calling Algorithm $\mathcal{A}$. In this step, it replaces a subset of "hard" operators by lambda expressions that *partially interpret* those operators. The resulting formula is then bit blasted to SAT.

For example, UCLID replaces the multiplication operator $*_w$ of width w (for $w > 4$, chosen according to the capacity of current SAT engines) by the following lambda expression involving the freshly introduced uninterpreted function symbol $\mathtt{mul}_w$:

$$\lambda x.\lambda y.ITE(x = 0 \vee y = 0, 0, ITE(x = 1, y, ITE(y = 1, x, \mathtt{mul}_w(x, y))))$$

This expression can be seen as partially interpreting multiplication, as it models precisely the behavior of this operator when one of the arguments is 0 or 1, but is uninterpreted otherwise.

4   Experimental Results

The new procedure is now incorporated within the UCLID verification system [24], which is implemented in Moscow ML [25] (a dialect of Standard ML). Mini-iSat [22] was used as the SAT solver to solve over-approximations, while Booleforce (written by Armin Biere) was used as a proof-generating SAT solver for under-approximations. The initial value of s_i is set to $\min(4, w_i)$ for benchmarks not involving hard operators (like multiplication) while it is set to $\min(2, w_i)$ otherwise.

Table 1. Comparison of run-time of abstraction-based approach (UCLID) with bit-blasting, STP, Yices. The best run-time is highlighted in **bold font**. A "TO" indicates a timeout of 3600 seconds was reached. An "err" indicates that the solver could not handle bit-vectors of width as wide as those in the benchmark or quit with an exception. Bit-blasting used MiniSat. UCLID used Booleforce for proof generation and MiniSat on the abstraction. STP is based on MiniSat. "Ans" indicates whether the formula was satisfiable (SAT) or not (UNSAT). "Enc" indicates time for translation to SAT, and "SAT" indicates the time taken by the SAT solver (both calls).

Formula	Ans.	Bit-Blasting Run-time (sec.)			UCLID Run-time (sec.)			STP (sec.)	Yices (sec.)
		Enc.	SAT	Total	Enc.	SAT	Total		
Y86-std	UNSAT	17.91	TO	TO	23.51	987.91	**1011.42**	2083.73	TO
Y86-btnft	UNSAT	17.79	TO	TO	26.15	1164.07	**1190.22**	err	TO
s-40-50	SAT	6.00	33.46	39.46	106.32	10.45	116.77	**12.96**	65.51
BBB-32	SAT	37.09	29.98	67.07	19.91	1.74	**21.65**	38.45	183.30
rfunit_flat-64	SAT	121.99	32.16	154.15	19.52	1.68	**21.20**	873.67	1312.00
C1-P1	SAT	2.68	45.19	47.87	2.61	0.58	**3.19**	err	err
C1-P2	UNSAT	0.44	TO	TO	2.24	2.12	**4.36**	TO	TO
C3-OP80	SAT	14.96	TO	TO	14.54	349.41	**363.95**	TO	3242.43
egt-5212	UNSAT	0.064	0.003	0.067	0.163	0.001	0.164	0.018	**0.009**

Table 1 shows experimental results obtained on a set of bit-vector formulas. We compare the run-time of UCLID against bit blasting to MiniSat, and the STP [10] and Yices [11] decision procedures. (The latter two procedures jointly won the bit-vector division of the recent SMT-COMP'06 competition, and we compare against the versions that were entered in the competition.) All results were obtained on a system with a 2.8 GHz Xeon processor and 2 GB RAM. The benchmarks are drawn from a wide range of sources, arising from verification and testing of both hardware and software:[3]

- Verification of word-level versions of an x86-like processor model [26] (Y86-std, Y86-btnft);
- Detection of format-string vulnerabilities in C programs [27] (s-40-50);
- Hardware verification benchmarks obtained from Intel, slightly modified (BBB-32, rfunit_flat-64);
- Word-level combinational equivalence checking benchmarks obtained from a CAD company[4] (C1-P1, C1-P2, C3-OP80); and
- Directed random testing of programs [10] (egt-5212). This represents the set of benchmarks used in SMT-COMP'06, which are easily solved within a fraction of a second. (As the run-times on this benchmark was so small, we state them to three decimal places, unlike the others.)

---

[3] All benchmarks that we have permission to make publicly available are online at http://www.cs.cmu.edu/~uclid/tacas07-examples.tgz

[4] Name withheld on their request.

Table 2. Statistics on the abstraction-based approach (UCLID). "$\max_i s_i$" indicates the maximum value of s_i generated in the entire run. "Num. Iter" indicates the number of iterations of the abstraction-refinement loop where an iteration is counted if at least one of the SAT solver calls is made. The second to last column compares the size of the largest abstraction $\bar{\phi}$ created as a fraction of the size of the original formula ϕ, where sizes are measured as the number of nodes in the DAG representations of the formulas. "Speedup" indicates the factor by which the abstraction-based approach is faster than its nearest competitor, or slower than the best solver.

Formula	Ans.	$\max_i s_i$	$\max_i w_i$	Num. Iter	$\max \frac{|\bar{\phi}|}{|\phi|}$	Speedup
Y86-std	UNSAT	4	32	1	0.18	2.06
Y86-btnft	UNSAT	4	32	1	0.20	> 3.01
s-40-50	SAT	32	32	8	0.12	0.11
BBB-32	SAT	4	32	1	−	1.78
rfunit_flat-64	SAT	4	64	1	−	7.27
C1-P1	SAT	2	65	1	−	15.00
C1-P2	UNSAT	2	14	1	1.00	> 825.69
C3-OP80	SAT	2	9	1	−	8.91
egt-5212	UNSAT	8	8	1	0.13	0.06

The first three sets of benchmarks involve only (finite-precision) linear arithmetic. The combinational equivalence checking benchmarks involve finite-precision multiplication with large widths (e.g., C1-P1 and C1-P2 involve 65-bit, 49-bit, and 30-bit multiplication), apart from bitwise operations including extraction and concatenation. The last set includes linear arithmetic and bitwise operations.

An analysis of UCLID's performance on the benchmarks is given in Table 2. We observe the following: 1) Only very few iterations of the abstraction-refinement loop are required, just 1 in most cases; 2) The abstractions generated are small in most cases; and 3) UCLID yields a speed-up in all but one case when the number of iterations is 1. In the 2 other cases, where some s_i reached the maximum w_i, it performs worse.

We look more closely at two benchmarks. UCLID's performance is orders of magnitude better than the other solvers on the C1-P2 benchmark: this involves multiplication as noted earlier, and the abstraction described in Section 3.3 was particularly effective. However, on the benchmark s-40-50, it is 10 times worse than STP, with most of the time spent in encoding. This problem is mainly due to re-generation of the SAT instance in each step, which an incremental implementation can fix.

The results indicate a complementarity amongst the solvers with respect to this set of benchmarks: either bit-blasting (with rewrites as explained in §3.3) is effective, or the problem is unsatisfiable with a small UNSAT core, or there is a satisfying solution within a small range at the high and low ends of the bit-vector's value domain. In the latter two cases, our abstraction-based approach is effective.

5   Conclusion

We have demonstrated the utility of an abstraction-based approach for deciding the satisfiability of finite-precision bit-vector arithmetic. The speed-ups we have obtained, especially on benchmarks involving non-linear arithmetic operations, indicate the promise of the proposed approach. The algorithm is applicable in many areas in formal verification (e.g., word-level bounded model checking) and can be extended to handle floating-point arithmetic. Ongoing and future work includes generalizing the form of over- and under-approximations beyond those we have proposed herein, and making the encoding to SAT incremental.

References

1. Biere, A., Cimatti, A., Clarke, E., Yhu, Y.: Symbolic model checking without BDDs. In: TACAS. (1999) 193–207
2. Clarke, E., Kroening, D.: Hardware verification using ANSI-C programs as a reference. In: Proceedings of ASP-DAC 2003, IEEE Computer Society Press (2003) 308–311
3. Xie, Y., Aiken, A.: Scalable error detection using Boolean satisfiability. In: Proc. 32nd ACM Symposium on Principles of Programming Languages (POPL). (2005) 351–363
4. Arons, T., Elster, E., Fix, L., Mador-Haim, S., Mishaeli, M., Shalev, J., Singerman, E., Tiemeyer, A., Vardi, M.Y., Zuck, L.D.: Formal verification of backward compatibility of microcode. In: Proc. Computer-Aided Verification (CAV'05). LNCS 2404 (2005) 185–198
5. Kroening, D., Ouaknine, J., Seshia, S.A., Strichman, O.: Abstraction-based satisfiability solving of Presburger arithmetic. In: Proc. CAV. Volume 3114 of LNCS. (2004) 308–320
6. McMillan, K., Amla, N.: Automatic abstraction without counterexamples. In: Proceedings of TACAS 03. Volume 2619., Springer LNCS (2003) 2–17
7. Cook, B., Kroening, D., Sharygina, N.: Cogent: Accurate theorem proving for program verification. In: Proceedings of CAV 2005, Springer (2005) 296–300
8. Berezin, S., Ganesh, V., Dill, D.: A decision procedure for fixed-width bit-vectors. Technical report, Computer Science Department, Stanford University (2005)
9. Wedler, M., Stoffel, D., Kunz, W.: Normalization at the arithmetic bit level. In: Proc. DAC, ACM Press (2005) 457–462
10. Cadar, C., Ganesh, V., Pawlowski, P.M., Dill, D.L., Engler, D.R.: EXE: Automatically generating inputs of death. In: 13th ACM Conference on Computer and Communications Security (CCS '06), ACM (2006) 322–335
11. Dutertre, B., de Moura, L.: The Yices SMT solver. Available at http://yices.csl.sri.com/tool-paper.pdf (2006)
12. Cyrluk, D., Möller, M.O., Rueß, H.: An efficient decision procedure for the theory of fixed-sized bit-vectors. In: Computer-Aided Verification (CAV '97). (1997) 60–71
13. Barrett, C.W., Dill, D.L., Levitt, J.R.: A decision procedure for bit-vector arithmetic. In: Proceedings of DAC'98, ACM Press (1998) 522–527
14. Babić, D., Musuvathi, M.: Modular Arithmetic Decision Procedure. Technical report, Microsoft Research, Redmond (2005)
15. Brinkmann, R., Drechsler, R.: RTL-datapath verification using integer linear programming. In: Proceedings of VLSI Design. (2002) 741–746

16. Parthasarathy, G., Iyer, M.K., Cheng, K.T., Wang, L.C.: An efficient finite-domain constraint solver for circuits. In: Design Automation Conference (DAC). (2004) 212–217
17. Huang, C.Y., Cheng, K.T.: Assertion checking by combined word-level ATPG and modular arithmetic constraint-solving techniques. In: Proc. DAC. (2000) 118–123
18. Gupta, A., Ganai, M., Yang, Z., Ashar, P.: Iterative abstraction using SAT-based BMC with proof analysis. In: ICCAD. (2003)
19. Lahiri, S., Mehra, K.: Interpolant based decision procedure for quantifier-free Presburger arithmetic. Technical Report 2005-121, Microsoft Research (2005)
20. Tseitin, G.: On the complexity of proofs in poropositional logics. In Siekmann, J., Wrightson, G., eds.: Automation of Reasoning: Classical Papers in Computational Logic 1967–1970. Volume 2., Springer-Verlag (1983) Originally published 1970.
21. zChaff. http://www.ee.princeton.edu/~chaff/zchaff.php.
22. MiniSat. http://www.cs.chalmers.se/Cs/Research/FormalMethods/MiniSat/.
23. Zhang, L., Malik, S.: Extracting small unsatisfiable cores from unsatisfiable Boolean formulas. In: Proceedings of SAT 03. (2003)
24. UCLID verification system. http://www.cs.cmu.edu/~uclid.
25. Moscow ML. http://www.dina.dk/~sestoft/mosml.html.
26. Bryant, R.E.: Term-level verification of a pipelined CISC microprocessor. Technical Report CMU-CS-05-195, Computer Science Department, Carnegie Mellon University (2005)
27. Wisconsin Safety Analyzer Project. http://www.cs.wisc.edu/wisa.

Abstraction Refinement of Linear Programs with Arrays

Alessandro Armando[1], Massimo Benerecetti[2], and Jacopo Mantovani[1]

[1] AI-Lab, DIST, Università di Genova, Italy
[2] Dip. di Scienze Fisiche, Università di Napoli "Federico II", Italy

Abstract. In previous work we presented a model checking procedure for linear programs, i.e. programs in which variables range over a numeric domain and expressions involve linear combinations of the variables. In this paper we lift our model checking procedure for linear programs to deal with arrays via iterative abstraction refinement. While most approaches are based on predicate abstraction and therefore the abstraction is relative to sets of predicates, in our approach the abstraction is relative to sets of variables and array indexes, and the abstract program can express complex correlations between program variables and array elements. Thus, while arrays are problematic for most of the approaches based on predicate abstraction, our approach treats them in a precise way. This is an important feature as arrays are ubiquitous in programming. We provide a detailed account of both the abstraction and the refinement processes, discuss their implementation in the EUREKA tool, and present experimental results that confirm the effectiveness of our approach on a number of programs of interest.

1 Introduction

We present an abstraction refinement procedure for linear programs with arrays, i.e. programs in which variables and array elements range over a numeric domain and expressions involve linear combinations of variables and array elements. Unlike the approaches based on predicate abstraction in which the abstraction is relative to sets of predicates, in our approach the abstraction is relative to sets of program variables and array indexes. Thus while predicate abstraction uses Boolean programs as the target of the abstraction, in our approach we use linear programs for the same purpose. This is particularly attractive as linear programs can directly and concisely represent complex correlations among program variables and a small number of iterations of the abstraction refinement loop usually suffice to either prove or disprove that the original program enjoys the desired properties.

In previous work [1] we proposed a model checking procedure for linear programs. In [2] we extended our procedure to deal with undefined values and conditional expressions, thereby paving the way to the model checking procedure for linear programs with arrays described in this paper.

The ability to analyse linear programs with arrays is particularly important as arithmetic and arrays are ubiquitous in programming and many real-world

O. Grumberg and M. Huth (Eds.): TACAS 2007, LNCS 4424, pp. 373–388, 2007.

programs belong to this class. Moreover, most predicate abstraction techniques suffer from a severe lack of precision when dealing with arrays. For instance, SLAM [3] and BLAST [4] treat all the elements of an array as they were a single element and this makes their analysis grossly inaccurate for all programs that access or manipulate arrays even in a trivial way. In addition, as the theory of arrays does not offer suitable interpolants, the approaches in which the refinement step is based on interpolation (see, e.g., [5,6]) have difficulties in the discovery of useful predicates when traces involve arrays. On the other hand, the procedure described in this paper efficiently handles linear programs with arrays in a sound and precise way.

We have implemented our procedure in the EUREKA tool and carried out several experiments using a number of linear programs of interest including string manipulation and sorting algorithms. We compared the results of our experiments with two state-of-the-art tools that adopt predicate abstraction, namely BLAST and SATABS [7]. On all problems considered BLAST detects spurious errors, and our procedure scales better than SATABS as the size of the arrays handled by the programs increases. We also compared EUREKA with CBMC [8], a well-known bounded model checker for C programs, with largely favourable results.

In the next section we present our procedure through a worked out example. In Section 3 we define the syntax and the semantics of linear programs with arrays. In Section 4 we define our abstraction and state its fundamental properties. In Section 5 we discuss how spurious error traces are detected. In Section 6 we present the refinement process. In Section 7 we describe the implementation of our ideas in EUREKA and discuss the results of our experiments.

2   Model Checking Linear Programs with Arrays

Our approach to model checking linear programs with arrays is based on the idea of abstracting away all program variables and array elements from the initial program, and then incrementally refining the abstract program obtained in this way by including program variables and array elements as suggested by the refinement process.

Let P be the linear program with arrays in the leftmost column of Table 1. We start by abstracting P into program $\widehat{P}_0$ by replacing every occurrence of array expressions with the symbol u (denoting an arbitrary value of numeric type) and by replacing every assignment to array elements with a skip statement (;). (For the sake of simplicity in our example we do not abstract away the program variable i which therefore occurs in $\widehat{P}_0$.)

By applying a model checker for linear programs to $\widehat{P}_0$ we get the execution trace 1, 2, 3, 4, 5, 3, 4, 5, 3, 6, 0 witnessing the violation of the assertion at line 6, where 0 is an additional node which is reached if and only if an assertion fails. This trace corresponds to the execution of two iterations of the while loop (lines 3–5) which leaves variable i with value 2 and therefore leads to a violation of the assertion at line 6.

Table 1. A simple program (P), the initial abstraction $(\widehat{P}_0)$ and its refinement $(\widehat{P}_1)$

Line	P	$\widehat{P}_0$	$\widehat{P}_1$
	`void main() {`	`void main() {`	`void main() {`
	`  int i, a[30];`	`  int i;`	`  int i, a`^{1}`;`
[1]	`  a[1] = 9;`	`  ;`	`  a`^{1}` = (1==1)?9:a`^{1}`;`
[2]	`  i = 0;`	`  i = 0;`	`  i = 0;`
[3]	`  while(a[i]!=9) {`	`  while(u!=9) {`	`  while(((i==1)?a`^{1}`:u)!=9) {`
[4]	`    a[i] = 2*i;`	`    ;`	`    a`^{1}` = (i==1)?2*i:a`^{1}`;`
[5]	`    i = i+1; }`	`    i = i+1; }`	`    i = i+1; }`
[6]	`  assert(i<=1); }`	`  assert(i<=1); }`	`  assert(i<=1); }`

The feasibility check of the above trace w.r.t. P is done by generating a set of quantifier-free formulae whose satisfying valuations correspond to all possible executions of the sequence of statements of P corresponding to the trace under consideration. This is done by first putting the trace in Single Assignment Form [9] and then by generating quantifier-free formulæ encoding the behaviour of the statements. Table 2 shows the sequence of the original statements, the trace in Single Assignment Form, and the associated formulæ for the above trace.

Table 2. Checking the trace for feasibility

Step	Line	Original Statement	Renamed Statement	Formula
1	[1]	`a[1]=9;`	`a`$_1$`[1]=9;`	$a_1 = \text{store}(a_0, 1, 9)$
2	[2]	`i=0;`	`i`$_1$`=0;`	$i_1 = 0$
3	[3]	`assume(a[i]!=9);`	`assume(a`$_1$`[i`$_1$`]!=9);`	$\text{select}(a_1, i_1) \neq 9$
4	[4]	`a[i]=2*i;`	`a`$_2$`[i`$_1$`]=2*i`$_1$`;`	$a_2 = \text{store}(a_1, i_1, 2 * i_1)$
5	[5]	`i=i+1;`	`i`$_2$`=i`$_1$`+1;`	$i_2 = i_1 + 1$
6	[3]	`assume(a[i]!=9);`	`assume(a`$_2$`[i`$_2$`]!=9);`	$\text{select}(a_2, i_2) \neq 9$
7	[4]	`a[i]=2*i;`	`a`$_3$`[i`$_2$`]=2*i`$_2$`;`	$a_3 = \text{store}(a_2, i_2, 2 * i_2)$
8	[5]	`i=i+1;`	`i`$_3$`=i`$_2$`+1;`	$i_3 = i_2 + 1$
9	[3]	`assume(!(a[i]!=9));`	`assume(!(a`$_3$`[i`$_3$`]!=9));`	$\neg(\text{select}(a_3, i_3) \neq 9)$
10	[6]	`assume(!(i<=1));`	`assume(!(i`$_3$`<=1));`	$\neg(i_3 \leq 1)$

The resulting set of formulæ is then fed to a theorem prover. If it is found unsatisfiable (w.r.t. a suitably defined background theory) then the trace is not executable in P, whereas if it is found satisfiable then we can conclude that the trace is also executable in P. In our example the set of formulæ (see rightmost column in Table 2) is found to be unsatisfiable. The formulæ that contributed to the proof of unsatisfiability are those associated with steps 1, 2, 4, 5, and 6. Moreover, the only term of the form $\text{select}(a, e)$ occurring in these formulæ is $\text{select}(a_2, i_2)$ (with $i_2 = 1$ given by the context). As we will see later in the paper, this suffice to conclude that in order to rule out the above trace we must refine $\widehat{P}_0$ by including the element of a at position 1. The resulting program, $\widehat{P}_1$, is obtained by replacing every expression of the form `a[e]` with the conditional expression $(e == 1\,?\,a^1 : u)$ and every assignment of the form $a[e_1] = e_2$; with the assignment

$$a^1 = (e_1 == 1\,?\,e_2 : a^1);$$

where a^1 is a new variable of numeric type corresponding to the array element of index 1. The application of the model checking procedure for linear programs to $\widehat{P_1}$ reveals that the error state cannot be reached in $\widehat{P_1}$ and from this it is possible to conclude that the error state is not reachable in P.

In the sequel, if P is a linear program with arrays, then by V_P and A_P we denote the set of numeric and array variables (resp.) of P. Moreover we assume that each array $a \in A_P$ is equipped with a positive integer $\dim(a)$ indicating the size of the array. Finally by R_P we denote the function mapping each $a \in A_P$ into the set $\{0, \ldots, \dim(a) - 1\}$.

A complete account of our abstraction refinement procedure for linear programs with arrays is given in Figure 1. The procedure takes as input a linear

procedure $AR(P,V,R)$
1. $\widehat{P} \leftarrow \text{abstract}(P, V, R)$;
2. $Trace \leftarrow \text{model-check}(\widehat{P})$;
3. if $Trace = \text{none}$ then return SAFE;
4. if $(V = V_P \text{ and } R = R_P)$ then return $Trace$;
5. $Formula \leftarrow \text{encode}(Trace, P)$;
6. $Result \leftarrow \text{decide}(Formula)$;
7. if $SAT?(Result)$ then return $Trace$;
   /* $Result$ contains a proof of the unsatisfiability of $Formula$ */
8. $\langle V', R' \rangle \leftarrow \text{refine}(Trace, Result, V, R)$;
9. return $AR(P,V',R')$;

Fig. 1. Abstraction refinement of linear programs with arrays

program with arrays P, a subset $V \subseteq V_P$ and a function R mapping each array $a \in A_P$ into a subset of $R_P(a)$. Initially V is set to the empty set and R is set to the function that maps every $a \in A_P$ into the empty set. The procedure starts by abstracting P w.r.t. V and R. The resulting abstract program $\widehat{P}$ is then fed to the model checker for linear programs at line 2. If no execution trace violating an assertion is found in $\widehat{P}$, then the procedure halts at line 3 reporting that the original program is safe. Otherwise (i.e. if $Trace$ contains an execution trace of $\widehat{P}$ that violates an assertion), the procedure checks at line 4 whether further refinement is possible. If this is not the case (this happens when $V = V_P$ and $R = R_P$), the procedure halts and returns $Trace$ as an execution trace of P witnessing an assertion violation. Otherwise (i.e. if further refinement is possible) the procedure builds at line 5 a quantifier-free formula whose unsatisfiability implies the infeasibility of $Trace$ w.r.t. P. The formula is then fed to a theorem prover at line 6. If the formula is found to be satisfiable by the theorem prover, then the procedure halts and returns $Trace$ as an execution trace of P witnessing an assertion violation. Otherwise $Result$ contains a proof of the unsatisfiability of the formula and the refinement procedure is invoked at line 8 with the task of extending the set of program variables and the sets of array indexes to be used for the construction of a new, refined abstraction of the original program. This is done by the recursive call to the AR procedure at line 9.

3 Linear Programs and Linear Programs with Arrays

A *linear program with arrays* is a program with the usual control-flow constructs (if, while, assert) procedural abstraction with call-by-value parameter passing and recursion, plus an additional assume statement. Variables and array elements range over a numerical domain $\mathcal{D}$, e.g. $\mathbb{R}$, $\mathbb{Z}$, or $\mathbb{Z}_n$ (i.e. the integers modulo n) for $n \in \mathbb{N}$; moreover, conditions and assignments to variables and array elements involve linear expressions with arrays. The sets E of *generalised linear expressions with arrays* (henceforth, simply *linear expression with arrays*) and the set B of *Boolean linear expressions with arrays* are defined by the following BNF production rules:

$$E ::= \mathfrak{u} \mid \mathbb{Z} \mid V_P \mid \mathbb{Z} * E \mid E + E \mid (B ? E : E) \mid A_P[E] \qquad B ::= (E \; op \; E)$$

where $op \in \{>=, <=, <, >, ==, !=\}$ and $\mathfrak{u}$ is a symbol representing an undefined value.

The definition of *generalised (Boolean, resp.) linear expression without arrays* (*(Boolean, resp.) linear expression*, for short) and of *linear programs without arrays* are subsumed by the above.

In the following we will consider only linear programs with arrays with no nested occurrences of arrays. This is without loss of generality, as nested occurrences of arrays can always be eliminated by introducing fresh variables. Moreover, we assume that the program is decorated with assertions in such a way to ensure that possible out-of-bounds array accesses always lead to an assertion violation.

For the sake of space, in the following we only present the semantics of linear programs with arrays without procedure calls and returns. We refer the reader to [2] for a complete account of the semantics that includes (recursive) procedures.

The *control flow graph* (CFG) of a program P is a directed graph $G_P = (N_P, \text{Succ}_P)$, where $N_P = \{0, 1, \ldots, n\}$ is the set of vertexes[1] and $\text{Succ}_P : N_P \to 2^{N_P}$ maps each vertex in the set of its successors. For every vertex i such that $1 \leq i \leq n$, s_i denotes the program statement corresponding to i. If s_i is if(e), while(e), or assert(e); then $\text{Succ}_P(i) = \{\text{Tsucc}_P(i), \text{Fsucc}_P(i)\}$, where $\text{Tsucc}_P(i)$ ($\text{Fsucc}_P(i)$) denotes the successor of i when e evaluates to true (false, resp.). If s_i is assert(e);, then $\text{Fsucc}_P(i) = 0$, while if s_i is assume(e);, then $\text{Succ}_P(i) = \{Tsucc_P(i)\}$. Finally, if $\text{Succ}_P(i_1) = \{i_2\}$, we define $\text{sSucc}_P(i_1) = i_2$.

Given a program P, Globals_P denotes the set of global variables of P and, for every $i \in N_P$, $\text{Locals}_P(i)$ is the set of the local variables in scope at vertex i. Moreover, we define $\text{InScope}_P(i) = \text{Globals}_P \cup \text{Locals}_P(i)$.

Let $W_P = V_P \cup A_P$ be the set of program variables of P, a *valuation* ω over W_P is a total function mapping V_P into $\mathcal{D}$ and each $a \in A_P$ into a finite

---

[1] Vertexes from 1 to n are associated with program statements and vertex 0 models the failure of assert statements.

$$\overline{\omega}(e) = \begin{cases} \{e\} & \text{if } e \in \mathbb{Z} \\ \{\omega(e)\} & \text{if } e \in V \\ \{d \in \omega(a)(d_1) : d_1 \in \overline{\omega}(e_1)\} & \text{if } e = a[e_1] \\ & \text{and } \overline{\omega}(e_1) \subseteq \{0, \dots, \dim(a) - 1\} \\ \{c \cdot d_1 : d_1 \in \overline{\omega}(e_1)\} & \text{if } e = c * e_1 \\ \{d_1 \ op \ d_2 : d_1 \in \overline{\omega}(e_1) \text{ and } d_2 \in \overline{\omega}(e_2)\} & \text{if } e = e_1 \ op \ e_2 \\ & \text{with } op \in \{\text{>=}, \text{<=}, \text{<}, \text{>}, \text{==}, \text{!=}, \text{+}\} \\ \overline{\omega}(e_1) \cup \overline{\omega}(e_2) & \text{if } e = (b\,?\,e_1 : e_2) \text{ and } \{0, d\} \subseteq \overline{\omega}(b) \\ & \text{for some } d \neq 0 \\ \overline{\omega}(e_1) & \text{if } e = (b\,?\,e_1 : e_2) \text{ and } 0 \notin \overline{\omega}(b) \\ \overline{\omega}(e_2) & \text{if } e = (b\,?\,e_1 : e_2) \text{ and } \overline{\omega}(b) = \{0\} \\ \mathcal{D} & \text{otherwise} \end{cases}$$

Fig. 2. Semantics of linear expressions

mapping from $\{0, \dots, \dim(a) - 1\}$ into $\mathcal{D}$. A *state of a linear program with arrays* P is a pair $\langle i, \omega \rangle$, where i is a vertex of the control flow graph of P and ω is a valuation over $W_P \cap \mathrm{InScope}_P(i)$. Thus, ω is a total function over $\mathrm{InScope}_P(i)$. The definition of *state of a linear program* is subsumed by the above.

We lift ω to a total function $\overline{\omega} : E \longrightarrow 2^{\mathcal{D}}$ over linear expressions with arrays defined as reported in Figure 2. The intuition is that $\overline{\omega}(e)$ collects the set of all the values of e which are compatible with the valuation ω. All the occurrences of the u symbol, as well as those corresponding to an out-of-range access to an array, within an expression e are modelled by non-deterministically assigning an arbitrary element in $\mathcal{D}$ to the corresponding sub-expression. $\overline{\omega}$ is extended to k–tuples **e** of expressions in the obvious way.

State transitions in P are denoted by $\langle i_1, \omega_1 \rangle \longrightarrow_P \langle i_2, \omega_2 \rangle$, where the valuation ω_k is such that $\omega_k : \mathrm{InScope}_P(i_k) \to \mathcal{D}$, for $k = 1, 2$. We use bold letters such as **x** to denote vectors of variables, elements or expressions. We also allow for parallel assignments, denoted by **x**=**e**;. Moreover, let $\mathbf{c} = \langle c_1, c_2, \dots, c_n \rangle$ and $\mathbf{d} = \langle d_1, d_2, \dots, d_n \rangle$ be n–tuples of values in a set X and in $\mathcal{D}$ respectively; for any function $f : X \to \mathcal{D}$ by $f[\mathbf{d}/\mathbf{c}]$ we denote the function f' such that $f'(c_k) = d_k$ for all $k = 1, 2, \dots, n$, and $f'(c) = f(c)$ for all $c \neq c_k$ and $k = 1, 2, \dots, n$. State transitions of a program P are defined as follows:

- if s_{i_1} is a skip (;), then $\langle i_1, \omega_1 \rangle \longrightarrow_P \langle \mathrm{sSucc}_P(i_1), \omega_1 \rangle$;
- if s_{i_1} is a parallel assignment **y**=**e**; then $\langle i_1, \omega_1 \rangle \longrightarrow_P \langle \mathrm{sSucc}_P(i_1), \omega_1[\mathbf{d}/\mathbf{y}] \rangle$, for $\mathbf{d} \in \overline{\omega}_1(\mathbf{e})$;
- if s_{i_1} is an assignment $a[e_1] = e_2$; then $\langle i_1, \omega_1 \rangle \longrightarrow_P \langle \mathrm{sSucc}_P(i_1), \omega_1[(\omega(a)[d_2/d_1]) /a] \rangle$, for $d_1 \in \overline{\omega}_1(e_1)$ and $d_2 \in \overline{\omega}_1(e_2)$;
- if i_1 corresponds to assume(e);, then $\langle i_1, \omega_1 \rangle \longrightarrow_P \langle i_2, \omega_1 \rangle$, where $i_2 = \mathrm{sSucc}_P(i_1)$ if $d \in \overline{\omega}_1(e)$ for some $d \neq 0$;
- if s_{i_1} is a statement of the form if(e), while(e), or assert(e);, then $\langle i_1, \omega_1 \rangle \longrightarrow_P \langle i_2, \omega_1 \rangle$, where $i_2 = \mathrm{Fsucc}_P(i_1)$ if $0 \in \overline{\omega}_1(e)$ and $i_2 = \mathrm{Tsucc}_P(i_1)$ if $d \in \overline{\omega}_1(e)$ for some $d \neq 0$.

Let $\longrightarrow_P^*$ denote the reflexive and transitive closure of $\longrightarrow_P$. A state $\langle i, \omega \rangle$ is *reachable* if and only if there exists a valuation ω_0 such that $\langle 1, \omega_0 \rangle \longrightarrow_P^* \langle i, \omega \rangle$. A vertex $i \in N_P$ is *reachable* if and only if there exist two valuations ω_0 and ω such that $\langle 1, \omega_0 \rangle \longrightarrow_P^* \langle i, \omega \rangle$. A *trace of P* is a sequence of nodes $i_0 i_1 \cdots i_n$ such that $\langle 1, \omega_0 \rangle \longrightarrow_P \langle i_1, \omega_1 \rangle \longrightarrow_P \cdots \longrightarrow_P \langle i_n, \omega_n \rangle$ for some valuations $\omega_0, \omega_1, \ldots, \omega_n$. By traces($P$) we denote the set of traces of P. An *error trace of P* is any trace of P ending with vertex 0.

In [1] we proposed a symbolic model checking procedure for linear programs based on the tabulation algorithm defined in [10]. In [2] we extended our procedure to support the analysis of linear programs with the u symbol and conditional expressions. The resulting procedure can be used to implement the model checker (model-check) invoked by the AR procedure of Figure 1. For the purpose of this paper it suffices to know that model-check(P_0) is capable to detect and return an error trace (if any) of the linear program P_0 given as input.

It is worth pointing out that the framework described in this paper is independent from the domain of computation. On the other hand, the decidability of the model checking problem clearly depends on it: if $\mathcal{D} = \mathbb{R}$ or $\mathcal{D} = \mathbb{Z}$, then the problem is undecidable, whereas if $\mathcal{D} = \mathbb{Z}_n$ (for $n \geq 0$), then the problem is decidable.

4 Abstracting Linear Programs with Arrays into Linear Programs

Let R be a function mapping each array $a \in A_P$ into a subset of $R_P(a)$, and let $V \subseteq V_P$. The *set of abstractions of P w.r.t. R and V*, in symbols abstract(P, V, R), is the set of linear programs defined as follows. The set of program variables of $\widehat{P} \in$ abstract(P, V, R) is $\widehat{V} = V \cup \{a^k : a \in A_P, k \in R(a)\}$. Intuitively, a^k is a new variable representing in $\widehat{P}$ the $(k+1)$-th element of the array a. Given any linear expression e in P, an abstract version $\widehat{e}$ is obtained from e by replacing *(i)* every occurrence of the variables not in V with the undefined symbol u, *(ii)* every expression of the form $a[e]$ with abs($a[e], [k_1, \ldots, k_n]$), where $[k_1, \ldots, k_n]$ is some permutation of $R(a)$ and:

$$\text{abs}(a[e], []) = \mathsf{u}$$
$$\text{abs}(a[e], [k_1, k_2, \ldots, k_n]) = (\widehat{e} == k_1 \,?\, a^{k_1} : \text{abs}(a[e], [k_2, \ldots, k_n])),$$

and *(iii)* every conditional expression of the form $e' \,?\, \mathsf{u} : \mathsf{u}$, possibly occurring in the expression resulting from step *(i)*, with the equivalent expression u.

Fixed a permutation of $R(a)$ for each $a \in A_P$, the linear program $\widehat{P} \in$ abstract(P, V, R) is then obtained from P by replacing all the expressions e occurring in P with $\widehat{e}$, and then by replacing each assignment of the form $x = e$; with the skip statement (;) if $x \notin V$, with $x = \widehat{e}$; otherwise, and by replacing each assignment of the form $a[i] = e$; with the (parallel) assignment

$$a^{k_1}, \ldots, a^{k_n} = (\widehat{i} == k_1 \,?\, \widehat{e} : a^{k_1}), \ldots, (\widehat{i} == k_n \,?\, \widehat{e} : a^{k_n});$$

that we abbreviate with $a[i] \mathrel{\hat=} e;$. If $n = 0$ (i.e. if $R(a) = \emptyset$), the assignment above reduces to a skip $(;)$ statement.

If θ and θ' are two permutations of $R(a)$,then $\overline{\omega}(\text{abs}(a[e],\theta))=\overline{\omega}(\text{abs}(a[e],\theta'))$. From this it readily follows that all programs in abstract(P, V, R) are semantically equivalent.

It is worth noticing that computing an abstraction of a program P w.r.t. V and R can be done in time linear in the size of P and the cardinality of R, where by cardinality of a mapping R we mean the cardinality of the set $\bigcup_{a \in A_P} R(a)$. This contrasts with approaches based on predicate abstraction, where theorem provers [3] or SAT solvers [7] are needed to compute abstractions.

We now show that the abstraction defined above is conservative (i.e. sound), namely that every node reachable in the concrete program P is also reachable in the abstract program $\widehat{P}$. The *abstraction of ω w.r.t. R and V* is the valuation $\widehat{\omega}$ over $\widehat{V}$ such that $\widehat{\omega}(v) = \omega(v)$ for all $v \in V$ and $\widehat{\omega}(a^k) = \omega(a)(k)$ for all $a \in A_P$ and $k \in R(a)$. The following result states the relation between abstract and concrete valuations on linear and Boolean expressions.

Lemma 1. *The following facts hold:*

1. *if ω is a valuation over V_P and A_P, then $\overline{\omega}(e) \subseteq \overline{\widehat{\omega}}(\widehat{e})$, for every expression e;*
2. *if ω is a valuation over V_P and A_P and $\widehat{\omega}$ is a valuation over $V_P \cup \{a^k : a \in A_P, k \in R_P(a)\}$, then $\overline{\omega}(e) = \overline{\widehat{\omega}}(\widehat{e})$, for every expression e.*

The first statement of the lemma ensures that when a concrete expression e is abstracted to its corresponding abstract expression $\widehat{e}$ all concrete values compatible with the concrete valuations are preserved by the abstract ones. This is the key property in order to prove that the abstraction is conservative. The second statement of the lemma guarantees the equivalence of the concrete and abstract semantics when the abstraction is relative to all the variables V_P and all the array indexes R_P of the concrete program.

Let S_P be the set of states of program P. The abstraction of valuations is lifted to abstraction of states by means of the function $h : S_P \to S_{\widehat{P}}$ such that $h(\langle i, \omega \rangle) = \langle i, \widehat{\omega} \rangle$ for all $\langle i, \omega \rangle \in S_P$.

Let $S \subseteq S_P$, we define the abstraction $\alpha[h](S) = \{h(s) : s \in S\}$; conversely, for all $\widehat{S} \subseteq S_{\widehat{P}}$, the concretisation is defined by $\gamma[h](\widehat{S}) = \{s \in S_P : h(s) \in \widehat{S}\}$. It can be proved that the pair $\langle \alpha[h], \gamma[h] \rangle$ forms a Galois connection.

We define $R \subseteq R'$ if and only if $R(a) \subseteq R'(a)$ for all $a \in A_P$. We define $\langle V, R \rangle \preceq \langle V', R' \rangle$ if and only if $V \subseteq V'$ and $R \subseteq R'$. Moreover we define $\langle V, R \rangle \prec \langle V', R' \rangle$ if and only if $\langle V, R \rangle \preceq \langle V', R' \rangle$, and $V' \neq V$ or $R' \neq R$. If P and P' are programs with the same control-flow graph, then we define $P' \sqsubseteq P$ if and only if traces$(P') \subseteq$ traces(P), $P' \sqsubset P$ if and only if traces$(P') \subset$ traces(P), and $P' \equiv P$ if and only if $P' \sqsubseteq P$ and $P \sqsubseteq P'$, i.e. traces$(P') =$ traces(P).

Let S be a set of states S of a program P. We define post$_P^*(S) = \{s' : s \longrightarrow_P^* s'$ and $s \in S\}$, i.e. the set of states reachable from S. We can now state the soundness of the abstraction.

Theorem 1 (Soundness). *Let* $\langle V, R \rangle \preceq \langle V_P, R_P \rangle$ *and* $\widehat{P} \in$ abstract(P, V, R). *Then,* post$^*_P \subseteq (\gamma[h] \circ$ post$^*_{\widehat{P}} \circ \alpha[h])$ *and* $P \sqsubseteq \widehat{P}$. *Moreover if* $\widehat{P} \in$ abstract(P, V_P, R_P) *then* post$^*_P = (\gamma[h] \circ$ post$^*_{\widehat{P}} \circ \alpha[h])$ *and* $P \equiv \widehat{P}$.

The following result is key to prove the completeness of the AR procedure.

Theorem 2. *Let* $\widehat{P} \in$ abstract(P, V, R) *and* $\widehat{P}' \in$ abstract(P, V', R'). *If* $\langle V, R \rangle \preceq \langle V', R' \rangle$, *then* $\widehat{P}' \sqsubseteq \widehat{P}$.

5   Checking Trace Feasibility

We now turn our attention to the problem of determining whether a trace $\tau = i_0 \cdots i_n$ of the abstract program $\widehat{P}$ is also a trace of the corresponding concrete program P. We show how this problem can be reduced to the problem of determining the satisfiability of a set of quantifier-free formulae (henceforth called *trace formulae*) in the decidable theory resulting from the combination of Linear Arithmetic and the theory of arrays. By Linear Arithmetic we mean standard arithmetic (over $\mathcal{D}$) with addition (i.e. $+$) and the usual relational operators (e.g. $=, <, \leq, >, \geq$) but without multiplication. (Multiplication by a constant, say $n * x$ where n is a numeral, is usually allowed but it is just a notational shorthand for the (linear) expression $x + \cdots + x$ with n occurrences of the variable x.). The theory of arrays we consider models arrays as data structures representing arbitrary associations of elements to a set of indexes. Unlike arrays available in standard programming languages, the arrays modelled by the theory of arrays need not have finite size. Let INDEX, ELEM and ARRAY be sorts for indexes, elements, and arrays (resp.), and select : ARRAY $\times$ INDEX $\rightarrow$ ELEM and store : ARRAY $\times$ INDEX $\times$ ELEM $\rightarrow$ ARRAY be function symbols. We also assume that the language of the theory of arrays includes a conditional term constructor that allows for terms of the form $(w ? t_1 : t_2)$, for every formula w and terms t_1 and t_2. Then the following is a concise presentation of the theory of arrays:

$$\forall a, i, j, e. \ \text{select}(\text{store}(a, i, e), j) = (j = i ? e : \text{select}(a, j)) \tag{1}$$

In the sequel we will denote Linear Arithmetic with $\mathcal{T}_0$ and the union of Linear Arithmetic with the theory of arrays with $\mathcal{T}_1$.

Let $s_{i_1} \cdots s_{i_n}$ the sequence of statements associated with $\tau = i_0 \cdots i_n$. The sequence of statements is put in Single Assignment Form [9], i.e. the program variables are renamed in such a way that each variable is assigned exactly once in the resulting program. This is done in the following way. Let v be a program variable and i a program location. We define $\alpha(v, i)$ to be the number of assignments made to v prior to location i. Let e be a program expression. With $\varrho(e)$ we denote the expression obtained from e by substituting every variable v in e with $v_{\alpha(v,i)}$. Every assignment to a variable x at a given location i, say $x = e;$, is replaced by $x_{\alpha(x,i)+1} = \varrho(e);$. Every assignment to an array element, say $a[e_1] = e_2;$, is replaced by $a_{\alpha(a,i)+1}[\varrho(e_1)] = \varrho(e_2);$. Every condition c (also called *guard*) is replaced by $\varrho(c)$.

The set of *trace formulae for* τ *w.r.t.* P is the set of quantifier-free formulae $\Phi(\tau, P) = \bigcup_{k=1}^{n} \phi(s_{i_k})$, where $\phi(s_{i_k})$ is defined in Table 3. We define $\Phi_{\mathcal{T}_i}(\tau, P) = \mathcal{T}_i \cup \Phi(\tau, P)$ for $i = 0, 1$. The following theorem holds:

Table 3. Encoding

s_{i_k}	$\phi(s_{i_k})$	condition
if(c), assert(c);, while(c);	$\{c\}$	if $i_{k+1} = \text{Tsucc}_P(i_k)$
if(c), assert(c);, while(c);	$\{\neg c\}$	if $i_{k+1} = \text{Fsucc}_P(i_k)$
$v_{j+1} = e$;	$\{v_{j+1} = e'\}$	
$a_{j+1}[e_1] = e_2$;	$\{a_{j+1} = \text{store}(a_j, e_1', e_2')\}$	
;	$\emptyset$	

Theorem 3. *Let P_0 be a linear program and let P_1 be a linear program with arrays, then $\tau \in \text{traces}(P_i)$ if and only if $\Phi_{\mathcal{T}_i}(\tau, P_i)$ is satisfiable, for $i = 0, 1$.*

In the AR procedure of Figure 1 the task of checking whether the trace for $\widehat{P}$ found by the model-checker is also a trace for P is jointly carried out by the functions encode and decide. If the variable *Trace* is set to τ, then the function call encode(*Trace, P*) at line 5 computes and returns the set of trace formulae $\Phi(\tau, P)$. If the variable *Formula* is set to the set of trace formulae $\Phi(\tau, P)$, then the function call decide(*Formula*) at line 6 checks the satisfiability of $\Phi_{\mathcal{T}_1}(\tau, P)$.

If $\Phi_{\mathcal{T}_1}(\tau, P)$ is unsatisfiable, then decide(*Formula*) returns a proof of this fact in a sequent calculus for first order logic with equality, i.e. it returns a proof of the sequent $\Phi_{\mathcal{T}_1}(\tau, P) \vdash \perp$, namely a tree whose root is labelled by the sequent $\Phi_{\mathcal{T}_1}(\tau, P) \vdash \perp$ and whose leaves are labelled by sequents of the form $\Phi_{\mathcal{T}_1}(\tau, P) \vdash \varphi$ with $\varphi \in \Phi_{\mathcal{T}_1}(\tau, P)$.

6   Refinement

Let $\widehat{P} \in \text{abstract}(P, V, R)$ with $V \subseteq V_P$ and $R \subseteq R_P$, let τ be a trace of $\widehat{P}$ such that $\Phi_{\mathcal{T}_1}(\tau, P)$ is unsatisfiable and let Π be a proof of $\Phi_{\mathcal{T}_1}(\tau, P) \vdash \perp$. The procedure refine($\tau, \Pi, V, R$) computes V' and R' such that $\langle V, R \rangle \prec \langle V', R' \rangle$ and $\tau \notin \text{traces}(\widehat{P'})$ for all $\widehat{P'} \in \text{abstract}(P, V', R')$. From this is it is easy to conclude that $\widehat{P'} \sqsubset \widehat{P}$. This fact, which is formally stated and proved below, is key to establish the completeness of the AR procedure of Figure 1.

The definition of the procedure refine(τ, Π, V, R) is given in Figure 3. The procedure exploits the fact that every term of the form select(a, e) occurring in Π has a corresponding representation in the abstract program $\widehat{P'}$ only if $e = k$ for $k \in R'(a)$. The set V' is obtained by extending V with all the program variables occurring in Π. The computation of R' is based on the idea of turning Π into a proof of the unsatisfiability of $\Phi_{\mathcal{T}_0}(\tau, \widehat{P'})$. This is done in step 1 by adding to the premises of each leaf sequent $\Phi_{\mathcal{T}_1}(\tau, P) \vdash \varphi$ of Π a formula $Q(e, a)$ for each term of the form select(a_k, e) occurring in φ. Informally a formula of the form $Q(e, a)$ is a placeholder for the formula $\bigvee_{k \in R'(a)} e = k$. However, since $R'(a)$ is unknown

procedure refine(τ, Π, V, R)

1. $V' \leftarrow V \cup \{x \in V_P : x_j \text{ occurs in } \Pi \text{ for some } j \geq 0\}$;
2. $\Pi' \leftarrow$ the sequent tree obtained from Π by
   - (a) replacing every leaf sequent $\Phi_{T_1}(\tau, P) \vdash \varphi$ with $\Phi_{T_1}(\tau, P), \{Q(e, a) : \text{select}(a, e) \text{ occurs in } \varphi\} \vdash \varphi$, where Q is a newly introduced binary predicate symbol added to the signature of T_1 and
   - (b) updating the sequents associated with the non-leaves nodes of the proof by re-applying all the inference rules.
3. Let $\Phi_{T_1}(\tau, P), Q(e_1', a), \ldots, Q(e_q', a) \vdash \bot$ be the root node of Π'. Choose an R' such that $R \subseteq R'$ and

$$\Phi_{T_0}(\tau, \widehat{P}') \models \bigvee_{k \in R'(a)} e_j' = k \qquad (2)$$

   for all $\widehat{P}' = \text{abstract}(P, V', R')$ and $j = 1, \ldots, q$.
4. **return** $\langle V', R' \rangle$

Fig. 3. The refinement procedure

at this stage, we use $Q(e, a)$ in place of its expanded version $\bigvee_{k \in R'(a)} e = k$. The sequent tree obtained in this way is then updated by re-applying all the inference rules of Π on the new leaf sequents. This leaves us with a sequent tree Π' whose root sequent is of the form $\Phi_{T_1}(\tau, P), Q(e_1', a_{k_1}), \ldots, Q(e_q', a_{k_q}) \vdash \bot$, where $a_{k_i} \in A_P$ for $i = 1, \ldots, q$. We are then left with the problem of defining R' in such a way that (2) holds. This is the task of step 2 of the procedure. Notice that (2) always admits $R' = R_P$ as (trivial) solution. However, as the size of $\widehat{P}'$ grows (linearly) with the cardinality of R', we are interested in finding a solution R' with the smallest possible cardinality. Since this problem is intractable in the general case, an alternative approach which works well in practice is to choose R' in such a way that $R'(a_j) = R(a_j) \cup \{e_i' : k_i = j \text{ and } i = 1, \ldots, q\}$ if $e_1', \ldots, e_q'$ are all numerals and $R' = R_P$ otherwise.

The following result states that if V' and R' are computed as described above, then the sequent tree Π' can be turned into a proof of the unsatisfiability of $\Phi_{T_0}(\tau, \widehat{P}')$. From this it readily follows the unsatisfiability of $\Phi_{T_0}(\tau, \widehat{P}')$.

Lemma 2. *The sequent tree Π' computed at step 2 of the refine(τ, Π, V, R) procedure of Figure 3 can be transformed into a proof of the unsatisfiability of $\Phi_{T_0}(\tau, \widehat{P}')$ for all $\widehat{P}' \in \text{abstract}(P, V', R')$. Hence $\Phi_{T_0}(\tau, \widehat{P}')$ is unsatisfiable for all $\widehat{P}' \in \text{abstract}(P, V', R')$.*

Example 1. If τ is the trace of Table 2 relative to the program P of Table 1, then $\Phi_{T_1}(\tau, P)$ comprises the set of formulae in the rightmost column of Table 2. The sequent tree corresponding to a proof of the unsatisfiability of $\Phi_{T_1}(\tau, P)$ after applying step 2 of the refine procedure and omitting the formulae $\Phi_{T_1}(\tau, P)$ in the left hand sides of the sequents is as follows:

$$\dfrac{\dfrac{\dfrac{\dfrac{\dfrac{\dfrac{Q(i_2,a) \vdash \text{select}(a_2,i_2) \neq 9 \ \vdash i_2 = i_1 + 1}{Q(i_1+1,a) \vdash \text{select}(a_2,i_1+1) \neq 9 \qquad \vdash a_2 = \text{store}(a_1,i_1,2 * i_1)}}{Q(i_1+1,a) \vdash \text{select}(\text{store}(a_1,i_1,2 * i_1),i_1+1) \neq 9 \qquad (1)}}{Q(i_1+1,a) \vdash (i_1+1 = i_1 \ ? \ 2 * i_1 : \text{select}(a_1,i_1+1)) \neq 9}}{Q(i_1+1,a) \vdash \text{select}(a_1,i_1+1) \neq 9 \qquad\qquad \vdash i_1 = 0}}{Q(1,a) \vdash \text{select}(a_1,1) \neq 9 \qquad\qquad \vdash a_1 = \text{store}(a_0,1,9)}}{Q(1,a) \vdash \text{select}(\text{store}(a_0,1,9),1) \neq 9 \qquad (1)}$$

$$\dfrac{}{\dfrac{Q(1,a) \vdash (1 = 1 \ ? \ 9 : \text{select}(a_0,1)) \neq 9}{Q(1,a) \vdash \bot}}$$

In this case—as we anticipated in Section 2—it thus suffices to refine the program using an R' such that $R'(a) = \{1\}$.

The following result states the key properties of the refinement process: if $\widehat{P}' \in \text{abstract}(P,V',R')$, where V' and R' are the sets of variables returned by the procedure $\text{refine}(\tau,\Pi,V,R)$, then $\widehat{P}'$ is a refinement of $\widehat{P}$ and $\langle V,R \rangle \prec \langle V',R' \rangle \preceq \langle V_P,R_P \rangle$.

Theorem 4. *Let $\widehat{P} \in \text{abstract}(P,V,R)$, $\tau \in \text{traces}(\widehat{P})$ such that $\Phi_{T_1}(\tau,P)$ is unsatisfiable, Π be a proof of $\Phi_{T_1}(\tau,P) \vdash \bot$ and $\widehat{P}' \in \text{abstract}(P,V',R')$, where V' and R' are the sets of variables returned by the procedure $\text{refine}(\tau,\Pi,V,R)$. Then $\widehat{P}' \sqsubset \widehat{P}$ and $\langle V,R \rangle \prec \langle V',R' \rangle \preceq \langle V_P,R_P \rangle$.*

We are now in a position to prove the soundness and (relative) completeness of the AR procedure.

Corollary 1 (Soundness). *Let $V \subseteq V_P$ and $R \subseteq R_P$. If $AR(P,V,R)$ returns SAFE, then P has no error trace.*

Corollary 2 (Relative Completeness). *Let $V \subseteq V_P$ and $R \subseteq R_P$. If P has no error trace and all the calls to the model-check procedure terminate, then $AR(P,V,R)$ terminates and returns SAFE.*

7   Implementation and Experimental Results

We have developed a prototype implementation of the techniques described in this paper in the EUREKA tool [1,2]. The EUREKA tool itself has been completely re-engineered: now it features *(i)* a new implementation of our model checking procedure for linear programs based on the Parma Polyhedra Library [11] for handling linear arithmetic constraints in an efficient way and *(ii)* a tight interface with CVC Lite [12] which is used as a decision procedure for the combination of linear arithmetic and the theory of arrays.

We have tested the abstraction refinement procedure described in this paper by running EUREKA against a variety of C programs featuring a non trivial interplay between array manipulation and arithmetic.[2] The programs we considered are implementations of well-known algorithms for string manipulation such as

---

[2] The current version of our tool checks for reachability properties and/or assertion violations.

string-copy, for coding (i.e. the (n, k)-Gray code, a generalisation of the binary Gray code [13]), and sorting (namely bubble sort, selection sort, and the partitioning phase of the quick sort). The string copy algorithm copies an array of char into another and checks that the '\0' character is eventually reached in the source array. The (n, k)-Gray code algorithm is a significantly more complex benchmark as it involves the simultaneous manipulation of four arrays and four loops, two of which are nested. The (n, k)-Gray code encodes integers using n different values and k digits (the length of the code). Adjacent elements of a (n, k)-Gray code differ in only one digit and the difference is either $+1$ or -1. (An assertion in the source code verifies this property.) The partitioning of the quick sort involves a single array and four loops, two of which—as in the Gray code algorithm—are nested. Finally, both sorting algorithms we considered involve a single array, two nested loops, and a third loop that checks the correctness through a sequence of assertions.

For each algorithm considered we have automatically generated a family of programs parametric in a positive integer N such that the size of the arrays occurring in the programs and/or the number of iterations carried out by the loops increase as N increases. Thus the higher is the value of N, the bigger is the search space to be analysed. This has allowed us to assess quantitatively the scalability of the tools we experimented with.

Besides EUREKA we have also run BLAST, SATABS, and CBMC on our benchmark programs. All the experiments have been carried out by using a 2.4GHz Pentium IV, running Linux with memory limit set to 800MB and time limit set to 30 minutes. The results of our experiments are summarised in Table 4. EUREKA performs very well on the string copy program: it scales up smoothly to program instances with arrays comprising hundreds of elements, the reason lying in that only a single element of the arrays out of the $2N$ is introduced by the refinement step (namely the one involved by the property, that is, the '\0' character). EUREKA is also able to analyse all the instances of the Gray code

Table 4. A summary of the results of our experiments. Every element of the table shows the greatest instance the tools are able to analyse and, in brackets, the time in seconds. The EUREKA column also shows the number of array elements found during the refinement and the sum of the sizes of the arrays involved in the programs. Numbers with * indicate that the tool can analyse greater instances than the one shown. Numbers with [1] and [2] are obtained by enabling interpolants with option -craig 1 (that eliminates variables not in scope) and -craig 2 (that applies a precise analysis) respectively. The choices were made in order to obtain the best results from the tool.

Benchmark	EUREKA			BLAST		SATABS		CBMC	
	Inst.	(Time)	refined/total array elements	Inst.	(Time)	Inst.	(Time)	Inst.	(Time)
String copy	1000*	(153.78)	1/2N	Incorrect[2]		10	(144.69)	221	(32.5)
Gray code	25	(230.26)	16/28	Incorrect[2]		Inconclusive		48	(83.65)
Partition	40	(178.02)	1/N	Incorrect[2]		Inconclusive		7	(157.14)
Bubble sort	8	(91.92)	N/N	Incorrect[1]		2	(30.42)	12	(1213.18)
Selection sort	6	(104.42)	N/N	Incorrect[2]		2	(115.86)	6	(432.60)

algorithm and of the partitioning algorithm up to $N = 25$ and $N = 40$ respectively. For the Gray code 16 out of the 28 elements of the arrays are introduced by the refinement step, whereas for the partitioning only 1 out of the N array elements suffices. The bubble sort and the selection sort algorithms proved more challenging as the largest instances EUREKA succeeded to analyse are with $N = 8$ and $N = 6$ respectively. This is due to the fact that all the N array elements are introduced by the refinement step. As a matter of fact, the assertions in the code check that every pair of adjacent elements is sorted. Therefore, every element of the array counts and needs to be modelled. In general, in the refinement step EUREKA introduces as many new *array variables* as the number of array elements required by the property to check. When all arrays are fully *expanded* then the abstraction is the most precise in the sense that the linear program is an exact approximation of the linear program with arrays.

BLAST has been used with all the recommended[3] optimisations (option -predH 7) and Craig interpolation [5] (options -craig 1 and -craig 2) enabled. BLAST wrongly returns error traces on all benchmarks. This is due to its lack of precision in handling arrays: all the elements of an array are indistinguishable for BLAST [14].

SATABS has been used with Cadence SMV as symbolic model checker. While the default maximum number of iterations of the abstraction refinement loop is set to 50, we increased this number to 100 (option --iterations 100) as this was necessary in most cases for the tool to succeed.[4] SATABS handles arrays with more precision than BLAST and thus it never returns a wrong answer. However, our experiments indicate that it scales poorly on all benchmarks considered.

CBMC generates a boolean formula that encodes all the computation paths of bounded length. It therefore explicitly represents all the elements of the arrays occurring in the input program. Being a *bounded* model checker, CBMC may return incomplete results. By default CBMC adopts so-called *unwinding assertions* in order to try to automatically determine the minimum bound for a complete analysis of the input program. However, this is an undecidable problem, as shown by the fact that on three families of benchmarks out of five the tool was not able to compute the proper bound and the analysis diverged. The minimum bound had to be set by hand on the string copy, the Gray code and the partitioning benchmarks (option --unwind). That said, CBMC shows good scalability results wrt. BLAST and SATABS, and compares favourably with EUREKA.

In order to overcome the limitations of BLAST in handling arrays, we generated a new set of benchmarks obtained by abstracting the programs of Table 4 w.r.t. all array indexes. These are linear programs having a distinguished variable for each array element in the corresponding original programs. Since in this case the input programs do not contain arrays anymore, BLAST performs slightly

---

[3] In BLAST's user manual, http://mtc.epfl.ch/software-tools/blast/doc

[4] SATABS also features an option for the detection of looping counterexamples from the abstract model. This option, when enabled, heavily affected the performance of SATABS on all benchmarks, and hence we disabled it.

better by returning correct results on some benchmarks (e.g. in the string copy and in the partitioning benchmarks), but it still suffers from scalability issues as it handles very small instances (e.g. it already fails for $N = 14$ and $N = 15$ of the string copy and the partitioning algorithms resp.). We also run CBMC and SATABS on these new problems. CBMC exhibits a varied behaviour: for example, while the largest instance of the original string copy it analyses is $N = 221$ in 32.5 s. (cf. Table 4), in this case the largest instance is $N = 47$ in $241, 46$ s.. On the other hand, CBMC analyses the Bubble sort algorithm up to $N = 38$, while in the original version it fails for $N = 13$. The reason of this behaviour needs to be further investigated. SATABS fails on most benchmarks (e.g. the string copy, the bubble sort, the Gray coding, and the partitioning), reporting the inability of discovering new predicates.

In conclusion, our experiments indicate the potential of EUREKA in handling a variety of linear programs with arrays. At the same time they confirm the difficulties that the approaches based on predicate abstraction have in handling this important class of programs. The experiments also confirm that the effectiveness of our procedure does not depend on the size of the arrays manipulated by the input programs, but it depends on the number of elements introduced by the refinement step.

8   Conclusions

Most of the procedures based on predicate abstraction refinement show difficulties when dealing with arrays: either the abstractions built are too coarse, or the refinements fail to determine suitable predicates for building a new, more precise abstract version of the program. In this paper we have proposed a novel abstraction refinement scheme for software analysis that employs sets of variables and array indexes instead of predicates as done traditionally. We have showed that our approach allows for a precise and efficient analysis of a wide class of programs. Moreover, we presented a number of experimental results that indicate that a prototype implementation of our ideas compares favourably with—and on a number of programs of interest outperforms—state-of-the-art software model checkers based on predicate abstraction refinement.

References

1. Armando, A., Castellini, C., Mantovani, J.: Software model checking using linear constraints. In: ICFEM'04. Volume 3308 of LNCS., Springer (2004)
2. Armando, A., Benerecetti, M., Mantovani, J.: Model checking linear programs with arrays. In: SoftMC'05. Volume 144 of ENTCS., Elsevier (2005)
3. Ball, T., Rajamani, S.K.: Automatically validating temporal safety properties of interfaces. In: Proc. of SPIN'01, Springer New York, Inc. (2001) 103–122
4. Henzinger, T., Jhala, R., Majumdar, R., Sutre, G.: Software Verification with Blast. In: Proc. of SPIN '03. Volume 2648 of LNCS., Springer (2003) 235–239
5. Henzinger, T.A., Jhala, R., Majumdar, R., McMillan, K.L.: Abstractions from proofs. In: POPL'04, New York, NY, USA, ACM Press (2004) 232–244

6. Jhala, R., McMillan, K.L.: A practical and complete approach to predicate refinement. In Hermanns, H., Palsberg, J., eds.: TACAS. Volume 3920 of LNCS., Springer (2006) 459–473
7. Clarke, E., Kroening, D., Sharygina, N., Yorav, K.: SATABS: SAT-based predicate abstraction for ANSI-C. In: TACAS'05. Volume 3440 of LNCS., Springer (2005) 570–4
8. Kroening, D., Clarke, E., Yorav, K.: Behavioral consistency of C and Verilog programs using bounded model checking. In: Proc. of DAC 2003, ACM Press (2003) 368–371
9. Aho, A.V., Sethi, R., Ullman, J.D.: Compilers: Principles, Techniques, and Tools. Addison-Wesley, Reading, MA (1986)
10. Reps, T., Horwitz, S., Sagiv, M.: Precise interprocedural dataflow analysis via graph reachability. In: Proc. of POPL '95, ACM Press (1995) 49–61
11. Bagnara, R., Ricci, E., Zaffanella, E., Hill, P.M.: Possibly not closed convex polyhedra and the Parma Polyhedra Library. In Hermenegildo, M.V., Puebla, G., eds.: SAS'02. Volume 2477 of LNCS., Madrid, Spain, Springer (2002) 213–229
12. Barrett, C., Berezin, S.: CVC Lite: A new implementation of the cooperating validity checker. In: CAV. (2004) 515–518
13. Black, P.E.: Gray code, in dictionary of algorithms and data structures. See http://www.nist.gov/dads/HTML/graycode.html (2005)
14. Henzinger, T.A., Jhala, R., Majumdar, R., Sutre, G.: Lazy abstraction. In: POPL 2002. (2002) 58–70

Property-Driven Partitioning for Abstraction Refinement

Roberto Sebastiani[1,*], Stefano Tonetta[2], and Moshe Y. Vardi[3,**]

[1] DIT, Università di Trento, Italy
rseba@dit.unitn.it
[2] University of Lugano, Switzerland
tonettas@lu.unisi.ch
[3] Dept. of Computer Science, Rice University, USA
vardi@cs.rice.edu

Abstract. Partitioning and abstraction have been studied extensively both in hardware and in software verification. The abstraction is typically partitioned according to the system design in the case of hardware or the control graph in the case of software. In this work we build on previous work on Property-Driven Partitioning (PDP), a hybrid Symbolic Model-Checking (SMC) technique for ω-regular properties in which the state space is partitioned according to the states of the property automaton. We investigate a new paradigm for abstraction refinement in SMC, which combines abstraction and PDP: each PDP partition may contain a different abstraction, so that it can be refined independently from the others; in case of a spurious counterexample π, the system is refined only in those partitions that are necessary to rule out π. We performed a preliminary experimental evaluation comparing standard Counterexample-Guided Abstraction Refinement (CEGAR) with its partitioned counterpart, which confirmed that the partitioned technique always allows for using coarser abstractions. While earlier work has shown that PDP almost always improves the performance of SMC, our experiments here show that this is not always the case for partitioned abstraction refinement, as in some cases the overhead due to the localization of the abstraction is too high.

1 Introduction

Verifying properties of finite-state machines is a fundamental problem in formal design verification. *Symbolic Model Checking* (SMC) [2] has been successful at verifying temporal specifications. In particular, LTL model checking is solved by building an automaton A with the complementary language of the property, computing the product of A with the system M and checking for emptiness [17]. Typically, the product is represented either explicitly, by enumerating its elements, or symbolically, by means of propositional formulas. The main obstacle to model checking is the *state-space explosion*, that is, the state-space is often too large to be handled.

* Supported in part by ORCHID, a project sponsored by Provincia Autonoma di Trento, and by a grant from Intel Corporation.
** Supported in part by NSF grants CCR-9988322, CCR-0124077, CCR-0311326, and ANI-0216467, by BSF grant 9800096, and by Texas ATP grant 003604-0058-2003.

O. Grumberg and M. Huth (Eds.): TACAS 2007, LNCS 4424, pp. 389–404, 2007.

One of the most efficient technique to reduce the state-space in SMC is *abstraction* [6]. An abstract system is simply an approximation of the original one. A *conservative* abstraction preserves all the behaviors of the concrete system. This way, if a universal property is satisfied by an abstract model, then the property is correct also in the concrete model. On the contrary, false negatives may be produced. An abstract counterexample that does not correspond to any concrete behavior is called *spurious*. When such a counterexample is found, the abstraction is *refined*, i.e., we add enough information to the system in order to rule out the spurious counterexample. This process is repeated until the property is proved correct or a concrete counterexample is found. Such a loop is known as *Counterexample-Guided Abstraction Refinement* (CEGAR) [5].

Partitioning and abstraction have been extensively studied both in hardware and in software verification. For hardware, the abstraction is typically partitioned according to the design that usually is composed of submodules (see, e.g., [3,14]). For software, the partitioning is guided by the control-flow graph of the program. In particular, *Lazy Abstraction* (LA) [11] produces different levels of precision in different parts of the program. The abstraction can be refined locally to some control paths [11] or to some control locations [10].

In [15,16], motivated by previous work on *Generalized Symbolic Trajectory Evaluation* (GSTE) [20], *Property-Driven Partitioning* (PDP) has been proposed as a new hybrid approach to LTL model checking. In this approach, the property automaton A is constructed explicitly, but its product with the system is represented in a partitioned fashion. If the state space of the system is S and that of the property automaton is $\mathcal{B}$, then PDP maintains a subset $Q \subseteq S \times \mathcal{B}$ of the product space as a collection $\{Q_b : b \in \mathcal{B}\}$ of sets, where each $Q_b = \{s \in S \mid (s,b) \in Q\}$ is represented symbolically. Thus, PDP maintains an array of BDDs instead of a single BDD to represent a subset of the product space. Based on extensive experimentation, it has been shown that the hybrid approach of PDP is superior to pure symbolic model checking.

In GSTE, this partitioning technique is embedded into a quaternary-abstraction framework. Each partition stores a quaternary assignment (or a set of quaternary assignments, if we use *symbolic indexing* [19]). Quaternary abstraction, also known as Cartesian abstraction, is a powerful mechanism that merges a set of states into an abstract state: the value "unknown" is used for variables that have different assignments in the set. The use of this "unknown" value gives different levels of approximation. By combining PDP with quaternary abstraction, GSTE has a different abstraction precision for each partition.

Building on the ideas of LA and GSTE, we explore in this paper the combination of PDP with predicate abstraction. We investigate a localized-abstraction framework, called *partitioned abstraction*, where each partition of PDP may contain a different abstraction. This way, we allow a flexible abstraction where every partition can be refined independently from the others. Intuitively, the state of the automaton corresponds to a particular phase of the operation of the circuit, and we expect that different partitions contain the appropriate abstractions for different phases.

We adapted the CEGAR loop to this framework. In PDP, a counterexample is a sequence of state-partition pairs. When the counterexample is spurious, the failure of the concretization must happen in some partition. Thus, we tuned the refinement in order to refine the system only in those partitions that are necessary to rule out the spurious counterexample.

Although *partitioned abstraction* is independent of any specific abstraction technique, we implemented it in NUSMV [4] in combination with localization reduction and the score-based refinement heuristic of [18]. We performed an experimental evaluation providing a comparison between the standard non-partitioned refinement loop with its partitioned counterpart. We evaluated the trade-off between the disadvantages of dealing with several abstractions at the same moment and the advantages of using coarser abstractions when possible. Our testing shows that this technique can be very efficient and can solve model-checking problems where the non-partitioned version fails. Unlike SMC, however, where partitioning always improved the performance of verification, here, partitioning the abstraction may involve high overhead. These experiments, for the first time[1] , compare an abstraction-localization technique with a uniform one. The results show that abstraction partitioning is successful at allowing verification with coarser abstractions. In some cases this may lead to an order-of-magnitude improvement in running time. Nevertheless, in many cases the improvement in the coarseness of the abstractions does not compensate for the overhead of having to compute many abstractions. Overall, abstraction partitioning, in spite of its initial promise, does not lead to a consistent improvement in running time.

2 Background

2.1 Symbolic Model Checking

Given a system M and a property φ, the model checking problem consists of checking if M is a model of φ. The semantics of M and φ are based on a shared set *PROP* of atomic propositions. Both the system and the property define languages over finite or infinite words. The alphabet of such languages is $\Sigma = 2^{PROP}$.

The system M is described with a set $\mathcal{V}$ of state variables. We use $\mathcal{V}'$ to denote the set of next state variables $\{v'\}_{v \in \mathcal{V}}$, where v' represents the next value of v. We represent the system M as a symbolic finite-state machine (FSM), i.e., a tuple $\langle \mathcal{V}, I, T, \mathbb{L} \rangle$, where $\mathcal{V}$ is a set of state variables, $I(\mathcal{V})$ is a formula that represents the initial condition, $T(\mathcal{V}, \mathcal{V}')$ is a formula that represents the transition relation, $\mathbb{L} = \{L_a(\mathcal{V})\}_{a \in PROP}$ is a set of formulas that associate the atomic propositions with states.

The set $\mathcal{S}_{\mathcal{V}}$ of states is given by all truth assignments to the variables $\mathcal{V}$. Given a state s, we use s' to denote the corresponding truth assignment to the next state variables, i.e. $s' = s[\mathcal{V}'/\mathcal{V}]$. A state s is labeled with the atomic proposition a iff $s \models L_a(\mathcal{V})$. A state s is initial iff $s \models I(\mathcal{V})$. Given two states s_1 and s_2, there exists a transition between s_1 and s_2 iff $s_1, s_2' \models T(\mathcal{V}, \mathcal{V}')$.

A finite (resp., infinite) path of the FSM is a finite (resp. infinite) sequence of states $\pi = s_1, ..., s_k$ (resp. $\pi = s_1, s_2, ...$) such that s_1 is an initial state and, for $1 \leq i < k$ (resp.

---

[1] Henzinger et al. [10] compared BLAST with and without the technique of predicate localization and showed that it led to a running-time improvement in one case out of six. Since BLAST itself uses lazy abstraction, which can be viewed as a weak form of abstraction localization, it is hard to draw conclusions from that work about the advantage of abstraction localization.

$i \geq 1$), there exists a transition between s_i and s_{i+1}. A lasso-shape path is a finite path π with a point l, $1 \leq l < |\pi|$ (called loop-back point), such that $s_l = s_{|\pi|}$. Thus, a lasso-shape path represents an infinite path (though, not all infinite paths are lasso shaped).

An infinite word $w \in \Sigma^\omega$ is accepted by the FSM M if there exists a path π of M such that $\pi(i) \models L_{w(i)}(\mathcal{V})$, for all $i \geq 1$. The language $\mathcal{L}_M$ of M is defined as the set of all infinite words accepted by M. Given the language $\mathcal{L}_\varphi$ of the property φ, we say that the system M satisfies the property φ ($M \models \varphi$) iff $\mathcal{L}_M \subseteq \mathcal{L}_\varphi$. In other words, all paths of the system must correspond to a word accepted by the property.

LTL model checking. A Büchi automaton (BA) is a tuple $\langle \mathcal{B}, b_0, \Sigma, \delta, F \rangle$, where $\mathcal{B}$ is a set of states, $b_0 \in \mathcal{B}$ is the initial state, $\delta \in \mathcal{B} \times \Sigma \times \mathcal{B}$ is the transition relation, and $F \subseteq \mathcal{B}$ is the fairness condition. A fair run of a BA A over the infinite word $w = l_1, l_2, \ldots \in \Sigma^\omega$ is an infinite sequence of states $\pi = b_1, b_2, \ldots$ such that $b_1 = b_0$ and, for $i \geq 1$, $(b_i, l_i, b_{i+1}) \in \delta$, and $\pi(i) \in F$ for infinitely many i. The word w belongs to the language $\mathcal{L}_A$ of A iff there exists a fair run over w.

If φ is an LTL property, the model checking problem is usually solved by building a BA $A_{\neg\varphi}$ with the complementary language of the property, computing its product with the system, and then checking for emptiness [17]. Extant model checkers use either a pure explicit-state approach, e.g., in SPIN [12], or a pure symbolic approach, e.g., in NuSMV [4]. To check language containment, a symbolic model checker implements a fixpoint algorithm [2]. Sets of states are manipulated by using basic set operations such as intersection, union, complementation, and the preimage and postimage operations. Since sets are represented by predicates on Boolean variables, intersection, union and complementation are translated into $\wedge$, $\vee$ and $\neg$ respectively. The preimage and postimage operations are translated into the following formulas:

$$preimage(Q) = \exists \mathcal{V}''((Q[\mathcal{V}''/\mathcal{V}])(\mathcal{V}') \wedge T(\mathcal{V}, \mathcal{V}')),$$
$$postimage(Q) = (\exists \mathcal{V}(Q(\mathcal{V}) \wedge T(\mathcal{V}, \mathcal{V}')))[\mathcal{V}/\mathcal{V}'].$$

2.2   Abstraction

Given two systems $M = \langle \mathcal{V}, I, T, \{L_a\}_{a \in PROP} \rangle$ and $\hat{M} = \langle \hat{\mathcal{V}}, \hat{I}, \hat{T}, \{\hat{L}_a\}_{a \in PROP} \rangle$, a relation $H(\mathcal{V}, \hat{\mathcal{V}})$ is a *simulation relation* iff the following conditions hold:

- every initial state of M corresponds to an initial state of $\hat{M}$; namely, if $s \models I(\mathcal{V})$, then there exists a state $\hat{s}$ of $\hat{M}$ such that $\hat{s} \models \hat{I}(\hat{\mathcal{V}})$ and $s, \hat{s} \models H(\mathcal{V}, \hat{\mathcal{V}})$;
- every transition of M corresponds to a transition of $\hat{M}$; namely, if $s_1, \hat{s}_1 \models H(\mathcal{V}, \hat{\mathcal{V}})$, and $s_1, s_2' \models T(\mathcal{V}, \mathcal{V}')$, then there exists a state $\hat{s}_2$ of $\hat{M}$ such that $s_2, \hat{s}_2 \models H(\mathcal{V}, \hat{\mathcal{V}})$ and $\hat{s}_1, \hat{s}_2' \models \hat{T}(\mathcal{V}, \mathcal{V}')$;
- if two states are related by H, they must have the same labels; namely, if $s, \hat{s} \models H(\mathcal{V}, \hat{\mathcal{V}})$ then $s \models L_a(\mathcal{V})$ iff $\hat{s} \models \hat{L}_a(\hat{\mathcal{V}})$, for all $a \in PROP$.

If such relation exists, we say that $\hat{M}$ is an *abstraction* of M, or M refines $\hat{M}$ ($M \preceq_H \hat{M}$). Intuitively, every path π of M is "simulated" by some path $\hat{\pi}$ of $\hat{M}$ that accepts the same infinite word. In terms of languages, if $M \preceq_H \hat{M}$, then $\mathcal{L}_M \subseteq \mathcal{L}_{\hat{M}}$. Thus, simulation preserves properties, so that if $M \preceq_H \hat{M}$ and $\hat{M} \models \varphi$ then $M \models \varphi$ (though, in general, the reverse does not hold).

Given the relation H, we define the *abstraction function* $\alpha_H : S_{\mathcal{V}} \to 2^{S_{\hat{\mathcal{V}}}}$ and the *concretization function* $\gamma_H : S_{\hat{\mathcal{V}}} \to 2^{S_{\mathcal{V}}}$ as follows:

- $\alpha_H(s) = \{\hat{s} \in S_{\hat{\mathcal{V}}} \mid s, \hat{s} \models H(s, \hat{s})\}$,
- $\gamma_H(\hat{s}) = \{s \in S_{\mathcal{V}} \mid s, \hat{s} \models H(s, \hat{s})\}$.

We extend these functions to paths: if $\hat{\pi} = \hat{s}_1, \hat{s}_2, \dots$ is a path of $\hat{M}$ then $\gamma_H(\hat{\pi})$ is a set of paths of M such that $\pi \in \gamma_H(\hat{\pi})$ iff $\pi = s_1, s_2, \dots$ is a path of M and $s_i \in \gamma_H(\hat{s}_i)$ for $1 \le i \le |\hat{\pi}|$ (similarly for α_H).

In *predicate abstraction* [9], the abstract state-space is described with a set of predicates; each predicate is represented by an abstract variable. Given an FSM M, we select a set $\mathbb{P}$ of predicates, such that each predicate P is a formula over the variables $\mathcal{V}$ that characterizes relevant facts of the system. For every $P \in \mathbb{P}$, we introduce a new abstract variable v_P. H is defined as follows: $H(\mathcal{V}, \mathcal{V}_{\mathbb{P}}) = \bigwedge_{P \in \mathbb{P}} v_P \leftrightarrow P(\mathcal{V})$, i.e., for every concrete state s, the corresponding abstract state $\hat{s}$ assigns v_P to true iff $s \models P(\mathcal{V})$. In the *minimal* (or *most accurate*) abstraction (wrt. $\mathbb{P}$), every abstract transition corresponds to at least one concrete transition. This involves a quantification of the concrete variables that may be computationally expensive. The usual technique to get an approximation of the minimal abstraction is *early quantification* [6]: the existential quantifications are pushed inside conjunctions; in this way, we simplify the expressions by losing precision.

Localization reduction. A particular case of abstraction uses the *localization reduction* technique [13]: suppose the system is defined functionally, i.e., $M = \langle \mathcal{V}, I, T, \mathbb{L} \rangle$, where

- $I(\mathcal{V}) = \exists \mathcal{W}(\bigwedge_{v \in \mathcal{V}} v = f_v^I(\mathcal{W}))$ for some functions f_v^I and input variables $\mathcal{W}$,
- $T(\mathcal{V}, \mathcal{V}') = \exists \mathcal{W}(\bigwedge_{v \in \mathcal{V}} v' = f_v^T(\mathcal{V}, \mathcal{W}))$ for some functions f_v^T and input variables $\mathcal{W}$.

Localization reduction consists in choosing a set of state variables, removing the corresponding constraints, and considering them as input variables. Let $\hat{\mathcal{V}} \subseteq \mathcal{V}$, and $\check{\mathcal{W}} = \mathcal{V} \setminus \hat{\mathcal{V}}$. We can build the abstraction $\hat{M} = \langle \hat{\mathcal{V}}, \hat{I}, \hat{T}, \hat{\mathbb{L}} \rangle$ where:

- $\hat{I}(\hat{\mathcal{V}}) = \exists \mathcal{W}(\bigwedge_{v \in \hat{\mathcal{V}}} v = f_v^I(\mathcal{W}))$,
- $\hat{T}(\hat{\mathcal{V}}, \hat{\mathcal{V}}') = \exists \check{\mathcal{W}} \exists \mathcal{W}(\bigwedge_{v \in \hat{\mathcal{V}}} v' = f_v^T(\hat{\mathcal{V}}, \check{\mathcal{W}}, \mathcal{W}))$,
- $\hat{\mathbb{L}} = \{\hat{L}^a\}_{a \in PROP}$, where $\hat{L}^a(\hat{\mathcal{V}}) = \exists \check{\mathcal{W}}(L_a(\hat{\mathcal{V}}, \check{\mathcal{W}}))$.

We call $\check{\mathcal{W}}$ *invisible variables* (also known as *abstracted* or *freed* variables).

Remark 1. Note that localization reduction is a particular case of predicate abstraction with early quantification, where the set of predicates is given by the visible variables themselves, namely $\mathbb{P} = \{v\}_{v \in \hat{\mathcal{V}}}$.

2.3 Counterexample-Guided Abstraction Refinement

Counterexample-guided Abstraction Refinement (CEGAR) is an iterative abstraction refinement methodology that starts from a very coarse abstraction and incrementally refine it until a result is yielded [5]. Every iteration corresponds to a false negative (spurious counterexample), which is removed from the abstract system by refining the abstraction. Given an FSM M and a property φ, the CEGAR method is based on the following steps:

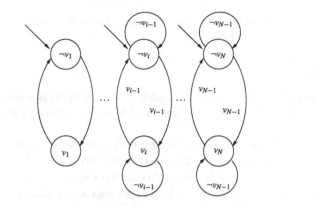

Fig. 1. N-bit counter

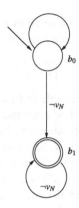

Fig. 2. BA for $!GFv_N$

1. **[Initial Abstraction]** build an initial abstraction $\hat{M}$ ($M \preceq_H \hat{M}$);
2. **[Model Checking]** check if $\hat{M} \models \varphi$: if it does, conclude that $M \models \varphi$; otherwise, produce a counterexample π;
3. **[Concretization]** check if the counterexample is concretizable (namely, $\gamma_H(\pi) \neq \emptyset$): if it does, conclude that $M \not\models \varphi$; otherwise, call it *spurious*;
4. **[Refinement]** build a new abstraction $\tilde{M}$ that refines $\hat{M}$ (namely, $M \preceq_{\tilde{H}} \tilde{M} \preceq_{\tilde{H}} \hat{M}$) and rules out π ($\gamma_{\tilde{H}}(\pi) = \emptyset$); turn $\hat{M}$ into $\tilde{M}$ and go to step 2

Numerous techniques have been conceived for the refinement of the abstract FSM. Typically, they analyze the reason why a spurious counterexample cannot be concretized, and they find a set of variables that may be used to eliminate it.

The purpose of the following example is twofold: on the one hand, we show how standard refinement works; on the other hand, we present a major limitation of this approach.

Example 1. Consider a system with N symbolic variables, which represents a N-bit counter (Fig. 1). The system can be thought of as the composition of N modules, one for every variable. (The labels on the arcs represent values triggering the transition.) A property of the system is that the most significant bit v_N becomes true infinitely often. The BA A, corresponding to the negation of the property, is shown in Fig. 2.

Since only the most significant bit v_N occurs in the property, the initial abstract system contains only one module (the rightmost module of Fig. 1); all the other variables are considered as inputs. The model checking procedure will produce a counterexample in which the abstract system eventually loops on the abstract state $\neg v_N$. This counterexample is spurious because it does not correspond to any concrete path. In order to refine the abstraction and kill the spurious counterexample, we need to add v_{N-1}, because v_N becomes true only when v_{N-1} is true. Similarly we have to add v_{N-2} and so on. This way, standard refinement techniques end up into the concrete system. More generally, notice that, in the context of localization reduction, it is not possible to prove the property, if even one of the variable is made invisible.

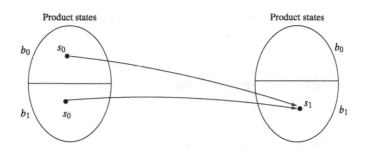

Fig. 3. Preimage in PDP

3   Property-Driven Partitioning for Abstraction Refinement

Property-driven partitioning. In *property-driven partitioning* (PDP), the property automaton, whose state space is often quite manageable, is represented explicitly, while the system, whose state space is typically exceedingly large, is represented symbolically. PDP partitions the symbolic state space according to an explicitly compiled property automaton.

Let $M = \langle \mathcal{V}, I, T, \{L_a\}_{a \in PROP} \rangle$ be the FSM to be verified and $A = \langle \mathcal{B}, b_0, \Sigma, \delta, F \rangle$ the BA for the complemented property. The product between M and a A is the BA $\langle \mathcal{P}, \mathcal{P}_0, \Sigma, \delta^{\mathcal{P}}, F^{\mathcal{P}} \rangle$, where

- $\mathcal{P} = S_{\mathcal{V}} \times \mathcal{B}$,
- $p \subset \mathcal{P}_0$ iff $p = (s, b_0)$ and $s \models I(\mathcal{V})$,
- $(p_1, l, p_2) \in \delta^{\mathcal{P}}$ iff $p_1 = (s_1, b_1)$, $p_2 = (s_2, b_2)$, $s_1, s_2' \models T(\mathcal{V}, \mathcal{V}')$, $(b_1, a, b_2) \in \delta$, and $s_1 \models L_a(\mathcal{V})$ for every $a \in l$,
- $F^{\mathcal{P}} = \{S_{\mathcal{V}} \times F\}$.

We consider the partitioning of the product state space $\mathcal{P}$: $\{\mathcal{P}_b\}_{b \in \mathcal{B}}$, where $\mathcal{P}_b = \{p \in \mathcal{P} : p = (s, b)\}$. Thus, a subset Q of $\mathcal{P}$ can be represented by the following set of states of M: $\{Q_b\}_{b \in \mathcal{B}}$, where $Q_b = \{s : (s, b) \in Q\}$. If $Q^1 = \{Q_b^1\}_{b \in \mathcal{B}}$ and $Q^2 = \{Q_b^2\}_{b \in \mathcal{B}}$, we translate the set operations used in symbolic algorithms into:

$$Q^1 \wedge Q^2 := \{Q_b^1 \wedge Q_b^2\}_{b \in \mathcal{B}},$$
$$Q^1 \vee Q^2 := \{Q_b^1 \vee Q_b^2\}_{b \in \mathcal{B}},$$
$$\neg Q := \{\neg Q_b\}_{b \in \mathcal{B}},$$
$$preimage(Q) := \{\textstyle\bigvee_{(b,a,b') \in \delta} preimage(Q_{b'}) \wedge a\}_{b \in \mathcal{B}},$$
$$postimage(Q) := \{\textstyle\bigvee_{(b',a,b) \in \delta} postimage(Q_{b'} \wedge a)\}_{b \in \mathcal{B}}.$$

Example 2. Consider the model checking problem of Example 1. The property automaton A has two states, which yield two partitions in PDP. We use s_i to denote the state of M where the counter has value i. Consider the product of state s_1 with the state b_1 of A. Suppose we want to compute the preimage of such a state. First, we compute the preimage of s_1 in M, which yields $\{s_0\}$. Then, we propagate this state to the other partitions. The result is shown in Fig. 3.

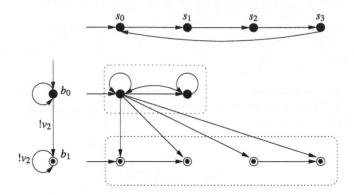

Fig. 4. Example of partitioned abstraction

All symbolic model-checking algorithms that operate on the product can be partitioned according to the property automaton, operating on a BDD array rather than on a single BDD (see [15,16]).

3.1 Combining PDP with Abstraction

Given an FSM $M = \langle \mathcal{V}, I, T, \mathbb{L} \rangle$ and a BA $A = \langle \mathcal{B}, b_0, \Sigma, \delta, F \rangle$, we define the *abstract partitioned product* $\mathcal{P}$ between M and A as a collection of FSMs $\{M_b\}_{b \in \mathcal{B}}$, one for every state b of the automaton A, with $M \preceq_{H_b} M_b$. We use $\langle \mathcal{V}_b, I_b, T_b, \{L_b^a\}_{a \in PROP} \rangle$ to denote the abstraction M_b. A state of $\mathcal{P}$ is a pair (s, b) where the state s of M is in the partition corresponding to state b of A (namely, $s \in S_{\mathcal{V}_b}$). A state (s, b) is initial if $b = b_0$ and $s \models I_b(\mathcal{V}_b)$. There exists a transition between two states (s_1, b_1) and (s_2, b_2) iff

1) there exists $l \in \Sigma$ such that $(b_1, l, b_2) \in \delta$, and $s \models L_{b_1}^a(\mathcal{V}_{b_1})$ for all $a \in l$, and
2) there exists $s_3 \in S_{\mathcal{V}_{b_1}}$ such that $s_1, s_3' \models T_{b_1}(\mathcal{V}_{b_1}, \mathcal{V}_{b_1}'')$ and $s_2 \in \alpha_{H_{b_2}}(\gamma_{H_{b_1}}(s_3))$.

Intuitively, given two partitions b_1 and b_2, there is a mapping $(\alpha_{H_{b_2}} \circ \gamma_{H_{b_1}})$ between the abstract states of the partition b_1 and the abstract states of the partition b_2: the transitions from states of the partition b_1 to states of the partition b_2 are given by the composition of T_{b_1} with the mapping $\alpha_{H_{b_2}} \circ \gamma_{H_{b_1}}$. Finally, a state (s, b) is fair iff b is fair.

Note that the combination of partitioning with abstraction is independent of the particular abstraction technique used. In fact, in principle, you may use different abstraction techniques in different partitions.

Example 3. Consider the model checking problem of Example 1 with $N = 2$. We drew a possible abstract partitioned product in Fig. 4: we used the abstract system described in the Example 1 in the partition corresponding to b_0, while the partition b_1 contains the concrete system.

Theorem 1. *If $L(\mathcal{P}) = \emptyset$, then $L(M) \cap L(A) = \emptyset$.*

Proof. Suppose $L(M) \cap L(A) \neq \emptyset$ and $w \in L(M) \cap L(A)$. Then, there exists a path $\pi_M = s_1, s_2, \ldots$ of M and a fair path $\pi_A = b_1, b_2, \ldots$ of A over some word $w = l_1, l_2, \ldots$. For every state b of A, $M \preceq M_b$ so that there exists a path $\pi_M^b \in \alpha_{H_b}(\pi_M)$ and π_M^b accepts

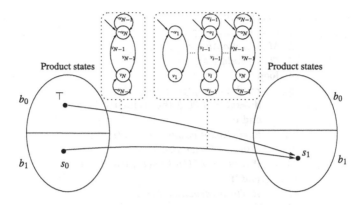

Fig. 5. Preimage in partitioned abstraction

w. Let $\pi_M^b = s_1^b, s_2^b, \ldots$ for every state b of A. Consider the sequence $\pi_\mathcal{P}$ of states of $\mathcal{P}$ where $\pi_\mathcal{P}(i) = (s_i^{b_i}, b_i)$. It is sufficient to prove that $\pi_\mathcal{P}$ is a fair path of $\mathcal{P}$. First, $\pi_\mathcal{P}(1)$ is initial since $b_1 = b_0$ and $s_1^{b_1} \models I_{b_1}(\mathcal{V}_{b_1})$. Second, for all $i \geq 1$, $(\pi_\mathcal{P}(i), \pi_\mathcal{P}(i+1))$ is a transition. In fact, 1) $(b_i, l_i, b_{i+1}) \in \delta$, and $s_i^{b_i} \models L_{b_i}^a(\mathcal{V}_{b_i})$, for all $a \in l_i$, and 2) $s_i^{b_i}, s_{i+1}^{b_i}{}' \models T_{b_i}(\mathcal{V}_{b_i}, \mathcal{V}'_{b_i})$, and $s_{i+1}^{b_{i+1}} \in \alpha_{H_{b_{i+1}}}(\gamma_{H_{b_i}}(s_{i+1}^{b_i}))$. Finally, $\pi_\mathcal{P}$ is fair since π_A is fair.

Notice that, if $M_b = M$ for every $b \in \mathcal{B}$, $\mathcal{P}$ is the hybrid structure we use in PDP. In this case, indeed, the opposite direction of Theorem 1 holds too.

We generalize the preimage and postimage computation defined for PDP as follows:

$$preimage(Q) := \{\bigvee_{(b,a,b') \in \delta} preimage_{T_b}(\alpha_{H_b}(\gamma_{H_{b'}}(Q_{b'}))) \wedge a\}_{b \in \mathcal{B}}$$
$$postimage(Q) := \{\bigvee_{(b',a,b) \in \delta} postimage_{T_b}(\alpha_{H_b}(\gamma_{H_{b'}}(Q_{b'} \wedge a)))\}_{b \in \mathcal{B}}.$$

Example 4. Consider the partitioned preimage computation of Example 2. Now, we re-computed the same preimage with a partitioned abstraction product: we will use the abstract system described in the Example 1 in the partition corresponding to b_0, while the partition b_1 will contain the concrete system. In this case, before computing the component b_0 of the preimage, we have to map the state s_1 of partition b_1 to the abstraction of partition b_0. s_1 corresponds to the abstract state $\neg v_N$, whose preimage (in the abstract system) yields the whole abstract state-space (denoted with $\top$). The result is shown in Fig. 5.

3.2 Property-Driven Partitioned Refinement

We investigated a new technique that combines refinement with PDP. We call such technique Property-driven Partitioned Refinement (PDPR). The idea is that, instead of refining the abstraction globally, we localize the refinement to some partition. This way, at every iteration of the CEGAR loop, we refine the abstraction trying to keep it coarser than standard refinement.

First, we adapted the standard refinement loop to LTL model checking (see Fig. 6). The LTL formula $\neg \varphi$ (the negation of the property) is translated into a *BA* A (line 1).

```
        Check(M,φ)
 1: A := LTL2BA(¬φ);
 2: M̂ := InitialAbsctraction(M,φ)
 3: P := Product(M̂,A);
 4: loop
 5:     result := EmptyLanguage(P);
 6:     if result = TRUE then return M ⊨ φ
 7:     end if
 8:     π := GenerateCounterexample(P);
 9:     result := Concretizable(π,M);
10:     if result = TRUE then return M ⊭ φ
11:     end if
12:     RefineAbstraction(P,π);
13: end loop
```

Fig. 6. The procedure for checking if $M \models \varphi$

The system is abstracted so that $\hat{M}$ contains all the information related to the variables that occur in the property. The product $\mathcal{P}$ between $\hat{M}$ and A is built (line 3). The emptiness of $\mathcal{P}$ is checked with the Emerson-Lei algorithm [8] (line 5). If a counterexample is found, we check if it corresponds to a concrete path (line 9) with Bounded Model Checking (BMC) [1], as proposed by [7]. Since the counterexample may be infinite, we consider lasso-shape paths. This way, if the counterexample is given by the abstract states $\hat{s}_1, ..., \hat{s}_k$ with $\hat{s}_l = \hat{s}_k$, we then generate the BMC formula

$$I(\mathcal{V}_0) \wedge \bigwedge_{1 \leq i < k} T(\mathcal{V}_i, \mathcal{V}_{i+1}) \wedge \bigwedge_{1 \leq i \leq k} S_i(\mathcal{V}_i) \wedge \bigwedge_{v \in \mathcal{V}} v_l = v_k$$

where the predicates S_i identify the abstract states $\hat{s}_i$. If the formula is not satisfiable, we refine the abstraction (line 12). Note that this concretization step is sound but not complete: we are fixing a specific lasso shape, so it may happen that the above formula is not satisfiable, but the counterexample is concretizable. The completeness of the whole algorithm is guaranteed by the fact that the refinement procedure is monotone, since at every iteration we add some information; eventually, the concrete counterexample will be found.

PDPR follows the same schema, though the product is handled differently. The main difference between the standard framework and PDPR consists of the refinement procedure, which refines the abstract system only in some partitions. The refinement depends on the type of abstraction we are considering. In the following, we adopt the framework of localization reduction.

The refinement (Fig. 7) consists in computing the score of each invisible variable (line 5). We pick the best scored variable (line 7) and we add it to the system (line 8). We repeat the procedure until the refined abstraction rules out the spurious counterexample. This is checked with a symbolic fix-point simulation (line 12). In the case of PDPR, the refinement is similar (Fig. 8). The only difference is that we score pairs of variables and partitions (line 8): if (v,b) is the best scored pair, we add v to the system of partition b (line 13).

$RefineAbstraction(\mathcal{P}, \pi)$
// $\mathcal{P}$ is the partitioned product
   of $\{\hat{M}_b\}_{b \in \mathcal{B}}$ and A
1: **repeat**
2:    **for all** $b \in \mathcal{B}$ **do**
3:       $\tilde{\mathcal{V}}_b := \emptyset$;
4:    **end for**
5:    **while** $|\cup_{b \in \mathcal{B}} \tilde{\mathcal{V}}_b| < threshold$ **do**
6:       **for all** $b \in \mathcal{B}$ **do**
7:          **for all** $v \in \check{\mathcal{V}}_b$ **do**
8:             $ComputeScore(v, b, \hat{M}, \pi)$;
9:          **end for**
10:       **end for**
11:       $v := BestVar$;
12:       $b := BestPartition$;
13:       $\tilde{\mathcal{V}}_b := \tilde{\mathcal{V}}_b \cup \{v\}$;
14:    **end while**
15:    **for all** $b \in \mathcal{B}$ **do**
16:       $\hat{M}_b := Abstract(\hat{M}_b, \tilde{\mathcal{V}}_b)$;
17:    **end for**
18:    $\mathcal{P} := PartitionedProduct(\{\hat{M}_b\}_{b \in \mathcal{B}}, A)$;
19:    $result := Simulate(\mathcal{P}, \pi)$;
20: **until** $result = FALSE$

$RefineAbstraction(\mathcal{P}, \pi)$
// $\mathcal{P}$ is the product of $\hat{M}$ and A
1: **repeat**
2:    $\tilde{\mathcal{V}} := \emptyset$;
3:    **while** $|\tilde{\mathcal{V}}| < threshold$ **do**
4:       **for all** $v \in \check{\mathcal{V}}$ **do**
5:          $ComputeScore(v, \hat{M}, \pi)$;
6:       **end for**
7:       $v := BestVar$;
8:       $\tilde{\mathcal{V}} := \tilde{\mathcal{V}} \cup \{v\}$;
9:    **end while**
10:    $\hat{M} := Abstract(\hat{M}, \tilde{\mathcal{V}})$;
11:    $\mathcal{P} := Product(\hat{M}, A)$;
12:    $result := Simulate(\mathcal{P}, \pi)$;
13: **until** $result = FALSE$

Fig. 7. Refinement function   **Fig. 8.** Partitioned version of the refinement function

Example 5. Consider the model checking problem of Example 1. PDPR starts with two identical systems, which is the system containing only the constraints of v_N. Thus, PDPR will produce the same spurious counterexample described in the Example 1, which was obtained with the standard abstraction. The refinement heuristic finds that we have to add v_{N-1} in the partition b_1, in order to force v_N to become true. Similarly, we have to add v_{N-2} and all the other variables to partition b_1. PDPR ends the refinement loop with the concrete system in partition b_1. Though, the abstract system of partition b_0 is never touched. In the subsequent emptiness checking, we use the partitioned abstraction described in Example 4. This abstraction is coarser than the concrete system (necessary for a standard refinement), but it is sufficiently fine to prove the property.

4 Experimental Results

We now evaluate the efficiency of PDPR in practice by testing it over some scalable verification models. The purpose of this experimental evaluation is to provide a comparison between the standard non-partitioned refinement approach and PDPR. Thus, we fix an abstraction refinement setting, in which we use PDP as representation of the product, and we compare the partitioned versus the non-partitioned refinement loop. Our tests do not provide a direct comparison with the numerous state-of-the-art refinement techniques because the partitioned abstraction is orthogonal to them. Rather, we try to

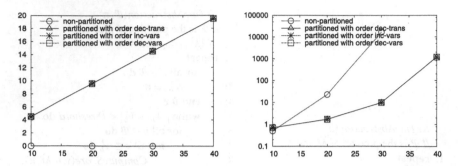

Fig. 9. Experiments on the *N*-bit-counter example. X axis: *N*. Y axis: Left plot: average number of invisible variables; Right plot: CPU time (secs).

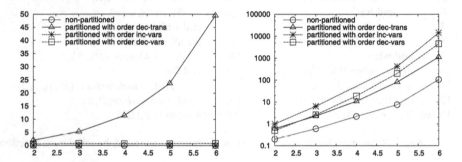

Fig. 10. Experiments on the memory example. X axis: number of bits for memory addresses. Y axis: Left plot: average number of invisible variables; Right plot: CPU time (secs).

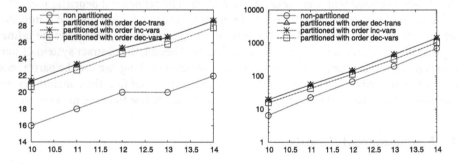

Fig. 11. Experiments on the stack example. X axis: stack's capacity. Y axis: Left plot: average number of invisible variables; Right plot: CPU time (secs).

evaluate the trade-off between the disadvantages of dealing with several abstractions at the same moment and the advantages of using coarser abstractions when possible.

NuSMVPDP is an extension of NuSMV [4] that uses a PDP representation to perform the emptiness checking of the product. We have enhanced NuSMVPDP with an abstraction refinement technique that implements localization abstraction with the

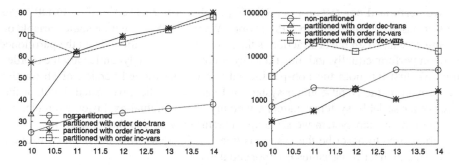

Fig. 12. Experiments on the gas-station example. X axis: number of customers. Y axis: Left plot: average number of invisible variables; Right plot: CPU time (secs).

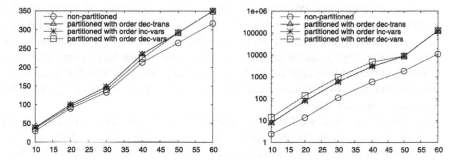

Fig. 13. Experiments on the mutual-exclusion example. X axis: number of processes. Y axis: Left plot: average number of invisible variables; Right plot: CPU time (secs).

refinement heuristic of [18][2]. In these settings, at every refinement iteration, a new abstract system is computed and composed with the property automaton; then, a PDP-based search checks the emptiness of the product.

We tested this standard abstraction refinement technique against its partitioned counterpart. In the partitioned refinement, we fixed an ordering of the partitions. This gives a priority to the partition to be refined when two invisible variables of different partitions get the same score. We selected three relevant orderings:

– **[inc-vars]** an increasing ordering according to the number of invisible variables in each partitions; this way, we prefer refining the abstraction in those partitions that had already been refined (thus, previously guilty of other spurious counterexample);
– **[dec-vars]** a decreasing ordering according to the number of invisible variables in each partitions; this way, we prefer refining the coarsest abstraction;
– **[dec-trans]** a decreasing ordering according to the number of outgoing transitions in the property automaton; this tries to alleviate the cost of the mapping between abstractions: every time we have to traverse backwardly a transition that starts from b, we have to quantify over the invisible variables of the partition b.

---

[2] Unlike [18], we use one counterexample per refinement iteration.

We performed our tests on the Rice Terascale Cluster (RTC)[3], a TeraFLOP Linux cluster based on Intel Itanium 2 Processors. We run NUSMV with a static variable ordering so that, when the abstraction is the same, the non-partitioned and the partitioned version perform equally and the efficiency is not biased by a dynamic variable reordering. We first run both the non-partitioned and the partitioned version of abstraction refinement on the N-bit-counter system of Example 1. Then, we tested the algorithm over other scalable systems: namely, memory, stack, mutual-exclusion example, and gas station. In each system we scale up a parameter N so that the number of symbolic variables used to describe the system is linear in N (apart from the memory example where the number of variables is exponential in N).

- The memory example implements standard read and write functionalities. In order to be able to scale up the verification, we use just one bit for the data so that we can write and read only two values. We scale up the number N of bits used for the memory addresses. We verify that if we write a value on a particular address, next time we read from it we obtain the same value, unless another write operation was performed in the meanwhile. Inspired by the work on GSTE of [20], we express the property by enumerating each address case so that the property automaton contains different subgraph for each case. The partitioned abstraction should take benefit from this, by keeping in each subgraph only the information regarding that particular memory address.
- In the stack example, we have the standard pop and push functions. In this case, scalability is given by the maximum size N of the stack. The property says that whenever we push an element on the stack, and later the stack results empty, there must be a pop call in the middle
- In the mutual-exclusion example, N processes non-deterministically try to access the critical session. The access is controlled by the main module, which guarantees that a process does not wait forever. The property says that, if a process is the only one that is waiting, then it accesses the critical session in one step.
- In the gas-station example, there are N customers who want to use one pump. They have to prepay an operator who then activates the pump. When the pump has charged, the operator give the change to the customer. The property says the if a customer pays before another one, then she must be server first.

We verified many other properties, but the initial abstraction was fine enough to prove the property; in one case the final abstraction coincided (with both techniques) with the concrete system. We reported only the other cases, where the refinement had been effectively useful to prove the property.[4] The results are shown in Figures 9, 11, 12, and 13. In every plot, we scale up the size of the system. The plots on the left of each figure present the number of invisible variables (the average in the case of partitioned abstraction) of the final abstraction. The plots on the right show the time in seconds plotted in log scale.

These results show that partitioned abstraction is successful at allowing verification with significantly coarser abstractions. The coarsest abstraction is obtained when the

---

[3] http://rcsg.rice.edu/rtc/

[4] All data available at www.inf.unisi.ch/postdoc/tonetta/TACAS07-PDP

states of the property automaton correspond to particular phases of the circuit, like in the case of the memory example (Fig. 10). In some cases (Figs. 9 and 12), this leads to an order-of-magnitude improvement in running time. Nevertheless, in some cases (Figs. 10, 11 and 13), the coarser abstractions do not compensate for the overhead of having to refine several abstractions. It is interesting to note that no single refinement order dominates in our experiments; the best refinement order seems model and property specific. For lack of space we did not show the plots with space performances but they present the same pattern of time plots. The only exception is the memory example, which is particularly interesting because the number of invisible variables grows exponentially (hiding an exponential amount of design with an order of magnitude improvement in space), but the verification time degrades by an order of magnitude.

5 Conclusions

We investigated a new approach for abstraction refinement, in which the abstraction is not uniform; rather, like in [10], the abstraction is localized and presents different precisions in different parts of the state space. We combined this idea with property-driven partitioning, which partitions the product state space for efficient LTL model checking. We presented a new refinement algorithm that exploits this approach by refining the abstraction only in those partitions where it is necessary. This way, as our tests confirmed, we can prove the correctness of a system with a higher level of abstraction, leading, in some cases, to dramatic performance improvement. Unlike, however, in SMC, where the partitioning almost always speeds up the verification time, here the use of partitioning is less compelling, as the overhead of having to refine multiple abstractions is in some cases too high, leading to performance degradation. This conclusion is consistent with the results in [10], where predicate localization improves performance only in a small number of test cases.

We note that most of time is spent in the refinement step, meaning that, the coarser abstractions do not compensate for the overhead of having to refine several abstractions. Since the partitioned abstractions are much coarser, we conjecture that we could afford to use less accurate but faster refinement techniques in order to speed up the overall verification time. This is left for future research.

References

1. A. Biere, A. Cimatti, E. M. Clarke, and Y. Zhu. Symbolic Model Checking without BDDs. In *Proceedings of TACAS'99*, pages 193–207, 1999.
2. J.R. Burch, E.M. Clarke, K.L. McMillan, D.L. Dill, and L.J. Hwang. Symbolic Model Checking: 10^{20} States and Beyond. *Information and Computation*, 98(2):142–170, 1992.
3. H. Cho, G.D. Hachtel, E. Macii, M. Poncino, and F. Somenzi. Automatic state space decomposition for approximate FSM traversal based on circuit analysis. *IEEE Trans. on CAD of Integrated Circuits and Systems*, 15(12):1451–1464, 1996.
4. A. Cimatti, E.M. Clarke, F. Giunchiglia, and M. Roveri. NUSMV: a new Symbolic Model Verifier. In *Proceedings of CAV'99*, pages 495 - 499, 1999.
5. E.M. Clarke, O. Grumberg, S. Jha, Y. Lu, and H. Veith. Counterexample-Guided Abstraction Refinement. In *Proceedings of CAV'00*, pages 154 - 169, 2000.

6. E.M. Clarke, O. Grumberg, and D.E. Long. Model Checking and Abstraction. *ACM Trans. Program. Lang. Syst.*, 16(5):1512–1542, 1994.

7. E.M. Clarke, A. Gupta, J.H. Kukula, and O. Strichman. SAT Based Abstraction-Refinement Using ILP and Machine Learning Techniques. In *Proceedings of CAV'02*, pages 265–279, 2002.

8. E.A. Emerson and C.L. Lei. Efficient Model Checking in Fragments of the Propositional μ-Calculus. In *Proceedings of the LICS'86*, pages 267 - 278, 1986.

9. S. Graf and H. Saïdi. Construction of Abstract State Graphs with PVS. In *Proceedings of CAV'97*, pages 72 - 83, 1997.

10. T.A. Henzinger, R. Jhala, R. Majumdar, and K.L. McMillan. Abstractions from proofs. In *Proceedings of POPL'04*, pages 232 - 244, 2004.

11. T.A. Henzinger, R. Jhala, R. Majumdar, and G. Sutre. Lazy abstraction. In *Proceedings of POPL'02*, pages 58 - 70, 2002.

12. G.J. Holzmann. *The SPIN model checker: Primer and reference manual*. Addison Wesley, 2003.

13. R.P. Kurshan. *Computer Aided Verification of Coordinating Processes*. Princeton University Press, 1994.

14. M.D. Nguyen, D. Stoffel, M. Wedler, and W. Kunz. Transition-by-Transition FSM Traversal for Reachability Analysis in Bounded Model Checking. In *Proceedings of ICCAD'05*, 2005.

15. R. Sebastiani, E. Singerman, S. Tonetta, and M. Y. Vardi. GSTE is Partitioned Model Checking. In *Proceedings of CAV'04*, pages 229 - 241, 2004.

16. R. Sebastiani, S. Tonetta, and M.Y. Vardi. Symbolic Systems, Explicit Properties: On Hybrid Approaches for LTL Symbolic Model Checking. In *Proceedings of CAV'05*, pages 350 - 363, 2005.

17. M.Y. Vardi and P. Wolper. An Automata-Theoretic Approach to Automatic Program Verification. In *Proceedings of LICS'86*, pages 332 - 344. IEEE Computer Society, 1986.

18. C. Wang, B. Li, H.S. Jin, G.D. Hachtel, and F. Somenzi. Improving Ariadne's Bundle by Following Multiple Threads in Abstraction Refinement. In *Proceedings of ICCAD'03*, pages 408 - 415, 2003.

19. J. Yang and C.-J. H. Seger. Introduction to Generalized Symbolic Trajectory Evaluation. *IEEE Transactions on Very Large Scale Integration Systems*, 11(3), 2003.

20. J. Yang and C.-J.H. Seger. Generalized Symbolic Trajectory Evaluation - Abstraction in Action. In *Proceedings of FMCAD'02*, pages 70 - 87, 2002.

Combining Abstraction Refinement and SAT-Based Model Checking

Nina Amla and Kenneth L. McMillan

Cadence Design Systems

Abstract. Unbounded model checking methods based on Boolean satisfiability (SAT) solvers are proving to be a viable alternative to BDD-based model checking. These methods include, for example, interpolation based and sequential ATPG-based approaches. In this paper, we explore the implications of using abstraction refinement in conjunction with interpolation-based model checking. Based on experiments using a large industrial benchmark set, we conclude that when using interpolation-based model checking, measures must be taken to prevent the overhead of abstraction refinement from dominating runtime. We present two new approaches to this problem. One is a hybrid approach that decides heuristically when to apply abstraction. The other is a very coarse but inexpensive abstraction method based on ideas from ATPG. This approach can produce order-of-magnitude reductions in memory usage, allowing significantly larger designs to be verified.

1 Introduction

Model checking [9,26,7], which is a widely used formal verification technique, is traditionally implemented with Binary Decision Diagrams (BDDs) [6]. Due to recent advances in tools that solve the Boolean satisfiability problem (SAT), formal reasoning based on SAT is proving to be an effective alternative to BDDs. At the core of these algorithms is Bounded Model Checking (BMC) [5], where a system is unfolded k times and encoded as a SAT problem to be solved by a SAT solver. A satisfying assignment returned by the SAT solver corresponds to a counterexample of length k. If the problem is determined to be unsatisfiable, the SAT solver produces a proof of the fact that there are no counterexamples of length k. BMC, while successful in finding errors, is incomplete: there is no efficient way to decide that a property is *true*.

Nonetheless, there are many Unbounded Model Checking (UMC) techniques that make use of SAT-based BMC in some way (see [25] for a comprehensive survey). Two methods, proof-based [23] and interpolation [22], were found to be the most robust in a recent experimental study [1] that compared many SAT-based UMC techniques. The proof-based algorithm is an iterative abstraction refinement method that typically uses a traditional BDD-based model checker to prove properties of the abstract models. It starts with a short BMC run and if the problem is satisfiable then an error has been found. However, if the problem is unsatisfiable, the resulting proof of unsatisfiability is used to guide

O. Grumberg and M. Huth (Eds.): TACAS 2007, LNCS 4424, pp. 405–419, 2007.

the formation of a new conservative abstraction. The algorithm terminates if the BDD-based model checker proves the property on the abstraction; otherwise the length of the counterexample generated by the model checker is used as the next BMC length.

The interpolation-based model checking algorithm is a purely SAT-based unbounded model checking method that does not rely on abstraction refinement, though like abstraction methods, it tends to work well on properties that are localizable, and is fairly insensitive to the addition of irrelevant logic. This method uses BMC to find failures and proves properties by doing a SAT-based approximate reachability analysis. The results in [1] show that the proof-based method does better on problems where BDDs are particularly effective. On the other hand the interpolation method has the advantage on larger problems. That paper also shows that model checking algorithms based on sequential Automatic Test Pattern Generation (ATPG) [15,16] are competitive with BDD UMC. These findings suggest that combining the strengths of these different techniques may yield more general and robust methods.

This paper explores experimentally the issue of whether abstraction can be fruitfully combined with SAT-based UMC methods. In particular, we consider the question of how best to combine abstraction with interpolation-based UMC. Since the latter is already fairly insensitive to the inclusion of irrelevant logic, a naïve approach to localization abstraction spends more time in the refinement phase than is gained in the UMC phase. We report on two approaches to solve this problem. The first is to judiciously apply proof-based abstraction with BDDs only when it is likely to improve performance. The second is to apply a very coarse but inexpensive refinement method based on ideas from ATPG. The latter approach avoids the concretization phase that applies BMC to the concrete model, and thus results in an order-of-magnitude savings of space, though the abstractions obtained are far from optimal.

There is a fair amount of related work on integrating BDDs and various SAT-based techniques. In [12], conflict clauses that were learned from BDDs are used to improve the performance of SAT BMC. The method proposed in [8] uses BDDs to compute an over-approximation of the reachable states and applies these constraints to the SAT BMC problem. The technique described in [3] uses BDD-based reachability analysis to compute lower bounds on reachable states to accelerate SAT-based induction. Proof-based and counterexample-based abstraction methods have been combined in different phases of an iterative abstraction refinement process in [13]. The hybrid method in [2] use a single abstraction phase that is intermediate between the proof-based and counterexample-based abstraction refinement. Abstraction refinement has also been used with BMC [14] to find failures more effectively. A recent technique [18], that is closest to our work, combines abstraction refinement and interpolation in a manner which is similar to using interpolation as the UMC in a proof-based technique. The differences between this approach and the ones presented in this paper will be discussed in detail in Section 3.

The paper is organized as follows: Section 2 gives a brief overview of the algorithms, Section 3 describes the two new interpolation-based techniques, Section 4 briefly describes the experimental framework, and discusses the experimental results and Section 5 summarizes our findings.

2 Overview of the Algorithms

2.1 Preliminaries

A model $M = (S, I, T, L)$ has a set of states S, a set of initial states $I \subseteq S$, a transition relation $T \subseteq S \times S$, and a labeling function $L : S \to 2^A$ where A is a set of atomic propositions. For the purposes of this paper, we consider properties specified in the logic LTL. The construction given in [17] can be used to reduce model checking of safety properties to checking invariant properties. We use the liveness to safety construction in [4] for methods, like interpolation based model checking, which do not support liveness checks. The syntax and semantics of LTL and other temporal logics is not given here but can be found in [10].

Given a finite state model M and a safety property p, the model checking algorithm checks that M satisfies p, written $M \models p$. The forward reachability algorithm starts at the initial states and computes the *image*, which is the set of states reachable in one step. This procedure is continued until either the property is falsified in some state or no new states are encountered (a fixed point). The backward reachability algorithm works similarly but starts from the states where the property is *false* and computes the *preimage*, which is the set of states that can reach the current states in one step. The representation and manipulation of the sets of states can be done explicitly or with BDDs.

2.2 DPLL-Style SAT Solvers

The Boolean satisfiability problem (SAT) determines if a given Boolean formula has a satisfying assignment. This is generally done by converting the formula into a satisfiability-equivalent formula in Conjunctive Normal Form (CNF), which can be solved by a SAT solver. A key operation used in SAT solvers is *resolution*, where two clauses $(a \lor b)$ and $(\neg a \lor c)$ can be resolved to give a new clause $(b \lor c)$. Modern DPLL-style SAT solvers [21,24,11] make assignments to variables, called *decisions*, and generate an implication graph that records the decisions and the effects of Boolean constraint propagation. When all the variables are assigned, the SAT solver terminates with the satisfying assignment. But if there is a *conflict*, which is a clause where the negation of every literal already appears in the implication graph, a conflict clause is generated through resolution. This conflict clause is added to the formula to avoid making those assignments again. The SAT solver then backtracks to undo some of the conflicting assignments. The SAT solver terminates with an *unsatisfiable* answer when it derives the empty clause, ruling out out all possible assignments. The resolution steps used in generating the empty clause can now be used to produce a *proof of unsatisfiability*.

2.3   SAT-Based Bounded Model Checking

Bounded Model Checking (BMC) [5] is a restricted form of model checking, where one searches for a counterexample (cex) in executions bounded by some length k. In this approach the model is unfolded k times, conjoined with the negation of the property, and then encoded as a propositional satisfiability formula. Given a model M and an invariant property p, the BMC problem is encoded as follows:

$$BMC(M, p, k) = I(s_0) \wedge \bigwedge_{i=0}^{k-1} T(s_i, s_{i+1}) \wedge \bigvee_{i=0}^{k} \neg p(s_i)$$

The formula can be converted into CNF and solved by a SAT solver. If the formula is satisfiable, then the property is *false*, and the SAT solver has found a satisfying assignment that corresponds to a counterexample of length k. In the unsatisfiable case, there is no counterexample of length k and a proof of unsatisfiability can be obtained from the SAT solver.

2.4   Proof-Based Abstraction Refinement

The proof-based abstraction refinement algorithm in [23] iterates through SAT-based BMC and BDD-based MC. It starts with a short BMC run, and if the problem is satisfiable, an error has been found. If the problem is unsatisfiable, the proof of unsatisfiability is used to guide the formation of a new conservative abstraction on which BDD-based MC is run. In the case that the BDD-based model checker proves the property then the algorithm terminates; otherwise the length of the counterexample generated by the model checker is used as the next BMC length. This procedure, shown in Figure 1, is continued until either a failure is found in the BMC phase or the property is proved in the BDD-based MC phase.

2.5   Interpolation-Based Model Checking

An *interpolant* $\mathcal{I}$ for an unsatisfiable formula $A \wedge B$ is a formula such that: (1) $A \Rightarrow \mathcal{I}$ (2) $\mathcal{I} \wedge B$ is unsatisfiable and (3) $\mathcal{I}$ refers only to the common variables of

procedure PBABDD(M,p)
1. initialize k
2. while *true* do
3.   if BMC(M, p, k) is SAT then return *cex*
4. M' = new abstraction derived from proof
5.   if BDDMC(M', p) holds then return *true*
6.   let k = length of abstract *cex*
7. end while
end

Fig. 1. Proof-based procedure

procedure INTERPOLATION(M, p, k)
1. while *true* do
2.   if BMC(M, p, k) is SAT then return *cex*
3.   if ARC(M, p, k) then return *true*
4.   increase k
5. end while
end

Fig. 2. Interpolation procedure

A and B. Intuitively, $\mathcal{I}$ is the set of facts that the SAT solver considers relevant in proving the unsatisfiability of $A \wedge B$.

The interpolation-based algorithm [22] uses interpolants to derive an over-approximation of the reachable states with respect to the property. This is done as follows (Figures 2 and 3). The BMC problem $BMC(M, p, k)$ is solved for an initial depth k. If the problem is satisfiable, a counterexample is returned, and the algorithm terminates. If $BMC(M, p, k)$ is unsatisfiable, the formula representing the problem is partitioned into $Pref(M, p, k) \wedge Suff(M, p, k)$, where $Pref(M, p, k)$ is the conjunction of the initial condition and the first transition, and $Suff(M, p, k)$ is the conjunction of the rest of the transitions and the final condition. The interpolant $\mathcal{I}$ of $Pref(M, p, k)$ and $Suff(M, p, k)$ is computed. Since $Pref(M, p, k) \Rightarrow \mathcal{I}$, it follows that $\mathcal{I}$ is *true* in all states reachable from $I(s_0)$ in one step. This means that $\mathcal{I}$ is an over-approximation of the set of states reachable from $I(s_0)$ in one step. Also, since $\mathcal{T} \wedge Suff(M, p, k)$ is unsatisfiable, it also follows that no state satisfying $\mathcal{I}$ can reach an error in $k - 1$ steps. If $\mathcal{I}$ contains no new states, that is, $\mathcal{I} \Rightarrow I(s_0)$, then a fixed point of the reachable set of states has been reached, thus the property holds. If $\mathcal{I}$ has new states then R' represents an over-approximation of the states reached so far. The algorithm then uses R' to replace the initial set I, and iterates the process of solving the BMC problem at depth k and generating the interpolant as the over-approximation of the set of states reachable in the next step. The property is determined to be *true* when the BMC problem with R' as the initial condition is unsatisfiable,

procedure ARC(M, p, k)
1. $R = I$, *steps* $= 0$
2. while true do
3. $M' = (S, R, T, L)$
4.   let $C = Pref(M', p, k) \wedge Suff(M', p, k)$
5.   if C is SAT then return *false*
6.   compute interpolant $\mathcal{I}$ of C
7. $R' = \mathcal{I}$
8.   if $R \Rightarrow R'$ then return *true*
9. $R = R' \vee R$
10.   *steps* = *steps* + 1;
11. end while

Fig. 3. Approximate Reachable states Computation

and its interpolant leads to a fixed point of reachable states. However, if the
BMC problem is satisfiable, the counterexample may be spurious since R' is an
over-approximation of the reachable set of states. In this case, the value of k is
increased, and the procedure is continued. We use the optimization in [20] that
sets the new value of k to be old value of k plus the number of approximate
image steps done in ARC.

3   Combining Interpolation and Abstraction Refinement

3.1   Using Proof-Based Abstraction in Interpolation

On certain problems BDDMC can be far more effective than the interpolation-
based algorithm. In particular, on problems where one needs to go deep to find
proofs or failures, BDDMC can be significantly faster. This is the motivation for
using proof-based abstraction (lines 4-5 in Figure 1) in the interpolation method
as shown in Figure 4.

This method works just like the INTERPOLATION procedure if *condition* is
set to *false*. However, when *condition* is *true* then a proof-based abstraction is
constructed and BDDMC is done on this abstraction. Thus this hybrid technique
makes a choice between two possible UMC methods for proving properties with
the aim of using the more efficient UMC method more often than not. The
key idea being that if the INTERPOLATION procedure was doing poorly, which
typically happens at larger depths, then one would use proof-based abstraction
with BDDMC. However, the inability to predict when BDDs will do poorly could
cause BDDMC to be the bottleneck on problems that can be proved fairly easily
with just interpolation. An optimization that worked well in avoiding wasted
effort was setting an effort limit on the BDDMC phase. We found that setting
the limit based on the effort taken by the ARC procedure in the previous iteration
was adequate. Note that there is no effort limit for the ARC procedure.

Clearly choosing the appropriate condition in Figure 4 is crucial. We use a
simple progress measure for BDDMC that is based on the number of image steps
completed divided by the effort needed by the BDDMC procedure. A similar
measure can be computed for the ARC procedure that uses the number of approximate image steps and effort. The INTERPHYBRID algorithm starts with
basic interpolation and the first time that k is greater than some predetermined
limit, a proof-based abstraction is created and BDDMC is run on this abstraction
with an effort limit. At the end of BDDMC step, if we detect that reachability
analysis did not start within the effort limit then BDDMC is never used again.
If BDDMC does reachability, whether it completes or not, the number of image
steps is used to compute the progress measure. If the progress of the ARC procedure becomes much slower than the progress of previous BDDMC run, then
BDDMC is tried again. Thus the heuristic attempts to use the UMC technique
which is doing better at that point and in the worst case, when the BDDs are
blowing up, we do only one BDDMC run with a low effort bound.

Combining abstraction refinement with interpolation has been explored in
[18]. This approach is similar to using interpolation instead of BDDMC as the

procedure INTERPHYBRID(M, p)
1. initialize k
2. while *true* do
3.   if BMC(M, p, k) is SAT then return *cex*
4.   if *condition* then
5.   derive abstraction M' from proof
6.   if BDDMC(M', p) then return *true*
7. k = length of abstract *cex*
8.   else
9.   if ARC(M, p, k) then return *true*
10.   increase k
11.   end if
12.   update *condition*
13. end while
end

Fig. 4. Hybrid Interpolation and BDD-based PBA procedure

UMC procedure in the proof-based method. However there are a number of differences between this framework [19,18] and the one in Figure 1. In proof-based abstraction (Figure 1), a new abstraction is derived from the proof of unsatisfiability in each iteration, while the method in [19] starts with an initial abstraction and refines this abstraction in each iteration. Another difference is the way the counterexample is concretized. In proof-based abstraction, BMC at the depth of the abstract counterexample is done on the concrete model to check if the counterexample is real. In contrast, the method in [19] takes an incremental approach that attempts to concretize the counterexample on abstract models and successively refines the abstraction until either the counterexample is eliminated or is determined to be real on the concrete model. In [18], they find that combining abstraction refinement with interpolation results in performance gains over the basic interpolation method, but they also observe the technique was not an effective way to improve the performance of interpolation without optimizations, like refinement prediction and minimization, that are focused on reducing the size of the abstraction.

3.2   Incremental Interpolation

Unlike BDD-based model checking, the interpolation-based method is fairly robust with respect to the addition of irrelevant state variables. For this reason, we can use fairly coarse and inexpensive methods of abstraction refinement. In particular, if the model is large (with greater that a few thousand state variables) it may not be practical to concretize abstract counterexamples using a SAT solver because of the space requirement of the BMC unfolding. Here, we will consider one method that avoids this concretization step, by borrowing some ideas from ATPG methods. Sequential ATPG methods search for input sequences to a circuit that test for the presence of a given fault.

On obtaining an abstract counterexample, we will attempt to produce a minimal justification of the abstract counterexample by assigning Boolean values to a subset of the free variables (that is, the primary inputs and the hidden state variables). A *justification* is a partial assignment that is sufficient to imply that the property is false in the abstraction $\hat{M}$. The set of hidden state variables H that are assigned in this justification at any time frame will be called the *justification frontier*.

Refinement consists of choosing some subset of the justification frontier and adding these state variables to the abstraction. Heuristically, these variables are more likely to be useful in eliminating the abstract counterexample, since those not occurring in the justification frontier are not relevant to the falsehood of the property in the cex. There is no guarantee, however, that the set of variables we choose is sufficient to eliminate the counterexample. Moreover, we may add many irrelevant variables in this way. We rely on the fact that adding irrelevant variables does not greatly effect the performance of the interpolation-based model checking method, so long as there is sufficient space to build the BMC unfolding.

Thus, the main intent of this approach is to prevent failure due to lack of space. If, for example, for a model with 100,000 state variables, we select 5000 state variables, out of which only 100 are actually necessary to prove the property, then we may succeed in preventing memory exhaustion and successfully prove the property, even though concretization is not feasible in such a large model.

Moreover, if at some point the justification frontier contains no hidden variables, then we have obtained a concrete counterexample, since the abstract counterexample fully justifies the falsehood of the property in the concrete model. This makes it possible to find concrete counterexamples without unfolding the concrete model, and in fact we will see cases where concrete counterexamples are obtained, but a BMC unfolding is infeasible due to lack of space.

The overall refinement procedure is outlined in Figure 5. We begin with an empty abstraction, and check the abstract model. If an abstract counterexample

procedure INTERPINC(M, p, k)
1. choose initial abstraction $\hat{M}$
2. while *true* do
3.   if ARC($\hat{M}, p, k$) return *true*
4.   let C be the abstract *cex*
5.   let $J = $ JUSTIFYCEX($C, \hat{M}, p, k$)
6.   let $H = \{r \mid r$ is hidden in $\hat{M}\}$
7.   let $JF = \{r \in H \mid r_i \in \text{dom}(J), \text{for some } i \in 0..k\}$
8.   if $JF = \emptyset$ then return *cex* C
9.   choose a non-empty subset of JF
10.   add these variables to $\hat{M}$
11. end while
end

Fig. 5. Incremental Interpolation procedure

is obtained, we produce a justification. This is a subset of the assignments in the abstract counterexample that is sufficient to imply falsehood of the property. That is, if C is the abstract counterexample, then a justification $J \subseteq C$ is an assignment to the free variables over time, such that

$$J \wedge \text{BMC}(\hat{M}, p, k) \Rightarrow \bigvee_{i \in 0 \ldots k} \neg p(s_i)$$

Procedure JUSTIFYCEX computes a justification by a simple greedy approach that traverses the circuit unfolding depth-first from the property, justifying the output of each gate by choosing a sufficient subset of its inputs. We first apply all assignments to the primary inputs, and propagate the implications of these assignments in the unfolding. Then we complete the justification by traversing the unfolding in a depth-first manner from its output (the property node), justifying the output of each gate by choosing a sufficient subset of its inputs. We have also modified the SAT solver to terminate with a partial assignment when the truth of the formula is justified. More sophisticated methods of finding a small justification are possible [27], though this may or may not provide a performance benefit.

The procedure then computes the justification frontier, and picks a subset of the state variables on the frontier to add to the abstraction. We choose a fixed number N of variables that have the highest aggregate VSIDS score in the SAT solver [24] for the BMC run that produced the abstract counterexample. Again, more sophisticated heuristics may be possible here. If the justification frontier is empty, we have a concrete counterexample, and we terminate. Note this procedure is terminating, since it adds at least one variable at each iteration.

The INTERPINC procedure can be more expensive than the INTERPOLATION procedure on the smaller problems hence we chose to be conservative in applying this method. This can be done within the INTERPOLATION procedure by checking the size of the unfolding each time k is increased and switching to INTERPINC only when a predetermined threshold limit is reached. By setting a very large threshold limit we invoke this procedure only if the size of the model or the value of k is large.

4   Experimental Analysis

In order to measure the relative performance of the algorithms described in the previous sections, we used the same BDD-based model checker and SAT solver. The SAT solver is incremental [28], in the sense that it is possible to add/delete clauses and restart the solver, while maintaining all previously inferred conflict clauses that were not derived from deleted clauses.

The benchmark set used has 1205 problems that were derived from 85 hardware designs which ranged in size from a few hundred to more than 100,000 lines of HDL code. Each design in our benchmark set contained from one up to a few hundred properties to check. The set contained some liveness properties but about 98% of properties were safety checks. There were 799 passing properties, 312 failures and 94 problems with unknown results. We partitioned the problems into three sets (BM1-BM3) based on size and difficulty of the problem. The set MOUT contains problems from BM1-BM3 where some algorithm ran out of memory. Table 1 characterizes the types of problems in each set. The Table shows the number of problems and the time limit used in each set. The average size of the problems in terms of the number of state variables, combinational variables and inputs is also given. For our experiments we used identical Redhat Enterprise Linux machines, each with an AMD Opteron CPU at 2GHZ and 2.6GB of available memory.

Table 1. Characterization of the benchmark sets

Benchmark	# Probs.	Time Limit (seconds)	Avg. Size		
			State	Comb.	Inputs
BM1	394	100	78	989	154
BM2	494	1000	307	2364	198
BM3	317	3600	2210	19363	1067
MOUT	29	10000	19055	151557	8018

We ran each problem with the specified time limit and measured the number of problems solved by each method. For all the tables and plots in the sequel, the time reported for any unresolved problem is the time limit for that problem even if the method ran out of memory in far less time. The tables present data for the five algorithms: the original proof-based method with BDDMC (PBABDD), the proof-based method in Figure 1 with ARC(M', p, k) instead of BDDMC(M', p) (PBAINTERP), the interpolation method (INTERPOLATION), the hybrid method that combines interpolation with BDD-based proof-based abstraction (INTERPHYBRID) and the new incremental interpolation method (INTERPINC). Table 2 reports the number of problems resolved (fin) and average time taken per problem (Av time) for benchmark sets BM1-BM3. For the entire set of problems (ALL), we also report the geometric mean (Gmean) of the run time. Table 3 presents results for the entire set partitioned into passes and failures. Table 3 report the average terminal BMC depth, and the number of "wins" with respect to time, where a win is attributed to a particular algorithm if it does better than all others with respect to runtime. In the case of a tie, which we defined to be two runs where the difference was less than 5% of the run time, we award a win for both methods.

Table 2 shows INTERPOLATION by itself is more robust overall than either PBABDD or PBAINTERP. The fact that PBAINTERP performs worse than INTERPOLATION can be explained by observing in Table 3 that the terminal BMC depth for the PBABDD and PBAINTERP methods is on average longer than INTERPOLATION. This is consistent with the observation in [18] that just replacing INTERPOLATION as the UMC in a proof-based abstraction framework does not necessarily improve the performance of interpolation. The fact that, within the proof-based abstraction framework, BDDMC is more effective overall than INTERPOLATION is somewhat surprising since in general INTERPOLATION

Table 2. Results for benchmark sets (BM1-BM3)

Algorithm	ALL			BM1		BM2		BM3	
	# fin	Av time	Gmean	# fin	Av time	# fin	Av time	# fin	Av time
PBABDD	1010	345.2	29.2	393	14.6	398	220.3	219	950.6
PBAINTERP	951	486.1	40.7	360	26.8	389	252.2	202	1421.7
INTERPOLATION	1032	339.5	24.2	389	16.3	399	227.2	244	916.2
INTERPHYBRID	1068	272.1	21.4	394	14.6	411	203.9	263	698.4
INTERPINC	1047	324.7	24.6	389	17.0	401	224.8	257	863.0

dominates BDDMC[1]. One possible reason is that BDDs do well on most small models and the abstractions derived in the proof-based method tend to be small. A second reason, which is the argument made in [23], is that SAT solvers do better when the number of relevant variables is small in comparison to the total number of variables. Since the abstractions are derived from proof generated by the SAT solver, the number of relevant variables is likely to be higher than usual, which could cause INTERPOLATION to be less effective.

As we can see in Table 2 the INTERPHYBRID is the most robust method on all three benchmarks and more so on the larger examples. On the 138 problems that could not be resolved by the INTERPOLATION method, the INTERPHYBRID procedure resolved 26% of these problems and the INTERPINC procedure resolved 12% of them. On the 766 problems that were verified by INTERPHYBRID, approximately 20% were resolved using BDDMC while the rest were resolved with ARC procedure. Table 4 presents the same data as Table 3 but partitions the problems into two sets: one with problems that were resolved by all five methods (All resolved) and the other with problems that were unresolved by some method (Some unresolved). As shown in Table 4, the INTERPHYBRID method is faster than the INTERPOLATION on both sets. It appears that the simple heuristic in INTERPHYBRID is fairly effective in choosing the appropriate UMC, and we find that the overhead of using BDDMC is minimal. This leads us to conclude that since BDDMC works better as the UMC for PBA, it is better to add PBABDD to INTERPOLATION rather than use INTERPOLATION within the proof-based abstraction refinement method.

The INTERPINC procedure has the same performance on BM1 and BM2 but is slightly more robust on the harder problems in BM3. The incremental

Table 3. Results partitioned into passes and failures

Algorithm	Passes				Failures			
	# fin	# wins	depth	Av. time	# fin	# wins	depth	Av. time
PBABDD	720	129	27	213.1	290	121	25	236.0
PBAINTERP	671	49	21	386.9	280	70	20	335.6
INTERPOLATION	735	153	13	211.7	297	14	20	217.9
INTERPHYBRID	766	341	17	132.7	302	85	24	159.7
INTERPINC	746	112	13	192.3	301	13	20	210.3

Table 4. Summary table for resolved problems

Algorithm	All Resolved				Some Unresolved			
	# fin	# wins	depth	Av. time	# fin	# wins	depth	Av. time
PbaBdd	887	138	14	28.5	123	61	96	266.8
PbaInterp	887	57	14	52.5	64	6	56	386.8
Interpolation	887	132	8	27.5	145	35	47	236.6
InterpHybrid	887	376	8	21.3	181	60	95	218.4
InterpInc	887	87	8	28.7	160	38	75	352.9

interpolation method, however, was intended to be efficient with respect to space. Therefore we consider the results for the 29 problems where some algorithm ran out of memory in Table 5. The Table presents the number of problems that passed, failed, exceeded the time limit (TO), ran out of memory (MO), the average time and the number of state variables in the last abstraction (Abs. size). We increased the time limit for these problems to 10000 seconds to gauge whether the incremental algorithm could solve additional problems with more time. The data indicates that the incremental interpolation approach is very effective in resolving these problems. The average memory usage of the INTERPINC procedure on these problems is 623 Megabytes which indicates that the method is highly efficient with respect to memory usage. Table 5 shows that although the INTERPINC method yields larger abstractions, it is still more efficient in terms of performance than PBAINTERP. This demonstrates that a very coarse but fast abstraction refinement heuristic can be effective with interpolation. Our ATPG-style heuristic gives a small overall improvement in robustness of interpolation with a large improvement in space.

Table 5. Results for the 29 Memory Intensive Examples (MOUT)

Algorithm	# Pass	# Fail	TO	MO	Avg. Time	Abs. size
PbaBdd	0	0	5	24	10000.0	38
PbaInterp	0	0	11	18	10000.0	70
Interpolation	1	1	13	14	9349.4	-
InterpHybrid	1	2	5	21	9013.1	-
InterpInc	8	6	13	2	6527.0	999

Figures 6 and 7 contain scatter plots of runtime in seconds. We see in Figure 6 that INTERPOLATION and its two variants, INTERPHYBRID and INTERPINC, are highly correlated but both variants have an advantage on problems that are hard for INTERPOLATION to solve. Figure 7 is interesting since it shows that, but for a few cases, PBAINTERP does far worse than INTERPOLATION. The right plot in 7) shows the run time of PBAINTERP versus a parallel run of INTERPOLATION and PBA (i.e. the best result of both methods). We see that PBAINTERP is slower in general but does resolve some problems that the parallel runs could not.

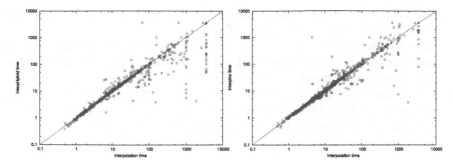

Fig. 6. Plot of time in seconds. Left: X-axis is Interpolation and Y-axis is InterpHybrid. Right: X-axis is Interpolation and Y-axis is InterpInc.

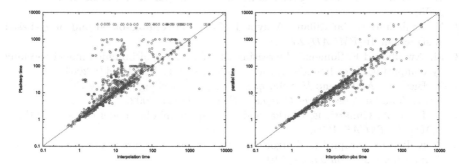

Fig. 7. Plot of time in seconds. Left: X-axis is Interpolation and Y-axis is PbaInterp. Right: X-axis is InterpHybrid and Y-axis is a parallel run of Interpolation and Proof-based abstraction.

5 Conclusions

This paper focused on combining abstraction refinement with interpolation-based UMC, with the goal of making this method more general and robust. First, we added a proof-based abstraction step to interpolation in order to use BDDs when they prove to be effective. This method was found to be very efficient on the problems in our benchmark set. Next, we describe a new incremental interpolation method that is designed to be memory efficient. This technique uses ATPG style justification in the concretization step which is generally the bottleneck with respect to space. A conservative application of this method was very effective on memory intensive problems and competitive with the interpolation method in general. Our findings can be summarized as follows.

1. The basic interpolation method is more robust overall than proof-based abstraction, with either interpolation or BDDs as the UMC.
2. Simple proof-based abstraction is not an effective way to improve the performance of interpolation as observed in [18]. We found that the terminal

BMC depth for PBAINTERP is on average longer than interpolation which in part explains the performance differences.

3. Since the data shows that BDDMC is more effective as the UMC in PBA, one can conclude that adding PBABDD to the interpolation method is better than using interpolation as the UMC in PBA.

4. A very coarse but fast abstraction refinement heuristic can be effective with interpolation. Our ATPG-style heuristic gives a small overall improvement in robustness of interpolation with a large improvement in space.

References

1. N. Amla, X. Du, A. Kuehlmann, R. Kurshan, and K. McMillan. An analysis of SAT-based model checking techniques in an industrial environment. In *CHARME*, 2005.
2. N. Amla and K. McMillan. A hybrid of counterexample-based and proof-based abstraction. In *FMCAD*, 2004.
3. M. Awedh and F. Somenzi. Increasing the robustness of bounded model checking by computing lower bounds on the reachable states. In *FMCAD*, 2004.
4. A. Biere, C. Artho, and V. Schuppan. Liveness checking as safety checking. *Electronic Notes in Theoretical Computer Science*, 66(2), 2002.
5. A. Biere, A. Cimatti, E. Clarke, and Y. Zhu. Symbolic model checking without BDDs. In *TACAS*, 1999.
6. R. E. Bryant. Graph-based algorithms for boolean function manipulations. *IEEE Transactions on Computers*, 1986.
7. J. R. Burch, E. M. Clarke, K. L. McMillan, D.L. Dill, and J. Hwang. Symbolic model checking: 10^{20} states and beyond. In *LICS*, 1990.
8. G. Cabodi, S. Nocco, and S. Quer. Improving SAT-based bounded model checking by means of bdd-based approximate traversals. In *DATE*, 2003.
9. E.M. Clarke and E. A. Emerson. Design and synthesis of synchronization skeletons using branching time temporal logic. In *Workshop on Logics of Programs*, 1981.
10. E. A. Emerson. Temporal and modal logic. In *Handbook of Theoretical Computer Science, Volume B: Formal Models and Sematics*, 1990.
11. E. Goldberg and Y. Novikov. BerkMin: A fast and robust SAT-solver. In *DATE*, 2002.
12. A. Gupta, M. Ganai, C. Wang, Z. Yang, and P. Ashar. Learning from BDDs in SAT-based bounded model checking. In *DAC*, 2003.
13. A. Gupta, M. Ganai, Z. Yang, and P. Ashar. Iterative abstraction using SAT-based BMC with proof analysis. In *ICCAD*, 2003.
14. A. Gupta and O. Strichman. Abstraction refinement for bounded model checking. In *CAV*, 2005.
15. C.Y. Huang, B. Yang, H.C. Tsai, and K.T. Cheng. Static property checking using atpg versus bdd techniques. In *ITC*, 2000.
16. M. Iyer, G. Parthasarathy, and K.T. Cheng. SATORI- an efficient sequential SAT solver for circuits. In *ICCAD*, 2003.
17. O. Kupferman and M. Vardi. Model checking of safety properties. In *Formal Methods in System Design*, 2001.
18. B. Li and F. Somenzi. Efficient abstraction refinement in interpolation-based unbounded model checking. In *TACAS*, 2006.

19. B. Li, C. Wang, and F. Somenzi. Abstraction refinement in symbolic model checking using satisfiability as the only decision procedure. In *STTT*, 2005.
20. J. Marques-Silva. Improvements to the implementation of interpolant-based model checking. In *CHARME*, 2005.
21. J. Marques-Silva and K. Sakallah. GRASP: A search algorithm for propositional satisfiability. *IEEETC: IEEE Transactions on Computers*, 48, 1999.
22. K. McMillan. Interpolation and SAT-based model checking. In *CAV*, 2003.
23. K. McMillan and N. Amla. Automatic abstraction without counterexamples. In *TACAS*, 2003.
24. M. W. Moskewicz, C. F. Madigan, Y. Zhao, L. Zhang, and S. Malik. Chaff: Engineering an Efficient SAT Solver. In *DAC*, 2001.
25. M. Prasad, A. Biere, and A. Gupta. A survey of recent advances in SAT-based formal verification. In *STTT*, 2005.
26. J.P. Queille and J. Sifakis. Specification and verification of concurrent systems in CESAR. In *Proc. of the 5th International Symposium on Programming*, 1982.
27. K. Ravi and F. Somenzi. Minimal assignments for bounded model checking. In *TACAS*, 2004.
28. J. Whittemore, J. Kim, and K. Sakallah. SATIRE: A new incremental satisfiability engine. In *DAC*, 2001.

Detecting Races in Ensembles of Message Sequence Charts

Edith Elkind[1], Blaise Genest[2], and Doron Peled[3]

[1] Department of Computer Science, University of Liverpool
Liverpool L69 3BX, United Kingdom
[2] CNRS & IRISA, Campus de Beaulieu, 35042 Rennes Cedex, France
[3] Department of Computer Science, Bar Ilan University, Ramat Gan 52900, Israel

Abstract. The analysis of message sequence charts (MSCs) is highly important in preventing common problems in communication protocols. Detecting race conditions, i.e., possible discrepancies in event order, was studied for a single MSC and for MSC graphs (a graph where each node consists of a single MSC, also called HMSC). For the former case, this problem can be solved in quadratic time, while for the latter case it was shown to be undecidable. However, the prevailing real-life situation is that a collection of MSCs, called here an *ensemble*, describing the different possible scenarios of the system behavior, is provided, rather than a single MSC or an MSC graph. For an ensemble of MSCs, a potential race condition in one of its MSCs can be compensated by another MSC in which the events occur in a different order. We provide a polynomial algorithm for detecting races in an ensemble. On the other hand, we show that in order to prevent races, the size of an ensemble may have to grow exponentially with the number of messages. Also, we initiate the formal study of the standard MSC *coregion* construct, which is used to relax the order among events of a process. We show that by using this construct, we can provide more compact race-free ensembles; however, detecting races becomes NP-complete.

1 Introduction

Software verification is an inherently difficult task. It is well known that it is undecidable for general domains. Moreover, even for finite domains many problems in this area are computationally intractable. In particular, this is often the case for problems that deal with concurrent processes. Another difficulty in applying verification methods for software is the technology transfer, i.e., providing the users (which are programmers and software engineers) with an easy-to-use and intuitive notation. It is thus beneficial to be able to analyze a notation that is already in use by software developers.

Message sequence charts (MSCs) is a formalism that is widely used in software engineering community and is formally described in [8]. This standard specification formalism consists of a textual notation, and a corresponding graphical notation. One MSC represents the relative order between message send and receive events (and sometimes also local events). A collection of charts represents alternative executions, which can also be organized into a graph, where each node is an MSC. The latter construction is called an MSC graph, or a High-level MSC (HMSC).

In recent years, several algorithms for analyzing MSCs and HMSCs have been suggested [4,6,10,11,12,13]. Perhaps the first problem to be analyzed was that of detecting

O. Grumberg and M. Huth (Eds.): TACAS 2007, LNCS 4424, pp. 420–434, 2007.

race conditions [2]. This problem arises because in the MSC notation, the events of each process must be totally ordered. On the other hand, because of limited control on speed of message propagation, messages do not always arrive in the order specified by the MSC. In other words, there are two partial orders associated with each MSC: the *visual order*, which corresponds to the graphical description of the MSC, and the *causal order*, i.e., the order that is under the control of the programmer (e.g., sending a message after receiving another one, but on the other hand, not the order between two messages received from different processes). A race condition is defined as a discrepancy between the two orders.

A polynomial-time transitive closure-based algorithm for race detection was proposed in [2]. This algorithm is used in various tools, in particular in Bell Labs' uBET tool [7]. In [15], the authors generalize this problem to HMSCs and show that in this setting, it becomes undecidable. This is also the case for many other problems for HMSCs, such as HMSC intersection and LTL model checking of HMSCs [3,14]. Intuitively, these undecidability results follow from the fact that the HMSC notation describes a system with no bound on the number of messages in transit. This complication can be avoided either by fixing a bound on the process queues, or by imposing various structural restrictions. The latter approach is taken by [3,14]; their proofs proceed by bounding the size of the queues as a function of the HMSC.

Alur et al. [1] analyze several decision problems for a set of MSCs, rather than for a single MSC or an HMSC. In particular, they consider the problem of deciding whether a combination of behaviors for different processes specified by different MSCs is covered in the MSC collection. This is a very natural setting, as in many cases, the actual objects that software engineers have to deal with are collection of scenarios (described as MSCs), rather than a single MSC or an HMSC (one reason for this is that the semantics of HMSCs is not quite clear due to different ways of defining the concatenation of MSCs [15,5]).

In this paper, we consider the problem of detecting race conditions in an ensemble of MSCs, i.e., a collection of MSCs over the same set of events. In this setting, even if in one of the MSCs the messages arrive in an order different from the one specified, another MSC in the collection may capture this alternative order. Thus, avoiding race conditions corresponds to *covering* alternative orders of events for one MSC by other MSCs in the collection. More precisely, race conditions can be defined in terms of the sets of linearizations (completions to total orders) of both orders associated with each MSC. Namely, for each MSC the visual order and the causal order typically produce different sets of linearizations (with the latter set including the former set). We say that an ensemble of MSCs contains a race if there is a linearization of the causal order of some MSC that is not a linearization of the visual order of any MSC in the ensemble.

We describe an efficient algorithm for finding race conditions, which extends the one of [2] for a single MSC. The running time of our algorithm is cubic in the representation size of the problem, i.e, the number of MSCs in the collection and the size of each MSC. However, in many cases one would need a large number of MSCs to avoid races: we describe some natural scenarios such that in any race-free collection that represents them the number of MSCs in the collection is exponential in the number of messages. Sometimes this problem can be alleviated by using *coregions*, which can be used to bundle together events in a single MSC. To the best of our knowledge, this paper provides the first formal study of the complexity and succinctness of this notational primitive, though it was already defined in [9] (see also [5,16] for coregions in LSCs and in TMSCs). Intuitively, it removes restrictions on the relative order of events that appear in it. We provide examples in which using coregions results in an exponentially smaller race-free collection. However, the more compact representation comes at a cost, as the problem of detecting races becomes NP-complete, even for the most restrictive definition of a coregion.

2 Preliminaries

In this section, we formally define message sequence charts (MSCs) as well as two partial orders that are associated with them. Intuitively, a message sequence chart can be graphically represented as a collection of process lines, where messages are depicted as arcs that link the sending process with the receiving process. This representation implies an ordering over all events that belong to the same process, as well as between send and receive events that correspond to the same message.

Definition 1. *A message sequence chart (MSC) $M = (E, <^M, \mathcal{P}, \ell, S, R, r)$ is given by a set of events E, a partial order $<^M$ on E, a set $\mathcal{P}$ of processes, and a mapping $\ell : E \mapsto \mathcal{P}$ that associates each event in E with a process. For each process P, the set $\ell^{-1}(P)$ is totally ordered by $<_P =<^M |_P$. The event set is partitioned as $E = S \cup R$, where S and R are the sets of send and receive events, respectively. Furthermore, $r : S \mapsto R$ is a bijective mapping that relates each send with a unique receive. We assume that a process cannot send a message to itself, i.e., for any $e \in S$ we have $\ell(e) \neq \ell(r(e))$.*

Set $e <_c f$ for every e, f such that $r(e) = f$. It is required that $<^M$ is equal to the transitive closure of $<_c \cup \bigcup_{P \in \mathcal{P}} <_P$. The relation $<^M$ is called the visual order *of the message sequence chart M.*

In practical systems, there is often no way to ensure that two messages from different processes arrive in the same order. This means that the visual order may provide more ordering over events that is achievable in practice. This issue can be tackled by introducing a weaker partial order, which only orders two events if they necessarily happen in that order in any execution. There are three classes of such events. First, it is clear that each send occurs before the corresponding receive. Second, a process can condition sending a message on sending or receiving some other messages. This means that each send event always happens after all send and receive events of the same process that precede it in the visual order. Finally, we assume that processes communicate through a fifo channel, which guarantees that any two messages sent by one process to another always arrive in the correct order. This set of requirements can be formalized as follows.

Definition 2. *Given a message sequence chart $M = (E, <, \mathcal{P}, \ell, S, R, r)$, its* causal order $\prec^M$ *is a transitive closure of the precedence relation $\prec_0^M$, where for two events $e, f \in E$ we have $e \prec_0^M f$ if one of the following conditions holds:*

- *e and f are a matching send-receive pair, i.e., $r(e) = f$;*
- *$\ell(e) = \ell(f) = P$, $e <_P f$, and $f \in S$;*

- $\ell(e) = \ell(f) = P$, $e, f \in R$, $r^{-1}(e) = e'$, $r^{-1}(f) = f'$, $\ell(e') = \ell(f') = P'$, and $e' <_{P'} f'$.

Let $\mathcal{L}(X)$ be the set of all linearizations (i.e., completions to total order) of a partial order X. Clearly, for any message sequence chart M, $e \prec^M f$ implies $e <^M f$; however, the converse does not hold. In other words, we have $\mathcal{L}(<^M) \subseteq \mathcal{L}(\prec^M)$. To simplify notation, we write $\mathcal{L}_<(M)$ instead of $\mathcal{L}(<^M)$ and $\mathcal{L}_\prec(M)$ instead of $\mathcal{L}(\prec^M)$.

Definition 3. *We say that a message sequence chart M contains a* race *condition if there are two events $e, f \in E$ such that $e <^M f$, but e, f are unordered by $\prec^M$.*

Intuitively, a race condition means that the causal order allows more executions than the visual order, i.e., by restricting our attention to scenarios prescribed by the visual order, we may miss some (unexpected) executions. This situation is illustrated in Figure 1: in each MSC, the order of the two receive events of the second process is specified by the visual order, but not by the causal order. Hence, it is desirable to have an algorithm that detects races.

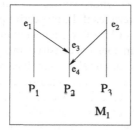 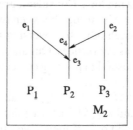

Fig. 1. Each of M_1, M_2 admits a race. In M_1, we have $e_3 <^{M_1} e_4$, but e_3 and e_4 are unordered by $\prec^{M_1}$. In M_2, we have $e_4 <^{M_2} e_3$, but e_3 and e_4 are unordered by $\prec^{M_2}$. However, taken together, M_1 and M_2 cover all possible executions.

An equivalent definition of a race is to say that the set of all linearizations of $<^M$ is strictly contained in the set of all linearizations of $\prec^M$. As we have $\mathcal{L}_<(M) \subseteq \mathcal{L}_\prec(M)$ for any M, it follows that M contains a race if and only if $\mathcal{L}_\prec(M) \neq \mathcal{L}_<(M)$. The advantage of this definition is that it is easier to generalize it to collections of MSCs, defined below.

3 Race Detection in Multiple MSCs

We start by introducing the notion of an *ensemble* of message sequence charts. Intuitively, it is a collection of several message sequence charts describing acceptable behaviors of the system. Consequently, the message sequence charts in an ensemble describe different partial orders (both visual and causal) on the same set of events.

Definition 4. *An ensemble of MSCs is a set $\mathbb{M} = \{M_1, \ldots, M_m\}$ such that*

- $E_1 = \cdots = E_m = E$;
- $\mathcal{P}_1 = \cdots = \mathcal{P}_m = \mathcal{P}$;

- *for any $e \in E$, it holds that $\ell_1(e) = \cdots = \ell_m(e) = \ell(e)$;*
- $S_1 = \cdots = S_m = S$, $R_1 = \cdots = R_m = R$;
- *for any $e \in S$, it holds that $r_1(e) = \cdots = r_m(e) = r(e)$.*

Remark 1. Note that in general the admissible executions may not share the same set (and type) of events, i.e., the MSCs given in the input do not necessarily form an ensemble. However, in this case one can easily decompose the input into a collection of ensembles. Therefore, checking ensembles rather than arbitrary collections of MSCs does not lead to a loss of generality.

For an ensemble $\mathbb{M} = \{M_1, \ldots, M_m\}$ of message sequence charts, we define $\mathcal{L}_<(\mathbb{M}) = \cup_{i=1,\ldots,m} \mathcal{L}_<(M_i)$, $\mathcal{L}_\prec(\mathbb{M}) = \cup_{i=1,\ldots,m} \mathcal{L}_\prec(M_i)$. Similarly to the case of a single message chart, we have $\mathcal{L}_<(\mathbb{M}) \subseteq \mathcal{L}_\prec(\mathbb{M})$. We say that there is a race if $\mathcal{L}_<(\mathbb{M}) \neq \mathcal{L}_\prec(\mathbb{M})$. It may be the case that each MSC in $\mathbb{M}$ is not race-free, but $\mathbb{M}$ is: for example, the two MSCs of Figure 1 form a race-free ensemble.

In the remainder of this section, we describe an algorithm that detect races in time polynomial in the total size of the message sequence charts in $\mathbb{M}$. Our approach is based on the following idea. Consider a graph G whose vertices are all permutations of events in E, and there is an edge between two vertices if the respective permutations can be obtained from each other by reversing the order of two adjacent events. Clearly, if $|E| = N$, then G has $N!$ vertices. Our algorithm does not construct this graph explicitly; however, it will be useful in proving correctness of our algorithm. It easy to see that each of the sets $\mathcal{L}_\prec(M_i)$, $\mathcal{L}_<(M_i)$, $i = 1, \ldots, m$, forms a connected subgraph of this graph. Note also that $\mathcal{L}_<(M_i) \subseteq \mathcal{L}_\prec(M_i)$ for all $i = 1, \ldots, m$. Moreover, if $M_i \neq M_j$, then the sets $\mathcal{L}_<(M_i)$ and $\mathcal{L}_<(M_j)$ are disjoint. To see this, note that the visual orders $<^{M_i}$ and $<^{M_j}$ differ if and only if they have different projections on some process line P_k, i.e., some events e_x and e_y with $\ell(e_x) = \ell(e_y) = P_k$ are ordered differently by $<^{M_i}$ and $<^{M_j}$. This means that for any $L_i \in \mathcal{L}_<(M_i)$ and $L_j \in \mathcal{L}_<(M_j)$ the events e_x and e_y will be ordered differently in L_i and L_j as well, i.e., $\mathcal{L}_<(M_i) \cap \mathcal{L}_<(M_j) = \emptyset$.

Proposition 1. *The ensemble $\mathbb{M}$ contains a race if and only if for some $i, j \in \{1, \ldots, m\}$ and a permutation L_1 the following conditions hold: (1) $L_1 \in \mathcal{L}_\prec(M_i)$; (2) L_1 is adjacent in G to some permutation $L_2 \in \mathcal{L}_<(M_j)$; (3) $L_1 \notin \mathcal{L}_<(\mathbb{M})$.*

Proof. Clearly, if $\mathbb{M}$ does not contain a race, no such i, j and L_1 can exist, as any permutation in $\mathcal{L}_\prec(M_i)$ will be contained in $\mathcal{L}_<(\mathbb{M})$.

For the opposite direction, suppose that $\mathbb{M}$ contains a race, that is, for some $i \in \{1, \ldots, m\}$ there is a permutation L such that $L \in \mathcal{L}_\prec(M_i)$, $L \notin \mathcal{L}_<(\mathbb{M})$. Consider the subgraph of G induced by $\mathcal{L}_<(\mathbb{M})$, and let $\hat{\mathcal{L}}$ be the maximal connected component of this subgraph that contains $\mathcal{L}_<(M_i)$. Clearly, we have $L \notin \hat{\mathcal{L}}$. On the other hand, as $\mathcal{L}_<(M_i) \subseteq \mathcal{L}_\prec(M_i)$, there is another permutation $L' \in \mathcal{L}_\prec(M_i)$ such that $L' \in \mathcal{L}_<(M_i) \subseteq \hat{\mathcal{L}}$. Since the set $\mathcal{L}_\prec(M_i)$ is connected, there is a path in G that stays within $\mathcal{L}_\prec(M_i)$ and leads from L to L'. The last vertex on this path is in $\hat{\mathcal{L}}$, while the first one is not. Therefore, there exist two adjacent vertices (i.e., permutations) L_1 and L_2 on this path such that (i) both L_1 and L_2 are in $\mathcal{L}_\prec(M_i)$ and (ii) L_2 is in $\hat{\mathcal{L}}$, while L_1 is not. Moreover, we have $L_2 \in \mathcal{L}_<(M_j) \subseteq \hat{\mathcal{L}}$ for some $j \in \{1, \ldots, m\}$. It remains to show that $L_1 \notin \mathcal{L}_<(M_k)$ for any $k = 1, \ldots, m$. For any k such that $\mathcal{L}_<(M_k) \subseteq \hat{\mathcal{L}}$, this holds since $L_1 \notin \hat{\mathcal{L}}$. Now, suppose $L_1 \in \mathcal{L}_<(M_k)$ for some k such that $\mathcal{L}_<(M_k) \not\subseteq \hat{\mathcal{L}}$. Then $\mathcal{L}_<(M_k)$ contains an element (i.e., L_1) that is adjacent to $\hat{\mathcal{L}}$. This means that the set $\hat{\mathcal{L}} \cup \mathcal{L}_<(M_k)$ is connected. However, $\hat{\mathcal{L}}$ was defined as the largest connected component of $\mathcal{L}_<(\mathbb{M})$ that contains $\mathcal{L}_<(M_i)$, a contradiction. ∎

Hence, to check for races, it is sufficient to verify if the condition of Proposition 1 holds. The straightforward approach of checking this condition for each linearization requires superpolynomial time. However, it turns out that we can partition candidate linearizations in a polynomial number of classes that correspond to certain partial orders, and check all linearizations in the same class simultaneously. Namely, consider the following algorithm DetectRace(M).

```
DetectRace(M);
forall M = M₁,...,Mₘ do
      forall P = P₁,...,Pₙ do
          K := |ℓ⁻¹(P)|;
          for j = 1,...,K − 1 do
              <′ₚ= Swap(M,P,j);
              <′ᴹ=<c ∪⋃ₚ′≠ₚ <ₚ′ ∪ <′ₚ;
              if PO(<′ᴹ) and Disjoint(<′ᴹ) then
                  forall N = M₁,...,Mₘ do
                      if PO(<′ᴹ ∪ ≺ᴺ) return true;
return false;
```

The function $\text{Swap}(M, P, j)$ returns the total order obtained from the order of the events that belong to process P in message sequence chart M by switching the order of the jth and the $(j + 1)$st event. The function $\text{PO}(X)$ checks if its input relation X is a partial order, i.e., contains no cycles. The function $\text{Disjoint}(<'^M)$ checks that the set of linearizations of $<'^M$ is disjoint from $\mathcal{L}_<(\mathbb{M})$; its implementation is given below. All other functions are straightforward to implement.

```
Disjoint(<′ᴹ);
forall N = M₁,...,Mₘ do
      forall P = P₁,...,Pₙ do
          if <′ᴹₚ≠<ᴺₚ break;
      return false;
return true;
```

In words, for each message sequence chart $M \in \{M_1, \ldots, M_m\}$, we consider the visual orders of all MSCs that can be obtained from M by switching the order of two consecutive events of some process. For each MSC obtained in this way, we check if it is valid, i.e., contains no cycles, using the function PO. If this is indeed the case, we check whether the linearizations of this MSC are not contained in $\mathcal{L}_<(\mathbb{M})$ (function Disjoint), and whether the union of the visual order of this MSC with the causal order of some other MSC in $\mathbb{M}$ is a partial order. If both of these conditions hold, our algorithm returns true, which means that $\mathbb{M}$ contains a race.

The correctness of our algorithm is proved via a sequence of lemmas.

Lemma 1. *For any $i, j = 1, \ldots, m$ and any $L \in \mathcal{L}_{\prec}(M_i)$, if L is adjacent to some $L' \in \mathcal{L}_{<}(M_j)$ in G, then L can be obtained as a linearization of one of the partial orders $<'^{M_j}$ constructed by* DetectRace.

Proof. Consider a linearization $L \in \mathcal{L}_{\prec}(M_i) \setminus \mathcal{L}_{<}(M_j)$ that is adjacent to some $L' \in \mathcal{L}_{<}(M_j)$. Let e_x and e_y be the two events that are ordered differently in L and L'; assume without loss of generality that e_x precedes e_y in L'. If e_x and e_y are not ordered by $<^{M_j}$, then changing their order will result in another linearization of $<^{M_j}$. Hence, we assume that $e_x <^{M_j} e_y$.

By construction of the graph G, e_x and e_y have to be adjacent events in L'. Recall that in $<^{M_j}$ the event e_x has at most two immediate successors: $e_t = r(e_x)$ if $e_x \in S$, and the event e_z that immediately follows e_x on the same process line. Hence, $e_y \in \{e_z, e_t\}$. If $e_y = e_t$, i.e., e_x and e_y are a matching send–receive pair, then $e_x \prec^{M_i} e_y$; as $L \in \mathcal{L}_{\prec}(M_i)$, e_y cannot precede e_x in L. Hence, e_x and e_y are consecutive events of some process. Consequently, $L \in \mathcal{L}(<'^M)$ for $M = M_j$, $P = \ell(e_x) = \ell(e_y)$ and j equal to the position of e_x in $<_P$. ∎

Lemma 2. *For any $j = 1, \ldots, m$ and any partial order $<'^{M_j}$ constructed by the algorithm* DetectRace *such that* PO$(<'^{M_j})$ = true, *either the set of all linearizations of $<'^{M_j}$ is disjoint from $\mathcal{L}(\mathbb{M})$ or $<'^{M_j} = <^{M_i}$ for some $i = 1, \ldots, m$.*

Proof. The partial order $<'^{M_j}$ is obtained from $<^{M_j}$ by changing the order of two consecutive events of the same process. Hence, $<'^{M_j}$ also provides a total ordering on the events of each process. If some other $M_i \in \mathbb{M}$ has the same projections on all process lines, then by definition we have $<'^{M_j} = <^{M_i}$. Otherwise, for each $M_i \in \mathbb{M}$ there is a pair of events ordered differently by $<'^{M_j}$ and $<^{M_i}$. In this case, the sets $\mathcal{L}(<'^{M_j})$ and $\mathcal{L}_{<}(M_i)$ are disjoint. ∎

Lemma 3. *For any two partial orders X and Y on the same set of events, we have $\mathcal{L}(X) \cap \mathcal{L}(Y) \neq \emptyset$ if and only if $X \cup Y$ is a partial order.*

Proof. If $X \cup Y$ is a partial order, we have $\mathcal{L}(X \cup Y) \neq \emptyset$. As $\mathcal{L}(X \cup Y) \subseteq \mathcal{L}(X) \cap \mathcal{L}(Y)$, we have $\mathcal{L}(X) \cap \mathcal{L}(Y) \neq \emptyset$.

Conversely, if $X \cup Y$ is not acyclic, assume for the sake of contradiction that $\mathcal{L}(X) \cap \mathcal{L}(Y) \neq \emptyset$ and let L be a linearization in $\mathcal{L}(X) \cap \mathcal{L}(Y)$. Consider some cycle $\mathcal{C} = \{(e_1, e_2), \ldots, (e_{t-1}, e_t), (e_t, e_1)\}$ in $X \cup Y$; there are two events e and f such that $(e, f) \in \mathcal{C}$, but f precedes e in L. Clearly, either $(e, f) \in X$, in which case $L \notin \mathcal{L}(X)$, or $(e, f) \in Y$, in which case $L \notin \mathcal{L}(Y)$. Hence, $L \notin \mathcal{L}(X) \cap \mathcal{L}(Y)$, a contradiction. ∎

Theorem 1. *The algorithm* DetectRace$(\mathbb{M})$ *returns* true *if and only if $\mathbb{M}$ admits a race. Moreover,* DetectRace$(\mathbb{M})$ *runs in time $O(m^2|E|^3)$, where $|E|$ is the number of events in any MSC in $\mathbb{M}$ and m is the number of message sequence charts in $\mathbb{M}$.*

Proof. By Proposition 1, detecting a race is equivalent to finding a permutation that satisfies conditions (1)–(3) in the statement of Proposition 1. By Lemma 1, for each $j = 1, \ldots, m$, the algorithm DetectRace$(\mathbb{M})$ considers all linearizations that lie in the 1-neighborhood of $\mathcal{L}_{<}(M^j)$. By Lemma 2, the function Disjoint correctly decides if any of these linearizations is not covered by $\mathcal{L}(\mathbb{M})$. Finally, by Lemma 3, the last loop correctly determines if any of them can be a linearization of some causal order $\prec^{M_i}$, $i = 1, \ldots, m$. Hence, our algorithm never fails to detect a race. Conversely, DetectRace($\mathbb{M}$) returns true only if it finds a linearization that lies in some $\prec^{M_i}$, $i = 1, \ldots, m$, but is not contained in $\mathcal{L}_<(\mathbb{M})$.

It remains to analyze the running time of our algorithm. For each triple M, P, j, we call PO once to check if $<'^M$ is acyclic, call Disjoint to compare $<'^M$ with all MSCs in $\mathbb{M}$, and then for each MSC in $\mathbb{M}$ compute a union of two partial orders and use PO again to check if it is acyclic. The function PO is based on computing the transitive closure. As each event has at most two immediate successors, the transitive closure computation can be done in time $O(|E|^2)$ [2]. Comparing the visual orders of two MSCs can be done in time $|E|$. Hence, we use $O(m|E|^2)$ operations for each triple M, P, j. As our algorithm only attempts to permute events that are adjacent on some process line for some MSC, we only consider $m|E|$ such triples. Hence, the running time of DetectRace is $O(m^2|E|^3)$, i.e., cubic in the size of the input. ∎

4 Number of MSCs Needed for Closedness

In the previous section, we give an algorithm that checks whether an ensemble of message sequence charts contains a race. Our algorithm is polynomial in the representation size of the ensemble, that is, the number of events and the number of MSCs in the ensemble. In this section, we investigate the relationship between these two parameters.

Two processes. Consider a message sequence chart M_2 given in Figure 2. It consists of two processes P_1 and P_2 and $n = 4k$ events $e_1, \ldots, e_n$, and describes the scenario when each process sends k messages to the other one, independently of the information it receives. Clearly, the causal order of M_2 induces a total order on all send events of each process. Because of the fifo assumption it also induces a total order on all receive events of the same process. However, the sends and receives of each process can be interleaved in an arbitrary way.

Theorem 2. *For any ensemble $\mathbb{M}$ that contains M_2, if $\mathbb{M}$ is race-free, then $\mathbb{M}$ contains $2^{\Omega(n)}$ message sequence charts.*

Proof. Recall that for any linearization L of $\prec^{M_2}$, its projection onto P_1 is a total order on the events $e_1, \ldots, e_k, e_{2k+1}, \ldots, e_{3k}$. Consider a collection of indices $I =$

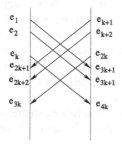
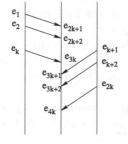
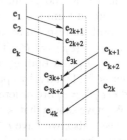

Fig. 2. An MSC with 2 processes whose causal order corresponds to $2^{\Omega(n)}$ visual orders

Fig. 3. An MSC with 3 processes whose causal order corresponds to $2^{\Omega(n)}$ visual orders

Fig. 4. A race-free MSC with a coregion of type 2

$\{i_1, \ldots, i_k\}$, where $1 \le i_1 < \cdots < i_k \le 2k$. We claim that for any such I, there exists a linearization L_I of $\prec^{M_2}$ such that its projection onto P_1 has the jth receive event of P_1, i.e., e_{2k+j}, in the i_jth position. Indeed, we can construct L_I by putting all send events of P_2 first, followed by all events of P_1, where the jth receive event of P_1 is in the position $k + i_j$, followed by all receive events of P_2. Formally, it can be described as a permutation $L_I = (e'_1, \ldots, e'_{4k})$ of the events in E such that for $i = 1, \ldots, k$ we have $e'_i = e_{k+i}$, $e'_{3k+i} = e_{3k+i}$, and for $i, \ldots, 2k$ we have $e'_{k+i} = e_{2k+j}$ if and only if $i = i_j \in I$, and the remaining events in $\{e'_{k+1}, \ldots, e'_{3k}\}$ are events from $\{e_1, \ldots, e_k\}$, ordered so that e_i precedes e_j whenever $1 \le i < j \le k$.

Now, consider any ensemble $\mathbb{M}$ that contains M_2. The visual order of any MSC in $\mathbb{M}$ provides a total order on the events of P_1. Hence, for $\mathbb{M}$ to be race-free, for each set I of the form described above, it has to contain an MSC whose visual order of the events in P_1 is the same as the one given by L_I: otherwise, L_I is not contained in $\mathcal{L}_<(\mathbb{M})$. There are $\binom{2k}{k} = \Theta(2^{2k}/\sqrt{k})$ ways to choose the set I. Hence, to be race-free, $\mathbb{M}$ has to contain at least $\Theta(2^{2k}/\sqrt{k}) = 2^{\Omega(n)}$ message sequence charts. ∎

The proof of Theorem 2 depends on a subtle property of our definition of causal order. Namely, for two events $x \in R$, $y \in S$, $\ell(x) = \ell(y) = P$, we assume that if x precedes y in the visual order, then the same is true for the causal order. However, if x *follows* y in the visual order, we do not require that they are ordered in the causal order (they may still be ordered, of course, because of their causal relationships with other events). An alternative definition of causal order requires that two events are ordered in the causal order whenever they belong to the same process and at least one of them is a send event. In other words, two $x, y \in E$ such that $\ell(x) = \ell(y)$ may be unordered by the causal order only if $x, y \in R$. Of course, we still require the other properties of the causal order, i.e., ordering a send and the corresponding receive, and fifo. It is easy to see that under this definition of causal order, the argument of Theorem 2 no longer applies. Moreover, it turns out that in this case, any message sequence chart with at most two processes is race-free.

Proposition 2. *For any message sequence chart M that contains exactly two processes P_1 and P_2, we have $<^M \equiv \prec'^M$, where $\prec'$ is the variation of causal order defined above.*

Proof. Consider two events e_i and e_j of P_1 (the argument for P_2 is identical). If one of them is a send event, then, by definition, they are ordered in $\prec'^M$. Now, suppose that both of them are receive events and e_i precedes e_j in the visual order $<^M$. Then they both correspond to messages sent by P_2, i.e., $r^{-1}(e_i) = e_{i'}$, $r^{-1}(e_j) = e_{j'}$, and $\ell(e_{i'}) = \ell(e_{j'}) = P_2$. The visual order has to obey the fifo property, i.e., we have $e_{i'} <_{P_2} e_{j'}$. As both $e_{i'}$ and $e_{j'}$ are send events, they are also ordered in the causal order $\prec'^M$. Finally, by applying the fifo property to $\prec'^M$, we conclude that $r(e_{i'}) = e_i$ and $e(e_{j'}) = e_j$ are ordered in $\prec'^M$.

We have shown that $\prec'^M$ imposes an order on any two events that belong to the same process. Also, we have $e \prec'^M r(e)$ for an $e \in S$. It follows that $\prec'^M$ and $<^M$ order exactly the same events, i.e., $<^M \equiv \prec'^M$. ∎

Three processes. We will now show that with three processes we may need an exponential number of message sequence charts to avoid race conditions, even for the modified definition of causal order $\prec'$.

Theorem 3. *For any ensemble* $\mathbb{M}$ *that contains the MSC* M_3 *given in Figure 3, if* $\mathbb{M}$ *is race-free, then* $\mathbb{M}$ *contains* $2^{\Omega(n)}$ *message sequence charts.*

The proof of this theorem is similar to that of Theorem 2 and is omitted. It relies on the number of possible orderings of the events of the second process. As all of them are receive events, it does not depend on which version of the causal order we use.

5 MSCs with Coregions

One can represent admissible orderings of events more compactly using *coregions*. A coregion is a notational primitive that covers two or more events. To the best of our knowledge, this paper is the first attempt to provide a formal analysis of the succinctness of this notation. Intuitively, by putting events in a coregion we say that they can happen in any order. There are several ways to formalize this intuition, depending on what classes of events are allowed to appear in the same coregion.

Coregions that do not affect the causal order. The most restrictive approach is to only allow events not ordered by the causal order within a coregion.

Definition 5. *Given a MSC* M *on a set of processes* $\mathcal{P} = \{P_1, \ldots, P_n\}$, *a coregion of type 1 for* M *is a set of events* $C = \{e_1, \ldots, e_k\}$ *such that* $e_1, \ldots, e_k$ *are consecutive events of some process* $P_i \in \mathcal{P}$ *and no two events in* C *are ordered by* $\prec^M$. *The causal order* $\prec^{(M,C)}$ *of the pair* (M, C) *is the same as the causal order of* M. *To describe the visual order* $<^{(M,C)}$ *of the pair* (M, C), *we define the relation* $<'_{P_i} = <_{P_i} \setminus \{(e_x, e_y) \mid e_x, e_y \in C\}$ *and let* $<^{(M,C)}$ *be the partial order induced by the relation* $<_c \cup \bigcup_{j \neq i} <_{P_j} \cup <'_{P_i}$.

This definition can be extended to a message sequence chart with several coregions $C_1, \ldots, C_t$ in an obvious way. Namely, each coregion is required to consist of consecutive events of some process, and the visual order of the resulting message sequence chart is obtained from the original one by deleting all pairs (e_x, e_y) such that both e_x and e_y appear in the same coregion. We do not require that all coregions of a particular MSC are disjoint. We will sometimes abuse notation and use M to denote an MSC with one or more coregions. Also, we may refer to an MSC with coregions simply as an MSC. The exact meaning will always be clear from the context.

It is easy to see that this construction can be used to decrease the number of MSCs needed to avoid a race by exponential factor. An obvious example is provided by an MSC with $n + 1$ processes $P_0, P_1, \ldots, P_n$, in which each of $P_1, \ldots, P_n$ sends a single message to P_0. In the absence of coregions, the visual order of P_0 imposes a total order on all n receive events, while the causal order allows for any ordering of them. Hence, we need $n!$ message sequence charts to avoid races, one for each possible permutation of the receive events. On the other hand, if we are allowed to use coregions, we can simply put all receive events inside a coregion, thus covering all linearizations admitted by the causal order. The savings are not limited to MSCs with unbounded number of processes: one can construct an example in which using coregions leads to an exponentially more compact race-free ensemble for three processes.

Unfortunately, the more compact representation has a computational cost. Namely, in Section 6 we show that for ensembles of MSCs with coregions detecting races becomes

NP-hard. This result holds even if in all MSCs in the ensemble each process has at most two coregions, all coregions are of type 1, and coregions of any process do not overlap.

Coregions that may affect the causal order. In some settings, the requirement that all events in a coregion are not ordered by the causal order can be too restrictive. To increase the expressive power, we can use coregions to also express indifference about the causal order of certain events. For example, we may want to say that given two messages m_1 and m_2 from P_1 to P_2 and P_1 to P_3, respectively, it does not matter in which order they are sent. To capture this meaning, we eliminate the restriction that all events in a coregion must be independent with respect to $\prec$.

Definition 6. *Given a MSC M on a set of processes $\mathcal{P} = \{P_1, \ldots, P_n\}$, a coregion of type 2 for M is a set of events $C = \{e_1, \ldots, e_k\}$ such that $e_1, \ldots, e_k$ are consecutive events of some $P_i \in \mathcal{P}$.*

However, it turns out that for this definition of coregion, we cannot describe the set of all linearizations implied by an MSC by a single partial order.

Example 1. Consider an MSC that corresponds to one process sending two messages to another one. Formally, we set $M = (E, <^M, \mathcal{P}, \ell, S, R, r)$, where $S = \{s_1, s_2\}$, $R = \{r_1, r_2\}$, $E = S \cup R$, $\mathcal{P} = \{P_1, P_2\}$, $\ell(s_1) = \ell(s_2) = P_1$, $\ell(r_1) = \ell(r_2) = P_2$. Suppose that we would like to use coregions to express that the messages can be sent in any order. A natural way to do this is to set $<_{P_1} = (s_1, s_2)$, $<_{P_2} = (r_1, r_2)$, $C_1 = \{s_1, s_2\}$, $C_2 = \{r_1, r_2\}$. Because of the fifo rule, the set $\mathcal{L}$ of all linearizations that correspond to the causal order of this MSC consists of 4 elements, namely $L_1 = (s_1, s_2, r_1, r_2)$, $L_2 = (s_1, r_1, s_2, r_2)$, $L_3 = (s_2, s_1, r_2, r_1)$, and $L_4 = (s_2, r_2, s_1, r_1)$. We will now show that this set of linearizations cannot correspond to a single partial order. For the sake of contradiction, suppose that there is a partial order X with this set of linearizations. Clearly, if for some $e, f \in E$, e precedes f in some $L_i \in \mathcal{L}$, then $(f, e) \notin X$. This allows us to derive $(s_i, s_j) \notin X$, $(r_i, r_j) \notin X$, $(r_i, s_j) \notin X$ for any $i, j = 1, 2$, and also $(s_2, r_1) \notin X$, $(s_1, r_2) \notin X$. Hence, X can contain at most two elements, namely, (s_1, r_1) and (s_2, r_2). But then (s_1, s_2, r_2, r_1) would be a linearization of X, which is a contradiction.

Note also that, in contrast to the case of MSCs with coregions of type 1, the set L is not connected.

Consequently, the definition of the set of all linearizations of an MSC with coregions of type 2 is more complicated than that for a simple MSC.

Definition 7. *Given a message sequence chart M and a collection $C_1, \ldots, C_t$ of coregions of type 2 for M, let $\mathbb{M}$ be the ensemble of all valid message sequence charts that can be obtained from M by permuting the events in each of the coregions arbitrarily. Let $\mathcal{L}_{\prec}(M, C_1, \ldots, C_t)$ denote the set of all linearizations of the causal order of $(M, C_1, \ldots, C_t)$, and let $\mathcal{L}_{<}(M, C_1, \ldots, C_t)$ denote the set of all linearizations of the visual order of $(M, C_1, \ldots, C_t)$. We define $\mathcal{L}_{\prec}(M, C_1, \ldots, C_t) = \mathcal{L}_{\prec}(\mathbb{M})$, $\mathcal{L}_{<}(M, C_1, \ldots, C_t) = \mathcal{L}_{<}(\mathbb{M})$.*

One can verify that the informal argument in Example 1 is consistent with Definition 7, i.e., the set $\mathcal{L} = \{L_1, L_2, L_3, L_4\}$ is exactly the set of all linearizations that correspond to $\mathcal{L}_{\prec}(M, C_1, C_2)$. Moreover, for an MSC that only contains coregions of type 1, the two definitions result in the same set of linearizations, both for causal and for visual order. We will say that an MSC M with coregions $C_1, \ldots, C_t$ *captures* an ordinary MSC M' if $M' \in \mathbb{M}$, where $\mathbb{M}$ is the ensemble of message sequence charts constructed from M as in Definition 7.

By generalizing Example 1 to the case when P_1 sends n messages to P_2, we can see that, compared to MSCs with coregions of type 1, using coregions of type 2 may result in exponentially smaller race-free ensembles. Indeed, one can represent this scenario by a single race-free MSC and two coregions of type 2: one for all send events, and one for all receive events. On the other hand, an ensemble of MSCs with coregions of type 1 needs $n!$ MSCs to be race-free. Another example is given by MSC in Figure 4, which is obtained from the MSC in Theorem 3 by putting all events of P_2 in a coregion. This MSC is race-free; however, some of the events inside the coregion are ordered because of the fifo rule, so we cannot use a coregion of type 1. Nevertheless, the worst-case complexity of race detection is the same in both cases: in the next section, we show that race detection is NP-complete for ensembles of MSCs with coregions of both types.

6   Hardness Results

Formally, an instance of the problem of race detection is given by an ensemble $\mathbb{M}$ whose elements are MSCs with coregions, i.e., each element of $\mathbb{M}$ is a list of the form $(M, C_1, \ldots, C_t)$, where M is a message sequence chart, and each C_i, $i = 1, \ldots, t$, is a coregion for M. We say that $\mathbb{M}$ is a "yes"-instance if and only if it admits a race.

Theorem 4. *The problem of race detection in ensembles of MSCs with coregions is NP-complete, even if each MSC in the ensemble only has coregions of type 1, each process has at most two coregions, and no two coregions can overlap.*

Proof. It is easy to see that this problem is in NP for coregions of both types: given an ensemble $\mathbb{M}$, a candidate linearization L and an MSC $M_i \in \mathbb{M}$, we can check that $L \in \mathcal{L}_{\prec}(M_i)$ and $L \notin \mathcal{L}_{<}(M_j)$ for all $M_j \in \mathbb{M}$.

For the opposite direction, the proof is by reduction from HAMILTONIAN PATH problem. Recall that an instance of HAMILTONIAN PATH is given by a graph $G = (V, E)$, $|V| = n$. It is considered to be a "yes"-instance if and only if it contains a simple path of length $n - 1$, i.e., there is an ordering $v_{i_1}, \ldots, v_{i_n}$ of the elements of V such that $(v_{i_j}, v_{i_{j+1}}) \in E$ for all $j = 1, \ldots, n - 1$.

Given an instance $G = (V, E)$ of HAMILTONIAN PATH, we construct an ensemble $\mathbb{M}$ of MSCs that corresponds to it. Consider an MSC M_0 that contains $2n + 1$ processes, which are partitioned into two sets $\mathcal{P}_1 = \{P_0, \ldots, P_n\}$ and $\mathcal{P}_2 = \{P_v \mid v \in V\}$. Intuitively, M_0 describes the scenario where each of the processes in $\mathcal{P}_1$ sends a single message to each process in $\mathcal{P}_2$. Formally, we set $S = \{s_i^v\}_{i=0,\ldots,n,v \in V}$, $R = \{r_i^v\}_{i=0,\ldots,n,v \in V}$, $\mathcal{P} = \mathcal{P}_1 \cup \mathcal{P}_2$. Also, for all $i = 0, \ldots, n, v \in V$ we define $r(s_i^v) = r_i^v, \ell(s_i^v) = P_i, \ell(r_i^v) = P_v$. Fix an ordering $<^V$ on the vertices of V. In M_0, all events of each process are ordered lexicographically, i.e., for any $P_i \in \mathcal{P}_1$ we have $s_i^u <_{P_i} s_i^v$ if and only if $u <^V v$ and for any $P_v \in \mathcal{P}_2$ we have $r_i^v <_{P_v} r_j^v$ if and only if $i < j$. We will now construct an ensemble $\mathbb{M}$ that contains M_0. By definition, each $M \in \mathbb{M}$ has the same set of processes, the same sets of send and receive events, and the same mappings r and ℓ as M_0. We will also require that all $M \in \mathbb{M}$ order events in

S in exactly the same way as M_0. Hence, to fully specify each $M \in \mathbb{M}$, we will only have to describe the order of the receive events for each process. Note that the causal order of M_0 imposes no restrictions on the relative order of the receives of any process. Hence, for $\mathbb{M}$ to be race-free, the linearizations of the visual orders of MSCs in $\mathbb{M}$ must cover all possible permutations of the receives.

To simplify notation, when describing the ordering of events on P_v, we will write i instead of r_i^v for $i = 1, \ldots, n$ and $\#$ instead of r_0^v. Consider a MSC M_{HP} that satisfies the following three conditions:

(1) for any $P_v \in \mathcal{P}_2$, there exists some $i \in \{1, \ldots, n\}$ such that the ordering of the receives on P_v is $(1, \ldots, i, \#, i+1, \ldots, n)$. This value of i is denoted by $i(v)$;
(2) for all $v \neq w \in V$, $i(v) \neq i(w)$;
(3) for any $v \in V$ such that $i(v) \neq n$, there exists an edge $(v, w) \in E$ such that $i(w) = i(v) + 1$.

Intuitively, M_{HP} describes a Hamiltonian path ρ in G: a vertex v is the ith vertex on ρ if $i(v) = i$. As $|V| = n$, conditions (1) and (2) imply that for any $i \leq n$, there exists a unique vertex v_i such that $i(v_i) = i$, and condition (3) means that for every $i < n$, (v_i, v_{i+1}) is an edge. Hence, $\rho = v_1 \cdots v_n$ is a Hamiltonian path. Therefore, if M_{HP} exists, then G has a Hamiltonian path; clearly, the converse is also true. We will now construct a polynomial ensemble $\mathbb{M}'$ of MSCs with coregions that captures all MSCs that violate at least one of the conditions (1), (2), or (3). Set $\mathbb{M} = \mathbb{M}' \cup \{M_0\}$; a race condition in $\mathbb{M}$ is equivalent to the existence of an MSC M_{HP} satisfying (1), (2) and (3), and hence to the existence of a Hamiltonian path in G.

The ensemble $\mathbb{M}'$ consists of three classes of MSCs with coregions: *bad order* MSCs (ones that capture MSCs that violate condition (1)), *no path* MSCs (ones that capture MSCs that violate condition (2)), and *bad path* MSCs (ones that capture MSCs that violate condition (3)).

Consider a message sequence chart that violates condition (1) for some P_v. If the first event of P_v is $\#$, then this MSC can be captured by a message sequence chart $M_{v,\#}$. In this MSC P_v starts with $\#$, followed by a coregion containing all other events of P_v in arbitrary order. For each P_w, $w \neq v$, the events of P_w are ordered arbitrarily, and there is a coregion that covers all of them. If P_v does not start with $\#$, let k be the first position in which the visual order of P_v deviates from the form prescribed by condition (1). As all events j, $j < k$, appear in their prescribed positions, the event in the position k must be l, $l > k$. We consider two cases, namely, $k \leq i(v)$ and $k > i(v)$.

All MSCs that violate condition (1) for P_v with $k \leq i(v)$ and event l in the kth position are captured by a message sequence chart $M_{(v,k,l)}^-$ defined as follows. For all P_w, $w \neq v$, the events of P_w are ordered arbitrarily, and there is a coregion that covers all of them. Moreover, the ordering of the first k events of P_v is $(1, \ldots, k-1, l)$, followed by all other events (including $\#$) in arbitrary order, and there is a coregion that consists of all events that appear after l.

Similarly, all MSCs that violate condition (1) for P_v with $k > i(v)$ and event l in the kth position are captured by a message sequence chart $M_{(v,k,l)}^+$ defined as follows. For all P_w, $w \neq v$, the events of P_w are ordered arbitrarily, and there is a coregion that covers all of them. The ordering of the first $k + 1$ events of P_v is $(1, \ldots, k - 1, \#, l)$, followed by all other events in arbitrary order. Also, there are two coregions for P_v: one that consists of all events that appear before l (including $\#$), and another one that consists of all events that appear after l. Observe that $M^+_{(v,k,l)}$ may also capture some MSCs where the first violation of condition (1) happens before k; nevertheless, all MSCs covered by $M^+_{(v,k,l)}$ violate condition (1) for P_v in position k.

Now, consider an MSC that satisfies condition (1), but violates condition (2). This happens if there are two vertices u and w such that $\#$ appears in the same position k in P_u and P_v. Hence, all such MSCs can be captured by n^3 *no path* MSCs $(M_{(u,v,k)})_{u\neq v\in V, k\leq n}$, defined as follows. In any $M_{(u,v,k)}$, for all P_w, $w \neq u,v$, the events of P_w are ordered arbitrarily, and there is a coregion that covers all of them. Furthermore, the events of P_u and P_v are ordered as $(1,\dots,k,\#,k+1,\dots,n)$.

Finally, we need to cover all MSCs that satisfy conditions (1) and (2), but violate condition (3). This happens if there is a pair of vertices $u,v \in V$ such that $(u,v) \notin E$, $i(u) = k$, $i(v) = k+1$. All such MSCs can be captured by at most n^3 *bad path* MSCs $(N_{(u,v,k)})_{(u,v)\notin E, k<n}$, defined as follows. In any $N_{(u,v,k)}$, for all P_w, $w \neq u,v$, the events of P_w are ordered arbitrarily, and there is a coregion that covers all of them. Furthermore, the events of P_u are ordered as $(1,\dots,k,\#,k+1,\cdots,n)$, and the events of P_v are ordered as $(1,\dots,k,k+1,\#,k+2,\cdots,n)$. Set

$$\mathbb{M}' = \bigcup_{v\in V} M_{v,\#} \cup \bigcup_{\substack{v\in V \\ k\neq l\leq n}} M^-_{(v,k,l)} \cup \bigcup_{\substack{v\in V \\ k\neq l\leq n}} M^+_{(v,k,l)} \cup \bigcup_{\substack{u\neq v\in V \\ k\leq n}} M_{(u,v,k)} \cup \bigcup_{\substack{(u,v)\notin E \\ k<n}} N_{(u,v,k)}.$$

Recall that $\mathbb{M} = \mathbb{M}' \cup \{M_0\}$, and observe that M_0 violates condition (1). The causal order of any $M \in \mathbb{M}$ is $\prec^{M_0}$, i.e., it puts no restrictions on the relative ordering of different receive events. For any MSCs M whose visual order violates (1), (2), or (3), there is an MSC M' in $\mathbb{M}$ (with or without coregions) such that $\mathcal{L}_<(M) \subseteq \mathcal{L}_<(M')$. On the other hand, any $M \in \mathbb{M}$ violates at least one of the conditions (1), (2), and (3).

Now, suppose that G contains a Hamiltonian path. Then there exists an MSC M_{HP} described above, which satisfies all three conditions. The set $\mathcal{L}_<(M_{HP})$ is not covered by $\mathcal{L}_<(\mathbb{M})$, i.e., there is a race. Conversely, suppose that G contains no Hamiltonian path, and let L be an arbitrary linearization of $\prec^{M_0}$. Consider the MSC M_L that is obtained by projecting L onto processes in $\mathcal{P}$. This MSC violates one of the conditions (1), (2), or (3), so we have $\mathcal{L}_<(M_L) \subseteq \mathcal{L}_<(\mathbb{M})$. As $L \in \mathcal{L}_<(M_L)$, the result follows. ∎

7 Conclusions

The MSC notation is important in describing scenarios of protocols. Its analysis allows one to detect common design errors. One of the most basic problems in MSCs is that of race conditions; the occurrence of events in an order that is different from the order of their appearance in the MSC. Race conditions are defined for a single MSC as the discrepancies between the visual order between events as they appear in the MSC, and the causal order, which takes into account only the order that is under the control of the system (e.g., excluding the order between receives from different processes). Equivalently, this can be defined as the discrepancy between the corresponding sets of linearizations. This relationship between partial orders and linearizations allows us to extend the problem beyond checking a single MSC. The classical algorithm for MSCs was described in [2] and was implemented in the uBET system. For a graph of MSCs (HMSC), this problem was shown to be undecidable [15].

In this paper we studied MSC ensembles, i.e., collections of MSCs for the same set of messages. In this case, a race in a single MSC of the ensemble may be compensated by another MSC with a different order of events. We describe a polynomial algorithm for race detection, which extends the algorithm of [2]. On the other hand, the existence of a polynomial algorithm can be attributed to the fact that a race-free ensemble of MSCs may need to have an exponential (in the number of events) number of MSCs.

We also studied the *coregion* construct, a part of the standard which has not been formally treated before. It allows encapsulating events (sends, receives) of a process within a box, denoting the lack of any particular order between the events in the box. We showed that by using this construct, one may achieve an exponential reduction in the size of race-free ensembles; however, race detection becomes NP-complete.

References

1. R. Alur, K. Etessami, and M. Yannakakis, Inference of message sequence charts. IEEE Transactions on Software Engineering, July 2003, Volume 29, 623–633
2. R. Alur, G. Holzmann, and D. Peled, An analyzer for message sequence charts. In *Software Concepts and Tools*, 17(2):70–77, 1996
3. R. Alur and M. Yannakakis, Model checking of message sequence charts. In *Proc. of CONCUR'99*, LNCS 1664, Springer, 114–129, 1999
4. H. Ben-Abdulla and S. Leue, Symbolic detection of process divergence and non-local choice in message sequence charts. In *Proc. of TACAS'97*, LNCS 1217, Springer, 259–274, 1997
5. W. Damm, D. Harel, LSCs: breathing life into message sequence charts. Formal Methods in System Design, Volume 19, July 2001, 45–80
6. L. Hélouët and C. Jard, Conditions for synthesis of communicating automata from HMSCs. In *5th International Workshop on Formal Methods for Industrial Critical Systems*, 2000
7. G. Holzmann, D. Peled, M. Redberg, Design tools for requirements engineering. Bell Labs Technical Journal, volume 2, 86–95, 1997
8. ITU-T Recommendation Z.120, Message Sequence Chart (MSC), Geneva, 1996
9. I. Krueger, Distributed system design with message sequence charts. Ph.D. Thesis, TU Munchen, 2000.
10. D. Kuske, Regular sets of infinite message sequence charts. *Information and Computation*, (187):80–109, 2003
11. M. Lohrey. Safe realizability of high-level message sequence charts. In *Proc. of CONCUR'02*, LNCS 2421, Springer-Verlag, 177–192, 2002
12. P. Madhusudan, Reasoning about sequential and branching behaviours of message sequence graphs. In *Proc. of ICALP'01*, LNCS 2076, Springer-Verlag, 809–820, 2001
13. M. Mukund, K. Narayan Kumar, and M. Sohoni, Synthesizing distributed finite-state systems from MSCs. In *Proc. of CONCUR'00*, LNCS 1877, Springer-Verlag, 521–535, 2000
14. A. Muscholl and D. Peled, Message sequence graphs and decision problems on Mazurkiewicz traces. In *Proc. of MFCS'99*, LNCS 1672, Springer-Verlag, 81–91, 1999
15. A. Muscholl, D. Peled, and Z. Su, Deciding properties of message sequence charts. In *Proc. of FoSSaCS'98*, LNCS 1378, Springer-Verlag, 226–242, 1998
16. B. Sengupta and R. Cleaveland, Triggered message sequence charts. *TSE* , IEEE, 2006.

Replaying Play In and Play Out: Synthesis of Design Models from Scenarios by Learning

Benedikt Bollig[1], Joost-Pieter Katoen[2], Carsten Kern[2], and Martin Leucker[3]

[1] LSV, CNRS UMR 8643 & ENS de Cachan, France
[2] Software Modeling and Verification Group, RWTH Aachen University, Germany
[3] Institut für Informatik, TU München, Germany

Abstract. This paper is concerned with bridging the gap between requirements, provided as a set of scenarios, and conforming design models. The novel aspect of our approach is to exploit *learning* for the synthesis of design models. In particular, we present a procedure that infers a message-passing automaton (MPA) from a given set of positive and negative scenarios of the system's behavior provided as message sequence charts (MSCs). The paper investigates which classes of regular MSC languages and corresponding MPA can (not) be learned, and presents a dedicated tool based on the learning library *LearnLib* that supports our approach.

1 Introduction

The elicitation of requirements is the main initial phase in the typical software engineering development cycle. A plethora of elicitation techniques for requirement engineering exist. Popular requirement engineering methods, such as the Inquiry Cycle and CREWS [26], exploit use cases and scenarios to specify the system's requirements. Sequence diagrams are also at the heart of the UML. A scenario is a partial fragment of the system's behavior, describing the system components, their message exchange and concurrency. Their intuitive yet formal nature has resulted in a broad acceptance. Scenarios can be positive or negative, indicating a desired or unwanted system behavior, respectively. Different scenarios together form a more complete description of the system behavior.

The following design phase in software engineering is a major challenge as it is concerned with a paradigm shift between the *requirement* specification—a partial, overlapping and possibly inconsistent description of the system's behavior—and a conforming *design model*, a complete behavioral description of the system (at a high level of abstraction). During the synthesis of design models, usually automata-based models that are focused on intra-agent communication, conflicting requirements will be detected and need to be resolved. Typical resulting changes to requirements specifications include adding or deleting scenarios, and fixing errors that are found by a thorough analysis (e.g., model checking) of the design model. Obtaining a complete and consistent set of requirements together with a related design model is thus a highly iterative process.

This paper proposes a novel technique that is aimed to be an important stepping stone towards bridging the gap between scenario-based requirement specifications and design models. The novel aspect of our approach is to exploit *learning* algorithms for the synthesis of *distributed* design models from scenario-based specifications. Since

O. Grumberg and M. Huth (Eds.): TACAS 2007, LNCS 4424, pp. 435–450, 2007.
© Springer-Verlag Berlin Heidelberg 2007

message-passing automata (MPA, for short) [10] are a commonly used model to realize the behavior as described by scenarios, we adopt MPA as design model. We present a procedure that interactively infers an MPA from a given set of positive and negative scenarios of the system's behavior provided as message sequence charts (MSCs). This is achieved by generalizing Angluin's learning algorithm for deterministic finite-state automata (DFA) [4] towards specific classes of bounded MPA, i.e., MPA that can be used to realize MSCs with channels of finite capacity. An important distinctive aspect of our approach is that it naturally supports the *incremental generation* of design models. Learning of initial sets of scenarios is feasible. On adding or deletion of scenarios, MPA are adapted accordingly in an automated manner. Thus, synthesis phases and analysis phases, supported by simulation or analysis tools such as *MSCan* [7], complement each other in a natural fashion. Furthermore, on establishing the inconsistency of a set of scenarios, our approach mechanically provides *diagnostic feedback* (in the form of a counterexample) that can guide the engineer to evolve his requirements. This paper investigates which classes of regular MSC languages and corresponding MPA can (not) be learned, and presents *Smyle*, a dedicated tool based on the learning library *LearnLib* [27] that supports our approach.

Generating automata-based models from scenarios has received a lot of attention. These works include algorithms to generate statechart models from MSCs [19], formalization and undecidability results for the synthesis for a simple variant of live sequence charts (LSCs) [9], and Harel's play-in, play-out approach for LSCs [11,12]. Another approach is proposed by Alur *et al.* in [2,3]. Uchitel *et al.* [29] present an algorithm for synthesizing transition systems from high-level MSCs. An executable variant of LSCs, triggered MSCs, are presented in [28]. All approaches are based on a rather complete, well-elaborated specification of the system to be, such as MSCs with loops or conditions, high-level MSCs, triggered MSCs, or LSCs, whereas for our synthesis approach only simple MSCs have to be provided as examples, simplifying the requirements specification task.

Applying learning yields an incremental approach, and facilitates the generation of diagnostic feedback. An alternative approach to using learning for inferring design models from UML sequence diagrams has been proposed in [23]. This approach focuses on learning DFA (from words) representing the global system and only considers synchronous communication. The use of learning for model-based testing in [18] has similar characteristics. Using our technique, collections of MSCs (in fact, partial orders or words with partial commutation) are learned and yield an MPA that explicitly reflects the composite structure of the system together with the asynchronous message exchange between the individual components.

After an introduction into MSCs and MPA (Sections 2 and 3), we formally define the general learning setting and describe the extension of Angluin's learning algorithm, cf. Section 4. We then consider existentially and universally bounded MPA, i.e., MPA for which some (all) possible event orderings can be realized with finite channels. It is shown (in Section 5) that universally bounded MPA and safe product MPA, as well as existentially bounded MPA with an a priori fixed channel capacity are learnable. Section 6 presents the basic functionality of our tool and some initial case study results.

2 Message Sequence Charts

Let Σ^* denote the set of finite words over a finite alphabet Σ. A Σ-*labeled partial order* is a triple $\mathcal{P} = (E, \leq, \ell)$ where E is a finite set, $\leq$ is a partial-order relation on E, i.e., it is reflexive, transitive, and antisymmetric, and $\ell : E \rightarrow \Sigma$ is a *labeling function*. A *linearization* of $\mathcal{P}$ is an extension $(E, \leq', \ell)$ of $\mathcal{P} = (E, \leq, \ell)$ such that $\leq' \supseteq \leq$ is a total order. As we will consider partial orders up to isomorphism, the set of linearizations of $\mathcal{P}$, denoted $Lin(\mathcal{P})$, is a subset of Σ^*.

We fix a finite set *Proc* of at least two *processes*, which exchange messages from a finite set *Msg* by executing communication actions. Let *Ch* denote the set $\{(p, q) \mid p, q \in Proc, p \neq q\}$ of reliable FIFO *channels*. For $p \in Proc$, Act_p denotes the set of actions of p, i.e., $\{!(p, q, a) \mid (p, q) \in Ch$ and $a \in Msg\} \cup \{?(p, q, a) \mid (p, q) \in Ch$ and $a \in Msg\}$. The action $!(p, q, a)$ is to be read as "p sends the message a to q", while $?(q, p, a)$ is the complementary action of receiving a sent from p to q (which is thus executed by q). Moreover, let $Act = \bigcup_{p \in Proc} Act_p$.

Definition 1 (Message Sequence Chart (MSC)). *An MSC (over Proc and Msg) is a structure $(E, \{\leq_p\}_{p \in Proc}, <_{\mathrm{msg}}, \ell)$ with:*

- *E is a finite set of events,*
- *$\ell : E \rightarrow Act$ is a labeling function,*
- *for any $p \in Proc$, $\leq_p$ is a total order on $E_p = \ell^{-1}(Act_p)$,*
- *$<_{\mathrm{msg}} \subseteq E \times E$ such that, for any $e \in E$, $e <_{\mathrm{msg}} e'$ or $e' <_{\mathrm{msg}} e$ for some $e' \in E$, and, for any $(e_1, e_1') \in <_{\mathrm{msg}}$, there are $p, q \in Proc$ and $a \in Msg$ satisfying:*
  - *$\ell(e_1) = !(p, q, a)$ and $\ell(e_1') = ?(q, p, a)$,*
  - *for any $(e_2, e_2') \in <_{\mathrm{msg}}$ with $\ell(e_2) = !(p, q, b)$ for some $b \in Msg$: $e_1 \leq_p e_2$ iff $e_1' \leq_q e_2'$ (which guarantees FIFO behavior), and*
  - *$\leq = (<_{\mathrm{msg}} \cup \bigcup_{p \in Proc} \leq_p)^*$ is a partial-order relation on E.*

Let $M = (E, \{\leq_p\}_{p \in Proc}, <_{\mathrm{msg}}, \ell)$ be an MSC. A *prefix* of M is a structure $(E', \{\leq_p'\}_{p \in Proc}, <_{\mathrm{msg}}', \ell')$ such that $E' \subseteq E$ with $e \in E'$ and $e' \leq e$ implies $e' \in E'$, $\leq_p' = \leq_p \cap (E' \times E')$ for any $p \in Proc$, $<_{\mathrm{msg}}' = <_{\mathrm{msg}} \cap (E' \times E')$, and ℓ' is the restriction of ℓ to E'. We write $P \preceq M$ if P is a prefix of the MSC M.

The set of MSCs is denoted by $\mathbb{MSC}$. A set of MSCs, $\mathcal{L} \subseteq \mathbb{MSC}$, is called an *MSC language*. For $\mathcal{L} \subseteq \mathbb{MSC}$, we let $Pref(\mathcal{L})$ denote $\{P \mid P \preceq M$ for some $M \in \mathcal{L}\}$ (a similar notation will be used in the context of words). Note that $\mathbb{MSC} \subseteq Pref(\mathbb{MSC})$.

Let $M = (E, \{\leq_p\}_{p \in Proc}, <_{\mathrm{msg}}, \ell) \in \mathbb{MSC}$. We set $Lin(M)$ to be $Lin((E, \leq, \ell))$ (canonically extended for prefixes of M); the linearizations of $\mathcal{L} \subseteq \mathbb{MSC}$ are defined by $Lin(\mathcal{L}) = \bigcup_{M \in \mathcal{L}} Lin(M)$. Note that $\mathcal{L} \subseteq \mathbb{MSC}$ is uniquely determined by $Lin(\mathcal{L})$, i.e., for any $\mathcal{L}, \mathcal{L}' \subseteq \mathbb{MSC}$, $Lin(\mathcal{L}) = Lin(\mathcal{L}')$ implies $\mathcal{L} = \mathcal{L}'$. A word $w \in Act^*$ is an *MSC word* if $w \in Lin(M)$ for some $M \in \mathbb{MSC}$; for $B \in \mathbb{N}$, w is *B-bounded* if, for any prefix v of w and any $(p, q) \in Ch$, $\sum_{a \in Msg} |v|_{!(p,q,a)} - \sum_{a \in Msg} |v|_{?(q,p,a)} \leq B$ where $|v|_\sigma$ denotes the number of occurrences of σ in v. For $B \in \mathbb{N}$, let $Lin^B(M)$ denote $\{w \in Lin(M) \mid w$ is B-bounded$\}$, and $Lin^B(\mathcal{L}) = \bigcup_{M \in \mathcal{L}} Lin^B(M)$ for $\mathcal{L} \subseteq \mathbb{MSC}$.

Definition 2 (Boundedness). *Let $M \in \mathbb{MSC}$. We call M universally B-bounded (i.e., $\forall B$-bounded) if $Lin(M) = Lin^B(M)$. We call it* existentially B-bounded *(i.e., $\exists B$-bounded) if $Lin(M) \cap Lin^B(M) \neq \emptyset$.*

The sets of $\forall B$-bounded MSCs and $\exists B$-bounded MSCs are denoted by $\mathsf{MSC}_{\forall B}$ and $\mathsf{MSC}_{\exists B}$, respectively. In an $\exists B$-bounded MSC, the events can be scheduled such that, during its execution, any channel contains at most B messages. In a $\forall B$-bounded MSC, any scheduling is within the channel bound B. A set $\mathcal{L} \subseteq \mathsf{MSC}$ is $\forall B$-bounded if $\mathcal{L} \subseteq \mathsf{MSC}_{\forall B}$, and $\exists B$-bounded if $\mathcal{L} \subseteq \mathsf{MSC}_{\exists B}$. It is is $\forall$-/$\exists$-bounded if it is $\forall B$-/$\exists B$-bounded for some $B \in \mathbb{N}$, respectively.

Example 1. The MSC word $w = \,!(1, 2, \mathsf{req})\,(!(1, 2, \mathsf{req})\,?(2, 1, \mathsf{req}))^4\,?(2, 1, \mathsf{req})$ is in $Lin(M)$ with M the MSC from Fig. 1c. Note that w is 2-bounded, but not 1-bounded. But M has a 1-bounded linearization, and $Lin^1(M) = \{(!(1, 2, \mathsf{req})\,?(2, 1, \mathsf{req}))^5\}$. In fact, M is $\exists 1$-bounded and $\forall B$-bounded for $B \geq 5$. The MSC in Fig. 1a is $\forall 4$-bounded and thus $\exists 4$- bounded. It is even $\exists 2$-bounded, but not $\exists 1$-bounded. The MSC in Fig. 1b is $\forall 3$-and $\exists 1$-bounded, but not $\forall 2$-bounded. Finally, we note that the set of MSCs where arbitrarily many messages are sent from 1 to 2 is $\exists 1$-bounded, but not $\forall$-bounded.

3   Message-Passing Automata

An MPA [10] is a collection of finite automata (called processes) that share a single global initial state and a set of global final states. Bilateral communication between the processes takes place via unbounded reliable FIFO buffers. Process transitions are labeled with send or receive actions. Action $!(p, q, a)$ puts the message a at the end of the channel from p to q. Receive actions are enabled only if the requested message is found at the head of the channel. The expressive power of MPA is extended by allowing components to exchange *synchronization messages*.

Definition 3 (Message-passing automaton (MPA)). *An MPA is a tuple* $((\mathcal{A}_p)_{p\in Proc}, Sync, \overline{s}^{in}, F)$ *with:*

- *Sync is a nonempty finite set of* synchronization messages,
- *for each* $p \in Proc$, $\mathcal{A}_p$ *is a pair* (S_p, Δ_p) *where* S_p *is a finite set of* local states *and* $\Delta_p \subseteq S_p \times Act_p \times Sync \times S_p$ *is a set of* local transitions,
- $\overline{s}^{in} \in S_{\mathcal{A}} = \prod_{p\in Proc} S_p$ *is the* global initial state, *and*
- $F \subseteq S_{\mathcal{A}}$ *is a set of* global final states.

As in [17,24], we consider the linearizations of MSCs that are obtained from the global automaton induced by an MPA. For an MPA $\mathcal{A} = ((\mathcal{A}_p)_{p\in Proc}, Sync, \overline{s}^{in}, F)$, where $\mathcal{A}_p = (S_p, \Delta_p)$, this global automaton is defined as follows. The set of *configurations* of $\mathcal{A}$, denoted by $Conf_{\mathcal{A}}$, consists of pairs $(\overline{s}, \chi)$ with $\overline{s} \in S_{\mathcal{A}}$ and $\chi : Ch \rightarrow (Msg \times Sync)^*$, indicating the channel contents. The *global transition relation* of $\mathcal{A}$, $\Longrightarrow_{\mathcal{A}} \subseteq Conf_{\mathcal{A}} \times Act \times Sync \times Conf_{\mathcal{A}}$, is defined by the following two inference rules ($\overline{s}[p]$ refers to the p-component of a global state $\overline{s} \in S_{\mathcal{A}}$):

$$\frac{(\overline{s}[p], !(p, q, a), m, \overline{s}'[p]) \in \Delta_p \quad \wedge \quad \text{for all } r \neq p, \overline{s}[r] = \overline{s}'[r]}{((\overline{s}, \chi), !(p, q, a), m, (\overline{s}', \chi')) \in \Longrightarrow_{\mathcal{A}}}$$

where $\chi' = \chi[(p, q) := (a, m) \cdot \chi((p, q))]$, i.e., χ' maps (p, q) to the concatenation of (a, m) and $\chi((p, q))$; for all other channels, it coincides with χ.

$$\frac{(\overline{s}[p], ?(p, q, a), m, \overline{s}'[p]) \in \Delta_p \quad \wedge \quad \text{for all } r \neq p, \overline{s}[r] = \overline{s}'[r]}{((\overline{s}, \chi), ?(p, q, a), m, (\overline{s}', \chi')) \in \Longrightarrow_{\mathcal{A}}}$$

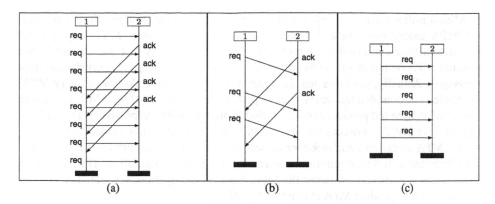

Fig. 1. Example message sequence charts

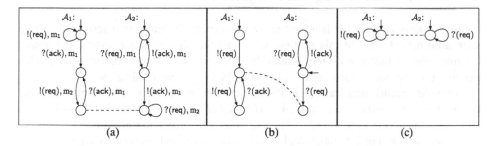

Fig. 2. Example message-passing automata

where $\chi((q,p)) = w \cdot (a,m)$ and $\chi' = \chi[(q,p) := w]$. The initial and final configurations of the global automaton are $(\overline{s}^{in}, \chi_\varepsilon)$ and $F \times \{\chi_\varepsilon\}$, respectively, where χ_ε maps each channel onto the empty word.

Now MPA $\mathcal{A}$ defines the word language $L(\mathcal{A}) \subseteq Act^*$, i.e., the set of words accepted by the global automaton of $\mathcal{A}$ while ignoring synchronization messages. The MSC language of $\mathcal{A}$, denoted by $\mathcal{L}(\mathcal{A})$, is the (unique) set $\mathcal{L}$ of MSCs such that we have $Lin(\mathcal{L}) = L(\mathcal{A})$. The notions of boundedness on MSCs carry over to MPA in a natural way, e.g., MPA $\mathcal{A}$ is $\forall$-bounded if its MSC language is $\forall$-bounded. The set of $\forall$-bounded and $\exists B$-bounded MPA is denoted by $MPA_\forall$ and $MPA_{\exists B}$, respectively.

Example 2. Fig. 2a shows a not $\exists$-bounded MPA with set of synchronization messages $\{m_1, m_2\}$ (and simplified action alphabet). Its only global final state is indicated by a dashed line. Its MSC language, which contains MSCs such as in Fig. 1a, cannot be recognized with less than two synchronization messages. For the MPA in Fig. 2b, specifying a part of the alternating-bit protocol (ABP), a single synchronization message suffices (which is therefore omitted). It is $\forall 3$-bounded (cf. Fig. 1b). The MPA in Fig. 2c has no synchronization messages either. Its accepted MSCs are as in Fig. 1c and form an $\exists 1$-bounded MSC language that, however, is not $\forall$-bounded.

An MPA $\mathcal{A} = ((\mathcal{A}_p)_{p \in Proc}, Sync, \overline{s}^{in}, F)$, with $\mathcal{A}_p = (S_p, \Delta_p)$, is a *product MPA* if $|Sync| = 1$ and $F = \prod_{p \in Proc} F_p$ for some $F_p \subseteq S_p$, $p \in Proc$. The acceptance condition is thus *local*, i.e., any process autonomously decides to halt. Moreover, product MPA cannot distinguish between synchronization messages. MSC languages of product MPA are referred to as *realizable* [24,21]. The MPA in Figs. 2b and 2c are product MPA, whereas the MPA in Fig. 2a is not, as it employs two synchronization messages. Actually, the latter has no equivalent product MPA. As for ordinary MPA, the notions of boundedness carry over to product MPA; let $\text{MPA}_\forall^p$ and $\text{MPA}_{\exists B}^p$ denote the set of $\forall$-bounded product and $\exists B$-bounded product MPA, respectively. The MPA in Fig. 2b is in $\text{MPA}_\forall^p$, whereas the MPA in Fig. 2c is in $\text{MPA}_{\exists 1}^p$, but not in $\text{MPA}_\forall^p$.

An MPA is called *deadlock-free* or *safe* if, from any configuration that is reachable from the initial configuration, one can reach a final configuration. The MPA from Figs. 2b and 2c are safe, whereas the MPA depicted in Fig. 2a is not safe. The class of $\forall$-bounded safe product MPA is denoted by $\text{MPA}_\forall^{sp}$.

4   An Extension of Angluin's Algorithm

Angluin's algorithm L^* [4] is a well-known algorithm for learning deterministic finite state automata (DFA). In this section, we recall the algorithm and extend it towards learning objects that can be *represented* by DFA in a way made precise shortly. This extension allows us to learn various classes of MPA, as described below.

Let us first recall some basic definitions. Let Σ be an alphabet. A deterministic finite automaton (DFA) over Σ is a tuple $\mathcal{A} = (Q, q_0, \delta, F)$, where Q is its finite set of *states*, $q_0 \in Q$ is the *initial state*, $\delta : Q \times \Sigma \to Q$ is its *transition function*, and $F \subseteq Q$ is the set of *final states*. The language of $\mathcal{A}$ is defined as usual and denoted by $L(\mathcal{A})$.

4.1   The Basic Algorithm

A *Learner*, who initially knows nothing about a given DFA $\mathcal{A}$, is trying to learn $\mathcal{A}$ by asking queries to a *Teacher*, who knows $\mathcal{A}$. There are two kinds of queries:

- A *membership query* consists in asking whether a string $w \in \Sigma^*$ is in $L(\mathcal{A})$.
- An *equivalence query* consists in asking whether a *hypothesized* DFA $\mathcal{H}$ is correct, i.e., whether $L(\mathcal{H}) = L(\mathcal{A})$. The *Teacher* will answer *yes* if $\mathcal{H}$ is correct, or else supply a counterexample w, either in $L(\mathcal{A}) \setminus L(\mathcal{H})$ or in $L(\mathcal{H}) \setminus L(\mathcal{A})$.

The *Learner* maintains a prefix-closed set $U \subseteq \Sigma^*$ of prefixes, which are candidates for identifying states, and a suffix-closed set $V \subseteq \Sigma^*$ of suffixes, which are used to distinguish such states. The sets U and V are increased when needed during the algorithm. The *Learner* makes membership queries for all words in $(U \cup U\Sigma)V$, and organizes the results into a *table* T which maps each $u \in (U \cup U\Sigma)$ to a mapping $T(u) : V \to \{+, -\}$ where $+$ represents accepted and $-$ not accepted. In [4], each function $T(u)$ is called a *row*. When T is

- *closed*: for any $u \in U$ and $a \in \Sigma$, there is a $u' \in U$ with $T(ua) = T(u')$, and
- *consistent*: for any $u, u' \in U$ and $a \in \Sigma$, $T(u) = T(u')$ implies $T(ua) = T(u'a)$,

the *Learner* constructs a hypothesized DFA $\mathcal{H} = (Q, q_0, \delta, Q^+)$, where $Q = \{T(u) \mid u \in U\}$ is the set of distinct rows, q_0 is the row $T(\varepsilon)$ (with ε denoting the empty word),

δ is defined by $\delta(T(u), a) = T(ua)$, and $Q^+ = \{T(u) \mid u \in U$ and $T(u)(\varepsilon) = +\}$. After that, the *Learner* submits $\mathcal{H}$ in an equivalence query. If the answer is *yes*, the learning procedure is completed, otherwise the returned counterexample is used to extend U and V, and subsequent membership queries are performed until arriving at a new hypothesized DFA.

4.2   Learning Objects Represented by Subclasses of Regular Word Languages

Our goal is to learn MPA from examples given as MSCs. To avail Angluin's algorithm, we need to establish a correspondence between MPA and regular word languages. As we will consider several classes of MPA with corresponding representations in the next section, let us first elaborate on general properties of representations for learning *objects* of a fixed arbitrary set of objects $\mathcal{O}$. These objects might be classified into equivalence classes of an equivalence relation $\sim \, \subseteq \mathcal{O} \times \mathcal{O}$. In our setting, the objects will be MPA, and two MPA are considered to be equivalent if they recognize the same MSC language.

We now have to *represent* elements from $\mathcal{O}$ (or, rather, their equivalence classes) by regular word languages, say over an alphabet Σ. For MPA $\mathcal{A}$, we might consider regular languages L over Act such that L corresponds to the set $Lin(\mathcal{L}(\mathcal{A}))$. But not every regular word language over Act gives rise to an MPA. In particular, it might contain words that are not MSC words, i.e., do not correspond to some MSC. Thus, in general, it is necessary to work within a subset $\mathcal{D}$ of Σ^*, i.e., we learn regular subsets of $\mathcal{D}$. For learning MPA, e.g., it is reasonable to set $\mathcal{D} = Lin(\mathbb{MSC})$.

It is not always sufficient to restrict to $\mathcal{D}$ in order to obtain a precise correspondence between $\mathcal{O}$ and regular word languages. Often, regular word languages are required to be closed under some *equivalence relation* and/or *inference rule*. E.g., an MPA always gives rise to an MSC word language that contains either any linearization of some given MSC, or none. Similarly, languages of product MPA are closed under inference (to be made precise later) imposing similar requirements on the representing language. So let us consider an equivalence relation $\approx \, \subseteq \mathcal{D} \times \mathcal{D}$ and, moreover, a relation $\vdash \, \subseteq 2^{\mathcal{D}} \times 2^{\Sigma^*}$ where $L_1 \vdash L_2$ intuitively means that L_1 still requires at least one element from L_2.

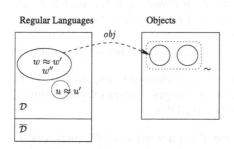

Fig. 3. Representing objects by regular languages

We say that $L \subseteq \mathcal{D}$ is $\approx$-*closed* (or, closed under $\approx$) if, for any $w, w' \in \mathcal{D}$ with $w \approx w'$, we have $w \in L$ iff $w' \in L$. Moreover, L is said to be $\vdash$-*closed* (or, closed under $\vdash$) if, for any $(L_1, L_2) \in \, \vdash$, we have that $L_1 \subseteq L$ implies $L \cap L_2 \neq \emptyset$.[1] Consider Fig. 3. The larger ellipse is closed under $\approx$ ($w \approx w'$) and under $\vdash$ (assuming $\{w, w'\} \vdash \{w''\}$), whereas the smaller circle is not.

Naturally, $\mathcal{D}$, $\approx$, and $\vdash$ determine a particular class $\mathfrak{R}_{\text{minDFA}}(\Sigma, \mathcal{D}, \approx, \vdash) = \{L \subseteq \mathcal{D} \mid L$ is regular and closed under both $\approx$

---

[1] Technically, $\approx$ and $\vdash$ could be encoded as a single relation. As they will serve a different purpose, we separate them in the general framework, to simplify the forthcoming explanations.

and ⊢} of regular word languages over Σ (where any language is understood to be given by its minimal DFA). Suppose a language of this class $\mathfrak{R}_{\mathrm{minDFA}}(\Sigma, \mathcal{D}, \approx, \vdash)$ can be learned in some sense that will be made precise. For learning elements of $\mathcal{O}$, we still need to derive an object from a language in $\mathfrak{R}_{\mathrm{minDFA}}(\Sigma, \mathcal{D}, \approx, \vdash)$. To this aim, we suppose a computable bijective mapping $obj : \mathfrak{R}_{\mathrm{minDFA}}(\Sigma, \mathcal{D}, \approx, \vdash) \to [\mathcal{O}]_\sim = \{[o]_\sim \mid o \in \mathcal{O}\}$ (where $[o]_\sim = \{o' \in \mathcal{O} \mid o' \sim o\}$). Again, Fig. 3 illustrates a typical situation.

As Angluin's algorithm works within the class of arbitrary DFA over Σ, its *Learner* might propose DFA whose languages are neither a subset of $\mathcal{D}$ nor satisfy the closure properties for $\approx$ and $\vdash$. To rule out and fix such hypotheses, the language inclusion problem and the closure properties in question are required to be *constructively decidable*, meaning that they are decidable and if the property fails, a *reason* of its failure can be computed. Now, let us formally define what we understand by a *learning setup*:

Definition 4. *Let $\mathcal{O}$ be a set of* objects *and* $\sim \subseteq \mathcal{O} \times \mathcal{O}$ *be an equivalence relation. A* learning setup *for $(\mathcal{O}, \sim)$ is a quintuple $(\Sigma, \mathcal{D}, \approx, \vdash, obj)$ where*

- *Σ is an alphabet,*
- *$\mathcal{D} \subseteq \Sigma^*$ is the* domain,
- *$\approx \subseteq \mathcal{D} \times \mathcal{D}$ is an equivalence relation such that, for any $w \in \mathcal{D}$, $[w]_\approx$ is finite,*
- *$\vdash \subseteq 2^{\mathcal{D}} \times 2^{\Sigma^*}$ such that, for any $(L_1, L_2) \in \vdash$, L_1 is both finite and $\approx$-closed, and L_2 is a nonempty decidable language,*
- *$obj : \mathfrak{R}_{\mathrm{minDFA}}(\Sigma, \mathcal{D}, \approx, \vdash) \to [\mathcal{O}]_\sim$ is a bijective effective mapping in the sense that, for $L \in \mathfrak{R}_{\mathrm{minDFA}}(\Sigma, \mathcal{D}, \approx, \vdash)$, a representative of $obj(L)$ can be computed.*

Furthermore, we require that the following hold for DFA $\mathcal{A}$ over Σ:

(D1) *The problem whether $L(\mathcal{A}) \subseteq \mathcal{D}$ is decidable. If, moreover, $L(\mathcal{A}) \not\subseteq \mathcal{D}$, one can compute $w \in L(\mathcal{A}) \setminus \mathcal{D}$. We then say that* INCLUSION$(\Sigma, \mathcal{D})$ *is constructively decidable.*

(D2) *If $L(\mathcal{A}) \subseteq \mathcal{D}$, it is decidable whether $L(\mathcal{A})$ is $\approx$-closed. If not, one can compute $w, w' \in \mathcal{D}$ such that $w \approx w'$, $w \in L(\mathcal{A})$, and $w' \notin L(\mathcal{A})$. We then say that the problem* EQCLOSURE$(\Sigma, \mathcal{D}, \approx)$ *is constructively decidable.*

(D3) *If $L(\mathcal{A}) \subseteq \mathcal{D}$ is closed under $\approx$, it is decidable whether $L(\mathcal{A})$ is $\vdash$-closed. If not, we can compute $(L_1, L_2) \in \vdash$ (hereby, L_2 shall be given in terms of a decision algorithm that checks a word for membership) such that $L_1 \subseteq L(\mathcal{A})$ and $L(\mathcal{A}) \cap L_2 = \emptyset$. We then say that* INFCLOSURE$(\Sigma, \mathcal{D}, \approx, \vdash)$ *is constructively decidable.*

Let us generalize Angluin's algorithm to cope with the extended setting, and let $(\Sigma, \mathcal{D}, \approx, \vdash, obj)$ be a learning setup for $(\mathcal{O}, \sim)$. The main changes concern the processing of membership queries and the treatment of hypothesized DFA:

- Once a membership query has been processed for a word $w \in \mathcal{D}$, queries $w' \in [w]_\approx$ must be answered equivalently. They are thus not forwarded to the *Teacher* anymore. We might think of an *Assistant* in between the *Learner* and the *Teacher* that checks if an equivalent query has already been performed. Queries for $w \notin \mathcal{D}$ are not forwarded to the *Teacher* either but answered negatively by the *Assistant*.
- When the table T is both closed and consistent, the hypothesized DFA $\mathcal{H}$ is computed as usual. After this, we proceed as follows:

1. If $L(\mathcal{H}) \not\subseteq \mathcal{D}$, compute a word $w \in L(\mathcal{H}) \setminus \mathcal{D}$, declare it a counterexample, and modify the table T accordingly (possibly involving further membership queries).
2. If $L(\mathcal{H}) \subseteq \mathcal{D}$ but $L(\mathcal{H})$ is not $\approx$-closed, then compute $w, w' \in \mathcal{D}$ such that $w \approx w'$, $w \in L(\mathcal{H})$, and $w' \notin L(\mathcal{H})$; perform membership queries for $[w]_\approx$.
3. If $L(\mathcal{H})$ is the union of $\approx$-equivalence classes but not $\vdash$-closed, then compute $(L_1, L_2) \in \vdash$ such that $L_1 \subseteq L(\mathcal{H})$ and $L(\mathcal{H}) \cap L_2 = \emptyset$; perform membership queries for any word from L_1; if all these membership queries are answered positively, the *Teacher* is asked to specify a word w from L_2, which will be declared "positive".

Actually, a hypothesized DFA $\mathcal{H}$ undergoes an equivalence test only if $L(\mathcal{H}) \subseteq \mathcal{D}$ and $L(\mathcal{H})$ is both $\approx$- and $\vdash$-closed. I.e., if, in the context of the extended learning algorithm, we speak of a hypothesized DFA, we actually act on the assumption that $L(\mathcal{H})$ is the union of $\approx$-equivalence classes and closed under $\vdash$.

Let the extension of Angluin's algorithm wrt. a learning setup as sketched above be called EXTENDEDANGLUIN (its pseudo code can be found in [6]). A careful analysis shows:

Theorem 1. *Let* $(\Sigma, \mathcal{D}, \approx, \vdash, obj)$ *be a learning setup for* $(\mathcal{O}, \sim)$. *If* $o \in \mathcal{O}$ *has to be learned, then invoking* EXTENDEDANGLUIN$((\mathcal{O}, \sim), (\Sigma, \mathcal{D}, \approx, \vdash, obj))$ *returns, after finitely many steps[2], an object* $o' \in \mathcal{O}$ *such that* $o' \sim o$.

The theorem suggests the following definition:

Definition 5. *Let* $\mathcal{O}$ *be a set of* objects *and* $\sim \subseteq \mathcal{O} \times \mathcal{O}$ *be an equivalence relation. We say that* $(\mathcal{O}, \sim)$ *is* learnable *if there is some learning setup for* $(\mathcal{O}, \sim)$.

5 Learning Message-Passing Automata

This section identifies some learnable classes of MPA, i.e, regular word languages that can be learned and generated by an MPA. It seems unlikely to find a reasonable learning approach for arbitrary MPA, which is suggested by negative results from [8]. We therefore propose to consider ∃- and ∀-regular MSC languages and study learnability for the class of MPA and product MPA.

5.1 Regular MSC Languages and Product MSC Languages

A word language is said to represent an MSC language $\mathcal{L}$ whenever it contains a linearization for each $M \in \mathcal{L}$, and no linearizations for $M' \notin \mathcal{L}$. Formally:

Definition 6 (Representative). $L \subseteq Act^*$ *is a* representative *for* $\mathcal{L} \subseteq \mathsf{MSC}$ *if* $L \subseteq Lin(\mathcal{L})$ *and, for any MSC M,* $M \in \mathcal{L}$ *iff* $Lin(M) \cap L \neq \emptyset$.

---

[2] When learning a DFA over Σ with n states, the number of membership queries in the worst case is $\mathcal{O}(|\Sigma| \cdot n^3)$.

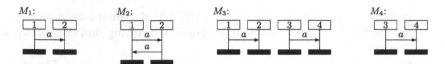

Fig. 4. Some MSCs

Example 3. Let $M_1 \cdot M_2$ denote the concatenation of MSCs M_1 and M_2, i.e., the unique MSC M such that $\{w_1 w_2 \mid w_1 \in Lin(M_1), w_2 \in Lin(M_2)\} \subseteq Lin(M)$. $\{M\}^*$ denotes the Kleene closure of $\cdot$. The MSC language $\{M_1\}^*$ for MSC M_1 in Fig. 4 is not regular in the sense of [17], as $Lin(\{M_1\}^*)$ is not a regular word language. However, $\{M_1\}^*$ can be represented by the regular word language $Lin^1(\{M_1\}^*) = \{(!(1,2,a) \ ?(2,1,a))^n \mid n \in \mathbb{N}\}$. Considering the MSC M_2 in Fig. 4, we even have that $Lin(\{M_2\}^*)$ is a regular representative for $\{M_2\}^*$.

The interesting case occurs when representatives are regular. But some MSC languages cannot be generated by MPA as their regular representatives require infinite channels.

Example 4. The $\exists 1$-bounded MSC language $\{M_3\}^*$ for MSC M_3 in Fig. 4 has the regular representative $\{(!(1,2,a) \ ?(2,1,a) \ !(3,4,a) \ ?(4,3,a))^n \mid n \in \mathbb{N}\}$, but there is no $B \in \mathbb{N}$ such that $Lin^B(\{M_3\}^*)$ is a regular representative for $\{M_3\}^*$. Thus, according to results from [16], it cannot be the language of some MPA.

Definition 7 (∀- and ∃-regular). $\mathcal{L} \subseteq \mathbb{MSC}$ is ∀-regular if $Lin(\mathcal{L}) \subseteq Act^*$ is regular. $\mathcal{L}$ is ∃-regular if, for some $B \in \mathbb{N}$, $Lin^B(\mathcal{L})$ is a regular representative for $\mathcal{L}$.

Any ∀-regular MSC language is ∀-bounded and any ∃-regular MSC language is ∃-bounded. Moreover, any ∀-regular MSC language is ∃-regular. An MPA is called ∀-regular, ∃-regular, etc., if so is its MSC language.

Example 5. The MPA in Fig. 2a is not ∃-regular, whereas the MPA in Fig. 2b is ∀-regular. In particular, only finitely many global configurations are reachable from the initial configuration. The MPA in Fig. 2c is ∃-regular, but not ∀-regular.

Regular MSC languages are of interest as they are realizable by MPA.

Theorem 2 ([16,17,20]). *Regular MSC languages versus bounded MPA:*

(a) *For any ∃-regular MSC language $\mathcal{L}$ (given as a regular representative), one can effectively compute an MPA $\mathcal{A}$ such that $\mathcal{L}(\mathcal{A}) = \mathcal{L}$. If $\mathcal{L}$ is ∀-regular, then $\mathcal{A}$ can be assumed to be deterministic.*
(b) *Let $B \in \mathbb{N}$. For $\mathcal{A} \in MPA_{\exists B}$, $Lin^B(\mathcal{L}(\mathcal{A}))$ is a regular representative for $\mathcal{L}(\mathcal{A})$ and $\mathcal{L}(\mathcal{A})$ is ∃-regular. For $\mathcal{A} \in MPA_\forall$, $Lin(\mathcal{L}(\mathcal{A}))$ is a regular representative for $\mathcal{L}(\mathcal{A})$ and $\mathcal{L}(\mathcal{A})$ is ∀-regular.*

A realization of $\{M_1, M_4\}$ (cf. Fig. 4) also infers M_3 provided the bilateral interaction between the processes is completely independent. A set of MSCs that is closed under such an inference is a *product* MSC language (it is called *weakly realizable* in [2]). For $M = (E, \{\leq_p\}_{p \in Proc}, <_{msg}, \ell) \in Pref(\mathbb{MSC})$, the behavior of M can be split into its components $M \upharpoonright p = (E_p, \leq_p, \ell_{|E_p})$, $p \in Proc$, each of which represents the behavior of a single agent, which can be seen as a word over Act_p. For finite set $\mathcal{L} \subseteq \mathbb{MSC}$ and $M \in \mathbb{MSC}$, let $\mathcal{L} \vdash^P_{MSC} M$ if, for any $p \in Proc$, there is $M' \in \mathcal{L}$ such that $M' \upharpoonright p = M \upharpoonright p$.

Definition 8 (Product MSC language [2]). $\mathcal{L} \subseteq \mathbb{MSC}$ *is a* product MSC language *if, for any $M \in \mathbb{MSC}$ and any finite $\mathcal{L}' \subseteq \mathcal{L}$, $\mathcal{L}' \vdash^P_{MSC} M$ implies $M \in \mathcal{L}$.*

For practical applications, it is desirable to consider so-called *safe* product languages. Those languages are implementable in terms of a safe product MPA, thus one that is deadlock-free. For a finite set $\mathcal{L} \subseteq \mathbb{MSC}$ and $P \in Pref(\mathbb{MSC})$, we write $\mathcal{L} \vdash^s_{MSC} P$ if, for any $p \in Proc$, there is $M \in \mathcal{L}$ such that $P \upharpoonright p$ is a prefix of $M \upharpoonright p$.

Definition 9 (Safe product MSC language [2]). *A product MSC language $\mathcal{L} \subseteq \mathbb{MSC}$ is called* safe *if, for any finite $\mathcal{L}' \subseteq \mathcal{L}$ and any $P \in Pref(\mathbb{MSC})$, $\mathcal{L}' \vdash^s_{MSC} P$ implies $P \preceq M$ for some $M \in \mathcal{L}$.*

Lemma 1 ([21], cf. [2,3]). $\mathcal{L} \subseteq \mathbb{MSC}$ *is a $\forall$-regular safe product MSC language (given in terms of $Lin(\mathcal{L})$) iff it is accepted by some $\mathcal{A} \in \text{MPA}^{sp}_\forall$. Both directions are effective.*

5.2   Learning $\forall$-Bounded Message-Passing Automata

Towards a learning setup for $\forall$-bounded MPA, we let

- $\sim_\forall - \{(\mathcal{A}, \mathcal{A}') \in \text{MPA}_\forall \times \text{MPA}_\forall \mid \mathcal{L}(\mathcal{A}) - \mathcal{L}(\mathcal{A}')\}$,
- $\approx_{MW} = \{(w, w') \in Lin(M) \times Lin(M) \mid M \in \mathbb{MSC}\}$, and
- $obj_\forall : \mathfrak{R}_{minDFA}(Act, Lin(\mathbb{MSC}), \approx_{MW}, \emptyset) \to [\text{MPA}_\forall]_{\sim_\forall}$ be an effective bijective mapping whose existence is stated by Theorem 2 *(a)*.

To prove that $(Act, Lin(\mathbb{MSC}), \approx_{MW}, \emptyset, obj_\forall)$ is indeed a learning setup for the pair $(\text{MPA}_\forall, \sim_\forall)$, we need to establish the corresponding decidability results.

Proposition 1. INCLUSION$(Act, Lin(\mathbb{MSC}))$ *and* EQCLOSURE$(Act, Lin(\mathbb{MSC}), \approx_{MW})$ *are constructively decidable.*

The decidability part stems from [17, Prop. 2.4] (see also [25]). The corresponding decision algorithm runs in time linear in the size of the transition function of the DFA. Counterexamples can be computed in linear time as well. For a detailed description, please consult [6]. Note that the question if the $\approx_{MW}$-closure of a regular set of MSC words is a regular language, too, is undecidable. For our learning approach, however, this problem does not play any role. For arbitrary finite automata $\mathcal{A}$ over Act with $L(\mathcal{A}) \subseteq Lin(\mathbb{MSC})$ (which are not necessarily deterministic), it was shown in [25] (for Büchi automata) that deciding if $L(\mathcal{A})$ is $\approx_{MW}$-closed is PSPACE complete. In our context of minimal DFA, however, the problem becomes much simpler.

Proposition 2. $(Act, Lin(\mathbb{MSC}), \approx_{MW}, \emptyset, obj_\forall)$ *is a learning setup for* $(\text{MPA}_\forall, \sim_\forall)$.

Theorem 3. $(\text{MPA}_\forall, \sim_\forall)$ *is learnable.*

5.3 Learning ∃-Bounded Message-Passing Automata

In this subsection, we are aiming at a learning setup for $\exists$-bounded MPA. As stated in Def. 7, we now have to provide a channel bound. So let $B \in \mathbb{N}$ and set

- $\sim_{\exists B} = \{(\mathcal{A}, \mathcal{A}') \in \mathrm{MPA}_{\exists B} \times \mathrm{MPA}_{\exists B} \mid \mathcal{L}(\mathcal{A}) = \mathcal{L}(\mathcal{A}')\}$,
- $\approx_{\exists B} = \{(w, w') \in Lin^B(M) \times Lin^B(M) \mid M \in \mathbb{MSC}\}$, and
- $obj_{\exists B} : \mathfrak{R}_{\mathrm{minDFA}}(Act, Lin^B(\mathbb{MSC}), \approx_{\exists B}, \emptyset) \to [\mathrm{MPA}_{\exists B}]_{\sim_{\exists B}}$ to be an effective bijective mapping whose existence is stated by Theorem 2.

In the following, we will see that $(Act, Lin^B(\mathbb{MSC}), \approx_{\exists B}, \emptyset, obj_{\exists B})$ is indeed a learning setup for $(\mathrm{MPA}_{\exists B}, \sim_{\exists B})$. Adapting Prop. 1, we can establish the corresponding decidability result (see [6] for the proof):

Proposition 3. *For any $B \in \mathbb{N}$, the problems* INCLUSION$(Act, Lin^B(\mathbb{MSC}))$ *and* EQCLOSURE$(Act, Lin^B(\mathbb{MSC}), \approx_{\exists B})$ *are constructively decidable.*

Proposition 4. *For any $B \in \mathbb{N}$, $(Act, Lin^B(\mathbb{MSC}), \approx_{\exists B}, \emptyset, obj_{\exists B})$ is a learning setup for* $(\mathrm{MPA}_{\exists B}, \sim_{\exists B})$.

Theorem 4. *For any $B \in \mathbb{N}$, $(\mathrm{MPA}_{\exists B}, \sim_{\exists B})$ is learnable.*

5.4 Learning ∀-Bounded Safe Product Message-Passing Automata

Let us set the scene for learning $\forall$-bounded safe product MPA. In this case, we have to create an inference rule $\vdash \neq \emptyset$ (cf. Definitions 8 and 9). We first define relations $\vdash^P_{\mathrm{MW}}$ and $\vdash^s_{\mathrm{MW}}$ for word languages, which correspond to $\vdash^P_{\mathrm{MSC}}$ and $\vdash^s_{\mathrm{MSC}}$, respectively:

- $\vdash^P_{\mathrm{MW}} = \{(Lin(\mathcal{L}), \{w\}) \mid \mathcal{L} \subseteq \mathbb{MSC}$ is finite and $\exists\, M \in \mathbb{MSC}: \mathcal{L} \vdash^P_{\mathrm{MSC}} M \wedge w \in Lin(M)\}$
- $\vdash^s_{\mathrm{MW}} = \{(Lin(\mathcal{L}), L_2) \mid \mathcal{L} \subseteq \mathbb{MSC}$ is finite and $\exists P \in Pref(\mathbb{MSC})$ and $u \in Lin(P)$ such that $\mathcal{L} \vdash^s_{\mathrm{MSC}} P$ and $L_2 = \{w \in Lin(\mathbb{MSC}) \mid w = uv$ for some $v \in Act^*\}\}$ (note that L_2 is a decidable language).

Given these relations, we can define our learning setup as follows:

- $\sim^{\mathrm{sp}}_{\forall} = \{(\mathcal{A}, \mathcal{A}') \in \mathrm{MPA}^{\mathrm{sp}}_{\forall} \times \mathrm{MPA}^{\mathrm{sp}}_{\forall} \mid \mathcal{L}(\mathcal{A}) = \mathcal{L}(\mathcal{A}')\}$,
- $\approx_{\mathrm{MW}} = \{(w, w') \in Lin(M) \times Lin(M) \mid M \in \mathbb{MSC}\}$ (as before),
- $\vdash^{\mathrm{sp}}_{\mathrm{MW}} = \vdash^P_{\mathrm{MW}} \cup \vdash^s_{\mathrm{MW}}$,
- $obj^{\mathrm{sp}}_{\forall} : \mathfrak{R}_{\mathrm{minDFA}}(Act, Lin(\mathbb{MSC}), \approx_{\mathrm{MW}}, \vdash^{\mathrm{sp}}_{\mathrm{MW}}) \to [\mathrm{MPA}^{\mathrm{sp}}_{\forall}]_{\sim^{\mathrm{sp}}_{\forall}}$ be an effective bijective mapping, as guaranteed by Lemma 1.

Proposition 5. INFCLOSURE$(Act, Lin(\mathbb{MSC}), \approx_{\mathrm{MW}}, \vdash^{\mathrm{sp}}_{\mathrm{MW}})$ *is constructively decidable.*

Proof. Decidability of INFCLOSURE$(Act, Lin(\mathbb{MSC}), \approx_{\mathrm{MW}}, \vdash^{\mathrm{sp}}_{\mathrm{MW}})$ has been shown in [3, Theorem 3], where an EXPSPACE-algorithm for bounded high-level MSCs is given, which reduces the problem to finite automata with a $\approx_{\mathrm{MW}}$-closed language. From such a $\approx_{\mathrm{MW}}$-closed DFA $\mathcal{H}$, we compute a (componentwise) minimal, reduced (i.e., without local sink states), and deterministic product MPA $\mathcal{A}$, by simply taking the projections of $\mathcal{H}$ onto Act_p for any $p \in Proc$, minimizing and determinizing them. Then, the MSC language $\mathcal{L}$ associated with $\mathcal{H}$ is a safe product language iff $\mathcal{A}$ is a safe product MPA realizing $\mathcal{L}$. From $\mathcal{H}$, we can moreover compute a bound B such that any run of $\mathcal{A}$ exceeding the buffer size B cannot correspond to a prefix of some MSC word in $L(\mathcal{H})$. Thus, a run through $\mathcal{A}$ (in terms of a prefix of an MSC word) that either

- exceeds the buffer size B (i.e., it is not B-bounded), or
- does not exceed the buffer size B, but results in a deadlock configuration

gives rise to a prefix u (of an MSC word) that is implied by $\mathcal{H}$ wrt. $\vdash^{s}_{MW}$, i.e., $L(\mathcal{H})$ must actually contain a completion $uv \in Lin(\mathsf{MSC})$ of u. Obviously, one can decide if a word is such a completion of u. The completions of u form one possible L_2. It remains to specify a corresponding set L_1 for u. By means of $\mathcal{H}$, we can, for any $p \in Proc$, compute a word $w_p \in L(\mathcal{H})$ such that the projection of u onto Act_p is a prefix of the projection of w_p onto Act_p. Observe that w_p can be computed in polynomial time. We set $L_1 = \bigcup_{p \in Proc}[w_p]_{\approx_{MW}}$.

Finally, suppose that, in $\mathcal{A}$, we could neither find a prefix exceeding the buffer size B nor a reachable deadlock configuration in the B-bounded fragment. Then, we still have to check if $\mathcal{A}$ recognizes $\mathcal{L}$. If not, one can compute a (B-bounded) MSC word $w \in L(\mathcal{A}) \setminus L(\mathcal{H})$ whose MSC is implied by $\mathcal{L}$ wrt. $\vdash^{p}_{MSC}$. Setting $L_2 = \{w\}$, a corresponding set L_1 can be specified as the union of sets $[w_p]_{\approx_{MW}}$, as above.   □

Together with Prop. 1, we obtain the following two results:

Proposition 6. *The quintuple* $(Act, Lin(\mathsf{MSC}), \approx_{MW}, \vdash^{sp}_{MW}, obj^{sp}_{\forall})$ *is a learning setup for* $(\mathrm{MPA}^{sp}_{\forall}, \sim^{sp}_{\forall})$.

Theorem 5. $(\mathrm{MPA}^{sp}_{\forall}, \sim^{sp}_{\forall})$ *is learnable.*

5.5   Learning ∀-Bounded Product Message-Passing Automata

Finally, we study the problem of learning ∀-bounded product MPA. Unfortunately, we are in the situation that the canonical definition of a learning setup does not work:

Proposition 7 ([3]). INFCLOSURE$(Act, Lin(\mathsf{MSC}), \approx_{MW}, \vdash^{p}_{MW})$ *is not constructively decidable. More specifically, it is undecidable if the language of a* $\approx_{MW}$*-closed DFA over Act is closed under* $\vdash^{p}_{MW}$.

Similar decision problems were considered in [24,2,3,21]. Most of them are, however, concerned with translating a *high-level MSC* into a product MPA.

6   Tool Description and Future Work

We have implemented the learning approach presented in the preceding sections in the tool *Smyle* (Synthesizing Models bY Learning from Examples), which can be freely downloaded at http://smyle.in.tum.de. It is written in Java and makes use of the LearnLib library [27], which implements *Angluin's algorithm*, and the libraries Grappa [5] and JGraph [22] for visualization purposes. For computing linearizations of MSCs we use the algorithm given in [30] running in $\mathcal{O}(n \cdot e(\mathcal{P}))$ time, where n is the number of elements of the partial order $\mathcal{P}$ and $e(\mathcal{P}) = |E(\mathcal{P})|$ is the number of linear extensions of $\mathcal{P}$. The tool is capable of learning universally regular and existentially regular MSC languages. The framework contains the following three main components:

- the *Teacher*, representing the interface between the GUI (user) and the *Assistant*
- the *Learner*, containing the LearnLib part
- the *Assistant*, keeping track of membership queries that were not yet asked, checking for B-boundedness as well as the language type ($\exists/\forall$)

The learning chain: Initially, the user is asked to specify the learning setup. After having selected a language type (existentially/universally) and a channel bound B, the user provides a set of MSCs. These MSC specifications must then be divided into *positive* (i.e., MSCs contained in the language to learn) and *negative* (i.e., MSCs not contained in the language to learn). After submitting these examples, all linearizations are checked for consistency with respect to the properties of the learning setup. Violating linearizations are stored as negative examples. Now the learning algorithm starts. The *Learner* continuously communicates with the *Assistant* in order to gain answers to membership queries. This procedure halts as soon as a query cannot be answered by the *Assistant*. In this case, the *Assistant* forwards the inquiry to the user, displaying the MSC in question on the screen. The user must classify the MSC as positive or negative (cf. Fig. 5 (1)).

The *Assistant* checks the classification for validity wrt. the learning setup. Depending on the outcome of this check, the linearizations of the current MSC are assigned to the positive or negative set of future queries. Moreover, the user's answer is passed to the *Learner*, which then continues his question-and-answer game with the *Assistant*. If the LearnLib proposes a possible automaton, the *Assistant* checks whether the learned model is consistent with all queries that have been categorized but not yet been asked. If he encounters a counter-example, he presents it to the learning algorithm which, in turn, continues the learning procedure until the next possible solution is found. In case there is no further evidence for contradicting samples, a new frame appears (cf. Fig. 5 (2, 3)). Among others, it visualizes the currently learned DFA (2, 4) and a panel for displaying MSCs (3) of runs of the system described by the automaton. The user is then asked if he agrees with the solution and may either stop or introduce a new counter-example proceeding with the learning procedure.

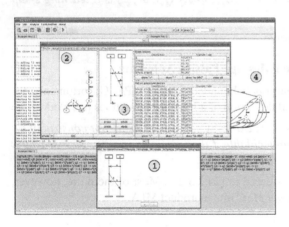

Fig. 5. *Smyle* screenshot

Case studies: We applied *Smyle* to the *simple negotiation protocol* from [13], the *continuous update protocol* from [14], a protocol being part of USB 1.1 mentioned in [15], and a variant of the ABP. For the first one, *Smyle* was provided with 6 positive MSCs and performed 9675 membership and 65 user-queries. It resulted in an automaton consisting of 9 states. The second protocol (giving 4 sample MSCs as input) was learned after 5235 membership and 43 user queries resulting in an automaton containing 8 states. The third protocol was learned after 1373 membership and 12 user-queries, providing it with 4 sample MSCs. The inferred automaton was composed of 9 states. The ABP was realized by an automaton with 15 states after 19276 membership and 105 user queries, providing 4+1 positive examples. For further details such as the input MSCs and inferred automata, we refer to [6] and the webpage of our tool.

Future work: There are other interesting classes of learnable MPA, and our setting applies to the *causal* closure by Adsul et al. [1]. We plan to provide high-level MSCs as a means to predefine patterns of positive or negative examples. Moreover, *MSCan* [7] will be integrated into *Smyle* to support formal analysis of a suggested model.

Smyle is freely available for exploration at http://smyle.in.tum.de.

References

1. B. Adsul, M. Mukund, K. N. Kumar, and V. Narayanan. Causal closure for MSC languages. In *FSTTCS 2005*, volume 3821 of *LNCS*, pages 335–347. Springer, 2005.
2. R. Alur, K. Etessami, and M. Yannakakis. Inference of message sequence charts. *IEEE Trans. Softw. Eng.*, 29(7):623–633, 2003.
3. R. Alur, K. Etessami, and M. Yannakakis. Realizability and verification of MSC graphs. *Th. Comp. Sc.*, 331(1):97–114, 2005.
4. D. Angluin. Learning regular sets from queries and counterexamples. *Inf. Comput.*, 75(2):87–106, 1987.
5. AT&T. *Grappa - A Java Graph Package.* http://www.research.att.com/ john/Grappa/.
6. B. Bollig, J.-P. Katoen, C. Kern, and M. Leucker. Replaying play in and play out: Synthesis of design models from scenarios by learning. Research Report AIB-2006-12, RWTH Aachen, 2006.
7. B. Bollig, C. Kern, M. Schlütter, and V. Stolz. MSCan: A tool for analyzing MSC specifications. In *TACAS 2006*, volume 3920 of *LNCS*, pages 455–458. Springer, 2006.
8. B. Bollig and M. Leucker. Message-passing automata are expressively equivalent to EMSO logic. *Th. Comp. Sc.*, 358(2-3):150–172, 2006.
9. Y. Bontemps, P. Heymand, and P.-Y. Schobbens. From live sequence charts to state machines and back: a guided tour. *IEEE Trans. Softw. Eng.*, 31(12):999–1014, 2005.
10. D. Brand and P. Zafiropulo. On communicating finite-state machines. *J. of the ACM*, 30(2):323–342, 1983.
11. W. Damm and D. Harel. LSCs: Breathing life into message sequence charts. *Formal Methods in System Design*, 19:1:45–80., 2001.
12. D.Harel and R. Marelly. *Come, Let's Play: Scenario-Based Programming Using LSCs and the Play-Engine.* Springer, 2003.
13. U. Endriss, N. Maudet, F. Sadri, and F. Toni. Logic-based agent communication protocols. In *Workshop on Agent Communication Languages*, pages 91–107, 2003.
14. U. Endriss, N. Maudet, F. Sadri, and F. Toni. Protocol conformance for logic-based agents. In *IJCAI 2003*, pages 679–684, 2003.
15. B. Genest. Compositional message sequence charts (CMSCs) are better to implement than MSCs. In *TACAS 2005*, volume 3440 of *LNCS*, pages 429–444. Springer, 2005.
16. B. Genest, D. Kuske, and A. Muscholl. A Kleene theorem and model checking algorithms for existentially bounded communicating automata. *Inf. Comput.*, 204(6):920–956, 2006.
17. J. G. Henriksen, M. Mukund, K. N. Kumar, M. Sohoni, and P. S. Thiagarajan. A theory of regular MSC languages. *Inf. and Comput.*, 202(1):1–38, 2005.

18. H. Hungar, O. Niese, and B. Steffen. Domain-specific optimization in automata learning. In *CAV 2003*, volume 2725 of *LNCS*, pages 315–327. Springer, 2003.

19. I. Krüger, R. Grosu, P. Scholz, and M. Broy. From MSCs to statecharts. In *DIPES 1998*, volume 155 of *IFIP Conf. Proc.*, pages 61–72. Kluwer, 1998.

20. D. Kuske. Regular sets of infinite message sequence charts. *Inf. Comput.*, 187:80–109, 2003.

21. M. Lohrey. Realizability of high-level message sequence charts: closing the gaps. *Th. Comp. Sc.*, 309(1-3):529–554, 2003.

22. J. Ltd. *JGraph - Java Graph Visualization and Layout*. http://www.jgraph.com/.

23. E. Mäkinen and T. Systä. MAS – An interactive synthesizer to support behavioral modeling in UML. In *ICSE 2001*, pages 15–24. IEEE Computer Society, 2001.

24. R. Morin. Recognizable sets of message sequence charts. In *STACS 2002*, volume 2285 of *LNCS*, pages 523–534. Springer, 2002.

25. A. Muscholl and D. Peled. From finite state communication protocols to high-level message sequence charts. In *ICALP 2001*, volume 2076 of *LNCS*, pages 720–731. Springer, 2001.

26. B. Nuseibeh and S. Easterbrook. Requirements engineering: a roadmap. In *ICSE 2000*, pages 35–46. ACM, 2000.

27. H. Raffelt and B. Steffen. LearnLib: A library for automata learning and experimentation. In *FASE 2006*, volume 3922 of *LNCS*, pages 377–380, 2006.

28. B. Sengupta and R. Cleaveland. Triggered message sequence charts. *IEEE Trans. Softw. Eng.*, 32(8):587–607, 2006.

29. S. Uchitel, J. Kramer, and J. Magee. Synthesis of behavioral models from scenarios. *IEEE Trans. Softw. Eng.*, 29(2):99–115, 2003.

30. Y. L. Varol and D. Rotem. An algorithm to generate all topological sorting arrangements. *Comput. J.*, 24(1):83–84, 1981.

Improved Algorithms for the Automata-Based Approach to Model-Checking[*]

Laurent Doyen[1] and Jean-François Raskin[2]

[1] I&C, Ecole Polytechnique Fédérale de Lausanne (EPFL), Switzerland
[2] CS, Université Libre de Bruxelles (ULB), Belgium

Abstract. We propose and evaluate new algorithms to support the automata-based approach to model-checking: algorithms to solve the universality and language inclusion problems for nondeterministic Büchi automata. To obtain those new algorithms, we establish the existence of pre-orders that can be exploited to efficiently evaluate fixed points on the automata defined during the complementation step (that we keep implicit in our approach). We evaluate the performance of our new algorithm to check for universality of Büchi automata experimentally using the random automaton model recently proposed by Tabakov and Vardi. We show that on the difficult instances of this probabilistic model, our algorithm outperforms the standard ones by several orders of magnitude. This work is an extension to the infinite words case of new algorithms for the finite words case that we and co-authors have presented in a recent paper [DDHR06].

1 Introduction

In the automata-based approach to model-checking [VW86, VW94], programs and properties are modeled by finite automata. Let A be a finite automaton that models a program and let B be a finite automaton that models a specification that the program should satisfy: all the traces of the program (executions) should be traces of the specification, that is $\mathcal{L}(A) \subseteq \mathcal{L}(B)$. To solve the inclusion problem, the classical automata-theoretic solution consists in complementing the language of the automaton B and then to check that $\mathcal{L}(A) \cap \mathcal{L}^c(B)$ is empty (the later intersection being computed as a product).

In the finite case, the program and the specification are finite automata over finite words (NFA) and the construction for the complementation is conceptually simple: it is achieved by a classical subset construction. In the case of infinite words, the program and (or at least) the specification are nondeterministic Büchi automata (NBW). The NBW are also complementable; this was first proved by Büchi in the late sixties [BL69]. However, the result is much harder to obtain than in the case of NFA. The orginal construction of Büchi has a $O(2^{2^n})$ worst case complexity (where n is the size of the automaton to complement) which is not optimal. In the late eighties Safra in [Saf88], and later Kupferman and Vardi in [KV97], have given optimal complementation procedures that have $O(2^{n \log n})$ complexity (see [Mic88] for the lower bound). While for finite words, the classical algorithm has been implemented and shown practically usable, for infinite words, the theoretically optimal solution is difficult to implement

---

[*] Supported by the FRFC project "Centre Fédéré en Vérification" funded by the Belgian National Science Foundation (FNRS) under grant nr 2.4530.02.

O. Grumberg and M. Huth (Eds.): TACAS 2007, LNCS 4424, pp. 451–465, 2007.

and very few results are known about their practical behavior. The actual attemps to implement them have shown very limited in the size of the specifications that can be handled: automata with more than around ten states are intractable [Tab06, GKSV03]. Such sizes are clearly not sufficient in pratcice. As a consequence, tools like SPIN [RH04] that implement the automata-theoretic approach to model-checking ask either that the complement of the specification is explicitly given or they limit the specification to properties that are expressible in LTL.

In this paper, we propose a new approach to check $\mathcal{L}(A) \subseteq \mathcal{L}(B)$ that can handle much larger Büchi automata. In a recent paper, we have shown that the classical subset construction can be avoided and kept implicit for checking language inclusion and language universality for NFA and their alternating extensions [DDHR06]. Here, we adapt and extend that technique to the more intricate automata on infinite words.

To present the intuition behind our new techniques, let us consider a simpler setting of the problem. Assume that we are given a NBW B and we want to check if $\Sigma^\omega \subseteq \mathcal{L}(B)$, that is to check if $\mathcal{L}(B)$ is universal. First, remember that $\mathcal{L}(B)$ is universal when $\mathcal{L}^c(B)$ is empty. The classical algorithm first complements B and then checks for emptiness. The language of a NBW is nonempty if there exists an infinite run of the automaton that visits accepting locations infinitely often. The existence of such a run can be established in polynomial time by computing the following fixed point $\mathcal{F} \equiv \nu y \cdot \mu x \cdot (\mathsf{Pre}(x) \cup (\mathsf{Pre}(y) \cap \alpha))$ where Pre is the predecessor operator of the automaton (given a set L of locations it returns the set of locations that can reach L in one step) and α is the set of accepting locations of the automaton. The automaton is non-empty if and only if its initial location is a member of the fixed point $\mathcal{F}$. This well-known algorithm is quadratic in the size of the automaton. Unfortunately, the automaton that accepts the language $\mathcal{L}^c(B)$ is usally huge and the evaluation of the fixed point is unfeasable for all but the smallest specifications B. To overcome this difficulty, we make the following observation: if $\preceq$ is a *simulation* pre-order on the locations of B^c ($\ell_1 \preceq \ell_2$ means ℓ_1 can simulate ℓ_2) which is compatible with the accepting condition (if $\ell_1 \preceq \ell_2$ and $\ell_2 \in \alpha$ then $\ell_1 \in \alpha$), then the sets that are computed during the evaluation of $\mathcal{F}$ are all $\preceq$-*closed* (if an element ℓ is in the set then all $\ell' \preceq \ell$ are also in the set). Then $\preceq$-closed sets can be represented by their $\preceq$-maximal elements and if operations on such sets can be computed directly on their representation, we have the ingredients to evaluate the fixed point in a more efficient way. For an automaton B over finite words, set inclusion would be a typical example of a simulation relation for B^c [DDHR06].

We show that the classical constructions for Büchi automata that are used in the automata-theoretic approach to model-checking are all equipped with a simulation pre-order that exists by construction and does not need to be computed. On that basis we propose new algorithms to check universality of NBW, language inclusion for NBW, and emptiness of alternating Büchi automata (ABW).

We evaluate an implementation of our new algorithm for the universality problem of NBW and on a randomized model recently proposed by Tabakov and Vardi. We show that the performance of the new algorithm on this randomized model outperforms by several order of magnitude the existing implementations of the Kupferman-Vardi algorithm [Tab06, GKSV03]. When the classical solution is limited to automata of size 8 for some parameter values of the randomized model, we are able to handle automata with more than one hundred locations for the same parameter values. We have identified the hardest instances of the randomized model for our algorithms and show that we can still handle problems with several dozens of locations for those instances.

Structure of the paper In Section 2, we recall the Vardi-Kupferman and Miyano-Hayashi constructions that are used for complementation of NBW. In Section 3, we recall the notion of simulation pre-order for a Büchi automaton and prove that the fixed point needed to establish emptiness of nondeterministic Büchi automata handles only closed sets for such pre-orders. We use this observation in Section 4 to define a new algorithm to decide emptiness of ABW. In Section 5, we adapt the technique for the universality problem of NBW. In Section 6, we report on the performances of the new algorithm for universality. In Section 7, we extend those ideas to obtain a new algorithm for language inclusion of NBW. The omitted technical proofs can be found in [DR06].

2 Büchi Automata and Classical Algorithms

An *alternating Büchi automaton* (ABW) is a tuple $\mathcal{A} = \langle \mathsf{Loc}, \iota, \Sigma, \delta, \alpha \rangle$ where:

- Loc is a finite set of states (or locations). The *size* of $\mathcal{A}$ is $|\mathcal{A}| = |\mathsf{Loc}|$;
- $\iota \in \mathsf{Loc}$ is the *initial* state;
- Σ is a finite *alphabet*;
- $\delta : \mathsf{Loc} \times \Sigma \to \mathcal{B}^+(\mathsf{Loc})$ is the *transition function* where $\mathcal{B}^+(\mathsf{Loc})$ is the set of positive boolean formulas over Loc, *i.e.* formulas built from elements in $\mathsf{Loc} \cup \{\mathsf{true}, \mathsf{false}\}$ using the boolean connectives $\wedge$ and $\vee$;
- $\alpha \subseteq \mathsf{Loc}$ is the acceptance condition.

We say that a set $X \subseteq \mathsf{Loc}$ *satisfies* a formula $\varphi \in \mathcal{B}^+(\mathsf{Loc})$ (noted $X \models \varphi$) iff the truth assignment that assigns true to the members of X and assigns false to the members of $\mathsf{Loc} \backslash X$ satisfies φ.

A *run* of $\mathcal{A}$ on an infinite word $w = \sigma_0 \cdot \sigma_1 \ldots$ is a DAG $T_w = \langle V, v_\iota, \to \rangle$ where:

- $V = \mathsf{Loc} \times \mathbb{N}$ is the set of nodes. A node (ℓ, i) represents the state ℓ after the first i letters of the word w have been read by $\mathcal{A}$. Nodes of the form (ℓ, i) with $\ell \in \alpha$ are called α-*nodes*;
- $v_\iota = (\iota, 0)$ is the root of the DAG;
- and $\to \subseteq V \times V$ is such that (i) if $(\ell, i) \to (\ell', i')$ then $i' = i + 1$ and (ii) for every $(\ell, i) \in V$, the set $\{\ell' \mid (\ell, i) \to (\ell', i + 1)\}$ satisfies the formula $\delta(\ell, \sigma_i)$. We say that $(\ell', i+1)$ is a *successor* of (ℓ, i) if $(\ell, i) \to (\ell', i+1)$, and we say that (ℓ', i') is *reachable* from (ℓ, i) if $(\ell, i) \to^* (\ell', i')$.

A run $T_w = \langle V, v_\iota, \to \rangle$ of $\mathcal{A}$ on an infinite word w is *accepting* iff all its infinite paths π rooted at v_ι (thus $\pi \in \mathsf{Loc}^\omega$) visit α-nodes infinitely often. An infinite word $w \in \Sigma^\omega$ is *accepted* by $\mathcal{A}$ iff there exists an accepting run on it. We denote by $\mathcal{L}(\mathcal{A})$ the set of infinite words accepted by $\mathcal{A}$, and by $\mathcal{L}^c(\mathcal{A})$ the set of infinite words that are not accepted by $\mathcal{A}$.

A *nondeterministic Büchi automaton* (NBW) is an ABW whose transition function is restricted to disjunctions over Loc. Runs of NBW reduce to (linear) traces. The transition function of NBW is often seen as a function $[Q \times \Sigma \to 2^Q]$ and we write

$\delta(\ell, \sigma) = \{\ell_1, \ldots, \ell_n\}$ instead of $\delta(\ell, \sigma) = \ell_1 \vee \ell_2 \vee \cdots \vee \ell_n$. We note by $\mathsf{Pre}_\sigma^{\mathcal{A}}(L)$ the set of predecessors by σ of the set L: $\mathsf{Pre}_\sigma^{\mathcal{A}}(L) = \{\ell \in \mathsf{Loc} \mid \exists \ell' \in L : \ell' \in \delta(\ell, \sigma)\}$. Let $\mathsf{Pre}^{\mathcal{A}}(L) = \{\ell \in \mathsf{Loc} \mid \exists \sigma \in \Sigma : \ell \in \mathsf{Pre}_\sigma^{\mathcal{A}}(L)\}$.

Problems. The *emptiness problem* for NBW is to decide, given an NBW $\mathcal{A}$, whether $\mathcal{L}(\mathcal{A}) = \emptyset$. This problem is solvable in polynomial time. The symbolic approach through fixed point computation is quadratic in the size of $\mathcal{A}$.

The *universality problem* for NBW is to decide, given an NBW $\mathcal{A}$ over the alphabet Σ whether $\mathcal{L}(\mathcal{A}) = \Sigma^\omega$ where Σ^ω is the set of all infinite words on Σ. This problem is PSPACE-complete [SVW87]. The classical algorithm to decide universality is to first complement the NBW and then to check emptiness of the complement. The difficult step is the complementation as it may cause an exponential blow-up in the size of the automaton. There exists two types of construction, one is based on a determinization of the automaton [Saf88] and the other uses ABW as an intermediate step [KV97]. We review the second construction below.

The *language inclusion problem* for NBW is to decide, given two NBW $\mathcal{A}$ and $\mathcal{B}$, whether $\mathcal{L}(\mathcal{A}) \subseteq \mathcal{L}(\mathcal{B})$. This problem is central in model-checking and it is PSPACE-complete in the size of $\mathcal{B}$. The classical solution consists in checking the emptiness of $\mathcal{L}(\mathcal{A}) \cap \mathcal{L}^c(\mathcal{B})$, which again requires the expensive complementation of $\mathcal{B}$.

The *emptiness problem* for ABW is to decide, given an ABW $\mathcal{A}$, whether $\mathcal{L}(\mathcal{A}) = \emptyset$. This problem is also PSPACE-complete and it can be solved using a translation from ABW to NBW that preserves the language of the automaton [MH84]. Again, this construction involves an exponential blow-up that makes straight implementations feasible only for automata limited to around ten states. However, the emptiness problem for ABW is very important in practice for LTL model-checking as there exist efficient polynomial translations from LTL formulas to ABW [GO01]. The classical construction is presented below.

Kupferman-Vardi construction. Complementation of ABW is straightforward by dualizing the transition function (by swapping $\wedge$ and $\vee$, and swapping true and false in each formulas) and interpreting the accepting condition α as a co-Büchi condition, *i.e.* a run T_w is accepted if all its infinite paths have a suffix that contains no α-nodes.

The result is an alternating co-Büchi automaton (ACW). The accepting runs of ACW have a layered structure that has been studied in [KV97], where the notion of *ranks* is defined. The rank is a positive number associated to each node of a run T_w of an ACW on a word w. Let $G_0 = T_w$. Nodes of rank 0 are those nodes from which only finitely many nodes are reachable in G_0. Let G_1 be the run T_w from which all nodes of rank 0 have been removed. Then, nodes of rank 1 are those nodes of G_1 from which no α-node is reachable in G_1. For $i \geq 1$, let G_i be the run T_w from which all nodes of rank $0, \ldots, i-1$ have been removed. Then, nodes of rank $2i$ are those nodes of G_{2i} from which only finitely many nodes are reachable in G_{2i}, and nodes of rank $2i + 1$ are those nodes of G_{2i+1} from which no α-node is reachable in G_{2i+1}. Intuitively, the rank of a node (ℓ, i) hints how difficult it is to prove that all the paths of T_w that start in (ℓ, i) visit α-nodes only finitely many times. It can be shown that every node has a rank between 0 and $2(|\mathsf{Loc}| - |\alpha|)$, and all α-nodes have an even rank [GKSV03].

The layered structure of the runs of ACW induces a construction to complement ABW [KV97]. We present this construction directly for NBW. Given a NBW $\mathcal{A} =$

$\langle \text{Loc}, \iota, \Sigma, \delta, \alpha \rangle$ and an even number $k \in \mathbb{N}$, let $\text{KV}(\mathcal{A}, k) = \langle \text{Loc}', \iota', \Sigma, \delta', \alpha' \rangle$ be an ABW such that:

- $\text{Loc}' = \text{Loc} \times [k]$ where $[k] = \{0, 1, \ldots, k\}$. Intuitively, the automaton $\text{KV}(\mathcal{A}, k)$ is in state (ℓ, n) after the first i letters of the input word w have been read if it guesses that the rank of the node (ℓ, i) in a run of $\mathcal{A}$ on w is at most n;
- $\iota' = (\iota, k)$;
- $\delta'((\ell, i), \sigma) = \text{false}$ if $\ell \in \alpha$ and i is odd, and otherwise $\delta'((\ell, i), \sigma) = \bigvee_{i' \leq i}(\ell_1, i') \wedge \bigvee_{i' \leq i}(\ell_2, i') \wedge \cdots \wedge \bigvee_{i' \leq i}(\ell_n, i')$ if $\delta(\ell, \sigma) = \ell_1 \vee \ell_2 \vee \cdots \vee \ell_n$; For example, if $\delta(\ell, \sigma) = \ell_1 \vee \ell_2$ then $\delta'((\ell, 2), \sigma) = ((\ell_1, 2) \vee (\ell_1, 1) \vee (\ell_1, 0)) \wedge ((\ell_2, 2) \vee (\ell_2, 1) \vee (\ell_2, 0))$.
- $\alpha' = \text{Loc} \times [k]^{odd}$ where $[k]^{odd}$ is the set of odd numbers in $[k]$.

The ABW that the Kupferman-Vardi construction specifies accepts the complement language and its size is quadratic in the size of the original automaton.

Theorem 1 ([KV97]). *For all NBW* $\mathcal{A} = \langle \text{Loc}, \iota, \Sigma, \delta, \alpha \rangle$, *for all* $0 \leq k' \leq k$, *we have* $\mathcal{L}(\text{KV}(\mathcal{A}, k')) \subseteq \mathcal{L}(\text{KV}(\mathcal{A}, k))$ *and for* $k = 2(|\text{Loc}| - |\alpha|)$, *we have* $\mathcal{L}(\text{KV}(\mathcal{A}, k)) = \mathcal{L}^c(\mathcal{A})$.

Miyano-Hayashi construction. Classically, to check emptiness of ABW, a variant of the subset construction is applied that transforms the ABW into a NBW that accepts the same language [MH84]. Intuitively, the NBW maintains a set s of states of the ABW that corresponds to a whole level of a guessed run DAG of the ABW. In addition, the NBW maintains a set o of states that "owe" a visit to an accepting state. Whenever the set o gets empty, meaning that every path of the guessed run has visited at least one accepting state, the set o is initiated with the current level of the guessed run. It is asked that o gets empty infinitely often in order to ensure that every path of the run DAG visits accepting states infinitely often. The construction is as follows.

Given an ABW $\mathcal{A} = \langle \text{Loc}, \iota, \Sigma, \delta, \alpha \rangle$, let $\text{MH}(\mathcal{A}) = \langle 2^{\text{Loc}} \times 2^{\text{Loc}}, (\{\iota\}, \emptyset), \Sigma, \delta', \alpha' \rangle$ be a NBW where $\alpha' = 2^{\text{Loc}} \times \{\emptyset\}$ and δ' is defined, for all $\langle s, o \rangle \in 2^{\text{Loc}} \times 2^{\text{Loc}}$ and $\sigma \in \Sigma$, as follows:

- If $o \neq \emptyset$, then $\delta'(\langle s, o \rangle, \sigma) = \{\langle s', o' \setminus \alpha \rangle \mid o' \subseteq s', s' \models \bigwedge_{\ell \in s} \delta(\ell, \sigma)$ and $o' \models \bigwedge_{\ell \in o} \delta(\ell, \sigma)\}$;
- If $o = \emptyset$, then $\delta'(\langle s, o \rangle, \sigma) = \{\langle s', s' \setminus \alpha \rangle \mid s' \models \bigwedge_{\ell \in s} \delta(\ell, \sigma)\}$.

The size of the Miyano-Hayashi construction is exponential in the size of the original automaton.

Theorem 2 ([MH84]). *For all ABW* $\mathcal{A}$, *we have* $\mathcal{L}(\text{MH}(\mathcal{A})) = \mathcal{L}(\mathcal{A})$.

The size of the automaton obtained after the Kupferman-Vardi and the Miyano-Hayashi construction is an obstacle to the straight implementation of the method. In Section 3, we propose a new approach that circumvents this problem.

Direct complementation. In our solution, we implicitly use the two constructions to complement Büchi automata but, as we will see, we do not construct the automata. For the sake of clarity, we give below the specification of the automaton that would result from the composition of the two constructions. In the definition of the state space, we omit the states (ℓ, i) for $\ell \in \alpha$ and i odd, as those states have no successor in the Kupferman-Vardi construction.

Definition 3. Given a NBW $\mathcal{A} = \langle \mathsf{Loc}, \iota, \Sigma, \delta, \alpha \rangle$ and an even number $k \in \mathbb{N}$, let $\mathsf{KVMH}(\mathcal{A}, k) = \langle Q_k \times Q_k, q_\iota, \Sigma, \delta', \alpha' \rangle$ be a NBW such that:

- $Q_k = 2^{(\mathsf{Loc} \times [k]) \setminus (\alpha \times \mathbb{N}^{odd})}$ where $\mathbb{N}^{odd}$ is the set of odd natural numbers;
- $q_\iota = (\{(\iota, k)\}, \emptyset)$;
- Let $\mathsf{odd} = \mathsf{Loc} \times [k]^{odd}$; δ' is defined for all $s, o \in Q_k$ and $\sigma \in \Sigma$, as follows:
  - If $o \neq \emptyset$, then $\delta'(\langle s, o \rangle, \sigma)$ is the set of pairs $\langle s', o' \setminus \mathsf{odd} \rangle$ such that:
    - (i) $o' \subseteq s'$;
    - (ii) $\forall (\ell, n) \in s \cdot \forall \ell' \in \delta(\ell, \sigma) \cdot \exists (\ell', n') \in s' : n' \leq n$;
    - (iii) $\forall (\ell, n) \in o \cdot \forall \ell' \in \delta(\ell, \sigma) \cdot \exists (\ell', n') \in o' : n' \leq n$.
  - If $o = \emptyset$, then $\delta'(\langle s, o \rangle, \sigma)$ is the set of pairs $\langle s', s' \setminus \mathsf{odd} \rangle$ such that:
    $\forall (\ell, n) \in s \cdot \forall \ell' \in \delta(\ell, \sigma) \cdot \exists (\ell', n') \in s' : n' \leq n$.
- $\alpha' = 2^{\mathsf{Loc} \times [k]} \times \{\emptyset\}$;

We write $\langle s, o \rangle \xrightarrow{\sigma}_{\delta'} \langle s', o' \rangle$ to denote $\langle s', o' \rangle \in \delta'(\langle s, o \rangle, \sigma)$.

Theorem 4 ([KV97, MH84]). *For all NBW $\mathcal{A} = \langle \mathsf{Loc}, \iota, \Sigma, \delta, \alpha \rangle$, for all $0 \leq k' \leq k$, we have $\mathcal{L}(\mathsf{KVMH}(\mathcal{A}, k')) \subseteq \mathcal{L}(\mathsf{KVMH}(\mathcal{A}, k))$ and for $k = 2(|\mathsf{Loc}| - |\alpha|)$, we have $\mathcal{L}(\mathsf{KVMH}(\mathcal{A}, k)) = \mathcal{L}^c(\mathcal{A})$.*

3   Simulation Pre-orders and Fixed Points

Let $\mathcal{A} = \langle \mathsf{Loc}, \iota, \Sigma, \delta, \alpha \rangle$ be a NBW. Let $\langle 2^{\mathsf{Loc}}, \subseteq, \cup, \cap, \emptyset, \mathsf{Loc} \rangle$ be the powerset lattice of locations. The fixed point $\mathcal{F}_\mathcal{A} \equiv \nu y \cdot \mu x \cdot (\mathsf{Pre}^\mathcal{A}(x) \cup (\mathsf{Pre}^\mathcal{A}(y) \cap \alpha))$ can be used to check emptiness of $\mathcal{A}$ as we have $\mathcal{L}(\mathcal{A}) \neq \emptyset$ iff $\iota \in \mathcal{F}_\mathcal{A}$.

Let $\preceq \subseteq \mathsf{Loc} \times \mathsf{Loc}$ be a pre-order and let $\ell_1 \prec \ell_2$ iff $\ell_1 \preceq \ell_2$ and $\ell_2 \not\preceq \ell_1$.

Definition 5. A pre-order $\preceq$ is a *simulation*[1] for $\mathcal{A}$ iff the following properties hold:

- for all $\ell_1, \ell_2, \ell_3 \in \mathsf{Loc}$, for all $\sigma \in \Sigma$, if $\ell_3 \preceq \ell_1$ and $\ell_2 \in \delta(\ell_1, \sigma)$ then there exists $\ell_4 \in \mathsf{Loc}$ such that $\ell_4 \preceq \ell_2$ and $\ell_4 \in \delta(\ell_3, \sigma)$;
- for all $\ell \in \alpha$, for all $\ell' \in \mathsf{Loc}$, if $\ell' \preceq \ell$ then $\ell' \in \alpha$.

A set $L \subseteq \mathsf{Loc}$ is $\preceq$-*closed* iff for all $\ell_1, \ell_2 \in \mathsf{Loc}$, if $\ell_1 \preceq \ell_2$ and $\ell_2 \in L$ then $\ell_1 \in L$. The $\preceq$-*closure* of L, is the set $\downarrow L = \{\ell \in \mathsf{Loc} \mid \exists \ell' \in L : \ell \preceq \ell'\}$. We denote by $\mathsf{Max}(L)$ the set of $\preceq$-maximal elements of L: $\mathsf{Max}(L) = \{\ell \in L \mid \nexists \ell' \in L : \ell \prec \ell'\}$. When the context is ambiguous, we sometimes write $\downarrow_{\preceq}$ and $\mathsf{Max}_{\preceq}$ with the intended pre-order in subscript. For any $\preceq$-closed set $L \subseteq \mathsf{Loc}$, we have $L = \downarrow \mathsf{Max}(L)$. Furthermore, if $\preceq$ is a partial order, then $\mathsf{Max}(L)$ is an antichain of elements and it is a canonical representation of L. The following lemma states interesting properties of $\preceq$-closed sets of locations.

---

[1] Several notions of simulation pre-orders have been defined for Büchi automata, see [EWS05] for a survey.

Lemma 6. *For all NBW* $\mathcal{A} = \langle \mathsf{Loc}, \iota, \Sigma, \delta, \alpha \rangle$, *for all simulations* $\preceq$ *for* $\mathcal{A}$, *the following properties hold:*

1. *for all* $\preceq$-*closed set* $L \subseteq \mathsf{Loc}$, *for all* $\sigma \in \Sigma$, $\mathsf{Pre}_\sigma^{\mathcal{A}}(L)$ *is* $\preceq$-*closed;*
2. *for all* $\preceq$-*closed sets* $L_1, L_2 \subseteq \mathsf{Loc}$, $L_1 \cup L_2$ *and* $L_1 \cap L_2$ *are* $\preceq$-*closed;*
3. *the set* α *is* $\preceq$-*closed.*

We can take advantage of Lemma 6 to compute the fixed point $\mathcal{F}_{\mathcal{A}}$ more efficiently in terms of space consumption and execution time. First, we represent $\preceq$-closed sets by their maximal elements. This way, the size of the sets is usually drastically reduced. As we will see later, this can potentially save an exponential factor. Second, the union of $\preceq$-closed sets can be computed efficiently using this representation as we have $\mathsf{Max}(L_1 \cup L_2) = \mathsf{Max}(\mathsf{Max}(L_1) \cup \mathsf{Max}(L_2))$. Third, we will see that the NBW that we have to analyze in the automata-based approach to model-checking are all equipped with a simulation pre-order that can be exploited to compute efficiently the intersection and the predecessors of $\preceq$-closed sets of locations.

Intuitively, when computing the sequence of approximations for $\mathcal{F}_{\mathcal{A}}$, we can concentrate on maximal elements for a simulation pre-order as those locations are such that if they have an accepting run in $\mathcal{A}$, then all the locations that are smaller for the pre-order also have an accepting run in $\mathcal{A}$.

4 Emptiness of ABW

We now show how to apply Lemma 6 to check more efficiently the emptiness of ABW. Let $\mathcal{A}_1 = \langle \mathsf{Loc}_1, \iota_1, \Sigma, \delta_1, \alpha_1 \rangle$ be an ABW for which we want to decide whether $\mathcal{L}(\mathcal{A}_1) = \emptyset$. We know that the (exponential) Miyano-Hayashi construction gives a NBW $\mathcal{A}_2 - \mathsf{MH}(\mathcal{A}_1)$ such that $\mathcal{L}(\mathcal{A}_2) = \mathcal{L}(\mathcal{A}_1)$. We show that the emptiness of $\mathcal{A}_1$ (or equivalently of $\mathcal{A}_2$) can be decided more efficiently by computing the fixed point $\mathcal{F}_{\mathcal{A}_2}$ and without constructing explicitly $\mathcal{A}_2$. To do so, we show that there exists a simulation for $\mathcal{A}_2$ for which we can compute $\cup$, $\cap$ and Pre by manipulating only maximal elements of closed sets of locations.

Let $\mathsf{MH}(\mathcal{A}_1) = \langle \mathsf{Loc}_2, \iota_2, \Sigma, \delta_2, \alpha_2 \rangle$. Remember that $\mathsf{Loc}_2 = 2^{\mathsf{Loc}_1} \times 2^{\mathsf{Loc}_1}$. Define the pre-order $\preceq_{\mathsf{alt}} \subseteq \mathsf{Loc}_2 \times \mathsf{Loc}_2$ such that for all $\langle s, o \rangle, \langle s', o' \rangle \in \mathsf{Loc}_2$, we have $\langle s, o \rangle \preceq_{\mathsf{alt}} \langle s', o' \rangle$ iff (i) $s \subseteq s'$, (ii) $o \subseteq o'$, and (iii) $o = \emptyset$ iff $o' = \emptyset$. Note that this pre-order is a partial order. As a consequence, given a set of pairs $L = \{\langle s_1, o_1 \rangle, \langle s_2, o_2 \rangle, \ldots, \langle s_n, o_n \rangle\}$, the set $\mathsf{Max}(L)$ is an antichain and identifies L.

Lemma 7. *For all ABW* $\mathcal{A}_1$, *the partial order* $\preceq_{\mathsf{alt}}$ *is a simulation for* $\mathsf{MH}(\mathcal{A}_1)$.

Proof. Let $\mathcal{A}_1 = \langle \mathsf{Loc}_1, \iota_1, \Sigma, \delta_1, \alpha_1 \rangle$ and $\mathsf{MH}(\mathcal{A}_1) = \langle \mathsf{Loc}_2, \iota_2, \Sigma, \delta_2, \alpha_2 \rangle$. First, let $\sigma \in \Sigma$ and $\langle s_1, o_1 \rangle, \langle s_2, o_2 \rangle, \langle s_3, o_3 \rangle \in \mathsf{Loc}_2$ be such that $\langle s_1, o_1 \rangle \xrightarrow{\sigma}_{\delta_2} \langle s_2, o_2 \rangle$ and $\langle s_3, o_3 \rangle \preceq_{\mathsf{alt}} \langle s_1, o_1 \rangle$. We show that there exists $\langle s_4, o_4 \rangle \in \mathsf{Loc}_2$ such that $\langle s_3, o_3 \rangle \xrightarrow{\sigma}_{\delta_2} \langle s_4, o_4 \rangle$ and $\langle s_4, o_4 \rangle \preceq_{\mathsf{alt}} \langle s_2, o_2 \rangle$. First, let us consider the case where $o_1 = \emptyset$. In this case, we have $o_3 = \emptyset$ by definition of $\preceq_{\mathsf{alt}}$ and $\delta_2(\langle s_1, o_1 \rangle, \sigma) = \{\langle s', s' \setminus \alpha_1 \rangle \mid s' \models \bigwedge_{l \in s_1} \delta_1(l, \sigma)\}$, this set being contained in $\delta_2(\langle s_3, o_3 \rangle, \sigma) = \{\langle s', s' \setminus \alpha_1 \rangle \mid s' \models \bigwedge_{l \in s_3} \delta_1(l, \sigma)\}$ as s_3 puts less constraints than s_1 since $s_3 \subseteq s_1$. A similar reasoning

---

Algorithm 1. Algorithm for $\text{Pre}_{\text{alt}}(\cdot)$.

> **Data** : An ABW $\mathcal{A}_1 = \langle \text{Loc}_1, \iota_1, \Sigma, \delta_1, \alpha_1 \rangle$, $\sigma \in \Sigma$ and $\langle s', o' \rangle \in 2^{\text{Loc}_1} \times 2^{\text{Loc}_1}$
> such that $o' \subseteq s'$.
>
> **Result** : The $\preceq_{\text{alt}}$-antichain $\text{Pre}_\sigma^{\text{alt}}(\langle s', o' \rangle)$.
>
> **begin**
>
> 1 $\quad L_{\text{Pre}} \leftarrow \emptyset$;
>
> 2 $\quad o \leftarrow \{\ell \in \text{Loc}_1 \mid o' \cup (s' \cap \alpha_1) \models \delta_1(\ell, \sigma)\}$;
>
> 3 $\quad$ **if** $o' \not\subseteq \alpha_1 \vee o' = \emptyset$ **then**
>
> 4 $\quad\quad \lfloor L_{\text{Pre}} \leftarrow \{\langle o, \emptyset \rangle\}$;
>
> 5 $\quad$ **if** $o \neq \emptyset$ **then**
>
> 6 $\quad\quad | \quad s \leftarrow \{\ell \in \text{Loc}_1 \mid s' \models \delta_1(\ell, \sigma)\}$;
>
> 7 $\quad\quad \lfloor L_{\text{Pre}} \leftarrow L_{\text{Pre}} \cup \{\langle s, o \rangle\}$;
>
> 8 $\quad$ **return** L_{Pre};
>
> **end**

---

holds if $o_1 \neq \emptyset$. Second, let $\langle s_1, o_1 \rangle \in \alpha_2$ and let $\langle s_2, o_2 \rangle \preceq_{\text{alt}} \langle s_1, o_1 \rangle$. By definition of α_2, we know that $o_2 = \emptyset$, and by definition of $\preceq_{\text{alt}}$ we have $o_2 = \emptyset$ and so $\langle s_2, o_2 \rangle \in \alpha_2$. ∎

So, we know according to Lemma 6 that all the sets that we compute to evaluate $\mathcal{F}_{\mathcal{A}_2}$ are $\preceq_{\text{alt}}$-closed. So, we explain now how to compute intersections and pre-operations by manipulating maximal elements only. Given $\langle s_1, o_1 \rangle, \langle s_2, o_2 \rangle$, we can compute $\langle s, o \rangle$ such that $\downarrow \langle s, o \rangle = \downarrow \langle s_1, o_1 \rangle \cap \downarrow \langle s_2, o_2 \rangle$ as follows. If $o_1 \cap o_2 \neq \emptyset$ then $\langle s, o \rangle = \langle s_1 \cap s_2, o_1 \cap o_2 \rangle$, and if $o_1 = o_2 = \emptyset$ then $\langle s, o \rangle = \langle s_1 \cap s_2, \emptyset \rangle$; otherwise the intersection is empty. Algorithm 1 computes the predecessors of a $\preceq_{\text{alt}}$-closed set by just manipulating its maximal elements. It runs in time $O(|\text{Loc}_1| \cdot \|\delta_1\|)$ where $\|\delta_1\|$ is the size of the transition relation, defined as the maximal number of boolean connectives in a formula $\delta_1(\ell, \sigma)$.

Theorem 8. *Given an ABW $\mathcal{A}_1 = \langle \text{Loc}_1, \iota_1, \Sigma, \delta_1, \alpha_1 \rangle$, $\sigma \in \Sigma$ and $\langle s', o' \rangle \in 2^{\text{Loc}_1} \times 2^{\text{Loc}_1}$ such that $o' \subseteq s'$, the set $L_{\text{Pre}} = \text{Pre}_\sigma^{\text{alt}}(\langle s, o \rangle)$ computed by Algorithm 1 is an $\preceq_{\text{alt}}$-antichain such that $\downarrow L_{\text{Pre}} = \text{Pre}_\sigma^{\mathcal{A}_2}(\downarrow\{\langle s', o' \rangle\})$ where $\mathcal{A}_2 = \text{MH}(\mathcal{A}_1)$.*

Proof. Let $\mathcal{A}_2 = \text{MH}(\mathcal{A}_1) = \langle \text{Loc}_2, \iota_2, \Sigma, \delta_2, \alpha_2 \rangle$. We show that (1) $L_{\text{Pre}} \subseteq \text{Pre}_\sigma^{\mathcal{A}_2}(\downarrow \{\langle s', o' \rangle\})$ and (2) for all $\langle s_1, o_1 \rangle \in \text{Pre}_\sigma^{\mathcal{A}_2}(\downarrow\{\langle s', o' \rangle\})$, there exists $\langle s, o \rangle \in L_{\text{Pre}}$ such that $\langle s_1, o_1 \rangle \preceq_{\text{alt}} \langle s, o \rangle$. This entails that $\downarrow L_{\text{Pre}} = \text{Pre}_\sigma^{\mathcal{A}_2}(\downarrow\{\langle s', o' \rangle\})$.

To prove (1), we first show that $\langle s, o \rangle \xrightarrow{\sigma}_{\delta_2} \langle s', o' \rangle$ where $\langle s, o \rangle$ is added to L_{Pre} at line 7 of Algorithm 1. By the test of line 5, we have $o \neq \emptyset$. According to the definition of $\text{MH}(\cdot)$ (see Section 2), we have to check that there exists a set $o'' \subseteq s'$ such that $o' = o'' \setminus \alpha_1$ (we take $o'' = o' \cup (s' \cap \alpha_1)$), and the following conditions hold:

(i) $s' \models \bigwedge_{\ell \in s} \delta_1(\ell, \sigma)$ since we have $s' \models \delta_1(\ell, \sigma)$ for all $\ell \in s$ by line 6 of Alg. 1.

(ii) $o'' \models \bigwedge_{\ell \in o} \delta_1(\ell, \sigma)$ since we have $o'' \models \delta_1(\ell, \sigma)$ for all $\ell \in o$ by line 2 of Alg. 1.

Second, we show that $\langle o, \emptyset \rangle \xrightarrow{\sigma}_{\delta_2} \langle s'', o'' \rangle$ for some $\langle s'', o'' \rangle \preceq_{\text{alt}} \langle s', o' \rangle$ where $\langle o, \emptyset \rangle$ is added to L_{Pre} at line 4 of Algorithm 1.

We take $s'' = o' \cup (s' \cap \alpha_1)$ and $o'' = s'' \setminus \alpha_1$. Since $o' \subseteq s'$, we have (a) $s'' \subseteq s'$, and we have (b) $o'' = o' \setminus \alpha_1 \subseteq o'$. Let us establish that (c) $o' = \emptyset$ iff $o'' = \emptyset$. If $o' = \emptyset$ then $o'' = \emptyset$ since $o'' \subseteq o'$. If $o' \neq \emptyset$ then by the test of line 3, we have $o' \not\subseteq \alpha_1$ and thus $o'' = o' \setminus \alpha_1 \neq \emptyset$. Hence we have $\langle s'', o'' \rangle \preceq_{\mathsf{alt}} \langle s', o' \rangle$, and by line 2 of the algorithm, we have $s'' \models \delta_1(\ell, \sigma)$ for all $\ell \in o$, and thus $s'' \models \bigwedge_{\ell \in o} \delta_1(\ell, \sigma)$. Therefore $\langle o, \emptyset \rangle \xrightarrow{\sigma}_{\delta_2} \langle s'', o'' \rangle$.

To prove (2), assume that there exist $\langle s_1, o_1 \rangle$ and $\langle s_1', o_1' \rangle$ such that $\langle s_1, o_1 \rangle \xrightarrow{\sigma}_{\delta_2}$ $\langle s_1', o_1' \rangle$ and $\langle s_1', o_1' \rangle \preceq_{\mathsf{alt}} \langle s', o' \rangle$. We have to show that there exists $\langle s, o \rangle \in L_{\mathsf{Pre}}$ such that $\langle s_1, o_1 \rangle \preceq_{\mathsf{alt}} \langle s, o \rangle$.

First, assume that $o_1 \neq \emptyset$. Since $\langle s_1, o_1 \rangle \xrightarrow{\sigma}_{\delta_2} \langle s_1', o_1' \rangle$, we have:

(i) for all $\ell \in s_1$, $s_1' \models \delta_1(\ell, \sigma)$ and since $s_1' \subseteq s'$ also $s' \models \delta_1(\ell, \sigma)$. Let s be the set defined at line 6 of Algorithm 1. For all $\ell \in \mathsf{Loc}$, if $s' \models \delta_1(\ell, \sigma)$ then $\ell \in s$. Hence, $s_1 \subseteq s$.

(ii) for all $\ell \in o_1$, $o_1'' \models \delta_1(\ell, \sigma)$ for some $o_1'' \subseteq s_1'$ such that $o_1' = o_1'' \setminus \alpha_1$. Hence necessarily $o_1'' \subseteq o_1' \cup (s_1' \cap \alpha_1) \subseteq o' \cup (s' \cap \alpha_1)$ and thus for all $\ell \in o_1$, $o' \cup (s' \cap \alpha_1) \models \delta_1(\ell, \sigma)$. Let o be the set defined at line 2 of Algorithm 1. For all $\ell \in \mathsf{Loc}$, if $o' \cup (s' \cap \alpha_1) \models \delta_1(\ell, \sigma)$ then $\ell \in o$. Hence, $o_1 \subseteq o$ and $o \neq \emptyset$.

Hence, $\langle s, o \rangle$ which is added to L_{Pre} by Alg. 1 at line 7 satisfies $\langle s_1, o_1 \rangle \preceq_{\mathsf{alt}} \langle s, o \rangle$.

Second, assume that $o_1 = \emptyset$. Since $\langle s_1, o_1 \rangle \xrightarrow{\sigma}_{\delta'} \langle s_1', o_1' \rangle$ and $o_1 = \emptyset$, we know that for all $\ell \in s_1$, $s_1' \models \delta_1(\ell, \sigma)$ and $o_1' = s_1' \setminus \alpha_1$. Let $s'' = o' \cup (s' \cap \alpha_1)$ so we have (a) $s_1' \cap \alpha_1 \subseteq s' \cap \alpha_1 \subseteq s''$ and (b) $s_1' \setminus \alpha_1 = o_1' \subseteq o' \subseteq s''$. Hence, $s_1' \subseteq s''$ and thus for all $\ell \in s_1$, $s'' \models \delta_1(\ell, \sigma)$. Let o be the set defined at line 2 of Algorithm 1. For all $\ell \in \mathsf{Loc}$, if $s'' \models \delta_1(\ell, \sigma)$ then $\ell \in o$. Hence, $s_1 \subseteq o$ and $\langle s_1, \emptyset \rangle \preceq_{\mathsf{alt}} \langle o, \emptyset \rangle$ where $\langle o, \emptyset \rangle$ is added to L_{Pre} by Algorithm 1 at line 4. Notice that the test at line 3 is satisfied because $o_1' = s_1' \setminus \alpha_1$ implies that $o_1' \not\subseteq \alpha_1 \vee o_1' = \emptyset$ and since $\langle s_1', o_1' \rangle \preceq_{\mathsf{alt}} \langle s', o' \rangle$, we have $o' \not\subseteq \alpha_1 \vee o' = \emptyset$. ∎

5   Universality of NBW

Given the NBW $\mathcal{A} = \langle \mathsf{Loc}, \iota, \Sigma, \delta, \alpha \rangle$, we define the pre-order $\preceq_{\mathsf{univ}} \subseteq (2^{\mathsf{Loc} \times \mathbb{N}} \times 2^{\mathsf{Loc} \times \mathbb{N}}) \times (2^{\mathsf{Loc} \times \mathbb{N}} \times 2^{\mathsf{Loc} \times \mathbb{N}})$ as follows: for $s, s', o, o' \subseteq \mathsf{Loc} \times \mathbb{N}$, let $\langle s, o \rangle \preceq_{\mathsf{univ}} \langle s', o' \rangle$ iff the following conditions hold:

– for all $(\ell, n) \in s$, there exists $(\ell, n') \in s'$ such that $n' \leq n$;
– for all $(\ell, n) \in o$, there exists $(\ell, n') \in o'$ such that $n' \leq n$;
– $o = \emptyset$ iff $o' = \emptyset$.

This relation formalizes the intuition that it is easier to accept a word in $\mathsf{KVMH}(\mathcal{A}, k)$ from a given location with a high rank than with a low rank. This is because the rank is always decreasing along every path of the runs of $\mathsf{KV}(\mathcal{A}, k)$, and so a rank is always simulated by a greater rank. Hence essentially the minimal rank of s and o is relevant to define the pre-order $\preceq_{\mathsf{univ}}$. The third condition requires that only accepting states simulate accepting states.

The relation $\preceq_{\mathsf{univ}}$ is a simulation for the NBW $\mathsf{KVMH}(\mathcal{A}, k)$ (with state space $Q_k \times Q_k$) defined in Section 2.

Lemma 9. *For all NBW $\mathcal{A}$, for all even numbers $k \in \mathbb{N}$, the restriction of $\preceq_{\text{univ}}$ to $(Q_k \times Q_k) \times (Q_k \times Q_k)$ is a simulation for the NBW KVMH$(\mathcal{A}, k)$ of Definition 3.*

According to Lemma 6, all the intermediate sets that are computed by the fixed point $\mathcal{F}_{\mathcal{A}^c}$ to check emptiness of $\mathcal{A}^c = \text{KVMH}(\mathcal{A}, k)$ for $k = 2(|\text{Loc}| - |\alpha|)$ (and thus universality of $\mathcal{A}$) are $\preceq_{\text{univ}}$-closed.

Before computing $\cup$, $\cap$ and Pre for $\preceq_{\text{univ}}$-closed sets, we make the following useful observation. Given a set $s \in Q_k$, define its *characteristic function* $f_s : \text{Loc} \rightarrow \mathbb{N} \cup \{\infty\}$ such that $f_s(\ell) = \inf\{n \mid (\ell, n) \in s\}$ with the usual convention that $\inf \emptyset = \infty$.

Lemma 10. *For all sets $s, s', o, o' \in Q_k$, if $f_s = f_{s'}$ and $f_o = f_{o'}$, then $\langle s, o \rangle \preceq_{\text{univ}} \langle s', o' \rangle$ and $\langle s', o' \rangle \preceq_{\text{univ}} \langle s, o \rangle$.*

Let f, g, f', g' be characteristic functions. We write $f \le f'$ iff for all $\ell \in \text{Loc}$, $f(\ell) \le f'(\ell)$ and we write $\langle f, g \rangle \le \langle f', g' \rangle$ iff $f \le f'$ and $g \le g'$. Let $\max(f, f')$ be the function f'' such that $f''(\ell) = \max\{f(\ell), f'(\ell)\}$ for all $\ell \in \text{Loc}$. We write $f_\emptyset$ for the function such that $f_\emptyset(\ell) = \infty$ for all $\ell \in \text{Loc}$. Given an even number $k \in \mathbb{N}$, define the set $[\![f]\!]_k = \{s \in Q_k \mid f_s = f\}$ and the set $[\![\langle f, g \rangle]\!]_k = \{\langle s, o \rangle \mid s \in [\![f]\!]_k \wedge o \in [\![g]\!]_k \wedge o \subseteq s\}$. Observe that $f \le f'$ iff $[\![f']\!]_k \subseteq [\![f]\!]_k$. We extend the operator $[\![\cdot]\!]_k$ to sets of pairs of characteristic functions as expected. According to Lemma 10, the set $[\![\langle f, g \rangle]\!]_k$ is an equivalence class for the equivalence relation induced by $\preceq_{\text{univ}}$, and a $\preceq_{\text{univ}}$-closed set (as well as its $\preceq_{\text{univ}}$-maximal elements) is a union of equivalence classes, so it can be equivalently seen as a union of pairs of characteristic functions.

Now, we show how to compute efficiently $\cup$, $\cap$ and Pre for $\preceq_{\text{univ}}$-closed sets that are represented by characteristic functions. Let L_1, L_2 be two sets of pairs of characteristic functions, let $L_\cup$ be the set of $\le$-minimal elements of $L_1 \cup L_2$, and let $L_\cap = \{\langle \max(f_s, f_{s'}), \max(f_o, f_{o'}) \rangle \mid \langle f_s, f_o \rangle \in L_1 \wedge \langle f_{s'}, f_{o'} \rangle \in L_2 \wedge \max(f_o, f_{o'}) \ne f_\emptyset\} \cup \{\langle \max(f_s, f_{s'}), f_\emptyset \rangle \mid \langle f_s, f_\emptyset \rangle \in L_1 \wedge \langle f_{s'}, f_\emptyset \rangle \in L_2\}$. Then, we have $[\![L_\cup]\!]_k = \text{Max}(\downarrow [\![L_1]\!]_k \cup \downarrow [\![L_2]\!]_k)$ and $[\![L_\cap]\!]_k = \text{Max}(\downarrow [\![L_1]\!]_k \cap \downarrow [\![L_2]\!]_k)$.

To compute $\text{Pre}_\sigma(\cdot)$ of a single pair of characteristic functions, we propose Algorithm 2 whose correctness is established by Theorem 11. Computing the predecessors of a set of characteristic functions is then straightforward using the algorithm for union of sets of pairs of characteristic functions since

$$\text{Pre}^{\text{KVMH}(\mathcal{A},k)}(L) = \bigcup_{\sigma \in \Sigma} \bigcup_{\ell \in L} \text{Pre}_\sigma^{\text{KVMH}(\mathcal{A},k)}(\ell)$$

Theorem 11. *Given a NBW $\mathcal{A} = \langle \text{Loc}, \iota, \Sigma, \delta, \alpha \rangle$, $\sigma \in \Sigma$, an even number k, and a pair of characteristic functions $\langle f_{s'}, f_{o'} \rangle$ such that $f_{s'} \le f_{o'}$, the set $L_{\text{Pre}} = \text{Pre}_\sigma^{\text{univ}}(\langle f_{s'}, f_{o'} \rangle)$ computed by Algorithm 2 is such that $\downarrow [\![L_{\text{Pre}}]\!]_k = \text{Pre}_\sigma^{\text{KVMH}(\mathcal{A},k)}(\downarrow [\![\langle f_{s'}, f_{o'} \rangle]\!]_k)$ and $\forall \langle f_s, f_o \rangle \in L_{\text{Pre}} : f_s \le f_o$.*

In Algorithm 2, we represent ∞ by any number strictly greater than k, and we adapt the definition of $\le$ as follows: $f \le f'$ iff for all $\ell \in \text{Loc}$, either $f(\ell) \le f'(\ell)$ or $f'(\ell) > k$. In the algorithm, we use the notations $\lceil n \rceil^{\text{odd}}$ for the least odd number n' such that $n' \ge n$, and $\lceil n \rceil^{\text{even}}$ for the least even number n' such that $n' \ge n$.

The structure of Algorithm 2 is similar to Algorithm 1, but the computations are expressed in terms of characteristic functions, thus in terms of ranks. For example,

Algorithm 2. Algorithm for $\mathsf{Pre}_\sigma^{\mathsf{univ}}(\cdot)$.

Data	: A NBW $\mathcal{A} = \langle \mathsf{Loc}, \iota, \Sigma, \delta, \alpha \rangle$, $\sigma \in \Sigma$, an even number k and a pair $\langle f_{s'}, f_{o'} \rangle$ of characteristic functions.
Result	: The set $\mathsf{Pre}_\sigma^{\mathsf{univ}}(\langle f_{s'}, f_{o'} \rangle)$.

begin

1   **foreach** $\ell \in \mathsf{Loc}$ **do**

2      $f_o(\ell) \leftarrow 0$;

3   **foreach** $\ell' \in \delta(\ell, \sigma)$ **do**

4   **if** $\ell' \in \alpha$ **then** $f_o(\ell) \leftarrow \max\{f_o(\ell), f_{o'}(\ell')\}$;

5   **else** $f_o(\ell) \leftarrow \max\{f_o(\ell), \min\{f_{o'}(\ell'), \lceil f_{s'}(\ell') \rceil^{\mathsf{odd}}\}\}$;

6   **if** $\ell \in \alpha$ **then** $f_o(\ell) \leftarrow \lceil f_o(\ell) \rceil^{\mathsf{even}}$;

7    $L_{\mathsf{Pre}} \leftarrow \{\langle f_o, f_\emptyset \rangle\}$;

8   **if** $\exists \ell : f_o(\ell) \leq k$ *(i.e. $o \neq \emptyset$)* **then**

9   **foreach** $\ell \in \mathsf{Loc}$ **do**

10        $f_s(\ell) \leftarrow \max\{f_{s'}(\ell') \mid \ell' \in \delta(\ell, \sigma)\}$;

11   **if** $\ell \in \alpha$ **then** $f_s(\ell) \leftarrow \lceil f_s(\ell) \rceil^{\mathsf{even}}$;

12      $L_{\mathsf{Pre}} \leftarrow L_{\mathsf{Pre}} \cup \{\langle f_s, f_o \rangle\}$;

13   **return** L_{Pre};

end

lines 4-5 compute the equivalent of line 2 in Algorithm 1, where α_1 corresponds here to the set of odd-ranked locations, and thus contains no α-nodes. Details are given in the proof of Theorem 11. Algorithm 2 runs in time $O(|\mathsf{Loc}|^2)$, which is no more computationally expensive than the classical Pre. However, there is often an exponential factor between the number of elements in the argument of Pre in the two approaches. For example, the set $\alpha' = 2^{\mathsf{Loc} \times [k]} \times \{\emptyset\}$ with an exponential number of elements is represented by the unique pair $\langle f_s, f_\emptyset \rangle$ where $f_s(\ell) = 0$ for all $\ell \in \mathsf{Loc}$, which makes the new approach much more efficient in practice.

6   Implementation and Practical Evaluation

The randomized model. To evaluate our new algorithm for universality of NBW and compare with the existing implementations of the Kupferman-Vardi and Miyano-Hayashi constructions, we use a random model to generate NBW. This model was first proposed by Tabakov and Vardi to compare the efficiency of some algorithms for automata in the context of finite words automata [TV05] and more recently in the context of infinite words automata [Tab06]. In the model, the input alphabet is fixed to $\Sigma = \{0, 1\}$, and for each letter $\sigma \in \Sigma$, a number k_σ of different state pairs $(\ell, \ell') \in \mathsf{Loc} \times \mathsf{Loc}$ are chosen uniformly at random before the corresponding transitions (ℓ, σ, ℓ') are added to the automaton. The ratio $r_\sigma = \frac{k_\sigma}{|\mathsf{Loc}|}$ is called the *transition density* for σ. This ratio represents the average outdegree of each state for σ. In all

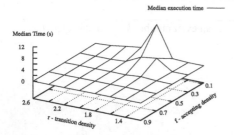
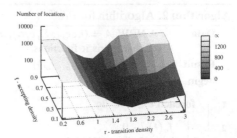

Fig. 1. Median time to check universality of 100 automata of size 30 for each sample point

Fig. 2. Automata size for which the median execution time to check universality is less than 20 seconds (log scale)

experiments, we choose $r_0 = r_1$, and denote the transition density by r. The model contains a second parameter: the *density f of accepting states*. There is only one initial state, and the number m of accepting states is linear in the total number of states, as determined by $f = \frac{m}{|Loc|}$. The accepting states themselves are chosen uniformly at random. Observe that since the transition relation is not always total, automata with $f = 1$ are not necessarily universal.

Tabakov and Vardi have studied the space of parameter values for this model and argue that "interesting" automata are generated by the model as the two parameters r and f vary. They also study the density of universal automata in [Tab06].

Performance comparison. We have implemented our algorithm to check the universality of randomly generated NBW. The code is written in C with an explicit representation for characteristic functions, as arrays of integers. All the experiments are conducted on a biprocessor Linux station (two 3.06Ghz Intel Xeons with 4GB of RAM).

Fig. 1 shows as a function of r (transition density) and f (density of accepting states) the median execution times for testing universality of 100 random automata with $|Loc| = 30$. It shows that the universality test was the most difficult for $r = 1.8$ and $f = 0.1$ with a median time of 11 seconds. The times for $r \leq 1$ and $r \geq 2.8$ are not plotted because they were always less than 250ms. A similar shape and maximal median time is reported by Tabakov for automata of size 6, that is for automata that are five times smaller [Tab06]. Another previous work reports prohibitive execution times for complementing NBW of size 6, showing that explicitly constructing the complement is not a reasonable approach [GKSV03].

To evaluate the scalability of our algorithm, we have ran the following experiment. For a set of parameter values, we have evaluated the maximal size of automata (measured in term of number of locations) for which our algorithm could analyze 50 over 100 instances in less than 20 seconds. We have tried automata sizes from 10 to 1500, with a fine granularity for small sizes (from 10 to 100 with an increment of 10, from 100 to 200 with an increment of 20, and from 200 to 500 with an increment of 30) and a rougher granularity for large sizes (from 500 to 1000 with an increment of 50, and from 1000 to 1500 with an increment of 100).

The results are shown in Fig. 2, and the corresponding values are given in Table 1. The vertical scale is logarithmic. For example, for $r = 2$ and $f = 0.5$, our algorithm

Table 1. Automata size for which the median execution time for checking universality is less than 20 seconds. The symbol $\propto$ means *more than 1500*.

r f	0.2	0.4	0.6	0.8	1.0	1.2	1.4	1.6	1.8	2.0	2.2	2.4	2.6	2.8	3.0
0.1	$\propto$	$\propto$	$\propto$	550	200	120	60	40	30	40	50	50	70	90	100
0.3	$\propto$	$\propto$	$\propto$	500	200	100	40	30	40	70	100	120	160	180	200
0.5	$\propto$	$\propto$	$\propto$	500	200	120	60	60	90	120	120	120	140	260	500
0.7	$\propto$	$\propto$	$\propto$	500	200	120	70	80	100	200	440	1000	$\propto$	$\propto$	$\propto$
0.9	$\propto$	$\propto$	$\propto$	500	180	100	80	200	600	$\propto$	$\propto$	$\propto$	$\propto$	$\propto$	$\propto$

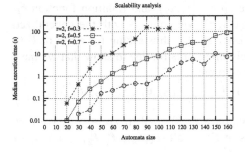

Fig. 3. Median time to check universality (of 100 automata for each sample point)

Fig. 4. Execution time to check universality of 100 automata, 57 of which were universal

was able to handle at least 50 automata of size 120 in less than 20 seconds and was not able to do so for automata of size 140. In comparison, Tabakov and Vardi have studied the behavior of Kupferman-Vardi and Miyano-Hayashi constructions for different implementation schemes. We compare with the performances of their symbolic approach which is the most efficient. For the same parameter values ($r = 2$ and $f = 0.5$), they report that their implementation can handle NBW with at most 8 states in less than 20 seconds [Tab06].

In Fig. 3, we show the median execution time to check universality for relatively difficult instances ($r = 2$ and f vary from 0.3 to 0.7). The vertical scale is logarithmic, so the behavior is roughly exponential in the size of the automata. Similar analyzes are reported in [Tab06] but for sizes below 10.

Finally, we give in Fig. 4 the distribution of execution times for 100 automata of size 50 with $r = 2.2$ and $f = 0.5$, so that roughly half of the instances are universal. Each point represents one automaton, and one point lies outside the figure with an execution time of 675s for a non universal automaton. The existence of very few instances that are very hard was often encountered in the experiments, and this is why we use the median for the execution times. If we except this hard instance, Fig. 4 shows that universal automata (average time 350ms) are slightly easier to analyze than non-universal automata (average time 490ms). This probably comes from the fact that we stop the computation of the (greatest) fixed point whenever the initial state is no more $\preceq_{univ}$-less than the successive approximations. Indeed, in such case, since the approximations are

$\preceq_{univ}$-decreasing, we know that the initial state would also not lie in the fixed point. Of course, this optimization applies only for universal automata.

7 Language Inclusion for Büchi Automata

Let $\mathcal{A}_1 = \langle \mathsf{Loc}_1, \iota_1, \Sigma, \delta_1, \alpha_1 \rangle$ and $\mathcal{A}_2$ be two NBW defined on the same alphabet Σ for which we want to check language inclusion: $\mathcal{L}(\mathcal{A}_1) \subseteq^? \mathcal{L}(\mathcal{A}_2)$. To solve this problem, we check emptiness of $\mathcal{L}(\mathcal{A}_1) \cap \mathcal{L}^c(\mathcal{A}_2)$. As we have seen, we can use the Kupferman-Vardi and Miyano-Hayashi construction to specify a NBW $\mathcal{A}_2^c = \langle \mathsf{Loc}_2, \iota_2, \Sigma, \delta_2, \alpha_2 \rangle$ that accepts the complement of the language of $\mathcal{A}_2$.

Using the classical product construction, let $\mathcal{B}$ be a finite automaton with set of locations $\mathsf{Loc}_{\mathcal{B}} = \mathsf{Loc}_1 \times \mathsf{Loc}_2$, initial state $\iota_{\mathcal{B}} = (\iota_1, \iota_2)$, and tranition function $\delta_{\mathcal{B}}$ such that $\delta_{\mathcal{B}}((\ell_1, \ell_2), \sigma) = \delta_1(\ell_1, \sigma) \times \delta_2(\ell_2, \sigma)$. We equip $\mathcal{B}$ with the generalized Büchi condition $\{\beta_1, \beta_2\} = \{\alpha_1 \times \mathsf{Loc}_2, \mathsf{Loc}_1 \times \alpha_2\}$, thus asking for a run of $\mathcal{B}$ to be accepting that it visits β_1 and β_2 infinitely often. It is routine to show that we have $\mathcal{L}(\mathcal{B}) = \mathcal{L}(\mathcal{A}_1) \cap \mathcal{L}(\mathcal{A}_2^c)$. The following fixed point

$$\mathcal{F}'_{\mathcal{B}} \equiv \nu y \cdot \left(\mu x_1 \cdot \left[\mathsf{Pre}^{\mathcal{B}}(x_1) \cup (\mathsf{Pre}^{\mathcal{B}}(y) \cap \beta_1) \right] \cap \mu x_2 \cdot \left[\mathsf{Pre}^{\mathcal{B}}(x_2) \cup (\mathsf{Pre}^{\mathcal{B}}(y) \cap \beta_2) \right] \right)$$

can be used to check emptiness of $\mathcal{B}$ as we have $\mathcal{L}(\mathcal{B}) \neq \emptyset$ iff $\iota_{\mathcal{B}} \in \mathcal{F}'_{\mathcal{B}}$. We now define the pre-order $\preceq_{inc}$ over the locations of $\mathcal{B}$: for all $(\ell_1, \ell_2), (\ell'_1, \ell'_2) \in \mathsf{Loc}_{\mathcal{B}}$, let $(\ell_1, \ell_2) \preceq_{inc} (\ell'_1, \ell'_2)$ iff $\ell_1 = \ell'_1$ and $\ell_2 \preceq_{univ} \ell'_2$.

Lemma 12. *The relation $\preceq_{inc}$ is a simulation for $\mathcal{B}$.*

As a consequence of the last lemma, we know that all the sets that we have to manipulate to solve the language inclusion problem using the fixed point $\mathcal{F}'_{\mathcal{B}}$ are $\preceq_{inc}$-closed. The operators $\cup$, $\cap$ and Pre can be thus computed efficiently, using the same algorithms and data structures as for universality. In particular, let $\mathsf{Pre}_\sigma^{inc}(\ell'_1, \ell'_2) = \mathsf{Pre}_\sigma^{\mathcal{A}_1}(\ell'_1) \times \mathsf{Pre}_\sigma^{univ}(\ell'_2)$ where $\mathsf{Pre}_\sigma^{univ}$ is computed by Algorithm 2 (with input $\mathcal{A}_2$). It is easy to show as a corollary of Theorem 11 that $\downarrow \mathsf{Pre}_\sigma^{inc}(\ell'_1, \ell'_2) = \mathsf{Pre}_\sigma^{\mathcal{B}}(\downarrow \{(\ell'_1, \ell'_2)\})$.

8 Conclusion

We have shown that the expensive complementation constructions for nondeterministic Büchi automata can be avoided for solving classical problems like universality and language inclusion. Our approach is based on fixed points computation and the existence of simulation relations for the (exponential) constructions used in complementation of Büchi automata. Those simulations are used to dramatically reduce the amount of computations needed to decide classical problems. Their definition relies on the structure of the original automaton and do not require explicit complementation.

The resulting algorithms evaluate a fixed point formula and avoid redundant computations by maintaining sets of maximal elements according to the simulation relation. In practice, the computation of the predecessor operator, which is the key of the approach, is efficient because it is done on antichain of elements only. Eventhough the classical approaches (as well as ours) have the same worst case complexity, our prototype implementation outperforms those approaches where complementation is explicit. The huge gap of performances holds over the entire parameter space of the randomized model proposed by Tabakov and Vardi.

Applications of this paper go beyond universality and language inclusion for NBW, as we have shown that the methodology applies to alternating Büchi automata for which efficient translations from LTL formula are known [GO01]. The hope rises then that significant improvements can be brought to the model-checking problem of LTL.

References

[BL69]   J. Richard Büchi and Lawrence H. Landweber. Definability in the monadic second-order theory of successor. *J. Symb. Log.*, 34(2):166–170, 1969.

[DDHR06]   M. De Wulf, L. Doyen, T. A. Henzinger, and J.-F. Raskin. Antichains: A new algorithm for checking universality of finite automata. In *Proceedings of CAV 2006, LNCS* 4144, pp. 17–30. Springer.

[DR06]   L. Doyen and J.-F. Raskin. Improved Algorithms for the Automata-Based Approach to Model-Checking (extended version) Tech. Rep. 76, U.L.B. – Federated Center in Verification, 2006. http://www.ulb.ac.be/di/ssd/cfv/publications.html.

[EWS05]   K. Etessami, T. Wilke, and R. A. Schuller. Fair simulation relations, parity games, and state space reduction for bu"chi automata. *SIAM J. Comput.*, 34(5):1159–1175, 2005.

[GKSV03]   S. Gurumurthy, O. Kupferman, F. Somenzi, and M. Y. Vardi. On complementing nondeterministic büchi automata. In *Proc. of CHARME 2003, LNCS* 2860, pp. 96–110. Springer.

[GO01]   P. Gastin and D. Oddoux. Fast LTL to Büchi automata translation. In *Proc. of CAV 2001, LNCS* 2102, pp. 53–65. Springer.

[KV97]   O. Kupferman and M. Y. Vardi. Weak alternating automata are not that weak. In *Proceedings of ISTCS'97*, pp. 147–158. IEEE Computer Society Press.

[MH84]   Satoru Miyano and Takeshi Hayashi. Alternating finite automata on omega-words. In *CAAP*, pages 195–210, 1984.

[Mic88]   Max Michel. Complementation is more difficult with automata on infinite words. CNET, Paris, 1988.

[RH04]   Theo C. Ruys and Gerard J. Holzmann. Advanced spin tutorial. In *SPIN, LNCS* 2989, pp. 304–305. Springer, 2004.

[Saf88]   Shmuel Safra. On the complexity of ω-automata. In *Proc. of FOCS: Foundations of Computer Science*, pages 319–327. IEEE, 1988.

[SVW87]   A. P. Sistla, M. Y. Vardi and P. Wolper. The Complementation Problem for Büchi Automata with Applications to Temporal Logic. *Theor. Comput. Sci.*, 49:217–237, 1987.

[Tab06]   D. Tabakov. Experimental evaluation of explicit and symbolic approaches to complementation of non-deterministic buechi automata. *Talk at "Games and Verification" workshop, Newton Institute for Math. Sciences.* July 2006.

[TV05]   D. Tabakov and M. Y. Vardi. Experimental evaluation of classical automata constructions. In *LPAR* 2005, *LNCS* 3835, pp. 396–411. Springer.

[VW86]   M. Y. Vardi and P. Wolper. An automata-theoretic approach to automatic program verification (prelim. report). In *LICS* 1986, pp. 332–344. IEEE.

[VW94]   Moshe Y. Vardi and Pierre Wolper. Reasoning about infinite computations. *Inf. Comput.*, 115(1):1–37, 1994.

GOAL: A Graphical Tool for Manipulating Büchi Automata and Temporal Formulae[*]

Yih-Kuen Tsay, Yu-Fang Chen, Ming-Hsien Tsai, Kang-Nien Wu, and Wen-Chin Chan

Department of Information Management, National Taiwan University, Taiwan

1 Introduction

In this paper, we present a tool named GOAL (an acronym derived from "Graphical Tool for Omega-Automata and Logics") whose main functions include (1) drawing and testing Büchi automata, (2) checking the language equivalence between two Büchi automata, (3) translating quantified propositional linear temporal logic (QPTL) formulae into equivalent Büchi automata, and (4) exporting Büchi automata as Promela code. The GOAL tool, available at http://goal.im.ntu.edu.tw, can be used for educational purposes, helping the user get a better understanding of how Büchi automata work and how they are related to linear temporal logics. It may also be used, as we shall explain below, to construct correct and smaller specification automata, supplementing model checkers that adopt the automata-theoretic approach, such as SPIN [5].

The automata-theoretic approach [11,1] to linear temporal logic model checking works as follows. Suppose A is the Büchi automaton modeling the system and B the Büchi automaton specifying a desired property. The problem of model checking translates into that of testing language containment $L(A) \subseteq L(B)$, which is equivalent to $L(A) \cap \overline{L(B)} = \emptyset$. As Büchi automata are closed under complementation and intersection, this reduces to testing if $L(A \times \overline{B}) = \emptyset$, namely the emptiness problem of Büchi automata. Because of the difficulty and high complexity in complementing a Büchi automaton, in practice, an automata-theoretic model checker typically assumes that the specification is given as a propositional linear temporal logic (PTL) formula. The model checker first negates a specification formula φ and then translates it into an automaton $B_{\neg\varphi}$ that represents all behaviors disallowed by φ, i.e., $L(B_{\neg\varphi}) = \overline{L(B_\varphi)}$ (where B_φ is a Büchi automaton equivalent to formula φ). Checking if $L(A) \cap \overline{L(B_\varphi)} = L(A \times \overline{B_\varphi}) = \emptyset$ is therefore the same as checking if $L(A \times B_{\neg\varphi}) = \emptyset$, where one only needs to construct the intersection (product) of A and $B_{\neg\varphi}$, and complementation is avoided.

Assuming that the specification is given as a PTL formula has two disadvantages. *First, it limits the type of properties that can be specified and checked.* An ideal automata-theoretic model checker would support some extension of PTL such as QPTL that is expressively equivalent to Büchi automata. The SPIN

[*] This work was supported in part by the National Science Council of Taiwan (R.O.C.) under grants NSC95-2221-E-002-127 and NSC95-3114-P-001-001-Y02 (iCAST).

O. Grumberg and M. Huth (Eds.): TACAS 2007, LNCS 4424, pp. 466–471, 2007.

model checker offers the user instead the possibility of directly defining $B_{\neg\varphi}$ in Promela. However, it provides no assist for the user to check the "correctness" of the defined automaton, i.e., if the automaton describes what is intended. Büchi automata are in general harder to get right than temporal formulae. *Second, the machine-translated automaton $B_{\neg\varphi}$ may be larger than an optimal and equivalent one.* Many algorithms exist for translating a PTL formula into an equivalent Büchi automaton, e.g., [3,4], but none of them guarantee optimality. As the emptiness checking of $A \times B_{\neg\varphi}$ requires time proportional to the size of the system automaton A and to that of the specification automaton $B_{\neg\varphi}$, a larger $B_{\neg\varphi}$ would mean a longer verification time. To reduce verification time, it may be worthwhile to construct a smaller $B_{\neg\varphi}$ manually. But again, a way for checking the correctness of a user-defined $B_{\neg\varphi}$ is needed.

This is one typical situation where the GOAL tool can be useful. First of all, GOAL is graphical, making a user-defined automaton easier for human inspection. More importantly, the correctness of a user-defined specification automaton can be checked against an easier-to-understand QPTL formula, by translating the specification formula into an equivalent automaton and testing the equivalence between the user-defined and the machine-translated automata. QPTL is expressively equivalent to Büchi automata [9]. GOAL also supports past temporal operators which make some specifications easier to write. In addition, GOAL provides a repository that contains common patterns of temporal formulae and their corresponding optimized and machine-checked Büchi automata. Once the specification automaton of an ideal size has been successfully constructed and checked, it can be exported as Promela code which can then be fed into the SPIN model checker.

GOAL was originally designed for learning/teaching Büchi automata and linear temporal logics. Despite the possibility of mechanical translation, a temporal formula and its equivalent Büchi automaton are two very different artifacts and their correspondence is not easy to grasp. Temporal formulae describe temporal dependency without explicit references to time points and are in general more abstract and easier to understand, while Büchi automata "localize" temporal dependency to relations between states and tend to be of lower level and harder to understand. Nonetheless, Büchi automata and their relation with linear temporal logics can be better understood by going through some translation algorithm with different input temporal formulae or simply by examining more examples of temporal formulae and their equivalent Büchi automata. This learning process, unfortunately, is tedious and prone to mistakes for the students, while preparing the material is very time-consuming for the instructor. Tool support is needed.

An earlier version of GOAL has been introduced and suggested for educational purposes in [10]. However, its inability in handling quantified temporal formulae limited the kind of Büchi automata that could be explored. It also lacked the exporting function that allows its use in combination with an automata-theoretic model checker. To the best of our knowledge, GOAL is the first graphical interactive tool for manipulating Büchi automata and temporal formulae that supports past temporal operators and quantification over propositions. There are other tools that provide translation of temporal formulae into Büchi automata, e.g., LTL2BA [3]. However, none of them provide facilities for visually manipulating automata and the temporal logics they support are less expressive. The operations and tests on Büchi automata provided by GOAL are also more comprehensive than those by other tools.

2   Main Functions

Below is a brief description of the main functions of GOAL, followed by some implementation highlights.

- **Drawing and Testing Büchi Automata:** The user can easily point-and-click and drag-and-drop to create a Büchi automaton and test it. To get a feel of what kind of inputs the automaton accepts, the user can run it through some input words. More interestingly, an automaton can be tested for emptiness and two automata can be tested for language containment and equivalence, as well as simulation equivalence.
- **Checking the Language Equivalence between Two Büchi Automata:** This is a particularly useful test function. The equivalence test between two Büchi automata is built on top of the language containment test which in turns relies on the intersection and complementation operations and the emptiness test. If two automata are not equivalent, an infinite word which is contained in the difference of the two automata will be displayed as a counter example.
- **Translating QPTL Formulae into Equivalent Büchi Automata:** The user can type in a QPTL formula and ask GOAL to translate it into an equivalent Büchi automaton, as shown in Figure 1(a). Currently, GOAL imposes a restriction that a quantifier must not fall in the scope of a temporal operator. This restriction does not sacrifice expressiveness, as QPTL with the restriction is as expressive as the original unrestricted QPTL, which is expressively equivalent to Büchi automata [9]. Machine-translated Büchi automata are usually not optimal in terms of size, yet they are useful for verifying the correctness of user-defined automata (by the equivalence test). GOAL also supports past temporal operators which make some specifications easier to write, helping the user convey his intuition without much hacking.
- **The Automata Repository:** This repository contains a collection of frequently used QPTL formulae and their corresponding equivalent Büchi automata, which have been optimized by hand and checked by GOAL; see Figure 1(b) for an example.
- **Exporting Büchi Automata as Promela Code:** Once an automaton has been defined and tested, the user can export it in the Promela syntax on the screen or as a file, as shown in Figure 1(b). This makes it possible to use GOAL as a graphical specification definition frontend to an automata-theoretic model checker like SPIN.

GOAL is implemented in Java for the ease of installation. Its automata and graph modules were adapted from those of JFLAP [7], a tool for classic theory of computation. The most complicated algorithms in GOAL are those for

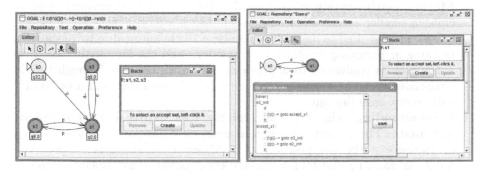

Fig. 1. Two equivalent Büchi automata that describe the property *"p* is true at every even position", which can also be expressed as a QPTL formula

translating temporal formulae into automata and for complementing automata. Our translation algorithm combines an adaptation of the tableau construction described in Manna and Pnueli's book [6] and the approach described in [9] for handling quantification. For automata complementation, we adopted the algorithm by Safra [8]. From inputs of a moderate size, these algorithms may produce very large automata, which are difficult to display and usually impossible to understand intuitively. However, this is not a serious problem, as on the one hand we intend GOAL to be used for educational purposes or for specification definition, where the input temporal formulae or automata tend to be small. On the other hand, the machine-generated automata are often used for equivalence tests, not for human inspection. Nonetheless, we did implement several methods for state reduction, for example, removing redundant states detected by simulation [2]. We have planned to include implementations of other translation and complementation algorithms, which would be useful for comparative studies.

3   Use Cases

We describe a number of use cases that illustrate how the GOAL functions may be combined and used in particular as a tool for learning/teaching Büchi automata and linear temporal logics or for specification development:

- **Checking correctness of a hand-drawn Büchi automaton:** Understanding a Büchi automaton is in general harder than understanding an equivalent temporal formula. Consequently, defining or drawing a Büchi automaton that conveys one's intention is also harder than writing a temporal formula for the same purpose. Whether a hand-drawn automaton is correct, i.e., if it conveys the specifier's intention, can be verified using GOAL by following these steps: (1) Write a QPTL (or PTL if it suffices) formula that specifies the same thing. (2) Translate the formula into an equivalent Büchi automaton. (3) Test the equivalence between the machine-translated and the hand-drawn automata. If the equivalence test is positive, then one can be assured that the hand-drawn Büchi automaton is indeed what is intended.

- **Manual optimization of a specification Büchi automaton:** In principle, a smaller specification automaton makes a model checker run faster. GOAL may be used to manually optimize a Büchi automaton by repeatedly merging or removing its states or transitions and checking if the resulting automaton is equivalent to a previous correct automaton. Though this is essentially a trial-and-error process, the equivalence test provided by GOAL will greatly ease the pain.
- **Understanding why PTL is strictly less expressive than Büchi automata:** The property "p is true at every even position" (an infinite word or sequence starts with position 0), or "Even p" for short, is a typical example for showing that PTL is strictly less expressive than Büchi automata. A plausible PTL formula for "Even p" would be "$p \wedge \Box(p \to \bigcirc\bigcirc p)$". Using GOAL, one can translate the formula into a Büchi automaton and compare it with the one for "Even p" from the repository. An equivalence test will show that the two automata are not equivalent and display a counter example. Indeed, the formula $p \wedge \Box(p \to \bigcirc\bigcirc p)$ is overly restrictive. Once p holds at some odd position, this formula forces p to hold at all subsequent odd positions, which is not required by "Even p". The property can, however, be expressed by a QPTL formula, e.g., $\exists t : t \wedge \Box(t \leftrightarrow \bigcirc\neg t) \wedge \Box(t \to p)$.
- **Combining GOAL with SPIN:** In the SPIN model checker, the specification can either be given as a PTL formula (without past operators) or directly as a Büchi automaton in Promela code. For a property that is not expressible in PTL, defining a suitable Büchi automaton becomes necessary. In this case, GOAL supplements SPIN by providing a convenient graphical interface for drawing and manipulating Büchi automata. Once the (negative) specification automaton of an ideal size has been successfully constructed and checked, it can be exported as Promela code. One can then copy-and-paste the Promela code to SPIN's model file as the "never claim" and continue the model checking procedure as usual.

4   Concluding Remarks

The GOAL tool will continue to be improved and extended. As the source of the acronym "GOAL" suggests, our long-term goal is for the tool to handle the common variants of omega-automata and the logics that are expressively equivalent to these automata. Currently, as by-products of Safra's complementation construction, GOAL already inlcudes Büchi to Rabin and Streett to Büchi translations. Although these variants of omega-automata do not necessarily have a direct impact on model-checking efficiency, they are powerful intermediaries for automata-based algorithms development. A tool that can visually manipulate these variants and perform their translations will be helpful in such developments. It is also of educational value, which should not be overlooked.

Acknowledgment. We thank Susan H. Rodger, the creator of JFLAP, at Duke University for granting us the permission to use and modify the JFLAP source code.

References

1. E.M. Clarke, O. Grumberg, and D.A. Peled. *Model Checking*. The MIT Press, 1999.
2. K. Etessami and G. Holzmann. Optimizing Büchi automata. In *Proceedings of the 11th International Conference on Concurrency Theory (CONCUR 2000), LNCS 1877*, pages 153–167. Springer, 2000.
3. P. Gastin and D. Oddoux. Fast LTL to Büchi automata translation. In *Proceedings of the 13th International Conference on Computer-Aided Verification (CAV 2001), LNCS 2102*, pages 53–65. Springer, 2001.
4. R. Gerth, D. Peled, M.Y. Vardi, and P. Wolper. Simple on-the-fly automatic verification of linear temporal logic. In *Protocol Specification, Testing, and Verification*, pages 3–18. Chapman & Hall, 1995.
5. G.J. Holzmann. *The SPIN Model Checker: Primer and Reference Manual*. Addison-Wesley, 2003.
6. Z. Manna and A. Pnueli. *Temporal Verification of Reactive Systems: Safty*. Springer, 1995.
7. S. Rodger and T. Finley. JFLAP. http://www.jflap.org/.
8. S. Safra. On the complexity of ω-automta. In *Proceedings of the 29th Annual IEEE Symposium on Foundations of Computer Science (FOCS 1988)*, pages 319–327, 1988.
9. A.P. Sistla, M. Vardi, and P. Wolper. The complementation problem for Büchi automata with applications to temporal logic. *Theoretical Computer Science*, 49:217–237, 1987.
10. Y.-K. Tsay, Y.-F. Chen, and K.-N. Wu. Tool support for learning Büchi automata and linear temporal logic. Presented at the Formal Methods in the Teaching Lab Workshop, Hamilton, Canada, August 2006.
11. M.Y. Vardi and P. Wolper. An automata-theoretic approach to automatic program verification. In *Proccedings of the 1st Annual IEEE Symposium on Logic in Computer Science (LICS 1986)*, pages 332–344, 1986.

Faster Algorithms for Finitary Games[*]

Florian Horn

LIAFA, Université Paris 7, Case 7014, 2 place Jussieu, F-75251 Paris 5, France
horn@liafa.jussieu.fr

Abstract. The theory of games is a prominent tool in the controller synthesis problem. The class of ω-regular games, in particular, offers a clear and robust model of specifications, and present an alternative vision of several logic-related problems. Each ω-regular condition can be expressed by a combination of safety and liveness conditions. An issue with the classical definition of liveness specifications is that there is no control over the time spent between two successive occurrences of the desired events. Finitary logics were defined to handle this problem, and recently, Chatterjee and Henzinger introduced games based on a finitary notion of liveness. They defined and studied finitary parity and Streett winning conditions. We present here faster algorithms for these games, as well as an improved upper bound on the memory needed by Eve in the Streett case.

1 Introduction

Games are one of the most practical tools to study the controller synthesis problem in open systems. The setting of the problem is translated into an arena, while the controller and the environment are the players that make decisions based on the current state of the system and the former actions of their opponent. The desired behaviour of the system is given as a constraint over the sequence of system states, usually in the form of an ω-regular condition [MP92]. The study of these ω-regular games is the subject of a very large part of the games theory (two out of many, [Tho95, AHK02]). These games also present the advantage of giving alternate tools to solve problems of model-checking and verification. However, they present some weaknesses when they are used in actual synthesis of controllers. Each ω-regular condition can be expressed by a combination of liveness and safety conditions. Safety specifications are sound in terms of controller synthesis: they ask for the controller to prevent the occurrence of undesirable events, as long as some other condition does not change. Liveness specifications, however, are not as satisfying. The classical definition asks only for the desired event to happen *eventually*, without any constraints on the number of transitions it may take. This allows more robust specifications, in the sense that they do not depend on the way a system is represented. In one-shot liveness (reachability), this is perfectly natural: the actual number of transitions

---

[*] Work supported by the EU-TMR network GAMES. Some of this work was done in RWTH, Aachen.

depends more on the particular representation we use than on the actual properties of the system studied. But as soon as we consider Büchi conditions, there exists behaviours compatible with these specifications in which the number of transitions between two visits to the target set is unbounded. On finite graphs, one can always take shortcuts to avoid these cases. When we consider parity conditions in open systems, however, there are cases where there is no bounded solution. Finitary conditions, in which the unbounded behaviours are forbidden were introduced in [AH94]. More recently, [BC06] proposed a logic based on a variant of the notion of ω-regularity that introduced bounds on the size of the set of states considered. A fragment of this logic, where the bounds concerns only the distance between events, express the finitary conditions.

In [CH06], Chatterjee and Henzinger introduced finitary games and studied the cases of parity and Streett specifications. They proved that both games were determined and provided algorithms computing the winning regions. The finitary parity problem was also proved to be in NP ∩ co-NP. We present here faster algorithms for both games, using Turing reductions to other variations on these games. The finitary parity game problem is proved to be in P, with a time complexity of $m \cdot n^2$, where n is the number of states in the arena and m is the number of edges. In comparison, the original algorithm of [CH06] had a time complexity of $O(n^{2c-3} \cdot c \cdot m)$ (c is the number of colors in the parity condition). The finitary Streett algorithm is faster than the original reduction to finitary parity with a complexity of $O(4^k \cdot k^2 \cdot m^2 \cdot n)$, where n and m still denotes the numbers of states and edges, and k is the number of pairs in the Streett condition. The algorithm of [CH06], based on a reduction to finitary parity games, had a complexity of $O((n \cdot k! \cdot k^2)^{2k-3} \cdot m \cdot k! \cdot k^3))$. In addition, our algorithm yields a strategy for Eve that uses $2^k \cdot k$ memory states, instead of $k! \cdot k^2$ in the strategy derived from the reduction.

Outline of the Paper. Section 2 defines the general notions on games we use in all the paper. Sections 3 defines several variants of parity games, including finitary ones, and gives algorithms that solve them. Section 4 does the same for Streett games. Finally, section 5 summarizes the results and presents some ideas about future work in this domain.

2 Definitions

A 2-player game is a tuple (V, E, Win) consisting of a graph (V, E) containing a token, and a winning condition $Win \subseteq V^\omega$. The token is always in one of the states and can only move along the edges. The set of states V is partitioned into Eve's states (V_E, represented by circles) and Adam's states (V_A, represented by squares). The owner of the state containing the token chooses the next state. An infinite play $\rho = q_1, q_2, \ldots$ is a sequence of states visited by the token, respecting the edge relation: $(q_i, q_{i+1}) \in E$ for all $i > 0$. We consider only infinite plays, by assuming that every state has at least one successor. A play in *Win* is winning for Eve. Otherwise, it is winning for Adam. For complexity computations, we will always denote by n the total number of states, and by m the total number of edges.

In this paper, we will only consider games on finite graphs. Most of the notions presented in this section also exist on infinite graphs, but our algorithms are not adapted to those. We will now introduce several definitions and tools used to solve games. See [Tho95, Zie98] for more detailed proofs.

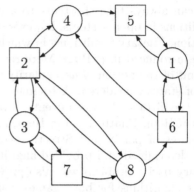

Definition 1. *A subgame of a game $G = (V, E, Win)$ is a game defined on a subset V' of V such that each state in V' has a successor in V'. The edges*

Fig. 1. A game graph

and the wining set are restrictions of E and Win to V'.

The *arena* of a game is the graph (V, E), including the partition between V_A and V_E. A *sub-arena* of an arena is the arena of a subgame. Many notions about games depend only on the arena of the game, and this allows us to export them from a game to another, as long as they are played on the same arena. The central notion of play, in particular, depends only of the arena.

A strategy for Eve (resp. Adam) is a function σ from V^*V_E (resp. V^*V_A) to V such that for any finite prefix w and any state q, there is an edge between q and $\sigma(w.q)$. Informally, a strategy for player P is a method of extending any finite prefix ending in a state of P. A strategy is positional if σ depends only on the current state. It has a finite memory if it can be realized by a finite-state transducer. A play is consistent with a strategy σ for P if $\forall i \in \mathbb{N}, \rho_i \in V_P \Rightarrow \rho_{i+1} = \sigma(\rho_{1..i})$. All these notions depend only on the arena of the game.

A strategy for P is winning for P from a state q if each play starting in q and consistent with it is won by P. The winning region of a player P in a game G, denoted by $Win_P(G)$, is the set of states from where P has a winning strategy.

The *attractor of W for player P in the game G*, denoted $Attr_P^G(W)$, is the set of states from which P can ensure that the token will reach the set W in a finite number of moves. It is computed inductively as usual:

$$W_0 = W$$
$$W_{n+1} = W_n$$
$$\cup \{q \in V_P \mid \exists q' \in W_n, (q, q') \in E\}$$
$$\cup \{q \in V \mid \forall q', (q, q') \in E \Rightarrow q' \in W_n\}$$

The *attractor strategy* for player P is positional, and consists in always going from a state of W_n to a state in W_{n-1}, thus getting closer to W. The complexity of the computation of either the attractor set or the attractor strategy is $O(m)$.

A *trap* is the dual of an attractor, and hence is a set from which one of the players cannot escape: A trap $T \subseteq V$ for player P is a region such that each state belonging to the other player has a successor in T, and each state in V_P has *all* its successors in T. Note that the complement of an attractor is a trap for the same player, and that a trap is always a sub-arena. Once again, the notions of attractor and trap depend only on the arena of the game.

In this paper, we will study the relations between several winning conditions defined on the same arena.

3   Parity Games

3.1   Parity Conditions

A parity coloring p is a function that associates an integer to each state of an arena $\mathcal{A}$. A parity arena is an arena equipped with a parity coloring. All the parity games that we define depend only on the parity arena they are played on. It is thus legitimate to talk about *the weak parity game on the arena $\mathcal{A}_p$* without further precision. In complexity computations, we will denote the number of colors in a parity arena by c.

The study of parity games is usually concerns one of the two following kind:

Weak parity games: A play is winning for Eve if the least color appearing in the play is even.

(Classical) parity games: A play is winning if the least color appearing infinitely often in the play is even.

In this paper, we will study another kind of parity games, called finitary parity. These games were introduced by Chatterjee and Henzinger in [CH06]. Intuitively, a play is winning for Eve in finitary parity if for each odd color that occurs infinitely often, a smaller even color occurs infinitely often, as in classical parity, with the added constraint that the delay between an occurrence of an odd color and the next smaller even color must be ultimately bounded.

The formal definition uses the notion of delay sequence of a play:

Definition 2. *The delay sequence $d(\rho)$ of a play ρ on a parity arena $\mathcal{A}_p$ is defined as follows:*

- *If $p(\rho_i)$ is even, then $d(\rho)_i = 0$.*
- *If $p(\rho_i)$ is odd, then $d(\rho)_i$ is the smallest j such that $p(\rho_{i+j})$ is even and $p((\rho)_{i+j}) < p(\rho_i)$. Note that if there is no such j, $d(\rho)_i = \infty$.*

A play ρ on a parity arena $\mathcal{A}_p$ is winning for Eve in the finitary parity game if and only if $d(\rho)$ is ultimately bounded. Note that, as the delay function can take infinite values, *ultimately bounded* is a weaker property than simply *bounded*.

Figure 2 gives some examples of how these games work. In arena 2(a), Adam can control the time between occurrences of 1, but an occurrence of 0 always comes immediately after. The delay sequence is made only of 0's and 1's. Thus Eve wins in the finitary parity game. In arena 2(b), Adam can control the time

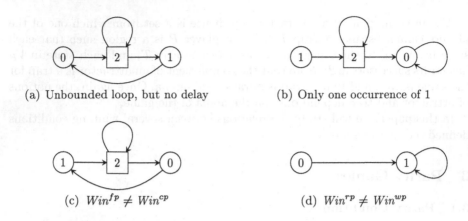

(a) Unbounded loop, but no delay

(b) Only one occurrence of 1

(c) $Win^{fp} \neq Win^{cp}$

(d) $Win^{rp} \neq Win^{wp}$

Fig. 2. Examples of parity games

spent between the first 1 and the next 0, or even choose to never go to 0. The first element of the sequence can thus be as high as Adam wants, or even infinite. But all following values will be equal to 0, so Eve wins in the finitary parity game. In the weak-parity game, Adam would have won if the play had begun in the state 1. In arena 2(c), however, Adam can delay the time between a 1 and the next 0 as long as he wants before allowing the loop to go on. Thus he can make the delay function unbounded and win the finitary game. Notice that he would not win in the classical parity game.

In [CH06], Chatterjee and Henzinger proved the following results about finitary parity games:

- Finitary parity games are determined ($Win_A^{fp}(\mathcal{A}) \cup Win_E^{fp}(\mathcal{A}) = \mathcal{A}$).
- In her winning region, Eve has a positional winning strategy.
- Adam may need strategies with infinite memory in order to win.
- Winning regions can be computed in time $O(n^{2c-3} \cdot c \cdot m)$.
- Deciding the winner in a given state is in NP ∩ co-NP.

Our algorithm for finitary games uses yet another kind of parity games, that we call repeating parity game. These games are also defined in terms of delay sequence: A play ρ is winning if the associated delay sequence only takes finite values. Intuitively, it means that for each occurrence of an odd color, there is later an occurrence of a smaller even color.

These games are different from the other parity games we defined. In figure 2(b), Adam will win if the play starts in state 1, by blocking the token in state 2, while Eve would have won a finitary or classical game. In figure 2(d), he wins again, even if the play starts in state 0, while Eve would have won a weak game. The definition does not supposes that the delay function is bounded. On finite arenas, however, it is easy to see that Eve can bound the delay function to n in her winning region : If she can reach a smaller even color, then she can reach it in less than n moves.

3.2   Algorithms

Another way of thinking about repeating parity games is to consider them as weak-parity games where Adam can reset the set of visited states whenever he wants, but will lose if he does so infinitely often. This intuition is formalized in the lemma 3.

Lemma 3. α : *The winning region of Adam in the weak-parity game on an arena $\mathcal{A}_p$ is also winning for him in the repeating parity game on the same arena. The attractor of this region is also winning for him in this game.*

  β : *If Eve wins everywhere in the weak-parity game on an arena $\mathcal{A}_p$, then she wins everywhere in the repeating parity game on the same arena.*

Before we give the proof for this lemma, a short review of how the winning regions are computed in a weak-parity game is in order. The full algorithm comes from [LT00]. It works by removing attractors for each players alternatively. We consider that the smallest color is 0^1. The region labeled by 0 is immediately winning for Eve, as any play starting from this region will have 0 as smallest occurring color. For the same reason, any state in Eve's attractor to this region will be winning for her. All these states are winning for Eve, and can now be removed from the game in order to compute the winning regions in the rest of the game: Eve cannot go to these states, and Adam will never want to go there, as Eve could force the token to visit a state labeled 0. The remainder of the arena is a (parity) sub-arena, as it is a trap, and its size is strictly smaller. We can thus use the same algorithm to get the winning regions of both players in this new game.

   An illustration of how this algorithm works is given in figure 3(a). Notice that all the attractors and regions are relative to earlier computation: there could be 1's in the region $Attr_E(0)$, for example. However, there cannot be a 0 in the region $Attr_A(1)$, as it would belong to $Attr_E(0)$ which was defined earlier. In the same way, the attractors are computed relatively to the subgames. $Attr_A(1)$, for example, is the region where Adam can force the token to a state labeled 1 without crossing $Attr_E(0)$. Figure 3(b) shows the special case where Eve wins everywhere. It is computed in the same way, but the odd regions and attractor happens to be empty (which is fitting, since they are regions winning for Adam). Obviously, there could be odd colors in the arena, but each belongs to attractors of smaller even colors.

   A naïve study of this algorithm leads to a worst-case time complexity of $O(c \cdot m)$. However, a careful use of data structures reduces this time to $O(m)$ [Cha06].

   We will now give the proof of lemma 3.

Proof. α : A play is winning for Adam in the weak parity game if the smallest color visited is odd. Obviously, a smaller even color cannot occur later. Thus

---

[1] If this is not the case, just replace 0 by the smallest color present in the arena, and Eve by Adam this color is odd

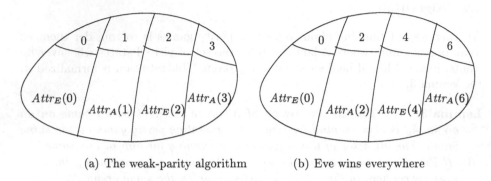

(a) The weak-parity algorithm   (b) Eve wins everywhere

Fig. 3. An arena where Eve wins everywhere in weak-parity

$Win_A^{wp}(\mathcal{A}) \subseteq Win_A^{rp}(\mathcal{A})$. The case of the attractor is solved by the following observation: If a play ρ is winning for Adam in the repeating parity game, then each play of the form $w \cdot \rho$ is also winning for him in this game. Thus $Attr_A(Win_A^{wp}(\mathcal{A})) \subseteq Win_A^{rp}(\mathcal{A})$. $\square$

β : An arena where Eve wins everywhere in the weak-parity game looks like figure 3(b). In this game, Eve needs only to play according to the attractors' strategies whenever the token is not in one of the top-most regions. This guarantees that the token will get to an even state in the top-most regions without crossing a smaller odd color. Thus Eve also wins everywhere in the repeating parity game. On a finite arena with n states, using this strategy also guarantees that the delay between an odd color and the next smaller even color is at most n. $\square$

This lemma leads directly to algorithm 1[2].

Algorithm 1. Algorithm computing the winning regions of Adam and Eve for the repeating parity game

---

Require: Algorithm for computing the winning regions in a weak-parity game
   input $\mathcal{A}, p$
   $\mathcal{B} \leftarrow \mathcal{A}$
   repeat
      $\mathcal{B} \leftarrow \mathcal{B} \setminus Attr_A(Win_A^{wp}(\mathcal{B}, p))$
   until $Win_A^{wp}(\mathcal{B}, p) = \emptyset$
   return $\mathcal{A} \setminus \mathcal{B}, \mathcal{B}$

The termination of the algorithm 1 is guaranteed by the fact that in each **repeat** loop, $\mathcal{B}$ loses at least one state. This limits the number of times the loop can be repeated to n. As weak-parity games are solved in time $O(m)$, the global complexity of our algorithm is $O(m \cdot n)$.

---

[2] In this algorithm, as in the others, the first component returned is Adam's winning region, while the second is Eve's winning region.

The validity of this algorithm derives directly from lemma 3.

We will now solve finitary games using the same kind of construction. Lemma 4 relates the winning regions of repeating parity and finitary parity, in a way very similar to lemma 3.

Lemma 4. α : *The winning region of Eve in the repeating parity game on an arena $\mathcal{A}_p$ is also winning for her in the finitary parity game on the same arena. The attractor of this region is also winning for her in this game.*

β : *If Adam wins everywhere in the repeating parity game on an arena $\mathcal{A}_p$, then he wins everywhere in the finitary parity game on the same arena.*

Proof. α : Eve's winning region in the repeating parity game is the region from where she can guarantee that the delay function remains finite. On this region, she can use the strategy described in the proof of lemma 3 which guarantees that the delay function will be bounded by n. The finitary parity game asks only for this function to be ultimately bounded. Thus $Win_E^{rp}(\mathcal{A}_p) \subseteq Win_E^{fp}(\mathcal{A}_p)$. As the finitary parity condition is prefix independent, we can conclude that $Attr_E(Win_E^{rp}(\mathcal{A}_p)) \subseteq Win_E^{fp}(\mathcal{A}_p)$ □

β : The second part of the proof is more complex. Adam has a strategy π that is winning everywhere in repeating parity. From it, we derive the following strategy π':
1. Set b to 1.
2. Play the strategy π with initial memory from the state where the token is now until there is a sequence with an odd priority followed by b moves without seeing a smaller even priority.
3. Increment b.
4. Go back to step 2.

It is immediate that if a play consistent with this strategy behaves in a way such that Adam goes infinitely often through the loop, then it is winning for Adam in the finitary parity game. The only point that could cause trouble is to get out of step 2. But a play that would get stuck in this state would be a play consistent with π where for each occurrence of an odd color, there is an occurrence of a smaller even color in the next b moves. This would be a contradiction to the hypothesis that π is winning for Adam in the repeating parity game. Thus π' is winning for Adam in the finitary parity game. □

As we did for repeating parity, we use this lemma to build Algorithm 2, computing the winning regions in finitary parity games.

As in Algorithm 1, the termination and complexity are guaranteed by the fact that the **repeat** loop removes one state from $\mathcal{B}$. Likewise, the complexity is n times the complexity of the former algorithm, or $O(m \cdot n^2)$. This complete the proof of the following theorem:

Theorem 5. *Deciding the winner of a state in a finitary parity game can be done in polynomial time. In particular, Algorithm 2 computes the winning regions of a game with n states and m edges in time $O(m \cdot n^2)$.*

To give a comparison, the algorithm of [CH06] was running in time $O(n^{2c-3} \cdot c \cdot m)$. Chaterjee and Henzinger also proved that the problem was in NP ∩ co-NP.

Algorithm 2. Algorithm computing the winning regions of Adam and Eve for the finitary parity game

---

Require: Algorithm for computing the winning regions in a repeating parity game
   input $\mathcal{A}, p$
   $\mathcal{B} \leftarrow \mathcal{A}$
   repeat
      $\mathcal{B} \leftarrow \mathcal{B} \setminus Attr_E(Win_E^{rp}(\mathcal{B}, p))$
   until $Win_E^{rp}(\mathcal{B}, p) = \emptyset$
   return $\mathcal{B}, \mathcal{A} \setminus \mathcal{B}$

---

4 Streett Games

4.1 Streett Conditions

A Streett coloring s over an arena $\mathcal{A}$ is a set of pairs of sets of states of $\mathcal{A}$. The first element of a pair is usually called a *request*, and the second element is the corresponding *response*. A Streett arena $\mathcal{A}_s$ is an arena equipped with a Streett coloring. The rank of a Streett arena is the number of pairs that constitute the Streett coloring. The rank of a Streett game is the rank of its arena. In complexity computation, the rank of the Streett condition will be denoted by k. As was the case for parity games, all the variants of Streett games that we will define depend only on the Streett arena they are played on. Again, there are two classical versions of the Streett games:

Weak Streett games: A play is winning for Eve if for each request that occurs in the play, the corresponding response also occurs.

(Classical) Streett games: A play is winning for Eve if for each request occurring infinitely often in the play, the corresponding response also occurs infinitely often.

Chatterjee and Henzinger also introduced a finitary version of the Streett games in [CH06]. Intuitively, a play is winning for Eve in finitary Streett if for each request that occurs infinitely often, the corresponding response occurs infinitely often, as in classical Streett, with the added constraint that the delay between an occurrence of a request and the next corresponding response must be ultimately bounded.

The formal definition also uses a notion of delay sequence derived from a play:

Definition 6. *The delay sequence $d(\rho)$ of a play ρ on a Streett arena $\mathcal{A}_p$ is defined as follows:*

- *If ρ_i does not belong to a request, then $d(\rho)_i = 0$.*
- *If ρ_i belongs to the request of only one pair, then $d(\rho)_i$ is the smallest j such that ρ_{i+j} belong to the corresponding response. Note that if there are no such j, $d(\rho)_i = \infty$.*
- *If ρ_i belong to several requests, then $d(\rho)_i$ is the maximum of the values computed with the method above for each request.*

A play ρ on a Streett arena $\mathcal{A}_p$ is winning for Eve in the finitary Streett game if and only if $d(\rho)$ is ultimately bounded.

In [CH06], Chatterjee and Henzinger proved the following results about finitary Streett games:

- Finitary Streett games are determined. ($Win_A^{fs}(\mathcal{A}) \cup Win_E^{fs}(\mathcal{A}) = \mathcal{A}$)
- In her winning region, Eve has a strategy that uses no more than $k! \cdot k^2$ memory states.
- Adam may need strategies with infinite memory in order to win.
- Winning regions can be computed in time $O((n \cdot k! \cdot k^2)^{2k-3} \cdot m \cdot k! \cdot k^3)$.

As for parity games, we will use another kind of Streett games in our algorithm, called request-response games. These games will have the same place in the Streett algorithm than repeating parity had in the parity algorithm. However, there are two significant differences: there is no relation[3] between these games and weak-parity games, and they were defined and studied by Wallmeier, Thomas and Hutten in [WHT03]. Even if these games do not bear the name Streett, they are defined by a Streett arena:

A play is winning in a request-response game if its delay sequence takes only finite values, $i.e.$ if for each occurrence of a request, there is later an occurrence of a corresponding response.

Wallmeier et al. present an algorithm to solve request-response games in [WHT03]. It is based on a reduction to generalized Büchi games. The time complexity of their algorithm is $O(4^k \cdot k^2 \cdot m^2)$. The strategy for Eve that is derived from this algorithm has the property that in each play consistent with it, each request is matched by a corresponding response in the next $k \cdot n$ moves.

The following lemma relates finitary Streett games and request-response games:

Lemma 7. α : *The winning region of Eve in the request-response game on an arena $\mathcal{A}_s$ is also winning for her in the finitary Streett game on the same arena. The attractor of this region is also winning for her in this game.*

β : *If Adam wins everywhere in the request-response game on an arena $\mathcal{A}_s$, then he wins everywhere in the finitary Streett game on the same arena.*

Proof. α : In the winning region of Eve in the request-response game, she can use the strategy derived from [WHT03]. It guarantees that each request is matched by a corresponding response in the next $k \cdot n$ moves, and thus that the delay sequence is bounded. Thus $Win_E^{rr}(\mathcal{A}_s)) \subseteq Win_E^{fs}(\mathcal{A}_p)$. As the finitary condition is prefix-independent, we get $Attr_E(Win_E^{rr}(\mathcal{A}_s)) \subseteq Win_E^{fs}(\mathcal{A}_p)$. $\quad\square$

β : The construction of a winning strategy for Adam for finitary Streett from a strategy winning everywhere for him in request-response is similar to the one used to build a winning strategy for him in finitary parity. If π is a winning strategy for Adam in the request-response game, the strategy π' is defined by:

---

[3] At least, none that we were able to find.

1. Set b to 1.
2. Play the strategy π with initial memory from the state where the token is now until there is a sequence with a request followed by b moves without seeing the corresponding response.
3. Increment b.
4. Go back to step 2.

Once again a play that does not get stuck in step 2 is clearly winning for Adam. And a play that would get stuck in the step 2 would be a play consistent with π where each request is followed by a response, in contradiction with the fact that π is winning in request-response. Thus π' is winning for Adam everywhere in $\mathcal{A}_s$. □

From this lemma we derive Algorithm 3.

Algorithm 3. Algorithm computing the winning regions of Adam and Eve for the finitary Streett game

---

Require: Algorithm computing the winning regions in a request-response game
  input $\mathcal{A}, p$
  $\mathcal{B} \leftarrow \mathcal{A}$
  repeat
    $\mathcal{B} \leftarrow \mathcal{B} \setminus Attr_E(Win_E^{rr}(\mathcal{B}, p))$
  until $Win_E^{rr}(\mathcal{B}, p) = \emptyset$
  return $\mathcal{B}, \mathcal{A} \setminus \mathcal{B}$

As in the other algorithms, the number of times the loop is repeated is bounded by the number of states in the arena. The complexity is thus n times the complexity of the algorithm for request-response games, or $O(4^k \cdot k^2 \cdot m^2 \cdot n)$. This complete the proof of the following theorem:

Theorem 8. *Computing the winning regions in a finitary Streett game can be done in time* $O(4^k \cdot k^2 \cdot m^2 \cdot n)$.

In comparison, the reduction to a finitary parity game showed in [CH06] was running in time $O((n \cdot k! \cdot k^2)^{2k-3} \cdot m \cdot k! \cdot k^3)$. This reduction was based on the indexes of appearance records from [BLV96]. It also implies that the winning strategy of Eve in her region could use up to $k! \cdot k^2$ memory states. This makes the following corollary to our algorithm interesting:

Corollary 9. *There are winning strategies for Eve in her winning region that use no more than* $k \cdot 2^k$ *memory states.*

Proof. The strategy for Eve that derives from our algorithm is a combination of request-response strategies and attractors strategies. The request-response strategies use at most $k \cdot 2^k$, while the attractors strategies are memoryless. Furthermore, these strategies are combined in a *spatial* fashion: when the token goes from a region to another, the memory can be reseted. Thus Eve needs only as much memory as she needs to win the request-response games, *i.e.* $k \cdot 2^k$. □

Interestingly, the weak-Streett strategies for Eve need less memory, with 2^k memory states [NSW02], while classical Streett games need $k!$ memory states [DJW97, Hor05].

5 Conclusion and Developments

We gave algorithms that solve finitary parity and Streett games. They are much faster than their counterpart in the original paper by Chatterjee and Henzinger. The finitary parity problem, in particular, was proved to be in P, improving the former result of NP ∩ co-NP. The algorithm for Streett games represents a good improvement in time complexity, and yields more compact strategies for Eve. We had hoped to solve finitary Streett games with a Turing-reduction starting from weak-Streett games, which may have made the solution a PSPACE problem. However, if there is such a reduction, it eluded us so far.

Our next interests in this field of research are an extension of the notion of finitary games to Muller conditions, and the study of links between these games and a fragment of the ωBS-regular logic of Bojanczyk and Colcombet.

Acknowledgments. I wish to thank Olivier Serre for introducing me to finitary games and then helping me in the construction of the algorithms. Also, special thanks to Claire David, whithout whom I would never have met the deadline.

References

[AH94]   R. Alur and T.A. Henzinger. Finitary Fairness In proceedings of *Logic In Computer Science*, LICS'94, p. 52–61. IEEE Computer Society, 1994.

[AHK02]   R. Alur, T.A. Henzinger and O. Kupferman. Alternating-time temporal logic. In *Journal of the ACM*, volume 49, p.672–713. 2002.

[BC06]   M. Bojanczyk and T. Colcombet. Bounds in ω-regularity In proceedings of *Logic In Computer Science*, LICS'06, p. 285–296, IEEE Computer Society, 2006.

[BLV96]   N. Buhrke, H. Lescow and J. Vöge. Strategy Construction in Infinite Games with Streett and Rabin Chain Winning Conditions. In proceedings of *Tools and Algorithms for Construction and Analysis of Systems*, volume 1055 of *Lecture Notes in Computer Science*, TACAS'96, p. 207–224, Springer, 1996.

[CH06]   K. Chatterjee and T.A. Henzinger. Finitary Winning in omega-Regular Games. In proceedings of *Tools and Algorithms for the Construction and Analysis of Systems*, volume 3920 of *Lecture Notes in Computer Science*, TACAS'06, p. 257–271, Springer, 2006.

[Cha06]   K. Chatterjee. Linear Time Algorithm for Weak Parity Games Technical Report No. UCB/EECS-2006-153. University of California at Berkeley, 2006.

[DJW97]   S. Dziembowski, M. Jurdziński and I. Walukiewicz. How Much Memory Is Needed to Win Infinite Games ? In proceedings of *Logic In Computer Science*, LICS'97, p. 99–110, IEEE Computer Society, 1997.

484   F. Horn

[Jur00]   M. Jurdziński Small Progress Measures for Solving Parity Games. In proceedings of *Symposium on Theoretical Aspects of Computer Science*, STACS'00, volume 1770 of *Lecture Notes in Computer Science*, p. 290–301, Springer, 2000

[Hor05]   F. Horn. Streett Games on Finite Graphs. *Games in Design and Verification*, Workshop collocated with *Computer Aided Verfication*, 2005

[LT00]   C. Löding and W. Thomas. Alternating Automata and Logics over Infinite Words. In proceedings of the *IFIP International Conference on Theoretical Computer Science*, IFIP TCS'00, volume 1872 of *Lecture Notes in Computer Science*, p. 521–535. Springer, 2000.

[MP92]   Z. Manna and A. Pnueli. The Temporal Logic of Concurrent and Reactive System Springer, 2002.

[NSW02]   J. Neumann, A. Szepietowski and I. Walukiewicz. Complexity of weak acceptance conditions in tree automata. In *Information Processing Letters*, volume 84, p181–187, Elsevier, 2002.

[Tho95]   W. Thomas. On the Synthesis of Strategies in Infinite Games. In proceedings of *Symposium on Theoretical Aspects of Computer Science*, STACS'95, volume 900 of *Lecture Notes in Computer Science*, p. 1–13, Springer, 1995.

[VJ00]   J. Vöge and M. Jurdziński. A Discrete Strategy Improvement Algorithm for Solving Parity Games. In proceedings of *Computer Aided Verfication*, CAV'00, volume 1855 of *Lecture Notes in Computer Science*, p. 202–215, Springer, 2000.

[WHT03]   N. Wallmeier, P. Hutten and W. Thomas. Symbolic Synthesis of Finite-State Controllers for Request-Response Specifications. In proceedings of *Conference on Implementation and Application of Automata*, CIAA'03, volume 2759 of *Lecture Notes in Computer Science*, p. 11–22, Springer, 2003.

[Zie98]   W. Zielonka. Infinite Games on Finitely Coloured Graphs with Applications to Automata on Infinite Trees. In *Theoretical Computer Science*, volume 200(1-2), p. 135–183, 1998

Planned and Traversable Play-Out:
A Flexible Method for Executing
Scenario-Based Programs*,**

David Harel and Itai Segall

The Weizmann Institute of Science, Rehovot, Israel
{david.harel,itai.segall}@weizmann.ac.il

Abstract. We introduce a novel approach to the smart execution of
scenario-based models of reactive systems, such as those resulting from
the multi-modal inter-object language of live sequence charts (LSCs).
Our approach finds multiple execution paths from a given state of the
system, and allows the user to interactively traverse them. The method
is based on translating the problem of finding a superstep of execution
into a problem in the AI planning domain, and issuing a known planning
algorithm, which we have had to modify and strengthen for our purposes.

1 Introduction

Scenario-based modeling appears to be a promising approach to system and software design and development, and has resulted in intensive research efforts in
the last few years. One of the most widely used languages for capturing inter-
object scenario-based specifications is that of *message sequence charts* (MSCs)
proposed by the ITU [21], or its UML variant, *sequence diagrams* [28]. Recently,
an extension of MSCs has been proposed, called *live sequence charts* (LSCs)
[4]. LSCs are multi-modal charts that distinguish between behaviors that may
happen (existential, cold) and those that must happen (universal, hot).[1] The
language is highly expressive and can also specify negative behavior, and more,
and it has been extended to include, among other things, time, forbidden elements, and symbolic instances (i.e., the ability to talk also about classes, rather
than only object instances) [14]. An LSC is divided into two parts, a prechart
and a main chart. A prechart is a precondition for the main chart, i.e., if the
prechart of an LSC is satisfied, then its main chart must be satisfied as well.

In [15,14], the *play-in/play-out approach* is introduced, in which the user specifies scenarios by playing them in directly from a graphical user interface of the
system to be developed. When a scenario is played in, the *Play-Engine* tool

---

* This research was supported by the John von Neumann Minerva Center for the
  Development of Reactive Systems at the Weizmann Institute of Science.
** This is a somewhat shortened conference version of the paper. The full version [16]
  can be obtained by emailing one of the authors.

[1] A variant of LSCs has also been defined, called *modal sequence diagrams*, or MSDs,
  which adheres to the UML 2.0 standard; see [12].

O. Grumberg and M. Huth (Eds.): TACAS 2007, LNCS 4424, pp. 485–499, 2007.
© Springer-Verlag Berlin Heidelberg 2007

translates it on the fly into an LSC. Play-out is the complementary idea, in which the Play-Engine uses the operational semantics of the language in order to execute a set of LSCs. In this stage, the user again interacts directly with the GUI, and the system responds to each user action with a *superstep*, which is a set of actions, *steps*, that are dictated by the LSC specification as the result of the action.

Here now is a simple example of an LSC specification for a three-story elevator, as shown in Figure 1. LSC Check1, shown in Figure 1(a), states that if the user presses the Close-Doors button then the elevator sends the message Check1 to itself. The specification includes three such LSCs, with messages Check1, Check2, Check3. LSC Goto1, shown in Figure 1(b), states that if the elevator sends Check1 to itself, then the system checks whether the elevator is not on floor 1 and the Floor1 button is pressed. If so, the elevator closes its doors, moves to floors 2 and 1 and then opens its doors. The Floor1 button is turned off as well. According to the LSC semantics, partial order is defined only among locations in the same lifeline (denoted by vertical lines). Therefore, in this example, there is no explicit order between turning off Floor1 and the other four actions. At the bottom of the figure, two forbidden elements are specified, which state that the elevator may *not* send the message Check2 or Check3 to itself, as long as the main chart is active. Similar charts exist in the system specifying movement to floors 2 and 3. Finally, the LSC TestCase of Figure 1(c) is a test case, stating that if the elevator visits floors 3, 2 and 1, in that order, then the Floor2 button is enabled.

The play-out mechanism described in [14] is naïve, in the sense that at each given point the system selects a single action that is enabled at that point and executes it. This approach might lead to violations in the future, which could have been avoided by selecting the action more wisely from the set of enabled actions. In our example, assume the elevator has visited floors 3 and 2, and is now moving to floor 1 according to the LSC Goto1 of Figure 1(b). Once the set Floor(1) message is sent from the elevator to itself, the TestCase LSC in Figure 1(c) becomes active too. Note that the elevator doors are closed at that point in time. Now the system has two options: either open the doors as specified in the Goto1 chart, or enable the Floor2 button as specified in the TestCase chart. If the system chooses to open the doors first, and only then enables the button, a violation will occur, since TestCase states that after enabling the button the doors must be closed, but the doors are already open and should not be closed again. Had the system chosen to enable the button first, this problem would have been avoided.

One way to tackle this problem is by using *smart play-out* [10,11], in which play-out is translated into a model-checking problem. A model-checker is then handed the claim "no legal superstep exists", and if it delivers a counter-example, which is really a legal superstep, it is then fed into the Play-Engine for execution.

Often it is useful to know more than a single legal superstep, but model checkers are usually unable to provide more than one counter-example. In [14], this issue is addressed in a rather crude way. The first-found superstep is turned by the Play-Engine into a negative (forbidden) scenario. The resulting LSC is then added to the specification and smart play-out is rerun. A different superstep will then be found, if one exists. In this approach, the model-checker must be employed repeatedly for each new superstep to be found, and the specification keeps growing with another chart at each such run.[2]

In this paper we describe a new approach to the play-out problem, termed *planned play-out*, which uses AI planning algorithms and finds many legal supersteps in a single run. As we show, this approach can also be used to support interactive play-out, where the user is allowed to backtrack, and to choose between possible steps, in the quest for an acceptable superstep.

Technically, finding a legal superstep is translated into a planning problem, and a planner is employed in order to solve it. The resulting plans are then translated back into supersteps. We have chosen to use the IPP planner [25,20], an iterative Graphplan-like algorithm. Graphplan planners use a data structure called a *planning graph*, which is a polynomial-sized graph that represents some of the constraints in the planning problem, and which is used to reduce the search for a legal plan. The resulting plan is a partial-order, in the sense that it is divided into timesteps such that two actions in the same timestep are unordered in time. Planning problems, Graphplan and IPP are all discussed in Section 3.

2 LSCs

A more detailed description of the LSC language is omitted from this version of the paper; see [16].

3 Planning

Planning is a field of research central to AI, in which algorithms are designed to generate a list of actions that lead to a predefined goal. Planning is appropriate whenever a number of actions must be performed in a coherent manner to achieve a goal — for example, a robot trying to reach a destination without bumping into walls or getting into dead ends. The algorithms usually consider in advance the consequences of their actions, and decide on the entire plan before performing it.

A *planning problem* typically consists of three inputs: (1) a description of the current state of the world — the *initial conditions*, (2) a description of the desired state after performing the plan — the *goals*, and (3) a set of possible actions — the *domain theory*. An action typically has a *precondition*, describing when it is allowed, and an *effect*, describing the consequence of performing it. An *output plan* is then a multiset of actions from the domain theory, with a partial (or total) order, such that if performed in a manner consistent with the order, starting in a state consistent with the initial conditions, the goals will be achieved.

---

[2] In addition, the new superstep might be very similar to those already found, as the only requirement is for it not to be identical to them.

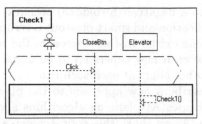

(a) The Check1 LSC, stating that if the user presses the **Close-Doors** button, the elevator sends the message **Check1** to itself.

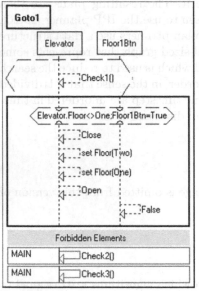

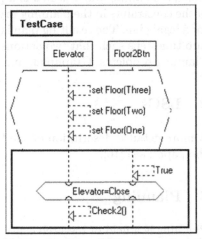

(b) The Goto1 LSC, describing how the elevator moves to floor 1.

(c) The TestCase LSC, stating that if the elevator goes to floors 3, 2 and 1, in that order, then the button for floor 2 is pressed.

Fig. 1. Sample LSCs from the three-story elevator example

There is a wide range of languages for representing the initial conditions, the goals and the possible actions. We shall focus on the classic STRIPS representation [7], and its extension, ADL [27]. The propositional STRIPS representation describes initial conditions and goals as a conjunction of positive boolean predicates. Actions consist of conjunctive preconditions, add effects (predicates that are true after performing the action) and delete effects (predicates that become false).

An example is given in Figure 2. It is similar to the rocket domain introduced in [29], and involves two objects, A and B, and a bag. The purpose is to move the objects from room R1 to R2, but only the bag can be moved directly between

Initial conditions: At(A, R1) ∧ At(B, R1) ∧ At(Bag, R1)
Goal: At(A, R2) ∧ At(B, R2)
Actions:
    Insert(object, room):
            Precondition: At(object, room) ∧ At(Bag, room)
            Effects: In(object) ∧ ¬At(object, room)
    Remove(object, room):
            Precondition: In(object) ∧ At(Bag, room)
            Effects: ¬In(object) ∧ At(object, room)
    Move(from, to):
            Precondition: At(Bag, from)
            effects: ¬At(Bag, from) ∧ At(Bag, to)

Fig. 2. A STRIPS problem example

the rooms. The initial conditions are that both objects and the bag are in room R1, and the goal is to have both the objects in room R2. The **insert** action represents inserting an object into the bag; its preconditions are that the object and the bag are in the same room, and the effect is that the object is in the bag and no longer in the room. Similarly, the **remove** action removes an object from the bag. Finally, the **move** action moves the bag from one room to the other; its precondition is the bag being in the **from** room, and its effect is removing it from the **from** room, and placing it in the **to** room. A simple legal plan in this example is to insert both objects into the bag, then move the bag, and then remove both objects.

The ADL [27] language is an extension of STRIPS [7], in which conditional and universally quantified effects are added, as well as negative goals. Our main interest in ADL, as we explain later, is in the conditional effects and negative goals.

3.1   Main Approaches to Planning

There are three main approaches to solving planning problems in the STRIPS representation: (1) translation into a different problem, e.g., a formula in propositional logic, which is then solved by an external black-box algorithm, e.g., a SAT solver [5,22,23], (2) heuristic-based state-space search [3,?], and (3) Graphplan and its descendants.

Tha Graphplan approach [2], which we will use, calls for constructing a polynomial-sized graph in a way that encodes many of the inherent constraints of the problem. This graph and the constraints that arise from it are used in order to significantly reduce the amount of search needed.

Graphplan's main data structure is a *planning graph*, a polynomial-sized graph that represents some of the constraints in the planning problem. Nodes in the planning graph represent either propositions or actions, and are divided into levels depicting timesteps. Two actions in the same timestep have no order between them, but all actions in a specific timestep must occur before those in the following one.

An important part of the graph analysis is detecting pairs of actions that can never appear in a plan in the same timestep, and propositions that can never be true together in the same timestep, and mark them as mutual exclusions (*mutexes*).

3.2 Planning Graphs

For lack of space, we omit from this version of the paper the more detailed description of the planning graph, its construction, and its usage in plan extraction; see [16].

3.3 IPP

An important feature that ADL adds to STRIPS is the notion of conditional effects. This allows actions to have different effects according to the state in which they are performed. One of the algorithms that support this feature in a Graphplan-like fashion is IPP [25,20]. Negative goals and negative preconditions are also supported by IPP.

4 Translating Play-Out into Planning

Our approach to finding legal supersteps is to represent play-out as a planning problem and to solve it using the IPP planner [25,20]. The domain theory is derived from the LSC specification, whereas the initial conditions are derived from the current system state. The goals are independent of the specification, and call simply for finishing the superstep safely. We have enhanced the IPP algorithm so that multiple plans are generated in a single run. These plans are then translated back into supersteps and are fed into the Play-Engine.

Even though we describe here the usage of the IPP planner, the problem is represented in the ADL language, and cen be fed to any planner that supports the relevant subset of ADL. The translation of play-out into planning is done so that a plan exists if and only if a legal superstep exists, and plans can be translated back into supersteps.

Each LSC is represented by an object, and its state is captured by various predicates. An LSC can be either active or not (i.e., its main chart is active or not) — a property represented by the predicate *active*. Each location in the LSC can be enabled or disabled (according to the cut at any given moment), represented by *enabled_loc_X*, for each location X in the LSC.

We assume that only a single copy of each LSC can be active at any given moment, hence a single object per LSC is sufficient. In the future, we plan (no pun intended. . .) to support multiple running copies by creating multiple objects of the same class, where the class represents the LSC.

4.1 Initial Conditions

The initial conditions of the planning problem are derived directly from the initial LSC state. Similarly to the smart play-out mechanism of [10], our translation is invoked after an external event has occurred, in a state in which some LSCs are active. The initial values of all the predicates are therefore determined according to the set of active LSCs and their enabled locations in the given initial configuration.

In the elevator example, suppose the superstep starts in a state where the buttons for floors 1 and 3 are on, the elevator is on floor 2, and the Close-Doors button is pressed. This causes charts Check1, Check2 and Check3 to be activated and the superstep to start. The initial condition will therefore be $active(Check1) \land active(Check2) \land active(Check3)$ and the *enabled* predicates corresponding to the location of the cut are true as well (any predicate not explicitly true is assumed to be false). In addition, the predicates representing the light in button floors 1 and 3 being on are both true.

4.2   The Goal

A legal superstep is a sequence of actions that the LSCs take, after which all LSCs are inactive. Hence the goal is:
$(\neg active(o_1)) \land \cdots \land (\neg active(o_n))$.
This is similar to the way it is done for smart play-out [10].

4.3   Actions

Actions represent the possible transitions of the LSC system. Each action stands for a possible step in a superstep, e.g., sending a message, advancing a condition, etc. For each action we formulate its precondition and effect.

There are two types of steps, local and global. Global steps are message sending and receiving, and are global in the sense that many charts must be considered when deciding to perform them. Other steps, such as conditions, are local, in the sense that only a single chart is relevant to them.

Conditions. We now describe the translation of conditions. Other constructs, such as if-then-else and unbounded loops are translated in a similar fashion.

Both hot and cold conditions have an action for advancing them, and cold conditions have an additional action for violation. A condition in an LSC is synchronized with one or more lifelines, for each of which there is one location that is *relevant* to the condition, and which must be active in order for the condition to be advanced. Therefore, the precondition for the action of advancing a condition is that all the relevant locations are enabled and that the condition holds. The effect of this action is that the previous locations become disabled and those subsequent to the condition become enabled.

For example, the action representing the hot condition of the doors being closed in the TestCase LSC (which is at location 4 in the Floor2Btn lifeline, and at location 6 in the Elevator lifeline) is:

Action advance_condition_1_TestCase (TestCase, Elevator)
 Precondition: enabled_loc_Floor2Btn_4(TestCase)$\land$
  enabled_loc_Elevator_6(TestCase)$\land$
  Doors_Closed(Elevator)

Effect: $(\neg enabled\_loc\_Floor2Btn\_4(TestCase))\wedge$
$(\neg enabled\_loc\_Elevator\_6(TestCase))\wedge$
$enabled\_loc\_Floor2Btn\_5(TestCase)\wedge$
$enabled\_loc\_Elevator\_7(TestCase)$

One slightly more delicate case is that in which the condition appears at the end of the main chart or the prechart, respectively. In this case, the effect is conditional: (1) if all other lifelines are already in their final location, terminate the LSC or enable the main chart, respectively, and (2) otherwise advance the locations as described above.

As mentioned earlier, cold conditions have an additional action for violation. It has similar preconditions, but if the condition does not hold then if it is in a subchart the effect is to move to locations subsequent to the subchart and otherwise the chart is deactivated and all locations are restarted.

Messages. Messages are not local: when one formalizes the action of sending a message (both its precondition and its effect), many charts must be considered. For simplicity, assume each message appears at most once in each LSC, and that the message is synchronous. Asynchronous messages are also supported, but are not described in this version of the paper.

In our translation, each message is transformed into an action. According to the LSC semantics, a message must be triggered, i.e., there must be at least one universal chart that causes it to be sent. Therefore, the precondition for the action of sending a message is that at least one of the charts that contain the message in their main chart is active, and that the message is enabled in it.

Upon sending a message that is enabled in an LSC, the cut is advanced past it. If the sent message appears in an LSC but is not enabled in it, the LSC is assumed to have a cold violation, so it is deactivated and the cut is reset to its initial location. Thus, for each LSC containing the message, there are two conditional effects: one stating that if the message is enabled the cut is forwarded, and the second stating that if the message is not enabled the chart is inactivated and the cut is reset to its initial location. Similarly to the case of conditions, if the message is, or can be, the last action in the main chart (or the prechart), the first effect must be divided into two different conditional effects, according to the locations of the other lifelines.

Note that the only difference between prechart and main chart messages is in the precondition: only main chart locations are considered in the precondition (that is, only they affect the decision of sending a message).

For example, the message `Set floor(2)` sent from the elevator to itself appears in the main charts of *Goto1, Goto2* and *Goto3* (in all of them at location 7 of lifeline *Elevator*) and in the prechart of *TestCase* (though it will never be the last message in that prechart). Its translation is as follows (and similarly for charts *Goto2, Goto3* and *TestCase*):[3]

---

[3] This translation can be made more efficient. For example, when violating a chart, it is sufficient to disable only main chart locations if the chart is necessarily active. These optimizations are not discussed in this version of the paper.

Action send_Floor2_Elevator_Elevator(Goto1, Goto2, Goto3, TestCase)
Precondition: enabled_loc_Elevator_7(*Goto*1)∨
                enabled_loc_Elevator_7(*Goto*2)∨
                enabled_loc_Elevator_7(*Goto*3)
Effect: when (enabled_loc_Elevator_7(*Goto*1) :
                ¬enabled_loc_Elevator_7(*Goto*1)∧
                enabled_loc_Elevator_8(*Goto*1)
        when ¬(enabled_loc_Elevator_7(*Goto*1) :
                enabled_loc_Elevator_3(*Goto*1)
                ¬enabled_loc_Elevator_4(*Goto*1)∧¬enabled_loc_Elevator_5(*Goto*1)∧
                ¬enabled_loc_Elevator_6(*Goto*1)∧¬enabled_loc_Elevator_7(*Goto*1)∧
                ¬enabled_loc_Elevator_8(*Goto*1)∧¬enabled_loc_Elevator_9(*Goto*1)∧
                ¬enabled_loc_Elevator_10(*Goto*1)∧
                enabled_loc_Floor2Btn_2(*Goto*1)∧
                ¬enabled_loc_Floor2Btn_3(*Goto*1)∧¬enabled_loc_Floor2Btn_4(*Goto*1)∧
                ¬enabled_loc_Floor2Btn_5(*Goto*1)

A slightly simpler translation can be made if the user chooses not to allow messages to violate main charts (which is sufficient in many cases). In this case, the precondition of the action is that each LSC that contains the message in its main chart is either inactive or else the message is enabled in it. Moreover, the conditional effect that violates the main chart can be skipped.

4.4   More Formally

The formal definition of the translation is omitted in this version of the paper; see [16].

5   Extending IPP

5.1   Forced Mutexes

In some cases, especially when conditional effects are used, not all mutexes inherent in the problem arise from IPP's planning graph. We introduce the notion of *forced mutexes* into the ADL language. These are facts that the user knows should always be mutex, and he/she can therefore explicitly specify them in the problem description, adding them to those discovered by the standard IPP algorithm. We have used this feature to specify that every two locations on the same lifeline should always be mutex. Surprisingly, this small addition results in huge performance improvements, causing problems that caused devastating performance issues in an earlier implementation of our algorithm to be solved within seconds. Further performance issues are discussed in section 6.3.

Mutexes in IPP are implemented using the efficient bit-vector idea introduced in [26]. We adopt these ideas in the implementation of forced mutexes as well. The result of this efficient implementation is that checking whether two facts are mutex is performed in constant time, which does *not* depend on the number of forced mutexes.

5.2 Finding Many Plans

IPP is a Graphplan-based planner that supports conditional effects, negative preconditions and negative goals. Like most Graphplan-based planners, IPP is an iterative process that halts once a solution is found. In order to be able to find multiple supersteps we have enhanced the IPP planner to find multiple plans in a single run. This is achieved by changing the halting condition and by adding memoization of positive results.

The new halting condition is as follows. The user states in advance the number of timesteps he/she wishes to continue calculating beyond the shortest plan. IPP will then find the shortest plan as before, but will keep iterating until all plans bounded by the specified length are found.

In order to keep the running time feasible, one must memoize positive results. IPP introduces an efficient memoization mechanism, as described in [17]. This mechanism is used for memoizing negative results (i.e., unachievable subgoals in the backtracking stage), in order to avoid re-checking them. Now that the process is not halted upon finding the first plan, positive results (i.e., achievable subgoals and subplans achieving them) must be memoized as well, since they could be useful for other plans. We have implemented this using the same mechanism as in the original IPP planner, with the addition that subgoals are augmented with all subplans that achieve them.

The output of the extended IPP algorithm is a leveled DAG representing multiple plans that achieve the goals. In it, nodes on level i represent states achievable in i timesteps and edges represent the actions that drive the system from one state to another. If an edge is labeled with more than one action, there is no explicit order between them.

A snippet of the DAG generated in our example can be seen in Figure 3.

6 Results

6.1 Traversable Play-Out

Once the play-out problem has been translated into a planning one and multiple plans have been found, this information can be used for what we call *traversable play-out* (TPO). In the TPO mode, play-out is performed interactively: at each step, a list of possible actions is given to the user, who is then allowed to choose his/her preferred action. The user can also undo previous steps and explore other paths of execution. Note that only "smart" steps are allowed, i.e., only those that can lead to a successful superstep. If a certain action is enabled at some given time, yet performing it will cause all future runs to fail (i.e., there is no legal way to finish all the LSCs), then the action will *not* be presented as a possible valid action at that time.

In the TPO mode the user can explore various possibilities, find new supersteps not considered earlier, and get a general feeling for all the options the LSC system provides. We feel that these abilities are one of the most significant advantages of our method.

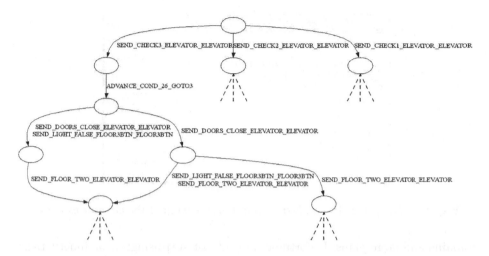

Fig. 3. Part of the DAG generated for the elevator example. In the first timestep, the elevator sends Check1, Check2 or Check3 to itself. If Check3 was sent, then the condition in the Goto3 chart is advanced, and then the doors close and the floor3 button turns off (with no explicit order between the last two).

Figure 4 demonstrates the dialog box for TPO with the valid steps at the beginning of the example. A video demonstrating the traversable play-out mode can be downloaded from [19].

6.2   Cut-Queries

Another feature that is part of our method is that of *cut-queries*, which query for locations of cuts during the run. The user can, for example, state that he/she wishes to see runs in which either a specific case in a switch-case statement is chosen, or two specific locations in an LSC are simultaneously enabled. Note that in general such queries cannot be described by simply adding an LSC to the specification, since one cannot directly describe by an LSC the requirement that a specific location should be enabled in another LSC.

Each such query can be described as an AND/OR combination of a set of atomic queries (those describing simultaneous locations of a cut). The query is then translated into the planning domain along with the play-out problem in a way that ensures that only compliant supersteps are found. For each atomic query, a predicate is added, together with an action. The precondition is that the cut is at the correct locations, and the effect is to enable the predicate. The AND/OR combination of the atomic queries can then be added to the goals as a similar combination of the corresponding predicates.

6.3   Performance

Planning is known to be NP-complete or worse under most reasonable assumptions [6]. Moreover, Graphplan-based planners usually do not scale up to large

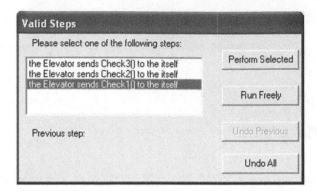

Fig. 4. Valid options for the first step in the superstep of the elevator example

domains and large plans. Unfortunately (but not surprisingly), we inherit these limitations.

Still, for the very simple elevator example discussed here, all supersteps (19 timesteps) were found in 300 milliseconds on a standard PC. A different elevator example, in which the "Goto" LSCs are more than twice the size of the ones described in this paper (and all the GUI buttons are takein into account), where 44 timesteps are needed for all plans, the full execution takes about 4 seconds. These results raise the hope that finding all supersteps in much larger specifications will also become eventually feasible. But, of course, the jury is not in on this yet.

It is important to note that finding all supersteps is usually not expected to be a run-time feature, but rather a design-time tool. Therefore, a running time on the scale of a few minutes for a large specification is quite satisfactory.

7   Future Work

We have described a framework in which supersteps of LSC specifications are calculated in advance using planning techniques, thus allowing users to interact with the system during play-out. The system lets the user choose steps during the run, but in a way that guarantees completion of the superstep: whatever the user chooses is legal and will lead to a successful completion of all LSCs. We also introduced cut-queries that allow the user to define in advance which of the supersteps are of interest.

A subset of the full LSC language of [14] is currently supported in our implementation of planned and traversable play-out, including synchronous and asynchronous messages, hot and cold conditions, switch-cases, infinite loops and main chart-scoped forbidden elements. Thus, for example, we do not yet support time and symbolic instances.

There are two main issues to be resolved in the context of finding all supersteps: supporting the full LSC language and finding a representation of *all* supersteps.

As mentioned above, only a subset of the features of the LSC language is currently supported, and we have described some assumptions made along the way. This subset should be extended to support the full language, and the assumptions should be removed. In our opinion, some of the constructs will turn out to be easier to support than others. For example, we feel that symbolic instances will not pose a serious problem. A predicate can determine to which object the instance is bound and this predicate should be checked in each relevant action. Similarly, multiple running copies of an LSC can be represented by multiple objects, all derived from the same LSC class. On the other hand, constructs that have a numeric essence, like time, numeric variables, and bounded loops, might be more difficult. This can perhaps be solved using *planning with resources* (see, e.g., [24]), but then the Graphplan solution might not be a good approach.

Our implementation finds many supersteps in a single run, but usually not all of them. In general, there can be infinitely many different supersteps, but these often have a finite representation. For example, a loop that can be iterated any number of times is often an adequate finite representation of infinitely many different supersteps. Future research should address this issue.

8   Related Work

In [30], a symbolic simulation engine for LSC specifications is described. It uses constraint logic programming, which in turn uses a form of backtracking in order to find a solution, and can be used to find many supersteps. It is noteworthy that this approach finds full-order supersteps only, hence the backtracking stage will be slower when trying to find interestingly-different supersteps (i.e., ones that differ not only in the order of the steps). Moreover, the approach is used mainly for simulation and finding violations in specifications, whereas our approach is intended for execution and finding many valid supersteps.

There has been an attempt, carried out recently in our group, of representing partial orders derived from LSCs as digraphs [8]. These digraphs were then merged in a way that represented all possible supersteps appropriate for a set of LSCs. The approach, however, was never implemented in the Play-Engine or extended to support more than messages.

In another piece of recent work in our group, LSC specifications are compiled into AspectJ code [13]. This code can then be compiled using any AspectJ Java compiler into a stand-alone application. The current compilation implements naïve play-out, yet stronger and more sophisticated play-out mechanisms can probably be adopted too.

In several projects, model checkers have been augmented to produce multiple counter-examples. In [1], a heuristic BDD-based algorithm for finding multiple behavior paths is introduced, in order to explore and debug hardware design. In [9], a model checker is used iteratively in order to refine an abstracted model.

Acknowledgments. We'd like to thank Orna Kupferman for suggesting to us the possible relevance of planning and AI, and Ron Merom for the idea of the elevator example.

References

1. S. Barner, S. Ben-David, A. Gringauze, B. Sterin and Y. Wolfsthal, "An Algorithmic Approach to Design Exploration", *Proc. International Symposium of Formal Methods Europe on Formal Methods - Getting IT Right* (FME'02), 2002, pp. 146-162.
2. A. Blum and M. Furst, "Fast Planning Through Planning Graph Analysis", *Proc. 14th Intl. Joint Conf. on Artificial Intelligence* (IJCAI'95), 1995, pp. 1636-1642 (Extended version appears in *Artificial Intelligence*, **90**(1-2), 1997, pp. 281-300)
3. B. Bonet and H. Geffner, "HSP: Heuristic Search Planner", *Proc. 4th Intl. Conf. on Artificial Intelligence Planning Systems (AIPS'98) Planning Competition*, Pittsburgh, 1998.
4. W. Damm and D. Harel, "LSCs: Breathing life into message sequence charts", *Formal Methods in System Design*, **19(1):45/22680**, 2001. Preliminary version appeared in *Proc. 3rd IFIP Int. Conf. on Formal Methods for Open Object-Based Distributed Systems* (FMOODS'99).
5. M. Ernst, T. Millstein and D. Weld, "Automatic SAT-Compilation of Planning Problems", *Proc. 15th Intl. Joint Conf. on Artificial Intelligence* (IJCAI'97), 1997, pp. 1169-1176.
6. K. Erol, D. S. Nau and V. S. Subrahmanian, "Complexity, Decidability and Undecidability Results for Domain-Independent Planning", *Artificial Intelligence*, **76**(1-2), July 1995, pp. 75-88.
7. R. Fikes and N. Nilsson, "STRIPS: A New Approach to the Application of Theorem Proving to Problem Solving", *Journal of Artificial Intelligence*, **2**(3/4), 1971, pp. 189-208.
8. Amos Gilboa, MSC Thesis, The Weizmann Institute of Science, 2003, "Finding all Possible Supersteps in LSCs".
9. M. Glusman, G. Kamhi, S. Mador-Haim, R. Fraer and M. Y. Vardi, "Multiple-Counterexample guided Iterative Abstraction Refinement: An Industrial Evaluation", *9th Intl. Conf. on Tools and Algorithms for the Construction and Analysis of Systems* (TACAS'03), 2003, pp. 176-191.
10. D. Harel, H. Kugler, R. Marelly and A. Pnueli, "Smart Play-Out of Behavioral Requirements", *Proc. 4th Int. Conf. on Formal Methods in Computer-Aided Design* (FMCAD'02), November 2002, pp. 378-398.
11. D. Harel, H. Kugler and A. Pnueli, "Smart Play-Out Extended: Time and Forbidden Elements", *Proc. 4th Int. Conf. on Quality Software* (QSIC'04), IEEE Computer Society Press, 2004, pp. 2-10.
12. D. Harel and S. Maoz, "Assert and Negate Revisited: Modal Semantics for UML Sequence Diagrams", *Proc. 5th Int. Workshop on Scenarios and State Machines: Models, Algorithms and Tools* (SCESM'06), 2006, pp. 13-20.
13. D. Harel and S. Maoz, "From Multi-Modal Scenarios to Code: Compiling LSCs into AspectJ", *14th ACM SIGSOFT Symp. on Foundations of Software Engineering (FSE'14)*, Portland, November 2006.
14. D. Harel and R. Marelly, *Come, Let's Play: Scenario-Based Programming Using LSCs and the Play-Engine*, Springer-Verlag, 2003.
15. D. Harel and R. Marelly, "Specifying and Executing Behavioral Requirements: The Play-In/Play-Out Approach", *Software and Systems Modeling* (SoSyM) **2**, 2003, pp. 82-107.
16. D. Harel and I. Segall, "Planned and Traversable Play-Out: A Flexible Method for Executing Scenario-Based Programs", Technical Report MCS07-01, The Weizmann Institute of Science, 2007.

17. J. Hoffmann and J. Koehler, "A new Method to Query and Index Sets", *Proc. 16th Intl. Joint Conf. on Artificial Intelligence* (IJCAI'99), 1999, pp. 462-467.
18. J. Hoffmann and B. Nebel, "The FF Planning System: Fast Plan Generation Through Heuristic Search", *J. Artificial Intelligence Research*, **14**, 2001, pp. 253-302.
19. http://www.wisdom.weizmann.ac.il/~itais/video/TPO-Example.avi
20. IPP website, http://www.informatik.uni-freiburg.de/~koehler/ipp.html.
21. ITU-TS Recommendation Z.120: "Message Sequence Chart (MSC)". ITU-TS, Geneva, 1996.
22. H. Kautz and B. Selman, "Pushing the Envelope: Planning, Propositional Logic, and Stochastic Search", *Proc. 13th National Conf. on Artificial Intelligence* (AAAI'96), Portland, 1996, pp. 1194-1201.
23. H. Kautz and B. Selman, "Blackbox: A New Approach to the Application of Theorem Proving to Problem Solving", *Workshop on Planning as Combinatorial Search, Artificial Intelligence Planning Systems* (AIPS'98), June 1998, pp. 58-60.
24. J. Koehler, "Planning under Resource Constraints", *13th biennial European Conf. on Artificial Intelligence* (ECAI'98), 1998, pp. 489-493.
25. J. Koehler, B. Nebel, J. Hoffmann and Y. Dimopoulos, "Extending Planning Graphs to an ADL Subset", *Proc. 4th European Conf. on Planning* (ECP'97), Springer LNAI, **1348**, 1997, pp. 273-285.
26. D. Long and M. Fox, "Efficient Implementation of the Plan Graph in STAN", *Journal of Artificial Intelligence Research*, **10**(1999), pp. 87-115.
27. E. P. D. Pednault, "ADL: Exploring the Middle Ground Between STRIPS and the Situation Calculus," *Proc. 1st Intl. Conf. on Principles of Knowledge Representation and Reasoning*, Toronto, 1989, pp. 324-332.
28. UML. Documentation of the unified modeling language (UML). Available from the Object Management Group (OMG), http://www.omg.org.
29. M. M. Veloso, "Nonlinear problem solving using intelligent casual-commitment", Technical Report CMU-CS-89-210, School of Computer Science, Carnegie Mellon University, 1989.
30. T. Wang, A. Roychoudhury, R.H.C. Yap and S.C. Choudhary, "Symbolic Execution of Behavioral Requirements", *Proc. 6th Intl. Symp. on Practical Aspects of Declarative Languages* (PADL'04), 2004, pp. 178-192.

MOTOR: The MODEST Tool Environment

Henrik Bohnenkamp[1], Holger Hermanns[2],
and Joost-Pieter Katoen[1,3]

[1] Software Modeling and Verfication Group, Informatik 2
RWTH Aachen University, 52056 Aachen, Germany
[2] Department of Computer Science
Saarland University, D-66123 Saarbrücken, Germany
[3] Formal Methods and Tools Group, Department of Computer Science
University of Twente, P.O. Box 217, 7500 AE Enschede, The Netherlands

Abstract. The MODEST Tool Environment (MOTOR) is a tool to facilitate the transformation, analysis and validation of MODEST models.
MODEST is a modelling language to describe stochastic real-time systems. MOTOR implements the formal semantics of MODEST and is designed to transform and abstract MODEST specifications such that analysis can be carried out by third-party tools. For the time being, a fragment of MODEST can be model-checked using CADP. The main analytical
workhorse behind MOTOR is discrete-event simulation, which is provided
by the MÖBIUS performance evaluation environment. We are experimenting with prototypical connections to the real-time model checker UP-
PAAL.

1   The MODEST Approach

The *Modeling and Description Language for Stochastic and Timed Systems*
(MODEST) [2] is a specification formalism for describing stochastic real-time systems. The language is rooted in classical process algebra, *i.e.* the specification of
models is compositional. Basic activities are expressed with atomic actions, more
complex behaviour with constructs for sequential composition, nondeterministic choice, parallel composition with CSP-style synchronisation, looping and
exception handling. A special construct exists to describe probabilistic choice.
Clocks, variables and random variables are used to describe stochastic real-time
aspects. All constructs and language concepts have a pleasant syntax, inspired
by Promela, LOTOS, FSP, and Java. The screen shot in Fig. 2 gives an impres-
sion of the language syntax. MODEST is equipped with a structural operational
semantics mapping on so-called stochastic timed automata (STA). The MODEST
semantics is described in full detail in [2]. MODEST allows one to describe a very
large spectrum of models, including: ordinary labelled transition systems, timed
automata, probabilistic automata, stochastic automata [8], Markov decision processes, and various combinations thereof (*cf.* [2]). Remarkably, the language is
designed in a way that all these models correspond to syntactic subsets of the
language, and can thus be identified while parsing a MODEST specification.

With MODEST, we take a *single-formalism, multi-solution* approach, similar
to [1]. Our view is to have a single specification that addresses various aspects

O. Grumberg and M. Huth (Eds.): TACAS 2007, LNCS 4424, pp. 500–504, 2007.
© Springer-Verlag Berlin Heidelberg 2007

of the system under consideration. This is contrary to the more common approach to construct different models to describe different aspects of a system and then analyse these models. Generally, no guarantee of consistency between these models can be given, be it for lack of a rigorous semantics or because a proper relation between the different model classes is not known. Thus, the validity of results w.r.t. the original system under study is often questionable.

Instead, with MODEST we advocate an approach to describe a system with *one* model and analyse it by extracting simpler models that are tailored to the specific properties of interest. For instance, for checking reachability properties, a possible strategy is to *distill* an automaton from the MODEST specification and feed it, *e.g.,* into an existing model checker. For carrying out an evaluation of the stochastic process underlying a MODEST specification, a discrete-event simulator can be used. This approach has the advantage that the modelling itself takes less time, since only one model has to be specified. Moreover, if the abstractions used to derive sub-models are sound, the *multi-solution* approach can ensure validity of the respective analysis results and thus significance for the modelled system.

2 MOTOR

In order to facilitate the analysis of the different models, tool support is essential. The MODEST Tool Environment (MOTOR) is a software tool that implements the MODEST semantics and is the central vehicle in the multi-solution analysis of MODEST models. The fundamental idea behind MOTOR is to simplify specifying MODEST models (e.g. by providing a macro-preprocessor), and to translate or adapt the models in a way such that the actual analysis work can be carried out by third-party state-of-the-art tools, such as PRISM [12], UPPAAL [13], or CADP [10].

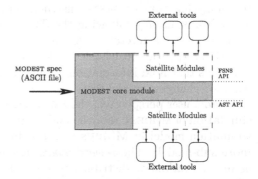

Fig. 1. The MOTOR architecture [4]

MOTOR is designed to facilitate easy access to all language features of MODEST, and thus to allow easy extraction of all imaginable model classes from a specification. The design allows straightforward extensibility of the tool. To realise this, MOTOR provides two programming interfaces, see Fig. 1: the AST API, which gives the programmer access to the abstract syntactic representation of the MODEST specification, and the FSNS API, which allows a programmer access to a first-state/next-state interface, and which allows convenient state-space exploration of the MODEST-specification. It provides the access to the STA defined by the MODEST semantics. The kernel of the tool is thus quite small: it comprises a parser and the implementation of the functionality behind the two interfaces. These two APIs enable modular design and extendability of MOTOR, the former for translation-oriented transformations, the latter for state-oriented approaches. This particular tool architecture is described in [4], and has since been actively developed. A prototype connection to the CADP tool box exists, which allows model-checking of untimed, non-probabilistic MODEST models. We are currently experimenting with another prototypical connection targeting at the UPPAAL model-checker for timed automata. The most interesting tool we connected MOTOR to is the MÖBIUS performance evaluation environment [7].

3   MOTOR and MÖBIUS

The by now most mature connection of MOTOR is the link with the MÖBIUS performability evaluation environment. MÖBIUS has been developed independently from MODEST and MOTOR at the University of Illinois at Urbana-Champaign [7]. MÖBIUS is designed as an integrated tool environment for the analysis of performability and dependability models. It allows specification of models in different formalisms, based on, for instance, Petri net-like formalisms or Markovian process algebra. The tool provides efficient discrete-event simulation capabilities and numerical solvers, such as Markov chain solvers.

The integration of MOTOR into the MÖBIUS framework is established by a direct mapping from MODEST-constructs onto the programming interface available for MÖBIUS, closely following the STA semantics as implemented in the FSNS API [4]. More concretely, a MODEST specification is interpreted as a so-called *atomic model*, the most basic model within MÖBIUS, which is made up of state variables that hold information about the state of a model and actions that are used for changing model state.

From a user perspective, the MOTOR/MÖBIUS tandem enables one to perform simulation of MODEST models, and to gather performability results. A complete simulation model in MÖBIUS consists, in addition to the atomic model, of two more sub-models. The *reward model* defines which performance measures (such as means, variances, distributions etc.) are to be estimated with the simulation. These rewards are based on the global variables of the atomic MODEST model. The *study model* defines intervals or sets of values as parameters for which the MODEST model is to be simulated. Experiment parameters are declared inside MODEST as special *external* constants. For each set of parameters an *experiment*, *i.e.* simulation process is started (in parallel or sequentially, depending on the configuration and number of available processors), where the external constants of the MODEST model are preset with the respective values defined in the study model.

Atomic MODEST models are entered in a dedicated MÖBIUS text-editor. MOTOR is called from MÖBIUS to translate the model into a C++ program, which is then compiled and linked together with an implementation of the MODEST semantics and the simulator libraries of MÖBIUS. Fig. 2 shows a screen shot of the different MÖBIUS editors, the MODEST editor in the center.

The reason to choose simulation as the prime analysis method of MODEST models to integrate into MOTOR is that simulation covers the largest language

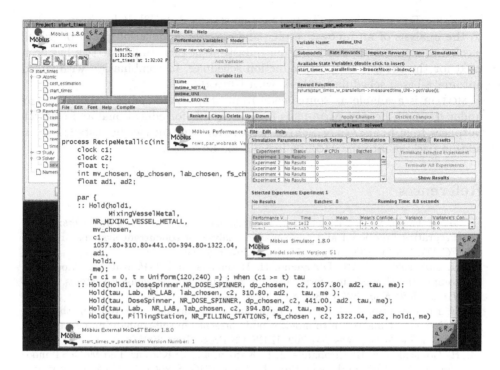

Fig. 2. MÖBIUS with MODEST editor

fragment of MODEST: the only concept that can not be supported by simulation is nondeterminism, in particular of delay durations and non-deterministic choice between actions. We exclude the former by assuming maximal-progress with respect to delays. We do not restrict action nondeterminism, since it is a convenient modelling instrument. However, no mechanisms, like a well-specified-check [9], is implemented yet to ensure validity of the simulation statistics when action nondeterminism is present.

Given that discrete-event simulation (DES) is supported by many tools, one may question what the benefits are of using MODEST. The main difference with existing simulation notations is that MODEST has a formal semantics. Consequently, the underlying stochastic model for simulation is well-defined and obtained simulation results—given that DES is a well-understood technique—is trustworthy. In commercially available simulation tools it is often unclear how simulation models are obtained from the modelling language. This is recently witnessed in e.g.,. [6] by obtaining significant different results from models that were fed into different simulators.

4 Status and Availability

MOTOR and its connection to MÖBIUS is mature and has been tested in a number of non-trivial case studies. In [11], it has been used for reliability analysis of the upcoming European Train Control System standard. In [3], it has been applied to the analysis of an innovative plug-and-play communication protocol, which has led to a patent application of our industrial partner. In [5], MOTOR has been used for the optimisation of production schedules, in combination with timed automata-based schedule synthesis with UPPAAL.

MOTOR is available as source code from http://www.purl.org/net/motor under the GPL license. MÖBIUS is freely available for educational and research purposes from http://www.mobius.uiuc.edu/. MOTOR can be installed as an add-on package into the MÖBIUS installation directory.

References

1. M. Bernardo, W.R. Cleaveland, S.T. Sims, and W.J. Stewart. TwoTowers: A tool integrating functional and performance analysis of concurrent systems. In *Proc. FORTE/PSTV 1998*, pages 457–467. Kluwer, 1998.
2. H. Bohnenkamp, P.R. D'Argenio, H. Hermanns, and J.-P. Katoen. Modest: A compositional modeling formalism for real-time and stochastic systems. *IEEE Trans. Soft. Eng.*, 32(10):812–830, 2006.
3. H. Bohnenkamp, J. Gorter, J. Guidi, and J.-P. Katoen. Are you still there? — A lightweight algorithm to monitor node presence in self-configuring networks. In *Proc. DSN 2005*, pages 704–709. IEEE CS Press, June 2005.
4. H. Bohnenkamp, H. Hermanns, J.-P. Katoen, and J. Klaren. The MoDeST modeling tool and its implementation. In *Proc. TOOLS 2003*, LNCS 2794. Springer, 2003.
5. H. Bohnenkamp, H. Hermanns, J. Klaren, A. Mader, and Y. Usenko. Synthesis and stochastic assessment of schedules for lacquer production. In *Proc. QEST '04*. IEEE CS Press, 2004.
6. D. Cavin, Y. Sasson, and A. Schiper. On the accuracy of MANET simulators. In *ACM Workshop On Principles Of Mobile Computing*, pages 38–43, 2002.
7. D. Daly, D. D. Deavours, J. M. Doyle, P. G. Webster, and W. H. Sanders. Möbius: An extensible tool for performance and dependability modeling. In *Proc. TOOLS 2000*, LNCS 1786. Springer, 2000.
8. P. R. D'Argenio and J.-P. Katoen. A theory of stochastic systems. Part I. Stochastic automata. *Inf. & Comp.*, 203:1–38, 2005.
9. D. D. Deavours and W. H. Sanders. An efficient well-specified check. In *Proceedings PNPM '99*, pages 124–133. IEEE Computer Society, 1999.
10. H. Garavel. OPEN/CÆSAR: An open software architecture for verification, simulation, and testing. In *Proc. TACAS '98*, volume 1384 of *LNCS*, 1998.
11. H. Hermanns, D. N. Jansen, and Y. S. Usenko. From StoCharts to MoDeST: a comparative reliability analysis of train radio communications. In *Proc. WOSP '05*. ACM Press, 2005.
12. M. Kwiatkowska, G. Norman, and D. Parker. Probabilistic symbolic model checking with PRISM. In *Proc. TACAS '02*, LNCS 2280. Springer, 2002.
13. Kim G. Larsen, Paul Pettersson, and Wang Yi. UPPAAL in a Nutshell. *Int. Journal on Software Tools for Technology Transfer*, 1(1–2):134–152, October 1997.

Syntactic Optimizations for PSL Verification

Alessandro Cimatti[1], Marco Roveri[1], and Stefano Tonetta[2]

[1] ITC-irst Trento, Italy
{cimatti,roveri}@itc.it
[2] University of Lugano, Lugano, Switzerland
tonettas@lu.unisi.ch

Abstract. The IEEE standard Property Specification Language (PSL) allows to express all ω-regular properties mixing Linear Temporal Logic (LTL) with Sequential Extended Regular Expressions (SEREs), and is increasingly used in many phases of the hardware design cycle, from specification to verification.

In recent works, we propose a modular and symbolic PSL compilation that is extremely fast in conversion time and outperforms by several orders of magnitude translators based on the explicit construction and minimization of automata. Unfortunately, our approach creates rather redundant automata, which result in a penalty in verification time.

In this paper, we propose a set of syntactic simplifications that enable to significantly improve the verification time without paying the price of automata simplifications. A thorough experimental analysis over large sets of paradigmatic properties shows that our approach drastically reduces the overall verification time.

1 Introduction

The IEEE standard Property Specification Language PSL [1] is increasingly used in several phases of the design flows: it is a means to describe behavioral requirements, such as assumptions about the environment in which the design is expected to operate, internal behavioral requirements, and further constraints that arise during the design process from specification to verification.

The most important fragment of PSL combines Linear Temporal Logic (LTL) [2] with Sequential Extended Regular Expressions (SERE), a variant of classical regular expressions [1]. This combination results in ω-regular expressiveness, and enables to express many properties of practical interest in a compact and readable way.

The conversion from PSL to Nondeterministic Büchi Automata (NBAs) is an enabling factor for the the adaptation of standard verification tools, and has been recently investigated in several works (e.g. [3,4,5,6,7]).

[3] describes a classical approach based on Alternating Büchi Automata (ABA): the SEREs occurring in the PSL formula are first translated into minimum Nondeterministic Finite Automata (NFA); the NFAs are then combined bottom up and the overall PSL formula is translated into an ABA; the ABA is finally translated into an NBA by means of the Miyano-Hayashi (MH) construction [8]. [4] specializes this approach to SAT-based bounded model checking, exploiting the fact that alternating automata are weak. In [5], a symbolic encoding, based on MH, of the NBA corresponding to the ABA of

O. Grumberg and M. Huth (Eds.): TACAS 2007, LNCS 4424, pp. 505–518, 2007.
© Springer-Verlag Berlin Heidelberg 2007

the PSL property is proposed. Both approaches try to limit the encoding size (delaying the explosion until search time), but are based on a library that tries to carry out some optimizations in order to minimize the ABA. However, the minimization of ABA is very expensive these approaches are often unable to carry out the conversion in acceptable time, even for PSL specifications of moderate size.

The works in [7] and in [6] independently propose direct encodings of PSL into symbolically represented NBA. Both approaches are compositional, and neither requires the generation of ABA. The former is based on the notion of transducer, while the latter proposes a reduction to Suffix Operator Normal Form (SONF). The experimental evaluation in [6] shows that the SONF construction is extremely fast in the construction of the NBA, thus enabling the verification in cases where the automaton construction blows up.

The results in [6], however, show that the verification times are often in favor of the approaches in [5] and [4]. In fact, the semantic simplifications implemented in the ABA library, though costly, are often able to construct optimized automata, that can then be verified more effectively. This is similar to what happens in LTL model checking, where semantic simplifications on the automaton recognizing the violation, though costly, can often pay off in overall verification time [9].

We notice that some specifications contain obvious forms of redundancy, since designers heavily rely on syntactic sugaring, and redundant specifications may enable reusability. A typical example is length matching between a fixed-length expression, and an expression containing stars. Thus, it is an important practical problem to devise means to deal with redundant specifications, without paying a price in performance. In principle, redundancies can be removed with automata minimization techniques; however, such reductions can be expensive and produce large intermediate automata.

In this paper, we propose a *syntactic* approach to improving PSL verification: rather than simplifying the automaton at a semantic level, we propose a number of syntactic rewriting rules on the formula. After the preprocessing, the SONF-based method result in more compact NBA, which in turn results in much faster verification. The rewrite rules are based on the following ideas. First, we try to minimize the size of the arguments to the SERE language intersection operators, given that they are associated with an exponential blow up. Second, whenever possible we convert the SEREs into LTL, in order to limit as much as possible Suffix operators, and to enable the use of specialized algorithms for LTL. Third, some Suffix Operator Subformulas resulting from the conversion into SONF can be eliminated by taking into account their structure. Finally, we also apply syntactic simplifications to the LTL component of the formula resulting from the conversion into SONF.

We experimentally evaluate our method on the test cases proposed in [6] on a large test suite with formulas identified and classified in [10] to be of practical relevance. The experiments show that the simplifications are computationally cheap, and substantially pay off in terms of verification time. The result is that overall the new method is vastly superior to [6] and to [5]. A final remark in favor of the proposed approach is that it is open and customizable with respect to typical patterns in the application at hand.

The paper is structured as follows. In Section 2 we present the syntax and semantics of PSL. In Section 3 we overview the approaches to PSL conversions into NBA, and discuss the performance issues. In Sections 4 we describe the various classes of rewriting rules. In Section 5 we experimentally evaluate the impact of our optimizations. Finally, in Section 6 we draw some conclusions and discuss directions for future research.

2 The Property Specification Language PSL

PSL is a very rich language [1]. We consider the subset of PSL that combines Linear Temporal Logic [2] (LTL) and Sequential Extended Regular Expressions (SERE), a variant of classical regular expressions [1]. This subset provides ω-regular expressiveness [11], it is the mostly used in practice and constitutes *the core* of the PSL temporal layer [1]. We will not deal with PSL "clocked" expressions that are not part of the core since any clocked expression can be rewritten into an equivalent un-clocked one [1]. The same applies for the PSL "abort" operator that can be efficiently rewritten into pure LTL as shown in [12].

In the following, we assume as given a set $\mathcal{A}$ of atomic propositions. Let $\Sigma := 2^{\mathcal{A}}$. We denote a letter over the alphabet Σ by ℓ, a word from Σ by v or w, and the concatenation of v and w by vw. We denote with $|w|$ the length of word w. A finite word $w = \ell_0\ell_1 \ldots \ell_n$ has length $n+1$, an infinite word has length ω. If $w = \ell_0\ell_1 \ldots$, for $0 \le i < |w|$, we use w^i to denote the letter ℓ_i, and we denote with $w^{i\cdots}$ the suffix of w starting at w^i. When $i \le j \le |w|$, we denote with $w^{i\cdots j}$ the finite sequence of letters starting from w^i and ending in w^j ($w^{i\cdots j} := w^i w^{i+1} \ldots w^j$).

SEREs are the PSL version of regular expressions. In particular, they extend the standard regular expressions with language intersection. This allows for a greater succinctness, but it implies a possible exponential blow-up in the conversion to automata. Moreover, the atoms of SEREs are Boolean expressions enabling efficient determinization of automata. Formally,

Definition 1 (SEREs syntax)

- *if b is Boolean expression, then b is a* SERE*;*
- *if r is a* SERE*, then* r[*] *is a* SERE*;*
- *if* r_1 *and* r_2 *are* SEREs*, then the following are* SEREs

$$r_1 \; ; r_2 \qquad r_1 : r_2 \qquad r_1 \mid r_2 \qquad r_1 \; \& \; r_2 \qquad r_1 \; \&\& \; r_2.$$

SEREs can be concatenated with the operators ; and : , the former for the consecutive concatenation of two sequences, the latter for one-state overlapping concatenation. The conjunction operators & and && can be used to specify overlapping sequences, the latter for length-matching sequences. Disjunction can be specified using the | operator. The [*] operator specifies finite consecutive repetitions. We use r[*n] as an abbreviation of $r \; ; r \; ; \ldots \; ; r$, where r is repeated n times.

The semantics of SEREs is formally defined over *finite* words using, as the base case, the semantics of Boolean expressions over letters in Σ, denoted with $\models_B$ hereafter.

Definition 2 (SEREs semantics). *Given a Boolean expression b, a* SERE *r, and a* finite word *w, we define the satisfaction relation* $w \models r$ *as follows:*

- $w \models b$ iff $|w| = 1$ and $w^0 \models_B b$;
- $w \models r_1 ; r_2$ iff $\exists w_1, w_2$ s.t. $w = w_1 w_2$, $w_1 \models r_1$, $w_2 \models r_2$;
- $w \models r_1 : r_2$ iff $\exists w_1, w_2, \ell$ s.t. $w = w_1 \ell w_2$, $w_1 \ell \models r_1$, $\ell w_2 \models r_2$;
- $w \models r_1 \mid r_2$ iff $w \models r_1$ or $w \models r_2$;
- $w \models r_1 \,\&\, r_2$ iff $w \models r_1$ and $\exists w_1, w_2$ s.t. $w = w_1 w_2$, $w_1 \models r_2$,
  or $w \models r_2$ and $\exists w_1, w_2$ s.t. $w = w_1 w_2$, $w_1 \models r_1$;
- $w \models r_1 \,\&\&\, r_2$ iff $\exists w_1, w_2$ s.t. $w = w_1 w_2$, $w_1 \models r_1$, $w_1 \models r_2$;
- $w \models r[^*]$ iff $|w| = 0$ or $\exists w_1, w_2$ s.t. $|w_1| \neq 0$, $w = w_1 w_2$, $w_1 \models r$, $w_2 \models r[^*]$.

In the definition of the PSL syntax, for technical reasons, we introduce the "releases" operator (that is the dual of the "until" operator), and also we introduce the "suffix conjunction" connective as a dual of the suffix implication. Moreover, we consider only the strong version of the temporal operators (the weak operators can be rewritten in terms of the strong ones [1]) and the strong version of the SEREs (though our approach can be easily extended to deal also with the weak semantics).

Definition 3 (PSL syntax). *We define the PSL formulas over $\mathcal{A}$, as follows:*

- *if $p \in \mathcal{A}$, p is a PSL formula;*
- *if ϕ_1 and ϕ_2 are PSL formulas, then $\neg\phi_1$, $\phi_1 \wedge \phi_2$, $\phi_1 \vee \phi_2$ are PSL formulas;*
- *if ϕ_1 and ϕ_2 are PSL formulas, then $\mathbf{X}\,\phi_1$, $\phi_1 \,\mathbf{U}\, \phi_2$, $\phi_1 \,\mathbf{R}\, \phi_2$ are PSL formulas;*
- *if r is a SERE and ϕ is a PSL formulas, then $r \Diamond\!\!\rightarrow \phi$ and $r \mapsto \phi$ are PSL formulas;*
- *if r is a SERE, then r is a PSL formula.*

The **X** ("next-time"), the **U** ("until"), and the **R** ("releases") operators are called *temporal operators*. We call the $\Diamond\!\!\rightarrow$ ("suffix conjunction"), and the $\mapsto$ ("suffix implication"), *suffix operators*. Notice that, the r not occurring in the left side of a suffix operator is the *strong* version of a SERE ($r!$ in the PSL notation). In the following, we will consider such r as an abbreviation for $r \Diamond\!\!\rightarrow True$ [1,3]. We also use $\mathbf{G}\,\phi$ as an abbreviation for *False* $\mathbf{R}\,\phi$. LTL can be seen as a subset of PSL in which the suffix operators and the SEREs are suppressed.

We interpret PSL expressions over *infinite* words:

Definition 4 (PSL semantics). *Let $w \in \Sigma^\omega$.*

- $w \models p$ *iff $w^0 \models_B p$;*
- $w \models \neg\phi$ *iff $w \not\models \phi$;*
- $w \models \phi \wedge \psi$ *iff $w \models \phi$ and $w \models \psi$;*
- $w \models \phi \vee \psi$ *iff either $w \models \phi$ or $w \models \psi$;*
- $w \models \mathbf{X}\,\phi$ *iff $|w| > 1$ and $w^{1\cdot\cdot} \models \phi$;*
- $w \models \phi \,\mathbf{U}\,\psi$ *iff, for some $j \geq 0$, $w^{j\cdot\cdot} \models \psi$ and, for all $0 \leq k < j$, $w^{k\cdot\cdot} \models \phi$;*
- $w \models \phi \,\mathbf{R}\,\psi$ *iff, for all $j \geq 0$, either $w^{j\cdot\cdot} \models \psi$ or, for some $0 \leq k < j$, $w^{k\cdot\cdot} \models \phi$;*
- $w \models r \Diamond\!\!\rightarrow \phi$ *iff, for some $j \geq 0$, $w^{0\cdot\cdot j} \models r$ and $w^{j\cdot\cdot} \models \phi$;*
- $w \models r \mapsto \phi$ *iff, for all $j \geq 0$, if $w^{0\cdot\cdot j} \models r$, then $w^{j\cdot\cdot} \models \phi$.*

Notice that we can build Boolean expressions by means of atomic formulas and Boolean connectives. The language of a PSL formula ϕ over the alphabet Σ is defined as the set $\mathcal{L}(\phi) := \{w \in \Sigma^\omega \mid w \models \phi\}$.

Example 1. Consider the PSL formula $\mathbf{G}\,(\{\{a ; b[^*] ; c\} \,\&\&\, \{d[^*] ; e\}\} \mapsto \{f ; g\})$. It encodes the property for which every sequence that matches both regular expressions $\{a ; b[^*] ; c\}$ and $\{d[^*] ; e\}$ must be followed by $\{f ; g\}$.

3   From PSL to NBA: Previous Approaches

In this section, we overview recent approaches to dealing with PSL verification. In the *monolithic* approaches, the first step is the conversion from PSL in a monolithic alternating Büchi automaton; during the conversion, semantic simplification steps (such as the elimination of unreachable states, and restricted forms of minimization by observational equivalence) are applied. The ABA is then converted into a symbolically represented NBA. In [5], this is done by means of a symbolic encoding of MH, and can be applied both to BDD-based and SAT-based verification. In [4], an encoding of the ABA that is specialized for bounded model checking is proposed.

The conversion proposed in [6] is based on the so called Suffix Operator Normal Form (SONF). The idea is to partition the translation, by first converting a PSL formula ϕ into an equisatisfiable formula in SONF, structured as follows

$$\overbrace{\bigwedge_i \phi_i}^{\Psi_{LTL}} \wedge \overbrace{\bigwedge_j \mathbf{G}\,(p_I^j \rightarrow (r_j \mapsto\!\!\!\leftarrow p_F^j))}^{\Psi_{PSL}}$$

where ϕ_i are LTL formulas, r_j are SEREs, p_I^j and p_F^j are propositional atoms, and $\mapsto\!\!\!\leftarrow$ is either $\mapsto$ or $\Diamond\!\!\!\rightarrow$. Formulae of the form $\mathbf{G}\,(p_I^j \rightarrow (r_j \mapsto\!\!\!\leftarrow p_F^j))$ are called *Suffix Operator Subformulas* (SOS's).

The translation first converts the formula in NNF, and then "lifts out" the occurrences of suffix operators, by introducing fresh variables (intuitively, the p^j in the formula above), together with the corresponding SOS. For lack of space, we omit the details regarding the conversion of SOS into NBA. We only mention that the translation is specialized to exploit the structure of SOS (see [6] for details).

Example 2. The SONF of the PSL formula of Example 1 is $\mathbf{G}\,p_1 \wedge \mathbf{G}\,(p_1 \rightarrow \{\{a\,;\,b[*]\,;\,c\}\,\&\&\,\{d[*]\,;\,e\}\} \mapsto p_2) \wedge \mathbf{G}\,(p_2 \rightarrow \{f\,;\,g\}\,\Diamond\!\!\!\rightarrow p_3)$.

In [6], a substantial experimental evaluation is carried out, both on PSL satisfiability problems (denoted with LE for language emptiness) and on Model Checking (MC) problems. The modular approach results in dramatic improvements in PSL compilation time. However, on those problems where the ABA library is able to build an automaton within the time limit, the search time is typically in favor of the monolithic approach. This is mainly due to the fact that in certain examples the semantic simplifications are extremely effective. We notice that, the loss of efficiency in search is often compensated by the much faster compilation; yet, in the rest of the paper we show how to enhance our approach even further, by proposing a similar simplification mechanism.

4   Syntactic Optimizations for PSL

In this section, we describe an optimized approach, which extends the SONF-based conversion with the integration of the following simplifications. Before the SONF conversion, we apply two steps: (*i*) we simplify the SEREs in order to reduce the subformulas in the scope of SERE conjunction operators; (*ii*) we simplify occurrences of

$$r \;\&\&\; (r_1 \mid r_2) \;\Rightarrow\; (r \;\&\&\; r_1) \mid (r \;\&\&\; r_2)$$
$$b_1 \;\&\&\; b_2 \;\Rightarrow\; b_1 \wedge b_2$$
$$b \;\&\&\; \{r_1 \;\&\&\; r_2\} \;\Rightarrow\; \{b \;\&\&\; r_1\} \;\&\&\; r_2$$
$$b \;\&\&\; \{r_1 \;;\; r_2\} \;\Rightarrow\; \begin{cases} \textit{False} \text{ if } \varepsilon \notin L(r_1), \varepsilon \notin L(r_2) \\ b \;\&\&\; r_1 \text{ if } \varepsilon \notin L(r_1), \varepsilon \in L(r_2) \\ b \;\&\&\; r_2 \text{ if } \varepsilon \in L(r_1), \varepsilon \notin L(r_2) \\ b \;\&\&\; r_1 \mid b \;\&\&\; r_2 \text{ otherwise} \end{cases}$$
$$b \;\&\&\; \{r_1 \;:\; r_2\} \;\Rightarrow\; \{b \;\&\&\; r_1\} \;\&\&\; r_2$$
$$b \;\&\&\; r[^*] \;\Rightarrow\; b \;\&\&\; r$$
$$b[^*] \;\&\&\; \{r_1 \;;\; r_2\} \;\Rightarrow\; \{b[^*] \;\&\&\; r_1\} \;;\; \{b[^*] \;\&\&\; r_2\}$$
$$b[^*] \;\&\&\; \{r_1 \;:\; r_2\} \;\Rightarrow\; \{b[^*] \;\&\&\; r_1\} \;:\; \{b[^*] \;\&\&\; r_2\}$$
$$b[^*] \;\&\&\; r[^*] \;\Rightarrow\; \{b[^*] \;\&\&\; r\}[^*]$$
$$\{b_1 \;;\; r_1\} \;\&\&\; \{b_2 \;;\; r_2\} \;\Rightarrow\; \{b_1 \wedge b_2\} \;;\; \{r_1 \;\&\&\; r_2\}$$
$$\{b_1 \;:\; r_1\} \;\&\&\; \{b_2 \;:\; r_2\} \;\Rightarrow\; \{b_1 \wedge b_2\} \;:\; \{r_1 \;\&\&\; r_2\}$$
$$\{r_1 \;;\; b_1\} \;\&\&\; \{r_2 \;;\; b_2\} \;\Rightarrow\; \{r_1 \;\&\&\; r_2\} \;;\; \{b_1 \wedge b_2\}$$
$$\{r_1 \;:\; b_1\} \;\&\&\; \{r_2 \;:\; b_2\} \;\Rightarrow\; \{r_1 \;\&\&\; r_2\} \;:\; \{b_1 \wedge b_2\}$$
$$\{b_1[^*] \;;\; r_1\} \;\&\&\; \{b_2 \;;\; r_2\} \;\Rightarrow\;$$
$$\{r_1 \;\&\&\; \{b_2 \;;\; r_2\}\} \mid \{\{b_1 \wedge b_2\} \;;\; \{\{b_1[^*] \;;\; r_1\} \;\&\&\; r_2\}\}$$
$$\{b_1[^*] \;;\; r_1\} \;\&\&\; \{b_2[^*] \;;\; r_2\} \;\Rightarrow\;$$
$$\{b_1 \wedge b_2\}[^*] \;;\; \{\{r_1 \;\&\&\; \{b_2[^*] \;;\; r_2\}\} \mid \{\{b_1[^*] \;;\; r_1\} \;\&\&\; r_2\}\}$$
$$r_1[^*] \;\&\&\; r_2[^*] \;\Rightarrow^* \; \{r_1[^*n_2] \;\&\&\; r_2[^*n_1]\}[^*]$$

*) where r_1 and r_2 have "fixed length", n_1 and n_2 are the least integers
such that $n = (|r_1| \cdot n_2) = (|r_2| \cdot n_1)$.

Fig. 1. Rules for **&&**

suffix operators by converting as much as possible the regexps to which they are applied to into LTL. Then, after the conversion in SONF, we apply two other steps: (iii) we simplify the Suffix Operator Subformulas by means of rules that strengthen the ones in (ii) by exploiting the specific structure of SOSs; (iv) the LTL component is rewritten in order to minimize the overall automaton and reduce the number of resulting fairness constraints. In the rest of this section we describe the first three sets of rewriting rules, which regard SEREs and PSL formulas and are an original contributions of this paper. For lack of space, we do not report a detailed description of the LTL simplification rules, which follow [13,14].

In the following, we write $b, b_1, b_2, \ldots$ for boolean formulas, and $r, r_1, r_2, \ldots$ for SEREs. We notice that we can check if the empty word ε belongs to the language of r by parsing: if $r = [\text{*0}]$, then *True*; if $r = b$, then *False*; if $r = r_1 \; ; \; r_2$, then *True* if both r_1 and r_1 accept ε, *False* otherwise; if $r = r_1 : r_2$, then *False*; if $r = r_1[^*]$, then *True*; if $r = r_1 \;\&\&\; r_2$ or $r = r_1 \;\&\; r_2$, then *True* if both r_1 and r_2 accept ε, *False* otherwise; if $r = r_1 \mid r_2$, then *True* if either r_1 or r_2 accept ε, *False* otherwise.

(i) Simplifying Regular Expressions. Step (i) of our simplification flow is implemented by the rules of Figures 1 and 2. For lack of space, Figure 2 only contains some of the rules for **&** ; other rules based on the commutativity and associativity of the operators are also omitted.

$$r \mathbin{\&} (r_1 \mid r_2) \Rightarrow (r \mathbin{\&} r_1) \mid (r \mathbin{\&} r_2)$$
$$b_1 \mathbin{\&} b_2 \Rightarrow b_1 \wedge b_2$$
$$b \mathbin{\&} \{r_1 \mathbin{\&} r_2\} \Rightarrow \{b \mathbin{\&} r_1\} \mathbin{\&} r_2$$

$$b \mathbin{\&} \{r_1 \,;\, r_2\} \Rightarrow \begin{cases} b : \{r_1 \,;\, r_2\} \text{ if } \varepsilon \notin \mathcal{L}(r_1), \varepsilon \notin \mathcal{L}(r_2) \\ b : \{r_1 \,;\, r_2\} \mid b \mathbin{\&\&} r_1 \\ \qquad \text{if } \varepsilon \notin \mathcal{L}(r_1), \varepsilon \in \mathcal{L}(r_2) \\ b : \{r_1 \,;\, r_2\} \mid b \mathbin{\&\&} r_2 \\ \qquad \text{if } \varepsilon \in \mathcal{L}(r_1), \varepsilon \notin \mathcal{L}(r_2) \\ b : \{r_1 \,;\, r_2\} \mid b \text{ otherwise} \end{cases}$$

$$b \mathbin{\&} \{r_1 : r_2\} \Rightarrow b : \{r_1 : r_2\}$$
$$b \mathbin{\&} r[^*] \Rightarrow b \mid \{b : r[^*]\}$$
$$b[^*] \mathbin{\&} r \Rightarrow r \mid \{b[^*] \mathbin{\&\&} r\} \,;\, b[^*]$$
$$r_1[^*] \mathbin{\&} r_2 \Rightarrow r_2 \mid r_1[^*] \mathbin{\&\&} \{r_2 \,;\, \top[^*]\}$$
$$\{b_1 \,;\, r_1\} \mathbin{\&} \{b_2 \,;\, r_2\} \Rightarrow \{b_1 \wedge b_2\} \,;\, \{r_1 \mathbin{\&} r_2\}$$
$$\{b_1 \,;\, r_1\} \mathbin{\&} \{b_2 : r_2\} \Rightarrow \{b_1 \wedge b_2\} : \{r_1 \mathbin{\&} r_2\}$$
$$\{r_1 \,;\, b_1\} \mathbin{\&} \{r_2 \,;\, b_2\} \Rightarrow \{r_1 \mathbin{\&} r_2\} \,;\, \{b_1 \wedge b_2\}$$
$$\{r_1 : b_1\} \mathbin{\&} \{r_2 : b_2\} \Rightarrow \{r_1 \mathbin{\&} r_2\} : \{b_1 \wedge b_2\}$$
$$r_1[^*] \mathbin{\&} r_2[^*] \Rightarrow r_1[^*] \mid r_2[^*]$$

Fig. 2. Rules for **&**

Example 3. The rewriting rules of Figure 1 apply to the SERE in the PSL formula of Example 1, as follows:

$$\{a \,;\, b[^*] \,;\, c\} \mathbin{\&\&} \{d[^*] \,;\, e\} \Rightarrow \{\{a \,;\, b[^*]\} \mathbin{\&\&} d[^*]\} \,;\, c \wedge e$$
$$\Rightarrow \{a \mathbin{\&\&} d[^*]\} \,;\, \{b[^*] \mathbin{\&\&} d[^*]\} \,;\, c \wedge e$$
$$\Rightarrow \{a \mathbin{\&\&} d\} \,;\, \{b[^*] \mathbin{\&\&} d\}[^*] \,;\, c \wedge e$$
$$\Rightarrow a \wedge d \,;\, \{b \mathbin{\&\&} d\}[^*] \,;\, c \wedge e$$
$$\Rightarrow a \wedge d \,;\, \{b \wedge d\}[^*] \,;\, c \wedge e.$$

(ii) Simplifying Suffix Operations In order to reduce a PSL formula to LTL "as much as possible", we define the rules in Figure 3. The rewritings are mostly effective on those expressions where iterations are applied to boolean expressions, as shown in the following example.

Example 4. Consider the formula of Example 1. After applying the rules of Figure 1 as in the Example 3, the formula becomes $\mathbf{G}\,(\{a \wedge d \,;\, \{b \wedge d\}[^*] \,;\, c \wedge e\} \mapsto \{f \,;\, g\})$. The rewriting rules of Figure 3 apply as follows:

$$\mathbf{G}\,(\{a \wedge d \,;\, \{b \wedge d\}[^*] \,;\, c \wedge e\} \mapsto \{f \,;\, g\}) \Rightarrow$$
$$\mathbf{G}\,((a \wedge d) \to \{\{b \wedge d\}[^*] \,;\, c \wedge e\} \mapsto (f \wedge \mathbf{X}\,\{g\})) \Rightarrow$$
$$\mathbf{G}\,((a \wedge d) \to (\neg(b \wedge d)\,\mathbf{R}\,(\{c \wedge e\} \mapsto (f \wedge \mathbf{X}\,g))) \Rightarrow$$
$$\mathbf{G}\,((a \wedge d) \to (\neg(b \wedge d)\,\mathbf{R}\,((c \wedge e) \to (f \wedge \mathbf{X}\,g))).$$

(iii) Rewriting Suffix Operator Subformulas After the simplifications described in previous sections, the SONF conversion is carried out [6], so that the occurrences of suffix operators have the fixed structure of SOS, and can be further rewritten. The aim is to

$$
\begin{aligned}
(\{[\mathbf{*0}]\} \Diamond\!\!\rightarrow \phi) &\Rightarrow \quad \textit{False} \\
(\{b\} \Diamond\!\!\rightarrow \phi) &\Rightarrow \quad b \wedge \phi \\
\{r_1 : r_2\} \Diamond\!\!\rightarrow \phi &\Rightarrow \quad \{r_1\} \Diamond\!\!\rightarrow (\{r_2\} \Diamond\!\!\rightarrow \phi) \\
\{r_1 ; r_2\} \Diamond\!\!\rightarrow \phi &\Rightarrow^* \quad \{r_1\} \Diamond\!\!\rightarrow \mathbf{X} (\{r_2\} \Diamond\!\!\rightarrow \phi) \\
(\{r_1 \mid r_2\} \Diamond\!\!\rightarrow \phi) &\Rightarrow \quad (\{r_1\} \Diamond\!\!\rightarrow \phi) \vee (\{r_2\} \Diamond\!\!\rightarrow \phi) \\
(\{r ; b[^*]\} \Diamond\!\!\rightarrow \phi) &\Rightarrow^{**} \quad \{r\} \Diamond\!\!\rightarrow ((\mathbf{X} b) \mathbf{U} \phi) \\
(\{b[^*] ; r\} \Diamond\!\!\rightarrow \phi) &\Rightarrow^{**} \quad b \mathbf{U} (\{r\} \Diamond\!\!\rightarrow \phi) \\
(\{[\mathbf{*0}]\} \mapsto \phi) &\Rightarrow \quad \textit{True} \\
(\{b\} \mapsto \phi) &\Rightarrow \quad b \rightarrow \phi \\
\{r_1 : r_2\} \mapsto \phi &\Rightarrow \quad \{r_1\} \mapsto (\{r_2\} \mapsto \phi) \\
\{r_1 ; r_2\} \mapsto \phi &\Rightarrow^* \quad \{r_1\} \mapsto \mathbf{X} (\{r_2\} \mapsto \phi) \\
(\{r_1 \mid r_2\} \mapsto \phi) &\Rightarrow \quad (\{r_1\} \mapsto \phi) \wedge (\{r_2\} \mapsto \phi) \\
(\{b[^*] ; r\} \mapsto \phi) &\Rightarrow^{**} \quad \neg b \mathbf{R} (\{r\} \mapsto \phi) \\
(\{r ; b[^*]\} \mapsto \phi) &\Rightarrow^{**} \quad \{r\} \mapsto ((\mathbf{X} \neg b) \mathbf{R} \phi)
\end{aligned}
$$

*) if $\varepsilon \notin L(r_1)$ and $\varepsilon \notin L(r_2)$
**) if $\varepsilon \notin L(r)$

Fig. 3. Rules for suffix operators

$$
\mathbf{G} (P \rightarrow (\{r[^*]\} \mapsto P')) \Rightarrow^* \quad \mathbf{G} (P \rightarrow (\{r\} \mapsto (P' \wedge \mathbf{X} P)))
$$

*) if $\varepsilon \notin L(r)$

Fig. 4. Rules for SOS

apply the suffix operators to smaller SERE. This way, we partition further the automaton representation, and we enable the sharing of subformulas representations. The rule in Figure 4 push the occurrences of suffix implication inside the SEREs, while keeping the overall formula in SONF. Note that, in general, the transformation is not correct: it preserves the satisfiability only if the global formula is the result of the SONF-ization process described in [6] so that there is a fixed structure for SOS. Unfortunately, no similar transformation is possible for suffix conjunction.

5 Experimental Evaluation

The rewrite rules have been implemented within the NuSMV model checker [15]. We compared their effectiveness with the same experimental setting as [6]. [1] We compare three methods: MONO [5], FMCAD06 [6], and TACAS07 (the method presented in this paper). We preliminarily compare the methods in encoding. We use the test suite of 1000 properties proposed in [6]. The set of properties has been obtained by filling in, with randomly generated SEREs, typical patterns extracted from industrial case studies [10]. Then, we used both Boolean combinations and single and double implications

---

[1] All the experiments and files to reproduce the experimental analysis described in this paper can be downloaded from the url: http://sra.itc.it/people/roveri/tacas07/tacas07.tar.gz.

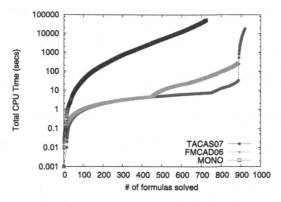

Fig. 5. Problem encoding on 1000 properties

between big conjunctions of typical properties. The latter cases model problems arising in requirements engineering setting, i.e. refinement and equivalence among specifications. For each of the methods (MONO, FMCAD06 and TACAS07), we report the time needed to construct the corresponding representation. All experiments were run on a 3GHz Intel CPU equipped with 4GB of memory running Linux; for each run, we used a timeout of 900 seconds and a memory limit of 1GB. Figure 5 reports the plot of the number of problems generated in a given amount of time (the samples are ordered by increasing computation time). The comparison between FMCAD06 and MONO, just as stated in [6], shows that the monolithic approach has a much harder time than FM-CAD06 in completing the generation. The plots also show that the TACAS07 rewriting, in addition to causing negligible overhead in the simple cases, seems to pay off in the harder cases. There are several samples where the construction time is substantially reduced, and (by looking carefully at the data) we see that TACAS07 completes the 884 samples that FMCAD06 can solve one order of magnitude faster; in addition, we see that TACAS07 can solve 36 hard problems where FMCAD06 times out. The speed up typically occurs in examples where SERE automata have to be determinized both in MONO and FMCAD06, while for TACAS07 the rules manage to generate smaller SERE.

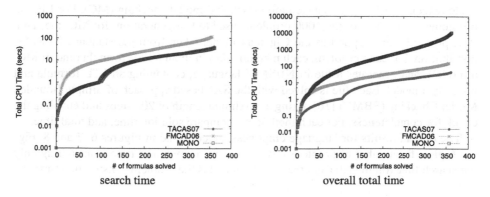

search time   overall total time

Fig. 6. Language emptiness using SBMC on 400 formulas

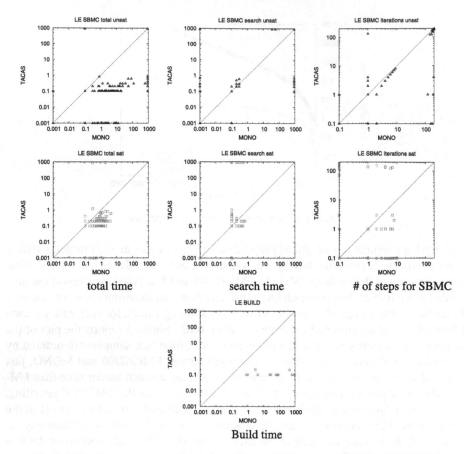

total time   search time   # of steps for SBMC

Build time

Fig. 7. LE — Experimental evaluation results on 400 formulas: MONO vs TACAS07

We then focus on the effect of the rewriting on the search, by considering, as in [6], a test suite of 400 selected problems for which the ABA library is able to complete the generation within the time limit. The test suite contains two kinds of problems, fair cycle detection (LE, for language emptiness), and model checking (MC). For LE, the problems are a subset of the 1000 problems used to test generation; for MC, the same PSL properties are applied to the Gigamax model taken from the standard NuSMV distribution. For each problem, each method takes in input a PSL formula (and, if MC, a model), and generates a file in NuSMV language, containing an LTL formula and possibly a model. Each file is solved with the SAT-based approach of Simple Bounded Model Checking (SBMC) [16], fixing a maximum length of 200 steps and enabling the check for completeness. For each method we compare solution time, and total time.

The overall results for language emptiness are collected in Figures 6, 7 and 8. Figure 6 plots the number of problem solved in a given amount of time, considering only the search time (on the left) and the search time plus the problem construction time (on

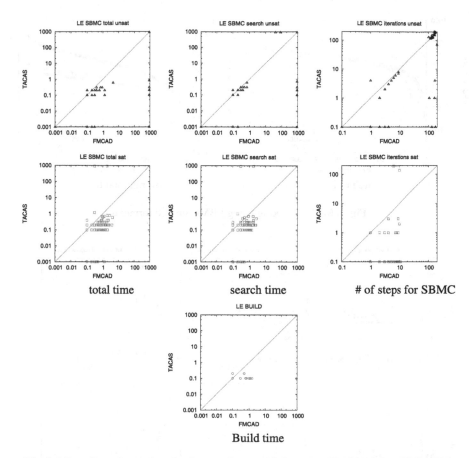

Fig. 8. LE — Experimental evaluation results on 400 formulas: FMCAD06 vs TACAS07

the right). We remark that, TACAS07 plot is under the MONO plot. The plot clearly shows that the search time for MONO and TACAS07 are comparable, i.e. the rewriting proposed in this paper are as effective as the semantic ones of MONO; the improvement with respect to FMCAD06 in terms of search time is also evident. When considering the total time, we notice that these advantages come without paying the price of the semantic simplification. In fact, this price is often so high that also FMCAD06 is superior to MONO. These claims are also confirmed by the scatter plots reported in Figure 7 (comparing MONO with TACAS07) and in Figure 8, where it is clear that TACAS07 is almost uniformly superior to FMCAD06. It is also interesting to notice that while MONO and TACAS07 have overall similar performance, they are not simplifying in the same way, and sometimes the semantic simplifications are unable to achieve as much reduction as rewriting.

The overall results for model checking are collected in Figures 9, 10 and 11. Figure 9 plots the number of model checking problems solved in a given amount of time, considering only the search time (on the left) and the search time plus the problem construction time (on the right). The plot of search time shows that the three methods,

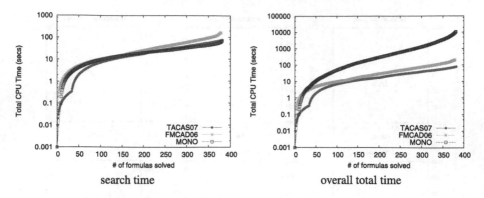

search time   overall total time

Fig. 9. Model checking using SBMC on 400 formulas

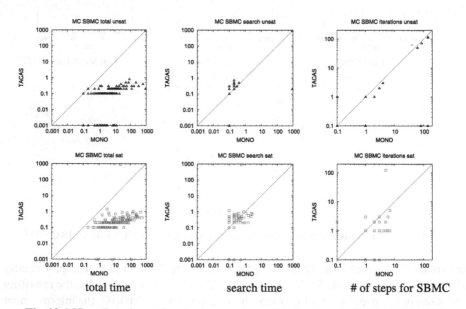

total time   search time   # of steps for SBMC

Fig. 10. MC — Experimental evaluation results on 400 formulas: MONO vs TACAS07

while tackling these model checking problems, are almost comparable; this is probably due to the presence of the model that here is predominant. However, if the total time is taken into account, it appears that MONO is outperformed by both FMCAD06 and TACAS07, and that TACAS07 is better than FMCAD06 as in the language emptiness case (again, here the difference is less evident because of the presence of the model). Also in this case the scatter plots in Figure 10 (comparing MONO with TACAS07) and in Figure 11 (comparing FMCAD06 with TACAS07) confirm that for the search TACAS07 is able to achieve substantial simplifications, although not exactly the same as MONO. The cost of semantic simplification is however substantial.

We restricted our experimental evaluation only to SBMC, even though in [6] the same experiments where carried out also using BDDs. Preliminary experiments showed

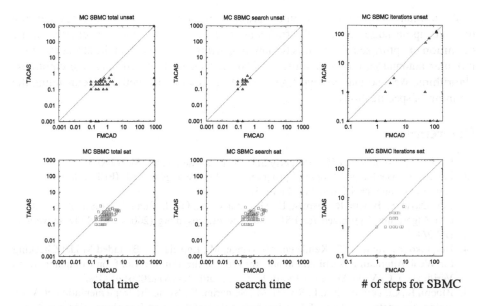

total time   search time   # of steps for SBMC

Fig. 11. MC — Experimental evaluation results on 400 formulas: FMCAD06 vs TACAS07

us that FMCAD06 and TACAS07 with the BDD engine are incomparable. The reason is that the optimizations we proposed produce a large number of fairness constraints so that the results are highly influenced by several factors (BDD variable ordering, order in which the fairness conditions are considered, algorithms for language emptiness). A fair comparison requires an improvement of language emptiness with multiple fairness conditions and a deep tuning of possible options. We plan to carry out this analysis later on to better support the new proposed approach.

Another relevant approach is the one by Heljanko et al. [4], in the following referred to as CAV06: basically, it takes in input an ABA and instead of using a symbolic MH for generating an NBA, a partitioning of the ABA is carried out by exploiting the fact that PSL will result in weak ABAs [3]. Given that the approach is substantially different, it would be worth to carry out a comparison with it. Since [4] implements its own format for reading in ABA, and we do not yet have a complete translator available, we leave the comparison to future work. We expect that the results would be biased by the fact that the approach implemented in [4] is not complete, so that we have to disable the completeness check. Since CAV06 must rely on the ABA library of MONO, it is easy to predict that it will inherit the same bottleneck in construction.

6 Conclusions and Future Work

In this paper, we proposed an approach based on syntactic rewriting to improve the verification times for PSL specifications. The approach improves on [6], greatly reducing the redundancies of the generated automata. Although the optimizations have negligible run-times, the benefit in verification and overall time is substantial.

In the future we plan to work on the problem of the analysis of requirements, trying to scale up on large sets of PSL formulas. In particular, we will concentrate on the definition of optimized algorithms for language emptiness, based on the structure of the modular automaton, on the definition of specialized BDD-based language emptiness algorithms. We also plan to investigate rewriting as a tool for better understanding the meaning of specifications.

References

1. IEEE: IEEE standard 1850 – Property Specification Language (PSL) (2005)
2. Pnueli, A.: The temporal logic of programs. In: Proceedings of 18th IEEE Symp. on Foundation of Computer Science. (1977) 46–57
3. Ben-David, S., Bloem, R., Fisman, D., Griesmayer, A., Pill, I., Ruah, S.: Automata Construction Algorithms Optimized for PSL. http://www.prosyd.org (2005) PROSYD deliverable D 3.2/4.
4. Heljanko, K., Junttila, T., Keinänen, M., Lange, M., Latvala, T.: Bounded Model Checking for Weak Alternating Büchi Automata. In: Proc. of the 18th Int. Conf. on Computer Aided Verification, CAV'06. Volume 4144 of LNCS., Seattle (USA) (2006) 95–108
5. Bloem, R., Cimatti, A., Pill, I., Roveri, M., Semprini, S.: Symbolic Implementation of Alternating Automata. In: Proc. of 11th International Conference on Implementation and Application of Automata (CIAA06). Volume 4094 of LNCS. (2006) 208–218
6. Cimatti, A., Roveri, M., Semprini, S., Tonetta, S.: From PSL to NBA: a Modular Symbolic Encoding. In: Procs. of FMCAD06. (2006)
7. Pnueli, A., Zaks, A.: PSL Model Checking and Run-time Verification via Testers. In: Proc. of 14th International Symposium on Formal Methods (FM'06). Volume 4085 of LNCS., Hamilton, Ontario, Canada (2006) 573–586
8. Miyano, S., Hayashi, T.: Alternating finite automata on omega-words. Theor. Comput. Sci. **32** (1984) 321–330
9. Sebastiani, R., Tonetta, S., Vardi, M.: Symbolic Systems, Explicit Properties: On Hybrid Approaches for LTL Symbolic Model Checking. In: Proceedings of the 16th International Conference on Computer-Aided Verification (CAV'05). (2005) 350–363
10. David, S.B., Orni, A.: Property-by-Example guide: a handbook of PSL/Sugar examples. http://www.prosyd.org (2005) PROSYD deliverable D 1.1/3.
11. Beer, I., Ben-David, S., Eisner, C., Fisman, D., Gringauze, A., Rodeh, Y.: The temporal logic sugar. In Berry, G., Comon, H., Finkel, A., eds.: Computer Aided Verification, 13th International Conference (CAV 2001). Volume 2102 of LNCS., Springer (2001) 363–367
12. Armoni, R., Bustan, D., Kupferman, O., Vardi, M.Y.: Resets vs. aborts in linear temporal logic. In: TACAS. (2003)
13. Somenzi, F., Bloem, R.: Efficient Büchi Automata from LTL Formulae. In: Proceedings of the 12th International Conference on Computer-Aided Verification. Volume 1855 of LNCS., Springer-Verlag (2000) 247–263
14. Etessami, K., Holtzmann, G.: Optimizing Büchi Automata. In: Proceedings of CONCUR'2000. Volume 1877 of LNCS. (2000) Springer.
15. Cimatti, A., Clarke, E., Giunchiglia, F., Roveri, M.: NuSMV: a new Symbolic Model Verifier. In: Proc. of the 11th International Conference on Computer-Aided Verification. Volume 1633 of LNCS., Springer-Verlag (1999) 495 – 499
16. Heljanko, K., Junttila, T.A., Latvala, T.: Incremental and complete bounded model checking for full PLTL. In: Proc. of the 17th Int. Conf. on Computer Aided Verification (CAV'05). Volume 3576 of LNCS., Springer (2005) 98–111

The Heterogeneous Tool Set, HETS *

Till Mossakowski[1], Christian Maeder[1], and Klaus Lüttich[2]

[1] DFKI Lab Bremen and Department of Computer Science, University of Bremen, Germany
[2] SFB/TR 8 and Department of Computer Science, University of Bremen, Germany

1 Introduction

Heterogeneous specification becomes more and more important because complex systems are often specified using multiple viewpoints, involving multiple formalisms (see Fig. 1). Moreover, a formal software development process may lead to a change of formalism during the development.

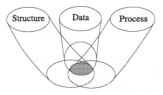

Fig. 1. Multiple viewpoints

Some of the current heterogeneous approaches deliberately stay informal, like UML. Current formal integration approaches have the drawback that they are uni-lateral in the sense that typically there is one logic (and one theorem prover) which serves as the central integration device, even if this central logic may not be needed or desired in particular applications.

By contrast, the heterogeneous tool set is a both flexible, multi-lateral *and* formal (i.e. based on a mathematical semantics) integration tool, providing parsing, static analysis and proof management for heterogeneous multi-logic specifications by combining various tools for individual specification languages. Unlike other tools, it treats logic translations (e.g. codings between logics) as first-class citizens. The architecture of the heterogeneous tool set is shown in Fig. 2. In the sequel, we will explain the details of this figure.

2 Logics in Hets

The notion of *institution* [2] captures in a very abstract and flexible way the essence of a logical system. *Institution morphisms* or *comorphisms* relate institutions.

In HETS, each logic (institution) is realized in the programming language Haskell [7] by a list of types (e.g. for signatures, signature morphisms, sentences) and functions (e.g. for parsing, static analysis and theorem proving, see the left column of Fig. 2). In Haskell jargon, the interface is called a multiparameter type class with functional dependencies.

The following logics have been integrated in HETS so far, with varying degree of support (see the middle column of Fig. 2 and [4,1] for more details and references).

CASL [1] extends many sorted first-order logic with partial functions and subsorting. It also provides induction sentences, expressing the (free) generation of datatypes.

---

* This work has been supported by the *Deutsche Forschungsgemeinschaft* unders grants KR 1191/5-2 and KR 1191/7-2 and in the project I4-SPIN in the SFB/TR8 "Spatial Cognition". We thank Stefan Wölfl for providing the first heterogeneous verification example.

Architecture of the heterogeneous tool set Hets

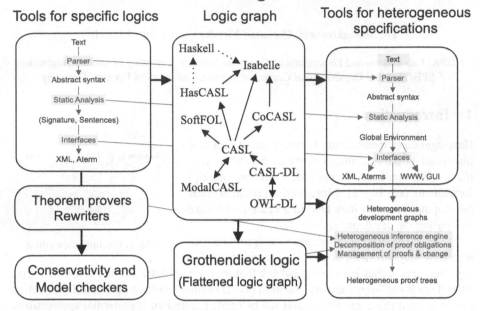

Fig. 2. Architecture of the heterogeneous tool set

CoCASL is a coalgebraic extension of CASL, suited for the specification of process types and reactive systems. The central proof method is coinduction.

ModalCASL is an extension of CASL with multi-modalities and term modalities. It allows the specification of modal systems with Kripke's possible worlds semantics.

HasCASL is a higher order extension of CASL allowing polymorphic datatypes and functions, closely related to the programming language Haskell.

Haskell [7] is a modern, pure and strongly typed functional programming language.

OWL DL is the Web Ontology Language (OWL) recommended by the World Wide Web Consortium (W3C, http://www.w3c.org). It is used for knowledge representation and the Semantic Web.

CASL-DL is an extension of a restriction of CASL, realizing a strongly typed variant of OWL DL in CASL syntax.

SoftFOL [3] offers three automated theorem proving systems (ATP) for first-order logic with equality: (1) SPASS [9]; (2) Vampire [8]; and (3) MathServe Broker [10]. These together comprise some of the most advanced theorem provers for first-order logic.

Isabelle [6] is an interactive theorem prover for higher-order logic, and (jointly with others) marks the frontier of current research in interactive higher-order provers.

3   Heterogeneous Specification

Heterogeneous specification is parameterized over some arbitrary graph of logics (institutions) and logic translations (comorphisms). The graph of currently supported logics is shown in Fig. 2. However, this graph is just a parameter: indeed, the HETS modules implementing the logic graph can be compiled independently of the HETS modules implementing heterogeneous specification, and this separation of concerns is essential to keep the tool manageable from a software engineering point of view.

Heterogeneous CASL (HETCASL; see [4]) includes the structuring constructs of CASL, such as union and translation. A key feature of CASL is that syntax and semantics of these constructs are formulated over an arbitrary institution (i.e. also for institutions that are possibly *completely different* from first-order logic resp. the CASL institution). HETCASL extends this with constructs for choosing the current logic and translating specifications along logic translations (i.e. comorphisms).

4 Proof Management

The central device for structured theorem proving and proof management in HETS is the formalism of *heterogeneous development graphs* [5,4]. Development graphs have been used for large industrial-scale applications with hundreds of specifications. They also support management of change. The graph structure provides a direct visualization of the structure of specifications and the open proof obligations.

The *proof calculus* for development graphs [5,4] is given by rules that allow for decomposing proof obligations into simpler ones, until they can be proved by turning them into *local proof goals*. The latter can be discharged using a logic-specific theorem prover. This can be done using a graphical user interface (GUI), which allows for selecting the prover and the subset of axioms that is sent to the prover. Also, provers

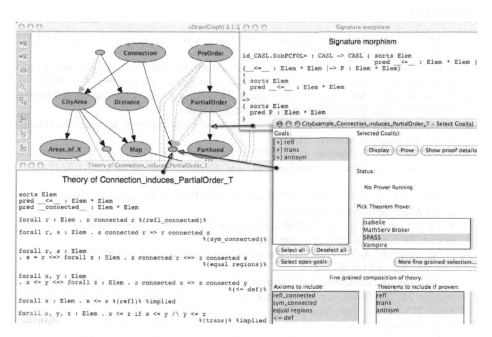

Fig. 3. A sample HETS session

for other logics than that of the current theory may be used, if there is a comorphism linking the two logics. In this way, theorem provers can be *borrowed* for other logics (e.g. a first-order prover can be also used for modal first-order logic). A typical session with HETS is shown in Fig. 3.

5 Conclusion

The Heterogeneous Tool Set (HETS) is available at http://www.cofi.info/ Tools. A sample heterogeneous proof concerns the correctness of the composition table of a qualitative spatial calculus. This involves two different provers and logics: an automated first-order prover solving the vast majority of the goals, and an interactive higher-order prover used to prove a few bridge lemmas. The corresponding heterogeneous specification is found under Calculi/Space/RCCVerification.het in the repository available at http://www.cofi.info/Libraries.

It may appear that HETS just provides a combination of some first-order provers and Isabelle. But already now, HETS provides proof support for modal logic (via the translation to CASL, and then further to either SPASS or Isabelle), as well as for CoCASL. Hence, it is quite easy to provide proof support for new logics by just implementing logic translations, which is at least an order of magnitude simpler than integrating a theorem prover. Future work will integrate more logics (such as CSP-CASL and other process calculi) and interface more existing theorem proving tools (such as CSP-Prover) with specific institutions in HETS, and provide more sample applications.

References

1. CoFI (The Common Framework Initiative). CASL *Reference Manual.* LNCS 2960 (IFIP Series). Springer, 2004.
2. J. A. Goguen and R. M. Burstall. Institutions: Abstract model theory for specification and programming. *Journal of the Association for Computing Machinery,* 39:95–146, 1992.
3. K. Lüttich and T. Mossakowski. Reasoning Support for CASL with Automated Theorem Proving Systems. WADT 2006, Springer LNCS, to appear.
4. T. Mossakowski. Heterogeneous specification and the heterogeneous tool set. Habilitation thesis, University of Bremen, 2005.
5. T. Mossakowski, S. Autexier, and D. Hutter. Development graphs – proof management for structured specifications. *Journal of Logic and Algebraic Programming,* 67(1-2):114–145, 2006.
6. T. Nipkow, L. C. Paulson, and M. Wenzel. *Isabelle/HOL — A Proof Assistant for Higher-Order Logic.* Springer Verlag, 2002.
7. S. Peyton-Jones, editor. *Haskell 98 Language and Libraries — The Revised Report.* Cambridge, 2003. also: J. Funct. Programming **13** (2003).
8. A. Riazanov and A. Voronkov. The design and implementation of VAMPIRE. *AI Communications,* 15(2-3):91–110, 2002.
9. C. Weidenbach, U. Brahm, T. Hillenbrand, E. Keen, C. Theobalt, and D. Topic. SPASS version 2.0. In Andrei Voronkov, editor, *Automated Deduction – CADE-18,* LNCS 2392, pages 275–279. Springer-Verlag, 2002.
10. J. Zimmer and S. Autexier. The MathServe System for Semantic Web Reasoning Services. In U. Furbach and N. Shankar, editors, *3rd IJCAR,* LNCS 4130. Springer, 2006.

Searching for Shapes in Cryptographic Protocols*

Shaddin F. Doghmi, Joshua D. Guttman, and F. Javier Thayer

The MITRE Corporation
shaddin@stanford.edu,
{guttman,jt}@mitre.org

Abstract. We describe a method for enumerating all essentially different executions possible for a cryptographic protocol. We call them the *shapes* of the protocol. Naturally occurring protocols have only finitely many, indeed very few shapes. Authentication and secrecy properties are easy to determine from them, as are attacks. CPSA, our Cryptographic Protocol Shape Analyzer, implements the method.

In searching for shapes, CPSA starts with some initial behavior, and discovers what shapes are compatible with it. Normally, the initial behavior is the point of view of one participant. The analysis reveals what the other principals must have done, given this participant's view.

1 Introduction

The executions of cryptographic protocols frequently have very few essentially different forms, which we call *shapes*. By enumerating these shapes, we may ascertain whether they all satisfy a security condition such as an authentication or confidentiality property. We may also find other anomalies, which are not necessarily counterexamples to the security goals, such as involving unexpected participants, or involving more local runs than expected.

In this paper, we describe a complete method for enumerating the shapes of a protocol within a pure Dolev-Yao model [7]. If the protocol has only finitely many essentially different shapes, the enumeration will terminate. From the shapes, we can then read off the answers to secrecy and authentication questions and observe other anomalies. Our software implementation of this method is called a Cryptographic Protocol Shapes Analyzer (CPSA).

We use the strand space theory [10]. A *skeleton* represents regular (non-penetrator) behavior that might make up part of an execution, and a *homomorphism* is an information-preserving map between skeletons. Skeletons are partially-ordered structures, like fragments of Lamport diagrams [13] or fragments of message sequence charts [12]. A skeleton is *realized* if it is nonfragmentary, i.e. it contains exactly the regular behavior of some execution. A realized skeleton is a *shape* if it is minimal in a sense we will make precise. We *search*

---

* Supported by the National Security Agency and by MITRE-Sponsored Research.

O. Grumberg and M. Huth (Eds.): TACAS 2007, LNCS 4424, pp. 523–537, 2007.

for shapes using the authentication tests [10] to find new strands to add when a skeleton is not large enough to be realized.

The main technical result underlying CPSA is *completeness*, in the sense that— for any protocol—our authentication test search eventually discovers every shape for that protocol. It cannot terminate for every protocol [8]. It does, however, terminate for reasonably inclusive classes [4,19].

The type-and-effect system for spi calculus [9] is related to the authentication tests, but differs from our work in two ways. First, we do not use the syntactically-driven form of a type system, but instead a direct analysis of behaviors. Second, type-and-effect systems aim at a sound approximation, whereas our work provides actual counterexamples when a security goal is not met. Blanchet's ProVerif [1] is also based on a sound approximation, and may thus refuse to certify a protocol even though there are no counterexamples.

CPSA's search is related to the second version of Athena [18], which adopted the authentication tests from [10]. However, CPSA differs from Athena in several ways. First, it involves the regular behaviors alone; we never represent adversary activity within a shape. Second, the notion of shape defines a criterion for which possible executions should be considered, among the infinitely many executions (of unbounded size) of any protocol. Third, we introduce strong versions of the authentication tests, for which completeness is true.

The shapes describe protocol executions of all sizes; we do not follow the widely practiced *bounded* protocol analysis (e.g. [2,15]).

Structure of this paper. We develop the CPSA search strategy from examples, leaving precise definitions, theorems, and proofs to an extended version [6]. Section 2 shows a protocol and its shapes, and introduces terminology. Section 3 introduces the Yahalom protocol [17], a more substantial example. The search for shapes is guided by the authentication test principles (Section 4), which we apply to analyze Yahalom's protocol in Section 5. This analysis illustrates almost every aspect of the CPSA search method. In Section 6, we define the search's control structure. The CPSA implementation is the subject of Section 7.

2   Shapes: The Core Idea

In practice, protocols have remarkably few shapes. The Needham-Schoeder-Lowe [16,14] protocol has only one. A responder B, asking what global behavior must have occurred when B has had a local run of the protocol, finds the initiator A must have had a matching run. An initiator A knows that B must have had a matching run, although the last message may not have been received.

Uniqueness of shape is unsurprising for so strong a protocol. However, even a flawed protocol such as the original Needham-Schroeder may have a unique shape, shown in Fig. 1.

Terminology. Newly introduced terminology is in **boldface**.
B's local behavior is represented by the right-hand column in Fig. 1, consisting of nodes connected by double arrows $\bullet \Rightarrow \bullet$. A's local behavior is represented

$$A \xrightarrow{\quad \{\!|N_a \,\hat{}\, A|\!\}_{\mathsf{pubk}(C)} \quad} \qquad \xrightarrow{\quad \{\!|N_a \,\hat{}\, A|\!\}_{\mathsf{pubk}(B)} \quad} B$$

$$\downarrow \xleftarrow{\quad \{\!|N_a \,\hat{}\, N_b|\!\}_{\mathsf{pubk}(A)} \quad} \succ \xleftarrow{\quad \{\!|N_a \,\hat{}\, N_b|\!\}_{\mathsf{pubk}(A)} \quad} \downarrow$$

$$\downarrow \xrightarrow{\quad \{\!|N_b|\!\}_{\mathsf{pubk}(C)} \quad} \prec \xrightarrow{\quad \{\!|N_b|\!\}_{\mathsf{pubk}(B)} \quad} \downarrow$$

Fig. 1. Needham-Schroeder Shape for B ($\mathsf{privk}(A)$ uncompromised, N_b fresh)

by the left-hand column. We call such a column a **strand**. The **nodes** represent message transmission or reception events, and the double arrows represent succession within a single linearly ordered local activity. The message transmitted or received on a node n is written $\mathsf{msg}(n)$. A **regular strand** is a strand that represents a principal executing a single local session of a protocol; it is called a regular strand because the behavior follows the protocol rules. A *local behavior* as used so far refers to a regular strand.

We use $\{\!|t|\!\}_K$ to refer to the encryption of t with key K, and $t \,\hat{}\, t'$ means the pair of messages t and t'. Messages are constructed freely from atomic values such as principal names A, nonces N_a, keys K, etc., via these two operations.

The **subterm** relation is the least reflexive, transitive relation such that t is a subterm of $\{\!|t|\!\}_K$, t is a subterm of $t \,\hat{}\, t'$, and t is a subterm of $t' \,\hat{}\, t$ (for all K, t'). We write $t \sqsubseteq t'$ if t is a subterm of t'. Thus, $K \not\sqsubseteq \{\!|t|\!\}_K$ unless (anomalously) $K \sqsubseteq t$. Instead, K contributed to *how* $\{\!|t|\!\}_K$ was produced. This terminology has an advantage: Uncompromised long-term keys are never subterms of messages transmitted in a protocol; they are used by regular principals to encrypt, decrypt, or sign messages, but are never transmitted. A value a **originates at** a node n if (1) n is a transmission node; (2) $a \sqsubseteq \mathsf{msg}(n)$; and (3) if m is any earlier node on the same strand, then $a \not\sqsubseteq \mathsf{msg}(m)$.

Adversary behavior is represented by strands too. **Penetrator strands** codify the basic abilities that make up the Dolev-Yao model. They include transmitting an atomic value such as a nonce or a key; transmitting an encrypted message after receiving its plaintext and key; and transmitting a plaintext after receiving ciphertext and decryption key. The adversary can pair two messages, or separate the pieces of a paired message. Since a penetrator strand that encrypts or decrypts must receive the key as one of its inputs, keys used by the adversary—compromised keys—have always been transmitted by some participant. The penetrator strands are independent of the protocol under analysis.

Let $\mathcal{B}$ be a finite, directed acyclic graph whose nodes lie on regular and penetrator strands, and whose edges are either (a) strand succession edges $n_0 \Rightarrow n_1$, or else (b) message transmission edges $n \rightarrow m$ where $\mathsf{msg}(n) = \mathsf{msg}(m)$, n is a transmission node, and m is a reception node. $\mathcal{B}$ is a **bundle** if (1) if $n_0 \Rightarrow n_1$ and $n_1 \in \mathcal{B}$, then $n_0 \in \mathcal{B}$, and (2) for every reception node $m \in \mathcal{B}$, there is a unique transmission node $n \in \mathcal{B}$ such that the edge $n \rightarrow m$ is in $\mathcal{B}$. The conditions (1,2) ensure that $\mathcal{B}$ is causally well founded. A *global behavior* or *execution*, as used so far, refers to a bundle.

The NS Shape. Suppose B's nonce N_b has been freshly chosen, and A's private key privk(A) is uncompromised. In this protocol, privk(A), privk(B) are used only to destructure incoming messages, never to construct messages. Given that—on a particular occasion—B received and sent the messages in the strand shown at the right in Fig. 1, what must have occurred elsewhere in the network?

A must have had a partially matching strand, with the messages sent and received in the order indicated by the arrows of both kinds and the connecting symbols $\prec$. These symbols mean that the endpoints are ordered, but that other behavior may intervene, whether adversary strands or regular strands. A's strand is only partially matching, because the principal A meant to contact is some C which may or may not equal B. There is no alternative: Any diagram containing the responder strand of Fig. 1 must contain at least an instance of the initiator strand, with the events ordered as shown, or it cannot have happened.

Such a diagram is a *shape*. A shape consists of the regular strands of some bundle, forming a *minimal* set containing initial regular strands (in this case, the right-hand column). Possible bundles may freely add adversary behavior.

Each shape is relative to assumptions about keys and freshness, in this case that privk(A) is uncompromised and N_b freshly chosen. Nothing useful would follow without any such assumptions.

Although there is a single shape, there are two ways that this shape may be realized in bundles. Either (1) C's private key may be compromised, in which case we may complete this diagram with adversary activity to obtain the Lowe attack [14]; or else (2) $C = B$, leading to the intended run.

Some protocols have more than one shape, Otway-Rees, e.g., having four. In searching for shapes, one starts from some initial set of strands. Typically, the initial set is a singleton, which we refer to as the "point of view" of the analysis.

Skeletons, Homomorphisms, Shapes. A **skeleton** $\mathbb{A}$ is (1) a finite set of regular nodes, equipped with additional information. The additional information consists of (2) a partial order $\preceq_{\mathbb{A}}$ on the nodes indicating causal precedence; (3) a set of keys non$_{\mathbb{A}}$; and (4) a set of atomic values unique$_{\mathbb{A}}$. Values in non$_{\mathbb{A}}$ must originate nowhere in $\mathbb{A}$, whereas those in unique$_{\mathbb{A}}$ originate at most once in $\mathbb{A}$.[1]

$\mathbb{A}$ is **realized** if it has precisely the regular behavior of some bundle $\mathcal{B}$. Every message received by a regular participant either should have been sent previously, or should be constructable by the adversary using messages sent previously. Fig. 1 shows a skeleton $\mathbb{A}_{ns}$, indeed a realized one.

A **homomorphism** is a map H from $\mathbb{A}_0$ to $\mathbb{A}_1$, written $H\colon \mathbb{A}_0 \mapsto \mathbb{A}_1$. We represent it as a pair of maps (ϕ, α), where ϕ maps the nodes of $\mathbb{A}_0$ into those of $\mathbb{A}_1$, and α is a **replacement** mapping atoms to atoms. We write $t \cdot \alpha$ for the result of applying a replacement α to all the atoms mentioned in a message t. $H = (\phi, \alpha)$ is a homomorphism iff: (1) ϕ respects strand structure, and for all $n \in \mathbb{A}_0$, msg(n) $\cdot \alpha = $ msg($\phi(n)$); (2) $m \preceq_{\mathbb{A}_0} n$ implies $\phi(m) \preceq_{\mathbb{A}_1} \phi(n)$; (3) non$_{\mathbb{A}_0} \cdot \alpha \subseteq$ non$_{\mathbb{A}_1}$; and (4) unique$_{\mathbb{A}_0} \cdot \alpha \subseteq$ unique$_{\mathbb{A}_1}$.

Homomorphisms are *information-preserving* transformations. Each skeleton $\mathbb{A}_0$ describes the realized skeletons reachable from $\mathbb{A}_0$ by homomorphisms. Since

---

[1] When $n \Rightarrow^* n'$ and $n' \in \mathbb{A}$, we require $n \in \mathbb{A}$ and $n \preceq_{\mathbb{A}} n'$.

homomorphisms compose, if $H: \mathbb{A}_0 \mapsto \mathbb{A}_1$ then any realized skeleton accessible from $\mathbb{A}_1$ is accessible from $\mathbb{A}_0$. Thus, $\mathbb{A}_1$ preserves the information in $\mathbb{A}_0$: $\mathbb{A}_1$ describes a subset of the realized skeletons described by $\mathbb{A}_0$.

A homomorphism may supplement the strands of $\mathbb{A}_0$ with additional behavior in $\mathbb{A}_1$; it may affect atomic parameter values; and it may identify different nodes together, if their strands are compatible in messages sent and positions in the partial ordering. For instance, consider the map H_{ns} embedding a single strand of Fig. 1 (e.g. $\mathbb{A}_b$ containing only B's strand on the right side) into $\mathbb{A}_{ns}$. This is a homomorphism $H_{ns}: \mathbb{A}_b \mapsto \mathbb{A}_{ns}$. Likewise if we embed the first two nodes of B's strand (rather than all of $\mathbb{A}_b$) into $\mathbb{A}_{ns}$. Another homomorphism H_i rewrites each occurrence of C in $\mathbb{A}_{ns}$ to B, hence each occurrence of $\mathsf{pubk}(C)$ to $\mathsf{pubk}(B)$. It yields the Needham-Schroeder intended run $\mathbb{A}_{nsi}$.

A homomorphism $H = (\phi, \alpha)$ is **nodewise injective** if the function ϕ on nodes is injective. The nodewise injective homomorphisms determine a partial order on homomorphisms: If for some nodewise injective H_1, $H_1 \circ H = H'$, we write $H \leq_n H'$. If $H \leq_n H' \leq_n H$, then H and H' are isomorphic.

A homomorphism $H: \mathbb{A}_0 \mapsto \mathbb{A}_1$ is a **shape** iff (a) $\mathbb{A}_1$ is realized and (b) H is $\leq_n$-minimal among homomorphisms from $\mathbb{A}_0$ to realized skeletons. If H is a shape, and we can factor H into $\mathbb{A}_0 \overset{H_0}{\mapsto} \mathbb{A}' \overset{H_1}{\mapsto} \mathbb{A}_1$, where $\mathbb{A}'$ is realized, then $\mathbb{A}'$ cannot contain fewer nodes than $\mathbb{A}_1$, or identify fewer atomic values. $\mathbb{A}_1$ is as small and as general as possible.

We call a *skeleton* $\mathbb{A}_1$ a shape when the homomorphism H (usually an embedding) is understood. In this looser sense, Fig. 1 shows the shape $\mathbb{A}_{ns}$. Strictly, the embedding $H_{ns}: \mathbb{A}_b \mapsto \mathbb{A}_{ns}$ is the shape. The embedding $H_{nsi}: \mathbb{A}_b \mapsto \mathbb{A}_{nsi}$, with target the Needham-Schroeder intended run $\mathbb{A}_{nsi}$, is not a shape. $\mathbb{A}_{ns}$ identifies fewer atoms, and the map replacing C with B is a nodewise injective $H_i: \mathbb{A}_{ns} \mapsto \mathbb{A}_{nsi}$, so $H_{ns} \leq_n H_i \circ H_{ns} = H_{nsi}$.

Shapes exist below realized skeletons: If $H: \mathbb{A}_0 \mapsto \mathbb{A}_1$ with $\mathbb{A}_1$ realized, then the set of shapes H_1 with $H_1 \leq_n H$ is finite and non-empty.

3   The Yahalom Protocol Definition

The Yahalom protocol (Fig. 2 [17]) provides a session key K to principals sharing long-term symmetric keys with a key server. We let $\mathsf{ltk}(\cdot)$ map each principal A to its long term shared key $\mathsf{ltk}(A)$. We assume that all participants agree on the server, which does not also participate as a client.

The protocol contains three roles, the initiator, the responder, and the server. Each is described by one strand in Fig. 2, and each role is parametrized by A, B, N_a, N_b, K. The parameters are atomic values, and the instances of each role are constructed by replacing them with other atomic values. The behavior Init of the initiator consists in transmitting $A \,\hat{}\, N_a$ followed by receiving some message of the form $\{\!|B \,\hat{}\, K \,\hat{}\, N_a \,\hat{}\, N_b|\!\}_{\mathsf{ltk}(A)}$ and finally transmitting $\{\!|N_b|\!\}_K$. The other roles are also self-explanatory. The key server is trusted to generate a fresh, uniquely originating session key K in each run. By this, we mean that if a skeleton $\mathbb{A}$ contains a server strand with session key K, then $K \in \mathsf{unique}_{\mathbb{A}}$.

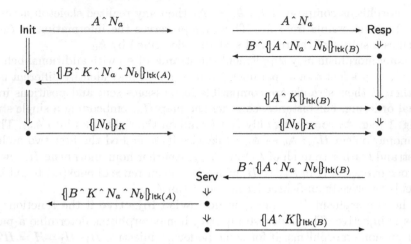

Fig. 2. Yahalom protocol (forwarding removed)

4   Search Steps

The authentication tests are the basic steps leading from a particular initial skeleton to its shapes. The Yahalom protocol requires both types of step, and relies on the strong outgoing test we give here. The older form [10] does not suffice.

Terminology. A **protocol** is a finite set of regular strands, called the **roles**. For instance, the Yahalom roles include the three strands shown in Fig. 2. Roles have atoms as parameters, namely A, B, N_a, N_b, K for each role of Fig. 2. A parameter may be distinguished by the assumption that it is always uniquely originating, like the session key K in the Yahalom server role. The instances of roles under replacements are regular strands.

We assume that each protocol also includes **listener strand** roles, by which we mean a regular strand with a single node receiving an atomic message. We write $\mathsf{Lsn}[a]$ for the strand $\xrightarrow{a} \bullet$ that receives the atom a. If $\mathbb{A}$ containing $\mathsf{Lsn}[a]$ is realized, then a is available without protection in $\mathbb{A}$, i.e. a is **compromised**. We use listener strands to test whether atoms are safe secrets. Suppose a skeleton $\mathbb{A}'$ is the result of adding $\mathsf{Lsn}[a]$ to $\mathbb{A}$, and there is no homomorphism mapping $\mathbb{A}'$ to any realized $\mathbb{A}''$. Then A is safe in $\mathbb{A}$, as no execution described by $\mathbb{A}$ is compatible with a being compromised. Listener strands, lacking transmission nodes, need never precede anything else; we always let them be maximal in $\preceq_{\mathbb{A}}$.

If $\mathbb{A}, \mathbb{A}'$ are both realized, and differ only in which listener strands they contain, then we regard them as similar and write $\mathbb{A} \sim_{\mathsf{L}} \mathbb{A}'$. In this case, the skeleton $\mathbb{A}''$ that contains all listener strands from both $\mathbb{A}, \mathbb{A}'$ is also realized, and $\mathbb{A}'' \sim_{\mathsf{L}} \mathbb{A} \sim_{\mathsf{L}} \mathbb{A}'$. We will ignore differences between homomorphisms $H: \mathbb{A}_0 \mapsto \mathbb{A}$ and $H': \mathbb{A}_0 \mapsto \mathbb{A}'$ that agree but have distinct, similar targets. Each may be extended by an embedding to yield the same homomorphism $H'': \mathbb{A}_0 \mapsto \mathbb{A}''$.

A homomorphism is a **contraction** if it identifies at least one pair of atoms and is surjective on nodes. A contraction replaces C with B in Fig. 1 to produce the Needham-Schroeder intended run.

Suppose that S is a set of encrypted messages and the atom $a \in \mathsf{unique}_A$ originates at n_0. The pair of nodes n_0, n_1, where n_1 is a reception node, form an **outgoing test pair** for a and S iff all a's occurrences in $\mathsf{msg}(n_0)$ are within messages in set S, but a has at least one occurrence in n_1 outside the messages in S.[2] The second and fourth nodes on the responder strand, for instance, form an outgoing test pair for N_b and $S_0 = \{\{|A \hat{\ } N_a \hat{\ } N_b|\}_{\mathsf{ltk}(B)}\}$, or for any $S_0' \supseteq S_0$. The set of keys used for outermost encryptions in any S is called $\mathsf{used}(S)$, i.e. $\mathsf{used}(S) = \{K \colon \exists t . \{|t|\}_K \in S\}$. So $\mathsf{used}(S_0) = \{\mathsf{ltk}(B)\}$.

The nodes m_0, m_1, with m_1 a transmission node, are an **outgoing transforming edge** for a, S if (1) they lie on the same regular strand $\ldots \Rightarrow^* m_0 \Rightarrow^+ m_1 \Rightarrow^* \ldots$; (2) a occurs in $\mathsf{msg}(m_0)$ but no earlier node; (3) a occurs outside S in $\mathsf{msg}(m_1)$ but not in any earlier node. In the Yahalom protocol, the second and third nodes of the server role are an outgoing transforming edge for N_b, S_0, although not for the larger set $S_0' = \{\{|A \hat{\ } N_a \hat{\ } N_b|\}_{\mathsf{ltk}(B)}, \{|B \hat{\ } K \hat{\ } N_a \hat{\ } N_b|\}_{\mathsf{ltk}(A)}\}$. However, the second and third nodes of the initiator role are an outgoing transforming edge for N_b, S_0'.

Types of Search Step. There are two types of search steps, *outgoing steps* and *incoming steps*. The *outgoing* step states that each outgoing test pair n_0, n_1 must be solved, either by contracting atoms, or else by adding an outgoing transforming edge or a listener strand.

Outgoing test principle. *Let $H \colon \mathbb{A}_0 \mapsto \mathbb{A}_1$ with $\mathbb{A}_1$ realized, and let $n_0, n_1 \in \mathbb{A}_0$ be an outgoing test pair for a and S. If $\mathbb{A}_0$ contains no outgoing transforming edge for a, S that precedes n_1, then, for some H'', $H = H'' \circ H'$ where either:*

1. *H' is a contraction; or*
2. *$H' \colon \mathbb{A}_0 \mapsto \mathbb{A}'$ is an embedding adding $m_0 \Rightarrow^+ m_1$, an outgoing transforming edge for a, S, where $n_0 \preceq_{\mathbb{A}'} m_0$ and $m_1 \preceq_{\mathbb{A}'} n_1$; or*
3. *H' is an embedding adding $\mathsf{Lsn}[K^{-1}]$, for some $K \in \mathsf{used}(S)$.*

Clause 1 is used when $H(n_0), H(n_1)$ is no longer an outgoing test pair for $H(S)$. It is also sometimes needed to prepare for an application of Clause 2, if (n_0, n_1) is more general than some transforming edge in a protocol role. Then the contraction H *unifies* a member of S with a subterm of a role. Clause 1 is needed *only* in these two cases. Clause 3 uses the inverse K^{-1} because in public-key (asymmetric) algorithms, the adversary would use the inverse key K^{-1} to extract a from an occurrence within a message $\{|t|\}_K \in S$. We regard $\mathsf{pubk}(A), \mathsf{privk}(A)$ as inverses; symmetric keys are self-inverse.

---

[2] A message t_0 *occurs only within S in t_1* if, in the abstract syntax tree for t_1, every path to an occurrence of t_0 as a subterm traverses some member of S. A message t_0 *occurs outside S in t_1* if $t_0 \sqsubseteq t_1$ and t_0 does not occur only within S in t_1 [6]. In our terminology (Section 2), the K in $\{|t|\}_K$ is not an occurrence as a subterm.

The older outgoing test [10] lacked the set parameter S and applied (in effect) only to singleton S. The Yahalom analysis requires a non-singleton S. Only finitely many homomorphisms (to within isomorphism) can satisfy an instance of Clauses 1–3, because only finitely many atoms are mentioned in $\mathbb{A}_0$ and only finitely many transforming edges exist in one protocol. In particular, there is a finite set of most general homomorphisms. A set of homomorphisms $\{H_k\}_{k \leq j}$ is an **outgoing cohort** if, for some instance of Clauses 1–3, each H_k satisfies a clause, and for every H' satisfying one of those clauses, there is some $k \leq j$ and some H'' such that $H' = H'' \circ H_k$.

In a simple though not quite complete version, the *incoming* step states that if $\{t\}_K$ is received, either K is compromised or a regular strand transmitted it.

Incoming test principle. *Let $H \colon \mathbb{A}_0 \mapsto \mathbb{A}_1$ with $\mathbb{A}_1$ realized, and let $n_1 \in \mathbb{A}_0$ receive message $\{t\}_K$. If $\mathbb{A}_0$ contains (preceding n_1) no m_1 transmitting $\{t\}_K$, then, for some H'', $H = H'' \circ H'$ where either:*

1. *H' is a contraction; or*
2. *$H' \colon \mathbb{A}_0 \mapsto \mathbb{A}'$ is an embedding adding an $m_1 \preceq_{\mathbb{A}'} n_1$ transmitting $\{t\}_K$; or*
3. *H' is an embedding adding $\mathsf{Lsn}[K]$.*

We use Clause 1 only to prepare for an application of Clause 2, when n_1 is more general than a node in a role of the protocol. Again, there are finite sets $\{H_k\}_{k \leq j}$ that satisfy Clauses 1–3 in a most general way; we call them **incoming cohorts**. We call the skeletons $\{\mathbb{A}_k\}_{k \leq j}$ a cohort if each $H_k \colon \mathbb{A} \mapsto \mathbb{A}_k$ for some outgoing or incoming cohort $\{H_k\}_{k \leq j}$. In practice, for protocols that occur naturally, the size of the cohorts is very small, no more than four in the Yahalom protocol.

5   Yahalom: Shapes for the Responder

Suppose an execution contains a local run s_r of the responder's role as in the upper right column of Fig. 2. We assume the long term keys $\mathsf{ltk}(A), \mathsf{ltk}(B)$ are uncompromised, as no authentication can be achieved otherwise. Similarly, we assume the responder's nonce N_b to be fresh and unguessable.

So let the initial skeleton $\mathbb{A}_0$ consist of s_r, with $\mathsf{non}_{\mathbb{A}_0} = \{\mathsf{ltk}(A), \mathsf{ltk}(B)\}$ and $\mathsf{unique}_{\mathbb{A}_0} = \{N_b\}$. What skeletons are shapes for $\mathbb{A}_0$? Or more precisely, for what realized skeletons $\mathbb{A}$ is there a shape $H \colon \mathbb{A}_0 \mapsto \mathbb{A}$?

We will find only one possibility, the skeleton $\mathbb{A}_4$ (Fig. 5). Any realized $\mathbb{A}$ containing any responder strand s_r'—with uncompromised long-term keys and a fresh nonce—has a subskeleton $\mathbb{A}'$ containing s_r', with $J \colon \mathbb{A}_4 \mapsto \mathbb{A}'$. J is both nodewise injective and surjective, i.e. an isomorphism on nodes, although it may identify atoms. The portion of $\mathbb{A}$ containing s_r' resembles $\mathbb{A}_4$.

Transforming the Nonce. B chooses a fresh nonce N_b in node n_0 (see Fig. 3), and transmits it within the encrypted unit $\{A \char`^ N_a \char`^ N_b\}_{\mathsf{ltk}(B)}$. In B's node n_2, it is received outside that unit, in the form $\{N_b\}_K$. So n_0, n_2 is an outgoing test pair for N_b, S_1 where $S_1 =$

$$\{\{A \char`^ N_a \char`^ N_b\}_{\mathsf{ltk}(B)}\} \cup \{\{B \char`^ K' \char`^ N_a \char`^ N_b\}_{\mathsf{ltk}(A)} \colon K' \text{ a key}\}.$$

1. The only outgoing transforming edges for N_b, S_1 lie on initiator strands. Unifying node 2 of the role with messages in S_1 shows that the parameters must be A, B, N_a, N_b, and some K'. We ask later whether $K' = K$.
2. Alternatively some decryption key may be compromised. Since $\mathsf{used}(S_1) = \{\mathsf{ltk}(A), \mathsf{ltk}(B)\}$ contains symmetric (self-inverse) keys, this means we consider adding $\mathsf{Lsn}[\mathsf{ltk}(A)]$ or $\mathsf{Lsn}[\mathsf{ltk}(B)]$.

No contraction is relevant. Thus, these three embeddings—adding to $\mathbb{A}_0$ an initiator strand s_i, a listener strand $\mathsf{Lsn}[\mathsf{ltk}(A)]$, or one of the form $\mathsf{Lsn}[\mathsf{ltk}(B)]$—form an outgoing cohort. When adding s_i, we know that $n_0 \prec (s_i \downarrow 2) \Rightarrow (s_i \downarrow 3) \prec n_2$.

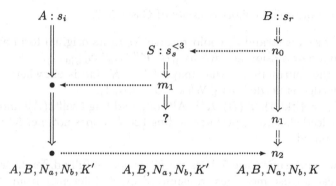

$A : s_i$ $\qquad\qquad\qquad$ $B : s_r$

$S : s_s^{<3}$

m_1

?

n_0

n_1

n_2

$A, B, N_a, N_b, K' \qquad A, B, N_a, N_b, K' \qquad A, B, N_a, N_b, K$

Fig. 3. Skeleton $\mathbb{A}_1$, with $\mathsf{non}_{\mathbb{A}_1} = \{\mathsf{ltk}(A), \mathsf{ltk}(B)\}$ and $\mathsf{unique}_{\mathbb{A}_1} = \{N_b, K'\}$

Since $\mathsf{non}_{\mathbb{A}_0} = \{\mathsf{ltk}(A), \mathsf{ltk}(B)\}$, we also know that $\mathbb{A}_0 \cup \mathsf{Lsn}[\mathsf{ltk}(A)]$ and $\mathbb{A}_0 \cup \mathsf{Lsn}[\mathsf{ltk}(B)]$ are unrealizable. No bundle $\mathcal{B}$ can ever contain a listener strand for a value that originates nowhere. Thus, the embeddings of Case 2 are *dead* in the sense that no homomorphism from $\mathbb{A}_0$ to a realized skeleton can begin this way. Thus, every homomorphism from $\mathbb{A}_0$ to a realized skeleton factors through the embedding $\mathbb{A}_0 \mapsto \mathbb{A}_0 \cup \{s_i\}$.

We again have an outgoing test edge between n_0 and $s_i \downarrow 2$, for N_b, S_2 where

$$S_2 = \{\!\{A \,\hat{}\, N_a \,\hat{}\, N_b\}\!\}_{\mathsf{ltk}(B)}\} \cup \{\!\{B \,\hat{}\, K'' \,\hat{}\, N_a \,\hat{}\, N_b\}\!\}_{\mathsf{ltk}(A)} : K'' \neq K'\}.$$

N_b originates only at n_0, where it occurs only within S_2; however, in $\mathsf{msg}(s_i \downarrow 2)$, N_b occurs outside S_2 in the form $\{\!\{B \,\hat{}\, K' \,\hat{}\, N_a \,\hat{}\, N_b\}\!\}_{\mathsf{ltk}(A)}$.

3. The only outgoing transforming edges for N_b, S_2 lie on server strands s_s. Unifying node 1 of the role with messages in S_2 shows that the parameters must be A, B, N_a, N_b, and some K''. Since N_b must occur outside S_2 in $s_s \downarrow 2$, we have $K'' = K'$; so that the last parameter is K'. The last node $s_s \downarrow 3$ may not be included; we will write $s_s^{<3}$ for the initial segment of s_s.
4. Alternatively a decryption key in $\mathsf{used}(S_1) = \{\mathsf{ltk}(A), \mathsf{ltk}(B)\}$ may be compromised. However, neither listener strand produces a live skeleton.

Thus, any homomorphism from $\mathbb{A}_0$ to a realized skeleton must factor through the embedding $\mathbb{A}_0 \mapsto \mathbb{A}_0 \cup s_r \cup s_s^{\leq 3}$. We call this skeleton $\mathbb{A}_1$, shown in Fig 3, which also shows how the ordering relation extends. Since the server always provides a fresh session key, we also have $K' \in \mathsf{unique}_{\mathbb{A}_1}$.

Does $K' = K$?. The server generated K' on strand s_s and delivers it to A on $s_i \downarrow 2$. B receives K on n_1, and on n_2 finds K also used to encrypt the nonce N_b. Must the keys K', K be the same, or could they be distinct?

Nodes n_0, n_2 form an outgoing test pair for N_b and the set

$$S_3 = \{\ \{\!|A \hat{\ } N_a \hat{\ } N_b|\!\}_{\mathsf{ltk}(B)}, \{\!|B \hat{\ } K' \hat{\ } N_a \hat{\ } N_b|\!\}_{\mathsf{ltk}(A)}, \{\!|N_b|\!\}_{K'}\ \}.$$

The resulting outgoing cohort consists of Cases 5–7:

5. Another server strand s'_s could receive N_b in its original form and transmit N_b and a new session key K'' as $\{\!|B \hat{\ } K'' \hat{\ } N_a \hat{\ } N_b|\!\}_{\mathsf{ltk}(A)}$.
6. Under the contraction β that maps $K' \mapsto K$ and is elsewhere the identity, no new edge is needed, as $\{\!|N_b|\!\}_{K'} \cdot \beta = \{\!|N_b|\!\}_K \cdot \beta$.
7. $\mathsf{used}(S_3) = \{\mathsf{ltk}(A), \mathsf{ltk}(B), K'\}$. Although adding $\mathsf{Lsn}[\mathsf{ltk}(A)]$ and $\mathsf{Lsn}[\mathsf{ltk}(B)]$ lead to dead skeletons, perhaps adding $\mathsf{Lsn}[K']$ does not, i.e. K' may become compromised.

However, we can prune Case 5, because K'' is not usefully different from K'. The adversary cannot use messages transmitted by s'_s differently from the messages transmitted by the existing s_s. Discarding Case 5, there are two live possibilities: either $K' = K$ or else K' becomes compromised. We consider Case 7 next.

Case 7: K' becomes compromised. Consider the skeleton $\mathbb{A}_1 \cup \mathsf{Lsn}[K']$. K' originates uniquely at m_1, so $m_1, (\mathsf{Lsn}[K'] \downarrow 1)$ is an outgoing transformed pair for K' and $S_4 = \{\ \{\!|B \hat{\ } K' \hat{\ } N_a \hat{\ } N_b|\!\}_{\mathsf{ltk}(A)}, \{\!|A \hat{\ } K'|\!\}_{\mathsf{ltk}(B)}\ \}$. Thus, some case in the cohort 8–9 must hold:

8. Some role $\mathsf{Init}, \mathsf{Resp}, \mathsf{Serv}$ provides a transforming edge for K', S_4. However, no Yahalom role retransmits it as a subterm of any new message. The initiator uses K' to encrypt a message, but in our model, this discloses nothing. For finer models, see e.g. [3,5].
9. One of the keys that protects K' in S_4, i.e. a key $K_0 \in \mathsf{used}(S_4)$, becomes compromised; but $\mathsf{used}(S_4) = \{\ \mathsf{ltk}(A), \mathsf{ltk}(B)\ \}$.

So neither Case 8 nor Case 9 is possible. We discard Case 7, as the whole cohort 8–9 is unrealizable or "dead."

Hence, all homomorphisms to realized skeletons must factor through Case 6. Let $\mathbb{A}_2 = \mathbb{A}_1 \cdot \beta$ be the result of replacing K' by K wherever mentioned in $\mathbb{A}_1$. If any homomorphism $H: \mathbb{A}_0 \mapsto \mathbb{A}'$ has $\mathbb{A}'$ realized, then H factors through the embedding $\mathbb{A}_0 \mapsto \mathbb{A}_2$.

B's Source for K. The responder B receives $\{\!|A \hat{\ } K|\!\}_{\mathsf{ltk}(B)}$ on node n_1. We apply the *Incoming Test Principle*, with cohort:

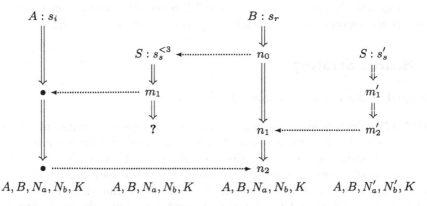

A, B, N_a, N_b, K A, B, N_a, N_b, K A, B, N_a, N_b, K A, B, N'_a, N'_b, K

Fig. 4. $\mathbb{A}_3$, with $\mathsf{non}_{\mathbb{A}_3} = \{\mathsf{ltk}(A), \mathsf{ltk}(B)\}$ and $\mathsf{unique}_{\mathbb{A}_3} = \{N_b, K\}$

10. A server strand s'_s, with parameters A, B, K, transmits $\{\!|A \,\hat{}\, K|\!\}_{\mathsf{ltk}(B)}$; possibly different nonces appear in s'_s. The embedding yields $\mathbb{A}_3$ in Fig. 4.
11. Alternatively, $\mathsf{ltk}(B)$ has been compromised and $\{\!|A \,\hat{}\, K|\!\}_{\mathsf{ltk}(B)}$ is generated by the adversary. However, $\mathsf{ltk}(B) \in \mathsf{non}_{\mathbb{A}_2}$, excluding this case.

$\mathbb{A}_3$ is not a skeleton because of an anomaly, however. $K \in \mathsf{unique}_{\mathbb{A}_3}$ is intended to originate at just one node, but in fact originates at both m_1 and m'_1. Therefore, in any skeleton obtained by a homomorphism $H = [\phi, \alpha]$ jointly from the union $\mathbb{A}_2 \cup \{s'_s\} = \mathbb{A}_3$, necessarily $\phi(m_1) = \phi(m'_1)$, equating the strands s_s and s'_s. H must then factor through skeleton $\mathbb{A}_4$ (Fig. 5), where consequently $N_a \cdot \alpha = N'_a \cdot \alpha$ and $N_b \cdot \alpha = N'_b \cdot \alpha$, and the height of $\phi(s_s)$ is 3.

Skeleton $\mathbb{A}_4$ is *realized*: every message received is sent, even without adversary activity. Moreover, $\mathbb{A}_4$ is a *shape*. First, if we leave out any nodes, then either B's original strand is no longer embedded in the result, or else the result is no longer realized. Second, we cannot make it more general: If two different strands share a parameter, and we alter that parameter in one of the strands, then the result is no longer realized. For instance, the diagram would no longer be realized if

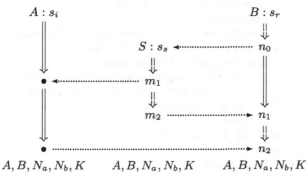

A, B, N_a, N_b, K A, B, N_a, N_b, K A, B, N_a, N_b, K

Fig. 5. Skeleton $\mathbb{A}_4$, with $\mathsf{non}_{\mathbb{A}_4} = \{\mathsf{ltk}(A), \mathsf{ltk}(B)\}$ and $\mathsf{unique}_{\mathbb{A}_4} = \{N_b, K\}$

A's parameter N_b were altered to some N_b'. Since all homomorphisms from $\mathbb{A}_0$ to realized skeletons factor through $\mathbb{A}_4$, it is the only shape for $\mathbb{A}_0$.

6   Search Strategy

The goal of CPSA is defined using the following terms:

step$(\mathbb{A}, C)$, which holds if the finite set C of skeletons is an outgoing or incoming cohort for $\mathbb{A}$. Any homomorphism from $\mathbb{A}$ to a realized skeleton passes through some $\mathbb{A}_k \in C$. The principles of Section 4 imply that the tests and their cohorts may be used in any order, while still finding all shapes.

realized$(\mathbb{A})$, which holds if $\mathbb{A}$ is realized; we can determine this directly.

min_real$_{\mathbb{A}_0}(\mathbb{A}')$, which is defined if $\mathbb{A}'$ is realized. Its value is the finite, non-empty set of shapes $\mathbb{A}$ such that (1) there is a homomorphism from $\mathbb{A}_0$ to $\mathbb{A}$; (2) $\mathbb{A}$ is realized; (3) there is a nodewise injective homomorphism from $\mathbb{A}$ to $\mathbb{A}'$; and (4) $\mathbb{A}$ is $\leq_n$-minimal among skeletons satisfying (1–3).

We say child$(\mathbb{A}, \mathbb{A}')$ if for some C, step$(\mathbb{A}, C)$ and $\mathbb{A}' \in C$. Let descendent be the reflexive, transitive closure of child. The goal of the search, given a starting skeleton $\mathbb{A}_0$, is to determine the set

$$\text{shapes}(\mathbb{A}_0) = \{\mathbb{A}_2 \colon \exists \mathbb{A}_1 \,.\, \text{descendent}(\mathbb{A}_0, \mathbb{A}_1) \,\wedge\, \mathbb{A}_2 \in \text{min\_real}_{\mathbb{A}_0}(\mathbb{A}_1)\}.$$

To do so, we use the search algorithm in Fig 6. We also need some auxiliaries:

dead$(\mathbb{A})$ means $\mathbb{A}$ cannot be realized, i.e. there is no realized $\mathbb{A}'$ with $H \colon \mathbb{A} \mapsto \mathbb{A}'$. Dead$(\mathbb{A})$ follows from any of the following: (1) $\mathbb{A}$ contains $\text{Lsn}[a]$ where $a \in \text{non}_{\mathbb{A}}$; (2) dead$(\mathbb{A}_0)$ and $H \colon \mathbb{A}_0 \mapsto \mathbb{A}$; or (3) step$(\mathbb{A}, C)$ where C consists of dead skeletons. Condition (1) was used repeatedly and condition (3) was used to discard Case 7, as the cohort 8–9 led only to dead skeletons.

```
F := {A₀};    shapes_found := ∅;    seen := F;
while F ≠ ∅ begin
        A := select(F);    F := F \ {A};
        if realized(A)
            then shapes_found := shapes_found ∪ min_real_A₀(A)
        else if redundant_strand(A) then skip
        else if step_applies(A) then begin
                let new = targets(apply_step(A)) \ seen in
                F := F ∪ new;    F := F \ (filter dead F);
                seen := seen ∪ new
            end
        else fail "Impossible."
    end;
return shapes_found
```

Fig. 6. CPSA Search Algorithm

redundant_strand($\mathbb{A}$) tests whether $\mathbb{A}$ contains a redundant strand that can be
   identified with some other strand by a homomorphism from $\mathbb{A}$ to a proper
   subskeleton. We discarded a redundant strand in Case 5.
step_applies($\mathbb{A}$) tests if an unsolved outgoing or incoming step exists in $\mathbb{A}$.
apply_step($\mathbb{A}$) selects an unsolved step, finds a cohort, updates the step relation,
   and then returns the cohort (assuming step_applies($\mathbb{A}$) is true).
targets(H) $= \{\mathbb{A}_k: k \leq j\}$, if H is a set of j homomorphisms $H_k: \mathbb{A} \mapsto \mathbb{A}_k$.

We assume select $\mathcal{S}$ selects a member of $\mathcal{S}$ if it is non-empty; and filter p $\mathcal{S}$ takes
the subset of $\mathcal{S}$ satisfying p. The failure marked "Impossible" in Fig. 6 cannot
be reached, because completeness [6] ensures that when $\mathbb{A}$ is not realized, then
some authentication test step applies.

7 Implementing CPSA

We discuss here three aspects of the CPSA implementation. They are: finding
candidate transforming edges in protocols, and using unification in applying
them; choosing sets S for outgoing tests, and representing the sets; and a few
items for future work.

Finding transforming edges. When CPSA reads a protocol description in its
input format, it identifies all the potential transforming edges. For the outgoing
tests, it locates all candidate pairs of a reception node m_0 and a transmission
node m_1 later on the same role such that a key or nonce is received in one or
more encrypted forms on m_0 and retransmitted outside these forms in m_1. For
incoming tests, CPSA notes all transmission nodes m_1 that send encrypted units.

   To find outgoing transforming edges for $a \in$ unique$_\mathbb{A}$ and a set S, CPSA considers each candidate edge $m_0 \Rightarrow^+ m_1$. Suppose an encrypted sub-message t
of msg(m_0) unifies with a member of S using a replacement α. If $a \cdot \alpha$ occurs
in msg(m_0) $\cdot \alpha$, but only within $S \cdot \alpha$, then we check msg(m_1) $\cdot \alpha$. If it occurs
outside $S \cdot \alpha$ in msg(m_1) $\cdot \alpha$, then $m_0 \Rightarrow^+ m_1$ is a successful candidate. If α
contracts atoms, then we apply the Outgoing Test Principle twice, once to apply
this contraction, and once to add the instance of $m_0 \Rightarrow^+ m_1$.[3] We also check
whether a contraction eliminates the outgoing test edge entirely, as in Case 6.

   For incoming tests, we do a unification on the candidate nodes m_1.

Selecting sets S for outgoing tests. To select sets S in the outgoing test
principle, we use a trick we call the "forwards-then-backwards" technique. CPSA
plans a sequence of applications of the outgoing test until no further transforming
edge is found, as in Yahalom cases 3 and 1. It follows the transmission of the
uniquely originating value—N_b in that case—forwards. Newly introduced atoms
like K' are implicitly universal. Originally, N_b occurs only in $\{\!|A \,\hat{}\, N_a \,\hat{}\, N_b|\!\}_{\mathsf{ltk}(B)}$;
after a server strand it also occurs in $\{\!|B \,\hat{}\, K' \,\hat{}\, N_a \,\hat{}\, N_b|\!\}_{\mathsf{ltk}(A)}$. After an initiator
strand, no other transforming edges can succeed.

---

[3] This is the only aspect of the authentication test search that does not occur in the
   Yahalom analysis.

Protocol	Point of view	Runtime	Shapes
ISO reject	responder	0.193s	2
Kerberos	client	1.443s	1
Needham-Schroeder	responder	0.055s	1
Needham-Schroeder-Lowe	responder	0.124s	1
Yahalom	responder	2.709s	1

Fig. 7. Protocols with CPSA runtimes

CPSA uses the sets in the opposite order. The set $S_1 = \{\{\!|A \hat{} N_a \hat{} N_b|\!\}_{\mathsf{ltk}(B)}\} \cup \{\{\!|B \hat{} K' \hat{} N_a \hat{} N_b|\!\}_{\mathsf{ltk}(A)} : K' \text{ a key}\}$ is used first to introduce the initiator transforming edge. Then the smaller set $\{\{\!|A \hat{} N_a \hat{} N_b|\!\}_{\mathsf{ltk}(B)}\}$ is used to introduce the (earlier) server transforming edge.[4]

The forwards-then-backwards technique suggested CPSA's representation for the sets S. These sets are not necessarily finite; S_1 e.g. is not. The family is closed under union and set difference. The primitive members are singletons $\{t_0\}$ and sets that represent all the instances of a term t_1 as some of t_1's parameters vary. Thus, we can represent all candidate sets are as finite unions and differences of values of the form $\lambda v . t$, where the vector v binds 0 or more atoms in t. Completeness requires only sets S representable in this form.

This representation fits also nicely with our use of unification to provide an extremely focused search, leading to good runtimes on a variety of protocols. Samples run on a Thinkpad X31, with a 1.4 GHz Pentium M processor and 1 GB store, under Linux, are shown in Fig. 7. CPSA is implemented in OCaml.

Future work. The soundness of the search algorithm does not require the barebones Dolev-Yao model used here. One can augment CPSA with Diffie-Hellman operations, as studied in [11]. One can also allow keys to be complex messages, typically the result of hashing. In our current framework, replacements map atoms to other atoms only, but it should be possible to map atoms to terms in general, at the cost of using more sophisticated methods to check whether skeletons are realized (e.g. [15]). The skeletons-and-homomorphisms approach may remain useful in a cryptographic, asymptotic probabilistic context.

Acknowledgments. We thank Lenore Zuck and John D. Ramsdell for their comments. Larry Paulson suggested the Yahalom protocol as a challenge.

References

1. Martín Abadi and Bruno Blanchet. Analyzing security protocols with secrecy types and logic programs. *Journal of the ACM*, 52(1):102–146, January 2005.
2. Roberto M. Amadio and Denis Lugiez. On the reachability problem in cryptographic protocols. In *Concur*, number 1877 in LNCS, pages 380–394, 2000.

---

[4] The cleverer set S_2 we used in Case 3 is an optimization. To ensure that the server and initiator agree on the session key, CPSA uses instead a cohort similar to Cases 5–7.

3. Michael Backes and Birgit Pfitzmann. Relating cryptographic and symbolic key secrecy. In *Proceedings, 26th IEEE Symposium on Security and Privacy*, May 2005. Extended version, http://eprint.iacr.org/2004/300.

4. Bruno Blanchet and Andreas Podelski. Verification of cryptographic protocols: Tagging enforces termination. In *Foundations of Software Science and Computation Structures*, LNCS, pages 136–152, April 2003.

5. Ran Canetti and Jonathan Herzog. Universally composable symbolic analysis of mutual authentication and key exchange protocols. In *Proceedings, Theory of Cryptography Conference (TCC)*, March 2006.

6. Shaddin F. Doghmi, Joshua D. Guttman, and F. Javier Thayer. Searching for shapes in cryptographic protocols (extended version). URL:http://eprint.iacr.org/2006/435, November 2006.

7. Daniel Dolev and Andrew Yao. On the security of public-key protocols. *IEEE Transactions on Information Theory*, 29:198–208, 1983.

8. Nancy Durgin, Patrick Lincoln, John Mitchell, and Andre Scedrov. Multiset rewriting and the complexity of bounded security protocols. *Journal of Computer Security*, 12(2):247–311, 2004.

9. Andrew D. Gordon and Alan Jeffrey. Types and effects for asymmetric cryptographic protocols. *Journal of Computer Security*, 12(3/4):435–484, 2003.

10. Joshua D. Guttman and F. Javier Thayer. Authentication tests and the structure of bundles. *Theoretical Computer Science*, 283(2):333–380, June 2002. Conference version appeared in *IEEE Symposium on Security and Privacy*, May 2000.

11. Jonathan C. Herzog. The Diffie-Hellman key-agreement scheme in the strand-space model. In *16th Computer Security Foundations Workshop*, pages 234–247, Asilomar, CA, June 2003. IEEE CS Press.

12. ITU. Message sequence chart (MSC). Recommendation Z.120, 1999.

13. Leslie Lamport. Time, clocks and the ordering of events in a distributed system. *CACM*, 21(7):558–565, 1978.

14. Gavin Lowe. Breaking and fixing the Needham-Schroeder public-key protocol using FDR. In *Proceeedings of* TACAS, volume 1055 of *Lecture Notes in Computer Science*, pages 147–166. Springer Verlag, 1996.

15. Jonathan K. Millen and Vitaly Shmatikov. Constraint solving for bounded-process cryptographic protocol analysis. In *8th ACM Conference on Computer and Communications Security (CCS '01)*, pages 166–175. ACM, 2001.

16. Roger Needham and Michael Schroeder. Using encryption for authentication in large networks of computers. *Communications of the ACM*, 21(12), 1978.

17. Lawrence C. Paulson. Relations between secrets: Two formal analyses of the Yahalom protocol. *Journal of Computer Security*, 2001.

18. Adrian Perrig and Dawn Xiaodong Song. Looking for diamonds in the desert: Extending automatic protocol generation to three-party authentication and key agreement protocols. In *Proceedings of the 13th IEEE Computer Security Foundations Workshop*. IEEE Computer Society Press, July 2000.

19. R. Ramanujam and S. P. Suresh. Decidability of context-explicit security protocols. *Journal of Computer Security*, 13(1):135–166, 2005. Preliminary version appeared in WITS '03, *Workshop on Issues in the Theory of Security*, Warsaw, April 2003.

Automatic Analysis of the Security
of XOR-Based Key Management Schemes

Véronique Cortier[1],*, Gavin Keighren[2], and Graham Steel[2],**

[1] Loria UMR 7503 & CNRS & INRIA Lorraine projet Cassis, France
Veronique.Cortier@loria.fr
http://www.loria.fr/~cortier
[2] School of Informatics, University of Edinburgh, Scotland
Graham.Steel@ed.ac.uk
http://homepages.inf.ed.ac.uk/gsteel

Abstract. We describe a new algorithm for analysing security protocols that use XOR, such as key-management APIs. As a case study, we consider the IBM 4758 CCA API, which is widely used in the ATM (cash machine) network. Earlier versions of the CCA API were shown to have serious flaws, and the fixes introduced by IBM in version 2.41 had not previously been formally analysed. We first investigate IBM's proposals using a model checker for security protocol analysis, uncovering some important issues about their implementation. Having identified configurations we believed to be safe, we describe the formal verification of their security. We first define a new class of protocols, containing in particular all the versions of the CCA API. We then show that secrecy after an unbounded number of sessions is decidable for this class. Implementing the decision procedure requires some improvements, since the procedure is exponential. We describe a change of representation that leads to an implementation able to verify a configuration of the API in a few seconds. As a consequence, we obtain the first security proof of the fixed IBM 4758 CCA API with unbounded sessions.

1 Introduction

Security protocols are small programs that aim to secure communications over a public network like the Internet. The design of such protocols is notoriously difficult and error-prone. Formal methods have proved their usefulness in the rigorous analysis of security protocols. Methods developed for security protocol analysis can also be useful for analysing other security-critical designs: for example, the security APIs of hardware security modules (HSMs). HSMs are essentially cryptographic co-processors encased in tamper-proof enclosures, and are widely used in security critical systems such as electronic payment and automated teller machine (ATM) networks. Use of the HSM is governed by the API, which can be thought of as a set of two-party security protocols, each describing an exchange between the HSM and the user, which may be

---

* This work has been partially supported by the ACI-SI project SATIN and the RNTL project POSE.
** Supported by EPSRC Grant number GR/S98139/01, 'Automated Analysis of Security Critical Systems'.

O. Grumberg and M. Huth (Eds.): TACAS 2007, LNCS 4424, pp. 538–552, 2007.
© Springer-Verlag Berlin Heidelberg 2007

used in any order. The IBM 4758 CCA[1] is an important example of such an API. In 2001, Bond discovered flaws in the CCA key management scheme that allowed an intruder to obtain access to PINs [2, §5.1]. The attack requires the intruder to exploit the algebraic properties of the XOR operation, which is used extensively in the CCA. Bond proposed changes to the API, which have been shown to be secure, [8], but these changes would not have been backward-compatible. IBM made changes of their own in version 2.41 of the API, and provided several procedural recommendations to prevent the attack. Though previous formal work has been able to rediscover the flaws in the old version [12,15], the new version of the API had not been formally analysed before.

In this paper, we propose a thorough analysis of the security of the revised IBM protocol, combining a case study with the development of a new tool for analysing protocols with XOR. Our first main contribution is the analysis of the IBM recommendations using the CL-AtSe protocol analysis tool [13], during which we discovered a possible attack, that we reported to IBM (see §2.3). For all the other versions, CL-AtSe concludes that the IBM protocol is safe. However, CL-AtSe only checks security for a finite number of *sessions*, or runs of the protocol. Furthermore, because the complexity of the API is greater than a standard key-exchange protocol, the number of sessions checked is often very small, usually only three. This means that there is no guarantee of security if the protocol is executed more than three times. In addition, the IBM CCA API lies outside both the existing classes of protocols using XOR which have been previously shown to be decidable [5,14] for an unbounded number of sessions. Other decidable classes of protocols with XOR have been proposed [6,4] but they only model a finite number of sessions.

To address this problem, our second main contribution is the development of a new class of protocols, called WFX-class, that includes the IBM CCA API. We show this class to be decidable. Our proof is considerably simpler that the corresponding proofs for the two previously treated classes, but the resulting decision procedure still has an exponential complexity. For example, in our application, our decision procedure may require us to compute about 2^{26} terms. We describe a change of representation that leads to an implementation able to verify a configuration of the API in a few seconds. As a consequence, we obtain the first security proof of the fixed IBM 4758 CCA API with unbounded sessions. To the best of our knowledge, this implementation is the first tool for automatically verifying protocols with XOR, for an unbounded number of sessions, albeit for a particular class of protocols.

The paper is organised as follows: in §2, we analyse each of IBM's recommendations for patching the CCA key management protocol, using CL-AtSe (thus for a bounded number of sessions). In §3, we define our class of well-formed protocols, and prove the decidability of security of protocols in the class for an unbounded number of sessions. We explain how to implement our procedure in §4, and provide our results for the CCA key management scheme. Concluding remarks can be found in §5. A longer version of the paper, containing full proofs and more details of the CCA command modelling, has been issued as a technical report [7].

---

[1] CCA stands for 'Common Cryptographic Architecture', while 4758 is the model number of the HSM. See http://www-3.ibm.com/security/cryptocards/pcicc.shtml

2 Analysing the IBM Recommendations Using CL-AtSe

HSMs typically consist of a cryptoprocessor and a small amount of memory inside a tamper-proof enclosure. They are designed so that should an intruder open the casing or insert probes to try to read the memory, it will auto-erase in a matter of nanoseconds. In a typical ATM network application, HSMs are used, for example, to decrypt, encrypt and verify PINs. Many different keys may are used for these operations. IBM's Common Cryptographic Architecture (CCA) API [3] supports various key types, such as data keys, key encryption keys, import keys and export keys. Each type is represented by a public 'control vector' which is XOR-ed with the security module's master key (which is stored inside the HSM), before being used to encrypt the particular key. For example, a data key would be encrypted under KM⊕DATA.[2] Keys encrypted in this manner are known as *working keys* and are stored outside of the security module. They can then only be used by sending them back into the HSM under the desired API command. Only particular types of keys will be accepted by the HSM for particular operations. For example, data keys can be used to encrypt arbitrary messages, but so-called 'PIN Derivation Keys' (PDKs, with control vector PIN) cannot, which is critical for security: a customer's PIN is just his account number encrypted under a PIN derivation key. In Bond's attack, the intruder uses API commands to change the type of a key, exploiting the algebraic properties of XOR. This allows a PIN derivation key to be converted into a data key, which can then be used to encrypt data. Hence the attack allows a criminal to generate a PIN for any account number. For more details of Bond's 'Chosen Key Difference' attack, see [2, §5.1].

2.1 CCA Key Management Commands

Following previous work [15,12], our experiments consider a number of key management commands from the CCA API. We ignore commands which do not generate key material and commands that are subsumed by more general ones. A full list of commands, including the ones not modelled and our justification for leaving them out, can be found in [7]. The modelled rules of the IBM 4758 CCA API are represented in Figure 1. For each command, the terms on the left of the arrow represent the user's input to the HSM, and the term on the right represents the HSM's output. For example, we have seen that data keys should be encrypted under KM⊕DATA. Thus the **Encipher** rule corresponds to a data encryption command which allows data keys to be used to encrypt any given plaintext. **Decipher** allows data keys to be used for decryption. **Key Import** allows a key from another 4758 module, encrypted for transport under a 'key encrypting key' (KEK), to be made into a working key for this HSM. **Key Export** is used to encrypt a working key under a key encrypting key for transport to another HSM. Note the division of types of KEK: IMP for import and EXP for export. In order to transport encrypted keys to a new HSM, an importer KEK must first be established as a working key at the destination HSM. In order to do this without giving away the value of the KEK, which would be a considerable security risk, the KEK is decomposed into three parts, which XOR together to give the final KEK. The three **Key Part Import**

---

[2] ⊕ represents bitwise XOR.

x, $\{xkey\}_{KM\oplus DATA} \rightarrow \{x\}_{xkey}$ **Encipher**

$\{x\}_{xkey}$, $\{xkey\}_{KM\oplus DATA} \rightarrow x$ **Decipher**

$\{xkey\}_{xkek\oplus xtype}$, $xtype$, $\{xkek\}_{KM\oplus IMP} \rightarrow \{xkey\}_{KM\oplus xtype}$ **Key Import**

$\{xkey\}_{KM\oplus xtype}$, $xtype$, $\{xkek\}_{KM\oplus EXP} \rightarrow \{xkey\}_{xkek\oplus xtype}$ **Key Export**

$xkpNew$, $xtype \rightarrow \{xkpNew\}_{KM\oplus xtype\oplus KPART}$ **Key Part Import 1**

$xkpNew$, $xtype$, $\{xkpOld\}_{KM\oplus xtype\oplus KPART} \rightarrow \{xkpNew\oplus xkpOld\}_{KM\oplus xtype\oplus KPART}$

Key Part Import 2

$xkpNew$, $xtype$, $\{xkpOld\}_{KM\oplus xtype\oplus KPART} \rightarrow \{xkpNew\oplus xkpOld\}_{KM\oplus xtype}$

Key Part Import 3

$\{xkey\}_{xkek1\oplus xtype}$, $xtype$, $\{xkek1\}_{KM\oplus IMP}$, $\{xkek2\}_{KM\oplus EXP} \rightarrow \{xkey\}_{xkek2\oplus xtype}$

Key Translate

Variables are prefixed by x. The term $\{m\}_k$ represents the message m encrypted with the key k (using symmetric encryption).

Fig. 1. Modelled rules of the IBM 4758 CCA API

commands can then be used one after the other, by three different security officers, each in possession of one key part, to create the working import key. It is this process that is subverted in Bond's attack to change the type of a key. **Key Translate** is used to translate a key from encryption under one KEK (of import type) to encryption under another (of export type). For a full description of all these rules, see [10].

2.2 Modelling the API

We chose to use CL-AtSe [13] to check the API since unlike most protocol analysis tools, it has built-in support for the XOR operator. CL-AtSe is a 'Dolev-Yao'[3] style protocol analyser, part of the AVISPA tool set [16]. It accepts models written in a special-purpose protocol specification language called HLPSL [17], and implements a variant of the Baader-Schulz unification algorithm [1], optimised for XOR. The HLPSL is initially converted into a transition relation, which CL-AtSe uses to generate a set of constraints describing the protocol. Each protocol step is modelled by constraints on the intruder's knowledge, with the execution of such steps simulated by adding new constraints to the system and by reducing or eliminating existing constraints. Security properties are checked against the system state at each step. See [17, §3.2.1] for more details of the operation of CL-AtSe.

Each of the commands were modelled as a separate 'role' containing exactly one transition. The intruder's initial knowledge includes an unknown working key of each

---

[3] This refers to the nature of the intruder being modelled, who may decompose and re-assemble message parts, but not perform any cryptanalytic attacks.

type, to reflect that fact that even if he does not already have such keys, he can always 'conjure' one by repeatedly trying random values against a command, [2, §3.4]. In addition, he is given all the initial knowledge assumed by Bond in his attacks, [2], which includes a key part K3, a partially completed importer key $\{\!|\text{KEK}\oplus\text{K3}|\!\}_{\text{KM}\oplus\text{KP}\oplus\text{IMP}}$, a PIN derivation key PDK encrypted under transport key KEK, and a customer's account number PAN. For standard security protocols, we would be interested in model checking properties such as the secrecy of a newly agreed session key, i.e. that a term representing the session key is unknown to the intruder. In the case of security APIs, we are interested in the secrecy of the cleartext value of the sensitive keys managed by the HSM. Additionally, we assume that the intruder knows a customer's account number, since these are not kept secret in the system. We can now also check the secrecy of the customer's PIN, i.e. the account number encrypted under the PIN derivation key, that is a message of the form $\{\!|\text{PAN}|\!\}_{\text{PDK}}$. This accounts for attacks where the intruder is able to encrypt arbitrary data under the PDK, without learning the key's cleartext value, as is the case in several of Bond's attacks.

Full details of the CL-AtSe modelling can be found in [10]. Having established that CL-AtSe can very quickly re-discover Bond's attack on the original API, we proceeded to investigate IBM's recommendations for preventing it.

2.3   Analysing IBM's Recommendations

In response to Bond's attacks [2, §5.1], IBM released a set of three recommendations designed to prevent it [9], covering command usage, the access control system, and general procedural safeguards. However, it was unclear which of the recommendations are necessary, or sufficient, to prevent the attack. We investigated all the recommendations using our CL-AtSe model.

Recommendation 1 – Use Public Key Techniques. Instead of transferring the initial key encryption key (KEK) using key parts in clear, IBM recommend that it is transferred encrypted under the destination HSM's public key. This ensures that the KEK is never present in clear, and thus cannot be modified. Using this method, the KEK is wrapped in a key block which is subsequently encrypted and provided as input to the **PKA Symmetric Key Import** command, defined as follows:

$$\{\!|xkey.xtype|\!\}_{\text{PK}} \rightarrow \{\!|xkey|\!\}_{\text{KM}\oplus xtype} \qquad \textbf{PKA Symmetric Key Import}$$

However, the format and encryption procedure for the key block is given in the manual, and it is therefore possible for a block containing an arbitrary key to be created, thus allowing a known key to be introduced into the security module. CL-AtSe quickly discovered that an attacker could introduce a known exporter key k,[4] and obtain the transported PIN derivation key encrypted under this key (see Figure 2). We reported this vulnerability to IBM. They conceded that the attack was possible, and intend to change the documentation to reflect this. They argue the attack would have to be carried out by an insider, and that the vulnerability is intrinsic to public key schemes. We

---

[4] Our experiments found that, even if the **PKA Symmetric Key Import** command does not accept export-type KEKs, it is still possible to obtain such a key (see [10] for details).

$$\{\!|kek.\mathtt{IMP}|\!\}_{\mathtt{PK}} \rightarrow \{\!|kek|\!\}_{\mathtt{KM}\oplus\mathtt{IMP}} \qquad\qquad\qquad \textbf{PKA Symmetric Key Import}$$

$$\{\!|k.\mathtt{EXP}|\!\}_{\mathtt{PK}} \rightarrow \{\!|k|\!\}_{\mathtt{KM}\oplus\mathtt{EXP}} \qquad\qquad\qquad \textbf{PKA Symmetric Key Import}$$

$$\{\!|pdk|\!\}_{kek\oplus\mathtt{PIN}}, \mathtt{PIN}, \{\!|kek|\!\}_{\mathtt{KM}\oplus\mathtt{IMP}} \rightarrow \{\!|pdk|\!\}_{\mathtt{KM}\oplus\mathtt{PIN}} \qquad \textbf{Key Import}$$

$$\{\!|pdk|\!\}_{\mathtt{KM}\oplus\mathtt{PIN}}, \mathtt{PIN}, \{\!|k|\!\}_{\mathtt{KM}\oplus\mathtt{EXP}} \rightarrow \{\!|pdk|\!\}_{k\oplus\mathtt{PIN}} \qquad \textbf{Key Export}$$

Fig. 2. A known-exporter attack. The attacker first imports the import-type KEK as intended, then imports an export-type key k which he knows. Then, he imports the PDK as intended, but then can export it under $k\oplus\mathtt{PIN}$, and since $\mathtt{PIN}$ is a public value, he can decrypt this packet and obtain the PDK.

suggest that access control should be used to restrict any single insider from having access to both the **PKA Symmetric Key Import** and **Key Import** commands. We created two models, each one allowing access to only one of these functions, and checked them with CL-AtSe, which discovered no further attacks, up to the bounds shown in the table below:

Available Command	Bound*	Analysed States	Reachable States	Run-Time (s)
Key Import	10#	76	10	0.08
PKA Symmetric Key Import	3	8751	1749	514.27

\# This bound could be set much higher, but informal analysis showed that the intruder was never able to obtain any useful new terms.

* Bound on the number of sessions.

Recommendation 2 – Use the Access Control System. Users of IBM's 4758 HSM are assigned to roles that determine which commands they are allowed to execute. The goal is to prevent one single individual from having access to all the commands required to mount Bond's attack. This is enforced using access controls. IBM provide an example of the KEK transfer process involving five roles (A – E) such that no single role is able to mount the attack (see Figure 3).

In the original attack, the intruder played the roles C and E together. Note that roles A and D do not have any access privileges at the destination security module. IBM state in their recommendation that roles A and B could actually be played by the same individual. This does not hold since that person has access to all the key parts, and thus the completed KEK, so she could decrypt the key in transit, and obtain its clear value.

In our experimental model, the intruder was actually given a greater range of API commands than as suggested by IBM, with still the restriction that at least one of the three requirements for the attack were missing. That is, none of them gave the intruder access to a **Key Part Import** command, the **Key Import** command, and the key being transferred. The reason for this was that we were trying to discover the minimum

Person	Responsibilities	Commands
A	Generates and distributes the clear key parts, as well as the key verification pattern (KVP) for the complete KEK.	N/A
B	Enters the first key part into the destination security module.	Key Part Import 1
C	Enters the second key part, and verifies that the completed KEK is correct by checking the KVP.	Key Part Import 3 Key Test
D	Distributes the PIN derivation key (PDK) encrypted under KEK.	N/A
E	Verifies that the KEK is correct, then imports the PDK.	Key Test Key Import

Fig. 3. Roles described by IBM in their 2nd recommendation

restrictions that are sufficient to prevent the attack. CL-AtSe reported no attacks up to the bounds shown below:

Person	Bound	Analysed States	Reachable States	Run-Time (s)
B	6	34	6	333.02
C	3	413	68	58.22
E	10*	54	10	0.03

* This bound could be set much higher, but informal analysis showed that the intruder was never able to obtain any useful new terms.

Recommendation 3 – Use Procedural Controls. IBM's third recommendation is to ensure that no single individual involved in the key transfer process has the opportunity to modify the KEK used. If the KEK is not modified, then the type of the key being transferred cannot be altered when it is imported. With respect to the API commands, this translates to restricting the **Key Import** command to only accept the unmodified KEK. CL-AtSe found no attack on this version of the API:

Bound	Analysed States	Reachable States	Run-Time (s)
3	13133	2625	2827.35

The large number of reachable states reflects the fact that the intruder is still able to generate a large number of modified KEKs, even though they cannot be used to import the PDK. IBM now seem to intend that Recommendation 3 is always followed, in addition to any of the other recommendations, in order to ensure a high level of security. The points outlined by the recommendation have since been expanded and included in the current version of the CCA Manual [3, Appendix H] as general principles for secure operation.

All the model files used in our experiments are available from `http://home pages.inf.ed.ac.uk/gsteel/CCA-experiments/`. The CL-AtSe tool may be downloaded from `http://www.avispa-project.org/`.

3   Theoretical Results for XOR-Based Key-Management APIs

Having investigated IBM's recommendations with a model checker, and adjusting them where necessary to produce what seemed to be secure configurations, we proceed towards verifying them secure. As we have seen, both protocols and intruder behaviours can be modelled symbolically using rules over terms with variables. We observe that the IBM 4758 CCA API can actually be modelled using what we call *well-formed* rules. We then show that reachability of a term is decidable for any set of well-formed rules.

3.1   Definitions

Cryptographic primitives are represented by functional symbols. More specifically, we consider the *signature* Σ containing an infinite number of constants including some special constant 0 and two non constant symbols $\{\_\}\_$ and $\oplus$ of arity 2. We also assume an infinite set of variables $\mathcal{V}$. The set of *terms or messages* is defined inductively by

$$
\begin{array}{llll}
T ::= & & \text{terms} \\
& \mid & x & \text{variable } x \\
& \mid & f(T_1, \ldots, T_k) & \text{application of symbol } f \in \Sigma \text{ of arity } k \geq 1 \\
& \mid & c & \text{constant } c \in \Sigma
\end{array}
$$

A term is *ground* if it has no variable.

As in §2, the term $\{m\}_k$ is intended to represent the message m encrypted with the key k (using symmetric encryption). The term $m_1 \oplus m_2$ represents the message m_1 XORed with the message m_2. The constants may represent agent identities, nonces or keys for example. Substitutions are written $\sigma = \{x_1 = t_1, \ldots, x_n = t_n\}$ with $dom(\sigma) = \{x_1, \ldots, x_n\}$. σ is *ground* iff all of the t_i are ground. The application of a substitution σ to a term t is written $\sigma(t) = t\sigma$. The *size* of a term t, denoted by $|t|$, is defined as usual by the total number of symbols used in t. More formally, $|a| = 1$ if a is a constant or a variable and $|f(t_1, \ldots, t_n)| = 1 + \sum_{i=1}^{n} |t|$ if f is of arity $k \geq 1$. The size of a set of terms S is the sum of the size of the terms in S.

We equip the signature with an equational theory E that models the algebraic properties of the XOR operator:

$$
\begin{array}{ll}
x \oplus (y \oplus z) = (x \oplus y) \oplus z & \quad x \oplus y = y \oplus x \\
x \oplus x = 0 & \quad x \oplus 0 = x
\end{array}
$$

It defines an equivalence relation that is closed under substitutions of terms for variables and under application of contexts. In particular, we say that two terms t_1 and t_2 are equal, denoted by $t_1 = t_2$ if they are equal modulo the equational theory E. If two terms are equal using only the equations of the first line, we say that they are equal modulo Associativity and Commutativity (AC).

Intruder capabilities and the protocol behaviour are described using *rules* of the form $t_1, \ldots, t_n \rightarrow t_{n+1}$ where the t_i are terms.

Example 1. The intruder capabilities are represented by the following set of three rules:

$$x, y \rightarrow \{x\}_y \qquad \text{encryption}$$
$$\{x\}_y, y \rightarrow x \qquad \text{decryption}$$
$$x, y \rightarrow x \oplus y \qquad \text{xoring}$$

The set of deducible terms is the reflexive and transitive closure of the rewrite rules.

Definition 1. *Let $\mathcal{R}$ be a set of rules. Let S be a set of ground terms. The term u is one-step deducible from S if there exists a rule $t_1, \ldots, t_n \rightarrow t \in \mathcal{R}$ and a ground substitution θ such that $t_i\theta \in S$ and $u = t\theta$.*

A term u is deducible *from S, denoted by $S \vdash_{\mathcal{R}} u$, if $u \in S$ or there exist ground terms $u_1, \ldots, u_n$ such that $u_n = u$ and u_i is one-step deducible from $S \cup \{u_1, \ldots, u_{i-1}\}$ for every $1 \leq i \leq n$. The sequence $u_1, \ldots, u_n$ is a* proof *that $S \vdash_{\mathcal{R}} u$.*

We write $\vdash$ instead of $\vdash_{\mathcal{R}}$ when $\mathcal{R}$ is clear from the context.

Example 2. Let $\mathcal{R}$ be the set of rules described in Example 1. Let $S = \{\{n\}_a, a \oplus b, b\}$. Then n is deducible from S and $\{n\}_a, a \oplus b, b, a$ is a proof of $S \vdash n$. Indeed a is one-step deducible from $\{a \oplus b, b\}$ using the rule $x, y \rightarrow x \oplus y$ and the fact that $(a \oplus b) \oplus b = a$ and n is one-step deducible from $\{\{n\}_a, a\}$ using the rule $\{x\}_y, y \rightarrow x$.

3.2 Well-Formed Protocols

Rather than restricting the use of variables in protocol rules, we take advantage of the form of API-like protocols, noticing that they only perform simple operations.

Definition 2. *A term t is an* XOR *term if $t = \bigoplus_{i=1}^{n} u_i$, $n \geq 1$ where each u_i is a variable or a constant.*

A term t is an encryption *term if $t = \{u\}_v$ where u and v are XOR terms.*

A term t is a well-formed *term if it is either an encryption term or an XOR term. In particular, a well formed term contains no nested encryption.*

A rule $t_1, \ldots, t_n \rightarrow t_{n+1}$ is well formed *if*

- *each t_i is a well-formed term.*
- *$Var(t_{n+1}) \subseteq \bigcup_{i=1}^{n} Var(t_i)$ (no variable is introduced in the right-hand-side of a rule).*

A proof is well-formed *if it only uses well-formed terms.*

Definition 3. *The* WFX-*class protocol consists of a pair $(\mathcal{R}, S)$, where $\mathcal{R}$ is a finite set of well-formed rules, and S is a finite set of ground, well-formed terms.*

Intuitively, the rules in $\mathcal{R}$ represent the commands of the API and the intruder capabilities, and the ground terms S the initial knowledge of the intruder. We call our class WFX since these are well-formed protocols using the XOR operator. In particular, the rules representing the intruder capabilities (defined in Example 1) and the rules representing the 4758 CCA API protocol (introduced in §2 are all well-formed.

The remaining of the section is devoted to the decidability of deducibility of a term, which can be used to encode secrecy preservation of a protocol. To the best of our knowledge, there exist only two decidable classes [5,14] for secrecy preservation for protocols with XOR, for an unbounded number of sessions. In both cases, the main difference with our class is that we make restrictions on the combination of functional symbols rather than on the occurrences of variables. As a consequence, our class is incomparable to the two existing ones. A more detailed discussion may be found in [7].

3.3   Proof of Decidability

The key idea of our decidability result is to show that only well-formed terms need to be considered when checking for the deducibility of a (well-formed) term. In particular, there is no need to consider nested encryption. This allows us to consider only a finite number of terms: we have a finite number of atoms in the initial set of rules which can only be combined by encryption and XORing, and XORing identical atoms results in cancellation. At the end of the proof, we comment on the complexity of the resulting decision procedure.

We first prove that whenever an encryption occurs in a deducible term, the encryption is itself deducible.

Proposition 1. *Let $\mathcal{R}$ be a set of well-formed rules. Let S be a set of ground well-formed terms (intuitively the initial knowledge). Let u be a term such that $S \vdash u$ and let $\{u_1\}_{u_2}$ be a subterm of u. Then $S \vdash \{u_1\}_{u_2}$.*

The proof is by induction on the number of steps needed to obtain u. The full proof is in [7].

Our main result states that only well-formed terms need to be considered when checking for deducibility.

Proposition 2. *Let $\mathcal{R}$ be a set of well-formed rules and S be a set of ground well-formed terms such that*

- *$\mathcal{R}$ contains the rule $x, y \rightarrow x \oplus y$;*
- *S contains 0 (the null element for XOR should always be known to an intruder).*

Let u be a ground well formed term deducible from S. Then there exists a well-formed proof of $S \vdash u$.

We briefly sketch the proof of this key proposition (the full proof appears in [7]). Taking advantage of the form of the rules, the main idea is to show that, considering a proof of a well-formed term u and removing all inside encrypted terms, we obtain a (well-formed) proof of u. We define a function $t \mapsto \bar{t}$ that removes inside encryption. For example, we have $\overline{\{a \oplus \{a\}_b\}_c \oplus \{c\}_b} = \{a\}_c \oplus \{c\}_b$. Roughly, we show by induction on the length of the proof that whenever $u_1, \ldots, u_n$ is a proof then $\overline{u_1}, \ldots, \overline{u_n}$ is a proof. Assume $u_1, \ldots, u_n, u_{n+1}$ is a proof and $t_1, \ldots, t_k \rightarrow t$ is the last rule been applied. There is a substitution θ such that $t\theta = u_{n+1}$ and $t_i\theta = u_{j_i}$. Since t is a well-formed term, any inside encryption e of u_{n+1} must appear under a variable x in t thus e also appears in some u_{j_i}. Intuitively, there is a case analysis depending on whether x also appears under an encryption in t_i. If x does not appear under an encryption, that is $t = x \oplus t'$, we use the fact that (Proposition 1) e is deducible thus $u_{j_i} \oplus e$ is also deducible and we could have chosen $x\theta' = x\theta \oplus e$, removing the encryption from u_{n+1}.

Using Proposition 2, we can now easily conclude the decidability of deducibility.

Theorem 1. *The following problem*

- *Given a finite set of well-formed rules $\mathcal{R}$ containing the rule $x, y \to x \oplus y$, a finite set S of ground well-formed terms containing 0 and a ground well-formed term u,*
- *Does $S \vdash_{\mathcal{R}} u$?*

is decidable in exponential time in the size of $\mathcal{R}$, S and u.

Let $a_1, \ldots, a_n$ be the constants that occur in $\mathcal{R}$, S or u. Let k be the maximal number of terms in the left-hand side of a rule in $\mathcal{R}$. For any $t_1, \ldots, t_l \to t \in \mathcal{R}$, we have $l \leq k$. We show that $S \vdash_{\mathcal{R}} u$ can be decided in $\mathcal{O}(2^{(k+1)(2n+1)})$.

The decision procedure is as follows: we saturate S by adding any well-formed deducible terms. We obtain a set S^*. By Proposition 2, $S \vdash_{\mathcal{R}} u$ if and only if $u \in S^*$. In S^* there are at most

- 2^n XOR terms
- and $2^n \times 2^n = 2^{2n}$ encryption terms

thus $|S^*| \leq 2^{2n+1}$. Note that we consider here terms modulo AC which means that we only consider one concrete representation for each class of terms equal modulo AC. This can be done for example by fixing an arbitrary order on the constants and using it to normalise terms.

Now, at each iteration, For each rule $t_1, \ldots, t_l \to t \in \mathcal{R}$ we consider any tuple of terms $(u_1, \ldots, u_l)$ with u_i in the set that is being saturated and compute the set $\mathcal{M}$ of most general unifiers of $(u_1, \ldots, u_l) = (t_1, \ldots, t_l)$ (which can be done in polynomial time for well-formed terms, see [7]). Then we add any well-formed instance of $t\sigma$ for any $\sigma \in \mathcal{M}$. We consider at most $|S^*|^k \leq 2^{k(2n+1)}$ tuples at each iteration. All together, we need at most $\mathcal{O}(2^{(k+1)(2n+1)})$ operations to compute S^*.

4   Implementation and Results

Our efforts to implement the decision procedure using existing tools such as theorem provers (Vampire and E) and model finders (Paradox and Darwin) were unsuccessful. The combinatorial complexity caused by the XOR operation prevents any of the tools from finding a saturation. Since our models have a finite Herbrand universe, and hence are effectively propositional, we considered a manual encoding as a Boolean satisfiability problem, for use with a SAT solver. Unfortunately, for n atoms (our models typically have $n = 13$), we will need 2^n (possible XOR terms) $+ 2^n \times 2^n$ (possible encryption terms) propositional variables to represent the intruder's knowledge. Additionally, writing out ground versions of the 8 well formed rules in the API will result is an enormous problem, far too large for any SAT solver. In the end, we solved the problem by making a change of representation, and writing an ad-hoc decision procedure for that representation.

4.1   Representation of XOR Terms

The representation consists of encoding an XOR term as a binary string, accomplished by assigning an (arbitrary) order to the finite set of atoms (or *base terms*). For example, if we have the ordered set of base terms KM, KP, KEK, IMP, EXP, DATA, PIN, we would represent KEK⊕PIN⊕DATA as

$$
\begin{array}{ccccccc}
\text{KM} & \text{KP} & \text{KEK} & \text{IMP} & \text{EXP} & \text{DATA} & \text{PIN} \\
\end{array}
$$

$$
\text{KEK} \oplus \text{PIN} \oplus \text{DATA} \rightarrow \quad 0 \quad 0 \quad 1 \quad 0 \quad 0 \quad 1 \quad 1
$$
$$
\downarrow
$$
$$
19
$$

Hence KEK⊕PIN⊕DATA is represented by the decimal integer 19. Notice the order of the atoms in the term does not matter - we still get the same integer - so our representation effectively normalises the term with respect to the properties of XOR. Notice further that if we have two terms $x1$ and $x2$, that are represented by integers l and m, then the integer representing $x1 \oplus x2$ is just $l \oplus m$. So, we represent XOR using XOR, which is an attractive feature of the representation. For example, we can write the intruder rule

$$
x1, x2 \rightarrow x1 \oplus x2
$$

as

$$
l, m \rightarrow l \oplus m
$$

For encryption terms, which consist of one XOR term encrypted by another, we simply shift the bits of the integer representing the message term n places to the left (where n is the number of base terms), and add the integer representing the key. We obtain a unique number in the range $0 \ldots 2^{2n}$ for each encryption term. For example, the term $\{\!|\text{KEK} \oplus \text{PIN} \oplus \text{DATA}|\!\}_{\text{KM} \oplus \text{DATA}}$ is represented by

$$
\begin{array}{ccccccc} \quad \begin{array}{ccccccc}
\text{KM} & \text{KP} & \text{KEK} & \text{IMP} & \text{EXP} & \text{DATA} & \text{PIN} \\
0 & 0 & 1 & 0 & 0 & 1 & 1
\end{array} & \quad & \begin{array}{ccccccc}
\text{KM} & \text{KP} & \text{KEK} & \text{IMP} & \text{EXP} & \text{DATA} & \text{PIN} \\
1 & 0 & 0 & 0 & 0 & 1 & 0
\end{array} \end{array}
$$
$$
\downarrow
$$
$$
2498
$$

4.2   The Implemented Procedure

Our decision procedure starts by allocating enough space in memory for $2^{2n} + 2^n$ integers, and setting all these memory locations to 0. Then, all locations corresponding to the intruder's initial knowledge S are set to 1, indicating that the intruder can obtain these terms. For each rule r_i in $\mathcal{R}$, with k terms on the left hand side, encode the operation as a partial function $f_i : \mathbb{N}^k \rightarrow \mathbb{N}$. As a simple example, for the 'Encipher' rule:

$$
x, \{\!|xkey|\!\}_{\text{KM} \oplus \text{DATA}} \rightarrow \{\!|x|\!\}_{xkey} \qquad\qquad \textbf{Encipher}
$$

Assuming KM⊕DATA is represented by the integer value p, we write

$$
f : x, [xkey|p], \rightarrow [x|xkey]
$$

where the braces $[|]$ denote composition of the two n-long bitstrings into a single $2n$-long bitstring. A more complicated example is the **Key Import** command:

$$\{|xkey|\}_{xkek \oplus xtype}, xtype, \{|xkek|\}_{\mathrm{KM} \oplus \mathrm{IMP}} \rightarrow \{|xkey|\}_{\mathrm{KM} \oplus xtype} \qquad \textbf{Key Import}$$

Assuming $\mathrm{KM} \oplus \mathrm{IMP}$ is represented by the integer q, and KM is represented by r, we write

$$f : [xkey|x], xtype, [xkek|q] \rightarrow [xkey|q \oplus xtype] \quad \text{IF} \quad x = xkek \oplus xtype$$

It will always be possible to write WFX class API rules as integer functions in this way provided the rules are executable, that is provided the HSM itself can work out the values of the bitstrings it needs to carry out the XORing or encryption/decryption required by the command. This leads directly to the integer formula required.

To obtain the fixpoint of the intruder's knowledge, we apply each rule exhaustively, looking for combinations of k suitable integers that the intruder already knows, and setting to 1 any location that we can now reach using these rules. We do this for all the rules in an iterative manner until no more rules apply. We check to see if any of the secret terms are now set to 1. If so, we have found an attack. If not, we have verified the API secure. Note that in the case where we find an attack, we cannot immediately return the trace of steps required to obtain the secret term, as CL-AtSe can. It would be possible to extend our procedure to keep track of the operations required to obtain each term, for example by outputting a list of terms obtained and post-processing the list to obtain the trace for the attack.

At each iteration of our decision procedure, it is possible to obtain terms we have already deduced, by repeating the original command application which returned the term in the first place. To avoid rediscovering existing terms, we mark the freshly obtained terms at each iteration, and require that a rule is applied only if it makes use of at least one fresh term. One final feature of our procedure is that is allows us to treat the value of the DATA control vector as zero, since this is its actual value, a fact which is exploited in an attack on the unrevised API presented by IBM themselves [9].

The full source code for our decision procedure, together with documentation and the files used for the experiments below, can be downloaded from http://homepages.inf.ed.ac.uk/gsteel/CCA-experiments/.

4.3   Results

Our WFX class does not account for public key encryption, nor the concatenation of key and type required by the **PKA Symmetric Key Import** command. So we modelled recommendation 1 by effectively pre-processing this command. We observe that the encrypted key blocks which it imports can either be legitimate (i.e. the intended KEK), or generated by the intruder from known unencrypted terms. Since the only operation the intruder can perform on the legitimate block is to execute **PKA Symmetric Key Import** on it, we provide him with the result of this, $\{|xKey|\}_{\mathrm{KM} \oplus xType}$, in his initial knowledge. This means that the **PKA Symmetric Key Import** command can be modelled such that it will only consider ways in which the intruder could use it to import self-generated encrypted blocks. Such blocks consist of a known unencrypted term and

Table 1. Results using our decision procedure to verify the recommendations

Model	Base Terms	Iterations	Terms Derived	Run-Time
Recommendation1_KeyImp	13	3	17015	0.23
Recommendation1_SymKeyImp	11	3	13045	3.04
Recommendation2_PersonB	14	2	4473	8.09
Recommendation2_PersonC	14	3	4413	12.10
Recommendation2_PersonE	13	2	1089	2.02
Recommendation3	14	3	83317	1.16

a key type control vector, so the command just becomes a way to turn a known unencrypted term into a working key of any type, i.e. the rule:

$$xkey, xtype \rightarrow \{\!|xkey|\!\}_{KM\oplus xtype} \qquad \textbf{Pre-Processed PKA Symmetric Key Import}$$

Apart from this change, all our models have the same initial knowledge and security goals as the CL-AtSe models. Table 1 summarises our results. We conclude that after our modifications described in §2.3 have been made, any one of the three recommendations is sufficient to secure the scheme against Dolev-Yao intruder attacks.

5   Conclusion

We have obtained a new decidable class of security protocols with XOR, for an unbounded number of sessions. The decision procedure has been implemented, yielding the first tool for automatically analysing a protocol with XOR and an unbounded number of sessions. As a case study, we have formally analysed the revised IBM 4758 CCA API protocol. We first discovered possible attacks using CL-AtSe, and refined IBM's recommendations to produce safe configurations. Our decision procedure then verified these configurations.

Related work includes that of Courant, who verified Bond's own suggestions for fixing the API in the interactive theorem prover Coq, [8]. His proof used normalisation functions to deal with XOR, and most of the proof effort was in showing these functions to be sound. Other work has looked at rediscovering Bond's attacks on the old API, [12,15], the latter work using (without proof) a heuristic that splits intruder knowledge into an encrypted and unencrypted part. We believe that our theoretical results show that their heuristic preserves attack-completeness.

In future we intend to try to extend our theoretical results to deal with asymmetric cryptography and pairing, so that we can analyse public-key management schemes, and to establish a formal theory that deals with so-called 'key-conjuring', [2, §3.4].

References

1. F. Baader and K. Schulz. Unification in the Union of Disjoint Equational Theories: Combining Decision Procedures. In D. Kapur, editor, *CADE-11: Eleventh International Conference on Automated Deduction*, volume 607, pages 50–65, June 1992.
2. M. Bond. Attacks on cryptoprocessor transaction sets. In Ç. K. Koç, D. Naccache, and C. Paar, editors, *Cryptographic Hardware and Embedded Systems - CHES 2001*, volume 2162 of *Lecture Notes in Computer Science*, pages 220–234. Springer, 2001.

3. *CCA Basic Services Reference and Guide*, October 2006.   Available online at http://www-03.ibm.com/security/cryptocards/pdfs/bs327.pdf.
4. Y. Chevalier, R. Küsters, M. Rusinowitch, and M. Turuani. An NP decision procedure for protocol insecurity with XOR. In *Proc. of 18th Annual IEEE Symposium on Logic in Computer Science (LICS '03)*, pages 261–270, 2003.
5. H. Comon-Lundh and V. Cortier. New decidability results for fragments of first-order logic and application to cryptographic protocols. In *Proceedings of the 14th International Conference on Rewriting Techniques and Applications (RTA'2003)*, volume 2706 of *LNCS*, pages 148–164, Valencia, Spain, June 2003. Springer-Verlag.
6. H. Comon-Lundh and V. Shmatikov. Intruder deductions, constraint solving and insecurity decision in presence of exclusive or. In *Proc. of 18th Annual IEEE Symposium on Logic in Computer Science (LICS '03)*, pages 271–280, 2003.
7. V. Cortier, G. Keighren, and G. Steel. Automatic analysis of the security of XOR-based key management schemes. Inf. Research Report EDI-INF-RR-0863, U. of Edinburgh, 2006.
8. J. Courant and J.-F. Monin. Defending the bank with a proof assistant. In *Proceedings of Workshop on Issues in the Theory of Security (WITS '06)*, Vienna, March 2006.
9. IBM Comment on "A Chosen Key Difference Attack on Control Vectors", January 2001. Available from http://www.cl.cam.ac.uk/~mkb23/research.html.
10. G. Keighren. Model checking IBM's common cryptographic architecture API. Informatics Research Report EDI-INF-RR-0862, University of Edinburgh, 2006.
11. R. Nieuwenhuis, editor. *Automated Deduction - CADE-20, 20th International Conference on Automated Deduction, Tallinn, Estonia, July 22-27, 2005, Proceedings*, volume 3632 of *Lecture Notes in Computer Science*. Springer, 2005.
12. G. Steel. Deduction with XOR constraints in security API modelling. In Nieuwenhuis [11], pages 322–336.
13. M. Turuani. The CL-Atse Protocol Analyser. In *Proceedings of the 17th International Conference on Rewriting Techniques and Applications (RTA'06)*, volume 4098 of *Lecture Notes in Computer Science*, pages 277–286, Seattle, WA, USA, 2006.
14. K. N. Verma, H. Seidl, and T. Schwentick. On the complexity of equational Horn clauses. In Nieuwenhuis [11], pages 337–352.
15. P. Youn, B. Adida, M. Bond, J. Clulow, J. Herzog, A. Lin, R. Rivest, and R. Anderson. Robbing the bank with a theorem prover. Technical Report UCAM-CL-TR-644, University of Cambridge, August 2005.
16. AVISPA Tool Set. Available from http://www.avispa-project.org/.
17. *AVISPA User Manual, version 1.1*, June 2006. Available online at http://www.avispa-project.org/package/user-manual.pdf.

State of the Union:
Type Inference Via Craig Interpolation[*]

Ranjit Jhala[1], Rupak Majumdar[2], and Ru-Gang Xu[2]

[1] UC San Diego
[2] UC Los Angeles

Abstract. The ad-hoc use of unions to encode disjoint sum types in
C programs and the inability of C's type system to check the safe use
of these unions is a long standing source of subtle bugs. We present
a dependent type system that rigorously captures the ad-hoc protocols
that programmers use to encode disjoint sums, and introduce a novel
technique for automatically inferring, via Craig Interpolation, those dependent types and thus those protocols. In addition to checking the safe
use of unions, the dependent type information inferred by interpolation
gives programmers looking to modify or extend legacy code a precise understanding of the conditions under which some fields may safely be accessed. We present an empirical evaluation of our technique on 350KLOC
of open source C code. In 80 out of 90 predicated edges (corresponding
to 1472 out of 1684 union accesses), our type system is able to infer
the correct dependent types. This demonstrates that our type system
captures and explicates programmers' informal reasoning about unions,
without requiring manual annotation or rewriting.

1 Introduction

We present a type system and inference algorithm for statically checking the
safety of downcasts in imperative programs. Our type system is motivated by
the problem of checking the safety of union accesses in C programs. C programmers extensively use unions to encode disjoint sum types in an ad-hoc
manner. The programmer uses the *value* of a *tag field* to determine which element of the union an instance actually corresponds to. For example, Figure 1
shows networking code that manipulates packets represented as a C structure
(`packet`) which contains an union (`icmp_hun`) representing different types of
packets. The packet is interpreted as a *parameter* message (field `ih_gwaddr`)
when the field `icmp_type` = 12, as a *redirect* message (field `ih_pptr`) when the
field `icmp_type` = 5, and as an *unreachable* message (field `ih_pmtu`) when the
field `icmp_type` = 3. This ad-hoc protocol determining the mapping between tag
values and the union elements is informally documented in the protocol description, but not enforced by the type system. The absence of static checking for the
correctness of these accesses can be a source of subtle bugs.

---

[*] This research was funded in part by the grants NSF-CCF-0427202 and NSF-CCF-
0546170.

O. Grumberg and M. Huth (Eds.): TACAS 2007, LNCS 4424, pp. 553–567, 2007.

The problem of checking the safety of union accesses is an instance of the more general problem of checking the safety of *downcasts* in a language with subtyping —consider each possible "completion" of a structure with the different elements of the union as subtypes of that structure, and view union accesses as downcasts to the appropriate completion. At run-time, each instance of a supertype corresponds to an instance of *one* of its immediate subtypes. To ensure safety, programmers typically associate with each subtype, a *guard predicate* over some tag fields. The predicates for the different subtypes are pairwise inconsistent. Before performing a downcast (*i.e.,* accessing the union), the programmer tests the tag fields to ensure that the corresponding subtype's guard predicate holds, and similarly before performing an upcast (*i.e.,* constructing the union), the programmer sets the tag field to ensure the guard predicate holds.

We formalize this idiom in a type system comprising two ingredients. The first ingredient is a type hierarchy corresponding to a directed tree of types, where the nodes correspond to types, and children to immediate subtypes. The second is a *predicated refinement* of the hierarchy, where the edges of the type hierarchy tree are labeled with *edge predicates* that hold when a supertype can be safely downcast to the subtype corresponding to the target of the edge, and conversely, must be established when the subtype is upcast to the supertype. By requiring that the edge predicates for the different children of a supertype be pairwise inconsistent, we ensure that there is a single subtype of which the supertype is an instance at runtime.

Given a predicated refinement for the subtype hierarchy of the program, we can statically type check the program by verifying that at each occurrence of an upcast or downcast, the edge predicate for the cast holds. Instead of a general invariant generator, we present a simple *syntax-directed* system that is scalable, captures the idiomatic ways in which programmers test fields, and concisely specifies the set of programs that are accepted by our type system. The technique converts the programs to SSA form, and then *conjoins* the statements *dominating* each cast location to obtain a *access predicate* that is an invariant at the cast location. Our type checking algorithm verifies that at each cast location the edge predicate corresponding to the cast holds by using a decision procedure to check that the access predicate *implies* the edge predicate.

We eliminate the burden of explicitly providing the predicated type refinement by devising a technique to infer types via interpolation. Our inference algorithm generates a system of *predicate constraints* with variables representing the unknown edge predicates. These constraints force the solutions for the variables to have the following key properties: (1) they are over the fields of the structure, (2) the edge predicates for the subtypes are pairwise inconsistent, and, (3) the edge predicates hold at each cast point, *i.e.,* at each (up- or down-) cast point, the cast predicate implies the edge predicate. We use *pairwise Craig interpolation*, a variant of Craig interpolation [3,16], to solve these constraints. We show that a predicated refinement exists if for each type, the cast predicates for its subtypes are pairwise inconsistent. Thus, to solve the predicate constraints and infer the predicated refinement, we compute the edge predicates for the subtypes of each type as pairwise interpolants of the corresponding cast predicates.

```
struct packet{
  u_char  icmp_type;
  u_char  icmp_code;
  u_short icmp_cksum;
  union {
    int ih_gwaddr;
    short ih_pptr;
    short ih_pmtu
  } icmp_hun; };
00 int type, dest, code;
01 struct packet icp;
02 . . .
03 type = icp.icmp_type;
04 if (type == 5) {
05   icp.icmp_hun.ih_gwaddr = dest;
06 }
07 else {
08   if (type == 12) {
09     icp.icmp_hun.ih_pptr = 0;
10     code = 0;
11   } else if (type == 3) {
12     icp icmp hun ih pmtu = 0; } }
```

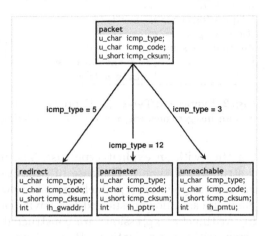

Fig. 1. (a) ICMP Example   (b) (Union) Subtype Hierarchy and its Predicated Refinement

We have implemented the predicated subtype inference algorithm for C, and used it to infer the edge predicates for subtype hierarchies obtained from unions, for a variety of open source C programs totaling 350K lines of code. We empirically show that our inference algorithm is effective. In 80 out of 90 predicated edges (corresponding to 1472 out of 1684 union access points), our algorithm finds the correct predicate guards (which we then manually verified).

2   Language and Type System

We formalize our approach with a core imperative language with simple types. We first describe the language, then define our type system. Our core language capture C programs such as Figure 1(a). In the converted program, union fields are accessed after casting the lvalue down to the subtype containing the field. Thus, the problem of checking the correct use of unions is reduced to that of checking the safety of downcasts.

2.1   Syntax and Semantics

Types. Figure 2(b) shows the types in our language. The set of types include base types **bool** and **int**, and structure types where each structure is defined by a list of fields that are pairs of a label l and a type t. We write **void** as an abbreviation for the type **s**{}. The set of types is equipped with a partial order: we say $t' \preceq t$, or t' is a *subtype* of t, if both t, t' are structures and fields of t are a prefix of the fields of t'. Note that every structure type is a subtype of **void**.

Syntax. Figure 2(a) shows the grammar for expressions and statements in our imperative language. An *lvalue lv* is either an integer, structure or a field access,

```
Lvalues lv      ::= (t)lv.l | (t)v
Expressions e ::= n | new(t) | lv | e₁ ⊕ e₂
Boolean p       ::= e₁ ~ e₂
Statements s ::= skip | lv := e | s₁; s₂
                | if p then s₁ else s₂
                | while p do s₁
```

Types t	$::=$ int $\mid$ bool $\mid s\{m_1, ..., m_k\}$
Fields m	$::= (l, t)$
Declarations	$::= t\ v$

Fig. 2. Syntax and Types. (a) Expressions and Statements (b) Types and Declarations. n is an integer constant, v a variable, l a string label, $\sim \in \{<, >, \leq, \geq, =, \neq\}$.

together with an explicit type cast. The $\text{new}(t)$ statement is used to allocate a structure of type t. For ease of exposition, in our language every lvalue lv includes a type-cast (t) which specifies how lv is interpreted. This captures explicit upcasts, downcasts and the trivial cast to the statically declared type of lv. Arithmetic expressions are constructed from constants and integer lvalues using arithmetic operations. Boolean expressions comprise arithmetic comparisons. Statements are skip (or no-op), assignments, sequential composition, conditionals, and while loops. A program P is a tuple (T, Γ_0, s) where T is a set of types, Γ_0 is a map from the program lvalues to their declared types, and s is a statement corresponding to the body of the program. While we present the intraprocedural, pointer-free case, our implementation, described in Section 5, handles both procedures and pointers.

Static Single Assignment Form. For convenience in describing the type checking and type inference rules, we shall assume that the programs are converted to static single assignment (SSA) form [4], where each variable in the program is written exactly once. Programs in SSA form have special Φ-assignment operations of the form $lv := \Phi(lv_1, \ldots, lv_\ell)$ that capture the effect of control flow joins. A Φ-assignment $lv := \Phi(lv_1, \ldots, lv_n)$ for lvalues $lv, lv_1, \ldots, lv_n$ at a node $\mathbf{n}$ implies: (1) $\mathbf{n}$ has exactly n predecessors in the control flow graph, (2) if control arrives at $\mathbf{n}$ from its jth predecessor, then lv has the value lv_j at the beginning of $\mathbf{n}$. Formally, we extend the syntax with Φ-assignments:

$$\text{Statements } s ::= \ldots \mid lv := \Phi(lv_1, \ldots, lv_n)$$

We assume that the program has first been transformed into SSA form. We describe type checking and inference on programs in this form.

Semantics. We define the operational semantics of the language using a store and a memory in the standard way but additionally taking into account the run-time type information [15]. We assume a *store* Σ mapping variables to values, a partial mapping *memory* M from addresses to values, and a partial mapping *run-time type information* (RTTI) W from variables and addresses to types. When a structure is created during execution using the $\text{new}(t)$ operation, it is tagged with the (leaf) type t that remains with it during the remainder of the execution. This value can be cast up or down along the path from the leaf t to the root type void, and any attempt to downcast it to a type not along this path leads the program into a "stuck" state. The (small step) operational semantics is defined using a relation $(\Sigma, M, W; s) \to (\Sigma', M', W'; s')$. The rules take into account the RTTI W, and execution gets "stuck" if a bad cast is made (i.e., an lvalue is cast to a type incompatible with its RTTI). We write $\to^*$ for the reflexive transitive closure of $\to$. For store Σ, memory M, RTTI W, and statement s, we say $(\Sigma, M, W; s)$ *diverges* if there is an infinite sequence $(\Sigma, M, W; s) \to (\Sigma_1, M_1, W_1; s_1) \to \ldots$. We say $(\Sigma, M, W; s)$ is *stuck* if (1) s is not skip, and (2) there is no $(\Sigma', M', W'; s')$ such that $(\Sigma, M, W; s) \to (\Sigma', M', W'; s')$.

2.2 Predicated Refinements of Subtype Hierarchies

Programs in our language are type checked by the standard typing rules dealing with booleans, integers and structures. However, we also want to show that each runtime downcast executes safely. To do so, we assume we are given a *predicated refinement* of the subtype hierarchy of the program.

Subtype Hierarchy. A *Subtype Hierarchy* is a forest (T, E) where *nodes* correspond to a set of types T, and *edges* $E \subseteq T \times T$ are such that $(t, t') \in E$ if t' is the immediate subtype of t, i.e., $t' \preceq t$ and there is no t'' such that $t' \preceq t''$ and $t'' \preceq t$. Consider the structure definition of the program in Figure 1(a). We can "unroll" the union definition to obtain three subtypes of the type packet, namely redirect, parameter and unreachable, which correspond, respectively to instances of packet where the union field is a ih_gwaddr, ih_pptr or ih_pmtu. Thus, as shown in Figure 1(b), each of the subtypes is a structure containing all the fields of the supertype packet together with the extra field from the union. In this setting, $l' \preceq l$ if the fields of l form a prefix of the fields of l'.

Therefore, we reduce the problem of checking the safety of union accesses to checking the safety of *downcasts* in our system by converting each union access into a downcast to the subtype containing the particular union field being accessed, followed by a standard field access on the subtype. Next, we see how to *refine* the subtype hierarchy to enable the static checking of the safety of downcasts and thus, union accesses.

Predicated Refinement and Tags. We say that (T, E, ϕ) is a *predicated (refinement of the) subtype hierarchy* (T, E) if ϕ is a map from the edges E to first-order *edge predicates* such that:

R1. For each edge $(t, t') \in E$, the edge predicate $\phi(t, t')$ has one free variable this that refers to a structure of type t, i.e., all variables are fields of the structure of type t.

R2. For each node $t \in T$, for each pair of its children t', t'' the predicates $\phi(t, t')$ and $\phi(t, t'')$ are inconsistent, i.e., $\phi(t, t') \wedge \phi(t, t'')$ is *unsatisfiable*.

The tag fields of a type t are the fields that occur in the edge predicates for any edge in the subtree rooted at t in the subtype hierarchy. Formally, the *tag fields* of $t \in T$ are defined as $\mathrm{tag}(t, \phi) \equiv \{l \mid \exists t' \preceq t : this.l$ occurs in $\phi(\cdot, t')\}$.

We use the predicate refinement to statically check the safety of downcasts and thus, union accesses. A predicated refinement captures the intuition that the programmer performs a downcast from t to t' only when a certain "tag" condition on the fields of t is met, and this tag condition is disjoint from the conditions under which downcasts are made from t to subtypes other than t'. Our type system checks that the first time a leaf type structure is upcast, the edge predicate for the structure holds, and that subsequently, the fields occurring in the edge predicate are not modified. As this is done for all structures, and the edge predicates for different downcasts are disjoint, we can statically deduce that if the edge predicate for that subtype holds at the downcast point, the downcast is safe. In Figure 1(b) each edge of the subtype hierarchy is labeled with its edge predicate. For example, `ih_gwaddr` field can be safely accessed only after the `packet` structure has been downcast to `redirect`, which is permissible only when the `icmp_type` field equals 5.

3   Type Checking

Informally, a program is type safe when all structures of type t (created by $new(t)$) are accessed only as the type t or a supertype of t. Given a predicated subtype hierarchy (T, E, ϕ), a program is type safe if the hierarchy meets requirements **R1**, **R2**, and at each point in the program where an expression **e** of type t is cast to the type t', we have: (1) either t' is a supertype of t, *i.e.,* we have an upcast, or (2) t' is a subtype of t, *i.e.,* we have a downcast. In either case, the predicate obtained by substituting **this** with the variable **e** in the edge predicate $\phi(t, t')$ holds at that point. Thus, to type check the program, the edge predicates must satisfy:

R3. The edge predicate $\phi(t, t')$ with **this** substituted with **e** must hold at each program location where an expression **e** is downcast from a type t to a subtype t', or upcast from t' to t.

R4. The tag fields of the structure t are not modified.

Our type checking algorithm proceeds in three steps. First, we use standard type checking to verify that each field access is to a field in the type of the expression, and that each cast conforms to the subtype hierarchy, *i.e.,* is either an upcast to a supertype or a downcast to a subtype. Second, we use a decision procedure to check that the edge predicates satisfy requirements **R1**, **R2**. Third, we perform a flow sensitive analysis to check that the edge predicates hold at each upcast or downcast. We now describe the last step in detail.

Judgments. A *judgment* in the type system for a statement s is of the form $\Gamma, \phi, I \vdash s \triangleright I'$. The judgment states: using the edge predicate map ϕ from the predicated subtype hierarchy (T, E, ϕ), we can deduce that if the program begins execution from a state satisfying the type environment Γ and the precondition I, the execution of a statement s proceeds without getting stuck (cast errors) and results in a state satisfying postcondition I'.

Our syntax-directed *derivation rules* for inferring type judgments are shown in Figure 3. At each cast point, the rules check, using a decision procedure, that the invariants imply the corresponding edge predicate. A typing rule transforms the invariant by adding the effect of the current statement on the invariant. Since our program is in SSA form, we have an invariant by taking the conjunction of the predicate representing the current statement with the previous derived invariant [12,6]. Assignments are represented by equality as shown in rules Var-Assign and Field-Assign in Figure 3). The latter rule also stipulates that tag fields should not be assigned to, once the structure has been upcast. The rule permits the usual C idiom of appropriately "initializing" the structure by setting the data and tag fields *before* casting up to the supertype, as the tag field only appears on the parent edge of the subtype, and not in the edges of the subtree rooted at the subtype. Conditionals on some predicate p are represented by p on **then** branch and $\neg p$ on the else branch (rule If in Figure 3).

Example 1. In Figure 1, consider the implicit cast (at the union access) from **packet** (t) to the redirect message (t') at line **05**. The statement 05 is dominated by the **then** branch at 04 and the assignment 03, and so the invariant at 05 is:

$$(\texttt{icp.icmp\_type} = \texttt{type}) \wedge (\texttt{type} = 5) \tag{1}$$

Similarly, the invariants at 09 and 11 are respectively:

$$(\texttt{icp.icmp\_type} = \texttt{type}) \wedge (\texttt{type} \neq 5) \wedge (\texttt{type} = 12), \text{ and,}$$
$$(\texttt{icp.icmp\_type} = \texttt{type}) \wedge (\texttt{type} \neq 5) \wedge (\texttt{type} \neq 12) \wedge (\texttt{type} = 3)$$

Thus, for each statement s where a downcast or upcast occurs, we compute, using the constraints generated by the type checking rules, the invariant at s.

Checking using Access Predicates. From the invariant, we construct an *access predicate* $\psi_s(t, t')$ by syntactically renaming all local variables in the invariant to fresh names, and renaming the cast expression with **this**. By replacing icp with **this** and type with a fresh, subscripted version, we have the access predicate $\psi_{05}(\texttt{packet}, \texttt{redirect})$:

$$\texttt{this.icmp\_type} = \texttt{type}_1 \wedge \texttt{type}_1 = 5 \tag{2}$$

To ensure that condition **R3** is met, we use a decision procedure[5] to check that at each downcast s of t to a subtype t', or upcast of t' to t, the access predicate $\psi_s(t, t')$ *implies* the edge predicate $\phi(t, t')$ (Rules Var-Up, Var-Down in Figure 3). So, for the downcast of icp from **packet** to **redirect** at line 05, we use a decision procedure to check the validity of the implication: $\texttt{this.icmp\_type} = \texttt{type}_1 \wedge \texttt{type}_1 = 5 \Rightarrow (\texttt{this.icmp\_type} = 5)$. In the given code snippet, at each downcast statement (there are no upcasts), the access predicate implies the corresponding edge predicate and so we conclude that the program is type safe.

Intuitively, the soundness of our type system follows from the following observations. First, we ensure that every new structure is a "leaf" of the type hierarchy. Thus, at run time, any instance that is ever downcast, must have been upcast to at some point in the past. Second, our type system ensures that the tag fields are not altered, and therefore, any edge predicate that held at the upcast in the past, will continue to hold till the downcast. Thus, by checking the edge predicates at upcasts, and by requiring that edge predicates for sibling

$$\frac{\Gamma(x) = t \qquad t' \preceq t \qquad \boxed{I[\texttt{this}/x] \Rightarrow \phi(t, t')}}{\Gamma, \phi, I \vdash_l (t')x : t'} \text{ Var-Down}$$

$$\frac{\Gamma(x) = t' \qquad t' \preceq t \qquad \boxed{I[\texttt{this}/x] \Rightarrow \phi(t, t')}}{\Gamma, \phi, I \vdash_l (t)x : t} \text{ Var-Up}$$

$$\frac{\Gamma, \phi, I \vdash_e e : t \qquad \Gamma, \phi, I \vdash_l (t)x : t}{\Gamma, \phi, I \vdash (t)x := e \triangleright I \wedge (lv = e)} \text{ Var-Assign}$$

$$\frac{\Gamma, \phi, I \vdash_e e : t}{\Gamma, \phi, I \vdash_e (t)lv.l : t \qquad \Gamma', \phi, I \vdash_l lv : t' \qquad l \notin \mathsf{tag}(t', \phi)}{\Gamma, \phi, I \vdash (t)lv.l := e \triangleright I \wedge (lv.l = e)} \text{ Field-Assign}$$

$$\frac{\Gamma, \phi, I \vdash_l lv_i : t \text{ for all } i \qquad \Gamma, \phi, I \vdash_l lv : t}{\Gamma, \phi, I \vdash lv := \Phi(lv_1, \dots, lv_n) \triangleright I} \text{ Assign-}\Phi$$

$$\frac{\Gamma, \phi, I \vdash_e p : \texttt{bool} \qquad \Gamma, \phi, I \wedge p \vdash s \triangleright I' \qquad \Gamma, \phi, I \wedge \neg p \vdash s' \triangleright I''}{\Gamma, \phi, I \vdash \texttt{if } p \texttt{ then } s \texttt{ else } s' \triangleright I} \text{ If}$$

$$\frac{\Gamma, \phi, I \vdash_e p : \texttt{bool} \qquad \Gamma, \phi, I \wedge p \vdash s \triangleright I'}{\Gamma, \phi, I \vdash \texttt{while } p \texttt{ do } s \triangleright I \wedge \neg p} \text{ While}$$

Fig. 3. Relevant type checking rules. Hypotheses in boxes correspond to queries to the decision procedure made in the checking phase, or the predicate constraints in the inference phase. A complete set of rules is in [11].

edges be pairwise inconsistent, our type system ensures there is an unique subtype that each supertype value is an instance of (and therefore, can be safely downcast to), namely the subtype whose edge predicate holds at the downcast point.

4   Type Inference Via Interpolation

In the previous section, we assumed that we were *given* a predicated refinement of the subtype hierarchy with which the program could be type checked to ensure statically that all casts were safe. In practice, these annotations are not available. We now present an algorithm that given a program and the subtype hierarchy, *automatically infers* a predicated refinement of the hierarchy such that the program type checks, if indeed the program is type safe. In other words, given a program (T, Γ_0, s), the inference algorithm computes an edge predicate map ϕ that satisfies conditions **R1-R4** or reports that no such map exists, *i.e.*, the program is not type safe.

To find the predicate map ϕ, we introduce, for each edge (t, t') induced by $\preceq$, a *predicate variable* $\pi_{t,t'}$. Next, using the syntax-directed type checking rules, we generate a set of *predicate constraints* on the predicate variables, such that a solution for the constraints will give us edge predicates that satisfy **R1-R4**. Finally, we describe how to solve the constraints and thus infer ϕ.

4.1 Generating Predicate Constraints

We use the syntax-directed typing rules of Figure 3 to generate the predicate constraints. The constraint generation is done in two phases.

In the first phase, we make a syntax-directed pass over the program to compute the set of fields that *cannot* be tag fields because they are modified *after* an upcast. This information is captured by computing a map $\overline{\mathsf{tag}}(t)$ from types t to the sets of fields that cannot be used in the edge predicates for edges $(t, \cdot)$.

In the second phase, we use type checking rules to compute the invariants at each access point. For a predicate I and a set of field names F, and a location s, define $\mathsf{rename}(I, F, s)$ as the predicate where all occurrences of free variables x other than `this` are substituted with a fresh name x_s and all occurrences of field names $l \in F$ are substituted with a fresh name l_s. At each downcast and upcast location s, *i.e.,* where one of the rules Var-Down, Var-Up (Figure 3) applies, instead of checking that the access predicate $I[\mathtt{this}/lv]$ implies the edge predicate for the cast, we introduce a predicate constraint:

$$\mathsf{rename}(I[\mathtt{this}/lv], \overline{\mathsf{tag}}(t), s) \Rightarrow \pi_{t,t'}$$

We call the LHS of the constraint above the *renamed access predicate* at location s. The renaming does not get in the way of inferring appropriate ϕ as the fields in $\overline{\mathsf{tag}}(t)$ cannot appear in $\phi(t, t')$. Instead, it will force the inferred predicates to not contain the fields in $\overline{\mathsf{tag}}(t)$, thus yielding a ϕ that suffices to type check the program, if one exists. Given a program $P \equiv (T, \Gamma_0, s)$, let $\mathsf{Cons}(P)$ be the set of predicate constraints generated by the algorithm described above.

We can always make the only upcasts and downcasts in the program be between immediate subtypes. Thus, the constraint generation introduces predicate constraints for $\pi_{t,t'}$ for edges $(t, t') \in E$.

Example 2. The downcast on line 05 in Figure 1(a) generates the constraint:

$$(\mathtt{type}_{05} = \mathtt{this.icmp\_type} \wedge \mathtt{type}_{05} = 5) \Rightarrow \pi_{\mathtt{packet},\mathtt{redirect}}$$

Similarly, the downcasts on line 09 and 12 generate constraints:

$$(\mathtt{type}_{09} = \mathtt{this.icmp\_type} \wedge \mathtt{type}_{09} \neq 5 \wedge \mathtt{type}_{09} = 12) \Rightarrow \pi_{\mathtt{packet},\mathtt{parameter}}$$
$$(\mathtt{type}_{12} = \mathtt{this.icmp\_type} \wedge \mathtt{type}_{12} \neq 5 \wedge \mathtt{type}_{12} \neq 12 \wedge \mathtt{type}_{12} = 3) \Rightarrow \pi_{\mathtt{packet},\mathtt{unreachable}}$$

Notice that the substitution renames `icp` to `this` and the variable `type` in each constraint.

Solutions. A *solution* to a set of constraints $\mathsf{Cons}(P)$ is a mapping Π from each predicate variable $\pi_{t,t'}$ to a predicate such that:

S1. For each predicate variable $\pi_{t,t'}$, the predicate $\Pi(\pi_{t,t'})$ has a single free variable `this`.

S2. For each triple t, t', t'', the predicates $\Pi(\pi_{t,t'})$ and $\Pi(\pi_{t,t''})$ are inconsistent.

S3. For each constraint $\psi_s \Rightarrow \pi_{t,t'}$ in $\mathsf{Cons}(P)$, the implication $\psi_s \Rightarrow \Pi(\pi_{t,t'})$ is valid.

S4. For each t, t', the predicate $\Pi(\pi_{t,t'})$ should not contain any field name in $\overline{\mathsf{tag}}(t)$.

Every solution Π for the set of constraints $\mathsf{Cons}(P)$, yields a predicated subtype hierarchy for P with which we can prove the safety of P.

Theorem 1 [Soundness of Constraint Generation]. *For every program* $P \equiv (T, \Gamma_0, s)$, *if* Π *is a solution for the constraints* $\mathsf{Cons}(P)$ *then* $\phi \equiv \lambda(t, t').\Pi(\pi_{t,t'})$ *is such that:* $\Gamma_0, \phi, true \vdash s \rhd \cdot$.

4.2 Solving Predicate Constraints

We now give an algorithm to find a solution to a set of constraints $\mathsf{Cons}(P)$ if one exists. We define for each edge $(t, t') \in E$ a *cast predicate* $\psi(t, t')$ as:

$$\psi(t, t') \equiv \bigvee_{\psi_s \Rightarrow \pi_{t,t'} \in \mathsf{Cons}(P)} \psi_s$$

The cast predicate for an edge is the disjunction over all the renamed access predicates ψ_s for the locations where a t is downcast to t' or a t' is upcast to t. Note that by the properties of disjunction and implication, a map Π from the type variables to predicates is a solution for the constraints $\mathsf{Cons}(P)$ iff it satisfies conditions **S1, S2** and **S4**, and in addition

S3' For each (t, t') we have $\psi(t, t') \Rightarrow \Pi(\pi_{t,t'})$.

For each $\psi_s \Rightarrow \pi_{t,t'}$ we have $\psi_s \Rightarrow \psi(t, t')$ as the RHS cast predicate is the disjunction of all the corresponding access predicates ψ_s. Thus, by the properties of disjunction and implication, any solution Π satisfies requirement **S3'** iff it satisfies **S3**.

Existence of a Solution. A solution can only exist if for each triple t, t', t'', the conjunction $\psi(t, t') \wedge \psi(t, t'')$ is unsatisfiable. If not, *i.e.*, if there are t, t', t'' such that: $\psi(t, t') \wedge \psi(t, t'')$ is satisfiable, then for any candidate solution such that $\psi(t, t') \Rightarrow \Pi(\pi_{t,t'})$ and $\psi(t, t'') \Rightarrow \Pi(\pi_{t,t''})$, the conjunction $\Pi(\pi_{t,t'}) \wedge \Pi(\pi_{t,t''})$ is satisfiable, thus violating **S2**. Intuitively, if the conjunction of the cast predicates for t', t'' is satisfiable, it means that there is some condition under which the program casts to (or from) type t' as well as to (or from) t'' thus one of those casts may be unsafe, or depends on a modified field *i.e.*, a field in $\overline{\mathsf{tag}}(t)$. In this case, the type inference fails with an error message declaring a *conflict* and pointing out the two conflicting casts.

Constraint Solving Via Interpolation. Dually, we show that if for each triple t, t', t'' the cast predicates $\psi(t, t')$ and $\psi(t, t'')$ are inconsistent, then

---

Algorithm 1. PredTypeInference

Input: Program $P = (T, \Gamma_0, s)$
Output: Refinement (T, E, ϕ) or ERROR
$E =$ edges induced by $\preceq$ on T; $C = \text{Cons}(P)$
for all $(t, t') \in E$ **do** $\psi(t, t') = \vee\{\psi_s \mid \psi_s \Rightarrow \pi_{t,t'} \in C\}$
for all $t \in T$ with immediate subtypes $t_1, \ldots, t_n$ **do**
  if $\psi(t, t_1) \wedge \ldots \wedge \psi(t, t_n)$ is unsatisfiable **then**
    $\phi(t, t_1), \ldots, \phi(t, t_n) := \text{ITP}(\psi(t, t_1), \ldots, \psi(t, t_n))$
  else return ERROR
return (T, E, ϕ)

---

through Craig interpolation [3] we can infer a solution to the constraints, and thus a predicated subtype hierarchy that suffices to type check the program. Given a sequence of predicates $A_1, \ldots, A_n$ such that for all i, j, the predicate $A_i \wedge A_j$ is unsatisfiable, a *pairwise interpolant* for the sequence is the sequence $\hat{A}_1, \ldots, \hat{A}_n \equiv \text{ITP}(A_1, \ldots, A_n)$ such that **(I1)** For each i, the variables of $\hat{A}_i$ occur in each of $A_1, \ldots, A_n$, **(I2)** for each pair i, j, the predicate $\hat{A}_i \wedge \hat{A}_j$ is unsatisfiable, and **(I3)** for each i, the implication $A_i \Rightarrow \hat{A}_i$ is valid. For predicates over theories of equality and arithmetic, pairwise interpolants can be computed from the *proof of unsatisfiability* of conjunctions of two predicates [16].

For each node $t \in T$ with immediate subtypes $t_1, \ldots, t_n$, we define:

$$\Pi(t, t_1), \ldots, \Pi(t, t_n) \equiv \text{ITP}(\psi(t, t_1), \ldots, \psi(t, t_n))$$

The properties of pairwise interpolants suffice to show that Π is indeed a solution to the constraints $\text{Cons}(P)$. The only variable common to $\psi(t, t_1), \ldots, \psi(t, t_n)$ is `this` and hence, by **I1** each $\Pi(t, t')$ contains the sole free variable `this`, thus enforcing requirement **S1**. In addition, as we renamed all the fields in $\overline{\text{tag}}(t)$, there is no field name in $\overline{\text{tag}}(t)$ that is in any $\psi(t, t')$ and thus Π meets condition **S4**. Property **I2** of interpolants ensure requirement **S2**. Finally, property **I3** of interpolants ensures requirement **S3'** and hence, **S3**.

By Theorem 1, we have inferred an edge map ϕ and thus, a predicated subtype hierarchy that suffices to show that all casts are safe. The inference algorithm runs in time linear in the number of constraints, and thus, the program, and makes linear (in the size of T) calls to an interpolating decision procedure.

We summarize the predicated type inference algorithm PredTypeInference in Algorithm 1. The correctness of the algorithm is stated in the following theorem.

Theorem 2 [Correctness of Type Inference]. *For every program* $P \equiv (T, \Gamma_0, s)$, PredTypeInference$(P)$ *terminates. If* PredTypeInference(P) *returns* (T, E, ϕ) *then* $\Gamma_0, \phi, true \vdash s \rhd \cdot$. *If* PredTypeInference$(P)$ *returns* ERROR *then there is no* ϕ *such that* $\Gamma_0, \phi, true \vdash s \rhd \cdot$.

Example 3. For the constraints from Example 2, we get the cast predicates:

$\psi(\texttt{packet}, \texttt{redirect})$ $\texttt{type}_{05} = \texttt{this.icmp\_type} \wedge \texttt{type}_{05} = 5$
$\psi(\texttt{packet}, \texttt{unreachable})$ $\texttt{type}_{09} = \texttt{this.icmp\_type} \wedge \texttt{type}_{09} \neq 5 \wedge \texttt{type}_{09} = 12$
$\psi(\texttt{packet}, \texttt{parameter})$ $\texttt{type}_{12} = \texttt{this.icmp\_type} \wedge \texttt{type}_{12} \neq 5 \wedge \texttt{type}_{12} \neq 12 \wedge \texttt{type}_{12} = 3$

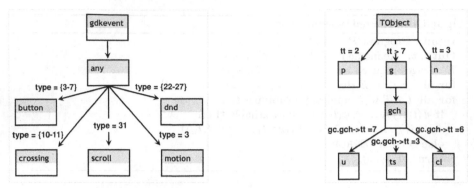

Fig. 4. Predicate subtype hierarchy for (a)gdkevent (b)lua

The only common names are `this` and the allowed fields. The pairwise interpolant of these predicates yields the edge predicates: `this.type` = 5, `this.type` = 12 and `this.type` = 3.

5 Implementation and Experiences

Implementation. We have implemented the predicated type inference algorithm for C. We use CIL [17] to parse and manipulate the C program, the structural invariant package [12] to generate constraints, and the theorem prover FOCI [16] to generate interpolants and check implications at cast locations. We first use physical subtyping [20] to get subtyping hierarchy based on structural prefixes. Next we model union accesses as casts. We add types representing each field in an union. If a structure t contains a union $t.u$ with fields f_i, we create a immediate subtype t'_i representing the same structure t but only allowing access to $t.u.f_i$. In the implementation, access to the union field $t.u.f_i$ is the same as a downcast from t to t'_i. We extend the invariants generation algorithm as described previously with pointers and functions using the techniques in [12].

Experimental Results. We summarize our experimental results on nine open source programs in Table 1. Our algorithm identified 1,684 downcasts requiring predicate guards. These accesses were determined by a predicated subtyping hierarchy of 90 edges. We were able to infer 77 predicate edges corresponding to union fields correctly. We also correctly inferred the 3 predicate edges corresponding to explicit C type casts in `moapsource`. Our tool can derive complex predicated subtyping hierarchies. Figure 4 shows partially the two predicated subtyping hierarchies for `gdkevent` and `lua`. Some subtypes are dropped because of space. Note that predicate edges are not simply single tag assignments but rather more complex predicates involving ranges.

Conflicts and Bugs. There are two sources of conflicts: casts on edges for which the predicated access idiom is not followed, and casts on edges where a predicate was inferred but where the generated access predicate was not strong enough to establish the edge predicate.

Table 1. Experimental Results: **LOC** is lines of code. **Time** is the number of seconds spent on inference. **Predicate Edges** is the number of predicated edges in the predicated subtype hierarchy. **Inferred** is the number such edges for which our tool inferred an edge predicate, and **Actual** is the number of edges constructed by manual inspection of the code. **Accesses** is the number of predicated cast points. Experiments were run on a Dell PowerEdge 1800 with two 3.6GHz processors and 5GB memory.

Program	Description	LOC	Predicate Edges		Accesses	Time
			Inferred	Actual		
ip_icmp	FreeBSD ICMP	7K	7	7	15	1s
xl	SPEC Lisp interpreter	12K	8	8	428	875s
moapsource	Emstar packet processor	14K	3	3	5	1s
gdkevent	GDK events	16K	12	13	90	38s
lua	Lua compiler	18K	13	15	274	151s
snort	Intrusion detector	42K	7	7	26	12s
sendmail	Mail server	106K	17	24	406	995s
ssh	Secure shell	35K	0	0	0	12s
bash	Bourne again shell	101K	13	13	440	1157s
Total		351K	80	90	1684	3242s

For the first case, we use the following heuristic to determine which edges have no predicates. Given a type node, if *all* cast instances of an outgoing predicate edge conflict with all cast instance of any other outgoing predicate edge, then we conclude that type node has no guards. An example of this is the memset macro which uses a union to access different bytes in memory. Our heuristic correctly distinguishes all such accesses from predicated casts.

For the second case, when the access predicate was not strong enough to imply the edge predicate, the downcast instance typically conflicted with many other downcast instances. Here either our generated invariant was too weak, the predicate guard used variables that were not allowed, or there was a bug. For the cases where our invariants are too weak, more precise invariant generators (e.g., Blast [10]) can be used to statically verify that the edge predicates hold at the cast points, or alternatively, dynamic checking can be inserted to ensure type-safety at runtime [18,7,15]. One bug is when the programmer forget to check the predicate before the access, leaving the possibility of an unsafe access. For example, there are 23 cases in Lua where two different variables are assumed to have the same predicate hold. An union field in one of those variables is accessed after the appropriate predicate is checked. However, the same union field in the other variable is also accessed without checking if the appropriate predicate holds as well. That is, there is an unchecked assumption that two different variables always satisfy the same predicate.

6   Related Work

Language support. Functional programming languages like ML and Haskell provide disjoint sum types within the language. The Cyclone language [13] provides mechanisms such as sum types and subtyping within C, allowing safer programs to be written within a C-like language. Our goal on the other hand is to check for safe usage in a large body of legacy code written in C or in low level code where bytes "off the wire" must be cast to proper data types (as in networking code).

Static analysis. There is a large body of recent work on statically proving memory safety of C programs (augmented with adding runtime checks) to make them execute safely [15,18,2]. CCured [18] performs a pointer-kind inference and adds runtime checks to make C programs memory safe. However, CCured leaves open the question of statically checking proper usage of unions or downcasts of pointers: either putting in additional tags or removing unions altogether and replacing them with structures. The former technique ignores checks the programmer already has in place, the latter technique may not work for applications such as network packet processors where the data layout cannot be changed. Runtime type information has been used for bug finding and providing debugging information for bad casts or union access [15], but the inference problem was not studied. Identifying correct use of datatypes in the presence of memory layout and casts has been studied in [2,20]. However, these type systems do not correlate guards to ensure correctness of downcasts.

Dependent types. There is substantial previous work in dependent types [22,9,21]. The predicate subtyping scheme of PVS [19] is more general than our system. All these systems require interactive theorem proving as the type systems are undecidable. By restricting our target properties and proof strategies, we provide an automatic mechanism. Closer to our work, [9] provides dependent record types to encode safety properties such as array bound checks and null pointer dereferences. The type system of [8] infers dependent types for representing ML values passed to C programs through the foreign language interface. Unlike our algorithm, they fix a set of dataflow facts for the guards.

Our type system is closest to the type systems in [1] and [14]. The type system in [1] only tracks the evaluation of ML-style pattern-matching statements. Our type system tracks all assignments and conditionals dominating the access. In [14], the authors consider the problem of identifying record types and guarded disjoint unions in COBOL programs. However, both approaches infer types by using a dataflow analysis to track equalities between variables and constants appearing in branch statements. In many of our experiments we have found that this simple language of guards is insufficient (because, for example, programmers use guards of the form $tag \geq 5$). Further, the problem of identifying guards in terms of the *in scope* fields is not considered.

Acknowledgments. We thank Todd Millstein and Pat Rondon for carefully reading drafts and providing valuable feedback.

References

1. A. Aiken, E. Wimmers, and T.K. Lakshman. Soft typing with conditional types. In *POPL 94*, pages 163–173. ACM, 1994.
2. S. Chandra and T. Reps. Physical type checking for c. In *PASTE 99*, pages 66–75. ACM, 1999.
3. W. Craig. Linear reasoning. *J. Symbolic Logic*, 22:250–268, 1957.
4. R. Cytron, J. Ferrante, B.K. Rosen, M.N. Wegman, and F.K. Zadek. Efficiently computing static single assignment form and the program dependence graph. *ACM TOPLAS*, 13:451–490, 1991.
5. D. Detlefs, G. Nelson, and J.B. Saxe. Simplify: a theorem prover for program checking. *J. ACM*, 52(3):365–473, 2005.
6. Y. Fang. *Translation validation of optimizing compilers*. PhD thesis, New York University, 2005.
7. C. Flanagan. Hybrid type checking. In *POPL 06*, pages 245–256. ACM, 2006.
8. M. Furr and J. Foster. Checking type safety of foreign function calls. In *PLDI 05*, pages 62–72. ACM, 2005.
9. M. Harren and G.C. Necula. Using dependent types to certify the safety of assembly code. In *SAS 05*, LNCS 3672, pages 155–170. Springer, 2005.
10. T.A. Henzinger, R. Jhala, R. Majumdar, and G. Sutre. Lazy abstraction. In *POPL 02*, pages 58–70. ACM, 2002.
11. R. Jhala, R. Majumdar, and R. Xu. Type inference using Craig interpolation. Technical Report. UCLA Computer Science Department, 2007.
12. R. Jhala, R. Majumdar, and R. Xu. Structural invariants. In *SAS 06*, LNCS 4134, pages 71–87. Springer, 2006.
13. T. Jim, J.G. Morrisett, D. Grossman, M.W. Hicks, J. Cheney, and Y. Wang. Cyclone: A safe dialect of C. In *Usenix Tech. Conf.*, pages 257–288. 2002.
14. R. Komondoor, G. Ramalingam, S. Chandra, and J. Fields. Dependent types for program understanding. In *TACAS 05*, LNCS 3440, pages 157–173. Springer, 2005.
15. A. Loginov, S. Yong, S. Horwitz, and T. Reps. Debugging via run-time type checking. In *FASE 01*, LNCS 2029, pages 217–232. Springer, 2001.
16. K.L. McMillan. An interpolating theorem prover. *TCS*, 345:101–121, 2005.
17. G. C. Necula, S. McPeak, S. P. Rahul, and W. Weimer. CIL: Intermediate language and tools for analysis and transformation of C programs. In *CC 02*, LNCS 2304, pages 213–228. Springer, 2002.
18. G.C. Necula, J. Condit, M. Harren, S. McPeak, and W. Weimer. CCured: type-safe retrofitting of legacy software. *ACM TOPLAS*, 27(3):477–526, 2005.
19. J.M. Rushby, S. Owre, and N. Shankar. Subtypes for specifications: Predicate subtyping in PVS. *IEEE Trans. Software Eng.*, 24(9):709–720, 1998.
20. M. Siff, S. Chandra, T. Ball, K. Kunchithapadam, and T. Reps. Coping with type casts in C. In *ESEC/FSE 99*, pages 180–198. ACM, 1999.
21. H. Xi and R. Harper. A dependently typed assembly language. In *ICFP 01*, pages 169–180. ACM, 2001.
22. H. Xi and F. Pfenning. Dependent types in practical programming. In *POPL 99*, pages 214–227. ACM, 1999.

Hoare Logic for Realistically Modelled Machine Code

Magnus O. Myreen and Michael J.C. Gordon

Computer Laboratory, University of Cambridge, Cambridge, UK

Abstract. This paper presents a mechanised Hoare-style programming logic framework for assembly level programs. The framework has been designed to fit on top of operational semantics of realistically modelled machine code. Many *ad hoc* restrictions and features present in real machine-code are handled, including finite memory, data and code in the same memory space, the behavior of status registers and hazards of corrupting special purpose registers (e.g. the program counter, procedure return register and stack pointer). Despite accurately modeling such low level details, the approach yields concise specifications for machine-code programs without using common simplifying assumptions (like an unbounded state space). The framework is based on a flexible state representation in which functional and resource usage specifications are written in a style inspired by separation logic. The presented work has been formalised in higher-order logic, mechanised in the HOL4 system and is currently being used to verify ARM machine-code implementations of arithmetic and cryptographic operations.

1   Introduction

Computer programs execute on machines where stacks have limits, integers are bounded and programs are stored in the same memory as data. However, verification of computer programs is almost without exception done using highly simplified models, where stacks and memory are unbounded, integers are arbitrarily large and the compilers are trusted to keep code and data apart. Proving properties of programs with respect to realistic models is generally avoided, since it is tedious as many of the common simplifying assumptions made by high-level programming logics tend to fit badly with realities of accurate low-level models. In this paper we present a programming logic that has been designed to fit on top of accurate models of machine languages.

We present a Hoare logic that has been carefully designed to accommodate many of the *ad hoc* restrictions and features of machine code: finite memory, data and code in the same memory space, the behaviour of status register, hazards of corrupting special purpose registers and some details that arise from hardware implementations. As an example of a restriction imposed by the underlying hardware, consider the following two seemingly equivalent implementations of the factorial program in ARM assembly. The example uses the ARM instructions "MOV b, #1" (set register b to 1), "MUL c, a, b" (put the product of

O. Grumberg and M. Huth (Eds.): TACAS 2007, LNCS 4424, pp. 568–582, 2007.

the contents of registers a and b into register c, but see restrictions discussed shortly), "SUBS a, a, #1" (subtract 1 from register a and update status bits so that status bit Z is assigned the boolean expression a-1=0) and "BNE L" (jump to L if status bit Z is 0).

```
       MOV   b, #1                MOV   b, #1
  L:   MUL   b, a, b         L:   MUL   b, b, a
       SUBS  a, a, #1             SUBS  a, a, #1
       BNE   L                    BNE   L
```

The first implementation terminates with the factorial of a (modulo 2^{32}) in b, while the other one has an unpredictable outcome, "MUL b, b, a" is specified as 'unpredictable' for ARM in order to accommodate hardware optimisations [15]. Thus "MUL c, a, b" cannot be modelled as $c := a \times b$ without a side condition.

The judgments of our framework are total-correctness specifications that state the functional behaviour and resource usage of machine-code programs. We use a separating conjunction, similar to that of separation logic [13], in order to write concise specifications about resource usage as well as to avoid unwanted aliasing between special purpose registers (and normal registers as motivated above). Our specifications allow multiple code segments and use positioning functions to enable reasoning about mixtures of position independent code and position dependent code. As a result, procedures and procedural recursion is readily handled (without assuming an unbounded stack).

The Hoare triples described in this paper have been defined in higher-order logic. Rules for reasoning about them have been derived from the formal definitions of the Hoare triples, using the HOL4 system [6] (thus the rules are sound). We can reason about ARM machine code by instantiation of our framework's Hoare triples to a high-fidelity model of the ARM machine language. The specialisation of our framework to ARM machine code is presented in a companion paper [10]. Here we concentrate on the core ideas of our approach.

This paper is not the first to address the problem of verifying realistically modelled machine code. Some early work was done by Maurer [9], Clutterbuck and Carré [5] and Bevier [3]. Boyer and Yu [4] did impressive pioneering work on verifying machine code written for a commercial processor: they verified programs using the bare operational semantics of a model of the Motorola MC68020. Projects on proof-carrying code (PCC) [11] and particularly foundation PCC [1] have ignited new interest in verification of low-level code. Of work on PCC, Tan and Appel's work [16] is particularly relevant to this paper: they use a Hoare logic to reason about a detailed model of the Sparc machine language. As for most work on PCC, their aim is to address safety properties that can be proved automatically (e.g. type safety). Tan and Appel's approach is hampered by the requirement of an extensive soundness proof. Hardin, Smith and Young [7] verify machine code for Rockwell Collins AAMP7G using a form of symbolic simulation. Work by Klein, Tuch and Norrish [8] has similar goal as ours, but they reason at a higher level about realistically modelled C programs.

The remainder of this paper is organised as follows. Section 2 gives an overview of how our specifications relate to those of standard Hoare-triples and motivates our design decisions. Section 3 contains the bulk of the material: it defines a Hoare triple for machine code, presents an example and shows how rules can be derived for procedures and procedure calls. Section 4 demonstrates how the framework can be instantiated to a given operational semantics of a machine language. Section 5 concludes with a summary.

2   Approach

This section motivates some key design decisions informally and gives an overview of the main ideas. The detailed definitions are given in the next section.

2.1   Basic Specifications

Our framework supports code specifications with multiple entries, multiple exits and multiple code segments, but for simplicity we start by considering specifications having single entry, single exit and single code segment. The full generality is described in Section 3.

Consider the ARM implementation of the factorial function given in the introduction. In classical Hoare logic, its specification could be written as follows with a side-condition:

$$\{(a = x) \land (x \neq 0)\} \qquad \textit{Side condition:}$$
$$\text{FACTORIAL} \qquad\qquad \text{The registers associated with}$$
$$\{(a = 0) \land (b = x!)\} \qquad a \text{ and } b \text{ are distinct.}$$

This specification is not satisfactory because it leaves many aspects unspecified. For example, it does not say whether the code modifies the status bits or what happens to the program counter.

We require specifications to mention each component of the state that might be altered during execution. That way we can easily see what is changed and what is not. Our approach is similar to that of separation logic [13,12], which assigns a memory footprint to each assertion. We make a stricter requirement: every state component (e.g. register, memory location, status bit) must appear in the footprint of an assertion. In our framework, the factorial program has the following specification where, for now, informally read $R\, a\, x$ as "register a has value x", $S\, b$ as "the status bits have value b", underscore (_) as "some value" and $P * Q$, following separation logic, as "P and Q are true for disjoint parts of the state" (precise definitions of these concepts are given later).

$$\{R\, a\, x * R\, b\, \_ * S\, \_ * \langle x \neq 0 \rangle\}$$
$$\text{FACTORIAL}$$
$$\{R\, a\, 0 * R\, b\, x! * S\, \_ \}^{+4}$$

The superscript $^{+4}$ specifies that FACTORIAL increments the program counter by 4. The separating conjunction $*$ avoids the need for the side-condition, since the side condition is implied by the occurrence of $*$ between $R\, a\, x$ and $R\, b\, \_$ in the precondition.

2.2 Heterogeneous Specifications

Machine-code programs depend on a variety of different resources. Even in a simple setting we encounter registers, special registers, memory locations and various status bits. For this reason we treat all types of resources uniformly. Consider for instance the specification of the instructions STR (store) and DSTR (decrement-and-store). Read $M\,x\,y$ as "memory location x has value y".

$$\{R\,a\,x * R\,b\,y * M\,y\,_-\}$$
$$\text{STR }b\,a$$
$$\{R\,a\,x * R\,b\,y * M\,y\,x\}^{+1}$$

$$\{R\,a\,x * R\,b\,y * M\,(y{-}1)\,_-\}$$
$$\text{DSTR }b\,a$$
$$\{R\,a\,x * R\,b\,(y{-}1) * M\,(y{-}1)\,x\}^{+1}$$

These specifications have a similar form to that of the factorial program, even though they specify the behavior of different types of resources.

Hoare-style reasoning can be applied to specifications. For example, DSTR given above can implement a stack push for a descending stack. We can state this with a specification $stack(sp, xs, n)$ defined to assert that the stack pointer (taken to be register 13) has value sp, that xs is on the stack and that there are n unused slots on top of the stack. We will use the HOL list notation $[x_0; \ldots; x_m]$ and the cons function defined by cons $x_0\,[x_1; \ldots; x_m] = [x_0; x_1; \ldots; x_m]$. In order to define $stack(sp, xs, n)$, recursively define $ms(a, [x_0; x_1; \ldots; x_m])$ to mean "$M\,a\,x_0 * M\,(a{+}1)\,x_1 * \cdots * M\,(a{+}m)\,x_m$" and similarly $blank(a, n)$ to mean "$M\,a\,_- * M\,(a{-}1)\,_- * \cdots * M\,(a{-}(n{-}1))\,_-$". The specification $stack(sp, xs, n)$ is then defined to be $R\,13\,sp * ms(sp, xs) * blank(sp{-}1, n)$.

Using this specification of a stack segment we are able to derive a specification for stack push from the specification of DSTR:

$$\{R\,a\,x * stack(sp, xs, n{+}1)\}$$
$$\text{DSTR }b\,a$$
$$\{R\,a\,x * stack(sp{-}1, \text{cons }x\,xs, n)\}^{+1}$$

2.3 Positioning Functions

We use positioning functions to make our Hoare triple general. These functions are written as superscripts in our notation: $\{P\}^f\,cs\,^g\,\{Q\}^h$. We omit superscripts that are the identity function $(\lambda x.x)$. The positioning functions specify entry points, exit points and code placement with respect to a variable base address. More concretely, $\{P\}^f\,cs\,^g\,\{Q\}^h$ states the following: for any address p, if the program counter points at address $f(p)$, the code sequence cs is stored at address $g(p)$ and P holds, then some time later the program counter will reach address $h(p)$ in a state where Q holds.

The positioning functions can be used to make position-independent specifications, position dependent specifications and mixtures of the two. A specification is position independent if the positioning functions describe offsets: we use $+n$ to abbreviate $\lambda x.x{+}n$, $-k$ to abbreviate $\lambda x.x{-}k$ and write nothing to mean a null offset, i.e. $\lambda x.x$. A specification is position dependent if it ignores its argument: e.g. $\lambda x.5$ and $\lambda x.y$.

```
sum:    CMP     a,#0            ; test: a = 0
        MOVEQ   r15,r14         ; return, if a = 0
        STR     a,[r13,#-4]!    ; push a
        STR     r14,[r13,#-4]!  ; push link-register
        LDR     r14,[a]         ; temp := node value
        ADD     s,s,r14         ; s := s + temp
        LDR     a,[a,#4]        ; a := address of left
        BL      sum             ; s := s + sum of a
        LDR     a,[r13,#4]      ; a := initial a
        LDR     a,[a,#8]        ; a := address of right
        BL      sum             ; s := s + sum of a
        LDR     r15,[r13],#8    ; pop two and return
```

Fig. 1. BINARY_SUM: ARM code to sum the values at the nodes of a binary tree

These positioning functions are useful as they can capture some of the non-trivial control structures used in machine-code. For example, the control structure of a procedure is easy to define: procedures are given a return address to which they must jump on completion. If we suppose that register 14 holds the return address, then we have the following format for procedure specifications:

$$\{P * R\ 14\ y\}\ cs\ \{Q * R\ 14\ \_\}^{\lambda x.y}$$

The superscript $\lambda x.y$ specifies that the value of the program counter is y on exit from cs no matter what it was on entry to cs. Section 3.6 presents a derivation of a call rule that evaluates the effect of a call to such a procedure.

The call rule and stack assertion, from above, have been used in the verification of recursive procedures in ARM code. An example of such a procedure is the code called BINARY_SUM shown in Figure 1. BINARY_SUM calculates the sum of values attached to the nodes of a binary tree. The trees we consider have nodes consisting of a value and addresses of two subtrees. Address 0 refers to the empty subtree. A predicate stating that tree t is stored with root at address x:

$$
\begin{aligned}
tree(x, \mathsf{Leaf}) &= \langle x = 0 \rangle \\
tree(x, \mathsf{Node}(z, l, r)) &= \exists x_1\ x_2.\ M\ x\ z * M\ (x{+}1)\ x_1 * M\ (x{+}2)\ x_2 * \\
&\quad tree(x_1, l) * tree(x_2, r) * \langle x \neq 0 \rangle
\end{aligned}
$$

The specification of BINARY_SUM states that BINARY_SUM adds to register s the sum of the nodes of a tree that is addressed by register a. The specification also states that no more than $2 \times depth(t)$ words of stack space is required during execution. ([ ] is the empty list and $stack(sp, [\,], n) = R\ 13\ sp * blank(sp-1, n)$).

$$
\begin{aligned}
&\{R\ a\ x * R\ s\ z * S\ \_ * \\
&\quad tree(x, t) * stack(sp, [\,], 2 \times depth(t)) * R\ 14\ y\} \\
&\qquad\qquad \text{BINARY\_SUM} \\
&\{R\ a\ \_ * R\ s\ (z + sum(t)) * S\ \_ * \\
&\quad tree(x, t) * stack(sp, [\,], 2 \times depth(t)) * R\ 14\ \_\}^{\lambda x.y}
\end{aligned}
$$

The formal ARM specification of BINARY_SUM requires some of the entities to be aligned addresses. Such details appear as slight variations of predicates M and R, for details see the companion paper [10].

2.4 Excessive Separation

The separating conjunction $*$ is set up in such a way that an occurrence of $R\,a\,x * R\,b\,y$ in a precondition will always imply $a \neq b$. This is both a weakness and a strength of our approach. It is a weakness since we will need many specifications for what seems to be special cases of a single operation. For instance, binary operators are given 5 different specifications.

$$\{R\,a\,x * R\,b\,y * R\,c\,\_\}$$
$$\text{MUL } c\,a\,b$$
$$\{R\,a\,x * R\,b\,y * R\,c\,(x \times y)\}^{+1}$$

$$\{R\,a\,x\}$$
$$\text{MUL } a\,a\,a$$
$$\{R\,a\,(x \times x)\}^{+1}$$

$$\{R\,a\,x * R\,b\,y\}$$
$$\text{MUL } b\,a\,b$$
$$\{R\,a\,x * R\,b\,(x \times y)\}^{+1}$$

$$\{R\,a\,x * R\,b\,\_\}$$
$$\text{MUL } b\,a\,a$$
$$\{R\,a\,x * R\,b\,(x \times x)\}^{+1}$$

$$\{R\,a\,x * R\,b\,y\}$$
$$\text{MUL } b\,b\,a$$
$$\{R\,a\,x * R\,b\,(y \times x)\}^{+1}$$

What appears to be an excessive use of $*$ is actually often a benefit. As mentioned earlier, not all the specifications above are true in every case. Furthermore, and particularly important, the separating conjunction makes the mechanisation significantly easier, as technicalities concerning register name aliasing diminish.

3   Hoare Triple for Machine Code

This section defines a Hoare triple for machine code and formalises what was informally presented in the previous section. This section ends with an example of how proof rules can be derived for procedure calls.

3.1   State Representation

We assume that a state is represented as one large set of basic state elements, where each element is an assertion specifying the state of a particular resource. State sets are required to enumerate all the resources of the observable state. In this presentation concrete states are enumerations of the following form:

{ Reg 0 820, Reg 1 540, Reg 2 412, $\cdots$, Reg 15 512,
  Mem 0 34, Mem 1 82, Mem 2 11, $\cdots$, Mem $(2^{32} - 1)$ 40,
  Status F }

Such sets contain 16 register elements Reg r x (register r holds value x), 2^{32} memory elements Mem a y (memory address a holds value y) and one status bit Status b (the status bit is b). No state is allowed to duplicate a basic state element, e.g. register 3 must not occur, in any state, as both Reg 3 34 and Reg 3 45. We will denote the set of all well-formed states by Σ, thus members of Σ represent states. Issues regarding restrictions on Σ are discussed further in Section 4.

The basic assertions described informally in the previous section can now be defined as predicates on states.

$$R\,r\,x \;=\; \lambda s.\,(s = \{\mathsf{Reg}\,r\,x\})$$
$$M\,a\,y \;=\; \lambda s.\,(s = \{\mathsf{Mem}\,a\,y\})$$
$$S\,b \;=\; \lambda s.\,(s = \{\mathsf{Status}\,b\})$$

Let *split* s (u,v) mean that the pair of sets (u,v) partitions the set s, i.e. *split* s $(u,v) = (u \cup v = s) \wedge (u \cap v = \emptyset)$. Separating conjunction ($*$) and the notion of "some value" (written as a postfixed operator $_-$) are then defined by:

$$P * Q \;=\; \lambda s.\,\exists u\,v.\;\textit{split}\;s\;(u,v) \wedge P\,u \wedge Q\,v$$
$$P_- \;=\; \lambda s.\,\exists x.\;P\,x\,s$$

3.2 Execution Predicate

The judgments of our Hoare logic are based on assertions about processor executions. We define the execution assertion $P \rightsquigarrow Q$ to mean that execution starting from any state which has a part satisfying P, *will reach* a state where *only* the part initially satisfying P has been changed and satisfies Q. Note that this incorporates a 'frame assumption'. The formal definition assumes a next-state function $next : \Sigma \to \Sigma$ and then uses $run(s,n)$ to denote the state reached after n steps starting from s (i.e. run is defined recursively by $run(s,0) = s$ and $run(s,n+1) = run(next(s),n)$).

$$P \rightsquigarrow Q \;=\; \forall s \in \Sigma.\,\forall F.\;(P * F)\,s \;\Rightarrow\; \exists k.\;(Q * F)\,(run(s,k))$$

The following frame-rule, similar to that of separation logic, easily follows.

$$\frac{P \rightsquigarrow Q}{\forall F.\;(P * F) \rightsquigarrow (Q * F)}$$

3.3 Code Assertion

The basic execution predicate determines how the underlying processor executes on a bare state. In order to specify how code executes we need first to specify how code is located in memory and what the value of the program counter has.

Asserting the value of the program-counter is generally simple, say $R\;15\;p$ if register 15 is the program counter. Let $pc(p)$ be such an assertion. Making a general assertion about the code in memory is more difficult. The idea is to use a kind of assertion we call a *code-pool*, which asserts that a union of possibly overlapping code sequences are part of the memory. Our approach is similar to that of Saabas and Uustalu [14] and Tan and Appel [16].

The definition of code-pool assertions uses a set-based separating conjunction operator $\circledast$ expressing the $*$-combination of the elements of an arbitrary set. Informally: $\circledast\,\{P_1,\cdots,P_n\} = P_1 * \cdots * P_n$ (when $P_1 \cdots P_n$ are distinct). The formal definition is based on a partial bijection between predicates P_i and partitions of the state set. The definition is straightforward, but has a few subtle details which are not particularly interesting. It is omitted due to lack of space.

A code pool is an assertion obtained by applying $\circledast$ to the union of sets of basic instruction assertions $M\ p\ c$, where $M\ p\ c$ specifies that instruction c is executed if the program counter has value p (this is a special case of the notion of basic instruction assertion that we actually use). If cs is a sequence of instructions, then $Mset(p, cs)$ denotes the set of assertions stating that the sequence starts at position p and runs consecutively from there.

$$Mset(p, cs) = \{\ M\ (p+k)\ (cs[k])\ |\ k < length(cs)\ \}$$

A pair (cs, f) is a code sequence cs together with a specification f of where to position it relative to a base address (see Section 2.3 for a discussion of positioning functions). We use $\mathcal{C}$ to range over sets of such pairs, and then define:

$$mpool(p, \mathcal{C}) = \circledast\,(\ \bigcup \{\ Mset(f(p), cs)\ |\ (cs, f) \in \mathcal{C}\ \}\,)$$

The intuition is that $mpool(p, \{(cs_1, f_1), \cdots, (cs_n, f_n)\})$ is the same as the expansion of $ms(f_1(p), cs_1) * \cdots * ms(f_n(p), cs_n)$ with the duplicated M-assertions removed by the set union. The benefit of using such a code pool is that it allows code sequences to overlap and builds into the representation the removal of duplicate sequences. This benefit is particularly apparent in the rule for procedural recursion, Section 3.6.

At the end of a verification of concrete code one can of course not have distinct sequences of code that overlap. Such an arrangement makes the precondition(s) of the machine-code Hoare-triple (defined in the next section) false and hence the specification trivially true. The following two equivalences simplify a code-pool into a simple sequence assertion.[1] Note that in the equation below and later, $+length(cs)$ denotes the function that adds the length of cs, thus $+length(cs) \circ f$ is the function $\lambda n.\ length(cs) + f(n)$.

$$mpool(p, \{(cs, f)\}) = ms(f(p), cs)$$
$$mpool(p, \{(cs, f), (cs', +length(cs) \circ f)\} \cup \mathcal{C}) = mpool(p, \{(cs; cs', f)\} \cup \mathcal{C})$$

3.4   Hoare Triple

In Section 2 we discussed a Hoare triple $\{P\}^f\ cs^{\,g}\ \{Q\}^h$. We will shortly generalise this to have sets of preconditions, sets of code sequences and sets of postconditions, but first we give a formal semantics of the simple case.

$$\{P\}^f\ cs^{\,g}\ \{Q\}^h\ =\ \forall p.\ (P * ms(g(p), cs) * pc(f(p))) \rightsquigarrow$$
$$(Q * ms(g(p), cs) * pc(h(p)))$$

We can read $\{P\}^f\ cs^{\,g}\ \{Q\}^h$ as asserting that if the processor is started from a state satisfying P and (for any p) if $f(p)$ is in the program counter and the

---

[1] The first of these equalities is only true under the assumption that the length of cs does not exceed the length of the address space.

code cs stored as a sequence from address $g(p)$ onwards, then it will reach a state satisfying Q. The specification also guarantees termination with the code unchanged and the program counter updated to $h(p)$. The functions f and g are frequently the identity function, in which case the program counter points at the first instruction in the sequence of instructions cs. Notice that the meaning of $*$ ensures that the precondition $P * ms(g(p), cs) * pc(f(p))$ only holds when P does not mention the program counter or any memory location where cs is stored.

We generalise the simple case to multiple preconditions, code segments and postconditions, each with positioning functions f_i, g_i and h_i, respectively:

$$\{P_1\}^{f_1} \cdots \{P_n\}^{f_n} \; cs_1{}^{g_1} \cdots cs_m{}^{g_m} \; \{Q_1\}^{h_1} \cdots \{Q_k\}^{h_k}$$

The intuition is the following: if all the code segments are present in memory, then whenever one of the preconditions $\{P_i\}^{f_i}$ is true, some time later (at least) one of the postconditions $\{Q_j\}^{h_j}$ will be true.

For the definition of the general Hoare-triple collect the preconditions, code segments and postconditions into respective sets $\mathcal{P} = \{(P_1, f_1), \cdots, (P_n, f_n)\}$, $\mathcal{C} = \{(cs_1, g_1), \cdots, (cs_m, g_m)\}$ and $\mathcal{Q} = \{(Q_1, h_1), \cdots, (Q_k, h_k)\}$. The machine-code Hoare-triple, which is written here as $\mathcal{P} \mid \mathcal{C} \mid \mathcal{Q}$, is defined using disjunction over as set of predicates $\bigvee$ (formally: $\bigvee \mathcal{X} = \lambda s. \exists P \in \mathcal{X}. \, P \, s$).

$$\mathcal{P} \mid \mathcal{C} \mid \mathcal{Q} = \forall p. \, (\bigvee \{ P * mpool(p, \mathcal{C}) * pc(f(p)) \mid (P, f) \in \mathcal{P} \}) \rightsquigarrow$$
$$(\bigvee \{ Q * mpool(p, \mathcal{C}) * pc(f(p)) \mid (Q, f) \in \mathcal{Q} \})$$

A variety of rules have been derived from this definition of Hoare triple. Some of the rules are presented in Figure 2. The rules for frame, shift and compose are used when joining specifications (as illustrated in the next section). Strengthen, weaken and merge are used when specifications are simplified. Contraction, extension and loop elimination add/remove entry points, exit points and code segments. The rule for loop elimination removes any number of interconnected exit points that match some set of entry point for a decreasing variant. The equivalences are mainly used in derivations of new rules.

3.5   Example: Composition

The rule for composition given in Figure 2 is quite abstract. We demonstrate its use by composing a specification of a decrement instruction and a branch instruction (c.f. the instructions of the factorial program). The branch instruction has two exit points, thus two postconditions. We illustrate the three possible compositions below.

$$\{R\ a\ x * S\ \_\}$$
$$\text{SUBS } a\ a\ 1$$
$$\{R\ a\ (x{-}1) * S\ (x{-}1 = 0)\}^{+1}$$

$$\{S\ b\}$$
$$\text{BNE } k$$
$$\{S\ \text{T} * \langle b\rangle\}^{+1}$$
$$\{S\ \text{F} * \langle\neg b\rangle\}^{+k}$$

Composition is commonly done in three stages: first the scope of the specifications is extended so that the footprints match, then the positioning functions

Let ":" denote insertion into a set and "$\prec$" denote any well-found relation.
Let $\mathcal{P} \bar{*} F = \{ (P * F, f) \mid (P, f) \in \mathcal{P} \}$ and $\mathcal{P} \bar{\circ} g = \{ (P, f \circ g) \mid (P, f) \in \mathcal{P} \}$.
Let $\langle b \rangle = \lambda s. \ (s = \emptyset) \wedge b$.

Frame, shift and compose.

$$\frac{\mathcal{P} \mid \mathcal{C} \mid \mathcal{Q}}{\forall F. \ \mathcal{P} \bar{*} F \mid \mathcal{C} \mid \mathcal{Q} \bar{*} F} \qquad \frac{\mathcal{P} \mid \mathcal{C} \mid \mathcal{Q}}{\forall g. \ \mathcal{P} \bar{\circ} g \mid \mathcal{C} \bar{\circ} g \mid \mathcal{Q} \bar{\circ} g}$$

$$\frac{\mathcal{P} \mid \mathcal{C} \mid \mathcal{Q} \cup \mathcal{M} \qquad \mathcal{M} \cup \mathcal{P}' \mid \mathcal{C}' \mid \mathcal{Q}'}{\mathcal{P} \cup \mathcal{P}' \mid \mathcal{C} \cup \mathcal{C}' \mid \mathcal{Q} \cup \mathcal{Q}'}$$

Contract, extend, strengthen and weaken.

$$\frac{\mathcal{P} \cup \mathcal{P}' \mid \mathcal{C} \mid \mathcal{Q}}{\mathcal{P} \mid \mathcal{C} \mid \mathcal{Q}} \qquad \frac{\mathcal{P} \mid \mathcal{C} \mid \mathcal{Q}}{\mathcal{P} \mid \mathcal{C} \cup \mathcal{C}' \mid \mathcal{Q}} \qquad \frac{\mathcal{P} \mid \mathcal{C} \mid \mathcal{Q}}{\mathcal{P} \mid \mathcal{C} \mid \mathcal{Q} \cup \mathcal{Q}'}$$

$$\frac{P' \Rightarrow P \qquad (P, f) : \mathcal{P} \mid \mathcal{C} \mid \mathcal{Q}}{(P', f) : \mathcal{P} \mid \mathcal{C} \mid \mathcal{Q}} \qquad \frac{Q \Rightarrow Q' \qquad \mathcal{P} \mid \mathcal{C} \mid (Q, f) : \mathcal{Q}}{\mathcal{P} \mid \mathcal{C} \mid (Q', f) : \mathcal{Q}}$$

Merge rules.

$$\frac{(P, f) : (P', f) : \mathcal{P} \mid \mathcal{C} \mid \mathcal{Q}}{(P \vee P', f) : \mathcal{P} \mid \mathcal{C} \mid \mathcal{Q}} \qquad \frac{\mathcal{P} \mid \mathcal{C} \mid (Q, f) : (Q', f) : \mathcal{Q}}{\mathcal{P} \mid \mathcal{C} \mid (Q \vee Q', f) : \mathcal{Q}}$$

$$\frac{\mathcal{P} \mid (cs, f) : (cs', +length(cs) \circ f) : \mathcal{C} \mid \mathcal{Q}}{\mathcal{P} \mid (cs \mathbin{+\!\!+} cs', f) : \mathcal{C} \mid \mathcal{Q}}$$

Loop elimination.

$$\frac{\forall v. \ I(v) \cup \mathcal{P} \mid \mathcal{C} \mid \mathcal{Q} \cup \{ i \mid i \in I(v') \wedge v' \prec v \}}{\forall v. \ I(v) \cup \mathcal{P} \mid \mathcal{C} \mid \mathcal{Q}}$$

Various equivalences.

$$\mathcal{P} \mid \mathcal{C} \mid (\exists x. \ Q(x) * \langle b(x) \rangle, f) : \mathcal{Q} = \mathcal{P} \mid \mathcal{C} \mid \mathcal{Q} \cup \{ (Q(x), f) \mid b(x) \}$$

$$(\exists x. \ P(x) * \langle b(x) \rangle, f) : \mathcal{P} \mid \mathcal{C} \mid \mathcal{Q} = \{ (P(x), f) \mid b(x) \} \cup \mathcal{P} \mid \mathcal{C} \mid \mathcal{Q}$$

$$\mathcal{P} \mid \mathcal{C} \mid \mathcal{Q} = \forall p. \ \mathcal{P} \bar{\circ} (\lambda x.p) \mid \mathcal{C} \bar{\circ} (\lambda x.p) \mid \mathcal{Q} \bar{\circ} (\lambda x.p)$$

Fig. 2. Rules for the machine-code Hoare triple

are made to match by a shift and finally the composition rule is applied followed by an application of a code merge if applicable.

We start by constructing a specification for "SUBS $a\,a\,1$; BNE k". The frame rule is used to extend the specification of BNE and b is instantiated:

$$\{R\,a\,(x{-}1) * S\,(x{-}1 = 0)\}$$
$$\text{BNE } k$$
$$\{R\,a\,(x{-}1) * S\,\mathsf{T} * \langle x{-}1 = 0\rangle\}^{+1}$$
$$\{R\,a\,(x{-}1) * S\,\mathsf{F} * \langle x{-}1 \neq 0\rangle\}^{+k}$$

A shift by $+1$ makes the precondition of BNE match the postcondition of SUBS:

$$\{R\,a\,(x{-}1) * S\,(x{-}1 = 0)\}^{+1}$$
$$\text{BNE } k^{+1}$$
$$\{R\,a\,(x{-}1) * S\,\mathsf{T} * \langle x{-}1 = 0\rangle\}^{+2}$$
$$\{R\,a\,(x{-}1) * S\,\mathsf{F} * \langle x{-}1 \neq 0\rangle\}^{+(k+1)}$$

An application of the composition rule followed by a code merge yields:

$$\{R\,a\,x * S\,_-\}$$
$$\text{SUBS } a\,a\,1; \text{ BNE } k$$
$$\{R\,a\,(x{-}1) * S\,\mathsf{T} * \langle x{-}1 = 0\rangle\}^{+2}$$
$$\{R\,a\,(x{-}1) * S\,\mathsf{F} * \langle x{-}1 \neq 0\rangle\}^{+(k+1)}$$

Alternatively, the specification for SUBS can be tacked onto either branch of BNE. The compositions are done with shifts $+1$ and $+k$, respectively. The composition with shift $+k$ results in a specification with two code segments.

$$\{R\,a\,x * S\,b\} \qquad\qquad \{R\,a\,x * S\,b\}$$
$$\text{BNE } k; \text{ SUBS } a\,a\,1 \qquad\qquad \text{SUBS } a\,a\,1^{+k} \quad \text{BNE } k$$
$$\{R\,a\,(x{-}1) * S\,(x{-}1 = 0) * \langle b\rangle\}^{+2} \qquad \{R\,a\,x * S\,\mathsf{T} * \langle b\rangle\}^{+1}$$
$$\{R\,a\,x * S\,\mathsf{F} * \langle \neg b\rangle\}^{+k} \qquad \{R\,a\,(x{-}1) * S\,(x{-}1 = 0) * \langle \neg b\rangle\}^{+(k+1)}$$

3.6   Example: Procedures and Procedural Recursion

This section illustrates how specifications for procedures and procedure calls fit into our framework. We define the control-flow contract of a procedure and a procedure call, derive a rule stating the effect of a procedure call and finally present a rule that we have found useful when proving recursive procedures.

The standard contract of a procedure can be captured easily within our framework. Commonly a procedure is given a return address to which it must jump upon completion. Given a resource, say, lr that holds the return address we can specify a reasonably general contract as follows:

$$\text{PROC}(f, P, C, Q) = \forall p.\ \{P * lr\,p\}^f\ C\ \{Q * lr\,_-\}^{\lambda x.p}$$

Specifying a general procedure call is slightly more involved in our framework. We define a call to be a jump that starts with the program counter set to $h(p)$, for any p, stores the address $g(p)$ in lr and jumps to address $f(p)$.

$$\text{CALL}(f, C, h, g) = \forall p.\ \{lr\,_-\}^{\lambda x.h(p)}\ (C \bar{\circ} (\lambda x.p))\ \{lr(g(p))\}^{\lambda x.f(p)}$$

$$\frac{\mathrm{CALL}(f,\mathcal{C},h,g)}{\dfrac{\forall p.\ \{(lr\_,\lambda x.h(p))\}\mid \mathcal{C}\,\bar{\mathrm{o}}\,(\lambda x.p)\mid \{(lr(g(p)),\lambda x.f(p))\}}{\dfrac{\{(lr\_,\lambda x.h(p))\}\mid \mathcal{C}\,\bar{\mathrm{o}}\,(\lambda x.p)\mid \{(lr(g(p)),\lambda x.f(p))\}}{\{(P*lr\_,\lambda x.h(p))\}\mid \mathcal{C}\,\bar{\mathrm{o}}\,(\lambda x.p)\mid \{(P*lr(g(p)),\lambda x.f(p))\}}}} \tag{1}$$

$$\frac{\mathrm{PROC}(f,P,\mathcal{C}',Q)}{\dfrac{\forall p.\ \{(P*lr(p),f)\}\mid \mathcal{C}'\mid \{(Q*lr\_,\lambda x.p)\}}{\dfrac{\{(P*lr(g(p)),f)\}\mid \mathcal{C}'\mid \{(Q*lr\_,\lambda x.g(p))\}}{\dfrac{\{(P*lr(g(p)),f\circ\lambda x.p)\}\mid \mathcal{C}'\,\bar{\mathrm{o}}\,(\lambda x.p)\mid \{(Q*lr\_,\lambda x.g(p)\circ\lambda x.p)\}}{\{(P*lr(g(p)),\lambda x.f(p))\}\mid \mathcal{C}'\,\bar{\mathrm{o}}\,(\lambda x.p)\mid \{(Q*lr\_,\lambda x.g(p))\}}}}} \tag{2}$$

$$\frac{(1)\qquad(2)}{\dfrac{\{(P*lr\_,\lambda x.h(p))\}\mid (\mathcal{C}\,\bar{\mathrm{o}}\,(\lambda x.p))\cup(\mathcal{C}'\,\bar{\mathrm{o}}\,(\lambda x.p))\mid \{(Q*lr\_,\lambda x.g(p))\}}{\dfrac{\{(P*lr\_,h)\}\,\bar{\mathrm{o}}\,(\lambda x.p)\mid (\mathcal{C}\cup\mathcal{C}')\,\bar{\mathrm{o}}\,(\lambda x.p)\mid \{(Q*lr\_,g)\}\,\bar{\mathrm{o}}\,(\lambda x.p)}{\dfrac{\forall p.\ \{(P*lr\_,h)\}\,\bar{\mathrm{o}}\,(\lambda x.p)\mid (\mathcal{C}\cup\mathcal{C}')\,\bar{\mathrm{o}}\,(\lambda x.p)\mid \{(Q*lr\_,g)\}\,\bar{\mathrm{o}}\,(\lambda x.p)}{\{(P*lr\_,h)\}\mid \mathcal{C}\cup\mathcal{C}'\mid \{(Q*lr\_,g)\}}}}}$$

Fig. 3. A derivation of the call rule

The ARM instruction for branch-and-link BL satisfies a specification that is essentially the same as $\mathrm{CALL}(+k,\{(\mathrm{BL}\ k,+0)\},+0,+1)$.

The effect of executing a call $\mathrm{CALL}(f,\mathcal{C},h,g)$ to a procedure $\mathrm{PROC}(f,P,\mathcal{C}',Q)$ is described by the call rule, derived in Figure 3.

$$\frac{\mathrm{CALL}(f,\mathcal{C},h,g)\qquad \mathrm{PROC}(f,P,\mathcal{C}',Q)}{\{P*lr\_\}^h\ \mathcal{C}\cup\mathcal{C}'\ \{Q*lr\_\}^g}$$

The call rule is quite general. It does not restrict the procedure body or the call statement to be position dependent or independent. This was achieved by the inclusion of positioning functions h, g and f. Of these functions f has an artificial role when the procedure is position independent. Why should the procedure specification have a positioning function in common with the call specification, if the procedure specification is position independent?

In order to remove this oddity a special rule can be proved for calls to procedures that have the positioning function set to $\lambda x.x$.

$$\frac{\mathrm{PROC}(\lambda x.x,P,\mathcal{C}',Q)}{\dfrac{\forall p.\ \{(P*lr(p),\lambda x.x)\}\mid \mathcal{C}'\mid \{(Q*lr\_,\lambda x.p)\}}{\dfrac{\forall p.\ \{(P*lr(p),(\lambda x.x)\circ f)\}\mid \mathcal{C}'\,\bar{\mathrm{o}}\,f\mid \{(Q*lr\_,(\lambda x.p)\circ f)\}}{\dfrac{\forall p.\ \{(P*lr(p),f)\}\mid \mathcal{C}'\,\bar{\mathrm{o}}\,f\mid \{(Q*lr\_,\lambda x.p)\}}{\mathrm{PROC}(f,P,\mathcal{C}'\,\bar{\mathrm{o}}\,f,Q)}}}} \tag{3}$$

$$\frac{\mathrm{CALL}(f,\mathcal{C},h,g)\qquad(3)}{\{P*lr\_\}^h\ \mathcal{C}\cup(\mathcal{C}'\,\bar{\mathrm{o}}\,f)\ \{Q*lr\_\}^g}$$

Informally this rule can be understood as follows: A call with jump function f executes a position-independent procedure with code $\mathcal{C}'$, if code $\mathcal{C}'$ is placed using function f.

Procedural recursion of one or more procedures is proved by induction over a bounded variant function that decreases strictly on each recursive call. The observation that each recursive call pushes at least one value (the return address) onto the stack[2], suggests that induction over the natural number is sufficient. The remaining stack space[3] is a natural number that decreases for each recursive call. We have found the following induction rule useful in proofs of recursive procedures. Let v be some variant function, $<$ be less-than over the natural numbers and ψ be any boolean-valued function.

$$\frac{\forall x\ \mathcal{C}'.\ (\forall y.\ v(y) < v(x) \Rightarrow \psi(y,\mathcal{C}')) \Rightarrow \psi(x, \mathcal{C} \cup \mathcal{C}')}{\forall x.\ \psi(x,\mathcal{C})}$$

The parameter $\mathcal{C}$ is intended to hold a set of code segments. Notice that $\mathcal{C}$ does not occur in the assumption of the premise. The absence of $\mathcal{C}$ makes the rule easier to use, as one does not need to assume the code one is constructing.

The definitions and theorems of this section were used in the verification of BINARY_SUM, Section 3.6. The verification of BINARY_SUM was done as a case analysis over the structure of the tree. The case of a leaf was trivial as it exits on the second instruction. The case of a branch required more work. For it we assumed that there is some code $\mathcal{C}'$ that performs the desired function for the subtrees. We used the second version of the call rule to extract specifications for the BL instructions that perform the recursive calls. The specifications for all twelve instructions were then composed and the cases (leaf and branch) were merged. The induction rule, from above, was specialised to trees by setting v to *depth* (depth of a binary tree) and then used to eliminate the assumed specifications and imaginary code $\mathcal{C}'$. The same induction was also used in proving a variant of BINARY_SUM that has the last call replaced by a tail-recursive call. The details of both proofs are given in [10].

4   Formalisation and Specialisation

Section 3.1 made restrictions on the format of the sets that are members of the set of valid states Σ. Restrictions are needed in order to ensure the intended meaning of separation for separating conjunction $*$. This section describes how we avoid such issues in our formalisation of the general case and also how we address them when the general theory is specialised and used.

The general theory, which consists of the definition of the machine-code Hoare triple and its rules, can be proved without any restrictions on the structure of the state sets[4]. The machine-code Hoare triple can be defined and all its rules proved for any set of state sets Σ, given a next-state function $next : \Sigma \to \Sigma$ [5],

---

[2] We consider tail-recursive-call as a loop, not as a call.

[3] We will not assume an infinite stack as we do not assume an infinite state space.

[4] In the HOL mechanisation the type of a state element is parametrised by a type variable. The type of a state set is "α set".

[5] Alternatively, one can use a next-state relation $next : \Sigma \times \Sigma$, for this redefine $\rightsquigarrow$.

a program-counter assertion $pc : \alpha \rightarrow \Sigma \rightarrow \mathbb{B}$ and a basic instruction assertion $inst : \alpha \times \beta \rightarrow \Sigma \rightarrow \mathbb{B}$, for some set α of instruction addresses and some set β of instructions. These abstractions ease the proof effort. All the definitions and rules are parametrised by a 6-tuple $(\Sigma, \alpha, \beta, next, pc, inst)$.

When the general theory is instantiated and one wants to prove basic specifications for the elementary operations of a specific language (examples of basic specification: Section 2.2, 2.4 and 3.5), then one has to restrict the shape of Σ so that $*$ has its intended meaning. We have found that a practical method for restricting the shape of the state sets is to have them produced by a function. We define Σ to be the range of a function tr, i.e. $\Sigma = \{ \, tr(x) \mid \text{any } x \, \}$, for some function tr that produces state sets of a specific form.

The function tr can be a translation function from a different state representation. If this is the case and the translation is accurate enough to also have an inverse $\bar{tr}$ (i.e. $\forall x.\ \bar{tr}(tr(x)) = x$), then one can define the next-state function for the set-based representation $(next)$ using a next-state function over the other state representation (say $next_{sem}$): $next(s) = tr(next_{sem}(\bar{tr}(s)))$. The benefit of defining $next$ according to a next-state function over a different state-representation is a practical one. The detailed semantics of a machine-code language might be more readily defined using a state-representation different from the set-based representation that our approach requires. This is the case in the application of our framework to the ARM processor: we generate members of Σ formally from the representations of states used by the ARM model.

5 Summary

This paper has presented a Hoare logic that has been carefully designed to fit on top of accurately modelled operational semantics of machine languages. Specifications are built on a separating conjunction, that allows concise resource usage specifications and also helps avoid unwanted aliasing. Multiple code segments and positioning functions make our specifications support control flow that allows specifications of procedures and procedure calls, as well as general control flow between position independent and position dependent code. We build on previous work on separation logic [13] and unstructured control-flow [2,16].

Our framework has been fully formalised in higher-order logic, mechanised using the HOL4 system and has been applied to ARM machine-code using an existing high-fidelity model of the ARM processor [10]. We have not yet applied our framework to other architectures nor large case studies, but we think we have a methodology and implemented tools that will scale. Demonstrating this is the next phase of our research.

Acknowledgments. We would like to thank Anthony Fox, Joe Hurd, Konrad Slind, Thomas Tuerk, Matthew Parkinson, Josh Berdine, Nick Benton and Richard Bornat for research discussions, comments and substantial constructive criticism. The first author is funded by Osk.Huttusen Säätiö and EPSRC.

References

1. Andrew W. Appel. Foundational proof-carrying code. In *Proc. 16th IEEE Symposium on Logic in Computer Science (LICS)*. IEEE Computer Society, 2001.
2. Michael A. Arbib and Suad Alagic. Proof rules for gotos. *Acta Informatica*, 11:139–148, 1979.
3. William R. Bevier. *A verified operating system kernel*. PhD thesis, University of Texas at Austin, 1987.
4. Robert S. Boyer and Yuan Yu. Automated proofs of object code for a widely used microprocessor. *J. ACM*, 43(1):166–192, 1996.
5. D. L. Clutterbuck and B. A. Carré. The verification of low-level code. *Software Engineering Journal*, 3:97–111, 1988.
6. The HOL4 System (Description). http://hol.sourceforge.net/documentation.html.
7. David S. Hardin, Eric W. Smith, and William D. Young. A robust machine code proof framework for highly secure applications. In Panagiotis Manolios and Matthew Wilding, editors, *Sixth International Workshop on the ACL2 Theorem Prover and Its Applications*, 2006.
8. Gerwin Klein, Harvey Tuch, and Michael Norrish. Types, bytes, and separation logic. To appear in Martin Hofmann and Matthias Felleisen, editors, *Proceedings of the 34th ACM SIGPLAN-SIGACT Symposium on Principles of Programming Languages (POPL)*. Springer, 2007.
9. W. D. Maurer. Proving the correctness of a flight-director program for an airborne minicomputer. In *Proceedings of the ACM SIGMINI/SIGPLAN interface meeting on Programming systems in the small processor environment*. ACM Press, 1976.
10. Magnus O. Myreen, Anthony C. J. Fox, and Michael J. C. Gordon. Hoare logic for ARM machine code. To appear in *Proceedings of the IPM International Symposium on Fundamentals of Software Engineering (FSEN)*. Springer, 2007.
11. George C. Necula. Proof-carrying code. In *Proceedings of the 28th ACM SIGPLAN-SIGACT Symposium on Principles of Programming Languages (POPL)*, 1997.
12. Peter O'Hearn, John Reynolds, and Hongseok Yang. Local reasoning about programs that alter data structures. In *Proceedings of Computer Science Logic*, 2001.
13. John Reynolds. Separation logic: A logic for shared mutable data structures. In *Proceedings of 17th IEEE Symposium on Logic in Computer Science (LICS)*, 2002.
14. Ando Saabas and Tarmo Uustalu. A compositional natural semantics and hoare logic for low-level languages. *Electronic Notes in Theoretical Computer Science*, 156(1):151–168, 2006.
15. David Seal. *ARM Architecture Reference Manual*. Addison-Wesley, 2000.
16. Gang Tan and Andrew W. Appel. A compositional logic for control flow. In *Proceedings of Verification, Model Checking and Abstract Interpretation (VMCAI)*, volume 3855 of *Lecture Notes in Computer Science*. Springer, 2006.

VCEGAR: Verilog CounterExample Guided Abstraction Refinement*

Himanshu Jain[1], Daniel Kroening[2], Natasha Sharygina[1,3],
and Edmund Clarke[1]

[1] Carnegie Mellon University, School of Computer Science
[2] ETH Zuerich, Switzerland
[3] Informatics Department, University of Lugano

Abstract. As first step, most model checkers used in the hardware industry convert a high-level register transfer language (RTL) design into a netlist. However, algorithms that operate at the netlist level are unable to exploit the structure of the higher abstraction levels, and thus, are less scalable. The RTL level of a hardware description language such as Verilog is similar to a software program with special features for hardware design such as bit-vector arithmetic and concurrency. We describe a hardware model checking tool, VCEGAR, which performs verification at the RTL level using software verification techniques. It implements predicate abstraction and a refinement loop as used in software verification. The novel aspects are the generation of new word-level predicates, an efficient predicate image computation in presence of a large number of predicates, and precise modeling of the bit-vector semantics of hardware designs.

1 Introduction

Most new hardware designs are implemented at a high level of abstraction, e.g., using *register transfer language (RTL)*, or even at the system-level. The RTL level of a hardware description language such as Verilog is very similar to a software program in ANSI-C, and offers special features for hardware designers such as bit-vector arithmetic and concurrency. However, most model checkers used in hardware industry still operate on a low-level design representation called a *netlist*. This is due to lack of automated verification techniques at the RTL level. Converting a high-level RTL design into a netlist results in a significant loss of structure present at the RTL level. This makes verification at the netlist level inherently more difficult and less scalable.

VCEGAR, the tool presented in this paper, is a hardware model checker that performs verification at the RTL level directly. In order to reduce the state space explosion problem during model checking, VCEGAR performs abstraction. Abstraction techniques reduce the state space by mapping the set of states

---

* This research was sponsored by the Gigascale Systems Research Center (GSRC), Semiconductor Research Corporation (SRC), the National Science Foundation (NSF), the Office of Naval Research (ONR), the Naval Research Laboratory (NRL), the Defense Advanced Research Projects Agency, the Army Research Office (ARO), and the General Motors Collaborative Research Lab at CMU.

O. Grumberg and M. Huth (Eds.): TACAS 2007, LNCS 4424, pp. 583–586, 2007.

of the actual, concrete system to an abstract, and smaller, set of states in a way that preserves the relevant behaviors of the system. Since high-level hardware designs are similar to concurrent software, it implements abstraction algorithms that have been devised for software verification. VCEGAR employs predicate abstraction [1], a key technique used in the SLAM software verification project [2]. Predicate abstraction removes data by only keeping track of certain predicates on the data. Each predicate is represented by a Boolean variable in the abstract model, while the original data paths are eliminated.

The abstract model is computed as a *conservative* over-approximation of the original circuit. This implies that if the abstraction satisfies the property, the property also holds on the original circuit. The drawback of the conservative abstraction is that when model checking of the abstraction fails, it may produce a counterexample that does not correspond to any concrete counterexample. This is usually called a *spurious counterexample*. The basic idea of abstraction refinement techniques [3,4,2] is to create a new abstract model that contains more detail in order to prevent the spurious counterexample. This process is iterated until the property is either proved or disproved. It is known as the *Counterexample Guided Abstraction Refinement* framework [4].

VCEGAR is geared towards application by hardware designers. It accepts Verilog, a popular hardware description language, as input. VCEGAR checks safety properties of the hardware designs.

Related Work. In the hardware domain, the most commonly used abstraction technique is *localization reduction* [3]. The abstract model is created from a given netlist level circuit by removing a large number of latches together with the logic required to compute their next state. During refinement, some of the removed latches may be added back to make the abstract model more precise. While localization reduction is a special case of predicate abstraction, predicate abstraction can result in a much smaller abstract model. As an example, assume a circuit contains two sets of latches, each encoding a number. Predicate abstraction can keep track of a numerical relation between the two numbers using a single predicate, and thus, using a single state bit in the abstract model. Localization reduction typically turns all bits of the two words into visible latches, and thus, the abstraction is identical to the original model.

Clarke et al. introduce a SAT-based technique for predicate abstraction of circuits given in Verilog [5]. The first step is to obtain predicates from the control flow guards in the Verilog file. The circuit is then synthesized into netlist level. Any refinement steps are carried out at the netlist level, new word-level predicates are never introduced. VCEGAR operates at the RTL level also during refinement and uses weakest pre-conditions to derive new word-level predicates.

2 Word-Level Circuit Verification with VCEGAR

This section provides a short overview of ideas implemented in VCEGAR. For more information, we refer the reader to [6,7]. The abstraction step in VCEGAR is performed by computing a predicate image. Two problems arise when applying predicate abstraction to RTL level circuits: 1) The computation of the abstract model is hard in presence of large number of predicates, and 2) discovery of suitable word-level predicates for abstraction refinement.

In order to address the first problem, the tool divides the set of predicates into *clusters* of related predicates. The abstraction is computed separately with respect to the predicates in each cluster. Since each cluster contains only a small number of predicates, the computation of the abstraction becomes more efficient. We refer to this technique as *predicate clustering*. We do not require the clusters to be disjoint, that is, they can have common predicates.

Example: Let x, y denote the current state and x', y' denote the next state of a hardware design. Let the transition relation $R(x, y, x', y')$ be $x' = y \wedge y' = x$. Let the set of predicates be $\{x = 1, y = 1, x' = 1, y' = 1\}$. The value of the predicate $y' = 1$ is affected by the value of x (as y' equals x). Note that the value of $y' = 1$ is not affected by the value of y. Thus, we keep $x = 1$ and $y' = 1$ together in a cluster C_1. Similarly, the other cluster $C_2 := \{y = 1, x' = 1\}$ is obtained.

The tool provides various options for predicate clustering. These options control the precision of the abstraction and the time required to compute the abstraction. The tool uses a SAT solver to compute the abstract model [8].

Due to predicate clustering, additional spurious counterexamples are introduced, which have to be removed during the refinement phase. When a spurious counterexample is encountered, we first check whether each transition in the counterexample can be simulated on the original program. This is done by creating a SAT instance for the simulation of each abstract transition. If the SAT instance for an abstract transition is unsatisfiable, then the abstract transition is spurious. In this case, we refine the abstraction by adding constraints on the abstract transition relation, which eliminate the spurious transition. We make use of the *unsatisfiable core* of the SAT instance to identify a small subset of the existing predicates that are causing the transition to be spurious. The fewer predicates are found, the more spurious transitions are eliminated in one step.

When all SAT instances for the simulation of abstract transitions are satisfiable, it means that none of the abstract transitions is spurious due to the predicate clustering. The immediate conclusion is that the spurious counterexample is caused by a lack of appropriate predicates. For this case, VCEGAR uses a refinement technique employed in software verification tools. It first determines a set of predicates that causes the simulation to fail. Subsequently, it computes the weakest precondition of these predicates with respect to the transition function given by the circuit in order to obtain new word-level predicates. *Example:* Let the property be $x < 3$, and the next state function for the register x be $((x < 5)?(x + 2) : x)$, where ? denotes a conditional operator. Suppose we obtain a spurious counterexample of length equal to 1. The weakest precondition wp of $x < 3$ is given as $(((x < 5) ? (x+2) : x) < 3)$. Refinement corresponds to adding the Boolean expressions occurring in wp to the existing set of predicates.

In case of a long spurious counterexample, the weakest precondition computation may become expensive due to a blowup in the size of weakest pre-conditions. We address this problem by applying a syntactic *simplification* to the weakest preconditions at each step. The simplification uses data from the abstract error trace. We exploit the fact that many of the control flow guards in the Verilog file are also present in the current set of predicates. The abstract trace assigns truth values to these predicates in each abstract state. In order to simplify the weakest preconditions, we substitute the guards in the weakest preconditions with their truth values. Furthermore, we only add the atomic predicates in the simplified weakest precondition as the new predicates (more details in [6]).

Example: Suppose the guard $x < 5$ is present in the current set of predicates. Let the value of $x < 5$ in an abstract state $\bar{s}$ be **true**. The weakest precondition given as $(((x < 5) ? (x + 2) : x) < 3)$ can be simplified in $\bar{s}$ by substituting the value of $x < 5$. This results in a new atomic predicate $x + 2 < 3$ (or $x < 1$).

VCEGAR was used to check safety properties of Instruction Cache Unit and Instruction Cache RAM (ICRAM) of Sun PicoJava II microprocessor in [7]. It has also been applied to examples from the opencores (www.opencores.org), and the Texas97 and VIS benchmark suites.

3   Conclusion

This paper describes a hardware model checker, VCEGAR, that implements counterexample guided abstraction and a refinement loop for RTL Verilog designs. It uses the idea of predicate abstraction from software verification tools. VCEGAR provides various options for balancing the precision of abstraction and the time required for abstraction computation. For abstraction-refinement new word-level predicates are discovered by computing syntactic weakest preconditions of predicates with respect to Verilog statements. This technique has not been applied to RTL circuits before. A user of the tool needs to provide the input program, property to check, and a few options. Given these inputs, the tool performs all the steps of the CEGAR loop automatically.

References

1. Graf, S., Saïdi, H.: Construction of abstract state graphs with PVS. In: CAV. Volume 1254 of LNCS., Springer (1997) 72–83
2. Ball, T., Rajamani, S.: Boolean programs: A model and process for software analysis. Technical Report 2000-14, Microsoft Research (2000)
3. Kurshan, R.: Computer-Aided Verification of Coordinating Processes. Princeton University Press, Princeton (1995)
4. Clarke, E.M., Grumberg, O., Jha, S., Lu, Y., Veith, H.: Counterexample-guided abstraction refinement. In: CAV. (2000) 154–169
5. Clarke, E., Talupur, M., Wang, D.: SAT based predicate abstraction for hardware verification. In: SAT. (2003)
6. Clarke, E., Jain, H., Kroening, D.: Predicate Abstraction and Refinement Techniques for Verifying Verilog. Technical Report CMU-CS-04-139 (2004)
7. Jain, H., Kroening, D., Sharygina, N., Clarke, E.M.: Word level predicate abstraction and refinement for verifying RTL In: DAC. (2005) 445–450
8. Clarke, E., Kroening, D., Sharygina, N., Yorav, K.: Predicate abstraction of ANSI–C programs using SAT. Formal Methods in System Design:25 (2004) 105–127

Alloy Analyzer+PVS in the Analysis and Verification of Alloy Specifications

Marcelo F. Frias*, Carlos G. Lopez Pombo, and Mariano M. Moscato

Department of Computer Science, FCEyN,
Universidad de Buenos Aires and CONICET
{mfrias,clpombo,mmoscato}@dc.uba.ar

Abstract. This article contains two main contributions. On the theoretical side, it presents a novel complete proof calculus for Alloy. On the applied side we present Dynamite, a tool that combines the semiautomatic theorem prover PVS with the Alloy Analyzer. Dynamite allows one to prove an Alloy assertion from an Alloy specification using PVS, while using the Alloy Analyzer for the automated analysis of hypotheses introduced during the proof process. As a means to assess the usability of the tool, we present a complex case-study based on Zave's Alloy model of addressing for interoperating networks.

1 Introduction

Alloy [7] is a formal modeling language with a simple syntax based on notations ubiquitous in object orientation, and semantics based on relations. Part of its appeal comes from the existence of the Alloy Analyzer, which allows one to analyze Alloy specifications in a fully automatic way. The analysis process relies on a translation of Alloy specifications (where domains are bounded to finite sizes) to a propositional formula, which is then analyzed using off-the-shelf SAT-solvers. Bounding the size of domains has a direct impact on the conclusions we can draw from the analysis process. If a counterexample for a given assertion is found, then the model is for sure flawed. On the other hand, if no counterexample is found, we can only conclude that no counterexamples exist when domain sizes are constrained to the given bounds. Choosing larger bounds may show the existence of previously unforeseen errors. This limited analyzability offered by the Alloy Analyzer is essential in order to analyze Alloy models and get rid of most errors introduced in the modeling process. At the same time, models for critical applications can also benefit from usage of the Alloy Analyzer, but one cannot entirely rely on that.

Lightweight formal methods with the limitations of the Alloy Analyzer cannot be entirely trusted when dealing with critical models. An alternative is the use of heavyweight formal methods, as for instance semi-automatic theorem provers,

---

* A preliminary version of this paper has been published in the ACM Digital Library as part of the proceedings of the First Alloy Workshop, colocated with 14th ACM Symposium on Foundations of Software Engineering, 2006 [6].

O. Grumberg and M. Huth (Eds.): TACAS 2007, LNCS 4424, pp. 587–601, 2007.

and among these, PVS [10]. Theorem provers have limitations too. First, they require an expertise from the user that many times discourages their use. Also, theorem provers use their own languages which are seldom close to lightweight modeling languages. This detracts from their usability by lightweight users, and is also a source of errors in case lightweight models have to be translated. Equally important, minor errors in a model may require to redo proofs that were using wrong hypotheses. Much the same as errors overlooked during software requirement elicitation have a greater impact the more advanced the development stage, model errors have greater impact the more auxiliary lemmas have been proved. Therefore, getting rid of as many errors as possible from the model before starting the theorem proving process is a must.

The previous paragraphs show that a marriage between simple automatically analyzable formal modeling languages and semiautomatic theorem provers is in fact necessary when analyzing critical models. The goal of this paper is to present Dynamite, a tool that marries Alloy and PVS.

Dynamite is an extension of PVS that incorporates the following features:

1. Sound automatic translation of Alloy models to PVS, preventing the introduction of errors in the translation process.
2. Novel complete proof calculus for Alloy. Therefore, valid Alloy properties can be proved (although this requires interaction with the user).
3. Modified PVS pretty-printer that shows proof steps in Alloy language (thus bridging the gap between Alloy and PVS).
4. Fluid automatic interaction with the Alloy Analyzer in order to automatically analyze hypotheses introduced during the theorem proving process.

The contributions of this paper are the following:

1. We present a novel complete calculus for Alloy by interpreting Alloy theories to fork algebra [3] theories.
2. We present Dynamite, the tool that incorporates the previously enumerated features.
3. We give a brief description of a case study where we prove several assertions introduced in Zave's Alloy model of addressing for interoperating networks [12], and present some conclusions regarding the usability and limitations of Dynamite.

The article is organized as follows. In Section 2 we present the Alloy modeling language by means of an example, as well as its supporting tool, the Alloy Analyzer. In Section 3 we present the complete calculus for Alloy. In Section 4 we describe our tool, Dynamite. In Section 5 we discuss a complex case-study. Finally, in Section 6 we discuss related work, conclusions about the contributions of this article, and some proposals for further work.

2   Alloy and the Alloy Analyzer

In this section we introduce the Alloy modeling language by means of an example. In [12] Zave presents a formal model of addressing for interoperating networks. These networks connect *agents* (which might be hardware devices or other software systems). Agents can be divided between *client agents* (users of the networking infrastructure), or *server agents* (part of the infrastructure). Agents can use resources from domains, to which they must be *attached*. In order to be able to reach clients from domains, pairs ⟨*address, domain*⟩ are assigned to clients. Different sorts of objects can be distinguished in the previous description. Signatures (akin to classes in object orientation), are the means to declare object domains. Figure 1 presents a (simplified[1] description of the signatures for this model.

```
sig Address{ }
sig Agent{ attachments: set Domain }
sig Server extends Agent { }
sig Client extends Agent { knownAt: Address -> Domain }
sig Domain{ space: set Address, map: space -> Agent }
```

Fig. 1. Simplified model for addresses, agents and domains

Signature **Address** denotes a unary relation (set) whose objects are atomic. According to Alloy's formal semantics, signature **Agent** declares a set of objects *Agent*, and field **attachments** denotes a binary relation *attachments* ⊆ *Agent* × *Domain* (where *Domain* is the set denoted by signature **Domain**). Notice that without the modifier **set** in the declaration of field **attachments**, relation *attachments* would instead be a total function. Signature extension allows us to model single inheritance between signatures. Signature **Server** singles out some agents as *servers*. Signature **Client**, besides distinguishing some agents as *clients*, introduces a new field. Field **knownAt** allows us to retrieve the pairs ⟨*address, domain*⟩ mentioned above. Following Alloy's semantics, field **knownAt** denotes a *ternary* relation *knownAt* ⊆ *Client* × *Address* × *Domain*.

Axioms are included in a model under the form of *facts*. Recalling that dot (.) stands for composition of relations (called *navigation* in Alloy), an axiom saying that "whenever an agent appears in the range of the **map** attribute it is because the agent is attached to that domain", is written in Alloy as:

```
fact { all d: Domain, g: Agent |
            g in Address.(d.map) => d in g.attachments }
```

Besides navigation, the relational logic underlying Alloy [7] includes operations for union of relations (+), intersection (&), difference (−), transposition (which flips pairs ⟨x, y⟩ of a binary relation to ⟨y, x⟩ and is denoted by ∼) and reflexive-transitive closure (∗). Also, *iden* denotes the binary identity relation, and *univ* denotes the unary universal relation (the set holding the union of all the domains from the model).

---

[1] The complete Alloy model can be obtained from http://www.research.att. com/∼pamela/svcrte.html

Once a model has been provided, it can be analyzed by looking for counterexamples of properties that are expected to hold in the model. These properties are called *assertions*. For instance, the (not necessarily valid) assertion that the `map` field targets only client agents, is written in Alloy as:

```
assert mapTargetsClients { all d:Domain, s:d.space |
                                        s.(d.map) in Client }
```

Command `check mapTargetsClients for 5` allows one to search for counterexamples in which domains have up to 5 elements, using the Alloy Analyzer. The Alloy Analyzer translates the model and the negation of the assertion to a propositional formula. Of course, the translation heavily depends on the bounds declared in the `check` command. Once a propositional formula has been obtained, the Alloy Analyzer employs off-the-shelf SAT-solvers, and in case a model of the formula is obtained, it is translated back to a counterexample of the source model and presented to the user using different visualization algorithms.

3   A Novel Complete Calculus for Alloy

Among the extensions of PVS included in Dynamite, an essential one is the inclusion of a complete calculus for Alloy. The calculus is obtained by translating Alloy theories (specifications) to fork algebraic theories (to be introduced in Section 3.1). Since:

1. the translation is semantics-preserving, and
2. there is a complete calculus for the fork algebras we will use in this article,

we will prove a theorem stating that an assertion α (semantically) follows from an Alloy specification Σ if (and only if) its translation $T(\alpha)$ can be proved from the translation of the theory using the complete calculus for fork algebras. In symbols, $\Sigma \models \alpha \iff \{T(\sigma) : \sigma \in \Sigma\} \vdash T(\alpha)$. This kind of theorems relating two logics are often called interpretation theorems.

The following question is now likely to arise:

> *Is the fork algebra language substantially different from the Alloy language (therefore reducing the usability of the proposed calculus by current Alloy users)?*

This section is then structured as follows. In Section 3.1 we introduce the class of point-dense omega closure fork algebras (also noted as PDOCFA), as well as their complete calculus. In Section 3.2 we present the translation from Alloy formulas to formulas in the language of PDOCFA, and provide a proof sketch of the interpretation theorem. Since we aim at defining a translation that yields algebraic formulas as close to Alloy formulas as possible, in Section 3.3 we give an answer to the previous question and analyze the similarities and differences between the Alloy language and the fork algebraic language.

3.1 Point-Dense Omega Closure Fork Algebras

Proper Point-Dense Omega Closure Fork Algebras. These algebras are structures whose domain is a set of binary relations built on top of a base set B. We denote by $Pw(A)$ the powerset of set A. If we call R the domain of such an algebra (notice that $R \subseteq Pw(B \times B)$), R has to be closed under the following operations for sets: *union* $(+)$, *intersection* $(\&)$, *complement* (denoted, for a binary relation r, by $\bar{r}$), the *empty* binary relation $(\emptyset)$, and the *universal* binary relation, (usually $B \times B$, and denoted by 1).

Besides the previous operations for sets, R has to be closed under the following operations for binary relations: *transposition* $(\sim)$, *navigation* $(.)$, and *reflexive–transitive closure* $(*)$. The *identity* relation (on B), is denoted by *iden*.

A binary operation called *fork* (∇) is included, which requires set B to be closed under an injective function $\star$. This means that there are elements x in B that are the result of applying the function $\star$ to elements y and z (i.e., $x = y \star z$). Since $\star$ is injective, x can be seen as an encoding of the pair $\langle y, z \rangle$. Those elements that <u>do not</u> encode pairs, are called *urelements*. Operation fork is defined by:

$$r \nabla s = \{ \langle a, b \star c \rangle : \langle a, b \rangle \in r \text{ and } \langle a, c \rangle \in s \} \ .$$

Finally, we require set R to be *point-dense*. A point is a relation of the form $\{ \langle a, a \rangle \}$. Point-density requires set R to have plenty of these relations. More formally speaking, for each nonempty relation I contained in the identity relation there must be a point $p \in R$ satisfying $p \subseteq I$.

A Complete Calculus for Point-Dense Omega Closure Fork Agebras. Introducing a calculus requires presenting its axioms and inference rules. Before doing so, we introduce some notation. In a proper PDOCFA the relations π and ρ defined by $\pi =\sim (iden \nabla 1)$ and $\rho =\sim (1 \nabla iden)$ behave as projections with respect to the encoding of pairs induced by the injective function $\star$. Their semantics in a proper PDOCFA $\mathfrak{A}$ whose binary relations range over a set B, is given by $\pi = \{ \langle a \star b, a \rangle : a, b \in B \}$, $\rho = \{ \langle a \star b, b \rangle : a, b \in B \}$.

The operation *cross* $(\otimes)$ performs a parallel product. Its set-theoretical definition is given by $r \otimes s = \{ \langle a \star c, b \star d \rangle : \langle a, b \rangle \in r \text{ and } \langle c, d \rangle \in s \}$. In algebraic terms, operation cross is defined by $r \otimes s = (\pi.r) \nabla (\rho.s)$.

We can characterize points as nonempty relations that satisfy the property $x.1.x \subseteq iden$. If we denote the inclusion relation by "in" (as in Alloy), the predicate "Point" defined by "Point$(p) \iff p != \emptyset \ \&\& \ p.1.p \text{ in } iden$" determines those relations that are points. The axioms and inference rules for the calculus are then:

1. Axioms for Boolean algebras defining the meaning of $+$, $\&$, $^-$, $\emptyset$ and 1.
2. Formulas defining composition of binary relations, transposition, reflexive–transitive closure and the identity relation:
   $x.(y.z) = (x.y).z$,
   $x.iden = iden.x = x$,
   $(x.y) \& z = \emptyset$ iff $(z. \sim y) \& x = \emptyset$ iff $(\sim x.z) \& y = \emptyset$,
   $*x = iden + (x.*x)$,
   $*x.y.1 \text{ in } (y.1) + (*x.(\overline{y.1} \& (x.y.1)))$.

3. Formulas defining the operator ∇:
$x \nabla y = (x. \sim \pi) \& (y. \sim \rho)$,
$(x \nabla y). \sim (w \nabla z) = (x. \sim w) \& (y. \sim z)$,
$\pi \nabla \rho$ in $iden$.

4. A formula enforcing point-density:
all $x \mid (x \mathrel{!=} \emptyset \&\& x$ in $iden) \Longrightarrow (\text{some } p \mid \text{Point}(p) \&\& p$ in $x)$,

5. Term $\overline{1}. \overline{(1 \nabla 1)} \& iden$ (to be abbreviated as $iden_\cup$) defines a partial identity on the set of urelements. Then, the following formula forces the existence of a nonempty set of urelements:
$1. iden_\cup . 1 = 1$

The inference rules for the closure fork calculus are those for classical first-order logic (choose you favorite ones), plus the following equational (but infinitary) proof rule for reflexive-transitive closure. Given $i > 0$, by x^i we denote the relation inductively defined as follows: $x^1 = x$, and $x^{i+1} = x.x^i$.

$$\frac{\vdash iden \text{ in } y \quad x^i \text{ in } y \vdash x^{i+1} \text{ in } y}{\vdash *x \text{ in } y} \quad (\Omega \text{ Rule})$$

The axioms and rules given above define a class of models. Proper PDOCFA satisfy the axioms [4], and therefore belong to this class. It could be the case that there are models for the axioms that are not proper PDOCFA. Fortunately, the following theorem (which follows from [4], [3, Thm. 4.2], [9, Thm. 52]), states that if a model is not a proper PDOCFA then it is isomorphic to one.

Theorem 1. *Every* PDOCFA $\mathfrak{A}$ *is isomorphic to a proper* PDOCFA $\mathfrak{B}$. *Moreover, there exist relations* $\{ \langle a_0, a_0 \rangle \}, \ldots, \{ \langle a_i, a_i \rangle \} \ldots$ *(possibly infinitely many of them) that belong to* $\mathfrak{B}$, *such that* $iden = \{ \langle a_0, a_0 \rangle, \ldots, \langle a_i, a_i \rangle, \ldots \}$.

Constraining Quantifiers to Atoms. Alloy quantifiers range over relations of the form $\{ a \}$, i.e., over unary singletons. On the other hand, relational quantifiers range over the elements of a PDOCFA, which are not even required to be relations (recall that PDOCFAs are just models of a set of axioms). But, since PDOCFAs are all isomorphic to proper ones, a relational quantifier can always be seen as ranging over all binary relations from a proper PDOCFA. Still a big distance remains between unary singletons and arbitrary binary relations. It is at least obvious that there are many more of the latter, than there are of the former. Point-density, by forcing the existence of all singletons, allows us to establish a one-one correspondence between $\{ a \}$ and $\{ \langle a, a \rangle \}$. Therefore, we will mimic the behavior of Alloy quantifiers by constraining relational quantifiers to range over points. Notice that some points hold urelements, but others do not. In this case, since Alloy atoms do not have structure (the structure is modeled through fields), we will employ points holding urelements.

We will now consider the restricted part of the first-order language of PDOCFAs defined by the following grammar:

$$\text{F} ::= \text{Equation} \mid !\text{F} \mid \text{F1} \parallel \text{F2} \mid \text{F1} \&\& \text{F2} \mid$$
$$::= \text{all p} / (\text{Point(p)} \&\& \text{p in } iden_\cup) \text{ implies F}$$

Actually, in a PDOCFA we will have different sub relations of $iden_U$, namely $iden_1, \ldots, iden_k$, representing each one a different Alloy signature $sig_1, \ldots, sig_k$. We will then use the following abbreviated notation for formulas. The formula "all p | (Point(p) && p in $iden_i$) implies F" is denoted as "all p : sig_i | F". Similar abbreviations are used for the "some" quantifier.

3.2   A Complete Calculus for Alloy

In this section we introduce a mapping from Alloy formulas to formulas in the language defined in Section 3.1. The mapping keeps the structure of Alloy formulas almost unchanged, thus simplifying the understanding of the resulting formulas by casual Alloy users. Since PDOCFAs only contain binary relations, we will show how to model relations of arbitrary rank as binary ones, with the aid of fork. We then prove that the resulting calculus is complete for Alloy.

Handling Relations of Rank Greater Than Two. Recall that due to the fork operator, the underlying domain of a proper PDOCFA is closed under an injective operation $\star$. Given a n-ary relation $R \subseteq A_1 \times \cdots \times A_n$, we will represent it by the binary relation

$$\{ \langle a_1, a_2 \star \cdots \star a_n \rangle : \langle a_1, \ldots, a_n \rangle \in R \} \ .$$

This will be an invariant in the representation of n-ary relations by binary ones. For instance, ternary relation knownAt is encoded as a binary relation knownAt whose elements are pairs of the form $\langle c, a \star d \rangle$ for c : *Client*, a : *Address* and d : *Domain*. We will in general denote the encoding of a relation C as a binary relation, by C. Given a point c : *Client*, the navigation of the relation knownAt through c should result in a binary relation contained in *Address* $\times$ *Domain*. Given a point a : t and a binary relation R encoding a relation of rank higher than 2, we define the navigation operation $\bullet$ by

$$a \bullet R = \sim \pi . Ran\,(a.R)\,.\rho \ . \tag{1}$$

Operation Ran in (1) returns the range of a relation as a partial identity. It is defined by $Ran\,(x) = (x.1)\,\&iden$. Its semantics in terms of binary relations is given by $Ran\,(R) = \{ \langle a, a \rangle : \text{some } b \mid \langle b, a \rangle \in R \}$.

For a binary relation R representing a relation of rank less than or equal to 2, navigation is easier. Given a point a : t, we define

$$a \bullet R = Ran\,(a.R) \ .$$

It still remains to define navigation whenever the relation on the left-hand side is not a point, i.e., it has rank greater than 1. The definition is as follows:

$$R \bullet S = \begin{cases} R.\,(iden \otimes (iden \otimes (\cdots \otimes ((iden \otimes S)\,.\pi)))) & \text{if rank}(S) = 1 \\ R.\,(iden \otimes (iden \otimes (\cdots \otimes (iden \otimes S)))) & \text{if rank}(S) > 1 \end{cases}$$

Going back to our example about agents, it is easy to check that for a point c' : *Client* such that $c' = \{ \langle c, c \rangle \}$,

$$c' \bullet \text{knownAt} = \{ \langle a, d \rangle : a \in Address, d \in Domain \text{ and } \langle c, a \star d \rangle \in \text{knownAt} \} \ .$$

Translating Alloy Formulas to Relational Formulas. In this section we present a translation of Alloy formulas to formulas in the language of PDOCFAs. Prior to that, it is necessary to translate Alloy terms to fork-algebra terms.

$$
\begin{array}{ll}
T(C) \ \ = \mathsf{C}, & T(r+s) = T(r) + T(s), \\
T(x_i) \ = X_i, (X_i \text{ variable ranging over points}) & T(r\&s) \ = T(r)\&T(s), \\
T(\sim r) = \ \sim T(r), & T(r-s) = T(r)\&\overline{T(s)}, \\
T(*r) \ = *T(r), & T(r.s) \ \ = T(r) \bullet T(s)
\end{array}
$$

We are now in the right conditions for translating formulas. The translation differs from the one previously presented in [5] in that the target of the translation is a first-order language rather than an equational language, and therefore it is no longer necessary to encode quantified variables because these are kept explicit. This will greatly improve the understandability of the translation by a casual Alloy user.

$$
\begin{array}{ll}
F(t_1 \text{ in } t_2) = T(t_1) \text{ in } T(t_2), & F(\alpha \ \&\& \ \beta) \qquad = F(\alpha) \ \&\& \ F(\beta), \\
F(!\alpha) \qquad = !F(\alpha), & F(\text{all } x : S \mid \alpha) \ \ = \text{all } x : S \mid F(\alpha), \\
F(\alpha \mid\mid \beta) \ \ = F(\alpha) \mid\mid F(\beta), & F(\text{some } x : S \mid \alpha) = \text{some } x : S \mid F(\alpha).
\end{array}
$$

Recall that quantifications in the right-hand side are abbreviations for formulas where quantifiers range over points of the appropriate signature. Notice that formulas are undistinguishable from Alloy formulas.

Completeness of the Alloy Calculus. Formal semantics of Alloy assigns semantics to expressions and formulas in a given *environment*. An environment is a function that assigns sets to signatures, adequate relations to relational constants (those arising from signature fields), and values to variables over individuals. From an Alloy environment e we build a PDOCFA $\mathfrak{F}_e$ and a relational environment e' as follows:

- Let $\text{sig}_1, \dots, \text{sig}_k$ be the Alloy signatures. Let $A = \bigcup_{1 \le i \le k} e\,(\text{sig}_i)$. Let $\mathfrak{T}(A)$ be the set of finite binary trees with information in the leaves, and whose information are elements from A.
- Let $\mathfrak{F}_e$ be the omega closure fork algebra with universe $Pw\,(\mathfrak{T}(A) \times \mathfrak{T}(A))$. If we denote the tree constructors by: $\mathsf{leaf} : A \to \mathfrak{T}(A)$ and $\mathsf{bin} : \mathfrak{T}(A) \times \mathfrak{T}(A) \to \mathfrak{T}(A)$, the fork operation is defined by

$$
R \nabla S = \{ \langle a, \mathsf{bin}(b,c) \rangle : \langle a, b \rangle \in R \ \wedge \ \langle a, c \rangle \in S \} \ .
$$

Notice that the remaining operations have their meaning fixed once the domain $Pw\,(\mathfrak{T}(A) \times \mathfrak{T}(A))$ is fixed.
- Let e' be the environment satisfying:
  - $e'(\text{sig}_i) = \{ p \in \mathfrak{F}_e : \text{Point}(p) \wedge p \le iden_{e(\text{sig}_i)} \}$,
  - $e'(R) = \mathsf{R}$ (the binary encoding of relation $e(R)$),
  - $e'(v_i) = \{ \langle e(v_i), e(v_i) \rangle \}$.

Similarly, given a proper PDOCFA, and a relational environment e, we define an Alloy environment e' as follows:

- $e'(\text{sig}_i) = \{\, a : \langle a, a \rangle \in iden_{\text{sig}_i} \,\}$,
- $e'(R) = \{\, \langle a_1, \ldots, a_n \rangle : \langle a_1, a_2 \star \cdots \star a_n \rangle \in e(R) \,\}$,
- $e'(v_i) = a$ such that $e(v_i) = \{\, \langle a, a \rangle \,\}$.

From the previous definitions, the following lemmata can be proved by induction on the structure of Alloy formulas. The proofs are not included due to the lack of space, but follow the lines of previous interpretability results by the authors [3,5].

Lemma 1. *Given an Alloy environment* e, $\models \varphi[e] \iff \mathfrak{F}_e \models F(\varphi)[e']$.

Lemma 2. *Given a* PDOCFA $\mathfrak{F}$ *and a relational environment* e, *there exists an Alloy environment* e' *such that for every Alloy formula* φ, $\mathfrak{F} \models F(\varphi)[e] \iff \models \varphi[e']$.

We then prove the following completeness theorem. The turnstile symbol $\vdash$ stands for derivability in the calculus for PDOCFAs.

Theorem 2. *Let* $\Sigma \cup \{\varphi\}$ *be a set of Alloy formulas. Then,*

$$\Sigma \models \varphi \iff \{\, F(\sigma) : \sigma \in \Sigma \,\} \vdash F(\varphi).$$

Proof. $\Longrightarrow$) If $\{\, F(\sigma) : \sigma \in \Sigma \,\} \nvdash F(\varphi)$, then there exists a PDOCFA $\mathfrak{F}$ such that $\mathfrak{F} \models \{\, F(\sigma) : \sigma \in \Sigma \,\}$ and $\mathfrak{F} \nvDash F(\varphi)$. From Thm. 1 there exists a proper PDOCFA $\mathfrak{F}'$ isomorphic to $\mathfrak{F}$. Clearly, $\mathfrak{F}' \models \{\, F(\sigma) : \sigma \in \Sigma \,\}$ and $\mathfrak{F}' \nvDash F(\varphi)$. Then, there is a relational environment e such that $\mathfrak{F}' \models \{\, F(\sigma) : \sigma \in \Sigma \,\}[e]$ and $\mathfrak{F}' \nvDash F(\varphi)[e]$. From Lemma 2, there exists an Alloy environment e' such that $\models \Sigma[e']$ and $\nvDash \varphi[e']$. Thus, $\Sigma \nvDash \varphi$.
$\Longleftarrow$) If $\Sigma \nvDash \varphi$, then there exists an Alloy environment e such that $\models \Sigma[e]$ and $\nvDash \varphi[e]$. From Lemma 1 there exist a proper PDOCFA $\mathfrak{F}_e$ and a relational environment e' such that $\mathfrak{F}_e \models \{\, F(\sigma) : \sigma \in \Sigma \,\}[e']$ and $\mathfrak{F}_e \nvDash F(\varphi)[e']$. Then, $\{\, F(\sigma) : \sigma \in \Sigma \,\} \nvdash F(\varphi)$.

3.3   Comparing the Source and Target Formalisms

If the calculus introduced in Section 3.2 is to be used by Alloy users, then the language should be as close as possible to Alloy. The translation of formulas shows that the formulas result of applying the translation (we are not discussing terms yet) are indeed Alloy formulas. It is clear that Alloy operations have a direct algebraic counterpart. Thus, from a syntactical point of view, terms result of the translation are also Alloy terms. There are a few points that need to be addressed, though. Namely:

1. Atoms (which in Alloy are modeled as unary singletons $\{\, a \,\}$) are modeled in the algebraic setting as singleton binary relations $\{\, \langle a, a \rangle \,\}$.
2. More generally, relations that may have rank greater than 2 in Alloy, are modeled in the algebraic setting as binary relations.

In our experience it is seldom the case that two relations having rank greater than 2 are composed. The most common situation arises when an atom is composed with a relation of higher rank $(a.R)$. We provide in Dynamite a theory for fork algebras that includes proofs of the usual properties of composition, as for instance

all R, S, T | R in S implies $(R \bullet T$ in $S \bullet T)$ && $(T \bullet R$ in $T \bullet S)$monotonicity
all R, S, T | !Set(S) implies $(R \bullet S) \bullet T = R \bullet (S \bullet T)$ associativity

Proving these properties requires using the full power of the calculus, including quantifications over relations, which cannot even be expressed in Alloy. These are part of the infrastructure provided by Dynamite. A user can prove particular instances of (for example) monotonicity with respect to fields F_1, F_2, F_3 (provided by the Alloy model) by instantiating the previous properties. She can also prove the property from scratch for the particular instances using Dynamite.

4   The Dynamite Tool

PVS [10] interacts with its users through the highly customizable text editor EMACS. Dynamite is a tool developed by customizing both EMACS and PVS. In Sections 4.1 and 4.2 we describe these customizations. In Section 4.3 we describe the proof process a user would go through, showing how these adaptations make the proof process more amenable.

4.1   Customizations Made on EMACS

EMACS is a highly customizable text editor. It is possible to run other applications from within EMACS. It is now possible to run the Alloy Analyzer on a specific model in order to analyze a provided assertion. While the standard scope for domains is 3, it is also possible for the user to choose new scopes. This is extremely useful when adding lemmas whose proof has not yet been developed, to a theory. The new lemma can be checked within the theory both for counterexamples and consistency with the aid of the Alloy Analyzer. Once PVS has been started, it is possible to choose an Alloy model (a .als file) and an extension of EMACS allows one to translate the Alloy model to an appropriate PVS theory.

4.2   Customizations Made on PVS

PVS reads theories and shows proofs in its specific syntax. Even properties written in Alloy, if one wants to prove them with the support of PVS, have to be rewritten using the syntax PVS recognizes. We have modified the PVS pretty printer in order to exhibit formulas using Alloy syntax. This will be shown with an example in Section 5.

The PVS rule "case", which allows one to introduce new hypotheses along a proof, has also been modified. According to [10], if the current sequent is of the form $\Gamma \vdash \Delta$, then the rule "(case A)" generates the subgoals $A, \Gamma \vdash \Delta$ and

$\varGamma \vdash A, \varDelta$. The rule allows to use formula A as an extra hypothesis along the proof of $\varDelta$, which has to be discharged later through a proof. Executing the modified rule "case", besides performing its regular duty of generating the appropriate subgoals, also automatically analyzes formula A using the Alloy Analyzer.

4.3 A Proof Scenario

A development team has built an Alloy model for a critical domain, and has already debugged it by automatically analyzing (using the Alloy Analyzer) some appropriate assertions. Since the model will serve as a basis for the development of a critical system, bounded analysis is not enough. The team then faces the need to prove a given property about their model. Upon starting Dynamite, they choose to upload the Alloy model. This generates (although they do not need to know about it), the corresponding PVS theory, and the user can choose an assertion to prove. Facts from the model are now available as axioms to be used in proofs.

The proof then proceeds until a new hypothesis has to be introduced using the PVS command "case", in whose case the Alloy Analyzer is launched in the background in order to check the hypothesis for counterexamples and consistency. If a new lemma has to be added to the theory, then the Alloy Analyzer can be used from within the framework in order to check for the existence of counterexamples and for consistency, too.

5   A Case Study: A Formal Model of Addressing for Interoperating Networks

In her paper [12], Zave presents a formal model of addressing for interoperating networks. Part of the model is presented in Fig. 1. Domains can create persistent connections between agents. Such connections are called *hops*. Besides the domain that created it, a hop contains information about the initiator and acceptor agents taking part in the connection, and also source and target addresses. A fact forces these addresses to correspond to the agents (according to the domain map).

```
sig Hop{ domain: Domain,
         initiator, acceptor: Agent,
         source, target: Address }
```

Multi-hop connections are enabled by the servers. These connections are called *links*. Links contain information about the server enabling the connection, and about the connected hops.

```
abstract sig End { }
one sig Init, Accept extends End { }
sig Link{ agent:Server, oneHop,anotherHop:Hop, oneEnd,anotherEnd:End }
{  oneHop != anotherHop
   oneEnd in Init => agent=oneHop.initiator
   oneEnd in Accept => agent=oneHop.acceptor
   anotherEnd in Init => agent=anotherHop.initiator
   anotherEnd in Accept => agent=anotherHop.acceptor }
```

The reflexive-transitive closure of the accessibility relation determined by links is kept by an object "Connections", which also keeps the relation established by the links.

```
one sig Connections{ atomConnected, connected: Hop -> Hop }
```

Interoperation is considered a *feature* of networks. Features are installed in domains and have a set of servers from that domain that implement them. Among the facts related to features, we find that each feature has at least one server, and that each server implements exactly one feature.

```
abstract sig Feature { domain: Domain, servers: set Server }
```

Interoperation features are then characterized as follows:

```
sig InteropFeature extends Feature{
    toDomain: Domain,
    exported, imported, remote, local: set Address,
    interTrans: exported some -> some imported }
{   domain != toDomain
    exported in domain.space    && remote in exported
    imported in toDomain.space && local in imported
    remote.interTrans = local }
```

An interoperation feature translates addresses (through relation interTrans) between different domains. This is necessary because whenever a client from the feature's domain wishes to connect to a client attached to a different domain, it must have a target address it can use in its own domain space. Of course, the target client must have an address in each domain from which it is to be reached. Different facts are introduced in [12] in order to fully understand an interoperation feature behavior, and the following assertions are singled out:

- ConnectedIsEquivalence, asserting that field connected is indeed an equivalence relation (reflexive, symmetric and transitive).
- UnidirectionalChains, asserting that two hops are connected through a link in an ordered manner (one can be identified as *initiator* and the other one as *acceptor*).
- Reachability, asserting that whenever a client c publishes an address a in a domain d ($\langle a, d \rangle \in c.\text{knownAt}$), clients c' from domain d can effectively connect to c.
- Returnability, asserting that if a client c accepted a connection from another client c', then a hop from c can be extended to a complete connection to client c'.

We proved these properties from the Alloy model using Dynamite. Without using the modified pretty printer from PVS, the PVS specification of the returnability predicate looks like this:

```
FAL_Returnability :

        |-------
  {1}    FORALL (hDm: (hop_domain), fDm: (feature_domain),
              tDm: (toDomain), tar: (target), rem: (remote),
              aCn: (atomConnected), con: (connected), oHp: (oneHop),
              aHp: (anotherHop), rBy: (reachedBy), map: (map),
              acc: (acceptor), srv: (servers), exp: (exported),
              imp: (imported), loc: (local), iTr: (interTrans),
              spc: (space), agn: (agent), oEd: (oneEnd),
              aEd: (anotherEnd), ini: (initiator),
[!t]          att: (attachments), src: (source)):
          FORALL (g1, g2: (Client), h1, h2, h3: (Hop)):
            Navigation_2(h1, ini)=g1 AND Navigation_2(h2, acc)=g2
            AND Leq(composition(composition(h1, one), h2),
                        Navigation(cConnections, con))
            AND Navigation_2(h3, ini)=g2
            AND Navigation_2(h3, hDm)=Navigation_2(h2, hDm)
            AND Navigation_2(h3, tar)=Navigation_2(h2, src)
            IMPLIES
            (EXISTS (h4: (Hop)):
              Navigation_2(h4, acc)=g1 AND
              Leq(composition(composition(h3, one), h4),
                        Navigation(cConnections, con)))
```

The modified pretty printer displays the same predicate to the user as follows:

```
FAL_Returnability :

        |-------
  {1}    all g1,g2: Client, h1,h2,h3: Hop |
          (h1.ini)=g1 AND (h2.acc)=g2 AND
          (h1->h2) in (cConnections.con) AND
          (h3.ini)=g2 AND (h3.hDm)=(h2.hDm) AND (h3.tar)=(h2.src)
          IMPLIES
          (some h4: Hop |
              (h4.acc)=g1 AND (h3->h4) in (cConnections.con))
```

Notice that the pretty printed version closely resembles the Alloy definition. Furthermore, it can even be compiled with the Alloy Analyzer.

We have shown that it is possible to make proofs within the presented calculus with the aid of Dynamite. We now present some empirical data that will allow readers to have a better understanding of the usability of the tool.

The proofs were carried on by a student who had just graduated, and had no previous experience neither with Alloy, nor with PVS. The estimated time he spent in order to master the proof process is the following. 5 days to learn Alloy's syntax and semantics. 15 days to learn PVS, including the understanding of the proof rules. 40 days to prove all the assertions contained in the Alloy model. 15 days to prove the non trivial required lemmas about PDOCFAs. These lemmas can be considered as *infrastructure* lemmas, that will be reused in future proofs.

Recall that relations of rank greater than 2 are encoded as binary ones. Therefore, it may be necessary to prove properties that deal with the representation. These are the only proofs that would not be completely natural to an Alloy user. The proof of all the assertions in the model comprises 285 lemmas, of which only 12 use this kind of properties. Moreover, the 12 lemmas use actually 8 different properties of the representation because 3 properties are used at least twice.

Table 1. Distribution of the workload

Assertion	Total Lemmas	Model Lemmas	Algebra Lemmas	Time (days)
ConnectedIsEquivalence	79	4	75	10
UnidirectionalChains	52	28	24	5
Reachability	121	62	59	23
Returnability	113	66	47	17

Table 1 shows some numerical information about the proofs of the specific assertions. Notice that the sum of the total of lemmas amounts to 365. Therefore, $365 - 285 = 80$ lemmas were re-used in the proof of different assertions.

6   Discussion

Abstracting from Alloy and PVS, our work can be described as a combination of a counterexample extractor with a semi-automatic theorem prover. This topic has been addressed by several researchers. Among the most relevant contributions we cite [8]. In [8], rather than focusing on providing theorem-proving capabilities to a lightweight formal method, the authors use model checking in order to look for counterexamples before (and during) the theorem proving process. This covers part (but not all) of our intentions when combining Alloy and PVS. In [11], alternative and more ambitious ways of combining model checking and theorem proving are presented. Model checkers and theorem provers interact using the latter for local deductions and propagation of known properties, while the former are employed in order to calculate new properties from reachability predicates or their approximations. Being Alloy models static, it is not clear how to employ these techniques, but it is clearly a road that we will explore in the near future. There are two approaches that we are aware of in what respects to theorem proving of Alloy assertions. One is the theorem prover Prioni [2]. Prioni translates Alloy specifications to first-order formulas characterizing their first-order semantics, and then the first-order logic theorem prover Athena [1] is used in order to prove the resulting theorem. While the procedure is sound, it is not completely amenable to Alloy users. Switching from a relational to a non relational language poses an overhead on the user. The other theorem prover is the one presented in [5]. This theorem prover translates Alloy specifications to a close relational language based on binary relations (the calculus for omega closure fork algebras [3]). Since the resulting framework is an equational calculus, quantifiers were removed from Alloy formulas in the translation process. This lead to very complicated equations, far from what an Alloy user would expect.

References

1. Arkoudas K., *Type-ω DPLs*, MIT AI Memo 2001-27, 2001.
2. Arkoudas K., Khurshid S., Marinov D. and Rinard M., *Integrating Model Checking and Theorem Proving for Relational Reasoning*, in Proceedings of RelMiCS'03 (Relational Methods in Computer Science), LNCS, Springer, 2003.

3. Frias M., *Fork Algebras in Algebra, Logic and Computer Science*, World Scientific Publishing Co., Series Advances on Logic, 2002.
4. Frias, M. F., Haeberer, A. M. and Veloso, P. A. S., *A Finite Axiomatization for Fork Algebras*, Logic Journal of the IGPL, Vol. 5, No. 3, 311–319, 1997.
5. Frias M.F., López Pombo C.G. and Aguirre N., *A Complete Equational Calculus for Alloy*, in Proceedings of Internacional Conference on Formal Engineering Methods (ICFEM'04), Seattle, USA, November 2004, Lecture Notes in Computer Science 3308, Springer-Verlag, 2004, pp. 162–175.
6. Frias M.F., López Pombo C.G. and Moscato M.M., *Dynamite: Alloy Analyzer+PVS in the Analysis and Verification of Alloy Specifications*, in Proceedings of the First Alloy Workshop (Daniel Jackson and Pamela Zave Eds.), colocated with 14th ACM Symposium on Foundations of Software Engineering, 2006, to appear.
7. Jackson, D., Shlyakhter, I., and Sridharan, M., *A Micromodularity Mechanism.* Proc. ACM SIGSOFT Conf. Foundations of Software Engineering/European Software Engineering Conference (FSE/ESEC '01), Vienna, September 2001.
8. Kong W., Ogata K., , Seino T., and Futatsugi K., *A Lightweight Integration of Theorem Proving and Model Checking for System Verification*, in Proc. of APSEC'05, IEEE.
9. Maddux, R. D., *Pair-Dense Relation Algebras*, Transactions of the AMS, Vol. 328, N. 1, 1991.
10. Shankar N., Owre S., Rushby J. M., and Stringer-Calvert D. W. J., *PVS Prover Guide.* Computer Science Laboratory, SRI International, Menlo Park, CA, September 1999.
11. Shankar N., *Combining Theorem Proving and Model Checking through Symbolic Analysis*, in Proc. of CONCUR 2000, LNCS, Springer, 2000.
12. Zave, P., *A Formal Model of Addressing for Interoperating Networks*, in Proceedings of the Thirteenth International Symposium of Formal Methods Europe, Springer-Verlag LNCS 3582, pages 318-333, 2005.

Combined Satisfiability
Modulo Parametric Theories

Sava Krstić[1], Amit Goel[1], Jim Grundy[1], and Cesare Tinelli[2]

[1] Strategic CAD Labs, Intel Corporation
[2] Department of Computer Science, The University of Iowa

Abstract. We give a fresh theoretical foundation for designing comprehensive SMT solvers, generalizing in a practically motivated direction. We define *parametric theories* that most appropriately express the "logic" of common data types. Our main result is a combination theorem for decision procedures for disjoint theories of this kind. Virtually all of the deeply nested data structures (lists of arrays of sets of . . .) that arise in verification work are covered.

1   Introduction

Formal methods for hardware or software development require checking validity (or, dually, satisfiability) of formulas in logical theories modeling relevant datatypes. Satisfiability procedures have been devised for the basic ones—reals, integers, arrays, lists, tuples, queues, and so on—especially when restricted to formulas in some some quantifier-free fragment of first-order logic. Thanks to a seminal result by Nelson and Oppen [11], these basic procedures can often be modularly combined to cover formulas that mingle several datatypes.

Most research on *Satisfiability Modulo Theories (SMT)* has traditionally used classical first-order logic as a foundation for defining the language of satisfiability procedures, or *SMT solvers*, and reasoning about their correctness. However, the untypedness of this most familiar logic is a major limitation. It unnecessarily complicates correctness arguments for combination methods and restricts the applicability of sufficient conditions for their completeness. Thus, researchers have recently begun to frame SMT problems directly in terms of richer typed logics and to develop combination results for these logics [21,4,24,15,3,6]. Ahead of the theory, solvers supporting the PVS system [19], solvers of the CVC family [2], and some others adopted a typed setting early on.

The SMT-LIB initiative, an international effort aimed at developing common standards for the SMT field, proposes a version of many-sorted first-order logic as an initial underlying logic for SMT [16]. We see this as a step in the right direction, but only the first one, because the many-sorted logic's rudimentary type system is still inadequate for describing and working with typical cases of combined theories and their solvers. For example, in this logic one can define a generic theory of lists using a sort List for the lists and the sort E for the list elements. Then, a theory of integer lists can be defined formally as the union

O. Grumberg and M. Huth (Eds.): TACAS 2007, LNCS 4424, pp. 602–617, 2007.

of the list theory with the integer theory, modulo the identification of the sort E with the integer sort of the second theory. This combination mechanism gets quickly out of hand if we want to reason about, say, lists of arrays of lists of integers, and it cannot be used at all to specify *arbitrarily* nested lists. Because of the frequent occurrence of such combined datatypes in verification practice, this is a serious shortcoming.

Fortunately, virtually all structured datatypes arising in formal methods are *parametric*, the way arrays or lists are. Combined datatypes like those mentioned above are constructed simply by parameter instantiation. For this reason, we believe that any logic for SMT should directly support parametric types and, consequently, parametric polymorphism. The goal of this paper is to provide a Nelson-Oppen-style framework and results for theories combinable by parameter instantiation.

The key concept of *parametric theory* can likely be defined in various logics with polymorphic types. We adopt the higher-order logic of the theorem provers *HOL* [7], *HOL Light* [9], and *Isabelle/HOL* [14]. It is well studied and widely used, and has an elegant syntax and intuitive set-theoretic semantics.

Integration of SMT solvers with other reasoning tools, in particular with interactive provers, is a topic of independent interest [5,1] with a host of issues, including language compatibility [8]. This paper contributes a solid theoretical foundation for the design of *HOL*-friendly SMT solvers.

Finally, a striking outcome of this work is that in practically oriented (that is, dealing with common datatypes) SMT research, the vexatious stable infiniteness condition of the traditional Nelson-Oppen approach does not need to be mentioned. Its role is played by a milder flexibility condition that, by our results, is automatically satisfied for all *fully parametric* theories.

Related Work. Observations that the congruence closure algorithm of [12] effectively translates a first-order goal into *HOL* via currying, and that the solver for algebraic datatypes of [3] actually works for lists of lists and the like, were key to the unveiling of parametric *HOL* theories.

Like all other work on combining SMT solvers for disjoint theories, from [11] on, our approach is based on inter-solver propagation of constraints over a common language. Similarly to [22], the constraints also involve cardinalities, so our method can manage both infinite and finite datatypes. The purification procedure that transforms the input query in the mixed language of several solvers into pure parts is more involved here than anywhere else because of the complexity brought by the rich type system.

We give model-theretical correctness arguments, analogous to those used in other modern treatments of Nelson-Oppen combination, from [18,20] to the recent work [6] which also tackles some non-disjoint combinations. However, in the completeness proof, we rely on the parametricity of the types modeled by the component theories, not on the theories' stable infiniteness. This difference has important practical consequences. While our results do not subsume existing results nor are subsumed by them, they apply more widely because most of the datatypes relevant in applications are described by theories that satisfy our parametricity requirements without necessarily satisfying the stable infiniteness requirements of other combination methods.

In this, our approach is closely related to the recent work of Ranise *et al.* [15]. They present an extension of the Nelson-Oppen method in which a many-sorted theory S modeling a data structure like lists or arrays can be combined with an arbitrary theory T modeling the elements of the data structure. The theory S is required to satisfy a technical condition ("politeness") for each element sort. This corresponds to our requiring that the data structure be a parametric type with flexibility conditions. (More specifically, the "smoothness" and "finite witnessability" parts of politeness correspond to our up-flexibility and down-flexibility, the latter being significantly weaker than its counterpart in [15].) The results in [15] can be extended in principle to more than two theories by incremental pairwise combinations. However, as we argued, many-sorted logic is not well-suited for working with elaborate combinations of theories, while in a logic with parametric types such combinations are straightforward. In particular, our main result about combination of multiple pairwise disjoint parametric theories, would be difficult even to state in the language of [15]. Yet, the important insight that it is parametricity and not stable infiniteness that justifies Nelson-Oppen cooperation of common solvers is already in [15]; we have given it full expression.

Outline. In Section 2, reviewing the standard *HOL* material, we define the syntactic concept of signatures, and their semantic counterpart, structures. In Section 3, we introduce the crucial (fully) parametric structures, which are essentially collections of polymorphic constants with uniform behavior specified by relational parametricity. In Section 4, we discuss satisfiability in parametric structures and a process that corresponds to the familiar reduction of satisfiability of arbitrary quantifier-free formulas to sets of literals. In Section 5, we describe the algorithm for combining solvers and identify conditions under which it is complete. All proofs, omitted for lack of space, can be found in the accompanying technical report [10].

2   Syntax and Semantics of Higher Order Logic

We give a brief account of the standard syntax and semantics of higher-order logic, similar to that given by Pitts for the logic of the *HOL* theorem prover [7]. Much of it has been formalized by Harrison in a *"HOL* in *HOL"* fashion [9].

2.1   Syntax of *HOL* Types and Terms

The syntactic world of *HOL* TYPES is built using TYPE OPERATORS and TYPE VARIABLES. Each type operator has a non-negative ARITY. Given a set O of type operators, the set Type_O is the smallest set containing all type variables and expressions of the form $F(\sigma_1, \ldots, \sigma_n)$, where $F \in O$ has arity n and $\sigma_i \in \mathsf{Type}_O$. The set of type variables occurring in σ will be denoted $\mathtt{tyvar}(\sigma)$.

A TYPE INSTANTIATION is a finite map from type variables to types. The notation $[\sigma_1/\alpha_1, \ldots, \sigma_n/\alpha_n]$ is for the finite map that takes $\alpha_1, \ldots, \alpha_n$ to $\sigma_1, \ldots, \sigma_n$.

For any type σ and type instantiation θ, $\theta(\sigma)$ denotes the simultaneous substitution of every occurrence of α_i in σ with σ_i. We say that τ is an INSTANCE of σ and write $\tau \preceq \sigma$ if there is some θ such that $\tau = \theta(\sigma)$. Clearly, $\theta(\sigma) = \theta'(\sigma)$ holds if and only if θ and θ' agree on $\mathtt{tyvar}(\sigma)$. Thus, if $\tau \preceq \sigma$, then there is a unique minimal type instantiation that maps σ to τ; its domain is $\mathtt{tyvar}(\sigma)$ and it will be denoted $[\tau/\!\!/\sigma]$.

A *HOL* SIGNATURE $\Sigma = \langle O \mid K \rangle$ consists of a set O of type operators and a set K of TYPED CONSTANTS. Each constant $k^\sigma \in K$ is a pair of a symbol k and a type $\sigma \in \mathsf{Type}_O$, with no two constants sharing the same symbol. Let K^+ be the set of all pairs (also called constants) k^τ where $k^\sigma \in K$ and $\tau \preceq \sigma$.

The standard boolean connectives and equality make up the signature Σ_{Eq}:[1]

$$\Sigma_{\mathsf{Eq}} = \langle \mathsf{Bool}, \Rightarrow \mid =^{\alpha^2 \Rightarrow \mathsf{Bool}}, \mathsf{true}^{\mathsf{Bool}}, \mathsf{false}^{\mathsf{Bool}}, \neg^{\mathsf{Bool} \Rightarrow \mathsf{Bool}}, \wedge^{\mathsf{Bool}^2 \Rightarrow \mathsf{Bool}}, \dots \rangle$$

The constants of Σ_{Eq} will be called LOGICAL. From now on we will assume that every signature we consider includes Σ_{Eq}. When—as in the following examples— we write a concrete signature $\Sigma = \langle O \mid K \rangle$, we will tacitly assume that the Σ_{Eq}-part is there, even if it is not explicitly shown.

Example 1. Here are some familiar signatures.

$\Sigma_{\mathsf{Int}} = \langle \mathsf{Int} \mid 0^{\mathsf{Int}}, 1^{\mathsf{Int}}, (-1)^{\mathsf{Int}}, \dots, +^{\mathsf{Int}^2 \Rightarrow \mathsf{Int}}, -^{\mathsf{Int}^2 \Rightarrow \mathsf{Int}}, \times^{\mathsf{Int}^2 \Rightarrow \mathsf{Int}}, \leq^{\mathsf{Int}^2 \Rightarrow \mathsf{Bool}}, \dots \rangle$

$\Sigma_{\mathsf{Array}} = \langle \mathsf{Array} \mid \mathsf{mk\_arr}^{\beta \Rightarrow \mathsf{Array}(\alpha, \beta)}, \mathsf{read}^{[\mathsf{Array}(\alpha, \beta), \alpha] \Rightarrow \beta}, \mathsf{write}^{[\mathsf{Array}(\alpha, \beta), \alpha, \beta] \Rightarrow \mathsf{Array}(\alpha, \beta)} \rangle$

$\Sigma_{\mathsf{List}} = \langle \mathsf{List} \mid \mathsf{cons}^{[\alpha, \mathsf{List}(\alpha)] \Rightarrow \mathsf{List}(\alpha)}, \mathsf{nil}^{\mathsf{List}(\alpha)}, \mathsf{head}^{\mathsf{List}(\alpha) \Rightarrow \alpha}, \mathsf{tail}^{\mathsf{List}(\alpha) \Rightarrow \mathsf{List}(\alpha)} \rangle$

$\Sigma_{\mathsf{Monoid}} = \langle \mathsf{Monoid} \mid 1^{\mathsf{Monoid}}, *^{\mathsf{Monoid}^2 \Rightarrow \mathsf{Monoid}} \rangle$

The ARITY of a constant $k^\sigma \in K$ is the number m from the unique expression of σ in the form $[\sigma_1, \dots, \sigma_m] \Rightarrow \tau$, where τ is not a function type. If all σ_i are non-function types too, we will say that the constant is ALGEBRAIC. All signatures in Example 1 are algebraic in the sense that all their constants are such.

The set Term_Σ of *HOL* TERMS over a signature Σ is defined by the rules in Figure 1. The four rules classify terms into VARIABLES, CONSTANTS, APPLICATIONS, and ABSTRACTIONS. The rules actually define the set of term-type pairs $M{:}\sigma$, which we read as "term M has type σ". By structural induction, every term has a unique type. Non-typeable expressions like $v^\sigma u^\sigma$ are not considered to be terms at all.

Each occurrence of a variable in a term is FREE or BOUND, by the usual inductive definition. We regard two terms M and N as equal if they are equal up to renaming of bound variables. The set of free variables occurring in M is denoted $\mathtt{var}(M)$. We define $\mathtt{tyvar}(M)$ to be the set of type variables occurring in the type of any variable or constant subterm of M.

2.2 Semantics of Types

Type operators of arity n are interpreted as n-ary set operations—functions $\mathcal{U}^n \to \mathcal{U}$, where $\mathcal{U}$ is a suitably large universe of sets. Fixing such an

---

[1] By convention, $[\alpha^2, \beta] \Rightarrow \gamma$ is $\alpha \Rightarrow \alpha \Rightarrow \beta \Rightarrow \gamma$, and $\Rightarrow$ associates to the right.

$$\frac{}{v^\sigma : \sigma} \qquad \frac{k^\tau \in K^+}{k^\tau : \tau} \qquad \frac{M : \sigma \Rightarrow \tau \quad N : \sigma}{M\,N : \tau} \qquad \frac{M : \tau}{\lambda v^\sigma.\,M : \sigma \Rightarrow \tau}$$

Fig. 1. Typing rules for *HOL* terms

interpretation that associates with every $F \in O$ a set operation $[F]$, we define the INTERPRETATION OF $\sigma \in \mathsf{Type}_O$ in Figure 2. The interpretation of a type σ in a TYPE ENVIRONMENT ι—a finite map from type variables to $\mathcal{U}$ —is a set $[\![\sigma]\!]\,\iota$, "the meaning of σ in ι". The set $[\![\sigma]\!]\,\iota$ is defined when $\mathsf{tyvar}(\sigma) \subseteq \mathsf{dom}(\iota)$ and will be unchanged if ι is replaced with ι' as long as ι and ι' agree on $\mathsf{tyvar}(\sigma)$. (Here and in what follows, dom is used to denote the domain of a finite map.)

$$[\![\alpha]\!]\,\iota = \iota(\alpha) \quad \text{for every } \alpha \in \mathsf{dom}(\iota)$$

$$[\![F(\sigma_1, \ldots, \sigma_n)]\!]\,\iota = [F]([\![\sigma_1]\!]\,\iota, \ldots, [\![\sigma_n]\!]\,\iota)$$

Fig. 2. Interpretation of *HOL* types

Common type operators usually come with a unique intended interpretation, so it becomes awkward to make a notational distinction between F and $[F]$. But, for the sake of clarity, we will distinguish syntax from the semantics. For constant types (0-ary type operators) Unit, Bool and Int we will use $[\mathsf{Unit}] = \mathbb{U} = \{*\}$, $[\mathsf{Bool}] = \mathbb{B} = \{\mathit{true}, \mathit{false}\}$ and $[\mathsf{Int}] = \mathbb{Z}$. The symbols $\Rightarrow$ and $\twoheadrightarrow$ will be used for the syntactic type operator and the full function space set operation it represents; that is, we have $[\Rightarrow] = \twoheadrightarrow$. Similar convention holds for the Cartesian product and disjoint sum operators $\times$ and $+$, and operations $\boldsymbol{\times}$, $\boldsymbol{+}$. The unary type operator List is interpreted as the set operation **List**, where $\mathbf{List}(A)$ is the set of finite lists with elements in the set A.

The meaning of an instantiated type in some environment is the same as that of the original type in an appropriately updated environment. Precisely, if $\tau = \theta(\sigma)$, then $[\![\tau]\!]\,\iota = [\![\sigma]\!]\,\iota'$, where ι' is defined by $\iota'(\alpha) = [\![\theta(\alpha)]\!]\,\iota$. The environment ι' will be denoted $\theta \cdot \iota$. (See Figure 3 for its use.) For example, if $\sigma = (\alpha \Rightarrow \beta)$, $\tau = (\gamma \Rightarrow \gamma \Rightarrow \mathsf{Bool})$, and $\iota = [X/\gamma]$, then $\iota' = [X/\alpha, (X \twoheadrightarrow \mathbb{B})/\beta]$.

2.3 Semantics of Terms

Suppose now an interpretation $[\![\sigma]\!]$ for $\sigma \in \mathsf{Type}_O$ is given as in Section 2.2. We define an INDEXED ELEMENT of $[\![\sigma]\!]$ to be a family of elements $a\,\iota$ indexed by type environments ι whose domains contain $\mathsf{tyvar}(\sigma)$; the requirements are that $a\,\iota \in [\![\sigma]\!]\,\iota$ and and that $a\,\iota = a\,\iota'$ when ι and ι' agree on $\mathsf{tyvar}(\sigma)$. For example, the list length function *len* is an indexed element of $[\![\mathsf{List}(\alpha) \Rightarrow \mathsf{Int}]\!]$; for every ι with $\iota(\alpha) = A$, *len* ι is the concrete length function len_A, an element of $\mathbf{List}(A) \twoheadrightarrow \mathbb{Z}$. Similarly, the identity function is an indexed element of $[\![\alpha \Rightarrow \alpha]\!]$, but note that there are no "natural" indexed elements of $[\![\alpha \Rightarrow \beta]\!]$.

Given an arbitrary signature $\Sigma = \langle O \mid K \rangle$, a Σ-STRUCTURE $\mathcal{S}$ consists of

- an arity-respecting assignment $\mathcal{S}_{\mathsf{typeop}}$ that maps every F in O to a set operation $[F]$, as in Section 2.2;
- an assignment $\mathcal{S}_{\mathsf{const}}$ of an indexed element $[k^\sigma]$ of $[\![\sigma]\!]$ to every k^σ in K.[2]

We stipulate that the type operators Bool and $\Rightarrow$, as well as boolean connectives and the equality predicate be always assigned their standard meanings. For example, $[\wedge^{\mathsf{Bool}^2 \Rightarrow \mathsf{Bool}}] \iota$ is the conjunction operation on booleans for all type environments ι. Also, $[=^{\alpha^2 \Rightarrow \mathsf{Bool}}] \iota$ is always the identity relation on the set $\iota(\alpha)$. In other words, there is only one Σ_{Eq}-structure we care about, and it is "part of" all Σ-structures that include it.

Example 2. For signatures associated with datatypes, we normally associate a unique structure. Referring to Example 1, this is clear for Σ_{Int}. For Σ_{Array}, we define $[\mathsf{Array}](X, Y)$ to be the set of functions from X to Y that give the same result for all but finitely many arguments; the interpretation of the constants is obvious. For Σ_{List} there is an issue with partiality of head and tail, which can be resolved, for example, by defining $[\mathsf{head}^{\mathsf{List}(\alpha) \Rightarrow \alpha}] \iota$ to be an arbitrary element of $\iota(\alpha)$. (See Example 5 below for better solutions.) Unlike these examples, there are multiple Σ_{Monoid}-structures of interest; every monoid gives us one.

Interpretation of terms requires two environments: one for type variables and one for the free term variables. For example, the meaning of the Σ_{Eq}-term $\lambda u^{\alpha \Rightarrow \beta}. u^{\alpha \Rightarrow \beta} v^\alpha$ in the pair of environments $\langle [\mathbb{Z}/\alpha, \mathbb{Z}/\beta], [0/v^\alpha] \rangle$ is the function that maps its argument $f \in (\mathbb{Z} \Rightarrow \mathbb{Z})$ to $f(0)$. To make this precise, define first, for a given type environment ι, a TERM ENVIRONMENT OVER ι to be any finite map that associates to each variable v^σ in its domain an element of the set $[\![\sigma]\!] \iota$. Then, for any term M, an ENVIRONMENT FOR M is a pair $\langle \iota, \rho \rangle$, where ι is a type environment such that $\mathtt{tyvar}(M) \subseteq \mathrm{dom}(\iota)$ and ρ is a term environment over ι such that $\mathtt{var}(M) \subseteq \mathrm{dom}(\rho)$.

Given a Σ-structure, a Σ-term M of type σ, and an environment $\langle \iota, \rho \rangle$ for M, the INTERPRETATION OF M is an element $[\![M]\!] \langle \iota, \rho \rangle$ of the set $[\![\sigma]\!] \iota$ defined inductively by the equations in Figure 3. The interpretation of a variable v^τ is found by consulting the term environment ρ. To interpret a constant k^τ, which must be an instance of a unique $k^\sigma \in K$, we transform ι from a type environment for τ to the type environment $[\tau /\!\!/ \sigma] \cdot \iota$ for σ (see the last paragraph of Section 2.2), whereupon we can find the interpretation for k^τ using the function $[k^\sigma]$ supplied by the Σ-structure. The interpretations of applications and abstractions are straightforward. The notation $\rho[v^\sigma \mapsto x]$ is for the environment that maps v^σ to x, and is otherwise equal to ρ. It is easy to check that $[\![M]\!] \langle \iota, \rho \rangle$ is determined by the restriction of ι and ρ to $\mathtt{tyvar}(M)$ and $\mathtt{var}(M)$ respectively.

---

[2] The proper notation would be $[F]_\mathcal{S}$, $[k^\sigma]_\mathcal{S}$, $[\![\sigma]\!]_\mathcal{S}$, but the structure $\mathcal{S}$ will always be understood from the context.

$$[\![v^\tau]\!]\langle \iota, \rho \rangle = \rho(v^\tau) \qquad\qquad [\![M\,N]\!]\langle \iota, \rho \rangle = ([\![M]\!]\langle \iota, \rho \rangle)([\![N]\!]\langle \iota, \rho \rangle)$$

$$[\![k^\tau]\!]\langle \iota, \rho \rangle = [k^\sigma]([\tau /\!\!/ \sigma] \cdot \iota) \qquad [\![\lambda v^\sigma.\,M]\!]\langle \iota, \rho \rangle = \lambda x \in [\![\sigma]\!]\,\iota.\,[\![M]\!]\langle \iota, \rho[v^\sigma \mapsto x] \rangle$$

Fig. 3. Interpretation of *HOL* terms

3   Parametric Structures

The uniformity exhibited by commonly used polymorphic type operators and constants is not captured by the semantics in Section 2, but has been formalized by the notion of *relational parametricity* [17,23]. It leads us to the concept of *fully parametric structures* and gives us powerful techniques, based on the *Abstraction Theorem* [17] to reason about them. See [10] for full statements and proofs of results needed in this paper.

3.1   Relational Semantics

A PARAMETRIC SET OPERATION is a pair consisting of a set operation G and an operation $G^\sharp$ on relations such that if $R_1 \colon A_1 \leftrightarrow B_1, \ldots, R_n \colon A_n \leftrightarrow B_n$, then $G^\sharp(R_1, \ldots, R_n) \colon G(A_1, \ldots, A_n) \leftrightarrow G(B_1, \ldots, B_n)$. It is also required that $G^\sharp$ be functorial on bijections: $G^\sharp(R_1, \ldots, R_n)$ must be a bijection if the R_i are all bijections, and the identities $G^\sharp(R_1, \ldots, R_n) \circ G^\sharp(S_1, \ldots, S_n) = G^\sharp(R_1 \circ S_1, \ldots, R_n \circ S_n)$ and $G^\sharp(id_{A_1}, \ldots, id_{A_n}) = id_{G(A_1, \ldots, A_n)}$ must hold, where $R_i \colon A_i \leftrightarrow B_i$ and $S_i \colon B_i \leftrightarrow C_i$ are arbitrary bijections and id_A denotes the identity relation on A. Note that the conditions are meaningful when $n = 0$: every set G together with $G^\sharp = id_G$ is a parametric 0-ary set operation.

Informally, we will say that a set operation G is parametric if there is a $G^\sharp$ such that $(G, G^\sharp)$ is a parametric set operation.

Example 3. **List** is parametric: for a given relation $R \colon A \leftrightarrow B$, the relation $\mathsf{List}^\sharp(R) \colon \mathsf{List}(A) \leftrightarrow \mathsf{List}(B)$ is the generalization of the familiar *map* function. The binary set operations $\times$ and $\Rightarrow$ are also parametric: given relations $R_1 \colon A_1 \leftrightarrow B_1$ and $R_2 \colon A_2 \leftrightarrow B_2$, the relation $R_1 \times^\sharp R_2 \colon A_1 \times A_2 \leftrightarrow B_1 \times B_2$ relates $\langle x_1, x_2 \rangle$ with $\langle y_1, y_2 \rangle$ iff $\langle x_1, y_1 \rangle \in R_1$ and $\langle x_2, y_2 \rangle \in R_2$; the relation $R_1 \Rightarrow^\sharp R_2 \colon (A_1 \Rightarrow B_1) \leftrightarrow (A_2 \Rightarrow B_2)$ relates f_1 with f_2 iff for every x_1, x_2, $\langle x_1, x_2 \rangle \in R_1$ implies $\langle f_1(x_1), f_2(x_2) \rangle \in R_2$.

Let ι_1 and ι_2 be two type environments with equal domains. An ENVIRONMENT RELATION $R \colon \iota_1 \leftrightarrow \iota_2$ is a collection of relations $R(\alpha) \colon \iota_1(\alpha) \leftrightarrow \iota_2(\alpha)$, for each α in the domain of ι_1 and ι_2. The identity relation $id_\iota \colon \iota \leftrightarrow \iota$ is defined by $id_\iota(\alpha) = id_{\iota(\alpha)}$.

Suppose O is a set of type operators, and that for each $F \in O$ the set operation $[F]$ is parametric, with the relational part denoted $[F]^\sharp$. Then for any type σ and a relation $R \colon \iota_1 \leftrightarrow \iota_2$ between type environments whose domain contains $\mathtt{tyvar}(\sigma)$, there is an induced relation $[\![\sigma]\!]^\sharp R \colon [\![\sigma]\!]\,\iota_1 \leftrightarrow [\![\sigma]\!]\,\iota_2$, defined in Figure 4. It is easy to prove that $[\![\sigma]\!]^\sharp id_\iota = id_{[\![\sigma]\!]\,\iota}$ holds for every σ, the result known as *Identity Extension Lemma* [17].

$$\llbracket \alpha \rrbracket^\sharp R = R(\alpha)$$

$$\llbracket F(\sigma_1, \dots, \sigma_n) \rrbracket^\sharp R = [F]^\sharp (\llbracket \sigma_1 \rrbracket^\sharp R, \dots, \llbracket \sigma_n \rrbracket^\sharp R)$$

Fig. 4. Relational type semantics

An indexed element a of $\llbracket \sigma \rrbracket$ is called PARAMETRIC if

$$\langle a \, \iota_1, a \, \iota_2 \rangle \in \llbracket \sigma \rrbracket^\sharp R \quad \text{for every relation } R \colon \iota_1 \leftrightarrow \iota_2. \tag{1}$$

Example 4. Let us check that *len* is a parametric indexed element of $\llbracket \mathsf{List}(\alpha) \Rightarrow \mathsf{Int} \rrbracket$. Pick a relation $R \colon [A/\alpha] \leftrightarrow [B/\alpha]$ between type environments, i.e., $R(\alpha)$ is some relation $r \colon A \leftrightarrow B$. By definition *len* $[A/\alpha]$ is the concrete length function $len_A \in \mathsf{List}(A) \Rightarrow \mathbb{Z}$; and similarly *len* $[B/\alpha] = len_B$. To verify the condition (1), we need to check that $\langle len_A, len_B \rangle \in \llbracket \mathsf{List}(\alpha) \Rightarrow \mathsf{Int} \rrbracket^\sharp R$. By the equations in Figure 4, the relation on the right is equal to $map(r) \Rightarrow^\sharp id_\mathbb{Z}$. By the definition of $\Rightarrow^\sharp$, we need to check that for every $x \in \mathsf{List}(A), y \in \mathsf{List}(B)$ such that $\langle x, y \rangle \in map(r)$ one must have $len_A(x) = len_B(y)$—which is true.

Example 5. Standard interpretations of constants in Σ_{List} and Σ_{Array} are parametric, except for the partiality of **head** and **tail**. This can be fixed by giving **head** the type $\mathsf{List}\,\alpha \Rightarrow \alpha + \mathsf{Unit}$ or $\mathsf{List}\,\alpha \Rightarrow \alpha \Rightarrow \mathsf{Bool}$, and similarly for **tail**.

3.2   Fully Parametric Structures

Polymorphic equality is not parametric! Indeed, given $R \colon A \leftrightarrow B$, condition (1) says: if $\langle x, y \rangle, \langle x', y' \rangle \in R$, then $(x =_A x') \Leftrightarrow (y =_B y')$ [23]. This condition is not true in general, but holds if and only if R is a partial bijection. To account for this limited parametricity of equality, we define a set operation G to be FULLY PARAMETRIC if $G^\sharp$ is functorial on partial bijections. We also define an indexed element a to be FULLY PARAMETRIC if (1) holds for all partial bijections R. (Thus, to specify a fully parametric set operation G, one need define $G^\sharp(R_1, \dots, R_n)$ only for the case where all the R_i are partial bijections.)

Note that the "Reynolds parametricity" defined in Section 3.1 and full parametricity are incomparable: to get from the former to the latter, we strengthened the functoriality condition and weakened the condition (1) on elements.

The following definition is crucial. An $\langle O \mid K \rangle$-structure S is FULLY PARAMETRIC if $S_{\mathsf{typeop}}(F)$ is a fully parametric set operation for every $F \in O - \{\Rightarrow\}$ and $S_{\mathsf{const}}(k^\sigma)$ is a fully parametric indexed element for every $k^\sigma \in K$.

The function space operation $\Rightarrow$ is not fully parametric; for example, if $R \colon A \to A'$ is an injection, then $R \Rightarrow^\sharp id_B \colon (A \Rightarrow B) \leftrightarrow (A' \Rightarrow B)$ is not a partial bijection. Fortunately, this is an exception.

Lemma 1. *The structures corresponding to the following datatypes are fully parametric: datatypes with 0-ary type constructors (such as* Bool, Int, *etc.); all algebraic datatypes (including sums, products, lists); arrays; sets; and multisets.*

In Section 5, we will see that full parametricity legitimizes structures' participation in the Nelson-Oppen combination algorithm.

4   *HOL* Theories and Satisfiability

In *HOL*, FORMULAS are simply terms of type Bool. If ϕ is a Σ-formula, S is a Σ-structure, and $e = \langle \iota, \rho \rangle$ is an environment for ϕ, we write $e \models \phi$ as an abbreviation for $[\![\phi]\!]\, e = true$. We say that ϕ is S-SATISFIABLE if $e \models \phi$ for some e, in which case we also say that the environment e is a MODEL for ϕ. When Φ is a set of formulas (for which we will use the term QUERY), we write $e \models \Phi$ to mean that $e \models \phi$ holds for all $\phi \in \Phi$.

We will need to discuss satisfiability in models with specified cardinality, so let the "equality" $\sigma \doteq n$ denote a CARDINALITY CONSTRAINT: by $\langle \iota, \rho \rangle \models \sigma \doteq n$ we mean that the set $[\![\sigma]\!]\, \iota$ has n elements.

Similarly, we will consider TYPE CONSTRAINTS of the form $\alpha \doteq \sigma$ and VARIABLE CONSTRAINTS of the form $u^\sigma \doteq v^\tau$. By definition, $\langle \iota, \rho \rangle \models \alpha \doteq \sigma$ holds iff $\iota(\alpha) = [\![\sigma]\!]\, \iota$, and $\langle \iota, \rho \rangle \models u^\sigma \doteq v^\tau$ holds iff $[\![\sigma]\!]\, \iota = [\![\tau]\!]\, \iota$ and $\rho(u^\sigma) = \rho(v^\tau)$.

Example 6. Consider the S_{Eq}-queries $\{f(f(f\, x)) = x, f(f\, x) = x, f\, x \neq x\}$ and $\{f\, x = g\, x, g\, x = h\, x, f \neq g, g \neq h, h \neq f\}$, where f, g, h are variables of type $\alpha \Rightarrow \alpha$ and x is one of type α. The first query is unsatisfiable. The second query is satisfiable, but is not simultaneously satisfiable with the cardinality constraint $\alpha \doteq 2$. (E.g., there are only two functions $\mathbb{B} \to \mathbb{B}$ that map *true* to *false*.)

A Σ-THEORY is a set of Σ-structures. If T is a Σ-theory, we say that a formula ϕ is T-SATISFIABLE if it is S-satisfiable for some $S \in T$.

The theories $T_{\mathsf{Int}}, T_{\mathsf{List}}, T_{\mathsf{Array}}$ (Examples 1 and 2) are each the theory of a single structure: $S_{\mathsf{Int}}, S_{\mathsf{List}}, S_{\mathsf{Array}}$ respectively. On the other hand, T_{Monoid} is the theory of all monoids. From now on, we assume that *every theory is defined by a single algebraic structure*, since such theories are of greatest practical interest.

By a SOLVER we will mean a sound and complete satisfiability procedure for Σ-queries whose formulas belong to a specified subset (FRAGMENT) of Term$_\Sigma$. For example, integer linear arithmetic is the Σ_{Int}-fragment consisting of boolean combinations of linear equalities and inequalites, and the integer linear programming algorithms can be seen as solvers for this fragment. Solvers that can check satisfiability with cardinality constraints will be called STRONG.

We will concern ourselves only with subfragments of the APPLICATIVE FRAGMENT of theories, where a Σ-term is called applicative if it contains no subterms that are abstractions and all occurrences of constants are fully applied. The latter means that every occurrence of a constant k^τ is part of a subterm of the form $k^\tau M_1 \cdots M_m$, where m is the constant's arity. Define also the ALGEBRAIC FRAGMENT to consist of all applicative terms that do not contain any occurrences of subterms of the form $x\, N$, where x is a variable ("uninterpreted function").

In the rest of this section we will narrow down the applicative fragment to a subfragment whose queries have a particularly simple form. First, we minimize the size of the formulas occurring in the query at the price of increasing the number of formulas in the query. Second, we do away with the propositional complexity of the query by case splitting over boolean variables. Finally, with a substitution, we remove equalities between variables from the query. This reduction will further ease our reasoning, and will incur no cost in generality.

Lemma 2. *Every applicative query over* $\langle O \mid K \rangle$ *is equisatisfiable with a query all of whose formulas are* ATOMIC, *i.e. have one of the following forms:*

(A) $x_0 = k\, x_1 \ldots x_n$, *where* $k \in K^+$ *has arity* n
(B) $x_0 = x_1\, x_2$

where the x_i *are variables. Also, an algebraic query is equisatisfiable with a query whose formulas all have the form (A).*

Transforming an applicative formula into a set of atomic formulas is done simply by introducing proxy variables for subterms, a process often called *variable abstraction*. For example, $(f\, x\, 1 \geq 1) \vee (x = 1)$ is equisatisfiable with: *(A)* $y = 1, p = (z \geq y), q = (x = y), r = p \vee q, r = \text{true}$; *(B)* $g = f\, x, z = g\, y$.

An ARRANGEMENT is a query determined by a set V of variables of the same type and an equivalence relation $\sim$ on V. For every $x, y \in V$, the arrangement contains either $x = y$ or $x \neq y$, depending on whether $x \sim y$ holds or not. The arrangement that forces all variables in V to be distinct will be denoted $\text{Dist}(V)$.

Suppose now Φ is a set of atomic formulas and let X^σ be the set of variables of type σ that occur in Φ. Let E^σ be the subset of Φ consisting of formulas of the form $z = (x = y)$, where $x, y \subset X^\sigma$. We can assume that E^{Bool} is empty by using the alternative way $z = (x \Leftrightarrow y)$ of writing $z = (x = y)$. We can also assume that for every $\sigma \neq \text{Bool}$ and every $x, y \in X^\sigma$ there exists z such that $z = (x = y)$ occurs in E^σ; just add this equality with a fresh z if necessary.

There are finitely many substitutions $\xi \colon X^{\text{Bool}} \to \{\text{true}, \text{false}\}$ and Φ is satisfiable iff some $\xi(\Phi)$ is. Let Φ_0 be the subset of Φ consisting of formulas *(A)* in which k is a boolean connective. Note that for any ξ, the query $\xi(E^\sigma)$ is either unsatisfiable, or equivalent to an arrangement on X^σ. Searching for a model for Φ, we can enumerate all ξ such that $\xi(\Phi_0)$ is satisfiable, and every $\xi(E^\sigma)$ is an arrangement. Thus, we will have a solver for all applicative $\mathcal{T}$-queries as soon as we have a solver for ALMOST-REDUCED queries that consist of

- arrangements Δ^σ for every type $\sigma \neq \text{Bool}$ that occurs in the query
- the set Δ^{Bool} containing $x = \text{true}$ or $x = \text{false}$ for every $x \in X^{\text{Bool}}$
- non-logical atomic formulas (where constants k in *(A)* are not logical)

Observe finally that for every almost-reduced query there is an equisatisfiable REDUCED query in which (1) $\Delta^\sigma = \text{Dist}(X^\sigma)$ for every $\sigma \neq \text{Bool}$ and (2) there are only two variables of type Bool—say $\mathfrak{t}$ and $\mathfrak{f}$—and two equations in Δ^{Bool}, namely $\mathfrak{t} = \text{true}$ and $\mathfrak{f} = \text{false}$. Indeed, we can bring a given almost-reduced query to this simpler form by choosing a representative for each class of the arrangements Δ^σ and then replacing every occurrence of $x \in X^\sigma$ with its representative.

Example 7. Let $\mathcal{T} = \mathcal{T}_1 + \mathcal{T}_2$, where $\mathcal{T}_1 = \mathcal{T}_{\mathsf{Int}}$ and $\mathcal{T}_2 = \mathcal{T}_{\times}$ is the simple parametric theory of pairs over the signature

$$\Sigma_{\times} = \langle \times \mid \langle \text{-}, \text{-} \rangle^{[\alpha, \beta] \Rightarrow \alpha \times \beta}, \mathsf{fst}^{\alpha \times \beta \Rightarrow \alpha}, \mathsf{snd}^{\alpha \times \beta \Rightarrow \beta} \rangle.$$

Consider the query $\Phi = \{x_2 = \langle \mathsf{snd}(\mathsf{snd}\, x_3), x_1\, x_2 \rangle, \mathsf{fst}(\mathsf{snd}\, x_3) > 0\}$ whose variables are typed as follows: $x_1 \colon \omega \times \mathsf{Bool} \Rightarrow \mathsf{Bool}; x_2 \colon \omega \times \mathsf{Bool}; x_3 \colon \omega \times (\mathsf{Int} \times \omega)$, where ω is a type variable. The types of instances of fst and snd can be inferred, so we leave them implicit. Variable abstraction produces $\Phi' = \{x_4 = x_1\, x_2, x_5 = \mathsf{snd}\, x_3, x_6 = \mathsf{snd}\, x_5, x_2 = \langle x_6, x_4 \rangle, x_7 = \mathsf{fst}\, x_5, x_8 = 0, x_9 = (x_7 > x_8), x_9 = \mathsf{true}\}$. Proxy variables have the following types: $x_4, x_9 \colon \mathsf{Bool};$ $x_7, x_8 \colon \mathsf{Int}; x_5 \colon \mathsf{Int} \times \omega; x_6 \colon \omega$. The assignment $\xi = [\mathsf{false}/x_4, \mathsf{true}/x_9]$ to propositional variables and the arrangement $\mathrm{Dist}\{x_7, x_8\}$ produce the reduced query $\Phi'' = \Delta^{\mathsf{Bool}} \cup \mathrm{Dist}\{x_7, x_8\} \cup \Phi_0 \cup \Phi_1 \cup \Phi_2$, where $\Phi_0 = \{\mathfrak{f} = x_1\, x_2\}$, $\Phi_1 = \{x_8 = 0, \mathfrak{t} = (x_7 > x_8)\}$, $\Phi_2 = \{x_5 = \mathsf{snd}\, x_3, x_6 = \mathsf{snd}\, x_5, x_2 = \langle x_6, \mathfrak{f} \rangle, x_7 = \mathsf{fst}\, x_5\}$.

5   Nelson-Oppen Cooperation

The signatures $\Sigma_1 = \langle O_1 \mid K_1 \rangle, \ldots, \Sigma_n = \langle O_N \mid K_N \rangle$ are DISJOINT if each *properly* contains Σ_{Eq} and the only constants and type operators that any two have in common are those of Σ_{Eq}. Their SUM SIGNATURE is $\Sigma = \Sigma_1 + \cdots + \Sigma_N = \langle O_1 \cup \cdots \cup O_N \mid K_1 \cup \cdots \cup K_N \rangle$. If each $\mathcal{T}_i$ is a Σ_i-theory determined by the structure $\mathcal{S}_i$, the SUM THEORY $\mathcal{T}$ is defined by the SUM Σ-STRUCTURE $\mathcal{S} = \mathcal{S}_1 + \cdots + \mathcal{S}_N$ that interprets every $F \in O_i$ and every $k^\sigma \in K_i$ the same way the structure $\mathcal{S}_i$ does it.

Our main result is the construction of a strong solver for the applicative fragment of $\mathcal{T}$, assuming the existence of strong solvers for the *applicative* fragment of $\mathcal{T}_{\mathsf{Eq}}$ and the *algebraic* fragment of every $\mathcal{T}_i$. The construction follows the original Nelson-Oppen approach [11], as revised by Tinelli and Harandi [20]. The completeness proof, however, is radically different and relies essentially on the parametricity of the component structures $\mathcal{S}_i$.

5.1   The Combined Solver

Let Σ and $\mathcal{T}$ be a sum signature and sum theory as above; for convenience, from now on, Σ_0 will stand for Σ_{Eq}. Given an input applicative Σ-query Φ_{in} and a set of cardinality constraints Γ, the combined solver proceeds as follows.

1. Create, as described in Section 4, a set $\mathcal{F}$ of reduced queries such that $\Phi_{\mathsf{in}}, \Gamma$ is $\mathcal{T}$-satisfiable iff Φ, Γ is $\mathcal{T}$-satisfiable for some $\Phi \in \mathcal{F}$.[3]
2. Processing a $\Phi \in \mathcal{F}$, partition it into subqueries $\Delta^{\mathsf{Bool}} = \{\mathfrak{t} = \mathsf{true}, \mathfrak{f} = \mathsf{false}\}$, $\mathrm{Dist}(X^\sigma)$ for all $\sigma \neq \mathsf{Bool}$, and $\Phi_0, \Phi_1, \ldots, \Phi_N$, where Φ_0 is a set of atomic formulas of the form *(B)*, and Φ_i is a set of non-logical atomic formulas of the form *(A)* with the constant k taken from K_i^+. (See Example 7.)

---

[3] The terrible inefficiency of enumerating propositional assignments and arrangements can be alleviated with techniques involving the use of a SAT solver, but is not our concern here. See, e.g., [13].

3. *Purify* each Φ_i into a reduced Σ_i-query Ψ_i, algebraic for $i > 0$, and a set of constraints Γ_i that are all together $\mathcal{T}$-equisatisfiable with Φ, Γ. (See Example 8 below.)

4. Use strong solvers for $\mathcal{T}_i$ to check the joint $\mathcal{T}_i$-satisfiability of Ψ_i and the cardinality constraints in Γ_i. Return "Φ, Γ satisfiable" iff all solvers return "satisfiable".

Purification in 3. is a four-step procedure:

1. Proxying types. Let T be the set of types containing the types of all subterms of formulas in Φ, and all types that occur as subexpressions of these. Partition T into the set of type variables T^{var}, the set T_0 of function types, and the sets T_i ($i = 1, \ldots, N$) of types of the form $F(\sigma_1, \ldots, \sigma_n)$ where $F \in O_i - \{\Rightarrow\}$. For every $\sigma \in T_i$, let α_σ be a fresh (proxy) type variable, and let σ° be the type obtained from σ by replacing each maximal alien (i.e., element of T_j for $j \neq i$) type τ that occurs as a subexpression in σ with the proxy α_τ.

2. Proxying variables. Partition the set X of variables occurring in Φ into $\{\mathsf{t}, \mathsf{f}\}$, X^{var}, $X_0, \ldots, X_N$, where $x \in X^{\mathrm{var}}$ iff the type of x is in T^{var}, and $x \in X_i$ iff the type of x is in T_i. For convenience, let us assume that the elements of X are $x_1, x_2, \ldots$. Introduce sets of fresh variables $Y_i = \{y_j \mid x_j \in X_i\}$ and $Z_i = \{z_j \mid x_j \in X_i\}$. By definition, the type of each y_j is σ°, and the type of z_j is α_σ, where σ is the type of x_j. Let $Y^\sigma = \{y_j \mid x_j \in X^\sigma\}$ and $Z^\sigma = \{z_j \mid x_j \in X^\sigma\}$. Let Y be the union of all the Y_i and Z be the union of the Z_i. Finally, let $\Delta_i = \Delta^{\mathrm{Bool}} + \bigcup_{\sigma \notin T_i} \mathrm{Dist}(Y^\sigma) + \bigcup_{\sigma \in T_i} \mathrm{Dist}(Z^\sigma)$—a union of arrangements.

3. Generating constraints. Let Γ_i^{card} be the union of Γ and cardinality constraints $\alpha_\sigma \doteq n$, where $\sigma \in T_j$, $j \neq i$, and $\sigma \doteq n$ is implied by Γ. Let also Γ_i^{type} be the set of type constraints $\alpha_\sigma \doteq \sigma^\circ$, where σ is an i-type. Note that these type constraints imply $\alpha_\sigma \doteq \sigma$ for every non-variable type σ. Let Γ_i^{var} be the set of variable constraints $z_j \doteq y_j$, where $x_j \in X_i$. Finally, let Γ_i be the union of Γ_i^{card}, Γ_i^{type}, and Γ_i^{var}.

4. Purifying atomic formulas. For every $x \in X$ and $i = 0, \ldots, N$ define

$$x_j^{[i]} = \begin{cases} x_j & \text{if } x_j \in \{\mathsf{t}, \mathsf{f}\} \cup X^{\mathrm{var}} \\ y_j & \text{if } x_j \in X_i \\ z_j & \text{if } x_j \in X_{i'} \text{ and } i' \neq i \end{cases}$$

and then (with k' and k in (3) being appropriately typed instances of the same constant in K_i)

$$\Psi_0 = \Delta_0 \cup \{u_0^{[0]} = u_1^{[0]} u_2^{[0]} \mid (u_0 = u_1 u_2) \in \Phi_0\} \tag{2}$$

$$\Psi_i = \Delta_i \cup \{u_0^{[i]} = k' u_1^{[i]} \ldots u_n^{[i]} \mid (u_0 = k u_1 \ldots u_n) \in \Phi_i\} \quad (i > 0) \tag{3}$$

Lemma 3 (Purification). *Every Ψ_i is a well-defined Σ_i-query and Γ_i is a set of Σ_i-constraints. The union of all the Ψ_i and Γ_i is $\mathcal{T}$-equisatisfiable with Φ, Γ.*

Example 8. Continuing with Example 7, purification of $\Phi_0 \cup \Phi_1 \cup \Phi_2$ produces:

$$\Psi_0 = \Delta^{\mathsf{Bool}} \cup \{\mathbb{f} = y_1\,z_2\} \qquad \Gamma_0 = \{\alpha_{\omega \times \mathsf{Bool} \Rightarrow \mathsf{Bool}} \doteq \alpha_{\omega \times \mathsf{Bool}} \Rightarrow \mathsf{Bool},\ z_1 \doteq y_1\}$$

$$\Psi_1 = \Delta^{\mathsf{Bool}} \cup \{y_7 \neq y_8;\ y_8 = 0,\ \mathbb{t} = (y_7 > y_8)\}\ \Gamma_1 = \{\alpha_{\mathsf{Int}} \doteq \mathsf{Int},\ z_7 \doteq y_7,\ z_8 \doteq y_8\}$$

$$\Psi_2 = \Delta^{\mathsf{Bool}} \cup \{y_5 = \mathsf{snd}\,y_3,\ x_6 = \mathsf{snd}\,y_5,\ z_7 = \mathsf{fst}\,y_5,\ y_2 = \langle x_6, \mathbb{f}\rangle\}$$

$$\Gamma_2 = \{\alpha_{\omega \times \mathsf{Bool}} \doteq \omega \times \mathsf{Bool},\ z_2 \doteq y_2;\ \alpha_{\omega \times (\mathsf{Int} \times \omega)} \doteq \omega \times (\alpha_{\mathsf{Int}} \times \omega),\ z_3 \doteq y_3;$$
$$\alpha_{\mathsf{Int} \times \omega} \doteq \alpha_{\mathsf{Int}} \times \omega,\ z_5 \doteq y_5\}$$

where each type constraint $\alpha_\sigma \doteq \sigma^\circ$ in Γ_i is followed by variable constraints $z_j \doteq y_j$ with $z_j \colon \alpha_\sigma$ and $y_j \colon \sigma^\circ$.

5.2   The Combination Theorem

Lemma 3 implies that the combined solver is sound: the input $\Phi_{\mathsf{in}}, \Gamma$ is unsatisfiable if the solver says so. Completeness is less clear because it requires that a $\mathcal{T}$-model be assembled from a collection of $\mathcal{T}_i$-models. When the theories satisfy a flexibility condition *à la* Löwenheim-Skolem, completeness follows immediately from the following theorem.

Theorem 1. *Assume the notation is as in the previous section and that the theories $\mathcal{T}_1, \ldots, \mathcal{T}_n$ are flexible for reduced algebraic queries. Then: Φ, Γ is $\mathcal{T}$-satisfiable if and only if $\Psi_i, \Gamma_i^{\mathrm{card}}$ is $\mathcal{T}_i$-satisfiable for every $i = 0, \ldots, N$.*

Here are the requisite definitions. An environment $\langle \iota, \rho \rangle$ is SEPARATING if ρ maps all variables of the same type to distinct elements. A theory is FLEXIBLE for a fragment $\mathcal{F}$ if for every separating model $\langle \iota, \rho \rangle$ for an $\mathcal{F}$-query Ψ and every $\alpha \in \mathrm{dom}(\iota)$, there exist separating models $\langle \iota^{\mathrm{up}(\kappa)}, \rho^{\mathrm{up}(\kappa)} \rangle$ and $\langle \iota^{\mathrm{down}}, \rho^{\mathrm{down}} \rangle$ for Ψ such that $\iota^{\mathrm{up}(\kappa)}(\beta) = \iota(\beta) = \iota^{\mathrm{down}}(\beta)$ for every $\beta \neq \alpha$, and

1. [UP-FLEXIBILITY] $\iota^{\mathrm{up}(\kappa)}(\alpha)$ has any prescribed cardinality κ greater than the cardinality of $\iota(\alpha)$
2. [DOWN-FLEXIBILITY] $\iota^{\mathrm{down}}(\alpha)$ is countable

Lemma 4. *Every fully parametric structure is up-flexible for reduced algebraic queries. It is also down-flexible for this fragment if it satisfies the following condition: for every type operator F and every element $a \in [F](A_1, \ldots, A_n)$, there exist countable subsets A_i' of A_i such that $a \in [F](A_1', \ldots, A_n')$.*

We have proved that $\mathcal{T}_{\mathsf{Eq}}$ is flexible for reduced queries [10]. Also, by Lemma 4, the theories of common datatypes mentioned in Lemma 1 all qualify for complete Nelson-Oppen cooperation. The mild condition in Lemma 4 required for down-flexibility is probably unnecessary. We conjecture (but are unable to prove without informal reference to the downward Löwenheim-Skolem Theorem) that down-flexibility for algebraic queries holds for all fully parametric theories.

The lemma below follows from parametricity theorems [10] and is central for the proof of Theorem 1. We use it to incrementally modify the members of a given family of $\mathcal{T}_i$-models so that at each step they agree more on the intersections of their domains; at the end, a $\mathcal{T}$-model is obtained by amalgamating the modified $\mathcal{T}_i$-models.

Lemma 5 (Remodeling). *Suppose $\langle \iota, \rho \rangle$ is a separating model for an algebraic query Ψ in a fully parametric structure, and $f \colon \iota(\alpha) \to \iota(\alpha)$ is a bijection for some $\alpha \in \mathrm{dom}(\iota)$. Then there exists a separating model $\langle \iota, \rho' \rangle$ for Ψ such that*

(a) $\rho'(x) = f(\rho(x))$ for every variable $x \in \mathrm{dom}(\rho)$ of type α
(b) $\rho'(y) = \rho(y)$ for every $y \in \mathrm{dom}(\rho)$ whose type does not depend on α

Example 9. To illustrate the proof of Theorem 1, let us continue with Example 8. Starting with T_i-models $\langle \iota_i, \rho_i \rangle$ for Ψ_i $(i = 0, 1, 2)$, we build a model $\langle \iota, \rho \rangle$ for the union of the Ψ_i and Γ_i. Let us order the types in T with respect to their complexity as in the first row of the table below. Let ι be a type environment that maps the original type variable ω and the proxy type variables α_σ for $\sigma \in T$ to sets in the second row of the table. Here $\mathbb{I} = \{\star, \dagger, \ddagger, \ldots\}$ is an arbitrary infinite set. Using the up- or down-flexibility of T_i and a simple consequence of parametricity ("permutational invariance"), we first modify the given models to achieve $\iota_0 = \iota_1 = \iota_2 = \iota$; this will satisfy all type constraints too. Then we modify the environments ρ_i in six steps, corresponding to the six types in T, so that after the step related to $\sigma \in T$, the ρ_i agree on their variables associated with σ and all types preceding σ. (For each $x_m \in X^\sigma$, one of the ρ_i has y_m in its domain, while the others have z_m.) These changes are possible by Lemma 5. The top half of the table shows the ρ_i's after the second step, where we have agreement on variables associated with ω and $\omega \times \mathsf{Bool}$ (the shaded area). Turning to the type Int, the pivot values $4, 0$ (underlined) are picked from the "owner" model ρ_1, and ρ_0, ρ_2 adjust to it, with appropriate changes at "higher" types. The table also shows the pivot value $\langle 4, \dagger \rangle$ for the next step.

σ	ω	$\omega \times \mathsf{Bool}$		Int	$\mathsf{Int} \times \omega$	$\omega \times (\mathsf{Int} \times \omega)$	$\omega \times \mathsf{Bool} \Rightarrow \mathsf{Bool}$
$[\![\sigma]\!]\iota$	$\mathbb{I}$	$\mathbb{I} \times \mathbb{B}$		$\mathbb{Z}$	$\mathbb{Z} \times \mathbb{I}$	$\mathbb{I} \times (\mathbb{Z} \times \mathbb{I})$	$\mathbb{I} \times \mathbb{B} \Rightarrow \mathbb{B}$
	x_6	y_2 or z_2	y_7 or z_7	y_8 or z_8	y_5 or z_5	y_3 or z_3	y_1 or z_1
ρ_0	$\dagger$	$\langle \dagger, \mathsf{false} \rangle$	1	5	$\langle 10, \ddagger \rangle$	$\langle \dagger, \langle 11, \star \rangle \rangle$	$\lambda u.\,\mathsf{false}$
ρ_1	$\dagger$	$\langle \dagger, \mathsf{false} \rangle$	$\underline{4}$	$\underline{0}$	$\langle 12, \star \rangle$	$\langle \star, \langle 13, \dagger \rangle \rangle$	$\lambda u.\,\mathsf{true}$
ρ_2	$\dagger$	$\langle \dagger, \mathsf{false} \rangle$	3	7	$\langle 3, \dagger \rangle$	$\langle \ddagger, \langle 3, \dagger \rangle \rangle$	$\lambda u.\,\mathsf{true}$
ρ_0'	$\dagger$	$\langle \dagger, \mathsf{false} \rangle$	4	0	$\langle 10, \ddagger \rangle$	$\langle \dagger, \langle 11, \star \rangle \rangle$	$\lambda u.\,\mathsf{false}$
ρ_1'	$\dagger$	$\langle \dagger, \mathsf{false} \rangle$	4	0	$\langle 12, \star \rangle$	$\langle \star, \langle 13, \dagger \rangle \rangle$	$\lambda u.\,\mathsf{true}$
ρ_2'	$\dagger$	$\langle \dagger, \mathsf{false} \rangle$	4	0	$\underline{\langle 4, \dagger \rangle}$	$\langle \ddagger, \langle 4, \dagger \rangle \rangle$	$\lambda u.\,\mathsf{true}$

6   Conclusion and Future Work

We contend that the base logic for SMT should have parametric types and polymorphic functions. These features make it possible to easily model typical datatypes by single parametric structures and to model (unbounded) combinations of several datatypes by simple parameter instantiation. of several datatypes by simple parameter instantiation.

Our revision of the Nelson-Oppen method relies just on the parametricity of the datatypes modeled by the component theories and on the existence of *strong solvers* for them. Parametricity requirements hold for virtually all datatypes of interest, so to make our method widely applicable it remains to enhance the existing satisfiability procedures into efficient strong solvers. This can likely be done in ways similar to [15], and is the subject of future work.

Acknowledgments. Thanks to John O'Leary for discussions on *HOL* semantics, and to Levent Erkök, John Harrison, John Matthews, Albert Oliveras, and Mark Tuttle for reading parts of the manuscript and commenting on it.

References

1. N. Ayache and J.-C. Filliâtre. Combining the Coq proof assistant with first-order decision procedures. (unpublished), 2006.
2. C. Barrett and S. Berezin. CVC Lite: A new implementation of the cooperating validity checker. In *Computer Aided Verification (CAV)*, vol. 3114 of *LNCS* , pp. 515–518. 2004.
3. C. Barrett, I. Shikanian, and C. Tinelli. An abstract decision procedure for satisfiability in the theory of recursive data types. In *Pragmatics of Decision Procedures in Automated Deduction (PDPAR)*, 2006.
4. P. Fontaine and E. P. Gribomont. Combining non-stably infinite, non-first order theories. In *Pragmatics of Decision Procedures in Automated Deduction*, 2004.
5. P. Fontaine et al. Expressiveness + automation + soundness: Towards combining SMT solvers and interactive proof assistants. In *Tools and Algorithms for the Construction and Analysis of Systems)*, vol. 3920 of *LNCS*, pp. 167–181. 2006.
6. S. Ghilardi, E. Nicolini, and D. Zucchelli. A comprehensive combination framework. *ACM Transactions on Computational Logic*, 2007. (to appear).
7. M. J. C. Gordon and T. F. Melham, editors. *Introduction to HOL: A Theorem Proving Environment for Higher Order Logic*. Cambridge University Press, 1993.
8. J. Grundy et al. Tool building requirements for an API to first-order solvers. *ENTCS*, 144(2):15–26, 2006.
9. J. Harrison. Towards self-verification in HOL Light. In *Automated Reasoning (IJCAR)*, vol. 4130 of *LNAI*. 2006.
10. S. Krstić et al. Combined satisfiability modulo parametric theories. Tech. report, Oct. 2006. (ftp://ftp.cs.uiowa.edu/pub/tinelli/papers/KrsGGT-RR-06.pdf).
11. G. Nelson and D. C. Oppen. Simplification by cooperating decision procedures. *ACM Transactions on Programming Languages and Systems*, 1(2):245–257, 1979.
12. R. Nieuwenhuis and A. Oliveras. Congruence closure with integer offsets. In *Logic for Programming, AI and Reasoning (LPAR)*, vol. 2850 of *LNCS*, pp. 78–90. 2003.
13. R. Nieuwenhuis, A. Oliveras, and C. Tinelli. Solving SAT and SAT Modulo Theories: From an abstract Davis-Putnam-Logemann-Loveland procedure to DPLL(T). *Journal of the ACM*, 2006. (to appear).
14. T. Nipkow, L. C. Paulson, and M. Wenzel. *Isabelle/HOL: A Proof Assistant for Higher-Order Logic*, vol. 2283 of *LNCS*. 2002.
15. S. Ranise, C. Ringeissen, and C. G. Zarba. Combining data structures with non-stably infinite theories using many-sorted logic. In *Frontiers of Combining Systems (FroCoS)*, vol. 3717 of *LNCS*, pp. 48–64. 2005.

16. S. Ranise and C. Tinelli. The SMT-LIB standard: Version 1.2. Technical report.
17. J. C. Reynolds. Types, abstraction and parametric polymorphism. In *Information Processing: 9th World Computer Congress*, pp. 513–523. North-Holland, 1983.
18. C. Ringeissen. Cooperation of decision procedures for the satisfiability problem. In *Frontiers of Combining Systems (FroCoS)*, vol. 3 of *Applied Logic*, pp. 121–140.
19. N. Shankar. Using decision procedures with a higher-order logic. In *Theorem Proving in Higher Order Logics (TPHOLS)*, vol. 2152 of *LNCS*, pp. 5–26, 2001.
20. C. Tinelli and M. Harandi. A new correctness proof of the Nelson-Oppen combination procedure. In *Frontiers of Combining Systems (FroCoS)*, vol. 3 of *Applied Logic*, pp. 103–120. Kluwer, 1996.
21. C. Tinelli and C. Zarba. Combining decision procedures for sorted theories. In *Logic in Artificial Intelligence (JELIA)*, vol. 3229 of *LNAI*, pp. 641–653. 2004.
22. C. Tinelli and C. Zarba. Combining nonstably infinite theories. *Journal of Automated Reasoning*, 34(3):209–238, 2005.
23. P. Wadler. Theorems for free! In *Functional Programming Languages and Computer Architecture (FPCA)*, pp. 347–359. ACM Press, 1989.
24. C. G. Zarba. Combining sets with elements. In *Verification: Theory and Practice*, vol. 2772 of *LNCS*, pp. 762–782. 2004.

A Gröbner Basis Approach to
CNF-Formulae Preprocessing*

Christopher Condrat and Priyank Kalla

Department of Electrical and Computer Engineering
University of Utah, Salt Lake City, UT, USA
chris@g6net.com, kalla@eng.utah.edu

Abstract. This paper presents a CNF SAT-formulae transformation technique employing Gröbner bases as a means to analyze the problem structure. Gröbner-bases have been applied in the past for SAT; however, their use was primarily restricted to analyzing entire problems for proof-refutation. In contrast, this technique analyzes limited subsets of problems, and uses the derived Gröbner bases to yield new constraint-information. This information is then used to reduce problem structure, provide additional information about the problem itself, or aid other preprocessing techniques. Contrary to the precepts of contemporary techniques, the transformation often increases the problem size. However, experimental results demonstrate that our approach often improves SAT-search efficiency in a number of areas, including: solve time, conflicts, number of decisions, etc.

1 Introduction

The Boolean Satisfiability Problem (SAT) is formulated as finding solutions satisfying a set of Boolean equations, or to show that no such solutions exist (UNSAT). Such problems are often represented in Conjunctive Normal Form (CNF), whereby sets of literal-disjunctions (clauses) must be simultaneously satisfied through some variable assignment.

Solving for SAT-problems involves SAT-solvers. Most are based on the Davis-Putnam [1] and Davis-Logemann-Loveland [2] procedures (DPLL), which performs recursive branching and unit propagation over clauses. This technique is aided by concepts such as constraint-propagation [3], conflict analysis [4], and learning [5], which enable non-chronological backtracking [4] [6] [7], pruning the search space and reducing overall search time.

The SAT solving-time is not, however, merely a function of the variables and constraints that form the core SAT problem. Problem-representation, especially in CNF, can affect how SAT-solving performs. This is especially true when SAT-instances are transformed from system designs, for validation purposes. In automated conversion, utilities can produce "unoptimized" instances for CNF—those with constraints and variables that do not provide useful information. As a result, time and resources are wasted.

A recent area of research has therefore formed around CNF-formula transformation and simplification. This approach diverges from, or should be said, *complements*

---

* This work is supported, in part, by a Faculty Early Career Development (CAREER) grant from the US National Science Foundation, contract No. CCF-546859.

O. Grumberg and M. Huth (Eds.): TACAS 2007, LNCS 4424, pp. 618–631, 2007.

"classical" approaches to SAT-solving, those based on DPLL-solving [2] [4] [6] [7], by attacking the SAT problem at its source: the constraints. Algorithms and techniques such as [8] [9] [10] simplify and transform CNF-constraints through methods such as clause subsumption, hyper-resolution, and variable elimination. The applicability of such approaches varies between problems; however, most problems can benefit from at least some level of CNF preprocessing.

The goal of the preprocessor is to make the problem easier to solve, not necessarily reduce the problem size. A smaller problem implies, at the very least, that there is less the SAT-solver needs to process. However, this does not necessarily imply it is easier to solve. Indeed, some of the hardest problems, are those which have no "redundant" information present in the problem [11]. Additional information may also help clue the solver into the actual purpose of the structures in the problem represent, especially in Hybrid solvers [12]. Even the abilities of rewrite-rule-based CNF-preprocessors can be affected if constraints do not fit their simplification templates.

Preprocessing approaches have traditionally concentrated on reducing the overhead—the time needed to consider constraint information—of SAT problems prior to performing the SAT search. This "overhead" comes in the form of constraints and variables that can be represented in simpler forms, or eliminated altogether. Techniques such as Hypre [8], NiVER [9], and SatELite [10] reduce this overhead through resolution-based preprocessing.

1.1 Contemporary Preprocessing Approaches

HyPre [8] employs a form of binary reasoning, called "hyper-binary resolution," in addition to the techniques found in previous preprocessors such as 2-Simplify [13]. Hyper-binary resolution performs a resolution step involving more than two input clauses. A single size-n clause and $(n-1)$-binary clauses are resolved to a form that aids in SAT-search. HyPre's ability to resolve sets of clauses to simpler forms has been relatively successful, but at the same time it can be slow.

NiVER and SatELite use resolution to eliminate variables from a SAT-instance. Variable elimination, the older cousin to DPLL, finds itself on the other end of SAT solving from DPLL, where space, as opposed to time, increases exponentially.

Given a variable x, and two clauses, containing the variable and its negation respectively, performing resolution on x represents the following:

$$(x \vee a_1 \vee \ldots \vee a_n) \bigotimes (x' \vee b_1 \vee \ldots \vee b_m) = (a_1 \vee \ldots \vee a_n \vee b_1 \vee \ldots \vee b_m) \quad (1)$$

where $\bigotimes$ is the **resolution operator**. Variable elimination is performed by resolving for a variable on all clauses that contain it as follows (for variable v):

$$C_v = ClausesContainingLiteral(v)$$
$$C_{v'} = ClausesContainingLiteral(v') \quad (2)$$
$$C_v \bigotimes_v C_{v'} = \{c_1 \bigotimes c_2 \mid c_1 \in C_v, \ c_2 \in C_{v'}\}$$

The variable is eliminated, but at the cost of more constraints than the original set, increasing the problem size in the general case.

NiVER [9] stands for "Non-Increasing Variable Elimination Resolution." This technique attempts to overcome the size-explosion problem associated with variable elimination by only eliminating variables in a way that does not increase problem size. Some constraint-sets resulting from variable elimination contain tautologies, which may be removed, resulting in a constraint set equal to or smaller than the original—hence "non-increasing" variable elimination.

SatELite [10] improves on NiVER by combining binary clause resolution simplification with non-increasing variable-elimination, adding new resolution rules for clause subsumption. Clause subsumption proves to be useful for simplifying clauses resulting from variable elimination, enabling an efficient clause-variable simplification procedure which can be repeated until no more reductions are possible.

2 Gröbner Bases for CNF-Transformation

This paper presents a new CNF-formula transformation approach, exploiting the power of polynomial ring algebra, particularly Gröbner bases, to transform CNF-constraints. Gröbner bases provide a computational means to derive reduced bases of sets of polynomials. The resulting polynomials better represent the solution-set and while this process can introduce new constraints and new variables, but the problem itself is simplified—easier to solve. We show that deriving extra constraint information during preprocessing may actually improve performance.

The application of Gröbner bases for SAT is nothing new. Proof-systems, such as the Nullstellensatz [14] and Gröbner/Polynomial Calculus [15] proof-systems, introduced in the mid-90s, used Gröbner bases as a means to derive proof-refutations, by generating a unit ideal from the polynomials representing the problem [16]. However, refuting an entire problem using Gröbner bases can be a time consuming, and often infeasible, task. Despite the many improvements to computation algorithms, Gröbner bases systems still have potential exponential time and space complexity, especially when analyzing large problems.

Analogous to the techniques forming the foundation of Hypre, NiVER, and SatELite, a single, partial application of Gröbner bases to a SAT instance may improve solving and problem performance. By only transforming parts of the CNF-structure, the problem, as a whole, can benefit from the reduction capabilities of Gröbner bases, while leaving alone parts which are computationally infeasible. This overall strategy fits well into a CNF-SAT transformation framework, through assisting dedicated SAT-solving tools, much as contemporary CNF-preprocessors do.

2.1 Methodology

Our CNF-transformation process is divided into phases: 1) the problem structure is first analyzed, and partitions identified; 2) CNF clauses are converted into polynomials over $\mathbb{Z}_2$; 3) the polynomials are then transformed using a Gröbner basis engine using a suitable monomial ordering derived from the partition information; 4) finally, the transformed polynomials are converted back into CNF to be used in SAT-solving. To evaluate the performance of the approach, we compare the SAT-solving results for the untransformed instances with those of the transformed versions.

A detailed explanation of the process and the concepts introduced above is the subject of the following sections.

3   Preliminaries

Boolean algebra is isomorphic to polynomial ring algebra over $\mathbb{Z}_2$. Therefore, a one-to-one mapping of operators between the two algebras is defined as follows:

$$f : B \rightarrow \mathbb{Z}_2 : \tag{3}$$

$$\neg n \rightarrow n + 1 \qquad a \wedge b \rightarrow a \cdot b$$
$$a \vee b \rightarrow a + b + a \cdot b \quad a \oplus b \rightarrow a + b$$

Addition and multiplication operations are performed mod 2 so no coefficients greater than 1 will be present. The property of idempotency ($x^2 = x$) is also present, ensuring that the polynomials will remain multi-linear.

Given a set of CNF-clauses $C = \{C_0, \ldots, C_n\}$ we can transform these clauses into a set of polynomials over $\mathbb{Z}_2$ using (Func.3):

$$C' = \{C'_0 = 1, \ldots, C'_n = 1\} \tag{4}$$

which is equivalent to the following polynomial equations over $\mathbb{Z}_2$:

$$C' = \{C'_0 + 1 = 0, \ldots, C'_n + 1 = 0\} \tag{5}$$

The latter form will be used throughout this paper, and for notational purposes, we will assume and omit the zero-equality ($= 0$) for the equations.

The polynomial-set generates an **ideal**—the set of all linear combinations of the polynomials—and therefore is called a **generating set** for the ideal. The individual polynomials are referred to as **generators**. In commutative algebra/algebraic geometry the set of all solutions for a set of equations is referred to as a **variety**.

What is interesting to note, is that the variety is defined, not so much by a set of polynomial equations, but rather by the *ideal* spanned by them. The effect of this is that different sets of generators can represent the same ideal, and therefore the same variety. Furthermore, some generating sets may be "better" than the original, in the sense that they are simpler or easier to solve—a better representation of the ideal. Techniques exist to find such representations. For linear equations, the well-known Gaussian Elimination technique is one such method to reduce sets of polynomials into a form which is easier to solve. However, for non-linear systems of polynomials, a generalization of this type of reduction procedure is necessary. The solution is: Gröbner bases.

3.1   Gröbner Bases

Introduced by Bruno Buchberger in 1965 [17], the theory of Gröbner bases provides a *computational framework* for deriving a special kind of generating subset of an ideal, where dividing any polynomial in the ideal by the Gröbner basis gives zero. While there are many equivalent definitions of a Gröbner basis, we choose this one as most suitable:

Definition 1. [**Gröbner Basis**] (From Def.1.6.1 of [18]): *For a set monomial ordering $>$, a set of of non-zero polynomials, $G = \{g_1, \ldots, g_t\}$, contained in an ideal I, is called a* **Gröbner basis** *for I if and only if for all $f \in I$ such that $f \neq 0$, there exists $i \in \{1, \ldots, t\}$ such that $lp(g_i)$ (lp = leading power-product) divides $lp(f)$.*

$$G = Gr\ddot{o}bnerBasis(I) \iff \forall f \in I : f \neq 0, \exists g_i \in G : lp(g_i)|lp(f) \qquad (6)$$

This definition of a Gröbner basis allows the basis to be derived through relatively efficient computational methods akin to deriving the greatest-common-divisor for a set of multi-variate polynomials.

Deriving a Gröbner basis generally relies on a variant of the Buchberger algorithm [17], the precise details of which can be found in [18]. The Gröbner basis begins as the initial set of polynomials to be reduced. A monomial ordering is fixed to ensure that polynomials are represented in a consistent manner (detailed in subsequent sections). Buchberger's algorithm then takes pairs of the polynomials in the basis and combines them into "S-polynomials" to cancel leading terms. An S-polynomial is defined as:

$$S(f, g) = \frac{L}{lt(f)} \cdot f - \frac{L}{lt(g)} \cdot g \quad where \quad L = lcm(lt(f), lt(g)) \qquad (7)$$

The $lt(p)$ is the *leading term* of p, and $lcm(f, g)$ is the *least common multiple* of f and g. For example, consider a set of polynomials F:

$$F = \left\{ \begin{array}{ll} f_1 = abcf + abc & f_3 = bf + f, \\ f_2 = af + f, & f_4 = cf + f \end{array} \right\} \qquad (8)$$

Deriving the S-polynomial for polynomials f_1 and f_2 results in:

$$lcm(f_1, f_2) = abcf$$
$$S(abcf + abc, af + f) = \frac{abcf}{abcf}(abcf + abc) - \frac{abcf}{af}(af + f) \qquad (9)$$
$$= abc + bcf$$

The S-polynomial is then reduced by all elements in F to a remainder r. Reduction of a polynomial p, by a single element $f_i \in F$, is denoted $p \xrightarrow{f_i} r$, and reduction by the entire set F is denoted $p \xrightarrow{F}_+ r$. The method for reduction is multivariate polynomial division. Reducing the S-polynomial in (Eqn.9) by elements of F is shown below:

$$S(f_1, f_2) \xrightarrow{bf+f} h_1 \qquad\qquad h_1 \xrightarrow{cf+f} h_2$$

$$
\begin{array}{r}
c \\
\hline
bf + f) \,\overline{abc + bcf} \\
- \quad\quad bcf + cf \\
\hline
abc \quad\quad + cf = h_1
\end{array}
\qquad
\begin{array}{r}
1 \\
\hline
cf + f) \,\overline{abc + cf} \\
- \quad\quad cf + f \\
\hline
abc \quad\quad + f = h_2
\end{array}
\qquad (10)
$$

No other members of F can reduce h_2 further, therefore $S(f_1, f_2) \xrightarrow{F}_+ (abc + f)$. As a non-zero polynomial, $abc + f$ is then added to the basis F as a new element. The Buchberger algorithm has therefore discovered a new element of the Gröbner basis.

This process is repeated for all unique pairs of polynomials (including those created by newly added elements), constructing the Gröbner basis. A Gröbner basis is considered **reduced** or *minimal* if no leading terms of differing polynomials in the set divide each other and the leading-term coefficient is 1. For example, a Gröbner basis

$$G = \left\{ \begin{array}{ll} f_1 = abcf + abc & f_4 = bf + f, \\ f_2 = af + f, & f_5 = cf + f \\ f_3 = abc + f, & \end{array} \right\} \tag{11}$$

is not a *reduced* Gröbner basis, as f_1 contains a leading term that is divisible by the leading term of other polynomials. Unreduced Gröbner bases contain redundant elements, and therefore this transformation approach only works with reduced Gröbner bases.

The result of the computation is a set of polynomials that should be easier to solve than the original set, while representing the same ideal. This improved set of polynomials can then be translated to CNF form, aiding SAT-solving. This forms the basic premise of the CNF-transformation approach presented. How this is effectively implemented is the subject of the next section.

4   Transformation Process

Computing a Gröbner basis using a Buchberger-variant algorithm can exhibit exponential worst-case time and computational complexity [19], and for this reason that many different techniques have been developed [15] [18] [20] [21] [22] for improving the algorithm, often for specific applications. However, while these techniques deal with the inner-workings of algorithm itself, outside the algorithm there is less control. What control there is comes in the form of polynomial selection (i.e. partitioning) and monomial ordering. For this reason, these two aspects of the computation process are an important part of the transformation process.

4.1   Partitioning

The generators of an ideal may be separated, manipulated, and then remerged with the original set in the same manner as clauses in a CNF-instance. This can be used for parallelizing Gröbner basis computations [23] or, in this case, operating only on specific subsets of the problem.

The first stage of partitioning involves removing sets of clauses that are too computationally intensive for a Gröbner basis engine to operate on. The multi-linear form of clauses may have up to $(2^n - 1)$ monomials for n literals. Therefore large clauses are avoided. In addition, sets of small clauses, taken together, may form into very large polynomials during the process of reduction. Finally, these large and small clauses may actually be components of constraint structures represented in CNF, such as large conjunctions (logical AND)—the form of which is depicted below:

$$f = \bigwedge_{i=0}^{n-1} x_i \iff \left(f \vee \bigvee_{i=0}^{n-1} \neg x_i \right) \wedge \bigwedge_{i=0}^{n-1} (x_i \vee \neg f) \tag{12}$$

An example is:

$$f = a \land b \land c \iff (a \lor \neg f) \land (b \lor \neg f) \land (c \lor \neg f) \land (\neg a \lor \neg b \lor \neg c \lor f) \quad (13)$$

Directly computing for such structures can cause a large intermediate expression swell [24], and because the final form is known and easily extracted, there is no point in direct computation.

Structures such as conjunctions can be quickly isolated and removed prior to transformation. For this implementation, only conjunction-like structures were targeted (disjunctions being of similar form). Conveniently, what often remains after conjunction-removal is the "glue" that connects the conjunctions—clusters of 3-literal clauses with relatively well-connected variables, which are good candidates for transformation. These clusters of clauses can be partitioned easily by collecting all clauses associated with a single variable. This works well for industrial-type SAT-instances. However, in cases where this approach may yield clusters which are too small, repeatedly collecting all clauses which are connected to a group of clauses by two or more variables also works. This ensures that clauses are connected to the group by at least two variables, while not requiring an overly high level of connectivity which could limit applicability. This also prevents, to a great extent, random CNF structures from being clustered, which are hard for polynomial calculus [25].

4.2 Generating the Gröbner Basis

A wide variety of Gröbner basis computation-engines are available due to widespread interest in their use. Our transformation engine uses CoCoA [26], specifically its C++ library, for performing Gröbner basis reductions. The output is a reduced Gröbner basis.

The CNF-clauses are converted into polynomials using (Func.3), and converted to the form found in (Eqn.5). These polynomials form the initial generating set from which a Gröbner bases will be derived. However, if the Gröbner basis is computed directly, unexpected results may appear. Take for example a set of polynomials in $\mathbb{Z}_2$, and its corresponding Gröbner basis on the right:

$$\left\{ \begin{array}{l} abc + ac + bc + c + 1 \\ bcd + bd + cd + d + 1 \\ acd + ad + cd + d + 1 \end{array} \right\} \longrightarrow \left\{ \begin{array}{l} a + b \\ b^2 d + b + 1 \\ bc + cd + c + d \\ cd^2 + bd + d^2 + d + 1 \end{array} \right\} \quad (14)$$

The second and fourth Gröbner-basis polynomials contain powered terms which should not appear due to the Boolean-ring property of idempotency. Furthermore, the monomials $d^2 + d$ maps to zero, and should not appear in the fourth equation at all.

To account for idempotency we use Fermat's Little Theorem, generalized in [27] as:

Theorem 1. [Fermat's Little Theorem] *If p is a prime number, and x is an integer, the following holds:*

$$x^p \equiv x \ (mod \ p) \quad (15)$$

The above equation can be rearranged in the following manner:

$$x^p - x \equiv 0 \ (mod \ p) \tag{16}$$

$$x^2 + x \equiv 0 \ (mod \ 2) \tag{17}$$

The above are the forms of a **vanishing polynomial** in the ring $\mathbb{Z}_p[x]$ and $\mathbb{Z}_2[x]$ respectively. The set of all such polynomial equations generates the **ideal of all vanishing polynomials** in their corresponding rings. When present during a Gröbner bases derivation, the basis elements that map to this ideal are eliminated during the reduction process.

Therefore, when using Gröbner bases for transformation, the generating set must contain a polynomial equation of form (Eqn.17) for every variable found in the generating set. The result is such that any polynomial in the resulting Gröbner basis will be in multi-linear form. Furthermore, no element of the basis will contain a redundant (i.e. zero) term.

4.3 Monomial Ordering

In the actual creation of a Gröbner basis, the results may be unimpressive: a set of polynomial equations larger than the original set, often with more monomials. While a larger basis may yield useful information, finding a smaller basis reduces the number of constraints that must be satisfied, affecting performance. One way to reduce the size of a Gröbner basis is through an efficient monomial ordering.

Monomial orders determine how the Gröbner basis is generated by affecting how leading terms—which the basis is formed upon—are ordered. The ordering-methodologies are explained in standard textbooks such as [18]. There are three general-purpose orderings: pure lexicographic (*lex*), degree-lexicographic (*deglex*), taking into account the degree of the polynomial, and a degree-reverse-lexicographic (*revdeglex*), a reversed-lexicographically ordered version of the *deglex* ordering. Our transformation approach uses a *deglex* ordering.

The *lex* / *deglex* / *revdeglex* orderings only affect the *global* monomial ordering. However, these orderings can be further refined at a *local* level by taking into account the properties of the constraint set over which the transformation is applied, notably its variables. Variables in many SAT-instances are often localized, and as a result a global variable ordering may be sub-optimal. Therefore, a variable-ordering is generated specifically for each constraint set.

During initial experiments, it was observed that the later in the variable-order a high-activity variable appeared, the smaller the Gröbner basis (activity being how often a variable appears in a set of clauses). Compared to ordering such variables first, the difference in size was often orders-of-magnitude smaller. For example, consider the following set of clauses where a is the most highly active variable:

$$(a' \vee b' \vee c) \wedge (a \vee b' \vee c') \wedge (a' \vee d' \vee e) \wedge (a \vee d' \vee e') \tag{18}$$

Using an *lex* ordering $a \prec e \prec c \prec d \prec b$ the resulting Gröbner basis is formed of three polynomials (omitting the Fermat $x^2 + x$ form elements):

$$ab + cb, \quad ad + ed, \quad edb + cdb \tag{19}$$

However, if the ordering is reversed, $b \prec d \prec c \prec e \prec a$, a different Gröbner basis is computed, one with only two polynomials:

$$de + da, \quad bc + ba \tag{20}$$

For larger sets of polynomials, the variable-ordering can have pronounced effects on the size of the resulting Gröbner bases—often by orders-of-magnitude. Our transformation approach therefore seeks to minimize the size of the Gröbner bases through an effective lexicographic ordering.

To understand how a variable order affects Gröbner bases the concepts of an **elimination ideal** and an **elimination theorem** for Gröbner basis are necessary. The consequences of these two will be described later.

Definition 2. [**Elimination Ideal**] From [28]: *Given* $I = \langle f_1, \ldots, f_s \rangle \subset k[x_1, \ldots, x_n]$, *the ith* **elimination ideal** I_i *is the ideal of* $k[x_{i+1}, \ldots, x_n]$ *defined by*

$$I_i = I \cap k[x_{i+1}, \ldots, x_n] \tag{21}$$

A ith elimination ideal does not contain variables $x_1, \ldots, x_i$, and neither does the basis that generates it. The basis of an elimination ideal can be a Gröbner basis by using the elimination theorem:

Theorem 2. [**Elimination Theorem**] From [28]: *Let* $I \subset k[x_1, \ldots, x_n]$ *be an ideal and let* G *be a Gröbner basis of* I *with respect to a lex ordering where* $x_1 \prec x_2 \prec \cdots \prec x_n$. *Then for every* $0 \leq i \leq n$, *the set*

$$G_i = G \cap k[x_{i+1}, \ldots, x_n] \tag{22}$$

is a Gröbner basis of the ith elimination ideal I_i.

The proof for (Thm.2) can be found in [28].

When a Gröbner basis G in variables $x_1, \ldots, x_n$ is generated using an *lex* order, the resulting Gröbner basis contains, as subsets, all Gröbner bases $G_0, \ldots, G_n$ for elimination ideals $I_0, \ldots, I_n$. As variables are progressively eliminated, the subsequent Gröbner bases containing the uneliminated variables must generate ideals in the absence of those variables. This can cause many additional elements to be generated. The Gröbner basis G can therefore have exponential size-complexity [29].

The more frequent a variable appears in a set of polynomials, and the earlier it is eliminated, the larger the Gröbner basis generally is. However, ordering higher-activity variables later in the order (accending activity) allows the variables to remain present in more elements of the Gröbner basis. The result is that it is not necessary to represent those variables—in their absence—with additional polynomials, producing a smaller basis.

Therefore, our transformation approach orders variables, on a per-set basis, by accending variable-activity. Despite the fact that a *deglex* monomial ordering is not an elimination order by nature, the Gröbner basis it generates is still reduced in overall size through this variable ordering. The computation is also fast, and the overall size of the transformed set is smaller.

The effects of variable-elimination in Gröbner bases parallels variable-elimination using resolution. In the example (Ex.18), the last polynomial in (Eqns.19) represents the SAT-instance in the absence of the variable a. Using the resolution on (Eqns.18) to eliminate a results in:

$$C_a \otimes C_{a'} = \left\{ \begin{array}{ll} (a' \vee b' \vee c) \otimes (a \vee b' \vee c') = (b' \vee c \vee c') & = \text{T}, \\ (a' \vee d' \vee e) \otimes (a \vee b' \vee c') = (b' \vee d' \vee c' \vee e), \\ (a' \vee b' \vee c) \otimes (a \vee d' \vee e') = (b' \vee c \vee d' \vee e'), \\ (a' \vee d' \vee e) \otimes (a \vee d' \vee e') = (d' \vee e \vee e') & = \text{T} \end{array} \right\}$$
$$= (b' \vee c' \vee d' \vee e) \wedge (b' \vee c \vee d' \vee e') \tag{23}$$

which is exactly equivalent to the constraints implied by the third polynomial of (Eqns.19):

$$edb + cdb = 0 \tag{24}$$

NiVER and SatELite use resolution to perform variable-elimination, while seeking to avoid the size-complexity problems associated with it. Avoiding the complexity problems associated with variable-elimination is also the goal of this approach. Our variable-ordering reduces this effect to a great degree.

4.4 Transforming Polynomials into CNF Clauses

After reduction by the Gröbner basis engine, the polynomials are converted back into CNF form using for use in SAT solving using the reverse function of (Func.3). Prior to conversion, "1" is added to each polynomial to convert the polynomials back into the form in (Eqn.4).

Final Recombination — After transforming the polynomials into CNF, the transformed clauses are merged with the original problem. The SAT-instance is then ready for solving by a SAT solver.

5   Results

The transformation technique was applied to various SAT-benchmarks. The testbench system for SAT-solving was an AMD Athlon 64 2800+ (1.6Mhz) processor with 2GB of memory, running Ubuntu Linux 6.06 x86-64. zChaff version 2004.11.15 Simplified was designated as the standard solving tool for all problems. No other preprocessing was applied for the initial set of benchmarks.

5.1   Categories of SAT-Instances

The SAT-instances used for transforming and solving were, for the most part, from industrial-category benchmarks. In other words, the benchmarks were converted from EDA designs, or other sources, into CNF for validation purposes. Proving UNSAT for such instances validates the design, whereas variants with bugs will have a SAT solution. A mix of the both SAT and UNSAT benchmarks were used. Other benchmarks include instances generated using a Bounded Model Checker [30], specifically the 12-12-barrel and longmult15 benchmarks, and a coloring benchmark.

By and large, the industrial SAT-instances dominate the results table. This is because the structure of such problems lend themselves to meaningful partitioning, where clauses can be partitioned into well-connected sets. Furthermore, some classes of SAT instances simply do not perform well using a transformation approach which relies on reducing polynomials with each other. Random SAT instances are a good example. The paper [25] showed that random CNFs are hard for Polynomial Calculus, and though this research was carried out over non-Boolean rings, in experiments, this appears to be true for Boolean rings as well.

The problems below reflect the types of problems that can be effectively processed by the Gröbner basis transformation engine. All times are measured in seconds.

Benchmark	S	Variables		Clauses		N	PPT	Solve Time	
		Orig	Trans	Orig	Trans			Orig	Trans
12-12-barrel	U	20114	0	83619	+34752	192576	123	545	488
engine_4_nd	U	7000	+2111	67586	+6787	1269	4.09	611	574
longmult15	U	7807	+2026	24351	+8531	180	4.54	364	218
9dlx_vliw_at_b_iq1	U	24604	+2665	261473	+8675	1536	2.88	410	326
manol-pipe-c10b	U	43517	+4967	129265	+19661	453	71.38	668	621
manol-pipe-c6id	U	82022	+12873	242044	+49707	3820	236	513	504
6pipe.sat03-414	U	15800	+1266	394739	+4724	680	17.61	142	138
7pipe_q0_k	U	26512	+2174	536414	+6648	1460	3.19	235	222
8pipe_q0_k	U	39434	+2707	887706	+8324	1812	4.55	672	634
9pipe_q0_k	U	55996	+1830	1468197	+6736	1246	29.44	872	838
12pipe_bug1_q0	S	138917	+25836	4678756	+83529	15190	502	2507	1696
color-10-3-1483	S	300	+371	6475	+1593	388	4.18	115	11.86
2dlx_cc_ex_bp_f_bug1	S	171648	+43490	2614355	+139196	26094	74.83	809	367
grieu-vmpc-s05-05s	S	625	+16046	76775	+54185	6981	8.06	1010	881
grieu-vmpc-s05-27r	S	729	+34364	96849	+110258	21498	39.72	480	167

S = SAT/UNSAT; N = number of clauses processed; PPT = Preprocessing time.

Benchmark	Decisions		Net Conflicts		Implications	
	Orig	Trans	Orig	Trans	Orig	Trans
12pipe_bug1_q0	2,959,248	1,883,240	59,419	39,077	1,666,102,113	1,100,747,357
2dlx_cc_ex_bp_f_bug1	924,583	317,972	25,512	22,580	874,876,875	301,397,803
grieu-vmpc-s05-27r	264,743	69,240	152,700	34,193	32,565,075	78,017,191
color-10-3-1483	436,772	92,283	182,689	45,396	9,734,635	3,237,651

Some results have more clauses processed than are present in the original problem. In such cases, clause sets were partitioned by their connection to variables. As some clauses may have simultaneously belonged to multiple sets, this represented a form of clause "cross-fertilization" [31]. Also, the lack of additional variables in the 12-12-barrel was a result of variable elimination from polynomial equations of form:

$$a + b = 0 \quad \text{or} \quad a + b + 1 = 0 \tag{25}$$

which imply $a = b$ and $a = \neg b$, respectively.

5.2 Combining SAT Preprocessors

In addition to applying the Gröbner basis transformation technique alone, the technique was combined with another preprocessor SatELite 1.13 [10] to test how two transformation engines complemented each other's abilities. With SatELite's ability to simplify CNF files at the clause-level, much of the overhead "clutter"created by the Gröbner basis transformations could be reduced. However, "cleanup" was not the only purpose of using SatELite: the additional constraint-information produced by the Gröbner basis transformation could be used to improve SatELite performance.

Benchmark	S	Processing Time			Solve Time			
		SatEL	GBT	Comb	Orig	SatEL	GBT	Comb
7pipe	U	41.70	3.28	45.17	333	411	382	305
9pipe_q0_k	U	70.85	29.44	113	872	594	838	539
2dlx_cc_ex_bp_f_bug1	S	194	74.83	316	809	594	367	117

SatEL = SatELite; GBT = Gröbner Basis Transformation; Comb = Combined

In all cases, the Gröbner basis engine was applied first, and then SatELite. Some benchmarks, such as the above, were able to derive benefits from a combination of preprocessors. In one instance, the solve time of the transformed problem was only less when both techniques were combined.

5.3   Interpreting the Results

The results are mixed. On many, the benefits obtained are far outweighed by the time spent during preprocessing. Furthermore, the processing varied greatly, with some problems benefiting from large numbers of clauses processed, and others very few. Also the time saved during solving varied from only marginal improvement to significant savings.

The purpose, however, is not to present a comprehensive solution, but to show the potential that lies in this approach. One stand-out result is that, despite the number of additional constraints and variables produced, in many cases the SAT solver could still find solutions in less time. Such results are encouraging, and can lead to a more refined approach, overcoming inefficiencies such as those caused by the polynomial-to-CNF translation.

6   Conclusion

We have presented a polynomial ring algebra approach to CNF-formulae transformation, using Gröbner bases as the core technique to transform polynomials. By applying this approach in an effective manner, sets of constraints, represented as polynomials can be simplified, making the problem easier to solve. We have shown that when a SAT instance is properly partitioned, and a partition-specific monomial ordering derived, this approach can perform relatively well. Also, despite the large number of clauses and variables added to the problem, extra constraint information, provided as a result of processing, can actually improve SAT solving. This technique is not fully refined; however, it shows promise and has a firm grounding in commutative ring algebra. We conclude that SAT-solving can benefit from this alternative approach to CNF-formulae transformation for preprocessing and, with additional improvements, may prove to be a viable technique for SAT preprocessing.

References

1. M. Davis and H. Putnam, "A Computing Procedure for Quantification Theory", *Journal of the ACM*, vol. 7, pp. 201–215, 1960.
2. M. Davis, G. Logemann, and D. Loveland, "A machine program for theorem proving", *in Communications of the ACM, 5:394-397*, 1962.
3. R. Zabih and D. A. McAllester, "A Rearrangement Search Strategy for Determining Propositional Satisfiability", *in Proc. Natl. Conf. on AI*, 1988.
4. J. Marques-Silva and K. A. Sakallah, "GRASP - A New Search Algorithm for Satisfiability", *in International Conference on Computer Aided Design (ICCAD)*, pp. 220–227, Nov. 1996.
5. W. Kunz and D.K. Pradhan, "Recursive Learning: A New Implication Technique for Efficient Solutions to CAD Problems – Test, Verification and Optimization", *IEEE Tr. on CAD*, vol. 13, pp. 1143–1158, Sep. 1994.
6. M. Moskewicz, C. Madigan, L. Zhao, and S. Malik, "CHAFF: Engineering an Efficient SAT Solver", *in In Proc. Design Automation Conference*, pp. 530–535, June 2001.
7. E. Goldberg and Y. Novikov, "BerkMin: A Fast and Robust Sat-Solver", *in Design, Automation and Test in Europe (DATE), pp 142-149*, 2002.
8. F. Bacchus and J. Winter, "Effective Preprocessing with Hyper-Resoluton and Equality Reduction", *in Proc. Intl Colloquium Automata, Languages, and Programming*, June 2003.
9. S. Subbarayan and D. Pradhan, "NiVER: Non Increasing Variable Elimination Resolution for Preprocessing SAT instances", *in International Conference on Theory and Applications of Satisfiability Testing (SAT2004)*, May 2004.
10. N. Eén and A. Biere, "Effective Preprocessing in SAT through Variable and Clause Elimination", *in International Conference on Theory and Applications of Satisfiability Testing*, June 2005.
11. E.A. Hirsch, "Random generator hgen8 of unsatisfiable formulas in CNF - SAT 2003 benchmark competition winner", http://logic.pdmi.ras.ru/~hirsch/benchmarks/hgen8.html
12. J. P. Warners and H. V. Maaren, "A Two Phase Algorithm for Solving a Class of Hard Satisfiability Problems", *in 90*, p. 10. Centrum voor Wiskunde en Informatica (CWI), ISSN 1386-369X, 30 1998.
13. R. I. Brafman, "A Simplifier for Propositional Formulas with Many Binary Clauses", *in Proceedings of the International Joint Conferences on Artificial Intelligence (IJCAI)*, pp. 515–522, 2001.
14. P. Beame, R. Impagliazzo, J. Kraj'icek, T. Pitassi, and P. Pudl'ak, "Lower bounds on Hilbert's Nullstellensatz and propositional proofs", *in Proceedings of the London Mathematical Society*, pp. 73:1–26, 1996.
15. M. Clegg, J. Edmonds, and R. Impagliazzo, "Using the Gröbner basis algorithm to find proofs of unsatisfiability", *in Proc. 28th ACM Symposium on Theory of Computing*, pp. 174–183, 1996.
16. J. Buresh-Oppenheim, M. Clegg, R. Impagliazzo, and T. Pitassi, "Homogenization and the Polynomial Calculus", *Comput. Complex.*, vol. 11, pp. 91–108, 2003.
17. B. Buchberger, *Ein Algorithmus zum Aunden der Basiselemente des Restklassenringes nach einem Nulldimensionalen Polynomideal*, PhD thesis, Institute of Mathematics. University of Innsbruck, Austria, 1965.
18. W. Adams and P Loustaunau, *An Introduction to Gröbner Bases*, American Mathematical Society, 1994.
19. D. Bayer and D. Mumford, "What can be computed in algebraic geometry", *in Computational Algebraic Geometry and Commutative Algebra, Cambridge University Press, 1993, pp. 1–48, Symposia Mathematica XXXIV.*, 1993.

20. O. Bachmann and H. Schönemann, "Monomial representations for Gröbner bases computations", *in ISSAC '98: Proceedings of the 1998 international symposium on Symbolic and algebraic computation*, pp. 309–316, New York, NY, USA, 1998. ACM Press.
21. A. Giovini, T. Mora, G. Niesi, L. Robbiano, and C. Traverso, ""One sugar cube, please" or Selection Strategies in the Buchberger Algorithm", *in ISSAC '91: Proceedings of the 1991 international symposium on Symbolic and algebraic computation*, pp. 49–54, New York, NY, USA, 1991. ACM Press.
22. M. Caboara, "A dynamic algorithm for Gröbner basis computation", *in ISSAC '93: Proceedings of the 1993 international symposium on Symbolic and algebraic computation*, pp. 275–283, New York, NY, USA, 1993. ACM Press.
23. H. Shah and j. Fortes, "Tree Structured Gröbner Basis Computation on Parallel Machines", *ECE Technical Reports, Purdue Libraries*, vol. TR-EE 94-30, October 1994.
24. J. Moses, "Algebraic simplification a guide for the perplexed", *in SYMSAC '71: Proceedings of the second ACM symposium on Symbolic and algebraic manipulation*, pp. 282–304, New York, NY, USA, 1971. ACM Press.
25. E. Ben-Sasson and R. Impagliazzo, "Random CNF's are Hard for the Polynomial Calculus", *in FOCS '99: Proceedings of the 40th Annual Symposium on Foundations of Computer Science*, p. 415, Washington, DC, USA, 1999. IEEE Computer Society.
26. CoCoATeam, "CoCoA: a system for doing Computations in Commutative Algebra", Available at http://cocoa.dima.unige.it.
27. I. Niven and J. L. Warren, "A Generalization of Fermat's Theorem", *Proceedings of American Mathematical Society*, vol. 8, pp. 306–313, 1957.
28. D. Cox, J. Little, and D. O'Shea, *Ideals, Varieties, and Algorithms : An Introduction to Computational Algebraic Geometry and Commutative Algebra (Undergraduate Texts in Mathematics)*, Springer, July 2005.
29. D. Castro, M. Giusti, J. Heintz, G. Matera, and L. Pardo, "The hardness of polynomial equation solving", *in Found. Comput. Mathematics, 2003.*, 2003.
30. A. Biere, A. Cimatti, E.M. Clarke, and Y. Zhu, "Symbolic Model Checking without BDDs", *in TACAS '99: Proceedings of the 5th International Conference on Tools and Algorithms for Construction and Analysis of Systems*, pp. 193–207, London, UK, 1999. Springer-Verlag.
31. N. Dershowitz, J. Hsiang, G-S. Huang, and D. Kaiss, "Boolean Ring Satisfiability", *in International Conference on Theory and Applications of Satisfiability Testing (SAT 2004)*, May 2004.

Kodkod: A Relational Model Finder

Emina Torlak and Daniel Jackson

MIT Computer Science and Artificial Intelligence Laboratory
{emina,dnj}@mit.edu

Abstract. The key design challenges in the construction of a SAT-based
relational model finder are described, and novel techniques are proposed
to address them. An efficient model finder must have a mechanism for
specifying partial solutions, an effective symmetry detection and breaking scheme, and an economical translation from relational to boolean
logic. These desiderata are addressed with three new techniques: a symmetry detection algorithm that works in the presence of partial solutions,
a sparse-matrix representation of relations, and a compact representation
of boolean formulas inspired by boolean expression diagrams and reduced
boolean circuits. The presented techniques have been implemented and
evaluated, with promising results.

1 Introduction

Many computational problems can be expressed declaratively as collections of
constraints, and then solved using a constraint-solving engine. A variety of such
engines have been developed, each tailored for a particular language: resolution
engines for Prolog, Simplex for linear inequalities, SAT solvers for boolean formulas, etc. This paper concerns the design of a general purpose *relational engine*:
that is, a model finder for a constraint language that combines first order logic
with relational algebra and transitive closure.

A relational engine is well-suited to solving a wide range of problems. For
example,

- Design analysis. A software design, modeled as a state machine over structured states (expressed as relations), can be checked, within finite bounds, for
  preservation of invariants by presenting the engine with a constraint of the
  form $S \land \neg P$, whose solutions are counterexamples satisfying the description
  of the system (S) but violating the expected property (P).
- Code analysis. A procedure can be checked against a declarative specification
  using the same method, by translating its code to a relational constraint.
- Test case generation. Unit tests for modules implementing intricate datatypes, such as red-black trees, with complex representation invariants, can
  be generated by a relational engine from the invariants.
- Scheduling and planning. For example, given the overall requirements and
  prerequisite dependences of a degree program, information about which
  terms particular courses are offered in, and a set of courses already taken, a
  relational engine can plan a student's course schedule.

O. Grumberg and M. Huth (Eds.): TACAS 2007, LNCS 4424, pp. 632–647, 2007.

We have established the feasibility of using a relational engine for design analysis [1], code analysis [2,3] and test case generation [4] in earlier work. The prototype tool that we describe in this paper has been applied to design analysis, code analysis [5], and course scheduling [6]; it is also a mean Sudoku player.

Our earlier work involved the development of the Alloy modeling language [1] and its analyzer. The Alloy Analyzer was designed for the analysis of software models, and attempts to use it as a generic relational engine have been hampered by its lack of a mechanism for exploiting a priori knowledge about a problem's solution. The user provides only a constraint to be solved, and if a partial solution—or, a *partial instance*—is available which the obtained solution should extend, it can be provided only in the form of additional constraints. Because the solver must essentially rediscover the partial instance from the constraints, this strategy does not scale well.

Kodkod is a new tool that, unlike the Alloy Analyzer, is suitable as a generic relational engine. Kodkod outperforms the Analyzer dramatically on problems involving partial instances, and, due to improvements in the core technology that we describe, outperforms Alloy even on the problems for which Alloy was designed. It also outperforms other SAT-based logic engines (such as Paradox [7] and MACE [8]) on a variety of TPTP [9] benchmarks.

The underlying technology involves translation from relational to boolean logic, and the application of an off-the-shelf SAT solver on the resulting boolean formula. The contributions of this paper are:

- A new symmetry-breaking scheme that works in the presence of partial instances; the inability of Alloy's scheme to accommodate partial instances was a key reason for not supporting them.
- A new sparse-matrix representation of relations that is both simpler to implement and better performing than the 'atomization' used in Alloy [10].
- A new scheme for detecting opportunities for sharing in the constraint abstract syntax tree inspired by boolean expression diagrams [11] and reduced boolean circuits [12].

Another major difference between the new tool and Alloy is its implementation as an API rather than as a standalone application. Alloy can in fact be accessed as an API, but the interface is string-based and awkward to use. The new tool is designed to be a plugin component that can easily be incorporated as a backend of another tool. These considerations, however, while crucial motivations of the project [13], are not the topic of the present paper.

2   Related Work

A variety of tools have been developed for finding finite models of first order logic (FOL) formulas [7,8,14,15,16,17,18,19]. Several of these [16,17,18,19] implement specialized search algorithms for exploring the space of possible interpretations of a formula. The rest [7,8,14,15] are essentially compilers. Given a FOL formula and a finite universe of uninterpreted atoms, they construct an equivalent propositional satisfiability problem and delegate the task of solving it to a SAT solver.

Most research on model finding has focused on producing high-performance tools for group-theoretic investigations. LDPP [14], MACE [8], FALCON [18], and SEM [19] have all been used to solve open problems in abstract algebra. Formulation of group-theoretic problems requires only a minimal logic. SEM and FINDER, for example, work on a quantifier-free many-sorted logic of uninterpreted functions. MACE and Paradox [7] support quantifiers, but none of these tools handle relational operators directly, which are indispensable for succinct description of systems whose state has a graph-like shape (such as networks or file systems) or for modeling programs with graph-like data structures (such as red-black trees or binomial heaps). Furthermore, lack of a closure operator, which cannot be encoded using first order constructs, makes it impossible to express common reachability constraints.

Nitpick [16] was the first model finder to handle binary relations and transitive closure in addition to quantifier-free FOL. This made it an attractive choice for analyzing small problems that involve structured state [20,21]. The usefulness of Nitpick was, however, limited by its poor scalability and lack of support for quantifiers and higher-arity relations.

The Alloy language and its analyzer [15] addressed both the scalability and expressiveness limitations of Nitpick. The underlying logic supports first order quantifiers, connectives, arbitrary-arity relations, and transitive closure. Alloy has been applied to a wide variety of problems, including the design of an intentional naming scheme [22], the safety properties of the beam scheduler for a proton therapy machine [23], code analysis [2,3], test-case generation [4], and network configuration [24].

Alloy's main deficiency as a general-purpose problem description language is its lack of support for partial instances. Logic programming languages such as Prolog [25] and Oz [26] provide mechanisms for taking advantage of partial knowledge to speed up constraint solving, but they lack quantifiers, relational operators, and transitive closure. The logic presented in this paper is a superset of the Alloy language that provides a mechanism for specifying partial instances. Its accompanying model finder, Kodkod, takes advantage of known information, scaling much better than the Alloy Analyzer in the presence of partial instances. Kodkod outperforms the Alloy Analyzer even on the problems without partial solutions, due to the new translation to propositional satisfiability based on sparse matrices and a new data structure, Compact Boolean Circuits (CBCs).

Compact Boolean Circuits, described in Section 4.3, are a hybrid between Reduced Boolean Circuits (RBCs) [12] and Boolean Expression Diagrams (BEDs) [11]. Like RBCs, CBCs are a representational form for a quantifier-free logic, and they restrict variable vertices to the leaves of the graph. Like BEDs, CBCs use a more extensive set of operators and rules than RBCs to maximize subformula sharing. CBCs differ from both RBCs and BEDs in that their sharing detection algorithm is parameterized by a user-controlled variable. In particular, the user controls the trade-off between the speed of circuit construction and the size of the resulting circuit by determining the depth d to which syntactically distinct sub-circuits are checked for semantic equivalence. All three circuit representations can be straightforwardly converted one to another.

3   Model Finding Basics

A *formula* in relational logic is a sentence over an alphabet of relational variables. A *model*, or an *instance*, of a formula is a binding of the formula's free variables to *relational constants* which makes the formula true. A relational constant is a set of *tuples* drawn from a universe of uninterpreted atoms. An engine that searches for models of a formula in a finite universe is called a *finite model finder* or, simply, a model finder.

3.1   Abstract Syntax

A Kodkod *problem* (Fig. 1) consists of a *universe declaration*, a set of *relation declarations*, and a *formula* in which the declared relations appear as free variables. Each relation declaration specifies the arity of a relational variable and bounds on its value. The lower bound contains the tuples which the variable's value *must* include in an instance of the formula; the union of all relations' lower bounds forms a problem's *partial instance*. The upper bound holds the tuples which the variable's value *may* include in an instance. The elements of the tuples in a constant are drawn from the problem's universe.

To illustrate, consider the following formulation of the pigeonhole principle—n pigeons cannot be placed into $n - 1$ holes with each pigeon having a hole to itself—for the case of 3 pigeons and 2 holes:

{P1, P2, P3, H1, H2}

Pigeon :$_1$ [{⟨P1⟩⟨P2⟩⟨P3⟩}, {⟨P1⟩⟨P2⟩⟨P3⟩}]
Hole   :$_1$ [{⟨H1⟩⟨H2⟩}, {⟨H1⟩⟨H2⟩}]
nest   :$_2$ [{}, {⟨P1, H1⟩⟨P1, H2⟩⟨P2, H1⟩⟨P2, H2⟩⟨P3, H1⟩⟨P3, H2⟩}]

(all p : Pigeon | one p.nest) and
(all h : Hole | one nest.h or no nest.h)

The first line declares a universe of five uninterpreted atoms. We arbitrarily chose the first three of them to represent pigeons and the last two to represent holes. Because formulas cannot contain constants, a relational variable $v :_k [C, C]$ with the same upper and lower bound is declared for each k-arity constant C that needs to be accessed in a problem's formula. The variables Pigeon and Hole, for example, serve as handles to the unary constants {⟨P1⟩⟨P2⟩⟨P3⟩} and {⟨H1⟩⟨H2⟩}, which represent the sets of all pigeons and holes respectively. The variable nest ⊆ Pigeon × Hole encodes the placement of pigeons into holes. Its value is constrained to be an injection by the problem's formula.

The syntactic productions other than the universe and relation declarations define a standard relational logic with transitive closure, first order quantifiers, and connectives. The closure (^) and transpose (˜) operators can only be applied to binary expressions. Mixed and zero arity expressions are not allowed. The arity of a relation variable and its declared bounds must match. The arity of the empty set constant, {}, is polymorphic, making it a valid bound in the context of any declaration.

problem := univDecl relDecl* formula

univDecl := { atom[, atom]* }
relDecl := rel :_arity [constant, constant]
varDecl := var : expr

constant := {tuple*}
tuple := ⟨atom[, atom]*⟩

arity := 1 | 2 | 3 | 4 | ...
atom := identifier
rel := identifier
var := identifier

expr := rel | var | unary | binary | comprehension
unary := unop expr
unop := ˜ | ^
binary := expr binop expr
binop := + | & | - | . | ->
comprehension := {varDecl | formula}

formula := elementary | composite | quantified
elementary := expr in expr | mult expr
mult := **some** | **no** | **one**
composite := **not** formula | formula logop formula
logop := **and** | **or**
quantified := quantifier varDecl | formula
quantifier := **all** | **some**

Fig. 1. Abstract syntax

P : problem → binding → boolean
R : relDecl → binding → boolean
M : formula → binding → boolean
X : expr → binding → constant
binding : (var ∪ rel) → constant

$P[\![A\ d_1\ ...\ d_n\ F]\!]b =$
$\quad R[\![d_1]\!]b \wedge ... \wedge R[\![d_n]\!]b \wedge M[\![F]\!]b$

$R[\![r : [c_L, c_U]]\!]b = c_L \subseteq b(r) \subseteq c_U$

$M[\![p\ in\ q]\!]b = X[\![p]\!]b \subseteq X[\![q]\!]b$
$M[\![some\ p]\!]b = X[\![p]\!]b \supset \emptyset$
$M[\![one\ p]\!]b = |X[\![p]\!]b| = 1$
$M[\![no\ p]\!]b = X[\![p]\!]b \subseteq \emptyset$
$M[\![not\ F]\!]b = \neg\ M[\![F]\!]b$
$M[\![F\ and\ G]\!]b = M[\![F]\!]b \wedge M[\![G]\!]b$
$M[\![F\ or\ G]\!]b = M[\![F]\!]b \vee M[\![G]\!]b$

$M[\![all\ v: p\ |\ F]\!]b = \bigwedge(M[\![F]\!](b \oplus v \mapsto X[\![p]\!]b))$
$M[\![some\ v: p\ |\ F]\!]b = \bigvee(M[\![F]\!](b \oplus v \mapsto X[\![p]\!]b))$

$X[\![p + q]\!]b = X[\![p]\!]b \cup X[\![q]\!]b$
$X[\![p\ \&\ q]\!]b = X[\![p]\!]b \cap X[\![q]\!]b$
$X[\![p - q]\!]b = X[\![p]\!]b \setminus X[\![q]\!]b$
$X[\![p\ .\ q]\!]b = \{\langle p_1,..., p_{n-1}, q_2,..., q_m\rangle\ |$
$\quad \langle p_1,..., p_n\rangle \in X[\![p]\!]b \wedge \langle q_1,..., q_m\rangle \in X[\![q]\!]b$
$\quad \wedge\ p_n = q_1\}$
$X[\![p -> q]\!]b = \{\langle p_1,..., p_n, q_1,..., q_m\rangle\ |$
$\quad \langle p_1,..., p_n\rangle \in X[\![p]\!]b \wedge \langle q_1,..., q_m\rangle \in X[\![q]\!]b\}$
$X[\![˜p]\!]b = \{\langle p_2, p_1\rangle\ |\ \langle p_1, p_2\rangle \in X[\![p]\!]b\}$
$X[\![^p]\!]b = \{\langle x, y\rangle\ |\ \exists\ p_1,..., p_n\ |$
$\quad \langle x, p_1\rangle, \langle p_1, p_2\rangle,..., \langle p_n, y\rangle \in X[\![p]\!]b\}$
$X[\![\{v: p\ |\ F\}]\!]b = \{\langle x\rangle : (X[\![p]\!]b)\ |$
$\quad M[\![F]\!](b \oplus (v \mapsto x))\}$
$X[\![r]\!]b = b(r)$
$X[\![v]\!]b = b(v)$

Fig. 2. Semantics

3.2   Semantics

The meaning of a problem (Fig. 2) is determined by recursive application of four meaning functions: P, R, M and X. The functions R and M evaluate relation declarations and formulas with respect to a *binding* of variables to constants. The function P deems a problem true with respect to a given binding if and only if its declarations and formula are true under that binding. The function X interprets expressions as sets of tuples. Atoms, tuples, and constants have their standard set-theoretic interpretations. That is, the meaning of an atom is its name, the meaning of a tuple is a sequence of atoms, and the meaning of a constant is a set of tuples.

4 Analysis

The analysis of a Kodkod problem P involves four steps:

1. Detecting P's symmetries.
2. Translating P into a Compact Boolean Circuit, $CBC(P)$.
3. Computing $SBP(P)$, a symmetry breaking predicate [27,28] for P.
4. Transforming $CBC(P) \wedge SBP(P)$ into conjunctive normal form, $CNF(P)$.
5. Applying a SAT solver to $CNF(P)$, and, if $CNF(P)$ is satisfiable, interpreting its model as an instance of P.

The first two steps are the focus of this section. The third step is done in a standard way (e.g. [28]), by computing a simple lex-leader symmetry breaking predicate for the symmetry classes detected in the first step. The fourth step is performed using the standard translation from boolean logic to conjunctive normal form (see, for example, [29]). The last step is delegated to an off-the-shelf SAT solver, such as zchaff [30] or MiniSat [31].

4.1 Symmetry Detection

Many problems exhibit symmetries. For example, the pigeons in the pigeonhole problem are symmetric, as are the pigeonholes; if there were a solution with a particular assignment of pigeons to holes, exchanging two pigeons or two holes would yield another solution. More formally, we define the symmetries of a problem as follows.

Definition 1. *Let $\mathcal{A}=\{a_0,\ldots,a_n\}$ be a universe, D a set of declarations over $\mathcal{A}$, and F a formula over D. Let $l : \mathcal{A} \rightarrow \mathcal{A}$ be a permutation, and define $l(t)$ to be $\langle l(a_{i_0}),\ldots,l(a_{i_k})\rangle$ for all tuples $t=\langle a_{i_0},\ldots,a_{i_k}\rangle$, $l(c)$ to be $\{l(t)|t \in c\}$ for all constants $c \subseteq \mathcal{A}^k$, etc. The permutation l is a symmetry of the problem $P = (\mathcal{A}, D, F)$ if and only if, for all bindings B, the binding $l(B) : \text{rel} \rightarrow \text{constant}$ is a model of P, written $l(B) \models P$, whenever $B \models P$, and $l(B) \not\models P$ whenever $B \not\models P$. The bindings B and $l(B)$ are said to be isomorphic.*

The set of symmetries of P, denoted by $Sym(P)$, induces an equivalence relation on the bindings that map the variables declared in D to sets of tuples drawn from $\mathcal{A}$. Two bindings B and B' are equivalent if $B' = l(B)$ for some $l \in Sym(P)$. Because each $l \in Sym(P)$ maps bindings that are models of P to other models of P and bindings that do not satisfy P to other non-models, it is sufficient to test one binding in each equivalence class induced by $Sym(P)$ to find a model of P. Isomorph elimination (a.k.a. *symmetry breaking*), using either a symmetry-aware model finder on P [18,19,16] or a SAT solver on $CNF(P \wedge SBP(P))$ [7,32], typically speeds up the model search by orders of magnitude. Many interesting problems are intractable without symmetry breaking [27,33].

In the case of a standard typed logic such as the Alloy language or SEM's logic, symmetry detection in a universe of uninterpreted atoms is straightforward: $Sym(P)$ is the set of all permutations that map an atom of $\mathcal{A}$ to itself or to another atom of the same type. Atoms of the same type are interchangeable because neither logic provides a means of referring to individual atoms. The Kodkod logic does, however, so even if it were typed, atoms of the same type would not necessarily be interchangeable.

Here, for example, is a toy specification of a traffic lights system showing a case where the conceptual typing of atoms does not partition $\mathcal{A}$ into equivalence classes:

> {N, E, G, Y, R}
>
> Green :$_1$ [{⟨G⟩}, {⟨G⟩}]
> Light :$_1$ [{⟨N⟩⟨E⟩}, {⟨N⟩⟨E⟩}]
> display :$_2$ [{}, {⟨N, G⟩⟨N, Y⟩⟨N, R⟩⟨E, G⟩⟨E, Y⟩⟨E, R⟩}]
>
> (all light: Light | one light.display) and
> (one Light.display & Green or no Light.display & Green)

The traffic-system universe consists of five atoms that are conceptually partitioned into two 'types': the atoms representing the stop lights at an intersection (north-south and east-west) and the atoms representing the colors green, yellow, and red. The formula constrains each light to display a color and requires that at most one of the displayed colors be Green. The stop-light atoms form an equivalence class, but the color atoms do not. In particular, only Y and R are interchangeable. To see why, consider the following model of the problem:

$$B = \{\text{Green} \mapsto \{\langle G \rangle\}, \text{Light} \mapsto \{\langle N \rangle \langle E \rangle\}, \text{display} \mapsto \{\langle N, Y \rangle \langle E, G \rangle\}\}.$$

Applying the permutations $l_1 = $ (N E)(Y R) and $l_2 = $ (G Y R)[1] to B, we get

$$l_1(B) = \{\text{Green} \mapsto \{\langle G \rangle\}, \text{Light} \mapsto \{\langle E \rangle \langle N \rangle\}, \text{display} \mapsto \{\langle E, R \rangle \langle N, G \rangle\}\},$$
$$l_2(B) = \{\text{Green} \mapsto \{\langle Y \rangle\}, \text{Light} \mapsto \{\langle N \rangle \langle E \rangle\}, \text{display} \mapsto \{\langle N, R \rangle \langle E, Y \rangle\}\}.$$

The binding $l_1(B)$ is a model of the problem, but $l_2(B)$ is not because it violates the constraint $\{\langle G \rangle\} \subseteq \text{Green} \subseteq \{\langle G \rangle\}$ imposed by the declaration of Green.

The traffic lights example reveals two important properties of declarations and formulas.[2] First, a permutation l is a symmetry of a set of declarations D if it *fixes* the constants in D, i.e. if $l(c) = c$ for each c occurring in D. The permutation l_1, for example, is a symmetry of the traffic-lights declarations. Second, *any* permutation is a symmetry of a formula. The binding $l_2(B)$ is a model of the traffic-lights formula even though it is not a model of the problem.

These observations lead to a simple criterion for deciding whether a permutation l is a symmetry of a problem: $l \in \text{Sym}(P)$ for all $P = (\mathcal{A}, D, F)$ if and only if l maps each constant that occurs in D to itself.

Theorem 1 (Symmetry Criterion). *Let $\mathcal{A}$ be the universe of discourse and $D = \{r_1 :_{k_1} [c_1, c_2], r_2 :_{k_2} [c_3, c_4], \ldots, r_m :_{k_m} [c_{2m-1}, c_{2m}]\}$ a set of declarations over $\mathcal{A}$. The permutation $l : \mathcal{A} \to \mathcal{A}$ is a symmetry for all problems P and formulas F such that $P = (\mathcal{A}, D, F)$ if and only if l fixes $c_1, c_2, \ldots, c_{2m}$.*

---

[1] Recall that cycle notation for permutations [34] indicates that each element in a pair of parenthesis is mapped to the one following it, with the last element being mapped to the first. The elements that are fixed under a permutation are not mentioned, i.e. (N E)(Y R)=(N E)(Y R)(G).

[2] The proofs of all assertions and theorems stated in this section can be found in the technical report on Kodkod [35], available at http://hdl.handle.net/1721.1/34218.

Because every relational constant is isomorphic to a graph, Thm. 1 equates the task of finding Sym(P) to that of computing the automorphisms of the graphs that correspond to the constants in D—a problem with no known polynomial time solution [36]. So, we use the algorithm in Fig. 3 to find a polynomially computable subset of Sym(P) that is equal to Sym(P) for many problems, including the pigeonhole, traffic lights, and all problems in Section 5.

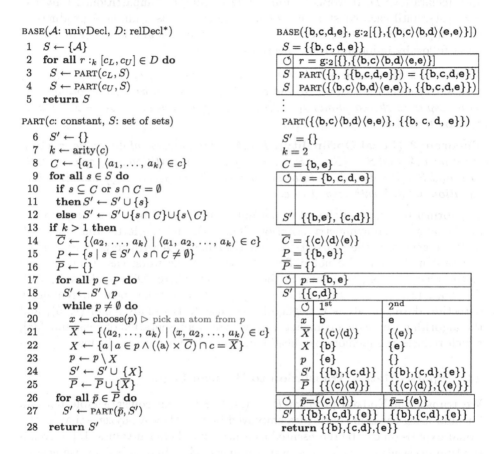

Fig. 3. Symmetry detection algorithm and a sample trace. Trace events are horizontally aligned with the pseudocode. Loops are shown as tables, with a column per iteration.

The intuition behind the algorithm is the observation that constants in most problem declarations are expressible as unions of products of 'types' with zero or more 'distinguished' atoms. For example, the bounds on the variables in the traffic lights problem can be expressed as Green $= T_{\{G\}}$, Light $= T_{\text{light}}$, and display $\subseteq T_{\text{light}} \times T_{\{R,Y\}} \cup T_{\text{light}} \times T_{\{G\}}$, where the 'types' are $T_{\text{light}} = \{N, E\}$ with no distinguished atoms and $T_{\text{color}} = T_{\{R,Y\}} \cup T_{\{G\}} = \{G, Y, R\}$ with the distinguished atom G. We call the sets $\{R, Y\}$, $\{G\}$ and $\{N, E\}$ a *base partitioning* of the traffic-lights universe with respect to the problem's declarations.

Definition 2. *Let $\mathcal{A}$ be a universe, c a constant over $\mathcal{A}$, and $S = \{S_1, \ldots, S_n\}$ a set of sets that partition $\mathcal{A}$. S is a* base partitioning *of $\mathcal{A}$ with respect to c if c can be expressed as a union of products of elements in $S \cup \{\emptyset\}$, i.e.: $\exists x \geq 1 \mid \exists s_1, \ldots, s_{xk} \in S \cup \{\emptyset\} \mid c = \bigcup_{j=0}^{x-1} (s_{jk+1} \times \ldots \times s_{jk+k})$, where $k = $ arity(c).*

The algorithm BASE finds the coarsest base partitioning for a given universe $\mathcal{A}$ and declarations D. It works by minimally refining the unpartitioned universe, $S = \{\mathcal{A}\}$, until each constant in D can be expressed as a union of products of the computed partitions (lines ??-??). The correctness and local optimality of BASE follow by induction from Theorems 2 and 3:

Theorem 2 (Soundness). *Let $D = \{r_1 :_{k_1} [c_1, c_2], \ldots, r_m :_{k_m} [c_{2m-1}, c_{2m}]\}$ be a set of declarations over $\mathcal{A}$ and $S = \{S_1, \ldots, S_n\}$ a base partitioning of $\mathcal{A}$ with respect to the constants $c_1, \ldots, c_{2m}$. If a permutation $l : \mathcal{A} \to \mathcal{A}$ fixes all $S_i \in S$, then it also fixes $c_1, \ldots, c_{2m}$.*

Theorem 3 (Local Optimality). *Let $\mathcal{A}$ be the universe of discourse, c a constant over $\mathcal{A}$, and $S = \{S_1, \ldots S_n\}$ a set of sets that partition $\mathcal{A}$. Applying PART to c and S will subdivide S into the coarsest $S' = \{S'_1, \ldots, S'_m\}$ that is a base partitioning of $\mathcal{A}$ with respect to c.*

The former tells us that the set of permutations induced by a base partitioning for D satisfies the symmetry criterion (Thm. 1), and the latter that each call to PART generates the coarsest base partitioning of $\mathcal{A}$ with respect to a given constant in D. It is also not difficult to see that the worst case running time of the algorithm is polynomial in the size of D, where $|D| = O(K|\mathcal{A}|^K)$ with $K = max(k_1, \ldots, k_m)$. In practice, the proportion of time spent on symmetry detection during analysis is negligible because K is usually small (< 5), and the algorithm works on a compact, interval tree representation of constants [35], which reduces the memory overhead exponentially for most problems.

4.2   Sparse-Matrix Translation to Boolean Logic

We translate a Kodkod problem $P = (\mathcal{A}, D, F)$ to an equisatisfiable boolean formula using the same basic idea employed by the Alloy Analyzer—that a relational expression can be represented as a matrix of boolean values [15]. Given a relation declaration $r :_k [c_L, c_U]$ over a universe $\mathcal{A} = \{a_0, \ldots, a_{n-1}\}$, we encode r as a k-dimensional boolean matrix m with

$$m[i_1, \ldots, i_k] = \begin{cases} \text{true} & \Leftrightarrow \langle a_{i_1}, \ldots, a_{i_k} \rangle \in c_L \\ \text{freshVar()} & \Leftrightarrow \langle a_{i_1}, \ldots, a_{i_k} \rangle \in c_U - c_L \\ \text{false} & \text{otherwise} \end{cases}$$

where $i_1, \ldots, i_k \in [0 .. n)$ and freshVar() returns a fresh boolean variable. Expressions are then translated using matrix operations, and formulas become constraints over matrix entries (Fig. 4). For example, the join of two expressions, p.q, is translated as the matrix product of the translations of p and q, and the non-emptiness formula, some p, is translated as the disjunction of the entries in the matrix translation of p.

T_P: problem → bool
T_R: relDecl → univDecl → matrix
T_M: formula → env → bool
T_X: expr → env → matrix
env: (quantVar ∪ relVar) → matrix
freshVar: boolVar
bool := true | false | boolVar |
¬ bool | bool ∧ bool | bool ∨ bool
boolVar := identifier

$\overrightarrow{x}, \overrightarrow{y}, \langle i_1, ..., i_k \rangle$ ▷ vectors
$\lfloor \rfloor$: matrix→⟨int⟩ ▷ minimum index
$\lceil \rceil$: matrix→⟨int⟩ ▷ maximum index
$||$: matrix→dim ▷ dimensions

$\mathcal{M}$: dim→(⟨int⟩→bool)→matrix ▷ constructor
$\mathcal{M}(s^d, f) = \{m \mid |m| = s^d \wedge$
$\forall \overrightarrow{x} \in \{0, ..., s-1\}^d, m[\overrightarrow{x}] = f(\overrightarrow{x})\}$

$\mathcal{M}$: dim→⟨int⟩→matrix ▷ constructor
$\mathcal{M}(s^d, \overrightarrow{x}) = \mathcal{M}(s^d,$
$\lambda \overrightarrow{y}.$ if $\overrightarrow{y} = \overrightarrow{x}$ then true else false)

$T_P[\mathcal{A} \; d_1 \; ... \; d_n \; F] =$
$T_M[F](\bigcup_{i=1}^m (r_i \mapsto T_R[d_i]\mathcal{A}))$
$T_R[r :_k [c_L, c_U]]\mathcal{A} = \mathcal{M}(|\mathcal{A}|^k, \lambda[i_1, ..., i_k].$
if $\langle a_{i_1}, ..., a_{i_k} \rangle \in c_L$ then true
else if $\langle a_{i_1}, ..., a_{i_k} \rangle \in c_u - c_L$ then freshVar()
else false)

$T_M[p$ in $q]e = \bigwedge(\neg T_X[p]e \vee T_X[q]e)$
$T_M[$some $p]e = \bigvee(T_X[p]e)$
$T_M[$one $p]e = $ let $(m = T_X[p]e)$ in
$\bigvee_{\overrightarrow{x}=\lfloor m \rfloor}^{\lceil m \rceil} (\bigwedge(\neg \mathcal{M}(|m|, \overrightarrow{x}) \oplus m))$
$T_M[$no $p]e = \bigwedge(\neg T_X[p]e)$
$T_M[!F]e = \neg \; T_M[F]e$
$T_M[F \; \&\& \; G]e = T_M[F]e \wedge T_M[G]e$
$T_M[F \; || \; G]e = T_M[F]e \vee T_M[G]e$
$T_M[$all $v: p \mid F]e = $ let $(m = T_X[p]e)$ in
$\bigwedge_{\overrightarrow{x}=\lfloor m \rfloor}^{\lceil m \rceil} (\neg m[\overrightarrow{x}] \vee T_M[F](e{:}v \mapsto \mathcal{M}(|m|, \overrightarrow{x})))$
$T_M[$some $v: p \mid F]e = $ let $(m = T_X[p]e)$ in
$\bigvee_{\overrightarrow{x}=\lfloor m \rfloor}^{\lceil m \rceil} (m[\overrightarrow{x}] \wedge T_M[F](e{:}v \mapsto \mathcal{M}(|m|, \overrightarrow{x})))$

$T_X[p + q]e = T_X[p]e \vee T_X[q]e$
$T_X[p \; \& \; q]e = T_X[p]e \wedge T_X[q]e$
$T_X[p \; \text{-} \; q]e = T_X[p]e \wedge \neg T_X[q]e$
$T_X[p \; . \; q]e = T_X[p]e \cdot T_X[q]e$
$T_X[p{\text{-}}{>}q]e = T_X[p]e \times T_X[q]e$
$T_X[\tilde{\;} p \;]e = (T_X[p]e)^T$
$T_X[\hat{\;} p \;]e = $ iterative-square$(T_X[p]e)$
$T_X[\{v: p \mid F\}]e = $ let $(m = T_X[p]e)$ in
$\mathcal{M}(|m|, \lambda \overrightarrow{x}. m[x] \wedge T_M[F](e{:}v \mapsto \mathcal{M}(|m|, \overrightarrow{x})))\}$

Fig. 4. Translation rules

A key difference between the Kodkod and Alloy [15] translation algorithms is that the latter is based on types. The Alloy Analyzer encodes a k-arity relation r of type $T_1 \rightarrow ... \rightarrow T_k$ as a boolean matrix with dimensions $|T_1| \times ... \times |T_k|$. Since operands of many matrix operators must have particular dimensions, the operands of their corresponding relational operators are forced to have specific types. For example, in a world with three women and three men, the Alloy Analyzer would reject the perfectly reasonable attempt to form the maternalGrandmother relation by joining the relation mother: Person → Woman with itself, because a 6×3 matrix cannot be multiplied by itself. There are two ways to remedy this problem: (1) force the type of mother up to Person → Person, doubling the size of its boolean representation, or (2) *atomize* mother into two pieces, mother$_w$: Woman → Woman and mother$_m$: Man → Woman, and split the expression mother.mother into mother$_w$.mother$_w$ + mother$_m$.mother$_w$ before handing it to the translator [10]. AA takes the latter approach which has not worked well in practice because of its awkward handling of transitive closure expressions [10].

We avoid the problems of a type-based translation by encoding all k-arity relations over $\mathcal{A}$ as k-dimensional sparse matrices $|\mathcal{A}| \times ... \times |\mathcal{A}|$. A sparse translation matrix is represented as a sorted map from *flat indices* [35] to boolean formulas. Each k-tuple, and its corresponding matrix index, is encoded as an integer in the range $[0 ... |\mathcal{A}|^k)$. A sparse matrix maps a tuple's integer representation only if it is non-false. For example, the sparse matrix representation of the display relation from the traffic-lights problem maps the flat indices of the upper bound tuples $\{\langle N, G \rangle \langle N, Y \rangle \langle N, R \rangle \langle E, G \rangle \langle E, Y \rangle \langle E, R \rangle\}$ to boolean variables, and leaves the indices of the remaining tuples in $\mathcal{A} \times \mathcal{A}$ unmapped (i.e. false). Consecutive indices that map to true are encoded using a run-length encoding, enabling a compact representation of lower bounds.

4.3 Sharing Detection with Compact Boolean Circuits

Formal specifications make frequent use of quantified formulas whose ground form contains many identical subcomponents. Detection and exploitation of this and other kinds of structural redundancy can greatly reduce the size of a problem's boolean encoding, leading to a more scalable analysis. Equivalent subformulas can be detected either at the problem level or at the boolean level. The Alloy Analyzer takes the former approach [37]. Our implementation uses Compact Boolean Circuits to detect sharing at the boolean level.

A Compact Boolean Circuit (CBC) is a partially canonical, directed, acyclic graph (V, E, d). The set V is partitioned into operator vertices $V_{\text{op}} = V_{\text{AND}} \cup V_{\text{OR}} \cup V_{\text{NOT}}$ and leaves $V_{\text{leaf}} = V_{\text{VAR}} \cup \{T, F\}$. An AND or an OR vertex has two children, and a NOT vertex has one child. The degree of canonicity is determined by an equivalence relation on vertices (which embodies standard properties of the logical operators, such as commutativity, associativity, etc.) and the circuit's *compaction depth* $d \geq 1$. In particular, no vertex $v \in V$ can be transformed into another vertex $w \in V$ by applying an equivalence transformation to the top $d \geq 1$ levels of the subgraph rooted at v.

An example of a non-compact boolean circuit and its compact equivalents is shown in Fig. 5. Fig. 5(a) contains the formula $(x \wedge y \wedge z) \Leftrightarrow (v \wedge w)$ encoded using the operators $\{\text{AND}, \text{OR}, \text{NOT}\}$ as $(\neg((x \wedge y) \wedge z) \vee (v \wedge w)) \wedge (\neg(v \wedge w) \vee (x \wedge (y \wedge z)))$. Fig. 5(b) shows an equivalent CBC with the minimal compaction depth of $d = 1$, which enforces partial canonicity at the level of inner nodes' children. That is, the depth of $d = 1$ ensures that all nodes in the circuit are syntactically distinct, forcing the subformula $(v \wedge w)$ to be shared. Fig. 5(c) shows the original circuit represented as a CBC with the compaction depth of $d = 2$, which enforces partial canonicity at the level of nodes' grandchildren. The law of associativity applies to the subformulas $((x \wedge y) \wedge z)$ and $(x \wedge (y \wedge z))$, forcing $((x \wedge y) \wedge z)$ to be shared.

The partial canonicity of CBCs is maintained in our implementation by a factory data structure which synthesizes and caches CBCs. The factory creates a new circuit from given components only if it does not find an equivalent (up to depth d) one in its cache. This ensures that all *syntactically* equivalent ground formulas and expressions are translated into the same circuit. *Semantically* equivalent nodes are encoded using the same circuit if their equivalence can be established by looking at the top $d \geq 1$ levels of their subgraphs. CBCs also end up catching structural redundancies in the boolean representation itself that could not be detected at the problem level. The net result is a tighter encoding than can be generated using a problem-level detection mechanism.

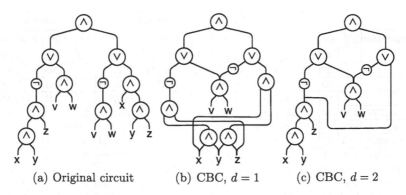

(a) Original circuit   (b) CBC, $d = 1$ (c) CBC, $d = 2$

Fig. 5. A non-compact boolean circuit and its compact equivalents

5   Results

We have compared the performance of Kodkod to that of three other tools, the Alloy Analyzer (version 3), MACE (version 4), and Paradox (version 1.3)[3] on two sets of problems:

- SYMMETRIC PROBLEMS include the pigeonhole problem and the 'Ceilings and Floors' problem from the Alloy 3 distribution. Like the pigeonhole problem, 'Ceilings and Floors' is unsatisfiable and highly symmetric.
- TPTP PROBLEMS consist of twelve TPTP [9] benchmarks from various problem domains. Because the TPTP problems had to be translated to our logic by hand (in the obvious way, by translating predicates and functions as relations, predicate application as membership testing, function application as join, etc.), the overriding criterion for benchmark selection was syntactic succinctness. Other selection criteria were a high difficulty rating (> 0.6), complex relationships between predicates and functions (geo, med, and set problems), prevalence of unit equalities (alg212 and num374), and presence of partial instances (alg195 and num378).

The results are given in Fig. 6. The table shows each problem's rating, if any, the size of its universe ($|\mathcal{A}|$), and the model finders' performance on it. For symmetric problems, we use two different universe sizes to demonstrate how changing search bounds impacts model finders' performance. For TPTP problems, the shown universe size is the largest universe for which at least three of the model finders produced a result in five minutes. The performance data for Alloy 3, Kodkod, and Paradox includes the analysis time, rounded to the nearest second, and the size of the generated CNF, given as the total number of variables and clauses. MACE4 does not report CNF statistics. All analyses were performed on a 3.6 GHz Pentium 4 with 3 GB RAM. Alloy 3, Kodkod and Paradox were configured with MiniSat [31] as their SAT engine; MACE4 uses its own internal SAT solver. Kodkod's sharing detection parameter d was set to 3. Analyses that did not

---

[3] Paradox 2.0b, the latest version, does not perform as well as 1.3 on our benchmarks.

| | PROBLEM | RAT-ING | $|A|$ | ALLOY ANALYZER 3 | | | KODKOD | | | PARADOX 1.3 | | | MA CE4 |
				SEC	VARS	CLAUSES	SEC	VARS	CLAUSES	SEC	VARS	CLAUSES	SEC
SYMMETRIC PROBLEMS	ceil		12	1	2,723	11,704	0	1,749	3,289	0	299	1,373	4
	ceil		20	16	9,987	46,740	14	6,477	12,449	–	695	4,850	–
	pigeon		39	2	15,703	76,994	0	6,953	12,648	–	1,041	9,889	0
	pigeon		99	33	92,191	576,554	5	82,613	156,843	–	5,901	143,344	0
TPTP PROBLEMS	alg195	0.89	14	31	195,408	834,508	3	77,240	254,239	22	30,771	982,467	–
	alg212	1.00	7	277	395,297	6,432,170	64	301,725	1,012,808	1	20,747	135,588	14
	com008	0.67	11	6	15,384	77,378	6	8,565	14,624	94	6,467	31,275	–
	geo091	1.00	8	72	81,267	587,728	16	33,463	73,292	84	19,146	145,373	–
	geo158	1.00	6	8	29,831	185,038	2	12,574	26,552	9	8,262	49,955	–
	med007	0.67	15	10	19,052	108,454	2	15,072	31,476	36	7,981	48,449	–
	med009	0.67	17	12	25,177	144,968	3	20,198	42,263	28	11,850	66,758	–
	num374	1.00	5	50	70,229	291,573	55	63,661	200,238	3	6,763	52,671	9
	num378	1.00	21	–	–	–	1	0	0	193	74,736	1,692,990	1
	set943	1.00	7	159	25,124	101,040	20	18,883	43,694	11	8,648	46,977	–
	set948	1.00	7	7	40,776	159,735	1	24,970	60,787	61	16,226	86,932	–
	top020	1.00	9	–	–	–	48	1,378,863	2,343,728	54	96,232	1,545,950	6

Fig. 6. Results for symmetric and TPTP problems. Gray shading indicates the fastest time(s) for each problem; dashes indicate timeouts.

complete within five minutes are indicated by dashes. The fastest analysis time for each problem is highlighted with gray shading.

The data on symmetric problems demonstrates the effectiveness of our symmetry detection algorithm compared to that of Alloy 3, which derives optimal symmetry information from Alloy's type system, and Paradox, which employs a sort inference algorithm to find symmetry classes. MACE4 performs no symmetry breaking, but, interestingly, its internal simplifications allow it to determine that the pigeonhole problem is unsatisfiable apparently without performing any search. The TPTP data shows that Kodkod's performance is competitive with Paradox's and MACE4's on a variety of classical logic problems. Kodkod outperforms MACE4 and Paradox on problems describing complex relationships between predicates and functions (e.g. geo091 or set948) and on problems with partial instances (alg195 and num378). MACE4 and Paradox, however, are superior on problems that contain many unit equalities or deeply nested universal quantifiers, such as alg212 and num374. These results are consistent with our overall experience using Alloy 3, Kodkod, MACE4 and Paradox.

The above problems were chosen to compare Kodkod to other SAT-based model finders, but they are in fact not representative of the class of problems for which Kodkod and Alloy were developed. Software design problems, in contrast to these mathematical problems, tend to have less regular structure, despite the grounding out of quantifiers. We compared Kodkod to Alloy 3 on three design problems: Dijkstra's mutual exclusion scheme [38], leader election in a ring [39], and the transfer protocol of the Mondex smart card [40].

The results are shown in Fig. 7. For the mutual exclusion and leader election problems, we use two different universe sizes; for the Mondex problem, we check

		ALLOY ANALYZER 3						KODKOD					
PROBLEM	$|\mathcal{A}|$	VARS	CLAUSES	FOL →CNF	BERK MIN	MINI SAT	ZCH AFF	VARS	CLAUSES	FOL →CNF	BERK MIN	MINI SAT	ZCH AFF
exclusion	30	74,818	722,236	20	7	1	10	20,080	120,097	3	0	0	1
	45	357,253	4,874,911	142	150	9	–	67,695	543,597	19	13	5	10
election	15	14,272	78,031	2	1	1	1	8,665	29,590	1	0	0	0
	24	91,594	662,188	16	143	109	–	45,136	183,484	3	62	76	–
mondex A241	51	50,926	416,744	10	27	90	52	35,791	86,402	1	4	87	9
OpTotal	51	43,256	381,458	7	3	2	1	0	0	0	0	0	0
IgnoreInv	51	43,413	386,812	6	7	4	4	28,243	57,604	1	2	22	2
TransferInv	51	50,902	419,094	7	174	–	173	35,761	83,172	1	46	–	53

Fig. 7. Results for design problems. Gray shading indicates the fastest SAT solving time(s) for each problem; dashes indicate timeouts.

a variety of assertions in the same universe. The performance data includes the size of the generated CNF and the time, in seconds, taken to generate and solve it using various SAT engines [41,31,30]. In all cases, Kodkod produces smaller formulas, which are solved faster by BerkMin [41] and zChaff [30]. Interestingly, on the Mondex problem (and a few others we encountered), MiniSat actually performs worse on Kodkod's formulas than on Alloy 3's larger formulas. Note that translation time is dramatically lower in Kodkod than in Alloy 3; the translation scheme in Alloy 3 used a more complicated (and apparently less effective) template mechanism for detecting sharing.

References

1. Jackson, D., Shlyakhter, I., Sridharan, M.: A micromodularity mechanism. In: ESEC / SIGSOFT FSE. (2001) 62–73
2. Vaziri, M., Jackson, D.: Checking properties of heap-manipulating procedures with a constraint solver. In: TACAS. (2003) 505–520
3. Taghdiri, M.: Inferring specifications to detect errors in code. In: ASE. (2004) 144–153
4. Khurshid, S., Marinov, D.: TestEra: Specification-based testing of java programs using sat. ASE **11**(4) (2004) 403–434
5. Dennis, G., Chang, F., Jackson, D.: Modular verification of code. In: ISSTA, Portland, Maine (2006)
6. Yeung, V.: Declarative configuration applied to course scheduling. Master's thesis, Massachusetts Institute of Technology, Cambridge, MA (2006)
7. Claessen, K., Sörensson, N.: New techniques that improve MACE-style finite model finding. In: CADE-19 Workshop on Model Computation, Miami, FL (2003)
8. McCune, W.: A Davis-Putnam program and its application to finite first-order model search: quasigroup existence problem. Technical report, ANL (1994)
9. Sutcliffe, G., Suttner, C.: The TPTP Problem Library: CNF Release v1.2.1. Journal of Automated Reasoning **21**(2) (1998) 177–203
10. Edwards, J., Jackson, D., Torlak, E., Yeung, V.: Faster constraint solving with subtypes. In: ISSTA '04, New York, NY, USA, ACM Press (2004) 232–242
11. Andersen, H.R., Hulgaard, H.: Boolean expression diagrams. In: LICS, Warsaw, Poland (1997)

12. Abdulla, P.A., Bjesse, P., Eén, N.: Symbolic reachability analysis based on sat-solvers. In: TACAS '00, London, UK, Springer-Verlag (2000) 411–425
13. Torlak, E., Dennis, G.: Kodkod for Alloy users. In: First ACM Alloy Workshop, Portland, Oregon (2006)
14. Fujita, M., Slaney, J., Bennett, F.: Automating generation of some results in finite algebra. In: 13th IJCAI, Chambéry, France (1993)
15. Jackson, D.: Automating first order relational logic. In: FSE, San Diego, CA (2000)
16. Jackson, D., Jha, S., Damon, C.A.: Isomorph-free model enumeration: a new method for checking relational specifications. ACM TPLS 20(2) (1998) 302–343
17. Slaney, J.K.: Finder: Finite domain enumerator - system description. In: CADE-12, London, UK, Springer-Verlag (1994) 798–801
18. Zhang, J.: The generation and application of finite models. PhD thesis, Institute of Software, Academia Sinica, Beijing (1994)
19. Zhang, J., Zhang, H.: SEM: a system for enumerating models. In: IJCAI95, Montreal (1995)
20. Jackson, D., Damon, C.A.: Elements of style: analyzing a software design feature with a counterexample detector. TOSEM (1996) 484–495
21. Ng, Y.C.: A Nitpick specification of IPv6. Senior Honors thesis, Computer Science Department, Carnegie Mellon University (1997)
22. Khurshid, S., Jackson, D.: Exploring the design of an intentional naming scheme with an automatic constraint analyzer. In: ASE. (2000) 13–22
23. Dennis, G., Seater, R., Rayside, D., Jackson, D.: Automating commutativity analysis at the design level. In: ISSTA. (2004) 165–174
24. Narain, S.: Network configuration management via model finding. In: ACM Workshop On Self-Managed Systems, Newport Beach, CA (2004)
25. O'Keefe, R.: The Craft of Prolog. Logic Programming. MIT Press, Cambridge, MA (1990)
26. Van Roy, P., Haridi, S.: Concepts, Techniques, and Models of Computer Programming. MIT Press (2004)
27. Crawford, J., Ginsberg, M.L., Luck, E., Roy, A.: Symmetry-breaking predicates for search problems. In: KR'96. Morgan Kaufmann, San Francisco (1996) 148–159
28. Shlyakhter, I.: Generating effective symmetry breaking predicates for search problems. Electronic Notes in Discrete Mathematics 9 (2001)
29. Eén, N., Sörensson, N.: Translating pseudo-boolean constraints into SAT. In: SBMC. Volume 2. (2006) 1–26
30. Mahajan, Y.S., Fu, Z., Malik, S.: zchaff2004: An efficient sat solver. In: SAT (Selected Papers). (2004) 360–375
31. Eén, N., Sörensson, N.: An extensible SAT-solver. In: SAT'03. Volume LNCS 2919. (2004) 502–518
32. Shlyakhter, I.: Declarative Symbolic Pure Logic Model Checking. PhD thesis, Massachusetts Institute of Technology, Cambridge, MA (2005)
33. Sabharwal, A.: SymChaff: A structure-aware satisfiability solver. In: 20th National Conference on Artificial Intelligence (AAAI), Pittsburgh, PA (2005) 467–474
34. Armstrong, M.A.: Groups and Symmetry. Springer-Verlag, New York (1988)
35. Torlak, E., Jackson, D.: The design of a relational engine. Technical Report MIT-CSAIL-TR-2006-068, MIT (2006)
36. Babai, L., Kantor, W.M., Luks, E.M.: Computational complexity and the classification of finite simple groups. In: IEEE SFCS, IEEE CSP (1983) 162–171
37. Shlyakhter, I., Sridharan, M., Seater, R., Jackson, D.: Exploiting subformula sharing in automatic analysis of quantified formulas. In: SAT, Portofino, Italy (2003)

38. Dijkstra, E.W.: Cooperating sequential processes. In Genuys, F., ed.: Programming Languages. Academic Press, New York (1968) 43–112
39. Chang, E.J.H., Roberts, R.: An improved algorithm for decentralized extrema-finding in circular configurations of processes. Commun. ACM **22**(5) (1979) 281–283
40. Ramananandro, T.: The Mondex case study with Alloy. http://www.eleves.ens.fr/home/ramanana/work/mondex/ (2006)
41. Goldberg, E., Novikov, Y.: BerkMin: A fast and robust SAT solver. In: Design Automation and Test in Europe. (2002) 142–149

Bounded Reachability Checking of Asynchronous Systems Using Decision Diagrams[⋆]

Andy Jinqing Yu[1], Gianfranco Ciardo[1], and Gerald Lüttgen[2]

[1] Department of Computer Science and Engineering, University of California,
Riverside, CA 92521, USA
{jqyu,ciardo}@cs.ucr.edu
[2] Department of Computer Science, University of York, York YO10 5DD, UK
luettgen@cs.york.ac.uk

Abstract. Bounded reachability or model checking is widely believed to work poorly when using decision diagrams instead of SAT procedures. Recent research suggests this to be untrue with regards to synchronous systems, particularly digital circuits. This paper shows that the belief is also a myth for asynchronous systems, such as models specified by Petri nets. We propose *Bounded Saturation*, a new algorithm to compute bounded state spaces using Multi-way Decision Diagrams (MDDs). This is based on the established Saturation algorithm which benefits from a non-standard search strategy that is very different from breadth-first search. To bound Saturation, we employ Edge-Valued MDDs and rework its search strategy. Experimental results show that our algorithm often, but not always, compares favorably against two SAT-based approaches advocated in the literature for deadlock checking in Petri nets.

1 Introduction

Bounded model checking is a well-established technique to reason about reactive systems [3]. Unlike conventional model checking based on explicit or symbolic representations of state spaces [13], bounded model checking takes a system, a bound B, and a safety property ϕ, unwinds the system's transition relation B times, and derives a propositional formula which is satisfiable if and only if there exists a path through the system of length at most B that demonstrates the violation of ϕ. Due to the impressive technology advances in *SAT solving* (see, e.g., [24]), such satisfiability problems can often be decided efficiently.

BDDs vs. SAT. Bounded model checking is an incomplete verification technique unless the bound exceeds the state space diameter. However, as many faults involve relatively short counterexamples in practice, the technique has proved itself an efficient debugging aid, and bounded model checkers are now used to verify *digital circuits* [12], *Petri nets* [17,25], and *software* [20,26]. Several studies

---

[⋆] Research supported by the NSF under grants CNS-0501747 and CNS-0501748 and by the EPSRC under grant GR/S86211/01.

O. Grumberg and M. Huth (Eds.): TACAS 2007, LNCS 4424, pp. 648–663, 2007.

have found such tools beneficial in industrial settings, especially when compared to symbolic model checkers using decision diagrams [14].

It is often believed that SAT methods are key to the performance of bounded model checkers. Recent research by Cabodi et al. [5], however, counters this suggestion. Their work proposes enhancements to standard techniques based on *Binary Decision Diagrams* (BDDs), making BDD-based bounded model checking competitive with SAT-based approaches. These results were obtained in the context of debugging synchronous systems and digital circuits, for which BDDs are known to work well. It has remained an open question whether the aforementioned belief is also a myth with regards to asynchronous systems governed by interleaving semantics, such as distributed algorithms expressed in Petri nets.

This paper. Our aim is to prove that decision diagrams are competitive with SAT solvers for the bounded model checking of *asynchronous* systems. To this end we propose a new approach for bounded reachability checking using decision diagrams based on *Saturation* [7], an established symbolic algorithm for generating the state space of asynchronous systems. By taking into account event locality and interleaving semantics and by using *Multi-way Decision Diagrams* (MDDs) instead of BDDs, Saturation is often orders of magnitude more efficient than breadth-first search algorithms implemented in popular model checkers [11].

The difficulty in adapting Saturation to bounded reachability checking lies in its non-standard search strategy that is completely different from breadth-first search. We then cope by storing not only the reachable states but also the distance of each state from the initial state(s), using the *edge-valued* decision diagrams of [9]. These extend EVBDDs [22] just as MDDs extend BDDs, and use a more general reduction rule. Each state stored in such a decision diagram corresponds to a path from the root to the only terminal node, whereas the distance of a state is the sum of the weights of the edges along that path.

The resulting *Bounded Saturation* algorithm comes in two variants. The first one computes all reachable states at distance no more than a user-provided bound B. The second one finds additional states at distance greater than B but at most $K \cdot B$, where K is the number of "components" of the underlying asynchronous system. Just as ordinary breadth-first search, both can find minimal-length counterexamples. However, the second variant is usually more efficient in terms of runtime and memory, even if it discovers more states. Such behavior, while counterintuitive at first, is not uncommon with decision diagrams.

Experiments and results. We evaluate Bounded Saturation against two SAT-based approaches for bounded reachability checking proposed by Heljanko [17] and Ogata, Tsuchiya, and Kikuno [25], both aimed at finding deadlocks in asynchronous systems specified by Petri nets. We implemented our algorithm in SMART [6], and ran it on the suite of examples used in both [17] and [25], first proposed by Corbett in [15], and on two models from the SMART release. The static variable ordering used in our algorithm was computed via a heuristic [27].

Our experiments show that Bounded Saturation performs better or at par with competing SAT-based algorithms, and is less efficient in only few cases.

Thus, it is a myth that decision diagrams are uncompetitive w.r.t. SAT solvers for bounded model checking; just as the roles of bounded and unbounded model checking are complementary, so are the use of SAT solving and decision diagrams.

2 Background

We consider a discrete-state model $\mathcal{M} = (\widehat{S}, S^{init}, \mathcal{R})$, where $\widehat{S}$ is a (finite) set of states, $S^{init} \subseteq \widehat{S}$ are the initial states, and $\mathcal{R} \subseteq \widehat{S} \times \widehat{S}$ is a transition relation. We assume the *global* model state to be a tuple $(x_K, ..., x_1)$ of K *local state* variables where, for $K \geq l \geq 1$, $x_l \in S_l = \{0, 1, ..., n_l - 1\}$ with $n_l > 0$, is the the lth *local state* variable. Thus, $\widehat{S} = S_K \times \cdots \times S_1$ and we write $\mathcal{R}(i[K], ..., i[1], j[K], ..., j[1])$, or $\mathcal{R}(\mathbf{i}, \mathbf{j})$, if the model can move from *current state* $\mathbf{i}$ to *next state* $\mathbf{j}$ in one step.

Computation of the reachable state space consists of building the smallest set of states $S \subseteq \widehat{S}$ satisfying $S \supseteq S^{init}$ and $S \supseteq Img(S, \mathcal{R})$, where the *image computation* function $Img(\mathcal{X}, \mathcal{R}) = \{\mathbf{j} : \exists \mathbf{i} \in \mathcal{X}, \mathcal{R}(\mathbf{i}, \mathbf{j})\}$ describes the successors to the set of states $\mathcal{X}$. In bounded model checking, only part of this state space is considered, the set of states within some distance bound B from S^{init}.

Most symbolic approaches encode x_l in b_l boolean variables, where b_l is either n_l or $\lceil \log n_l \rceil$ (*one-hot* or *binary* encoding), and a set of states using a BDD with $\sum_{K \geq l \geq 1} b_l$ levels. *Ordered multi-way decision diagrams* (MDDs) [21], instead map x_l to level l, whose nodes have n_l outgoing edges. MDDs can be implemented directly, as is done in our tool SMART [6], or as an interface to BDDs [16].

Symbolic technique for asynchronous models. A BFS-based approach, as used for example by NuSMV [11], computes the bounded state space with a simple image computation iteration. Set $\mathcal{X}^{[0]}$ is initialized to S^{init} and, after d iterations, set $\mathcal{X}^{[d]}$ contains the states at distance up to d from S^{init}. With MDDs, $\mathcal{X}^{[d]}$ is encoded as a K-level MDD and $\mathcal{R}$ as a $2K$-level MDD whose current and next state variables are normally interleaved for efficiency. The transition relation is often conjunctively partitioned into a set of *conjuncts* or disjunctively partitioned into a set of *disjuncts* [4], stored as a set of MDDs with shared nodes, instead of a single monolithic MDD. Heuristically, such partitions are known to be effective for synchronous and asynchronous systems, respectively.

Disjunctive partitioning and chaining. Our work focuses on the important class of systems exhibiting *globally-asynchronous locally-synchronous* behavior, and assumes that the high-level model specifies a set of asynchronous events $\mathcal{E}$, where each event $\alpha \in \mathcal{E}$ is further specified as a set of small synchronous components. We then write the transition relation as $\mathcal{R} \equiv \bigvee_{\alpha \in \mathcal{E}} \mathcal{D}_\alpha$, and further conjunctively partition each disjunct $\mathcal{D}_\alpha$ into conjuncts representing a synchronous component of α, finally expressing $\mathcal{R}$ as $\mathcal{R} \equiv \bigvee_{\alpha \in \mathcal{E}} \mathcal{D}_\alpha \equiv \bigvee_{\alpha \in \mathcal{E}} (\bigwedge_r \mathcal{C}_{\alpha,r})$.

For example, a guarded command language model consists of a set of commands of the form "*guard* $\rightarrow$ *assignment*$_1$ $\|$ *assignment*$_2$ $\| \cdots \|$ *assignment*$_m$", with the meaning that, whenever the boolean predicate *guard* evaluates to *true*, the m parallel atomic assignments can be executed concurrently (synchronously).

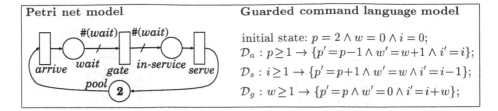

Fig. 1. A limited-arrival gated-service model with marking-dependent arc cardinalities

Commands are asynchronous events and, for each command, the corresponding parallel assignments are its synchronous components. Similarly, for a Petri net, the transitions are the asynchronous events, and the firing of a transition synchronously updates all the input and output places connected to it. We use extended Petri nets as the input formalism in SMART [6].

Running example. Fig. 1 shows a Petri net, and its equivalent guarded command language expression, modeling a gated-service queue with a limited pool of customers. New arrivals wait at the gate until it is opened, then all the waiting customers enter the service queue. Customers return to the pool after service. Each state of the model corresponds to a possible value of the integer variable vector (p,w,i), where p stands for *pool*, w for *wait*, and i for *in-service*. Assuming a pool of two customers, the model has an initial state $(2,0,0)$ and six reachable states: $S = \{(2,0,0), (1,1,0), (0,2,0), (1,0,1), (0,0,2), (0,1,1)\}$.

Event locality. In asynchronous models, the execution of each event usually modifies or depends on just a small subset of all the state variables. In the running example, for example, event *gate*, $\mathcal{D}_g$, depends only on variable w and modifies only variables w and i. Given an event α, we define the set of variables
- $\mathcal{V}_M(\alpha) = \{x_l : \exists \mathbf{i}, \mathbf{j} \in \widehat{S}, \mathcal{D}_\alpha(\mathbf{i}, \mathbf{j}) \wedge \mathbf{i}[l] \neq \mathbf{j}[l]\}$ and
- $\mathcal{V}_D(\alpha) = \{x_l : \exists \mathbf{i}, \mathbf{i}' \in \widehat{S}, \forall k \neq l, \mathbf{i}[k] = \mathbf{i}'[k] \wedge \exists \mathbf{j} \in \widehat{S}, \mathcal{D}_\alpha(\mathbf{i}, \mathbf{j}) \wedge \not\exists \mathbf{j}' \in \widehat{S}, \mathcal{D}_\alpha(\mathbf{i}', \mathbf{j}')\}$

that can be modified by α, or can disable α, respectively. Letting

$$Top(\alpha) = \max\{l : x_l \in \mathcal{V}_M(\alpha) \cup \mathcal{V}_D(\alpha)\}, Bot(\alpha) = \min\{l : x_l \in \mathcal{V}_M(\alpha) \cup \mathcal{V}_D(\alpha)\},$$

we can then partition the events according to the value of *Top*, into the subsets $\mathcal{E}_l = \{\alpha : Top(\alpha) = l\}$, for $K \geq l \geq 1$. In [8] we observed that a chaining [28] order where these subsets are applied to the MDD in bottom-up fashion results in good speedups with respect to a strict BFS symbolic state-space generation. The bounded version of chaining is shown in Fig. 3 and discussed in Sec. 3.

By exploiting this *event locality*, we can store $\mathcal{D}_\alpha$ in an MDD over just the current and next state variables with index k, for $Top(\alpha) \geq k \geq Bot(\alpha)$; variables outside this range undergo an *identity transformation*, i.e., remain unchanged.

Saturation-based symbolic fixpoint computation. The Saturation algorithm for computing the reachable state spaces of asynchronous systems was originally proposed in [7] for models in *Kronecker-product* form; it has since been extended to general models [10] and applied to shortest path computations

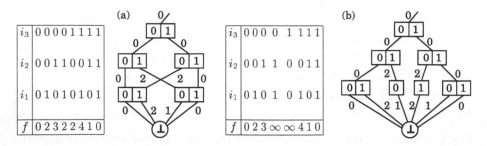

Fig. 2. Storing total (a) and partial (b) integer functions with EDDs

and CTL model-checking [9]. Saturation has been shown to reduce memory and runtime requirements by several orders of magnitude with respect to BFS-based algorithms, when applied to asynchronous systems.

Saturation is unique in that it does not perform fixpoint computations over a global decision diagram, as standard breadth-first iteration strategies do, but recursively computes (sub-)fixpoints at each decision diagram node. This exploits the locality of events inherent in asynchronous systems as well as the semantic concept of interleaving. The formal algorithm of Saturation on our variant of edge-valued decision diagrams is described in detail in Sec. 3. For details of the original Saturation algorithm on MDDs we refer the reader to [10].

To employ Saturation for bounded reachability checking we encode not just the reachable states, but also their distance from S^{init}. This can be achieved using either edge-valued decision diagrams (EDDs, called EV$^+$MDDs in [9]) or the ADDs of [2]. ADDs are a well-known variant of BDDs that can encode non-boolean functions by having an arbitrary set of terminal nodes instead of just the two terminal nodes corresponding to the boolean values *true* and *false*. In our discussion, we focus instead on EDDs since they can be exponentially more compact than ADDs; see also the results in Sec. 4.

Definition 1 (EDD [9]). An EDD on the *domain* $\widehat{S} = S_K \times \cdots \times S_1$ is a directed acyclic graph with labeled and weighted edges where:

- Each node p belongs to a *level* in $\{K, ..., 1, 0\}$, denoted $p.lvl$.
- Level 0 contains a single terminal node, $\perp$.
- A non-terminal node p at level $l > 0$ has $n_l \geq 2$ outgoing edges, labeled from 0 to $n_l - 1$. We write $p[i] = \langle v, q \rangle$ if the ith edge has weight $v \in \mathbb{N} \cup \{\infty\}$ and points to node q. We also write $p[i].val = v$ and $p[i].node = q$.
- If $p[i].val = \infty$, then $p[i].node = \perp$; otherwise, $p[i].node$ is at level $p.lvl-1$.
- There is a single root node, r^*, at level K, with an incoming "dangling" edge having weight $\rho \in \mathbb{Z}$. We write such edges as $\langle \rho, r \rangle$.
- Each non–terminal node has at least one outgoing edge labeled with 0.
- There are no *duplicate* nodes, i.e., if $\forall i, 0 \leq i < n_l, p[i].node = q[i].node$ and $p[i].val = q[i].val$, then $p = q$.

```
mdd BoundedBfsChain( )
 1  S ← S^init;
 2  for d = 1 to B do
 3     for l = 1 to K do
 4        foreach α ∈ E_l do
 5           S ← Union(S, Image(S, D_α))
 6  return S;
```

Fig. 3. Symbolic bounded BFS state-space generation with chaining

The function $f_{\langle v,p \rangle} : S_l \times \cdots \times S_1 \rightarrow \mathbb{Z} \cup \{\infty\}$ encoded by an edge $\langle v,p \rangle$, with $p.lvl = l > 0$ is $f_{\langle v,p \rangle}(i_l, \ldots, i_1) = v + f_{\langle p[i_l].val, p[i_l].node \rangle}(i_{l-1}, \ldots, i_1)$, where we let $f_{\langle x, \perp \rangle} = x$. Thus, the function encoded by the entire EDD is $f_{\langle \rho, r \rangle}$. □

As defined, EDDs can canonically encode *any* function of the form $\widehat{S} \rightarrow \mathbb{Z} \cup \{\infty\}$, except the constant ∞, for which we use a special EDD with $r = \perp$ and $\rho = \infty$. Fig. 2 shows two EDDs storing a total and partial function, respectively. Here, "partial" means that some of its values are ∞; whenever this is the case, we omit the corresponding value and edge from the graphical representation. We point out that EDDs allow for efficient implementations of standard operations on the functions they encode, including computing the EDD representing the pointwise *minimum* of two functions, needed in our reachability algorithm [9].

3 Bounded Reachability Checking Using Decision Diagrams

Given a model $\mathcal{M}$ and a property ϕ, a generic breadth-first bounded reachability checking algorithm starts with some initial guess for the bound B, computes the set of states S^B within distance B of the initial states S^{init}, and, if any state in S^B violates ϕ, returns *Error*. If no such state exists, B is increased and these steps are repeated except that, if S^B does not change between iterations, the *entire* state space has been explored, so one can stop and declare ϕ to hold.

MDDs with BFS-style event-locality-based chaining. Before presenting our main contribution, an algorithm for bounded reachability checking based on Saturation and EDDs, we first show how the above algorithm can be improved when dealing with MDD-encoded state spaces of event-based asynchronous systems, using ideas from *event locality* and *forward chaining*. This serves as one of the reference algorithms in our experimental studies of Sec. 4. The improved algorithm is displayed in Fig. 3.

Exploiting event locality for an event α, we can ignore MDD levels above $Top(\alpha)$ and modify *in-place* MDD nodes at level $Top(\alpha)$. Indeed, the call to *Image* in Fig. 3 does not even access nodes below $Bot(\alpha)$, only *Union* does. This has been shown to significantly reduce the peak number of MDD nodes [8].

Chaining [28] compounds the effect of multiple events within a single iteration. For example, if (i) the set of states known at iteration B is $\mathcal{X}^B$, (ii) $\mathbf{j} \notin \mathcal{X}^B$ can be reached from $\mathbf{i} \in \mathcal{X}^B$ by firing the sequence of events (α, β, γ), and (iii) we happen to explore events in that exact order, then $\mathbf{j}$ will be included in $\mathcal{X}^{B+1}$. Thus, $\mathcal{X}^B \supseteq \mathcal{S}^B$, since some states in $\mathcal{S}^{|\mathcal{E}| \cdot B} \setminus \mathcal{S}^B$ might be present in $\mathcal{X}^B$. Reducing the number of iterations does not guarantee greater efficiency, as the MDD for $\mathcal{X}^B$ can be much larger than that for $\mathcal{S}^B$; however, it has been shown experimentally that chaining often reduces both time and memory requirements [28].

It is well known that the variable order for the MDD representation is essential. Furthermore, in our setting, the variable order affects also the value of *Top* and *Bot* and the event order. In this paper we employ the heuristics reported in [27] to automatically generate a good order.

Bounded Saturation using EDDs. In several studies, Saturation has been shown superior to BFS-style iterations when symbolically computing least fixpoints for asynchronous models [8,9,10]. The challenge in adapting Saturation to bounded model checking lies in the need to bound the symbolic traversal in the nested fixpoint computations. We propose to use EDDs to encode both the bounded state space and the distance information in the same symbolic encoding. Thus, we bound the symbolic traversal during the EDD symbolic operations by using the distance information, instead of simply limiting the number of outermost iterations performed in a traditional BFS-style approach with or without chaining. Instead of EDDs, we could have used ADDs, but this can result in a performance penalty, as reported in Sec. 4.

Fig. 4 shows two EDD approaches differing in how they bound the symbolic traversal. They are obtained by replacing the *Truncate* call in procedure *BoundedImage* with either *TruncateExact* or *TruncateApprox*. The former computes the exact bounded state space $\mathcal{S}^B$; the latter computes a superset of $\mathcal{S}^B$ that may contain reachable states with distance at most $K \cdot B$, where K is the number of state variables, i.e., EDD levels. Recall that the transition relations are stored using MDDs, with $\mathbf{0}$ and $\mathbf{1}$ denoting an MDD's terminal nodes.

Both approaches start from an EDD where states in $\mathcal{S}^{init}$ have distance 0 and states in $\widehat{\mathcal{S}} \setminus \mathcal{S}^{init}$ have distance ∞ (line 1 in *BoundedSaturation*). Then, procedure *BoundedSaturate* is called on all EDD nodes, starting from those at level 1, to compute the bounded state space. Each EDD node p at level l encodes a set of (sub-)states and distance information consisting of variables at level l or below. When calling procedure *BoundedSaturate* on an EDD node p at level l, a least fixpoint encoding the (sub-)state space and distance with respect to the set $\mathcal{E}_l$ of events with top level l is computed. During the fixpoint computation of *BoundedSaturate* on node p at level l, each event in $\mathcal{E}_l$ is exhaustively fired to perform bounded forward traversal, until no more new reachable (sub-) states are found. *BoundedImage* performs bounded forward traversal by first computing the forward image, followed by either an exact truncation to prune all the (sub-)states exceeding bound B (procedure *TruncateExact*), or a faster but approximate truncation to prune only (sub-)states for which the edge value in the current EDD node would exceed B (procedure *TruncateApprox*). Procedures *BoundedSaturate* and *BoundedImage* are mutually recursive: *BoundedImage* performs a bounded forward traversal of the reachable state space, while all the

---

void *BoundedSaturation*()

1 $r^* \leftarrow$ root of the EDD encoding $f(\mathbf{i}) = 0$ if $\mathbf{i} \in \mathcal{S}^{init}$, and $f(\mathbf{i}) = \infty$ otherwise
2 **for** $l = 1$ **to** K **do foreach** node p at level l **do** *BoundedSaturate*(p);

---

node *BoundedSaturate*(node p)

1 $l \leftarrow p.lvl$;
2 **repeat**
3   choose $\alpha \in \mathcal{E}_l, i \in \mathcal{S}_l, j \in \mathcal{S}_l$ s.t. $p[i].val < B$ and $\mathcal{D}_\alpha[i][j] \neq 0$;
4      $\langle v,q \rangle \leftarrow BoundedImage(p[i], \mathcal{D}_\alpha[i][j])$;
5      $p[j] \leftarrow Minimum(p[j], Truncate(v+1, q))$;   ●*exact or approximate*
6 **until** p does not change;
7 **return** p;

---

edge *BoundedImage*(edge $\langle v,q \rangle$, mdd f)

1 **if** $f = 0$ **then return** $\langle \infty, \bot \rangle$; **if** $f = 1$ or $q = \bot$ **then return** $\langle v,q \rangle$;
2 $k \leftarrow q.lvl$;   ●*given our quasi-reduced form, $f.lvl = k$ as well*
3 $s \leftarrow NewNode(k)$;   ●*create EDD node at level k with edges set to $\langle \infty, \bot \rangle$*
4 **foreach** $i \in \mathcal{S}_k, j \in \mathcal{S}_k$ s.t. $q[i].val \leq B$ and $f[i][j] \neq 0$ **do**
5      $\langle w,o \rangle \leftarrow Truncate(BoundedImage(q[i], f[i][j]))$;   ●*exact or approximate*
6      $s[j] \leftarrow Minimum(s[j], \langle w,o \rangle)$;
7 $s \leftarrow BoundedSaturate(s)$;
8 $\langle \gamma,s \rangle \leftarrow Normalize(s)$;
9 **return** $\langle \gamma+v,s \rangle$;

---

edge *Minimum*(edge $\langle v,p \rangle$, edge $\langle w,q \rangle$)

1 **if** $v = \infty$ **then return** $\langle w,q \rangle$; **if** $w = \infty$ **then return** $\langle v,p \rangle$;
2 $k \leftarrow p.lvl$;   ●*given our quasi-reduced form, $q.lvl = k$ as well*
3 **if** $k = 0$ **then return** $\langle \min\{v, w\}, \bot \rangle$;   ●*the only node at level $k = 0$ is $\bot$*
4 $s \leftarrow NewNode(k)$;   ●*create EDD node at level k with edges set to $\langle \infty, \bot \rangle$*
5 $\gamma \leftarrow \min\{v, w\}$;
6 **foreach** $i \in \mathcal{S}_k$ **do**
7      $s[i] \leftarrow Minimum(\langle v-\gamma+p[i].val, p[i].node \rangle, \langle w-\gamma+q[i].val, q[i].node \rangle)$;
8 **return** $\langle \gamma,s \rangle$;

---

edge *Normalize*(node p)

1 $v \leftarrow \min\{p[i].val : i \in \mathcal{S}_{p.lvl}\}$;
2 **foreach** $i \in \mathcal{S}_{p.lvl}$ **do** $p[i].val \leftarrow p[i].val - v$;
3 **return** $\langle v,p \rangle$;

---

edge *TruncateExact*(edge $\langle v,p \rangle$)

1 **if** $v > bound$ **then return** $\langle \infty, \bot \rangle$;
2 **foreach** $i \in \mathcal{S}_{p.lvl}$ **do** $p[i] \leftarrow TruncateExact(\langle v+p[i].val, p[i].node \rangle)$;
3 **return** $\langle v,p \rangle$;

---

edge *TruncateApprox*(edge $\langle v,p \rangle$)

1 **if** $v > bound$ **then return** $\langle \infty, \bot \rangle$; **else return** $\langle v,p \rangle$;

Fig. 4. Bounded Saturation for state-space exploration using EDDs

newly created nodes in the new image are saturated by *BoundedSaturate* (line 7 in procedure *BoundedImage*). Procedure *Minimum* computes the pointwise minimum of the functions encoded by its two argument EDDs, i.e., computing the union of the state sets encoded by the arguments. Finally, procedure *Normalize* takes a node p and ensures that it has at least one outgoing edge with value 0, returning the excess in the edge value v.

We now examine the manipulation of the edge values in more detail. When an event α is fired, the distance of the image states is the distance of the corresponding "from" states incremented by 1. *BoundedSaturate* fires α by calling *BoundedImage* (line 4), which returns the root of the image, so that the "dangling" edge value must be incremented by 1 to account for the firing of α (line 5). The first portion of procedure *BoundedImage* (lines 1–6) performs the symbolic image computation of the same event α fired by *BoundedSaturate*, and the distance of the new image is incremented by the distance of the "from" states at the return statement (line 9). The distance of the image states can be greater than the distance of their "from" states by more than one, due to saturation of the image states (line 7). *BoundedSaturate* uses the test $p[i].value < B$ (line 3), but *BoundedImage* uses instead the test $q[i].val \leq B$, since the increment of the edge value by 1 is performed in the former, but not in the latter.

Comparing with BFS-style MDD approaches, our new proposed EDD approaches use Saturation, a more advanced iteration order, but at the cost of a more expensive symbolic data structure, EDDs (or ADDs). The experimental results of Sec. 4 show that this tradeoff is effective in both time and memory, as the new algorithms often outperform the BFS approach in our benchmarks.

Running example of the EDD approach. Fig. 5 shows the execution of bounded Saturation using *TruncateApprox* as the truncation procedure, on the running example of Fig. 1 with bound $B = 1$. In Fig. 5, snapshot (a) shows the $2K$-level MDDs for the disjunctively partitioned transition relation. $\mathcal{D}_a$ and $\mathcal{D}_g$ have identity transformations for variables i and g, respectively, thus the corresponding levels in the decision diagram are skipped to exploit event locality. Snapshots (b)–(f) show the evolution of the bounded state space encoded by the EDD, from the initial state to the final bounded state space, listing the key procedure calls. For readability, edges with value ∞ are omitted. We denote the nodes of the EDD encoding the state space with capital letters (A to E), two specific MDD nodes in the transition relation encoding with f and h, and color a node black once it is saturated. The algorithm starts by saturating nodes A and B, which are saturated immediately since no events are enabled in them (Snapshot (c)). Nodes E, D, and C are saturated in that order. The procedure stops when the root C becomes saturated. Not all procedure calls are shown, e.g., *BoundedImage*$(C[1], \mathcal{D}_s[1][2])$ is called in Snapshot (f) before node C becomes saturated, but it is not shown since this call does not generate new nodes (states).

Bounded Saturation using ADDs. A version of Saturation using ADDs can be obtained by extending the MDD-based Saturation algorithm of [10], so that it uses an ADD to store the states and their distances, instead of a simple MDD.

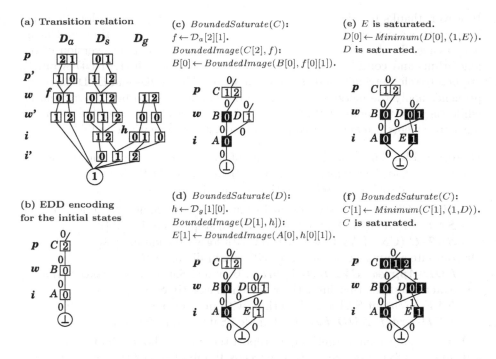

Fig. 5. Bounded Saturation applied to our running example

The ADD has $B + 1$ terminal nodes corresponding to the distances of interest, $\{0, 1, \ldots, B, \infty\}$. We omit this algorithm's details due to space limitations.

4   Experimental Results

We implemented Bounded Saturation in the verification tool SMART, which supports Petri nets as front-end. This section reports our experimental results on a suite of asynchronous Petri net benchmarks when checking for deadlock-freedom as an example of bounded reachability checking. For our symbolic algorithms, this check simply requires us to remove the set of states enabling α, i.e., $Img^{-1}(\widehat{\mathcal{S}}, \mathcal{D}_\alpha)$, for each event α, from the final bounded state space. We compare the performance of several decision-diagram-based methods and the SAT-based methods of Heljanko et al. [18,19] and Ogata et al. [25].

We conduct our experiments on a 3Ghz Pentium machine with 1GB RAM. Benchmarks *byzagr4, mmgt, dac, hs(hartstone), sentest, speed, dp, q, elevator, key* are taken from Corbett [15], and were translated into safe Petri nets by Heljanko [17]. Benchmarks *fms* and *kanban* are deadlocked versions of non-safe Petri net manufacturing system models in the SMART distribution, automatically translated into safe Petri nets by SMART. All benchmarks have deadlocks.

BDDs and EVBDDs are natural candidates for our decision-diagram-based approaches when models have binary variables, as is the case for safe Petri nets.

However, thanks to a heuristic to merge binary variables and exploit Petri net invariants, we can instead use MDDs and EDDs, and achieve time and memory savings. In the following, we thus present the multi-valued version of our algorithms and consider only one EVBDD-based approach (EVBDD-Approx), applied to safe Petri net models, for comparison. The MDD- and EDD-based approaches apply the merging heuristic to the safe nets of Corbett's benchmarks, while they use the non-safe Petri nets *fms* and *kanban* as-is. Variable orders for our experiments are automatically obtained using the heuristic in [27].

Result table. The first three columns of Table 1 show the model name and parameters, and the number of places (#P) and events (#E). The other columns are either "approximate" methods that use a difference definition of distance:

- **MDD-Chain** (BFS-style event-locality-based chaining technique of Fig. 3)
- **SAT-S** (circuit SAT-based method with step semantics [19])
- **SAT-C** (CNF SAT-based method with forward chaining [25])

Or compute a superset of the states S^B within distance B:

- **EDD-Approx/EVBDD-Approx** (Bounded Saturation: *TruncateApprox*)

Or "exact" methods that limit their search to exactly S^B:

- **SAT-I** (circuit SAT-based method with interleaving semantics [19])
- **EDD-Exact/ADD-Exact** (Bounded Saturation: *TruncateExact*).

For each approximate method, we report the smallest bound B at which either a deadlock is found or the runtime exceeds 10 minutes. For the exact methods, report the exact distance bound B of the deadlock, except for the cases marked "?", where none of the exact methods could find a deadlock within 10 minutes. All the decision-diagram-based methods are implemented in SMART, and their runtime and memory consumptions are reported in the table, while for the SAT-based tools, only the runtime is available and reported.

Corbett's benchmarks and the SAT-I and SAT-C tools are from [18]. In our experiments, SAT-S performs at least as well as the analogous approach using process semantics [17] (this is also confirmed by the results in Heljanko and Junttila's recent tutorial [18]), therefore we report only the former in Table 1. With Corbett's benchmarks, we show different bounds for SAT-C than those reported in [25]; this is due to using a different initial state, the same as the one considered in [18]. For SAT-I and SAT-C both the encoding time and the `bczchaff` circuit SAT-solver runtime are reported in Table 1. For a fair comparison, the runtime of SAT-C includes the preprocessing steps for scheduling events, encoding the safe Petri net into a boolean formula and then into a CNF formula, and querying the `zchaff` SAT-solver for deadlocks.

Discussion. From Table 1 we can roughly classify benchmarks *byzagr, hs, sentest, fms, kanban* as models with "deep" deadlocks, where the smallest bounds to detect deadlocks range from 30 to 500, and classify all the other benchmarks as models with "shallow" deadlocks, where the smallest bounds are less than 30. For benchmarks with "deep" deadlocks, the newly proposed EDD-Approx method achieves the best performance. For models with "shallow" deadlocks, it seems almost all the methods perform reasonably well, including our

Table 1. Experimental results (Time in sec, Mem in MB). ">600" indicates that runtime exceeds 600 sec or memory exceeds 1GB.

| | | | Approximate distance methods | | | | | | | | | | | | | Exact distance methods | | | | | |
| | | | EDD-Approx | | | EVBDD-Approx | | | MDD-Chain | | | SAT-S | | SAT-C | | SAT-I | | EDD-Exact | | ADD-Exact | |
Model	#P	#E	B	Time	Mem	B	Time	Mem	B	Time	Mem	B	Time	B	Time	B	Time	Time	Mem	Time	Mem
byzagr4(2a)	579	473	49	2.23	2.41	49	9.14	3.43	6	7.3	9.24	8	0.79	2	2.07	?	>600	>600	–	>600	–
mmgt(3)	122	172	9	0.11	0.2	8	1.28	0.34	5	0.07	0.16	7	0.09	3	1.04	10	1.37	0.32	0.55	0.41	0.33
mmgt(4)	158	232	17	1.22	1.15	17	2.15	1.67	3	0.11	0.2	8	0.23	4	5.52	20	1.24	4.36	3.12	12.87	3.61
dac(15)	105	73	4	0.01	0.0	4	0.03	0.01	2	0.01	0.01	3	0.01	2	0.04	20	0.01	0.03	0.05	0.06	0.04
hs(75)	302	152	151	0.01	0.03	151	0.36	0.05	93	0.08	0.53	151	5.84	1	0.07	151	7.94	0.15	0.03	0.13	0.34
hs(100)	402	202	201	0.03	0.04	201	0.78	0.07	116	0.14	0.78	201	14.85	1	0.13	201	20.31	0.3	0.04	0.23	0.58
sentest(75)	252	102	45	0.0	0.02	45	0.21	0.03	32	0.03	0.21	83	4.27	3	0.13	88	8.51	0.06	0.02	0.08	0.14
sentest(100)	327	127	61	0.01	0.03	61	0.34	0.05	73	0.07	0.47	108	10.71	4	0.29	113	21.85	0.12	0.03	0.22	0.25
speed(1)	29	31	4	0.01	0.02	2	0.24	0.01	3	0.01	0.04	4	0.01	2	0.03	7	0.02	0.02	0.04	0.02	0.01
dp(12)	72	48	2	0.01	0.02	2	0.02	0.03	1	0.0	0.01	1	0.0	1	0.02	12	0.06	0.96	1.77	0.33	0.12
q(1)	163	194	9	0.01	0.03	8	1.45	0.04	7	0.06	0.14	9	0.13	1	0.07	21	0.83	0.08	0.15	0.19	0.13
elevator(3)	326	782	8	15.07	9.46	7	28.5	9.83	6	0.87	0.58	8	0.42	2	3.77	20	2.74	>600	–	7.54	1.83
key(2)	94	92	13	0.06	0.14	18	0.16	0.19	14	0.07	0.2	36	2.88	2	0.05	50	>600	0.15	0.2	0.22	0.34
key(3)	129	133	17	0.2	0.48	17	0.55	0.71	14	0.21	0.52	37	4.39	2	0.10	50	>600	0.62	0.67	2.8	1.64
key(4)	164	174	17	0.69	1.48	15	2.4	1.39	17	0.67	1.54	38	4.21	2	0.18	50	>600	2.02	2.11	9.71	3.15
key(5)	199	215	17	2.04	4.15	17	5.97	6.66	15	1.73	3.37	39	8.07	2	0.25	50	>600	16.87	10.52	33.65	10.03
fms(3)	22	16	9	0.06	0.02	5	0.74	0.02	7	0.01	0.08	10	0.75	3	1.25	30	>600	0.07	0.06	0.05	0.14
fms(7)	22	16	19	0.07	0.26	11	4.4	0.69	15	0.24	2.58	18	>600	6	>600	70	>600	0.8	2.2	1.12	4.7
fms(10)	22	16	28	0.12	0.99	6	>600	–	21	1.35	14.75	16	>600	7	>600	100	>600	5.37	14.37	5.24	24.11
kanban(1)	17	16	28	0.04	0.0	27	0.33	0.01	13	0.0	0.01	19	0.05	5	0.09	40	16.56	0.08	0.0	0.01	0.01
kanban(3)	17	16	82	0.05	0.06	79	5.34	0.34	19	0.03	0.23	12	>600	3	>600	120	>600	0.1	0.07	0.27	0.64
kanban(10)	17	16	271	0.84	10.43	1	>600	–	54	2.83	29.29	1	>600	1	>600	400	>600	14.4	10.46	51.76	187.9

MDD-Chain method. Comparing EDD-Approx with EVBDD-Approx, we observe that the former always performs better than the latter. The comparison between EDD-Exact and ADD-Exact shows that they can complement each other. EDD-Approx is arguably the method with the best overall performance, except for the elevator model, where it performs much worse than the MDD-Chain method and the SAT-S method. This might be because a very large superset of S^B is computed, and the elevator model could be a case where doing so is not beneficial to the structure of the EDD. We also suspect that our variable order heuristic does not perform well on this model.

We also observe that the poor performance of SAT-solvers for unsatisfiable boolean formulas makes it hard to guess the bound B. If the guess is too large, the boolean formula is huge, if it is too small the formula is unsatisfiable, and both cases have severe performance penalties. For example, SAT-I finds a deadlock in benchmark $q(1)$ in less than 1 sec when $B = 21$ but, when $B = 20$, the formula is unsatisfiable and the runtime exceeds 600 sec. Decision-diagram-based methods tend instead to have "well-behaved" runtimes monotonically increasing in B.

5 Discussion and Related Work

SAT-solving for Petri nets. We first add some details to the two SAT-based approaches to deadlock checking of safe Petri nets [17,25], against which we compared ourselves in the previous section regarding run-time efficiency.

Heljanko's work [17] establishes the so-called *process semantics* of Petri nets as the 'best' net semantics for translating bounded reachability into a propositional satisfiability problem, in the sense that the resulting SAT problem can be solved more efficiently than for step or interleaving semantics. However, this technique can only be safely applied for safe Petri nets, i.e., finite nets, as otherwise these semantics may not coincide. In contrast, our technique is applicable to general Petri nets, even if they exhibit an infinite state space.

Ogata, Tsuchiya, and Kikuno's approach [25] focuses on the translation of Petri nets, which must again be safe, into propositional formulas. The ordinary encoding of safe nets into propositional formulas results in large formulas, thereby degrading the performance of SAT solving and hampering scalability. The authors suggest a more succinct encoding, albeit at the price of exploring not only states with a distance up to the considered bound but also some states with a larger distance. This is similar to our Bounded Saturation, for which it is also more efficient to collect some additional states. The authors leave a comparison to Heljanko's approach as future work; this comparison is now included in the previous section, and shows that neither method is superior in all cases.

BDD vs. SAT on synchronous systems. As mentioned before, the common belief that SAT-based model checking outperforms decision-diagram-based model checking was proved wrong by Cabodi, Nocco, and Quer [5] for a class of digital circuits that largely exhibits synchronous behavior. The advocated approach relies on improving standard BDD-based techniques by mixing forward and backward traversals, dovetailing approximate and exact methods, adopting guided and partitioned searches, and using conjunctive decompositions and generalized cofactor-based BDD simplifications.

Our research complements their findings for asynchronous systems. In a nutshell, our improvement over standard techniques lies in the local manipulation of decision diagrams by exploiting the event locality inherent in asynchronous systems, interleaving semantics, and disjunctive partitioning. These are the central ideas behind *Saturation* [7] on which our *Bounded Saturation* algorithm is based. Similar to the algorithm proposed in [5], we also achieve efficiency by including some states with a distance larger than the given bound B; such states have a distance of up to $K \cdot B$ in our approach and up to $E \cdot B$ in [5], where K and E are the number of components and events in the studied Petri net, respectively.

Together, the results of Cabodi et al. and ours, as well as further recent research [29], revise some of the claims made in the literature, especially regarding the performance of decision-diagram-based (bounded) model checking. It must be noted here that our results were obtained with static variable orders which have been computed using a simple heuristic [27]. Thus, no fine-tuning of models by hand was necessary, which was criticized in [14].

Petri net unfoldings. Both SAT-based and decision-diagram-based techniques are established techniques for addressing the state-space explosion problem. The Petri net community has developed another successful technique to address this problem, first suggested in a seminal paper by McMillan [23]. The idea is to finitely unfold a Petri net until the resulting prefix has exactly the same reachable markings as the original net. For certain Petri nets such finite prefixes exist and often prove to be small in practice. In contrast to bounded reachability checking, analysis techniques based on unfoldings are thus complete, as they capture a net's entire behavior. However, unfoldings are often limited to finite-state Petri nets, although recent work suggests an extension to some infinite-state systems [1].

6   Conclusions and Future Work

This paper explored the utility of decision diagrams for bounded reachability checking of asynchronous systems. To this end, we reconsidered *Saturation*, a state-space generation algorithm which is based on Multi-way Decision Diagrams (MDDs) and exploits the event locality and interleaving semantics inherent in asynchronous systems. As the search strategy in Saturation is unlike breadth-first search, bounding the search required us to employ *Edge-Valued MDDs*, which allow for storing states together with their distances from the initial states.

Our extensive experimental analysis of the resulting *Bounded Saturation* algorithm showed that it often compares favorably to the competing SAT-based approaches introduced in [17,18,25]. In many cases, Bounded Saturation could build bounded state spaces and check for deadlocks at least as fast and frequently faster, while using acceptable amounts of memory. Thus, decision-diagram-based techniques can well compete with SAT-based techniques for bounded reachability checking of asynchronous systems, and the widespread perception that decision diagrams are not suited for bounded model checking [14] is untrue.

Future work should investigate whether an efficient version of Bounded Saturation can be developed using standard decision diagrams, rather than decision diagrams with explicit distance counters built in. We also intend to investigate whether the event locality inherent in asynchronous systems can be exploited in SAT-based reachability checking.

Acknowledgements. We would like to thank K. Heljanko, T. Jussila, and T. Tsuchiya for providing their inputs and software tools used in our study.

References

1. P. Abdulla, S. Iyer, and A. Nylén. SAT-solving the coverability problem for Petri nets. *FMSD*, 24(1):25–43, 2004.
2. R. I. Bahar, et. al. Algebraic decision diagrams and their applications. *FMSD*, 10(2/3):171–206, 1997.
3. A. Biere, A. Cimatti, E. Clarke, Y. Zhu. Symbolic model checking without BDDs. *TACAS*, LNCS 1579, pp. 193–207, 1999. Springer.
4. J. R. Burch, E. M. Clarke, D. E. Long. Symbolic model checking with partitioned transition relations. *VLSI*, pp. 49–58, 1991.
5. G. Cabodi, S. Nocco, S. Quer. Are BDDs still alive within sequential verification? *STTT*, 7(2):129–142, 2005.
6. G. Ciardo, R. L. Jones, A. S. Miner, and R. Siminiceanu. Logical and stochastic modeling with SMART. *Perf. Eval.*, 63:578–608, 2006.
7. G. Ciardo, G. Lüttgen, R. Siminiceanu. Saturation: an efficient iteration strategy for symbolic state-space generation. *TACAS*, LNCS 2031, pp. 328–342, 2001. Springer.
8. G. Ciardo, R. Marmorstein, R. Siminiceanu. The saturation algorithm for symbolic state space exploration. *STTT*, 8(1):4–25, 2006.
9. G. Ciardo, R. Siminiceanu. Using edge-valued decision diagrams for symbolic generation of shortest paths. *FMCAD*, LNCS 2517, pp. 256–273, 2002. Springer.
10. G. Ciardo, A. Yu. Saturation-based symbolic reachability analysis using conjunctive and disjunctive partitioning. *CHARME*, LNCS 3725, pp. 146–161, 2005. Springer
11. A. Cimatti, E. Clarke, F. Giunchiglia, M. Roveri. NuSMV: A new symbolic model verifier. *CAV*, LNCS 1633, pp. 495–499, 1999. Springer.
12. E. Clarke, A. Biere, R. Raimi, Y. Zhu. Bounded model checking using satisfiability solving. *FMSD*, 19(1):7–34, 2001.
13. E. Clarke, O. Grumberg, D. Peled. *Model Checking*. MIT, 1999.
14. F. Copty, et. al. Benefits of bounded model checking at an industrial setting. *CAV*, LNCS 2102, pp. 436–453, 2001. Springer.
15. J. C. Corbett. Evaluating deadlock detection methods for concurrent software. *IEEE Trans. Softw. Eng.*, 22(3):161–180, 1996.
16. The VIS Group. VIS: A system for verification and synthesis. *CAV*, LNCS 1102, pp. 428–432, 1996. Springer.
17. K. Heljanko. Bounded reachability checking with process semantics. *CONCUR*, LNCS 2154, pp. 218–232, 2001. Springer.
18. K. Heljanko, T. Junttila. Advanced tutorial on bounded model checking, *ACSD/ICATPN*, 2006. http://www.tcs.hut.fi/~kepa/bmc-tutorial.html.

19. K. Heljanko, I. Niemelä. Answer set programming and bounded model checking. *Answer Set Programming*, 2001.
20. F. Ivančić, Z. Yang, M. Ganai, A. Gupta, P. Ashar. F-Soft: Software Verification Platform. *CAV*, LNCS 3576, 2005. Springer.
21. T. Kam, T. Villa, R. Brayton, A. Sangiovanni-Vincentelli. Multi-valued decision diagrams: Theory and applications. *Multiple-Valued Logic*, 4(1–2):9–62, 1998.
22. Y.-T. Lai, S. Sastry. Edge-valued binary decision diagrams for multi-level hierarchical verification. *DAC*, pp. 608–613, 1992. IEEE Press.
23. K. McMillan. A technique of state space search based on unfolding. *FMSD*, 6(1):45–65, 1995.
24. M. Moskewicz, C. Madigan, Y. Zhao, L. Zhang, S. Malik. Chaff: Engineering an efficient SAT solver. *DAC*, pp. 530–535, 2001. ACM Press.
25. S. Ogata, T. Tsuchiya, T. Kikuno. SAT-based verification of safe Petri nets. *ATVA*, LNCS 3299, pp. 79–92, 2004. Springer.
26. I. Rabinovitz, O. Grumberg. Bounded model checking of concurrent programs. *CAV*, LNCS 3576, pp. 82–97, 2005. Springer.
27. R. Siminiceanu, G. Ciardo. New metrics for static variable ordering in decision diagrams. *TACAS*, LNCS 3920, pp. 90–104, 2006. Springer.
28. M. Solé, E. Pastor. Traversal techniques for concurrent systems. *FMCAD*, LNCS 2517, pp. 220–237, 2002. Springer.
29. R. Tzoref, M. Matusevich, E. Berger, I. Beer. An optimized symbolic bounded model checking engine. *CHARME*, LNCS 2860, pp. 141–149, 2003. Springer.

Model Checking on Trees with Path Equivalences*

Rajeev Alur, Pavol Černý, and Swarat Chaudhuri

University of Pennsylvania

Abstract. For specifying and verifying branching-time requirements, a reactive system is traditionally modeled as a labeled tree, where a path in the tree encodes a possible execution of the system. We propose to enrich such tree models with "jump-edges" that capture observational indistinguishability: for an agent a, an a-labeled edge is added between two nodes if the observable behaviors of the agent a along the paths to these nodes are identical. We show that it is possible to specify information flow properties and partial information games in temporal logics interpreted on this enriched structure. We study complexity and decidability of the model checking problem for these logics. We show that it is PSPACE-complete and EXPTIME-complete respectively for fragments of CTL and μ-calculus-like logics. These fragments are expressive enough to allow specifications of information flow properties such as "agent A does not reveal x (a secret) until agent B reveals y (a password)" and of partial information games.

1 Introduction

Temporal logics have been successfully used for specifying and verifying requirements of reactive systems such as distributed protocols [6,12]. In particular, in the branching-time approach, a system is modeled as a labeled tree whose paths correspond to executions of the system; a specification describes a set of correct trees; and verification reduces to a membership question [10]. Typical branching-time specification languages include CTL, the μ-calculus, and tree automata [9,7]. The theoretical foundations of this approach are now well understood, and model checkers such as SMV implement highly optimized algorithms for verifying branching-time requirements of finite-state systems [3,5].

This paper is motivated by our interest in extending model checking to reasoning about secrecy requirements of software systems [14]. Informally, a variable x is not secret after an execution e of a process a if the value of x is the same after all executions that are equivalent to e, where two executions are considered equivalent if the "observable" behavior of the process a (such as messages sent and received by a) is identical along the two executions. Classical tree logics cannot relate distinct paths in the tree, and thus, secrecy is not specifiable in logics such as the μ-calculus [1].

To be able to specify properties such as secrecy, we propose to enrich the traditional tree model with "jump-edges" that capture observational

---

* This research was supported by NSF grants CPA 0541149 and CNS 0524059.

O. Grumberg and M. Huth (Eds.): TACAS 2007, LNCS 4424, pp. 664–678, 2007.

indistinguishability. More precisely, consider a tree T whose nodes are labeled with sets of atomic propositions. For an agent a, if the set of propositions $O(a)$ captures the observable behavior of a, then two tree nodes are considered a-equivalent if the paths from the root to these nodes agree on the propositions in $O(a)$ at every step. We convert the tree T into a graph $IG(T)$ by adding, for every agent a of interest, an a-labeled edge between every pair of a-equivalent nodes. One can view $IG(T)$ as a Kripke model, where both nodes and edges have labels, and interpret standard tree logics over it. For an agent a, we also define a stuttering (weak) equivalence on paths to make modeling of timing insensitive information flow properties possible. We define a graph $IG^w(T)$ similarly.

Tree logics interpreted over tree models augmented with equivalence edges have rich expressiveness. To specify that the agent a keeps the value of a variable x secret, we simply have to assert that for all tree nodes, the value of x is different from the value of x in one of the nodes connected by an a-labeled edge. One can integrate temporal reasoning with secrecy to specify requirements such as "agent a does not reveal x unless agent b reveals y." These examples, as well as the more specific examples in Section 2, lead us to conclude that a tree with path equivalences is a useful model for reasoning about information flow properties. The reason is that it contains just enough information so that these properties are specifiable in logics interpreted on this model.

Games are useful for specifying requirements as well as for formulating synthesis questions. In *partial information* games, the strategy can depend only on the sequence of observations, rather than the complete execution of the system. If a-labeled edges model the knowledge of player a (i.e. they connect two nodes in the tree iff along the paths leading to these nodes the sequence of observations of a is the same), then different versions of such partial information games are also expressible in our framework.

In our formulation, the model checking question is to decide whether $IG(T_K)$ satisfies a tree logic formula φ, where T_K is the tree unfolding of a finite-state model K. Keeping track of paths equivalent with respect to one agent requires a subset construction leading to PSPACE complexity. We show that this construction can be generalized, and the key parameter is the *nesting depth* of the specification. Informally, when we need to evaluate a formula φ after jumping across an a-labeled edge, then an additional layer of subset construction is required to process b-equivalence, for agents $b \neq a$. We show that, if we restrict the nesting depth to 1, as is the case for all our example specifications, the model checking problem for a CTL-like logic is PSPACE-complete, and EXPTIME-complete for a μ-calculus-like logic. When nesting depth is unbounded, model checking for CTL$\approx$ (the CTL-like logic) becomes nonelementary, and is undecidable for $\mu_\approx$-calculus (the μ-calculus-like logic).

2   Trees with Path Equivalences

Let P be a set of propositions. We consider labeled, unranked, unordered, infinite trees of the form $T = (V, E, \lambda, r)$, where V is an infinite set of nodes, $E \subseteq V \times V$

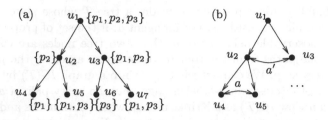

Fig. 1. (a) A labeled tree (b) Part of its equivalence graph

is a set of tree edges, $\lambda : V \to 2^P$ is a map labeling each node with the set of propositions holding there, and $r \in V$ is the root of the tree. A *path* in T is a sequence of nodes $\pi = v_0 v_1 v_2 \ldots$ such that $v_0 = r$ and for all i, v_i is the parent of v_{i+1}. Note that each node can be associated with a unique path (the path that leads from the root to this node) and vice-versa.

Let A be a fixed set of agents, and let us have a map $O : A \to 2^P$ defining the set of observables for an agent. We use the map O to define equivalences among paths in a tree T as follows. Let the map $Obs_a : V \to 2^P$, defined as $Obs_a(v) = \lambda(v) \cap O(a)$ for all v, return the observables of a at a node v of T. We lift this map to paths in T by defining $Obs_a(v_0 v_1 \ldots) = Obs_a(v_0) Obs_a(v_1) \ldots$. Let u and v be two nodes of T and let π be a path leading from the root to u and π' a path leading from the root to v. Nodes u and v are *a-equivalent* (written as $u \approx_a v$) iff $Obs_a(\pi) = Obs_a(\pi')$.

We define the *equivalence graph* $IG(T)$ of a tree T as the node and edge-labeled graph where: (1) the set of nodes is the set V of nodes of T; (2) the *root node* of $IG(T)$ is the root r of T; (3) the node-labeling map λ is the same as in T; (4) there is an *unlabeled edge* from node u to node v (in this case, we write $u \to v$) iff (u, v) is an edge in T; (5) for each agent a, there is an edge labeled a from u to v (we write $u \xrightarrow{a} v$) iff $u \approx_a v$. Intuitively, the structure $IG(T)$ uses a-labeled edges to capture equivalence and defined by the relation $\approx_a$. We can now view $IG(T)$ as a Kripke structure rooted at r. It is on this structure that we interpret our logics. Fig. 1-(a) depicts a tree T with path equivalences. We have two agents a and a' satisfying $O(a) = \{p_1, p_2\}$ and $O(a') = \{p_2, p_3\}$, and the nodes $u_1, u_2, \ldots$ are labeled as in the figure. Now it is easy to check that, for instance, $u_2 \approx_{a'} u_3$. Consequently, the edges of the equivalence graph $IG(T)$, part of which is shown in Fig. 1-(b), include $u_2 \xrightarrow{a'} u_3$ (and $u_3 \xrightarrow{a'} u_2$.)

The above definition of a-equivalence can be considered time sensitive in the sense that it can model an observer who knows that a transition has occurred even if the observation has not changed. We consider also the following time insensitive equivalence. Let $\equiv_w$ be the smallest congruence on sequences of sets of propositions such that $U \equiv_w UU$, where U is a set of propositions. This relation is sometimes called stuttering congruence. Once more, let u and v be two nodes of T and let π be a path leading from the root to u and π' a path leading from the root to v. Nodes u and v are *weakly a-equivalent* (written as

$u \approx_a^w v$) iff $Obs_a(\pi) \equiv_w Obs_a(\pi')$. The *weak-equivalence graph* $IG^w(T)$ graph is defined similarly as $IG(T)$, with $\approx_a^w$ replacing $\approx_a$.

3 Branching-Time Logics on Equivalence Graphs

In this section, we interpret branching-time temporal logics on equivalence graphs and apply this interpretation to express some natural information-flow and partial-information requirements.

$\mu_\approx$-**calculus.** The $\mu_\approx$-calculus has modalities to reason about edges labeled a, for any agent a, as well as unlabeled edges. For example, we have formulas such as $\langle a\rangle\varphi$, which holds at a node u iff there is a node v satisfying φ such that $u \xrightarrow{a} v$. In order to increase the expressiveness of the logic (without increasing the complexity of model checking), we add an operator $\langle \bar{a}\rangle$ to the syntax. The formula $\langle \bar{a}\rangle\varphi$ holds at a node u if there is another node v satisfying φ on the same level of $IG(T)$ (i.e., with the same distance from the root) that is not a-equivalent to u. See Example 4 below for an example of a property specified using the $\langle \bar{a}\rangle$ operator. To define the semantics of this operator, we will need to refer to nodes that are on the same level. This can be done using an agent sl such that $O(sl) = \emptyset$. Intuitively, this agent does not observe anything, and thus considers all the nodes at the same level to be equivalent.

Formally, let P be the set of propositions labeling our trees, and *Var* be a set of *variables*. Formulas in the $\mu_\approx$-calculus are given by the grammar: $\varphi = p \mid \neg\varphi' \mid X \mid \varphi_1 \vee \varphi_2 \mid \langle\rangle\varphi' \mid \langle a\rangle\varphi' \mid \langle \bar{a}\rangle\varphi' \mid \mu X.\varphi'(X)$, if X occurs in φ' only under an even number of negations, where $p \in P, a \in A$ and $X \in \textit{Var}$.

As for semantics, consider the equivalence graph $IG(T)$ of a tree T with path equivalences. A formula φ is interpreted in an *environment* $\mathcal{E}$ that interprets free variables of the formula as sets of nodes in $IG(T)$. The set $[\![\varphi]\!]_\mathcal{E}$ of nodes satisfying φ in environment $\mathcal{E}$ is defined inductively in a standard way. We state only a few cases: (1) $[\![\langle\rangle\varphi]\!]_\mathcal{E} = \{u : \text{for some } v, u \to v \text{ and } v \in [\![\varphi]\!]_\mathcal{E}\}$; (2) $[\![\langle a\rangle\varphi]\!]_\mathcal{E} = \{u : \text{for some } v, u \xrightarrow{a} v \text{ and } v \in [\![\varphi]\!]_\mathcal{E}\}$, (3) $[\![\langle \bar{a}\rangle\varphi]\!]_\mathcal{E} = \{u : \text{for some } v, u \xrightarrow{sl} v \text{ and } \neg(u \xrightarrow{a} v) \text{ and } v \in [\![\varphi]\!]_\mathcal{E}\}$. If φ is a closed formula, its satisfaction by u is independent of the environment. If u satisfies φ in this case, then we write $u \models \varphi$. If $IG(T)$ has root r, then T satisfies φ ($T \models \varphi$) iff $r \models \varphi$.

$\mu_\approx^w$-**calculus.** For reasoning on the model $IG^w(T)$, we use a fragment of $\mu_\approx$-calculus called $\mu_\approx^w$-calculus that does not contain the operator $\langle \bar{a}\rangle$, since in this case the same level predicate is not meaningful. If the root r of $IG^w(T)$ satisfies a closed $\mu_\approx^w$-calculus formula φ, then T satisfies φ (written $T \models \varphi$).

CTL≈ . As we shall see in Section 4, the full $\mu_\approx$-calculus over equivalence trees turns out to have an undecidable model checking problem[1]. Consequently,

---

[1] One may wonder if monadic second order logic (MSO) is of any interest in this context. It turns out that a single path equivalence relation suffices to encode the "same-level" predicate on trees studied in the literature [11]. This implies that model checking MSO on trees with path equivalences is undecidable even for single-agent systems.

we are interested in a simple fragment called CTL$\approx$ that is very similar to CTL interpreted on equivalence trees. Not only is this logic decidable, but it is also expressive enough for most of our illustrative examples.

Formulas of CTL$\approx$ are given by: $\varphi = p \mid \varphi_1 \vee \varphi_2 \mid \neg\varphi' \mid EX\,\varphi' \mid EI_a\,\varphi' \mid EI_{\bar{a}}\,\varphi' \mid \varphi_1\,EU\,\varphi_2 \mid EG\varphi'$, where $p \in P$ and $a \in A$ as before. Following CTL conventions, let us use the following abbreviations $EF\,\varphi$ and $AG\,\varphi$. We also write $AX\,\varphi$, $AI_a\,\varphi$ and $AI_{\bar{a}}\varphi$ as shorthand for $\neg EX\,\neg\varphi$, $\neg EI_a\,\neg\varphi$, and $\neg EI_{\bar{a}}\,\neg\varphi$. We define the semantics of CTL$\approx$ using a map $\Psi : \varphi \mapsto \psi$ that rewrites a CTL$\approx$ formula φ as a $\mu_{\approx}$-calculus formula ψ. The function Ψ is defined inductively in the standard way. We state the definition only for a few cases: $\Psi(EI_a\,\varphi') = \langle a \rangle \Psi(\varphi')$ and $\Psi(EI_{\bar{a}}\,\varphi') = \langle \bar{a} \rangle \Psi(\varphi')$. A tree T with path equivalences satisfies a CTL$\approx$ formula φ iff it satisfies $\Psi(\varphi)$.

CTL$\approx^w$. We also consider the logic CTL$\approx^w$ for reasoning on the model with weak path equivalences $IG^w(T)$. This logic does not contain the operator $EI_{\bar{a}}$, but otherwise is same as CTL$\approx$. Its semantics is defined on $IG^w(T)$.

Semantics on finite Kripke structures. We use finite Kripke structures to model finite-state systems. Formally, a Kripke structure K is a tuple $(Q, \to \subseteq Q \times Q, \lambda : Q \to 2^P, r)$, where Q is a finite set of states, $\to$ is a transition function, $\lambda : Q \to 2^P$ is a map labeling each state with the set of propositions, and $r \in Q$ is the initial state.

We want to define when a Kripke structure K satisfies a CTL$\approx$ (CTL$\approx^w$,$\mu_{\approx}$,$\mu_{\approx}^w$) formula φ. Note that it is not possible to define whether or not the formula holds in a particular state of K. The reason is that the equivalence relations are relations on paths in the structure, rather than on states of the structure. Thus, given a state s, it is not possible to determine which states are equivalent to s. This also implies that whether or not a given Kripke structure K satisfies φ can be defined inductively on the structure of φ on the tree unrolling of K. For a node in this tree, there is a unique path leading to it, so the set of equivalent nodes is well-defined. Given a Kripke structure K, let T_K be its tree unrolling. T_K can be seen as a tree with (weak) path equivalences (which are determined by the set of agents A). Then we define $K \models \varphi$ iff $T_K \models \varphi$.

Let us now see how logics on trees with path equivalences aid specification.

Example 1. Consider the game of Battleship. In our formulation, each player owns a grid whose cells are filled with 0's and 1's, and at each round, a player asks another player about the contents of a cell. A central requirement is that player a does not reveal information about the contents of a cell (i, j) at any time unless the opponent asks specifically for them. To see how this property may be unintentionally violated in an automated Battleship game, consider an implementation where rows in a's grid are represented as linked lists that a iterates through to answer a query about a cell. Now, if a is asked about an element in an empty row, it gives an answer immediately (as it has nothing to iterate over). If the row is non-empty, it must iterate through a non-empty list and spend more time "thinking". Thus, a's opponent may glean information about whether a row in a's board is nonempty by tracking the time a takes to answer a query.

We can write a requirement forbidding the above scenario in CTL≈ . Let propositions c_{ij} and ask_{ij} be true at points in a play respectively iff cell c_{ij} contains 1 and a receives a request to reveal the contents of cell (i, j). We omit the full definition of a-equivalence in this version; roughly, observables of a includes the requests a receives, the answers it gives, and a "silent proposition" τ that holds when a is "thinking". Now consider the CTL≈ property $\varphi = \neg(\neg ask_{ij} \, EU \, (AI_a \, c_{ij} \vee AI_a \, \neg c_{ij}))$, which asserts that there is no play with a node such that: (1) all behaviors a-equivalent to the play till this point lead to nodes where the content of (i, j) is the same, and (2) no explicit request for the contents of cell (i, j) is made by the opponent prior to this point. This ensures that the adversary cannot infer the contents of (i, j) by watching a's observables. On the contrary, in the case when $AI_a\varphi$ holds at any reachable node of the tree for some secret property φ, then an observer of a can infer the property φ by watching a's actions till that point. In other words, a *leaks* the secret φ.

Example 2. Logics on trees with path equivalences may be used to specify properties of systems where participants have partial information. Consider a Kripke structure representing a *blindfold reachability game* played by an agent a. At each round, an *active node* represents the current state of the game, and when a takes an action, a child of the current active node becomes the new active node. Because of partial information, however, a given action may cause different children of the current node to become active. We say that a has a winning strategy in this game if it can decide on a sequence of actions a priori, execute actions in it in succession, and no matter what actual path in the tree is taken, end in a node satisfying a target proposition p. Letting two paths be a-equivalent iff they agree on the sequence of actions of a, we find that a has a winning strategy in this game iff the tree satisfies the CTL≈ requirement $EF \, (AI_a \, p))$.

Now consider an *adaptive reachability game*, where a can choose actions to guide the game while it is in progress. Let some of the tree nodes be now labeled with a *control proposition* b. At each round, a is now able to pick, along with an action, one of the *control formulas* b and $\neg b$. At any given point, partial information may cause different children of the current node to become active; however, the new active node is guaranteed to satisfy the control formula chosen at the current round. Let us define a-equivalence as before. It can be shown that a has a strategy to reach a node satisfying a target proposition p iff the game tree satisfies the $\mu_\approx$-calculus formula $\varphi = \mu X.(p \vee [a][](b \wedge X) \vee [a][](\neg b \wedge X))$.

Example 3. In various protocols involving multiple agents, a need for properties involving secrecy and time arises often. For example in the case of auction protocols (studied in security literature, see e.g. [4]), the following property is important. Agent a's bid is not revealed before the auctioneer reveals all the bids. In order to illustrate how such requirements can be expressed in our logic, we present the following formula, which states that agent a does not reveal p (a secret) before agent b reveals q: $\varphi = \neg((EI_b \, q \wedge EI_b \, \neg q) \, EU \, (AI_a \, p \vee AI_a \, \neg p))$. The formula expresses it is not the case that: b does not reveal q ($EI_b \, q \wedge EI_b \, \neg q$) until a reveals p ($AI_a \, p \vee AI_a \, \neg p$). Now let us consider agents who make only time-insensitive observations, i.e. ones who cannot tell that an agent has performed an operation if the observables have not changed. This can be modeled using the weak-equivalence graph. The correctness of the protocol can thus be established by model checking the formula φ on $IG^w(T)$.

Example 4. Consider a system that is being observed by a low-security observer. We define low-security (low) and high-security (high) variables, where low variables are visible to the observer and high variables are not. We now show how to specify in CTL$\approx$ the following requirement R: " The sequence of valuations of the low variables is the same along all execution paths." Consider for example the case when there is a secret input, i.e. an input to a high variable. If the above requirement R is satisfied, the observer cannot infer any property of the secret input, since there cannot be any flow of information from the high input to low variables. (Note however that the requirement R is even stronger, it prevents e.g. inputs to low variables.)

The values of variables are encoded by propositions from a set P. We have one proposition for every bit of every variable. We will use only one agent a. The subset of propositions observable by the agent is the set of all those propositions that encode low variables. The requirement R is satisfied iff the following CTL$\approx$ formula holds: $AG\,AI_{\bar{a}}\,false$. This property says that for each node, there does *not* exist an a-nonequivalent node at the same level of the execution tree. This implies that all nodes at the same level are a-equivalent, and therefore have the same valuations of low variables. Notice that this property cannot be captured without the $AI_{\bar{a}}$ operator, since we need to refer to all nodes at the same level.

4   Model Checking

In this section we present a model checking algorithm for CTL$\approx$ and the $\mu_{\approx}$-calculus. We are given a finite state system, such as a program or a protocol and a CTL$\approx$ formula φ. We want to check whether the system satisfies the formula.

Recall that $K \models \varphi$ is defined in terms of an infinite state structure. However, we can still apply model checking on a finite state system. This is because for a given CTL$\approx$ formula φ and a given Kripke structure K, we can find a finite model $FM^\varphi(K)$ such that $FM^\varphi(K) \models \varphi$ iff $T_K \models \varphi$. Let A_φ be the set of agents that appear in φ.

The *nesting depth* of a CTL$\approx$ formula φ is intuitively the number of nestings between equivalence operators EI_a, $EI_{\bar{a}}$. The only exception is the nesting of EI_a operators for the same agent, which does not contribute to nesting depth. For example, the nesting depth of $EI_a\,p$ is 1, $(EI_a\,p)\,EU\,(EI_b\,r)$ is also 1, while for $EI_a\,EI_{\bar{a}}\,p$ it is 2. On the other hand, $EI_a\,EI_a\,p$ and $EI_a\,(\varphi_1\,EU\,EI_a\,\varphi_2)$ have a nesting depth of 1. The nesting depth of φ will be denoted by $nd(\varphi)$. Formally, the nesting depth is defined as follows. We will use an auxiliary function that takes two parameters: $nd(\varphi, a)$, where a is an agent. Let c be an agent that does not appear in φ. The function $nd(\varphi, a)$ is then defined as follows: (1) $nd(\varphi, a) = 0$ if $\varphi = p$, (2) $nd(\varphi, a) = nd(\varphi_1)$ if $\varphi = \neg(\varphi_1), EX\,\varphi_1, EI_a\,\varphi_1, EG\,\varphi_1$, (3) $nd(\varphi, a) = \max(nd(\varphi_1, a), nd(\varphi_2, a))$ if $\varphi = \varphi_1 \vee \varphi_2, \varphi_1\,EU\,\varphi_2$, (4) $nd(\varphi, a) =$

$nd(\varphi_1, b) + 1$ if $\varphi = EI_b \varphi_1$ where $b \neq a$, (5) $nd(\varphi, a) = nd(\varphi_1, c) + 1$ if $\varphi = EI_{\bar{a}} \varphi_1$. $nd(\varphi)$ can then be defined as $nd(\varphi, c)$.

The complexity of model checking of a CTL$\approx$ formula φ grows rapidly with the nesting depth of φ. However, as we show, the nesting of EI_a operators for the same agent does not contribute to the growth in complexity of the problem. This distinction is especially important in the case of the $\mu_\approx$-calculus, where the formulas with unbounded nesting depth are undecidable in general. However, formulas where only $\langle a \rangle$ operators for the same agent are nested unboundedly are in a decidable (EXPTIME-complete) fragment. This fragment allows e.g. specification of adaptive partial-information games (see Section 3).

Finite model $FM^\varphi(K)$. We first give the intuition behind the construction of the finite state model $FM^\varphi(K)$. The states of this model carry enough information so that the semantics of CTL$\approx$ formulas can be defined on these states in such a way that $FM^\varphi(K) \models \varphi$ iff $T_K \models \varphi$. Consider the case when φ is a CTL formula. To determine whether φ holds at a node s of T_K, we only need to know to which state of K the node s corresponds, because if two nodes in T_K correspond to the same state of K, they satisfy the same CTL formulas. Now consider $\varphi \equiv EI_a \varphi_1$, where φ_1 is a CTL formula. Let S be the set of a-equivalent nodes of T_K. In order to determine whether $EI_a\varphi_1$ holds at s, one needs to know to which state of K the node s corresponds and to which states of K the nodes in S correspond. The amount of information needed is thus finite, and can be stored as a pair (s, U) such that $s \in Q, U \subseteq Q$, where Q is the set of states of K. We also need to know how to update this information across transitions. There are two key ideas: First, the transition relation $(s, U) \rightarrow (t, V)$ on these pairs can be computed locally - the set of nodes V equivalent to t will be all those nodes v that have the same observation as t and that have predecessors equivalent to s, i.e. stored in U. Second, we can also define an a-transition ($\xrightarrow{a}$) on these tuples locally, since the tuple stores the set of nodes that are mutually a-equivalent. The transition is thus defined as follows: $(s, U) \xrightarrow{a} (t, U)$ for $t \in U$.

This construction lends itself to generalization in three ways: we can have multiple agents, we can store information needed for $\bar{a}$ transitions, and we can keep enough information to allow nesting of equivalence and nonequivalence operators. This leads to a definition of the finite-state model of $FM^\varphi(K)$. Note that in order to allow for nesting of equivalence operators, it is not enough to store only a set of a-equivalent nodes U for all agents a. In fact, for each node in U, we need to store the set of its b-equivalent nodes (where $b \neq a$), etc. We store this information as a tree whose nodes are labeled by states of K. Formally, we define $FM^\varphi(K)$ as follows:

States of $FM^\varphi(K)$: A state W of $FM^\varphi(K)$ is a tree of depth at most $nd(\varphi)$. The vertices of these trees are labeled by states of K and edges are labeled by a or $\bar{a}$, where a is in A_φ. We require that if a subtree is an a-child of its parent, then it itself does not have a-children. For all nodes in W, we require that no two of its a-children are isomorphic (similarly for $\bar{a}$-children). The state W is labeled by the same propositions as its root in the original Kripke structure K.

The intuition behind the definition is simple: a node s in T_K corresponds to a state W, if s is a root of W, the a-equivalent nodes of s correspond to a-children of W and this correspondence continues to depth $nd(\varphi)$. Such a state thus carries enough information to allow checking whether or not φ of nesting depth $nd(\varphi)$ holds. An example of a state W is in Figure 2. It stores the information about a node s, which has two a-equivalent nodes u and v, one a-nonequivalent node t and one b-equivalent node x.

If a subtree rooted at u is an a-child of its parent s, it does not need to have a-children, since the nodes that are a-equivalent to u are a-equivalent to s., thus we do not need to replicate these nodes as children of u. In fact, we do not replicate this information. The main reason is that for a subtree of depth d, the a-siblings store more information (they are trees of depths (at most) d) than would a-children - subtrees of depth (at most) $d - 1$. This is what allows arbitrary nesting of EI_a (or $\langle a \rangle$) operators for the same agent a.

We can bound the number of states in $FM^\varphi(K)$. To state an upper bound, we will use the following function exp: $\exp(a, b, 0) = a$, $\exp(a, b, n + 1) = a * b * 2^{\exp(a,b,n)}$. Considering how a state is constructed (it does not have isomorphic a-children), we can conclude that $FM^\varphi(K)$ has less than $\exp(|K|, 2*|A_\varphi|, nd(\varphi))$ states.

Transition relation of $FM^\varphi(K)$: We explained above how a transition function is determined locally for tuples of the form (s, U) representing the node and a set of its a-equivalent nodes. The construction can be generalized to states of $FM^\varphi(K)$. We abuse the notation slightly and use the same notation for transition relations $\rightarrow, \overset{a}{\rightarrow}, \overset{\bar{a}}{\rightarrow}$ as is used in T_K. Given a state W, $root(W)$ refers to its root (a node in K). a-child of W refers to the tree rooted at a node that is an a-child of the root of W. For a state W of depth n, transition relation $\rightarrow$ is defined recursively on n.

- $n = 0$: Trees W and W' are of depth 0, i.e. they contain only a root without any children. $W \rightarrow W'$ if $root(W) \rightarrow root(W')$ in the Kripke structure K.
- $n = k + 1$: $W \rightarrow W'$ iff $root(W) \rightarrow root(W')$ in K and
  - V is an a-child of W' iff $Obs_a(root(W')) = Obs_a(root(V))$ and there exists an a-child U of W, such that $U \rightarrow V$
  - V is an $\bar{a}$-child of W' iff either there exists an $\bar{a}$-child U of W, such that $U \rightarrow V$ or there exists an a-child U', such that $U' \rightarrow V$ and $Obs_a(root(W')) \neq Obs_a(root(V))$.

An example of a transition $W \rightarrow W'$ transition in $FM^\varphi(K)$ is in Figure 2. The figure captures the following situation: There is a transition in K from s (the root of W) to s', and from the a-equivalent node u to u' and the node u' is a-equivalent to s' (similarly for the b-equivalent node x). The node v is a-equivalent to s and it has a transition to v' in K. However, v' is not a-equivalent to s'. The node t is non-equivalent to s, thus its successor t' will be nonequivalent to s'. The subtrees T_u, T_v, T_t, T_x need to be transformed in a similar way.

We defined the structure $FM^\varphi(K)$ in order to keep information about a-equivalent nodes locally. Now we use this information to define a-transitions

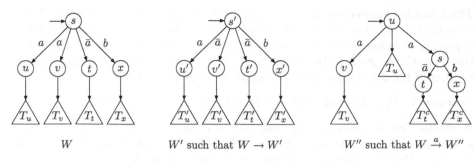

Fig. 2. States and transitions of $FM^\varphi(K)$

(transitions of the form $W \xrightarrow{a} W'$). The idea is that on an a-transition, we go from a state W to a state W' represented by an a-child of W. In general, this transition leads from a tree of depth n to a tree with depth $n-1$ (this is true for b-children where $b \neq a$ and all ($\bar{a}$)-children). However, for a-children we leverage the fact that a-children of a parent are mutually equivalent, which enables us to construct a tree such that the depth of a-children does not decrease. Transition relations $\xrightarrow{a}, \xrightarrow{\bar{a}}$ are defined as follows:

- $W \xrightarrow{a} W'$ iff W' can be constructed as follows: Let V be an a-child of W. Let V' be V with other a-children of W as a-children (note that V did not have a-children). Let V'' be W without all the a-children, and we remove the leaves for all the other children (to ensure that the depth of W' is smaller or equal to $nd(\varphi)$). Finally, let W' be V' with V'' as an a-child.
- $W \xrightarrow{\bar{a}} W'$ if W' is a $\bar{a}$-child of W

An example of an $\xrightarrow{a}$ transition in $FM^\varphi(K)$ $W \xrightarrow{a} W''$ is in Figure 2. The idea is that W'' will be a subtree rooted at an a-child of s, which in this case is the subtree rooted at u. However, as explained above, we add as a-children subtrees rooted at a-siblings of u (in this case, the subtree rooted at v) and the subtree rooted at the parent s and its subtrees (except the a-children). We modify these subtrees (T_t^c and T_x^c in the figure) by removing the leaves.

CTL$\approx$. We want to prove that the finite state model $FM^\varphi(K)$ is adequate for evaluating the formula φ, i.e. that for each node s of T_K there is a corresponding state W in $FM^\varphi(K)$, such that φ holds in s iff it holds in W. In order to state this claim, we need to define the correspondence between the states of T_K and $FM^\varphi(K)$. We will do so using a family of functions Ω^n. Each Ω^n is a function that relates a node in T_K to a node of $FM^\varphi(K)$. It is defined recursively as follows:

- $n = 0$: $\Omega^0(u)$ is a tree of depth 0, whose root is u.
- $n = k+1$: $\Omega^{k+1}(u) = W$ iff W can be constructed as follows: $root(W) = u$. Consider the set S of all a-equivalent nodes of u. For every node v in this set, compute $V = \Omega^k(v)$. Let V' be V without a-children. Add V' as an a-child to W. For every node r at the same depth as u, that is not a-equivalent to u, add $R = \Omega^k(r)$ as an $\bar{a}$-child to W.

The following lemma asserts that the construction of $FM^\varphi(K)$ is correct. It implies that model checking of CTL$\approx$ formula φ can be performed on $FM^\varphi(K)$. It is proven by induction on the nesting depth of the formula. However, the inductive hypothesis needs to be strengthened to account for the fact that arbitrary nesting of the EI_a operator for the same agent is allowed.

Lemma 1. $T_K, s \models \varphi$ iff $FM^\varphi(K), \Omega^n(s) \models \varphi$, where $n = nd(\varphi)$

A nesting-free formula is a formula with nesting depth at most 1. Thus it is a formula that can refer to operators EI_a, $EI_{\bar{a}}$ for different agents, but it can nest only the EI_a operators for the same agent. All of the example properties mentioned in Section 3 are expressed in this fragment.

Theorem 1. *The model checking problem for nesting-free formulas of CTL$\approx$ is PSPACE-complete.*

Proof. (Sketch) We show that the problem is in PSPACE using Lemma 1. The lemma shows that it is possible to reduce CTL$\approx$ model checking to CTL model checking on an exponentially larger structure $FM^\varphi(K)$, whose number of states is less than $|K| * 2 * |A| * 2^{|K|}$. Note however, that it is not necessary to construct the structure ahead of time, since the transition function can be computed locally. Thus the non-deterministic model checking algorithm for CTL [10] that uses only logarithmic space in terms of the size of the structure can be used. Therefore the model checking problem for nesting-free formulas is in PSPACE. The lower bound is obtained by reduction from equivalence checking of nondeterministic finite automata.   □

The reasoning that shows that the model checking for nesting-free formulas is in PSPACE can be extended to obtain the following result.

Theorem 2. *For a fixed CTL$\approx$ formula φ such that $nd(\varphi) \geq 2$, the model checking problem is decidable in space polynomial in $exp(|K|, 2 * |A|, nd(\varphi) - 1)$.*

In order to obtain a lower bound for the model checking problem for CTL$\approx$ formulas, we can encode Shilov and Garanina's Act-CTL-K_n [15] in CTL$\approx$ and use the fact that model checking for Act-CTL-K_n has a nonelementary lower bound. Act-CTL-K_n is a logic similar to CTL with actions augmented with knowledge operators that are given the perfect-recall semantics, i.e. an agent remembers the whole sequence of its past states. CTL with actions can be encoded into CTL in a standard way. If we define the equivalence relation $\approx_a$ to be such that two paths (sequences of the multiagent system) are equivalent iff the corresponding sequences of states of agent a are the same, then the knowledge operator K_i corresponding to agent a can be encoded as follows: $K_i\varphi = \neg EI_a \neg \varphi$. Therefore, defining the function $Tower(n, k)$ as $Tower(n, 1) = n$ and $Tower(n, k + 1) = 2^{Tower(n,k)}$, we have:

Theorem 3. *For every algorithm $\mathcal{A}$ for the model checking problem of CTL$\approx$, and each $i \geq 1$, there is a Kripke structure K with n states and a CTL$\approx$ formula φ such that $\mathcal{A}$ runs on K and φ in time $\Omega(Tower(n, i))$.*

$\mu_\approx$-**calculus** We now consider the model checking problem for $\mu_\approx$-calculus formulas on trees with path equivalences. In general, this problem is undecidable. We can prove it by encoding Shilov and Garanina's μ-calculus of knowledge - (μPLK_n)[15]. This logic can be encoded in $\mu_\approx$-calculus over trees with path equivalences in a similar way as as Act-CTL-K_n was encoded to CTL$\approx$. Since the model checking problem for μPLK_n is undecidable, we have:

Theorem 4. *The model checking problem for the $\mu_\approx$-calculus is undecidable.*

However, we identify a decidable fragment of the $\mu_\approx$-calculus as follows. Define the set $Subf(\varphi)$ of subformulas of a formula φ inductively as: (1) for $\varphi = p$ or $\neg p$, $Subf(\varphi) = \{\varphi\}$; (2) if φ equals $\varphi_1 \vee \varphi_2$ or $\varphi_1 \wedge \varphi_2$, then $Subf(\varphi) = \{\varphi\} \cup Subf(\varphi_1) \cup Subf(\varphi_2)$; (3) if φ equals $\langle\rangle\varphi'$, $[\ ]\varphi'$, $\langle a\rangle\varphi'$ or $[a]\varphi'$, for arbitrary a, we have $Subf(\varphi) = Subf(\varphi')$; and (4) for $\varphi = \mu X.\varphi'$ or $\nu X.\varphi'$, we have $Subf(\varphi) = \{X\} \cup Subf(\varphi')$. Now, let us only consider "well-named" formulas, i.e., closed formulas φ where for each variable X appearing in φ, there is a unique binding formula $\mu X.\varphi'$ or $\nu X.\varphi'$ in $Subf(\varphi)$ such that $X \in Subf(\varphi')$. As for the μ-calculus, every closed $\mu_\approx$-calculus formula can be rewritten in a well-named form. Now construct the graph G_φ with node set $Subf(\varphi)$ and edges as below:

1. for each node φ of the form $\langle\rangle\varphi'$, $[\ ]\varphi'$, $\langle a\rangle\varphi'$, $[a]\varphi'$, $\mu X.\varphi'$, or $\nu X.\varphi'$, add an edge from φ to φ'.
2. for each node X, where $X \in Var$, add an edge from X to the unique subformula of the form $\mu X.\varphi'$ or $\nu X.\varphi'$ that binds it.

Intuitively, G_φ captures the operational semantics of φ. If there is a path from φ' to φ'' in $G_{\varphi'}$, then evaluation of φ' requires the evaluation of φ'' (note that to evaluate $\varphi' = X$, we must recursively evaluate the formula φ'' binding X).

A formula is said to be a-modal (resp. $\bar{a}$-modal) if it is of the form $\langle a\rangle\varphi$ or $[a]\varphi$ (resp. $\langle\bar{a}\rangle\varphi$ or $[\bar{a}]\varphi$). Let $\pi = \psi_1\psi_2\ldots\psi_m$ be a path in G_φ. The *nesting distance* of π is k, where k is the length of the maximum subsequence $\pi' = \psi_1'\psi_2'\ldots\psi_k'$ in π such that: (1) each ψ_i' is an a-modal formula for some agent a; and (2) for each i, if ψ_i' is a-modal and ψ_{i+1}' is a'-modal, then $a \neq a'$. A formula φ has *nesting depth* k if k is the least upper bound on the nesting distance of any path in G_φ. Note that such a k may not exist—if it does, then φ is said to have a *bounded* nesting depth. For instance, the formula $\varphi_1 = \nu X.([a_1]\langle a_2\rangle p \wedge \langle a_1\rangle[\ ][a_1]X)$ is bounded, while $\varphi_2 = \mu X.(p \vee \langle\rangle[a_1]\langle a_2\rangle X)$ is not.

Using an argument similar to that for CTL$\approx$ and using the same structure $FM^\varphi(K)$ for formulas with nesting depth k, we can obtain a non-elementary model checking procedure for the fragment of the $\mu_\approx$-calculus with bounded nesting depth. In addition, this fragment can easily encode CTL$\approx$, so that it is non-elementary-hard. Then:

Theorem 5. *The model checking problem for a Kripke structure K and a $\mu_\approx$-calculus formula φ with nesting depth k is solvable in time $exp(|K|, 2*|A|, k)$. Also, for every algorithm $\mathcal{A}$ for this problem and every $i \geq 1$, there is a Kripke structure K with n states and a formula φ such that $\mathcal{A}$ runs on K and φ in time $\Omega(Tower(n, i))$.*

Now consider the model checking problem for *nesting-free formulas*, i.e., formulas with nesting depth 1. Recall that such formulas can express all properties involving a single agent. Now, given a Kripke structure K and a set of agents A, construct the structure $FM^\varphi(K)$ in exponential time; we can interpret nesting-free $\mu_\approx$-calculus formulas on $FM^\varphi(K)$ using the semantics of the classical μ-calculus. As above, we can show that K satisfies a nesting-free formula φ iff $FM^\varphi(K)$ satisfies φ.

For a lower bound, we turn to the model of *space-bounded private alternating Turing machines* introduced by Reif [13]. Let PALOGSPACE be the class of languages recognized by such machines using logarithmic space—Reif shows that PALOGSPACE = EXPTIME. Now recall that the alternation-free modal μ-calculus is complete for PTIME and consequently alternating LOGSPACE [10]. Augmenting this result, and encoding private tapes using the path equivalence relation induced by a single agent, we can reduce recognition by a PALOGSPACE-machine to the model checking problem for an alternation-free, single-agent $\mu_\approx$-calculus formula. The latter problem is thus EXPTIME-hard.

Theorem 6. *Model checking nesting-free $\mu_\approx$-calculus formulas is EXPTIME-complete. Model checking single-agent, alternation-free $\mu_\approx$-calculus formulas is EXPTIME-hard.*

Weak-equivalence graphs We now turn our attention to the model-checking problem on weak-equivalence graphs. The solution proceeds via the construction of $FM_w^\varphi(K)$, a finite state Kripke structure analogical to $FM^\varphi(K)$. The model checking algorithms are again based on state space exploration on the finite state model $FM_w^\varphi(K)$. For the model checking problem for CTL$\approx^w$ formulas, as well as for $\mu_\approx^w$ formulas, the same upper and lower bounds are obtained as those above for CTL$\approx$ and $\mu_\approx$ formulas.

5 Related Work

In some aspects, the logics we introduced are related to logic of knowledge [8]. The main semantic difference is that logics of knowledge are concerned about what an agent knows, whereas in the logics presented in this paper we are concerned about what an agent has revealed. However, from an intuitive point of view, it might be possible to capture what an agent a reveals by adding one "observer agent", who would observe a and record its observations (e.g. outputs and inputs of a) and then ask about the knowledge of this observer agent. However, in a finite state setting under the standard semantics for knowledge operators (the semantics is defined in terms of equivalence relations on states of the Kripke structure, not the paths), this is not possible.

The idea of introducing an observer agent would work in the case of *perfect recall* semantics [8], i.e. when an agent remembers the sequence of its past states. In this case, our equivalence operator $EI_a\varphi$ can be translated as $\neg K_{Obs_a}\neg\varphi$, where Obs_a is the agent introduced to record the observable actions of a. Note however, that the nonequivalence operator $EI_{\bar{a}}\varphi$ cannot be expressed in logic of knowledge with perfect recall, because this logic can express properties that some or all equivalent nodes have and there is no way to refer to nonequivalent nodes. In the setting of perfect recall semantics, van der Meyden and Shilov [17] have considered model checking of LTL with knowledge operators and Shilov and Garanina [15] consider model checking of CTL and μ-calculus with knowledge operators. The construction of our finite-state model is similar to "k-trees" used in these papers. However, note that the notions of nesting depths are different, and that our notion yields better complexity bounds. (In [16], a notion of nesting depth similar to ours is used, in a context without temporal operators). We argue that our logics are more suitable for specifying secrecy and information flow properties than logics of knowledge. First, we showed that it is possible to specify information flow properties using standard tree logics (CTL, μ-calculus), provided that we enrich the tree model with path equivalences. This approach can be readily extended to other tree logics, such as ATL [2]. Second, we are also able to model information flow properties directly, without the need to introduce an observer agent for each agent in the original system. Third, some information flow properties can be expressed naturally using the $EI_{\bar{a}}$ operator. This is not possible in logic of knowledge.

For $\mu_{\approx}$-calculus, we have identified an EXPTIME-complete fragment in which it is possible to specify partial-information adaptive games. For simplicity, we presented our approach using Kripke structures as a basic model. However, there are other models, such as alternating transition systems (see [2]), which are better suited for modeling games. We believe our results can be easily lifted to ATSs. Note that partial information games have also been studied in the context of ATL, but were proven undecidable for multiple players.

6 Conclusion

We have introduced a branching-time logics on trees with path equivalences. We have shown that extending the execution tree by adding equivalence (or "jump") edges allows us to specify partial information games and information flow properties in tree logics (the $\mu_{\approx}$-calculus and CTL$\approx$). We have presented a model checking algorithm for these logics, and identified fragments where the problem has reasonable complexity (PSPACE for the case of the nesting-free fragment of CTL$\approx$).

The work presented in this paper can be extended in several directions. We plan to investigate the extension of the logics on trees with path equivalences with boolean edge formulas (a generalization of $\langle a \rangle$ and $\langle \bar{a} \rangle$ operators). Given results presented in this paper, we expect that only a (small) fragment of this generalization will be decidable. However, there are tractable fragments not explored in this paper in which one can express other information flow properties, such as noninterference and its generalizations. Another interesting direction is to investigate automata on trees with path equivalences. We would also like to find an efficient way of implementing the model checking algorithm presented in Section 4, such as (SAT-based) bounded model checking. We plan to identify classes of applications where this implementation would prove useful and where the specifications involving multiple agents, information flow, and time are needed. Good candidates include cryptographic protocols and auction protocols. Furthermore, we would like to investigate the possibilities of extending this work for verifying information-flow properties for infinite-state systems, e.g. via abstractions that preserve information-flow properties.

References

1. R. Alur, P. Černý, and S. Zdancewic. Preserving secrecy under refinement. In *Proc. of ICALP '06*, pages 107–118, 2006.
2. R. Alur, T. Henzinger, and O. Kupferman. Alternating-time temporal logic. *Journal of the ACM*, 49(5):1–42, 2002.
3. J. Burch, E. Clarke, D. Dill, L. Hwang, and K. McMillan. Symbolic model checking: 10^{20} states and beyond. *Information and Computation*, 98(2):142–170, 1992.
4. S. Chong and A. Myers. Decentralized robustness. In *Proc. of CSFW'02*, pages 242–256, 2006.
5. A. Cimatti, E. Clarke, E. Giunchiglia, F. Giunchiglia, M. Pistore, M. Roveri, R. Sebastiani, and A. Tacchella. NuSMV Version 2: An OpenSource Tool for Symbolic Model Checking. In *Proc. of CAV'02*, pages 359–364, 2002.
6. E. Clarke and E. Emerson. Design and synthesis of synchronization skeletons using branching time temporal logic. In *Proc. Workshop on Logic of Programs*, pages 52–71, 1981.
7. H. Comon, M. Dauchet, R. Gilleron, F. Jacquemard, D. Lugiez, S. Tison, and M. Tommasi. Tree automata techniques and applications. Available on: http://www.grappa.univ-lille3.fr/tata, 1997.
8. R. Fagin, J. Halpern, Y. Moses, and M. Vardi. *Reasoning About Knowledge*. MIT Press, Cambridge, MA, USA, 1995.
9. D. Kozen. Results on the propositional μ-calculus. *Theoretical Computer Science*, 27:333–354, 1983.
10. O. Kupferman, M. Vardi, and P. Wolper. An automata-theoretic approach to branching-time model checking. *Journal of the ACM*, 47(2):312–360, 2000.
11. H. Lauchli and Ch. Savioz. Monadic second order definable relations on the binary tree. *J. Symb. Log.*, 52(1):219–226, 1987.
12. A. Pnueli. The temporal logic of programs. In *Proceedings of the 18th IEEE Symposium on Foundations of Computer Science*, pages 46–77, 1977.
13. J. Reif. Universal games of incomplete information. In *Proc. of STOC '79*, pages 288–308, 1979.
14. F. Schneider, editor. *Trust in Cyberspace*. National Academy Press, 1999.
15. N. Shilov and N. Garanina. Model checking knowledge and fixpoints. In *Proc. of FICS'02*, pages 25–39, 2002.
16. R. van der Meyden. Common knowledge and update in finite environments. *Information and Computation*, 140(2):115–157, 1998.
17. R. van der Meyden and N. Shilov. Model checking knowledge and time in systems with perfect recall. In *Proc. of FSTTCS'99*, pages 432–445, 1999.

UPPAAL/DMC – Abstraction-Based Heuristics for Directed Model Checking

Sebastian Kupferschmid[1], Klaus Dräger[2], Jörg Hoffmann[3], Bernd Finkbeiner[2],
Henning Dierks[4], Andreas Podelski[1], and Gerd Behrmann[5]

[1] University of Freiburg, Germany
{kupfersc,podelski}@informatik.uni-freiburg.de
[2] Universität des Saarlandes, Saarbrücken, Germany
{draeger,finkbeiner}@cs.uni-sb.de
[3] Digital Enterprise Research Institute, Innsbruck, Austria
joerg.hoffmann@deri.org
[4] OFFIS, Oldenburg, Germany
dierks@offis.de
[5] Aalborg University, Denmark
behrmann@cs.aau.dk

Abstract. UPPAAL/DMC is an extension of UPPAAL which provides generic heuristics for directed model checking. In this approach, the traversal of the state space is guided by a heuristic function which estimates the distance of a search state to the nearest error state. Our tool combines two recent approaches to design such estimation functions. Both are based on computing an abstraction of the system and using the error distance in this abstraction as the heuristic value. The abstractions, and thus the heuristic functions, are generated fully automatically and do not need any additional user input. UPPAAL/DMC needs less time and memory to find shorter error paths than UPPAAL's standard search methods.

1 Introduction

UPPAAL/DMC is a tool that accelerates the detection of error states by using the directed model checking approach [4,5]. Directed model checking tackles the state explosion problem by using a *heuristic function* to influence the *order* in which the search states are explored. A heuristic function h is a function that maps states to integers, estimating the state's distance to the nearest error state. The search then gives preference to states with lower h value. There are many different ways of doing the latter, all of which we consider the wide-spread method called *greedy search* [8]. There, search nodes are explored in ascending order of their heuristic values. Our empirical results show that this can drastically reduce memory consumption, runtime, and error path length.

Our tool combines two recent approaches to design heuristic functions. Both are based on defining an abstraction of the problem at hand, and taking the heuristic value to be the length of an abstract solution. It is important to note that both techniques are *fully automatic*, i.e., no user intervention is needed to generate the heuristic function. UPPAAL has a built-in heuristic mode, but the specification of the heuristic is entirely up to the user. Inventing a useful heuristic is a tedious job: it requires expert knowledge and a huge amount of time.

O. Grumberg and M. Huth (Eds.): TACAS 2007, LNCS 4424, pp. 679–682, 2007.
© Springer-Verlag Berlin Heidelberg 2007

2 Heuristics

The next two sections give a brief overview of the abstractions used to build our heuristics, and how heuristic values are assigned to search states.

2.1 Monotonicity Abstraction

Our first heuristic [7] adapts a technique from AI Planning, namely *ignoring delete lists* [1]. The idea of this abstraction is based on the simplifying assumption that *every state variable, once it obtained a value, keeps that value forever*. I.e., the value of a variable is no longer an element, but a *subset* of its domain. This subset grows monotonically over transition applications – hence the name of the abstraction.

When applying the monotonicity abstraction to a system of timed automata, then each automaton will (potentially) be in several locations in a state. The system's integer variables will have several possible values in a state. So far clocks are not included in the computation of heuristic values. If we included clocks in the obvious way, every guard or invariant involving a clock would be immediately satisfied. The reason for this is that clock value sets quickly subsume all possible time points.

Our heuristic h^{ma} assigns to each state encountered during search a heuristic value by solving an abstract problem. Such an abstract problem is obtained by applying the monotonicity abstraction to the current state. The length of a solution found in this abstraction is then used as the heuristic estimate for the state's distance to the nearest error state. In a nutshell, an abstract solution is computed by iteratively applying all enabled transitions to the initial abstract state (the state for which we want to estimate the distance), until either the enlarged state subsumes an error state, or a fixpoint is reached. In the former case, an abstract solution can be extracted by backtracking through the state enlargement steps. In case of reaching a fixpoint, we can exclude this state from further exploration: the monotonicity abstraction induces an over-approximation, i.e. so if there is no abstract error path, then there is no real one either.

2.2 Automata-Theoretic Abstraction

The second heuristic [3] aims at a close representation of the process synchronization required to reach the error. Each process is represented as a finite-state automaton. The heuristic h^{aa} estimates the error distance $d(s)$ of a system state s as the error distance of the corresponding abstract state $\alpha(s)$ in an abstraction that approximates the full product of all process automata. The approximation of the product of a set of automata is computed incrementally by repeatedly selecting two automata from the current set and replacing them with an abstraction of their product. To avoid state space explosion, the size of these intermediate abstractions is limited by a preset bound N: to reach a reduction to N states, the abstraction first merges bisimilar states and then states whose error distance is already high in the partial product. In this way, the precision of the heuristic is guaranteed to be high in close proximity to the error, and can, by setting N, be fine-tuned for states further away from the error. In our experiments, fairly low values of N, such as $N = 100$, already significantly speed up the search for the error, and therefore represent a good trade-off between cost and precision.

3   Results

We compare the performance of UPPAAL/DMC's[1] greedy search and UPPAAL's randomized depth first search (rDF), which is UPPAAL's most efficient standard search method across many examples. The results for rDF in Table 1 are averaged over 10 runs. The C_i examples stem from an industrial case study called "Single-tracked Line Segment" [6] and the M_i examples come from another case study, namely "Mutual Exclusion" [2]. An error state was made reachable by increasing an upper time bound in each example.

The results in Table 1 clearly demonstrate the potential of our heuristics. The heuristic searches consistently find the error paths much faster. Due to the reduced search space size and memory requirements, they can solve all problems. At the same time, they find, by orders of magnitude, *much* shorter error paths in *all* cases.

Table 1. Experimental results of UPPAAL's rDF and UPPAAL/DMC's greedy search with h^{ma} and h^{aa}. The results are computed on an Intel Xeon with 3 Ghz and 4 GB of RAM. Dashes indicate out of memory.

Exp	runtime in s			explored states			memory in MB			trace length		
	rDF	h^{ma}	h^{aa}	rDF	h^{ma}	h^{aa}	rDF	h^{ma}	h^{aa}	rDF	h^{ma}	h^{aa}
M_1	0.8	0.1	0.2	29607	5656	12780	7	1	11	1072	169	74
M_2	3.1	0.3	0.9	118341	30742	46337	10	11	11	3875	431	190
M_3	2.8	0.2	0.8	102883	18431	42414	9	10	11	3727	231	92
M_4	12.7	0.8	1.9	543238	76785	126306	22	13	14	15K	731	105
C_1	0.8	0.2	0.5	25219	2339	810	7	9	11	1065	95	191
C_2	1.0	0.3	1.0	65388	5090	2620	8	10	19	875	86	206
C_3	1.1	0.5	1.1	85940	6681	2760	10	10	19	760	109	198
C_4	8.4	2.5	1.8	892327	40147	25206	43	11	23	1644	125	297
C_5	72.4	13.2	4.0	8.0e+6	237600	155669	295	21	28	2425	393	350
C_6	–	10.1	14.9	–	207845	1.2e+6	–	20	67	–	309	404
C_7	–	169.0	162.4	–	2.7e+7	1.3e+7	–	595	676	–	1506	672
C_8	–	14.5	155.3	–	331733	1.2e+7	–	23	672	–	686	2210
C_9	–	1198.0	1046.0	–	1.3e+8	3.6e+7	–	2.5G	1.6G	–	18K	1020

Other heuristics, proposed by Edelkamp et al. [4,5] in the context of SPIN are based on graph distances. The underlying abstraction of these heuristics preserves only edges and locations of an automata system. For an automaton a let $d(a)$ be the distance of a's start location to its target location. Then, the h_{max}^{gd} heuristic is defined as $\max_a d(a)$. The h_{sum}^{gd} heuristic is defined as $\sum_a d(a)$.

Note that h_{max}^{gd} and h_{sum}^{gd} are rather crude approximations of the systems semantics. For example, they completely ignore variables and synchronization. In contrast, the

---

[1] Two different versions of UPPAAL/DMC (both Linux executables) are available under
http://www.informatik.uni-freiburg.de/~kupfersc/uppaal_dmc/. One
is optimized for Intel Pentium 4 processors, the other one was compiled with default optimization. The page also provides a short description of the used benchmarks, and *all* used model and query files.

h^{ma} and h^{aa} heuristics do *not* do this. Our approximations are more costly, i.e. one call of h^{ma} or h^{aa} takes more runtime than one call of h^{gd}_{max} or h^{gd}_{sum}. The additional effort typically pays off: for example, in the case studies shown in Table 1, greedy search with $\max_a d(a)$ and $\sum_a d(a)$ performs only slightly better than rDF, and much worse than our heuristics; e.g. it cannot solve any of C_6, C_7, C_8, and C_9.

4   Outlook

The most important piece of future work is to explore the value of our tool in the abstraction refinement life cycle. The basic idea is to use heuristics to address the intermediate iterations where (spurious) errors still exist. As our results show, this has the potential to speed up the process *and* yield shorter, and thus more informative error paths. Hence, our technique for error detection will be able to help with actual *verification*.

Acknowledgments

This work was partly supported by the German Research Council (DFG) as part of the Transregional Collaborative Research Center "Automatic Verification and Analysis of Complex Systems" (SFB/TR 14 AVACS). See http://www.avacs.org/ for more information.

References

1. Blai Bonet and Héctor Geffner. Planning as heuristic search. *Artificial Intelligence*, 129 (1–2):5–33, 2001.
2. Henning Dierks. Comparing model-checking and logical reasoning for real-time systems. *Formal Aspects of Computing*, 16(2):104–120, 2004.
3. Klaus Dräger, Bernd Finkbeiner, and Andreas Podelski. Directed model checking with distance-preserving abstractions. In *Proceedings of the 13th International SPIN Workshop on Model Checking of Software*, 2006.
4. Stefan Edelkamp, Alberto Lluch-Lafuente, and Stefan Leue. Directed explicit model checking with HSF-Spin. In *Proceedings of the 8th International SPIN Workshop on Model Checking of Software*, pages 57–79, 2001.
5. Stefan Edelkamp, Alberto Lluch-Lafuente, and Stefan Leue. Directed explicit-state model checking in the validation of communication protocols. *International Journal on Software Tools for Technology Transfer*, 2004.
6. Bernd Krieg-Brückner, Jan Peleska, Ernst-Rüdiger Olderog, and Alexander Baer. The Uni-ForM Workbench, a universal development environment for formal methods. In *FM'99 – Formal Methods*, volume 1709 of *LNCS*, pages 1186–1205. Springer, 1999.
7. Sebastian Kupferschmid, Jörg Hoffmann, Henning Dierks, and Gerd Behrmann. Adapting an AI planning heuristic for directed model checking. In *Proceedings of the 13th International SPIN Workshop on Model Checking of Software*, 2006.
8. Judea Pearl. *Heuristics: Intelligent search strategies for computer problem solving*. Addison-Wesley, 1984.

Distributed Analysis with μCRL: A Compendium of Case Studies

Stefan Blom[2], Jens R. Calamé[1], Bert Lisser[1], Simona Orzan[3], Jun Pang[4],
Jaco van de Pol[1,3], Mohammad Torabi Dashti[1], and Anton J. Wijs[1]

[1] CWI, Amsterdam, The Netherlands
[2] Institut für Informatik, Universität Innsbruck, Austria
[3] TU/e, Eindhoven, The Netherlands
[4] Carl von Ossietzky Universität, Oldenburg, Germany
Stefan.Blom@uibk.ac.at, {jens.calame,bertl,vdpol,dashti,a.j.wijs}@cwi.nl,
s.m.orzan@tue.nl, jun.pang@informatik.uni-oldenburg.de

Abstract. Models in process algebra with abstract data types can be analysed by state space generation and reduction tools. The μCRL toolset implements a suite of distributed verification tools for clusters of workstations. We illustrate their application to large case studies from a wide range of application areas, such as functional analysis, scheduling, security analysis, test case generation and game solving.

1 Introduction

The μCRL toolset (www.cwi.nl/~mcrl, [2,3]) is equipped with several tools to analyse models of industrial systems, comparable to CADP [8], SPIN [10], UPPAAL [1] and MURϕ [7]. Most techniques rely on explicit state space generation. In order to overcome memory problems of a single machine, we have constructed distributed implementations of the μCRL tools. With this paper we illustrate that these distributed analysis tools are essential in a wide range of application areas. In particular, we discuss applications in functional analysis, scheduling, test generation, security analysis, and game solving.

Before doing so, we shortly mention the distributed tools, which all run on a cluster of workstations. First of all, there is the *state space generator* [11]. Besides generating all possible behaviour of a μCRL-model, it can check for simple properties, e.g. deadlock freeness. One manager and n clients perform a distributed breadth-first exploration, where a hash function is used to assign states to the clients. This exploration is done level by level simultaneously on all clients, whereby the clients, which have finished their part of the task, communicate destination states to the other clients. The manager synchronises the clients, hence enforcing the breadth-first character of the exploration.

A GUI is provided with the toolset to monitor running jobs. A running job can be killed at any time, to be restarted later on. Some *minimisation tools* [4] reduce a state space modulo strong or branching bisimulation. There is also a *distributed SCC contraction tool* [12], which eliminates for instance all τ-cycles. Finally, it

O. Grumberg and M. Huth (Eds.): TACAS 2007, LNCS 4424, pp. 683–689, 2007.

is possible to deal with priced reachability problems. We implemented minimal-cost search (where the search order is determined by the costs associated with actions), and beam search (which uses heuristics to guide the search) [14,15]. In the latter case, state space generation is not exhaustive.

2   Applications of Distributed Analysis

Functional Analysis – A Cache Coherence Protocol. Jackal is a fine-grained distributed shared memory implementation of the Java programming language. It aims to implement Java's memory model and allows multithreaded programs to run unmodified on a distributed memory system. It employs a self-invalidation based, multiple-writer cache coherence protocol, which allows processors to cache a region created on another processor.

A μCRL specification of the protocol was extracted from an informal (C-like language) description. It contains parallel processes for components such as threads, processors, buffers, and regions. These components interact with each other via message communications. Our analysis [13] has revealed two unanticipated errors in the implementation, which were confirmed and corrected by the developers of Jackal. The μCRL distributed state space generation tool has played a central role for this case study. It was used to generate state spaces for several large instances of the protocol. One of the two errors found by analysing them with CADP can only be detected on these instances.

Test Case Generation – Common Electronic Purse Specifications. The Common Electronic Purse Specifications (CEPS) define a protocol for electronic payment using a chip card as a wallet. A complete electronic purse system covers three roles: A card user, a card issuer (e.g. bank institute) and a card reader as a connection between these two.

We generated parameterisable test cases from a μCRL model of the card application as follows [5]: We first applied a so-called chaos abstraction to limit the infinite behaviour due to unbounded input values. However, even the abstracted version was very large. The full state space was generated on a cluster of machines, while the minimised state space fitted in one machine. Finally, we applied enumerative test generation with the (sequential) tool TGV.

Scheduling – Clinical Chemical Analyser. Opposed to more traditional *qualitative* model checking, where properties are checked resulting in a "yes" or "no" answer, in *quantitative* model checking, measurements are performed on a model. Scheduling problems can be seen as priced reachability problems, where costs are associated with actions (and states), and the goal is to find a successful termination in a state space where the traces represent all possible schedules.

We used μCRL to model the scheduling problem of a Clinical Chemical Analyser [15], which is used to automatically analyse patient samples, designed by TNO Industry and TU/e. As naïve breadth-first search could not cope with costs and large problem instances, we developed a set of distributed techniques, incorporating minimal-cost search and several pruning techniques [14], building on the traditional notion of beam search. We were able to find solutions for several problem instances on-the-fly.

Security Analysis – Digital Rights Management. Digital Rights Management (DRM) schemes have recently attracted much research because of their essential role in enabling digital business in the entertainment market. However, sobering experiences, such as the recent Sony-BMG case, have shown that DRM systems are inherently complicated, hence error-prone, and if not applied with ample scrutiny and analysis can infringe on both vendors' and customers' rights. We extended an existing concept of DRM-preserving content redistribution in [9], where users double as content distributors.

We used μCRL to formally specify a finite model of this scheme. The resulting system is highly non-deterministic, mainly due to several fall back scenarios for suffered parties. Particularly when an intruder is included in the model, it easily hits the boundaries of single-machine state space generation. We therefore resorted to the distributed setting for generating and minimising the corresponding state space, to later on model check security goals of the scheme.

Game solving - Sokoban. A rather surprising application of our verification techniques is in solving instances of the one-player maze puzzles of Sokoban. Squares of a Sokoban instance may be occupied by stones, or marked as targets. A person can walk around or push stones, in order to move them all to the target squares, minimising the number of pushes. Walking steps are not counted.

To solve a screen, we generate its state space, and look for the shortest number of pushes leading to the goal state. However, as walk steps don't count, they should be eliminated first. Due to the large number of move options at every step, for most instances the state spaces could only be generated on a cluster of workstations. By *hiding* the walking actions, we get a state space with many τ-cycles, on which the *distributed SCC elimination tool* [12] was applied, and led to a significant reduction. In the reduced state space we can simply count the pushes in the shortest path to the success state.

3   Evaluation and Conclusion

The μCRL toolset has the capabilities to do distributed analysis on a cluster of computers. In a number of experiments we successfully applied the toolset to the areas, which have been described in the previous section. Thereby, the case studies we worked on, led to large state spaces.

In general, we used a cluster of 2.2GHz AMD Athlon 64 bit single CPU computers with 1 GB RAM each and SuSE Linux 9.3 installed. In those cases, where the number of machines is given as $n+1$, we used a cluster of 1.4GHz AMD Opteron 64 bit computers running under Debian 3.1. The first n machines had two CPUs and 2 GB RAM each while the extra machine had four CPUs and 16 GB main memory. As can be seen in Table 1, most problems could not have been solved on a single machine, because computation would have taken too long and would have consumed too much memory. Therefore, problems of this size can only be solved by a toolset supporting distributed analysis features.

Table 1. Performance Results

Case Study	States	Transitions	Machine(s)	Time (hours)
Functional Analysis	97,451,014	1,061,619,779	31	02:38:26
after minimisation	3,634,036	39,603,188	1	n/a
Test Generation	3,023,121	17,475,646	5	00:09:26
after minimisation	1,626	5,487	1	00:07:32
Scheduling	341,704,322	n/a	16	n/a
with beam search	7,408	n/a	1	00:00:08
Security Analysis	28,206,430	114,824,743	8+1	16:04:16
after minimisation	1,979	36,667	1	00:07:44
Game Solving	29,933,087	72,309,227	9+1	00:51:54
after τ-cycle elimination	2,583,703	7,167,175	10	00:02:01

References

1. G. Behrmann, T. Hune, and F.W. Vaandrager. Distributing Timed Model Checking - How the Search Order Matters. In *Proc. CAV'00*, volume 1855 of *LNCS*, pages 216–231, 2000.
2. S.C.C. Blom, W.J. Fokkink, J.F. Groote, I. van Langevelde, B. Lisser, and J.C. van de Pol. μCRL: A Toolset for Analysing Algebraic Specifications. In *Proc. CAV'01*, volume 2102 of *LNCS*, pages 250–254, 2001.
3. S.C.C. Blom, J.F. Groote, I. van Langevelde, B. Lisser, and J.C. van de Pol. New developments around the μCRL tool set. *ENTCS*, 80, 2003.
4. S.C.C. Blom and S.M. Orzan. A distributed algorithm for strong bisimulation reduction of state spaces. *STTT*, 7(1):74–86, 2005.
5. J.R. Calamé, N. Ioustinova, and J.C. van de Pol. Towards Automatic Generation of Parameterized Test Cases from Abstractions. Technical Report SEN-E0602, CWI, March 2006.
6. T. Chothia, S.M. Orzan, J. Pang, and M. Torabi Dashti. A framework for automatically checking anonymity with μCRL. In *Proc. TGC'06*, LNCS, 2007.
7. D. Dill. The Murφ Verification System. In *Proc. CAV'96*, volume 1102 of *LNCS*, pages 390–393, 1996.
8. H. Garavel, R. Mateescu, D. Bergamini, A. Curic, N. Descoubes, C. Joubert et al. DISTRIBUTOR and BCG_MERGE: Tools for Distr. Explicit State Space Generation. In *TACAS'06*, volume 3920 of *LNCS*, pages 445–449, 2006.
9. H. Jonker, S. Krishnan Nair, and M. Torabi Dashti. Nuovo DRM paradiso. Technical Report SEN-R0602, CWI, Amsterdam, 2006.
10. F. Lerda and R. Sista. Distributed-Memory model checking with SPIN. In *Proc. SPIN'99*, volume 1680 of *LNCS*, pages 22–39, 1999.
11. B. Lisser. Distributed State Space Generator (preliminary). http://www.cwi.nl/~mcrl/instantiators.pdf, 2006.
12. S.M. Orzan and J.C. van de Pol. Detecting strongly connected components in large distributed state spaces. Technical Report SEN-E0501, CWI, 2005.
13. J. Pang, W. J. Fokkink, R. F.H. Hofman, and R. Veldema. Model checking a cache coherence protocol of a Java DSM implementation. *JLAP*, 71:1–43, 2007.
14. A.J. Wijs and B. Lisser. Distributed Extended Beam Search for Quantitative Model Checking. In *MoChArt'06*, LNAI, 2007.
15. A.J. Wijs, J.C. van de Pol, and E. Bortnik. Solving Scheduling Problems by Untimed Model Checking. In *Proc. FMICS '05*, pages 54–61. ACM Press, 2005.

A   Appendix

Security Analysis - Anonymity. Anonymity is a non-standard security property, in the sense that it is not verifiable by model checking directly, but requires special techniques, where state space minimisation is essential [6].

The powerful *distributed state space generation* and *minimisation* tools of the μCRL toolset allowed us to automatically check anonymity for large instances of known protocols. For instance, the Dining Cryptographers protocol, used as case study for many tools, has so far been verified for a maximum of 8 participants. We succeed in verifying it for 15 participants in a few hours. Moreover, the anonymity property of the FOO voting protocol has never before been established in an automatic framework. Our toolset supports its verification for up to 7 voters.

For this second security analysis case study, we generated a state space of 65,282,690 states and 221,299,564 transitions. It could then be minimised to 3,676,249 states and 9,628,686 transitions. On a cluster with 16 machines as described in Section 3, this took us 4 hours and 48 minutes.

The Toolset in Action. The toolset described in the paper is used on a regular basis in the area of computer science research. The toolset is available in open source from the website http://www.cwi.nl/~mcrl/tacas2007/.

The presentation of the toolset is planned as follows: First, we will give an introduction to the toolset in general before discussing its technical aspects. These aspects will be shown by an exemplary execution of the beam search example. This execution will be given as an animation as follows:

1. Starting a job on the cluster (Figure 1).

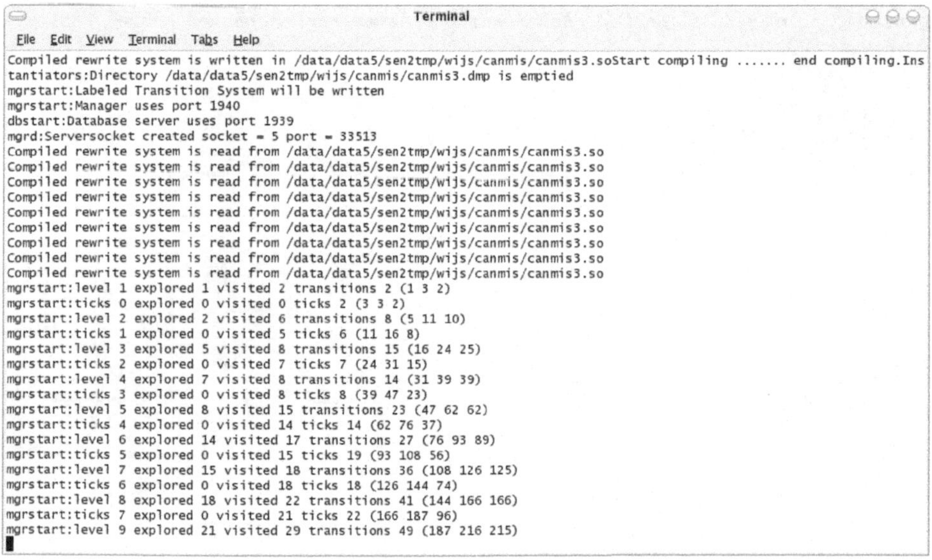

Fig. 1. Starting a job

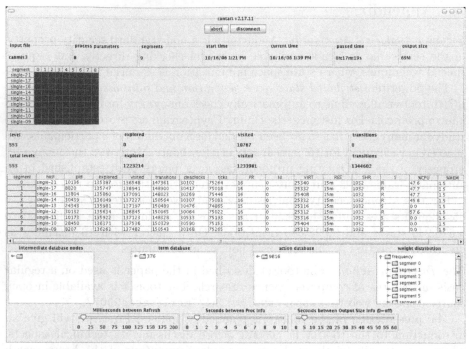

Fig. 2. All processors calculating

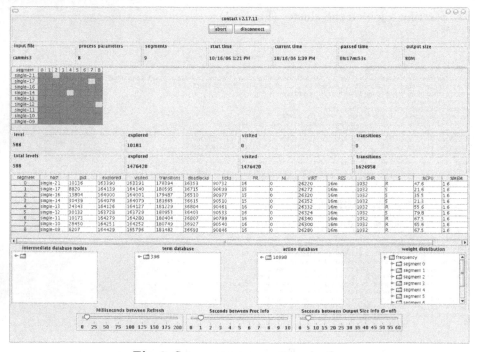

Fig. 3. Some processors communicating

2. Starting the tool *contact*, a monitoring GUI for the toolset.
3. Discussion of the different states of job execution: *idle* (color white), *busy* (color red, see Figure 2), *communicating* (color yellow, see Figure 3) and *finished* (color green, ibid).
4. Interpretation of the results (showing output files, e.g. the state space directory, and explaining their meaning).

Afterwards, we will give a short introduction into each of the given case studies. This introduction will contain some information about the case study itself and about the results we achieved in the experiments.

A Generic Framework for Reasoning About Dynamic Networks of Infinite-State Processes

Ahmed Bouajjani, Yan Jurski, and Mihaela Sighireanu

LIAFA, University of Paris 7, Case 7014, 2 place Jussieu, 75251 Paris 05, France
{abou,jurski,sighirea}@liafa.jussieu.fr

Abstract. We propose a framework for reasoning about unbounded dynamic networks of infinite-state processes. We propose Constrained Petri Nets (CPN) as generic models for these networks. They can be seen as Petri nets where tokens (representing occurrences of processes) are colored by values over some potentially infinite data domain such as integers, reals, etc. Furthermore, we define a logic, called CML (colored markings logic), for the description of CPN configurations. CML is a first-order logic over tokens allowing to reason about their locations and their colors. Both CPNs and CML are parametrized by a color logic allowing to express constraints on the colors (data) associated with tokens.

We investigate the decidability of the satisfiability problem of CML and its applications in the verification of CPNs. We identify a fragment of CML for which the satisfiability problem is decidable (whenever it is the case for the underlying color logic), and which is closed under the computations of post and pre images for CPNs. These results can be used for several kinds of analysis such as invariance checking, pre-post condition reasoning, and bounded reachability analysis.

1 Introduction

The verification of software systems requires in general the consideration of infinite-state models. The sources of infinity in software models are multiple. One of them is the manipulation of variables and data structures ranging over infinite domains (such as integers, reals, arrays, etc). Another source of infinity is the fact that the number of processes running in parallel in the system can be either a parameter (fixed but arbitrarily large), or it can be dynamically changing due to process creation. While the verification of parameterized systems requires reasoning uniformly about the infinite family of (static) networks corresponding to any possible number of processes, the verification of dynamic systems requires reasoning about the infinite number of all possible dynamically changing network configurations.

There are many works and several approaches on the verification of infinite-state systems taking into account either the aspects related to infinite data domains, or the aspects related to unbounded network structures due to parameterization or dynamism. Concerning systems with data manipulation, a lot of work has been devoted to the verification of, for instance, finite-structure systems with unbounded counters, clocks, stacks, queues, etc. (see, e.g., [1,11,30,7,5,27,26]). On the other hand, a lot of work has been done for the verification of parameterized and dynamic networks of boolean (or finite-data domain) processes, proposing either exact model-checking and reachability

O. Grumberg and M. Huth (Eds.): TACAS 2007, LNCS 4424, pp. 690–705, 2007.
© Springer-Verlag Berlin Heidelberg 2007

analysis techniques for specific classes of systems (such as broadcast protocols, multithreaded programs, etc) [24,25,22,16,15], or generic algorithmic techniques (which can be approximate, or not guaranteed to terminate) such as network invariants-based approaches [31,20], and (abstract) regular model checking [13,17,3,12]. However, only few works consider both infinite data manipulation and parametric/dynamic network structures (see the paragraph on related work).

In this paper, we propose a generic framework for reasoning about parameterized and dynamic networks of concurrent processes which can manipulate (local and global) variables over infinite data domains. Our framework is parameterized by a data domain and a first-order theory on it (e.g., Presburger arithmetics on natural numbers). It consists of (1) expressive models allowing to cover a wide class of systems, and (2) a logic allowing to specify and to reason about the configurations of these models.

The models we propose are called Constrained Petri Nets (CPN for short). They are based on (place/transition) Petri nets where tokens are colored by data values. Intuitively, tokens represent different occurrences of processes, and places are associated with control locations and contain tokens corresponding to processes which are at a same control location. Since processes can manipulate local variables, each token (process occurrence) has several colors corresponding to the values of these variables. Then, configurations of our models are markings where each place contains a set of colored tokens, and transitions modify the markings as usual by removing tokens from some places and creating new ones in some other places. Transitions are guarded by constraints on the colors of tokens before and after firing the transition. We show that CPNs allow to model various aspects such as unbounded dynamic creation of processes, manipulation of local and global variables over unbounded domains such as integers, synchronization, communication through shared variables, locks, etc.

The logic we propose for specifying configurations of CPN's is called Colored Markings Logic (CML for short). It is a first order logic over tokens and their colors. It allows to reason about the presence of tokens in places, and also about the relations between the colors of these tokens. The logic CML is parametrized by a first order logic over the color domain allowing to express constraints on tokens.

We investigate the decidability of the satisfiability problem of CML and its applications in verification of CPNs. While the logic is decidable for finite color domains (such as booleans), we show that, unfortunately, the satisfiability problem of this logic becomes undecidable as soon as we consider as a color domain the set of natural numbers with the usual ordering relation (and without any arithmetical operations). We prove that this undecidability result holds already for the fragment $\forall^* \exists^*$ of the logic (in the alternation hierarchy of the quantifiers over token variables) with this color domain.

On the other hand, we prove that the satisfiability problem is decidable for the fragment $\exists^* \forall^*$ of CML whenever the underlying color logic has a decidable satisfiability problem, e.g., Presburger arithmetics, the first-order logic of addition and multiplication over reals, etc. Moreover, we prove that the fragment $\exists^* \forall^*$ of CML is effectively closed under post and pre image computations (i.e., computation of immediate successors and immediate predecessors) for CPN's where all transition guards are also in $\exists^* \forall^*$. We show also that the same closure results hold when we consider the fragment $\exists^*$ instead of $\exists^* \forall^*$.

These generic decidability and closure results can be applied in the verification of CPN models following different approaches such as pre-post condition (Hoare triples based) reasoning, bounded reachability analysis, and inductive invariant checking. More precisely, we derive from our results mentioned above that (1) checking whether starting from a $\exists^*\forall^*$ pre-condition, a $\forall^*\exists^*$ condition holds after the execution of a transition is decidable, that (2) the bounded reachability problem between two $\exists^*\forall^*$ definable sets is decidable, and that (3) checking whether a formula defines an inductive invariant is decidable for boolean combinations of $\exists^*$ formulas.

These results can be used to deal with non trivial examples of systems. Indeed, in many cases, program invariants and the assertions needed to establish them fall in the considered fragments of our logic. We illustrate this by carrying out in our framework the parametric verification of a Reader-Writer lock with an arbitrarily large number of processes. This case study was introduced in [28] where the authors provide a correctness proof for the case of one reader and one writer.

For lack of space, proofs as well as the exposition of the Reader-Writer case study are omitted in this short version of the paper. They are provided in the full paper [14].

Related work: The use of unbounded Petri nets as models for parametrized networks of processes has been proposed in many existing works such as [29,24,22]. However, these works consider networks of *finite-state* processes and do not address the issue of manipulating infinite data domains. The extension of this idea to networks of infinite-state processes has been addressed only in very few works [4,21,18,2]. In [4], Abdulla and Jonsson consider the case of networks of 1-clock timed systems and show, using the theory of well-structured systems and well quasi orderings [1,27], that the verification problem for a class of safety properties is decidable. Their approach has been extended in [21,18] to a particular class of multiset rewrite systems with constraints (see also [2] for recent developments of this approach). Our modeling framework is actually inspired by these works. However, while they address the issue of deciding the verification problem of safety properties (by reduction to the coverability problem) for specific classes of systems, we consider in our work a general framework, allowing to deal in a generic way with various classes of systems, where the user can express assertions about the configurations of the system, and check automatically that they hold (using post-pre reasoning and inductive invariant checking) or that they do not hold (using bounded reachability analysis). Our framework allows to reason automatically about systems which are beyond the scoop of the techniques proposed in [4,21,18,2] (such as, for instance, the parametrized Reader-Writer lock system [14]).

In a series of papers, Pnueli et al. developed an approach for the verification of parameterized systems combining abstraction and proof techniques (see, e.g., [6]). This is probably one of the most advanced existing approaches allowing to deal with unbounded networks of infinite-state processes. We propose here a different framework for reasoning about these systems. In [6], the authors consider a logic on (parametric-bound) *arrays* of integers, and they identify a fragment of this logic for which the satisfiability problem is decidable. In this fragment, they restrict the shape of the formula (quantification over indices) to formulas in the fragment $\exists^*\forall^*$ similarly to what we do, and also the class of used arithmetical constraints on indices and on the associated values. In a recent work by Bradley and al. [19], the satisfiability problem of the logic of unbounded arrays with integers is investigated and the authors provide a new decidable fragment, which is incomparable to the one defined in [6], but again which imposes similar restrictions on the quantification alternation in the formulas, and on the kind of constraints that can be used. In contrast with these works, we consider a logic on *multisets* of elements with *any* kind of associated data values, provided that the used theory on the data domain is decidable. For instance, we can use in our logic general Presburger constraints whereas [6] and [19] allow limited classes of constraints. On the other hand, we cannot specify faithfully unbounded arrays in our decidable fragment because formulas of the form $\forall\exists$ are needed to express that every non extremal element has a successor/predecessor. Nevertheless, for the verification of safety properties and invariant checking, expressing this fact is not necessary, and therefore, it is possible to handle in our framework all usual examples of parametrized systems (such as mutual exclusion protocols) considered in the works mentioned above.

Let us finally mention that there are recent works on logics (first-order logics, or temporal logics) over finite/infinite structures (words or trees) over infinite alphabets (which can be considered as abstract infinite data domains) [9,8,23]. The obtained positive results so far concern logics with very limited data domain (basically infinite sets with only equality, or sometimes with an ordering relation), and are based on reduction to complex problems such as reachability in Petri nets.

2 Colored Markings Logic

2.1 Preliminaries

Consider an enumerable set of *tokens* and let us identify this set with the set of natural numbers $\mathbb{N}$. Intuitively, tokens represent occurrences of (parallel) processes. We assume that tokens may have colors corresponding for instance to data values attached to the corresponding processes. Let $\mathbb{C}$ be a (potentially infinite) *token color domain*. Examples of color domains are the set of natural numbers $\mathbb{N}$ and the set of real numbers $\mathbb{R}$.

Colors are associated with tokens through *coloring functions*. Let Γ be a finite set of *token coloring symbols*. Each element in Γ is interpreted as a mapping from $\mathbb{N}$ (the set of tokens) to $\mathbb{C}$ (the set of colors). Then, let a valuation of the token coloring symbols be a mapping in $[\Gamma \rightarrow (\mathbb{N} \rightarrow \mathbb{C})]$.

To express constraints on token colors, we use first-order logics over the considered color domains. In the sequel we refer to such logics as *color logics*. Presburger arithmetics $\mathsf{PA} = (\mathbb{N}, \{0, 1, +\}, \{\leq\})$ is an example of such a logic. It is well known that the satisfiability problem of Presburger arithmetics is decidable. An interesting sublogic of PA is the *difference logic* $\mathsf{DL} = (\mathbb{N}, \{0\}, \{\leq_k : k \geq 0\})$ where, for every $u, v, k \in \mathbb{N}$, $u \leq_k v$ holds if and only if $u - v \leq k$. The *order logic* on natural numbers is the sublogic of DL defined by $\mathsf{OL} = (\mathbb{N}, \{0\}, \leq)$. Another example of a decidable logic which can be used as a color logic is the first-order theory of reals $\mathsf{FO}_\mathbb{R} = (\mathbb{R}, \{0, 1, +, \times\}, \{\leq\})$.

We consider that tokens can be located at *places*. Let $\mathbb{P}$ be a finite set of such places. A *marking* is a mapping in $[\mathbb{N} \rightarrow \mathbb{P} \cup \{\bot\}]$ which associates with each token the unique place where it is located if it is defined, or $\bot$ otherwise. A *colored marking* is a pair $\langle M, \mu \rangle$ where M is a marking and μ is a valuation of the token coloring symbols.

2.2 Syntax and Semantics of CML

We define hereafter the syntax of the logic *colored markings logic* $\mathrm{CML}(L, \Gamma, \mathbb{P})$ which is parametrized with a color logic L, a finite set of token coloring symbols Γ, and a finite set of places $\mathbb{P}$. Then, let $L = (\mathbb{C}, \Omega, \Xi)$ be the first-order logic over the color domain $\mathbb{C}$ of the set of functions Ω and the set of relations Ξ. In the sequel, we omit all or some of the parameters of CML when their specification is not necessary.

Let T be set of *token variables* and let C be set of *color variables*, and assume that $T \cap C = \emptyset$. The set of CML terms (called *token color terms*) is given by the grammar:

$$t ::= z \mid \gamma(x) \mid \omega(t_1, \ldots, t_n)$$

where $z \in C$, $\gamma \in \Gamma$, $x \in T$, and $\omega \in \Omega$. Then, the set of CML formulas is given by:

$$\varphi ::= x = y \mid p(x) \mid \xi(t_1, \ldots, t_m) \mid \neg\varphi \mid \varphi \vee \varphi \mid \exists z.\ \varphi \mid \exists x.\ \varphi$$

where $x, y \in T$, $z \in C$, $p \in \mathbb{P} \cup \{\bot\}$, $\xi \in \Xi$, and $t_1, \ldots, t_m$ are token color terms. Boolean connectives such as conjunction ($\wedge$) and implication ($\Rightarrow$), and universal quantification ($\forall$) can be defined in terms of $\neg$, $\vee$, and $\exists$. We also use $\exists x \in p.\ \varphi$ (resp. $\forall x \in p.\ \varphi$) as an abbreviation of the formula $\exists x.\ p(x) \wedge \varphi$ (resp. $\forall x.\ p(x) \Rightarrow \varphi$). Notice that the set of terms (resp. formulas) of L is included in the set of terms (resp. formulas) of $\mathrm{CML}(L)$.

The notions of free/bound occurrences of variables in formulas and the notions of closed/open formulas are defined as usual in first-order logics. In the sequel, we assume w.l.o.g. that in every formula, each variable is quantified at most once.

We define a satisfaction relation between colored markings and CML formulas. For that, we need first to define the semantics of CML terms. Given valuations $\theta \in [T \to \mathbb{N}]$, $\delta \in [C \to \mathbb{C}]$, and $\mu \in [\Gamma \to (\mathbb{N} \to \mathbb{C})]$, we define a mapping $\langle\!\langle \cdot \rangle\!\rangle_{\theta, \delta, \mu}$ which associates with each color term a value in $\mathbb{C}$:

$$\langle\!\langle z \rangle\!\rangle_{\theta, \delta, \mu} = \delta(z)$$
$$\langle\!\langle \gamma(x) \rangle\!\rangle_{\theta, \delta, \mu} = \mu(\gamma)(\theta(x))$$
$$\langle\!\langle \omega(t_1, \ldots, t_n) \rangle\!\rangle_{\theta, \delta, \mu} = \omega(\langle\!\langle t_1 \rangle\!\rangle_{\theta, \delta, \mu}, \ldots, \langle\!\langle t_n \rangle\!\rangle_{\theta, \delta, \mu})$$

Then, we define inductively the satisfaction relation $\models_{\theta, \delta}$ between colored markings $\langle M, \mu \rangle$ and CML formulas as follows:

$$\langle M, \mu \rangle \models_{\theta, \delta} \xi(t_1, \ldots, t_m) \text{ iff } \xi(\langle\!\langle t_1 \rangle\!\rangle_{\theta, \delta, \mu}, \ldots, \langle\!\langle t_m \rangle\!\rangle_{\theta, \delta, \mu})$$
$$\langle M, \mu \rangle \models_{\theta, \delta} p(x) \text{ iff } M(\theta(x)) = p$$
$$\langle M, \mu \rangle \models_{\theta, \delta} x = y \text{ iff } \theta(x) = \theta(y)$$
$$\langle M, \mu \rangle \models_{\theta, \delta} \neg\varphi \text{ iff } \langle M, \mu \rangle \not\models_{\theta, \delta} \varphi$$
$$\langle M, \mu \rangle \models_{\theta, \delta} \varphi_1 \vee \varphi_2 \text{ iff } \langle M, \mu \rangle \models_{\theta, \delta} \varphi_1 \text{ or } \langle M, \mu \rangle \models_{\theta, \delta} \varphi_2$$
$$\langle M, \mu \rangle \models_{\theta, \delta} \exists x.\ \varphi \text{ iff } \exists t \in \mathbb{T}.\ \langle M, \mu \rangle \models_{\theta[x \leftarrow t], \delta} \varphi$$
$$\langle M, \mu \rangle \models_{\theta, \delta} \exists z.\ \varphi \text{ iff } \exists c \in \mathbb{C}.\ \langle M, \mu \rangle \models_{\theta, \delta[z \leftarrow c]} \varphi$$

For every formula φ, we define $[\![\varphi]\!]_{\theta, \delta}$ the be the set of markings $\langle M, \mu \rangle$ such that $\langle M, \mu \rangle \models_{\theta, \delta} \varphi$. A formula φ is *satisfiable* iff there exist valuations θ and δ s.t. $[\![\varphi]\!]_{\theta, \delta} \neq \emptyset$.

2.3 Syntactical Forms and Fragments

Prenex normal form: A formula is in *prenex normal form* (PNF) if it is of the form

$$Q_1 y_1 Q_2 y_2 \cdots Q_m y_m. \; \varphi$$

where (1) $Q_1, \ldots, Q_m$ are (existential or universal) quantifiers, (2) $y_1, \ldots, y_m$ are variables in $T \cup C$, and φ is a quantifier-free formula. It can be proved that for every formula φ in CML, there exists an equivalent formula φ' in prenex normal form.

Quantifier alternation hierarchy: We consider two families $\{\Sigma_n\}_{n \geq 0}$ and $\{\Pi_n\}_{n \geq 0}$ of fragments of CML defined according to the alternation depth of existential and universal quantifiers in their PNF:

- Let $\Sigma_0 = \Pi_0$ be the set of formulas in PNF where all quantified variables are in C,
- For $n \geq 0$, let Σ_{n+1} (resp. Π_{n+1}) be the set of formulas $Q y_1 \ldots y_m. \; \varphi$ in PNF where $y_1, \ldots, y_m \in T \cup C$, Q is the existential (resp. universal) quantifier $\exists$ (resp. $\forall$), and φ is a formula in Π_n (resp. Σ_n).

It is easy to see that, for every $n \geq 0$, Σ_n and Π_n are closed under conjunction and disjunction, and that the negation of a Σ_n formula is a Π_n formula and vice versa. For every $n \geq 0$, let $B(\Sigma_n)$ denote the set of all boolean combinations of Σ_n formulas. Clearly, $B(\Sigma_n)$ subsumes both Σ_n and Π_n, and is included in both Σ_{n+1} and Π_{n+1}.

Special form: The set of formulas in special form is given by the grammar:

$$\varphi ::= x = y \mid \xi(t_1, \ldots, t_n) \mid \neg \varphi \mid \varphi \vee \varphi \mid \exists z. \; \varphi \mid \exists x \in p. \; \varphi$$

where $x, y \in T$, $z \in C$, $p \in \mathbb{P} \cup \{\bot\}$, $\xi \in \Xi$, and $t_1, \ldots, t_n$ are token color terms. It is not difficult to see that for every closed formula φ in CML, there exists an equivalent formula φ' in special form. The transformation is based on the following fact: since variables are assumed to be quantified at most once in formulas, each formula $\exists x. \; \phi$ can be replaced by $\bigvee_{p \in \mathbb{P} \cup \{\bot\}} \exists x \in p. \; \phi_{x,p}$ where $\phi_{x,p}$ is obtained by substituting in ϕ each occurrence of $p(x)$ by *true*, and each occurrence of $q(x)$, with $p \neq q$, by *false*.

3 Satisfiability Problem

We investigate the decidability of the satisfiability problem of the logic $CML(L)$, assuming that the underlying color logic L has a decidable satisfiability problem.

Let us mention that in the case of a finite color domain, for instance for the domain of booleans with equality and usual operations, the logic CML is decidable. The result is a direct consequence of the decidability of the class of relational monadic formulae in first-order logic, also known as the Löwenheim class with equality [10].

Then, let us consider the case of infinite data domains. First, we prove that as soon as we consider natural numbers with ordering, the satisfiability problem of CML is undecidable already for the fragment Π_2. The proof is by a reduction of the halting problem of Turing machines. The idea is to encode a computation of a machine, seen as a sequence of tape configurations, using tokens with integer colors. Each token represents a cell in the tape of the machine at some computation step. Therefore the token has two integer colors, its position in the tape, and the position of its configuration in the computation (the corresponding computation step). The other informations such as the contents of the cell, the fact that a cell corresponds to the position of the head, and the control state, are encoded using a finite number of places. Then, using $\forall^*\exists^*$ formulas, it is possible to express that two consecutive configurations correspond indeed to a valid transition of the machine. Intuitively, this is possible because these formulas allow to relate each cell at some configuration to the corresponding cell at the next configuration.

Theorem 1. *The satisfiability problem of the fragment Π_2 of* CML(OL) *is undecidable.*

Nevertheless, we can prove the following generic decidability result for the fragment Σ_2 of our logic:

Theorem 2. *Let L be a colored tokens logic. If the satisfiability problem of L is decidable, then the fragment Σ_2 of* CML(L) *is decidable.*

The idea of the proof is to reduce the satisfiability problem of Σ_2 to the satisfiability problem of Σ_0 formulas (which are formulas in the color logic L). We proceed as follows: we prove first that the fragment Σ_2 has the small model property, i.e., every satisfiable formula φ in Σ_2 has a model of a bounded size (where the size is the number of tokens in each place). This bound corresponds actually to the number of existentially quantified token variables in the formula. Notice that this fact does not lead directly to an enumerative decision procedure for the satisfiability problem since the number of models of a bounded size is infinite in general (due to infinite color domains). Then, we use the fact that over a finite model, universal quantifications in φ can be transformed into finite conjunctions, in order to build a formula $\widehat{\varphi}$ in Σ_1 which is satisfiable if and only if the original formula φ is satisfiable. Actually, $\widehat{\varphi}$ defines precisely the upward-closure of the set of markings defined by φ (w.r.t. the inclusion ordering between sets of colored markings, extended to vectors of places). Finally, it can be shown that the Σ_1 formula $\widehat{\varphi}$ is satisfiable if and only if the Σ_0 obtained by transforming existential quantification over token into existential quantification over colors is decidable.

4   Constrained Petri Nets

Let T be a set of token variables and C be a set of color variables such that $T \cap C \neq \emptyset$. A *Constrained Petri Net* (CPN) is a tuple $S = (\mathbb{P}, L, \Gamma, \Delta)$ where $\mathbb{P}$ is a finite set of places, $L = (\mathbb{C}, \Omega, \Xi)$ is a colored tokens logic, Γ is a finite set of token coloring symbols, and Δ is a finite set of *constrained transitions* of the form:

$$\overrightarrow{x} \in \overrightarrow{p} \; \hookrightarrow \; \overrightarrow{y} \in \overrightarrow{q} \; : \; \varphi(\overrightarrow{x}, \overrightarrow{y}) \tag{1}$$

where $\overrightarrow{x} = (x_1, \ldots, x_n) \in T^n$, $\overrightarrow{y} = (y_1, \ldots, y_m) \in T^m$, $\overrightarrow{p} = (p_1, \ldots, p_n) \in \mathbb{P}^n$, $\overrightarrow{q} = (q_1, \ldots, q_m) \in \mathbb{P}^m$, and $\varphi(\overrightarrow{x}, \overrightarrow{y})$ is a CML($L, \Gamma, \mathbb{P}$) formula called the *transition guard*.

Given a fragment Θ of CML, we denote by CPN[Θ] the class of CPN where all transition guards are formulas in the fragment Θ. Due to the (un)decidability results of section 3, we focus in the sequel on the classes CPN[Σ_2] and CPN[Σ_1].

Configurations of CPN's are colored markings. Constrained transitions define transformation rules of these markings. Given a CPN S, we define a transition relation $\rightarrow_S$ between colored markings as follows: For every two colored markings $\langle M, \mu \rangle$ and $\langle M', \mu' \rangle$, we have $\langle M, \mu \rangle \rightarrow_S \langle M', \mu' \rangle$ iff there exists a constrained transition of the form (1), and there exist tokens $t_1, \ldots, t_n$ and $t'_1, \ldots, t'_m$ s.t. $\forall i, j \in \{1, \ldots, n\}.\, i \neq j \Rightarrow t_i \neq t_j$, and $\forall i, j \in \{1, \ldots, m\}.\, i \neq j \Rightarrow t'_i \neq t'_j$, and

1. $\forall i \in \{1, \ldots, n\}.\, M(t_i) = p_i$ and $M'(t_i) = \perp$,
2. $\forall i \in \{1, \ldots, m\}.\, M(t'_i) = \perp$ and $M'(t'_i) = q_i$,
3. $\forall t \in \mathbb{N}$, if $\forall i \in \{1, \ldots, n\}.\, t \neq t_i$ and $\forall j \in \{1, \ldots, m\}.\, t \neq t'_j$, then $M(t) = M'(t)$ and $\forall \gamma \in \Gamma.\, \mu(\gamma)(t) = \mu'(\gamma)(t)$,
4. $\langle M, \mu \cup \mu' \rangle \models_{\theta, \delta_0} \varphi(\vec{x}, \vec{y})$, where $\theta \in [T \rightarrow \mathbb{N}]$ is a valuation of the token variables such that $\forall i \in \{1, \ldots, n\}.\, \theta(x_i) = t_i$ and $\forall j \in \{1, \ldots, m\}.\, \theta(y_j) = t'_j$, δ_0 is the empty domain valuation of color variables, and $\mu \cup \mu'$ is such that: for every $\gamma \in \Gamma$, and every token $t \in \mathbb{T}$, if $t \in \{t_1, \ldots, t_n\}$ then $\mu \cup \mu'(\gamma)(t) = \mu(\gamma)(t)$, if $t \in \{t'_1, \ldots, t'_m\}$ then $\mu \cup \mu'(\gamma)(t) = \mu'(\gamma)(t)$, and $\mu \cup \mu'(\gamma)(t) = \mu(\gamma)(t) = \mu'(\gamma)(t)$ otherwise.

Intuitively, the definition above says that firing a transition means that n different tokens $t_1, \ldots, t_n$ are deleted from the places $p_1, \ldots, p_n$ (1), and m new different tokens $t'_1, \ldots, t'_m$ are added to the places $q_1, \ldots, q_m$ (2), provided that the colors of all these (old and new) tokens satisfy the formula φ, which may also involve constraints on other tokens in the whole marking M (4). Moreover, this operation does not modify the rest of the tokens (others than $t_1, \ldots, t_n$ and $t'_1, \ldots, t'_m$) in the marking (3).

Given a colored marking $\mathcal{M}$, let $\mathrm{post}_S(\mathcal{M}) = \{\mathcal{M}' : \mathcal{M} \rightarrow_S \mathcal{M}'\}$ be the set of its immediate successors, and let $\mathrm{pre}_S(\mathcal{M}) = \{\mathcal{M}' : \mathcal{M}' \rightarrow_S \mathcal{M}\}$ be the set of its immediate predecessors. These definitions can be generalized to sets of colored markings in the obvious way. Finally, for every set of colored markings $\mathbb{M}$, let $\widetilde{\mathrm{pre}}_S(\mathbb{M}) = \overline{\mathrm{pre}_S(\overline{\mathbb{M}})}$, where $(\overline{\cdot})$ denotes complementation (w.r.t. the set of all colored markings).

5 Modeling Power of CPN

We show in this section how CPN can be used to model (unbounded) dynamic networks of parallel processes. We assume w.l.o.g. that all processes are identically defined. We consider that a process is defined by a finite control state machine supplied with variables and data structures ranging over potentially infinite domains (such as integer variables, reals, etc). Processes running in parallel can communicate and synchronize using various kinds of mechanisms (rendez-vous, shared variables, locks, etc). Moreover, they can dynamically spawn new (copies of) processes in the network.

Dynamic networks of processes: Let L be the set of control locations of each of the processes. (Remember that this set is the same for all processes.) We associate with each process control location $\ell \in L$ a place. Then, each running process is represented by a token, and in every marking, a place contains precisely the tokens representing processes which are at the corresponding control location.

Assume for the moment that processes do not manipulate (infinite domain) data. Then, a basic action $\ell \longrightarrow \ell'$ of a process moving its control from a location ℓ to another location ℓ' is modeled by a transition: $x \in \ell \hookrightarrow y \in \ell' : true$. An action spawning a new process $\ell \xrightarrow{\text{spawn}(\ell_0)} \ell'$ is modeled using a transition which creates a new token in the initial control location of the new process: $x \in \ell \hookrightarrow y_1 \in \ell', y_2 \in \ell_0 : true$.

Local variables: Consider now that each process has a vector of n local variables $\overrightarrow{v} = (v_1, \ldots, v_n)$ over some (potentially infinite) data domain. Then, we consider a set of coloring symbols $\Gamma = \{\gamma_1, \ldots, \gamma_n\}$ associating with each token n colors (in the considered data domain) corresponding to the values of the local variables: for each process, represented by a token t, for each local variable v_i, $\gamma_i(t)$ defines the value of v_i.

A process action $\ell \xrightarrow{\overrightarrow{v} := \overrightarrow{f}(\overrightarrow{v})} \ell'$ which (in addition of changing the control location from ℓ to ℓ') performs the assignment $\overrightarrow{v} := \overrightarrow{f}(\overrightarrow{v})$, where $\overrightarrow{f}$ is a vector of expressions over the considered data domain, is modeled by the transition

$$x \in \ell \hookrightarrow y \in \ell' : \bigwedge_{i=1}^{n} \gamma_i(y) = f_i(\gamma_1(x), \ldots, \gamma_n(x))$$

For that, we use a token color logic which allows to express the effects of the actions. For instance, in the case of processes with integer variables and linear assignments, Presburger arithmetics (PA) can be used as colored tokens logic.

Global variables: Assume that processes share global variables $\overrightarrow{u} = \{u_1, \ldots, u_m\}$ (which are read and updated in a concurrent way). We associate with each global variable u_i a place g_i containing a single token t_i, and we associate with this token a color $\alpha(t_i)$ representing the value of u_i, where $\alpha \in \Gamma$ is a special coloring symbol. Then, a process action $\ell \xrightarrow{\overrightarrow{u} := \overrightarrow{f}(\overrightarrow{u}, \overrightarrow{v})} \ell'$ (assigning to global variables values depending on both global variables and local variables of the process) is modeled by the transition:

$$x \in \ell, x_1 \in g_1, \ldots, x_m \in g_m \hookrightarrow y \in \ell', y_1 \in g_1, \ldots, y_m \in g_m :$$

$$\left(\bigwedge_{i=1}^{n} \gamma_i(y) = \gamma_i(x) \right) \wedge \bigwedge_{i=1}^{m} \alpha(y_i) = f_i(\alpha(x_1), \ldots, \alpha(x_m), \gamma_1(x), \ldots, \gamma_n(x))$$

In the modeling above, we consider that the execution of the process action is atomic. When assignments are not atomic, we must transform each of assignment action into a sequence of atomic operations: read first the global variables and assign their values to local variables, then compute locally the new values to be assigned to global variables, and finally assign these values to global variables.

Rendez-vous synchronization: Synchronization between a finite number of processes can be modeled as in Petri nets. CPNs allow in addition to put constraints on the colors (data) of the involved processes.

Priorities: Various notion of priorities, such as priorities between different classes of processes (defined by properties of their colors), or priorities between different actions, can be modeled in CPNs. This can be done by imposing in transition guards that transitions (performed by processes or corresponding to actions) of higher priority are not enabled. These constraints can be expressed using Π_1 formulas. In particular, checking that a place p is empty can be expressed by $\forall x \in p. \, false$. (Which shows that as soon as universally quantified formulas are allowed in guards, our models are as powerful as Turing machines, even for color logics over finite domains.)

Process identities: It is possible to associate with each newly created process an identity defined by an integer number. For that, we consider a special coloring symbol $Id \in \Gamma$ associating to each token the identity of the process it represents. To ensure that different processes have different identities, we express in the guard of every transition which creates a process (i.e., adds a token to the place corresponding to its initial control location) the fact that the identity of this process does not exist already among tokens in places corresponding to control locations. This can easily be done using a universally quantified (Π_1) formula. Therefore, a spawn action $\ell \xrightarrow{\text{spawn}(\ell_0)} \ell'$ is modeled by:

$$x \in \ell \hookrightarrow y_1 \in \ell', y_2 \in \ell_0 :$$

$$Id(x) = Id(y_1) \wedge \left(\bigwedge_{i=1}^{n} \gamma_i(y_1) = \gamma_i(x) \right) \wedge \bigwedge_{loc \in \mathcal{L}} \forall t \in loc. \, \neg(Id(y_2) = Id(t))$$

and the modeling of other actions (such as local/global variables assignments) can be modified accordingly in order to propagate the process identity through the transition. Notice that process identities are different from token values. Indeed, in some cases (e.g., for modeling value passing as described below), we may use different tokens (at some special places representing buffers for instance) corresponding to the same Id.

Locks: Locks can be simply modeled using global variables storing the identity of the owner process, or a special value (e.g. -1) if it is free. A process who acquires the lock must check if it is free, and then write his identity:

$$x_1 \in \ell, x_2 \in lock \hookrightarrow y_1 \in \ell', y_2 \in lock : \alpha(x_2) = -1 \wedge \alpha(y_2) = Id(x_1) \wedge \dots$$

To release the lock, a process assigns -1 to the lock, which can be modeled in a similar way. Other kinds of locks, such as reader-writer locks, can also be modeled in our framework (see [14]). The modeling of such locks when the number of readers and writers can be arbitrarily large requires the use of universal quantification in guards.

Value passing, return values: Processes may pass/wait for values to/from other processes with specific identities. They can use for that shared arrays of data indexed by process identities. Such an array A can be modeled in our framework using a special place containing for each process a token. Initially, this place is empty, and whenever a new process is created, a token with the same identity is added to this place. Then, to model that a process read/write on $A[i]$, we use a transition which takes from the place associated with A the token with Id equal to i, read/modifies the value attached with this token, and put the token again in the same place. For instance, an assignment action $\ell \xrightarrow{A[k]:=e} \ell'$ executed by some process is modeled by the transition:

$$x_1 \in \ell, x_2 \in A \hookrightarrow y_1 \in \ell', y_2 \in A :$$

$$Id(x_1) = Id(y_1) \wedge \left(\bigwedge_{i=1}^{n} \gamma_i(x_1) = \gamma_i(y_1) \right) \wedge Id(x_2) = k \wedge \alpha(y_2) = e \wedge Id(y_2) = Id(x_2)$$

Notice that, while it is possible to model using CPNs systems manipulating parametric-size arrays (using multisets of tokens with integer colors), we cannot express in the decidable fragment Σ_2 of CML the fact that a multiset indeed encodes an array of elements indexed by integers in some given interval. The reason is that, while we can express in Π_1 the fact that each token has a unique color in the interval, we need to use Π_2 formulas to say that for each color in the interval there exists a token with that color. Nevertheless, for the verification of safety properties and checking invariants, it is not necessary to require the latter property.

6   Computing post and pre Images

We prove hereafter closure properties of CML fragments under the computation of immediate successors and predecessors for CPNs. The main result of this section is:

Theorem 3. *Let S be a $CPN[\Sigma_n]$, for $n \in \{1,2\}$. Then, for every closed formula φ in the fragment Σ_n of CML, it is possible to construct two closed formulas φ_{post} and φ_{pre} in the same fragment Σ_n such that $\llbracket \varphi_{post} \rrbracket = post_S(\llbracket \varphi \rrbracket)$ and $\llbracket \varphi_{pre} \rrbracket = pre_S(\llbracket \varphi \rrbracket)$.*

We give hereafter a sketch of the proof. Let φ be a closed formula, and let τ be a transition $\overrightarrow{x} \in \overrightarrow{p} \hookrightarrow \overrightarrow{y} \in \overrightarrow{q} : \psi$ of the system S. W.l.o.g., we suppose that φ and ψ are in special form. We define hereafter the formulas φ_{post} and φ_{pre} for this single transition. The generalization to the set of all transitions is straightforward.

The construction of the formulas φ_{post} and φ_{pre} is not trivial because our logic does not allow to use quantification over places and color mappings (associated with coloring symbols). Intuitively, the idea is to express first the effect of deleting/adding tokens, and then composing these operations to compute the effect of a transition.

Let us introduce two transformations $\ominus$ and $\oplus$ corresponding to deletion and creation of tokens. These operations are inductively defined on the structure of special form formulas in Table 1.

The operation $\ominus$ is parameterized by a vector $\overrightarrow{z}$ of token variables to be deleted, a mapping loc associating with token variables in $\overrightarrow{z}$ the places from which they will be deleted, and a mapping col associating with each coloring symbol in Γ and each token variable in $\overrightarrow{z}$ a fresh color variable in C. Intuitively, $\ominus$ projects a formula on all variables which are not in $\overrightarrow{z}$. Rule $\ominus_1$ substitutes in a color formula $\xi(\overrightarrow{t})$ all occurences of colored tokens in $\overrightarrow{z}$ by fresh color variables given by the mapping col. A formula $x = y$ is unchanged by the application of $\ominus$ is the token variables x and y are not in $\overrightarrow{z}$; otherwise, rule $\ominus_2$ replaces $x = y$ by true if it is trivially true (i.e., we have the same variable in both sides of the equality) or by false if x or y is in $\overrightarrow{z}$. Indeed, each token variable in $\overrightarrow{z}$ represents (by the semantics of CPN) a different token, and since this token is deleted by the transition rule, it cannot appear in the reached configuration. Rules $\ominus_3$ and $\ominus_4$ are straightforward. Finally, rule $\ominus_5$ does a case splitting according to the fact whether a deleted token is precisely the one referenced by the existential token quantification or not.

The operation $\oplus$ is parameterized by a vector $\overrightarrow{z}$ of token variables to be added and a mapping loc associating with each variable in $z \in \overrightarrow{z}$ a place (in which it will be added). Intuitively, $\oplus$ transforms a formula taking into account that the added tokens by the transition were not present in the previous configuration (and therefore not constrained by the original formula describing the configuration before the transition). Then, the application of $\oplus$ has no effect on color formulas $\xi(\overrightarrow{t})$ (rule $\oplus_1$). When equality of tokens is tested, rule $\oplus_2$ takes into account that all added tokens are distinct and different from the existing tokens. For token quantification, rule $\oplus_5$ says that quantified tokens of the previous configuration cannot be equal to the added tokens.

Then, we define φ_{post} to be the formula:

$$\exists \overrightarrow{y} \in \overrightarrow{q}.\, \exists \overrightarrow{c}.\, \left((\varphi \wedge \psi) \ominus (\overrightarrow{x}, \overrightarrow{x} \mapsto \overrightarrow{p}, \Gamma \mapsto (\overrightarrow{x} \mapsto \overrightarrow{c})) \right) \oplus (\overrightarrow{y}, \overrightarrow{y} \mapsto \overrightarrow{q})$$

In the formula above, we first delete the tokens corresponding to $\overrightarrow{x}$ from the current configuration φ intersected with the guard of the rule ψ. Then, we add tokens corresponding to $\overrightarrow{y}$. Finally, we close the formula by quantifying existentially the color variables and the token variables corresponding to the added tokens.

Similarly, we define φ_{pre} to be the formula:

$$\exists \overrightarrow{x} \in \overrightarrow{p}.\, \exists \overrightarrow{c}.\, \left((\varphi \oplus (\overrightarrow{x}, \overrightarrow{x} \mapsto \overrightarrow{p})) \wedge \psi \right) \ominus (\overrightarrow{y}, \overrightarrow{y} \mapsto \overrightarrow{q}, \Gamma \mapsto (\overrightarrow{y} \mapsto \overrightarrow{c}))$$

For predecessor computation, we add to the current configuration the tokens represented by the left hand side of the rule $\overrightarrow{x}$ in order to obtain a configuration on which the guard ψ can be applied. Then, we remove the tokens added by the rule using token variables $\overrightarrow{y}$. Finally, we close the formula by quantifying existentially the color variables and the token variables corresponding to the added tokens. It is easy to see that if φ and ψ are in a fragment Σ_n, for any $n \geq 1$, then both of the formulas φ_{post} and φ_{pre} are also in the same fragment Σ_n.

Corollary 1. *Let S be a* $\mathsf{CPN}[\Sigma_1]$. *Then, for every formula φ in Π_1, it is possible to construct a formula $\varphi_{\widetilde{\mathsf{pre}}}$ also in Π_1 s.t.* $[\![\varphi_{\widetilde{\mathsf{pre}}}]\!] = \widetilde{\mathsf{pre}}_S([\![\varphi]\!])$.

7 Applications in Verification

We show in this section how to use the results of the previous section to perform various kinds of analysis. Let us fix for the rest of the section a colored tokens logic L with a decidable satisfiability problem, and a CPN S defined over L and the logic $\mathsf{CML}(L)$.

7.1 Pre-post Condition Reasoning

Given a transition τ in S and given two formulas φ and φ', $\langle \varphi, \tau, \varphi' \rangle$ is a Hoare triple if whenever the condition φ holds, the condition φ' holds after the execution of τ. In other words, we must have $\mathsf{post}_\tau([\![\varphi]\!]) \subseteq [\![\varphi']\!]$, or equivalently that $\mathsf{post}_\tau([\![\varphi]\!]) \cap [\![\neg\varphi']\!] = \emptyset$. Then, by Theorem 3 and Theorem 2 we deduce the following:

Theorem 4. *If S is a* $\mathsf{CPN}[\Sigma_2]$, *then the problem whether $\langle \varphi, \tau, \varphi' \rangle$ is a Hoare triple is decidable for every transition τ of S, every formula $\varphi \in \Sigma_2$, and every formula $\varphi' \in \Pi_2$.*

Table 1. Definition of the $\oplus$ and $\ominus$ operators

$$\ominus_1: \quad \xi(\overrightarrow{t}) \ominus (\overrightarrow{z}, \texttt{loc}, \texttt{col}) = \xi(\overrightarrow{t})[\texttt{col}(\gamma)(z)/\gamma(z)]_{\gamma \in \Gamma, z \in \overrightarrow{z}}$$

$$\ominus_2: \quad (x = y) \ominus (\overrightarrow{z}, \texttt{loc}, \texttt{col}) = \begin{cases} x = y & \text{if } x, y \notin \overrightarrow{z} \\ \text{true} & \text{if } x \equiv y \\ \text{false} & \text{otherwise} \end{cases}$$

$$\ominus_3: \quad (\neg\varphi) \ominus (\overrightarrow{z}, \texttt{loc}, \texttt{col}) = \neg(\varphi \ominus (\overrightarrow{z}, \texttt{loc}, \texttt{col}))$$

$$\ominus_4: \quad (\varphi_1 \vee \varphi_2) \ominus (\overrightarrow{z}, \texttt{loc}, \texttt{col}) = (\varphi_1 \ominus (\overrightarrow{z}, \texttt{loc}, \texttt{col})) \vee (\varphi_2 \ominus (\overrightarrow{z}, \texttt{loc}, \texttt{col}))$$

$$\ominus_5: (\exists x \in p.\ \varphi) \ominus (\overrightarrow{z}, \texttt{loc}, \texttt{col}) = \exists x \in p.\ (\varphi \ominus (\overrightarrow{z}, \texttt{loc}, \texttt{col})) \vee$$
$$\bigvee_{z \in \overrightarrow{z}:\texttt{loc}(z)=p} (\varphi[z/x]) \ominus (\overrightarrow{z}, \texttt{loc}, \texttt{col})$$

$$\oplus_1: \quad \xi(\overrightarrow{t}) \oplus (\overrightarrow{z}, \texttt{loc}) = \xi(\overrightarrow{t})$$

$$\oplus_2: \quad (x = y) \oplus (\overrightarrow{z}, \texttt{loc}) = \begin{cases} x = y & \text{if } x, y \notin \overrightarrow{z} \\ \text{true} & \text{if } x \equiv y \\ \text{false} & \text{otherwise} \end{cases}$$

$$\oplus_3: \quad (\neg\varphi) \oplus (\overrightarrow{z}, \texttt{loc}) = \neg(\varphi \oplus (\overrightarrow{z}, \texttt{loc}))$$

$$\oplus_4: \quad (\varphi_1 \vee \varphi_2) \oplus (\overrightarrow{z}, \texttt{loc}) = (\varphi_1 \oplus (\overrightarrow{z}, \texttt{loc})) \vee (\varphi_2 \oplus (\overrightarrow{z}, \texttt{loc}))$$

$$\oplus_5: \quad (\exists x \in p.\ \varphi) \oplus (\overrightarrow{z}, \texttt{loc}) = \exists x \in p.\ (\varphi \oplus (\overrightarrow{z}, \texttt{loc})) \wedge \bigwedge_{z \in \overrightarrow{z}:\texttt{loc}(z)=p} \neg(x = z)$$

7.2 Bounded Reachability Analysis

An instance of the bounded reachability analysis problem is a triple $(Init, Target, k)$ where $Init$ and $Target$ are two sets of configurations, and k is a positive integer. The problem consists in deciding whether there exists a computation of length at most k which starts from some configuration in $Init$ and reaches a configuration in $Target$. In other words, the problem consists in deciding whether $Target \cap \bigcup_{0 \leq i \leq k} \texttt{post}_S^i(Init) \neq \emptyset$, or equivalently whether $Init \cap \bigcup_{0 \leq i \leq k} \texttt{pre}_S^i(Target) \neq \emptyset$. The following result is a direct consequence of Theorem 3 and Theorem 2.

Theorem 5. *If S is a $\text{CPN}[\Sigma_2]$, then, for every $k \in \mathbb{N}$, and for every two formulas $\varphi_I, \varphi_T \in \Sigma_2$, the bounded reachability problem $([\![\varphi_I]\!], [\![\varphi_T]\!], k)$ is decidable.*

7.3 Checking Invariance Properties

An instance of the *invariance checking problem* is given by a pair of sets of configurations (colored markings) $(Init, Inv)$, and consists in deciding whether starting from any configuration in $Init$, every computation of S can only visit configurations in Inv, i.e., $\bigcup_{k \geq 0} \texttt{post}_S^k(Init) \subseteq Inv$. This problem is of course undecidable in general. However, a deductive approach using inductive invariants (provided by the user) can be adopted. We show that our results allow to automatize the steps of this approach.

A set of configurations $\mathbb{M}$ is an *inductive invariant* if $\texttt{post}_S(\mathbb{M}) \subseteq \mathbb{M}$, or equivalently, if $\mathbb{M} \subseteq \widetilde{\texttt{pre}}_S(\mathbb{M})$. By Theorem 3 and Theorem 2, we have:

Theorem 6. *If S is a $\text{CPN}[\Sigma_2]$, then for every formula φ in $B(\Sigma_1)$, the problem of checking whether φ defines an inductive invariant is decidable.*

The deductive approach for establishing an invariance property considers the *inductive invariance checking problem* given by a triple $(Init, Inv, Aux)$ of sets of configurations, and which consists in deciding whether (1) $Init \subseteq Aux$, (2) $Aux \subseteq Inv$, and (3) Aux is an inductive invariant. Indeed, a (sound and) complete rule for solving an invariance checking problem $(Init, Inv)$ consists in finding a set of configurations Aux allowing to solve the inductive invariance checking problem $(Init, Inv, Aux)$. The following result follows directly from Theorem 3, Theorem 2, and the previous theorem.

Theorem 7. *If S is a $\mathsf{CPN}[\Sigma_2]$, then the inductive invariance checking problem is decidable for every instance $([\![\varphi_{Init}]\!], [\![\varphi]\!], [\![\varphi']\!])$ where $\varphi_{Init} \in \Sigma_2$, and $\varphi, \varphi' \in B(\Sigma_1)$.*

Of course, the difficult part in applying the deductive approach is to find useful auxiliary inductive invariants. One approach to tackle this problem is to try to compute the largest inductive invariant included in *Inv* which is the set $\bigcap_{k \geq 0} \widetilde{\mathsf{pre}}_S^k(Inv)$. Therefore, a method to derive auxiliary inductive invariants is to try iteratively the sets Inv, $Inv \cap \widetilde{\mathsf{pre}}_S(Inv)$, $Inv \cap \widetilde{\mathsf{pre}}_S(Inv) \cap \widetilde{\mathsf{pre}}_S^2(Inv)$, etc. In many practical cases, only few strengthening steps are needed to find an inductive invariant. (Indeed, the user is able in general to provide accurate invariant assertions for each control point of his system.) The result below implies that the steps of this iterative strengthening method can be automatized when $\mathsf{CPN}[\Sigma_1]$ models and Π_1 invariants are considered. This result is a direct consequence of Corollary 1.

Theorem 8. *If S is a $\mathsf{CPN}[\Sigma_1]$, then for every formula φ in Π_1 and every positive integer k, it is possible to construct a formula in Π_1 defining the set $\bigcap_{0 \leq i \leq k} \widetilde{\mathsf{pre}}_S^i([\![\varphi]\!])$.*

We show in the full paper the applicability of our framework on a nontrivial example. We present the verification of a Reader-Writer lock for an unbounded number of processes using the inductive invariant checking approach. This example has been considered in [28] for a fixed number of processes.

8 Conclusion

We have presented a framework for reasoning about dynamic/parametric networks of processes manipulating data over infinite domains. We have provided generic models for these systems and a logic allowing to specify their configurations, both being parametrized by a logic on the considered data domain. We have identified a fragment of this logic having a decidable satisfiability problem and which is closed under post and pre image computation, and we have shown the application of these results in verification.

The complexity of the decision procedure and of the post/pre computation is exponential in the size of the formula, and more precisely in the number of quantified variables. However, formulas which appear in the analysis of systems such as parametrized/dynamic networks (such as assertions expressing invariants at each particular control location) are naturally in special form (see definition in Section 2.3) where each token variable is bound to a unique place (this allows to avoid the case splitting according to all possible mappings between token variables and places), and moreover, new token variables introduced by post/pre computations are of a fixed small number (the number of synchronized processes by the considered transition which is in general equal to two). These facts reduce significantly the complexity in practice.

Our framework allows to deal in a uniform way with all classes of systems manipulating infinite data domains with a decidable first-order theory. In this paper, we have considered instantiations of this framework based on logics over integers or reals (which allows to consider systems with numerical variables). Different data domains can be considered in order to deal with other classes of systems such as multithreaded programs where each process (thread) has an unbounded stack (due to procedure calls). We will address in more details the issue of applying our framework to the verification of multithreaded programs in a forthcoming paper. Our future work includes also the extension of our framework to other classes of systems and features such as dynamic networks of timed processes, networks of processes with broadcast communication, interruptions and exception handling, etc.

References

1. P. A. Abdulla, K. Cerans, B. Jonsson, and Y.-K. Tsay. General decidability theorems for infinite-state systems. In *Proc. of LICS'96*, pages 313–321, 1996.
2. P. A. Abdulla and G. Delzanno. On the Coverability Problem for Constrained Multiset Rewriting. In *Proc. of AVIS'06, Satellite workshop of ETAPS'06*, Vienna, Austria, 2006.
3. P. A. Abdulla, B. Jonsson, M. Nilsson, and M. Saksena. A Survey of Regular Model Checking. In *Proc. of CONCUR'04*, volume 3170 of *LNCS*. Springer, 2004.
4. Parosh Aziz Abdulla and Bengt Jonsson. Verifying networks of timed processes (extended abstract). In Bernhard Steffen, editor, *Proc. of TACAS'98*, volume 1384 of *LNCS*, pages 298–312. Springer, 1998.
5. A. Annichini, E. Asarin, and A. Bouajjani. Symbolic techniques for parametric reasoning about counter and clock systems. In *Proc. of CAV'00*. LNCS 1855, 2000.
6. T. Arons, A. Pnueli, S. Ruah, J. Xu, and L.D. Zuck. Parameterized Verification with Automatically Computed Inductive Assertions. In *Proc. of CAV'01*, volume 2102 of *LNCS*. Springer, 2001.
7. Bernard Boigelot. *Symbolic Methods for Exploring Infinite State Space*. PhD thesis, Faculté des Sciences, Université de Liège, volume 189, 1999.
8. M. Bojanczyk, C. David, A. Muscholl, Th. Schwentick, and L. Segoufin. Two-variable logic on data trees and XML reasoning. In *Proc. of PODS'06*. ACM, 2006.
9. M. Bojanczyk, A. Muscholl, Th. Schwentick, L. Segoufin, and C. David. Two-variable logic on words with data. In *Proc. of LICS'06*. IEEE, 2006.
10. E. Börger, E. Grädel, and Y. Gurevich. *The Classical Decision Problem*. Perspectives of Mathematical Logic. Springer-Verlag, 1997. Second printing (Universitext) 2001.
11. A. Bouajjani, J. Esparza, and O. Maler. Reachability analysis of pushdown automata: Application to model-checking. In *Proc. of CONCUR'97*, volume 1243 of *LNCS*, pages 135–150. Springer, 1997.
12. A. Bouajjani, P. Habermehl, and T. Vojnar. Abstract Regular Model Checking. In *Proc. of CAV'04*, volume 3114 of *LNCS*. Springer, 2004.
13. A. Bouajjani, B. Jonsson, M. Nilsson, and T. Touili. Regular Model Checking. In *Proc. of CAV'00*, volume 1855 of *LNCS*. Springer, 2000.
14. A. Bouajjani, Y. Jurski, and M. Sighireanu. A generic framework for reasoning about dynamic networks of infinite-state processes. Technical Report 2007-01, LIAFA lab, January 2007. Available at http://www.liafa.jussieu.fr/~abou/publis.html.

15. A. Bouajjani, M. Müller-Olm, and T. Touili. Regular symbolic analysis of dynamic networks of pushdown systems. In *Proc. of CONCUR'05*, volume 3653 of *LNCS*. Springer, 2005.
16. A. Bouajjani and T. Touili. On computing reachability sets of process rewrite systems. In *Proc. of RTA'05*, volume 3467 of *LNCS*. Springer, 2005.
17. Ahmed Bouajjani. Languages, Rewriting systems, and Verification of Infinte-State Systems. In *Proc. of ICALP'01*, volume 2076 of *LNCS*. Springer Pub., 2001.
18. M. Bozzano and G. Delzanno. Beyond Parameterized Verification. In *Proc. of TACAS'02*, volume 2280 of *LNCS*, Grenoble, France, 2002. Springer Pub.
19. A. R. Bradley, Z. Manna, and H. B. Sipma. What's decidable about arrays ? In *Proc. of VMCAI'06*, volume 3855 of *LNCS*. Springer, 2006.
20. E. M. Clarke, O. Grumberg, and S. Jha. Verifying parameterized networks. *TOPLAS*, 19(5), 1997.
21. G. Delzanno. An assertional language for the verification of systems parametric in several dimensions. *Electr. Notes Theor. Comput. Sci.*, 50(4), 2001.
22. G. Delzanno, J.-F. Raskin, and L. Van Begin. Towards the automated verification of multi-threaded java programs. In *TACAS*, volume 2280 of *LNCS*, pages 173–187. Springer, 2002.
23. S. Demri and R. Lazic. LTL with the freeze quantifier and register automata. In *Proc. of LICS'06*. IEEE, 2006.
24. E. A. Emerson and K. S. Namjoshi. On model checking for non-deterministic infinite-state systems. In *LICS'98*. IEEE, 1998.
25. J. Esparza, A. Finkel, and R. Mayr. On the verification of broadcast protocols. In *Proceedings of LICS '99*, pages 352–359. IEEE Computer Society, 1999.
26. A. Finkel and J. Leroux. How to compose presburger-accelerations: Applications to broadcast protocols. In *Proc. of FST&TCS'02*, volume 2556 of *LNCS*. Springer, 2002.
27. A. Finkel and Ph. Schnoebelen. Well-structured transition systems everywhere! *Theor. Comput. Sci.*, 256(1-2):63–92, 2001.
28. C. Flanagan, S.N. Freund, and S. Qadeer. Thread-modular verification for shared-memory programs. In *Proc. of ESOP'02*, pages 262–277. LNCS 2305, 2002.
29. S. M. German and P. A. Sistla. Reasoning about systems with many processes. *JACM*, 39(3), 1992.
30. P. Wolper and B. Boigelot. Verifying systems with infinite but regular state spaces. In *Proc. of CAV'98*, volume 1427 of *LNCS*. Springer, 1998.
31. P. Wolper and V. Lovinfosse. Verifying properties of large sets of processes with network invariants. In *Proc. Intern. Workshop on Automatic Verification Methods for Finite State Systems*. LNCS 407, 1989.

Unfolding Concurrent Well-Structured Transition Systems*

Frédéric Herbreteau, Grégoire Sutre, and The Quang Tran

LaBRI, CNRS UMR 5800, Domaine Universitaire, Talence, France
{fh,sutre,tran}@labri.fr

Abstract. Our main objective is to combine partial-order methods with verification techniques for infinite-state systems in order to obtain efficient verification algorithms for concurrent infinite-state systems. Partial-order methods are commonly used in the analysis of finite systems consisting of many parallel components. In this paper we propose an extension of these methods to parallel compositions of infinite-state systems. We argue that it is advantageous to model each component by an event structure as this allows us to exhibit the concurrency present implicitly in some infinite-state systems such as automata with queues or counters. We generalize the notion of complete prefix from 1-safe Petri nets to all well-structured transition systems. We give an on-the-fly unfolding algorithm which given event structures representing the components produces an event structure representing their synchronized product. A prototype implementation demonstrates the benefits of our approach.

1   Introduction

Partial-order methods [God96, Val91, Pel93] are frequently used for the verification of programs, in particular for systems of concurrent processes. Indeed, proving that the computations of such systems meet some requirement often results in the well-known exponential blow-up due to interleaving of concurrent actions. Partial-order methods tackle this problem by selecting a hopefully small set of relevant computations that are sufficient to conclude. Selecting among the interleavings is sound because ordering concurrent (independent) actions is irrelevant. Hence, instead of considering totally ordered computations, one analyses *traces* [Maz86] that stand for all equivalent computations w.r.t. concurrency. As a consequence, the whole computation tree can be partially rather than totally ordered resulting in *event structures* [NPW81, NRT95]. Efficient exploration techniques, e.g. unfolding [McM95, NRT95], exist for partially-ordered structures.

Traditionally, partial-order methods have been applied to concurrent *finite-state* processes and proved to be successful. In this paper, we apply partial-order methods to parallel compositions of *infinite-state* systems such as counter machines and communicating finite-state machines. Verification of infinite-state systems is known to be

---

* This work was partially supported by the French Ministry of Research (Project PERSÉE of the ACI Sécurité et Informatique).

O. Grumberg and M. Huth (Eds.): TACAS 2007, LNCS 4424, pp. 706–720, 2007.

undecidable, however some classes of infinite-state systems enjoy nice decidability results. Well-Structured Transition Systems [Fin90, AČJT00, FS01] provide us with a nice framework based on weak simulation relations that are well-preorders. Since a well-preorder admits no infinite decreasing sequence, one can consider only a finite prefix of the computation tree in order to decide properties like boundedness, termination or covering.

Our contribution. Our goal is to analyse synchronized products of well-structured systems using a method similar to Petri net unfolding in order to obtain event structures. The most straightforward approach would be to consider that each component generates an (infinite) transition system, then use an on-the-fly variant of the unfolding method for parallel composition of finite automata. This turns out not to be satisfactory: imagine that one models a counter by an (infinite) automaton then if, say, three different processes want to increase the counter, their actions will get interleaved on the automaton modeling the counter. As in principle those actions are independent, we lose a good deal of concurrency present in the original system. Our solution is to model each component by an event structure, hence taking advantage of the intrinsic concurrency present in each component.

Our first contribution is an algorithm for constructing event structures for components modeling counters. It results in event structures with more concurrency than in [McM95]. We also present a general algorithm that works for all (infinite) transition systems. This is not trivial: one wants the most concurrent event structure whereas concurrency is not explicit in transition systems. Of course, our algorithm is less efficient than dedicated algorithms (e.g. for counter automata), however it exhibits a good deal of concurrency using local independence. For instance it produces the same event structures as those reported in [LI05] for queue automata.

Our second contribution is a generalization of the unfolding method of [ER99] to parallel composition of potentially infinite event structures. Our algorithm is both capable of exploiting concurrency in components as well as among them. In particular we show that modeling Petri nets as the parallel composition of its places (viewed as counters) results in very efficient analysis using our algorithms.

Of course there is no hope to have a notion of complete prefix for a parallel composition of infinite systems. There is hope though when the components are well-structured systems. We give a property-preserving truncation criterion for event structures of well-structured transition systems. The resulting (complete) prefix contains enough information to decide boundedness, termination and quasi-liveness. We also show preservation of well-structure under parallel composition for all variants of well-structure. Remark that these results cannot be directly obtained from previous techniques on well-structured systems, since the complete prefix is not a compact partial-order representation of the finite reachability tree of [FS01].

Related work. The unfolding technique [McM95] has been developed for several models of concurrency, e.g. synchronous products of transition systems [ER99], high-level Petri nets [KK03], extended finite state machines [LI05], symmetric Petri nets [CGP01]. However, all these techniques deal with finite-state models.

In [AJKP98], the authors address the coverability problem for infinite state systems by combining partial-order reductions and symbolic backward computations. The unfolding of unbounded Petri nets was recently considered. In [AIN00] Abdulla et al. propose a backward unfolding technique for coverability analysis, and [DJN04] presents an unfolding-based adaptation of Karp and Miller's algorithm. Our method generalizes these results: it analyses any (infinite) well-structured transition system [FS01], offering both forward and backward approaches, hence enabling to check covering, boundedness and termination properties.

Outline. Section 2 introduces notations and definitions for transition systems and event structures. In section 3 we prove well-structure properties for event structures. Then, in section 4 we introduce our algorithms for unfolding systems. Finally, in section 5 we give some experimental results showing the benefits of our approach, and we conclude on future work. Please note that some preliminary (standard) definitions along with all proofs had to be omitted due to space constraints. A long version of this paper can be obtained from the authors.

2 Labeled Transition Systems and Event Structures

A *binary relation* R on some set U is any subset of $U \times U$. We will sometimes view functions as relations. Given a subset $X \subseteq U$, we denote by $R[X]$ the *relational image* of X through R, defined by $R[X] = \{y \in U \mid \exists x \in X, x\,R\,y\}$. The *inverse* of R is the binary relation R^{-1} on U defined by $x\,R^{-1}\,x'$ iff $x'\,R\,x$. A *preorder* on some set U is any reflexive and transitive relation $\preceq$ on U. We let $x \prec x'$ denote $x \preceq x' \npreceq x$. Given a preorder $\preceq$ on U, the *inverse* relation $\preceq^{-1}$ is a preorder also written $\succeq$. For any subset $X \subseteq U$, the set $\preceq[X]$ (resp. $\succeq[X]$) is called the *upward closure* (resp. *downward closure*) of X with respect to $\preceq$. We say that X is *upward-closed* (resp. *downward-closed*) if X is equal to its upward closure (resp. downward closure). A *partial order* on U is any antisymmetric preorder on U. Given a partial order $\leq$ on U, a *maximal element* (resp. *minimal element*) of some subset $X \subseteq U$ is any $m \in X$ such that $m' \not\geq m$ (resp. $m' \not\leq m$) for all $m' \neq m$ in X. We write $\mathsf{Max}_{\leq}(X)$ (resp. $\mathsf{Min}_{\leq}(X)$) for the set of maximal elements (resp. minimal elements) of X with respect to $\leq$.

Given a set Σ, we denote by Σ^* (resp. Σ^ω) the set of all finite (resp. infinite) sequences $a_1, a_2, \ldots, a_k$ (resp. $a_1, a_2, \ldots, a_k, \ldots$) of elements in Σ. The empty sequence is written ε and we denote by Σ^+ the set $\Sigma^* \setminus \{\varepsilon\}$.

2.1 Labeled Transition Systems

Definition 2.1. *A labeled transition system (LTS) is a 4-tuple* $\mathcal{S} = (S, s^0, \Sigma, \rightarrow)$ *where S is a set of* states, $s^0 \in S$ *is an* initial state, Σ *is a set of* labels *and* $\rightarrow \subseteq S \times \Sigma \times S$ *is a* transition relation.

A transition $(s, a, s') \in \rightarrow$ is also written $s \xrightarrow{a} s'$. We also write $s \xrightarrow{a}$ whenever there exists s' such that $s \xrightarrow{a} s'$. A *finite path* (resp. *infinite path*) in $\mathcal{S}$ is any finite (resp. infinite) sequence $\pi = s_1 \xrightarrow{a_1} s_1', s_2 \xrightarrow{a_2} s_2', \ldots, s_k \xrightarrow{a_k} s_k', \ldots$ of transitions such that $s_{i-1}' = s_i$ for every index $i > 1$ in the sequence. We shortly write $\pi = s_1 \xrightarrow{a_1} s_2 \xrightarrow{a_2} s_3 \cdots s_k \xrightarrow{a_k} s_{k+1} \cdots$ and we say that π *starts in* s_1. A finite (resp. infinite) *execution* of $\mathcal{S}$ is any finite (resp. infinite) path starting in the initial state s^0 of $\mathcal{S}$. Slightly abusing notations, we will also write $s \xrightarrow{\varepsilon} s$ for every state s. The *reachability set* post$_{\mathcal{S}}^*$ of $\mathcal{S}$ is the set of states that are visited by some execution.

We now present the composition primitive that we use to build complex systems from basic components: the synchronized product of labeled transitions [Arn94]. In a synchronized product, components must behave according to so-called synchronization vectors. Consider n labeled transition systems $\mathcal{S}_1, \ldots, \mathcal{S}_n$ with $\mathcal{S}_i = (S_i, s_i^0, \Sigma_i, \rightarrow_i)$. A *synchronization vector* is any n-tuple v in $\Sigma_\otimes = (\Sigma_1 \cup \{\varepsilon\}) \times \cdots \times (\Sigma_n \cup \{\varepsilon\})$, and a *synchronization constraint* is any subset $V \subseteq \Sigma_\otimes$ of synchronization vectors. Intuitively, a label a in a synchronization vector means that the corresponding component must take a transition labeled by a, whereas an ε means that the component must not move.

Definition 2.2. *The synchronized product of n labeled transition systems $\mathcal{S}_1, \ldots, \mathcal{S}_n$ with respect to a synchronization constraint V is the labeled transition system $\mathcal{S}_\otimes = (S_\otimes, s^0_\otimes, \Sigma_\otimes, \rightarrow_\otimes)$ defined by: $S_\otimes = S_1 \times \cdots \times S_n$, $s^0{}_\otimes = \langle s_1^0, \ldots, s_n^0 \rangle$ and $s \xrightarrow{v}_\otimes s'$ iff $v \in V$ and $s(i) \xrightarrow{v(i)} s'(i)$ for every $1 \leq i \leq n$.*

2.2 Labeled Event Structures

Definition 2.3. *A labeled event structure (LES) is a 5-tuple $\mathcal{E} = (E, \leq, \#, \Sigma, l)$ where E is a set of events, $\leq$ is a partial order on E, $\#$ is a symmetric and irreflexive relation on E, Σ is a set of labels, and $l : E \to \Sigma$ is a labeling function satisfying:*

i) the downward closure $\geq[\{e\}]$ is finite for every $e \in E$, and
ii) $e\#e'$ and $e' \leq e''$ implies $e\#e''$ for every $e, e', e'' \in E$.

In the previous definition, relations $\leq$ and $\#$ are respectively called *causality* and *conflict* relations. Intuitively, an event e can occur when (1) every causal event e' with $e' \leq e$ has already occurred and (2) no conflicting event e' with $e'\#e$ has already occurred. Condition i) enforces that any event has finitely many causal events, and condition ii) expresses a *conflict inheritance* property.

A subset of E is called *conflict-free* if it does not contain any two events that are in conflict. A *configuration* is any conflict-free and downward-closed (w.r.t. causality) subset of E. We denote by $\mathcal{C}(\mathcal{E})$ (resp. $\mathcal{C}_f(\mathcal{E})$) the set of all configurations (resp. finite configurations) of a labeled event structure $\mathcal{E}$. For any event $e \in E$, the set $\geq[\{e\}]$ is called the *local configuration of e* (it is readily seen that this set is a finite configuration). We will shortly write $[e]$ the local configuration of e when the causality preorder is clear from the context. An event $e \in E$ is *enabled* at some configuration C, written $C \vdash e$, if $e \notin C$ and $C \cup \{e\}$ is a configuration. We say that a labeled event structure is *finitely-branching* if every finite configuration has finitely many enabled events. A variant of König's lemma applies to finitely-branching labeled event structures.

Definition 2.4. *A marking for a labeled event structure $\mathcal{E}$ is any function M from $\mathcal{C}_f(\mathcal{E})$ to some set S.*

A *marked LES* is any pair $(\mathcal{E}, M)$ consisting of a labeled event structure $\mathcal{E}$ and a marking M for $\mathcal{E}$. We denote by $\mathcal{S}_{\mathcal{E}}^{M}$ the labeled transition system *induced by* $(\mathcal{E}, M)$ and defined by $\mathcal{S}_{\mathcal{E}}^{M} = (M[\mathcal{C}_f(\mathcal{E})], M(\emptyset), \Sigma, \rightarrow)$ where $s \xrightarrow{a} s'$ iff there exists a finite configuration C and an event e enabled at C such that $s = M(C)$, $a = l(e)$ and $s' = M(C \cup \{e\})$. Given a labeled transition system $\mathcal{S}$, a *marked LES for* $\mathcal{S}$ is any marked LES $(\mathcal{E}, M)$ such that $\mathcal{S}_{\mathcal{E}}^{M}$ coincides with the restriction of $\mathcal{S}$ to $post_{\mathcal{S}}^{*}$. Remark that $(\mathcal{E}, M)$ is obviously a marked LES for $\mathcal{S}_{\mathcal{E}}^{M}$.

3 Truncation for Well-Structured Transition Systems

Well-Structured Transition Systems were introduced in [Fin90, AČJT00] as an abstract generalization of Petri nets satisfying the same *monotonicity* property, and hence enjoying nice decidability properties. It turns out that many classes of infinite-state systems are well-structured [FS01].

We will see in the next section how to algorithmically construct labeled event structures. However, a labeled event structure is infinite as soon as the underlying system has an infinite execution. Thus, we need property-preserving truncation techniques in order to decide verification problems using only a finite prefix of an event structure. In this section, we show how such techniques can be obtained when the underlying system is well-structured.

For simplicity we only focus, without loss of generality, on forward analysis techniques for well-structured transition systems. We show in the long version of this paper how known backward analysis results on well-structured transition systems can be captured by this forward analysis. Moreover, we do not discuss effectivity issues (such as whether preorders need to be decidable, whether successor states need to be computable, etc.) since they are basically the same as in [FS01].

3.1 Synchronized Product of Well-Structured Transition Systems

Recall that our main objective is to verify complex systems obtained by (potentially nested) synchronized products of basic components. Thus, we first show that well-structure is preserved under synchronized product. Our presentation of well-structured transition systems differs from (and generalizes) the standard (non-labeled) one as we need to take care of labels.

Until the end of this sub-section, we assume that each set of labels Σ is partitioned into a set Σ_τ of *local labels* (for internal transitions) and a set Σ_γ of *global labels* (for synchronizable transitions). In order to account for this separation between internal transitions and synchronizable ones, we assume (1) that every synchronization constraint V implicitly contains the set $V_\tau = \{\langle \tau, \varepsilon, \ldots, \varepsilon \rangle, \ldots, \langle \varepsilon, \ldots, \varepsilon, \tau, \varepsilon, \ldots, \varepsilon \rangle, \ldots, \langle \varepsilon, \ldots, \varepsilon, \tau \rangle \mid \tau \in \Sigma_\tau \}$ of synchronization vectors, and (2) that no local label $\tau \in \Sigma_\tau$ may appear in a synchronization vector of $V \setminus V_\tau$. Naturally V_τ becomes the set of local labels of any synchronized product w.r.t. V.

A *preordered LTS* is any LTS $\mathcal{S} = (S, s^0, \Sigma, \rightarrow)$ equipped with a preorder $\preceq$ on S. We say that $\preceq$ is *compatible* (resp. *transitively compatible*, *reflexively compatible*) with

$\rightarrow$ if for every transition $s \xrightarrow{a} s'$ and $t \succeq s$ there exists $t' \succeq s'$ such that $t \xrightarrow{\sigma} t'$ for some $\sigma \in \Sigma^*$ satisfying:

$$\begin{cases} \sigma \in \Sigma_\tau^* & \text{if } a \in \Sigma_\tau \\ \sigma \in \Sigma_\tau^* \, a \, \Sigma_\tau^* & \text{otherwise} \end{cases} \qquad \begin{cases} \sigma \in \Sigma_\tau^+ & \text{if } a \in \Sigma_\tau \\ \sigma \in \Sigma_\tau^* \, a \, \Sigma_\tau^* & \text{otherwise} \end{cases} \qquad \begin{cases} \sigma \in \{\varepsilon\} \cup \Sigma_\tau \text{ if } a \in \Sigma_\tau \\ \sigma = a \qquad\quad \text{otherwise} \end{cases}$$

$$\text{(compatibility)} \qquad\qquad \text{(transitive compatibility)} \qquad \text{(reflexive compatibility)}$$

Moreover we also say that $\preceq$ is *strictly compatible* with $\rightarrow$ if both $\preceq$ and $\prec$ are compatible with $\rightarrow$ (recall that $s \prec s'$ is defined by $s \preceq s' \not\preceq s$). Of course, this strictness notion may be combined with transitive and reflexive compatibilities.

Remark 3.1. The previous definitions of compatibility coincide with the definitions given in [FS01] when $\Sigma = \Sigma_\tau$ is a singleton.

Any synchronized product $S_\otimes$ of n preordered LTSs $(S_1, \preceq_1), \ldots, (S_n, \preceq_n)$ may be equipped with the *product preorder* $\preceq_\otimes$ defined by $s \preceq_\otimes s'$ iff $s(i) \preceq_i s'(i)$ for every $1 \leq i \leq n$. The following proposition shows that all six compatibility notions defined above are preserved under synchronized product.

Proposition 3.2. *Let $Cond$ denote any compatibility condition among $\{(non\text{-}strict), strict\} \times \{(standard), transitive, reflexive\}$. Any synchronized product of preordered LTSs with compatibility $Cond$ also has compatibility $Cond$.*

Recall that a *well-preorder* on some set U is any preorder $\preceq$ on U such that any infinite sequence $x_1, \ldots, x_k, \ldots$ of elements in U contains an increasing pair $x_i \preceq x_j$ with $i < j$. A *well-preordered LTS* is any preordered LTS $(S, \preceq)$ where $\preceq$ is a well-preorder on the state set S of S. Since the product preorder of any n well-preorders is also a well-preorder (from Higman's lemma), we obtain that well-preordering is preserved under synchronized product.

Proposition 3.3. *Any synchronized product of well-preordered LTSs is a well-preordered LTS.*

A *well-structured* LTS is any well-preordered LTS with (standard) compatibility. It follows from the two previous propositions that well-structure is preserved under synchronized product.

3.2 Finite Property-Preserving Truncation of Well-Structured LES

The intuition behind well-structure is that any state may be weakly simulated by any greater state, and thus we may forget about smaller states when performing reachability analysis. The well-preordering condition between states guarantees termination of the analysis [FS01]. We show in this sub-section how to extend these ideas to the partial-order verification of well-structured labeled transition systems.

Recall that any marked LES $(\mathcal{E}, M)$ induces a labeled transition system $S_\mathcal{E}^M$. We lift the well-structure notions defined in the previous sub-section from labeled transition systems to labeled event structures. A *preordered marked LES* (resp. *well-preordered marked LES*) is any marked LES $(\mathcal{E}, M)$ equipped with a preorder (resp. well-preorder)

$\preceq$ on $M[\mathcal{C}_f(\mathcal{E})]$. Given any preordered marked LES $(\mathcal{E}, M, \preceq)$, we say that $(\mathcal{E}, M, \preceq)$ has compatibility $Cond \in \{(\text{non-strict}), \text{strict}\} \times \{(\text{standard}), \text{transitive}, \text{reflexive}\}$ whenever $\mathcal{S}^M_{\mathcal{E}}$ has compatibility $Cond$.

Consider any preordered marked LES $(\mathcal{E}, M, \preceq)$ where $\mathcal{E} = (E, \leq, \#, \Sigma, l)$. A *cut-off event* is any $e_{cut} \in E$ such that $M([e_{cut}]) \succeq M([e])$ for some event e with $e < e_{cut}$. The *truncation* $\mathcal{T}(\mathcal{E}, M, \preceq)$ of $(\mathcal{E}, M, \preceq)$ is the set of events having no strictly causal cutoff event, formally $\mathcal{T}(\mathcal{E}, M, \preceq) = E \backslash \{e \in E \mid \exists\, e_{cut} \in E_{cut}, e_{cut} < e\}$ where E_{cut} denotes the set of cutoff events in $\mathcal{E}$. Observe that $\mathcal{T}(\mathcal{E}, M, \preceq)$ is downward-closed, and that any minimal cutoff event (i.e. any event in $\mathsf{Min}_<(E_{cut})$) is a maximal event of $\mathcal{T}(\mathcal{E}, M, \preceq)$ but the converse does not hold in general. In order to preserve termination and boundedness properties, this truncation criterion "respects" causality, and this leads to larger truncations than in [McM95] where the truncation only preserves reachability properties.

We will show in the rest of this sub-section how to use the truncation to decide several verification problems. Unfortunately the truncation may be infinite in general, as it may be "too deep" and/or "too wide". A well-preordering condition avoids the first possibility, and a branching finiteness assumption eliminates the second.

Proposition 3.4. *The truncation of any well-preordered finitely-branching marked LES is finite.*

Given any labeled transition system $\mathcal{S}$, we say that $\mathcal{S}$ *terminates* (resp. is *bounded*) if $\mathcal{S}$ has no infinite execution (resp. has a finite reachability set $\mathsf{post}^*_{\mathcal{S}}$). The two following propositions show that, assuming an adequate compatibility condition, the truncation defined above contains enough information to decide termination and boundedness. Remark that in these two propositions, the finiteness requirement on the truncation can be dropped when the marked LES is finitely-branching and well-preordered.

Proposition 3.5. *For any preordered finitely-branching marked LES $(\mathcal{E}, M, \preceq)$ with transitive compatibility, $\mathcal{S}^M_{\mathcal{E}}$ terminates iff $\mathcal{T}(\mathcal{E}, M, \preceq)$ is finite and contains no cutoff event.*

In order to decide boundedness, we will need "strict" cutoff events, and we will also require a partial-order $\preceq$. Formally, a *strict cutoff event* is any $e_{cut} \in E$ such that $M([e_{cut}]) \succ M([e])$ for some event e with $e < e_{cut}$. Observe that any strict cutoff event is also a cutoff event. A *partially-ordered marked LES* is any preordered marked LES $(\mathcal{E}, M, \preceq)$ where $\preceq$ is a partial order on $M[\mathcal{C}_f(\mathcal{E})]$. Notice that the following proposition does not hold for general preordered marked LES.

Proposition 3.6. *For any partially-ordered marked LES $(\mathcal{E}, M, \preceq)$ with strict compatibility, $\mathcal{S}^M_{\mathcal{E}}$ is bounded iff $M[\{C \in \mathcal{C}_f(\mathcal{E}) \mid C \subseteq \mathcal{T}(\mathcal{E}, M, \preceq)\}]$ is finite and $\mathcal{T}(\mathcal{E}, M, \preceq)$ contains no strict cutoff event.*

We now turn our attention to the quasi-liveness problem which, assuming an adequate compatibility condition, reduces to the computation of the upward closure of $\mathsf{post}^*_{\mathcal{S}^M_{\mathcal{E}}}$.

For any labeled transition system $\mathcal{S} = (S, s^0, \Sigma, \rightarrow)$, we say that a given label $a \in \Sigma$ is *quasi-live* if there is an execution in $\mathcal{S}$ containing a transition labeled with a.

The truncation that we have used so far would be sufficient to decide quasi-liveness, but in order to improve efficiency, we consider a refined notion of cutoff events which leads to smaller truncations (that still contain enough information to decide quasi-liveness). This refined notion is based on the size of configurations as in [McM95]. Formally, given any preordered marked LES $(\mathcal{E}, M, \preceq)$ where $\mathcal{E} = (E, \leq, \#, \Sigma, l)$, we denote by $\trianglelefteq$ the preorder on $C_f(\mathcal{E})$ defined by $C \trianglelefteq C'$ iff $\mathsf{Card}(C) \leq \mathsf{Card}(C')$. Note that $C \triangleleft C'$ means $\mathsf{Card}(C) < \mathsf{Card}(C')$. A $\triangleleft$-*cutoff event* is any $e_{cut} \in E$ such that $M([e_{cut}]) \succeq M([e])$ for some event e with $[e] \triangleleft [e_{cut}]$. The $\triangleleft$-*truncation* $\mathcal{T}_\triangleleft(\mathcal{E}, M, \preceq)$ of $(\mathcal{E}, M, \preceq)$ is the set of events having no strictly causal $\triangleleft$-cutoff event, formally $\mathcal{T}_\triangleleft(\mathcal{E}, M, \preceq) = E \setminus \{e \in E \,/\, \exists\, e_{cut} \in E_{cut}^\triangleleft, e_{cut} < e\}$ where $E_{cut}^\triangleleft$ denotes the set of $\triangleleft$-cutoff events in $\mathcal{E}$.

For clarity, any (standard) cutoff event will now be called a $\sqsubset$-cutoff event, and the (standard) truncation will now be called the $\sqsubset$-truncation and be denoted by $\mathcal{T}_\sqsubset(\mathcal{E}, M, \preceq)$. It is readily seen that $\mathcal{T}_\triangleleft(\mathcal{E}, M, \preceq) \subseteq \mathcal{T}_\sqsubset(\mathcal{E}, M, \preceq)$. Hence $\triangleleft$-truncations are also finite for well-preordered finitely-branching marked LESs. Notice that the following proposition requires reflexive compatibility of the inverse preorder $\succeq$ of $\preceq$ (this requirement was called "downward compatibility" in [FS01]).

Proposition 3.7. *For any preordered marked LES $(\mathcal{E}, M, \succeq)$ with reflexive compatibility, the two following assertions hold:*

i) *the sets $M[\{C \in C_f(\mathcal{E}) \,/\, C \subseteq \mathcal{T}_\triangleleft(\mathcal{E}, M, \preceq)\}]$ and $\mathsf{post}^*_{\mathcal{S}_\mathcal{E}^M}$ have the same upward closure w.r.t. $\preceq$.*

ii) *for any global label a, a is quasi-live in $\mathcal{S}_\mathcal{E}^M$ iff a labels an event in $\mathcal{T}_\triangleleft(\mathcal{E}, M, \preceq)$.*

Remark that the previous proposition also holds for the standard truncation (i.e. we may replace $\mathcal{T}_\triangleleft$ by $\mathcal{T}_\sqsubset$ in the proposition). We may even further refine the truncation by considering a preorder on $C_f(\mathcal{E})$ that refines $\trianglelefteq$ (i.e. a preorder that is contained in $\trianglelefteq$). However Proposition 3.7 may not hold for this refined preorder unless we assume stronger requirements on the preordered marked LES $(\mathcal{E}, M, \succeq)$. In particular, if every label is global then Proposition 3.7 still holds for the lexicographic preorder between configurations defined in [ERV02].

4   Compositional Unfoldings of Concurrent Systems

We now give algorithms for unfolding given systems into labeled event structures. Figure 4(a) depicts an LES $\mathcal{E}_a$ modeling a positive counter initialized to 1. Black (resp. white) events represent increasing ($+$) events (resp. decreasing ($-$) events) and arrows represent the causality relation. Since this counter is initialized to 1, both $-$ and $+$ are initially enabled, however one needs to first unfold a $+$ event before unfolding a second $-$, and so on. Thus, unfolding $\mathcal{E}_a$ is achieved by first building the lowest two events (initialization phase), and then extending every $+$ event with new $-$ and $+$ events (extension phase).

All our unfolding algorithms rely on this principle. The following Unfold builds on-the-fly LES for given systems:

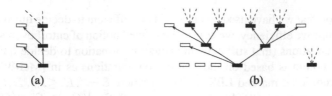

Fig. 1. LES for counters with: (a) $v_0 = 1$ and $k = 1$, (b) $v_0 = 3$ and $k = 2$

```
Unfold()
   PE:=Init()
   for (P,A) ∈ PE do
      NewPE:=Extend(P,A)
      PE:= (PE \ {(P,A)}) ∪ NewPE
   end
```

Pairs (P, A) correspond to new extensions: P is the preset of the new event (e.g. the lowest black event in Figure 4(a)) and A is the set of actions to extend with (e.g. $\{+, -\}$). Extending creates new events using the **NewEvent** function that also updates causality and conflict relations. Then **Unfold** computes new pending extensions. Notice that this algorithm terminates if **Extend** eventually always returns an empty set, which is the case for well-structured LESs if we do not extend cut-off events as defined in section 3.2.

In the sequel, we detail **Init** and **Extend** functions for three types of systems. We first consider *counters* for which we give dedicated functions. Ad hoc algorithms are always more efficient and can be defined for other datatypes for instance FIFO queues [LI05]. However, it is not always possible nor wanted to have specific algorithms, hence in section 4.2 we define functions that compute a concurrent marked LES for any given LTS. Finally, in section 4.3, we consider the unfolding of synchronized products of systems.

4.1   Unfolding Counters

A *counter* is a datatype with values ranging over the set of natural numbers $\mathbb{N}$, equipped with two operations: $+$ and $-$ that respectively increase and decrease its value, and initial value $v_0 \in \mathbb{N}$. It may be viewed as an LTS $\mathcal{S}_c = (\mathbb{N}, v_0, \{+, -\}, \rightarrow)$ where $n \xrightarrow{+} n + 1$ for any $n \in \mathbb{N}$ and $n \xrightarrow{-} n - 1$ for all $n > 0$. Places of Petri nets are examples of such counters.

We aim at defining **Init** and **Extend** functions that build an LES for a counter. Figure 4 depicts two different LESs $\mathcal{E}_a$ and $\mathcal{E}_b$ modeling a counter. The labeling l_c associates $+$ (resp. $-$) to every black (resp. white) event and the natural marking M_c associates to every $C \in \mathcal{C}_f(\mathcal{E})$ the value $v_0 + \mathrm{Card}(\{e \in C \,/\, l_c(e) = +\}) - \mathrm{Card}(\{e \in C \,/\, l_c(e) = -\})$. Both $(\mathcal{E}_a, M_c)$ and $(\mathcal{E}_b, M_c)$ are marked LESs for $\mathcal{S}_c$.

In these LESs, causality between $-$ and $+$ events correspond to intuitive constraints: a counter must be increased before being decreased. However, if $v_0 > 0$, it may be decreased v_0 times without any increasing. Also, $+$ events are concurrent since there is no constraint for increasing. Hence, labeled event structures $\mathcal{E}_a$ and $\mathcal{E}_b$ differ in the degree of concurrency between $+$ events. Choosing the degree $k \geq 1$ of concurrency is a matter of modeling leading to more or less concurrent truncations depending on the system that is analysed, in particular for synchronized products of LESs (see section 4.3).

Init creates v_0 $(\emptyset, \{-\})$ and k $(\emptyset, \{+\})$ pending extensions. Then, Extend simply follows the the principle depicted in Figures 4(a) and 4(b).

```
Extend (P, A)
    if  (− ∈ A)  e⁻ :=NewEvent (−, P)
    if  (+ ∈ A)  for  i ∈ [1; k]  do  eᵢ⁺ :=NewEvent (+, P)
    return  {({eᵢ⁺}, {+, −}) / i ∈ [1; k]}
```

Using our algorithm, one obtains the $(v_0 = 1, k = 1)$ counter LES in Figure 4(a), which corresponds to McMillan's unfolding of a counter [McM95]. However, Figure 4(b) shows that our approach yields the ability to choose more or less concurrent models using parameter k.

4.2   Unfolding Labeled Transition Systems

Defining the semantics of given systems as LESs or designing dedicated unfolding algorithms for those systems is often very hard. However, most systems can easily be described as LTSs. Hence, being able to compute a marked LES for any LTS is a solution to benefit from intrinsic concurrency in those systems.

A trivial LES for any LTS is its reachability tree, however every event in a reachability tree is either in causality or in conflict with any other event. We introduce an algorithm that computes a *concurrent* marked LES for any given LTS. Figure 2(b) depicts a prefix of the LES $\mathcal{E}_f$ computed by our algorithm for a FIFO queue LTS $\mathcal{S}_f$ over messages $\{a, b\}$. Concurrency essentially corresponds to independence diamonds in $\mathcal{S}_f$: whenever two or more actions are commutative. Moreover, our algorithm infers *local* concurrency: the same actions can be concurrent in some state of $\mathcal{S}_f$ and conflicting in some other state.

Init defines initially pending extension $(\emptyset, \Sigma)$ and marking $M(\emptyset) = s^0$ for the given LTS $(S, s^0, \Sigma, \rightarrow)$. Assume that e_0 in Figure 2(b) has not been extended so far: $P = \{e_0\}$ and $A = \{?a, ?b, !a, !b\}$. Extending P results in creating new events $\{e_2, e_3, e_4\}$ in causality with e_0 ($?b$ is not enabled in $M(\{e_0\})$). Now, extending $P = \{e_0, e_2\}$ with label $!a$ does not create any event since adding e_3 to P yields the expected extension. Hence, our Extend function first looks for concurrent events that can extend P, and

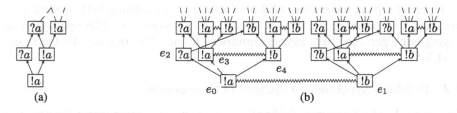

Fig. 2. LES for $\emptyset$-initialized FIFO channels with messages: (a) $\{a\}$ and (b) $\{a, b\}$

then creates new events only for the labels in $A \setminus l(X)$ that were not matched by this first step.

```
Extend (P, A)
   X:=∅
   for e ∈ E s.t. l(e) ∈ A and P ⊢ e do X:=X ∪ e
   for a ∈ A \ l(X) s.t. M(P) →ᵃ do e:=NewEvent(a, P); X:=X ∪ {e}
   for e ∈ X do C(ℰ):=C(ℰ) ∪ {P ∪ {e}}; M(C ∪ {e}):=→[M(P), l(e)]
   return {(P ∪ {e}, Σ) / e ∈ X}
```

Notice that in this algorithm, P is always a configuration: **Extend** explores the configuration space of the LES.

However, **Extend** is not correct so far as it does not add any conflict whereas Figure 2(b) clearly shows the need for it. Missing conflicts are detected as follows. Assume that $\mathcal{E}_f$ in Figure 2(b) only contains e_0 and e_1 without conflict so far. Extending $(\{e_0\}, !b)$ leads to configuration $\{e_0, e_1\}$ with $M(\{e_0, e_1\}) = \rightarrow[M(\{e_0\}), !b] = ab$. Next, extending $(\{e_1\}, !a)$, leads to associating e_0 to $\{e_1\}$ which results to be impossible since $\rightarrow[M(\{e_1\}), !a] = ba \neq M(\{e_0, e_1\})$. Hence, conflict must be added between e_0 and e_1 using the **CheckConflict** function below when **Extend** detects the problem.

```
CheckConflict (P, PE)
   for e ∈ E s.t. P ⊢ e and (M(P) ↛^{l(e)} or M(P ∪ {e}) ≠ →[M(P), l(e)]) do
      e':=choose in Max_≤(P)
      E:=E \ {e'' ∈ E / e ≤ e'' and e' ≤ e''}
      C(ℰ):=C(ℰ) \ {C ∈ C(ℰ) / {e, e'} ∈ C}
      PE:=(PE ∩ C(ℰ)) ∪ {(P', Σ) / P' ∈ C(ℰ), (e ∈ P', P' ⊢ e') or (e' ∈ P', P' ⊢ e)}
      #:=# ∪ {⟨e, e'⟩, ⟨e', e⟩}
   end
   return Sort (PE)
```

CheckConflict updates PE since whenever one needs to add conflict between 2 events e_0 and e_1, every configuration in $C(\mathcal{E})$ that contains both events must be discarded and every configuration that contains e_0 (resp. e_1) has potentially mistaken extensions. Notice that pending extensions (P, A) in PE are eventually sorted w.r.t increasing size of P. This is due to a natural hypothesis made by **Extend**: if P is to be extended, then all the extensions of any $P' \subset P$ are up-to-date.

Figure 2 depicts the marked LES obtained for LTS modeling FIFO queues in the standard way (one state per queue content, and transitions w.r.t. FIFO policy) by applying our algorithm. They exactly correspond to the LES computed by the method in [LI05].

4.3 Unfolding Synchronized Products of Components

Sections 4.1 and 4.2 present unfolding algorithms for single components. We now introduce an algorithm for unfolding complex systems built from synchronized components.

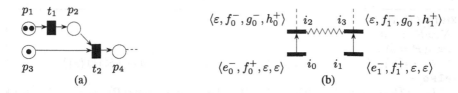

Fig. 3. A Petri net N (a) and a marked LES for N (b)

Consider Petri net N in Figure 3(a). In our framework, each place p_i is modeled by a counter LES and each transition t_j by a synchronization vector between actions of these counters. Since tokens in Petri nets are concurrent processes, we choose a $(v_0 = 2, k = 2)$ counter LES $\mathcal{E}_1$ for p_1 since it initially contains 2 tokens. Similarly we choose a $(1, 1)$ counter LES $\mathcal{E}_3$ for p_3. Place p_2 is initially empty and can simultaneously contain 2 tokens, thus we model it by a $(0, 2)$ counter LES $\mathcal{E}_2$. Finally, we choose a $(0, 1)$ counter LES $\mathcal{E}_4$ for p_4. In the case of unbounded places, one can choose k as the number of entering edges.

Let e_i^a (resp. f_i^a, g_i^a and h_i^a) denote the ith event labeled by $a \in \{+, -\}$ in $\mathcal{E}_1$ (resp. $\mathcal{E}_2$, $\mathcal{E}_3$ and $\mathcal{E}_4$) w.r.t. causality. The semantics of N is modeled in the synchronized product of $\mathcal{E}_1$, $\mathcal{E}_2$, $\mathcal{E}_3$ and $\mathcal{E}_4$ by the synchronization vectors $\langle -, +, \varepsilon, \varepsilon \rangle$ for t_1 and $\langle \varepsilon, -, -, + \rangle$ for t_2.

Figure 3(b) depicts LES $\mathcal{E}_N$ obtained for N using our unfolding algorithm. To each event in $\mathcal{E}_N$ is associated a tuple of components' events by mapping $\lambda : (E_1 \cup \{\varepsilon\}) \times \cdots \times (E_n \cup \{\varepsilon\}) \to E$, for instance $\lambda(i_0) = \langle e_0^-, f_0^+, \varepsilon, \varepsilon \rangle$. Conflict and causality relations in $\mathcal{E}_N$ are defined from components' ones. Basically, conflict appears when a components' event is used by two or more global events, e.g. g_0^- in i_2 and i_3, and causality inherits from components, e.g. $f_0^+ \to f_0^-$ entails $i_0 \to i_2$. Formally, let $\langle e_1, \ldots, e_n \rangle \# \langle e_1', \ldots, e_n' \rangle$ iff there exists i s.t. $e_i = e_i'$ or $e_i \# e_i'$. The global causality and conflict relations are respectively the smallest partial order $\leq$ and the smallest symmetric and irreflexive relation $\#$ satisfying for every global events e, e', e'':

- if $e \# e'$ and $e' \leq e''$ then $e \# e''$, and
- if $\lambda(e) \# \lambda(e')$ then $e \# e'$, and
- if there exists i s.t. $(\lambda(e))_i \leq_i (\lambda(e'))_i$ and we do not have $e \# e'$ then $e \leq e'$.

As Figure 3(b) shows, unfolding a synchronized product of LESs consists in associating components' events into global events w.r.t. synchronization vectors, conflict and causality relations. Since components' LES maybe infinite we use an on-the-fly algorithm that proceeds as follows. Init initializes every component (in particular PE_i) and extends *all* their initially pending extensions $(\emptyset, A_i)$. This is necessary due to synchronization. Next, extending (P, A) in the global LES consists, for every synchronization vector $v \in A$, in finding all tuples $\langle e_1, \ldots, e_n \rangle$ of components' events which are instances of v that extend P. A new global event e is created for each such instance $\langle e_1, \ldots, e_n \rangle$ and each conflict-free preset ps of global events that match the presets of every e_i. Finally, every component such that $e_i \neq \varepsilon$ is extended since the successors of e_i may be needed to extend further.

```
Extend (P, A)
   NewE := ∅
   if (P = ∅)
      E⊗ := {⟨e₁,...,eₙ⟩ / ⟨l(e₁),...,l(eₙ)⟩ ∈ A  and  eᵢ ∈ Min≤ᵢ(Eᵢ) ∪ {ε}}
   else
      E⊗ := {⟨e₁,...,eₙ⟩ / ⟨l(e₁),...,l(eₙ)⟩ ∈ A and ∃e′ ∈ Max≤(P), ∃i, eᵢ ∈ (λ(e′))ᵢ•}
   for ⟨e₁,...,eₙ⟩ ∈ E⊗ do
      for ps ∈ {E′ ∈ 2^E / ∀e,e′ ∈ E′, e #e′ and ∀i, (λ(E′))ᵢ = •eᵢ} do
         e := NewEvent(⟨l(e₁),...,l(eₙ)⟩, ps)
         λ(e) := ⟨e₁,...,eₙ⟩
         for i ∈ [1;n] s.t. l(eᵢ) ≠ ε and eᵢ• = ∅ do PEᵢ := Extendᵢ(PEᵢ, Σᵢ)
         NewE := NewE ∪ {e}
      end
   end
   return {(≥[e], Σ⊗) / e ∈ NewE}
```

In this algorithm, we denote by $\bullet e = \text{Max}_{\leq}((\geq[e]) \setminus \{e\})$ the preset of e w.r.t. causality, and by $e\bullet = \text{Min}_{\leq}((\leq[e]) \setminus \{e\})$ the postset of e. Σ_i denotes the set of actions of component i. Notice that $\text{Extend}_i(PE_i, \Sigma_i)$ is a slight abuse of notations as PE_i is a *set* of pending extensions.

Extend first checks that components' events have not been extended yet before doing so ($e_i\bullet = \emptyset$) since an event may be associated to many global events. The labeling of global events and configurations are defined component-wise, and global conflict and causality relations are computed as defined previously.

Using our algorithm, one can compute a marked unfolding $\mathcal{E}_{\otimes}$ of a synchronized product of components as depicted in Figure 3. Furthermore, $\mathcal{E}_{\otimes}$ can itself be used as a component, giving raise to hierarchical unfolding of systems and components.

5   Experimental Results

We have implemented the algorithms and truncation techniques presented in this paper in a tool called ESU. This tool is implemented in Objective Caml, and permits the verification of termination, boundedness and quasi-liveness for synchronized products of well-structured components. Components may be counters, queues or finite-state (control) automata. For the particular case of bounded systems such as bounded Petri nets, ESU is also able to compute reachability set.

To our knowledge, ESU is the first tool able to analyse infinite-state systems using forward unfolding techniques. Hence, in order to evaluate the benefits of our approach we have compared ESU with two tools for Petri nets: the PEP environment which provides an unfolding tool for bounded Petri nets [Pep], and the tool TINA which analyzes arbitrary Petri nets using structural analysis techniques and forward Karp-Miller reachability analysis [Tin]. Petri nets are modeled in ESU by synchronized counter components. Experiments were conducted on an Intel XEON 2.2 GHz station with 6 GB of RAM. In the following tables, E (resp. E_{cf}, N, S) denotes the number of events in the truncation (resp. of cutoff events, of nodes in TINA's tree, of markings in TINA's tree), and a '–' means that the analysis exhausted memory or did not finish within 10 minutes.

The Petri net depicted below represents a concurrent Producer/Consumer Petri Net with n independent production lines and m machines on each line. The products from these n lines are combined into another product that is then stored in place p_s. PEP's unfolder cannot analyze this Petri net as it is unbounded. ESU performs very well on this example, but this is not very surprising as this Petri net is extremely concurrent. Observe that the number of events in the truncation is approximately the number of transitions in the Petri net.

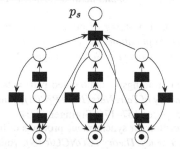

	TINA		ESU		
$m \times n$	N	T(s)	E	E_{cf}	T(s)
3×3	49	0.01	10	4	0.01
5×5	4636	0.04	25	5	0.01
7×7	1094241	24.41	50	8	0.01
7×10	–	–	71	8	0.03
10×10	–	–	96	6	0.04
20×25	–	–	491	11	1.4

We also experimented on a more challenging and well-known example: the swimming pool. The swimming pool has much less explicit concurrency as most transitions share places. We used TINA's bounded swimming pool Petri net which is a variant of the classical one with an additional place that limits the number of clients [Tin]. In the following table, the size denotes the number of resources in the swimming pool.

	PEP			TINA			ESU		
Size	E	E_{cf}	T(s)	N	S	T(s)	E	E_{cf}	T(s)
3	37593	18009	159.59	126	56	0.00	18	3	0.01
10	–	–	–	12012	3003	0.05	60	10	0.20
20	–	–	–	255024	53130	3.35	120	20	3.02
30	–	–	–	1669536	324632	44.74	180	30	20.64
40	–	–	–	6516048	1221759	297.19	240	40	64.04

Future work will focus on improving and extending our method to other frameworks for the analysis of infinite state systems. In particular we plan to focus on abstraction algorithms in order to build more compact and concurrent event structures that would abstract away causality and conflict information that is irrelevant w.r.t. to a desired property. We also plan to consider acceleration techniques as a tool for truncating unfoldings, hence enforcing the termination of our algorithms while preserving reachability properties.

Acknowledgements. The authors wish to thank Igor Walukiewicz for insightful comments and suggestions on a preliminary version of this paper.

References

[AČJT00] P. A. Abdulla, K. Čerāns, B. Jonsson, and Y. K. Tsay. Algorithmic analysis of programs with well quasi-ordered domains. *Information and Computation*, 160(1–2):109–127, 2000.

[AIN00]   P. A. Abdulla, S. P. Iyer, and A. Nylén. Unfoldings of unbounded petri nets. In *Proc. of 12th Int. Conf. on Computer Aided Verification (CAV'00)*, volume 1855 of *Lecture Notes in Computer Science*, pages 495–507. Springer, 2000.

[AJKP98]   P. A. Abdulla, B. Jonsson, M. Kindahl, and D. Peled. A general approach to partial order reductions in symbolic verification (extended abstract). In *Proc. of 10th Int. Conf. on Computer Aided Verification (CAV '98)*, volume 1427 of *Lecture Notes in Computer Science*, pages 379–390. Springer, 1998.

[Arn94]   A. Arnold. *Finite Transition Systems. Semantics of Communicating Systems*. Prentice Hall Int., 1994.

[CGP01]   J-M. Couvreur, S. Grivet, and D. Poitrenaud. Unfolding of products of symmetrical petri nets. In *Proc. 22nd Int. Conf. on Application and Theory of Petri Nets (ICATPN'01)*, volume 2075 of *Lecture Notes in Computer Science*, pages 121–143. Springer, 2001.

[DJN04]   J. Desel, G. Juhás, and C. Neumair. Finite unfoldings of unbounded petri nets. In *Proc. 25th Int. Conf. on Applications and Theory of Petri Nets (ICATPN'04)*, volume 3099 of *Lecture Notes in Computer Science*, pages 157–176. Springer, 2004.

[ER99]   J. Esparza and S. Römer. An unfolding algorithm for synchronous products of transition systems. In *10th Int. Conf. on Concurrency Theory (CONCUR'99)*, volume 1664 of *Lecture Notes in Computer Science*, pages 2–20. Springer, 1999.

[ERV02]   J. Esparza, S. Römer, and W. Vogler. An improvement of McMillan's unfolding algorithm. *Formal Methods in System Design*, 20(3):285–310, 2002.

[Fin90]   A. Finkel. Reduction and covering of infinite reachability trees. *Information and Computation*, 89(2):144–179, 1990.

[FS01]   A. Finkel and P. Schnoebelen. Well-structured transition systems everywhere! *Theoretical Computer Science*, 256(1–2):63–92, 2001.

[God96]   P. Godefroid. *Partial-order methods for the verification of concurrent systems: An approach to the state-explosion problem*, volume 1032 of *Lecture Notes in Computer Science*. Springer, New York, NY, USA, 1996.

[KK03]   V. Khomenko and M. Koutny. Branching processes of high-level petri nets. In *Proc. 9th Int. Conf. on Tools and Algorithms for the Construction and Analysis of Systems (TACAS'03)*, volume 2619 of *Lecture Notes in Computer Science*, pages 458–472. Springer, 2003.

[LI05]   Y. Lei and S. P. Iyer. An approach to unfolding asynchronous communication protocols. In *Proc. 13th Int. Symp. on Formal Methods (FM'05)*, volume 3582 of *Lecture Notes in Computer Science*, pages 334–349. Springer, 2005.

[Maz86]   A. W. Mazurkiewicz. Trace theory. In *Advances in Petri Nets*, volume 255 of *Lecture Notes in Computer Science*, pages 279–324. Springer, 1986.

[McM95]   K. L. McMillan. A technique of state space search based on unfolding. *Formal Methods in System Design*, 6(1):45–45, 1995.

[NPW81]   M. Nielsen, G. Plotkin, and G. Winskel. Petri nets, event structures and domains, part I. *Theoretical Computer Science*, 13:85–108, 1981.

[NRT95]   M. Nielsen, G. Rozenberg, and P. S. Thiagarajan. Transition systems, event structures and unfoldings. *Information and Computation*, 118(2):191–207, 1995.

[Pel93]   D. Peled. All from one, one for all: on model checking using representatives. In *Proc. of the 5th Int. Conf. on Computer Aided Verification (CAV'93)*, volume 697 of *Lecture Notes in Computer Science*, pages 409–423. Springer, 1993.

[Pep]   PEP tool. *Homepage:* http://peptool.sourceforge.net/.

[Tin]   TINA tool. *Homepage:* http://www.laas.fr/tina/.

[Val91]   A. Valmari. Stubborn sets for reduced state space generation. In *Proc. of 10th Int. Conf. on Applications and Theory of Petri Nets (ICATPN'90)*, number 483 in Lecture Notes in Computer Science. Springer, 1991.

Regular Model Checking Without Transducers (On Efficient Verification of Parameterized Systems)

Parosh Aziz Abdulla,[1] Giorgio Delzanno,[2] Noomene Ben Henda,[1]
and Ahmed Rezine[1]

[1] Uppsala University,
Sweden
parosh@it.uu.se, Noomene.BenHenda@it.uu.se, Rezine.Ahmed@it.uu.se
[2] Università di Genova, Italy
giorgio@disi.unige.it

Abstract. We give a simple and efficient method to prove safety properties for parameterized systems with linear topologies. A process in the system is a finite-state automaton, where the transitions are guarded by both local and global conditions. Processes may communicate via broadcast, rendez-vous and shared variables. The method derives an over-approximation of the induced transition system, which allows the use of a simple class of regular expressions as a symbolic representation. Compared to traditional regular model checking methods, the analysis does not require the manipulation of transducers, and hence its simplicity and efficiency. We have implemented a prototype which works well on several mutual exclusion algorithms and cache coherence protocols.

1 Introduction

In this paper, we consider analysis of safety properties for *parameterized systems*. Typically, a parameterized system consists of an arbitrary number of finite-state processes organized in a linear array. The task is to verify correctness of the system regardless of the number of processes inside the system. Examples of parameterized systems include mutual exclusion algorithms, bus protocols, telecommunication protocols, and cache coherence protocols.

One important technique which has been used for verification of parameterized systems is that of *regular model checking* [19,3,6]. In regular model checking, states are represented by words, sets of states by regular expressions, and transitions by finite automata operating on pairs of states, so called *finite-state transducers*. Safety properties can be checked through performing reachability analysis, which amounts to applying the transducer relation iteratively to the set of initial states. The main problem with transducer-based techniques is that they are very heavy and usually rely on several layers of computationally expensive automata-theoretic constructions; in many cases severely limiting their applicability. In this paper, we propose a much more light-weight and efficient

O. Grumberg and M. Huth (Eds.): TACAS 2007, LNCS 4424, pp. 721–736, 2007.

approach to regular model checking, and describe its application in the context of parameterized systems.

In our framework, a process is modeled as a finite-state automaton which operates on a set of local variables ranging over finite domains. The transitions of the automaton are conditioned by the local state of the process, values of the local variables, and by *global conditions*. A global condition is either *universally* or *existentially* quantified. An example of a universal condition is that all processes to the left of a given process i should satisfy a property θ. Process i is allowed to perform the transition only in the case where all processes with indices $j < i$ satisfy θ. In an existential condition we require that *some* (rather than *all*) processes satisfy θ. In addition, processes may communicate through broadcast, rendez-vous, and shared variables. Finally, processes may dynamically be created and deleted during the execution of the system.

The main idea of our method is to consider a transition relation which is an over-approximation of the one induced by the parameterized system. To do that, we modify the semantics of universal quantifiers by eliminating the processes which violate the given condition. For instance in the above example, process i is always allowed to take the transition. However, when performing the transition, we eliminate all processes which have indices $j < i$ and which violate the condition θ. The approximate transition system obtained in this manner is *monotonic* with respect to the subword relation on configurations (larger configurations are able to simulate smaller ones). In fact, it turns out that universal quantification is the only operation which does not preserve monotonicity and hence it is the only source of approximation in the model. Since the approximate transition relation is monotonic, it can be analyzed using symbolic backward reachability algorithm based on a generic method introduced in [1]. An attractive feature of this algorithm is that it operates on sets of configurations which are upward closed with respect to the subword relation. In particular, reachability analysis can be performed by computing predecessors of upward closed sets, which is much simpler and more efficient than applying transducer relations on general regular languages. Also, as a side effect, the analysis of the approximate model is always guaranteed to terminate. This follows from the fact that the subword relation on configurations is a *well quasi-ordering*. The whole verification process is fully automatic since both the approximation and the reachability analysis are carried out without user intervention. Observe that if the approximate transition system satisfies a safety property then we can safely conclude that the original system satisfies the property, too.

To simplify the presentation, we introduce the class of systems we consider in a stepwise manner. First, we consider a basic model where we only allow Boolean local variables together with local and global conditions. We describe how to derive the approximate transition relation and how to analyze safety properties for the basic model. Then, we introduce the additional features one by one. This includes using general finite domains, shared variables, broadcast and rendez-vous communication, dynamic creation and deletion of processes, and counters. For each new feature, we describe how to extend the approximate transition relation and the reachability algorithm in a corresponding manner.

Based on the method, we have implemented a prototype which works well on several mutual exclusion algorithms and cache coherence protocols, such as the Bakery and Szymanski algorithms, the Java Meta-locking protocol, the Future-bus+ protocol, German's directory-based protocol, etc.

Related work. Several recent works have been devoted to develop regular model checking, e.g., [19,9]; and in particular augmenting regular model checking with techniques such as widening [6,27], abstraction [7], and acceleration [3]. All these works rely on computing the transitive closure of transducers or on iterating them on regular languages.

A technique of particular interest for parameterized systems is that of *counter abstraction*. The idea is to keep track of the number of processes which satisfy a certain property. In [15] the technique generates an abstract system which is essentially a Petri net. Counter abstracted models with *broadcast communication* are proved to be *well-structured* in [14]. In [10,11] symbolic model checking based on real arithmetics is used to verify counter abstracted models of cache coherence protocols enriched with global conditions. The method works without guarantee of termination. The paper [24] refines the counter abstraction idea by truncating the counters at the value of 2, and thus obtains a finite-state abstract system. The method may require manual insertion of auxiliary program variables for programs that exploit knowledge of process identifiers (examples of such programs are the mutual exclusion protocols we consider in this paper). In general, counter abstraction is designed for systems with unstructured or clique architectures. Our method can cope with this kind of systems, since unstructured architectures can be viewed as a special case of linear arrays where the ordering of the processes is not relevant. In [18] and [26], the authors present a tool for the analysis and the verification of *linear parameterized hardware systems* using the *monadic second-order logic on strings*.

Other parameterized verification methods are based on reductions to finite-state models. Among these, the *invisible invariants* method [4,23] exploits *cut-off* properties to check invariants for mutual exclusion protocols like the Bakery algorithm and German's protocol. The success of the method depends on the heuristic used in the generation of the candidate invariant. This method sometimes (e.g. for German's protocol) requires insertion of auxiliary program variables for completing the proof. In [5] finite-state abstractions for verification of systems specified in WS1S are computed on-the-fly by using the weakest precondition operator. The method requires the user to provide a set of predicates on which to compute the abstract model. Heuristics to discover *indexed predicates* are proposed in [20] and applied to German's protocol as well as to the Bakery algorithm. In contrast to these approaches, we provide a uniform approximation scheme which is independent on the analyzed system. *Environment abstraction* [8] combines predicate abstraction with the counter abstraction. The technique is applied to the Bakery and Szymanski algorithms. The model of [8] contains a more restricted form of global conditions than ours, and also does not include features such as broadcast communication, rendez-vous communication, and dynamic behaviour. Other approaches tailored to snoopy cache protocols modeled with broadcast communication are presented in [13,21]. In [12] German's directory-based protocol is verified via a manual transformation into a snoopy protocol. It is important to remark that frameworks for finite-state abstractions [8] and those based on cutoff properties [4,23] can be applied to parameterized systems where each component itself contains counters and other unbounded data structures. This allows for instance to deal with a model of the Bakery algorithm which is more concrete (precise) than ours.

Finally, in [25] a parameterized version of the Java Meta-locking algorithm is verified by means of an induction-based proof technique which requires manual strengthening of the mutual exclusion invariant.

In summary, our method provides a uniform simple abstraction which allows fully automatic verification of a wide class of systems. We have been able to verify all benchmarks available to us from the literature (with the exception of the Bakery protocol, where we can only model an abstraction of the protocol). The benchmarks include some programs, e.g. the German protocol and Java Meta-locking algorithm, which (to our knowledge) have previously not been possible to verify without user interaction or specialized heuristics. On the negative side, the current method only allows the verification of safety properties, while most regular model checking and abstraction-based techniques can also handle liveness properties.

Outline. In the next Section we give some preliminaries and define a basic model for parameterized systems. Section 3 describes the induced transition system and introduces the coverability (safety) problem. In Section 4 we define the over-approximated transition system on which we run our technique. Section 5 presents a generic scheme for deciding coverability. In Section 6 we instantiate the scheme on the approximate transition system. Section 7 explains how we extend the basic model to cover features such as shared variables, broadcast and binary communications, and dynamic creation and deletion of processes. In Section 8 we report the results of our prototype on a number of mutual exclusion and cache coherence examples. Finally, in Section 9, we give conclusions and directions for future work. A detailed description of the case studies can be found in [2].

2   Preliminaries

In this section, we define a basic model of parameterized systems. This model will be enriched by additional features in Section 7.

For a natural number n, let $\overline{n}$ denote the set $\{1, \ldots, n\}$. We use $\mathcal{B}$ to denote the set $\{true, false\}$ of Boolean values. For a finite set A, we let $\mathbb{B}(A)$ denote the set of formulas which have members of A as atomic formulas, and which are closed under the Boolean connectives $\neg, \wedge, \vee$. A *quantifier* is either *universal* or *existential*. A universal quantifier is of one of the forms $\forall_{LR}, \forall_L, \forall_R$. An existential quantifier is of one of the forms $\exists_L, \exists_R$, or $\exists_{LR}$. The subscripts L, R, and LR

stand for *Left*, *Right*, and *Left-Right* respectively. A *global condition* over A is of the form $\Box\theta$ where $\Box$ is a quantifier and $\theta \in \mathbb{B}(A)$. A global condition is said to be *universal* (resp. *existential*) if its quantifier is *universal* (resp. *existential*). We use $\mathbb{G}(A)$ to denote the set of global conditions over A.

Parameterized Systems. A parameterized system consists of an arbitrary (but finite) number of identical processes, arranged in a linear array. Each process is a finite-state automaton which operates on a finite number of Boolean local variables. The transitions of the automaton are conditioned by the values of the local variables and by *global* conditions in which the process checks, for instance, the local states and variables of all processes to its left or to its right. A transition may change the value of any local variable inside the process. A parameterized system induces an infinite family of finite-state systems, namely one for each size of the array. The aim is to verify correctness of the systems for the whole family (regardless of the number of processes inside the system).

A *parameterized system* $\mathcal{P}$ is a triple (Q, X, T), where Q is a set of *local states*, X is a set of *local variables*, and T is a set of *transition rules*. A transition rule t is of the form

$$t : \begin{bmatrix} q \\ grd \rightarrow stmt \\ q' \end{bmatrix} \tag{1}$$

where $q, q' \in Q$ and $grd \rightarrow stmt$ is a *guarded command*. Below we give the definition of a guarded command. A *guard* is a formula $grd \in \mathbb{B}(X) \cup \mathbb{G}(X \cup Q)$. In other words, the guard grd constraints either the values of local variables inside the process (if $grd \in \mathbb{B}(X)$); or the local states and the values of local variables of other processes (if $grd \in \mathbb{G}(X \cup Q)$). A *statement* is a set of assignments of the form $x_1 = e_1; \ldots; x_n = e_n$, where $x_i \in X$, $e_i \in \mathcal{B}$, and $x_i \neq x_j$ if $i \neq j$. A *guarded command* is of the form $grd \rightarrow stmt$, where grd is a guard and $stmt$ is a statement.

Remark. We can extend the definition of the transition rule in (1) so that the grd is a *conjunction* of formulas in $\mathbb{B}(X) \cup \mathbb{G}(X \cup Q)$. All the definitions and algorithms which are later presented in this paper can easily be extended to the more general form. However, for simplicity of presentation, we only deal with the current form.

3   Transition System

In this section, we first describe the transition system induced by a parameterized system. Then we introduce the *coverability problem*.

Transition System. A *transition system* $\mathcal{T}$ is a pair $(D, \Longrightarrow)$, where D is an (infinite) set of *configurations* and $\Longrightarrow$ is a binary relation on D. We use $\overset{*}{\Longrightarrow}$ to denote the reflexive transitive closure of $\Longrightarrow$. We will consider several transition systems in this paper.

First, a parameterized system $\mathcal{P} = (Q, X, T)$ induces a transition system $\mathcal{T}(\mathcal{P}) = (C, \longrightarrow)$ as follows. A configuration is defined by the local states of the processes, and by the values of the local variables. Formally, a *local variable state* v is a mapping from X to $\mathcal{B}$. For a local variable state v, and a formula $\theta \in \mathbb{B}(X)$, we evaluate $v \models \theta$ using the standard interpretation of the Boolean connectives. A *process state* u is a pair (q, v) where $q \in Q$ and v is a local variable state. Sometimes, abusing notation, we view a process state (q, v) as a mapping $u : X \cup Q \mapsto \mathcal{B}$, where $u(x) = v(x)$ for each $x \in X$, $u(q) = true$, and $u(q') = false$ for each $q' \in Q - \{q\}$. The process state thus agrees with v on the values of local variables, and maps all elements of Q, except q, to *false*. For a formula $\theta \in \mathbb{B}(X \cup Q)$ and a process state u, the relation $u \models \theta$ is then well-defined. This is true in particular if $\theta \in \mathbb{B}(X)$.

A *configuration* $c \in C$ is a sequence $u_1 \cdots u_n$ of process states. Intuitively, the above configuration corresponds to an instance of the system with n processes. Each pair $u_i = (q_i, v_i)$ gives the local state and the values of local variables of process i. Notice that if c_1 and c_2 are configurations then their concatenation $c_1 \bullet c_2$ is also a configuration.

Next, we define the transition relation $\longrightarrow$ on the set of configurations as follows. We will define the semantics of global conditions in terms of two quantifiers $\forall$ and $\exists$. For a configuration $c = u_1 \cdots u_n$ and a formula $\theta \in \mathbb{B}(X \cup Q)$, we write $c \models \forall\theta$ if $u_i \models \theta$ for each $i : 1 \leq i \leq n$; and write $c \models \exists\theta$ if $u_i \models \theta$ for some $i : 1 \leq i \leq n$. For a statement $stmt$ and a local variable state v, we use $stmt(v)$ to denote the local variable state v' such that $v'(x) = v(x)$ if x does not occur in $stmt$; and $v'(x) = e$ if $x = e$ occurs in $stmt$. Let t be a transition rule of the form of (1). Consider two configurations $c = c_1 \bullet u \bullet c_2$ and $c' = c_1 \bullet u' \bullet c_2$, where $u = (q, v)$ and $u' = (q', v')$. We write $c \xrightarrow{t} c'$ to denote that the following three conditions are satisfied:

1. If $grd \in \mathbb{B}(X)$ then $v \models grd$, i.e., the local variables of the process in transition should satisfy grd.
2. If $grd = \Box\theta \in \mathbb{G}(X \cup Q)$ then one of the following conditions is satisfied:
   - $\Box = \forall_L$ and $c_1 \models \forall\theta$.
   - $\Box = \forall_R$ and $c_2 \models \forall\theta$.
   - $\Box = \forall_{LR}$ and $c_1 \models \forall\theta$ and $c_2 \models \forall\theta$.
   - $\Box = \exists_L$ and $c_1 \models \exists\theta$.
   - $\Box = \exists_R$ and $c_2 \models \exists\theta$.
   - $\Box = \exists_{LR}$ and either $c_1 \models \exists\theta$ or $c_2 \models \exists\theta$.

   In other words, if grd is a global condition then the rest of the processes should satisfy θ (in a manner which depends on the type of the quantifier).
3. $v' = stmt(v)$.

We use $c \longrightarrow c'$ to denote that $c \xrightarrow{t} c'$ for some $t \in T$.

Safety Properties. In order to analyze safety properties, we study the *coverability problem* defined below. Given a parameterized system $\mathcal{P} = (Q, X, T)$, we assume that, prior to starting the execution of the system, each process is in an (identical) *initial* process state $u_{init} = (q_{init}, v_{init})$. In the induced transition system $\mathcal{T}(\mathcal{P}) = (C, \longrightarrow)$, we use *Init* to denote the set of *initial* configurations, i.e., configurations of the form $u_{init} \cdots u_{init}$ (all processes are in their initial states). Notice that this set is infinite.

We define an ordering on configurations as follows. Given two configurations, $c = u_1 \cdots u_m$ and $c' = u'_1 \cdots u'_n$, we write $c \preceq c'$ to denote the existance of a strictly monotonic[1] injection h from $\overline{m}$ to $\overline{n}$ such that $u_i = u'_{h(i)}$ for each $i : 1 \leq i \leq m$. A set of configurations $D \subseteq C$ is *upward closed* (with respect to $\preceq$) if $c \in D$ and $c \preceq c'$ implies $c' \in D$. For sets of configurations $D, D' \subseteq C$ we use $D \longrightarrow D'$ to denote that there are $c \in D$ and $c' \in D'$ with $c \longrightarrow c'$. The *coverability problem* for parameterized systems is defined as follows:

PAR-COV
Instance
  - A parameterized system $\mathcal{P} = (Q, X, T)$.
  - An upward closed set C_F of configurations.
Question *Init* $\overset{*}{\longrightarrow} C_F$?

It can be shown, using standard techniques (see e.g. [28,16]), that checking safety properties (expressed as regular languages) can be translated into instances of the coverability problem. Therefore, checking safety properties amounts to solving PAR-COV(i.e., to the reachability of upward closed sets).

4   Approximation

In this section, we introduce an over-approximation of the transition relation of a parameterized system.

In Section 3, we mentioned that each parameterized system $\mathcal{P} = (Q, X, T)$ induces a transition system $\mathcal{T}(\mathcal{P}) = (C, \longrightarrow)$. A parameterized system $\mathcal{P}$ also induces an *approximate* transition system $\mathcal{A}(\mathcal{P}) = (C, \rightsquigarrow)$, where the set C of configurations is identical to the one in $\mathcal{T}(\mathcal{P})$. We define $\rightsquigarrow = (\longrightarrow \cup \rightsquigarrow_1)$, where $\longrightarrow$ is the transition relation defined in Section 3, and $\rightsquigarrow_1$, which reflects the approximation of universal quantifiers, is defined as follows. For a configuration c, and a formula $\theta \in \mathbb{B}(X \cup Q)$, we use $c \ominus \theta$ to denote the maximal configuration c' (with respect to $\preceq$) such that $c' \preceq c$ and $c' \models \forall \theta$. In other words, we derive c' from c by deleting all process states which do not satisfy θ. Consider two configurations $c = c_1 \bullet u \bullet c_2$ and $c' = c'_1 \bullet u' \bullet c'_2$, where $u = (q, v)$ and $u' = (q', v')$. Let t be a transition rule of the form of (1), such that $grd = \Box \theta$ is a universal global condition. We write $c \overset{t}{\rightsquigarrow}_1 c'$ to denote that the following conditions are satisfied:

1. if $\Box = \forall_L$, then $c'_1 = c_1 \ominus \theta$ and $c'_2 = c_2$.
2. if $\Box = \forall_R$, then $c'_1 = c_1$ and $c'_2 = c_2 \ominus \theta$.

---

[1] $h : \overline{m} \to \overline{n}$ strictly monotonic means: $i < j \Rightarrow h(i) < h(j)$ for all $i, j : 1 \leq i < j \leq m$.

3. if $\square = \forall_{LR}$, then $c_1' = c_1 \ominus \theta$ and $c_2' = c_2 \ominus \theta$.
4. $v' = stmt(v)$.

We use $c \rightsquigarrow c'$ to denote that $c \overset{t}{\rightsquigarrow} c'$ for some $t \in T$. We define the coverability problem for the approximate system as follows:

APRX-PAR-COV
Instance
  - A parameterized system $\mathcal{P} = (Q, X, T)$.
  - An upward closed set C_F of configurations.
Question $Init \overset{*}{\rightsquigarrow} C_F$?

Since $\longrightarrow \subseteq \rightsquigarrow$, a negative answer to APRX-PAR-COV implies a negative answer to PAR-COV.

5 Generic Scheme

In this section, we recall a generic scheme from [1] for performing symbolic backward reachability analysis.

Assume a transition system $(D, \Longrightarrow)$ with a set $Init$ of initial states. We will work with a set of constraints defined over D. A *constraint* ϕ denotes a potentially infinite set of configurations (i.e. $[\![\phi]\!] \subseteq D$). For a finite set Φ of constraints, we let $[\![\Phi]\!] = \bigcup_{\phi \in \Phi} [\![\phi]\!]$.

We define an *entailment relation* $\sqsubseteq$ on constraints, where $\phi_1 \sqsubseteq \phi_2$ iff $[\![\phi_2]\!] \subseteq [\![\phi_1]\!]$. For sets Φ_1, Φ_2 of constraints, abusing notation, we let $\Phi_1 \sqsubseteq \Phi_2$ denote that for each $\phi_2 \in \Phi_2$ there is a $\phi_1 \in \Phi_1$ with $\phi_1 \sqsubseteq \phi_2$. Notice that $\Phi_1 \sqsubseteq \Phi_2$ implies that $[\![\Phi_2]\!] \subseteq [\![\Phi_1]\!]$ (although the converse is not true in general).

For a constraint ϕ, we let $Pre(\phi)$ be a finite set of constraints, such that $[\![Pre(\phi)]\!] = \{c|\ \exists c' \in [\![\phi]\!].\ c \Longrightarrow c'\}$. In other words $Pre(\phi)$ characterizes the set of configurations from which we can reach a configuration in ϕ through the application of a single transition rule. For our class of systems, we will show that such a set always exists and is in fact computable. For a set Φ of constraints, we let $Pre(\Phi) = \bigcup_{\phi \in \Phi} Pre(\phi)$. Below we present a scheme for a symbolic algorithm which, given a finite set Φ_F of constraints, checks whether $Init \overset{*}{\Longrightarrow} [\![\Phi_F]\!]$.

In the scheme, we perform a backward reachability analysis, generating a sequence $\Phi_0 \sqsupseteq \Phi_1 \sqsupseteq \Phi_2 \sqsupseteq \cdots$ of finite sets of constraints such that $\Phi_0 = \Phi_F$, and $\Phi_{j+1} = \Phi_j \cup Pre(\Phi_j)$. Since $[\![\Phi_0]\!] \subseteq [\![\Phi_1]\!] \subseteq [\![\Phi_2]\!] \subseteq \cdots$, the procedure terminates when we reach a point j where $\Phi_j \sqsubseteq \Phi_{j+1}$. Notice that the termination condition implies that $[\![\Phi_j]\!] = (\bigcup_{0 \leq i \leq j} [\![\Phi_i]\!])$. Consequently, Φ_j characterizes the set of all predecessors of $[\![\Phi_F]\!]$. This means that $Init \overset{*}{\Longrightarrow} [\![\Phi_F]\!]$ iff $(Init \bigcap [\![\Phi_j]\!]) \neq \emptyset$.

Observe that, in order to implement the scheme (i.e., transform it into an algorithm), we need to be able to (i) compute Pre; (ii) check for entailment between constraints; and (iii) check for emptiness of $Init \bigcap [\![\phi]\!]$ for a given constraint ϕ. A constraint system satisfying these three conditions is said to be *effective*. Moreover, in [1], it is shown that termination is guaranteed in case the constraint system is *well quasi-ordered (WQO)* with respect to $\sqsubseteq$, i.e., for each infinite sequence $\phi_0, \phi_1, \phi_2, \ldots$ of constraints, there are $i < j$ with $\phi_i \sqsubseteq \phi_j$.

6   Algorithm

In this section, we instantiate the scheme of Section 5 to derive an algorithm for solving APRX-PAR-COV. We do that by introducing an effective and well quasi-ordered constraint system.

Throughout this section, we assume a parameterized system $\mathcal{P} = (Q, X, T)$ and the induced approximate transition system $\mathcal{A}(\mathcal{P}) = (C, \leadsto)$. We define a constraint to be a finite sequence $\theta_1 \cdots \theta_m$ where $\theta_i \in \mathbb{B}(X \cup Q)$. Observe that for any constraints ϕ_1 and ϕ_2, their concatenation $\phi_1 \bullet \phi_2$ is also a constraint. For a constraint $\phi = \theta_1 \cdots \theta_m$ and a configuration $c = u_1 \cdots u_n$, we write $c \models \phi$ to denote that there is a strictly monotonic injection h from $\overline{m}$ to $\overline{n}$ such that $u_{h(i)} \models \theta_i$ for each $i : 1 \leq i \leq m$. Given a constraint ϕ, we let $[\![\phi]\!] = \{c \in C \mid c \models \phi\}$. Notice that if $\phi = \theta_1 \cdots \theta_m$ and some θ_i is unsatisfiable then $[\![\phi]\!]$ is empty. Such a constraint can therefore be safely discarded in the algorithm.

An aspect of our constraint system is that each constraint characterizes a set of configurations which is upward closed with respect to $\preceq$. Conversely (by Higman's Lemma [17]), any upward closed set C_F of configurations can be characterized as $[\![\Phi_F]\!]$ where Φ_F is a finite set of constraints. In this manner, APRX-PAR-COV is reduced to checking the reachability of a finite set of constraints.

Below we show effectiveness and well quasi-ordering of our constraint system, meaning that we obtain an algorithm for solving APRX-PAR-COV.

Pre. For a constraint ϕ', we define $Pre(\phi') = \bigcup_{t \in T} Pre_t(\phi')$, i.e., we compute the set of predecessor constraints with respect to each transition rule $t \in T$. In the following, assume t to be a transition rule of the form (1). To compute $Pre_t(\phi')$, we define first the function $[t]$ on $X \cup Q$ as follows: for each $x \in X$, $[t](x) = stmt(x)$ if x occurs in $stmt$ and $[t](x) = x$ otherwise. For each $q'' \in Q$, $[t](q'') = true$ if $q'' = q'$, and $false$ otherwise. For $\theta \in \mathbb{B}(X \cup Q)$, we use $\theta[t]$ to denote the formula obtained from θ by substituting all occurrences of elements in θ by their corresponding $[t]$-images.

Now, we define two operators, $\otimes$ and $\oplus$, which we use to capture the effects of universal and existential quantifiers when computing *Pre*. We use $\otimes$ to handle universal quantifiers. For a constraint $\phi = \theta_1 \cdots \theta_m$ and a $\theta \in \mathbb{B}(X \cup Q)$, we define $\phi \otimes \theta$ to be the constraint $(\theta_1 \wedge \theta) \cdots (\theta_m \wedge \theta)$. We use $\oplus$ to deal with existential quantifiers. For a constraint $\phi = \theta_1 \cdots \theta_m$ and a $\theta \in \mathbb{B}(X \cup Q)$, we define $\phi \oplus \theta$ to be the set of constraints which are of one of the following forms:

- $\theta_1 \cdots \theta_{i-1}(\theta_i \wedge \theta)\theta_{i+1} \cdots \theta_m$ where $1 \leq i \leq m$; or
- $(\theta_1 \wedge \neg\theta) \cdots (\theta_i \wedge \neg\theta)\theta(\theta_{i+1} \wedge \neg\theta) \cdots (\theta_m \wedge \neg\theta)$ where $0 \leq i \leq m+1$.

In the first case, the constraint implies that there is at least one process satisfying θ. In the the second case, the constraint does not imply the existence of such a process, and therefore the formula θ is added explicitly to the representation of the constraint. Notice that in the second case the length of the resulting constraint is larger (by one) than the length of ϕ. This means that the lengths of the constraints which arise during the analysis are not *a priori* fixed. Nevertheless, termination is still guaranteed by well quasi-ordering of the constraints.

For a constraint ϕ' and a rule t of the form (1), we define $Pre_t(\phi')$ to be the set of all constraints ϕ such that ϕ (resp. ϕ') is of the form $\phi_1 \bullet \theta \bullet \phi_2$ (resp. $\phi'_1 \bullet \theta' \bullet \phi'_2$) and the following conditions are satisfied:

- If $grd \in \mathbb{B}(X)$ (i.e. grd is a local condition), then $\theta = \theta'[t] \wedge grd \wedge q$, $\phi_1 = \phi'_1$ and $\phi_2 = \phi'_2$;
- If $grd = \Box grd'$, where $grd' \in \mathbb{B}(X \cup Q)$, then $\theta = \theta'[t] \wedge q$ and depending on $\Box$ the following conditions hold:
  - If $\Box = \forall_L$ then $\phi_1 = \phi'_1 \otimes grd'$ and $\phi_2 = \phi'_2$.
  - If $\Box = \forall_R$ then $\phi_1 = \phi'_1$ and $\phi_2 = \phi'_2 \otimes grd'$.
  - If $\Box = \forall_{LR}$ then $\phi_1 = \phi'_1 \otimes grd'$ and $\phi_2 = \phi'_2 \otimes grd'$.
  - If $\Box = \exists_L$ then $\phi_1 \in \phi'_1 \oplus grd'$ and $\phi_2 = \phi'_2$.
  - If $\Box = \exists_R$ then $\phi_1 = \phi'_1$ and $\phi_2 \in \phi'_2 \oplus grd'$.
  - If $\Box = \exists_{LR}$ then either $\phi_1 \in \phi'_1 \oplus grd'$ and $\phi_2 = \phi'_2$; or $\phi_1 = \phi'_1$ and $\phi_2 \in \phi'_2 \oplus grd'$.

Entailment. The following Lemma gives a syntactic characterization which allows computing of the entailment relation.

Lemma 1. *For constraints $\phi = \theta_1 \ldots \theta_m$ and $\phi' = \theta'_1 \ldots \theta'_n$, we have $\phi \sqsubseteq \phi'$ iff there exists a strictly monotonic injection $h : \overline{m} \to \overline{n}$ such that $\theta'_{h(i)} \Rightarrow \theta_i$ for each $i \in \overline{m}$.*

Proof. ($\Rightarrow$) Assume there is no such injection. We derive a configuration c such that $c \in \llbracket \phi' \rrbracket$ and $c \notin \llbracket \phi \rrbracket$. To do that, we define the function g on $\overline{n}$ as follows: $g(1) = 1$, $g(i+1) = g(i)$ if $\theta'_i \not\Rightarrow \theta_{g(i)}$, and $g(i+1) = g(i) + 1$ if $\theta'_i \Rightarrow \theta_{g(i)}$. Observe that, since the above mentioned injection does not exist, we have either $g(n) < m$, or $g(n) = m$ and $\theta'_n \not\Rightarrow \theta_m$. We choose $c = u_1 \cdots u_n$, where u_i is defined as follows: (i) if $\theta'_i \not\Rightarrow \theta_{g(i)}$ let u_i be any process state such that $u_i \models \neg \theta_{g(i)} \wedge \theta'_i$; and (ii) if $\theta'_i \Rightarrow \theta_{g(i)}$ let u_i be any process state such that $u_i \models \theta'_i$.

($\Leftarrow$) Assume there exists a strictly monotonic injection $h : \overline{m} \to \overline{n}$ such that $\theta'_{h(i)} \Rightarrow \theta_i$ for each $i \in \overline{m}$. Let $c = u_1 \ldots u_p$ be a configuration in $\llbracket \phi' \rrbracket$. It follows that there exists a strictly monotonic injection $h' : \overline{n} \to \overline{p}$ such that $u_{h'(i)} \models \theta'_i$ for each $i \in \overline{n}$. By assumption, for each $j \in \overline{m}$, we have $\theta'_{h(j)} \Rightarrow \theta_j$. Therefore, for each $j \in \overline{m}$, $u_{h' \circ h(j)} \models \theta_j$. It is straightforward to check that $h' \circ h$ is a strictly monotonic injection from $\overline{m}$ to $\overline{p}$. It follows that $c \in \llbracket \phi \rrbracket$.

Intersection with Initial States. For a constraint $\phi = \theta_1 \ldots \theta_n$, we have $(Init \cap \llbracket \phi \rrbracket) = \emptyset$ iff $u_{init} \not\models \theta_i$ for some $i \in \overline{n}$.

Termination. We show that the constraint system is *well quasi-ordered (WQO)* with respect to $\sqsubseteq$. $(A, \preceq)$ is obviously a *WQO* for any finite set A and any *quasi-order* $\preceq$ on A. Let A^* be the set of words over A, and $\preceq^*$ be the subword relation.

Higman's Lemma [17] states that $(A^*, \preceq^*)$ is also a WQO. Take A to be the quotient sets of $\mathbb{B}(X \cup Q)$ under the equivalence relation. Let $\preceq$ be the implication relation on formulas in $\mathbb{B}(X \cup Q)$. By lemma 1, the relation $\sqsubseteq$ coincides with $\preceq^*$. We conclude that the constraint system is a WQO.

7 Extensions

In this section, we add a number of features to the model of Section 2. For each additional feature, we show how to modify the constraint system of Section 6 in a corresponding manner.

Shared Variables. We assume the presence of a finite set S of Boolean *shared variables* that can be read and written by all processes in the system. A guard may constraint the values of both the shared and the local variables, and a statement may assign values to the shared variables (together with the local variables). It is straightforward to extend the definitions of the induced transition system and the symbolic algorithm to deal with shared variables.

Variables over Finite Domains. Instead of Boolean variables, we can use variables which range over arbitrary finite domains. Below we describe an example of such an extension. Let Y be a finite set of variables which range over $\{0, 1, \ldots, k\}$, for some natural number k. Let $\mathbb{N}(A)$ be the set of formulas of the form $x \sim y$ where $\sim \in \{<, \leq, =, \neq, >, \geq\}$ and $x, y \in Y \cup \{0, 1, \ldots, k\}$. A guard is a formula $grd \in \mathbb{B}(X \cup \mathbb{N}(Y)) \cup \mathbb{G}(X \cup Q \cup \mathbb{N}(Y))$. In other words, the guard grd may also constraint the values of the variables in Y. Similarly, a statement may assign values in $\{0, 1, \ldots, k\}$ to variables in Y. A local variable state is a mapping from $X \cup Y$ to $\mathcal{B} \cup \{0, 1, \ldots, k\}$ respecting the types of the variables. The definitions of configurations, the transition relation, and constraints are extended in the obvious manner. Well quasi-ordering of the constraint system follows in a similar manner to Section 6, using the fact that variables in Y range over finite domains.

Broadcast. In a broadcast transition, an arbitrary number of processes change states simultaneously. A *broadcast rule* is a sequence of transition rules of the following form

$$\begin{bmatrix} q_0 \\ grd_0 \to stmt_0 \\ q_0' \end{bmatrix} \begin{bmatrix} q_1 \\ grd_1 \to stmt_1 \\ q_1' \end{bmatrix}^* \begin{bmatrix} q_2 \\ grd_2 \to stmt_2 \\ q_2' \end{bmatrix}^* \cdots \begin{bmatrix} q_m \\ grd_m \to stmt_m \\ q_m' \end{bmatrix}^* \quad (2)$$

where $grd_i \in \mathbb{B}(X)$ for each $i : 0 \leq i \leq m$. Below, we use t_i to refer to the ith rule in the above sequence. The broadcast rule is deterministic in the sense that either $grd_i \wedge grd_j$ is not satisfiable or $q_i \neq q_j$ for each $i, j : 1 \leq i \neq j \leq m$. The broadcast is initiated by a process, called the *initiator*, which is represented by t_0 (i.e., the leftmost transition rule). This transition rule has the same interpretation as in Section 2. That is, in order for the broadcast transition to take place, the initiator should be in local state q_0 and its local variables should satisfy the guard grd_0. After the completion of the broadcast, the initiator has changed state to q_0' and updated its local variables according to $stmt_0$. Together with the initiator, an arbitrary number of processes, called the *receptors*, change state simultaneously. The receptors are modeled by the transition rules $t_1, \ldots, t_m$ (each rule being marked by a * to emphasize that an arbitrary number of receptors may execute that rule). More precisely, if the local state of a process is q_i and its local variables satisfy grd_i, then the process changes its local state to q_i' and updates its local variables according to $stmt_i$. Notice that since the broadcast rule is deterministic, a receptor satisfies the precondition of at most one of the transition rules. Processes which do not satisfy the precondition of any of the transition rules remain passive during the broadcast. We define a transition relation $\longrightarrow_B$ to reflect broadcast transitions. The definition of $\longrightarrow_B$ can be derived in a straightforward manner from the above informal description. We extend the transition relation $\longrightarrow$ defined in Section 3, by taking its union with $\longrightarrow_B$. In a similar manner, we extend the approximate transition relation $\rightsquigarrow$ (defined in Section 4) by taking its union with $\longrightarrow_B$. This means that the introduction of broadcast transitions are interpreted exactly, and thus they do not add any additional approximation to $\rightsquigarrow$.

We use the same constraint system as the one defined for systems without broadcast; consequently checking entailment, checking intersection with initial states, and proving termination are identical to Section 6. Below we show how to compute *Pre*. Consider a constraint $\phi' = \theta_1' \cdots \theta_n'$ and a broadcast rule b of the above form. We define $Pre_b(\phi')$ to be the set of all constraints of the form $\theta_1 \cdots \theta_n$ such that there is $i : 1 \leq i \leq n$ and the following properties are satisfied:

- $\theta_i = \theta_i'[t_0] \wedge grd_0 \wedge q_0$. This represents the predecessor state of the initiator.
- For each $j : 1 \leq j \neq i \leq n$, one of the following properties is satisfied:
  - $\theta_j = \theta_j' \wedge \neg((q_1 \wedge grd_1) \vee (q_2 \wedge grd_2) \vee \cdots \vee (q_m \wedge grd_m))$. This represents a passive process (a process other than the initiator, is allowed to be passive if it does not satisfy the preconditions of any of the rules).
  - $\theta_j = \theta_j'[t_k] \wedge grd_k \wedge q_k$, for some $k : 1 \leq k \leq m$. This represents a receptor.

Binary Communication. In *binary communication* two processes perform a *rendez-vous* changing states simultaneously. A rendez-vous rule consists of two transition rules of the from

$$
\begin{bmatrix} q_1 \\ grd_1 \to stmt_1 \\ q_1' \end{bmatrix} \begin{bmatrix} q_2 \\ grd_2 \to stmt_2 \\ q_2' \end{bmatrix} \tag{3}
$$

where $grd_1, grd_2 \in \mathbb{B}(X)$. Binary communication can be treated in a similar manner to broadcast transitions (here there is exactly one receptor). The model definition and the symbolic algorithm can be extended in a corresponding way.

Dynamic Creation and Deletion. We allow dynamic creation and deletion of processes. A *process creation* rule is of the form

$$
\begin{bmatrix} grd \to \cdot \\ q' \end{bmatrix} \tag{4}
$$

where $q' \in Q$ and $grd \in \mathbb{B}(X)$. The rule creates a new process whose local state is q' and whose local variables satisfy grd. The newly created processes may be placed anywhere inside the array of processes.

We define a transition relation $\longrightarrow_D$ to reflect process creation transitions as follows. For configurations c and c', and a process creation rule d of the form of (4), we define $c \xrightarrow{d}_D c'$ to denote that c' is of the form $c'_1 \bullet u' \bullet c'_2$ where $c = c'_1 \bullet c'_2$, $u' = (q', v')$ and $v' \models grd$. We use the same constraint system as the one defined for systems without process creation and deletion. We show how to compute *Pre*. Consider a constraint ϕ' and a creation rule d of the form of (4). We define $Pre_d(\phi')$ to be the set of all constraints ϕ such that ϕ' (resp. ϕ) is of the form $\phi'_1 \bullet \theta' \bullet \phi'_2$ (resp. $\phi'_1 \bullet \phi'_2$) and $\theta'[t] \wedge grd$ is satisfiable. Notice that $\theta'[t]$ does not change the values of the local variables in θ'.

A *process deletion* rule is of the form

$$
\begin{bmatrix} q \\ grd \to \cdot \\ \cdot \end{bmatrix} \tag{5}
$$

where $q \in Q$ and $grd \in \mathbb{B}(X)$. The rule deletes a single process whose local state is q provided that the guard grd is satisfied. The definitions of the transition system and the symbolic algorithm can be extended in a similarly to the case with process creation rules. We omit the details here due to shortage of space.

Counters. Using deletion, creation, and universal conditions we can simulate counters, i.e., global unbounded variables which range over the natural numbers. For each counter c, we use a special local state q_c, such that the value of c is encoded by the number of occurrences of q_c in the configuration. Increment and decrement operations can be simulated using creation and deletion of processes in local state q_c. Zero-testing can be simulated through universal conditions. More precisely, $c = 0$ is equivalent to the condition that there is no process in state q_c. This gives a model which is as powerful as Petri nets with inhibitor arcs (or equivalently counter machines). Observe that the approximation introduced by the universal condition means that we replace zero-testing (in the original model) by resetting the counter value to zero (in the approximate model). Thus, we are essentially approximating the counter machine by the corresponding lossy counter machine (see [22] for a description of lossy counter machines). In fact, we can equivalently add counters as a separate feature (without simulation through universal conditions), and approximate zero-testing by resetting as described above.

8   Experimental Results

Based on our method, we have implemented a prototype tool and run it on a collection of mutual exclusion and cache coherence protocols. The results, using a Pentium M 1.6 Ghz with 1G of memory, are summarized in Tables 1 and 2. For each of the mutual exclusion protocols, we consider two variants; namely one with dynamic creation and deletion of processes (marked with a * in Table 1), and one without. Full details of the examples can be found in [2]. For each example,

Table 1. Mutual exclusion algorithms

	# iter	# constr	t(ms)
Bakery	2	2	4
Bakery*	2	2	4
Burns	14	71	230
Burns*	9	21	32
Java M-lock	5	24	30
Java M-lock*	5	17	30
Dijkstra	13	150	1700
Dijkstra*	8	57	168
Szymanski	17	334	3880
Szymanski*	17	334	4080

Table 2. Cache coherence protocols

	# iter	# constr	t(ms)
Synapse	3	3	4
Berkeley	2	6	8
Mesi	3	8	8
Moesi	1	12	12
Dec Firefly	3	11	16
Xerox P.D	3	20	52
Illinois	5	33	80
Futurebus	7	153	300
German	44	14475	3h45mn

we give the number of iterations performed by the reachability algorithm, the largest number of constraints maintained at any point during the execution of the algorithm, and the time (in milliseconds). The computation for each example required less than 15MB of memory.

9   Conclusion and Future Work

We have presented a method for verification of parameterized systems where the components are organized in a linear array. We derive an over-approximation of the transition relation which allows the use of symbolic reachability analysis defined on upward closed sets of configurations. Based on the method, we have implemented a prototype which performs favorably compared to existing tools on several protocols which implement cache coherence and mutual exclusion.

One direction for future research is to apply the method to other types of topologies than linear arrays. For instance, in the cache coherence protocols we consider, the actual ordering on the processes inside the protocol has no relevance. These protocols fall therefore into a special case of our model where the system can be viewed as set of processes (without structure) rather than as a linear array. This indicates that the verification algorithm can be optimized even further for such systems. Furthermore, since our algorithm relies on a small set of properties of words which are shared by other data structures, we believe that our approach can be lifted to a more general setting. In particular we aim to develop similar algorithms for systems whose behaviours are captured by relations on trees and on general forms of graphs.

References

1. P. A. Abdulla, K. Čerāns, B. Jonsson, and T. Yih-Kuen. General decidability theorems for infinite-state systems. In *Proc. LICS '96*, pages 313–321, 1996.
2. P. A. Abdulla, N. B. Henda, G. Delzanno, and A. Rezine. Regular model checking without transducers. Technical Report 2006-052, Uppsala University, Dec. 2006.
3. P. A. Abdulla, B. Jonsson, M. Nilsson, and J. d'Orso. Regular model checking made simple and efficient. In *Proc. CONCUR '02*, pages 116–130, 2002.
4. T. Arons, A. Pnueli, S. Ruah, J. Xu, and L. Zuck. Parameterized verification with automatically computed inductive assertions. In *CAV '01*, pages 221–234, 2001.
5. K. Baukus, Y. Lakhnech, and K. Stahl. Parameterized verification of a cache coherence protocol: Safety and liveness. In *VMCAI '02*, pages 317–330, 2002.
6. B. Boigelot, A. Legay, and P. Wolper. Iterating transducers in the large. In *Proc. CAV '03*, volume 2725 of *LNCS*, pages 223–235, 2003.
7. A. Bouajjani, P. Habermehl, and T. Vojnar. Abstract regular model checking. In *Proc. CAV '04*, LNCS, pages 372–386, Boston, July 2004.
8. E. Clarke, M. Talupur, and H. Veith. Environment abstraction for parameterized verification. In *Proc. VMCAI '06*, volume 3855 of *LNCS*, pages 126–141, 2006.
9. D. Dams, Y. Lakhnech, and M. Steffen. Iterating transducers. In *Proc. CAV' 01*, volume 2102 of *LNCS*, 2001.
10. G. Delzanno. Automatic verification of cache coherence protocols. In Emerson and Sistla, editors, *Proc. CAV '00*, volume 1855 of *LNCS*, pages 53–68, 2000.
11. G. Delzanno. Verification of consistency protocols via infinite-state symbolic model checking. In *Proc. FORTE/PSTV 2000*, pages 171–186, 2000.
12. E. Emerson and V. Kahlon. Exact and efficient verification of parameterized cache coherence protocols. In *CHARME 2003*, pages 247–262, 2003.
13. E. Emerson and V. Kahlon. Model checking guarded protocols. In *Proc. LICS '03*, pages 361–370, 2003.
14. J. Esparza, A. Finkel, and R. Mayr. On the verification of broadcast protocols. In *Proc. LICS '99*, pages 352–359, 1999.
15. S. M. German and A. P. Sistla. Reasoning about systems with many processes. *Journal of the ACM*, 39(3):675–735, 1992.
16. P. Godefroid and P. Wolper. Using partial orders for the efficient verification of deadlock freedom and safety properties. *FMSD*, 2(2):149–164, 1993.
17. G. Higman. Ordering by divisibility in abstract algebras. *Proc. London Math. Soc.*, 2:326–336, 1952.
18. P. Kelb, T. Margaria, M. Mendler, and C. Gsottberger. MOSEL: A flexible toolset for monadic second-order logic. In *Proc. TACAS '97*, pages 183–202, 1997.
19. Y. Kesten, O. Maler, M. Marcus, A. Pnueli, and E. Shahar. Symbolic model checking with rich assertional languages. *TCS, Volume 256*, pages 93–112, 2001.
20. S. K. Lahiri and R. E. Bryant. Indexed predicate discovery for unbounded system verification. In *CAV 2004*, pages 135–147, 2004.
21. M. Maidl. A unifying model checking approach for safety properties of parameterized systems. In *Proc. CAV '01*, pages 324–336, 2001.
22. R. Mayr. Undecidable problems in unreliable computations. *Theoretical Computer Science, Volume 297*, pages 337–354, 2003.

23. A. Pnueli, S. Ruah, and L. Zuck. Automatic deductive verification with invisible invariants. In *Proc. TACAS '01*, pages 82–97, 2001.
24. A. Pnueli, J. Xu, and L. Zuck. Liveness with (0,1,infinity)-counter abstraction. In *Proc. CAV '02*, volume 2404 of *LNCS*, 2002.
25. A. Roychoudhury and I. Ramakrishnan. Automated inductive verification of parameterized protocols. In *Proc. CAV '01*, pages 25–37, 2001.
26. C. Topnik, E. Wilhelm, T. Margaria, and B. Steffen. jMosel: A Stand-Alone Tool and jABC Plugin for M2L(Str). In *Model Checking Software: 13th International SPIN Workshop*, volume 3925 of *LNCS*, pages 293–298, 2006.
27. T. Touili. Regular Model Checking using Widening Techniques. *ETCS*, 50(4), 2001. Proc. VEPAS'01.
28. M. Y. Vardi and P. Wolper. An automata-theoretic approach to automatic program verification. In *Proc. LICS '86*, pages 332–344, June 1986.

Author Index

Lecture Notes in Computer Science

For information about Vols. 1–4307

please contact your bookseller or Springer